2001
BLUE JAYS
OFFICIAL GUIDE

T5-DHC-059

25th SEASON — A SUMMER TRADITION SINCE 1977

CONTENTS

FILLER INDEX

Trade edition published by Dan Diamond and Associates, Inc. (416) 531-6535.
Distributed by North 49 Books (416) 449-4000. Printed and bound in Canada by vistainfo.
Color separation and film work by Stafford Graphics.
Data management and page composition by Caledon Data Management.

ISBN 0-920445-72-1

SkyDome

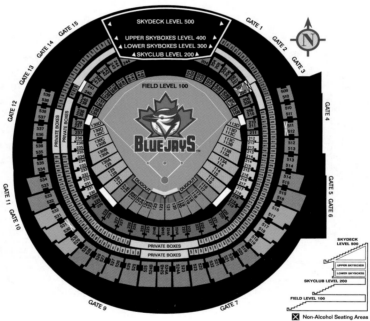

● In the Action	$150.00		● Field Level - Baselines	$29.00
● Club 200 Infield*	$44.00		● 200 Level - Outfield	$23.00
● Club 200 Baselines*	$41.00		● 100 Level - Outfield	$23.00
● Premium Dugout Level	$44.00		● SkyDeck - Infield	$23.00
● Field Level - Infield	$41.00		● SkyDeck - Bases	$16.00
● Field Level - Bases	$35.00		● SkyDeck - Baselines	$7.00

Ticket prices include a 25¢ stadium surcharge, 7% GST and 10% PAT. * Membership fees apply for Club 200 seats

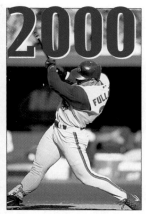

Home runs power Jays to third place finish

Manager	W	L	Pct.	Pos.	GB	Attendance
Jim Fregosi	**83**	**79**	**.512**	**3rd**	**-4.5**	**1,819,886**

THE TORONTO BLUE JAYS featured the American League's most explosive offense in 2000, leading the circuit in home runs (244) and extra-base hits (593). Seven different Jays hit at least 20 homers to tie an A.L. record, while Carlos Delgado (41), Tony Batista (41), Jose Cruz (31) and newcomer Brad Fulmer (32) all reached the 30-homer plateau to tie another American League mark. The power surge helped carry the club to its third consecutive winning season, finishing only 4½ games back of the New York Yankees. Carlos Delgado was the club's main offensive catalyst during much of the season, setting career-highs in average (.344), runs scored (115), doubles (57) and RBIs (137). On the mound, southpaw David Wells was the staff ace, notching 20 wins with an A.L. best nine complete games. He became the club's first lefthanded 20-game winner. Despite Wells's and Delgado's heroics, the team faltered heading down the stretch, due to injuries and inconsistent pitching. Raul Mondesi, who electrified fans with his energy and all-out effort, missed almost half of the season with a damaged elbow. The pitching staff was diminished by injuries as well, with Joey Hamilton and Frank Castillo both forced to the sidelines. Before his injury, Castillo was the surprise of the season, winning 10 games with an outstanding 3.59 ERA after having won a spot in the starting rotation after a strong training camp.

Brad Fullmer had 32 HRs and 104 RBIs as a designated hitter.

BATTER	Pos.	Avg.	G	AB	R	H	HR	RBI
BATISTA, Tony	3B	.263	154	620	96	163	41	114
BUSH, Homer	2B	.215	76	297	38	64	1	18
CASTILLO, Alberto	C	.211	66	185	14	39	1	16
CORDOVA, Marty	OF-DH	.245	62	200	23	49	4	18
CRUZ Jr., Jose	OF	.242	162	603	91	146	31	76
DELGADO, Carlos	1B	.344	162	569	115	196	41	137
DUCEY, Rob	OF	.154	5	13	2	2	0	1
FLETCHER, Darrin	C	.320	122	416	43	133	20	58
FULLMER, Brad	DH	.295	133	482	76	142	32	104
GONZALEZ, Alex	SS	.252	141	527	68	133	15	69
GREBECK, Craig	2B-SS	.295	66	241	38	71	3	23
GREENE, Charlie	C	.111	3	9	0	1	0	0
GREENE, Todd	DH-PH	.235	34	85	11	20	5	10
MARTINEZ, Dave	OF	.311	47	180	29	56	2	22
MONDESI, Raul	OF	.271	96	388	78	105	24	67
MORANDINI, Mickey	2B	.271	35	107	10	29	0	7
MOTTOLA, Chad	OF	.222	3	9	1	2	0	2
PHELPS, Josh	C	.000	1	1	0	0	0	0
STEWART, Shannon	OF	.319	136	583	107	186	21	69
THOMPSON, Andy	OF	.167	2	6	2	1	0	1
WELLS, Vernon	OF	.000	3	2	0	0	0	0
WISE, Dewayne	OF	.136	28	22	3	3	0	0
WOODWARD, Chris	IF	.183	37	104	16	19	3	14
Pitchers		.107	162	28	3	3	0	0
Designated Hitters		.285	153	606	92	173	39	120
Pinch Hitters		.333	–	51	6	17	0	8
2000 Totals		**.275**	**162**	**5677**	**861**	**1562**	**244**	**826**

PITCHER	ERA	W-L	SV	G	IP	H	ER	BB	SO
ANDREWS, Clayton	10.02	1-2	0	8	20.2	34	23	9	12
BALE, John	14.73	0-0	0	2	3.2	5	6	3	6
BORBON, Pedro	6.48	1-1	1	59	41.2	45	30	38	29
CARPENTER, Chris	6.26	10-12	0	34	175.1	204	122	83	113
CASTILLO, Frank	3.59	10-5	0	25	138.0	112	55	56	104
COCO, Pasqual	9.00	0-0	0	1	4.0	5	4	5	2
CUBILLAN, Darwin	8.04	1-0	0	7	15.2	20	14	11	14
DeWITT, Matt	8.56	1-0	0	8	13.2	20	13	9	6
ESCOBAR, Kelvim	5.35	10-15	2	43	180.0	186	107	85	142
ESTRELLA, Leoncio	5.79	0-0	0	2	4.2	9	3	0	3
FRASCATORE, John	5.42	2-4	0	60	73.0	87	44	33	30
GUNDERSON, Eric	7.11	0-1	0	6	6.1	15	5	2	2
GUTHRIE, Mark	4.79	0-2	0	23	20.2	20	11	9	20
HALLADAY, Roy	10.64	4-7	0	19	67.2	107	80	42	44
HAMILTON, Joey	3.55	2-1	0	6	33.0	28	13	12	15
KOCH, Billy	2.63	9-3	33	68	78.2	78	23	18	60
LOAIZA, Esteban	3.62	5-7	0	14	92.0	95	37	26	62
MUNRO, Pete	5.96	1-1	0	9	25.2	38	17	16	16
PAINTER, Lance	4.73	2-0	0	42	66.2	69	35	22	53
QUANTRILL, Paul	4.52	2-5	1	68	83.2	100	42	25	47
TRACHSEL, Steve	5.29	2-5	0	11	63.0	72	37	25	32
WELLS, David	4.11	20-8	0	35	229.2	266	105	31	166
2000 Totals	**5.14**	**83-79**	**37**	**162**	**1437.1**	**1615**	**821**	**560**	**978**

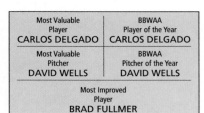

Most Valuable Player	BBWAA Player of the Year
CARLOS DELGADO	**CARLOS DELGADO**
Most Valuable Pitcher	BBWAA Pitcher of the Year
DAVID WELLS	**DAVID WELLS**

Most Improved Player
BRAD FULLMER

Carlos Delgado set a new Jays franchise record with 137 RBIs.

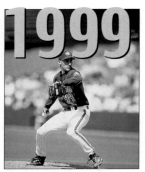

1999

Rookie reliever Billy Koch had 31 saves.

Awesome offense fuels hopes for post–season

Manager	W	L	Pct.	Pos.	GB	Attendance
Jim Fregosi	**84**	**78**	**.519**	**3rd**	**-20**	**2,163,473**

THE BLUE JAYS established two new franchise records in 1999 with a .280 team batting average and 883 runs scored. Shawn Green, who enjoyed a league-high 28-game hitting streak in July, blossomed into one of the A.L.'s premier power-hitters by crushing 42 homers during the campaign. Carlos Delgado led the club in home runs (44) and RBIs (134), while third baseman Tony Fernandez, second baseman Homer Bush and outfielder Shannon Stewart all hit above .300. Fire-balling freshman hurler Billy Koch set a new American League rookie record with 31 saves and was rewarded by being named the team's Pitcher-of-the-Year and Rookie-of-the-Year. Kelvim Escobar (14-11), Pat Hentgen (11-12) and David Wells (17-10) all reached double-digits in victories, helping the club stay in wild-card contention until the dog days of August.

BATTER	Pos.	Avg.	G	AB	R	H	HR	RBI
BATISTA, Tony	SS	.285	98	375	61	107	26	79
BERROA, Geronimo	DH-PH	.194	22	62	11	12	1	6
BLAKE, Casey	3B	.256	14	39	6	10	1	1
BORDERS, Pat	C-DH	.214	6	14	1	3	1	3
BROWN, Kevin	C	.444	2	9	1	4	0	1
BRUMFIELD, Jacob	OF	.235	62	170	25	40	2	19
BUSH, Homer	2B-SS	.320	128	485	69	155	5	55
BUTLER, Rich	DH-OF	.143	8	7	1	1	0	1
CRUZ Jr., Jose	OF	.241	106	349	63	84	14	45
DALESANDRO, Mark	C-DH-3B	.185	16	27	3	5	0	1
DELGADO, Carlos	1B	.272	152	573	113	156	44	134
FERNANDEZ, Tony	3B	.328	142	485	73	159	6	75
FLETCHER, Darrin	C	.291	115	412	48	120	18	80
GONZALEZ, Alex	SS	.292	38	154	22	45	2	12
GOODWIN, Curtis	OF	.000	2	8	0	0	0	0
GREBECK, Craig	IF-DH	.363	34	113	18	41	0	10
GREEN, Shawn	OF	.309	153	614	134	190	42	123
GREENE, Willie	DH-3B-OF	.204	81	226	22	46	12	41
HOLLINS, Dave	DH	.222	27	99	12	22	2	6
KELLY, Pat	2B	.267	37	116	17	31	6	20
LENNON, Patrick	OF	.207	9	29	3	6	1	6
MARTIN, Norberto	2B	.222	9	27	3	6	0	0
MATHENY, Mike	C	.215	57	163	16	35	3	17
McRAE, Brian	DH-OF	.195	31	82	11	16	3	11
OTANEZ, Willis	3B-1B	.252	42	127	21	32	5	13
SANDERS, Anthony	DH-OF	.286	3	7	1	2	0	2
SEGUI, David	DH-1B	.316	31	95	14	30	5	13
STEWART, Shannon	OF	.304	145	608	102	185	11	67
WELLS, Vernon	OF	.261	24	88	8	23	1	8
WITT, Kevin	DH-PH	.206	15	34	3	7	1	5
WOODWARD, Chris	SS	.231	14	26	1	6	0	2
Designated Hitters		.250	153	608	80	152	24	81
Pinch Hitters		.238	–	84	9	20	4	13
Pitchers		.053	162	19	0	1	0	0
1999 Totals		**.280**	**162**	**5642**	**883**	**1580**	**212**	**856**

PITCHER	ERA	W-L	SV	G	IP	H	ER	BB	SO
BALE, John	13.50	0-0	0	1	2.0	2	3	2	4
CARPENTER, Chris	4.38	9-8	0	24	150.0	177	73	48	106
DAVEY, Tom	4.70	1-1	1	29	44.0	40	23	26	42
ESCOBAR, Kelvim	5.69	14-11	0	33	174.0	203	110	81	129
FRASCATORE, John	3.41	7-1	1	33	37.0	42	14	9	22
GLOVER, Gary	0.00	0-0	0	1	0.0	0	0	1	0
HALLADAY, Roy	3.92	8-7	1	36	149.1	156	65	79	82
HAMILTON, Joey	6.52	7-8	0	22	98.0	118	71	39	56
HENTGEN, Pat	4.79	11-12	0	34	199.0	225	106	65	118
HUDEK, John	12.27	0-0	0	3	3.2	8	5	1	2
KOCH, Billy	3.39	0-5	31	56	63.2	55	24	30	57
LLOYD, Graeme	3.63	5-3	3	74	72.0	68	29	23	47
LUDWICK, Eric	27.00	0-0	0	1	1.0	3	3	2	0
MUNRO, Peter	6.02	0-2	0	31	55.1	70	37	23	38
PERSON, Robert	9.82	0-2	2	11	11.0	9	12	15	12
PLESAC, Dan	8.34	0-3	0	30	22.2	28	21	9	26
QUANTRILL, Paul	3.33	3-2	0	41	48.2	53	18	17	28
RODRIGUEZ, Nerio	13.50	0-1	0	2	2.0	2	3	2	2
ROMANO, Mike	11.81	0-0	0	3	5.1	8	7	5	3
SINCLAIR, Steve	12.71	0-0	0	3	5.2	7	8	4	3
SPOLJARIC, Paul	4.65	2-2	0	37	62.0	62	32	32	63
WELLS, David	4.82	17-10	0	34	231.2	246	124	62	169
1999 Totals	**4.93**	**84-78**	**39**	**162**	**1439.0**	**1582**	**788**	**575**	**1009**

Most Valuable Player	BBWAA Player of the Year
SHAWN GREEN	**SHAWN GREEN**
Most Valuable Pitcher	**BBWAA Pitcher of the Year**
BILLY KOCH	**BILLY KOCH**
Most Improved Player	**BBWAA Rookie of the Year**
HOMER BUSH	**BILLY KOCH**

Tony Batista slammed 26 homers in only 98 games.

1998

On July 4, 1998, Tony Fernandez became the club's all-time hits leader with his 1,320th hit as a Blue Jay.

Clemens and Canseco help vault Jays into third place

Manager	W	L	Pct.	Pos.	GB	Attendance
Tim Johnson	**88**	**74**	**.543**	**3rd**	**-26**	**2,454,283**

IT WAS A TALE OF TWO SEASONS for the Blue Jays in 1998, as the team struggled during the first half of the campaign before exploding into wild-card contention in August. Free agent Jose Canseco returned to the form that made him one of the A.L.'s most feared sluggers, slamming 46 homers and stealing 29 bases. Shannon Stewart, Jose Cruz Jr. and Shawn Green patrolled the outfield, combining speed with power in a manner that recalled the famed 1980s trifecta of Bell, Moseby and Barfield. The infield defense was solidified with the addition of Tony Fernandez who led the team with a career-best .321 batting average. Shawn Green served notice that he was among the A.L.'s elite by joining the exclusive 30-30 club with 35 homers and 35 stolen bases. Carlos Delgado led the Jays with 115 RBIs, while Canseco drove in 107. Roger Clemens earned his fifth Cy Young Award, going 20-6 and topping 3,000 career strikeouts.

BATTER	Pos.	Avg.	G	AB	R	H	HR	RBI
BROWN, Kevin	C	.264	52	110	17	29	2	15
CANSECO, Jose	DH-OF	.237	151	583	98	138	46	107
CRESPO, Felipe	OF-IF	.262	66	130	11	34	1	15
CRUZ Jr., Jose	OF	.253	105	352	55	89	11	42
DALESANDRO, Mark	C-3B-1B	.299	32	67	8	20	2	14
DELGADO, Carlos	1B	.292	142	530	94	155	38	115
EVANS, Tom	3B	.000	7	10	0	0	0	0
FERNANDEZ, Tony	2B-3B	.321	138	486	71	156	9	72
FLETCHER, Darrin	C	.283	124	407	37	115	9	52
GONZALEZ, Alex	SS	.239	158	568	70	136	13	51
GREBECK, Craig	IF	.256	102	301	33	77	2	27
GREEN, Shawn	OF	.278	158	630	106	175	35	100
LENNON, Patrick	OF	.500	2	4	1	2	0	0
PEREZ, Tomas	SS-2B	.111	6	9	1	1	0	0
PHILLIPS, Tony	OF	.354	13	48	9	17	1	7
SAMUEL, Juan	DH-OF	.180	43	50	14	9	1	2
SANTIAGO, Benito	C	.310	15	29	3	9	0	4
SPRAGUE, Ed	3B	.238	105	382	49	91	17	51
STANLEY, Mike	DH-1B	.240	98	341	49	82	22	47
STEWART, Shannon	OF	.279	144	516	90	144	12	55
WITT, Kevin	1B	.143	5	7	0	1	0	0
Designated Hitters		.228	155	597	94	136	43	101
Pinch Hitters		.204	–	54	4	11	1	5
Pitchers		.100	163	20	0	2	0	0
1998 Totals		**.266**	**163**	**5580**	**816**	**1482**	**221**	**776**

Most Valuable Player	BBWAA Player of the Year
CARLOS DELGADO	**CARLOS DELGADO**
Most Valuable Pitcher	BBWAA Pitcher of the Year
ROGER CLEMENS	**ROGER CLEMENS**
Most Improved Player	BBWAA Rookie of the Year
SHAWN GREEN	**KEVIN BROWN**

PITCHER	ERA	W-L	SV	G	IP	H	ER	BB	SO
ALMANZAR, Carlos	5.34	2-2	0	25	28.2	34	17	8	20
ANDUJAR, Luis	9.53	0-0	0	5	5.2	12	6	2	1
CARPENTER, Chris	4.37	12-7	0	33	175	177	85	61	136
CLEMENS, Roger	2.65	20-6	0	33	234.2	169	69	88	271
ESCOBAR, Kelvim	3.73	7-3	0	22	79.2	72	33	35	72
GUZMAN, Juan	4.41	6-12	0	22	145.0	133	71	65	113
HALLADAY, Roy	1.93	1-0	0	2	14.0	9	3	2	13
HANSON, Eric	6.24	0-3	0	11	49.0	73	34	29	21
HENTGEN, Pat	5.17	12-11	0	29	177.0	208	102	69	94
MYERS, Randy	4.46	3-4	28	41	42.1	44	21	19	32
PERSON, Robert	7.04	3-1	6	27	38.1	45	30	22	31
PLESAC, Dan	3.78	4-3	4	78	50.0	41	21	16	55
QUANTRILL, Paul	2.59	3-4	7	82	80.0	88	23	22	59
RISLEY, Bill	5.27	3-4	0	44	54.2	52	32	34	42
RODRIGUEZ, Nerio	9.72	1-0	0	7	8.1	10	9	8	3
SINCLAIR, Steve	3.60	0-2	0	24	15.0	13	6	5	8
STIEB, Dave	4.83	1-2	2	19	50.1	58	27	17	27
VAN RYN, Ben	9.00	0-1	0	10	4.0	6	4	2	3
WILLIAMS, Woody	4.46	10-9	0	32	209.2	196	104	81	151
WITHEM, Shannon	3.00	0-0	0	1	3.0	3	1	2	2
1998 Totals	**4.28**	**88-74**	**47**	**163**	**1465.0**	**1443**	**697**	**587**	**1154**

Shawn Green became the first Blue Jay to steal 30 bases and hit 30 home runs in the same season.

Rocket Roger soars but Jays finish sub-.500

Manager	W	L	Pct.	Pos.	GB	Attendance
Cito Gaston	**72**	**85**	**.459**			
Mel Queen	**4**	**1**	**.800**			
Total	**76**	**86**	**.469**	**5th**	**-22**	**2,589,297**

FREE AGENT ACQUISITION ROGER CLEMENS was the story of the Blue Jays' 1997 season. In addition to capturing his fourth Cy Young Award, Clemens tied a club record with 21 victories and established a new franchise mark with 292 strikeouts. By finishing the season with a league-low ERA of 2.05, Clemens also became the first Blue Jay to win the "Triple Crown" of pitching. Joe Carter reached the century mark in RBIs for the tenth time in his career and passed George Bell as the club's all-time home run leader when he hit his 203rd Blue Jay round-tripper in September. Carlos Delgado (30 HRs, 91 RBIs) and Shawn Green (16 HRs, 53 RBIs) emerged as the club's newest offensive weapons. Sophomore hurler Chris Carpenter chalked up 12 wins while Pat Hentgen continued to deliver victories (15) and innings pitched (264).

Roger Clemens won his 4th Cy Young Award with a 21-7 record.

BATTER	Pos.	Avg.	G	AB	R	H	HR	RBI
BRITO, Tilson	IF	.222	49	126	9	28	0	8
BRUMFIELD, Jacob	OF	.207	58	174	22	36	2	20
BUTLER, Rob	OF-DH	.286	7	14	3	4	0	2
CARTER, Joe	DH-OF-1B	.234	157	612	76	143	21	102
CRESPO, Felipe	3B-DH-2B	.286	12	28	3	8	1	5
CRUZ Jr., Jose	OF	.231	55	212	31	49	14	34
DELGADO, Carlos	1B-DH	.262	153	519	79	136	30	91
DUNCAN, Mariano	2B	.228	39	167	20	38	0	12
EVANS, Tom	3B	.289	12	38	7	11	1	2
GARCIA, Carlos	2B	.220	103	350	29	77	3	23
GONZALEZ, Alex	SS	.239	126	426	46	102	12	35
GREEN, Shawn	OF-DH	.287	135	429	57	123	16	53
MARTINEZ, Sandy	C	.000	3	2	1	0	0	0
MERCED, Orlando	OF	.266	98	368	45	98	9	40
MOSQUERA, Julio	C	.250	3	8	0	2	0	0
NIXON, Otis	OF	.262	103	401	54	105	1	26
O'BRIEN, Charlie	C	.218	69	225	22	49	4	27
PEREZ, Robert.	OF-DH	.192	37	78	4	15	2	6
PEREZ, Tomas	SS-2B	.195	40	123	9	24	0	9
SAMUEL, Juan	DH-1B-OF	.284	45	95	13	27	3	15
SANTIAGO, Benito	C	.243	97	341	31	83	13	42
SIERRA, Ruben	OF-DH	.208	14	48	4	10	1	5
SPRAGUE, Ed	3B	.228	138	504	63	115	14	48
STEWART, Shannon	OF	.286	44	168	25	48	0	22
Designated Hitters		.237	156	598	71	142	25	95
Pinch Hitters		.127	–	63	8	8	1	8
Pitchers		.118	162	17	1	2	0	0
1997 Totals		**.244**	**162**	**5473**	**654**	**1333**	**147**	**627**

	Most Valuable Player	BBWAA Player of the Year
	CARLOS DELGADO	**CARLOS DELGADO**
	Most Valuable Pitcher	BBWAA Pitcher of the Year
	ROGER CLEMENS	**ROGER CLEMENS**
	Most Improved Player	BBWAA Rookie of the Year
	PAUL QUANTRILL	**JOSE CRUZ Jr.**

PITCHER	ERA	W-L	SV	G	IP	H	ER	BB	SO
ALMANZAR, Carlos	2.70	0-1	0	4	3.1	1	1	1	4
ANDUJAR, Luis	6.48	0-6	0	17	50.0	76	36	21	28
CARPENTER, Chris	5.09	3-7	0	14	81.1	108	46	37	55
CLEMENS, Roger	2.05	21-7	0	34	264.0	204	60	68	292
CRABTREE, Tim	7.08	3-3	2	37	40.2	65	32	17	26
DAAL, Omar	4.00	1-1	0	9	27.0	34	12	6	28
ESCOBAR, Kelvim	2.90	3-2	14	27	31.0	28	10	19	36
FLENER, Huck	9.87	0-1	0	8	17.1	40	19	6	9
GUZMAN, Juan	4.95	3-6	0	13	60.0	48	33	31	52
HANSON, Eric	7.80	0-0	0	3	15.0	15	13	6	18
HENTGEN, Pat	3.68	15-10	0	35	264.0	253	108	71	160
JANZEN, Marty	3.60	2-1	0	12	25.0	23	10	13	17
PERSON, Robert	5.61	5-10	0	23	128.1	125	80	60	99
PLESAC, Dan	3.58	2-4	1	73	50.1	47	20	19	61
QUANTRILL, Paul	1.94	6-7	5	77	88.0	103	19	17	56
RISLEY, Bill	8.31	0-1	0	3	4.1	3	4	2	2
ROBINSON, Ken	2.70	0-0	0	3	3.1	1	1	1	4
SPOLJARIC, Paul	3.19	0-3	3	37	48.0	37	17	36	70
TIMLIN, Mike	2.87	3-4	9	38	47.0	41	15	15	36
WILLIAMS, Woody	4.35	9-14	0	31	194.2	201	94	66	124
1997 Totals	**3.92**	**76-86**	**34**	**162**	**1442.2**	**1453**	**628**	**497**	**1150**

Carlos Delgado reached the 30-homer plateau for the first time in 1997.

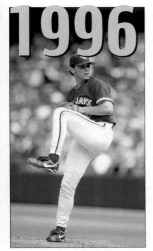

1996

Hentgen's Cy Young win highlights Jays' 20th season

Manager	W	L	Pct.	Pos.	GB	Attendance
Cito Gaston	**74**	**88**	**.457**	**4th**	**-18**	**2,559,563**

THE BLUE JAYS 20TH ANNIVERSARY season was highlighted by the performance of pitcher Pat Hentgen, who became the first Blue Jay to win the Cy Young Award. Hentgen posted a 20-10 record and led the A.L. with 10 complete games and 265.2 innings pitched. Third baseman Ed Sprague recorded career-best numbers, registering 36 home runs and driving in 101 runs, while Joe Carter rebounded from a sub-par 1995 season to top the 30 homer and 100 RBI plateaus for the ninth time in his career. Right-hander Juan Guzman also returned to the form that made him one of the junior circuit's top hurlers, leading the A.L. with a 2.93 ERA. Robert Perez led the team with a .327 average, while Jacob Brumfield supplied some well-needed punch to the offense by hitting 12 homers and delivering 52 RBIs. Youngsters like first baseman/DH Carlos Delgado, outfielder Shawn Green, and shortstop Alex Gonzalez showed both potential and improvement when they were given a chance to play every day. The result was an 18-win improvement over the club's 1995 record.

Pat Hentgen became the first Jay to capture the Cy Young Award.

BATTER	Pos.	Avg.	G	AB	R	H	HR	RBI
BRITO, Tilson	2B-SS	.238	26	80	10	19	1	7
BRUMFIELD, Jacob	OF-DH	.256	90	308	52	79	12	52
CAIRO, Miguel	2B	.222	9	27	5	6	0	1
CARTER, Joe	OF-1B-DH	.253	157	625	84	158	30	107
CEDENO, Domingo	2B-SS	.280	77	282	44	79	2	17
CRESPO, Felipe	IF	.184	22	49	6	9	0	4
DELGADO,Carlos	1B-DH	.270	138	488	68	132	25	92
GONZALEZ, Alex	SS	.235	147	527	64	124	14	64
GREEN, Shawn	OF	.280	132	422	52	118	11	45
HUFF, Mike	OF-3B	.172	11	29	5	5	0	0
MARTINEZ, Sandy	C	.227	76	229	17	52	3	18
MOSQUERA, Julio	C	.227	8	22	2	5	0	2
NIXON, Otis	OF	.286	125	496	87	142	1	29
O'BRIEN, Charlie	C	.238	109	324	33	77	13	44
OLERUD, John	1B-DH	.274	125	398	59	109	18	61
PEREZ, Robert	OF-DH	.327	86	202	30	66	2	21
PEREZ, Tomas	IF	.251	91	295	24	74	1	19
SAMUEL, Juan	DH-OF-1B	.255	69	188	34	48	8	26
SPRAGUE, Ed	3B-DH	.247	159	591	88	146	36	101
STEWART, Shannon	OF	.176	7	17	2	3	0	2
Designated Hitters		.260	162	628	95	163	32	109
Pinch Hitters		.204	–	113	15	23	2	14
1996 Totals		**.259**	**162**	**5599**	**766**	**1451**	**177**	**712**

Most Valuable Player	BBWAA Player of the Year
ED SPRAGUE	**ED SPRAGUE**
Most Valuable Pitcher	BBWAA Pitcher of the Year
PAT HENTGEN	**PAT HENTGEN**
Most Improved Player	BBWAA Rookie of the Year
JUAN GUZMAN	**PAUL SPOLJARIC**

PITCHER	ERA	W-L	SV	G	IP	H	ER	BB	SO
ANDUJAR, Luis	5.02	1-1	0	3	14.1	14	8	1	5
BOHANON, Brian	7.77	0-1	1	20	22.0	27	19	19	17
BROW, Scott	5.59	1-0	0	18	38.2	45	24	25	23
CARRARA, Giovanni	11.40	0-1	0	11	15.0	23	19	12	10
CASTILLO, Tony	4.23	2-3	1	40	72.1	72	34	20	48
CRABTREE, Tim	2.54	5-3	1	53	67.1	59	19	22	57
FLENER, Huck	4.58	3-2	0	15	70.2	68	36	33	44
GUZMAN, Juan	2.93	11-8	0	27	187.2	158	61	53	165
HANSON, Eric	5.41	13-17	0	35	214.2	243	129	102	156
HENTGEN, Pat	3.22	20-10	0	35	265.2	238	95	94	177
JANZEN, Marty	7.33	4-6	0	15	73.2	95	60	38	47
JOHNSON, Dane	3.00	0-0	0	10	9.0	5	3	5	7
QUANTRILL, Paul	5.43	5-14	0	38	134.1	172	81	51	86
RISLEY, Bill	3.89	0-1	0	25	41.2	33	18	25	29
SILVA, Jose	13.50	0-0	0	2	2.0	5	3	0	0
SPOLJARIC, Paul	3.08	2-2	1	28	38.0	30	13	19	38
TIMLIN, Mike	3.65	1-6	31	59	56.2	47	23	18	52
VIOLA, Frank	7.71	1-3	0	6	30.1	43	26	21	18
WARE, Jeff	9.09	1-5	0	13	32.2	35	33	31	11
WILLIAMS, Woody	4.73	4-5	0	12	59.0	64	31	21	43
1996 Totals	**4.57**	**74-88**	**35**	**162**	**1445.2**	**1476**	**734**	**610**	**1033**

Ed Sprague had a career year in 1996 with 36 homers and 101 RBIs.

Back to the drawing board: Jays look to rebuild

Manager	W	L	Pct.	Pos.	GB	Attendance
Cito Gaston	**56**	**88**	**.389**	**5th**	**-30**	**2,826,483**

DESPITE THE DISAPPOINTING RESULTS that were reflected in the standings, the 1995 season still featured its share of Blue Jays highlights. Joe Carter belted 25 HRs to lead the club in round-trippers for the fifth straight season while right-fielder Shawn Green set a club rookie record with 50 extra base hits. Freshman backstop Sandy Martinez jumped from AA to the major leagues in mid-season and led the team in RBIs in August. Southpaw Al Leiter posted career-highs in wins (11); ERA (3.64); innings pitched (183.0) and strikeouts (153). Domingo Cedeno and rookie Tomas Perez both helped solidify the defense and Ed Sprague (18 homers, 74 RBIs) emerged as a team leader and solid presence at third base. Also impressive was the resilience of left-hander Tony Castillo (3.22 ERA in 55 games) and the promising contributions of diminutive rookie pitcher Ken Robinson (3.69 ERA in 21 appearances) and split-finger special-ist Tim Crabtree (3.09 ERA in 31 appearances).

In his first full season as a Jay, Shawn Green hit 15 homers.

BATTER	Pos.	Avg.	G	AB	R	H	HR	RBI
ALOMAR, Roberto	2B	.300	130	517	71	155	13	66
BATTLE, Howard	3B	.200	9	15	3	3	0	0
CARTER, Joe	OF	.253	139	558	70	141	25	76
CEDENO, Domingo	SS-2B	.236	51	161	18	38	4	14
DELGADO, Carlos	OF-DH-1B	.165	37	91	7	15	3	11
GONZALEZ, Alex	SS	.243	111	367	51	89	10	42
GREEN, Shawn	OF	.288	121	379	52	109	15	54
HUFF, Michael	OF	.232	61	138	14	32	1	9
KNORR, Randy	C	.212	45	132	18	28	3	16
MALDONADO, Candy	OF	.269	61	160	22	43	7	25
MARTINEZ, Sandy	C	.241	62	191	12	46	2	25
MOLITOR, Paul	DH	.270	130	525	63	142	15	60
OLERUD, John	1B	.291	135	492	72	143	8	54
PARRISH, Lance	C	.202	70	178	15	36	4	22
PEREZ, Robert	OF	.188	17	48	2	9	1	3
PEREZ, Tomas	SS-2B	.245	41	98	12	24	1	8
SPRAGUE, Ed	3B	.244	144	521	77	127	18	74
STEWART, Shannon	OF	.211	12	38	2	8	0	1
WHITE, Devon	OF	.283	101	427	61	121	10	53
Designated Hitters		.262	144	584	68	153	16	69
Pinch Hitters		.192	–	73	6	14	1	8
1995 Totals		**.260**	**144**	**5036**	**642**	**1309**	**140**	**613**

PITCHER	ERA	W-L	SV	G	IP	H	ER	BB	SO
CARRARA, Giovanni	7.21	2-4	0	12	48.2	64	39	25	27
CASTILLO, Tony	3.22	1-5	13	55	72.2	64	26	24	38
CONE, David	3.38	9-6	0	17	130.1	113	49	41	102
CORNETT, Brad	9.00	0-0	0	5	5.0	9	5	3	4
COX, Danny	7.40	1-3	0	24	45.0	57	37	33	38
CRABTREE, Tim	3.09	0-2	0	31	32.0	30	11	13	21
DARWIN, Danny	7.62	1-8	0	13	65.0	91	55	24	36
GUZMAN, Juan	6.32	4-14	0	24	135.1	151	95	73	94
HALL, Darren	4.41	0-2	3	17	16.1	21	8	9	11
HENTGEN, Pat	5.11	10-14	0	30	200.2	236	114	90	135
HURTADO, Edwin	5.45	5-2	0	14	77.2	81	47	40	33
JORDAN, Ricardo	6.60	1-0	1	15	15.0	18	11	13	10
LEITER, Al	3.64	11-11	0	28	183.0	162	74	108	153
MENHART, Paul	4.92	1-4	0	21	78.2	72	43	47	50
ROBINSON, Ken	3.69	1-2	0	21	39.0	25	16	22	31
ROGERS, Jimmy	5.70	2-4	0	19	23.2	21	15	18	13
TIMLIN, Mike	2.14	4-3	5	31	42.0	38	10	17	36
WARD, Duane	27.00	0-1	0	4	2.2	11	8	5	3
WARE, Jeff	5.47	2-1	0	5	26.1	28	16	21	18
WILLIAMS, Woody	3.69	1-2	0	23	53.2	44	22	28	41
1995 Totals	**4.88**	**56-88**	**22**	**144**	**1292.2**	**1336**	**701**	**654**	**894**

Most Valuable Player	BBWAA Player of the Year
ROBERTO ALOMAR	**ROBERTO ALOMAR**
Most Valuable Pitcher	BBWAA Pitcher of the Year
AL LEITER	**AL LEITER**
Most Improved Player	BBWAA Rookie of the Year
ED SPRAGUE	**SHAWN GREEN**

Al Leiter led all Toronto starters with 11 wins and a 3.64 ERA.

1994

Jays improving when strike ends baseball season

Manager	W	L	Pct.	Pos.	GB	Attendance
Cito Gaston	**55**	**60**	**.478**	**3rd**	**-16**	**2,907,933**

THE 1994 BLUE JAYS STRUGGLED in May and June and finished under .500 for the first time since 1982. The club started strongly, thanks in large part to the efforts of two gifted sluggers. Carlos Delgado was an early-season sensation, tying a major-league rookie record with eight homers in April. World Series hero Joe Carter was also at his record-smashing best, establishing a new M.L. record with 31 RBIs in the first month of the campaign. While the Jays were setting individual milestones, the team struggled, winning just 18 games in the months of May and June combined. The club rebounded with 17 victories in July, but they were 16 games back when the season was halted due to a labour dispute. Inconsistency and injuries figured prominently in the team's disappointing result.

Rookie reliever Darren Hall saved 17 games for the Jays in 1994.

Veteran right-hander Juan Guzman struggled to find his control and bullpen ace Duane Ward injured his shoulder in spring training, underwent surgery and was lost for the season. Yet, in spite of the team's failure to finish above .500, there were numerous highlights. Veteran Paul Molitor hit .341. Mike Huff and Dick Schofield performed well, both in the field and at the plate. Pat Hentgen was named the Jays' Pitcher-of-the-Year, thanks to a team-leading 13 wins as well as an ERA of 3.40. The surprise of the season was the emergence of Darren Hall as the club's closer. The veteran minor leaguer recorded 17 saves to win team Rookie-of-the-Year honours.

BATTER	Pos.	Avg.	G	AB	R	H	HR	RBI
ALOMAR, Roberto	2B	.306	107	392	78	120	8	38
BORDERS, Pat	C	.247	85	295	24	73	3	26
BUTLER, Rob	OF	.176	41	74	13	13	0	5
CARTER, Joe	OF	.271	111	435	70	118	27	103
CEDENO, Domingo	2B-SS	.196	47	97	14	19	0	10
COLES, Darnell	OF-1B	.210	48	143	15	30	4	15
DELGADO, Carlos	OF	.215	43	130	17	28	9	24
GONZALEZ, Alex	SS	.151	15	53	7	8	0	1
GREEN, Shawn	OF	.091	14	33	1	3	0	1
HUFF, Mike	OF	.304	80	207	31	63	3	25
KNORR, Randy	C	.242	40	124	20	30	7	19
MOLITOR, Paul	DH	.341	115	454	86	155	14	75
OLERUD, John	1B	.297	108	384	47	114	12	67
PEREZ, Robert	OF	.125	4	8	0	1	0	0
SCHOFIELD, Dick	SS	.255	95	325	38	83	4	32
SPRAGUE, Ed	3B	.240	109	405	38	97	11	44
WHITE, Devon	OF	.270	100	403	67	109	13	49
Designated Hitters		.333	115	457	84	152	14	75
Pinch Hitters	.	.125	–	32	4	4	1	4
1994 Totals		**.269**	**115**	**3962**	**566**	**1064**	**115**	**534**

PITCHER	ERA	W-L	SV	G	IP	H	ER	BB	SO
BROW, Scott	5.90	0-3	2	18	29.0	34	19	19	15
CADARET, Greg	5.85	0-1	0	21	20.0	24	13	17	15
CASTILLO, Tony	2.51	5-2	1	41	68.0	66	19	28	43
CORNETT, Brad	6.68	1-3	0	9	31.0	40	23	11	22
COX, Danny	1.45	1-1	3	10	18.2	7	3	7	14
GUZMAN, Juan	5.68	12-11	0	25	147.1	165	93	76	124
HALL, Darren	3.41	2-3	17	30	31.2	26	12	14	28
HENTGEN, Pat	3.40	13-8	0	24	174.2	158	66	59	147
LEITER, Al	5.08	6-7	0	20	111.2	125	63	65	100
RIGHETTI, Dave	6.75	0-1	0	13	13.1	9	10	10	10
ST. CLAIRE, Randy	9.00	0-0	0	2	2.0	4	2	2	2
SMALL, Aaron	9.00	0-0	0	1	2.0	5	2	2	0
SPOLJARIC, Paul	38.57	0-1	0	2	2.1	5	10	9	2
STEWART, Dave	5.87	7-8	0	22	133.1	151	87	62	111
STOTTLEMYRE, Todd	4.22	7-7	1	26	140.2	149	66	48	105
TIMLIN, Mike	5.18	0-1	2	34	40.0	41	23	20	38
WILLIAMS, Woody	3.64	1-3	0	38	59.1	44	24	33	56
1994 Totals	**4.70**	**55-60**	**26**	**115**	**1025.0**	**1053**	**535**	**482**	**832**

Most Valuable Player	BBWAA Player of the Year
JOE CARTER	**JOE CARTER**
Most Valuable Pitcher	BBWAA Pitcher of the Year
PAT HENTGEN	**PAT HENTGEN**
Most Improved Player	BBWAA Rookie of the Year
RANDY KNORR	**DARREN HALL**

Pat Hentgen emerged as the staff ace, winning 13 games with an ERA of 3.40.

Sweet repeat:
Jays win second World Series

Manager	W	L	Pct.	Pos.	GB	Attendance
Cito Gaston	**95**	**67**	**.586**	**1st**	**+7**	**4,057,947**

THE BLUE JAYS became the first expansion team to win back-to-back World Series titles in 1993, downing the Chicago White Sox in the A.L. Championship Series before defeating the Philadelphia Phillies in six games to win their second world championship. Paul Molitor was brought in to replace the departed Dave Winfield and former Oakland ace Dave Stewart was signed to solidify the starting rotation. The Jays became the first team in modern baseball history to finish the season with a lineup that included the top three hitters in the League. John Olerud (.363), Paul Molitor (.332) and Robbie Alomar (.326) finished in that order. Joe Carter was as consistent as ever, hitting 33 homers and driving in 121 RBIs, and Tony Fernandez, brought aboard early in the season, hit .306. Eight Blue Jays drove home at least 50 runs. The pitching staff was anchored by Stewart and Jack Morris, but it was Pat Hentgen who emerged as the ace, winning 19 games. Juan Guzman was a marvellous 14-3 while Duane Ward established a new team record with 45 saves and an impressive ERA of 2.13.

World Series hero Joe Carter enjoys Canada's most famous home run trot.

BATTER	Pos.	Avg.	G	AB	R	H	HR	RBI
ALOMAR, Roberto	2B	.326	153	589	109	192	17	93
BORDERS, Pat	C	.254	138	488	38	124	9	55
BUTLER, Rob	OF	.271	17	48	8	13	0	2
CANATE, Willie	OF	.213	38	47	12	10	1	3
CARTER, Joe	OF	.254	155	603	92	153	33	121
CEDENO, Domingo	SS-2B	.174	15	46	5	8	0	7
COLES, Darnell	OF-3B	.253	64	194	26	49	4	26
DELGADO, Carlos	C	.000	2	1	0	0	0	0
FERNANDEZ, Tony	SS	.306	94	353	45	108	4	50
GREEN, Shawn	OF	.000	3	6	0	0	0	0
GRIFFIN, Alfredo	IF	.211	46	95	15	20	0	3
HENDERSON, Rickey	OF	.215	44	163	37	35	4	12
JACKSON, Darrin	OF	.216	46	176	15	38	5	19
KNORR, Randy	C	.248	39	101	11	25	4	20
MARTINEZ, Domingo	1B	.286	8	14	2	4	1	3
MOLITOR, Paul	DH-1B	.332	160	636	121	211	22	111
OLERUD, John	1B-DH	.363	158	551	109	200	24	107
SCHOFIELD, Dick	SS	.191	36	110	11	21	0	5
SOJO, Luis	IF	.170	19	47	5	8	0	6
SPRAGUE, Ed	3B	.260	150	546	50	142	12	73
WARD, Turner	OF	.192	72	167	20	32	4	28
WHITE, Devon	OF	.273	146	598	116	163	15	52
Designated Hitters		.308	162	639	116	197	20	101
Pinch Hitters		.185	–	27	1	5	1	5
1993 Totals		**.279**	**162**	**5579**	**847**	**1556**	**159**	**796**

PITCHER	ERA	W-L	SV	G	IP	H	ER	BB	SO
BROW, Scott	6.00	1-1	0	6	18.0	19	12	10	7
CASTILLO, Tony	3.38	3-2	0	51	50.2	44	19	22	28
COX, Danny	3.12	7-6	2	44	83.2	73	29	29	84
DAYLEY, Ken	0.00	0-0	0	2	0.2	1	0	4	2
EICHHORN, Mark	2.72	3-1	0	54	72.2	76	22	22	47
FLENER, Huck	4.05	0-0	0	6	6.2	7	3	4	2
GUZMAN, Juan	3.99	14-3	0	33	221.0	211	98	110	194
HENTGEN, Pat	3.87	19-9	0	34	216.1	215	93	74	122
LEITER, Al	4.11	9-6	2	34	105.0	93	48	56	66
LINTON, Doug	6.55	0-1	0	4	11.0	11	8	9	4
MORRIS, Jack	6.19	7-12	0	27	152.2	189	105	65	103
STEWART, Dave	4.44	12-8	0	26	162.0	146	80	72	96
STOTTLEMYRE, Todd	4.84	11-12	0	30	176.2	204	95	69	98
TIMLIN, Mike	4.69	4-2	1	54	55.2	63	29	27	49
WARD, Duane	2.13	2-3	45	71	71.2	49	17	25	97
WILLIAMS, Woody	4.38	3-1	0	30	37.0	40	18	22	24
1993 Totals	**4.21**	**95-67**	**50**	**162**	**1441.1**	**1441**	**674**	**620**	**1023**

Most Valuable Player	BBWAA Player of the Year
PAUL MOLITOR	**PAUL MOLITOR**

Most Valuable Pitcher	BBWAA Pitcher of the Year
DUANE WARD	**DUANE WARD**

Most Improved Player	BBWAA Rookie of the Year
JOHN OLERUD	**RANDY KNORR**

John Olerud (right), Paul Molitor (centre) and Robbie Alomar (left) finished 1-2-3 in the A.L. batting race.

1992

We can, we are, we will: Jays win World Series

Manager	W	L	Pct.	Pos.	GB	Attendance
Cito Gaston	**96**	**66**	**.593**	**1st**	**+4**	**4,028,318**

FROM THE START OF SPRING TRAINING, the Blue Jays focused on three objectives: to defend their A.L. East title ("We Can"), to capture their first American League pennant ("We Are"), and to win the World Series ("We Will"). Although the 1991 version of the Jays was a high quality team with all-stars at three positions, the squad still needed extra depth in four areas: defense, starting pitching, leadership and designated hitting. Veteran Alfredo Griffin was signed as infield insurance and Dave Winfield (.290, 108 RBIs), a respected leader with a potent bat, was inked to solidify the DH spot. Free agent Jack Morris (21-6), with two World Series rings to his credit, was the final piece of the puzzle. He went on to become the first 20-game winner in the history of the franchise. The Jays rolled through the regular season, gained a measure of revenge by ousting the Oakland A's in six games then became the first team outside the United States to win a World Series title with an exciting six-game series win over Atlanta. In addition to Winfield, the offensive heroes for the club were Joe Carter (34 HR, 119 RBIs), Robbie Alomar (.310, 76 RBIs), and Candy Maldonado (20 HR, 66 RBIs). Juan Guzman (16-5), Jimmy Key (13-13) and Todd Stottlemyre (12-11) all reached double digits in wins and the almost unstoppable tandem of Tom Henke and Duane Ward combined for 10 wins and 46 saves.

Duane Ward gives Candy Moldonado a victory ride after 1992 ALCS win.

BATTER	Pos.	Avg.	G	AB	R	H	HR	RBI
ALOMAR, Roberto	2B	.310	152	571	105	177	8	76
BELL, Derek	OF	.242	61	161	23	39	2	15
BORDERS, Pat	C	.242	138	480	47	116	13	53
CARTER, Joe	OF-DH	.264	158	622	97	164	34	119
DUCEY, Rob	OF-DH	.048	23	21	3	1	0	0
GRIFFIN, Alfredo	SS-2B	.233	63	150	21	35	0	10
GRUBER, Kelly	3B	.229	120	446	42	102	11	43
KENT, Jeff	IF	.240	65	192	36	46	8	35
KNORR, Randy	C	.263	8	19	1	5	1	2
LEE, Manuel	SS	.263	128	396	49	104	3	39
MAKSUDIAN, Mike	PH	.000	3	3	0	0	0	0
MALDONADO, Candy	OF	.272	137	489	64	133	20	66
MARTINEZ, Domingo	1B	.625	7	8	2	5	1	3
MULLINIKS, Rance	PH	.500	3	2	1	1	0	0
MYERS, Greg	C	.230	22	61	4	14	1	13
OLERUD, John	1B	.284	138	458	68	130	16	66
QUINLAN, Tom	3B	.067	13	15	2	1	0	2
SPRAGUE, Ed	C-IF	.234	22	47	6	11	1	7
TABLER, Pat	1B-OF	.252	49	135	11	34	0	16
WARD, Turner	OF	.345	18	29	7	10	1	3
WHITE, Devon	OF	.248	153	641	98	159	17	60
WINFIELD, Dave	DH-OF	.290	156	583	92	169	26	108
ZOSKY, Eddie	SS	.286	8	7	1	2	0	1
Designated Hitters		.267	162	619	95	165	29	112
Pinch Hitters		.273	–	55	8	15	0	9
1992 Totals		**.263**	**162**	**5536**	**780**	**1458**	**163**	**737**

PITCHER	ERA	W-L	SV	G	IP	H	ER	BB	SO
CONE, David	2.55	4-3	0	8	53.0	39	15	29	47
EICHHORN, Mark	4.35	2-0	0	23	31.0	35	15	7	19
GUZMAN, Juan	2.64	16-5	0	28	180.2	135	53	72	165
HENKE, Tom	2.26	3-2	34	57	55.2	40	14	22	46
HENGTEN, Pat	5.36	5-2	0	28	50.1	49	30	32	39
KEY, Jimmy	3.53	13-13	0	33	216.2	205	85	59	117
LEITER, Al	9.00	0-0	0	1	1.0	1	1	2	0
LINTON, Doug	8.63	1-3	0	8	24.0	31	23	17	16
MacDONALD, Bob	4.37	1-0	0	27	47.1	50	23	16	26
MORRIS, Jack	4.04	21-6	0	34	240.2	222	108	80	132
STIEB, Dave	5.04	4-6	0	21	96.1	98	54	43	45
STOTTLEMYRE, Todd	4.50	12-11	0	28	174.0	175	87	63	98
TIMLIN, Mike	4.12	0-2	1	26	43.2	45	20	20	35
TRLICEK, Ricky	10.80	0-0	0	2	1.2	2	2	2	1
WARD, Duane	1.95	7-4	12	79	101.1	76	22	39	103
WEATHERS, David	8.10	0-0	0	2	3.1	5	3	2	3
WELLS, David	5.40	7-9	2	41	120.0	138	72	36	62
1992 Totals	**3.91**	**96-66**	**49**	**162**	**1440.2**	**1346**	**626**	**541**	**954**

Most Valuable Player	BBWAA Player of the Year
ROBERTO ALOMAR	**ROBERTO ALOMAR**
Most Valuable Pitcher	BBWAA Pitcher of the Year
JACK MORRIS	**JACK MORRIS**
Most Improved Player	BBWAA Rookie of the Year
PAT BORDERS	**JEFF KENT**

Pumping his fist in delight, Ed Sprague celebrates his clutch pinch-hit homer in the second game of the World Series.

1991

New faces, record crowds and a third A.L. East crown

Manager	W	L	Pct.	Pos.	GB	Attendance
Cito Gaston	**91**	**71**	**.562**	**1st**	**+7**	**4,001,526**

IN A DRAMATIC REVERSAL OF STRATEGY, Pat Gillick completely rebuilt the roster of the Toronto Blue Jays with a flurry of off-season moves. He sent three players, including Junior Felix, to the California Angels for Devon White and Willie Fraser and then shocked all of baseball by sending Tony Fernandez and Fred McGriff to the San Diego Padres for Joe Carter and Roberto Alomar. The new additions helped the Jays win their third A.L. title, but once again the club faltered in the playoffs, losing in five games to the Minnesota Twins. The loss overshadowed the contributions of newcomer Juan Guzman (10-3), Robbie Alomar (.295, 53 steals), Joe Carter (33 HR, 108 RBIs), Tom Henke (32 saves) and Todd Stottlemyre (15-8, 219 innings, 3.78 ERA). Third baseman Ed Sprague, brought in to replace an injured Kelly Gruber, batted .391 in Gruber's absence, earning a full-time spot on the big club's roster for the remainder of the campaign.

Joe Carter lived up to his billing with 33 homers and 108 RBIs.

BATTER	Pos.	Avg.	G	AB	R	H	HR	RBI
ALOMAR, Roberto	2B	.295	161	637	88	188	9	69
BELL, Derek	OF	.143	18	28	5	4	0	1
BORDERS, Pat	C	.244	105	291	22	71	5	36
CARTER, Joe	OF	.273	162	638	89	174	33	108
DUCEY, Rob	OF	.235	39	68	8	16	1	4
GIANNELLI, Ray	3B	.167	9	24	2	4	0	0
GONZALES, Rene	IF	.195	71	118	16	23	1	6
GRUBER, Kely	3B	.252	113	429	58	108	20	65
HILL, Glenallen	DH-OF	.253	35	99	14	25	3	11
KNORR, Randy	C	.000	3	1	0	0	0	0
LEE, Manny	SS	.234	138	445	41	104	0	29
MALDONADO, Candy	OF	.277	52	177	26	49	7	28
MULLINIKS, Rance	DH	.250	97	240	27	60	2	24
MYERS, Greg	C	.262	107	309	25	81	8	36
OLERUD, John	1B	.256	139	454	64	116	17	68
PARKER, Dave	DH	.333	13	36	2	12	0	3
SNYDER, Cory	OF-1B	.143	21	49	4	7	0	6
SPRAGUE, Ed	3B-1B	.275	61	160	17	44	4	20
TABLER, Pat	DH-1B	.216	82	185	20	40	1	21
WARD, Turner	OF	.308	8	13	1	4	0	2
WHITE, Devon	OF	.282	156	642	110	181	17	60
WHITEN, Mark	OF	.221	46	149	12	33	2	19
WILLIAMS, Kenny	OF	.207	13	29	5	6	1	3
WILSON, Mookie	OF-DH	.241	86	241	26	58	2	28
ZOSKY, Eddie	SS	.148	18	27	2	4	0	2
Designated Hitters		.252	162	583	70	147	5	56
Pinch Hitters		.236	–	123	13	29	1	21
1991 Totals		**.257**	**162**	**5489**	**684**	**1412**	**133**	**649**

PITCHER	ERA	W-L	SV	G	IP	H	ER	BB	SO
ACKER, Jim	5.20	3-5	1	54	88.1	77	51	36	44
BOUCHER, Denis	4.58	0-3	0	7	35.1	39	18	16	16
CANDIOTTI, Tom	2.98	6-7	0	19	129.2	114	43	45	81
DAYLEY, Ken	6.23	0-0	0	8	4.1	7	3	5	3
FRASER, Willie	6.15	0-2	0	13	26.1	33	18	11	12
GUZMAN, Juan	2.99	10-3	0	23	138.2	98	46	66	123
HENKE, Tom	2.32	0-2	32	49	50.1	33	13	11	53
HENGTEN, Pat	2.45	0-0	0	3	7.1	5	2	3	3
HORSMAN, Vince	0.00	0-0	0	4	4.0	2	0	3	2
KEY, Jimmy	3.05	16-12	0	33	209.1	207	71	44	125
LEITER, Al	27.00	0-0	0	3	1.2	3	5	5	1
MacDONALD, Bob	2.85	3-3	0	45	53.2	51	17	25	24
STIEB, Dave	3.17	4-3	0	9	59.2	52	21	23	29
STOTTLEMYRE, Todd	3.78	15-8	0	34	219.0	194	92	75	116
TIMLIN, Mike	3.16	11-6	3	63	108.1	94	38	50	85
WARD, Duane	2.77	7-6	23	81	107.1	80	33	33	132
WEATHERS, David	4.91	1-0	0	15	14.2	15	8	17	13
WELLS, David	3.72	15-10	1	40	198.1	188	82	49	106
WESTON, Mickey	0.00	0-0	0	2	2.0	1	0	1	1
WILLS, Frank	16.62	0-1	0	4	4.1	8	8	5	2
1991 Totals	**3.50**	**91-71**	**60**	**162**	**1462.2**	**1301**	**569**	**523**	**971**

Labatt's Most Valuable Player	BBWAA Player of the Year
ROBERTO ALOMAR	**ROBERTO ALOMAR**
Labatt's Most Valuable Pitcher	BBWAA Pitcher of the Year
DUANE WARD	**DUANE WARD**
Most Improved Player	BBWAA Rookie of the Year
DEVON WHITE	**JUAN GUZMAN**

Righthander Juan Guzman came up from the minors to record 10 wins and a 2.99 ERA.

1990

September rally can't undo August slide

Manager	W	L	Pct.	Pos.	GB	Attendance
Cito Gaston	**86**	**76**	**.531**	**2nd**	**-2**	**3,885,284**

THE BLUE JAYS failed to defend their A.L. East title again by finishing in second place, two games behind the Boston Red Sox. The Jays were in first place in every month except August, when the club had its worst stretch of the season with eight losses in ten games. Still, the Jays managed to win 14 of their first 18 games in September and went into the final weekend of the season with a chance to win the division. Kelly Gruber had a career year, hitting 31 homers and delivering 118 RBIs. Fred McGriff reached the 30-homer plateau for the third straight season, finishing with 35. Young players John Olerud (14 homers, 48 RBIs) and Glenallen Hill (12 homers) each made fine contributions, while backstop Pat Borders set career highs in homers (15) and RBIs (49). The pitching staff was once again anchored by Dave Stieb, who won 18 games and recorded a sparkling 2.93 ERA. The southpaw combo of Jimmy Key (13-7) and David Wells (11-6) was augmented by Todd Stottlemyre, who won a career-high 13 games. Tom Henke and Duane Ward combined for 43 saves. The highlight of the season came on September 2, when Dave Stieb recorded the first no-hitter in Blue Jays history, a 3-0 win in front of a small crowd in Cleveland.

In the end, there were no excuses. The team simply didn't get the job done. And that meant changes.

Kelly Gruber was at home at third with a .274 average, 31 homers and 118 RBIs.

BATTER	Pos.	Avg.	G	AB	R	H	HR	RBI
BELL, George	OF-DH	.265	142	562	67	149	21	86
BORDERS, Pat	C	.286	125	346	36	99	15	49
DIAZ, Carlos	C	.333	9	3	1	1	0	0
DUCEY, Rob	OF	.302	19	53	7	16	0	7
EPPARD, Jim	PH	.200	6	5	0	1	0	0
FELIX, Junior	OF	.263	127	463	73	122	15	65
FERNANDEZ, Tony	SS	.276	161	635	84	175	4	66
GRUBER, Kelly	3B	.274	150	592	92	162	31	118
HILL, Glenallen	OF-DH	.231	84	260	47	60	12	32
LAWLESS, Tom	IF-OF	.083	15	12	1	1	0	1
LEE, Manny	2B	.243	117	391	45	95	6	41
LIRIANO, Nelson	2B	.212	50	170	16	36	1	15
McGRIFF, Fred	1B	.300	153	557	91	167	35	88
MULLINIKS, Rance	3B-DH	.289	57	97	11	28	2	16
MYERS, Greg	C	.236	87	250	33	59	5	22
OLERUD, John	DH-1B	.265	111	358	43	95	14	48
QUINLAN, Tom	3B	.500	1	2	0	1	0	0
SOJO, Luis	IF	.225	33	80	14	18	1	9
VIRGIL, Ozzie	C-DH	.000	3	5	0	0	0	0
WHITEN, Mark	OF	.273	33	88	12	24	2	7
WILLIAMS, Kenny	OF-DH	.194	49	72	13	14	0	8
WILSON, Mookie	OF	.265	147	588	81	156	3	51
Designated Hitters		.220	162	604	68	133	14	68
Pinch-Hitters		.216		97	4	21	0	14
1990 Totals		**.265**	**162**	**5589**	**767**	**1479**	**167**	**729**

PITCHER	ERA	W-L	SV	G	IP	H	ER	BB	SO
ACKER, Jim	3.83	4-4	1	59	91.2	103	39	30	54
BLACK, Bud	4.02	2-1	0	3	15.2	10	7	3	3
BLAIR, Willie	4.06	3-5	0	27	68.2	66	31	28	43
CANDELARIA, John	5.48	0-3	1	13	21.1	32	13	11	19
CERUTTI, John	4.76	9-9	0	30	140.0	162	74	49	49
CUMMINGS, Steve	5.11	0-0	0	6	12.1	22	7	5	4
FLANAGAN, Mike	5.31	2-2	0	5	20.1	28	12	8	5
GILLES, Tom	6.75	1-0	0	2	1.1	2	1	0	1
HENKE, Tom	2.17	2-4	32	61	74.2	58	18	19	75
KEY, Jimmy	4.25	13-7	0	27	154.2	169	73	22	88
KILGUS, Paul	6.06	0-0	0	11	16.1	19	11	7	7
LEITER, Al	0.00	0-0	0	4	6.1	1	0	2	5
LUECKEN, Rick	9.00	0-0	0	1	1.0	2	1	1	0
MacDONALD, Bob	0.00	0-0	0	4	2.1	0	0	2	0
STIEB, Dave	2.93	18-6	0	33	208.2	179	68	64	125
STOTTLEMYRE, Todd	4.34	13-17	0	33	203.0	214	98	69	115
WARD, Duane	3.45	2-8	11	73	127.2	101	49	42	112
WELLS, David	3.14	11-6	0	43	189.0	165	66	45	115
WILLS, Frank	4.73	6-4	0	44	99.0	101	52	38	72
1990 Totals	**3.84**	**86-76**	**48**	**162**	**1454.0**	**1434**	**620**	**445**	**892**

Labatt's Most Valuable Player	BBWAA Player of the Year
KELLY GRUBER	**KELLY GRUBER**
Labatt's Most Valuable Pitcher	BBWAA Pitcher of the Year
DAVE STIEB	**DAVE STIEB**
Most Improved Player	BBWAA Rookie of the Year
PAT BORDERS	**JOHN OLERUD**

Dave Stieb, 18-6 during the season, pitched a no-hitter against Cleveland.

1989

Hot when it counts, Jays win A.L. East by 2 games

Manager	W	L	Pct.	Pos.	GB	Attendance
Jimy Williams	**12**	**24**	**.333**			
Cito Gaston	**77**	**49**	**.611**			
Total	**89**	**73**	**.549**	**1st**	**+2**	**3,375,883**

THE TORONTO BLUE JAYS won their second A.L. East Division crown in 1989, enduring a slow start and a managerial change before putting together a strong second half. A serious injury to Tony Fernandez and a lack of clutch hitting left the Jays 12-24 in mid-May. Manager Jimy Williams was dismissed and replaced by batting coach Cito Gaston. The club responded immediately and started climbing the ladder to the top. A key moment in the season came during a three-game sweep of the Boston Red Sox, when the Jays rebounded from a 10-run deficit to win in extra innings. Exciting newcomers included Junior Felix (46 RBIs), Glenallen Hill (.288) and key mid-season acquisitions Mookie Wilson and Lee Mazzilli, all of whom helped carry the team to the title. George Bell rebounded from a sub-par 1988 season to drive in 104 runs while Fred McGriff finsihed with 36 homers. Dave Stieb was the ace of the staff again with a 3.35 ERA and a team-high 17 wins. Newcomers David Wells (7-4, 2.40), Todd Stottlemyre (7-7, 3.88) and Frank Wills (3-1) combined with the tandem of Tom Henke and Duane Ward (35 saves between them) to give the Jays a powerful bullpen. However, the Jays were no match for the powerhouse Oakland Athletics in the A.L. Championship Series. The A's used speed, power and an intimidating brand of baseball to cruise past the Jays in five games.

Tom Henke saved 20 games for the Blue Jays in 1989.

BATTER	Pos.	Avg.	G	AB	R	H	HR	RBI
BARFIELD, Jesse	OF	.200	21	80	8	16	5	11
BATISTE, Kevin	OF	.250	6	8	1	2	0	0
BELL, George	OF	.297	153	613	88	182	18	104
BORDERS, Pat	C-DH	.257	94	241	22	62	3	29
BRENLY, Bob	DH-C	.170	48	88	9	15	1	6
CABRERA, Francisco	DH	.167	3	12	1	2	0	0
DUCEY, Rob	OF	.211	41	76	5	16	0	7
FELIX, Junior	OF	.258	110	415	62	107	9	46
FERNANDEZ, Tony	SS	.257	140	573	64	147	11	64
GRUBER, Kelly	3B	.290	135	545	83	158	18	73
HILL, Glenallen	OF	.288	19	52	4	15	1	7
INFANTE, Alexis	IF	.167	20	12	1	2	0	0
LAWLESS, Tom	OF-IF	.229	59	70	20	16	0	3
LEE, Manny	IF	.260	99	300	27	78	3	34
LIRIANO, Nelson	2B	.263	132	418	51	110	5	53
MAZZILLI, Lee	DH-1B	.227	28	66	12	15	4	11
McGRIFF, Fred	1B	.269	161	551	98	148	36	92
MOSEBY, Lloyd	OF	.221	135	502	72	111	11	43
MULLINIKS, Rance	DH-3B	.238	103	273	25	65	3	29
MYERS, Greg	C-DH	.114	17	44	0	5	0	1
OLERUD, John	1B	.375	6	8	2	3	0	0
VIRGIL, Ozzie	DH-C	.182	9	11	2	2	1	2
WHITT, Ernie	C	.262	129	385	42	101	11	53
WILSON, Mookie	OF	.298	54	238	32	71	2	17
Designated Hitters		.216	162	589	66	127	8	55
Pinch-Hitters		.264	–	121	14	32	3	13
1989 Totals		**.260**	**162**	**5581**	**731**	**1449**	**142**	**685**

PITCHER	ERA	W-L	SV	G	IP	H	ER	BB	SO
ACKER, Jim	1.59	2-1	0	14	28.1	24	5	12	24
BUICE, DeWayne	5.82	1-0	0	7	17.0	13	11	13	10
CASTILLO, Tony	6.11	1-1	1	17	17.2	23	12	10	10
CERUTTI, John	3.07	11-11	0	33	205.1	214	70	53	69
CUMMINGS, Steve	3.00	2-0	0	5	21.0	18	7	11	8
FLANAGAN, Mike	3.93	8-10	0	30	171.2	186	75	47	47
GOZZO, Mauro	4.83	4-1	0	9	31.2	35	17	9	10
HENKE, Tom	1.92	8-3	20	64	89.0	66	19	25	116
HERNANDEZ, Xavier	4.76	1-0	0	7	22.2	25	12	8	7
KEY, Jimmy	3.88	13-14	0	33	216.0	226	93	27	118
LEITER, Al	4.05	0-0	0	1	6.2	9	3	2	4
MUSSELMAN, Jeff	10.64	0-1	0	5	11.0	19	13	9	3
NUNEZ, Jose	2.53	0-0	0	6	10.2	8	3	2	14
SANCHEZ, Alex	10.03	0-1	0	4	11.2	16	13	14	4
STIEB, Dave	3.35	17-8	0	33	206.2	164	77	76	101
STOTTLEMYRE, Todd	3.88	7-7	0	27	127.2	137	55	44	63
WARD, Duane	3.77	4-10	15	66	114.2	94	48	58	122
WELLS, David	2.40	7-4	2	54	86.1	66	23	28	78
WILLS, Frank	3.66	3-1	0	24	71.1	65	29	30	41
1989 Totals	**3.58**	**89-73**	**38**	**162**	**1467.0**	**1408**	**584**	**478**	**849**

Labatt's	BBWAA
Most Valuable Player	Player of the Year
GEORGE BELL	**GEORGE BELL**
Labatt's	BBWAA
Most Valuable Pitcher	Pitcher of the Year
DAVE STIEB	**TOM HENKE**
Most Improved Player	BBWAA Rookie of the Year
TODD STOTTLEMYRE	**JUNIOR FELIX**

Junior Felix hit the first major-league pitch he ever saw over the fence for a home run.

1988

Late-season streak sees Jays finish two back

Manager	W	L	Pct.	Pos.	GB	Attendance
Jimy Williams	**87**	**75**	**.537**	**T-3rd**	**-2**	**2,595,175**

A SLOW START that saw the club win only nine of its first 22 games played a key role in the Jays' third place finish in 1988. On almost every other level, the Jays had an exceptional year. The club led the league in home runs (158), triples (47) and slugging percentage (.419). The pitching staff also had a marvellous season, leading the league with 17 shutouts and a nifty 3.80 team ERA. Dave Stieb, who became the first pitcher in league history to lose back-to-back no-hitters with two outs in the ninth inning, rebounded to win 16 games and record an ERA of 3.04. Jimmy Key was superb once again, notching 12 wins and a 3.29 ERA, while another lefthander, Mike Flanagan, went 13-13 in his first full season as a Blue Jay. Tom Henke saved 25 games and was deftly assisted by Duane Ward, whose wicked slider helped him record 15 saves. On the offensive side of the ledger, the Jays had two new emerging stars. First baseman Fred McGriff produced 34 homers while third baseman Kelly Gruber knocked out 16 HRs and added 81 RBIs. In the outfield, George Bell, Jesse Barfield and Lloyd Moseby continued to produce, combining for 52 homers and 195 RBIs.

Reliever Duane Ward recorded 15 saves and nine victories in 1988.

BATTER	Pos.	Avg.	G	AB	R	H	HR	RBI
BARFIELD, Jesse	OF	.244	137	468	62	114	18	56
BELL, George	OF	.269	156	614	78	165	24	97
BENIQUEZ, Juan	DH	.293	27	58	9	17	1	8
BORDERS, Pat	C	.273	56	154	15	42	5	21
BUTERA, Sal	C	.233	23	60	3	14	1	6
CAMPUSANO, Sil	OF	.218	73	142	14	31	2	12
DUCEY, Rob	OF	.315	27	54	15	17	0	6
FERNANDEZ, Tony	SS	.287	154	648	76	186	5	70
FIELDER, Cecil	DH-1B	.230	74	174	24	40	9	23
GRUBER, Kelly	3B	.278	158	569	75	158	16	81
INFANTE, Alexis	IF	.200	19	15	7	3	0	0
LEACH, Rick	OF	.276	87	199	21	55	0	23
LEE, Manny	2B-SS	.291	116	381	38	111	2	38
LIRIANO, Nelson	2B	.264	99	276	36	73	3	23
McGRIFF, Fred	1B	.282	154	536	100	151	34	82
MOSEBY, Lloyd	OF	.239	128	472	77	113	10	42
MULLINIKS, Rance	DH	.300	119	337	49	101	12	48
THORNTON, Lou	OF	.000	11	2	1	0	0	0
WHITT, Ernie	C	.251	127	398	63	100	16	70
Designated Hitters		.288	162	612	90	176	25	95
Pinch-Hitters		.202	–	129	14	26	2	18
1988 Totals		**.268**	**162**	**5557**	**763**	**1491**	**158**	**706**

PITCHER	ERA	W-L	SV	G	IP	H	ER	BB	SO
BAIR, Doug	4.05	0-0	0	10	13.1	14	6	3	8
CASTILLO, Tony	3.00	1-0	0	14	15.0	10	5	2	14
CERUTTI, John	3.13	6-7	1	46	123.2	120	43	42	65
CLANCY, Jim	4.49	11-13	1	36	196.1	207	98	47	118
EICHHORN, Mark	4.19	0-3	1	37	66.2	79	31	27	28
FLANAGAN, Mike	4.18	13-13	0	34	211.0	220	98	80	99
HENKE, Tom	2.91	4-4	25	52	68.0	60	22	24	66
KEY, Jimmy	3.29	12-5	0	21	131.1	127	48	30	65
MUSSELMAN, Jeff	3.18	8-5	0	15	85.0	80	30	30	39
NUNEZ, Jose	3.07	0-1	0	13	29.1	28	10	17	18
ROSS, Mark	4.91	0-0	0	3	7.1	5	4	4	4
STIEB, Dave	3.04	16-8	0	32	207.1	157	70	79	147
STOTTLEMYRE, Todd	5.69	4-8	0	28	98.0	109	62	46	67
WARD, Duane	3.30	9-3	15	64	111.2	101	41	60	91
WELLS, David	4.62	3-5	4	41	64.1	65	33	31	56
WILLS, Frank	5.23	0-0	0	10	20.2	22	12	6	19
1988 Totals	**3.80**	**87-75**	**47**	**162**	**1449.0**	**1404**	**611**	**528**	**904**

Labatt's Most Valuable Player	BBWAA Player of the Year
FRED McGRIFF	**FRED McGRIFF**
Labatt's Most Valuable Pitcher	BBWAA Pitcher of the Year
DAVE STIEB	**DAVE STIEB**
Most Improved Player	BBWAA Rookie of the Year
KELLY GRUBER	**PAT BORDERS**

Fred McGriff's sweet stroke enabled him to hit 34 homers in 1988.

Duel with Detroit
sees Jays a close second

Manager	W	L	Pct.	Pos.	GB	Attendance
Jimy Williams	**96**	**66**	**.593**	**2nd**	**-2**	**2,778,459**

IN THE MOST EXCITING STRETCH RUN in franchise history, the Blue Jays and Detroit Tigers battled through seven gripping one-run games before the Tigers edged out the Jays for the 1987 A.L. East crown. The Jays, who won the first three games of a late season home-and-home series with Detroit, ended up losing their last seven games, four of which were against the Tigers. Key season-ending injuries to Tony Fernandez and Ernie Whitt played a large role in the club's collapse. Still, it was one of the greatest campaigns in club history. George Bell became the first Blue Jay to win the American League MVP award, setting team records with 47 homers and 134 RBIs. Lloyd Moseby also had a career year with 26 HRs and 96 RBIs. Rookie first sacker Fred McGriff knocked out 20 home runs and Jesse Barfield added another 28 HRs and 84 RBIs. The rookie sensation of the season was southpaw Jeff Musselman, who won 12 games and added three saves. In total, six different pitchers won at least 10 games. In addition to Musselman, Jimmy Key (17-8), Jim Clancy (15-11), Dave Stieb (13-9), John Cerutti (11-4) and Mark Eichhorn (10-6) all reached double figures in wins. The highlight of the season came on September 14 when the Jays established a major league record by hitting 10 home runs in a game against Baltimore.

George Bell became the first Blue Jays player named A.L. MVP.

	Labatt's		BBWAA
	Most Valuable Player		Player of the Year
	GEORGE BELL		**GEORGE BELL**
	Labatt's		BBWAA
	Most Valuable Pitcher		Pitcher of the Year
	JIMMY KEY		**JIMMY KEY**
	Most Improved		BBWAA
	Player		Rookie of the Year
	LLOYD MOSEBY		**JEFF MUSSELMAN**

BATTER	Pos.	Avg.	G	AB	R	H	HR	RBI
BARFIELD, Jesse	OF	.263	159	590	89	155	28	84
BELL, George	OF	.308	156	610	111	188	47	134
BENIQUEZ, Juan	DH-OF	.284	39	81	6	23	5	21
DEWILLIS, Jeff	C	.120	13	25	2	3	1	2
DUCEY, Rob	OF	.188	34	48	12	9	1	6
FERNANDEZ, Tony	SS	.322	146	578	90	186	5	67
FIELDER, Cecil	DH-1B	.269	82	175	30	47	14	32
GRUBER, Kelly	3B-SS	.235	138	341	50	80	12	36
INFANTE, Alexis	PR	.000	1	0	0	0	0	0
IORG, Garth	2B-3B	.210	122	310	35	65	4	30
LEACH, Rick	OF-DH	.282	98	195	26	55	3	25
LEE, Manny	2B-SS	.256	56	121	14	31	1	11
LIRIANO, Nelson	2B	.241	37	158	29	38	2	10
McGRIFF, Fred	DH-1B	.247	107	295	58	73	20	43
MOORE, Charlie	C	.215	51	107	15	23	1	7
MOSEBY, Lloyd	OF	.282	155	592	106	167	26	96
MULLINIKS, Rance	3B-DH	.310	124	332	37	103	11	44
MYERS, Greg	C	.111	7	9	1	1	0	0
SHARPERSON, Mike	2B	.208	32	96	4	20	0	9
STARK, Matt	C	.083	5	12	0	1	0	0
THORNTON, Lou	DH-OF	.500	12	2	5	1	0	0
UPSHAW, Willie	1B	.244	150	512	68	125	15	58
WHITT, Ernie	C	.269	135	446	57	120	19	75
Designated Hitters		.258	162	592	101	153	38	97
Pinch-Hitters		.234	–	167	0	39	3	28
1987 Totals		**.269**	**162**	**5635**	**845**	**1514**	**215**	**790**

PITCHER	ERA	W-L	SV	G	IP	H	ER	BB	SO
CERUTTI, John	4.40	11-4	0	44	151.1	144	74	59	92
CLANCY, Jim	3.54	15-11	0	37	241.1	234	95	80	180
EICHHORN, Mark	3.17	10-6	4	89	127.2	110	45	52	96
FLANAGAN, Mike	2.37	3-2	0	7	49.1	46	13	15	43
GORDON, Don	4.09	0-0	0	5	11.0	8	5	3	3
HENKE, Tom	2.49	0-6	34	72	94.0	62	26	25	128
JOHNSON, Joey	5.13	3-5	0	14	66.2	77	38	18	27
KEY, Jimmy	2.76	17-8	0	36	261.0	210	80	66	161
LAVELLE, Gary	5.53	2-3	1	23	27.2	36	17	19	17
MUSSELMAN, Jeff	4.15	12-5	3	68	89.0	75	41	54	54
NIEKRO, Phil	8.25	0-2	0	3	12.0	15	11	7	7
NUNEZ, Jose	5.01	5-2	0	37	97.0	91	54	58	99
STIEB, Dave	4.09	13-9	0	33	185.0	164	84	87	115
WARD, Duane	6.94	1-0	0	12	11.2	14	9	12	10
WELLS, David	3.99	4-3	1	18	29.1	37	13	12	32
1987 Totals	**3.74**	**96-66**	**43**	**162**	**1454.0**	**1323**	**605**	**567**	**1064**

Silky-smooth Jimmy Key won 17 games and compiled a 2.76 ERA in 1987.

1986

All-Star performances but a slow start hurts

Manager	W	L	Pct.	Pos.	GB	Attendance
Jimy Williams	**86**	**76**	**.531**	**4th**	**-9.5**	**2,445,477**

THE JAYS ENTERED THE 1986 SEASON with a new manager and a new goal: to defend their A.L. East title. Third base coach Jimy Williams replaced Bobby Cox, but the club was slow to respond to their new skipper. Despite all-star performances from Jesse Barfield, George Bell and Tony Fernandez, the club finished in fourth place. Barfield and Bell both had career years, with Bell slugging 31 homers and Barfield setting a team record with an A.L. leading 40 of his own. Both men established new club marks with 108 RBIs. Tony Fernandez, a wizard with the glove, was a magician with the bat as well, hitting .310 with a team-record 213 hits. While the position players all had sterling seasons, the pitching staff went through a difficult campaign. Dave Stieb (7-12) failed to win ten games, Jim Clancy (14-14) lost his last seven decisions and Doyle Alexander (5-4) was dispatched to Atlanta for Duane Ward. Only Jimmy Key (14-11, 3.57 ERA) managed to match his performance of the previous campaign. There were

Mark Eichhorn's unusual pitching style helped him win 14 games for the Blue Jays in 1986.

some fine performances from the bullpen staff. Tom Henke saved a team-record 27 games, lefty John Cerutti went 9-4 and submarine-styled rookie Mark Eichhorn won team Pitcher-of-the-Year honours by winning 14 games and compiling a 1.72 ERA.

BATTER	Pos.	Avg.	G	AB	R	H	HR	RBI
BARFIELD, Jesse	OF	.289	158	589	107	170	40	108
BELL, George	OF	.309	159	641	101	198	31	108
FERNANDEZ, Tony	SS	.310	163	687	91	213	10	65
FIELDER, Cecil	DH-1B	.157	34	83	7	13	4	13
GARCIA, Damaso	2B	.281	122	424	57	119	6	46
GRUBER, Kelly	IF	.196	87	143	20	28	5	15
HEARRON, Jeff	C	.217	12	23	2	5	0	4
IORG, Garth	3B-2B	.260	137	327	30	85	3	44
JOHNSON, Cliff	DH	.250	107	336	48	84	15	55
LEACH, Rick	DH-OF	.309	110	246	35	76	5	39
LEE, Manny	2B-SS	.205	35	78	8	16	1	7
MARTINEZ, Buck	C	.181	81	160	13	29	2	12
McGRIFF, Fred	1B-DH	.200	3	5	1	1	0	0
MOSEBY, Lloyd	OF	.253	152	589	89	149	21	86
MULLINIKS, Rance	3B	.259	117	348	50	90	11	45
SHEPHERD, Ron	OF	.203	65	69	16	14	2	4
UPSHAW, Willie	1B	.251	155	573	85	144	9	60
WHITT, Ernie	C	.268	131	395	48	106	16	56
Designated Hitters		.242	162	616	86	149	20	83
Pinch-Hitters		.277	–	155	19	43	4	32
1986 Totals		**.269**	**163**	**5716**	**809**	**1540**	**181**	**767**

PITCHER	ERA	W-L	SV	G	IP	H	ER	BB	SO
ACKER, Jim	4.35	2-4	0	23	60.0	63	29	22	32
ALEXANDER, Doyle	4.46	5-4	0	17	111.0	120	55	20	65
AQUINO, Luis	6.35	1-1	0	7	11.1	14	8	3	5
CAUDILL, Bill	6.19	2-4	2	40	36.1	36	25	17	32
CERUTTI, John	4.15	9-4	1	34	145.1	150	67	47	89
CLANCY, Jim	3.94	14-14	0	34	219.1	202	96	63	126
CLARKE, Stan	9.24	0-1	0	10	12.2	18	13	10	9
DAVIS, Steve	17.18	0-0	0	3	3.2	8	7	5	5
EICHHORN, Mark	1.72	14-6	10	69	157.0	105	30	45	166
GORDON, Don	7.06	0-1	1	14	21.2	28	17	8	13
HENKE, Tom	3.35	9-5	27	63	91.1	63	34	32	118
JOHNSON, Joe	3.89	7-2	0	16	88.0	94	38	22	39
KEY, Jimmy	3.57	14-11	0	36	232.0	222	92	74	141
LAMP, Dennis	5.05	2-6	2	40	73.0	93	41	23	30
MAHLER, Mickey	0.00	0-0	0	2	1.0	1	0	0	0
MUSSELMAN, Jeff	10.13	0-0	0	6	5.1	8	6	5	4
STIEB, Dave	4.74	7-12	1	37	205.0	239	108	87	127
WARD, Duane	13.50	0-1	0	2	2.0	3	3	4	1
1986 Totals	**4.08**	**86-76**	**44**	**163**	**1476.0**	**1467**	**669**	**487**	**1002**

Labatt's Most Valuable Player **GEORGE BELL**	BBWAA Player of the Year **JESSE BARFIELD**
Labatt's Most Valuable Pitcher **JIMMY KEY**	BBWAA Pitcher of the Year **MARK EICHHORN**
Most Improved Player **RICK LEACH**	

Jesse Barfield's bullet outfield arm and powerful stroke made him a fan favourite.

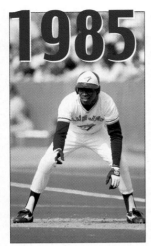

1985

A dream season: 99 wins and a championship

Manager	W	L	Pct.	Pos.	GB	Attendance
Bobby Cox	**99**	**62**	**.615**	**1st**	**+2**	**2,468,925**

THE TORONTO BLUE JAYS won their first American League East Division Championship on October 5, 1985 when Doyle Alexander pitched a complete game to beat the New York Yankees 5-1. They finished the season with 99 wins but lost a hard fought seven-game A.L. championship series to the Kansas City Royals.

In the off-season, the Jays attempted to improve their bullpen, trading Alfredo Griffin and Dave Collins to Oakland for bullpen ace Bill Caudill. Tony Fernandez replaced Griffin at shortstop and he responded by batting .289 and playing airtight defense. Jesse Barfield and George Bell were a potent 1-2 combo at the plate, combining to hit 55 home runs and drive in 179 runs. Once again, the club had four pitchers with at least 10 wins. Doyle Alexander topped the staff with 17 victories, while Dave Stieb (14-13), Jimmy Key (14-6) and reliever Dennis Lamp (11-0) all recorded key wins during the championship run. Stieb's 2.48 ERA was the lowest mark in the American League. The most surprising performance of the season was delivered by Tom Henke, who came up from the farm in mid-season and recorded 13 saves and a 2.03 ERA. Jim Acker chipped in with seven wins and 10 saves, while the third base tandem of Rance Mulliniks and Garth Iorg combined for 17 homers and 94 RBIs.

Smooth in the field and an effective baserunner, Tony Fernandez electrified fans.

BATTER	Pos.	Avg.	G	AB	R	H	HR	RBI
AIKENS, Willie	DH	.200	12	20	2	4	1	5
ALLENSON, Gary	C	.118	14	34	2	4	0	3
BARFIELD, Jesse	OF	.289	155	539	94	156	27	84
BELL, George	OF	.275	157	607	87	167	28	95
BURROUGHS, Jeff	DH	.257	86	191	19	49	6	28
FERNANDEZ, Tony	SS	.289	161	564	71	163	2	51
FIELDER, Cecil	1B	.311	30	74	6	23	4	16
GARCIA, Damaso	2B	.282	146	600	70	169	8	65
GRUBER, Kelly	3B	.231	5	13	0	3	0	1
HEARRON, Jeff	C	.143	4	7	0	1	0	0
IORG, Garth	3B-2B	.313	131	288	33	90	7	37
JOHNSON, Cliff	DH-1B	.274	24	73	4	20	1	10
LEACH, Rick	1B-OF	.200	16	35	2	7	0	1
LEE, Manny	IF	.200	64	40	9	8	0	0
MARTINEZ, Buck	C	.162	42	99	11	16	4	14
MATUSZEK, Len	DH-1B	.212	62	151	23	32	2	15
MOSEBY, Lloyd	OF	.259	152	584	92	151	18	70
MULLINIKS, Rance	3B	.295	129	366	55	108	10	57
NICOSIA, Steve	C	.267	6	15	0	4	0	1
OLIVER, Al	DH	.251	61	187	20	47	5	23
SHEPHERD, Ron	OF-DH	.114	38	35	7	4	0	1
THORNTON, Lou	OF-DH	.236	56	72	18	17	1	8
UPSHAW, Willie	1B	.275	148	501	79	138	15	65
WEBSTER, Mitch	OF-DH	.000	4	1	0	0	0	0
WHITT, Ernie	C	.245	139	412	55	101	19	64
Designated Hitters		.247	161	600	77	148	13	78
Pinch-Hitters		.222	–	167	18	37	4	29
1985 Totals		**.269**	**161**	**5508**	**759**	**1482**	**158**	**714**

	Labatt's	BBWAA
	Most Valuable Player	Player of the Year
	JESSE BARFIELD	**JESSE BARFIELD**
	Labatt's	BBWAA
	Most Valuable Pitcher	Pitcher of the Year
	DAVE STIEB	**DENNIS LAMP**
	Most Improved Player	
	DENNIS LAMP	

PITCHER	ERA	W-L	SV	G	IP	H	ER	BB	SO
ACKER, Jim	3.23	7-2	10	61	86.1	86	31	43	42
ALEXANDER, Doyle	3.45	17-10	0	36	260.2	268	100	67	142
CAUDILL, Bill	2.99	4-6	14	67	69.1	53	23	35	46
CERUTTI, John	5.40	0-2	0	4	6.2	10	4	4	5
CLANCY, Jim	3.78	9-6	0	23	128.2	117	54	37	66
CLARKE, Stan	4.50	0-0	0	4	4.0	3	2	2	2
DAVIS, Steve	3.54	2-1	0	10	28.0	23	11	13	22
FILER, Tom	3.88	7-0	0	11	48.2	38	21	18	24
HENKE, Tom	2.03	3-3	13	28	40.0	29	9	8	42
KEY, Jimmy	3.00	14-6	0	35	212.2	188	71	50	85
LAMP, Dennis	3.32	11-0	2	53	105.2	96	39	27	68
LAVELLE, Gary	3.10	5-7	8	69	72.2	54	25	36	50
LEAL, Luis	5.75	3-6	0	15	67.1	82	43	24	33
MUSSELMAN, Ron	4.47	3-0	0	25	52.1	59	26	24	29
STIEB, Dave	2.48	14-13	0	36	265.0	206	73	96	167
1985 Totals	**3.29**	**99-62**	**47**	**161**	**1448.0**	**1312**	**529**	**484**	**823**

Dennis Lamp never tasted defeat in 1985, rolling to a perfect 11-0 record.

1984

Unstoppable Tigers conceal Jays' strong season

Manager	W	L	Pct.	Pos.	GB	Attendance
Bobby Cox	**89**	**73**	**.549**	**2nd**	**-15**	**2,110,009**

THE TORONTO BLUE JAYS made a number of off-season moves in an attempt to improve the depth of their bullpen, which had been a key factor in their late-season collapse in 1983. The club signed free agent closer Dennis Lamp and sent Barry Bonnell to Seattle for left-hander Bryan Clark. Unfortunately, neither pitcher lived up to expectations. Lamp was inconsistent, finishing with an 8-8 record, nine saves and a 4.55 ERA. Clark tossed only 45.2 innings and registered an ERA of 5.91.

In hindsight, there was little the Jays could have done in 1984. The Detroit Tigers won 35 of their first 40 games and easily cruised to the Division crown. Despite bullpen troubles, the Jays did have a productive season, winning 89 games and climbing to second place in the A.L. East standings. George Bell established himself as the team's offensive leader, stroking 26 homers and driving in 87 runs. Speedy Dave Collins set a club record with 60 stolen bases while Lloyd Moseby continued to provide the team with tight defense and timely offense, matching a career-high with 18 home runs and a club-high 92 RBIs. Doyle Alexander was the ace of the pitching staff, tossing 11 complete games on his way to a 17-6 season with a sparkling ERA of 3.13. Dave Stieb (16-8, 2.83), Luis Leal (13-8, 3.89) and Jim Clancy (13-15, 5.12) all reached double digits in victories. Savvy rookie southpaw Jimmy Key set a Jays rookie record with 10 saves, a total matched by Roy Lee Jackson.

Doyle Alexander topped all Jays starters with 17 wins in 1984.

BATTER	Pos.	Avg.	G	AB	R	H	HR	RBI
AIKENS, Willie	DH	.205	93	234	21	48	11	26
BARFIELD, Jesse	OF	.284	110	320	51	91	14	49
BELL, George	OF	.292	159	606	85	177	26	87
COLLINS, Dave	OF	.308	128	441	59	136	2	44
FERNANDEZ, Tony	SS	.270	88	233	29	63	3	19
GARCIA, Damaso	2B	.284	152	633	79	180	5	46
GRIFFIN, Alfredo	SS-2B	.241	140	419	53	101	4	30
GRUBER, Kelly	3B	.063	15	16	1	1	1	2
HERNANDEZ, Toby	C	.500	3	2	1	1	0	0
IORG, Garth	3B	.227	121	247	24	56	1	25
JOHNSON, Cliff	DH	.304	127	359	51	109	16	61
LEACH, Rick	OF-1B	.261	65	88	11	23	0	7
MANRIQUE, Fred	2B	.333	10	9	0	3	0	1
MARTINEZ, Buck	C	.220	102	232	24	51	5	37
MOSEBY, Lloyd	OF	.280	158	592	97	166	18	92
MULLINIKS, Rance	IF	.324	125	343	41	111	3	42
PETRALLI, Geno	C	.000	3	3	0	0	0	0
SHEPHERD, Ron	OF	.000	12	4	0	0	0	0
UPSHAW, Willie	1B	.278	152	569	79	158	19	84
WEBSTER, Mitch	OF	.227	26	22	9	5	0	4
WHITT, Ernie	C	.238	124	315	35	75	15	46
Designated Hitters		.270	163	612	91	165	27	93
Pinch-Hitters		.284	–	215	29	61	6	39
1984 Totals		**.273**	**163**	**5687**	**750**	**1555**	**143**	**702**

PITCHER	ERA	W-L	SV	G	IP	H	ER	BB	SO
ACKER, Jim	4.38	3-5	1	32	72.0	79	35	25	33
ALEXANDER, Doyle	3.13	17-6	0	36	261.2	238	91	59	139
CLANCY, Jim	5.12	13-15	0	36	219.2	249	125	88	118
CLARK, Bryan	5.91	1-2	0	20	45.2	66	30	22	21
GOTT, Jim	4.02	7-6	2	35	109.2	93	49	49	73
JACKSON, Roy Lee	3.56	7-8	10	54	86.0	73	34	31	58
KEY, Jimmy	4.65	4-5	10	63	62.0	70	32	32	44
LAMP, Dennis	4.55	8-8	9	56	85.0	97	43	38	45
LEACH, Rick	27.00	0-0	0	1	1.0	2	3	2	0
LEAL, Luis	3.89	13-8	0	35	222.1	221	96	77	134
McLAUGHLIN, Joey	2.53	0-0	0	6	10.2	12	3	7	3
MUSSELMAN, Ron	2.11	0-2	1	11	21.1	18	5	10	9
STIEB, Dave	2.83	16-8	0	35	267.0	215	84	88	198
1984 Totals	**3.86**	**89-73**	**33**	**162**	**1464.0**	**1433**	**628**	**528**	**875**

Labatt's Most Valuable Player GEORGE BELL	BBWAA Player of the Year DAVE COLLINS
Labatt's Most Valuable Pitcher DAVE STIEB	BBWAA Pitcher of the Year DOYLE ALEXANDER
Most Improved Player DAVE COLLINS	BBWAA Rookie of the Year TONY FERNANDEZ

On August 5, Cliff Johnson hit his 19th career pinch home run to set a Major League record.

1983

Maturing Jays leave the cellar behind

Manager	W	L	Pct.	Pos.	GB	Attendance
Bobby Cox	**89**	**73**	**.549**	**4th**	**-9**	**1,930,415**

THE TORONTO BLUE JAYS became contenders in 1983, and much of Canada was gripped by Blue Jays fever in July and August. The Jays were fuelled by speed, timely hitting, strong defense and three excellent starting pitchers. The DH tandem of Jorge Orta and Cliff Johnson combined to hit 32 home runs and drive in 114 runs. Lloyd Moseby clicked on all cylinders, hitting .315, scoring 104 runs, stealing 27 bases, all while showing respectable power with 18 homers. Newcomer Dave Collins and Damaso Garcia both burned up the base paths, swiping 31 bases each to share the team lead. Willie Upshaw emerged as a top offensive weapon, clouting 27 home runs and becoming the first Jay to reach the century mark in RBIs by plating a team-record 104 runners. The terrific trio of Dave

\Willie Upshaw became the first Blue Jay to drive in 100 runs.

Stieb (17-12), Jim Clancy (15-11) and Luis Leal (13-12) continued to build on the momentum they had established the previous summer. Dave Stieb's 3.04 ERA established him as one of the top pitchers in the majors and set a new team record. Crafty Doyle Alexander, acquired by general manager Pat Gillick after he had been released by the Yankees, regained his confidence and control and reeled off six straight wins as the season drew to a close. Randy Moffitt saved 10 games and compiled a nifty 6-2 record to lead the bullpen crew. If there was one glaring weakness on the club, it was in the late innings where the Jays lacked an effective closer. The hunt for a ninth inning go-to pitcher was the main item on the Jays' summer shopping list.

BATTER	Pos.	Avg.	G	AB	R	H	HR	RBI
BARFIELD, Jesse	OF	.253	128	388	58	98	27	68
BELL, George	OF	.268	39	112	5	30	2	17
BONNELL, Barry	OF	.318	121	377	49	120	10	54
COLLINS, Dave	OF	.271	118	402	55	109	1	34
FERNANDEZ, Tony	SS	.265	15	34	5	9	0	2
GARCIA, Damaso	2B	.307	131	525	84	161	3	38
GRIFFIN, Alfredo	SS	.250	162	528	62	132	4	47
IORG, Garth	3B-2B	.275	122	375	40	103	2	39
JOHNSON, Cliff	DH	.265	142	407	59	108	22	76
KLUTTS, Mickey	3B	.256	22	43	3	11	3	5
MARTINEZ, Buck	C	.253	88	221	27	56	10	33
MOSEBY, Lloyd	OF	.315	151	539	104	170	18	81
MULLINIKS, Rance	3B-SS	.275	129	364	54	100	10	49
ORTA, Jorge	DH-OF	.237	103	245	30	58	10	38
PETRALLI, Geno	C	.000	6	4	0	0	0	0
POWELL, Hosken	OF	.169	40	83	6	14	1	7
UPSHAW, Willie	1B	.306	160	579	99	177	27	104
WEBSTER, Mitch	OF	.182	11	11	2	2	0	0
WHITT, Ernie	C	.256	123	344	53	88	17	56
Designated Hitters		.250	162	604	86	151	34	113
Pinch-Hitters		.290	–	200	26	58	5	42
1983 Totals		**.277**	**162**	**5581**	**795**	**1546**	**167**	**748**

PITCHER	ERA	W-L	SV	G	IP	H	ER	BB	SO
ACKER, Jim	4.33	5-1	1	38	97.2	103	47	38	44
ALEXANDER, Doyle	3.93	7-6	0	17	116.2	126	51	26	46
CLANCY, Jim	3.91	15-11	0	34	223.0	238	97	61	99
CLARKE, Stan	3.27	1-1	0	10	11.0	10	4	5	7
COOPER, Don	6.75	0-0	0	4	5.1	8	4	0	5
GEISEL, Dave	4.64	0-3	5	47	52.1	47	27	31	50
GOTT, Jim	4.74	9-14	0	34	176.2	195	93	68	121
JACKSON, Roy Lee	4.50	8-3	7	49	92.0	92	46	41	48
LEAL, Luis	4.31	13-12	0	35	217.1	216	104	65	116
McLAUGHLIN, Joey	4.45	7-4	9	50	64.2	63	32	37	47
MOFFITT, Randy	3.77	6-2	10	45	57.1	52	24	24	38
MORGAN, Mike	5.16	0-3	0	16	45.1	48	26	21	22
STIEB, Dave	3.04	17-12	0	36	278.0	223	94	93	187
WILLIAMS, Matt	14.63	1-1	0	4	8.0	13	13	7	5
1983 Totals	**4.12**	**89-73**	**32**	**162**	**1445.1**	**1434**	**662**	**517**	**835**

Labatt's Player of the Year	BBWAA Player of the Year
LLOYD UPSHAW WILLIE UPSHAW	WILLIE UPSHAW
Labatt's Pitcher of the Year	BBWAA Pitcher of the Year
DAVE STIEB	DAVE STIEB
Most Improved Player	BBWAA Rookie of the Year
LLOYD MOSEBY	JIM ACKER

Skipper Bobby Cox used an innovative platoon system to help the Jays finish above .500.

1982

Cox's platooning Jays on verge of contention

Manager	W	L	Pct.	Pos.	GB	Attendance
Bobby Cox	**78**	**84**	**.481**	**T-6th**	**-17**	**1,275,978**

A NEW MANAGER and a new attitude combined to give the Blue Jays their best-ever record and a taste of life outside the basement. Bobby Cox, former skipper of the Atlanta Braves, came aboard and immediately started molding the club in his image. Cox was an expert strategist who decided to use a platoon system at third base and behind the plate. Rance Mulliniks and Garth Iorg split the hot corner while Buck Martinez and Ernie Whitt shared duties behind the plate. Although rising new stars like first baseman Willie Upshaw (21 homers, 75 RBIs) and Jesse Barfield (18 homers, 58 RBIs) more than compensated for the departed John Mayberry, the real story of the Jays success in 1982 was on the mound. The club's ERA was a shining 3.95, with three hurlers, Luis Leal (12-15, 3.98), Jim Clancy (16-14, 3.71) and Dave Stieb (17-14, 3.25) reaching double digits in wins. Down in the bullpen, Dale Murray got the bulk of the work, appearing in a team-high 56 games and collecting 11 saves. The offense was sparked by Damaso Garcia, who stole 58 bases and batted a lofty .310, and Jesse Barfield, who had a strong arm and a sweet swing. Barfield's 15 outfield assists were the second most in the league. The Jays' 78 wins tied Cleveland for sixth place. The table was set for a wild ride through the 1980s.

Dale Murray was the Jays' bullpen ace in 1982, collecting 11 saves.

BATTER	Pos.	Avg.	G	AB	R	H	HR	RBI
ADAMS, Glenn	DH	.258	30	66	2	17	1	11
BAKER, Dave	3B	.250	9	20	3	5	0	2
BARFIELD, Jesse	OF	.246	139	394	54	97	18	58
BONNELL, Barry	OF	.293	140	437	59	128	6	49
DAVIS, Dick	OF-DH	.286	3	7	0	2	0	2
GARCIA, Damaso	2B	.310	147	597	89	185	5	42
GRIFFIN, Alfredo	SS	.241	162	539	57	130	1	48
HERNANDEZ, Pedro	3B	.000	8	9	1	0	0	0
IORG, Garth	3B-2B	.285	129	417	45	119	1	36
JOHNSON, Anthony	OF-DH	.235	70	98	17	23	3	14
MARTINEZ, Buck	C	.242	96	260	26	63	10	37
MAYBERRY, John	DH-1B	.273	17	33	7	9	2	3
MOSEBY, Lloyd	OF	.236	147	487	51	115	9	52
MULLINIKS, Rance	3B-SS	.244	112	311	32	76	4	35
NORDHAGEN, Wayne	DH-OF	.270	72	185	12	50	1	20
PETRALLI, Geno	C	.364	16	44	3	16	0	1
POWELL, Hosken	OF-DH	.275	112	265	43	73	3	26
REVERING, Dave	DH	.215	55	135	15	29	5	18
ROBERTS, Leon	OF-DH	.229	40	105	6	24	1	5
UPSHAW, Willie	1B	.267	160	580	77	155	21	75
VELEZ, Otto	DH	.192	28	52	4	10	1	5
WHITT, Ernie	C	.261	105	284	28	74	11	42
WOODS, Al	OF	.234	85	201	20	47	3	24
Designated Hitters		.238	162	596	52	142	8	56
Pinch-Hitters		.271	–	262	24	71	4	53
1982 Totals		**.262**	**162**	**5526**	**651**	**1447**	**106**	**605**

PITCHER	ERA	W-L	SV	G	IP	H	ER	BB	SO
BOMBACK, Mark	6.03	1-5	0	16	59.2	87	40	25	22
CLANCY, Jim	3.71	16-14	0	40	266.2	251	110	77	139
EICHHORN, Mark	5.45	0-3	0	7	38.0	40	23	14	16
GARVIN, Jerry	7.25	1-1	0	32	58.1	81	47	26	35
GEISEL, Dave	3.98	1-1	0	16	31.2	32	14	17	22
GOTT, Jim	4.43	5-10	0	30	136.0	134	67	66	82
JACKSON, Roy Lee	3.06	8-8	6	48	97.0	77	33	31	71
LEAL, Luis	3.93	12-15	0	38	249.2	250	109	79	111
McLAUGHLIN, Joey	3.21	8-6	8	44	70.0	54	25	30	49
MURRAY, Dale	3.16	8-7	11	56	111.0	115	39	32	60
SCHROM, Ken	5.87	1-0	0	6	15.1	13	10	15	8
SENTENEY, Steve	4.91	0-0	0	11	22.0	23	12	6	20
STIEB, Dave	3.25	17-14	0	38	288.1	271	104	75	141
1982 Totals	**3.95**	**78-84**	**25**	**162**	**1443.2**	**1428**	**633**	**493**	**776**

Labatt's Player of the Year **DAMASO GARCIA**	BBWAA Player of the Year **DAMASO GARCIA**
Labatt's Pitcher of the Year **DAVE STIEB**	BBWAA Pitcher of the Year **DAVE STIEB**
Most Improved Player **JIM CLANCY**	BBWAA Rookie of the Year **JESSE BARFIELD**

Second baseman Damaso Garcia led all Jays' with a .310 average and 185 hits.

1981

A split season
see the Jays turn it around

Manager	W	L	Pct.	Pos.	GB	Attendance
Bob Matick	**16**	**42**	**.276**	**7th**	**-19**	
(split season)	21	27	.438	7th	-7.5	755,083

Roy Lee Jackson nailed down seven saves in 1981.

IN A SEASON SPLIT IN TWO by a player's strike, the Jays combined the worst start and the strongest finish in the club's five-year history. Dave Stieb became the Jays' first regular starter to win more games than he lost, completing the campaign with an 11-10 record and a glittering ERA of 3.19. Although Jim Clancy struggled much of the season, righthander Luis Leal picked up the slack with a respectable 7-13 record and a fine 3.68 ERA. Joey McLaughlin anchored the bullpen by recording 10 saves and compiling a tidy 2.85 ERA. Roy Lee Jackson, acquired from the New York Mets for Bob Bailor, was solid as well, nailing down seven saves and an ERA of 2.61. Many of the faces that would go on to lead the Jays for the rest of the decade made appearances during this campaign. George Bell, Jesse Barfield, Lloyd Moseby, Ernie Whitt and Garth Iorg all saw playing time with the club. John Mayberry continued to be the club's top offensive star, leading the team with 17 homers while sharing the RBI lead with the flashy Moseby. The pieces were being put in place and the Blue Jays were about to leave the nest.

BATTER	Pos.	Avg.	G	AB	R	H	HR	RBI
AINGE, Danny	3B	.187	86	246	20	46	0	14
BARFIELD, Jesse	OF	.232	25	95	7	22	2	9
BEAMON, Charlie	DH-1B	.200	8	15	1	3	0	0
BELL, George	OF	.233	60	163	19	38	5	12
BONNELL, Barry	OF	.220	66	227	21	50	4	28
BOSETTI, Rick	OF	.234	25	47	5	11	0	4
COX, Ted	3B	.300	16	50	6	15	2	9
GARCIA, Damaso	2B	.252	64	250	24	63	1	13
GRIFFIN, Alfredo	SS	.209	101	388	30	81	0	21
IORG, Garth	2B-3B	.242	70	215	17	52	0	10
MACHA, Ken	3B-1B	.200	37	85	4	17	0	6
MANRIQUE, Fred	IF	.143	14	28	1	4	0	1
MARTINEZ, Buck	C	.227	45	128	13	29	4	21
MAYBERRY, John	1B	.248	94	290	34	72	17	43
MOSEBY, Lloyd	OF	.233	100	378	36	88	9	43
STIEB, Dave	PR	.000	1	0	1	0	0	0
UPSHAW, Willie	DH-1B-OF	.171	61	111	15	19	4	10
VELEZ, Otto	DH	.213	80	240	32	51	11	28
WELLS, Greg	1B-DH	.247	32	73	7	18	0	5
WHITMER, Dan	C	.111	7	9	0	1	0	0
WHITT, Ernie	C	.236	74	195	16	46	1	16
WOODS, Al	OF	.247	85	288	20	71	1	21
Designated Hitters		.212	106	363	45	77	13	36
Pinch-Hitters		.234	–	77	4	18	1	15
1981 Totals		**.226**	**106**	**3521**	**329**	**797**	**61**	**314**

PITCHER	ERA	W-L	SV	G	IP	H	ER	BB	SO
BARLOW, Mike	4.20	0-0	0	12	15.0	22	7	6	5
BERENGUER, Juan	4.31	2-9	0	12	71.0	62	34	35	29
BOMBACK, Mark	3.89	5-5	0	20	90.1	84	39	35	33
CLANCY, Jim	4.90	6-12	0	22	125.0	126	68	64	56
ESPINOSA, Nino	9.00	0-0	0	1	1.0	4	1	0	0
GARVIN, Jerry	3.40	1-2	0	35	53.0	46	20	23	25
JACKSON, Roy Lee	2.61	1-2	7	39	62.0	65	18	25	27
LEAL, Luis	3.68	7-13	1	29	129.2	127	53	44	71
McLAUGHLIN, Joey	2.85	1-5	10	40	60.0	55	19	21	38
MIRABELLA, Paul	7.36	0-0	0	8	14.2	20	12	7	9
MURRAY, Dale	1.17	1-0	0	11	15.1	12	2	5	12
STIEB, Dave	3.19	11-10	0	25	183.2	148	65	61	89
TODD, Jackson	3.96	2-7	0	21	97.2	94	43	31	41
WILLIS, Mike	5.91	0-4	0	20	35.0	43	23	20	16
1981 Totals	**3.81**	**37-69**	**18**	**106**	**953.1**	**908**	**404**	**377**	**451**

Labatt's Player of the Year	BBWAA Player of the Year
DAVE STIEB	DAVE STIEB

Labatt's Pitcher of the Year	BBWAA Pitcher of the Year
DAVE STIEB	DAVE STIEB

Most Improved Player
JOEY McLAUGHLIN

In only his third season as a M.L. pitcher, Dave Stieb fashioned an 11-10 record for the Jays.

1980

A new manager and the best season yet

Manager	W	L	Pct.	Pos.	GB	Attendance
Bob Mattick	**67**	**95**	**.414**	**7th**	**-36**	**1,400,327**

BOBBY MATTICK, the Jay's scouting supervisor, was selected as the team's new manager and the club responded with a franchise-best 67 victories. John Mayberry and Otto Velez were the team's top offensive weapons, with Big John becoming the first Jays slugger to notch 30 home runs. Second baseman Damaso Garcia, who came over from the New York Yankees, proved to be a solid addition to the inner defense, forming a top-notch double play tandem with Alfredo Griffin. Alvis Woods hit a team-high .300 while Barry Bonnell stroked 13 homers and plated 56 runners. The greatest improvement for the Jays was on the mound, where both Dave Stieb and Jim Clancy proved themselves to be among the league's top hurlers. Clancy rebounded from an injury-plagued 1979 campaign to win 13 games while Stieb collected 12 victories and a 3.71 ERA. Jerry Garvin was the top arm in the bullpen, saving eight games while recording a glowing 2.29 ERA.

Classy Jim Clancy tied a team record with 13 victories in 1980.

BATTER	Pos.	Avg.	G	AB	R	H	HR	RBI
AINGE, Danny	OF-IF	.243	38	111	11	27	0	4
AULT, Doug	1B-DH	.194	64	144	12	28	3	15
BAILOR, Bob	OF-IF	.236	117	347	44	82	1	16
BONNELL, Barry	OF	.268	130	463	55	124	13	56
BOSETTI, Rick	OF	.213	53	188	24	40	4	18
BRAUN, Steve	PH-DH	.273	37	55	4	15	1	9
CANNON, J.J.	PR-OF	.080	70	50	16	4	0	4
DAVIS, Bob	C	.216	91	218	18	47	4	19
GARCIA, Damaso	2B	.278	140	543	50	151	4	46
GRIFFIN, Alfredo	SS	.254	155	653	63	166	2	41
HODGSON, Paul	OF	.220	20	41	5	9	1	5
HOWELL, Roy	3B	.269	142	528	51	142	10	57
IORG, Garth	IF	.248	80	222	24	55	2	14
KELLY, Pat	C	.286	3	7	0	2	0	0
MACHA, Mike	3B-C	.000	5	8	0	0	0	0
MAYBERRY, John	1B	.248	149	501	62	124	30	82
MOSEBY, Lloyd	OF	.229	114	389	44	89	9	46
RAMOS, Domingo	IF	.125	5	16	0	2	0	0
STIEB, Dave	P-OF	.000	1	1	0	0	0	0
UPSHAW, Willie	1B-DH	.213	34	61	10	13	1	5
VELEZ, Otto	DH	.269	104	357	54	96	20	62
WHITT, Ernie	C	.237	106	295	23	70	6	34
WOODS, Al	OF	.300	109	373	54	112	15	47
Designated Hitters		.229	162	599	73	137	22	84
Pinch-Hitters		.280	–	100	10	28	3	15
1980 Totals		**.251**	**162**	**5571**	**624**	**1398**	**126**	**580**

PITCHER	ERA	W-L	SV	G	IP	H	ER	BB	SO
BAILOR, Bob	7.71	0-0	0	3	2.1	4	2	1	0
BARLOW, Mike	4.09	3-1	5	40	55.0	57	25	21	19
BUSKEY, Tom	4.46	3-1	0	33	66.2	68	33	26	34
CLANCY, Jim	3.30	13-16	0	34	250.2	217	92	128	152
GARVIN, Jerry	2.29	4-7	8	61	82.2	70	21	27	52
JEFFERSON, Jesse	5.47	4-13	0	29	121.2	130	74	52	53
KUCEK, Jack	6.75	3-8	1	23	68.0	83	51	41	35
LEAL, Luis	4.53	3-4	0	13	59.2	72	30	31	26
LEMANCZYK, Dave	5.40	2-5	0	10	43.1	57	26	15	10
McLAUGHLIN, Joey	4.51	6-9	4	55	135.2	159	68	53	70
MIRABELLA, Paul	4.34	5-12	0	33	130.2	151	63	66	53
MOORE, Balor	5.29	1-1	0	7	64.2	76	38	31	22
SCHROM, Ken	5.23	1-0	1	17	31.0	32	18	19	13
STIEB, Dave	3.71	12-15	0	34	242.2	232	100	83	108
TODD, Jackson	4.02	5-2	0	12	85.0	90	38	30	44
WILLIS, Mike	1.71	2-1	3	20	26.1	25	5	11	14
1980 Totals	**4.19**	**67-95**	**23**	**162**	**1466.1**	**1523**	**683**	**635**	**705**

Labatt's Player of the Year	BBWAA Player of the Year
JOHN MAYBERRY	**JOHN MAYBERRY**

Labatt's Pitcher of the Year	BBWAA Pitcher of the Year
JIM CLANCY	**JIM CLANCY**

BBWAA Rookie of the Year
DAMASO GARCIA

Big John Mayberry became the first Jays' slugger to hit 30 homers in a season.

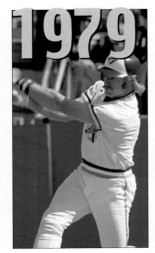

Youthful Jays: talent in the wings

Manager	W	L	Pct.	Pos.	GB	Attendance
Roy Hartsfield	**53**	**109**	**.327**	**7th**	**-50.5**	**1,431,651**

SHORTSTOP ALFREDO GRIFFIN, acquired from Cleveland for Victor Cruz, was a defensive wizard with a deft glove and quick bat for the Jays in 1979. Griffin's .287 average, 179 hits and 21 stolen bases were tops on the club and helped him win a share of the American League's Rookie-of-the-Year Award. Big John Mayberry was the team's top offensive power, leading the team in homers (21) and RBIs (74). Roy Howell established career-highs in home runs (15) and RBIs (72) while outfielder Otto Velez proved to be a pleasant surprise with a .288 average, 15 homers and 48 RBIs. Rick Cerone became the club's number-one catcher, appearing in 136 games and driving home 61 RBIs. The pitching staff was anchored by Tom Underwood (9-16) and a brash newcomer named Dave Stieb (8-8), who was 5-0 in "A" ball and 5-2 in "AAA" before earning his promotion to the big club. Stieb made it all the way to the major leagues less than a year after being converted from an outfielder to a pitcher.

Roy Howell was solid at third and at the plate, driving in 72 runs.

BATTER	Pos.	Avg.	G	AB	R	H	HR	RBI
AINGE, Danny	2B	.237	87	308	26	73	2	19
BAILOR, Bob	OF-3B	.229	130	414	50	95	1	38
BOSETTI, Rick	OF	.260	162	619	59	161	8	65
BROWN, Bobby	OF	.000	4	10	1	0	0	0
CANNON, J.J.	OF	.211	61	142	14	30	1	5
CARTY, Rico	DH	.256	132	461	48	118	12	55
CERONE, Rick	C	.239	136	469	47	112	7	61
DAVIS, Bob	C	.124	32	89	6	11	1	8
GOMEZ, Luis	IF	.239	59	163	11	39	0	11
GRIFFIN, Alfredo	SS	.287	153	624	81	179	2	31
HERNANDEZ, Pedro	PR	.000	3	0	1	0	0	0
HOWELL, Roy	3B	.247	138	511	60	126	15	72
JOHNSON, Tim	IF	.186	43	86	6	16	0	6
KUSICK, Craig	1B	.204	24	54	3	11	2	7
MAYBERRY, John	1B	.274	137	464	61	127	21	74
McKAY, Dave	2B	.218	47	156	19	34	0	12
ROBERTSON, Bob	1B	.103	15	29	1	3	1	1
SOLAITA, Tony	DH-1B	.265	36	102	14	27	2	13
VELEZ, Otto	OF	.288	99	274	45	79	15	48
WILBORN, Ted	OF	.000	22	12	3	0	0	0
WOODS, Al	OF	.278	132	436	57	121	5	36
Designated Hitters		.260	162	599	70	156	18	82
Pinch-Hitters		.231	–	52	5	12	4	14
1979 Totals		**.251**	**162**	**5423**	**613**	**1362**	**95**	**562**

Labatt's Player of the Year	BBWAA Player of the Year
ALFREDO GRIFFIN	**ALFREDO GRIFFIN**
Labatt's Pitcher of the Year	BBWAA Pitcher of the Year
TOM UNDERWOOD	**TOM UNDERWOOD**

PITCHER	ERA	W-L	SV	G	IP	H	ER	BB	SO
BUSKEY, Tom	3.43	6-10	7	44	78.2	74	30	25	44
CLANCY, Jim	5.51	2-7	0	12	63.2	65	39	31	33
EDGE, Butch	5.23	3-4	0	9	51.2	60	30	24	19
FREISLEBEN, Dave	4.95	2-3	3	42	91.0	101	50	53	35
GARVIN, Jerry	2.78	0-1	0	8	22.2	15	7	10	14
GRILLI, Steve	0.00	0-0	0	1	2.1	1	0	0	1
HUFFMAN, Phil	5.77	6-18	0	31	173.0	220	111	68	56
JEFFERSON, Jesse	5.51	2-10	1	34	116.0	150	71	45	43
KUSICK, Craig	4.91	0-0	0	1	3.2	3	2	0	0
LEMANCZYK, Dave	3.71	8-10	0	22	143.0	137	59	45	63
LEMONGELLO, Mark	6.29	1-9	0	18	83.0	97	58	34	40
LUEBBER, Steve	INF	0.00	0-0	0	1	0.0	2	1	1	0
MILLER, Dyar	10.57	0-0	0	10	15.1	27	18	5	7
MOORE, Balor	4.84	5-7	0	34	139.1	135	75	79	51
MURPHY, Tom	5.40	1-2	0	10	18.1	23	11	8	6
STIEB, Dave	4.31	8-8	0	18	129.1	139	62	48	52
TODD, Jackson	5.85	0-1	0	12	32.1	40	21	7	14
UNDERWOOD, Tom	3.69	9-16	0	33	227.0	213	93	95	127
WILLIS, Mike	8.44	0-3	0	17	26.2	35	25	16	8
1979 Totals	**4.81**	**53-109**	**11**	**162**	**1417.0**	**1537**	**758**	**594**	**613**

Alfredo Griffin is still the only Blue Jay to be named American League Rookie-of-the-Year.

1978

Player changes help but wins still scarce

Manager	W	L	Pct.	Pos.	GB	Attendance
Roy Hartsfield	**59**	**102**	**.366**	**7th**	**-40**	**1,562,585**

TWO EXPERIENCED HITTERS – Rico Carty and John Mayberry – joined the Jays for the 1978 season. Although each reached the 20 HR plateau and combined to drive in 138 runs, the team was outscored by 185 runs over the course of the campaign. There was marginal improvement as the Jays won 59 games, four more than they did in their opening season. Rookie centerfielder Rick Bosetti, whose laser-like arm nailed 17 opposition runners attempting to take an extra base, established what would prove to be a Jays tradition of fast, young outfielders. The infield was anchored by third baseman Roy Howell, who belted eight homers and drove in 61 runs. Boppin' Bob Bailor drove in 52 runs while backstop Alan Ashby captured the club's Most Improved Player award with his consistent play behind the plate. On the mound, Jim Clancy was the top starter in the rotation, winning 10 games with a modest 4.09 ERA. Victor Cruz was the bullpen ace, saving nine games, winning another seven with a sparkling 1.71 ERA.

Rico "Big Mon" Carty slugged 20 homers for the Jays in 1978.

BATTER	Pos.	Avg.	G	AB	R	H	HR	RBI
ALBERTS, Butch	DH	.278	6	18	1	5	0	0
ASHBY, Alan	C	.261	81	264	27	69	9	29
AULT, Doug	1B	.240	54	104	10	25	3	7
BAILOR, Bob	OF-IF	.264	154	621	74	164	1	52
BOSETTI, Rick	OF	.259	136	568	61	147	5	42
CARTY, Rico	DH	.284	104	387	51	110	20	68
CERONE, Rick	C	.223	88	282	25	63	3	20
EWING, Sam	DH-OF	.179	40	56	3	10	2	9
GOMEZ, Luis	SS	.223	153	413	39	92	0	32
HORTON, Willie	DH	.205	33	122	12	25	3	19
HOWELL, Roy	IF	.270	140	551	67	149	8	61
HUTTON, Tommy	OF-1B	.254	64	173	19	44	2	9
IORG, Garth	2B	.163	19	49	3	8	0	3
JOHNSON, Tim	SS-2B	.241	68	79	9	19	0	3
MAYBERRY, John	1B	.250	152	515	51	129	22	70
McKAY, Dave	2B	.238	145	504	59	120	7	45
MILNER, Brian	C	.444	2	9	3	4	0	2
NORDBROOK, Tim	SS	.000	7	0	1	0	0	0
UPSHAW, Willie	OF-DH	.237	95	224	26	53	1	17
VELEZ, Otto	OF	.266	91	248	29	66	9	38
WHITT, Ernie	C	.000	2	4	0	0	0	0
WOODS, Al	OF	.241	62	220	19	53	3	25
WOODS, Gary	OF	.158	9	19	1	3	0	0
Designated Hitters		.250	161	621	75	155	25	96
Pinch-Hitters		.236	–	123	11	29	2	18
1978 Totals		**.250**	**161**	**5430**	**590**	**1358**	**98**	**551**

Labatt's Player of the Year	BBWAA Player of the Year
ROY HOWELL	**BOB BAILOR**
Labatt's Pitcher of the Year	BBWAA Pitcher of the Year
JIM CLANCY **TOM UNERWOOD**	**JIM CLANCY** **VICTOR CRUZ**
Most Improved Player	BBWAA Rookie of the Year
ALAN ASHBY	**VICTOR CRUZ**

PITCHER	ERA	W-L	SV	G	IP	H	ER	BB	SO
BUSKEY, Tom	3.38	0-1	0	8	13.1	14	5	5	7
CLANCY, Jim	4.09	10-12	0	31	193.2	199	88	91	106
COLEMAN, Joe	4.60	2-0	0	31	60.2	67	31	30	28
CRUZ, Victor	1.71	7-3	9	32	47.1	28	9	35	51
GARVIN, Jerry	5.54	4-12	0	26	144.2	189	89	48	67
JEFFERSON, Jesse	4.38	7-16	0	31	211.2	214	103	86	97
KIRKWOOD, Don	4.24	4-5	0	16	68.0	76	32	25	29
LEMANCZYK, Dave	6.26	4-14	0	29	136.2	170	95	65	62
MOORE, Balor	4.93	6-9	0	37	144.1	165	79	54	75
MURPHY, Tom	3.93	6-9	7	50	94.0	87	41	37	36
UNDERWOOD, Tom	4.10	6-14	0	31	197.2	201	90	87	139
WALLACE, Dave	3.86	0-0	0	6	14.0	12	6	11	7
WILEY, Mark	6.75	0-0	0	2	2.2	3	2	1	2
WILLIS, Mike	4.56	3-7	7	44	100.2	104	51	39	52
1978 Totals	**4.54**	**59-102**	**23**	**161**	**1429.1**	**1529**	**723**	**614**	**758**

Victor Cruz was the ace of the bullpen, saving nine games with a 1.71 ERA.

Major League Baseball comes to Toronto

Manager	W	L	Pct.	Pos.	GB	Attendance
Roy Hartsfield	**54**	**107**	**.335**	**7th**	**-45.5**	**1,701,052**

Bob Bailor's smooth glove work made him a first-season fan favourite.

BIG-LEAGUE BASEBALL came to Toronto on April 7, 1977 when the Blue Jays defeated the Chicago White Sox 9-5. Doug Ault, a 27-year old rookie first baseman, homered twice in the Jays' first game. Otto Velez, who hit .442 for the month of April to earn American League Player-of-the-Month honours, became the first Jays' player to hit two-or-more home runs in a game twice, popping a pair against Boston and Oakland. Bob Bailor hit .310 for the season, the highest-ever mark for a player on an expansion team. Ron Fairly, a 20-year veteran who played with the great Los Angeles Dodgers teams in the 1960s, led the club with 19 HRs and became the first player since Stan Musial to play more than 1,000 games in both the infield and the outfield. On the mound, Dave Lemanczyk led the staff with 13 wins, another first-year expansion club record. Southpaw forkballer Jerry Garvin won 10 games and led the A.L. by picking 22 runners off base. Pete Vukovich, who finished the campaign with eight saves, a 7-7 record and a respectable ERA of 3.47, also tossed the first shutout in franchise history, a 2-0 whitewashing of the Baltimore Orioles on June 28. Other notable performers included third-sacker Roy Howell (.316, 44 RBIs); left-fielder Doug Rader (.240, 40 RBIs); and hurler Jesse Jefferson (9-17, 217 innings pitched). Although he wouldn't make an impact on the big club for a few more seasons, the Jays used their first ever "Rule 5" draft choice to select Willie Upshaw, who would later go on to wear the club's colours for nine seasons.

	Labatt's Most Valuable Player	BBWAA Player of the Year
	BOB BAILOR	**BOB BAILOR**
	BBWAA Pitcher of the Year	BBWAA Rookie of the Year
	DAVE LEMANCZYK	**BOB BAILOR**

BATTER	Pos.	Avg.	G	AB	R	H	HR	RBI
ASHBY, Alan	C	.210	124	396	25	83	2	29
AULT, Doug	1B-DH	.245	129	445	44	109	11	64
BAILOR, Bob	IF-OF	.310	122	496	62	154	5	32
BOWLING, Steve	OF	.206	89	194	19	40	1	13
CERONE, Rick	C	.200	31	100	7	20	1	10
EWING, Sam	OF-DH	.287	97	244	24	70	4	34
FAIRLY, Ron	DH-1B-OF	.279	132	458	60	128	19	64
GARCIA, Pedro	2B	.208	41	130	10	27	0	9
HOWELL, Roy	3B	.316	96	364	41	115	10	44
MASON, Jim	SS	.165	22	79	10	13	0	2
McKAY, Dave	IF	.197	95	274	18	54	3	22
NORDBROOK, Tim	SS	.175	24	63	9	11	0	1
RADER, Doug	3B-DH	.240	96	313	47	75	13	40
ROOF, Phil	C	.000	3	5	0	0	0	0
SCOTT, John	OF	.240	79	233	26	56	2	15
STAGGS, Steve	2B	.259	72	290	37	75	2	28
TORRES, Hector	IF	.241	91	266	33	64	5	26
VELEZ, Otto	OF-DH	.256	120	360	50	92	16	62
WHITT, Ernie	C	.171	23	41	4	7	0	6
WOODS, Al	OF	.284	122	440	58	125	6	35
WOODS, Gary	OF	.216	60	227	21	49	0	17
Designated Hitters		.269	161	583	75	157	22	87
Pinch-Hitters		.280		93	10	26	5	23
1977 Totals		**.252**	**161**	**5418**	**605**	**1367**	**100**	**553**

PITCHER	ERA	W-L	SV	G	IP	H	ER	BB	SO
BRUNO, Tom	7.85	0-1	0	12	18.1	30	16	13	9
BYRD, Jeff	6.18	2-13	0	17	87.1	98	60	68	40
CLANCY, Jim	5.05	4-9	0	13	76.2	80	43	47	44
DARR, Mike	33.75	0-1	0	1	1.1	3	5	4	1
DeBARR, Dennis	5.91	0-1	0	14	21.1	29	14	8	10
GARVIN, Jerry	4.19	10-18	0	34	244.2	247	114	85	127
HARGAN, Steve	5.22	1-3	0	6	29.1	36	17	14	11
HARTENSTEIN, Chuck	6.59	0-2	0	13	27.1	40	20	6	15
JEFFERSON, Jesse	4.31	9-17	0	33	217.0	224	104	83	114
JOHNSON, Jerry	4.60	2-4	5	43	86.0	91	44	54	54
LEMANCZYK, Dave	4.25	13-16	0	34	252.0	278	119	87	105
MURPHY, Tom	3.63	2-1	2	19	52.0	63	21	18	26
SINGER, Bill	6.79	2-8	0	13	59.2	71	45	39	33
VUKOVICH, Pete	3.47	7-7	8	53	148.0	143	57	59	123
WILLIS, Mike	3.94	2-6	5	43	107.1	105	47	38	59
1977 Totals	**4.57**	**54-107**	**20**	**161**	**1428.1**	**1538**	**726**	**623**	**771**

Dave Lemanczyk tied a major-league expansion team record with 13 victories in 1977.

TORONTO BLUE JAYS BASEBALL CLUB

1 BLUE JAYS WAY, SUITE 3200, SKYDOME
TORONTO, ONTARIO M5V 1J1
(416) 341-1000

INTERNET: www.bluejays.com

FAXES:

MEDIA RELATIONS (416) 341-1250
EXECUTIVE (416) 341-2323
COMMERCE COURT (416) 341-1090
FINANCE (416) 341-1096
TICKETS (416) 341-1177

BASEBALL (416) 341-1245
MARKETING/SALES (416) 341-1146
OPERATIONS (416) 341-1103
TBJ MERCHANDISING (416) 341-2910

TORONTO BLUE JAYS OWNERSHIP

On March 26, 1976, the American League granted an expansion franchise to a group consisting of Labatt Breweries, Imperial Trust Limited and The Canadian Imperial Bank of Commerce. Both Labatt Breweries and Imperial Trust each controlled 45% of the team. The C.I.B.C. had the other 10% of the club. Imperial Trust was a holding company set up by the late R. Howard Webster, who was instrumental in the granting of the franchise in 1976. The Webster family still maintained their share of the ownership until selling their 45% to Labatt in November, 1991. The ownership then consisted of John Labatt Limited, 90% and Canadian Imperial Bank of Commerce, 10%. In June of 1995 John Labatt Limited was purchased by Interbrew S.A., Belgium's leading brewer.

In September of 2000, local ownership returned to the Toronto Blue Jays as Rogers Communications Inc. purchased 80% control of the franchise. John Labatt Limited (Interbrew) maintains a 20% interest while The Canadian Imperial Back of Commerce relinquished their stake. Rogers Communications, headed by Ted Rogers, joins the ranks of North American communication companies such as Time Warner, Newscorp and Disney in their ownership of sports franchises.

The 2001 Toronto Blue Jays Media Guide

Data for the 2001 Toronto Blue Jays Media Guide was gathered through March 1.

Produced by:	Howard Starkman, Jay Stenhouse, Michael Shaw, Laura Ammendolia, Jennifer Morris, Leanna England
Research Assistance:	Matt Rutsey
Stats provided by:	Major League Baseball Information System, Elias Sports Bureau, Stats Inc and Howe Sportsdata International.
Creative Services:	Caledon Data Management (John Pasternak, Alex Dubiel)
Photo Credits:	Fred Thornhill

BOARD OF DIRECTORS

Chairman . . . . Herb Solway

Rudy Bratty, Albert Gnat, Paul Godfrey, Charles Hoffman, Phil Lind, Jeff Lyons, Edward Rogers,
Ted Rogers, David Smith, John Tory, Anthony Viner

EXECUTIVE OFFICE

President and CEO . . . . Paul Godfrey
Senior Vice-President and General Manager . . Gord Ash
Senior Vice-President, Finance . . . . . . Richard Wong
Senior Vice-President, Marketing and Sales Paul Allamby

Executive Assistant to the President & CEO Julie Stoddart
Executive Assistant, Baseball . . . . Fran Brown
Executive Assistant, Sales and Marketing . . Mary McCall

BASEBALL

Vice-President, Baseball Operations
& Assistant GM . . . . Tim McCleary
Assistant GM & Director, Player Personnel . Dave Stewart
Vice-President . . . . Bob Mattick
Vice-President . . . . Tim Wilken
Special Assistant to the General Manager . . Jim Fanning
Director, Florida Operations . . . . Ken Carson
Manager, Team Travel . . . . Bart Given
Manager, Amateur Baseball . . . . Kevin Briand
Head Trainer . . . . Scott Shannon
Assistant Trainer . . . . George Poulis
Strength and Conditioning Coordinator . . . . Jeff Krushell
Equipment Manager . . . . Jeff Ross
Clubhouse Manager, Blue Jays . . . . Kevin Malloy
Visiting Clubhouse Manager . . . . Len Frejlich

Video Operations . . . . Robert Baumander
Team Physician . . . . Dr. Ron Taylor
Medical Advisor . . . . Dr. Bernie Gosevitz
Consulting Orthopedic Surgeon . . . . . Dr. Allan Gross
Consulting Orthopedic Surgeon . . . Dr. Steve Mirabello
Consulting Orthopedic Surgeon . . . . . Dr. Erin Boynton
Consulting Orthopedic Surgeon . . . . . Dr. Tony Miniaci
Consulting Chiropractor . . . . Dr. Pat Graham
Employee Assistance Program Director . . . Tim Hewes
Cultural Diversity Coordinator . . . . . . Candice Henson
Baseball Assistant, Major
League Operations . . . . Heather Connolly
Baseball Assistant, Player Development . . Donna Kuzoff
Baseball Assistant, Player Development . Angie Van Evera

* For Minor League Player Development and Scouting please refer to page 366 of the 2001 Media Guide

FINANCE

Vice President, Finance & Administration . . Susan Brioux
Controller . . . . Cathy McNamara-MacKay
Manager, Payroll & Benefits . . . . Brenda Dimmer
Office Manager . . . . Anne Fulford
Director, Risk Management . . . . Suzanne Joncas
Financial Reporting Manager . . . . Jerry Chow
Accounts Receivable Coordinator . . . . Marion Sullivan
Accounts Payable Coordinator . . . . Andy Topolie

Accounting Analyst . . . . Sharon Labenski
Administrative Assistant . . . . Lisa Carpino
Assistant Manager, Payroll & Benefits . . George Gavros
Accounting Coordinator . . . . Shari Ralph
Ticket Office Receivable Coordinator . . . Joseph Roach
Receptionist . . . . Mary Anne Sturley
Receptionist . . . . Beth Wilson
Gate 9 Information . . . . Pete Gaskin

INFORMATION SYSTEMS

Manager, Information Systems . . . . . Peter Ferwerda
Systems Analyst . . . . Tony Miranda

Systems Administrator . . . . Spencer Lui
IS Support . . . . Vidal Abad

MARKETING

Director, Marketing . . . . Peter Cosentino
Director, Charitable Foundation & Corporate
Communications . . . . Brenda Maynard
Manager, Marketing & Player Relations . . Laurel Lindsay
Manager, Promotions . . . . Julian Franklin
Manager, Game Entertainment
& Productions . . . . Joan Mizzi Paley

Manager, Community Relations . . . Jennifer Santamaria
Mascot & Youth Outreach
Coordinator . . . . Brennan Anderson
Administrative Assistant . . . . Maria North
Marketing Assistant . . . . Mike Volpatti

STRATEGIC OPERATIONS

Director, Strategic Operations . . . . Meg Stokes

THE 25th ANNIVERSARY SEASON

In celebration of the 25th Anniversary Season of Blue Jays baseball in Toronto, the organization has planned many special events for the 2001 season. The following is brief synopsis of some of the highlights. In December of 2000, the Blue Jays commenced fan voting to select the 25th Anniversary All-Time Blue Jays Roster. In a similar selection process, the 25 greatest moments in club history will be selected. In-stadium giveaways will be highlighted by a commemorative coin set. The set of six coins will be given out over six games throughout the season. The Turn Back the Clock pin set is also going to be presented to fans as an in-stadium giveaway. On opening day a limited edition

25th Anniversary Season Toronto Blue Jays Stamp, commissioned by Canada Post, will be an in-stadium giveaway. The organization has created great interest in the April 29 and September 16 games as they announced those dates as Carlos Delgado & Billy Koch Bobblehead doll nights. On the field the Blue Jays will wear their original uniforms on May 21 when they take on their first ever opponent, the Chicago White Sox. Along with other 25th Anniversary theme giveaways and weekends, the Blue Jays will hold an Alumni Weekend in August with a Gala Dinner on the 16th.

CORPORATE PARTNERSHIPS & BUSINESS DEVELOPMENT

Vice-President, Corporate Partnerships/
Business Development . . . . Mark Lemmon
Senior Account Executive . . . . Robert MacKay

Coordinator, Corporate Partnerships . . Honsing Leung
Coordinator, Client Services . . . . Tara Murphy
Executive Assistant . . . . Darla McKeen

SALES and TICKET OPERATIONS

Manager, Ticket Office Sales . . . . Jan Marshall
Manager, Client Service and
Premium Seating . . . . Sheila Cantarutti
Administrator, Database and Ticket System . . Doug Barr
Manager, Season Ticket and Group Sales . Isabelle Frati
Manager, Mail Order Services
& Game Day Services . . . . Sandra Wilbur
Coordinator, Telephone Order Services . Cathie Caulfield
Supervisor Future Game Sales . . . . Vic Braknis
Client Service Representative . . . . . Adam Melanson
Client Service Representative . . . . . Vahak Veghoyan
Client Service Representative . . . . . . Sonia Privato
Account Representative . . . . Lynda Bauer
Account Representative . . . . Daniel Diaz
Account Representative . . . . Jason Diplock
Account Representative . . . . Paul Fruitman
Account Representative . . . . Terry Gaudet
Account Representative . . . . Ben Kelly
Account Representative . . . . Todd Merton
Account Representative . . . . Jamie Messina
Account Representative . . . . Regan Miles
Account Representative . . . . Tom Pell
Account Representative . . . . Kelley Richards
Account Representative . . . . Shelby Nelson
Account Representative . . . . Anne Wilson

Group Sales Representative . . . . Sue Mallabon
Group Sales Representative . . . . Matt Dougan
Ticket Office Representative . . . . Mark Myers
Call Centre Supervisor . . . . John Chumarow
Call Centre Supervisor . . . . Robert McGivney
Call Centre Supervisor . . . . Mark Nguyen
Call Centre Supervisor . . . . Tara-Leigh O'Brien
Call Centre Supervisor . . . . Kellie O'Leary
Call Centre Representative . . . . Paul Ainsworth
Call Centre Representative . . . . . Aisha Bandukwala
Call Centre Representative . . . . Gina Chin
Call Centre Representative . . . . Laila Gomes
Call Centre Representative . . . . . Elizabeth Gonzalez
Call Centre Representative . . . . Endre Kantor
Call Centre Representative . . . . Farrah Francis
Call Centre Representative . . . . Ai-Lin Ku
Call Centre Representative . . . . Wei-Lin Ku
Call Centre Representative . . . . Kelly Mattatall
Call Centre Representative . . . . Ursula Munoz
Call Centre Representative . . . . . Matthew Murdock
Call Centre Representative . . . . Miguel Perez
Call Centre Representative . . . . . Dwayne Schrader
Call Centre Representative . . . . Carmel Slade
Call Centre Representative . . . . Ann Viscardis
Call Centre Representative . . . . Liz Walsh

STADIUM OPERATIONS

Director, Operations . . . . Mario Coutinho
Game Security . . . . John Booth
Supervisor, Office Services . . . . Mick Bazinet
Administrative Assistant, Operations . . . . . . June Sym

Office Services Assistant . . . . Sam Platsis
Office Services Assistant . . . . Piero Aceto
Operations Assistant . . . . Marion Farrell
Head Grounds Keeper . . . . Tom Farrell

MEDIA RELATIONS

Vice President, Media Relations . . . . Howard Starkman
Manager, Media Relations . . . . Jay Stenhouse
Media Relations Coordinator . . . . Michael Shaw

Media Relations Coordinator . . . . Jennifer Morris
Media Relations Supervisor . . . . . Laura Ammendolia
Media Relations Assistant . . . . Leanna England

TBJ MERCHANDISING

General Manager . . . . Michael Andrejek
Manager, Purchasing & Mail Order Sales . Helen Maunder
Manager, Retail Operations . . . . . . Stephen Tolkunow
Manager, Stadium Events . . . . Linda Mykytshyn

Manager, Bullpen, Commerce Court . . . Diana Goucher
Manager, Bullpen, SkyDome . . . . . . Teresa Michalski
Coordinator, Warehouse Services . . . Adrian Veerman
Assistant Manager, Stadium Events . . . . . . Arto Emas

BLUE JAYS 2001 ROAD HOTELS

CLUB	HOTEL	PHONE	FAX
ANAHEIM	Anaheim Hilton & Towers	(714) 750-4321	(714) 740-4460
BALTIMORE	Marriott Waterfront, Trip #1 & #3	(410) 385-3000	(410) 385-0330
	Hyatt Inner Harbor, Trip #2	(410) 528-1234	(410) 685-3362
BOSTON	Boston Sheraton	(617) 236-2000	(617) 236-1702
CHICAGO	The Westin Hotel	(312) 943-7200	(312) 397-5580
CLEVELAND	Marriott Society Center	(216) 696-9200	(216) 696-0096
DETROIT	Ritz Carlton	(313) 441-2000	(313) 441-6035
KANSAS CITY	The Fairmont	(816) 756-1500	(816) 756-1635
MINNESOTA	Minneapolis Hyatt	(612) 370-1234	(612) 370-1233
MONTREAL	Le Centre Sheraton	(514) 878-2000	(514) 878-3958
NEW YORK	The Grand Hyatt	(212) 883-1234	(212) 697-3772
OAKLAND	The Westin St. Francis	(415) 397-7000	(415) 774-0124
PHILADELPHIA	The Ritz Carlton	(215) 735-7700	(215) 735-7710
SEATTLE	Crowne Plaza	(206) 464-1980	(206) 340-1617
TAMPA	Renaissance Vinoy	(813) 894-1000	(813) 822-2785
TEXAS	Arlington Wyndham	(817) 261-8200	(817) 548-2873

TED ROGERS
President & CEO of Rogers Communications Inc.

Is the President and Chief Executive Officer of Rogers Communications Inc... A pioneer in the communication industry as he had been involved in the start-up stage with numerous ventures in broadcasting, cable television and telecommunications, championing service and innovative engineering throughout... Earned a Bachelor of Arts from the University of Toronto in 1956 and earned his LLB from Osgoode Hall Law School in 1961... While articling with Tory, Tory, DesLauriers & Binnington, he created Rogers Radio Broadcasting Limited, which acquired the nation's pioneer FM station, CHFI-FM... Made significant contributions to wireless communications in Canada... Was a founding shareholder of Cantel Inc. which commenced service in 1985 to operate a national cellular telephone network... In October 1990 he was made an Officer of The Order of Canada and in April of 1994 was inducted into the Canadian Business Hall of Fame... Serves as director of many organizations including The Toronto-Dominion Bank; Canada Publishing Company; Telesystem International Wireless Inc.; Cable Television Labratories, Inc. and Canadian Cable Television Association; The Hull Group; Junior Achievement of Canada; Excite @ Home; and AT&T Canada Corporation... Also serves on the Board of Governors of The Lyford Cay Club and The Sigma Chi Foundation... Has obtained Doctorates from Clarkson University, University of Victoria, York University, University of Western Ontario and Trinity College of the University of Toronto.

PAUL GODFREY
President & CEO, Toronto Blue Jays

Born in Toronto and attended Bathurst Heights Collegiate... Graduated in 1962 as a Chemical Engineer from the University of Toronto... Began public life in 1964 when elected as a Councillor for the City of North York... Elected Alderman in 1967 and Controller in 1970... Appointed Chairman of Metropolitan Toronto in 1973 and served a record 11 years... In the 1960s, was active in working to obtain a MLB franchise for Toronto with the dream being realized in 1977... Joined The Toronto Sun in August of 1984 as Publisher and Chief Executive Officer... Was appointed President and Chief Operating Officer of The Toronto Sun Publishing Corporation (later known as Sun Media Corporation) in April, 1991 and was President and Chief Executive Officer from November, 1992 to June 30, 2000... In 1984, was appointed by the Ontario Premier to the Crown Corporation delegated with the selection, design and construction of a domed stadium for Toronto... Named President and Chief Executive Officer of the Toronto Blue Jays on September 1, 2000... Is active on numerous boards and associations including The Herbie Fund which he established at The Hospital for Sick Children Foundation in 1979... Was honoured by his appointment as a member of the Order of Canada in 1999... Has received many awards including the Civic Award of Merit (the City of Toronto's highest award), Professional Engineer Award, Outstanding Canadian by Canada's Jaycees and the Award of Merit from B'nai Brith Canada in 1998... Resides in Toronto with his wife Gina... Three sons, Rob, Noah and Jay.

GORD ASH
Senior Vice-President & General Manager

Born December 20, 1951 in Toronto, Ontario... Attended Vaughn Road Collegiate Institute... Graduated with a Bachelor of Arts Degree in History and Sociology from York University in 1974... Began working for the Canadian Imperial Bank of Commerce in May 1974... Following his tenure with the CIBC, he joined the Blue Jays organization in 1978 as a ticket office employee... The very next year, he left the ticket office to join the Operations Department as an Operations Supervisor responsible for the day-to-day supervision of the grounds crew... Promoted to Assistant Director, Operations in February, 1980... His new duties included stadium and game-day operations... In February of 1984, Gord was appointed Administrator, Player Personnel in the Baseball Department... His duties included minor league contracts and supervising the daily operation of the Blue Jays' farm clubs... Attended the University of Michigan in May of 1988 for seminar on human resource management... Also attended an industrial relations seminar at Queens University in May of 1990... Promoted to Assistant General Manager in January 1989... There he was instrumental in the negotiation of major league contracts and the daily operation of the club... Was promoted to Vice-President, Baseball and General Manager on October 14, 1994... Promoted to Executive Vice-President, General Manager in December 1997... Named President, Baseball on January 29, 1999... In February 2001 title was adjusted to Senior Vice-President and General Manager... Gord is one of only four Canadians to become a General Manager of a Major League team- others are: Doug Melvin- Texas Rangers (1994-), George Selkirk- Washington Senators (1964-69), Murray Cook- Montreal Expos (1985-87) and Cincinnati Reds (1988-89)... Serves as Chairman of the Major League Baseball General Managers Labor Committee... Member of the Advisory Board for the Canadian Special Olympics Foundation.

RICHARD WONG
Senior Vice-President, Finance

Raised in Toronto and attended George Vanier Secondary School... Attended the University of Western Ontario, graduating in 1989 with a Honours Bachelor of Science degree... Went on to obtain his Masters of Business Administration from Queens University in 1992... Began working in the Rogers Communications Group of Companies for Rogers Cable TV on a part time basis as an Underground Services/Installations Technician from 1985 to 1992 while completing his education... In 1992 joined Rogers Communications as an Investment Analyst... In August of 1994 was named as the Manager, Special Projects in the Corporate Development department... Was promoted again in August of 1996 to Director, Special Projects where he worked on investment and corporate business development... Joined the Toronto Blue Jays on January 8, 2001 as Senior Vice-President, Finance.

PAUL ALLAMBY
Senior Vice-President, Marketing & Sales

Born in London, England and was educated at St. Martins College, England and at York University... Was one of the first graduates of the Canadian Direct Marketing Associations' Certificate program at Humber College... Spent nine years in marketing and sales management with Union Carbide (Glad, Eveready, Energizer)... Led Padulo Integrated's Direct Marketing Division where he was a major force in the launch of many award winning, multi-million dollar advertising/ direct-response marketing programs including Club Z Visa and Ford Visa cards, CIBC Insurance Corp., management of CIBC's advertising campaign, Personalvision and the introduction of BMG Music Services into Canada... Spent five years with Rogers Communications during which time holding titles of Vice-President Customer Based Management, Vice-President Pricing and Research, Vice-President Marketing Services & Vice President Market Management... Joined the Toronto Blue Jays on December 8, 2000 as Senior Vice-President, Sales and Marketing... Is a member of the Direct Marketing Association of America, the DRTV council and the Canadian Direct Marketing Association... Has appeared as a featured speaker to many of these and other Associations.

BASEBALL OPERATIONS

BOBBY MATTICK
Vice-President, Baseball

Born December 5, 1915 at Sioux City, Iowa but grew up in St. Louis, Missouri... Father Wally "Chick" Mattick was a major league player with the Chicago White Sox (1912-1913) and the Cardinals (1918)... Signed first professional contract as a shortstop with Chicago Cubs in 1933... Best season was 1937 when he hit .279 with 66 RBI and 39 doubles for Los Angeles of the Pacific Coast League... After playing for both the Cubs and Cincinnati, he retired in 1942 finishing with a career major league average of .233 with 64 RBI in 206 games... Suffered a serious eye injury in 1936 (fractured skull above the right eye due to a foul ball) while with Los Angeles which seriously hampered his career... Resulted in double vision... Managed in Southern League, 1944-45... From 1946-1979 worked in administrative and scouting capacities for 10 different organizations including a 20 year association with Gabe Paul... Left Montreal in 1976 to join the Blue Jays as scouting supervisor... In 1978 was appointed Director, Player Development overseeing all minor league field activities... Replaced Roy Hartsfield as Blue Jays Field Manager in 1980 becoming the oldest rookie manager to start a season (64 years)... Served in that capacity for two seasons compiling a 104-164 record... Appointed Executive Co-ordinator, Baseball Operations with responsibilities including on-field, player personnel and field staff recruitment activities at all levels of the organization with emphasis at the major league level... Appointed Vice-President, Baseball, September 24, 1984... Oversaw the operation of the Blue Jays' entry in the Florida Instructional League from 1977-1988... Recruited, signed and developed several former major league talents including: Hall of Famer Frank Robinson, Curt Flood, Vada Pinson, Rusty Staub, Darrell Porter, Don Baylor, Tommy Harper, Gorman Thomas, Bobby Grich and Dave Stieb... Honoured in 1993 by the Baseball Hall of Fame in an exhibit dedicated to scouting... 68 years in professional baseball... Inducted into the Canadian Baseball Hall of Fame in 1999... Resides in Arizona.

Major League Baseball has designed special logos to commemorate the first 100 seasons of American League Baseball. The logos will be worn as uniform patches by every American League Club and will be used on special commemorative merchandise.

TIM McCLEARY
Vice-President, Baseball Operations & Assistant General Manager

Born August 28, 1964 in Queens, New York... Entering his sixth full season with the Blue Jays... Married the former Juli Roush on November 12, 1994... Has one child, Brogan... Graduated with a Bachelor of Science Degree in Athletic and Business Administration from St. John's University, NY, in 1986... Recipient of a Jackie Robinson Scholarship... Attended North Polytechnic School in London, England in the fall of 1985... Began his career in baseball as an intern in the Office of the Commissioner for Major League Baseball under Commissioner Peter Ueberroth in the spring of 1986... Worked for the American League and was named Manager, Waiver & Player Records in 1987... Named to Director, Waiver and Player records in 1988 responsible for reviewing and approving player contracts and transactions... In December 1992, he left to assume the position of Assistant General Manager, Baseball Operations for the New York Yankees under Gene Michael... Duties included the negotiation of major league contracts and arbitration cases... Coordinated major league scout coverage... Joined the Toronto Blue Jays as Assistant General Manager on November 30, 1995... Responsible for contract negotiations, budgeting, arbitration preparation as well as interpretation of Major League Rules, the Basic Agreement and American League Rules/Regulations... Appointed Vice-President, Baseball Operations & Assistant General Manager on December 20, 1999 and assists in overseeing all facets of the baseball operations.

DAVE STEWART
Assistant General Manager & Director, Player Personnel

Born February 19, 1957 in Oakland, CA... Attended St. Elizabeth High School where he was three sport star, was an All-American as a catcher in baseball and linebacker /tight end in football... Played small forward in basketball... Offered football scholarships but selected baseball his 16th round selection by the Los Angeles Dodgers in 1975... Went on to post four 20-win seasons and compile a 168-129 record with a 3.95 ERA during a 15 year Major League career (1981-1995) with the Dodgers, Rangers, Phillies, A's and Blue Jays... On three World Championship clubs including the 1993 Toronto Blue Jays... In ALCS play has a career record of 8-0 in ten starts with a 2.08 ERA and two ALCS MVP's... Has been a community activist during his entire professional career in every city he has played... The Dave Stewart Foundation has been involved in many community programs including Toronto where he has held Thanksgiving dinners and a Kids Christmas party at SkyDome for many years... Following playing career worked for the Oakland A's as a Special Assistant to GM Sandy Alderson in 1996... In 1997 joined the San Diego Padres as a special assistant to GM Kevin Towers and in 1998 was on field as the Padres pitching coach... On November 3, 1998 was named Assistant General Manager, Toronto Blue Jays... Has two children, Adrian and Alyse... On December 20, 1999 title was adjusted to Assistant General Manager and Director, Player Personnel... He will oversee both player development and scouting.

TIM WILKEN
Vice-President, Baseball

Born September 6, 1953 in Decatur, Illinois... Attended Dunedin High School in Dunedin, Florida- home of Toronto Blue Jays' Spring Training since 1977... Attended St. Petersburgh Junior College, Spring Hill College and the University of South Florida and studied child psychology... Father pitched in the St. Louis Browns and Washington Senators organizations and was a pitching instructor and scout with both the Phillies and Pirates... Began working for Toronto as a part-time Public Relations Assistant during spring training... Hired as an area scout in 1979 by Pat Gillick, assisting Wayne Morgan in California, Utah, Colorado, Oregon and Washington... Coached at Medicine Hat of the Pioneer League in 1980... Coached and managed the Bradenton Blue Jays of the Gulf Coast League in 1981... Continued to scout for Toronto in various areas of the United States and Caribbean... Named national cross-checker in 1989 responsible for assessing top U.S. prospects... Promoted to Director of U.S. Scouting on August 28, 1995... Appointed Vice-President, Baseball on October 31, 2000, his responsibilities will include scouting Major League talent and serving as chief advisor on player procurement... One daughter, Karis (1/22/93).

JIM FANNING
Special Assistant to the Senior Vice-President & General Manager

Born in Chicago, Illinois and was raised in Iowa... Obtained a Masters Degree in Physical Education from the University of Illinois... Signed with the Chicago Cubs and played four season in the Major Leagues beginning in 1954... The 2001 season will be his 52nd in professional baseball... Joined the Toronto Blue Jays on February 6, 2001 as a Special Assistant to Gord Ash, Senior Vice-President and General Manager... Was inducted into the Canadian Baseball Hall of Fame on June 24, 2000 for his lifetime service to Canadian baseball... Spent almost 25 years with the Montreal Expos... Joined the Expos after establishing and directing the Major League Scouting Bureau... Started as the Expos first General Manager in 1968 and later became Vice-President in 1973, responsible for the scouting and development programs while also being involved with community relations... As Montreal's Scouting Director his staff signed such stars as Larry Walker, Andres Galaraga and Randy Johnson... Had two stints as the field manager with the Expos, highlighted in his first season, when he led the club to their first-ever playoff appearance in 1981... Also managed the club in 1982 and 1984... Served as a colour commentator for the Expos radio and television broadcasts... Worked at CJAD, Montreal's largest English radio station, where he enjoyed a morning baseball show for eight years... Worked as a major league scout for the Colorado Rockies organization from 1994 to 1999... He and his wife Maria of Montreal, have two children, Cynthia and Frank.

BART GIVEN
Manager, Team Travel

Born October 26, 1973 in Brantford, Ontario... Attended Haliburton Highlands Secondary School... Graduated from York University with an hounour degree in Kinesiology and Health Sciences and a specialized certificate in Sports Administration... While at York University was an O.U.A.A. All-Star in Track and Field in 1995 & 1996... In 1996 was a C.I.A.U. bronze medallist in the 4 x 200 relay... In 1997 worked on the American Bowl Organizing Committee... In August of 1997 was hired by the Toronto Argonauts as Coordinator Special Events... Spent four months in 1998 as Communication Coordinator with the Toronto Blue Jays... Returned to the Argo's in June 1998 as Manager, Marketing and Game Entertainment... Joined the Toronto Blue Jays in January 2000 as the Manager, Game Entertainment and Promotions... Named Manager, Team Travel in January 2001.

TIM HEWES
Employee Assistance Program Director

Born August 8, 1947... Graduated from Bakersfield High School in 1965... Attended one season at Bakersfield J.C. before attending Biola College in Los Angeles... Drafted by California in 1967 and played in the minors from 1967 to 1971... Graduated from Biola College in 1972 with a degree in Psychology... Was a high school teacher in 1972-73... Attended Spanish Language Institute in San Jose, Costa Rica in 1974... Served as baseball Coach at Autonomous University of Guadalajara, Mexico from 1975-77... Obtained a masters in Psychology from Cal State in 1980... Served as a part-time scout with San Diego in 1983, Montreal in 1984 and then with the Blue Jays in 1986... Licensed Marriage, Family therapist in California where he has worked with families and children for 20 years... On October 25, 1996 was appointed Director, Employee Assistance Program for the Toronto Blue Jays... Also works in the area of performance enhancement/sports psychology with the organization.

BLUE JAYS MEDICAL AND TRAINING STAFF

DR. RON TAYLOR
Team Physician

A Toronto native, became the first former Major League player to return to the game in the capacity of team physician- February 1979... Spent 11 years in the Major Leagues with five teams before retiring from the game in 1972... Began his Major League career with the Cleveland Indians in 1962... Played the next 10 seasons with National League teams including 2 plus seasons with St. Louis and five with the New York Mets... Other teams were Houston and San Diego... Finished career with a 45-43 record, 72 saves and a 3.93 ERA... Pitched on two World Series teams- 1964 Cardinals and 1969 Mets... Obtained degree in electrical engineering from University of Toronto while playing baseball... Began medical studies in 1972 and graduated from University of Toronto in 1977... Served internship at Mount Sinai Hospital in Toronto and returned for a second year in 1978, specializing in sports medicine... Currently runs a sports medicine clinic at Mount Sinai Hospital... Elected to the Canadian Baseball Hall of Fame in 1985 and the Canadian Sports Hall of Fame in 1993... He and wife Rona have two sons, Drew (19) and Matthew (17).

DR. ALLAN GROSS
Consulting Orthopaedic Surgeon

Has been involved with the Blue Jays since 1979... Graduated from the University of Toronto in 1962 with his Doctor of Medicine Degree... Began working at Mt. Sinai Hospital in June of 1971... Interested in bone and cartilage transplantation, he established the Mount Sinai Hospital Bone Bank in 1972... Has pioneered many transplant surgery techniques... From 1975-1982 he was the Surgeon-In-Chief of Mt. Sinai Hospital... From 1982-1986 was the Head, Combined Division of Orthopaedic Surgery, Toronto General Hospital/Mt. Sinai Hospital... Is the Head of Orthopaedic Surgery at Mt. Sinai Hospital and the Bernie Ghert Professor of reconstructive surgery at Mt. Sinai Hospital... He is also a Fellow of The Royal College of Surgeons of Canada in Orthopaedic Surgery (1969)... Married, wife's name Penny Gross PhD... Has four children: Lowell, Tony, Robyn and Jeremy... Resides in Toronto.

TORONTO BLUE JAYS CHARITABLE FOUNDATION

The Toronto Blue Jays Charitable Foundation is a non-profit Foundation incorporated under the laws of the Government of Canada.

Established in March of 1992, the Foundation is funded by various means and programs. The Foundation is geared towards responding to requests from charitable organizations which contribute to the enrichment of the quality of life we can enjoy.

The Toronto Blue Jays Baseball Club has long supported many and various causes within our community. The Foundation enables the Club to expand and continue this goodwill into the future.

Our mission is simple: To contribute to the enrichment of the quality of life (of youth to seniors) in the community through means associated (directly or indirectly) with the Toronto Blue Jays Baseball Club. To date, the Foundation has helped numerous charities across Canada.

SCOTT SHANNON
Trainer

Entering his 14th season with the organization and his second as Head Trainer in Toronto... Graduated from Sheridan College with a degree in Sports Injury Management in 1987... Worked with the Toronto Blue Jays in the 1987 and 1988 seasons before becoming the Head Trainer in Medicine Hat in 1989... Worked with the St. Catharines Stompers of the New York Penn League from 1990 to 1995... In 1996 and 1997 served as Head Trainer for the Knoxville Smokies of the Southern League (AA)... Was the Assistant Trainer with Toronto in 1998 & 1999... The 37 year old resides in Toronto.

GEORGE POULIS
Assistant Trainer

Entering his second season in the Toronto Blue Jays organization... Graduated from Baldwin Wallace College with a Bachelor's degree in Sports Medicine... Began with the San Diego Padres in 1989 as the trainer for Waterloo (A)... After a season off in 1992 he returned to the Padres with their AA affiliate which was in Wichita in 1993 & 1994, Memphis in 1995 & 1996 and Mobile in 1997... In 1998 & 1999 was the trainer for the Las Vegas Stars (AAA) of the Pacific Coast League... After nine seasons with the Padres joined the Blue Jays as assistant trainer in Toronto... Married, wife's name is Jenny... Two daughters, Lainey and Evy.

JEFF KRUSHELL
Strength and Conditioning Coordinator

Born October 21, 1968... Entering his second season with Toronto... The 2001 season will be his fourth year in the organization after starting in 1998 as a roving minor league strength and conditioning coordinator... Is a member of the National Strength and Conditioning Association... Graduated from the University of Calgary with a Bachelors degree in Kinesiology... Served as strength and conditioning coach for various varsity teams at the University of Calgary... Moved to Edmonton in 1995 to assume the role of Director of Athletic Development at the Edmonton Sport Institute... Currently resides in Burlington with his wife Debbie and daughters Madison and Olivia.

BLUE JAYS BEHIND THE SCENES

JEFF ROSS
Equipment Manager

Jeff is entering his 24th season in the organization and his 21st season as Equipment Manager after succeeding John Silverman prior to the start of the 1981 season... Is a 47 year old Montreal native who now lives in Palm Harbor, Florida... Ran the visiting clubhouse at Exhibition Stadium during the Blue Jays first four seasons of operation... Responsibilities include maintenance of all uniforms and equipment as well as overseeing the transport of such items during the regular season... Graduated from Darcy McGee High School in Montreal... Attended Dawson College and worked part-time for the Montreal Expos as a member of their grounds crew and in the clubhouses... Enjoys golf and fishing... Married, wife's name is Sally.

KEVIN MALLOY
Clubhouse Manager

Kevin enters his sixth season as Clubhouse Manager and his 19th overall in the organization... Graduated from Seneca College in 1987 where he studied Marketing and Administration... Has worked for the Toronto Blue Jays since 1982 when he began as a seasonal assistant in the Blue Jays Clubhouse... In 1996 was appointed Clubhouse Manager... Responsible for co-ordinating the clubhouse responsibilities with Equipment Manager, Jeff Ross and overseeing and directing the seasonal clubhouse assistants... Married, wife's name Allison... Two children, Cody Christian (4/18/93) and Brendan Casey (1/16/96)... Enjoys ice hockey, downhill skiing and golf... Resides in Pickering, Ontario.

LEN FREJLICH
Visiting Clubhouse Manager

Len enters his sixth full season as the visiting clubhouse manager... Is an original employee of the Blue Jays and is now entering his 25th season... Began in the ticket office and was appointed Assistant Director, Tickets in the club's first season, 1977... For the 1986 season he joined the Operations department as the Assistant Director... In 1996 he began as Visiting Clubhouse Manager, where he is responsible for hosting all visiting clubs and their equipment and uniforms... Attended Michael Power Collegiate in Toronto before graduating from Wilfred Laurier University where he studied Business Administration... Married, wife's name is Angie... One son, Len Jr. (5)... Enjoys horse racing, ice hockey and golf.

THE HISTORY OF THE BLUE JAYS UNIFORM

In 1977 when the Toronto Blue Jays began play in the American League they sported the now familiar Blue Jays logo that was designed by Toronto-based Savage Sloan Ltd.

The lettering style that has become associated with the organization began in 1977. The uniform numbers and name BLUE JAYS on the home uniforms in 1977 were done with rounded corners and a thin white centered highlight line which is now so distinctly associated with the Toronto Blue Jays.

In 1977 the Blue Jays players wore pullover uniform tops and beltless waistband pants with decorative striping of blue, white and light blue on the sleeves, necks and pants. The caps were dark blue with two white panels in front and the team logo proudly displayed in the middle. Undersweaters and socks were solid dark blue.

The home uniforms were white with BLUE JAYS arched across the chest over the Blue Jay logo which was centered on the uniform top. The lettering was dark blue split with a white highlight line centered in the lettering. The uniform numbers on the back of the jersey were done in the same split style. The road uniforms were light blue with TORONTO across the chest in solid dark blue lettering.

In 1978 a white outline was added to highlight the solid blue lettering. TORONTO on the road uniform top. In 1981 the road uniform top adopted the split lettering style as white letters with a dark blue centering line. The letters now read BLUE JAYS instead of TORONTO as had appeared across the chest since 1977.

It was in 1980 that the players names first appeared on the backs of the uniforms. The names appeared on the home uniforms only and not on the road jerseys. Names first appeared on road uniforms in 1989 after the team had dropped the light blue uniform.

In 1989 the Blue Jays dropped the pullovers and waistband pants for buttoned shirts and belted pants. The home and road uniforms saw the logo move from the center of the uniform top to the left side of the chest below the lettering. The lettering and numbers remained in the distinctive split lettering style. The player names on both of the uniforms appeared in solid dark blue letters. The home uniform remained white but made the above changes and dropped the striping around the collar. The striping of dark blue, white and light blue remained on the sleeves and the sides of the pants.

The road uniform changed from medium blue pant and shirt to a grey uniform with dark blue, white and dark blue striping on the sleeves and pants only. The name BLUE JAYS was replaced with TORONTO in dark blue in the familiar split lettering style with a white centered highlight line arched across the chest. The logo shifted to the left breast below the lettering. The road cap was changed to a solid dark blue cap with the Blue Jays logo centered on the front.

In 1994 the solid dark blue road cap was adopted as both the home and road cap. As well in 1994 an alternate jersey was added for the first time in club history. The alternate jersey being a solid dark blue buttoned jersey.

In the twenty-two year history of the club the team has added patches to the sleeves for four different seasons. In 1986 a special 10 year anniversary patch was added which was displayed on the left arm. In 1991 the Blue Jays uniform added a patch to commemorate the hosting of the 1991 All-Star Game in Toronto. The third patch displayed on the uniform throughout the season was in 1996 when the Blue Jays displayed their commemorative 20th season logo. In 1997 the Blue Jays wore the Jackie Robinson 50th year Anniversary patch. Toronto had short term logos in 1992 and in 1993 when the World Series logo was displayed on the left arm.

In 1997 the Blue Jays uniform changed as they adopted a new team logo. The new/current logo was designed by Major League Properties and brings the colour red into prominence as the maple leaf serves as the backdrop for the bird logo. The Blue Jays maintained the split lettering style on the home white buttoned jersey's and the belted pants but added a light blue centering line to the letters instead of the plain white used in the past. The road uniforms remain grey with TORONTO across the chest but it now appeared in three colours. It along with players names and numbers are now dark blue, with a red centering line and a white outline. The striping on both the home and away pants was switched to blue, light blue and red. The Blue Jays also added an alternate jersey of solid blue with Toronto across the chest with the player number. The split style lettering and numbers are red with a blue centering line and a white outline. All three of the jerseys display the team logo on the left arm.

In 1999 the Blue Jays added a home white sleeveless buttoned jersey. The uniforms, accompanying by dark blue undershirts, have split letters of light blue with a dark blue dividing line. The front of the jersey vest displays BLUE JAYS along with the logo with the player names and numbers on the back. It is the only current jersey without the number on the front of the jersey.

In 2000 the Blue Jays will add an alternate logo on hats which will be used exclusively as spring training and batting practice caps. The logo features an animated Blue Jay holding a bat and reaching around a large red T to toss a ball in the air. The arm of the bird tossing the ball displays a red maple leaf.

In 2001 the Blue Jays will celebrate their 25th Season with a commemorative logo that will be displayed on the left arm of the jersey. In conjunction with the Anniversary logo, the Blue Jays have also made some changes to their uniform. The uniform changed from blue, light blue, and red striping around the sleeves and down the sides of the pants to dark blue piping that surrounds the sleeves, down the sides of the pants and throughout the middle of the jersey. The piping is the same for all the uniforms, except the alternate jersey, which displays red piping that surrounds the sleeves, down the sides of the pants and throughout the middle of the jersey. In addition, the solid gray road and the solid white alternate home jerseys have blue set-in sleeves. Also, the T-bird logo will be added to the front left side of the alternate home jersey, which replaces the number.

Buck
MARTINEZ

MANAGER

BIRTHDATE	November 7, 1948
OPENING DAY AGE	52
BIRTHPLACE	Redding, CA
RESIDENCE	Holmdel, NJ
BATS/THROWS	R/R
HEIGHT/WEIGHT	5-11/200

13

APPOINTED: Named Manager of the Toronto Blue Jays on November 3, 2000.

PERSONAL: John Albert (Buck) Martinez... Married, wife's name Arlene... One child, Casey (8/31/77)... Graduated from Elk Grove High School in California... Attended Sacramento City College, Sacramento State University and Southwestern Missouri State University... Resides in Holmdel, New Jersey... Son Casey was drafted in the 47th round (1384th overall) of the 2000 June Draft and is currently in the Blue Jays organization... Has written two books, both about seasons with the Toronto Blue Jays entitled "From Worst to First" (1985) and "The Last Out" (1986)... Enjoys golfing, hunting and fishing.

BROADCASTING CAREER: 1982-88 worked with the Telemedia Radio Network covering the American League Championship Series, the World Series and the All-Star Game... Began TV broadcast career in 1987 with The Sports Network (TSN)... Was the Colour Commentator for Blue Jays games televised on TSN... Worked radio and television for ESPN Baseball broadcasts beginning in 1992... Served as an analyst on ESPN's Wednesday night Game of the Week telecasts and on Baseball Tonight... Continued to work for both TSN and ESPN through the 2000 baseball season... In addition to his work in baseball, he was the host of the half hour special "The Boys of Winter" and "Knockout", a half-hour game show.

PLAYING CAREER: 1967: Originally signed by the Philadelphia Phillies organization after being selected in the 2nd round of the January Free Agent Draft... Batted .357 in his first professional season with Eugene of the Northwest League (A)... Led the league in games (77) and assists (48) by a catcher... **1968:** Split the season between Spartanburg (A) of the West Carolinas League and Tidewater (A) of the Carolina League where he combined to bat .304 in 44 games with one home run and 25 RBI... Drafted by the Houston Astros organization on December 2 in the minor league draft... Was traded to the Kansas City Royals along with IF Mickey Sinnerud and C Tommie Smith in exchange for C John Jones on December 16... **1969:** Batted .229 in 72 games with four home runs and 23 RBI in his first season in the major leagues... Shared catching duties with Ellie Rodriguez... Was on the restricted list from April 7 to June 17... **1970:** Played in just six games after spending most of the season in active duty in the Air National Guard... **1971:** Was the opening day catcher for the Royals... With Kansas City batted .152 in 22 games... Spent most of the season with Omaha (AAA) of the American Association where he batted .286 with five home runs and 39 RBI in 75 games... **1972:** Did not see any major league action after hitting .174 with four home runs and 12 RBI in 67 games with Omaha of the American Association... Spent much of the season on the disabled list from July 9 to August 25... **1973:** Started the season with Omaha and batted .272 with five home runs and 38 RBI in 82 games... Finished the season with the Royals, playing in 14 games and batted .250 with a home run and six RBI... **1974:** Spent the entire season in the major league for the first time and batted .215 with one home run and eight RBI... **1975:** Played in 80 games and hit three home runs and drove in 23 while batting .226... Caught 79

games, the most by a Royals' catcher that season, posting a .980 fielding percentage... Stole his first career base... **1976:** Caught 94 games and posted a .991 fielding percentage... Hit in a career high 11 straight from May 4-19... Was on the disabled list from May 20 to June 5... On the season batted .228 with five home runs and 34 RBI... In the post season vs. the Yankees batted .333 with five hits and four RBI in 15 at bats... **1977:** Played in just 29 games for the Royals and batted .225 with one home run and nine RBI... Traded to the St. Louis Cardinals along with RHP Mark Littell in exchange for LHP Al Hrabosky on December 8... Was traded that same day to the Milwaukee Brewers in exchange for RHP George Frazier... **1978:** Batted .219 in 89 games and had career highs in runs scored (26) and sacrifice hits (12)... **1979:** Batted a career high .270 with four home runs and 26 RBI in 69 games... Batted .330 in the second half of the season... Pitched in one game for the Brewers allowing one run in an inning of work (1H, BB)... **1980:** Hit .224 with three home runs and 17 RBI in 76 games for the Brewers... Had a .985 fielding percentage and threw out 42% of attempted base-stealers... **1981:** Was traded to the Blue Jays in exchange for OF Gil Kubski on May 11... Made his Blue Jays debut that same day (0-1) as a late inning substitution... Started the next night and picked up a two run double and scored the winning run... For the season batted .227 with four home runs and 21 RBI in 45 games... **1982:** Set career highs in hits (63), doubles (17), home runs (10) and RBI (37)... Batted .242 in 96 games and posted a .988 fielding percentage in 93 games behind the plate... **1983:** Platooned with Ernie Whitt seeing most of his action vs. left-handed pitching... Matched career high with 10 home runs... Seven of his 10 home runs came when catching Jim Clancy... Set career highs with 27 runs and 29 walks... Had a .989 fielding percentage in 85 games as catcher... **1984:** Batted .220 with five home runs and tied career high with 37 RBI... Played in a career high 102 games, 98 behind the plate where he posted a .995 fielding percentage which tied for the league lead (Jim Sundberg, TEX) among catchers with 95 games or more played... Had first career two homer game on June 23 at Boston's Fenway Park... Set club mark for sac flies in a season with nine... Batted .304 with runners in scoring position... Was hitless in 23 at bats from June 23 to July 3... **1985:** Played in just 42 games and batted .162 with four home runs and 14 RBI... Was hitless in 32 at bats from April 28 to May 29... Hit three home runs in 12 at bats... Injured in a collision at the plate with Phil Bradley in Seattle on July 9, where he recorded two putouts on the play... Sustained dislocated right ankle and broken right fibula and was placed on the 21-day disabled list from July 10 through the remainder of the season... Had corrective surgery on July 17... Finished the season writing a season-in-review book titled "From Worst to First"... **1986:** Played in 81 games for Toronto and batted .181 with two home runs and 12 RBI... On June 14 vs. Detroit's Willie Hernandez, hit his second career pinch hit home run (solo) to win the game 6-5 with two outs in the ninth inning... Recorded his 600th career hit on June 12 vs. Detroit and played in his 1000th career game on June 15 vs. Detroit... Wrote his second book called "The Last Out" which noted his final season in the majors as a player.

BUCK MARTINEZ — PLAYING RECORD

Year	Club & League	AVG	G	AB	R	H	2B	3B	HR	RBI	SH-SF	HP	BB	SO	SB-CS
1967	Eugene (NWST)	.357	77	269	53	96	16	4	2	46	4-1	1	25	33	4-4
1968	Spartanburg (WCL)	.393	8	28	6	11	4	0	0	11	0-0	0	4	1	0-1
1968	Tidewater (Caro)	.282	36	110	10	31	12	1	1	14	1-1	0	7	12	0-0
1969	KANSAS CITY (AL)	.229	72	205	14	47	6	1	4	23	1-0	0	8	25	0-0
1970	KANSAS CITY (AL)	.111	6	9	1	1	0	0	0	0	0-0	0	2	1	0-0
1971	Omaha (AmAs)	.286	75	269	34	77	23	1	5	39	3-4	4	35	40	0-0
1971	KANSAS CITY (AL)	.152	22	46	3	7	2	0	0	1	1-1	0	5	9	0-1
1972	Omaha (AmAs)	.174	67	195	23	34	9	0	4	12	1-1	0	4	34	0-1
1973	Omaha (AmAs)	.272	82	254	24	69	13	0	5	38	7-3	1	29	22	0-3
1973	KANSAS CITY (AL)	.250	14	32	2	8	1	0	1	6	1-0	0	4	5	0-0
1974	KANSAS CITY (AL)	.215	43	107	10	23	3	1	1	8	0-0	2	14	19	0-1
1975	KANSAS CITY (AL)	.226	80	226	15	51	9	2	3	23	6-1	1	21	28	1-0
1976	KANSAS CITY (AL)	.228	95	267	24	61	13	3	5	34	9-3	0	16	45	0-0
1977	KANSAS CITY (AL)	.225	29	80	3	18	4	0	1	9	2-0	0	3	12	0-1
1978	MILWAUKEE (AL)	.219	89	256	26	56	10	1	1	20	12-4	0	14	42	1-1
1979	MILWAUKEE (AL)	.270	69	196	17	53	8	0	4	26	8-2	0	8	25	0-1
1980	MILWAUKEE (AL)	.224	76	219	16	49	9	0	3	17	5-1	1	12	33	1-0
1981	TORONTO (AL)	.227	45	128	13	29	8	1	4	21	3-3	1	11	16	1-0
1982	TORONTO (AL)	.242	96	260	26	63	17	0	10	37	2-5	0	24	34	1-1
1983	TORONTO (AL)	.253	88	221	27	56	14	0	10	33	1-2	0	29	39	0-1
1984	TORONTO (AL)	.220	102	232	24	51	13	1	5	37	1-9	2	29	49	0-3
1985	TORONTO (AL)	.162	42	99	11	16	3	0	4	14	0-3	1	10	12	0-0
1986	TORONTO (AL)	.181	81	160	13	29	8	0	2	12	4-1	0	20	25	0-0
Minor Totals		.283	345	1125	150	318	77	6	17	160	16-10	6	104	142	4-9
TORONTO TOTALS		.221	454	1100	114	244	63	2	35	154	11-23	4	123	175	2-5
MAJOR TOTALS		.225	1049	2743	245	618	128	10	58	321	56-35	8	230	419	5-10

CHAMPIONSHIP SERIES RECORD

Year	Club & League	AVG	G	AB	R	H	2B	3B	HR	RBI	SH-SF	HP	BB	SO	SB-CS
1976	KANSAS CITY (AL)	.333	5	15	0	5	0	0	0	4	0-0	0	1	3	0-0

MARTINEZ — TRANSACTIONS

- Selected by the Philadelphia Phillies organization in the 7th round of the January 1967, Free Agent Draft.
- Drafted by the Houston Astros, December 2, 1968.
- Traded to the Kansas City Royals along with IF Mickey Sinnerud and C Tommie Smith in exchange for catcher John Jones on December 16, 1968.
- On restricted list April 7-June 17, 1969.
- On military list April 2-August 10, 1970.
- On disabled list July 9-August 25, 1972.
- On disabled list May 20-June 5, 1976.
- Traded to the St. Louis Cardinals along with RHP Mark Littell in exchange for LHP Al Hrabosky on December 8, 1977.
- Traded to the Milwaukee Brewers in exchange for RHP George Frazier on December 8, 1977.
- Traded to the Toronto Blue Jays in exchange for OF Gil Kubski on May 10, 1981.
- On disabled list (dislocated right ankle and broken right fibula) July 10-through remainder of the season, 1985.

BLUE JAYS MANAGERS

	G *	W	L	PCT	YEARS
Gaston, Cito	1316	681	635	.517	1989-97
Cox, Bobby	648	355	292	.549	1982-85
Williams, Jimy	523	281	241	.537	1986-89
Hartsfield, Roy	472	163	309	.345	1977-79
Fregosi, Jim	324	167	157	.515	1999-2000
Mattick, Bobby	268	104	164	.388	1980-81
Johnson, Tim	163	88	74	.543	1998
Tenace, Gene #$	36	21	15	.583	1991, 1994
Warner, Harry ‡	12	3	9	.250	1978
Queen, Mel †	5	4	1	.800	1997
Martinez, Buck	—	—	—	—	2001-

* Includes Tie Games.
# Served as Interim Manager, August 21 to September 26, 1991 in the absence of Manager Cito Gaston (ruptured disk in lower back).
$ Served as Interim Manager, May 27-29, 1994 in the absence of Manager Cito Gaston (suspension).
† Served as Interim Manager, September 24-28, 1997 after dismissal of Cito Gaston.
‡ Served as interim Manager, May 20 to 29, 1978 in the absence of Manager Ray Hartsfield (wife's illness).

AGE WHEN MANAGERS TOOK OVER THEIR FIRST GAME

MANAGER	FIRST GAME	AGE
ROY HARTSFIELD	April 7, 1977	51
HARRY WARNER*	May 20, 1978	49
BOBBY MATTICK	April 9, 1980	64
BOBBY COX	April 6, 1982	40
JIMY WILLIAMS	April 8, 1986	42
CITO GASTON	May 15, 1989	45
GENE TENACE*	August 21, 1991	45
MEL QUEEN*	September 24, 1997	55
TIM JOHNSON	April 1, 1998	48
JIM FREGOSI	April 6, 1999	57
BUCK MARTINEZ	April 1, 2001	52

*- denotes interim manager

Terry
BEVINGTON

THIRDBASE COACH

35

BIRTHDATE	July 27, 1956
OPENING DAY AGE	44
BIRTHPLACE	Akron, OH
RESIDENCE	Santa Monica, CA
BATS/THROWS	R/R
HEIGHT/WEIGHT	6-2/205

APPOINTED: Named Third Base Coach on March 31, 1999.

PERSONAL: Terry Paul Bevington... Married Cyndi Lochard... Has two children, Courtney Taylor (March 4, 1993) and Trevor Paul (October 22, 1996)... Older brother Zach was longtime minor league umpire and called games Terry managed... Lists Johnny Neun, a former Yankees manager and coach, Dee Fondy and Cal McLish, longtime members of the Brewers organization, as influences in his career... Attended Santa Monica (CA) HS and Santa Monica City College.

PLAYING CAREER: 1974: Began professional playing career as a catcher in the New York Yankees organization... Was selected in the fourth round of the June 1974 First Year Draft... **1975:** Named to New York-Penn League All-Star team in his second pro season... **1976:** Played in just two games and collected just three at-bats... **1977:** Was released on July 7 and then signed with Milwaukee as a free agent on February 2, 1978... **1978-1980:** Played three seasons in the Brewers organization before retiring following the 1980 season... Was a .247 (265-1074) hitter with 16 home runs in 368 career games.

COACHING/MANAGERIAL CAREER: Began his minor league managerial career in 1981 at the age of 24... Has managed 1245 minor-league games including 142 with the Syracuse SkyChiefs (AAA) in 1998, his first season in the Toronto Blue Jays organization... Won division titles in five of his nine seasons as a minor league manager and compiled a 691-554 (.555) career mark... Reached the playoffs in each of his last five seasons as a minor league manager (1985-88, 1998)... Managed in the Milwaukee Brewers organization for seven seasons before joining the Chicago White Sox organization in 1988... **1981:** Began his managerial career at Class A Burlington of the Midwest League... **1982:** Again managed in the Midwest League with Beloit... **1983:** Won the first half of the California League race at Class A Stockton... Lost to Redwood in the league semi-finals, (1-2)... **1984:** Managed El Paso in the Texas League to second place finishes in both halves of the season... **1985:** Was named Texas League Manager of the Year at Class AA El Paso... Lost to Jackson in league championships in four straight... **1986:** Took Vancouver to first place finishes in both halves of the season in the Northern Division... Lost in the finals to Las Vegas (2-3) after defeating Tacoma in the Division finals (3-0)... **1987:** Managed the Class AAA Denver of the American

Association and claimed a divisional title... Lost in the finals to Indianapolis (1-4) after defeating Oklahoma City in the semi-finals (3-2)... **1988:** Managed the White Sox Class AAA Vancouver affiliate to the Pacific Coast League Northern Division title in both halves of the season... Lost to Las Vegas in the finals (1-3) after defeating Portland (3-0) in the semifinals... Was his last season managing before he joined the Sox coaching staff in 1989 as first base coach... **1990-95:** Was the third base coach of the Chicago White Sox... Has been ejected three times in his career as a coach (April 29, 1989 at New York; October 4, 1991 at Seattle; September 6, 1992 at Kansas City)... **1995:** Became the White Sox 35th manager in club history on June 2, taking over for Gene Lamont... Took over when the club was 11-20, before leading them to a 57-56 record for the remainder of the season... Was the 16th White Sox manager to take over during the season and just the third to post a winning record in that campaign (excluding Interim managers)... Was the second manager in franchise history with no Major League playing experience... Was ejected four times (June 17, John Shulock at California; June 21, Tim McClelland at Seattle; July 23, Larry Young at Milwaukee; August 14, Ken Kaiser vs California)... Was suspended four games for ejection on July 23 by AL President Gene Budig, which was served from August 1 through 4... **1996:** Finished the season with an 85-77 mark and in second place behind the AL Central Division Champion, Cleveland Indians... Chicago led the AL Wild Card race for 52 days following the All-Star Break before being eliminated from playoff contention on the next to last day of the season... The White Sox posted the AL's third biggest improvement in winning percentage in 1996, in his first full season as manager... Was ejected twice, on May 9 by Jim Evans at Baltimore and on August 27 at Milwaukee by Larry Barnett... **1997:** Guided the White Sox to an 80-81 finish, second in the AL Central division, six games back of Cleveland... Was ejected by umpire Ed Hickox on April 20 for arguing balls and strikes... Was ejected automatically on June 4 after Bill Simas was ejected for throwing at Marquis Grissom... Compiled a record of 222 and 214 in 2 1/2 season as manager of the Chicago White Sox... **1998:** Joined the Blue Jays organization as the manager of Syracuse of the International League and led the SkyChiefs to a wildcard berth... Finished with a 80-62 record, second in the Northern Division, before losing three straight to Buffalo in the semifinals.

TERRY BEVINGTON — PLAYING CAREER

Year Club & League	AVG	G	AB	R	H	2B	3B	HR	RBI	BB	SO	SB
1974 Johnson City (Appy)	.198	63	222	33	44	10	0	2	30	34	26	2
1975 Oneonta (NYP)	.264	60	193	24	51	11	1	2	23	25	19	3
1976 Oneonta (NYP)	.000	2	3	0	0	0	0	0	0	0	0	0
1977 FtLauderdale (FSL)	.217	23	60	7	13	1	0	1	8	5	7	0
1978 Burlington (Mid)	.240	63	179	22	43	14	0	4	23	22	31	4
1979 Holyoke (East)	.252	85	214	26	54	12	0	4	21	31	31	8
1980 Burlington (Mid)	.265	39	117	14	31	7	0	2	11	13	9	11
1980 Vancouver (PCL)	.337	33	86	13	29	5	0	1	8	14	7	6
Minor Totals	.247	368	1074	139	265	60	1	16	124	144	130	38

BEVINGTON — TRANSACTIONS

- Selected by the New York Yankees organization in the fourth round of the June 1974 First Year Draft.
- On disabled list April 20-June 30, 1976.
- Released by the New York Yankees organization July 5, 1977.
- Signed by the Milwaukee Brewers organization February 7, 1978.

MANAGERIAL/COACHING CAREER

(Joined Blue Jays Organization in 1998)

1981	Manager, Burlington, Midwest League (Brewers)
1982	Manager, Beloit, Midwest League (Brewers)
1983	Manager, Stockton, California League (Brewers)
1984-85	Manager, El Paso, Texas League (Brewers)
1986	Manager, Vancouver, Pacific Coast League (Brewers)
1987	Manager, Denver, American Association (Brewers)
1988	Manager, Vancouver, Pacific Coast League (White Sox)
1989	First Base Coach, Chicago White Sox
1990-95	Third Base Coach, Chicago White Sox
1995-97	Manager, Chicago White Sox
1998	Manager, Syracuse, International League
1999-	Third Base Coach, Toronto Blue Jays

RECORD AS MANAGER

Year	Club & League	W-L	PCT	Finish
1981	Burlington (Mid)	54-81	.400	(3rd in Div., 2nd in Div.)
1982	Beloit (Mid)	71-68	.511	(2nd in Div.)
1983	Stockton (Cal)	79-59	.572	(1st in Div., 3rd in Div.)
1984	El Paso (Tex)	72-63	.533	(2nd in Div., 2nd in Div.)
1985	El Paso (Tex)	86-50	.632	(1st in Div., 1st in Div.)
1986	Vancouver (PCL)	85-53	.616	(1st in Div., 1st in Div.)
1987	Denver (AmAs)	79-61	.564	(1st in Div.)
1988	Vancouver (PCL)	85-57	.599	(1st in Div., 1st in Div.)
1995	CHICAGO (AL)	57-56	.504	(3rd in Div.)
1996	CHICAGO (AL)	85-77	.525	(2nd in Div.)
1997	CHICAGO (AL)	80-81	.497	(2nd in Div.)
1998	Syracuse (Int)	80-62	.563	(2nd in Div.)
Minor Totals		691-554	.555	
MAJOR TOTALS		222-214	.509	

POST-SEASON PLAY

Year	Club & League	W-L	PCT	Finish
1983	Stockton (Cal)	1-2	.333	(Lost to Redwood 2-1 in semi-finals)
1985	El Paso (Tex)	0-4	.000	(Lost to Jackson 4-0 in finals)
1986	Vancouver (PCL)	5-3	.625	(Defeated Tacoma 3-0 in semi-finals; lost to Las Vegas 3-2 in finals)
1987	Denver (AmAs)	4-6	.400	(Defeated Okla. City 3-2 in semi-finals; lost to Indianapolis 4-1 in finals)
1988	Vancouver (PCL)	4-3	.571	(Defeated Portland 3-0 in semi-finals; lost to Las Vegas 3-1 in finals)
1998	Syracuse (Int)	0-3	.000	(Lost to Buffalo 3-0 in semi-finals)
Totals		14-21	.400	

Mark
CONNOR
PITCHING COACH

BIRTHDATE	May 27, 1949
OPENING DAY AGE	51
BIRTHPLACE	Brooklyn, NY
RESIDENCE	Knoxville, TN
BATS/THROWS	R/R
HEIGHT/WEIGHT	6-2/205

53

APPOINTED: Named Pitching Coach for the Toronto Blue Jays on November 3, 2000.

PERSONAL: Mark Peter Connor... Married, wife's name is Katie... Three children, Jennie (9/14/76), Shannon (2/8/79) and Ryan (1/24/85)... Graduated from Chaminade High School in Mineola, NY, in 1967, then attended Belmont Abbey College... Earned a B.S. degree from Manhattan College in 1972 and received the Topps Award as a college All-Star in 1971... In 1971 he fanned 20 batters in a game vs. Columbia University... Earned his Masters Degree from the University of Tennessee in 1974-75 where he worked as a baseball coach... Mark's first coaching job came with the University where he worked as their pitching coach from 1974-78 while completing graduate school... During his stints at U.T., he had the opportunity to coach future big-league hurlers Rick Honeycutt, Mike Smithson and Greg McMichael... Credits Sammy Ellis, a Red Sox instructor, in having the biggest influence on his career... Off-field time is shared among his family, the golf course, coaching in clinics throughout the country, and closely following the gridiron adventures of the Tennessee Volunteers.

PLAYING CAREER: 1971: 1971: Was 4-5 with three saves and an ERA of 2.78 for the Minnesota Twins New York-Penn League Affiliate in Auburn... Started three of 20 games and tossed one complete game... **1972:** With Wisconsin Rapids was 3-3 in 32 relief appearances with five saves... Was his last season after suffering a career ending arm injury.

COACHING CAREER: 1978: Pitching Coach for Paintsville, the Yankees affiliate in the Appalachian League... **1980-1982:** Worked as the Pitching coach for Greensboro... **1983-1984:** Served as pitching coach for the Yankees AAA affiliate, the Columbus Clippers... **1998-1989:** Worked as the Head baseball coach for the University of Tennessee... **1990:** Was the bullpen coach for the New York Yankees... **1991-1992:** Moved to the position of Pitching coach for the New York Yankees... **1993:** Returned to position of Bullpen coach for the Yankees... **1994-1995:** Joined the Toronto Blue Jays organization where he served as the Pitching coach for the Knoxville Smokies of the Southern League (AA)... **1996-1997:** Joined the Arizona Diamondbacks and served as their Pitching coordinator... Spent much of his time scouting and researching for the expansion draft and inaugural season... **1998-2000:** Was the Pitching coach for the Arizona Diamondbacks... In 1999 the Diamondbacks posted the second best ERA in the majors and were highlighted by Randy Johnson who captured the NL Cy Young Award... In 2000 Randy Johnson captured his second consecutive Cy Young Award.

MARK CONNOR — PLAYING RECORD

Year	Club & League	W-L	ERA	G	GS	CG	ShO	SV	IP	H	R	ER	HR	HB	BB-IBB	SO	WP
1971	Auburn (NYP)	4-5	2.78	20	3	1	0	3	55.0	55	28	17	2	2	26-5	57	3
1972	Wisconsin Rapids (Mid)	3-3	3.83	32	0	0	0	5	54.0	49	29	23	1	4	25-1	51	6
Minor Totals		**7-8**	**3.31**	**52**	**3**	**1**	**0**	**8**	**109.0**	**104**	**57**	**40**	**3**	**6**	**51-6**	**108**	**9**

COACHING CAREER

1974-78	Pitching Coach, University of Tennessee
1978	Pitching Coach, Paintsville (Independent)
1979	Scout, New York Yankees
1980-82	Pitching Coach, Greensboro (Yankees)
1983-84	Pitching Coach, Columbus (Yankees)
1984-85	Pitching Coach, New York Yankees
1985	Pitching Coach, Ft. Lauderdale (Yankees)
1986-87	Pitching Coach, New York Yankees
1988-89	Head Baseball Coach, University of Tennessee
1990	Bullpen Coach, New York Yankees
1991-92	Pitching Coach, New York Yankees
1993	Bullpen Coach, New York Yankees
1994-95	Pitching Coach, Knoxville (Blue Jays)
1996-97	Pitching Coordinator, Arizona Diamondbacks
1998-2000	Pitching Coach, Arizona Diamondbacks

Cito GASTON

BATTING COACH

41

BIRTHDATE .... March 17, 1944
OPENING DAY AGE 56
BIRTHPLACE .... San Antonio, TX
RESIDENCE .... Oldsmar, FL
BATS/THROWS .... R/R
HEIGHT/WEIGHT 6-4/220

APPOINTED: Joined the Blue Jays' coaching staff on November 4, 1981... Appointed interim manager on May 15, 1989... Named to the permanent post on May 31, 1989... Released of duties on September 24, 1997... Hired as the Blue Jays' batting coach on October 12, 1999.

PERSONAL: Clarence Edwin Gaston... Two children, Rachell and Shawn... 1962 graduate of Holy Cross High School in Corpus Christi.

PLAYING CAREER: 1964: Originally signed by the Milwaukee Braves after an all-star career at Holy Cross High School (3 letters)... Collected hits in 43 of 60 games at Binghamton (NYP) and Greenville (WCL)... **1965:** Spent the season at the Class A level with West Palm Beach... Averaged 1 hit every 2 games... **1966:** Led the New York-Penn League in HR (28), RBI (104), TB (255) and was 4th in runs (84)... Named to the All-Star team and was the league MVP... **1967:** Made his ML debut, appearing in 9 games for the Atlanta Braves... Had started the season with Austin of the Texas League where he was named to the League's All-Star team... **1968:** Split the season between Richmond and Shreveport, batting .279 with the latter... **1969:** Was the Padres' 30th and final selection in the NL Expansion Draft... Hit .230 for the expansion Padres... **1970:** Set career best with 29 HR and 93 RBI while batting .318... Represented the Padres in the All-Star Game going 0-2... Was named the Padres' MVP... **1971:** Hit just .228 with 39 of 118 hits going for extra bases... **1972:** Hit .269 and averaged close to 1 hit per game (102/111)... On supplemental DL, May 17-June 2... Hit a PH grand slam HR vs the Cubs' Ferguson Jenkins on June 14, the 2nd in franchise history and the 1st time since May 2, 1969... **1973:** 38 of 119 hits were extra base hits... Marked 3rd time in 4 years that he had reached double figures in HR... **1974:** Final season with the Padres and had average drop to .213, his lowest for a full ML season... **1975:** Returned to the Braves organization after being traded for Danny Frisella on Nov. 7, 1974... Roomed with Home Run great Hank Aaron... Saw limited duty appearing in only 64 games... **1976:** Had best season since 1970 hitting .291 while appearing in 69 games... **1977:** Played in just 56 games and hit .271... Had three sacrifice flies... **1978:** Final season at ML level... Started the season with the Braves and was sold to the Pirates on Sept. 22... combined to hit .233 in 62 games... **1979:** Was granted free agency on Nov. 2, 1978 and invited to the Braves' spring training camp... Subsequently released and played in the Inter-American League before the league folded on June 30... Joined Leon (Mexican League) to finish season, batting .337 in 24 games... **1980:** Completed playing career with Leon while playing in 48 games and collecting 44 hits.

COACHING AND MANAGING CAREER: 1981: At the urging of Braves' VP of Player Personnel, Hank Aaron, he joined the Braves as a minor league hitting instructor... **1982-1989:** Hired by then-manager Bobby Cox as the club's first full-time batting instructor, replacing the part-time Bobby Doerr... Improved club's overall average in 1982 by 36 points... Club batting average while hitting instructor: 1982: (.262), 1983: (.277), 1984: (.273), 1985: (.269), 1986: (.269), 1987: (.269), 1988: (.268), 1989: (.260)... **1989:** Appointed interim manager on May 15 upon the dismissal of Jimy Williams... Posted an 8-7 record before assuming the full-time title on May 31... Club was 77-49 overall from May 15 through season's end- the best record in the Major Leagues... Became the 24th rookie manager since 1900 to finish in first place... Named Baseball Man of the Year in Canada by Toronto-Montreal BBWAA... **1990:** Led the Blue Jays to a second place finish in the AL East, 2.0 games behind the Red Sox... **1991:** Was his second full season at the helm of the Blue Jays posting an overall 72-57 won-lost record as the Blue Jays finished in first place, 7.0 games ahead of the Red Sox and Tigers... 1991 was his second AL East Division title in 3 seasons as Manager... Served as AL Coach at All-Star Game... Experienced lower back problems (compressed nerve root) and was hospitalized for 10 days (August 21-31) leaving behind a record of 66-54 with a 2.5 game lead... Hitting coach, Gene Tenace (19-14) assumed the managerial reigns on August 21 until Cito returned on September 27 vs the Twins... Had back surgery at Mt. Sinai Hospital in Toronto on January 7, 1992... **1992:** Was third full year at the controls for the Blue Jays and fourth overall since taking over in May of 1989 leading Toronto to their first ever World Series victory... **1993:** Won his fourth American League East Division crown and his third consecutive, becoming just the second AL East manager to win 3 consecutive divisional championships since divisional play started in 1969 (Earl Weaver- Baltimore)... Fourth Manager in AL annals to have accomplished the feat (Weaver- 1969-1971, Herzog- 1976-1978, LaRussa- 1988-1990)... Became just the third manager since 1969 to win 4 divisional crowns in 5 years (Earl Weaver- Baltimore: 1969, 1970, 1971, 1973 & Sparky Anderson- Cincinnati: 1972, 1973, 1975, 1976)... Cito became the winningest manager in Blue Jays history passing Bobby Cox with his 356th victory with a 4-1 win over Milwaukee on May 24... On June 20th vs the Red Sox, Gaston became the Blue Jays leader in games managed with his 649th surpassing Bobby Cox... Named "The Sporting News" Sportsman of the Year along with Blue Jays Executive Vice-President and General Manager Pat Gillick... **1994:** Received Honourary Doctor of Laws from the University of Toronto on June 10... Was first losing season as Toronto manager finishing in third place, 16.0 games behind the Yankees with a record of 55-60... Suspended for three games - May 27-29... Was his first ever suspension as a coach or manager... Named the first winner of the Rube Foster Character Award... Rube Foster Character Award presented to the Manager or Coach who exemplifies character, dedication and love of the game... **1995:** Suffered second straight losing season, 56-88, finishing tied for last in the American League... Ejected from six games... **1996:** 15th season on Blue Jays ML staff and seventh full

season as manager, eighth overall... Guided the team to a fourth place finish in the AL East with a 74-88 record, his third consecutive losing season... Received two ejections... Team winning percentage of .457 was .068 points higher than the 56-88, .389 Blue Jays of 1995... Managed his 1000th game on April 5 at Cleveland, a 7-1 win... Captured career win #600 on September 8, 4-2 over the Yankees in New York... **1997:** Led the club to a 72-85 record before being relieved of his duties as manager on September 24... Left as the longest serving manager in club history, managing 1,316 games from May 15 1989 to September 24... Was his 16th season on the Blue Jays ML staff... Was ejected from two games, July 20 at Anaheim by Mike Everitt and September 3 in New York against the Mets by Charlie Williams... **1999:** Returned to coaching as the batting coach in Toronto.

CAREER NOTES: Is one of four men on the Blue Jays Level of Excellence... He joins George Bell, Dave Stieb and Joe Carter and is the only non-player recognized... He and Joe Carter were enshrined in 1999... Leads the Blue Jays in games managed with 1,316 and wins with 681... Received honourary Doctor of Laws from University of Toronto on June 10, 1994... Named "The Sporting News" Sportsman of the Year in 1993 along with Blue Jays Executive Vice-President and General Manager, Pat Gillick... Named Rube Foster Award winner in 1994... Named Baseball Man of the Year in Canada in 1989 by the Toronto-Montreal BBWAA... American League All-Star Game manager in 1993 and 1994, and an All-Star coach in 1991.

POST SEASON EXPERIENCE: As a player, Gaston never participated in the post season (10 Major League seasons)... Was the Blue Jays' hitting instructor in 1985 when Toronto captured its first AL East crown... The club hit .269 vs the Royals in the 1985 ALCS; the same as the squads regular season mark... In the 1989 ALCS vs the Oakland Athletics- lost in 5 games with the lone win coming in Game #3... Lost 4-1 to the Twins in the 1991 ALCS... Since 1969 only 3 other managers have won back-to-back-to-back AL Divisional titles (Earl Weaver with Baltimore- 1969,1970,1971, Whitey Herzog with Kansas City- 1976,1977,1978 & Tony LaRussa with Oakland- 1988, 1989, 1990)... Became the 20th AL manager since 1903 to win a World Series in his first attempt as Toronto defeated the Braves 4 games to 2 in 1992... Guided the Blue Jays to their second consecutive World Series Championship in 1993 with a 4 games to 2 win over the Phillies... First manager to win back to back World Series Championships since Sparky Anderson with the Reds in 1975-1976 and the first AL Manager to accomplish the feat since Dick Williams with Oakland (1972-1973)... Is 18-16 lifetime as a manager in post-season play.

CITO GASTON — PLAYING RECORD

Year	Club & League	AVG	G	AB	R	H	2B	3B	HR	RBI
1964	Binghamton (NYP)	.238	11	21	1	5	2	0	1	4
1964	Greenville (Cal)	.230	49	165	15	38	6	3	0	16
1965	West Palm Beach (FSL)	.188	70	202	14	38	5	3	0	9
1966	Batavia (NYP)	.330	114	433	84	143	18	5	28	104
1966	Austin (Tex)	.300	4	10	2	3	1	1	0	4
1967	Austin (Tex)	.305	136	505	72	154	24	6	10	70
1967	ATLANTA (NL)	.120	9	25	1	3	0	1	0	1
1968	Richmond (Int)	.239	21	71	9	17	4	0	2	8
1968	Shreveport (Tex)	.279	96	340	49	95	15	4	6	57
1969	SAN DIEGO (NL)	.230	129	391	20	90	11	7	2	28
1970	SAN DIEGO (NL)	.318	146	584	92	186	26	9	29	93
1971	SAN DIEGO (NL)	.228	141	518	57	118	13	9	17	61
1972	SAN DIEGO (NL)	.269	111	379	30	102	14	0	7	44
1973	SAN DIEGO (NL)	.250	133	476	51	119	18	4	16	57
1974	SAN DIEGO (NL)	.213	106	267	19	57	11	0	6	33
1975	ATLANTA (NL)	.241	64	141	17	34	4	0	6	15
1976	ATLANTA (NL)	.291	69	134	15	39	4	0	4	25
1977	ATLANTA (NL)	.271	56	85	6	23	4	0	3	21
1978	ATL. PITTS (NL)	.233	62	120	6	28	1	0	1	9
1979	Santo Dom. (IntA)	.324	40	148	22	48	5	0	1	14
1979	Leon (Mex)	.337	24	83	5	28	2	0	1	8
1980	Leon (Mex)	.238	48	185	16	44	5	0	4	27
ML TOTALS		.256	1026	3120	314	799	106	30	91	387

ALL-STAR GAME RECORD

Year	Club & League	AVG	G	AB	R	H	2B	3B	HR	RBI
1970	NL at CIN	.000	1	2	0	0	0	0	0	0

GASTON — TRANSACTIONS

- Selected by San Diego Padres from Atlanta in expansion draft, October 14, 1968.
- On disabled list, May 17 to June 2, 1972.
- Traded to Atlanta Braves for Pitcher Danny Frisella, November 7, 1974.
- Sold to Pittsburgh Pirates, September 22, 1978.
- Granted free agency, November 2, 1978; signed by Santo Domingo of Mexican League, April 10, 1979.
- On suspended list, June 21 to July 21, 1979.
- Released, July 22, 1979; signed by Leon Of Mexican League, July 22, 1979.
- Minor League hitting instructor, Atlanta Braves, 1981.
- Coach, Toronto Blue Jays, 1982-1989.
- Appointed interim manager of Blue Jays, May 15, 1989.
- Named as manager of Blue Jays, May 31, 1989.
- Named as batting coach of Blue Jays, October 12, 1999.

MANAGERIAL RECORD

Year	Club & League	W-L	Position
1989	TORONTO (AL)	77-49	1st, East Division *
1990	TORONTO (AL)	86-76	2nd, East Division
1991	TORONTO (AL)	72-57	1st, East Division #
1992	TORONTO (AL)	96-66	1st, East Division, won World Series
1993	TORONTO (AL)	95-67	1st, East Division, won World Series
1994	TORONTO (AL)	53-59	3rd, East Division $
1995	TORONTO (AL)	56-88	5th, East Division
1996	TORONTO (AL)	74-88	4th, East Division
1997	TORONTO (AL)	72-85	5th, East Division**
TOTALS		681-635	

* Club finished overall at 89-73 and were 12-24 when the managerial change was made.
\# Missed 33 games due to lower back problems.
$ Suspended for three games May 27-29, 1994.
** Relieved of managerial duties on September 24, 1997.

Garth
IORG

FIRSTBASE COACH

BIRTHDATE . . . . October 12, 1954
OPENING DAY AGE 46
BIRTHPLACE . . . . Arcata, CA
RESIDENCE . . . . Palm Harbour, FL
BATS/THROWS . . . . R/R
HEIGHT/WEIGHT 5-11/170

16

APPOINTED: Named as First Base Coach on November 3, 2000.

PERSONAL: Garth Ray Iorg... Graduated from Arcata High School in California where he played shortstop in baseball, also played basketball and football... Attended College of the Redwoods in Eureka California... Older brother Dane Iorg played ten years in the major leagues with the Phillies, Cardinals, Royals and Padres... Another brother, Lee Iorg, played in the Mets farm system from 1974 to 1977.

COACHING CAREER: 1990: Began his managing career with the Medicine Hat Blue Jays of the Pioneer League (A)... **1991:** Moved to South Atlantic League (A) where he managed for Myrtle Beach... **1992-1995:** Moved to the Southern League (AA) with the Knoxville Smokies... In the 1993 season led the Smokies to post-season play as the second half division champions... Knoxville defeated Greenville, three games to two but fell to Birmingham in the SAL Championship finals, three games to one... In 1994 was named as the Best Managing Prospect in the Southern League by Baseball America... **1996:** Stayed in Knoxville, working as a coach... **1997:** Moved to AAA to manage the Syracuse Sky-Chiefs of the International League... **1998-2000:** Worked as a roving infield instructor in the Blue Jays organization.

PLAYING CAREER: 1973: Signed with the Yankees organization after being selected in the eighth round of the June Free agent draft... Assigned to Johnson City of the Appalachian League... **1974:** Spent first of two seasons at Fort Lauderdale where he recorded 20 sacrifice hits... **1975:** Appeared in only 50 games with Fort Lauderdale but increased his average 38 points from the previous season... Promoted to West Haven of the Eastern League (AA) where he hit .250 in 76 games with 21 RBI... **1976:** Opened the season with West Haven but appeared in only 76 games

after suffering a broken leg in a collision at second base in June... Was selected by the Toronto Blue Jays in the American League Expansion Draft on November 5, 1976, was Toronto's 21st selection... **1977:** Moved to AAA and hit .294 with 34 RBI in 70 games for Charleston... **1978:** Opened the season with the Blue Jays and made his ML debut on April 9 at Detroit, started at second base and was 1-3... Was optioned to Syracuse on May 20... Was on the disabled list with Syracuse, June 18 to 28... Suffered a broken left hand while playing winter ball in Venezuela... **1979:** Hit .281 in 121 games with Syracuse (AAA)... Had 46 walks and 44 strike-outs in 430 at bats... **1980:** Started the season in Syracuse and earned promotion to Toronto on May 24 after hitting .281 in 21 games... Hit his first ML home run on June 22 vs Texas' Sparky Lyle... Played all four infield positions and appeared in the outfield in 14 games... **1981:** Had his first full season in the ML and hit .242 in 70 games... Saw action primarily as a utility infielder until 2B Damaso Garcia was injured late in the season... Hit in nine straight games from August 29 to September 7 to match his then career high... **1982:** Experimented as a catcher in spring training... Opened the season with an eight game hit streak through April 21... Was platooned with Rance Mulliniks at third while also seeing action at second base... Posted a career high ten game hit streak from September 15 to 28... Matched a then club record with seven sacrifice flies... Lone HR came against Frank Viola of the Twins on September 28 (1st game)... **1983:** Again used in a platoon role with Mulliniks at third-base and hit .275 with 22 doubles and 39 RHO in 122 games... Hit over .300 until May 22... Posted first career four-hit game on August 9 at New York... Was 7-0 in stolen base attempts... **1984:** Hit .227 in 121 games... In the first half hit .261... On April 19 was 4-4 with two RBI vs Baltimore... Hit his first HR in 131 games on September 2 vs Minnesota's Frank Viola... Despite .227

average, hit .286 with runners in scoring position... **1985:** Hit a career high .313 in 131 games with 22 doubles, a career high seven home runs and 37 RBI... Again platooned with Mulliniks at third and also made 20 starts at second for the injured Damaso Garcia... Was second in the majors in most points added to 1985 batting average (.086), trailing only Wayne Tolleson (.100) of Texas... Appeared in 131 games, making 73 starts... Was 2-16 in the ALCS against Kansas City... **1986:** Set career highs in games (137) and RBI (44)... Starts 76 games and in those starts hit .245 with two home runs and 31 RBI... Delivered his first career pinch-hit home run on June 15, a three run shot against Detroit's Chuck Cary... Collected three RBI the next day, June 16 vs Milwaukee... Was ejected from three games... Made 90 appearances at third base and 52 times at second base... Tied for the club lead with ten pinch hits (Leach)... Selected as the Good Guy Award winner by the Toronto chapter of the BBWAA... **1987:** Hit .210 with 11 doubles, four home runs and 30 RBI in his final season... Played 91 games at second base, 28 at third base and five times at designated hitter... Hit .276 with runners in scoring position... Had a team leading six sacrifice hits.

GARTH IORG — PLAYING RECORD

Year	Club & League	AVG	G	AB	R	H	2B	3B	HR	RBI	BB	SO	SB
1973	Johnson City (Appy)	.237	51	169	20	40	3	0	3	13	8	29	3
1974	Ft. Lauderdale (FSL)	.215	102	325	30	70	11	4	0	38	29	49	7
1975	Ft. Lauderdale (FSL)	.253	50	186	10	47	4	2	0	16	12	14	14
1975	West Haven (East)	.250	76	236	19	59	6	2	0	21	22	30	8
1976	West Haven (East)	.275	78	273	31	75	17	1	1	24	16	15	15
1977	Charleston (Int)	.294	70	262	35	77	8	3	1	34	21	33	10
1978	TORONTO (AL)	.163	19	49	3	8	0	0	0	3	3	4	0
1978	Syracuse (Int)	.216	89	324	29	70	16	2	6	25	18	55	2
1979	Syracuse (Int)	.281	121	430	65	121	23	4	5	39	46	44	2
1980	Syracuse (Int)	.299	32	134	17	40	6	3	1	14	7	17	7
1980	TORONTO (AL)	.248	80	222	24	55	10	1	2	14	12	39	2
1981	TORONTO (AL)	.242	70	215	17	52	11	0	0	10	7	31	2
1982	TORONTO (AL)	.285	129	417	45	119	20	5	1	36	12	38	3
1983	TORONTO (AL)	.275	122	375	40	103	22	5	2	39	13	45	7
1984	TORONTO (AL)	.227	121	247	24	56	10	3	1	25	5	16	1
1985	TORONTO (AL)	.313	131	288	33	90	22	1	7	37	21	26	2
1986	TORONTO (AL)	.260	137	327	30	85	19	1	3	44	20	47	3
1987	TORONTO (AL)	.210	122	310	35	65	11	0	4	30	21	52	2
Minor Totals		.256	669	2339	256	599	94	21	17	224	179	286	68
MAJOR TOTALS		.258	931	2450	251	633	125	16	20	238	114	298	22

CHAMPIONSHIP SERIES RECORD

Year	Club & League	AVG	G	AB	R	H	2B	3B	HR	RBI	BB	SO	SB
1985	TORONTO (AL)	.133	6	15	1	2	0	0	0	0	1	3	0

IORG — TRANSACTIONS

- Selected by the New York Yankees as their 8th pick in the 1973 June Draft.
- Selected by the Toronto Blue Jays in the 4th round on November 5, 1976 in American League Expansion Draft.
- On disabled list, June 29-September 1, 1977.
- On disabled list, June 18-June 28, 1978.

MANAGERIAL/COACHING CAREER (All in Blue Jays Organization)

1990	Manager, Medicine Hat, Pioneer League
1991	Manager, Myrtle Beach, South Atlantic League
1992-95	Manager, Knoxville, Southern League
1996	Coach, Knoxville, Southern League
1997	Manager, Syracuse, International League
1998-2000	Roving Infield Instructor, Toronto Blue Jays organization

RECORD AS MANAGER

Year	Club & League	W-L	PCT	Finish
1990	Medicine Hat (Pio)	20-46	.303	(4th in Div.)
1991	Myrtle Beach (SAL)	60-79	.432	(6th in Div., 6th in Div.)
1992	Knoxville (Sou)	56-88	.389	(5th in Div., 5th in Div.)
1993	Knoxville (Sou)	71-71	.500	(4th in Div., 1st in Div.)
1994	Knoxville (Sou)	64-76	.457	(3rd in Div., 4th in Div.)
1995	Knoxville (Sou)	54-90	.375	(5th in Div., 5th in Div.)
1997	Syracuse (Int)	55-87	.387	(4th in Div.)
TOTALS		380-537	.414	

POST-SEASON PLAY

Year	Club & League	W-L	PCT	Finish
1993	Knoxville (Sou)	4-5	.444	(Def. Greenville 3G to 2 in semi-finals; lost to Birmingham 3G to 1 in championship finals)

CALL IT A DRAW

The Blue Jays have played three tie games in their history. The first one was on May 13, 1984 at Cleveland. With one out in the top of the 8th inning, the rains came and play could not resume with the score tied at four. The game had to be completely replayed as part of a TWDH on August 15. The second occurrence was at Cleveland on August 26, 1986. Play was halted after nine innings due to rain with the score notched at six. The game was completely replayed as part on an August 27 TWDH. The third time was on April 26, 1998 after six innings. The Blue Jays and White Sox were tied at five when the rains came and cancelled the game in Chicago. The game was completely replayed on July 15 as part of a TWDH. Though the games were rained out, the statistics from the games were entered into the books.

Gil
PATTERSON
BULLPEN COACH

BIRTHDATE . . . . September 5, 1955
OPENING DAY AGE 45
BIRTHPLACE . . . . Philadelphia, PA
RESIDENCE . . . . Lutz, FL
BATS/THROWS . . . . R/R
HEIGHT/WEIGHT 6-1/185

47

APPOINTED: Named as the Bullpen Coach on November 27, 2000.

PERSONAL: Gilbert Thomas Patterson... Married, wife's name is Honie... Four children, Brandy (5/18/77), Raquel (1/4/85), Kyle (4/13/87) and Gilbert Jr. (5/1/98)... Graduated from Miami Dade South Junior College where he pitched and DH'ed, was selected as the team MVP... Was drafted four times prior to signing with the Yankees... Was the Yankees #1 selection in the secondary phase of the June 1975 draft by Pat Gillick.

PLAYING CAREER: 1975: Made his pro debut with Oneonta where he was 8-4 with a 1.95 ERA and six complete games in his 14 appearances, 13 starts... Led the New York-Penn League (A) in strikeouts with 97 in his 106 innings of work... **1976:** Split the season between West Haven (AA) and Syracuse (AAA) and combined to post a 16-6 record in 23 games, 19 starts with eight complete games... Pitched a 1-0 no-hit victory against Williamsport on June 28... **1977:** Opened the year in Syracuse (AAA) before joining the Yankees at age 21... Appeared in ten games, six starts with the eventual World Series Champions and was 1-2 with a 5.45 ERA... Earned his first major league win over the Texas Rangers on May 25... Following a May 31 start against Boston, Carl Yastrzemski said he was the best young pitcher he's seen in the AL in some time... Was on the disabled list from June 15 to July 14... Did not pitch in the post-season... **1978:** Spent the season on the disabled list after surgery to repair a torn rotator cuff... **1979:** Was unable to pitch after surgery in 1978... Experimented pitching with his left hand during spring training... **1980:** Pitched in the Yankees organization for Bradenton where he was 5-2 with 1.58 ERA in eight starts with two complete games... **1981:** Made just seven appearances with the Yankees Class A affiliate in Fort Lauderdale, Florida... Was 1-4 with a 3.20 ERA... **1982:** Joined the San Fransisco Giants organization and made four starts with Fresno (A)... Was 1-1 with a complete game and a 1.33 ERA... **1983:** Attending spring training with manager Joe Torre and the Atlanta Braves... Had Tommy John surgery following spring training... Career note: In total had eight operations during his career.

COACHING CAREER: 1984: Began his coaching career with the New York Yankees Organization... Worked with Mark Connor in Columbus (AAA) for one half of the season and then moved to Oneonta of the New York-Penn League (A)... **1991:** Joined the Oakland A's organization and coached in the Arizona Rookie League with Scottsdale... **1992-1993:** Was a coach for the Madison Muskies of the Midwest League (A)... **1994:** Coached in the Midwest League (A) with the West Michigan Whitecaps... **1995:** Was a coach for the Scottsdale A's of the Rookie League... **1996:** Roving minor league pitching instructor for the A's organization... **1997-2000:** Spent four seasons with the Arizona Diamondbacks as their minor league pitching coordinator.

GIL PATTERSON — PLAYING CAREER

Year	Club & League	W-L	ERA	G	GS	CG	ShO	SV	IP	H	R	ER	HR	HB	BB	SO	WP
1975	Oneonta (NYP)	8-4	1.95	14	13	6	1	0	106.0	79	32	23	2	4	33	97	5
1976	West Haven (East)	9-2	2.07	13	13	6	2	0	100.0	67	35	23	2	3	27	64	3
1976	Syracuse (Int)	7-2	2.92	10	10	6	0	0	77.0	71	30	25	1	1	34	40	2
1977	Syracuse (Int)	2-1	4.82	7	7	0	0	0	28.0	30	15	15	3	2	10	19	1
1977	NEW YORK (AL)	1-2	5.45	10	6	0	0	0	33.0	38	20	20	3	3	20	29	3
1978	Tacoma (PCL)						INJURED — DID NOT PLAY										
1979							RETIRED										
1980	Bradenton (Gulf)	5-2	1.58	8	8	2	1	0	57.0	40	20	10	0	4	18	20	1
1981	Ft. Lauderdale (FSL)	1-4	3.20	7	7	0	0	0	45.0	31	22	16	2	3	29	28	0
1982	Fresno (Caro)	1-1	1.33	4	4	1	0	0	27.0	28	12	4	0	0	11	8	3
Minor Totals		33-16	2.37	63	62	21	4	0	440.0	346	166	116	10	17	162	276	15

PATTERSON — TRANSACTIONS

- Selected in the 1st round by the New York Yankees in the June 1975 Draft.
- On disabled list June 15-July 14, 1977.
- On disabled list the entire season (torn rotator cuff), 1978.

MANAGERIAL/COACHING CAREER

1984	Coach, Columbus, International League
1984	Coach, Oneonta, New York-Penn League
1991	Coach, Scottsdale, Arizona Rookie League
1992-93	Coach, Madison, Midwest League
1994	Coach, West Michigan, Midwest
1995	Coach, Scottsdale, Arizona Rookie League
1996	Roving pitching instructor, Oakland A's
1997-2000	Minor League Pitching Coordinator, Arizona

Cookie
ROJAS
BENCH COACH

BIRTHDATE	March 6, 1939
OPENING DAY AGE	62
BIRTHPLACE	Havana, Cuba
RESIDENCE	Aventura, FL
BATS/THROWS	R/R
HEIGHT/WEIGHT	5-10/165

1

APPOINTED: Joined the Blue Jays organization as bench coach on November 3, 2000.

PERSONAL: Octavio Victor "Cookie" Rojas... Married to the former Candy Rosa Boullon... Has four children Octavio Jr. (5/23/61), Miguel (4/18/63), Victor (2/3/68) and Bobby (11/11/69)... Graduated from La Luz High School in Havana, Cuba... Has sponsored the "Annual Cookie Rojas Golf Tournament" at Don Shula's Country Club in Miami for the National Cancer Society... In February, 1998 he received the Lifetime Achievement Award from the American Cuban Conference in Miami.

PLAYING CAREER: 1956: After signing with the Reds he made his pro debut with West Palm Beach and hit .275... **1957:** Moved to Wausua where he hit .260 with 25 doubles, four home runs and 49 RBI... **1958:** With Savannah was the third straight season he posted more walks (47) than strikeouts... Hit .254 and reached double figures in home runs for the only season in his career with 10... **1959:** Played in 99 games with Havana and hit .233 with 17 walks and 44 strikeouts... **1960:** Split his season between Havana and Jersey City and combined to hit .228 in 110 games with 24 RBI... **1961:** Played the entire season with Jersey City and hit .265 in 150 games with 25 doubles and 44 RBI... **1962:** Split his season between Cincinnati and Dallas/Fort Worth... Hit .221 in 39 games for the Reds... Played in the first game ever held at Dodger Stadium (April 10, 1962) and collected his first big league hit against Sandy Koufax... **1963:** Was traded to the Philadelphia Phillies where he hit .221 in 64 games... **1964:** Hit .291 for the Phillies in 109 games with 19 doubles and 31 RBI... **1965:** Hit a career high .303 in 142 games for the Phillies with 25 doubles, three home runs and 42 RBI... Walked 42 times while striking out just 33... Was named to the NL All-Star team and was 0-1 in the game which was held in Minnesota... **1966:** Hit .268 in 156 games with six home runs and 55 RBI... **1967:** Stole a then career high eight bases while hitting .259 in 147 games... **1968:** Despite a ML career high of nine home runs hit just .232 in 152 games with 48 RBI and his second straight season with more than 50 strikeouts... Were the only two seasons in his career with 50 strikeouts... **1969:** In his final season in Philadelphia hit just .228 in 110 games with 30 RBI... Following the season was traded to St. Louis along with Dick Allen and Jerry Johnson in exchange for Curt Flood, Tim McCarver, Joel Hoerner and Byron Browne... **1970:** Appeared in just 23 games with St. Louis and hit only .106 before being dealt to Kansas City where he teamed with Fred Patek to form the American league's top double-play combination for the next six seasons... With KC hit .260 in 98 games... **1971:** Hit .300 for KC in his first full season... Was one of two seasons in his career he would hit .300 (.303 in 1965)... Selected to the AL All-Star Team... Was his first of four straight All-Star game appearances... **1972:** Hit .261 with 25 doubles, three home runs and 53 RBI... Homered in his only at bat in the All-Star game held in Atlanta... Walked 41 times while striking out just 35... **1973:** Hit .273 and set career highs with 78 runs scored, 29 doubles, 69 RBI and 18 stolen bases... Heading in to 1973 had only 41 stolen bases in his first ten major leagues seasons and had never recorded ten in a season... Made his third straight All-Star game appearance and fourth overall... **1974:** Hit .271 and drove in 60 runs... Was his second straight 60 RBI season and also the second of his career... Collected 17 doubles, six home runs and eight stolen bases... Made his fourth consecutive All-Star team but did not play in the game... **1975:** Hit .254 in 120 games with 18 doubles and 37 RBI... Walked 30 times and struck out only 24... **1976:** Hit .242 in 63 games with 16 RBI... Hit .333 (3-9) with an RBI in the ALCS against New York... **1977:** In his final season he hit .250 in 64 games with nine doubles and ten RBI... In the ALCS hit .250 (1-4) with a stolen base.

PLAYING CAREER NOTES: Had a career average of .263 and struck out once every 12.90 at bats... Named to five All-Star games including four consecutive from 1971 through 1974... Became just the ninth player in history to play in an All-Star Game for both the American and National Leagues during his 19-year major league career... Named the Phillies' greatest second baseman in voting during baseball's centennial (1969)... Compiled a .263 batting average in 1,822 games... Hit .303 with the Phillies in 1965 and .300 with the Royals in 1971... Hit .308 (4-13) in two League Championship Series with Kansas City in 1976-1977... Is a member of the Kansas City Royals', Philadelphia Phillies' and Cuba's Baseball Hall of Fame.

MANAGING/COACHING/SCOUTING CAREER: 1978-1981: After playing in the 1977 season he went directly to coaching for the Cubs in 1978... **1982:** Joined the California Angels beginning as the advance scout... **1988:** Took over as Manager of the California Angels on March 26 and saw the team post a 75-79 record under his leadership... He was replaced as manager near the end of the season and remained as a special assignment scout... Was the third native Cuban to manage in the majors, joining Mike Gonzalez (Cardinals) and Preston Gomez (Astros, Cubs)... **1989-1991:** Served as a special assignment scout with the Angels... **1991-1992:** Joined the Florida Marlins on October 24, 1991 after a 10-year stint with the California Angels... Served as a major league scout and Special Assistant to the General Manager... **1993-1996:** Moved into uniform as the Marlins third base coach for their inaugural season... Was named to the position on November 12, 1992... **1997-2000:** Joined the New York Mets and spent four seasons as the third base and infield coach.

FORFEIT GAME

The Blue Jays have played one forfeit game, a 9-0 decision vs Baltimore on September 15, 1977... In that game Jim Clancy had held the Orioles to two-hits over five innings before Earl Weaver pulled his club off the field... His reason was that the tarps on the Blue Jays bullpen created a hazard for his players.

COOKIE ROJAS — PLAYING RECORD

Year	Club & League	AVG	G	AB	R	H	2B	3B	HR	RBI	BB	SO	SB
1956	West Palm Beach (FSL)	.275	129	476	75	131	19	5	1	43	49	35	28
1957	Wausau (Nor)	.260	116	443	46	115	25	8	4	49	41	34	6
1958	Savannah (SAL)	.254	134	527	74	134	24	2	10	44	47	37	10
1959	Havana (Int)	.233	99	318	30	74	12	1	3	13	17	44	6
1960	Havana/Jersey City (Int)	.228	110	276	19	63	8	1	1	24	18	20	1
1961	Jersey City (Int)	.265	150	567	62	150	25	6	1	44	25	36	11
1962	CINCINNATI (NL)	.221	39	86	9	19	2	0	0	6	9	4	1
1962	Dallas/Ft. Worth (AmAs)	.241	47	170	13	41	4	0	0	11	13	13	0
1963	PHILADELPHIA (NL)	.221	64	77	18	17	0	1	1	2	3	8	4
1964	PHILADELPHIA (NL)	.291	109	340	58	99	19	5	2	31	22	17	1
1965	PHILADELPHIA (NL)	.303	142	521	78	158	25	3	3	42	42	33	5
1966	PHILADELPHIA (NL)	.268	156	626	77	168	18	1	6	55	35	46	4
1967	PHILADELPHIA (NL)	.259	147	528	61	137	21	2	4	45	30	58	8
1968	PHILADELPHIA (NL)	.232	152	621	53	144	19	0	9	48	16	55	4
1969	PHILADELPHIA (NL)	.228	110	391	35	89	11	1	4	30	23	28	1
1970	ST. LOUIS (NL)	.106	23	47	2	5	0	0	0	2	3	4	0
1970	KANSAS CITY (AL)	.260	98	384	36	100	13	3	2	28	20	29	3
1971	KANSAS CITY (AL)	.300	115	414	56	124	22	2	6	59	39	35	8
1972	KANSAS CITY (AL)	.261	137	487	49	127	25	0	3	53	41	35	2
1973	KANSAS CITY (AL)	.276	139	551	78	152	29	3	6	69	37	38	18
1974	KANSAS CITY (AL)	.271	144	542	52	147	17	1	6	60	30	43	8
1975	KANSAS CITY (AL)	.254	120	406	34	103	18	2	2	37	30	24	4
1976	KANSAS CITY (AL)	.242	63	132	11	32	6	0	0	16	8	15	2
1977	KANSAS CITY (AL)	.250	64	156	8	39	9	1	0	10	8	17	1
Minor Totals		.255	785	2777	319	708	117	23	20	228	210	219	62
AL TOTALS		.268	880	3072	324	824	139	12	25	332	213	236	46
NL TOTALS		.258	942	3237	391	836	115	13	29	261	183	253	28
MAJOR TOTALS		.263	1822	6309	715	1660	254	25	54	593	396	489	74

LEAGUE CHAMPIONSHIP SERIES

Year	Club & League	AVG	G	AB	R	H	2B	3B	HR	RBI	BB	SO	SB
1976	KANSAS CITY (AL)	.333	4	9	2	3	0	0	0	1	0	0	1
1977	KANSAS CITY (AL)	.250	1	4	0	1	0	0	0	0	0	1	1
LCS TOTALS		.308	5	13	2	4	0	0	0	1	0	1	2

ALL-STAR GAMES

Year	Club & League	AVG	G	AB	R	H	2B	3B	HR	RBI	BB	SO	SB
1965	NL at MIN	.000	1	1	0	0	0	0	0	0	0	0	0
1971	AL at DET	.000	1	1	0	0	0	0	0	0	0	0	0
1972	AL at ATL	1.000	1	1	1	1	0	0	1	2	0	0	0
1973	AL at KC	.000	1	0	0	0	0	0	0	0	1	0	0
1974	AL at PIT					(Selected-Did not play)							
ALL-STAR TOTALS		.333	4	3	1	1	0	0	1	2	1	0	0

ROJAS — TRANSACTIONS

- Signed to a professional contract by Havana's Armando Llano, 1956.
- Sold to the Cincinnati Reds organization, 1956.
- Traded to the Philadelphia Phillies in exchange for RHP Jim Owens on November 27, 1962.
- Traded to the St. Louis Cardinals along with OF Richie Allen and RHP Jerry Johnson in exchange for OF Curt Flood, OF Bryon Browne, C Tim McCarver and LHP Joe Hoerner on October 7, 1969. OF Curt Flood refused to report and was replaced by 1B Willie Montanez and P James Browning on April 7, 1970.
- Traded to the Kansas City Royals in exchange for C/OF Fred Rice on June 13, 1970.

MANAGERIAL/COACHING CAREER

1978-81	Coach, Chicago Cubs
1988	Manager, California Angels
1993-96	3B Coach, Florida Marlins
1997-2000	3B Coach, New York Mets

RECORD AS MANAGER

Year	Club & League	W-L	PCT	Finish
1988	CALIFORNIA (AL)	75-79	.487	4th West

1-2-3 IN BATTING RACE

In 1993 John Olerud (.363), Paul Molitor (.332) and Roberto Alomar (.326) finished the year first, second and third respectively in the American League batting race... It was just the third time in Major League history that three teammates had finished in that order- and the first since 1893. Alomar was in fourth place trailing Cleveland's Kenny Lofton heading into the last day of the regular season... Alomar then went 3-4 on the final day to finish .001 ahead of Lofton (.325)... The two other times that this feat occurred were: 1893- Philadelphia A's (Billy Hamilton- .380, Sam Thompson- .370 and Ed Delahanty- .368) & 1891- Boston Reds (Dan Brouthers- .350, Hugh Duffy- .336 and Tom Brown- .321).

Ryan
BALFE
OUTFIELDER

66

BIRTHDATE	November 11, 1975
OPENING DAY AGE	25
BIRTHPLACE	Cornwall, NY
RESIDENCE	Cornwall, NY
BATS/THROWS	S/R
HEIGHT/WEIGHT	6-1/180
CONTRACT STATUS	signed thru 2001
M.L. SERVICE	0.000

PERSONAL: Ryan Ross Balfe... Attended Cornwall Central High School in Cornwall, New York.

LAST SEASON: Hit .262 in 130 games with Mobile (AA) and collected 21 doubles, four triples, 12 home runs and 66 RBI... Made 108 appearances in the outfield, 11 at designated hitter, seven at first base and two at third base... Hit .319 in April with seven doubles, two home runs and 20 RBI... On April 12 was 3-5 with a triple, a home run and five RBI... Was selected to the Southern League All-Star Game... Hit six of his 12 home runs in July... Hit .279 with runners in scoring position with five home runs and 54 RBI... Was 1-5 as a pinch-hitter.

PROFESSIONAL CAREER: 1994: Made his pro debut with Bristol in the Tigers organization... Hit .215 in 43 games... **1995:** Hit .261 in 113 games with Fayetteville of the South Atlantic League (A)... Had 32 extra-base hits, ten of which were home runs... **1996:** Hit .277 with 21 doubles, 11 home runs and 65 RBI for Lakeland of the Florida State League (A)... **1997:** Established a career-high with a combined 14 home runs between Lakeland (A) and the Gulf Coast League

Tigers (A)... Appeared in two games with the Gulf Coast League club hitting .571 with a home run... Hit .268 with Lakeland with 13 home runs and 48 RBI over 13 games from May 3-16... On May 9 connected for a triple, a home run and three RBI vs. Kissimmee... On the road hit .309 with six home runs and 25 RBI... On November 19 was acquired by the San Diego Padres along with RHP's Dan Miceli and Donne Wall in exchange for RHP Tim Worrell and OF Trey Beamon... **1998:** Spent the season with Mobile of the Southern League (AA)... Hit .232 in 23 games with two home runs and 11 RBI... **1999:** Set career highs with Mobile (AA) in most offensive categories, including batting average (.280), hits (112), RBI (70) and walks (50)... Ranked second on the club with 31 doubles... Started the season slowly after dislocating his left shoulder in the second game of the season, April 9 at Birmingham... Was on the disabled list from April 10-25... On June 24 hit two home runs in a 12-6 victory over Carolina 12-6... Hit .338 against left-handed pitchers... With runners in scoring position and two out hit .369 with three homers and 31 RBI.

RYAN BALFE

Year	Club & League	AVG	G	AB	R	H	TB	2B	3B	HR	RBI	SH-SF	HP	BB-IBB	SO	SB-CS	GIDP	SLG	OBP
1994	Bristol (Appy)	.215	43	121	12	26	32	3	0	1	11	1-1	1	23-0	38	2-4	1	.264	.342
1995	Fayetteville (SAL)	.261	113	398	53	104	158	20	2	10	49	0-1	9	48-0	85	1-1	11	.397	.353
1996	Lakeland (FSL)	.277	92	347	48	96	152	21	1	11	65	0-3	5	24-2	66	3-0	13	.438	.330
1997	Lakeland (FSL)	.269	86	312	40	84	140	13	2	13	48	1-6	3	24-3	75	1-1	7	.449	.322
1997	Tigers (Gulf)	.571	2	7	2	4	7	0	0	1	1	0-0	0	1-0	1	0-0	0	1.000	.625
1998	Mobile (Sou)	.232	23	69	9	16	29	5	1	2	11	0-0	0	8-0	10	1-0	3	.420	.312
1999	Mobile (Sou)	.280	111	400	69	112	182	31	3	11	70	0-3	4	50-4	95	0-1	18	.455	.363
2000	Mobile (Sou)	.262	130	462	61	121	186	21	4	12	66	0-4	9	46-2	120	3-3	12	.403	.338
Minor Totals		.266	600	2116	294	563	886	114	13	61	321	2-18	31	224-11	490	11-10	65	.419	.342

BALFE — TRANSACTIONS

- Selected by the Detroit Tigers in eighth round of the June 1994 First Year Player Draft.
- Traded to the San Diego Padres along with RHP Dan Miceli and RHP Donne Wall in exchange for RHP Tim Worrell and OF Trey Beamon on November 19, 1997.
- Signed by the Toronto Blue Jays on December 1, 2000.

Tony
BATISTA
INFIELDER

7

BIRTHDATE	December 9, 1973
OPENING DAY AGE	27
BIRTHPLACE	Puerto Plata, DR
RESIDENCE	Mao, DR
BATS/THROWS	R/R
HEIGHT/WEIGHT	6-0/205
CONTRACT STATUS	signed thru 2003
M.L. SERVICE	4.072

PERSONAL: Leocadio Francisco (Tony) Batista... Married, wife's name Australia... Two children, Willie (4) and Gina (1)... Resides in Mao, Dominican Republic... He was discovered and signed by former major league standout pitcher

Juan Marichal, signing as a non-drafted free agent with the Athletics in 1991... Was named to the Baseball America Winter League All-Star team for 1996-97, playing for Aguilas, tying for the league lead with 26 RBI...

LAST SEASON: Hit .263 in 154 games with career highs of 41 HR's and 114 RBI... The 41 home runs were tied for fourth in the AL and the club lead with Carlos Delgado... Established a new club record for HR's by a third baseman surpassing the previous mark of 31 held by Kelly Gruber (1990) and Ed Sprague (1996)... Now holds the club record for HR at two positions (26 as SS in 1999)... His totals of 322 total bases and 114 RBI both rank as the ninth highest single season totals in club history... Opened the year by hitting two home runs on opening day including a game ending HR in the bottom of the ninth vs KC... Wound up with four multi-HR games on the season to give him seven in his career... Was the first of four walk-off game winning hits, also did so with an RBI single in the ninth on May 16 vs Boston, an RBI single in the bottom of the 13th on June 25 vs Boston and an RBI single in the ninth against Oakland on September 1... Hit .301 in April with eight home runs and his highest RBI total for any month at 24... Raised his batting average to a season high .365 on April 19 after a 4-5 night with two doubles, a home run and three RBI vs Anaheim... Was his first of two four-hit games during the season... Hit .234 in May with four HR's and 13 RBI... Broke an 0-13 stretch, May 19 to 23, with a solo HR in Boston against Pedro Martinez... Missed eight games from May 31 to June 7 after suffering a strained left rib cage — had been the Blue Jay Iron Man up to that point playing in 151 consecutive games dating back to 1999... In June hit .316 with nine home runs and 23 RBI in only 19 games... On June 11 vs Montreal had a career high five RBI after hitting his second career grand slam in the eighth inning off Lira to give Toronto an 8-5 last at bat win... June 22 vs Detroit posted his second multi-HR game of the season, hitting two against Nomo... From June 25 to July 7 he hit in a season high 12 straight games... Hit home runs in the ninth inning of three straight games, June 29 vs Tampa Bay and June 30 & July 1 against Baltimore... Homered in five of six games from June 29 to July 4... July 3 hit his second grand slam of the season, in Baltimore against Jason Johnson... Made his first All-Star game appearance, was named as reserve and was 0-1 as a pinch-hitter... Posted third two-HR game to open the second half on July 13 vs Philadelphia... Homered in the eighth inning on July 20 for a last at bat win against Tampa Bay, his second last at bat eighth inning HR... The next day posted his fourth multi-HR game of the season hitting two solo HR's vs the Orioles on July 21 in Toronto... Finished July on an 0-27 stretch which ran from July 25 to Aug 1... Hit .270 in July with 10HR's and 23 RBI... Played in his 500th career game on August 11 at Minnesota... On August 30 reached 100 RBI for the second consecutive season as he hit HR #37 against Anaheim's Matt Wise... In August hit .300 (30-100) with six home runs and 17 RBI... Reached a career high 101 RBI on September 1 with a game winning single in the ninth against Oakland... On September 7 hit HR #38 off Seattle's Paniagua to give Toronto a new club record for HR's in a season at 222... On September 27 was 2-4 at Baltimore with a 3R-HR off Ponson to give him nine HR's against the O's in one season — nine is a Blue Jay club record for HR in a season series and it matches the Orioles club record against done once previous, in 1968 by Frank Howard of the Washington Senators... Hit .360 vs the O's with 16 RBI... Struggled in September hitting just .160 with three home runs and 14 RBI... Hit a solo HR on October 1 at Cleveland to finish the season with 41... Hit .273 vs RHP and .235 against LHP... 41HR, 35RHP, 6 vs LHP, 25 at Home and 16 on the Road... At the All-Star break was batting .289 with 24 HR and 72 RBI and following the break hit .234 with 17 HR and 42 RBI.

PROFESSIONAL CAREER: 1991: Played for the Athletics' club in the Dominican Summer League... **1992:** His first year in the U.S., played both second base and shortstop for Scottsdale, playing in 45 games... **1993:** Opened the year with Scottsdale (Rookie), and batted .327 with 17 RBI in 24 games... Was promoted to Tacoma (AAA) on July 25... Had season-ending surgery after suffering a fractured skull on July 28 in a collision with another player while fielding a groundball... **1994:** Earned California League All-Star honors as the everyday shortstop at Modesto (A)... Was also the league's top fielding shortstop with a .950 pct... Hit three grand slams... Hit .360 (9-for-25) while starting all seven games of the California League playoffs... **1995:** Spent the entire year at Huntsville (AA), finishing second on the club in home runs (16) and third in RBI (61)... Played 84 games at shortstop and 18 at second base... **1996:** Completed organizational climb, starting the year as the shortstop at Edmonton, before finishing the season as the Athletics' second baseman... Started final 33 games of the year with Oakland, hitting .317 (45-for-142) with four homers and 21 RBI, while also playing errorless defense... Was called up to the majors for first time on June 2 and picked up first big league hit on June 8 at Minnesota off Erik Bennett... Hit first major league home run on June 18 in Detroit off Tom Urbani... Had a pair of four-hit games, including August 26 in Baltimore, homering to open the game, then adding another blast in the 8th, finishing with four RBI... Was named the second baseman on the Topps Rookie All-Star team... **1997:** Was Oakland's opening day shortstop... Through 29 games hit .167 and was optioned to Edmonton on May 17... Recalled on July 1 when Rafael Bournigal was disabled, hit .269 (14-for-52) before going 2-for-24, and was optioned back to Edmonton on August 10... Returned to Oakland on August 21, participating in five games before going on the disabled list on August 27 with strained left quadriceps... Had a four-hit game on August 23 at Cleveland... After healing from the leg injury, was sent to Edmonton to participate in the final game of the PCL playoffs, going 2-for-4 with two RBI as the Trappers won the title... Was activated from the DL on September 12, but did not play until September 24... Started 54 games at shortstop, second on the club to Bournigal's 59, while also starting one game at second base... While with Edmonton, hit .315 in 33 games... **1998:** Set then career highs in nearly every offensive category after becoming an every day player in the second half of the season... Hit 18 HR in 293 AB, entered 1998 with 10 career HR in 426 AB... Had a 48-game stretch in which he hit 16 home runs from July 3 through September 13, spanning 156 at-bats, a 1 HR per 9.8 AB ratio... Hit first pinch-hit home run in Diamondbacks history, first of his career, a two-run blast in Wrigley Field on August 3 off Don Wengert in a 6-5 Arizona win... The pinch home run began a five-game, five-homer stretch for Batista, ending with a pair at home on August 11, his second career two homer contest... He had a season-high 10-game hitting streak from July 30-August 14... Hit nine home runs on the road and nine in Bank One Ballpark... Batted .296 (48-for-162) in his home park, and .244 (32-for-131) away from home... Defensively, he spent most of the season as the second baseman, until swapping spots on the diamond with Jay Bell on September 11, becoming the shortstop for the remainder of the season... Batted .277 for the Aguilas of Dominican in Winter League Ball, ranking 3rd in the league with eight home runs, 4th in RBI (33) and 4th in runs scored (34)... **1999:** Split the season between Arizona and Toronto, combined to hit .277 with a career high 31 home runs and 100 RBI... Acquired by Toronto on June 12 along with RHP John Frascatore in exchange for LHP Dan Plesac... With Arizona hit .257 in 44 games with five HR and 21 RBI... In 98 games with Toronto hit .285 with 26 home runs and 79 RBI... His 26 home runs and 79 RBI are a new Blue Jays record for a shortstop... Began Blue Jays career with a five game hit streak and homered in his debut on June 15 against Anaheim's Tim Belcher... After June 15 started every game the rest of the season... With Toronto averaged a HR every once 3.8 games and once every 14.4 at bats... Hit two game winning home runs in extra innings, on July 26 in Chicago in the 11th against the White Sox's Bob Howry & July 20 in the 10th inning at home against Atlanta's John Hudek... Had one two-HR game, the third of his career, on July 8 in Baltimore off Ponson (1R) and Coppinger (2R)... Hit in a career high 17 straight games from July 30 to August 16, hit .338 (23-68) with five HR and 15 RBI... Reached 100 RBI on the season with a Grand Slam in the final game of the season on October 3 at Cleveland against Mike Jackson, was the first slam of his career... Finished the season with 17 RBI and three HR's in the last 11 games... Of his 26 HR with Toronto, 16 were solo's, six were with one on base, three with two on and one with three on... Hit .230 (14-38) vs. left-handed pitching with three HR and 11 RBI and .296 (93-314) against right-handers with 23 HR's and 68 RBI... Hit .302 (35-116) with runners in scoring position... Posted a .975 fielding percentage

(12E/486TC) and participated in 72 double plays in 98 games.

CAREER NOTES: In 2000 joined with Delgado, Mondesi and Cruz to become the first four teammates in ML history to each hit 20 home runs prior to the All-Star break... Was one of Toronto's four players to hit 30 HR's during the 2000 season, just the second time in the history of the AL (Anaheim- 2000), and the ninth time in ML history that four teammates each finished the season with 30 home runs... One of seven Toronto players to hit 20 home runs during the 2000 season to match the ML record done once previously (Baltimore-1996)... Holds the Blue Jays HR record at two positions, 26 at shortstop (1999) & 41at third base (2000)... Is the fifth player to hold his franchise home run record at two positions (Cubs' Ernie Banks- 1B & SS, Twins' Harmon Killebrew- 1B, 3B & LF, Texas' Juan Gonzalez- LF, CF & RF and Texas' Rafael Palmeiro- 1B & DH)... Holds the Blue Jays club record for HR's against an opponent in one season with nine against Baltimore in 2000... In two seasons with Toronto has hit .271 (270-995) in 252 games with 157 runs, 57 doubles, 67 home runs and 193 RBI.

TONY BATISTA

Year	Club & League	AVG	G	AB	R	H	TB	2B	3B	HR	RBI	SH-SF	HP	BB-IBB	SO	SB-CS	GIDP	SLG	OBP
1991	Athletics (DSL)	.187	46	166	16	31	44	5	1	2	15	2-3	1	23-1	16	4-2	3	.265	.284
1992	Scottsdale (Ari)	.246	45	167	32	41	51	6	2	0	22	5-0	2	15-0	29	1-0	4	.305	.315
1993	Scottsdale (Ari)	.327	24	104	21	34	50	6	2	2	17	0-2	0	6-1	14	6-2	1	.481	.357
1993	Tacoma (PCL)	.167	4	12	1	2	3	1	0	0	1	0-0	1	1-0	4	0-0	0	.250	.286
1994	Modesto (Cal)	.281	119	466	91	131	214	26	3	17	68	5-2	4	54-1	108	7-7	10	.459	.359
1995	Huntsville (SOU)	.255	120	419	55	107	180	23	1	16	61	6-3	2	29-0	98	7-8	8	.430	.305
1996	Edmonton (PCL)	.322	57	205	33	66	115	17	4	8	40	1-1	2	15-0	30	2-1	8	.561	.372
1996	OAKLAND (AL)	.298	74	238	38	71	103	10	2	6	25	0-2	1	19-0	49	7-3	2	.433	.350
1997	OAKLAND (AL)	.202	68	188	22	38	62	10	1	4	18	3-0	2	14-0	31	2-2	8	.330	.265
1997	Edmonton (PCL)	.315	33	124	25	39	60	10	1	3	21	1-2	1	17-0	18	2-2	4	.484	.396
1998	ARIZONA (NL)	.273	106	293	46	80	152	16	1	18	41	0-4	3	18-0	52	1-1	7	.519	.318
1999	ARIZONA (NL)	.257	44	144	16	37	57	5	0	5	21	0-2	2	16-3	17	2-0	1	.396	.335
1999	TORONTO (AL)	.285	98	375	61	107	212	25	1	26	79	3-5	4	22-1	79	2-0	11	.565	.328
2000	TORONTO (AL)	.263	154	620	96	163	322	32	2	41	114	0-3	6	35-1	121	5-4	15	.519	.307
Minor Totals		.271	448	1663	274	451	717	94	14	48	245	20-13	13	160-3	317	29-22	38	.431	.337
TORONTO TOTALS		.271	252	995	157	270	534	57	3	67	193	3-8	10	57-2	200	7-4	26	.537	.314
AL TOTALS		.267	394	1421	217	379	699	77	6	77	236	6-10	13	90-2	280	16-9	36	.492	.313
NL TOTALS		.268	150	437	62	117	209	21	1	23	62	0-6	5	34-3	69	3-1	8	.478	.324
MAJOR TOTALS		.267	544	1858	279	496	908	98	7	100	298	6-16	18	124-5	349	19-10	44	.489	.316

ALL-STAR GAME RECORD

Year	Club & League	AVG	G	AB	R	H	TB	2B	3B	HR	RBI	SH-SF	HP	BB-IBB	SO	SB-CS	GIDP	SLG	OBP
2000	AL at ATL	.000	1	1	0	0	0	0	0	0	0	0-0	0	0-0	0	0-0	0	.000	.000

HOME RUN BREAKDOWN

				MEN ON				ONE GAME							
Total	H	A	0	1	2	3	2	3	4	LO	XN	IP	PH	RHP	LHP
100	45	55	58	31	8	3	7	0	0	1	3	0	1	80	20

BATISTA — TRANSACTIONS

- Signed by Oakland Athletics as a non-drafted free agent, February 8, 1991.
- On disabled list (fractured skull) July 29 through the end of the season, 1993.
- On disabled list (strained left quadricep) August 27 to September 12, 1997.
- Selected by Arizona Diamondbacks with their 14th pick in the 1st round of MLB Expansion Draft, November 18, 1997.
- Traded to the Toronto Blue Jays along with RHP John Frascatore in exchange for LHP Dan Plesac, June 12, 1999.

CAREER HIGHS — BATISTA, Tony

SEASON:

Games	154 - 2000
Avg.	.277 - 1999
Runs	96 - 2000
Hits	163 - 2000
Doubles	32 - 2000
Home Runs	41 - 2000
RBI	114 - 2000
Walks	38 - 1999
Strikeouts	121 - 2000
Stolen Bases	7 - 1996
Longest Hitting Streak	17G - Jul. 30-Aug. 16, 1999
Longest Hitless Streak	27 AB - Jul. 25-Aug. 1, 2000
Multi HR Games	4 - 2000

GAME:

ML Debut	Jun. 3, 1996 vs. KC
Runs	3 - 5 times, last Aug. 13, 2000 at MIN
Hits	5 - Apr. 10, 1999 at ATL
Doubles	2 - 9 times, last Sep. 17, 2000 at CWS
Home Runs	2 - 7 times, last Jul. 21, 2000 vs. BAL
RBI	5 - Jun. 11 vs. MON
Stolen Bases	1 - 19 times, last May 15, 2000 vs. BOS
Last ML Home Run	Oct. 1, 2000 at CLE

ML Franchise HR Leaders At More than One Position

Player	Team	Positions
Ernie Banks	Chicago Cubs	1B & SS
Harmon Killebrew	Minnesota Twins	1B, 3B & LF
Juan Gonzalez	Texas Rangers	LF, CF, RF
Rafael Palmeiro	Texas Rangers	1B & DH
TONY BATISTA	Toronto Blue Jays	SS & 3B

FIELDING

BATISTA, Tony—SS

Year	PCT	G	PO	A	E	TC	DP
1996 (AL)	1.000	4	4	11	0	15	1
1997 (AL)	.970	61	91	169	8	268	39
1998 (NL)	.971	34	43	93	4	140	13
1999 (NL)	.979	43	60	130	4	194	27
1999 (AL)	.975	98	165	309	12	486	72
Total	.975	240	363	712	28	1103	152

BATISTA, Tony—3B

Year	PCT	G	PO	A	E	TC	DP
1996 (AL)	.931	18	9	18	2	29	3
1997 (AL)	1.000	4	3	1	0	4	0
1998 (NL)	.974	15	9	28	1	38	1
1999 (NL)	.000	1	0	0	0	0	0
2000 (AL)	.963	154	120	318	17	455	35
Total	.962	191	141	365	20	526	39

BATISTA, Tony—2B

Year	PCT	G	PO	A	E	TC	DP
1996 (AL)	.988	52	84	162	3	249	36
1997 (AL)	1.000	1	2	4	0	6	0
1998 (NL)	.994	41	71	84	1	156	23
Total	.990	94	157	250	4	411	59

TONY BATISTA DETAILED HITTING

	2000									CAREER								
	Avg	AB	H	HR	RBI	BB	SO	OBP	SLG	Avg	AB	H	HR	RBI	BB	SO	OBP	SLG
Total	.263	620	163	41	114	35	121	.307	.519	.267	1858	496	100	298	124	349	.316	.489
vs. Left	.235	162	38	6	23	11	28	.287	.414	.258	500	129	20	67	46	84	.323	.442
vs. Right	.273	458	125	35	91	24	93	.314	.557	.270	1358	367	80	231	78	265	.314	.506
Home	.270	307	83	25	60	22	63	.324	.580	.268	927	248	45	137	73	169	.324	.474
Away	.256	313	80	16	54	13	58	.290	.460	.266	931	248	55	161	51	180	.309	.504
April	.301	103	31	8	24	3	18	.339	.631	.250	264	66	12	39	15	44	.302	.447
May	.234	107	25	4	13	8	21	.288	.383	.234	222	52	8	28	22	45	.307	.383
June	.316	79	25	9	23	4	13	.349	.696	.307	212	65	17	42	11	34	.344	.590
July	.270	111	30	10	23	6	25	.319	.586	.246	341	84	24	63	24	65	.302	.510
August	.300	110	33	6	17	5	15	.328	.527	.309	398	123	23	64	23	69	.344	.555
September	.160	106	17	3	13	9	29	.226	.311	.248	403	100	13	53	29	87	.302	.422
October	.500	4	2	1	1	0	0	.500	1.250	.333	18	6	3	9	0	5	.333	.833
Scoring Posn	.287	181	52	13	77	12	26	.333	.564	.298	487	145	32	212	39	82	.347	.565
Bases Loaded	.400	15	6	2	18	0	1	.375	.867	.283	46	13	3	34	1	12	.286	.500
DH	–	–	–	–	–	–	–	–	–	.200	5	1	0	1	2	1	.429	.400
PH	–	–	–	–	–	–	–	–	–	.121	33	4	1	4	4	14	.216	.212
vs. Ana	.340	47	16	4	11	3	6	.396	.681	.324	108	35	7	20	7	12	.373	.593
vs. Bal	.360	50	18	9	16	1	11	.373	.980	.360	100	36	15	30	6	19	.393	.870
vs. Bos	.302	53	16	3	12	1	11	.309	.528	.282	117	33	4	22	7	23	.328	.453
vs. CWS	.128	39	5	0	5	3	11	.190	.179	.174	86	15	4	16	10	23	.268	.384
vs. Cle	.255	51	13	2	4	3	13	.296	.451	.248	145	36	5	19	10	33	.297	.407
vs. Det	.261	46	12	3	8	2	10	.300	.478	.321	78	25	6	16	2	18	.337	.603
vs. KC	.317	41	13	5	10	2	4	.364	.756	.274	106	29	7	17	7	19	.328	.500
vs. Mil	–	–	–	–	–	–	–	–	–	.205	44	9	1	3	3	6	.286	.273
vs. Min	.296	27	8	0	1	2	2	.345	.333	.283	92	26	2	9	5	9	.316	.413
vs. NYY	.204	49	10	2	6	2	7	.235	.388	.227	128	29	3	14	7	33	.272	.367
vs. Oak	.195	41	8	1	7	1	11	.214	.341	.260	77	20	4	12	2	15	.278	.506
vs. Sea	.289	38	11	2	8	6	11	.400	.553	.283	106	30	4	15	12	26	.361	.472
vs. TB	.227	44	10	3	5	6	5	.320	.455	.213	80	17	5	10	6	11	.273	.425
vs. Tex	.159	44	7	2	4	0	13	.159	.318	.224	98	22	4	14	4	24	.252	.408
vs. Tor	–	–	–	–	–	–	–	–	–	.154	13	2	0	0	0	2	.154	.231
vs. Atl	–	–	–	–	–	–	–	–	–	.319	47	15	3	10	2	7	.347	.553
vs. ChC	–	–	–	–	–	–	–	–	–	.324	37	12	2	6	3	6	.366	.514
vs. Cin	–	–	–	–	–	–	–	–	–	.212	33	7	3	6	1	5	.235	.515
vs. Col	–	–	–	–	–	–	–	–	–	.387	31	12	2	3	3	4	.441	.581
vs. Fla	–	–	–	–	–	–	–	–	–	.143	14	2	0	1	2	5	.250	.143
vs. Hou	–	–	–	–	–	–	–	–	–	.300	20	6	1	5	2	4	.348	.500
vs. LA	–	–	–	–	–	–	–	–	–	.205	44	9	2	3	2	5	.250	.386
vs. Mon	.370	27	10	2	11	0	4	.393	.667	.295	61	18	5	15	3	11	.338	.623
vs. NYM	.167	12	2	0	1	2	2	.286	.167	.324	37	12	1	7	4	5	.395	.459
vs. Phi	.364	11	4	3	5	1	0	.417	1.182	.268	41	11	6	10	3	6	.318	.780
vs. Pit	–	–	–	–	–	–	–	–	–	.316	19	6	1	2	3	3	.409	.684
vs. StL	–	–	–	–	–	–	–	–	–	.000	7	0	0	0	0	1	.000	.000
vs. SD	–	–	–	–	–	–	–	–	–	.143	35	5	0	2	2	3	.205	.171
vs. SF	–	–	–	–	–	–	–	–	–	.315	54	17	3	11	6	11	.387	.630
Pre-All Star	.289	329	95	24	72	15	59	.328	.571	.265	804	213	47	137	54	138	.317	.493
Post-All Star	.234	291	68	17	42	20	62	.284	.460	.269	1054	283	53	161	70	211	.316	.486

TONY BATISTA HITTING AT ML PARKS

Park	Avg	G	AB	R	H	2B	3B	HR	RBI	SB	CS	BB	SO	OBP	Slg
Camden Yards	.308	14	52	10	16	2	0	9	20	0	0	2	8	.327	.865
Fenway Park	.339	17	56	6	19	5	0	3	14	2	2	6	11	.400	.589
Edison Field	.283	13	53	8	15	2	0	2	4	1	0	2	8	.309	.434
Comiskey Park	.222	16	54	10	12	4	0	4	13	0	0	7	11	.323	.519
Jacobs Field	.288	19	73	8	21	6	0	4	14	0	0	5	16	.333	.534
Tiger Stadium	.429	7	21	4	9	2	0	2	5	0	0	0	5	.429	.810
Kauffman Stadium	.286	9	35	2	10	1	0	1	4	0	1	1	5	.306	.400
County Stadium	.217	9	23	3	5	0	0	0	1	0	0	1	5	.308	.217
Metrodome	.350	11	40	5	14	2	0	1	4	1	0	1	6	.366	.475
Yankee Stadium	.221	17	68	7	15	3	0	1	6	2	0	1	20	.232	.309
Oakland-Alameda	.243	86	267	34	65	12	3	4	28	5	3	20	46	.300	.356
Kingdome	.308	7	26	3	8	3	0	1	3	0	0	0	5	.308	.538
Arlington	.167	16	60	9	10	3	0	3	10	0	0	2	13	.194	.367
SkyDome	.273	130	495	89	135	28	2	34	89	5	2	34	101	.322	.543
Wrigley Field	.294	5	17	3	5	1	0	2	5	0	0	0	3	.294	.706
Cinergy Field	.143	8	28	5	4	0	0	2	3	0	0	1	5	.172	.357
Astrodome	.273	5	11	1	3	0	0	1	4	0	0	2	1	.385	.545
Dodger Stadium	.000	5	17	1	0	0	0	0	1	0	0	1	2	.100	.000
Olympic Stadium	.273	11	33	4	9	3	0	2	6	0	0	2	5	.333	.545
Shea Stadium	.455	5	11	2	5	2	0	1	3	0	0	1	1	.500	.909
Veterans Stadium	.200	5	15	2	3	2	0	1	1	0	0	2	5	.294	.533
Three Rivers	.250	5	12	4	3	1	1	1	1	0	0	1	2	.308	.750
Busch Stadium	.000	2	3	0	0	0	0	0	0	0	0	0	1	.000	.000
Qualcomm Park	.125	6	16	0	2	0	0	0	1	0	0	0	1	.118	.125
3 Com Park	.346	8	26	2	9	3	1	2	6	0	0	1	4	.370	.769
Coors Field	.438	4	16	4	7	0	0	1	1	1	0	2	3	.500	.625
Pro Player Stadium	.000	3	1	2	0	0	0	0	0	0	0	2	1	.667	.000
Turner Field	.500	5	18	3	9	1	0	2	7	0	0	0	2	.500	.889
BankOne Ballpark	.288	74	219	32	63	11	0	10	29	2	1	19	31	.347	.475
Tropicana Field	.261	12	46	7	12	1	0	4	9	0	1	3	7	.314	.543
SAFECO Field	.043	6	23	4	1	0	0	1	2	0	0	3	10	.185	.174
Comerica Park	.304	6	23	5	7	0	0	1	4	0	0	2	5	.370	.435

Peter
BAUER
PITCHER

58

BIRTHDATE . . . . November 6, 1978
OPENING DAY AGE 22
BIRTHPLACE . . . . Washington, DC
RESIDENCE . . . . Hagerstown, MD
BATS/THROWS . . . . R/R
HEIGHT/WEIGHT 6-7/250
CONTRACT STATUS . . . . signed thru 2001
M.L. SERVICE 0.000

PERSONAL: Peter Josef Bauer... Name pronounced Bower... One of five children, three brothers, one sister... Graduated from Paint Branch High School where he lettered four years in baseball and three times in basketball... Was a USA Today and Gatorade Player of the Year for Maryland... Was selected by Seattle in the 1997 first year player draft but did not sign... Attended University of South Carolina where he was a Freshman All-American in 1998.

LAST SEASON: Made his pro debut with Hagerstown of the South Atlantic League (A) where he was 1-5 in five starts with a 5.06 ERA... Started the season going 0-4 in his first seven starts... Captured his first pro win on August 25 vs Macon after allowing three earned runs over 5.0 innings... Pitched a season high 5.0 innings in each of his last three starts... Held opponents to a .296 average, with left-handed batters at .189 and right-handers at .341... Allowed only two home runs in his 32.0 innings.

PETER BAUER

Year Club & League	W-L	ERA	G	GS	CG	ShO	SV	IP	H	R	ER	HR	HB	BB-IBB	SO	WP	BK	OBA
2000 Hagerstown (SAL)	1-5	5.06	9	9	0	0	0	32.0	37	27	18	2	3	8-0	22	4	0	.296

BAUER — TRANSACTIONS
- Selected by the Toronto Blue Jays in 2nd round (45th overall) of June 2000 First Year Player Draft.

Kevin
BEIRNE
PITCHER

40

BIRTHDATE .... January 1, 1974
OPENING DAY AGE 27
BIRTHPLACE .... Houston, TX
RESIDENCE .... The Woodlands, TX
BATS/THROWS .... L/R
HEIGHT/WEIGHT 6-4/210
CONTRACT STATUS .... signed thru 2001
M.L. SERVICE 0.135

PERSONAL: Kevin Patrick Beirne... Name pronounced Burn... Attended Texas A&M University where he pitched and played the outfield... Was a wide receiver on the football squad... Lettered two seasons in football... Made four starts at wide receiver in 1994 and caught 13 passes for 139 yards... Attended McCollough High School in The Woodlands, TX and was one of the top wide receivers in the state... Drafted by the Cincinnati Reds in 1992 but did not sign... His father Jim played professional football for the Houston Oilers from 1968 to 1976.

LAST SEASON: Split the season between Chicago and Charlotte (AAA) where he was 1-2 in seven starts with a 3.51 ERA... Was recalled from Charlotte on May 8... Made his major-league debut in relief on May 17 at Yankee Stadium tossing a scoreless inning... In that game recorded first strikeout, Bernie Williams... From June 14 to 21 he appeared in three games allowing one run over 7.2 innings... Earned his first ML win on June 14 at Cleveland with 3.2 scoreless innings (2H, 2BB, 3K)... On July 8 vs the Cubs pitched a scoreless 1.2 innings and struckout the side in the sixth inning... Suffered his first career loss and blown save on July 28 at Anaheim (3 ER/0.2 IP)... Struck out a career-high four on August 8 vs. Seattle (Gm 1)... Allowed one run over a career-high 4.1 innings in relief with three strikeouts on August 14 at Baltimore... Was optioned to Charlotte on August 24 and then recalled on September 4... Lost his first ML start on September 26 vs Boston, allowed three runs on three hits over 5.0 innings... Was 0-1 in save situations, stranded 11 of 21 inherited runners (52.4 percent) and first batters hit .200 (5-25).

PROFESSIONAL CAREER: 1995: Pitched for Sarasota, Bristol and Hickory and combined to go 1-0 with four saves and a 1.62 ERA in his first pro season... Averaged 10.3 strikeouts per 9.0 IP (19 SO/16.2 IP) while posting a 3.8 to 1, strikeout-to-walk ratio... **1996:** Was 4-11 in 26 games, 25 starts for South Bend (A) while posting a 4.15 ERA... Registered his only complete game on August 25 at Quad City... Allowed just six earned runs over four starts with a 1.98 ERA from July 25 to August 9... **1997:** Split the season between Class A Winston-Salem and Birmingham (AA), combining to go 10-8 in 26 games, 25 starts, with a 3.94 ERA... Pitched 157.2 innings which was fifth in the system and his 3.94 ERA was sixth... Averaged 8.2 strikeouts per 9.0 IP and held opponents to a .220 average at Winston-Salem... **1998:** Combined to go 13-9 with a 3.49 ERA and 159 strikeouts between Class AA Birmingham and Class AAA Calgary... Ranked as the sixth best prospect in the White Sox organization by Baseball America... The 159 strikeouts were second in the organization, fifth in the Southern League and ninth in the minors... Also tied for third in the league in wins and ranked fifth in ERA (3.44)... Tied for the organization lead in wins, starts (28) and shutouts (one)... Averaged 8.2 strikeouts per 9.0 IP... Selected to the SL Midseason All-Star Team and started for the American League squad on July 8 in New Haven, Connecticut, tossing 2.0 shutout innings... Posted a 9-3 record with a 2.08 ERA at home... Won six straight June 1 to July 12 allowing eight runs in 48.0 innings (1.50 ERA)... Struck out a season-high 10 batters on August 28 vs. Mobile... Promoted to Calgary on August 29 where he started a pair of games in the Pacific Coast League playoffs, going 0-0 with a 6.00 ERA (4ER/6.0 IP)... **1999:** Spent the entire season at Class AAA Charlotte... Was 5-2 with a 2.28 ERA (14 ER/55.1) on June 1... From that point on was 0-3 with an 8.43 ERA... Was placed on the disabled list August 6 with soreness on his right side and missed the remainder of the season... Was also on the disabled list from May 6 to 14 with a strain of the right lateral muscle... Named organizational Player of the Month in May after going 3-0 with 0.72 ERA... Went 4-1 with a 1.19 ERA in seven starts from April 23 to June 1, four of the starts were scoreless... Pitched six innings in 13 of 20 starts.

KEVIN BEIRNE

Year	Club & League	W-L	ERA	G	GS	CG	ShO	SV	IP	H	R	ER	HR	HB	BB-IBB	SO	WP	BK	OBA
1995	White Sox (Gulf)	0-0	2.45	2	0	0	0	2	3.2	2	2	1	0	1	1-0	3	0	0	.154
1995	Bristol (Appy)	1-0	0.00	9	0	0	0	2	9.0	4	0	0	0	0	4-0	12	0	0	.129
1995	Hickory (SAL)	0-0	4.50	3	0	0	0	0	4.0	7	2	2	0	0	0-0	4	0	0	.438
1996	South Bend (Mid)	4-11	4.15	26	25	1	0	0	145.1	153	85	67	5	9	60-0	110	12	3	.279
1997	Winston-Salem (Caro)	4-4	3.05	13	13	1	0	0	82.2	66	38	28	7	7	28-1	75	5	0	.220
1997	Birmingham (Sou)	6-4	4.92	13	12	0	0	0	75.0	76	51	41	4	4	41-0	49	2	1	.266
1998	Birmingham (Sou)	13-9	3.44	26	26	2	1	0	167.1	142	77	64	12	6	87-2	153	4	2	.238
1998	Calgary (PCL)	0-0	4.50	2	2	0	0	0	8.0	12	5	4	1	1	4-0	6	0	0	.387
1999	Charlotte (Int)	5-5	5.42	20	20	0	0	0	113.0	134	75	68	14	2	36-0	63	12	0	.296
2000	Charlotte (Int)	1-2	3.51	7	7	0	0	0	33.1	39	13	13	3	2	7-0	28	5	0	.293
2000	CHICAGO (AL)	1-3	6.70	29	1	0	0	0	49.2	50	41	37	9	4	20-1	41	1	0	.263
Minor Totals		34-35	4.04	121	105	4	1	4	641.1	635	348	288	46	32	268-3	503	40	6	.264

BEIRNE — TRANSACTIONS

- Selected by the Chicago White Sox in 11th round of the June 1995 First Year Player Draft.
- On disabled list (quadricep strain) July 3-25, 1995.
- On disabled list (strain of right lateral muscle) May 6-14, 1999.
- On disabled list (soreness on right side) August 6 through remainder of the season, 1999.
- Traded to the Toronto Blue Jays along with OF Brian Simmons, LHP Mike Sirotka and RHP Mike Williams in exchange for RHP Matt DeWitt and LHP David Wells on January 14, 2001.

CAREER HIGHS — BEIRNE, Kevin
GAME:

ML Debut	May 17, 2000 at NYY
Innings Pitched:	
Starter	5.0 - Sep. 26, 2000 vs. BOS
Reliever	4.1 - Aug. 14, 2000 at BAL
Walks:	
Starter	1 - Sep. 26, 2000 vs. BOS
Reliever	3 - Aug. 14, 2000 at BAL
Strikeouts:	
Starter	4 - Aug. 14, 2000 vs. BOS
Reliever	4 - Aug. 8, 2000 vs. SEA
Hits Allowed	6 - Aug. 8, 2000 vs. SEA
Runs Allowed	5 - Aug. 8, 2000 vs. SEA
ER Allowed	5 - Aug. 8, 2000 vs. SEA
HR Allowed	2 - Jul. 3, 2000 at KC
	2 - Sep. 26, 2000 vs. BOS
Low Hit CG	None
Last Win	Jun. 14, 2000 at CLE
Last Save	None
Last CG	None
Last ShO	None
Last Start	Sep. 26, 2000 vs. BOS
Last Relief App.	Oct. 1, 2000 vs. KC
Scoreless Innings Streak	5.2 - Jun. 14-18, 2000

FIELDING
BEIRNE, Kevin—P

Year	PCT	G	PO	A	E	TC	DP
2000	.857	29	2	4	1	7	0

KEVIN BEIRNE DETAILED PITCHING

	2000							CAREER						
	ERA	W-L-Sv	G	IP	H	ER	BB	SO	ERA	W-L-Sv	G	IP	H	ER	BB	SO
Total	6.70	1-3-0	29	49.2	50	37	20	41	6.70	1-3-0	29	49.2	50	37	20	41
ST	5.40	0-1-0	1	5.0	3	3	1	4	5.40	0-1-0	1	5.0	3	3	1	4
REL	6.85	1-2-0	28	44.2	47	34	19	37	6.85	1-2-0	28	44.2	47	34	19	37
Home	8.42	0-1-0	15	25.2	29	24	10	22	8.42	0-1-0	15	25.2	29	24	10	22
Away	4.88	1-2-0	14	24.0	21	13	10	19	4.88	1-2-0	14	24.0	21	13	10	19
May	6.75	0-0-0	4	5.1	7	4	2	2	6.75	0-0-0	4	5.1	7	4	2	2
June	5.84	1-0-0	8	12.1	11	8	8	9	5.84	1-0-0	8	12.1	11	8	8	9
July	6.97	0-1-0	7	10.1	12	8	1	11	6.97	0-1-0	7	10.1	12	8	1	11
August	9.90	0-0-0	4	10.0	12	11	6	9	9.90	0-0-0	4	10.0	12	11	6	9
September	5.06	0-2-0	5	10.2	7	6	3	9	5.06	0-2-0	5	10.2	7	6	3	9
October	0.00	0-0-0	1	1.0	1	0	0	1	0.00	0-0-0	1	1.0	1	0	0	1
vs. Ana	40.50	0-1-0	1	0.2	2	3	0	1	40.50	0-1-0	1	0.2	2	3	0	1
vs. Bal	2.08	0-0-0	1	4.1	3	1	3	3	2.08	0-0-0	1	4.1	3	1	3	3
vs. Bos	4.50	0-1-0	2	6.0	3	3	1	6	4.50	0-1-0	2	6.0	3	3	1	6
vs. Cle	4.09	1-0-0	4	11.0	7	5	5	7	4.09	1-0-0	4	11.0	7	5	5	7
vs. KC	3.38	0-0-0	4	5.1	6	2	0	4	3.38	0-0-0	4	5.1	6	2	0	4
vs. Min	3.38	0-1-0	3	2.2	1	1	0	3	3.38	0-1-0	3	2.2	1	1	0	3
vs. NYY	7.94	0-0-0	5	5.2	10	5	2	4	7.94	0-0-0	5	5.2	10	5	2	4
vs. Sea	12.27	0-0-0	1	3.2	6	5	1	4	12.27	0-0-0	1	3.2	6	5	1	4
vs. TB	33.75	0-0-0	1	1.1	3	5	2	2	33.75	0-0-0	1	1.1	3	5	2	2
vs. Tex	0.00	0-0-0	2	1.2	1	0	1	0	0.00	0-0-0	2	1.2	1	0	1	0
vs. Tor	0.00	0-0-0	1	1.0	0	0	0	2	0.00	0-0-0	1	1.0	0	0	0	2
vs. ChC	0.00	0-0-0	1	1.2	1	0	0	3	0.00	0-0-0	1	1.2	1	0	0	3
vs. Cin	99.00	0-0-0	1	0.0	2	4	2	0	99.00	0-0-0	1	0.0	2	4	2	0
vs. Hou	0.00	0-0-0	1	2.0	1	0	2	0	0.00	0-0-0	1	2.0	1	0	2	0
vs. StL	10.13	0-0-0	1	2.2	4	3	1	2	10.13	0-0-0	1	2.2	4	3	1	2
Pre-All Star	5.56	1-0-0	15	22.2	24	14	10	16	5.56	1-0-0	15	22.2	24	14	10	16
Post-All Star	7.67	0-3-0	14	27.0	26	23	10	25	7.67	0-3-0	14	27.0	26	23	10	25

KEVIN BEIRNE PITCHING AT ML PARKS

Park	ERA	W-L-Sv	SvO	G	GS	IP	H	R	ER	HR	BB	SO
Camden Yards	2.08	0-0-0	0	1	0	4.1	3	1	1	0	3	3
Fenway Park	0.00	0-0-0	0	1	0	1.0	0	0	0	0	0	2
Edison Field	40.50	0-1-0	1	1	0	0.2	2	3	3	1	0	1
Comiskey Park	8.42	0-1-0	0	15	1	25.2	29	26	24	5	10	22
Jacobs Field	2.70	1-0-0	0	2	0	6.2	4	2	2	0	3	6
Kauffman Stadium	5.40	0-0-0	0	2	0	3.1	5	2	2	2	0	2
Metrodome	13.50	0-1-0	0	1	0	0.2	1	1	1	1	0	0
Yankee Stadium	0.00	0-0-0	0	2	0	3.0	2	0	0	0	0	2
Arlington	0.00	0-0-0	0	1	0	0.2	0	0	0	0	0	0
Wrigley Field	0.00	0-0-0	0	1	0	1.2	1	0	0	0	0	3
Cinergy Field	99.00	0-0-0	0	1	0	0.0	2	4	4	0	2	0
Enron Field	0.00	0-0-0	0	1	0	2.0	1	2	0	0	2	0

Pedro BORBON

PITCHER

51

BIRTHDATE . . . . November 15, 1967
OPENING DAY AGE 33
BIRTHPLACE . . . . Mao, DR
RESIDENCE . . . . Houston, TX
BATS/THROWS . . . . L/L
HEIGHT/WEIGHT 6-1/224
CONTRACT STATUS . . . . signed thru 2002
M.L. SERVICE 6.045

PERSONAL: Pedro Felix Borbon... Two children, Ty Noel (11) and Isabella Nicole (5)... Graduated from Dewitt Clinton High School, Sioux, New Jersey in 1985... Attended Ranger Junior College in Ranger, Texas... Is the son of former major league pitcher Pedro Borbon Sr. who pitched for the Cincinnati Reds, California Angels, San Francisco Giants and St. Louis Cardinals from 1969 to 1980.

LAST SEASON: In his first season with Toronto was 1-1 with a save and a 6.48 ERA in 59 games... Collected 12 holds which was one short of the team lead... Started the season allowing three hits and an earned run without recording an out over his first two games... On April 12 collected his only win of the season in Anaheim (0.1IP, 1HB)... Was busiest in April appearing in 13 games and posting a 1-0 record with a 7.45 ERA over 9.2 innings... April 15 & 16 allowed grand slams to Seattle (Martinez & Rodriguez), were the first two slams he had allowed in his career... In May posted a 3.00 ERA over 12 games and recorded three holds... Posted a 0.00ERA in June when he appeared in 11 games (5.2IP)... Went from June 2 to July 3 without allowing a run, a span of 13 games and 7.0 innings pitched... Had an ERA of 3.86 at the end of the scoreless streak... Recorded holds in three straight appearances from June 17 to 23... At the All-Star break had a record of 1-0 with a 4.76 ERA in 41 games... In the second half of the season was 0-1 with a save and a 10.13 ERA... In July was 0-1 with an ERA of 12.27 and walked 12 batters in 7.1 innings... On August 11 pitched a season high 2.0 innings at Minnesota retiring six batters in order... Retired 11 straight batters faced from August 11 at KC to August 15 vs Anaheim... Matched season high 2.0 innings pitched on August 26 at Texas to record his only save of the season... Appeared in two September games allowing seven ER in a combined 1.1 innings before being shutdown with left elbow soreness... Following the season had surgery performed by Dr. James Andrews to remove bone chips from his left elbow... Had nine appearances in which he did not record an out... Left handed batters hit .209 (18-86) with two home runs while right handed batters hit .360 (27-75) with three home runs.

PROFESSIONAL CAREER: 1988: Began professional career in the Chicago White Sox organization with Sarasota and was 5-3 in 16 games, 11 starts with an ERA of 2.41... Posted 67 strikeouts with 17 walks in 75.0 innings pitched... Led Gulf Coast League pitchers with 19 assists... **1989:** Was released by the White Sox organization on April 1 and did not play the rest of the season... Was signed by the Atlanta Braves organization on August 25... **1990:** Started the season at Burlington- A and won seven straight decisions from May 10 to June 10... Allowed just 9.12 base-runners per nine innings, lowest among Midwest League starters... Promoted to Durham- A where he started 11 games and was 4-5... **1991:** Appeared in 37 games for Durham- A and posted a 4-3 record with a 2.28 ERA and five saves... Promoted to Greenville- AA where he started four games and was 0-1 with a 2.79 ERA... **1992:** Opened the season in the starting rotation for Greenville and was 5-2 with a 4.23 ERA in ten starts... Moved to the bullpen on June 10 and was 3-0 with three saves and a 1.40 ERA... Allowed one run in 25.1 innings from June 28 to August 31 (18 gms.)... Saved two games for Greenville in the Southern League Playoffs... Made his Major League debut on October 2 vs San Diego pitching a third of an inning... Played winter ball for Estrellas in the Dominican Republic and was 4-1 with a 1.32 ERA... **1993:** Spent most of the season with AAA Richmond where he was 5-5 with a

4.23 ERA in 52 games... Allowed only five of 36 inherited runners to score... Had 95 strikeouts in 76.2 innings and allowed only 71 hits... Recalled to Atlanta on September 10 and appeared in three games... **1994:** Played the entire season with Richmond and was 3-4 with four saves in 59 games with an ERA of 2.79... Left-handed batters hit just .200 (12-60)... Allowed only a .203 (14-69) opponents batting average with runners in scoring position... Did not allow a home run in his last 34.0 innings... In the International League play-offs did not allow a run in four games (3.2IP)... Struckout at least one batter in 47 of his 59 games, averaged 9.15 strikeouts per 9.0 innings pitched - 6th in the IL... Was eighth in the league appearing in 59 games... **1995:** In his first full season in the major leagues held left-handed batters to a .167 (7-42) average... Went 11 consecutive games from May 5 to June 10 without allowing a hit (7.2IP)... Earned his first ML victory on August 3 vs. Philadelphia... Saved his first ML game on May 13 vs the Reds, fanning the only batter he faced... The first career save gave him and his father the all-time saves record for a father-son team (each with at least one save)... Pedro Sr. recorded 80 saves in his 11 year career (1969-1980)... Struckout 33 batters in 32.0 innings... Just five of 29 inherited runners scored... Was 2-4 in save situations... In the post-season did not allow a run in his two games... Earned a save in Game 4 of the World Series, was the first save by a rookie since Todd Worrell of the Cardinals saved Game 1 in 1985... The Borbon's became only the third father-son team to pitch in a World Series joining the Bagby's (Jim Sr. and Jr.) and the Stottlemyre's (Mel and Todd)... **1996:** Was 3-0 with one save and an ERA of 2.75 in 43 games when season was cut short on August 22 vs. Cincinnati... Suffered a torn medial collateral ligament in his left elbow... Was placed on the 15-day disabled list and underwent reconstructive surgery on August 30 in Atlanta... Surgery was performed by Dr. Joe Chandler who took a tendon from one of Borbon's legs and used it to replace the elbow ligament... Recuperation time was estimated between nine months and two years... **1997:** Missed the entire season due to his elbow surgery... **1998:** Began to pitch after surgery and spent the entire season in the Atlanta Braves' minor league's system... Combined between three clubs was 0-3 in 39 games with an ERA of 5.52 (28ER/45.2IP)... **1999:** Signed as a free agent by the Los Angeles Dodgers on January 11... Made a successful comeback after missing two seasons due to elbow surgery... Appeared in a team and career high 70 games and was 4-3 with a 4.09 ERA... The 70 games tied for eighth in Dodgers single season games list with Ron Perranoski (1962, 1967) and Charlie Hough (1977)... Was the first Dodger pitcher whose father also played in the majors... Held opponents to a .209 batting average, .156 (14-90) vs. LH hitters and .258 (25-97) by RH hitters... Did not allow an earned run in 27 of 29 games from April 12 to June 25... In May was 1-1 in 12 games with an ERA of 0.93 which was his lowest of any month... Earned first win on May 30 at Atlanta, was his first win since August 21, 1996... Was 2-1 with a 1.64 ERA prior to the All-Star game and 2-2 with a 8.66 ERA in the second half... Earned first save in three years in a rain shortened game on September 19 at Colorado... Prior save was April 1, 1996 with Atlanta... Was 1-2 in save opportunities... Posted 15 holds and allowed only eight of 37 inherited runners to score.

POST-SEASON EXPERIENCE: 1995: Member of the World Champion Atlanta Braves... Made two post season appearances pitching a scoreless inning in the Division

Series vs Colorado (1H, 3K) and in the World Series earned a save in game four of the World Series vs. Cleveland (1.0IP, 2K)... Was the first World Series save by a rookie since Todd Worrell of the Cardinals saved game one of the 1985 Series... He and his father, Pedro Sr., are just the third father-son team to pitch in the World Series after the Bagby's (Jim Sr. and Jr.) and the Stottlemyre's (Mel and Todd).

CAREER NOTES: He and his father hold the all-time saves record for a father-son team (each with at least one save)... Pedro Sr. recorded 80 saves in his 11 year career (1969-1980)... Left hand batters enter the 2001 season with a .174 (46-264) career batting average against him, RH are at .283 (98-346)... On August 30, 1996 had reconstructive surgery on his left elbow to replace a torn medial collateral ligament with a tendon from his leg... Has made 218 career relief appearances, has never started a game.

PEDRO BORBON

Year	Club & League	W-L	ERA	G	GS	CG	ShO	SV	IP	H	R	ER	HR	HB	BB-IBB	SO	WP	BK	OBA
1988	White Sox (Gulf)	5-3	2.41	16	11	1	1	1	74.2	52	28	20	1	2	17-0	67	5	14	.190
1989									DID NOT PLAY										
1990	Burlington (Mid)	11-3	1.47	14	14	6	2	0	97.2	73	25	16	3	3	23-0	76	4	1	.206
1990	Durham (Caro)	4-5	5.43	11	11	0	0	0	61.1	73	40	37	8	2	16-0	37	2	1	.299
1991	Durham (Caro)	4-3	2.27	37	6	1	0	5	91.0	85	40	23	2	2	35-2	79	4	2	.249
1991	Greenville (Sou)	0-1	2.79	4	4	0	0	0	29.0	23	12	9	1	3	10-0	22	2	0	.217
1992	Greenville (SOU)	8-2	3.06	39	10	0	0	3	94.0	73	36	32	6	3	42-1	79	2	0	.218
1992	ATLANTA (NL)	0-1	6.75	2	0	0	0	0	1.1	2	1	1	0	0	1-1	1	0	0	.333
1993	Richmond (Int)	5-5	4.23	52	0	0	0	1	76.2	71	40	36	7	2	42-9	95	3	1	.247
1993	ATLANTA (NL)	0-0	21.60	3	0	0	0	0	1.2	3	4	4	0	0	3-0	2	0	0	.000
1994	Richmond (Int)	3-4	2.79	59	0	0	0	4	80.2	66	29	25	3	1	41-5	82	1	0	.228
1995	ATLANTA (NL)	2-2	3.09	41	0	0	0	2	32.0	29	12	11	2	1	17-4	33	0	1	.240
1996	ATLANTA (NL)	3-0	2.75	43	0	0	0	1	36.0	26	12	11	1	1	7-0	31	0	0	.203
1996	Greenville (Sou)	0-0	0.00	1	0	0	0	0	1.0	0	0	0	0	0	0-0	0	0	0	.000
1997									INJURED--DID NOT PLAY										
1998	Macon (SAL)	0-0	9.00	3	0	0	0	0	3.0	4	3	3	1	0	1-0	3	0	0	.308
1998	Greenville (Sou)	0-2	4.74	16	0	0	0	0	19.0	21	14	10	2	2	14-0	10	0	0	.288
1998	Richmond (Int)	0-1	5.70	20	0	0	0	0	23.2	29	17	15	1	2	8-0	15	0	0	.302
1999	LOS ANGELES (NL)	4-3	4.09	70	0	0	0	1	50.2	39	23	23	5	1	29-1	33	1	0	.209
2000	TORONTO (AL)	1-1	6.48	59	0	0	0	1	41.2	45	37	30	5	5	38-5	29	0	0	.280
Minor Totals		40-29	3.12	272	56	8	3	14	651.2	570	284	226	35	22	249-17	565	23	19	.236
NL TOTALS		9-6	3.70	159	0	0	0	4	121.2	99	52	50	8	3	57-6	100	1	1	.214
MAJOR TOTALS		10-7	4.41	218	0	0	0	5	163.1	141	89	80	13	8	95-11	129	1	1	.231

DIVISION SERIES RECORD

Year	Club & League	W-L	ERA	G	GS	CG	ShO	SV	IP	H	R	ER	HR	HB	BB-IBB	SO	WP	BK	OBA
1995	ATLANTA (NL)	0-0	0.00	1	0	0	0	0	1.0	1	0	0	0	0	0-0	3	0	0	.250

WORLD SERIES RECORD

Year	Club & League	W-L	ERA	G	GS	CG	ShO	SV	IP	H	R	ER	HR	HB	BB-IBB	SO	WP	BK	OBA
1995	ATLANTA (NL)	0-0	0.00	1	0	0	0	1	1.0	0	0	0	0	0	0-0	2	0	0	.000

BORBON — TRANSACTIONS

- Signed as non-drafted free agent by the Chicago White Sox on June 4, 1988.
- Released by the Chicago White Sox on April 1, 1989.
- Signed as a free agent by the Atlanta Braves on August 25, 1989.
- On disabled list April 8-26, 1996 (left shoulder tendinitis).
- On disabled list August 23-November 1, 1996 (torn medial collateral ligament in left elbow).
- On disabled list March 29, 1997 to end of the season (left elbow ligament).
- Granted free agency on October 1, 1998.
- Signed by the Los Angeles Dodgers on December 21, 1998.
- Traded to the Toronto Blue Jays along with OF Raul Mondesi in exchange for OF Shawn Green and IF Jorge Nunez on November 8, 1999.

FIELDING

BORBON, Pedro—P

Year	PCT	G	PO	A	E	TC	DP
1992 (NL)	.000	2	0	0	0	0	0
1993 (NL)	.000	3	0	0	0	0	0
1995 (NL)	1.000	41	1	6	0	7	1
1996 (NL)	.900	43	4	5	1	10	1
1999 (NL)	1.000	70	2	6	0	8	0
2000 (AL)	1.000	59	2	9	0	11	1
Total	.972	218	9	26	1	36	3

CAREER HIGHS — BORBON, Pedro

PEDRO BORBON DETAILED PITCHING

	2000								CAREER						
	ERA	W-L-Sv	G	IP	H	ER	BB	SO	ERA	W-L-Sv	G	IP	H	ER	BB	SO
Total	6.48	1-1-1	59	41.2	45	30	38	29	4.41	10-7-5	218	163.1	144	80	95	129
REL	6.48	1-1-1	59	41.2	45	30	38	29	4.41	10-7-5	218	163.1	144	80	95	129
Home	9.47	0-1-0	28	19.0	26	20	22	17	4.77	5-4-3	112	83.0	80	44	47	73
Away	3.97	1-0-1	31	22.2	19	10	16	12	4.03	5-3-2	106	80.1	64	36	48	56
April	7.45	1-0-0	13	9.2	15	8	5	3	5.09	1-0-1	27	23.0	25	13	14	10
May	3.00	0-0-0	12	9.0	6	3	5	10	1.17	1-1-2	38	30.2	10	4	9	26
June	0.00	0-0-0	11	5.2	4	0	3	5	3.00	2-1-0	41	27.0	22	9	11	27
July	12.27	0-0-0	12	7.1	14	10	12	8	4.94	0-1-0	45	31.0	34	17	22	25
August	2.08	0-0-1	9	8.2	4	2	7	3	5.73	4-1-1	44	33.0	32	21	20	25
September	47.25	0-0-0	2	1.1	2	7	6	0	8.44	2-2-1	19	16.0	18	15	18	13
October	–	–	–	–	–	–	–	–	3.38	0-1-0	4	2.2	3	1	1	3
vs. Ana	7.94	1-0-0	8	5.2	5	5	5	1	5.79	1-0-0	11	9.1	6	6	5	3
vs. Bal	2.08	0-0-0	6	4.1	4	1	5	5	2.08	0-0-0	6	4.1	4	1	5	5
vs. Bos	0.00	0-0-0	7	6.1	1	0	2	4	0.00	0-0-0	7	6.1	1	0	2	4
vs. CWS	0.00	0-0-0	2	1.1	0	0	0	2	0.00	0-0-0	2	1.1	0	0	0	2
vs. Cle	18.90	0-0-0	6	3.1	9	7	4	5	18.90	0-0-0	6	3.1	9	7	4	5
vs. Det	0.00	0-0-0	4	1.1	1	0	2	2	0.00	0-0-0	4	1.1	1	0	2	2
vs. KC	6.75	0-0-0	3	1.1	3	1	1	0	6.75	0-0-0	3	1.1	3	1	1	0
vs. Mil	–	–	–	–	–	–	–	–	5.40	0-1-0	5	3.1	2	2	2	5
vs. Min	3.38	0-0-0	3	2.2	2	1	2	2	3.38	0-0-0	3	2.2	2	1	2	2
vs. NYY	9.00	0-0-0	3	3.0	5	3	3	0	9.00	0-0-0	3	3.0	5	3	3	0
vs. Oak	36.00	0-0-0	2	1.0	2	4	4	0	18.00	0-0-0	3	2.0	2	4	5	1
vs. Sea	9.00	0-0-0	4	3.0	4	3	2	3	6.75	0-0-0	5	4.0	4	3	2	4
vs. TB	0.00	0-0-0	1	0.1	0	0	0	1	0.00	0-0-0	1	0.1	0	0	0	1
vs. Tex	2.25	0-0-1	4	4.0	3	1	2	1	1.93	0-0-1	5	4.2	4	1	3	1
vs. Ari	–	–	–	–	–	–	–	–	4.76	0-0-0	8	5.2	6	3	4	3
vs. Atl	0.00	0-0-0	2	0.2	1	0	2	0	1.42	1-0-0	7	6.1	4	1	6	4
vs. ChC	–	–	–	–	–	–	–	–	1.00	0-0-0	9	9.0	4	1	3	9
vs. Cin	–	–	–	–	–	–	–	–	1.13	1-1-1	11	8.0	5	1	2	8
vs. Col	–	–	–	–	–	–	–	–	2.84	0-0-2	13	6.1	6	2	3	6
vs. Fla	0.00	0-0-0	1	0.2	0	0	0	1	5.63	0-2-0	9	8.0	9	5	6	5
vs. Hou	–	–	–	–	–	–	–	–	2.84	0-0-0	10	6.1	7	2	1	8
vs. LA	–	–	–	–	–	–	–	–	4.50	1-0-0	5	6.0	4	3	1	4
vs. Mon	18.00	0-0-0	1	1.0	3	2	2	0	4.76	1-0-0	8	5.2	7	3	4	1
vs. NYM	13.50	0-1-0	1	1.1	2	2	2	1	7.62	2-1-0	14	13.0	19	11	6	10
vs. Phi	0.00	0-0-0	1	0.1	0	0	0	1	7.71	1-0-0	19	14.0	12	12	8	15
vs. Pit	–	–	–	–	–	–	–	–	3.86	1-0-0	7	4.2	4	2	5	4
vs. StL	–	–	–	–	–	–	–	–	1.80	0-0-0	9	5.0	2	1	2	3
vs. SD	–	–	–	–	–	–	–	–	2.08	0-1-0	14	8.2	8	2	5	5
vs. SF	–	–	–	–	–	–	–	–	1.93	1-1-1	11	9.1	4	2	3	9
Pre-All Star	4.76	1-0-0	41	28.1	33	15	17	22	3.09	4-2-3	120	93.1	70	32	39	75
Post-All Star	10.13	0-1-1	18	13.1	12	15	21	7	6.17	6-5-2	98	70.0	74	48	56	54

PEDRO BORBON PITCHING AT ML PARKS

Park	ERA	W-L-Sv	SvO	G	GS	IP	H	R	ER	HR	BB	SO
Camden Yards	0.00	0-0-0	0	3	0	2.1	2	0	0	0	1	2
Fenway Park	0.00	0-0-0	0	4	0	3.1	1	0	0	0	0	2
Edison Field	8.31	1-0-0	1	5	0	4.1	3	4	4	1	3	1
Comiskey Park	0.00	0-0-0	0	1	0	0.1	0	0	0	0	0	0
Jacobs Field	10.80	0-0-0	0	2	0	1.2	4	3	2	0	1	3
Kauffman Stadium	0.00	0-0-0	0	1	0	1.1	0	0	0	0	0	0
County Stadium	6.75	0-1-0	0	4	0	2.2	2	2	2	0	2	3
Metrodome	0.00	0-0-0	0	1	0	2.0	0	0	0	0	0	1
Yankee Stadium	13.50	0-0-0	0	2	0	2.0	3	3	3	0	3	0
Oakland-Alameda	0.00	0-0-0	0	2	0	1.1	0	0	0	0	2	1
Arlington	0.00	0-0-1	1	2	0	3.0	1	0	0	0	0	1
SkyDome	9.47	0-1-0	0	28	0	19.0	26	24	20	5	22	17
Atlanta-Fulton	3.46	3-1-3	4	52	0	41.2	35	18	16	2	12	41
Wrigley Field	3.86	0-0-0	0	4	0	2.1	3	1	1	0	1	4
Cinergy Field	3.38	0-1-0	1	3	0	2.2	2	1	1	1	0	3
Astrodome	6.75	0-0-0	0	3	0	1.1	4	1	1	0	1	2
Dodger Stadium	3.71	3-2-0	0	35	0	26.2	23	11	11	1	14	17
Olympic Stadium	4.15	0-0-0	0	6	0	4.1	5	4	2	0	4	1
Shea Stadium	4.05	2-0-0	0	8	0	6.2	7	3	3	0	3	4
Veterans Stadium	12.00	0-0-0	0	9	0	6.0	5	8	8	2	4	3
Three Rivers	6.00	0-0-0	0	5	0	3.0	4	2	2	0	4	2
Busch Stadium	0.00	0-0-0	0	1	0	0.1	0	0	0	0	0	0
Qualcomm Park	1.59	0-0-0	0	8	0	5.2	3	1	1	1	3	4
3 Com Park	2.25	0-0-0	0	6	0	4.0	1	1	1	0	1	5
Coors Field	0.00	0-0-1	1	5	0	2.1	0	0	0	0	1	3
Pro Player Stadium	4.91	0-1-0	0	4	0	3.2	5	2	2	0	5	4
Turner Field	0.00	1-0-0	0	4	0	3.1	1	0	0	0	3	1
BankOne Ballpark	0.00	0-0-0	0	4	0	4.1	2	0	0	0	2	2
Tropicana Field	0.00	0-0-0	0	1	0	0.1	0	0	0	0	0	1
SAFECO Field	0.00	0-0-0	0	2	0	0.1	1	0	0	0	1	0
Comerica Park	0.00	0-0-0	0	3	0	1.0	1	0	0	0	2	1

Homer
BUSH

INFIELDER

BIRTHDATE . . . . November 12, 1972
OPENING DAY AGE 28
BIRTHPLACE . . . . East St. Louis, IL
RESIDENCE . . . . Keller, TX
BATS/THROWS . . . . R/R
HEIGHT/WEIGHT 5-10/180
CONTRACT STATUS . . . . signed thru 2002
M.L. SERVICE 3.154

18

PERSONAL: Homer Giles Bush... Married, wife's name Monica... One daughter, Jailyn Danielle (4/22/99)... Was signed by Van Smith... Was a two-sport star in high school, earning All-Area, All-Metro, All-State and All-American honours in football during his senior season as a split end... Was second team All-Conference in baseball, batting .395 with 5 HR and 25 RBI in 1991.

LAST SEASON: Hit .215 in just 76 games with eight doubles, a home run and 18 RBI... Finished the season on the 60-day disabled list after having right hip (labrum) microsurgery on September 6 by Dr. Joe McCarthy in Boston... Started the season with just one hit in his first four games (1-14)... Missed five games due to a sore left hamstring, April 15-19... Had career hit #200 on April 26 at Oakland (single off Olivares)... Finished April with a .175 (14-80) average... Matched his career high of three RBI on May 4 vs Cleveland, was his sixth career three RBI game... Suffered a right hip strain and was placed on the disabled from May 22 to June 5... Struggled in June with an 0-19 stretch from June 12 to 21... Hit in a season high nine straight from July 3-14 (15-36/.417)... Had three 3-hit games including one on July 14 to raise his average to a season high .223... On July 14 hit HR #1 off Brantley-1R in the ninth to tie the game- first HR since Sept. 4, 1999 at KC... Best month of the season was in July when he hit .326 in 20 games with 17 runs scored, one home run and four RBI... On July 30 in Seattle was hit by a Jose Paniagua pitch and the following day was placed on the 15-day disabled list with a non-displaced hairline fracture of the 4th metacarpal in left hand... Was transferred to the 60-day disabled list on September 1... Hit .199 (51-

256) with one HR against right-handed pitchers and .317 (13-41) against left-handed pitchers... Had a .986 fielding percentage after committing six errors in 417 total chances.

PROFESSIONAL CAREER: 1991: Hit .323 with 16 RBI and 11 stolen bases in 32 games for Scottsdale of the Arizona Rookie League... **1992:** Spent his first full season of professional baseball at Class-A Charleston... Batted .234 and stole 14 bases in 108 games... **1993:** Named Padres' Minor League Player of the Year after leading the Midwest League with a .322 BA and 152 hits at Class-A Waterloo... Stole 39 bases to lead all Padres' minor leaguers... Played winter ball in Australia, earning MVP honours with .367 BA for the league-champion Brisbane Bandits... **1994:** Opened the season at Class-A Rancho Cucamonga and hit .335 in 39 games before being promoted to Double-A Wichita... Hit .298 in 59 games with the Wranglers... After starting the season 0-for-5, he hit safely in 19 of 21 games (.478), raising his average to .449... Recorded five hits on April 20 vs. Riverside... Had two stints on the disabled list with hamstring problems... Was placed on the disabled list on April 27 and activated on May 4... Batted .471 (8-for-17) before going on the disabled list for the second time from May 9-26... Hit safely in 11 of his first 14 games with Wichita (.328, 20-for-61) with 5 doubles, 2 triples, 3 HR and 11 RBI... Belted two homers in the second game of a doubleheader on June 25 vs. San Antonio... Shared the lead among Padres' farmhands with seven triples... Committed 15 errors in 422 total chances (.964)... **1995:** Batted .280 with 5 HR and 37 RBI in 108 games at Double-A Memphis... Stole 34 bases, tied for fourth in the organization... Ranked second on the club in hits (121) and total bases (158)... Had three four-hit games... Led the Chicks with seven post-season hits, batting .333 (7-for-21) with five doubles vs. Chattanooga... **1996:** Batted a team-high .362 in his first 32 games for Triple-A Las Vegas before breaking his right fibula on May 17 vs Calgary while sliding into second base... Did not play the remainder of the season... Had hit safely in 28 of 32 games... Began the season with a six-game hitting streak, batting .438 (8-for-17)... Had a 17-game hitting streak from April 19-May 13, batting .369 (24-for-65)... Hit safely in 21 of his final 22 games, batting .373 (31-for-83)... Contract was purchased by San Diego on May 20 and he was immediately placed on the 60-day disabled list... Played 27 games for Sun City of the Arizona Fall League and batted .278 with 10 RBI and three stolen bases... **1997:** Hit .364 in 10 games with the Yankees... Was recalled from Triple-A Columbus on August 15 to replace Luis Sojo on the 25-man roster... Made his Major League debut on August 16 vs. Texas, pinch-running for Strawberry in the eighth... Collected his first ML hit and RBI on August 26 at Oakland with a pinch-hit single off Don Wengert... Was optioned back to Columbus on August 29 to make room on the roster for Andy Fox... Was recalled on September 23 and made his first ML start that night at Cleveland, going 2-for-4 with 1R, 2 RBI and an error at second base... Hit .308 (44-for-143) with 5 HR and 18 RBI for Phoenix of the Arizona Fall League, leading the team with a .355 on-base percentage, .308 BA and 27 runs scored... **1998:** First full season in the Majors, batting .380 with 1 HR and 5 RBI in 45 games... Made 12 starts, 10 at second base and two at third base... Was 19-for-50 (.380) in his 12 starts... Used as a pinch runner in 13 of his 45 games... Was the only rookie on the Yankee's Opening-Day roster... Batted .294 (15-for-51) with 2 HR and 5 RBI in 25 games in the spring... Went 2-for-6 with 2R and a stolen base in his first start at second base on May 3 at Kansas City... Had his first career three-hit game on July 20 vs. Detroit, going 3-for-4 with a double and a sacrifice bunt... Hit his first ML home run on August 26 vs Anaheim (Game 2), a three-run shot off Steve

Sparks... Made his first career start at third base on August 27 vs. Anaheim... Had his second career three-hit game on September 16 at Tampa Bay, going 3-for-5 with a stolen base... **1999:** Traded to Toronto along with LHP's David Wells and Graeme Lloyd on February 18 in exchange for RHP Roger Clemens... Hit .320 with 26 doubles, four triples, five home runs and 55 RBI... Appeared in four games and hit .313 (5-16) before suffering a torn ligament in his right index finger... Was disabled from April 11 to May 13 during which time he played for Dunedin on a rehab assignment and hit .357 (5-14)... Returned to the lineup on May 15 and then started 18 straight games at shortstop from May 18 to June 16 due to an injury to Alex Gonzalez... Average reached a season high .354 following a 3-4, three RBI game on June 2 vs Chicago - 3RBI was a season high done four times... Hit his first home run with Toronto and the second of his career against Chris Fussell on June 21 vs KC... Hit in a then career high seven straight from June 22 to 28... August 9 had a career high four hits in Texas... Homered in back-to-back games, August 9 in Texas off LHP Doug Davis and August 10 in Minnesota off Brad Radke... In August hit .337 (32-95) with three HR and 11RBI... Posted a second seven game hit streak from September 15 to 23... Named AL Player of the Week for the final week of the season, Sept. 30- Oct 3, in six games hit .452 with .516 slugging percentage and a .452 on-base percentage... Stole 32 bases which ranked 10th in the league, was caught eight times... Was also tenth in stolen base success at 80% (32-40) and was third in the AL attempting to steal 27.2% of the time he was on base... Three of 32 steals were of third base... Hit .368 (28-76) against left-hand pitchers and .311 (127-409) against right-handers... Hit .333 (42-126) with runners in scoring position & .385 (5-13) with the bases loaded... Hit .286 with one HR and 25 RBI before the All-Star break and .344 with four HR's and 30 RBI after the break... Was fourth among AL second baseman in fielding percentage at .984 (9E/580TC)... Started 107 games at second and 18 at shortstop.

HOMER BUSH

Year	Club & League	AVG	G	AB	R	H	TB	2B	3B	HR	RBI	SH-SF	HP	BB-IBB	SO	SB-CS	GIDP	SLG	OBP
1991	Padres (Ariz)	.323	32	127	16	41	48	3	2	0	16	0-0	1	4-1	33	11-7	2	.378	.348
1992	Charlestn-SC (SAL)	.234	108	367	37	86	106	10	5	0	18	0-2	3	13-0	85	14-11	3	.289	.265
1993	Waterloo (Mid)	.322	130	472	63	152	192	19	3	5	51	1-1	1	19-0	87	39-14	10	.407	.349
1994	Rancho Cuca (Cal)	.335	39	161	37	54	70	10	3	0	16	1-1	4	9-0	29	9-2	2	.435	.383
1994	Wichita (Tex)	.298	59	245	35	73	101	11	4	3	14	1-0	3	10-0	39	20-7	6	.412	.333
1995	Memphis (Sou)	.280	108	432	53	121	158	12	5	5	37	4-0	2	15-0	83	34-12	6	.366	.307
1996	Las Vegas (PCL)	.362	32	116	24	42	61	11	1	2	3	5-0	2	3-1	33	3-5	2	.526	.388
1997	Las Vegas (PCL)	.277	38	155	25	43	64	10	1	3	14	1-4	2	7-0	40	5-1	1	.413	.310
1997	Columbus (Int)	.247	74	275	36	68	90	10	3	2	26	7-4	1	25-0	56	12-7	6	.327	.308
1997	NEW YORK (AL)	.364	10	11	2	4	4	0	0	0	3	0-0	0	0-0	0	0-0	0	.364	.364
1998	NEW YORK (AL)	.380	45	71	17	27	33	3	0	1	5	2-0	0	5-0	19	6-3	1	.465	.421
1999	Dunedin (FSL)	.357	4	14	3	5	7	2	0	0	1	1-0	1	1-0	1	1-0	0	.500	.438
1999	TORONTO (AL)	.320	128	485	69	155	204	26	4	5	55	8-3	6	21-0	82	32-8	9	.421	.353
2000	TORONTO (AL)	.215	76	297	38	64	75	8	0	1	18	4-1	5	18-0	60	9-4	10	.253	.271
Minor Totals		.290	624	2364	329	685	897	98	27	20	195	21-12	20	106-2	486	148-66	39	.379	.324
TORONTO TOTALS		.280	204	782	107	219	279	34	4	6	73	12-4	11	39-0	142	41-12	19	.356	.308
MAJOR TOTALS		.289	259	864	126	250	316	37	4	7	81	14-4	11	44-0	161	47-15	20	.366	.330

DIVISION SERIES RECORD

Year	Club & League	AVG	G	AB	R	H	TB	2B	3B	HR	RBI	SH-SF	HP	BB-IBB	SO	SB-CS	GIDP	SLG	OBP
1998	NEW YORK (AL)	.000	1	0	0	0	0	0	0	0	0	0-0	0	0-0	0	1-0	0	.000	.000

CHAMPIONSHIP SERIES RECORD

Year	Club & League	AVG	G	AB	R	H	TB	2B	3B	HR	RBI	SH-SF	HP	BB-IBB	SO	SB-CS	GIDP	SLG	OBP
1998	NEW YORK (AL)	.000	2	0	1	0	0	0	0	0	0	0-0	0	0-0	0	1-0	0	.000	.000

WORLD SERIES RECORD

Year	Club & League	AVG	G	AB	R	H	TB	2B	3B	HR	RBI	SH-SF	HP	BB-IBB	SO	SB-CS	GIDP	SLG	OBP
1998	NEW YORK (AL)	.000	2	0	0	0	0	0	0	0	0	0-0	0	0-0	0	0-0	0	.000	.000

HOME RUN BREAKDOWN

Total	H	A		MEN ON				ONE GAME			LO	XN	IP	PH	RHP	LHP
			0	1	2	3		2	3	4						
7	4	3	5	1	1	0		0	0	0	0	0	0	0	6	1

BUSH — TRANSACTIONS

- Selected by the San Diego Padres in seventh round of June 1991 First Year Player Draft.
- On disabled list (hamstring problems) April 27-May 4, 1994.
- On disabled list (hamstring problems) May 9-26, 1994.
- On disabled list (broken right fibula) May 17, 1996 through remainder of season.
- Traded by the San Diego Padres with OF Gordon Amerson, RHP Hideki Irabu and OF Vernon Maxwell to the New York Yankees for OF Ruben Rivera and RHP Rafael Medina, May 30, 1997.
- Traded by the New York Yankees along with LHP David Wells and LHP Graeme Lloyd to the Toronto Blue Jays in exchange for RHP Roger Clemens, February 18, 1999.
- On disabled list (right index finger — tear in ligament) April 11-May 14, 1999; including rahabilitation assignment at Dunedin (A) May 9-14.
- On disabled list (right hip) May 22-June 6, 2000.
- On disabled list (left hand) July 31 through remainder of season, 2000.

CAREER HIGHS — BUSH, Homer

SEASON:

Games	128 - 1999
Avg.	.320 - 1999
Runs	69 - 1999
Hits	155 - 1999
Doubles	26 - 1999
Home Runs	5 - 1999
RBI	55 - 1999
Walks	21 - 1999
Strikeouts	82 - 1999
Stolen Bases	32 - 1999
Longest Hitting Streak	9G - Jul. 3-14, 2000
Multi HR Games	None

GAME:

ML Debut	Aug. 16, 1997 vs. TEX
Runs	4 - Jul. 9, 2000 at MON
Hits	4 - Aug. 9, 1999 at TEX
Doubles	1 - 37 times, last Jul. 23, 2000 vs. BAL
Home Runs	1 - 7 times, last Jul. 14, 2000 vs. PHI
RBI	3 - 6 times, last May 4, 2000 vs. CLE
Stolen Bases	2 - May 25, 1999 at DET
	2 - Jun. 21, 1999 vs. KC
	2 - Jul. 16, 1999 vs. FLA
Last ML Home Run	Jul. 14, 2000 vs. PHI

FIELDING

BUSH, Homer—2B

Year	PCT	G	PO	A	E	TC	DP
1997	.913	8	8	13	2	23	2
1998	.971	24	37	29	2	68	4
1999	.984	109	220	350	9	579	81
2000	.986	75	165	246	6	417	68
Total	.983	216	430	638	19	1087	155

BUSH, Homer—3B

Year	PCT	G	PO	A	E	TC	DP
1998	1.000	3	1	6	0	7	0

BUSH, Homer—SS

Year	PCT	G	PO	A	E	TC	DP
1998	1.000	2	0	3	0	3	0
1999	.920	18	26	54	7	87	5
Total	.922	20	26	57	7	90	5

HOMER BUSH DETAILED HITTING

	2000									CAREER								
	Avg	AB	H	HR	RBI	BB	SO	OBP	SLG	Avg	AB	H	HR	RBI	BB	SO	OBP	SLG
Total	.215	297	64	1	18	18	60	.271	.253	.289	864	250	7	81	44	161	.330	.366
vs. Left	.317	41	13	0	5	4	7	.370	.341	.343	134	46	1	17	9	24	.386	.433
vs. Right	.199	256	51	1	13	14	53	.255	.238	.279	730	204	6	64	35	137	.320	.353
Home	.214	159	34	1	16	7	32	.254	.258	.292	435	127	4	52	24	82	.334	.375
Away	.217	138	30	0	2	11	28	.289	.246	.287	429	123	3	29	20	79	.327	.357
April	.175	80	14	0	2	5	19	.241	.200	.210	100	21	0	4	7	25	.275	.240
May	.229	70	16	0	9	3	14	.280	.271	.276	134	37	0	15	7	27	.326	.321
June	.180	61	11	0	3	3	10	.219	.213	.229	166	38	1	20	6	28	.261	.307
July	.267	86	23	1	4	7	17	.326	.314	.313	192	60	1	11	11	36	.354	.359
August	–	–	–	–	–	–	–	–	–	.333	135	45	4	16	3	21	.353	.489
September	–	–	–	–	–	–	–	–	–	.339	121	41	1	13	10	20	.391	.438
October	–	–	–	–	–	–	–	–	–	.500	16	8	0	2	0	4	.500	.625
Scoring Posn	.183	71	13	0	17	6	20	.244	.225	.305	218	61	1	72	11	47	.309	.349
Bases Loaded	.167	6	1	0	2	0	1	.167	.167	.318	22	7	0	14	0	4	.364	.364
DH	–	–	–	–	–	–	–	–	–	.000	2	0	0	0	1	1	.333	.000
PH	–	–	–	–	–	–	–	–	–	.500	4	2	0	1	0	1	.500	.500
vs. Ana	.200	15	3	0	1	1	2	.294	.267	.238	42	10	1	7	3	6	.304	.357
vs. Bal	.269	26	7	0	3	1	4	.321	.385	.228	57	13	0	5	3	14	.279	.281
vs. Bos	.154	26	4	0	2	1	5	.214	.154	.254	71	18	0	5	1	13	.274	.310
vs. CWS	.056	18	1	0	2	1	3	.105	.056	.294	68	20	0	10	2	14	.329	.397
vs. Cle	.300	40	12	0	4	5	10	.378	.325	.330	97	32	0	9	9	22	.387	.371
vs. Det	.125	24	3	0	0	1	6	.160	.125	.350	80	28	0	8	6	16	.402	.438
vs. KC	.071	14	1	0	0	2	3	.188	.071	.286	49	14	2	8	3	6	.321	.449
vs. Min	–	–	–	–	–	–	–	–	–	.281	32	9	1	3	0	2	.303	.438
vs. NYY	.160	25	4	0	0	0	6	.192	.200	.196	56	11	0	3	5	16	.274	.250
vs. Oak	.250	12	3	0	0	1	3	.308	.250	.378	45	17	0	4	2	7	.404	.444
vs. Sea	.200	20	4	0	0	0	5	.238	.200	.214	42	9	1	2	2	12	.267	.310
vs. TB	.316	19	6	0	0	1	3	.350	.421	.344	61	21	0	2	2	8	.375	.393
vs. Tex	.222	9	2	0	1	1	3	.300	.222	.357	42	15	1	4	1	5	.372	.476
vs. Tor	–	–	–	–	–	–	–	–	–	.600	5	3	0	0	0	1	.600	.800
vs. Atl	–	–	–	–	–	–	–	–	–	.214	14	3	0	1	1	4	.267	.286
vs. Fla	–	–	–	–	–	–	–	–	–	.333	12	4	0	0	0	2	.333	.333
vs. Mon	.360	25	9	0	2	3	2	.429	.360	.304	46	14	0	6	3	5	.340	.304
vs. NYM	.077	13	1	0	2	0	4	.071	.077	.095	21	2	0	2	1	5	.130	.095
vs. Phi	.364	11	4	1	1	0	1	.364	.636	.292	24	7	1	2	0	3	.320	.417
Pre-All Star	.214	243	52	0	14	16	50	.274	.243	.251	470	118	1	40	26	94	.299	.298
Post-All Star	.222	54	12	1	4	2	10	.259	.296	.335	394	132	6	41	18	67	.368	.447

Bush • 61

HOMER BUSH HITTING AT ML PARKS

Park	Avg	G	AB	R	H	2B	3B	HR	RBI	SB	CS	BB	SO	OBP	Slg
Camden Yards	.194	11	31	6	6	1	0	0	1	3	1	1	9	.219	.226
Fenway Park	.219	10	32	4	7	2	0	0	1	0	0	1	7	.242	.281
Edison Field	.095	6	21	2	2	1	0	0	0	1	0	1	3	.174	.143
Comiskey Park	.241	9	29	1	7	1	0	0	2	1	1	1	7	.290	.276
Jacobs Field	.429	13	42	9	18	2	0	0	5	2	0	4	9	.478	.476
Tiger Stadium	.444	11	27	8	12	1	2	0	5	5	0	3	5	.500	.630
Kauffman Stadium	.375	4	16	4	6	0	0	1	3	3	0	0	1	.353	.563
Metrodome	.333	5	21	1	7	2	0	1	2	0	0	0	2	.333	.571
Yankee Stadium	.317	31	63	10	20	4	0	1	4	4	3	3	13	.358	.429
Oakland-Alameda	.333	10	33	7	11	0	1	0	2	1	0	2	5	.371	.394
Kingdome	.000	2	1	1	0	0	0	0	0	0	0	0	1	.000	.000
Arlington	.423	6	26	7	11	1	0	1	4	0	1	1	3	.444	.577
SkyDome	.282	107	394	49	111	19	1	3	48	21	8	21	75	.324	.358
Olympic Stadium	.417	7	24	8	10	0	0	0	1	1	0	2	3	.462	.417
Shea Stadium	.125	2	8	0	1	0	0	0	0	1	0	1	1	.222	.125
Veterans Stadium	.250	3	12	2	3	0	0	0	1	0	0	0	2	.308	.250
Turner Field	.000	1	5	0	0	0	0	0	0	0	0	0	3	.000	.000
Tropicana Field	.298	12	47	7	14	3	0	0	2	2	1	1	6	.327	.362
SAFECO Field	.150	6	20	0	3	0	0	0	0	2	0	1	4	.227	.150
Comerica Park	.083	3	12	0	1	0	0	0	0	0	0	1	2	.154	.083

HOMER'S HOMERS: Research shows that 10 men named Homer have played Major League Baseball, seven hitters and three pitchers... When Homer Bush homered in August of 1998 for the Yankees it was the first homer by a Homer since 1933 when Homer Peel of the New York Giants homered at the Polo Grounds... That's 65 years between homers by a Homer... Here are the Homers and the number of homers they hit... Homer Thompson (0)-NY-AL, 1912, 1 game... Homer Summa (18)-1920-30-Pitts-NL, Clev-AL, Phi-AL, 840 games... Homer Smoot (15)-St. Louis-NL, Cinn-NL, 1902-06, 680 games... Homer Peel (2)-St. Louis-NL, PHIL-NL, NY-NL, 1927-34, 186 games... Homer Ezzell (0)-St. Louis-AL, Boston-AL-1923-25, 236 games... Homer Davidson (0)-Clev-AL, 1908, 9 games... HOMER BUSH (7)-NY-AL, TOR-AL, 1997-2000... The pitchers are Homer Spragins, Homer Hillebrand and Homer Blankenship.

Chris
CARPENTER

PITCHER

26

BIRTHDATE	April 27, 1975
OPENING DAY AGE	25
BIRTHPLACE	Exeter, NH
RESIDENCE	Bedford, NH
BATS/THROWS	R/R
HEIGHT/WEIGHT	6-6/225
CONTRACT STATUS	signed thru 2001
M.L. SERVICE	3.080

PERSONAL: Christopher John Carpenter... Married, wife's name Alyson... 1993 graduate of Trinity High School in Manchester, NH where he earned Athlete-of-the-Year honors as a senior... Selected All-State for three years in both baseball and hockey and was a member of the Globe All-Scholastic team as a senior... Captured state championship in baseball in 1992... Played American Legion, Babe Ruth and Little League ball.

LAST SEASON: Was 10-12 with a 6.26 ERA in 34 games, 27 starts... As a starter posted a record of 8-12 in 27 starts with a 6.55 ERA and two complete games... In relief was 2-0 in seven games with an ERA of 3.86... Opened the season losing his first three starts and posting an ERA of 7.31, 18 hits, six home runs and ten walks in 16.0 innings... Posted first win of the season with a complete game victory over the Yankees on April 21 in an 8-3 win — was his seventh career complete game... Was the first of three consecutive wins to even his record to 3-3 on May 1... Was 2-3 in April with a 5.25ERA in five starts and in May was 2-2 in six starts with a 5.59 ERA... Tossed second complete game (8.0) of the season in a 4-3 loss in Tampa Bay on May 12... Fell to 3-5 before defeating Pedro Martinez, 3-2 in Boston on May 23... Allowed runs in the first inning of five consecutive starts from May 6 to May 28... Posted second three game win streak of the season from May 23 to June 14... An 8-1 win on June 14 at Detroit left him with a winning record for the only time during the season at 6-5... The rest of the season would post a 3-7 record... On June 20 allowed a career high nine ER against the Tigers in 2.0 innings of work... Would match that two starts later in Baltimore in 4.2 innings... ERA as starter excluding those two starts drops from 6.55 to 5.76... Of his 27 starts had nine starts with six or more earned runs and

11 of five or more... At the All-Star break was 7-7 with a 6.13ERA and following the break was 3-5 with a 6.48 ERA... Made 20 consecutive starts before appearing in relief on July 22 against Baltimore... Then returned to rotation for two more starts and lasted 3.1 innings in both... Then five straight appearances in relief from August 6 to 23 and was a combined 2-0 with a 6.63ERA... Won two straight relief appearances on August 10 & 13... Collected win #8 on August 10 at KC after retiring 12 of 15 batters faced over 4.1 scoreless innings in relief... Win #9 came on August 13 at Minnesota after pitching 5.1 innings in relief, was the longest relief appearance by a Blue Jay in 2000 and also tied the AL season high for strikeouts in relief at seven... Returned to the rotation from August 29 to September 28... Lost start on August 29 at Anaheim in career game #200... Posted three straight quality starts from September 9 to September 16... On September 16 against the White Sox was hit on the right side of the face by a ball off the bat of Jose Valentin... Returned to the mound on September 28 in a start at Baltimore where he suffered his 12th loss of the season... Pitched in relief in Cleveland on October 1 to finish the season... Opponents finished the season batting .290 with a .294 average by left-handers and a .287 average by right handers... In his first inning pitched opponents hit .306... At home was 3-6 with a 7.53 ERA while on the road posted a winning record of 7-6 with a 5.25 ERA.

PROFESSIONAL CAREER: 1994: Finished third in Pioneer League in ERA (2.76), tied for fourth in starts (15) and was fourth in strikeouts per nine innings pitched (8.50)... Struck out a season-high nine in his pro debut, beating Great Falls June 18 (6.2 IP, 4 H, 1 R) and tossed six scoreless innings of one-hit ball... Also defeated Lethbridge to claim

Pitcher-of-the-Week honors ending July 2... **1995:** Opened the season with Dunedin of the Florida State League where he was 3-5 with a 2.17 ERA in 15 starts... Surrendered 3 earned runs or less in 13 of his 15 starts... Promoted to Knoxville (AA) on June 25 in just his second pro season... Was 3-7 in 12 starts with a 5.18 ERA... In his last seven starts he was 3-2 with a 2.86 ERA... **1996:** Spent the entire season with Knoxville in the Southern League (AA) and was 7-9 with a 3.94 ERA... Led the club with 28 starts, 171.1 innings pitched, and 150 strikeouts... The 150 strikeouts ties him for third in Knoxville club history (Alex Sanchez 166, 1988)... 150 K were also third in the organization... Knoxville Pitcher of the Month in May going 3-0 with a 1.91 ERA... Had 10 strikeouts in a 5-0 win at Carolina on May 17... He struck out six consecutive batters in the 6th & 7th innings... Of his nine losses allowed two earned runs or less in five of them... In 28 starts struck out eight or more batters nine times... Pitched for Phoenix in Arizona Fall League earning club MVP honours, was 2-0 in ten starts and finished second in the league with a 2.33 ERA and third in strikeouts with 43... Ranked third top prospect in organization by Baseball America... **1997:** Made seven starts with Syracuse, posted a 1-3 record with a 3.88 ERA... Contract was purchased by Toronto on May 10... Started and lost his major league debut on May 12 in Minnesota, L 12-2 (3.0IP, 8H, 7R, 5ER, 3BB, 5K)... First ML strikeout was Paul Molitor... In debut he became the sixth youngest Blue Jays pitcher to start a game- 22 years and 18 days old... Made two more appearances... Knoxville Pitcher returning to Syracuse, in three games was 0-2, 12.71 ERA... Made 12 more starts with Syracuse including a seven inning complete game shutout against Richmond on May 28... Totalled 19 starts with Syracuse and was 4-9 with a 4.50 ERA before being recalled to Toronto on July 29... Used exclusively as a starter in Toronto the rest of the season... Captured his first major league win on August 19 at Chicago in game one of two against the White Sox (6.0IP, 10H, 4R, 3ER, 4BB, 6th ML start)... Became the ninth Blue Jay rookie to throw a shutout on September 9 as he defeated the Anaheim Angels, 2-0 (9.0IP, 3H, 3BB, 4K, 1NP)... First Blue Jay rookie to toss a shutout since John Cerutti in 1986... Lowered his ERA in each of his last nine starts, over that time was 3-3 with a 3.30 ERA (22ER, 60IP)... Seven of his last nine starts were quality starts... Finished 10th in innings pitched for AL rookies, ninth in starts and was one of three rookies to record a shutout... Struck out season high eight batters on two occasions, August 24 at KC and September 14 at Seattle... **1998:** Finished 12-7 with a 4.37ERA in 33 games, 24 starts... As a starter was 11-7, 4.67 ERA with one complete game... In relief was 1-0 with a 2.38ERA in 22.2 innings pitched... Started first two games and then made nine relief appear-

ances... Pitched 4.0 shutout innings in relief on May 18 and struck out six batters - a season high for strikeouts for a Blue Jays reliever... From May 28 on made 21 consecutive starts to finish the season... Won three straight decisions for the first time in his career from June 7 to 23 over four starts... Was 3-2 in June with 5.14 ERA... Tossed a complete game four-hit shutout on July 4 vs Tampa Bay, his first complete game and shutout of the season and second of each in his career... Struck out a season high ten batters on July 16 in Chicago to set his career high... Walked a career high seven batters on August 4 at Texas in and 11-9 loss... Posted second three game win streak from August 11 to 21... In September was 3-0 in five starts with a 2.55ERA... All five starts were quality starts, in 35.1 innings walked just nine and struckout 26... In his last ten starts allowed more than three earned runs just twice... Finished 10th in the AL in strikeouts per 9.0 innings pitched at 6.99... In Toronto was 7-4 with a 3.66 ERA in 17 games, 11 starts and on the road was 5-3 with a 5.24 ERA in 16 games, 11 starts... Had 11 quality starts... **1999:** Was 9-8 in 24 starts with four complete games, a shutout and an ERA of 4.38 prior to season ending elbow surgery on September 16... Surgery performed by Dr. James Andrews to remove a bone spur... Last start was September 10, after not pitching since August 27 with right elbow pain, he lasted only three innings (ND)... The four complete games were second on the club and tied for fifth in the AL... Was second on the club with 14 Quality Starts... Allowed three earned runs or less in 16 of 24 starts... Did not allow more than three ER in each of his first nine starts but was 3-4 with a 3.02ERA... Lost first start of the season 1-0 in Baltimore to Mussina on April 10... Tossed a complete game two-hitter on April 15 against Tampa Bay in an 11-1 victory at home, his second start of the season and the first complete game of 1999 in the AL... Finished April 2-1 with a 2.55 ERA but then in May was 1-4 in six starts with a 4.50 ERA... Tossed complete game on May 6 in a 3-2 loss at home to Oakland... On the DL from June 3 to 28 with inflammation in his right elbow... Made one rehab start with St. Catharines of the New York Penn League (A) on June 23 vs Batavia (4.0IP, 5H, 2R/ER, 1BB, 6K)... Returned from the DL and won next five decisions over eight starts from June 28 to August 11... Tossed a CG shutout in second start after the DL on July 3 vs Tampa Bay, won 5-0 allowing just three hits for his 3rd career shutout... Was undefeated in June and July going 4-0 in eight starts with an ERA of 3.72 (29ER, 48.1)... Was 6-5 at the All-Star break with a 3.24 ERA but following the break 3 with a 6.31 ERA in 10 starts... Was 2-3 in August with a 6.46 ERA... Won his first two starts in August but then lost the next three... Opponents attempted to steal just nine times and were successful only three times.

CHRIS CARPENTER

Year	Club & League	W-L	ERA	G	GS	CG	ShO	SV	IP	H	R	ER	HR	HB	BB-IBB	SO	WP	BK	OBA
1994	Medicine Hat (Pio)	6-3	2.76	15	15	0	0	0	84.2	76	40	26	3	8	39-0	80	9	2	.243
1995	Knoxville (Sou)	3-7	5.18	12	12	0	0	0	64.1	71	47	37	4	1	31-1	53	9	0	.284
1995	Dunedin (FSL)	3-5	2.17	15	15	0	0	0	99.1	83	29	24	3	4	50-0	56	9	3	.229
1996	Knoxville (Sou)	7-9	3.94	28	28	1	0	0	171.1	161	94	75	13	8	91-4	150	8	2	.250
1997	Syracuse (Int)	4-9	4.50	19	19	3	2	0	120.0	113	64	60	16	3	53-0	97	8	0	.257
1997	TORONTO (AL)	3-7	5.09	14	13	1	1	0	81.1	108	55	46	7	2	37-0	55	7	1	.325
1998	TORONTO (AL)	12-7	4.37	33	24	1	1	0	175.0	177	97	85	18	5	61-1	136	5	0	.265
1999	St. Catharines (NYP)	0-0	4.50	1	1	0	0	0	4.0	5	2	2	0	0	1-0	6	1	0	.294
1999	TORONTO (AL)	9-8	4.38	24	24	4	1	0	150.0	177	81	73	16	3	48-1	106	9	1	.294
2000	TORONTO (AL)	10-12	6.26	34	27	2	0	0	175.1	204	130	122	30	5	83-1	113	3	0	.290
Minor Totals		23-33	3.71	90	90	4	2	0	543.2	509	276	224	38	24	265-5	442	44	7	.251
MAJOR TOTALS		34-34	5.04	105	88	8	3	0	581.2	666	363	326	71	15	229-3	410	24	2	.289

YOUNGEST PITCHERS TO START A GAME

PLAYER	BIRTHDATE	FIRST START	AGE	PLAYER	BIRTHDATE	FIRST START	AGE
Jeff Byrd	Nov. 11, 1956	June 20, 1977	20	Kelvim Escobar	Apr. 11, 1976	Aug. 5, 1998	22
Phil Huffman	June 20, 1958	Apr. 10, 1979	20	Pasqual Coco	Sept. 8, 1977	July 17, 2000	22
Jim Clancy	Dec. 18, 1955	July 26, 1977	21	Clayton Andrews	May 15, 1978	June 7, 2000	22
Mark Eichhorn	Nov. 21, 1960	Aug. 30, 1982	21	Butch Edge	July 18, 1956	Aug. 13, 1979	23
Dave Stieb	July 22, 1957	June 29, 1979	21	Luis Leal	Mar. 21, 1957	May 25, 1980	23
Roy Halladay	May 14, 1977	Sept. 20, 1998	21	Jose Nunez	Jan. 13, 1964	July 9, 1987	23
Chris Carpenter	Apr. 27, 1975	May 12, 1997	22	Luis Andujar	Nov. 22, 1972	Sept. 11, 1996	23
Marty Janzen	May 31, 1973	May 27, 1996	22				

CARPENTER — TRANSACTIONS

- Selected by the Toronto Blue Jays organization in the 1st round (15th overall) of the June 1993 First Year Player Draft.
- On disabled list June 13-28, 1999 (right elbow inflammation); included rehabilitation assignment at St. Catharines (A).

CAREER HIGHS — CARPENTER, Chris

SEASON:		GAME:	
Wins	12 - 1998	ML Debut	May 12, 1997 at MIN
Losses	12 - 2000	Innings Pitched:	
Saves	None	Starter	9.0 - 7 times, last Apr. 21, 2000 vs. NYY
ERA	4.37 - 1998	Reliever	6.0 - May 23, 1997 vs. ANA
Games	34 - 2000	Walks:	
Starts	27 - 2000	Starter	9 - Aug. 16, 1999 vs. SEA
Complete Games	4 - 1999	Reliever	3 - May 23, 1997 vs. ANA
Shutouts	1 - 1997, 98, 99	Strikeouts:	
Innings Pitched	175.1 - 2000	Starter	10 - Jul. 16, 1998 at CWS
Walks	83 - 2000	Reliever	7 - Aug. 13, 2000 at MIN
Strikeouts	136 - 1998	Hits Allowed	12 - May 28, 1999 vs. NYY
Longest Win Streak	6 - Jun. 2-Aug. 11, 1999	Runs Allowed	10 - Aug. 4, 1998 at TEX
Longest Losing Streak	5 - May 12-Aug. 9, 1997	ER Allowed	9 - Jun. 20, 2000 vs. DET
Scoreless Innings Streak	11.0 - Jul. 16-23, 1998		9 - Jul. 1, 2000 at BAL
		HR Allowed	3 - 5 times, last Jul. 1, 2000 at BAL
		Low Hit CG	2 - Apr. 15, 1999 vs. TB
		Last Win	Sep. 10, 2000 vs. DET
		Last Save	None
		Last CG	May 12, 2000 at TB (8.0)
		Last ShO	Jul. 3, 1999 vs. TB
		Last Start	Sep. 28, 2000 at BAL
		Last Relief App.	Oct. 1, 2000 at CLE

FIELDING

CARPENTER, Chris—P

Year	PCT	G	PO	A	E	TC	DP
1997	.923	14	7	5	1	13	1
1998	.971	33	20	13	1	34	2
1999	.962	24	10	15	1	26	3
2000	.950	34	7	12	1	20	2
Total	.957	105	44	45	4	93	8

CHRIS CARPENTER DETAILED PITCHING

		2000								CAREER					
	ERA	W-L-Sv	G	IP	H	ER	BB	SO	ERA	W-L-Sv	G	IP	H	ER	BB	SO
Total	6.27	10-12-0	33	173.2	203	121	82	111	5.04	34-34-0	104	580.0	665	325	228	408
ST	6.55	8-12-0	27	156.2	182	114	81	95	5.19	31-34-0	88	534.1	614	308	212	368
REL	3.71	2-0-0	6	17.0	21	7	1	16	3.35	3-0-0	16	45.2	51	17	16	40
Home	7.53	3-6-0	15	77.2	98	65	35	45	5.00	16-18-0	51	293.2	327	163	103	178
Away	5.25	7-6-0	18	96.0	105	56	47	66	5.09	18-16-0	53	286.1	338	162	125	230
April	5.01	2-3-0	5	32.1	28	18	12	13	4.04	5-4-0	15	78.0	65	35	33	51
May	5.59	2-2-0	6	38.2	44	24	12	26	5.68	3-9-0	21	111.0	150	70	39	79
June	5.93	2-2-0	5	27.1	34	18	22	16	5.63	7-3-0	13	72.0	93	45	32	45
July	11.75	1-4-0	6	28.1	44	37	17	18	6.01	5-7-0	18	103.1	121	69	39	74
August	5.96	2-1-0	7	22.2	32	15	6	24	5.73	8-9-0	22	119.1	152	76	49	94
September	3.33	1-1-0	4	24.1	21	9	13	14	2.80	6-2-0	15	96.1	84	30	36	65
vs. Ana	6.35	0-2-0	2	11.1	9	8	11	8	3.88	4-2-0	9	55.2	51	24	31	33
vs. Bal	12.66	0-2-0	3	10.2	15	15	5	8	5.98	3-3-0	8	40.2	47	27	13	26
vs. Bos	6.19	1-1-0	3	16.0	23	11	8	10	5.29	1-3-0	8	51.0	60	30	16	38
vs. CWS	1.80	1-0-0	2	15.0	9	3	4	9	2.30	6-0-0	8	47.0	35	12	17	31
vs. Cle	7.62	1-0-0	2	13.0	19	11	5	12	8.65	1-2-0	5	26.0	42	25	11	20
vs. Det	7.65	2-1-0	4	20.0	29	17	14	16	7.31	2-3-0	9	44.1	70	36	19	34
vs. KC	2.63	1-1-0	4	13.2	10	4	1	8	3.74	2-3-0	10	45.2	41	19	11	38
vs. Mil	–	–	–	–	–	–	–	–	3.18	0-1-0	1	5.2	10	2	1	6
vs. Min	3.38	1-0-0	1	5.1	5	2	1	7	6.65	2-2-0	4	21.2	28	16	7	24
vs. NYY	3.00	1-0-0	1	9.0	5	3	0	3	4.03	2-1-0	4	29.0	28	13	3	12
vs. Oak	5.06	1-0-0	2	10.2	13	6	4	7	6.00	1-2-0	6	27.0	33	18	12	18
vs. Sea	11.20	0-2-0	3	13.2	25	17	12	4	5.86	2-3-0	8	43.0	53	28	34	32
vs. TB	4.50	0-1-0	1	8.0	8	4	0	2	1.58	4-1-0	5	40.0	24	7	7	19
vs. Tex	10.80	0-0-0	1	1.2	7	2	0	2	7.18	1-4-0	8	36.1	59	29	21	38
vs. Atl	–	–	–	–	–	–	–	–	17.47	0-1-0	2	5.2	17	11	3	6
vs. Fla	0.00	0-0-0	1	7.0	5	0	4	3	2.57	0-1-0	3	21.0	19	6	8	4
vs. Mon	3.86	1-0-0	1	7.0	6	3	5	5	2.57	2-0-0	3	21.0	25	6	6	18
vs. NYM	15.75	0-1-0	1	4.0	5	7	6	3	15.75	0-1-0	1	4.0	5	7	6	3
vs. Phi	9.39	0-1-0	1	7.2	10	8	2	4	5.28	1-1-0	2	15.1	18	9	2	8
Pre-All Star	6.13	7-7-0	18	108.2	124	74	50	63	5.06	18-17-0	54	295.1	344	166	113	198
Post-All Star	6.51	3-5-0	15	65.0	79	47	32	48	5.03	16-17-0	50	284.2	321	159	115	210

CHRIS CARPENTER PITCHING AT ML PARKS

Park	ERA	W-L-Sv	SvO	G	GS	IP	H	R	ER	HR	BB	SO
Camden Yards	8.18	1-3-0	0	4	4	22.0	27	22	20	4	8	17
Fenway Park	4.26	1-1-0	0	3	3	19.0	23	11	9	1	9	13
Edison Field	5.04	1-2-0	0	4	4	25.0	22	14	14	3	18	13
Comiskey Park	2.09	4-0-0	0	6	5	38.2	25	11	9	2	13	28
Jacobs Field	6.97	1-0-0	0	2	1	10.1	18	8	8	2	2	8
Tiger Stadium	7.53	0-1-0	0	3	3	14.1	23	12	12	5	3	12
Kauffman Stadium	3.33	2-1-0	0	6	3	27.0	22	13	10	3	8	27
County Stadium	3.18	0-1-0	0	1	1	5.2	10	3	2	0	1	6
Metrodome	6.65	2-2-0	0	4	3	21.2	28	18	16	2	7	24
Yankee Stadium	2.45	1-0-0	0	2	2	14.2	11	6	4	0	3	7
Oakland-Alameda	7.50	1-1-0	0	5	3	18.0	27	15	15	3	11	11
Kingdome	3.09	1-0-0	0	2	2	11.2	13	4	4	1	9	11
Arlington	6.89	1-1-0	0	3	3	15.2	26	20	12	3	11	20
SkyDome	5.00	16-18-0	0	51	43	293.2	327	177	163	38	103	178
Olympic Stadium	3.00	0-0-0	0	1	1	6.0	11	2	2	0	1	8
Pro Player Stadium	0.00	0-0-0	0	1	1	7.0	5	0	0	0	4	3
Turner Field	23.14	0-1-0	0	1	1	2.1	8	7	6	0	2	3
Tropicana Field	4.15	1-1-0	0	2	2	13.0	15	6	6	1	3	7
SAFECO Field	16.20	0-1-0	0	1	1	3.1	8	6	6	0	5	1
Comerica Park	5.73	1-0-0	0	2	2	11.0	16	7	7	2	7	11

Hector
CARRASCO

PITCHER

72

BIRTHDATE	October 22, 1969
OPENING DAY AGE	31
BIRTHPLACE	San Pedro de Macoris, DR
RESIDENCE	San Pedro de Macoris, DR
BATS/THROWS	R/R
HEIGHT/WEIGHT	6-2/220
CONTRACT STATUS	signed thru 2001
M.L. SERVICE	6.147

PERSONAL: Hector Pacheco Pipo Carrasco... Married, wife's name is Tanya... Two children, son Hector Jr. (5) and daughter Gelen (8)... 1987 graduate of Liceo Matias High School in the Dominican Republic.

LAST SEASON: Split the season between Minnesota and Boston and combined to post a 5-4 record with a 4.69 ERA... Opened the season with Minnesota where he appeared in 61 games with a 4-3 record and a 4.25 ERA... Was 3-1 with a 0.98 ERA in his first 14 appearances from April 3 to May 2... Pitched a career-high 4.1 innings on April 12 at Boston... Had his third career four strikeout game on July 3 vs. Boston... Appeared in 14 July games and was 0-0 with a 1.23 ERA... In August was 1-1 with a 3.75 ERA... Was traded to Boston on September 10 in exchange for outfielder Lew Ford... With the Red Sox appeared in eight games making one start and was 1-1 with a 9.45 ERA... On the season had four holds and stranded 27 of 51 inherited runners... Opponents hit .291 with left-handed hitters at .281 and right-handed hitters at .297.

PROFESSIONAL CAREER: 1988: Made his professional debut with Gulf Port and was 0-2 with a 4.17 ERA... Had .248 batting-average-against... **1989:** Moved to Kingsport of the Appalachian League (A) where he was 1-6 in 12 games, ten starts with an ERA of 5.74... Averaged 9.28 strikeouts per 9.0 innings... **1990:** Limited to just three games due to right elbow injury... **1991:** With Pittsfield of the New York-Penn League was 0-1 in 12 games, one start... Averaged 7.71 strikeouts per 9.0 innings... **1992:** Given unconditional release on January 6... Signed by Houston on January 21 and spent the season with Asheville of the South Atlantic League (A)... Was 5-5 with a 2.99 ERA in 49 relief appearances... Averaged 7.70 strikeouts per 9.0 innings pitched... Traded along with pitcher Brian Griffiths to Florida in exchange for pitcher Tom Edens, November 17... **1993:** Led the Midwest league in starts (28) and tied for fourth in losses... Was 6-12 for Kane County with a 4.11 ERA... On September 10 was sent to Cincinnati to complete trade of March 27, in which Reds traded pitcher Chris Hammond to Florida for third baseman Gary Scott... **1994:** Spent the entire season with Cincinnati and was 5-6 with a 2.24 ERA in 45 games... Won his major league debut on April 4 vs. St. Louis... In his first

12 games, from April 4 to May 11, was 3-1 with four saves and a 0.60 ERA (15.0IP)... Earned his first career save on April 9 vs. Philadelphia... Career high three game win-streak, April 4-11... Was on the disabled list from May 12 to June 1 with a foot infection... Opponents hit .210 with lefties hitting .198 (19-96)... Established career best ERA and career-high for wins and saves... Finished eighth in the National League Rookie of the Year voting... **1995:** Was 2-7 with a 4.12 ERA in 64 games with five saves... From April 27 to September 6 was 2-5 with a 2.72 ERA... Then in the last 11 games of the season was 0-2 with a 13.50 ERA (11.1IP, 17ER) from September 8 to 30... Allowed no home runs in final 55.2 innings, June 14-September 30... Career-high four strikeouts on August 8 at Atlanta... Pitched a career-high 87.1 innings... Led the Reds in games and was second in innings pitched... **1996:** Appeared in 56 games for Cincinnati and was 4-3 with a 3.75 ERA... Pitched a season high 2.2 innings on April 11 vs. Houston... Was optioned to Indianapolis on April 16 and recalled on May 23... Was 1-1 with a 0.96 ERA in 14 appearances from June 5 to July 5... Had nine straight outings without an earned run from June 10 to 28... Singled off Joe Borowski for first major league hit on August 22 at Atlanta... Allowed just one earned run in final six appearances, September 1 to 18... Opponents hit .214 against him with right-handers hitting .181... **1997:** Started the season with Indianapolis appearing the three games before he was recalled on April 11... Was 1-0 with a 2.30 ERA in 13 appearances, April 11-May 4... Pitched a season high 3.0 innings on May 7 at Los Angeles... Has his second career four strikeout game on May 10 at San Diego... Was optioned on June 7 and then recalled on June 8... On July 15 was traded along with pitcher Scott Service to Kansas City in exchange for outfielders Chris Stynes and Jon Nunnally, July 15... Appeared in 28 games with KC and was 1-6 with a 5.45 ERA... Was selected by Arizona with their 11th pick in second round of MLB expansion draft on November 18... **1998:** Attended spring training with Arizona and was then claimed off waivers by Minnesota... Made his Twins' debut on April 7 vs. Toronto... Had a season high three strikeouts on May 10 vs. New York... Allowed one home run in 45 games from June 5 to September 26... Was 3-0 with a 1.20 ERA in 17 appearances from June 14 to July 22...

Recorded a save on June 21 at Chicago, was his first save since June 24, 1995 vs. Florida... Second career three game win streak from June 28 to July 18... Had a career high 4.0 innings pitched on August 6 vs. Kansas City... Did not allow a run in 10 appearances from August 12 to 27... First batters faced were 14-52 (.269)... Stranded 38 of 63 inherited runners (60.3%)... Opponents hit .304 against him with left-hand hitter at .309 with two homers and right-hand hitters at .301 with two homers... Averaged 6.71 strikeouts per 9.0 innings pitched... **1999:** Did not pitch until June after being disabled from April 3 to June 25 with a circulatory disorder in his right arm... Had rehab assignments at Ft. Myers and Salt Lake... Appeared in 39 games with the Twins and was 2-3 with a 4.96 ERA... Did not allow a run in seven appearances from August 2 to 13... Earned his only save of the season on August 8 at Kansas City... Was 1-1 with a 1.69 ERA in his final 15 appearances of the season, August 22 to October 1... Converted one of two save opportunities... First batters faced were 8-34 with nine strikeouts... Stranded 15 of 26 (58%) inherited runners... Opponents hit .261 against him with left-hand hitters at .297 and right-hand hitters at .242.

HECTOR CARRASCO

Year	Club & League	W-L	ERA	G	GS	CG	ShO	SV	IP	H	R	ER	HR	HB	BB-IBB	SO	WP	BK	OBA
1988	Mets (Gulf)	0-2	4.17	14	2	0	0	0	36.2	37	29	17	0	1	13-0	21	5	0	.248
1989	Kingsport (Appy)	1-6	5.74	12	10	0	0	0	53.1	69	49	34	6	1	34-1	55	4	5	.314
1990	Kingsport (Appy)	0-0	4.05	3	1	0	0	0	6.2	8	3	3	1	0	1-0	5	2	0	.308
1991	Pittsfield (NYP)	0-1	5.40	12	1	0	0	1	23.1	25	17	14	1	1	21-0	20	7	0	.263
1992	Asheville (SAL)	5-5	2.99	49	0	0	0	8	78.1	66	30	26	5	3	47-6	67	11	3	.237
1993	Kane County (Mid)	6-12	4.11	28	28	0	0	0	149.0	153	90	68	11	11	76-6	127	13	1	.266
1994	CINCINNATI (NL)	5-6	2.24	45	0	0	0	6	56.1	42	17	14	3	2	30-1	41	3	1	.210
1995	CINCINNATI (NL)	2-7	4.12	64	0	0	0	5	87.1	86	45	40	1	2	46-5	64	15	0	.257
1996	CINCINNATI (NL)	4-3	3.75	56	0	0	0	0	74.1	58	37	31	6	1	45-5	59	8	1	.214
1996	Indianapols (AmAs)	0-1	2.14	13	2	0	0	0	21.0	18	7	5	1	1	13-1	17	2	0	.222
1997	Indianapols (AmAs)	0-0	6.23	3	0	0	0	1	4.1	5	3	3	1	0	3-0	4	0	0	.294
1997	CINCINNATI (NL)	1-2	3.68	38	0	0	0	0	51.1	51	25	21	3	4	25-2	46	3	2	.250
1997	KANSAS CITY (AL)	1-6	5.45	28	0	0	0	0	34.2	29	21	21	4	4	16-3	30	8	0	.227
1998	MINNESOTA (AL)	4-2	4.38	63	0	0	0	1	61.2	75	30	30	4	1	31-1	46	8	0	.304
1999	Fort Myers (FSL)	0-0	4.50	1	1	0	0	0	2.0	2	1	1	0	0	1-0	1	0	0	.286
1999	Salt Lake (PCL)	1-0	0.00	3	0	0	0	1	4.1	3	0	0	0	0	1-0	3	0	0	.188
1999	MINNESOTA (AL)	2-3	4.96	39	0	0	0	1	49.0	48	29	27	3	1	18-0	35	4	0	.261
2000	MINNESOTA (AL)	4-3	4.25	61	0	0	0	1	72.0	75	38	34	6	3	33-0	57	14	0	.270
2000	BOSTON (AL)	1-1	9.45	8	1	0	0	0	6.2	15	8	7	2	1	5-1	7	0	1	.469
Minor Totals		13-27	4.06	138	45	0	0	11	379.0	386	229	171	26	18	210-14	320	44	9	.263
AL TOTALS		12-15	4.78	199	1	0	0	3	224.0	242	126	119	19	10	103-5	175	34	1	.278
NL TOTALS		12-18	3.54	203	0	0	0	11	269.1	237	124	106	13	9	146-13	210	29	4	.235
MAJOR TOTALS		24-33	4.10	402	1	0	0	14	493.1	479	250	225	32	19	249-18	385	63	5	.255

CHAMPIONSHIP SERIES RECORD

Year	Club & League	W-L	ERA	G	GS	CG	ShO	SV	IP	H	R	ER	HR	HB	BB-IBB	SO	WP	BK	OBA
1995	CINCINNATI (NL)	0-0	0.00	1	0	0	0	0	1.1	1	0	0	0	0	0-0	1	0	0	.200

CARRASCO — TRANSACTIONS

- Signed as non-drafted free agent by the New York Mets on March 20, 1988.
- Signed by the Houston Astros on January 29, 1992.
- Traded to the Florida Marlins along with RHP Brian Griffiths in exchange for RHP Tom Edens on November 17, 1992.
- Traded to the Cincinnati Reds on September 10, 1993, completing trade in which Reds sent LHP Chris Hammond to the Florida Marlins for 3B Gary Scott and a player to be named (March 27, 1993).
- Traded to the Kansas City Royals along with RHP Scott Service in exchange for OF Chris Stynes and OF Jon Nunnally on July 15, 1997.
- Selected by the Arizona Diamondbacks (49th overall) from the Kansas City Royals in expansion draft on November 18, 1997.
- Claimed on waivers by the Minnesota Twins on April 3, 1998.
- On disabled list (circulatory problem in right arm) April 3-June 25, 1999, including rehabilitation assignment at Fort Myers, June 16-17 and Salt Lake, June 18-25.
- Traded to the Boston Red Sox in exchange for OF Lew Ford on September 10, 2000.
- Signed by the Toronto Blue Jays on January 2, 2001.

FIELDING

CARRASCO, Hector—P

Year	PCT	G	PO	A	E	TC	DP
1994 (NL)	.909	45	3	7	1	11	0
1995 (NL)	.867	64	4	9	2	15	1
1996 (NL)	.882	56	3	12	2	17	1
1997 (NL)	.857	38	2	4	1	7	0
1997 (AL)	1.000	28	2	6	0	8	0
1998 (AL)	1.000	63	9	6	0	15	0
1999 (AL)	.833	39	5	0	1	6	0
2000 (AL)	.933	69	2	12	1	15	0
Total	.915	402	30	56	8	94	2

CAREER HIGHS — CARRASCO, Hector

SEASON:

Wins	5 - 1994, 2000
Losses	8 - 1997
Saves	6 - 1994
ERA	2.24 - 1994
Games	69 - 2000
Starts	1 - 2000
Complete Games	None
Shutouts	None
Innings Pitched	86.0 - 1997
Walks	46 - 1995
Strikeouts	76 - 1997
Longest Win Streak	3 - Apr. 4-11, 1994
	3 - Jun. 28-Jul. 18, 1998
Longest Losing Streak	5 - Aug. 10-Sep. 23, 1997
Scoreless Innings Streak	12.1 - Jul. 17-Aug. 8, 1995

GAME:

ML Debut	Apr. 4, 1994 vs. STL
Innings Pitched:	
Starter	2.0 - Oct. 1, 2000 at TB
Reliever	4.1 - Apr. 12, 2000 at BOS
Walks:	
Starter	1 - Oct. 1, 2000 at TB
Reliever	3 - 11 times, last Sep. 9, 2000 at SEA
Strikeouts:	
Starter	2 - Oct. 1, 2000 at TB
Reliever	4 - Aug. 8, 1995 at ATL
	4 - May 10, 1997 at SD
	4 - Jul. 30, 2000 vs. BOS
Hits Allowed	5 - May 4, 1995 vs. PHI
	5 - Jun. 14, 1995 at COL
	5 - Jun. 15, 1997 vs. CWS
	5 - Aug. 1, 1998 vs. TOR
Runs Allowed	5 - Sep. 8, 1995 at COL
	5 - Aug. 11, 1996 vs. LA
	5 - Jun. 15, 1997 vs. CWS
ER Allowed	5 - Sep. 8, 1995 at COL
	5 - Aug. 11, 1996 vs. LA
	5 - Jun. 15, 1997 vs. CWS
HR Allowed	2 - Jul. 26, 1997 at TOR
	2 - May 22, 1998 at ANA
	2 - Sep. 13, 2000 at CLE
Low Hit CG	None
Last Win	Sep. 23, 2000 vs. BAL
Last Save	May 12, 2000 at CWS
Last CG	None
Last ShO	None
Last Start	Oct. 1, 2000 at TB
Last Relief App.	Sep. 29, 2000 at TB

HECTOR CARRASCO DETAILED PITCHING

	2000								CAREER						
	ERA	W-L-Sv	G	IP	H	ER	BB	SO	ERA	W-L-Sv	G	IP	H	ER	BB	SO
Total	4.69	5-4-1	69	78.2	90	41	38	64	4.10	24-33-14	402	493.1	479	225	249	385
ST	0.00	0-0-0	1	2.0	4	0	1	2	0.00	0-0-0	1	2.0	4	0	1	2
REL	4.81	5-4-1	68	76.2	86	41	37	62	4.12	24-33-14	401	491.1	475	225	248	383
Home	3.48	4-2-0	35	41.1	47	16	15	38	3.48	12-13-6	206	258.2	238	100	115	188
Away	6.03	1-2-1	34	37.1	43	25	23	26	4.79	12-20-8	196	234.2	241	125	134	197
April	0.98	3-1-0	13	18.1	13	2	5	9	3.03	7-5-2	49	62.1	56	21	32	44
May	5.23	0-1-1	13	10.1	15	6	9	11	2.50	2-3-6	54	72.0	66	20	38	64
June	10.38	0-0-0	11	13.0	21	15	5	5	5.32	3-5-3	72	88.0	97	52	39	50
July	1.23	0-0-0	11	14.2	12	2	2	17	3.81	6-7-2	82	101.2	85	43	46	90
August	3.75	1-1-0	10	12.0	10	5	6	13	3.79	3-7-1	83	99.2	88	42	53	88
September	11.88	1-1-0	10	8.1	15	11	10	7	6.34	3-6-0	60	66.2	83	47	40	46
October	0.00	0-0-0	1	2.0	4	0	1	2	0.00	0-0-0	2	3.0	4	0	1	3
vs. Ana	10.38	0-0-0	4	4.1	9	5	2	2	8.44	0-1-0	9	10.2	17	10	6	4
vs. Bal	0.00	1-0-0	5	5.2	6	0	3	4	4.50	1-1-0	15	16.0	17	8	9	11
vs. Bos	1.13	0-0-0	3	8.0	3	1	4	6	2.08	1-1-0	12	17.1	11	4	8	19
vs. CWS	3.00	0-0-1	3	3.0	1	1	1	3	4.00	0-1-2	15	18.0	17	8	4	13
vs. Cle	5.87	0-0-0	9	7.2	13	5	3	10	7.20	0-1-0	17	15.0	25	12	6	15
vs. Det	7.71	1-1-0	5	4.2	6	4	2	5	4.85	1-1-0	16	13.0	16	7	4	17
vs. KC	2.45	1-0-0	6	7.1	6	2	4	6	1.93	1-0-1	12	18.2	14	4	6	13
vs. Mil	13.50	0-0-0	1	1.1	4	2	1	1	15.00	0-1-0	4	3.0	6	5	3	1
vs. Min	–	–	–	–	–	–	–	–	0.00	0-0-0	3	3.2	2	0	0	1
vs. NYY	3.00	0-0-0	4	3.0	1	1	2	4	1.80	0-0-0	16	15.0	10	3	8	12
vs. Oak	3.60	0-0-0	4	5.0	6	2	0	4	8.47	2-3-0	16	17.0	28	16	9	14
vs. Sea	9.95	0-0-0	7	6.1	8	7	10	4	5.71	1-0-0	15	17.1	17	11	12	16
vs. TB	4.26	1-2-0	6	6.1	10	3	2	5	6.75	2-2-0	14	12.0	20	9	7	9
vs. Tex	3.00	1-0-0	3	3.0	4	1	1	1	2.40	2-0-0	11	15.0	12	4	6	11
vs. Tor	3.86	0-1-0	3	4.2	5	2	2	4	4.60	0-2-0	11	15.2	15	8	6	11
vs. Atl	–	–	–	–	–	–	–	–	3.26	2-1-0	16	19.1	19	7	9	20
vs. ChC	0.00	0-0-0	2	1.2	0	0	0	2	4.28	0-1-0	21	27.1	24	13	15	24
vs. Cin	4.50	0-0-0	1	2.0	2	1	0	0	8.10	0-0-0	3	3.1	3	3	3	1
vs. Col	–	–	–	–	–	–	–	–	10.00	1-3-0	15	18.0	23	20	14	12
vs. Fla	–	–	–	–	–	–	–	–	1.29	1-2-2	17	28.0	18	4	14	25
vs. Hou	27.00	0-0-0	1	1.0	3	3	1	0	1.60	0-0-4	22	33.2	21	6	12	24
vs. LA	–	–	–	–	–	–	–	–	3.66	0-3-0	12	19.2	20	8	7	16
vs. Mon	–	–	–	–	–	–	–	–	7.36	2-1-1	16	14.2	25	12	5	8
vs. NYM	–	–	–	–	–	–	–	–	3.63	0-0-0	14	17.1	17	7	10	15
vs. Phi	–	–	–	–	–	–	–	–	4.60	1-1-1	12	15.2	19	8	9	10
vs. Pit	9.00	0-0-0	1	1.0	1	1	0	1	3.14	0-2-1	23	28.2	20	10	14	20
vs. StL	0.00	0-0-0	1	2.2	2	0	0	2	4.43	3-3-1	19	22.1	21	11	18	19
vs. SD	–	–	–	–	–	–	–	–	0.76	2-2-1	17	23.2	13	2	19	15
vs. SF	–	–	–	–	–	–	–	–	3.14	1-0-0	9	14.1	9	5	6	9
Pre-All Star	4.86	3-2-1	40	46.1	53	25	21	31	3.99	13-17-12	199	250.2	245	111	130	186
Post-All Star	4.45	2-2-0	29	32.1	37	16	17	33	4.23	11-16-2	203	242.2	234	114	119	199

HECTOR CARRASCO PITCHING AT ML PARKS

Park	ERA	W-L-Sv	SvO	G	GS	IP	H	R	ER	HR	BB	SO
Camden Yards	9.45	0-1-0	0	8	0	6.2	10	9	7	2	5	6
Fenway Park	3.18	1-1-0	0	9	0	11.1	13	4	4	0	5	10
Edison Field	12.71	0-0-0	0	4	0	5.2	8	8	8	3	2	1
Comiskey Park	1.00	0-0-2	2	8	0	9.0	5	1	1	0	1	7
Jacobs Field	9.95	0-1-0	0	8	0	6.1	8	7	7	2	4	6
Tiger Stadium	4.91	0-0-0	0	3	0	3.2	3	2	2	0	0	6
Kauffman Stadium	2.89	1-2-1	2	20	0	28.0	20	9	9	2	8	15
County Stadium	40.50	0-1-0	0	1	0	0.2	1	3	3	0	2	0
Metrodome	3.48	5-4-0	4	86	0	101.0	106	42	39	4	43	83
Yankee Stadium	2.84	0-0-0	0	8	0	6.1	5	2	2	0	5	5
Oakland-Alameda	7.71	2-2-0	0	8	0	7.0	12	6	6	2	6	9
Kingdome	0.00	0-0-0	0	3	0	3.1	1	0	0	0	0	5
Arlington	2.00	2-0-0	0	7	0	9.0	7	2	2	0	4	5
SkyDome	11.25	0-2-0	2	4	0	4.0	6	5	5	2	2	3
Atlanta-Fulton	1.86	2-1-0	0	7	0	9.2	10	2	2	0	5	10
Wrigley Field	8.74	0-1-0	1	11	0	11.1	16	12	11	1	8	11
Cinergy Field	3.62	5-7-6	11	108	0	139.1	118	65	56	10	69	94
Astrodome	0.59	0-0-1	1	9	0	15.1	7	2	1	0	4	14
Dodger Stadium	1.88	0-2-0	0	7	0	14.1	13	4	3	1	3	14
Olympic Field	4.32	1-0-1	1	8	0	8.1	12	4	4	0	2	5
Shea Stadium	7.50	0-0-0	0	6	0	6.0	9	6	5	0	4	4
Veterans Stadium	6.75	0-0-0	0	4	0	5.1	5	4	4	0	5	2
Three Rivers	4.61	0-1-0	0	12	0	13.2	11	7	7	1	9	11
Busch Stadium	3.12	1-1-1	1	7	0	8.2	7	3	3	0	6	9
Qualcomm Park	1.29	1-2-1	1	11	0	14.0	8	4	2	0	15	10
3 Com Park	4.50	1-0-0	0	4	0	6.0	7	3	3	1	4	3
Coors Field	12.19	1-2-0	2	7	0	10.1	17	15	14	1	9	9
Pro Player Stadium	0.69	0-1-1	2	7	0	13.0	7	3	1	0	8	15
Turner Field	0.00	0-0-0	0	1	0	1.0	1	0	0	0	0	3
Tropicana Field	7.56	1-1-0	0	9	1	8.1	16	8	7	0	4	7
SAFECO Field	6.75	0-0-0	0	4	0	4.0	5	3	3	0	5	3
Enron Field	27.00	0-0-0	0	1	0	1.0	3	4	3	0	1	0
Comerica Park	5.40	0-0-0	1	2	0	1.2	2	1	1	0	1	0

Alberto

CASTILLO

CATCHER

30

BIRTHDATE	February 10, 1970
OPENING DAY AGE	31
BIRTHPLACE	San Juan de la Magna, DR
RESIDENCE	Port St. Lucie, FL
BATS/THROWS	R/R
HEIGHT/WEIGHT	6-0/200
CONTRACT STATUS	signed thru 2001
M.L. SERVICE	3.171

PERSONAL: Alberto Therrero Castillo... Married, wife's name is Ingrid... Two children, Machael Gregg and Chelsea... Attended Mercedes Maria Mateo High School in the Dominican Republic.

LAST SEASON: Hit .211 with seven doubles, a home run and 16 RBI over 66 games in his first season with Toronto... Started 57 games for Toronto... The starting pitchers in those starts were Wells — 17 times, Frank Castillo- 10, Carpteter- 9, Escobar- 8, Loaiza- 5, Halladay- 4, Andrews- 2, Munro- 1 and Trachsel- 1... Opened the season batting .259 in April with a home run and three RBI... On April 14 vs Seattle matched his career high with three hits including a solo HR against Paul Abbott of Seattle, was his seventh career home run... Started nine of his 10 May games and hit only .148 with one RBI... Hit in a season high four straight games from May 28 to June 5... In June hit .233 with four doubles and nine RBI and saw action in 22 games as Fletcher was disabled... On June 6 at Atlanta was ejected by home plate umpire Jerry Layne for arguing balls and strikes as a batter... On July 27 matched his season and career high with three hits at Seattle, was his fourth career three-hit game and second of the season... Finished the season hitting .500 (7-14) against Seattle with six runs scored... Threw out 39% (16-41) of base-stealers.

PROFESSIONAL CAREER: 1987: Signed by the New York Mets as a non drafted free agent on April 15... Made pro debut at age 17 with Kingsport and hit .111 in seven games... **1988:** Split the season between the Gulf Coast Mets and Kingsport... In 24 games with Kingsport hit .293 with a home run and 14 RBI... **1989:** Split the season between three clubs, Kingsport, Pittsfield (A) and St. Lucie (A)... **1990:** Again played for three clubs, all Class-A: Columbia, Pittsfield and St. Lucie... **1991:** Spent the entire season with Columbia... Was seventh in batting (.277) among Mets minor league players... **1992:** Hit .204 with St. Lucie but season was cut short after a July 2 knee injury... Threw out 11 of 14 base-runners attempting to steal... **1993:** Established a St. Lucie (A) club record for catchers with a .983 fielding percentage... Made 12 errors in 696 total chances... Led the Florida State League with 604 putouts... On May 25 hit two home runs against Felix Rodriguez of Vero Beach and collected five RBI... **1994:** Moved to Binghamton (AA) and was selected to the Double-A All-Star Game... Caught 40% (28-of-70) of base runners who attempted to steal, seventh best percentage in the Eastern League... Hit .294 in the playoffs to help Binghamton to the Eastern League Championship... **1995:** Stared the season with Norfolk of the International League (AAA)... Was called up to the New York Mets on two occasions, from May 28 to June 4 and July 23 through the end of the season... Appeared in 13 games with nine starts... Made his ML debut on May 28 vs San Francisco and was 0-3 with a walk... First ML hit came on May 30 vs San Diego's Scott Sanders... With Norfolk hit .321 (9-28) in nine April games and in June hit .338 (23-68) in 23 games... Threw out 37% (19-of-33) runners who attempted to steal... **1996:** Opened the season with Norfolk... Threw out 44.8 (39-of-87) of would be base-runners... His 11 home runs were a high for his minor league career... Hit two HR's in the second game of an August 3 doubleheader vs Ottawa...

Was promoted to New York on September 8... Appeared in six games for the Mets and hit safely in three of four starts... First multi-hit game came on September 11 vs Florida as he was 2-3 with a run scored... **1997:** Made the Major League team out of spring training... Earned first ML RBI on June 1 vs. Philadelphia... Appeared in 34 games making 18 starts before being optioned to Norfolk on July 11... Appeared in 34 games and hit .217 prior to being recalled on September 2... First ML extra base hit was a game-winning RBI double in the bottom of the ninth on September 27 vs Atlanta... Had a career high four game hit streak to end the season... Played in Caribbean World Series with Aguilas of the Dominican Winter League... **1998:** Split the season between the Mets and Norfolk... Hit .205 in 38 games for the Mets... Hit his first ML home run on May 16 in San Francisco against Kirk Reuter... Hit second on June 5 in Boston against Pedro Martinez... Was designated for assignment on July 11...

Cleared waivers and was outrighted to Norfolk... Appeared in 21 games with the Tides and hit just .184 with a home run and six RBI... Signed as a free agent to a minor league contract with the Philadelphia Phillies in October... Was selected by the St. Louis Cardinals in the Rule V Draft on December 14... **1999:** Hit .263 in his first season with St. Louis and his first full season in the majors... Played in 93 games and was the Cardinals main starter in the second half... Threw out 44% (27-of-62) base runners who attempted to steal... Hit .308 against right-hand pitching and .174 against left-handers... Best months were July and August when he hit .351 (20-57) and .310 (18-58) respectively... Had a career high three hits on May 4 at Atlanta... Matched that with three on July 24 at Colorado... Hit in a career high ten straight from August 8-23 (13-34)... Had a career high three RBI on August 9 at Philadelphia... Hit .229 prior to the All-Star break and .292 after.

ALBERTO CASTILLO

Year	Club & League	AVG	G	AB	R	H	TB	2B	3B	HR	RBI	SH-SF	HP	BB-IBB	SO	SB-CS	GIDP	SLG	OBP
1987	Kingsport (Appy)	.111	7	9	1	1	1	0	0	0	0	1-0	0	5-0	3	1-0	0	.111	.429
1988	Mets (Gulf)	.265	22	68	7	18	22	4	0	0	10	2-3	2	4-0	4	2-0	3	.324	.312
1988	Kingsport (Appy)	.293	24	75	7	22	28	3	0	1	14	1-1	0	15-1	14	0-1	1	.373	.407
1989	Kingsport (Appy)	.257	27	74	15	19	32	4	0	3	12	0-0	1	11-1	14	2-1	2	.432	.360
1989	Pittsfield (NYP)	.236	34	123	13	29	40	8	0	1	13	2-2	1	7-0	26	2-0	3	.325	.278
1990	Columbia (SAL)	.233	30	103	8	24	37	4	3	1	14	2-2	0	10-0	21	1-1	2	.359	.296
1990	Pittsfield (NYP)	.219	58	187	19	41	63	8	1	4	24	1-2	5	26-1	35	3-3	8	.337	.327
1990	St. Lucie (FSL)	.364	3	11	4	4	7	0	0	1	3	0-0	0	1-0	1	0-0	2	.636	.417
1991	Columbia (SAL)	.277	90	267	35	74	109	20	3	3	47	5-5	5	43-0	44	6-5	6	.408	.381
1992	St. Lucie (FSL)	.204	60	162	11	33	48	6	0	3	17	3-2	2	16-0	37	0-0	4	.296	.280
1993	St. Lucie (FSL)	.258	105	333	37	86	122	21	0	5	42	2-7	3	28-1	46	0-2	5	.366	.315
1994	Binghamton (East)	.248	90	315	33	78	113	14	0	7	42	3-1	0	41-0	46	1-3	11	.359	.333
1995	Norfolk (Int)	.267	69	217	23	58	85	13	1	4	31	3-2	1	26-0	32	2-3	6	.392	.346
1995	NEW YORK (NL)	.103	13	29	2	3	3	0	0	0	0	0-0	1	3-0	9	1-0	0	.103	.212
1996	Norfolk (Int)	.208	113	341	34	71	118	12	1	11	39	7-3	4	39-1	67	2-2	3	.346	.295
1996	NEW YORK (NL)	.364	6	11	1	4	4	0	0	0	0	0-0	0	0-0	4	0-0	0	.364	.364
1997	NEW YORK (NL)	.203	35	59	3	12	13	1	0	0	7	2-1	0	9-0	16	0-1	3	.220	.304
1997	Norfolk (Int)	.217	34	83	4	18	22	1	0	1	8	3-1	0	17-1	16	1-0	3	.265	.347
1998	NEW YORK (NL)	.205	38	83	13	17	27	4	0	2	7	6-0	1	9-0	17	0-2	1	.325	.290
1998	Norfolk (Int)	.184	21	49	4	9	14	2	0	1	6	0-0	0	11-2	12	0-0	0	.286	.333
1999	ST. LOUIS (NL)	.263	93	255	21	67	87	8	0	4	31	5-4	2	24-1	48	0-0	6	.341	.326
2000	TORONTO (AL)	.211	66	185	14	39	49	7	0	1	16	2-3	0	21-0	36	0-0	3	.265	.287
Minor Totals		.242	787	2417	255	585	861	120	9	46	322	35-31	24	300-8	418	23-21	59	.356	.328
NL TOTALS		.236	185	437	40	103	134	13	0	6	45	13-5	4	45-1	94	1-3	10	.307	.310
MAJOR TOTALS		.228	251	622	54	142	183	20	0	7	61	15-8	4	66-1	130	1-3	13	.294	.303

HOME RUN BREAKDOWN

				MEN ON				ONE GAME							
Total	H	A	0	1	2	3	2	3	4	LO	XN	IP	PH	RHP	LHP
7	3	4	5	2	0	0	0	0	0	0	0	0	0	6	1

CASTILLO — TRANSACTIONS

- Signed as non-drafted free agent by the New York Mets on April 15, 1987.
- On disabled list July 3 to end of season, 1992 (knee injury).
- On disabled list June 1-July 13, 1994.
- Granted free agency on October 16, 1998.
- Signed by the Philadelphia Phillies on October 29, 1998.
- Selected by St. Louis Cardinals from the Philadelphia Phillies in the Rule 5 major league draft on December 14, 1998.
- Traded to the Toronto Blue Jays along with LHP Lance Painter and RHP Matt DeWitt in exchange for RHP Pat Hentgen and LHP Paul Spoljaric on November 11, 1999.

FIELDING

CASTILLO, Alberto—C

Year	PCT	G	PO	A	E	TC	DP
1995 (NL)	.974	12	66	9	2	77	0
1996 (NL)	1.000	6	23	0	0	23	0
1997 (NL)	.987	34	142	8	2	152	0
1998 (NL)	.990	35	193	15	2	210	3
1999 (NL)	.991	91	514	38	5	557	10
2000 (AL)	.993	66	372	31	3	406	2
Total	.990	244	1310	101	14	1425	15

Players

CAREER HIGHS — CASTILLO, Alberto

SEASON:

Games	93 - 1999
Avg.	.263 - 1999
Runs	21 - 1999
Hits	67 - 1999
Doubles	8 - 1999
Home Runs	4 - 1999
RBI	31 - 1999
Walks	24 - 1999
Strikeouts	48 - 1999
Stolen Bases	1 - 1995
Longest Hitting Streak	10G - Aug. 8-23, 1999
Multi HR Games	None

GAME:

ML Debut	May 28, 1995 vs. SF
Runs	2 - 9 times, last Jul. 27, 2000 at SEA
Hits	3 - Jul. 24, 1996 at COL
	3 - May 4, 1999 at ATL
	3 - Apr. 14, 2000 vs. SEA
	3 - Jul. 27, 2000 at SEA
Doubles	2 - May 4, 1999 at ATL
	2 - Jul. 27, 2000 at SEA
Home Runs	1 - 7 times, last Apr. 14, 2000 vs. SEA
RBI	3 - Aug. 9, 1999 at PHI
Stolen Bases	1 - Aug. 3, 1995 at CIN
Last ML Home Run	Apr. 14, 2000 vs. SEA

ALBERTO CASTILLO DETAILED HITTING

	2000									CAREER								
	Avg	AB	H	HR	RBI	BB	SO	OBP	SLG	Avg	AB	H	HR	RBI	BB	SO	OBP	SLG
Total	.211	185	39	1	16	21	36	.287	.265	.228	622	142	7	61	66	130	.303	.294
vs. Left	.197	71	14	0	3	12	14	.313	.211	.183	213	39	1	6	36	47	.299	.211
vs. Right	.219	114	25	1	13	9	22	.270	.298	.252	409	103	6	55	30	83	.305	.337
Home	.241	79	19	1	6	9	14	.315	.316	.260	289	75	3	31	34	60	.338	.325
Away	.189	106	20	0	10	12	22	.267	.226	.201	333	67	4	30	32	70	.272	.267
March	–	–	–	–	–	–	–	–	–	1.000	1	1	0	1	0	0	1.000	1.000
April	.259	27	7	1	3	1	1	.276	.370	.242	91	22	1	5	8	15	.300	.308
May	.148	27	4	0	1	3	4	.233	.185	.192	120	23	2	8	17	24	.302	.292
June	.233	73	17	0	9	7	17	.293	.288	.215	135	29	1	16	14	32	.281	.274
July	.269	26	7	0	2	5	6	.387	.346	.280	100	28	1	9	10	21	.345	.350
August	.095	21	2	0	0	1	6	.136	.095	.250	88	22	2	14	5	14	.292	.330
September	.182	11	2	0	1	4	2	.400	.182	.202	84	17	0	8	12	24	.306	.214
October	–	–	–	–	–	–	–	–	–	.000	3	0	0	0	0	0	.000	.000
Scoring Posn	.205	44	9	0	15	5	11	.269	.250	.244	168	41	2	56	15	41	.293	.315
Bases Loaded	.143	7	1	0	1	0	4	.143	.143	.261	23	6	0	13	0	9	.231	.304
DH	–	–	–	–	–	–	–	–	–	.000	0	0	0	0	0	0	.000	.000
PH	–	–	–	–	–	–	–	–	–	.375	8	3	0	1	1	0	.444	.375
vs. Ana	.091	11	1	0	0	0	0	.091	.091	.091	11	1	0	0	0	0	.091	.091
vs. Bal	.063	16	1	0	1	4	2	.238	.063	.056	18	1	0	1	4	2	.217	.056
vs. Bos	.192	26	5	0	0	3	4	.276	.231	.171	35	6	1	1	4	4	.256	.286
vs. CWS	.111	9	1	0	0	1	1	.200	.111	.200	15	3	0	0	1	2	.250	.267
vs. Cle	.273	11	3	0	1	1	5	.333	.273	.273	11	3	0	1	1	5	.333	.273
vs. Det	.240	25	6	0	5	1	5	.259	.280	.194	31	6	0	5	1	5	.212	.226
vs. KC	.000	4	0	0	0	0	1	.000	.000	.125	8	1	0	0	0	1	.125	.125
vs. Mil	–	–	–	–	–	–	–	–	–	.182	33	6	0	1	4	12	.289	.182
vs. Min	.111	9	1	0	0	1	3	.200	.111	.250	16	4	0	1	1	4	.294	.250
vs. NYY	.500	6	3	0	0	0	2	.500	.500	.500	6	3	0	0	0	2	.500	.500
vs. Oak	.143	7	1	0	2	3	0	.364	.143	.143	7	1	0	2	3	0	.364	.143
vs. Sea	.500	14	7	1	1	4	2	.611	.857	.500	14	7	1	1	4	2	.611	.857
vs. TB	.111	9	1	0	1	0	2	.111	.222	.111	9	1	0	1	0	2	.111	.222
vs. Tex	.091	11	1	0	0	0	2	.091	.091	.091	11	1	0	0	0	2	.091	.091
vs. Tor	–	–	–	–	–	–	–	–	–	.000	1	0	0	0	0	0	.000	.000
vs. Ari	–	–	–	–	–	–	–	–	–	.188	16	3	0	1	0	5	.176	.188
vs. Atl	.200	10	2	0	2	2	5	.333	.300	.267	45	12	0	9	5	13	.340	.356
vs. ChC	–	–	–	–	–	–	–	–	–	.217	23	5	0	2	2	2	.269	.261
vs. Cin	–	–	–	–	–	–	–	–	–	.167	36	6	0	4	3	9	.225	.250
vs. Col	–	–	–	–	–	–	–	–	–	.476	21	10	1	3	4	2	.577	.667
vs. Fla	.333	3	1	0	0	0	1	.333	.333	.194	31	6	1	5	3	8	.265	.290
vs. Hou	–	–	–	–	–	–	–	–	–	.303	33	10	0	2	4	9	.378	.303
vs. LA	–	–	–	–	–	–	–	–	–	.500	6	3	0	0	2	1	.625	.667
vs. Mon	.286	7	2	0	1	1	0	.375	.429	.226	31	7	1	4	4	4	.314	.355
vs. NYM	.500	4	2	0	1	0	0	.500	.500	.471	17	8	1	4	0	2	.474	.706
vs. Phi	.333	3	1	0	1	0	1	.333	.333	.233	30	7	0	8	0	9	.226	.267
vs. Pit	–	–	–	–	–	–	–	–	–	.148	27	4	0	0	8	6	.343	.148
vs. StL	–	–	–	–	–	–	–	–	–	.214	14	3	0	0	0	2	.214	.214
vs. SD	–	–	–	–	–	–	–	–	–	.161	31	5	0	3	3	7	.257	.194
vs. SF	–	–	–	–	–	–	–	–	–	.257	35	9	1	2	5	8	.350	.343
Pre-All Star	.211	133	28	1	13	13	23	.275	.271	.211	384	81	4	32	42	79	.289	.279
Post-All Star	.212	52	11	0	3	8	13	.317	.250	.256	238	61	3	29	24	51	.326	.319

ALBERTO CASTILLO HITTING AT ML PARKS

Park	Avg	G	AB	R	H	2B	3B	HR	RBI	SB	CS	BB	SO	OBP	Slg
Camden Yards	.067	7	15	0	1	0	0	0	1	0	0	4	1	.250	.067
Fenway Park	.190	7	21	2	4	0	0	1	1	0	0	2	2	.261	.333
Edison Field	.167	2	6	0	1	0	0	0	0	0	0	0	0	.167	.167
Comiskey Park	.000	2	3	1	0	0	0	0	0	0	0	1	0	.250	.000
Jacobs Field	.500	1	2	0	1	0	0	0	1	0	0	0	1	.500	.500
Tiger Stadium	.000	3	4	0	0	0	0	0	0	0	0	0	0	.000	.000
Kauffman Stadium	.167	3	6	0	1	0	0	0	0	0	0	0	1	.167	.167
County Stadium	.143	7	21	1	3	0	0	0	0	0	0	0	9	.182	.143
Metrodome	.000	1	3	0	0	0	0	0	0	0	0	0	2	.000	.000
Yankee Stadium	.500	2	6	0	3	0	0	0	0	0	0	0	2	.500	.500
Oakland-Alameda	.167	2	6	0	1	0	0	0	2	0	0	0	0	.143	.167
Arlington	.000	2	7	1	0	0	0	0	0	0	0	0	0	.000	.000
SkyDome	.237	31	80	6	19	3	0	1	6	0	0	9	14	.311	.313
Wrigley Field	.000	6	10	2	0	0	0	0	0	0	0	1	0	.091	.000
Cinergy Field	.059	10	17	1	1	0	0	0	1	1	0	2	7	.150	.059
Astrodome	.273	9	22	0	6	0	0	0	1	0	0	1	6	.304	.273
Dodger Stadium	.500	4	6	2	3	1	0	0	0	0	0	2	1	.625	.667
Olympic Stadium	.182	9	22	1	4	0	0	1	3	0	0	3	3	.280	.318
Shea Stadium	.277	46	94	13	26	4	0	1	13	0	2	14	23	.381	.351
Veterans Stadium	.176	7	17	0	3	1	0	0	3	0	0	0	6	.176	.235
Three Rivers	.273	3	11	1	3	0	0	0	0	0	0	1	2	.333	.273
Busch Stadium	.250	47	128	11	32	3	0	2	14	0	0	11	24	.307	.320
Qualcomm Park	.154	5	13	0	2	1	0	0	0	0	1	0	3	.154	.231
3 Com Park	.381	7	21	2	8	0	0	1	2	0	0	3	4	.458	.524
Coors Field	.571	2	7	2	4	1	0	0	2	0	0	2	1	.667	.714
Pro Player Stadium	.118	7	17	1	2	0	0	0	2	0	0	2	4	.211	.118
Turner Field	.300	7	20	2	6	3	0	0	3	0	0	4	6	.417	.450
BankOne Ballpark	.167	3	6	0	1	0	0	0	1	0	0	0	1	.143	.167
Tropicana Field	.111	3	9	0	1	1	0	0	1	0	0	0	2	.111	.222
SAFECO Field	.375	2	8	3	3	2	0	0	0	0	0	3	2	.545	.625
Comerica Park	.214	4	14	2	3	0	0	0	3	0	0	1	3	.267	.214

Pasqual

COCO

PITCHER

BIRTHDATE	September 8, 1977
OPENING DAY AGE	23
BIRTHPLACE	Santo Domingo, DR
RESIDENCE	Santo Domingo, DR
BATS/THROWS	R/R
HEIGHT/WEIGHT	6-1/180
CONTRACT STATUS	signed thru 2001
M.L. SERVICE	0.002

38

PERSONAL: Pasqual Reynoso Coco... Originally signed as an outfielder, converted to a pitcher in his first season in 1995.

LAST SEASON: Spent most of the season with Tennessee where he was 12-7 with a 3.76 ERA in 27 games, 26 starts... Was recalled to Toronto on July 17 and returned on July 18... Made his ML debut starting for Toronto on July 17 against the New York Mets (ND, 4.0IP, 4R/ER, 1HR, 1BB, 5K)... Led the Blue Jays organization in wins (12) and strikeouts (142)... His ERA was seventh in the organization (94IP min)... Struck out a season high 11 batters on May 2 in 7.0 innings against Jacksonville... Was consistent, posting three wins in May, June and July... Allowed two earned runs or less in five consecutive starts from July 22 through August 12... Won four consecutive starts from July 22 to August 6... Was winless in his last five starts posting an 0-3 record with a 5.22 ERA... Was 8-3 at home and on the road was 4-4 with a 4.25 ERA... Opponents hit .244, with right-handers at .263 and left-handers at .212... Rated by Baseball America as the eighth best prospect in the organization and fourth among pitchers... Named to the Southern League's year-end All-Star team.

PROFESSIONAL CAREER: 1995: Was 7-1 in 11 starts for the Blue Jays in the Dominican Summer League... Was third in the Santo Domingo division with an .875 winning percentage... **1996:** Was 7-2 for the Dominican Summer League Blue Jays with a .209 opponents batting average... Led the division in strikeouts (92) and was second in innings pitched

(102.2)... **1997:** Joined St. Catharines of the New York Penn League (A) and was 1-4 with a 4.89 ERA... Captured league Pitcher of the Week honours, July 7-13, after pitching 7.2 shutout innings vs Jamestown allowing just two hits and striking out a season high 11... Spent much of August on the disabled list with a strained right shoulder... **1998:** Was 3-7 for St. Catharines in 15 starts which tied for second most in the New York Pen League... Led Stompers in strikeouts with 84 and posted the best ERA of any of the clubs regular starters... Struckout ten in six innings on June 21 vs Erie for his first win of the season... Tossed an eight inning complete games no-hitter on August 16 against Jamestown but lost on three unearned runs... Pitched for Escogido in the Dominican Winter League... **1999:** Led the Blue Jays organization with a combined 15 wins which tied for second most in minor league baseball... Pitched a total of 172.2 innings which was eighth among class-A pitchers... Opened the season in Hagerstown of the South Atlantic League (A) and was 11-1 with a 2.21 ERA in 14 starts... Selected to the SAL All-Star game... Started 3-1 in six starts and then won eight consecutive starts from May 11 to June 18... On June 6 pitched 7.1 innings of no-hit ball with two hit-batters, one walk, and a season high 12 strikeouts... Promoted to Dunedin and made his Florida State League (A) debut with a no-decision on June 26... Was 4-6 with Dunedin after losing his final four starts... Pitched for Escogido of the Dominican Winter League and was 1-0 in 14 relief appearances with an ERA of 6.28.

PASQUAL COCO

Year	Club & League	W-L	ERA	G	GS	CG	ShO	SV	IP	H	R	ER	HR	HB	BB-IBB	SO	WP	BK	OBA
1995	Blue Jays (DSL)	7-1	2.78	11	11	0	0	0	58.1	51	30	18	2	8	36-0	38	2	1	.232
1996	Blue Jays (DSL)	7-2	2.99	17	16	2	0	0	96.1	77	46	32	1	0	53-0	92	8	2	.209
1997	St. Cathrines (NYP)	1-4	4.89	10	8	0	0	0	46.0	48	32	25	5	2	16-1	44	6	1	.271
1998	St. Cathrines (NYP)	3-7	3.20	15	15	1	0	0	81.2	62	52	29	4	9	32-0	84	10	3	.201
1999	Hagerstown (SAL)	11-1	2.21	14	14	0	0	0	97.2	67	29	24	4	8	25-1	83	2	0	.193
1999	Dunedin (FSL)	4-6	5.64	13	13	2	0	0	75.0	81	50	47	7	6	36-0	59	7	2	.279
2000	Tennessee (Sou)	12-7	3.76	27	26	2	0	0	167.2	154	83	70	16	17	68-0	142	6	3	.244
2000	TORONTO (AL)	0-0	9.00	1	1	0	0	0	4.0	5	4	4	1	1	5-0	2	1	0	.294
Minor Totals		45-28	3.54	107	103	7	0	0	622.2	540	322	245	39	50	266-2	542	41	12	.231

COCO — TRANSACTIONS

- Signed as non-drafted free-agent by the Toronto Blue Jays, August 10, 1994.
- On disabled list August 5-29, 1997.

FIELDING
COCO, Pasqual—P

Year	PCT	G	PO	A	E	TC	DP
2000	.000	1	0	0	0	0	0

Jose
CRUZ Jr.
OUTFIELDER

BIRTHDATE	April 19, 1974
OPENING DAY AGE	26
BIRTHPLACE	Arroyo, PR
RESIDENCE	Houston, TX
BATS/THROWS	S/R
HEIGHT/WEIGHT	6-0/200
CONTRACT STATUS	signed thru 2002
M.L. SERVICE	3.063

23

PERSONAL: Jose Cruz Jr... Married, wife's name is Sarah... Two sons, Trei (2) and Antonio (1)... Graduated from Bellaire (Houston) High School in 1992... Led Bellaire to a number one national ranking by USA Today... Attended Rice University where he was named co-Freshman of the Year in 1993... Set 15 school records including career average (.375), home runs (43), RBI (203) and slugging percentage (.674) which was a Southwest Conference record... Played with team USA in 1994... Was a three time All-American selection (1993-95)... Named conference Player of the Year in 1995 and a finalist for the Golden Spikes Award... Son of Houston Astro Coach Jose Cruz who played in the Major Leagues from 1970 to 1988 with St. Louis, Houston and the New York Yankees... Nephew of former Major League players Hector Cruz (1973, 1975-82) and Tommy Cruz (1973, '77).

LAST SEASON: Hit .242 with career highs of 146 hits, 32 doubles, five triples, 31 home runs, 76 RBI and 15 stolen bases... Played in all 162 games during the season and is the seventh Blue Jay to play every game in a season... Has the longest current consecutive games played streak on the team at 167... Opened the season batting just .179 with three home runs through the first 12 games... Moved to the lead-off spot for 25 of the next 26 games from April 17 to May 14 as Shannon Stewart was injured... Leading off the first hit .381 (8-21, 1-2B, 3HR, 4BB)... Had a season high eight-game hit streak from April 18 to 25... Hit his first career lead-off home run on April 19 vs Anaheim's Ken Hill... Then hit second lead-off home run on April 22 vs New York as part of his fifth career two-homer game, both home runs against David Cone... Was his first multi-HR game since his rookie season in 1997... Then hit his third lead-off home run the next day on April 23 against Orlando Hernandez... Is the second Blue Jay to hit lead-off HR's in consecutive games (Damaso Garcia, June 1 & 2, 1983)... Homered in three straight games on May 5, 6 & 7 in Cleveland... Hit in seven straight games from May 4 to 10... Was named the AL Player of the Week, May 1-7, after hitting .387 with nine runs, three doubles, four home runs, nine RBI and five walks... When batting first in the order finished with a .286 average over 112 at bats with

10 home runs and 23 RBI... Hit .272 in May with five HR's and 13 RBI... Went a season high 23 games between home runs from May 7 to June 3... Hit just .216 in June with five HR's and 13 RBI and then only .194 in July with four home runs and nine RBI... In July walked 15 times to post a .303 on-base percentage despite the .194 average... Hit his 20th home run in the second last game prior to the All-Star break to give Toronto the first four teammates in ML history to each hit 20 home runs prior to the All Star break... Best month for average was August at .286 with six home runs and 12 RBI... Did not go two games without a hit until the 29 & 30 of August... Homered in three consecutive games for the second time in 2000 on August 25 & 26 in Texas and the 28th in Anaheim... On September 14 at New York hit his second career extra-inning home run, a two-run HR vs Choate... Hit .290 against LHP with five home runs and .224 against RHP with 26 HR... Hit .250 at home with 15 HR and .235 on the road with 16HR... Hit .247 with runners in scoring position with seven HR's and 47 RBI... Was one of Toronto's four players to hit 30HR's in 2000 (Batista, Delgado, Fullmer) — it marks just the second time in AL history this has been done (Anaheim- 2000)... Was also one of the seven Toronto teammates to each hit 20 HR's during the season, only the second team to ever do so... When putting the first pitch seen in to play hit .333 (37-111) which was sixth in the AL.

PROFESSIONAL CAREER: 1995: Signed by the Mariners on July 20 after his first round selection, third overall in the June Draft... Made pro debut with Everett (A) of the Northwest League where he singled in his first professional at bat... After three games was promoted to Riverside (A) of the California League... Hit first pro HR on July 29 vs. Rancho Cucamonga... Drove in 29 runs and scored 34 in just 35 games for the Pilots... Played winter ball for Santurce in Puerto Rico, which was managed by his father... **1996:** Opened the season with Lancaster in the California League (A)... Singled in the JetHawks home opener which was the first game in their new stadium and the first minor league game played in Los Angeles county since Sept. 15, 1957... Captured league Player of the Week honours for the week April 4-13 (.442/19-43)... Hit in ten straight from April 6 to

16... Named to the mid season Cal League All-Star team... After hitting .325 with six home runs and 43 RBI was promoted to double-A Port City of the Southern League... In nine games from June 29 to July 7 hit .438 with two home runs and 15 RBI... Collected six RBI in a 19-10 win over the Greenville Braves on July 3... Promoted to Tacoma (AAA) where he finished the season batting .237 in 22 games with six home runs and 15 RBI... Walked 18 times and struck out 12... Combined on the season hit 17 doubles, 15 home runs and drove in 89 in 122 games... Named the Mariners Organizational Player of the Year... **1997:** Finished second in the AL Rookie of the Year voting behind Nomar Garciaparra (Boston)... Named to the Topps Rookie Team... Traded to the Toronto Blue Jays from the Seattle Mariners in exchange for RHP Mike Timlin and LHP Paul Spoljaric... Opened the season in Tacoma (AAA) hitting .268 in 50 games, 51-190, 33R, 16-2B, 2-3B, 6HR and 30 RBI... Recalled to Seattle on May 31 and made his ML debut that day vs Detroit in left field (0-4, 1RBI)... Collected first ML hit on June 2 vs Toronto, a double off Luis Andujar... June 3 hit his first ML home run against the Blue Jays RHP Woody Williams- 1R... Collected 1st career multi home run game on June 6 in Detroit, two 2R home runs against Omar Olivares... Second two HR game with Seattle came on July 1 vs San Francisco, a two run HR against Will Van Landingham and a three run HR off Joe Roa- the 5RBI established a new career high... Hit in a season high eight straight games from July 4 to 15... Batted .268 with Seattle with 12 doubles one triple, 12 home runs and 34 RBI... Hit .302 in July with six home runs and 20 RBI... Made Blue Jays debut in Detroit on August 1, was 1-4 with a 2R-HR off RHP Dan Miceli... Made 1st ML start in center field on August 10... On August 24 became the second player in Blue Jays history to homer from both sides of the plate, the other Roberto Alomar (5/10/91 vs CWS & 5/03/93 vs CWS)... In his first multi HR game as a Blue Jay, hit first HR batting left off Ricky Bones-1R and then batting right against Larry Casian- 2R... August 24 game was also his first career four hit game... Finished with four multi-HR games after hitting two on September 2 at the New York Mets, both off Turk Wendell (1R, 2R)... Against LHP hit .258 (25-97) with five HR and 18 RBI and against RHP hit .245 (73-298) with 21 HR's and 50 RBI... Finished second among AL rookies in home runs (26), RBI (68), extra base hits (46) and outfield assists (4), was third in multi-hit games (28), runs (59) and total bases (197)... **1998:** Hit .253 in 105 games with 11 home runs and 42 RBI... Split the season between Toronto and Syracuse (AAA)... Started the season with a 3-3, HR, 3RBI performance in the season opener... Next extra base hit was a HR on May 20 vs Tampa Bay, 96 at bats later...

Optioned to Syracuse June 13 with a .214 average, no doubles, one triple, and three home runs... At Syracuse appeared in 40 games and hit .298 (42-141) with 14-2B, 1-3B, 7HR, 23RBI, 32BB and 32K... Named IL player of the Week From July 20 to 26 after hitting .440 (11-25, 7R, 3-2B, 1-3B, 3HR, 7RBI)... Recalled to Toronto on July 30 and in August hit .366 (37-101) with 11 doubles, a triple, five home runs and 22 RBI... Career high 18 game hit streak from August 5 to 25... After re-call hit .285 (55-193) with eight home runs and 28 RBI... Started 96 games, 95 in center and one in left field... Was batting .274 on August 29, hit just .200 (18-90) in September with three HR's and six RBI... **1999:** Appeared in 106 games and hit .241 with 19 doubles, three triples, 14 home runs and 45 RBI... Opened the season hitting just .213 in April with three home runs and 11 RBI... Walked 16 times in the first 11 games of the season... Finished the season walking 64 times with 91 strikeouts... From May 8 to 16 delivered eight consecutive extra-base hits (5-2B, 1-3B, 2HR)... Homered in back-to-back games May 15 & 16... Also HR'ed in back-to-back games on June 8 & 9 at New York Mets... Was disabled from June 24 to July 8 after suffering a fracture to the tip of the middle finger of his left hand... During rehab with Syracuse (AAA) 6-14) with one home run and two RBI... Played 25 games between home runs from June 9 at the New York Mets to July 27 vs Boston... From June 9 to July 17 did not post an extra-base hit or RBI... In July hit .254 with two home runs and five RBI... Optioned to Syracuse on August 6 after going 4-31 in his previous 10 games... Recalled from Syracuse on September 6... With Syracuse hit .146 (13-89) with two HR and 12 RBI in August and September... Returned and appeared in 16 games making 11 starts... Hit in nine of the 11 starts... In September and October combined, hit .361 (13-36) with three home runs and 10 RBI... On October 1, playing left field in Cleveland, set a club record for an outfielder in a nine inning game with 10 putouts & 10 total chances - Lloyd Moseby (1983) and Shannon Stewart (1998) both have posted 10 putouts, total chances games, but they were extra inning games... Had a season high four RBI on October 3 at Cleveland... Started 88 games in center field and eight in left field.

CAREER NOTES: Is the second Blue Jay to hit lead-off HR's in consecutive games on April 22 & 23, 2000 against the Yankees David Cone and Orlando Hernandez — he joins Damaso Garcia who did so on June 1 & 2, 1983... On October 1, 1999 while playing left field in Cleveland set club records for an outfielder in a nine inning game with 10 putouts and 10 total chances.

JOSE CRUZ Jr.

Year	Club & League	AVG	G	AB	R	H	TB	2B	3B	HR	RBI	SH-SF	HP	BB-IBB	SO	SB-CS	GIDP	SLG	OBP
1995	Everett (NWST)	.455	3	11	6	5	5	0	0	0	2	0-0	0	3-0	3	1-0	0	.455	.571
1995	Riverside (Cal)	.257	35	144	34	37	67	7	1	7	29	0-2	0	24-1	50	3-1	1	.465	.359
1996	Lancaster (Cal)	.325	53	203	38	66	103	17	1	6	43	0-6	0	39-1	33	7-1	4	.507	.423
1996	Port City (Sou)	.282	47	181	39	51	74	10	2	3	31	0-1	0	27-4	38	5-0	8	.409	.373
1996	Tacoma (PCL)	.237	22	76	15	18	41	1	2	6	15	1-0	0	18-1	12	1-1	2	.539	.383
1997	Tacoma (PCL)	.268	50	190	33	51	89	16	2	6	30	1-0	1	34-1	44	3-0	4	.468	.382
1997	SEATTLE (AL)	.268	49	183	28	49	99	12	1	12	34	1-1	0	13-0	45	1-0	3	.541	.315
1997	TORONTO (AL)	.231	55	212	31	49	98	7	0	14	34	0-4	0	28-2	72	6-2	2	.462	.316
1998	Syracuse (Int)	.298	40	141	29	42	79	14	1	7	23	0-1	0	32-0	32	8-4	2	.560	.425
1998	TORONTO (AL)	.253	105	352	55	89	142	14	3	11	42	0-4	0	57-3	99	11-4	0	.403	.354
1999	Syracuse (Int)	.184	31	103	17	19	33	3	1	3	14	0-1	0	28-3	20	5-0	3	.320	.356
1999	TORONTO (AL)	.241	106	349	63	84	151	19	3	14	45	1-0	0	64-5	91	14-4	6	.433	.358
2000	TORONTO (AL)	.242	162	603	91	146	281	32	5	31	76	2-3	2	71-3	129	15-5	11	.466	.323
	Minor Totals	.276	281	1049	211	289	491	68	10	38	187	2-11	1	205-11	232	33-7	24	.468	.391
	TORONTO TOTALS	.243	428	1516	240	368	672	72	11	70	197	3-11	2	220-13	391	46-15	19	.443	.337
	MAJOR TOTALS	.245	477	1699	268	417	771	84	12	82	231	4-12	2	233-13	436	47-15	22	.454	.335

HOME RUN BREAKDOWN

Total	H	A	0	MEN ON 1	2	3	ONE GAME 2	3	4	LO	XN	IP	PH	RHP	LHP
82	38	44	44	30	8	0	5	0	0	3	2	0	0	68	14

Cruz Jr. — TRANSACTIONS

- Selected by the Atlanta Braves in the 15th round of the June 1992 First Year Player Draft; did not sign.
- Selected by the Seattle Mariners in the first round (3rd overall) of the June 1995 First Year Player Draft.
- Traded to the Toronto Blue Jays in exchange for RHP Mike Timlin and LHP Paul Spoljaric on July 31, 1997.
- On disabled list (fractured finger-tip - left hand) June 24-July 9, 1999; included rehabilitation at Syracuse July 5-9, 1999.

CAREER HIGHS — CRUZ Jr., Jose

FIELDING

CRUZ Jr., Jose—OF

Year	PCT	G	PO	A	E	TC	DP
1997	.974	104	181	4	5	190	1
1998	.984	105	247	7	4	258	1
1999	.990	106	277	8	3	288	2
2000	.993	162	405	9	3	417	1
Total	.987	477	1110	28	15	1153	5

JOSE CRUZ Jr. DETAILED HITTING

	2000									CAREER								
	Avg	AB	H	HR	RBI	BB	SO	OBP	SLG	Avg	AB	H	HR	RBI	BB	SO	OBP	SLG
Total	.242	603	146	31	76	71	129	.323	.466	.245	1699	417	82	231	233	436	.335	.454
vs. Left	.290	162	47	5	19	11	21	.339	.481	.280	429	120	14	53	53	77	.358	.459
vs. Right	.224	441	99	26	57	60	108	.317	.460	.234	1270	297	68	178	180	359	.327	.452
Home	.250	288	72	15	40	39	60	.341	.479	.254	838	213	38	126	128	206	.352	.462
Away	.235	315	74	16	36	32	69	.305	.454	.237	861	204	44	105	105	230	.318	.446
April	.235	98	23	8	18	13	18	.319	.520	.222	261	58	12	34	47	63	.338	.410
May	.272	114	31	5	13	14	30	.352	.456	.236	250	59	11	32	37	65	.333	.428
June	.216	102	22	5	13	11	17	.292	.441	.234	299	70	13	35	33	69	.309	.425
July	.194	93	18	4	9	15	22	.306	.430	.246	244	60	12	34	27	59	.320	.475
August	.286	98	28	6	12	11	20	.364	.520	.297	320	95	20	56	44	71	.379	.547
September	.245	94	23	3	11	7	20	.301	.436	.229	310	71	13	36	41	104	.319	.426
October	.250	4	1	0	0	0	2	.250	.250	.267	15	4	1	4	4	5	.421	.467
Scoring Posn	.271	133	36	7	47	24	33	.375	.496	.242	417	101	18	141	85	121	.362	.427
Bases Loaded	.444	9	4	0	8	1	1	.455	.556	.250	32	8	0	20	4	10	.316	.281
PH	–	–	–	–	–	–	–	–	–	.000	4	0	0	0	0	1	.000	.000
vs. Ana	.233	43	10	4	8	9	8	.365	.558	.236	127	30	7	23	20	21	.340	.465
vs. Bal	–	–	–	–	–	–	–	–	–	.189	90	17	1	4	13	26	.291	.278
vs. Bos	.277	47	13	1	5	5	10	.346	.383	.244	135	33	6	15	16	34	.325	.459
vs. CWS	.244	41	10	3	4	2	11	.279	.537	.200	105	21	3	9	17	26	.309	.352
vs. Cle	.304	46	14	4	9	9	13	.418	.717	.276	145	40	10	30	28	42	.389	.545
vs. Det	.146	41	6	2	3	6	5	.255	.293	.187	134	25	7	16	16	29	.272	.343
vs. KC	.273	33	9	2	4	6	6	.385	.485	.276	98	27	5	14	20	23	.395	.469
vs. Mil	–	–	–	–	–	–	–	–	–	.000	1	0	0	0	0	1	.000	.000
vs. Min	.343	35	12	1	4	1	5	.361	.543	.309	110	34	7	20	9	22	.358	.609
vs. NYY	.255	47	12	4	12	4	15	.302	.574	.237	131	31	8	21	17	44	.320	.489
vs. Oak	.250	36	9	0	1	3	10	.308	.306	.267	101	27	1	9	8	27	.321	.366
vs. Sea	.205	39	8	2	6	3	7	.273	.385	.267	101	27	7	17	7	28	.318	.515
vs. TB	.262	42	11	2	7	6	8	.354	.476	.260	77	20	4	13	19	19	.406	.494
vs. Tex	.275	40	11	3	6	2	7	.326	.575	.213	122	26	4	12	12	31	.283	.393
vs. Tor	–	–	–	–	–	–	–	–	–	.467	15	7	1	1	0	3	.467	.867
vs. Atl	.154	13	2	0	1	2	3	.267	.154	.304	23	7	0	2	5	4	.429	.348
vs. Col	–	–	–	–	–	–	–	–	–	.125	8	1	0	1	1	3	.222	.250
vs. Fla	.286	14	4	1	2	0	3	.286	.571	.326	46	15	2	5	2	10	.354	.500
vs. LA	–	–	–	–	–	–	–	–	–	.333	6	2	1	3	4	4	.600	.833
vs. Mon	.167	18	3	1	2	5	3	.348	.444	.225	40	9	1	4	6	12	.326	.350
vs. NYM	.400	10	4	1	1	3	2	.538	1.100	.313	32	10	5	6	8	14	.450	.938
vs. Phi	.100	10	1	0	0	1	1	.182	.200	.121	33	4	0	1	4	9	.216	.152
vs. SD	–	–	–	–	–	–	–	–	–	.000	6	0	0	0	0	1	.000	.000
vs. SF	–	–	–	–	–	–	–	–	–	.308	13	4	2	5	1	3	.357	.846
Pre-All Star	.240	346	83	20	47	42	73	.321	.477	.233	868	202	41	111	124	211	.327	.433
Post-All Star	.245	257	63	11	29	29	56	.325	.451	.259	831	215	41	120	109	225	.344	.475

IRON MAN STREAK

The all-time Blue Jays Iron Man streak is 403 games set by Tony Fernandez between September 21, 1984 and June 24, 1987. Alfredo Griffin has the second longest streak at 392. In 1999 Carlos Delgado had played in every inning of every game and had the third longest iron man streak in franchise history at 235 consecutive games before suffering a non-displaced fracture of the right tibia on September 22 at Boston. Ed Sprague is both fourth at 225 games and fifth at 223 games

Heading into the 2001 season, Blue Jays outfielder Jose Cruz Jr., has played in 167 consecutive games. First baseman Carlos Delgado has currently played in 162 consecutive games.

JOSE CRUZ Jr. HITTING AT ML PARKS

Park	Avg	G	AB	R	H	2B	3B	HR	RBI	SB	CS	BB	SO	OBP	Slg
Camden Yards	.176	10	34	3	6	1	1	0	0	0	0	6	6	.300	.265
Fenway Park	.267	17	60	10	16	2	2	2	9	2	0	6	13	.333	.467
Edison Field	.179	17	56	5	10	4	1	2	6	1	0	7	12	.270	.393
Comiskey Park	.185	15	54	8	10	3	0	3	4	1	0	9	13	.302	.407
Jacobs Field	.241	24	87	12	21	3	1	4	15	3	0	17	25	.362	.437
Tiger Stadium	.278	12	36	8	10	0	0	4	7	0	1	2	11	.316	.611
Kauffman Stadium	.314	13	51	12	16	4	0	3	6	1	1	5	12	.368	.569
County Stadium	.000	1	1	0	0	0	0	0	0	0	0	0	1	.000	.000
Metrodome	.259	14	54	9	14	3	0	4	9	1	2	5	14	.317	.537
Yankee Stadium	.235	22	85	12	20	4	1	4	10	2	1	11	32	.320	.447
Oakland-Alameda	.288	14	52	2	15	3	0	0	3	3	1	5	13	.351	.346
Kingdome	.282	36	142	24	40	7	0	12	31	2	1	9	43	.322	.585
Arlington	.172	15	58	9	10	3	0	3	5	0	0	4	14	.222	.379
SkyDome	.254	220	756	126	192	42	6	31	105	26	8	122	182	.357	.448
Olympic Stadium	.222	6	18	2	4	1	0	1	2	2	0	3	6	.333	.444
Shea Stadium	.273	6	22	7	6	1	0	4	5	0	0	5	12	.407	.864
Veterans Stadium	.083	3	12	0	1	0	0	0	0	0	0	0	3	.083	.083
Qualcomm Park	.000	2	6	0	0	0	0	0	0	0	0	0	1	.000	.000
3 Com Park	.000	1	3	0	0	0	0	0	0	0	0	1	1	.250	.000
Pro Player Stadium	.304	5	23	2	7	1	0	1	2	1	0	1	5	.333	.478
Turner Field	.154	3	13	2	2	0	0	0	1	0	0	2	3	.267	.154
Tropicana Field	.243	10	37	7	9	2	0	2	5	0	1	8	9	.378	.459
SAFECO Field	.222	5	18	2	4	0	0	1	4	0	0	1	4	.263	.389
Comerica Park	.190	6	21	6	4	0	0	1	2	0	1	4	1	.320	.333

JOSE CRUZ Jr. — MILESTONES

	DATE	OPP.	H/A	PITCHER		NOTES
HITS						
1	June 2, 1997	SEA vs TOR	H	Luis Andujar		double
HR						
1	June 3, 1997	SEA vs TOR	H	Woody Williams		1R
RBI						
1	May 31, 1997	SEA vs DET	H	Omar Olivares		fielder's choice
SB						
1	June 14, 1997	SEA vs LA	H	Ramon Martinez Catcher-Mike Piazza		2nd
MULTI-HR (5)						
2	June 6, 1997	SEA vs DET	A	Olivares-2R, 2R		2nd, 6th
2	July 1, 1997	SEA vs SF	H	Van Landingham-2R, Roa-3R		2nd, 3rd
2	Aug. 24, 1997	TOR vs KC	A	Bones-1R, Casian-2R		1st, 13th
2	Sept. 2, 1997	TOR vs NYM	A	Wendell-1R, 2R		7th, 9th
2	April 22, 2000	TOR vs NYY	H	Cone-1R, 1R		1st, 4th

Pat
DANEKER

PITCHER

70

BIRTHDATE . . . . January 14, 1976
OPENING DAY AGE 25
BIRTHPLACE . . . . Williamsport, PA
RESIDENCE . . . . Williamsport, PA
BATS/THROWS . . . . R/R
HEIGHT/WEIGHT 6-3/195
CONTRACT STATUS . . . . signed thru 2001
M.L. SERVICE 0.011

PERSONAL: Patrick Rees Daneker... Graduated from Loyalstock High School in Williamsport, PA, where as a senior was 8-0 with a 0.88 ERA... Attended University of Virginia where he was selected as a Mizuno Freshman All-American... Ranks second in school history in innings pitched (280.1) and games (40), third in strikeouts (213) and fifth in wins (16) and complete games (15).

LAST SEASON: Combined to post a 9-13 record in the International League (AAA) with a 5.54 ERA while pitching for Charlotte (White Sox) and Syracuse (Blue Jays)... Opened the season with Charlotte where he was 8-12 with a 5.75 ERA in 27 games, 25 starts... Posted 11 quality starts... Best month for ERA came in June when he was 2-2 with a 4.15 ERA in five starts... Pitched a season high 8.0 innings on July 16 vs Syracuse... Against Syracuse was 2-0 in two starts... On August 23 was claimed on waivers by Toronto and assigned to Syracuse... Won his SkyChiefs debut on

August 26 against Scranton as he matched his season high with 8.0 innings pitched... Lost his only other start with Syracuse to finish with a 1-1 record and a 3.29 ERA in two starts.

PROFESSIONAL CAREER: 1997: Made his pro debut with Bristol (rookie-A)... Was 3-6 with a 6.50 ERA... Was second on the club in starts (12) and innings (63.2)... Had 2.7:1 strikeout-to-walk ratio (53K/20BB)... Struck out 7.5 batters per nine innings pitched... **1998:** Split time between Hickory (A) and Winston-Salem (A) combining to go 11-6 with a 2.81 ERA with 138 strikeouts and four complete games... Rated as the ninth best prospect in the organization by Baseball America... Led the organization in complete games, was second in ERA, third in winning percentage (.647) and fourth in innings pitched (170.0)... 20 of his 27 starts were quality starts... Named the Player of the Week in the South Atlantic League from April 10-16 and in the Carolina League from

August 27 to September 2... Struck out a season high 12 batters in seven innings on July 11 at Greensboro... Lasted at least 7.0 innings in nine consecutive starts from July 5 to August 18... **1999:** Split the season between Chicago, Charlotte (AAA) and Birmingham (AA)... Opened the season with Birmingham before having his contract purchased by Chicago on July 1... Made his ML debut in relief on July 2 vs Boston, pitched 3.0 scoreless innings with two strikeouts... Next two appearances were starts, posting a 5.25 ERA with no-decisions on July 8 vs Kansas City and July 19 at Milwau-kee... Was optioned to Birmingham on July 20... Noted as having the Best Control in the Southern League by Baseball America... In eight starts from May 7 to June 13 posted a 1.99 ERA... Struckout a season high nine in a complete game win June 8 at Carolina... On July 24 was promoted to Charlotte (AAA) where he won three of his first four starts... Combined was 10-12 with a 4.26 ERA between Birmingham and Charlotte... Was second in the White Sox organization in complete games (4), fourth in wins (10) and innings pitched (158.1).

PAT DANEKER

Year	Club & League	W-L	ERA	G	GS	CG	ShO	SV	IP	H	R	ER	HR	HB	BB-IBB	SO	WP	BK	OBA
1997	Bristol (Appy)	3-6	6.50	12	12	0	0	0	63.2	83	55	46	5	5	20-1	53	4	5	.314
1998	Hickory (SAL)	6-6	3.15	17	17	2	0	0	117.0	115	50	41	14	1	16-0	95	2	6	.253
1998	Winston-Sal (Caro)	5-0	2.04	7	7	2	0	0	53.0	51	13	12	3	2	5-1	43	1	4	.254
1999	Birmingham (Sou)	6-8	3.22	16	16	3	0	0	109.0	106	46	39	6	2	30-1	71	4	2	.256
1999	CHICAGO (AL)	0-0	4.20	3	2	0	0	0	15.0	14	8	7	1	0	6-0	5	0	0	.255
1999	Charlotte (Int)	4-4	6.57	9	9	1	0	0	49.1	64	36	36	10	3	16-0	36	4	0	.308
2000	Charlotte (Int)	8-12	5.75	27	25	0	0	0	144.0	168	102	92	26	4	49-1	69	4	4	.292
2000	Syracuse (Int)	1-1	3.29	2	2	0	0	0	13.2	18	6	5	2	1	2-0	4	1	0	.333
Minor Totals		33-37	4.44	90	88	8	0	0	549.2	605	308	271	66	18	138-4	371	20	21	.279

DANEKER — TRANSACTIONS

- Selected by the Chicago White Sox in fifth round of the June 1997 First Year Player Draft.
- Claimed on waivers by the Toronto Blue Jays from the Chicago White Sox on August 23, 2000.

CAREER HIGHS — DANEKER, Pat
GAME:

ML Debut	Jul. 2, 1999 vs. BOS
Innings Pitched:	
Starter	7.0 - Jul. 8, 1999 vs. KC
Reliever	3.0 - Jul. 2, 1999 vs. BOS
Walks:	
Starter	3 - Jul. 19, 1999 at MIL
Reliever	1 - Jul. 2, 1999 vs. BOS
Strikeouts:	
Starter	2 - Jul. 8, 1999 vs. KC
Reliever	2 - Jul. 2, 1999 vs. BOS
Hits Allowed	7 - Jul. 8, 1999 vs. KC
Runs Allowed	5 - Jul. 19, 1999 at MIL
ER Allowed	4 - Jul. 19, 1999 at MIL
HR Allowed	1 - Jul. 19, 1999 at MIL
Low Hit CG	None
Last Win	None
Last Save	None
Last CG	None
Last ShO	None
Last Start	Jul. 19, 1999 at MIL
Last Relief App.	Jul. 2, 1999 vs. BOS

FIELDING
DANEKER, Pat—P

Year	PCT	G	PO	A	E	TC	DP
1999 (AL)	1.000	3	0	3	0	3	0

PAT DANEKER DETAILED PITCHING

	2000								CAREER						
	ERA	W-L-Sv	G	IP	H	ER	BB	SO	ERA	W-L-Sv	G	IP	H	ER	BB	SO
Total	–	–	–	–	–	–	–	–	4.20	0-0-0	3	15.0	14	7	6	5
ST	–	–	–	–	–	–	–	–	5.25	0-0-0	2	12.0	12	7	5	3
REL	–	–	–	–	–	–	–	–	0.00	0-0-0	1	3.0	2	0	1	2
Home	–	–	–	–	–	–	–	–	2.70	0-0-0	2	10.0	9	3	3	4
Away	–	–	–	–	–	–	–	–	7.20	0-0-0	1	5.0	5	4	3	1
July	–	–	–	–	–	–	–	–	4.20	0-0-0	3	15.0	14	7	6	5
vs. Bos	–	–	–	–	–	–	–	–	0.00	0-0-0	1	3.0	2	0	1	2
vs. KC	–	–	–	–	–	–	–	–	3.86	0-0-0	1	7.0	7	3	2	1
vs. Mil	–	–	–	–	–	–	–	–	7.20	0-0-0	1	5.0	5	4	3	1
Pre-All Star	–	–	–	–	–	–	–	–	2.70	0-0-0	2	10.0	9	3	3	4
Post-All Star	–	–	–	–	–	–	–	–	7.20	0-0-0	1	5.0	5	4	3	1

PAT DANEKER PITCHING AT ML PARKS

Park	ERA	W-L-Sv	SvO	G	GS	IP	H	R	ER	HR	BB	SO
Comiskey Park	2.70	0-0-0	0	2	1	10.0	9	3	3	0	3	4
County Stadium	7.20	0-0-0	0	1	1	5.0	5	5	4	1	3	1

Morrin
DAVIS

OUTFIELDER

BIRTHDATE	December 11, 1982
OPENING DAY AGE	18
BIRTHPLACE	Tampa, FL
RESIDENCE	Tampa, FL
BATS/THROWS	R/R
HEIGHT/WEIGHT	6-2/190
CONTRACT STATUS	signed thru 2001
M.L. SERVICE	0.000

63

PERSONAL: Morrin Antoine Davis... Graduated from Hillsborough High School in Florida... Was a State All-Star Game selection.

LAST SEASON: Made his professional debut with Medicine Hat of the Pioneer League (A)... Hit .222 in 40 games with six doubles, two triples, five home runs and 16 RBI... Hit in his first four pro games... Hit three home runs from July 26 to August 3... Season high three RBI on July 30 vs Helena and August 3 vs Missoula... Hit in a season high six straight August 13-19... Hit .225 at home with three home runs and 10 RBI and on the road hit .219 with two home runs and six RBI.

MORRIN DAVIS

Year	Club & League	AVG	G	AB	R	H	TB	2B	3B	HR	RBI	SH-SF	HP	BB-IBB	SO	SB-CS	GIDP	SLG	OBP
2000	Medicine Hat (Pio)	.222	40	162	17	36	61	6	2	5	16	0-0	1	11-1	59	2-1	3	.377	.276

DAVIS — TRANSACTIONS

- Selected by the Toronto Blue Jays in the 3rd round (88th overall) of the June 2000 First Year Player Draft.

Carlos
DELGADO

FIRST BASEMAN/DH

BIRTHDATE	June 25, 1972
OPENING DAY AGE	28
BIRTHPLACE	Aguadilla, PR
RESIDENCE	Aguadilla, PR
BATS/THROWS	L/R
HEIGHT/WEIGHT	6-3/230
CONTRACT STATUS	signed thru 2004
M.L. SERVICE	6.002

25

PERSONAL: Carlos Juan Delgado... Graduate of Jose de Diego High School in 1989 (Puerto Rico) where he participated in baseball, volleyball and track and field.

LAST SEASON: Set career highs with .344 average, 115 runs scored, 196 hits, 57 doubles, 137 RBI, 99 extra-base hits, 123 walks... Named as the Sporting News Player of the Year and earned his second straight Silver Slugger Award... Recipient of the AL Hank Aaron Award... Named the Player of the Year by the New York Chapter of the BBWAA... Led the American League in doubles, extra-base hits and total bases (378), was second in walks, on-base percentage (.470), slugging percentage (.644), batting with runners in scoring position (.384) and tied for second in intentional walks (18), third in extra-base hits, was fourth in the AL in average, tied for fourth in home runs and RBI, was sixth in hits and tied for seventh in runs scored... Set Blue Jays all-time single season records for RBI at 137, extra-base hits at 99, walks at 123 and slugging percentage at .664... The .344 average and .470 on-base percentage were second highest in franchise history (Olerud- .363 & .473 in 1993)... Was just the third Blue Jay to reach 100 walks in a season... Was twice named the AL Player of the Week, April 17 to 23 (.480/12-25, 11R, 4HR, 8RBI, 1.080SLG%) and June 5-11 (.556/10-18, 4HR, 13RBI, 25TB, 1.389Slg, 9BB)... Played in all 162 games, now done seven times in club history... Started the season with one hit in his first 19 at bats but finished April hitting .319 with eight home runs and 20 RBI... Had first of five multi-HR games in 2000 with two on April 16 vs Seattle to begin a nine game hit streak... Posted RBI in eight straight games from April 16 to 23 to tie the club record for consecutive games with an RBI... Hit eight home runs in 13 games from April 14 to 26... Hit .340 in May with 10 home runs and 26 RBI... Hit in ten straight games from May 3 to 13... Homered in three straight games May 4-6 in Cleveland... Collected second two home run game on May 28 at Detroit and totalled five RBI to match his then career high... Hit in 31 of 32 games from May 24 to June 29... Posted a career high 22 game hit streak from June 4-29 (35-79, 25RBI), was the second longest hit streak in the AL this season (Kapler-TEX 28)... Set a career high with six RBI on June 7 at Atlanta after collecting his third two-HR game and first grand slam of the season against John Burkett, was his sixth career slam - was the 12th Blue Jay to post a six RBI game... June 25 hit a two run HR against Boston's Pedro Martinez to tie the game, Toronto won that game for the fourth straight win and a sweep of Boston which moved the Blue Jays ahead of them for first in the AL East... For the month of June hit .411 (39-95) with six doubles, nine home runs and 26 RBI to pace Toronto to their best month of the season at 16-10... At the All-Star break had 80 RBI to tie Joe Carter (1994) for the club record and had 28 HR's, one short of George Bell's 29 in 1987... Was one of Toronto's four players to hit 20 HR's by the All-Star break for the first time in ML history... Made his first career ALL-STAR appearance and was 1-1 with a double... Collected third two HR game on July 20 against Tampa Bay and Steve Trachsel... Finished July hitting .368 (34-88, 5HR) with a club record 19 doubles and 24 extra-base hits (17 & 22-Olerud-June-93)... Walked 27 times in July to finish with a .538 on-base percentage for the month... Doubled in seven straight games from July 22-29 and hit in eight straight from July 22 to July 30... Opened August with an eight game hit streak... Aug 7 at KC had his 100th RBI, his 200th career double and 400th career walk... Hit a walk-off home run on August 16 against Anaheim's Lou Pote... Fourth two HR game came August 23 vs KC... On August 29 collected his 88th extra-base hit to break Shawn Green's club record of 87 set in 1999... In August hit .368 with nine doubles, a triple, seven home runs and 31 RBI... Went a season high 17 games with out a home run from August 28 to September 16 until belting his second grand slam of the season, seventh career on Sept. 17 at Chicago against Jesus Pena... September 18 set a new club mark with his 135th RBI passing the previous mark of 134 held by Delgado (1999) and George Bell (1987)... Managed just one hit in his final six games and three in his last ten games, all three hits were doubles to leave him with 99 extra base hits but a club record 57 doubles... Hit .256 in September with two home runs and 13 RBI... Hit .360 at home with 75 RBI and new club mark of 30 home runs (Canseco- 25 at home in 1997)... On the road hit .329 with 11 home runs and 62 RBI... Hit .319 vs LHP with six HR and 36 RBI and against RHP hit .357 with 35HR and 101 RBI... His 41 HR accounted for 64 RBI, 24 were solo's, 13-2R, 2-3R, 2 slams... Is part of the Blue Jays record seven 20HR hitters in a season (2nd time ML, both AL) and four 30-HR players in a season (nine times, twice in AL)... Had a .991 fielding percentage with 13 errors in a league high 1,511 total chances... Joined MLB All-Star team for the 2000 Japan Series in November.

PROFESSIONAL CAREER: 1989: Used primarily at the designated hitter position at St. Catharines in the New York-Penn League... **1990:** Earned his first R. Howard Webster Award as St. Catharines' MVP... Led club in doubles (13) and RBI (39)... Tied for team lead in runs (30)... Batted .326 in August (30-92) ending the season with a season high .281 average... Selected by Baseball America as the league's fourth best prospect... **1991:** Third in the South Atlantic League in HR (18), tied for fifth in walks (75) and seventh in slugging percentage (.397)... Homered once every 24.50 plate appearances- seocnd in the loop... Hit homers in consecutive games on three occasions... Hit .328 in April and .308 in August... Called up to Syracuse (AAA) of the International League at the end of the season going 0-3... **1992:** Won his second R. Howard Webster Award as the MVP of the Dunedin (A) club in the Florida State League... Led the league in HR (30) and RBI (100) and finished second in batting average (.324) to capture league MVP honours... USA Today's Baseball Weekly Minor League Player of the Year... Was first Florida State League player to reach the 100 RRI plateau since Mike Holcutt of West Palm Beach in 1984... Also led the circuit in total bases (281), walks (59), on base percentage (.402), hits (157), doubles (30), extra-base hits (62) and slugging percentage (.579)... Hit 3 HR in a game on May 8 becoming just the fifth player in Florida State League history to do so... Rated as the best power prospect in the league by Baseball America... **1993:** Won his third R. Howard Webster Award as team MVP at Double A Knoxville... Selected to both the regular and post season All-Star teams for the Southern League... He led the loop in home runs (25), RBI (102) and finished sixth in batting average (.303)... Posted a .524 slugging percentage while leading Knoxville with 53 extra-base hits... Second consecutive 100 RBI season... Southern League MVP... Played 107 games at catcher and threw out 34%(55-162) would be base stealers... Contract was purchased in September by Toronto... Made Major League debut on October 1 at Baltimore (defensive replacement)... **1994:** Started the spring at catcher but moved to left field on March 18 vs Montreal... All 39 starts at the Major League level came as an outfielder... Made one appearance at catcher- May 31 vs Oakland (defensive replacement)... Was leading the Majors in HR's on April 19 with 8 in 13 games... April 5 hit a 445 ft. homer off the glass of Windows Restaurant- only the second Blue Jays player to manage the feat (McGriff)... April 11 at Oakland, registered first career 2 homer game- (3R off Witt, 2R off Taylor)... Eight HR in April tied him with Hrbek for the most HR's ever in April by a rookie in the majors... 8th home run came April 19 vs Texas but did not hit #9 until May 30... Optioned to AAA Syracuse on June 10 where he spent the remainder of the season... International League Player of the Week for week ending July 9... Batted .351(39-111) with 11 HR and 30 RBI during August... Led Syracuse in HR (19) and slugging percentage (.541)... Returned to catcher position at Syracuse and caught 41 games with the Chiefs... Named MVP of the Puerto Rican Winter League after batting

.323 with 12 HR, 47 RBI and 50 walks in 51 games for San Juan... Named Baseball America Winter League Player of the Year... **1995:** Opened the season with Toronto making just 10 starts- all at DH... Hit a pinch-hit homer May 23 vs Kansas City... Was his first HR in the Majors since May 30 of 1994 vs New York... Optioned to AAA Syracuse of the International League June 1... Was the IL and Jays' organization Player of the Month for June (.308, 32-104, 8-2B, 1-3B, 6HR, 22RBI) and the Chiefs' Player of the Month for July (.326, 31-95, 8-2B, 1-3B, 5HR, 17RBI)... Hit a grand slam for Syracuse on June 27 (2nd game) against Charlotte... Was IL Player of the Week three times and was selected to the IL All-Star team... Led the IL in slugging percentage (.610), 3rd in BA (.318) & ex-base hits (49), T4th in HR (22), 5th in RBI (74)... Appeared in 79 games at first base... Recalled by Toronto on September 3 and played in 23 games batting .172 (10-58)... Made first career start at first base on September 23 (Game #2) at Boston... Ended 0-24 streak on September 30 with a single vs NYY... Hit .273 (3-11) vs LHP with Toronto... **1996:** First full season in the majors, hit .270 with 25 HR's and 92 RBI... Was third on the club in homers and RBI... In spring tied the club mark with 7 HR's and hit for the league lead with 61 total bases while hitting .333 with 22 RBI... In April hit .333 (30-90), 6 HR and 26 RBI... April 12 tied the club mark of 4 strikeouts in a game done many times previously... April 27 vs Cleveland posted his first career three hit game and tied his career mark for RBI with four... First career four hit game came May 30 vs Milwaukee (3RBI)... Homered in back-to-back games five times including four of five games from April 27 to May 2-April 27 & 28 vs Cleveland and May 1 & 2 vs Milwaukee... Season high nine game hit streak from May 21 to June 1 (14-38, 4-2B)... On July 6th had his second career 2-HR game and became the 29th player to clear Tiger Stadium with his 15th HR of the season off Omar Olivares- first visiting player to do so since George Brett in 1988... Also matched his season high of four RBI and tied the club record scoring four runs... July 28 drove in lone run in a 1-0 win vs Oakland with home run #18 off Ariel Prieto... September 24 hit HR #25 off C.J. Nitkowski, his second vs left-hand pitching... Of 25 HR's- 23 vs RHP, 2 vs LHP, 12 at home, 13 on the road, 13- 1R, 6-2R, 6- 3R... Started 125 games, 100 as the DH and 25 at first base... Pre All-Star game hit .288 (82-285) with 15 HR and 60 RBI - Post All-Star game hit .246 (50-203) with 10 HR and 32 RBI... Hit a team best .292 with RISP, also led club in average with bases loaded (.455), batting vs RHP (.298), batting at home (.282), pitches seen per plate appearance (4.09) and sacrifice flies (8)... Had artroscopic surgery on his right knee on December 11 by Dr. Tony Miniaci (Toronto) and on his right wrist on December 17 by Dr. Frank McCue (Charlottesville, VA)... **1997:** Posted then career highs and led the team with 42 doubles, 30 home runs and 274 total bases... Received the Neil MacCarl Award as the Blue Jays Player of the Year by the Toronto chapter of the BBWAA... The 42 doubles was the second highest single season total by a Blue Jay (Olerud 54)... Is now the seventh Blue Jay to reach 30 home runs... Hit three grand slams, the first three of his career... Is now the only player in franchise history to hit three grand slams in the same season... Slams came April 25 vs Seattle off Dennis Martinez, June 6 vs Oakland off Mike Oquist and July 24 vs Milwaukee off Jose Mercedes... Hit .345 (19-55) in April with five home runs and 15 RBI... Homered in four straight games June 3, 5, 6 & 7 to match the club record held by George Bell (1985) and Joe Carter (1991)... Career hit 200 was a home run on June 6 in Minnesota against Dan Naulty... Hit 30 HR's, 28 vs RHP and 2 vs LHP... First HR vs LHP was #24 of the season on August 8 vs Detroit's Mike Myers... Posted two multi-HR games... Collected five RBI twice to match career high, July 11 at Boston and July 17 at Texas... Hit .312 (29-93) in September with two home runs and nine RBI and ended the season on a then career high 16 game hit streak (20-56, 8-2B, 1HR)... Was the longest hit streak by a Blue Jay in 1997... Started 116 games at first base and 21 at DH... Also led the team in walks (64) and strikeouts (133)- 8th in the AL... Was tied for 2nd in the AL with three slams, fifth in extra base hits (75) and tied for fifth in doubles (42)... Hit .254 vs LHP (2HR, 16RBI) and .265 vs. RHP (28HR, 75 RBI)... **1998:** Despite starting the year on the DL set then career highs in runs (94), hits (155), doubles (43), home runs (38), RBI (115), total bases (314) and walks

(73) and was named the Neil MacCarl Award Winner as the Blue Jays Player of the Year as voted by the Toronto chapter of the BBWAA... Second consecutive season to win the award... Ranked fifth in the AL in doubles, tied for fourth in extra base hits (82), fifth in slugging pct. (.592) & strikeouts (139), sixth in HR/AB frequency (13.9AB) and ninth in home runs... Was second in the AL in both intentional walks (13) and pitches per plate appearance (4.14)... Had arthroscopic surgery performed January 19 on his right shoulder after suffering a torn labrum in winter ball... Activated from the DL on April 24 after rehab stints with Dunedin-A & Syracuse-AAA... Missed 20 games due to the DL and the club was 8-12 in those games... Hit .240 in his first 25 at bats in April before he rebounded to hit .324 (36-111) with four HR's and 21 RBI in May... May 7 posted first career 5-hit game in Seattle, 11th Blue Jay to accomplish the feat... Included in the five hits was his fourth career grand slam HR off LHP Jamie Moyer... Hit in a then career high 19 straight games from May 21 to June 9... Was the 5th longest hit streak in club history... Named AL Player of the Week, June 1-7, hit .407/11-27, 7R, 3-2B, 1-3B, 4HR & 9 RBI... June 1 vs Boston collected first of six multi HR games on the season... Matched career high with 5 RBI on July 4 vs Tampa Bay with a 3-4, 2HR night... Following the break collected one hit in his first eight games highlighted by a career high 0-29 stretch... July 19 vs NYY became the first player in the history of SkyDome to homer into the fifth deck in right field, was HR #19 off Pettitte-2R... On August 4 in Texas posted first career three HR game, only the sixth Blue Jay to do so... The three HR's came in consecutive at bats making him just the third Blue Jay to HR in three straight at bats and the first to do so in one game - George Bell and Cliff Johnson accomplished the feat over two games... August was the best RBI month driving in 28 while batting .308 (32-104)... Second grand slam of the year came August 12 off LHP Greg McCarthy of the Mariners... August 13 was appointed team Captain, the second in club history (Mayberry-'81)... Posted second five RBI game of the season on August 19 at Seattle with a two HR performance... Named AL Player of the Week for the second time in 1998... Set the club record for HR's in September with 11 breaking the previous mark of 10 (Barfield 2, Mayberry)... September 17 at Detroit posted his sixth multi-HR game of the season, the first HR off Bryce Florie was career HR #100... 38 HR's- 5 vs LHP/ 33 vs RHP/ 20 at SkyDome/ 18 on the road... Hit .303 vs LHP and .288 vs RHP... On the road was a .282 hitter and at SkyDome hit .304... With MISP posted a .302 (45-149) average... Prior to the All-Star break hit .308 with 17 HR's and 57 RBI, following the break hit .278 with 21 HR's and 58 RBI... Member of the Major League Baseball All-Star team which played a series of games in Japan in November... **1999:** Hit .272 with then career highs in hits (156), total bases (327), extra-base hits (83), home runs (44) and RBI (134)... The 134 RBI tie George Bell's single season RBI mark set in 1987... Became the fourth Blue Jay to reach 40 home runs and was followed by Shawn Green, they join Jesse Barfield (1986), George Bell (1987) & Jose Canseco (1998)... Broke his own club record for HR's by a left-handed hitter... Named to the Sporting News Silver Slugger team... Missed the final ten games of the season after fouling a ball off on September 22 and suffering a non displaced fracture of the right tibia... Had played every inning of every game in 1999 and had the third longest iron-man streak in club history at 235 consecutive games... Among AL leaders was second in extra-base hits, tied for third in HR and RBI, tied for ninth in doubles (39) and tenth in total bases... Hit HR #30 on August 8 in Texas to become the third player in franchise history to post three consecutive 30 HR seasons, joins Fred McGriff (1988-1990) and Joe Carter (1991-1993)... Homered on opening day in Minnesota, his third opening day home run which ties George Bell for most opening day HR's... April 30 at Seattle had the first of six multi-HR games on the season... May 3 at Seattle became the first player in club history to score five runs in a game, he also matched his career high of five RBI and hit two HR's... May 16 vs Boston hit a game ending three run HR vs. Kip Gross... June 16- 23 struggled through an 0-25 skid... Hit just .190 (20-105) in June - season average excluding June is .291... At the All-Star break had 77 RBI... Hit just .246 (30-122) with runners in scoring position prior to the All-Star break and .288 (21-73) after... Had 57 RBI in 62 games after the break... Batting average prior to the break was .244 (84-344) and after was .314 (72-229)... Hit in 12 straight from July 8 to 22... In July hit .273 with nine HR and 27 RBI... August 6 at Texas had second career 3-HR game, all solo's, two off Helling and one vs Zimmerman - both career three HR games have been in Texas... From August 6 to August 11 hit eight home runs in six games with 13 RBI... Established a club record for home runs in a month with 12 in August, the previous mark of 11 had been accomplished five times... In August also matched the club record for RBI in a month with 32 which was first set by Dave Winfield in August of 1992... Reached 100 RBI on August 10 in Minnesota after hitting two HR's... Tied a club record with four walks on September 18 vs Chicago... Had two four-hit games... Of the 44 home runs, 17 were at home, 27 on the road which was one short of the club record (George Bell 28 in 1987), 26 HR's were solo's, 11 with one on base and seven with two on base... Hit .309 (47-152) against left-handers with 12 HR's and 33 RBI and .259 (109-421) with 32 HR's and 101 RBI against right-handers.

CAREER NOTES: Is the franchise leader in slugging percentage (.557), multi-HR games (22) and tied for the lead in grand slams (7 with George Bell), is second in intentional walks (53), hit by pitch (61), is third in home runs (190), on-base percentage (.383) and strikeouts (728), is fourth in RBI (604), fifth in doubles (214), sixth in total bases (1,616), seventh in runs scored (493) and eighth in batting (.282)... Captured Sporting News Player of the Year honours in 2000... AL Hank Aaron Award winner in 2000... Captured consecutive Silver Slugger Awards in 1999 and 2000... Holds single season club records for doubles (57 in 2000), RBI (137 in 2000), walks (137 in 2000), total bases (378 in 2000), slugging percentage (.470) and home runs at home (30)... Holds the club mark for HR by a LH batter at 44 in 1999... Is the only Blue Jay to have two 40HR seasons... Only Blue Jay player in franchise history to post four consecutive 30 HR seasons and second with four 30 home run season (Joe Carter)... One of only two Blue Jays to hit three grand slams in a season (Fletcher in 2000)... Owns the third longest consecutive games playing streak in club history at 235 games over the 1998 & 1999 seasons... Is the only player in club history with more than one season of 130 RBI... Now ranks third in games played at first base at 600 trailing Willie Upshaw (950) and John Olerud (766)... Has now won four AL Player of the Week Awards in his career, two in 2000... Has a franchise high 22 multi-HR games, 20-2HR games and two 3HR... Has reached 100RBI for third straight season, club record is four consecutive seasons by Joe Carter from 1991 through 1994... Shares in ML record of four players to hit 20 home runs at the All-Star break in 2000 (Batista, Cruz and Mondesi)... One of seven Blue Jays in 2000 to hit 20 home runs to match the ML record for most 20HR team mates in a season (Baltimore- 1996)... Was one of Toronto's four players to hit 30HR's in 2000 (Batista, Cruz, Fullmer) — it marks just the second time in AL history this has been done (Anaheim- 2000)... Was the 29th player to clear the Tiger Stadium roof with a home run on July 6, 1996 against Omar Olivares and the first visiting player since George Brett in 1988... Tied Kent Hrbek's record for most HR in April by a rookie in the majors with eight in 1994... Was the 1992 USA Today's Baseball Weekly Minor League Player of the Year... One of seven Blue Jays to hit three home runs in a game, has done it twice — August 4, 1998 at Texas and August 6, 1999 at Texas... Is the third Blue Jays to ever HR in three consecutive at bats (George Bell and Cliff Johnson) and first to do so in the same game- August 4, 1998 at Texas... Holds the club record for HR's in September at 11 in 1998... Has seven 5-RBI games (April 11, 1994 at OAK; July 11, 1997 at BOS; July 17, 1997 at TEX; July 4, 1998 at TB; August 19, 1998 at SEA; May 3, 1999 at SEA; and May 28, 2000 at DET) and one 6-RBI game (June 7, 2000 at ATL).

CARLOS DELGADO

Year	Club & League	AVG	G	AB	R	H	TB	2B	3B	HR	RBI	SH-SF	HP	BB-IBB	SO	SB-CS	GIDP	SLG	OBP
1989	St. Catharines (NYP)	.180	31	89	9	16	21	5	0	0	11	0-1	0	23-1	39	0-0	4	.236	.345
1990	St. Catharines (NYP)	.283	67	226	29	64	95	13	0	6	39	1-4	5	35-2	65	2-7	2	.417	.382
1991	Myrtle Beach (SAL)	.286	132	441	72	126	202	18	2	18	70	1-3	8	75-2	97	9-10	7	.458	.397
1991	Syracuse (Int)	.000	1	3	0	0	0	0	0	0	0	0-0	0	0-0	0	0-0	0	.000	.000
1992	Dunedin (FSL)	.324	133	485	83	157	281	30	2	30	100	0-2	6	59-11	91	2-5	8	.579	.402
1993	Knoxville (Sou)	.303	140	468	91	142	245	28	0	25	102	0-5	6	102-18	98	10-3	11	.524	.430
1993	TORONTO (AL)	.000	2	1	0	0	0	0	0	0	0	0-0	0	1-0	0	0-0	0	.000	.500
1994	TORONTO (AL)	.215	43	130	17	28	57	2	0	9	24	0-1	3	25-4	46	1-1	5	.438	.352
1994	Syracuse (Int)	.319	85	307	52	98	166	11	0	19	58	0-2	3	42-8	58	1-0	3	.541	.404
1995	Syracuse (Int)	.318	91	333	59	106	203	23	4	22	74	0-4	5	45-7	78	0-4	8	.610	.403
1995	TORONTO (AL)	.165	37	91	7	15	27	3	0	3	11	0-2	0	6-0	26	0-0	1	.297	.212
1996	TORONTO (AL)	.270	138	488	68	132	239	28	2	25	92	0-8	9	58-2	139	0-0	13	.490	.353
1997	TORONTO (AL)	.262	153	519	79	136	274	42	3	30	91	0-4	8	64-9	133	0-3	6	.528	.350
1998	Dunedin (FSL)	.313	4	16	4	5	12	1	0	2	7	0-0	0	2-0	4	0-0	1	.750	.389
1998	Syracuse (Int)	.571	2	7	4	4	9	2	0	1	6	0-0	0	2-0	0	0-0	0	1.286	.667
1998	TORONTO (AL)	.292	142	530	94	155	314	43	1	38	115	0-6	11	73-13	139	3-0	8	.592	.385
1999	TORONTO (AL)	.272	152	573	113	156	327	39	0	44	134	0-7	15	86-7	141	1-1	11	.571	.377
2000	TORONTO (AL)	.344	162	569	115	196	378	57	1	41	137	0-4	15	123-18	104	0-1	12	.664	.470
Minor Totals		.302	686	2377	404	718	1234	131	8	123	467	2-21	33	385-49	532	24-30	44	.519	.403
MAJOR TOTALS		.282	829	2901	493	818	1616	214	7	190	604	0-32	61	436-53	728	5-6	56	.557	.383

ALL-STAR GAME RECORD

Year	Club & League	AVG	G	AB	R	H	TB	2B	3B	HR	RBI	SH-SF	HP	BB-IBB	SO	SB-CS	GIDP	SLG	OBP
2000	AL at ATL	1.000	1	1	0	1	2	1	0	0	0	0-0	0	0-0	0	0-0	0	2.000	1.000

HOME RUN BREAKDOWN

				MEN ON				ONE GAME									
Total	H	A	0	1	2	3		2	3	4	LO	XN	IP	PH	RHP	LHP
190	103	87	107	50	26	7		20	2	0	0	1	0	1	159	31

DELGADO — TRANSACTIONS

- Signed as a free agent by Blue Jays on October 9, 1988.
- On disabled list (right shoulder surgery) March 15-April 24, 1998; included rehabilitation assignment at Dunedin, April 17-21 and at Syracuse, April 21-23.

CAREER HIGHS — DELGADO, Carlos

SEASON:

Games	162 - 2000
Avg.	.344 - 2000
Runs	115 - 2000
Hits	196 - 2000
Doubles	57 - 2000
Home Runs	44 - 1999
RBI	137 - 2000
Walks	123 - 2000
Strikeouts	141 - 1999
Stolen Bases	3 - 1998
Longest Hitting Streak	22G - Jun. 4-29, 2000
Longest Hitless Streak	29AB - Jul. 9-16, 1998
Multi HR Games	6 - 1998, 1999

GAME:

ML Debut	Oct. 1, 1993 at BAL
Runs	5 - May 3, 1999 vs. SEA
Hits	5 - May 7, 1998 at SEA
Doubles	2 - 20 times, last Sep. 25, 2000 vs. TB
Home Runs	3 - Aug. 4, 1998 at TEX
	3 - Aug. 6, 1999 at TEX
RBI	6 - Jun. 7, 2000 at ATL
Stolen Bases	1 - 5 times, last Apr. 28, 1999 at ANA
Last ML Home Run	Sep. 21, 2000 vs. NYY

FIELDING

DELGADO, Carlos—C

Year	PCT	G	PO	A	E	TC	DP
1993	1.000	1	2	0	0	2	0
1994	1.000	1	1	0	0	1	0
1995	1.000	4	20	1	0	21	3
Total	1.000	6	23	1	0	24	3

DELGADO, Carlos—OF

Year	PCT	G	PO	A	E	TC	DP
1994	.966	41	55	2	2	59	0
1995	1.000	17	34	1	0	35	0
Total	.979	58	89	3	2	94	0

DELGADO, Carlos—1B

Year	PCT	G	PO	A	E	TC	DP
1995	1.000	4	20	1	0	21	3
1996	.983	27	221	13	4	238	21
1997	.988	119	962	67	12	1041	98
1998	.992	141	1165	87	10	1262	110
1999	.990	147	1306	84	14	1404	134
2000	.991	162	1416	82	13	1511	157
Total	.990	600	5090	334	53	5477	523

BLUE JAYS TOP 10 SEASONS

HR			RBI		
Bell	47	1987	DELGADO	137	2000
Canseco	46	1998	DELGADO	134	1999
DELGADO	44	1999	Bell	134	1987
Green	42	1999	Green	123	1999
DELGADO	41	2000	Carter	121	1993
Batista	41	2000	Carter	119	1992
Barfield	40	1986	Gruber	118	1990
DELGADO	38	1998	DELGADO	115	1998
Sprague	36	1996	Batista	114	2000
McGriff	36	1989	Molitor	111	1993

CARLOS DELGADO DETAILED HITTING

	2000 Avg	AB	H	HR	RBI	BB	SO	OBP	SLG	CAREER Avg	AB	H	HR	RBI	BB	SO	OBP	SLG
Total	.344	569	196	41	137	123	104	.470	.664	.282	2901	818	190	604	436	728	.383	.557
vs. Left	.319	188	60	6	36	29	37	.422	.537	.275	766	211	31	143	92	212	.365	.490
vs. Right	.357	381	136	35	101	94	67	.492	.727	.284	2135	607	159	461	344	516	.390	.581
Home	.360	283	102	30	75	59	42	.477	.777	.292	1448	423	103	305	228	368	.395	.595
Away	.329	286	94	11	62	64	62	.463	.552	.272	1453	395	87	299	208	360	.371	.519
April	.319	94	30	8	20	15	22	.430	.660	.292	432	126	33	107	67	116	.393	.572
May	.340	103	35	10	26	19	25	.439	.699	.285	579	165	28	96	75	162	.374	.527
June	.411	95	39	9	26	20	15	.517	.758	.276	478	132	34	101	75	132	.383	.561
July	.386	88	34	5	21	27	12	.538	.773	.279	452	126	32	100	78	120	.393	.586
August	.368	95	35	7	31	19	9	.487	.705	.311	485	151	37	129	64	93	.398	.629
September	.256	90	23	2	13	23	19	.424	.411	.252	468	118	26	71	76	102	.367	.483
October	.000	4	0	0	0	0	2	.000	.000	.000	7	0	0	0	1	3	.125	.000
Scoring Posn	.384	172	66	13	102	38	34	.495	.715	.294	837	246	59	435	150	199	.399	.578
Bases Loaded	.333	12	4	2	17	0	1	.267	.917	.295	78	23	7	79	8	16	.333	.628
DH	–	–	–	–	–	–	–	–	–	.264	512	135	26	87	63	136	.356	.480
PH	–	–	–	–	–	–	–	–	–	.140	43	6	1	2	1	7	.087	.190
vs. Ana	.400	45	18	4	16	8	9	.509	.778	.259	189	49	11	40	32	51	.383	.503
vs. Bal	.268	41	11	2	6	10	9	.412	.488	.232	224	52	10	34	32	55	.326	.442
vs. Bos	.326	46	15	3	10	8	6	.418	.587	.267	243	65	8	43	38	55	.360	.457
vs. CWS	.257	35	9	3	7	7	8	.395	.543	.277	177	49	10	34	33	46	.394	.508
vs. Cle	.381	42	16	3	14	12	9	.527	.762	.346	205	71	11	47	30	55	.436	.659
vs. Det	.357	42	15	3	12	9	10	.481	.595	.249	229	57	20	53	41	59	.369	.568
vs. KC	.317	41	13	2	7	2	4	.364	.585	.217	207	45	8	28	17	49	.296	.372
vs. Mil	–	–	–	–	–	–	–	–	–	.229	83	19	6	18	7	26	.297	.482
vs. Min	.385	26	10	4	8	10	5	.556	.962	.289	180	52	14	36	26	41	.376	.578
vs. NYY	.409	44	18	3	9	5	12	.481	.682	.265	189	50	8	24	25	60	.364	.439
vs. Oak	.300	30	9	1	2	9	7	.512	.500	.290	207	60	12	40	33	49	.412	.546
vs. Sea	.405	37	15	3	9	7	5	.511	.811	.376	194	73	21	62	34	41	.479	.809
vs. TB	.318	44	14	2	5	7	6	.412	.568	.248	133	33	7	25	18	29	.340	.466
vs. Tex	.289	38	11	1	11	7	3	.383	.500	.342	202	69	19	55	26	50	.419	.723
vs. Atl	.556	9	5	2	8	5	3	.733	1.333	.413	46	19	7	19	5	11	.491	.957
vs. Fla	.308	13	4	1	3	1	3	.357	.615	.283	46	13	3	9	7	15	.400	.565
vs. Mon	.474	19	9	2	6	8	1	.630	1.053	.344	61	21	7	17	16	11	.488	.803
vs. NYM	.250	8	2	1	2	6	1	.571	.750	.225	40	9	4	10	11	7	.389	.625
vs. Phi	.222	9	2	1	2	2	3	.417	.667	.261	46	12	4	10	5	18	.346	.652
Pre-All Star	.363	320	116	28	80	66	64	.476	.709	.285	1613	460	107	344	243	445	.386	.560
Post-All Star	.321	249	80	13	57	57	40	.462	.606	.278	1288	358	83	260	193	283	.380	.553

CARLOS DELGADO HITTING AT ML PARKS

Park	Avg	G	AB	R	H	2B	3B	HR	RBI	SB	CS	BB	SO	OBP	Slg
Camden Yards	.191	34	110	14	21	4	1	6	17	0	0	18	26	.298	.409
Fenway Park	.285	35	130	21	37	13	1	2	22	0	1	15	27	.351	.446
Edison Field	.267	31	101	14	27	5	0	6	22	1	0	13	35	.362	.495
Comiskey Park	.239	29	92	8	22	6	0	2	15	0	0	19	29	.379	.370
Jacobs Field	.280	25	93	13	26	10	0	2	18	0	0	14	26	.376	.452
Tiger Stadium	.204	25	93	17	19	4	0	9	20	0	0	15	22	.327	.538
Kauffman Stadium	.282	26	103	17	29	4	1	4	18	0	1	7	17	.348	.456
County Stadium	.125	9	32	2	4	0	0	2	4	0	0	1	8	.152	.313
Metrodome	.244	26	90	15	22	1	0	8	19	0	0	14	21	.340	.522
Yankee Stadium	.206	32	102	7	21	2	0	1	7	0	1	13	34	.302	.255
Oakland-Alameda	.301	27	93	14	28	8	0	5	22	0	0	16	20	.444	.548
Kingdome	.444	22	81	29	36	5	0	12	32	0	0	14	11	.529	.951
Arlington	.347	26	98	16	34	11	0	13	34	0	0	13	23	.426	.857
SkyDome	.292	421	1448	266	423	122	4	103	305	4	3	228	368	.395	.595
Olympic Stadium	.320	7	25	6	8	3	0	2	6	0	0	5	6	.469	.680
Shea Stadium	.182	6	22	1	4	2	0	1	4	0	0	4	2	.321	.409
Veterans Stadium	.217	6	23	5	5	2	0	2	5	0	0	3	9	.308	.565
Pro Player Stadium	.231	6	26	3	6	1	0	2	5	0	0	4	9	.355	.500
Turner Field	.524	6	21	6	11	3	0	3	11	0	0	5	4	.630	1.095
Tropicana Field	.175	16	63	7	11	2	0	0	2	0	0	8	18	.268	.206
Cashman Field	.444	2	9	1	4	0	0	1	4	0	0	1	2	.500	.778
SAFECO Field	.478	6	23	6	11	5	0	2	4	0	0	3	4	.556	.957
Comerica Park	.391	6	23	5	9	1	0	2	8	0	0	3	7	.462	.696

BLUE JAYS' RBI RECORDS BY POSITION

POSITION	PLAYER	RBI	YEAR
1B	Carlos Delgado	137	2000
2B	Roberto Alomar	93	1993
3B	Tony Batista	114	2000
SS	Tony Batista	79	1999
LF	George Bell	126	1987
CF	Lloyd Moseby	96	1987
RF	Shawn Green	123	1999
C	Darrin Fletcher	80	1999
DH	Brad Fullmer	104	2000

Players

CARLOS DELGADO — MILESTONES

	DATE	OPP.	H/A	PITCHER	DESCRIPTION
HITS					
1	April 4, 1994	TOR vs CWS	H	Jack McDowell	Single
500	May 13, 1999	TOR vs KC	A	Jose Rosado	Single
HR					
1	April 4, 1994	TOR vs CWS	H	Dennis Cook	2R
50	June 17, 1997	TOR vs ATL	H	Mike Bielecki	1R
100	Sept. 17, 1998	TOR vs DET	A	Bryce Florie	2R
RBI					
1	April 4, 1994	TOR vs CWS	H	Dennis Cook	HR
500	May23, 2000	TOR vs BOS	A	Pedron Martinez	SF
SB					
1	May 30, 1994	TOR vs OAK	H	Taylor Catcher-Steinbach	2nd
GM					
1	Oct. 1, 1993	TOR vs BAL	A	—	Defensively-C
500	Sept. 11, 1998	TOR vs NYY	A	—	1-4, HR, Start 1B
SLAMS (7)					
1	April 25, 1997	TOR vs SEA	H	Dennis Martinez	1st
2	June 6, 1997	TOR vs OAK	H	Mike Oquist	1st
3	July 24, 1997	TOR vs MIL	H	Jose Mercedes	1st
4	May 7, 1998	TOR vs SEA	A	Jamie Moyer	3rd
5	May 12, 1998	TOR vs SEA	H	Greg McCarthy	7th
6	June 7, 2000	TOR vs ATL	A	Kevin Millwood	5th
7	Sept. 17, 2000	TOR vs CWS	A	Jesus Pena	6th
MULTI HR (22)					
2	April 11, 1994	TOR vs OAK	A	Witt-3R, Taylor-2R	1st, 8th
2	July 6, 1996	TOR vs DET	A	Olivares-1R, Keagle-3R	3rd, 7th
2	July 17, 1997	TOR vs TEX	A	Burkett-1R, Hernandez-3R	1st, 7th
2	Aug. 8, 1997	TOR vs DET	H	Blair-2R, Myers-2R	3rd, 8th
2	Aug. 27, 1997	TOR vs CWS	H	Drabek-3R, Cruz-1R	1st, 7th
2	June 1, 1998	TOR vs BOS	A	Wakefield-3R, Corsi-1R	3rd, 8th
2	July 4, 1998	TOR vs TB	H	Ruebel-3R, Hernandez-1R	6th, 8th
3	Aug. 4, 1998	TOR vs TEX	A	Stottlemyre-2R, Gunderson-1R, Patterson-1R	5th, 7th, 8th
2	Aug. 19, 1998	TOR vs SEA	A	Cloude-2R, Ayala-2R	3rd, 5th
2	Aug. 21, 1998	TOR vs ANA	A	Juden-1R, 1R	2nd, 6th
2	Sept. 17, 1998	TOR vs DET	A	Florie-2R, 1R	1st, 6th
2	April 30, 1999	TOR vs SEA	A	Fassero-1R, Halama-1R	3rd, 8th
2	May 3, 1999	TOR vs SEA	A	Garcia-1R, Mesa-1R	2nd, 9th
2	July 19, 1999	TOR vs ATL	H	Chen-1R, Seanez-1R	3rd, 8th
3	Aug. 6, 1999	TOR vs TEX	A	Helling-1R, 1R Zimmerman-1R	2nd, 7th 8th
2	Aug. 10, 1999	TOR vs MIN	A	Radke-1R, Miller-1R	3rd, 9th
2	Sept. 8, 1999	TOR vs SEA	A	Moyer-1R, Mesa-2R	7th, 9th
2	April 16, 2000	TOR vs SEA	H	Garcia-2R, 1R	1st, 3rd
2	May 28, 2000	TOR vs DET	A	Blair-2R, McDill-3R	5th, 8th
2	June 7, 2000	TOR vs ATL	A	Millwood-GS, Renlinger-2R	5th, 9th
2	July 20, 2000	TOR vs TB	H	Trachsel-1R, 1R	2nd, 4th
2	Aug. 23, 2000	TOR vs KC	H	Wilson-1R, Larkin-1R	7th, 8th

REACHING BASE 300 TIMES

JOHN OLERUD and **CARLOS DELGADO** are the only Blue Jays to have reached base 300 times during a season (hits, walks and hit by pitch)... **OLERUD** reached base 321 times during the 1993 season when he notched 200 hits, 114 base on balls and seven hit by pitch... **DELGADO** reached base 334 times in the 2000 season collecting 196 hits, 123 base on balls and 15 hit by pitch... Since 1901 only 57 players have reached base 300 or more times during a season... 32 players in the American League have accomplished the feat 71 times, while 25 players in the National League have done so 44 times... Below is a list of players since 1977 who have reached base 300 or more times in a season.

YEAR	PLAYER	TOTAL	YEAR	PLAYER	TOTAL
1977	Rod Carew	311	1997	Edgar Martinez	309
1979	Pete Rose	305		Craig Biggio	309
1980	Rickey Henderson	301		Barry Bonds	308
1983	Wade Boggs	303		Jeff Bagwell	305
1985	Wade Boggs	340		Larry Walker	300
1986	Wade Boggs	312	1998	Mark McGwire	320
1987	Wade Boggs	307		Barry Bonds	305
	Tony Gwynn	303	1999	Jeff Bagwell	331
1988	Wade Boggs	342		Derek Jeter	322
1989	Wade Boggs	319		Chipper Jones	309
1991	Frank Thomas	317		John Olerud	309
1992	Frank Thomas	312		Bernie Williams	303
1993	Lenny Dykstra	325	2000	**Carlos Delgado**	**334**
	John Olerud	**321**		Todd Helton	323
	Tony Phillips	313		Jason Giambi	316
	Barry Bonds	309		Frank Thomas	308
1995	Edgar Martinez	306		Jeff Bagwell	305
1996	Chuck Knoblauch	314		Darrin Erstad	305
	Mo Vaughn	316			
	Jeff Bagwell	324			

Jason
DICKSON

PITCHER

34

BIRTHDATE	March 30, 1973
OPENING DAY AGE	28
BIRTHPLACE	London, ON
RESIDENCE	Chandler, AZ
BATS/THROWS	L/R
HEIGHT/WEIGHT	6-0/195
CONTRACT STATUS	signed thru 2001
M.L. SERVICE	4.029

PERSONAL: Jason Royce Dickson... Married, wife's name is Dana... Graduated from James M. Hill High School in 1991... Attended Northeastern Oklahoma A & M... Signed by Angels scout Steve Bowden.

LAST SEASON: Returned to action with the Angels after missing entire 1999 season due to surgery to repair torn labrum in right shoulder... Posted 2-2 record with 6.11 ERA (28 IP - 19 ER) in six starts... Allowed 39 hits and seven walks while striking out 18... Won his first start of the season 7-3 over Boston on April 7... Other win came on April at Toronto in 16-10 win... Pitched a season high seven innings on April 23 in a 1-0 loss in Tampa Bay and recorded a season best six strikeouts... Made five starts before being placed on 15-day disabled list from April 29 to May 14 with a strained left hip flexor... Made one start before returning to the 15-day DL on May 20 (retroactive to May 15) with tendinitis of left hip flexor and a stiff right shoulder... Made two rehabilitation starts for Edmonton (AAA) on June 11 and June 16, was 0-2 with 10.13 ERA (9ER, 8.0IP)... Did not pitch following June 16 and was transferred to the 60-day disabled list on August 16... On October 3 was designated for assignment and elected free agency on October 6.

PROFESSIONAL CAREER: 1994: Began his professional career with Boise of the Northwest League (A)... Was 3-1 with a 3.86 ERA in nine games, seven starts... Made one post-season start allowing one run over 5.0 innings for the Northwest League Champion Boise Hawks... **1995:** Posted a 14-6 record with a 2.86 ERA in 25 starts for Cedar Rapids of the Midwest League (A)... Led the league with nine complete games, was tied for second in wins, third in innings pitched (173.0), fifth in strikeouts (134), tied for fifth in shut-outs (1) and sixth in ERA (2.86)... Led Kernels' staff in wins, ERA, complete games, innings pitched and strikeouts (134)... Twice named Midwest League "Pitcher of the Week," June 18-25 and July 24-30... Appeared in one post-season game for Kernels, posting 1-0 record with 2.25 ERA (8 IP - 2 ER) while striking out seven... **1996:** Opened the season with Midland (AA) before moving up to Vancouver (AAA) and then the Angels... Made eight starts for Midland and posted a 5-2 record with three complete games and an ERA of 3.58... In 55.1 innings pitched he walked ten and struck out 40... Opened the season with a shutout in his first start on April 6 vs San Antonio (2nd game, 7.0IP, 5H)... Was promoted to Vancouver on May 16 where he made 18 starts and was 7-11 with seven complete games and an ERA of 3.80... Led the Pacific Coast League in complete games, was seventh in ERA and tied for fourth in losses... Won his triple-A debut with a complete game effort on May 17 vs Alburquerque... Contract was purchased by the Angels on August 21... Made seven starts and was 1-4 with a 4.57 ERA... Made his ML debut on August 21 and won 7-1 in Yankee Stadium (6.1IP, 1ER)... First ML hitter faced was Derek Jeter who homered... Was the first Angel to win his major league debut as starter since Scott Lewis on September 25, 1990 vs. Texas... **1997:** Completed rookie season with Anaheim, posting a 13-9 record with two complete games, one shutout and a 4.29 ERA (203.2 IP - 97 ER) in 33 appearances, 32 starts... Led the club in innings pitched (203.2) and tied with Chuck Finley for the team lead in wins and shutouts... Was the third rookie in Angels' history to lead club in wins joining Ricky Clark with 12 in 1967 and Ken McBride with 12 in

1961... On Angels' All-Time Rookie season list, ranked fourth in wins and tied for fourth in starts... Wins total was one shy of club best set by Frank Tanana (1974), Marcelino Lopez (1965) and Dean Chance (1962)... Finished third in AL Rookie of the Year balloting with 27 points (six 2nd place and nine 3rd place votes), behind Boston's Nomar Garciaparra (140 pts.) and Seattle-Toronto's Jose Cruz, Jr. (61 pts.)... Named to Topps (RHP), The Sporting News (AL Rookie Pitcher of the Year) and Baseball Digest All-Rookie teams... Among AL leaders, ranked tied for ninth in shutouts, ninth in hits allowed (236) and tied for third in home runs allowed (32)... Also ranked tied for ninth in GDPs induced (20), second in stolen base percentage allowed (41.7%; 5/12), fifth in SBs attempted per baserunner (12/223) and sixth in batting average allowed with runners in scoring position (.234)... Named as club's representative in the All-Star Game at Cleveland on July 8 but did not pitch in the AL victory... Was the Angels' first rookie selected to All-Star game since Wally Joyner who was voted in 1986... Also became first Angels' rookie pitcher named to All-Star squad since Mark Clear in 1979... Other Angels rookies to be selected to Major League Baseball All-Star game in club history are infielder Dave Chalk in 1974 and right-handed pitcher Ken McBride in 1961... Registered first career shut-out in first start of season, April 3 vs. Boston... Complete game shutout was first by Angel against Boston since June 4, 1991 in Anaheim (Chuck Finley; 3-0 score)... Other complete game came April 20 at Kansas City in an 11-1 win in which he posted his career low hit game at three... Won a season best four decisions over five starts to open the season from April 3-25, posted a 2.78 ERA... Struckout a career high eight batters on two occasions, June 15 vs. San Francisco (7 IP) and Sept. 13 vs. Kansas City (6.2 IP)... Made first relief appearance of major league career, Aug. 19 vs. New York, earning victory (6.1 IP, 4 H, 4 BB, 1 SO)... Recipient of Fred Haney Memorial Award for outstanding rookie during 1997 spring training... **1998:** Completed second season with Angels posting a 10-10 record and a 6.05 ERA in 27 games, 18 starts)... Allowed 147 hits, 17 of which were home runs while he walked 41 and struck out 61... Career-high 10 losses led all Angels' staff... First win came on April 28 at Baltimore to snap a seven-game losing streak and was his first win in 10 starts, previous win was August 23, 1997 vs. Boston... Won career-best seven straight decisions, May 16 to June 21, during which time he pitched in eight games, five starts, and posted a 3.83 ERA... Was the fifth longest streak in the AL... Was optioned to triple-A Vancouver on August 11 when Angels acquired Mike Fetters... Made four starts and was 2-1 with a 1.78 ERA... Recalled on September 1... Finished the season posting a 7-10 record in 18 starts with a 7.11 ERA... In relief was 3-0 with a 0.87 ERA in nine games and allowed 10 hits over 20.2 innings without a home run... **1999:** Missed entire season due to surgery to repair torn labrum in right shoulder... Surgery was performed March 25 by Angels' Medical Director, Dr. Lewis Yocum, at UCI Medical Center in Orange, CA... Placed on 15-day disabled list, April 4, and transferred to 60-day DL on July 7.

CAREER NOTES: Is 4-0 with 0.67 ERA (27 IP, 14 H, 2 R, 2 ER, 6 BB, 11 SO, 1 HB) in 10 career relief appearances.

JASON DICKSON

Year	Club & League	W-L	ERA	G	GS	CG	ShO	SV	IP	H	R	ER	HR	HB	BB-IBB	SO	WP	BK	OBA
1994	Boise (NWST)	3-1	3.86	9	7	0	0	1	44.1	40	22	19	3	2	18-1	37	3	2	.237
1995	Cedar Rapds (Mid)	14-6	2.86	25	25	9	1	0	173.0	151	71	55	12	8	45-0	134	7	2	.233
1996	Midland (Tex)	5-2	3.58	8	8	3	1	0	55.1	55	27	22	3	0	10-0	40	3	0	.255
1996	Vancouver (PCL)	7-11	3.80	18	18	7	0	0	130.1	134	73	55	9	5	40-1	70	4	4	.267
1996	CALIFORNIA (AL)	1-4	4.57	7	7	0	0	0	43.1	52	22	22	6	1	18-1	20	1	1	.306
1997	ANAHEIM (AL)	13-9	4.29	33	32	2	1	0	203.2	236	111	97	32	7	56-3	115	4	1	.289
1998	ANAHEIM (AL)	10-10	6.05	27	18	0	0	0	122.0	147	89	82	17	6	41-1	61	6	0	.303
1998	Vancouver (PCL)	2-1	1.78	4	4	0	0	0	25.1	26	5	5	2	1	4-0	18	0	1	.280
1999							Injured—DID NOT PLAY												
2000	ANAHEIM (AL)	2-2	6.11	6	6	0	0	0	28.0	39	20	19	5	1	7-0	18	0	0	.336
2000	Edmonton (PCL)	0-2	10.13	2	2	0	0	0	8.0	13	9	9	1	0	4-0	4	1	0	.382
Minor Totals		31-23	3.40	66	64	19	2	1	436.1	419	207	165	30	16	121-2	303	18	9	.252
MAJOR TOTALS		26-25	4.99	73	63	2	1	0	397.0	474	242	220	60	15	122-5	214	11	2	.299

DICKSON — TRANSACTIONS

- Selected by the California Angels in 6th round of the June 1994 First Year Player Draft.
- On disabled list (torn labrum right shoulder) March 25-October 13, 1999.
- On disabled list (strained left hip flexor) April 30-May 14, 2000.
- On disabled list (strained left hip flexor/ soreness right shoulder) May 15 through remainder of season, 2000.
- Signed by the Toronto Blue Jays on November 13, 2000.

CAREER HIGHS — DICKSON, Jason

SEASON:

Wins	13 - 1997
Losses	10 - 1998
Saves	None
ERA	4.29 - 1997
Games	33 - 1997
Starts	32 - 1997
Complete Games	2 - 1997
Shutouts	1 - 1997
Innings Pitched	203.2 - 1997
Walks	56 - 1997
Strikeouts	115 - 1997
Longest Win Streak	7 - May 16-June 21, 1998
Longest Losing Streak	4 - Aug. 26-Sep. 9, 1996
	4 - Aug. 28-Sep. 25, 1997
	4 - Jul. 17-Aug. 8, 1998
Scoreless Innings Streak	16.2 - May 24-June 11, 1998

GAME:

ML Debut	Aug. 21, 1996 at NYY
Innings Pitched:	
Starter	9.0 - Apr. 3, 1997 vs. BOS
	9.0 - Apr. 20, 1997 at KC
Reliever	6.1 - Aug. 19, 1997 vs. NYY
Walks:	
Starter	5 - Sep. 25, 1997 vs. TEX
	5 - Apr. 5, 1998 vs. CLE
	5 - Jul. 17, 1998 vs. BAL
Reliever	4 - Aug. 19, 1997 vs. NYY
Strikeouts:	
Starter	8 - Jun. 15, 1997 vs. SF
	8 - Sep. 13, 1997 vs. KC
Reliever	3 - May 31, 1998 at MIN
Hits Allowed	12 - Apr. 8, 1997 vs. NYY
Runs Allowed	8 - Jul. 31, 1997 vs. CWS
	8 - Aug. 28, 1997 at SD
	8 - Jul. 28, 1998 vs. NYY
	8 - Aug. 2, 1998 vs. BOS
ER Allowed	8 - Jul. 31, 1997 vs. CWS
HR Allowed	3 - 5 times, last Apr. 18, 2000 at TOR
Low Hit CG	3 - Apr. 20, 1997 at KC
Last Win	Apr. 18, 2000 at TOR
Last Save	None
Last CG	Apr. 20, 1997 at KC
Last ShO	Apr. 3, 1997 vs. BOS
Last Start	May 14, 2000 vs. TEX
Last Relief App.	Sep. 24, 1998 at OAK

FIELDING

DICKSON, Jason—P

Year	PCT	G	PO	A	E	TC	DP
1996	.889	7	3	5	1	9	0
1997	.933	33	8	20	2	30	1
1998	.950	27	9	10	1	20	0
2000	1.000	6	3	2	0	5	0
Total	.938	73	23	37	4	64	1

JASON DICKSON DETAILED PITCHING

| | 2000 | | | | | | | | CAREER | | | | | | | |
	ERA	W-L-Sv	G	IP	H	ER	BB	SO	ERA	W-L-Sv	G	IP	H	ER	BB	SO
Total	6.11	2-2-0	6	28.0	39	19	7	18	4.99	26-25-0	73	397.0	474	220	122	214
ST	6.11	2-2-0	6	28.0	39	19	7	18	5.30	22-25-0	63	370.0	460	218	116	203
REL	–	–	–	–	–	–	–	–	0.67	4-0-0	10	27.0	14	2	6	11
Home	8.62	1-1-0	4	15.2	26	15	6	7	5.67	12-16-0	40	211.0	266	133	73	120
Away	2.92	1-1-0	2	12.1	13	4	1	11	4.21	14-9-0	33	186.0	208	87	49	94
April	4.72	2-2-0	5	26.2	33	14	4	16	4.81	7-6-0	15	86.0	100	46	22	50
May	33.75	0-0-0	1	1.1	6	5	3	2	5.31	5-2-0	14	62.2	66	37	25	29
June	–	–	–	–	–	–	–	–	3.68	6-3-0	10	66.0	81	27	11	37
July	–	–	–	–	–	–	–	–	5.43	3-3-0	11	64.2	88	39	21	38
August	–	–	–	–	–	–	–	–	6.71	4-6-0	10	55.0	75	41	23	28
September	–	–	–	–	–	–	–	–	4.31	1-5-0	13	62.2	64	30	20	32
vs. Bal	–	–	–	–	–	–	–	–	2.20	3-1-0	5	28.2	22	7	13	10
vs. Bos	2.70	1-0-0	1	6.2	4	2	1	2	3.47	3-3-0	7	46.2	49	18	10	30
vs. CWS	–	–	–	–	–	–	–	–	14.04	0-3-0	5	16.2	31	26	9	6
vs. Cle	–	–	–	–	–	–	–	–	7.56	0-2-0	3	16.2	18	14	10	7
vs. Det	–	–	–	–	–	–	–	–	5.79	2-0-0	3	18.2	17	12	6	5
vs. KC	–	–	–	–	–	–	–	–	2.20	2-1-0	4	28.2	21	7	4	17
vs. Mil	–	–	–	–	–	–	–	–	5.40	1-0-0	2	11.2	16	7	3	3
vs. Min	–	–	–	–	–	–	–	–	2.86	2-1-0	5	28.1	26	9	7	20
vs. NYY	–	–	–	–	–	–	–	–	5.91	3-2-0	6	32.0	48	21	15	17
vs. Oak	–	–	–	–	–	–	–	–	3.91	3-1-0	5	23.0	25	10	4	16
vs. Sea	–	–	–	–	–	–	–	–	5.02	2-1-0	5	28.2	33	16	4	13
vs. TB	6.48	0-2-0	2	8.1	11	6	3	6	7.82	0-3-0	4	12.2	21	11	4	8
vs. Tex	33.75	0-0-0	1	1.1	6	5	3	2	4.93	2-2-0	6	34.2	45	19	15	21
vs. Tor	4.63	1-0-0	2	11.2	18	6	0	8	3.96	1-0-0	5	25.0	33	11	4	14
vs. Ari	–	–	–	–	–	–	–	–	6.75	1-0-0	1	6.2	9	5	0	3
vs. Col	–	–	–	–	–	–	–	–	4.22	1-1-0	2	10.2	12	5	5	4
vs. LA	–	–	–	–	–	–	–	–	1.50	0-0-0	1	6.0	11	1	0	5
vs. SD	–	–	–	–	–	–	–	–	10.61	0-2-0	2	9.1	18	11	5	6
vs. SF	–	–	–	–	–	–	–	–	7.30	0-2-0	2	12.1	19	10	4	9
Pre-All Star	6.11	2-2-0	6	28.0	39	19	7	18	4.70	18-12-0	41	226.0	267	118	60	122
Post-All Star	–	–	–	–	–	–	–	–	5.37	8-13-0	32	171.0	207	102	62	92

JASON DICKSON PITCHING AT ML PARKS

Park	ERA	W-L-Sv	SvO	G	GS	IP	H	R	ER	HR	BB	SO
Camden Yards	1.80	2-0-0	0	3	2	15.0	14	3	3	1	5	5
Fenway Park	4.50	0-1-0	0	2	2	10.0	16	9	5	2	3	7
Edison Field	5.67	12-16-0	0	40	35	211.0	266	143	133	34	73	120
Comiskey Park	9.82	0-2-0	0	3	2	11.0	17	12	12	1	4	3
Jacobs Field	5.84	0-1-0	0	2	2	12.1	11	9	8	2	5	4
Tiger Stadium	6.57	1-0-0	0	2	2	12.1	13	9	9	3	4	3
Kauffman Stadium	2.45	2-1-0	0	3	3	22.0	17	7	6	2	3	9
County Stadium	4.26	0-0-0	0	1	1	6.1	9	3	3	0	1	1
Metrodome	1.80	2-0-0	0	3	2	20.0	17	5	4	0	3	12
Yankee Stadium	1.35	2-0-0	0	2	2	13.1	15	2	2	1	5	8
Oakland-Alameda	2.16	2-0-0	0	2	2	8.1	6	2	2	2	2	9
Kingdome	6.00	1-1-0	0	2	2	12.0	18	9	8	5	1	7
Arlington	2.35	0-0-0	0	1	1	7.2	7	2	2	0	4	3
SkyDome	5.40	1-0-0	0	2	2	11.2	16	7	7	4	3	8
Qualcomm Park	10.61	0-2-0	0	2	2	9.1	18	14	11	1	5	6
BankOne Ballpark	6.75	1-0-0	0	1	1	6.2	9	5	5	2	0	3
Tropicana Field	0.00	0-1-0	0	2	1	8.0	5	1	0	0	1	6

Kelvim
ESCOBAR
PITCHER

47

BIRTHDATE .... April 11, 1976
OPENING DAY AGE 24
BIRTHPLACE .... La Guaria, VZ
RESIDENCE .... Caracas, VZ
BATS/THROWS .... R/R
HEIGHT/WEIGHT 6-1/210
CONTRACT STATUS .... signed thru 2001
M.L. SERVICE 3.040

PERSONAL: Kelvim Jose Escobar (Bolivar)... Name pronounced ES-KO-BAR... One child, Kelvim Jose (9/11/00)... Signed as a free agent by Blue Jays Epy Guerrero.

LAST SEASON: Was 10-15 with two saves and an ERA of 5.35 in 43 games, 24 starts... The 15 losses were a team high and tied for second most in the AL... Split the season between the starting rotation and the bullpen... First 25 appearances were all starts, as a starter was 7-13 with a 5.42 ERA... Appeared in relief on August 15 breaking a stretch of 30 consecutive starts dating back to August 28, 1999... In relief was 3-2 with two saves and a 4.94 ERA in 19 games... Lost his first two starts of the season allowing eight runs in 8.2 innings and then rebounded with two straight wins allowing three runs in 17.0 innings... Threw first complete game of the season on April 22 for a 8-2 win over the Yankees... Finished April 2-3 with a 3.98 ERA... In May was 2-3 with a 5.82 ERA... Won back-to-back starts on May 8 vs Baltimore and May 13 at Tampa Bay to improve to 4-4... Allowed first inning runs in five consecutive starts from May 24 to June 16, in those five innings he allowed 14 runs... Tossed his second complete game and struck out a season high ten batters on June 4 in Florida against the Marlins for a 7-2 win, both runs allowed were in the first inning... On June 10 vs Montreal allowed a career high seven earned runs, four in the first inning, in an 11-2 loss... Ended the first inning run streak by tossing his first career shutout on June 21 vs Detroit in a 6-0 win (9.0IP, 4H, 3BB, 6K, 1WP) - was his third complete game of the season, and fourth career... June 27 at Tampa Bay matched his season and career high allowing seven earned runs over 3.1 innings in an 11-1 loss... At the All-Star break was 6-9 with a 5.26 ERA in 18 starts... Won on July 19 vs Tampa Bay before losing his next four starts from July 25 to August 11 - in those four starts allowed 22 earned runs in 24.0 innings on 23 hits and 16 walks... Then moved to the bullpen and made his first appearance on August 15 vs Anaheim... Won consecutive relief appearances, posted win #8 on August 22 vs KC and win #9 on Aug 23 vs KC... Recorded saves on Sept 10 vs Detroit and September 14 at New York... Twice was tagged for four runs in relief - excluding those two outings, relief ERA was 2.52... Did not allow an earned run in 12 of 19 relief appearances... Posted three holds and stranded four of nine inherited runners... Retired 13 of 19 first batters faced in relief... Had three starts in which he walked seven batters to set his career high... Had decisions in 20 of 24 starts, 7-13... Pitched at least 7.0 innings in nine of 24 starts and 6.0 innings in 17 starts... Had 10 quality starts... At home was 7-7 with a save and a 4.32 ERA and on the road was 3-8 with a save and a 6.59 ERA.

PROFESSIONAL CAREER: 1993: Made professional debut with Blue Jays Santo Domingo team in Dominican Summer League... Was 2-1 with a 4.13 ERA and 31 strikeouts in 33.0 innings... **1994:** Recipient of R. Howard Webster Award as team MVP... Tied for tenth in Gulf Coast League in ERA at 2.35... Ranked fourth among starters in strikeouts per nine innings (9.00)... Led league pitchers with 12 putouts... In five July games, four starts, was 3-0 with a 1.50 ERA... **1995:** Began the year in the Dominican Summer League before joining Medicine Hat at the start of the Pioneer League season... Was fourth in the strikeouts (75), tied for fourth in complete games (1), tied for fifth in games started (14) and tied for the league lead in shutouts (1)... Struck out an average of 9.74 batters every nine innings, ranking second among league starters... Struck out a season-high 11 batters on July 2 in Lethbridge (6IP, 1H, 0R)... Threw a No-Hitter on July 20th (G1), a 2-0 win against Ogden (4BB, 7SO)... Was 2-1 with a 2.64 ERA through July 7... Started two Pioneer League playoff games (0-2, 1.50 ERA, 12IP, 11H, 2ER, 7BB, 15SO)... **1996:** Combined to post a 12-9 record with a 3.56 ERA between Dunedin (A) and Knoxville (AA) with 157 strikeouts in 164.1 innings... The 157 strikeouts tied for tops in the organization with Joe Young... Opened the season with Dunedin posting a 9-5 record with a 2.69 ERA in 18 starts... Earned organizational Pitcher of the Month award in May going 5-1, with a 2.72 ERA... Struckout 14 batters in a two-hit complete game on June 4 vs St. Petersburg in a 6-1 victory... In June recorded 41 strikeouts in 33.0 innings... Selected to the Florida State League All-Star team... Named second best prospect in the FSL by Baseball America... Second in FSL with 9.22 strikeouts per 9.0 innings... Promoted to AA Knoxville on July 11... Started ten games for the Smokies, 3-4, 5.33 ERA... At home was 2-1 with a 4.24 ERA... Struckout 44 in 54.0 innings... Selected to the Howe Sportsdata 1996 All-Teen Team... Selected as fourth best prospect in the organization by Baseball America... In winter ball was 5-0 with a 0.92 ERA for Lara in Venezuela... **1997:** Made ML debut posting a 3-2 record with a 2.90 ERA and 14 saves to lead all AL rookies... The 14 saves are the second most ever by a Blue Jays rookie- 17 by Darren Hall in 1994... Opened the season on the disabled list after arthroscopic surgery in March to remove loose bodies in his right elbow... First pitched in May with Dunedin (A) on a medical rehab assignment from the Knoxville Smokies (AA), was 0-1 in three games, two starts with a 3.75 ERA... Was recalled to Knoxville and activated from the disabled list on June 28... Started in five games (2-1, 3.70) before joining Toronto on June 28... Won ML debut on June 29 at Baltimore

allowing one run over 4.1 innings in relief of Guzman (2H, 1R/ER, 3BB, 5K)... First batter faced was Surhoff who walked... First strikeout was Brady Anderson... Prior to joining Toronto had made just three career appearances in relief in the minors, 69 games, 66 starts- appeared in relief once in 1993 with Santo Domingo, in 1994 with the Gulf Coast Blue Jays and with Dunedin on medical rehab earlier in the season... Was 2-0 in two games after pitching one hit ball over four shutout innings in relief against the New York Yankees on July 4... July 13 in Boston recorded first major league save in a 3-2 win (0.2IP)... Then recorded saves in his next seven games... Eight consecutive saves was two short of the club record ten held by Duane Ward (1991) and Darren Hall (1994)... First blown save came in his 11th opportunity on August 24 at KC in a 13 inning 11-8 win... Finished the season 14-17 in save opportunities... Did not enter a game with a man on base until his 26th appearance on September 25- stranded one of two, other scored on an error... Retired 21of 27 first batters faced... **1998:** Was 7-3 with a 3.73 ERA in 22 games, ten starts... Started the season in the bullpen... Allowed runs in five of his first six games and was placed on the disabled list on April 16 with right elbow inflammation, was 0-1 with a 18.00ERA (12ER, 6.0IP)... Joined Syracuse on a rehab assignment, was 0-0 with a save in two games (2.0IP, -ER)... Recalled and activated from the DL on May 6... Pitched in six May games and was 1-0 with a 5.79 ERA... Earned first win of the season on May 6 at Anaheim with 1.1 scoreless innings... Optioned to Syracuse on May 31... At Syracuse made one relief appearance and then joined the starting rotation making ten starts... In the ten starts was 2-2 with a 3.95 ERA and struck out 62 batters in 57.0 innings... Was recalled to Toronto on August 1 and inserted into the starting rotation... Received a no-decision in his first ML start on August 5 at Texas (2ER/7.0IP)... Did not allow more than two earned runs in his first six ML starts... First win as a starter was August 17 in a 4-2 win at Oakland... Struckout a career high 11 on August 22 in Anaheim but lost 5-1 (7.0IP, 2ER)... Won four consecutive starts from August 27 to September 20... Was two outs away from a complete game shutout on Sept. 2 in Kansas City, left with two on for Quantrill who preserved the 5-0 win... During that start struckout five consecutive batters during the fourth and fifth innings... As a starter was 6-2 with a 2.35 ERA and held opponents to a .210 average... In relief was 1-1 with a 12.66ERA, stranded six of nine inherited runners and retired nine of 12 first batters faced... Had five holds and was 0-1 in save situations... **1999:** Posted a career high 14 wins against 11 losses in 33 games, 30 starts with a 5.69 ERA... The 14 wins were second on the club to David Wells 17... Opened the season 2-0 in April despite posting a 5.52 ERA in five starts... On April 30 at Seattle had a no-decision despite allowing a career high seven earned runs and three home runs... In May was 2-2 with a 6.21 ERA after posting one quality start in five outings... In June was 3-3 with a 4.89 ERA... In four starts from June 6 to 22 was 3-1 with a 2.33 ERA (7ER, 27.0IP)... Made what was then his shortest career start of 2.0 innings on June 27 at Tampa Bay when he matched his career high of seven ER... His shortest career start would come on August 4 at Yankees Stadium, lost 8-3 and allowed five earned runs in 1.2 innings pitched... Tossed one complete game on July 30 at Detroit when he won 8-2 and threw a season high 132 pitches... Made three appearances in relief in August and was 0-0 with one earned run in 6.0 innings... Had made 34 consecutive starts since August 1998... Returned to the rotation to begin September and responded with a 4-2 record and an ERA of 4.64 which was the lowest of any month... Started on three days rest on September 5 and lost in KC (4.0IP, 4ER)... Left September 12 start at Detroit after allowing one run over 5.0 innings but suffered a cracked nail on the index finger of his right hand... Won his final two starts of the season.

CAREER NOTES: Has three ten strikeout games... In save situations is 16-21... Has pitched in 125 games in his career with Toronto, has made 64 starts and 61 appearances in relief.

KELVIM ESCOBAR

Year	Club & League	W-L	ERA	G	GS	CG	ShO	SV	IP	H	R	ER	HR	HB	BB-IBB	SO	WP	BK	OBA
1993	Santo Domingo (DSL)	2-1	4.13	8	7	0	0	0	32.2	34	17	15	2	1	25-0	31	4	0	.270
1994	Blue Jays (Gulf)	4-4	2.35	11	10	1	0	0	65.0	56	23	17	1	2	18-0	64	5	3	.237
1995	Santo Domingo (DSL)	0-1	1.72	3	2	0	0	0	16.0	14	3	3	0	0	5-0	20	0	0	.226
1995	Medicine Hat (Pio)	3-3	5.71	14	14	1	1	0	69.1	66	47	44	6	6	33-0	75	4	4	.253
1996	Dunedin (FSL)	9-5	2.69	18	18	1	0	0	110.1	101	44	33	5	3	33-0	113	6	2	.240
1996	Knoxville (Sou)	3-4	5.33	10	10	0	0	0	54.0	61	36	32	7	1	24-0	44	7	1	.288
1997	Dunedin (FSL)	0-1	3.75	3	2	0	0	0	12.0	16	9	5	0	1	3-0	16	1	0	.327
1997	Knoxville (Sou)	2-1	3.70	5	5	1	0	0	24.1	20	13	10	1	2	16-0	31	1	2	.222
1997	TORONTO (AL)	3-2	2.90	27	0	0	0	14	31.0	28	12	10	1	0	19-2	36	0	0	.237
1998	Syracuse (Int)	2-2	3.77	13	10	0	0	1	59.2	51	26	25	7	4	24-0	63	3	0	.229
1998	TORONTO (AL)	7-3	3.73	22	10	0	0	0	79.2	72	37	33	5	0	35-0	72	0	0	.237
1999	TORONTO (AL)	14-11	5.69	33	30	1	0	0	174.0	203	118	110	19	10	81-2	129	6	1	.293
2000	TORONTO (AL)	10-15	5.35	43	24	3	1	2	180.0	186	118	107	26	3	85-3	142	4	0	.267
Minor Totals		25-22	3.74	85	78	4	1	1	443.1	419	218	184	29	20	181-0	458	31	12	.249
MAJOR TOTALS		34-31	5.04	125	64	4	1	16	464.2	489	285	260	51	13	220-7	379	10	1	.270

ESCOBAR — TRANSACTIONS

- Signed as a non-drafted free agent July 3, 1992.
- On disabled list (right elbow surgery) April 3-May 18, 1997.
- On disabled list (right elbow inflammation) April 16-May 6, 1998; included rehabilitation assignment at Syracuse, May 1-5.

CAREER HIGHS — ESCOBAR, Kelvim

SEASON:

Wins	14 - 1999
Losses	15 - 2000
Saves	14 - 1997
ERA	5.35 - 2000
Games	43 - 2000
Starts	30 - 1999
Complete Games	3 - 2000
Shutouts	1 - 2000
Innings Pitched	180.0 - 2000
Walks	85 - 2000
Strikeouts	142 - 2000
Longest Win Streak	4 - Aug. 27-Sep. 13, 1998
Longest Losing Streak	4 - Jul. 25-Aug. 11, 2000
Scoreless Innings Streak	15.1 - Jul. 29-Aug. 8, 1997

GAME:

ML Debut	Jun. 29, 1997 at BAL
Innings Pitched:	
Starter	9.0 - Jul. 30, 1999 vs. DET
	9.0 - Apr. 22, 2000 vs. NYY
	9.0 - Jun. 4, 2000 at FLA
	9.0 - Jun. 21, 2000 vs. DET
Reliever	4.1 - Jun. 29, 1997 at BAL
Walks:	
Starter	7 - May 24, 2000 at BOS
	7 - Jul. 30, 2000 at SEA
Reliever	3 - Jun. 29, 1997 at BAL
	3 - Aug. 6, 1997 vs. CLE
Strikeouts:	
Starter	11 - Aug. 22, 1998 at ANA
Reliever	5 - Jun. 29, 1997 at BAL
Hits Allowed	12 - May 8, 2000 vs. BAL
Runs Allowed	9 - Jun. 27, 2000 at TB
	9 - Jul. 30, 2000 at SEA
ER Allowed	7 - Apr. 30, 1999 at SEA
	7 - Jun. 27, 1999 at TB
	7 - Jun. 10, 2000 vs. MON
	7 - Jun. 27, 2000 at TB
HR Allowed	3 - Apr. 30, 1999 at SEA
	3 - May 3, 2000 at CWS
Low Hit CG	4 - Jun. 21, 2000 vs. DET
Last Win	Sep. 15, 2000 at CWS
Last Save	Sep. 14, 2000 at NYY
Last CG	Jun. 21, 2000 vs. DET
Last ShO	Jun. 21, 2000 vs. DET
Last Start	Aug. 11, 2000 at MIN
Last Relief App.	Sep. 30, 2000 at CLE

FIELDING
ESCOBAR, Kelvim—P

Year	PCT	G	PO	A	E	TC	DP
1997	1.000	27	0	2	0	2	1
1998	1.000	22	2	4	0	6	0
1999	.944	33	6	11	1	18	1
2000	.963	43	11	15	1	27	1
Total	.962	125	19	32	2	53	3

KELVIM ESCOBAR DETAILED PITCHING

| | 2000 | | | | | | | | CAREER | | | | | | | |
	ERA	W-L-Sv	G	IP	H	ER	BB	SO	ERA	W-L-Sv	G	IP	H	ER	BB	SO
Total	5.35	10-15-2	43	180.0	186	107	85	142	5.04	34-31-16	125	464.2	489	260	220	379
ST	5.42	7-13-0	24	152.2	155	92	78	113	5.06	27-26-0	64	389.2	409	219	184	295
REL	4.94	3-2-2	19	27.1	31	15	7	29	4.92	7-5-16	61	75.0	80	41	36	84
Home	4.32	7-7-1	22	98.0	93	47	41	80	4.09	17-13-9	60	235.1	243	107	100	179
Away	6.59	3-8-1	21	82.0	93	60	44	62	6.00	17-18-7	65	229.1	246	153	120	200
April	3.98	2-3-0	5	31.2	39	14	12	17	5.91	4-4-0	16	67.0	90	44	29	46
May	5.82	2-3-0	6	38.2	38	25	30	28	5.97	5-5-0	17	72.1	78	48	44	55
June	5.94	2-3-0	5	33.1	38	22	10	28	5.20	6-6-0	12	72.2	84	42	26	55
July	4.42	1-2-0	6	38.2	26	19	21	32	4.83	4-4-5	18	78.1	63	42	45	63
August	7.45	2-2-0	8	19.1	23	16	8	19	4.59	5-5-5	27	80.1	78	41	41	75
September	5.40	1-2-2	13	18.1	22	11	4	18	4.12	10-7-6	35	94.0	96	43	35	85
vs. Ana	5.52	1-1-0	4	14.2	20	9	5	8	2.79	4-2-2	11	38.2	40	12	10	32
vs. Bal	4.20	1-0-0	3	15.0	20	7	6	12	4.28	5-0-1	9	40.0	50	19	18	33
vs. Bos	6.57	0-1-0	2	12.1	14	9	9	10	7.03	1-3-1	10	32.0	33	25	22	29
vs. CWS	8.59	1-3-0	4	14.2	13	14	11	11	8.63	1-6-1	8	32.1	38	31	21	20
vs. Cle	8.00	0-1-0	2	9.0	8	8	5	8	4.15	2-1-1	6	26.0	20	12	16	22
vs. Det	0.00	1-0-1	3	12.0	7	0	3	11	2.14	4-0-3	8	33.2	23	8	7	27
vs. KC	3.86	2-1-0	3	7.0	8	3	5	7	3.40	5-2-2	11	39.2	41	15	16	33
vs. Mil	—	—	—	—	—	—	—	—	0.00	0-0-0	2	2.0	1	0	0	2
vs. Min	7.84	0-2-0	2	10.1	14	9	9	10	6.66	2-3-0	7	25.2	30	19	18	18
vs. NYY	3.00	1-1-1	5	18.0	19	6	3	13	4.21	3-2-2	10	36.1	34	17	14	34
vs. Oak	0.00	0-0-0	1	1.0	1	0	0	1	4.50	1-3-0	7	20.0	28	10	15	15
vs. Sea	4.32	0-2-0	2	8.1	5	4	7	6	5.87	1-2-0	7	23.0	25	15	14	18
vs. TB	6.95	2-1-0	5	22.0	20	17	10	14	8.18	3-4-0	11	44.0	56	40	23	34
vs. Tex	6.30	0-1-0	3	10.0	11	7	5	8	4.50	0-1-1	9	24.0	20	12	9	21
vs. Atl	—	—	—	—	—	—	—	—	6.75	0-0-0	1	6.2	9	5	3	7
vs. Fla	2.00	1-0-0	1	9.0	8	2	1	10	1.80	1-0-0	2	10.0	9	2	1	11
vs. Mon	9.28	0-1-0	2	10.2	15	11	3	7	6.27	1-1-0	3	18.2	23	13	8	8
vs. NYM	—	—	—	—	—	—	—	—	9.00	0-0-0	1	1.0	1	1	0	2
vs. Phi	1.50	0-0-0	1	6.0	3	1	3	6	3.27	0-1-0	2	11.0	8	4	5	13
Pre-All Star	5.26	10-16-0	18	114.2	127	67	55	80	5.74	17-16-0	50	235.1	279	150	113	173
Post-All Star	5.51	4-6-2	25	65.1	59	40	30	62	4.32	17-15-16	75	229.1	210	110	107	206

KELVIM ESCOBAR PITCHING AT ML PARKS

Park	ERA	W-L-Sv	SvO	G	GS	IP	H	R	ER	HR	BB	SO
Camden Yards	3.38	3-0-0	0	5	3	24.0	24	9	9	0	12	23
Fenway Park	7.09	1-3-1	2	8	4	26.2	28	21	21	3	18	24
Edison Field	4.91	1-2-1	1	5	2	14.2	15	8	8	3	6	20
Comiskey Park	9.39	1-3-1	2	5	2	15.1	14	16	16	3	13	4
Jacobs Field	10.13	0-0-0	0	2	0	2.2	5	3	3	2	2	3
Tiger Stadium	4.63	2-0-1	1	3	2	11.2	10	6	6	3	2	10
Kauffman Stadium	4.30	2-1-1	2	6	3	23.0	26	11	11	0	8	17
Metrodome	9.82	1-1-0	0	3	2	11.0	15	12	12	3	7	8
Yankee Stadium	6.04	1-2-2	2	7	4	22.1	22	17	15	4	13	25
Oakland-Alameda	1.86	1-1-0	1	4	1	9.2	6	5	2	1	8	7
Kingdome	10.29	1-0-0	0	3	1	7.0	12	8	8	3	4	4
Arlington	3.75	0-0-0	0	4	1	12.0	11	5	5	0	4	9
SkyDome	4.09	17-13-9	10	60	30	235.1	243	116	107	16	100	179
Olympic Stadium	7.20	0-0-0	0	1	1	5.0	7	5	4	0	1	3
Shea Stadium	9.00	0-0-0	0	1	0	1.0	1	1	1	1	0	2
Veterans Stadium	5.40	0-1-0	0	1	1	5.0	5	4	3	2	2	7
Pro Player Stadium	2.00	1-0-0	0	1	1	9.0	8	2	2	0	1	10
Tropicana Field	9.00	2-3-0	0	5	5	23.0	33	27	23	5	12	19
SAFECO Field	5.68	0-1-0	0	1	1	6.1	4	9	4	2	7	5

Scott
EYRE

29

PITCHER

BIRTHDATE	May 30, 1972
OPENING DAY AGE	28
BIRTHPLACE	Inglewood, CA
RESIDENCE	Bradenton, FL
BATS/THROWS	L/L
HEIGHT/WEIGHT	6-1/200
CONTRACT STATUS	signed thru 2001
M.L. SERVICE	2.046

PERSONAL: Scott Alan Eyre... Married, wife's name is Laura... Has two children, Caleb Scott (8/14/98) and Jacob (9/11/00)... Graduated from Cyprus High School in Magna, Utah in 1990... Attended Southern Idaho Junior College.

LAST SEASON: Split the season between Chicago and Charlotte (AAA) after making his second opening day roster with the White Sox... With the Sox was 1-1 in 13 games with one start and a 6.63 ERA... Lone win came on April 7 at Oakland (2ER/2.0IP)... Made lone start on April 19 vs Seattle and had a no-decision after allowing two runs on five hits over 3.2 innings... Pitched 2.0 innings or more in four of 12 relief appearances... LH hitters posted a .393 (11-28) average and RH hitters a .360 (18-50) average... Was optioned to Charlotte on May 25... Appeared in 47 games with the Knights and was 3-2 with a 3.00 ERA (16ER/48.0IP)... Posted a team high 12 saves... Struck out 46 batters and allowed only one home run (July 4)... From July 6 on he posted a 3-1 record with eight saves and a 2.05 ERA in 27 games... On August 31 suffered a broken left hand when struck by a line drive at Norfolk, recorded the out after throwing the ball to first with his right hand.

POST SEASON EXPERIENCE: 1992: Topped Class A Butte in ERA (2.90), strikeouts (94), IP (80.2) and starts (14)... his seven wins tied for the team lead... His 94 strikeouts set a Rangers rookie league record... **1993:** Led Class A Charleston (S.C.) in victories (11) and strikeouts (154) despite two stints on the disabled list... **1994:** Made 19 appearances at Class A South Bend before his season ended due to an arm injury... Had 111 strikeouts to rank third on the team... Was 4-0 with a 1.37 ERA at home... Won all five of his decisions in July... Struck out seven or more in 11 of his 18 starts, including eight straight from June 24 to July 30... Tossed a complete-game, four-hitter with nine strikeouts on July 3 vs. Clinton... **1995:** Was limited by an arm injury to nine starts at Rookie Sarasota... Averaged 13.2 strikeouts per 9.0 IP (40 SO/27.1 IP) while allowing 5.3 hits per 9.0 IP (16 H)... **1996:** Tied for the team lead with 27 starts and ranked second with a career-high 12 wins and 137 strikeouts at Class AA Birmingham... Averaged 7.8 strikeouts per 9.0 IP (158.1 IP)... Was selected Birmingham's Player of the Month for August after going 4-1 with a 2.15 ERA (9 ER/37.2 IP)... Struck out seven or more batters eight times, including a season-high 10 on May 26 vs. Greenville... Won four straight starts from August 2-18, allowing four earned runs in 25.2 IP (1.40 ERA)... Made 12 quality starts... Ranked fifth in the Southern League with 79 walks... **1997:** Split the season between Birmingham (AA) and Chicago where he was 4-4 in 11 starts with a 5.04 ERA... Named the Southern League Pitcher of the Year and selected by Baseball America as the league's Most Outstanding Pitcher after going 13-5 with a 3.84 ERA (54 ER/126.2 IP) in 22 starts and recording 127 strikeouts for the Barons... Tied for the league lead in wins, ranked second in strikeouts and third in ERA... Named to both the SL mid-season and post-season All-Star teams... Was Birmingham's recipient of the Charles W. Lubin Award (MVP)... Averaged 9.0 strikeouts per 9.0 IP and limited opponents to a .231 average... Struck out seven or more batters 12 times, including a season-high nine on three occasions... Lasted 7.0 innings or more 10 times... Allowed one or no earned runs nine times... Went 8-2 with a 3.58 ERA (30 ER/75.1 IP) on the road... Went 5-1 with a 2.68 ERA (14 ER/47.0 IP) and 49 strikeouts in May... Won 11 of 12 decisions from May 6 to July 15 and went 6-0 with a 2.42 ERA (13 ER/48.1 IP) in seven starts from May 6 to June 8... Was recalled from Birmingham on July 31 and lost in his major-league debut on August 1 at Anaheim (6 ER/4.1 IP)... First major-league victory came on August 13 vs. Anaheim, allowing two runs (one earned) on six hits over 5.0 IP... Combined with rookie Keith Foulke on a four-hit shutout victory against the Mariners on August 18 at Comiskey Park, scattered three hits over 5.0 scoreless innings... Struck out a season-high six batters on September 3 at St. Louis and September 9 vs. Milwaukee... Went 4-0 with a 2.48 ERA (8 ER/29.0 IP) in five starts at Comiskey Park... Pitched a then career-high 7.0 IP in each of his last two starts, earning the win in Chicago's season finale on September 28 vs. Kansas City (3 ER/7.0 IP)... **1998:** Spent his first full season in the major leagues, appearing in 33 games and making 17 starts... Was 2-7 with a 5.79 ERA (56 ER/87.0 IP) as a starting pitcher and in relief was 1-1 with a 3.60 ERA (8 ER/20.0 IP)... Allowed 5.4 walks (64 BB/107.0 IP) and 2.0 home runs (24 HR) per 9.0 IP... Went 1-7 with a 5.42 ERA (50 ER/83.0 IP) before the All-Star Break and then 2-1 with a 5.25 ERA (14 ER/24.0 IP) after the break... 14 of his first 15 appearances were as a starter, was moved to the bullpen after June 17 start vs Boston and posting a 1-7 record with a 5.61 ERA... Second victory came in start on 8/12 vs. Oakland when he fired 5.0 hitless IP, walking one and striking out four — despite the no-hitter was removed after reaching his pitch limit... First win since April 25 vs. Toronto... From June 21 to August 21 went 1-0 with a 3.32 ERA (8 ER/21.2 IP) over 13 outings... Third victory, first career in relief, came in 17-16, extra-inning contest at Detroit on September 14 when he went the final 2.0 IP (0 ER)... Struck out a career-high seven twice in successive starts on April 14 at Baltimore and April 19 at Toronto... Lasted a career-high 7.2 IP (4 ER) on June 1 at New York... **1999:** Made 21 relief appearances for the White Sox before being sidelined with an impingement in his left rotator cuff on August 30... Returned in late September but did not pitch... Was recalled from Class AAA Charlotte on June 20... Pitched exclusively out of the bullpen for the first time in his career... Allowed six of 14 (42.3 percent) of inherited runners to score... Left-handers batted .279 (12-43)... Opponents hit .295 (13-44) with runners in scoring position... Went a season-high 3.1 IP on two occasions... Earned his only victory on July 24 v. Toronto, going 1.0 IP — first win since August 12, 1998 vs. Oakland... Struck out a season-high four on June 26 at Boston... Posted his first career hold on June 24 vs. Minnesota... Opened the season at Charlotte, where he was 6-4 with a 3.82 ERA in 12 games, 11 starts... Averaged 8.3 strikeouts per 9.0 IP (63 SO/68.1 IP)... Lowered his ERA each month from 4.42 in April to 3.83 in May and 2.70 in June.

SCOTT EYRE

Year	Club & League	W-L	ERA	G	GS	CG	ShO	SV	IP	H	R	ER	HR	HB	BB-IBB	SO	WP	BK	OBA
1992	Butte (Pio)	7-3	2.90	15	14	2	1	0	80.2	71	30	26	6	4	39-0	94	6	1	.241
1993	Chston-sc (SAL)	11-7	3.45	26	26	0	0	0	143.2	115	74	55	6	6	59-1	154	2	1	.220
1994	South Bend (Mid)	8-4	3.47	19	18	2	0	0	111.2	108	56	43	7	3	37-0	111	8	3	.248
1995	White Sox (Gulf)	0-2	2.30	9	9	0	0	0	27.1	16	7	7	0	1	12-0	40	2	0	.174
1996	Birmingham (Sou)	12-7	4.38	27	27	0	0	0	158.1	170	90	77	12	8	79-3	137	12	0	.277
1997	Birmingham (Sou)	13-5	3.84	22	22	0	0	0	126.2	110	61	54	14	5	55-2	127	9	1	.231
1997	CHICAGO (AL)	4-4	5.04	11	11	0	0	0	60.2	62	36	34	11	1	31-1	36	2	0	.267
1998	CHICAGO (AL)	3-8	5.38	33	17	0	0	0	107.0	114	78	64	24	2	64-0	73	7	0	.271
1999	Charlotte (Int)	6-4	3.82	12	11	0	0	0	68.1	75	32	29	3	1	23-1	63	5	2	.284
1999	CHICAGO (AL)	1-1	7.56	21	0	0	0	0	25.0	38	22	21	6	1	15-2	17	1	0	.339
2000	CHICAGO (AL)	1-1	6.63	13	1	0	0	0	19.0	29	15	14	3	1	12-0	16	0	0	.372
2000	Charlotte (Int)	3-2	3.00	47	0	0	0	12	48.0	33	18	16	1	0	20-3	46	2	0	.200
Minor Totals		60-34	3.61	177	127	4	1	12	764.2	698	368	307	49	28	324-10	772	46	8	.244
MAJOR TOTALS		9-14	5.66	78	29	0	0	0	211.2	243	151	133	44	5	122-3	142	10	0	.289

EYRE — TRANSACTIONS

- Selected by the Texas Rangers in the 9th round of June 1991 First Year Player Draft.
- On disabled list May 15-24, 1993.
- On disabled list July 5-15, 1993.
- Traded to the Chicago White Sox in exchange for SS Esteban Beltre on March 28, 1994.
- On disabled list (arm injury) April 8-27, 1994.
- On disabled list (arm injury) April 6-September 7, 1995.
- On disabled list (impingement left rotator cuff) August 31-September 26, 1999.
- Traded to the Toronto Blue Jays in exchange for RHP Gary Glover on November 7, 2000.

CAREER HIGHS — EYRE, Scott

SEASON:		GAME:	
Wins	4 - 1997	ML Debut	Aug. 1, 1997 at ANA
Losses	8 - 1998	Innings Pitched:	
Saves	None	Starter	7.2 - Jun. 1, 1998 at NYY
ERA	5.38 - 1998	Reliever	3.1 - Jun. 26, 1999 at BOS
Games	33 - 1998		3.1 - Aug. 15, 1999 vs. TEX
Starts	17 - 1998	Walks:	
Complete Games	None	Starter	8 - May 12, 1998 vs. ANA
Shutouts	None	Reliever	3 - Apr. 25, 2000 vs. BAL
Innings Pitched	107.0 - 1998	Strikeouts:	
Walks	64 - 1998	Starter	7 - Apr. 14, 1998 at BAL
Strikeouts	73 - 1998		7 - Apr. 19, 1998 at TOR
Longest Win Streak	2 - Aug. 13-18, 1997	Reliever	4 - Jun. 26, 1999 at BOS
	2 - Aug. 12-Sep. 14, 1998	Hits Allowed	9 - Apr. 4, 1998 at TB
Longest Losing Streak	5 - Apr. 30-Jun. 17, 1998		9 - Jun. 12, 1998 at MIN
Scoreless Innings Streak	10.1 - Aug. 2-Aug. 21, 1998	Runs Allowed	9 - Sep. 15, 1997 at MIL
			9 - Jun. 26, 1999 at BOS
		ER Allowed	9 - Sep. 15, 1997 at MIL
			9 - Jun. 26, 1999 at BOS
		HR Allowed	4 - May 5, 1998 at SEA
			4 - Jun. 26, 1999 at BOS
		Low Hit CG	None
		Last Win	Apr. 7, 2000 at OAK
		Last Save	None
		Last CG	None
		Last ShO	None
		Last Start	Apr. 19, 2000 vs. SEA
		Last Relief App.	May 24, 2000 vs. NYY

FIELDING

ERYE, Scott—P

Year	PCT	G	PO	A	E	TC	DP
1997	1.000	11	0	6	0	6	0
1998	.947	33	1	17	1	19	3
1999	1.000	21	0	1	0	1	0
2000	1.000	13	0	3	0	3	0
Total	.966	78	1	27	1	29	3

SCOTT EYRE DETAILED PITCHING

	2000							CAREER						
	ERA	W-L-Sv	G	IP	H	ER	BB	SO	ERA	W-L-Sv	G	IP	H	ER	BB	SO
Total	6.63	1-1-0	13	19.0	29	14	12	16	5.66	9-14-0	78	211.2	243	133	122	142
ST	4.91	0-0-0	1	3.2	5	2	1	5	5.47	6-11-0	29	151.1	158	92	88	102
REL	7.04	1-1-0	12	15.1	24	12	11	11	6.12	3-3-0	49	60.1	85	41	34	40
Home	5.23	0-0-0	7	10.1	16	6	7	10	4.29	7-3-0	41	107.0	114	51	59	64
Away	8.31	1-1-0	6	8.2	13	8	5	6	7.05	2-11-0	37	104.2	129	82	63	78
April	6.00	1-1-0	9	15.0	18	10	9	13	4.96	2-4-0	15	45.1	47	25	27	35
May	9.00	0-0-0	4	4.0	11	4	3	3	5.52	0-2-0	9	29.1	36	18	23	20
June	–	–	–	–	–	–	–	–	8.80	0-2-0	10	30.2	46	30	14	21
July	–	–	–	–	–	–	–	–	4.15	1-0-0	13	13.0	13	6	9	5
August	–	–	–	–	–	–	–	–	5.24	3-3-0	22	56.2	60	33	38	33
September	–	–	–	–	–	–	–	–	5.15	3-3-0	9	36.2	41	21	11	28
vs. Ana	9.00	0-0-0	2	2.0	3	2	1	2	4.95	1-1-0	7	20.0	21	11	17	13
vs. Bal	3.38	0-0-0	1	2.2	3	1	3	0	3.72	0-2-0	5	19.1	17	8	13	9
vs. Bos	–	–	–	–	–	–	–	–	8.84	0-1-0	6	18.1	26	18	8	10
vs. Cle	–	–	–	–	–	–	–	–	4.50	0-0-0	3	4.0	4	2	2	1
vs. Det	3.38	0-1-0	2	2.2	3	1	2	2	7.71	1-2-0	4	7.0	13	6	3	5
vs. KC	16.20	0-0-0	1	1.2	7	3	1	0	5.59	1-0-0	3	9.2	13	6	2	5
vs. Mil	–	–	–	–	–	–	–	–	7.82	1-1-0	4	12.2	16	11	6	10
vs. Min	–	–	–	–	–	–	–	–	6.75	0-1-0	4	8.0	14	6	4	5
vs. NYY	5.40	0-0-0	2	1.2	4	1	0	3	4.30	0-0-0	5	14.2	17	7	9	12
vs. Oak	12.00	1-0-0	2	3.0	4	4	2	3	4.67	2-1-0	8	17.1	12	9	8	14
vs. Sea	4.91	0-0-0	1	3.2	5	2	1	5	5.61	1-2-0	7	25.2	26	16	18	22
vs. TB	–	–	–	–	–	–	–	–	4.70	0-1-0	4	7.2	14	4	5	3
vs. Tex	0.00	0-0-0	1	1.0	0	0	0	1	7.82	0-0-0	6	12.2	16	11	7	5
vs. Tor	0.00	0-0-0	1	0.2	0	0	2	0	3.00	2-0-0	7	15.0	10	5	12	12
vs. ChC	–	–	–	–	–	–	–	–	9.00	0-1-0	2	7.0	10	7	3	7
vs. Hou	–	–	–	–	–	–	–	–	4.05	0-0-0	2	6.2	6	3	3	3
vs. StL	–	–	–	–	–	–	–	–	4.50	0-1-0	1	6.0	8	3	2	6
Pre-All Star	6.63	1-1-0	13	19.0	29	14	12	16	6.32	2-8-0	38	109.2	136	77	67	79
Post-All Star	–	–	–	–	–	–	–	–	4.94	7-6-0	40	102.0	107	56	55	63

SCOTT EYRE PITCHING AT ML PARKS

Park	ERA	W-L-Sv	SvO	G	GS	IP	H	R	ER	HR	BB	SO
Camden Yards	2.25	0-1-0	0	2	1	8.0	6	2	2	1	5	7
Fenway Park	8.53	0-0-0	0	4	1	12.2	17	12	12	4	5	6
Edison Field	12.46	0-1-0	0	1	1	4.1	6	6	6	1	5	4
Comiskey Park	4.29	7-3-0	0	41	15	107.0	114	64	51	14	59	64
Jacobs Field	4.50	0-0-0	0	2	0	2.0	3	1	1	0	1	1
Tiger Stadium	0.00	1-0-0	0	1	0	2.0	2	1	0	0	0	3
Kauffman Stadium	16.20	0-0-0	0	1	0	1.2	7	3	3	0	1	0
County Stadium	14.29	0-1-0	0	2	1	5.2	8	9	9	2	4	4
Metrodome	9.53	0-1-0	0	2	1	5.2	12	6	6	0	3	5
Yankee Stadium	4.32	0-0-0	0	2	1	8.1	7	4	4	3	3	5
Oakland-Alameda	11.57	1-1-0	0	5	0	4.2	7	6	6	1	5	5
Kingdome	6.28	0-2-0	0	3	3	14.1	13	11	10	7	13	10
Arlington	6.43	0-0-0	0	4	1	7.0	7	6	5	3	3	3
SkyDome	6.75	0-0-0	0	1	1	5.1	5	5	4	2	3	7
Wrigley Field	6.00	0-1-0	0	1	1	6.0	6	6	4	2	2	6
Astrodome	0.00	0-0-0	0	1	0	1.0	0	0	0	0	0	1
Busch Stadium	4.50	0-1-0	0	1	1	6.0	8	3	3	1	2	6
Tropicana Field	6.35	0-1-0	0	2	1	5.2	11	4	4	2	5	3
SAFECO Field	9.00	0-0-0	0	1	0	2.0	2	2	2	1	1	1
Comerica Park	3.86	0-1-0	0	1	0	2.1	2	1	1	0	2	1

Bob
FILE
PITCHER

BIRTHDATE	January 28, 1977
OPENING DAY AGE	24
BIRTHPLACE	Philadelphia, PA
RESIDENCE	Philadelphia, PA
BATS/THROWS	R/R
HEIGHT/WEIGHT	6-4/215
CONTRACT STATUS	signed thru 2001
M.L. SERVICE	0.000

36

PERSONAL: Robert Michael File... 1994 graduate of Father Judge High School in Philadelphia where he played baseball and was MVP of the Catholic League... 1998 graduate of Philadelphia College of Textiles and Science where he played baseball and was NYCAC Player-of-the-Year, a second-team All-American and All-Northeast Region selection... In 1998, he led NCAA Division II in batting (.542) while setting school records in homers (19) and RBI (68)... Was signed by Blue Jays Ben McLure in 1998 after his 19th round selection (No. 561 overall)... Converted to pitching full-time after tossing just six innings in college.

LAST SEASON: Split the season between Tennessee of the Southern League (AA) and Syracuse of the International League (AAA)... On the season was 6-3 with 28 saves in 56 games while posting a 2.33 ERA... Opened the season at Tennessee where he was 4-3 with 20 saves in 36 games with a 3.12 ERA... In 34.2 innings he recorded 40 strikeouts and held opponents to a .215 average... Had a 1.17 ERA in eight April games with six saves... On May 5 vs Greenville suffered first loss after being charged with four ER without recording an out... Was one of two occasions all season that he allowed more than one earned run in a game... In June was 1-1 with four saves and a 1.17 ERA in eight games... On July 15 vs Greenville pitched a season high 2.0 innings and allowed a solo HR, his first allowed all season... Pitched one inning or less in 31 of his 36 games... In Tennessee was 3-2 with eight saves with a 5.40 ERA in 17 games and on the road was 1-1 with 12 saves in 19 games with a 1.37 ERA... Was called up to Syracuse on July 28 and debuted with a scoreless inning on July 30 vs Indianapolis... After allowing an earned run on July 31 he posted 14 consecutive scoreless games from August 2 to August 26... From August 18 to September 2, he recorded saves in eight of nine games to finish the season...

With Syracuse was 2-0 with eight saves and a 0.93 ERA in 20 games... Following the season pitched for Scottsdale in the Arizona Fall League and was 2-1 with five saves and a 3.38 ERA in 15 games... Was selected to the 2000 Arizona Fall League All-Prospect Team as one of two right-handed relievers.

PROFESSIONAL CAREER: 1998: Made his pro debut with Medicine Hat and led Pioneer League (A) in saves (16), relief points (50), games finished (26) and was second in games (28)... Led league relievers in baserunners per 9.0IP ratio at 8.72 and placed third in walks per 9.0IP at 1.40... Did not allow an earned run in first 17 appearances, was 1-0 with nine saves... Allowed earned runs in only three of 28 appearances... Did not allow more than two runs, earned or unearned, in any outing... Held opponents to batting average of .211... **1999:** With Dunedin of the Florida State League was All-Star selection after posting a 4-1 record with 26 saves and a 1.70 ERA in 47 games... Led league in relief points (84), was second in league and fifth in all minor leagues among relievers in the opponents average allowed at .165... Was third in league among relievers in runners per 9.0IP at 8.15... Was fourth in league and second in the organization in saves (26), fourth in league in games finished (42)... Did not allow an earned run in first 13 appearances over 13.1 innings, allowing just four hits and three walks while striking out 15 to pick up eight saves... Closed season by allowing just one earned run in last 13 appearances spanning 14.2 innings and was 1-0 with nine saves... On the road was 1-0, with a 1.04 ERA and 12 saves... Right-handed hitters batted .134 (16-119)... With runners in scoring position hit just .115 (6-52)... Pitched for Rancho Cucamonga, California Fall League, compiling 1-0 record with a 3.45 ERA and three saves in 14 games.

NON-PITCHERS WHO PITCHED FOR THE BLUE JAYS

Player	Position	Pitched	W-L	ERA	G	GS	IP	H	BB	SO
Bailor, Bob	IF/OF	1980	0-0	7.71	3	0	2.1	4	1	0
Kusick, Craig	1B	1979	0-0	4.91	1	0	3.2	3	0	0
Leach, Rick	1B/OF	1984	0-0	27.00	1	0	1.0	2	2	0

BOB FILE

Year	Club & League	W-L	ERA	G	GS	CG	ShO	SV	IP	H	R	ER	HR	HB	BB-IBB	SO	WP	BK	OBA
1998	Medicine Hat (Pio)	2-1	1.41	28	0	0	0	16	32.0	24	7	5	1	2	5-0	28	1	0	.211
1999	Dunedin (FSL)	4-1	1.70	47	0	0	0	26	53.0	30	13	10	2	4	14-0	48	1	1	.165
2000	Tennessee (Sou)	4-3	3.12	36	0	0	0	20	34.2	29	20	12	1	2	13-0	40	0	1	.215
2000	Syracuse (Int)	2-0	0.93	20	0	0	0	8	19.1	14	2	2	1	1	2-0	10	0	0	.212
Minor Totals		12- 5	1.88	131	0	0	0	70	139.0	97	42	29	5	9	34-0	126	2	2	.195

FILE — TRANSACTIONS

- Selected by the Toronto Blue Jays in the 19th round (561st overall) of June 1998 First Year Player Draft.

Darrin
FLETCHER
CATCHER

BIRTHDATE	October 3, 1966
OPENING DAY AGE	34
BIRTHPLACE	Elmhurst, IL
RESIDENCE	Oakwood, IL
BATS/THROWS	L/R
HEIGHT/WEIGHT	6-2/205
CONTRACT STATUS	signed thru 2003
M.L. SERVICE	9.140

9

PERSONAL: Darrin Glen Fletcher...Married the former Sheila Draper...Two children, son Casey Thomas (1/1/93) and daughter Preslie Ann (10/22/96)...Graduated from Oakwood High School in Illinois were he lettered and earned all-conference honours in football, basketball and baseball...Attended University of Illinois where in 1987 he finished third in NCAA Division I batting at .497, 68 points ahead of Mo Vaughan and 69 ahead of Robin Ventura...Named Big Ten catcher and Player of the Year in 1987 and was a third team All-American...Son of pitcher Tom Fletcher, former Detroit Tiger in 1962 and grandson of Glen Fletcher who played 11 years in the Red Sox organization...Enjoys playing guitar.

LAST SEASON: Set new career highs with a .320 average and 20 home runs... Also had 19 doubles, a triple and 58 RBI in 122 games... Reported to spring training and then had surgery on February 28 performed by Dr. Steve Mirabello to repair some fraying of the meniscus in his right knee... Did not see game action until March 15... Was not slowed by the injury as he opened the season batting .329 in April with three home runs and 12 RBI... Hit in nine straight games from April 12 to 23... On April 20 matched his career high with his sixth career first RBI game after hitting his first grand slam of the season against Kent Mercker... Finished April with a four hit game on April 30 at New York to match his career high, fifth time... Posted a season high 11 game hit streak, one short of career high, from May 3 to 16... Hit second grand slam of the season on May 8 vs Baltimore (Johnson)... On May 26 hit his third grand slam, the sixth of his career, in Detroit against Doug Brocail... Three grand slams in one season matches the club record done once previously by Carlos Delgado in 1997... Hit .358 in May with six home runs and 16 RBI... On June 4 suffered a right shoulder strain... Appeared defensively on June 6... Next start was on June 9 and then on June 10 was forced to leave the game after aggravating his shoulder... Was placed on the disabled list from June 11 to July 3... Returned from the DL to hit in six straight games... On July 9 in Montreal he played his 1000th ML game and marked the occasion with his 6th career four hit game, second of 2000, and stole his second career base, other steal was July 18, 1997... At the All-Star break was batting .349 with 10 home runs and 33 RBI... Following the break hit .295 with 10 home runs and 25 RBI... Averaged slipped below .300 on August 27 for the first time since April... In August hit .256 with four home runs and seven RBI... On August 27 at Texas posted his seventh multi-HR game and hit first career 3HR game, all solo HR's off Helling... He is the seventh Blue Jay to hit three HR in a game and became the 9th catcher in the history of the AL... Last AL catcher to hit three was Ivan Rodriguez (Sept. 11, 1997)- others are Mickey Cochrane, Bill Dickey, Don Leppert, Bill Freehan, Ernie Whitt, Mike Stanley & Dan Wilson... Went on to hit .370 in September with three home runs and 13 RBI... Finished the season by hitting in 15 of the last 16 games... Had third four hit game of the season on September 22 vs Tampa Bay... On September 23 delivered a ninth inning double for a walk-off victory against Tampa Bay... Hit his 20th home run on September 28 at Baltimore against Pat Rapp - the HR gave the Blue Jays seven players with 20 home runs to tie the ML record done once previously by the 1996 Orioles... Hit .342 vs LHP with one home run and .315 against RHP with 19 HR... At home posted a .332 average with ten HR and 34 RBI and on the road hit .306 with ten HR and 24 RBI... Threw out 21.5% of base-stealers (20 of 93)... Led AL catchers with a .994 fielding percentage committing four errors in 664 total chances.

PROFESSIONAL CAREER: **1987:** Hit .266 in 43 games for Vero Beach of the Florida State League (A) after being drafted by the Expos in the sixth round of the June draft...**1988:** Hit .208 in 89 games with San Antonio of the Texas League...Led league catchers in fielding percentage at .992 and was tied for the lead with nine double plays...**1989:** Joined AAA Albuquerque where he led all Pacific Coast League catchers with a .987 fielding percentage...Hit .273 with five home runs and 44 RBI...Was promoted to Los Angeles in September and hit .500 in five games...Singled in his first at bat on September 10 in San Diego...Hit first ML home run, a pinch hit HR, on September 23 at San Diego...**1990:** Hit .291 for Albuquerque which was the highest average for a starting catcher in AAA baseball...Collected 23 doubles, 13 home runs and 65 RBI...Was recalled to Los Angeles and was 0-1 in pinch hitting appearances prior to being traded to the Philadelphia Phillies on Sept 13 in exchange for LHP Dennis Cook...Started six games with Phillies and collected first career multi-hit game in first start on September 19 at St. Louis...**1991:** Opened the season with Scranton (AAA) until being recalled to Philadelphia on May 6...In his 22nd ML game behind the plate on May 23 caught Tommy Greene's no-hitter at Olympic Stadium against the Expos...Collected a career high four RBI on May 28 after hitting a three run home run...Was returned to Scranton on June 18 and then returned to the Phillies on September 4...Hit .284 at Scranton with eight home runs and 50 RBI...December 9 was traded along with cash to the Montreal Expos in exchange for P Barry Jones...**1992:** Member of opening day ML roster for the first time...Caught eight of the Expos 14 shutouts despite starting in just 59 of 162 games...Expos posted a 2.97 ERA with Fletcher behind the plate...It tied for the second lowest ERA among catchers in the NL (min 225 innings)...Hit first HR as an Expo on April 30 vs the Padres...Was disabled from May 12 to June 15 after suffering from severe bronchitis...Joined Indianapolis (AAA) on a rehab assignment...Hit first career triple on July 24 vs Dodgers...Hit .268 after the All start break...**1993:** Played in a career high 133 games and hit .255 with 20 doubles, nine home runs and 60 RBI...Stared 105 games behind the plate posting a .988 fielding percentage...Was batting .252 through May 2 before seeing his average fall to a season low .228...Rebounded from June 25 to August 1 he hit .361 (35-97) with five doubles, four homers and 20 RBI to raise his average to .283...Started 64 of the clubs last 76 games...Was sixth among NL catchers in batting at .255 (min 350 at- bats)...Hit .260 against lefties and .254 against righties...As a PH was 7-16 including a home run on April 13 against the Astros Doug Jones...Set career high with a ten game hit streak from August 19 to 31 (19-41)...**1994:** Finished third in NL in catchers fielding with a .996 fielding mark...Set a then career high with ten home runs...Had first career two HR game on April 13 vs Cincinnati's Jose Rijo...The second HR was his 200th career hit...Named Expo player of the month in May hitting .300 with one home run and 19 RBI...Collected a career high five RBI's on May 24 vs the Marlins ...Matched that performance on June 24 again vs the Marlins...June 24 was his second career two HR game (Mike Jeffcoat, Jeff Mutis)...Named to the NL All-Star team where he caught the 10th inning for winning pitcher Doug Jones of the Phillies...Collected 48 RBI in this final 68 games...**1995:** Established what were new career highs in batting (.286), runs (42), doubles (21) and home runs (11)...Posted the third highest fielding percentage among NL catchers at (.994) trailing only Benito Santiago and Darren Daulton...Posted a four hit game on June 11 at San Francisco and hit a three-run homer off Will Van Landingham to highlight a five RBI game which matched his career high...Hit a game winning home run in the 10th inning on August 31 against San Diego's Ron Villone...Ended a streak of 119 games without a home run dating back to June 24, 1994...Of his 110 games he started 93 at catcher...Threw out 33.3% (36-119) of attempted steals...**1996:** Set then personal highs with hits (105) and doubles (22)... Also hit 11 home runs which at the time was a career high...Hit first career grand slam on April 20 against the Pirates Lee Hancock...Collected second career grand slam eight days later, April 28, in Colorado off Bryan Rekar...Matched career highs in RBI at five in both grand slam games...On April 29 was batting .348...Slumped from May 22 to June 8 going 3-34 to see average drop from .270 to .231...Hit .312 in June with 12 RBI in 20 games and then hit .325 in August with three home runs and nine RBI...Posted third career four hit game on June 25 vs Pittsburgh...Hit in an career high 12 straight games from July 25 to August 10 (18-45)...Posted third career two HR game on August 7 in Houston, had two 2R HR's off Donne Wall and Terry Clark...Hit .261 with 11 home runs and 45 RBI against right-handers and 295 with one HR and 12 RBI against right-handers...Was the Expos nominee for the Roberto Clemente Award for community involvement... **1997:** Hit .277 in 96 games with 55 RBI and a career high of 17 home runs...Opened the season with a six game hit streak...Hit .259 in April with three home runs and 13 RBI in 14 games...Homered in three straight games for the first time in his career on April 25 & 26 against the Mets and April 29 in Chicago (NL)...Hit in a season high ten straight games from April 19 to May 6 (14-41, 12RBI)...May was top month hitting .365 (23-63) with six home runs and 15 RBI...May 22 collected his 500th career hit, a home run off of Pittsburgh's Jon Lieber...Was disabled from June 18 to July 2 after suffering sprained ligaments in his right ankle in a home plate collision with Mike Bordick on June 17 in Baltimore...Collected first ML stolen base on July 18 vs Houston to end what was the longest stolen base-less streak in the majors at 659 games...August 23 in Chicago collected his fourth career two homer game against the Cubs Mark Clark and Bob Patterson, also set season high with four RBI...In August hit .282 with six home runs and 17 RBI...Ranked third in the NL with a .994 (4E/636TC) fielding percentage with four passed balls...With the exception of DL time caught every start for Cy Young Award winner Pedro Martinez,

caught 28 of 31 starts... Threw out just 16 of 88 stolen base attempts (18.2%)...Appeared in 83 games behind the plate, 79 starts...Hit .253 (19-75) with four HR's and 16 RBI against lefties and .285 (67-235) with 13 home runs and 39 RBI against right handers...**1998:** Hit .283 with nine home runs and 52 RBI in his first season in the AL...Set what were career highs with 115 hits and 23 doubles...Started the season 0-18, from that point on hit .296 (115-389) for the year...Finished April batting .194 (13-67) with no HR's and five RBI...From May 1 hit .300 (102-340)...First Blue Jay HR on May 3 in Oakland vs. Dave Telgheder...On the disabled list May 29 until June 14 with a left hamstring strain...Hit .319 (22-69) in May with three HR's and 15 RBI...In 12 June games hit .409 (18-44)... Posted fourth career four hit game on June 22 vs Montreal...Was 8-11, 1HR, 5RBI in three games against his former team, the Montreal Expos...After a 1-3 day on July 1 his batting average reached a season high .295...In September hit .333 (22-66) with two home runs and five RBI... Season high eight game hit streak was September 13 to 22...Hit .310 (31-100) with MISP...Hit .203 (12-59) with one HR and seven RBI against left-handed pitchers and .296 (103-348) with eight HR's and 45 RBI against right-handed pitching...Hit .311 (66-212) with six home runs on the road and .251 (49-195) with three home runs at home...Team posted a 3.94 ERA with him behind the plate...Threw out 23.5% of base-runners (31CS/101SB)...Starting catcher for all but two of Cy Young Award winner Roger Clemens 33 starts, on the DL for those two starts...Was the 29th man to play for the Expos and Blue Jays... **1999:** Posted then career highs with a .291 average, 120 hits, 26 doubles, 18 home runs, 44 extra-base hits and 80 RBI...The 80 RBI are a club mark for a Blue Jay catcher...Hit .308 in April with two HR and 15 RBI, had 5 RBI in April 11...In batting practice on May 1 in Seattle suffered a non-displaced fracture of the medial orbit of his right eye as the ball hit the frame of the cage and rebounded back...Was disabled from May 2-31 and joined Syracuse on rehab where he hit .267 (4-15) in four games...Upon his return, June 2, he homered on first pitch he saw off the White Sox John Snyder, went on to homer again off Bryan Ward to post his fifth career two HR game...Hit in a season high eight straight games from June 9 to 19...Finished June hitting .305 with team highs of seven home runs & 20 RBI...In Baltimore on June 30 delivered a three run HR in the tenth inning off Jesse Orosco...Average fell below .300 for the first time all season on July 6...At the All-Star break was batting .302 with nine HR and 37 RBI...In the second half hit .282 with nine HR and 43 RBI...On July 20 hit his third career grand slam against Mike Remlinger of the Atlanta Braves...Tied his career high with 5 RBI on August 20 in Oakland...On September 10 in Detroit had sixth career two HR game and second of the season as he homered off Moehler and Hiljus...Of the 18 home runs, seven were LHP, 11 vs. RHP, seven were solo's, eight were 2R, two were 3R and one slam...Ranked second in the AL in fielding percentage among catchers at .997 (679/681)...Threw out 21.8% of base-stealers...With runners in scoring position hit .314 (37-118).

CAREER NOTES: Is one of nine catchers in the history of the AL and the second Blue Jays catcher to hit three home runs in one game - hit three on August 27, 2000 at Texas to join Ivan Rodriguez, Mickey Cochrane, Bill Dickey, Don Leppert, Bill Freehan, Ernie Whitt, Mike Stanley & Dan Wilson... Is the seventh player in Blue Jay history to hit three home runs in a game... Has a career fielding percentage of .993... Is one of two Blue Jays players to ever hit three grand slams in a season, accomplished in the 2000 season... One of seven Toronto players to hit 20 home runs during the 2000 season to match the ML record done once previously (Baltimore-1996)... Was the 29th player to appear for both the Blue Jays and Expos.

DARRIN FLETCHER

Year	Club & League	AVG	G	AB	R	H	TB	2B	3B	HR	RBI	SH-SF	HP	BB-IBB	SO	SB-CS	GIDP	SLG	OBP
1987	Vero Beach (FSL)	.266	43	124	13	33	40	7	0	0	15	0-4	1	22-3	12	0-2	6	.323	.371
1988	San Antonio (Tex)	.208	89	279	19	58	69	8	0	1	20	6-2	3	17-5	42	2-6	6	.247	.259
1989	Albuquerque (PCL)	.273	100	315	34	86	119	16	1	5	44	2-6	2	30-0	38	1-5	12	.378	.334
1989	LOS ANGELES (NL)	.500	5	8	1	4	7	0	0	1	2	0-0	0	1-0	0	0-0	0	.875	.556
1990	Albuquerque (PCL)	.291	105	350	58	102	166	23	1	13	65	3-6	5	40-6	37	1-1	11	.474	.367
1990	LOS ANGELES (NL)	.000	2	1	0	0	0	0	0	0	0	0-0	0	0-0	1	0-0	0	.000	.000
1990	PHILADELPHIA (NL)	.136	9	22	3	3	4	1	0	0	1	0-0	0	1-0	5	0-0	0	.182	.174
1991	Scranton-WB (Int)	.284	90	306	39	87	126	13	1	8	50	1-6	3	23-4	29	1-3	7	.412	.334
1991	PHILADELPHIA (NL)	.228	46	136	5	31	42	8	0	1	12	1-0	0	5-0	15	0-1	2	.309	.255
1992	MONTREAL (NL)	.243	83	222	13	54	74	10	2	2	26	2-4	2	14-3	28	0-2	8	.333	.289
1992	Indianapolis (AmAs)	.255	13	51	2	13	18	2	0	1	9	0-0	0	2-0	10	0-0	0	.353	.283
1993	MONTREAL (NL)	.255	133	396	33	101	150	20	1	9	60	5-4	6	34-2	40	0-0	7	.379	.320
1994	MONTREAL (NL)	.260	94	285	28	74	124	18	1	10	57	0-12	3	25-4	23	0-0	6	.435	.314
1995	MONTREAL (NL)	.286	110	350	42	100	156	21	1	11	45	1-2	4	32-1	23	0-1	15	.446	.351
1996	MONTREAL (NL)	.266	127	394	41	105	163	22	0	12	57	1-3	6	27-4	42	0-0	13	.414	.321
1997	MONTREAL (NL)	.277	96	310	39	86	159	20	1	17	55	0-2	5	17-3	35	1-1	6	.513	.323
1998	TORONTO (AL)	.283	124	407	37	115	167	23	1	9	52	1-7	6	25-7	39	0-0	19	.410	.328
1999	Syracuse (Int)	.267	4	15	0	4	4	0	0	0	0	0-0	0	1-0	1	0-0	1	.267	.313
1999	TORONTO (AL)	.291	115	412	48	120	200	26	0	18	80	0-4	6	26-0	47	0-0	16	.485	.339
2000	TORONTO (AL)	.320	122	416	43	133	214	19	1	20	58	0-4	5	20-3	45	1-0	8	.514	.355
Minor Totals		.266	444	1440	165	383	542	69	3	28	203	12-24	14	135-18	169	5-17	43	.376	.330
TORONTO TOTALS		.298	361	1235	128	368	581	68	2	47	190	1-15	17	71-10	131	1-0	43	.470	.341
NL TOTALS		.263	705	2124	205	558	879	120	6	63	315	10-27	26	156-17	212	1-5	57	.414	.316
MAJOR TOTALS		.276	1066	3359	333	926	1460	188	8	110	505	11-42	43	227-27	343	2-5	100	.435	.326

HOME RUN BREAKDOWN

				MEN ON				ONE GAME							
Total	H	A	0	1	2	3	2	3	4	LO	XN	IP	PH	RHP	LHP
110	54	56	62	31	11	6	6	1	0	0	2	0	3	91	19

FLETCHER — TRANSACTIONS

- Selected by the Los Angeles Dodgers organization in the 6th round of the June 1987 First Year Player Draft.
- On disabled list August 1-22, 1988.
- On disabled list May 28-June 5, 1989.
- Traded to the Philadelphia Phillies for LHP Dennis Cook, September 13, 1990.
- Traded to the Montreal Expos along with cash for RHP Barry Jones, December 9, 1991.
- On disabled list May 12-June 15, 1992; included rehabilitation assignment to Indianapolis, May 31-June 14.
- On disabled list (stretched ligaments, right ankle) June 18-July 3, 1997.
- Elected free agency October 27, 1997.
- Signed by the Toronto Blue Jays November 26, 1997.
- On disabled list (left hamstring strain) May 30-June 14, 1998.
- On disabled list (right eye - medial orbit) May 2-31, 1999; included rehabilitation assignment at Syracuse, May 24-27.
- On disabled list (right shoulder) June 11-July 3, 2000.

CAREER HIGHS — FLETCHER, Darrin

SEASON:

Games	133 - 1993
Avg.	.320 - 2000
Runs	48 - 1999
Hits	133 - 2000
Doubles	26 - 1999
Home Runs	20 - 2000
RBI	80 - 1999
Walks	34 - 1993
Strikeouts	47 - 1999
Stolen Bases	1 - 1997, 2000
Longest Hitting Streak	12G - Jul. 25-Aug. 10, 1996
Multi HR Games	2 - 1994, 1999

GAME:

ML Debut	Sep. 10, 1989 at SD
Runs	3 - 6 times, last Aug. 27, 2000 at TEX
Hits	4 - 7 times, last Sep. 22, 2000 vs. TB
Doubles	2 - 14 times, last Apr. 16, 2000 vs. SEA
Home Runs	3 - Aug. 27, 2000 at TEX
RBI	5 - 6 times, last Apr. 26, 2000 vs. ANA
Stolen Bases	1 - Jul. 18, 1997 vs. HOU
	1 - Jul. 9, 2000 at MON
Last ML Home Run	Sep. 28, 2000 at BAL

FIELDING
FLETCHER, Darrin—C

Year	PCT	G	PO	A	E	TC	DP
1989 (NL)	1.000	5	16	1	0	17	0
1990 (NL)	1.000	7	30	3	0	33	0
1991 (NL)	.992	45	242	22	2	266	1
1992 (NL)	.995	69	360	33	2	395	3
1993 (NL)	.988	127	620	41	8	669	3
1994 (NL)	.996	81	479	20	2	501	4
1995 (NL)	.994	98	612	45	4	661	8
1996 (NL)	.992	112	721	30	6	757	5
1997 (NL)	.994	83	606	26	4	636	4
1998 (AL)	.991	121	832	51	8	891	1
1999 (AL)	.997	113	638	42	2	682	4
2000 (AL)	.994	117	621	39	4	664	7
Total	.993	978	5777	353	42	6172	40

DARRIN FLETCHER DETAILED HITTING

	2000 Avg	AB	H	HR	RBI	BB	SO	OBP	SLG	CAREER Avg	AB	H	HR	RBI	BB	SO	OBP	SLG
Total	.320	416	133	20	58	20	45	.355	.514	.276	3359	926	110	505	227	343	.326	.435
vs. Left	.342	79	27	1	12	4	15	.391	.468	.255	550	140	19	105	46	84	.325	.416
vs. Right	.315	337	106	19	46	16	30	.346	.525	.280	2809	786	91	400	181	259	.326	.438
Home	.332	220	73	10	34	10	21	.365	.518	.281	1586	445	54	249	111	159	.332	.447
Away	.306	196	60	10	24	10	24	.344	.510	.271	1773	481	56	256	116	184	.320	.424
April	.329	70	23	3	12	2	6	.356	.529	.281	495	139	17	84	29	41	.333	.444
May	.358	81	29	6	16	3	6	.376	.654	.276	519	143	19	90	36	58	.319	.445
June	.250	16	4	0	0	1	1	.333	.250	.285	494	141	20	89	37	45	.340	.478
July	.296	71	21	4	10	4	5	.346	.493	.280	603	169	17	83	49	56	.339	.423
August	.256	82	21	4	7	4	13	.299	.451	.272	618	168	24	98	35	69	.315	.447
September	.370	92	34	3	13	6	14	.400	.511	.271	586	159	13	60	35	69	.315	.394
October	.250	4	1	0	0	0	0	.250	.250	.159	44	7	0	1	6	5	.260	.250
Scoring Posn	.280	93	26	3	37	7	13	.343	.441	.262	928	243	28	381	103	113	.335	.417
Bases Loaded	.333	9	3	1	16	0	1	.333	1.333	.275	91	25	6	92	8	17	.306	.593
DH	.333	6	2	1	1	0	1	.333	.833	.200	10	2	1	1	0	1	.200	.500
PH	.308	13	4	0	2	1	2	.357	.385	.277	119	33	3	16	12	23	.348	.429
vs. Ana	.314	35	11	2	7	2	4	.368	.514	.320	100	32	4	24	4	10	.349	.500
vs. Bal	.321	28	9	3	7	0	2	.310	.643	.255	102	26	5	23	5	7	.291	.431
vs. Bos	.333	18	6	1	1	0	2	.333	.611	.296	71	21	3	10	3	14	.324	.479
vs. CWS	.357	28	10	2	4	2	7	.400	.643	.302	86	26	5	9	5	12	.341	.570
vs. Cle	.400	35	14	2	6	4	3	.463	.600	.298	104	31	4	18	7	14	.348	.462
vs. Det	.211	19	4	1	4	0	1	.211	.421	.324	74	24	3	14	6	4	.375	.500
vs. KC	.105	38	4	1	3	0	7	.105	.211	.208	77	16	1	8	5	12	.267	.299
vs. Min	.280	25	7	0	0	0	5	.280	.360	.266	94	25	1	12	2	12	.273	.372
vs. NYY	.385	39	15	1	5	1	5	.400	.487	.292	89	26	3	12	4	11	.340	.404
vs. Oak	.240	25	6	0	1	2	1	.296	.240	.222	72	16	2	9	7	3	.284	.375
vs. Sea	.304	23	7	1	3	1	3	.320	.522	.288	73	21	3	7	4	13	.321	.479
vs. TB	.406	32	13	1	5	2	2	.429	.563	.343	105	36	1	10	6	9	.391	.438
vs. Tex	.480	25	12	3	6	4	1	.567	1.000	.325	83	27	5	13	4	5	.364	.602
vs. Atl	.000	1	0	0	0	0	0	.000	.000	.193	119	23	2	12	9	26	.263	.277
vs. ChC	–	–	–	–	–	–	–	–	–	.236	178	42	6	27	14	20	.291	.393
vs. Cin	–	–	–	–	–	–	–	–	–	.302	139	42	4	17	9	14	.355	.460
vs. Col	–	–	–	–	–	–	–	–	–	.322	121	39	3	30	6	4	.356	.471
vs. Fla	.200	10	2	0	0	0	1	.273	.200	.247	154	38	4	28	19	16	.335	.396
vs. Hou	–	–	–	–	–	–	–	–	–	.284	155	44	9	24	6	17	.321	.516
vs. LA	–	–	–	–	–	–	–	–	–	.273	198	54	5	23	18	16	.329	.414
vs. Mon	.529	17	9	1	4	2	0	.600	.765	.387	75	29	4	18	8	5	.459	.613
vs. NYM	.300	10	3	1	2	0	1	.300	.700	.258	225	58	10	28	17	16	.313	.436
vs. Phi	.125	8	1	0	0	0	0	.125	.125	.215	177	38	2	21	12	19	.266	.316
vs. Pit	–	–	–	–	–	–	–	–	–	.312	170	53	8	40	9	16	.364	.541
vs. StL	–	–	–	–	–	–	–	–	–	.279	165	46	4	22	8	18	.310	.424
vs. SD	–	–	–	–	–	–	–	–	–	.277	177	49	6	24	22	11	.361	.429
vs. SF	–	–	–	–	–	–	–	–	–	.250	176	44	3	22	8	19	.285	.347
Pre-All Star	.349	189	66	10	33	9	14	.387	.571	.282	1700	479	63	295	124	158	.335	.455
Post-All Star	.295	227	67	10	25	11	31	.328	.467	.269	1659	447	47	210	103	185	.316	.414

DARRIN FLETCHER HITTING AT ML PARKS

Park	Avg	G	AB	R	H	2B	3B	HR	RBI	SB	CS	BB	SO	OBP	Slg
Camden Yards	.260	15	50	8	13	2	0	2	10	0	1	3	4	.296	.420
Fenway Park	.293	10	41	3	12	2	1	1	6	0	0	1	7	.310	.463
Edison Field	.280	13	50	4	14	6	0	2	8	0	0	1	4	.294	.520
Comiskey Park	.289	12	45	4	13	4	0	2	4	0	0	3	6	.333	.511
Jacobs Field	.269	15	52	4	14	1	0	1	10	0	0	4	10	.333	.346
Tiger Stadium	.344	9	32	5	11	1	0	2	6	0	0	3	1	.400	.563
Kauffman Stadium	.313	9	32	0	10	1	0	0	3	0	0	2	8	.361	.344
Metrodome	.306	14	49	4	15	2	0	1	8	0	0	2	9	.327	.408
Yankee Stadium	.265	17	49	5	13	0	0	1	4	0	0	2	7	.288	.327
Oakland-Alameda	.205	14	39	6	8	1	1	2	7	0	0	4	2	.273	.436
Kingdome	.364	6	22	3	8	1	0	2	2	0	0	2	3	.417	.682
Arlington	.306	13	49	6	15	4	0	4	6	0	0	2	2	.333	.633
SkyDome	.296	183	609	66	180	33	0	23	99	0	0	34	62	.341	.463
Atlanta-Fulton	.137	21	51	4	7	0	0	0	1	0	0	3	8	.214	.137
Wrigley Field	.241	24	79	10	19	1	1	5	15	0	0	8	5	.310	.468
Cinergy Field	.300	23	80	9	24	7	0	2	11	0	0	6	10	.356	.463
Astrodome	.200	28	85	5	17	3	0	3	9	0	0	3	10	.250	.341
Dodger Stadium	.268	37	112	10	30	4	0	3	13	0	0	9	6	.323	.384
Olympic Stadium	.281	323	941	98	264	67	2	30	152	2	0	77	88	.337	.452
Shea Stadium	.259	33	116	11	30	5	0	4	12	0	1	8	10	.307	.405
Veterans Stadium	.204	56	157	7	32	8	1	3	22	0	1	11	21	.253	.325
Three Rivers	.287	31	94	10	27	4	0	4	14	0	0	6	9	.350	.457
Busch Stadium	.283	28	92	10	26	8	0	2	10	0	1	2	12	.298	.435
Qualcomm Park	.316	30	95	10	30	4	1	4	13	0	1	11	8	.396	.505
3 Com Park	.302	30	106	9	32	5	0	2	13	0	0	3	12	.321	.406
Coors Stadium	.288	15	52	10	15	3	0	2	12	0	0	3	1	.333	.462
Pro Player Stadium	.230	25	74	4	17	5	1	1	16	0	0	8	7	.314	.365
Turner Field	.176	7	17	0	3	0	0	0	0	0	0	1	5	.222	.176
Tropicana Field	.372	12	43	4	16	4	0	0	4	0	0	4	3	.417	.465
Mile High Stadium	.318	7	22	2	7	1	0	0	9	0	0	1	1	.333	.364
SAFECO Field	.133	4	15	1	2	0	0	1	2	0	0	0	2	.133	.333
Comerica Park	.222	2	9	1	2	1	0	1	4	0	0	0	0	.222	.667

DARRIN FLETCHER — MILESTONES

	DATE	OPP.	H/A	PITCHER	DESCRIPTION
HITS					
1	Sept. 10, 1989	LA vs SD	A	Don Schultze	Single
500	May 22, 1999	MTL vs PIT	A	Jon Lieber	Home run
HR					
1	Sept. 23, 1989	LA vs SD	H	Calvin Schiraldi	Solo PH
100	July 7, 2000	TOR vs MTL	A	Julio Santana	Solo
RBI					
1	Sept. 23, 1989	LA vs SD	H	Calvin Schiraldi	Solo HR
500	May 3, 2000	TOR vs CWS	A	Baldwin	Solo HR
SB					
1	July 18, 1997	MTL vs HOU	H	Garcia Catcher-Ausmus	2nd
GM					
1	Sept. 10, 1989	LA vs SD	A	—	PH
1000	July 7, 2000	TOR vs MTL	A	—	C
SLAMS (6)					
1	April 20, 1996	MTL vs PIT	H	Lee Hancock	3rd
2	April 28, 1996	MTL vs COL	A	Bryan Rekar	1st
3	July 20, 1999	TOR vs ATL	H	Mike Remlinger	6th
4	April 20, 2000	TOR vs ANA	H	Kent Mercker	4th
5	May 8, 2000	TOR vs BAL	H	Jason Johnson	4th
6	May 26, 2000	TOR vs DET	A	Doug Brocail	8th
MULTI HR (7)					
2	April 13, 1994	MTL vs CIN	H	Jose Rio-1R, 1R	2nd, 7th
2	June 24, 1994	MTL vs FLA	H	Jeffcoat-1R, Mutis-3R	7th, 8th
2	August 7, 1996	MTL vs HOU	H	Wall-2R, Clark-2R	6th, 7th
2	August 23, 1997	MTL vs CHI (NL)	A	Clark-2R, Patterson-2R	2nd, 8th
2	June 2, 1999	TOR vs CWS	H	Snyder-1R, Ward-2R	2nd, 7th
2	Sept. 10, 1999	TOR vs DET	A	Moehler-1R, Hiljus-1R	2nd, 8th
3	August 27, 2000	TOR vs TEX	A	Helling-1R, 1R, 1R	2nd, 4th, 8th

John
FRASCATORE

PITCHER

52

BIRTHDATE	February 4, 1970
OPENING DAY AGE	31
BIRTHPLACE	Queens, NY
RESIDENCE	Brookeville, FL
BATS/THROWS	R/R
HEIGHT/WEIGHT	6-1/223
CONTRACT STATUS	signed thru 2002
M.L. SERVICE	4.057

PERSONAL: Name is pronounced FRASS-Kuh-TOR-ee... Married to the former Kandria McNamara... They have a son Gavin (5/1/95) and a daughter Kaylee Marie (3/10/99)... Attended C.W. Post University, where he played baseball and was named Diamond Conference Pitcher of the Week... Graduated in 1988 from Oceanside High School, where he played baseball and basketball, earning all-county honors... Enjoys building auto engines and monster trucks.

LAST SEASON: In his first full season with Toronto was 2-4 with a 5.42 ERA in 60 games... Tied for the club lead with 13 holds... Prior to the All-Star break was 1-3 with a 7.14 ERA, following the break was 1-1 with a 3.31 ERA... Opened the season with a 10.13 ERA in April after appearing in 12 games... In three games from April 15 to 18 allowed 11 earned runs over 3.2 innings, ERA for the month excluding those games was 2.00 (2ER.9.0IP)... Was ejected by home plate umpire Al Clark on April 18 after hitting Scott Spiezo... Last five outings of April were scoreless, 2.2 innings... Was tagged for back-to-back home runs by Thomas and Konerko in Chicago on May 3... Pitched a then season high 3.0 innings on May 20 vs the White Sox... Suffered first loss on May 24 in Boston after allowing a game ending three run HR to Brian Daubach... Rebounded with a win after 2.1 scoreless innings in his next outing at Detroit on May 26... In May was 1-1 with a 4.20 ERA... Struggled in June posting an 8.44 ERA in seven games after twice allowing four earned runs in an outing... On June 20 vs Detroit was tagged for four ER after allowing back-to-back home runs for the second time

(Fick & Becker)... ERA was a season high 7.86 following the June 20 game, from that point on posted an ERA of 3.26 (14ER/38.2IP)... Was ejected on July 30 in Seattle after an inside pitch to Alex Rodriguez... In July was 0-1 after appearing in 12 games posting an ERA of 2.45, had three save opportunities in July but was 0-3... In August was 0-0 with 3.12 ERA in ten games, club was 8-2... Pitched in seven straight wins from August 22 to September 15... Pitched a season high 3.1 innings on September 28 at Baltimore... Had four outings of 3.0 innings or more... Opponents hit .301 with a .289 mark by right-handers and a .324 average by left-handers... At home was 1-1 with a 6.09 ERA while on the road was 1-3 with 4.85 ERA in 33 games.

PROFESSIONAL CAREER: 1991: Picked up first win vs. Batavia on August 4... Finished 4th in NY-Penn League with 30 appearances... Pitched for Cards' instructional league club, with a 2-0 record and a 1.08 ERA... **1992:** Finish third in SAL Rolaids Relief award race and fourth in saves... In seven outings vs. Macon, picked up a win and six saves... Took part in three combined shutouts... Pitched as a starter for Cards' instructional league club, posting a 2-0 record, with, a 2.10 ERA... **1993:** In his first season as a starter, finished seventh among Cards' minor leaguers in innings pitched and strikeouts... Allowed just 1.90 UBB's/9IP, fifth-lowest among Midwest League starters... Hurled a CG 3-hitter on May 31, a 1-0 loss to Clinton... Fired a CG 1-hitter, with no walks and 12 Ks in a 1-0 win vs Waterloo... Pitched for Cards' instructional league club, finishing with a 4-0 record and a 1.06 ERA... **1994:** In first season above Class A level, ranked among Cards' farm system leaders in wins (third), innings (15th) and strikeouts (eighth)... Pitched four complete games at Class AA Arkansas to rank third in Texas League... Was 3-0 in his final three starts for the Travelers, posting a 1.11 ERA in 24.1 innings, including two complete games... Promoted to Class AAA Louisville, where he ranked third on the club with eight wins despite pitching only three months for Redbirds... Promoted to St. Louis to make July 21 emergency start when the Cards played consecutive doubleheaders against ATL... **1995:** Rookie pitcher had three separate stints with the Cardinals while also appearing in 28 games (10 starts) at Louisville (AAA)... Was recalled from Louisville on May 1 and went 1-1 in six games, including four starts... Earned his first ML win in May 13 start at LA when he allowed one run in five IP of 3-2 Cards' win... Was optioned to Louisville on May 31 and was recalled again on July 20... Made just two relief appearances before returning to Louisville on July 24... Completed the year at Louisville before being recalled on September 16 once the American Association Championship Series concluded... Finished the year with a 3.95 ERA at Louisville with five saves... Also had two saves during the playoffs for Louisville during the semi-final round vs Indianapolis... Owned an impressive 2.25 ERA in 10 relief outings for the Cards... Made his longest relief appearance on May 5 vs. Houston... Finished 2nd in the Arizona Fall League with six saves... **1996:** In third season at Class AAA Louisville, was fourth in American Association with three complete games... Threw one-hitter over eight innings, facing the minimum 24 hitters striking out six and walking none, April 17 vs Nashville before Matt Arrandale entered to save 1-0 win... Effort earned John AmAs Pitcher-of-the-Week honors for April 14-20... Gave one run in six innings to win next start April 26 vs Iowa... Beginning with those two efforts and through the month of May, a span of eight starts, posted a 2.48 ERA (16 ER/58 IP) and held opposing hitters to .233 average (50-215)... Tallied season-high eight strikeouts in five innings June 4 vs Omaha... Showed good control yielding 2.57 walks per nine innings (38 BB/133.1 IP) in his 21 starts, which lasted average six and one-third innings... Was moved to bullpen during late July series vs Nashville after winning two of previous 10 efforts... Walked just four and surrendered no home runs in 23 innings during his 15 relief outings, during which he recorded 3.91 ERA... Originally recalled September 9 but not to report, activated for season-ending series vs Cincinnati, but saw no action... **1997:** Led the Cardinals' bullpen corps with a 2.47 ERA, 58 strikeouts and five wins... Ranked fifth among NL relievers in ERA (minimum 54 IP)... Had his

best months in April (1.32 ERA/13.2 IP) and August (0.00 ERA/14.1 IP)... Surrendered only two home runs through July... Was touched for three homers in September... Worked two scoreless innings June 23 vs. Chicago and two shutout innings on June 10 at San Diego... Held left handed batters to a .214 average... After the All-Star break limited batters to a .193 average while going 2-0 with a 2.29 ERA... **1998:** Led the Cardinals' staff in games, a career-high 69, and the bullpen in innings, a personal-high 95.2, which ranked second among National League relievers... Pitched at least two innings in 25 of his 69 outings... Did not allow a run in six outings (11 IP) vs. the Cubs... After starting 0-2 with an 8.79 ERA in April, had a 3.26 ERA in May and 2.12 mark in June... Overall, opponents batted .256 against him (.245, 3 HRs vs.LH/.264, 8 HRs vs RH)... Gained his first win May 19 by Philly by retiring all five batters he faced... Logged a season-high four innings on June 24 at Cleveland, allowing two runs on six hits... Allowed three-straight homers (Derrek Lee, Cliff Floyd and Kevin Orie) in the ninth inning on August 26 vs. Florida after tossing a perfect eighth inning... Stroked his first career big-league hit on May 30 at San Diego, a single against Andy Ashby...**1999:** Had a combined record of 8-5 with a save and a 3.73 ERA between Arizona and Toronto... Attended spring training with St. Louis and was traded to Arizona on March 30 in exchange for RHP Clint Sodowsky... Appeared in 26 games with the Diamondbacks and was 1-4 with a 4.09 ERA, four holds and one blown save... Traded to Toronto on June 12 along with SS Tony Batista in exchange for LHP Dan Plesac... With Toronto appeared in 33 games and was 7-1 with a 3.41 ERA and a save... Started his Blue Jays career going 7-0 which tied him with Tom Filer (7-0) in 1985 for the third best start as a Blue Jay behind the 11-0 starts by Roger Clemens (1997) and Dennis Lamp (1985)... Equaled the major league record for wins in consecutive games by a reliever - was the winning pitcher in three consecutive games against Baltimore, June 29, 30 & July 1... Was the ninth Major League relief pitcher to win three straight and fifth in the AL... On September 4 in KC earned his first ML and professional save with a scoreless inning - was career game #127 in the majors and the 525th game of his pro career... Earned first loss on September 10 in Detroit after one ER in 0.1IP... With Toronto was 3-1 on the road with a 2.29 ERA and 4-0 at home with an ERA of 4.67... Posted six holds for Toronto and stranded 21 of 32 inherited runners... On the season had 10 holds combined and stranded 30 of 46 inherited runners.

CAREER NOTES: As a batter has one hit in 17 at bats with one walk and 12 strikeouts... Has appeared in 262 games and made five starts.

JOHN FRASCATORE

Year	Club & League	W-L	ERA	G	GS	CG	ShO	SV	IP	H	R	ER	HR	HB	BB-IBB	SO	WP	BK	OBA
1991	Hamilton (NYP)	2-7	9.20	30	1	0	0	1	30.1	44	38	31	3	2	22-1	18	1	2	.328
1992	Savannah (SAL)	5-7	3.84	50	0	0	0	23	58.2	49	32	25	4	3	29-2	56	4	5	.218
1993	Springfield (Mid)	7-12	3.78	27	26	2	1	0	157.1	157	84	66	6	3	33-0	126	2	3	.259
1994	Arkansas (Tex)	7-3	3.10	12	12	4	1	0	78.1	76	37	27	3	3	15-0	63	3	0	.251
1994	Louisville (AmAs)	8-3	3.39	13	12	2	1	0	85.0	82	34	32	3	2	33-2	58	2	0	.255
1994	ST. LOUIS (NL)	0-1	16.20	1	1	0	0	0	3.1	7	6	6	2	0	2-0	2	1	0	.438
1995	Louisville (AmAs)	2-8	3.95	28	10	1	0	5	82.0	89	54	36	5	3	34-3	55	5	0	.273
1995	ST. LOUIS (NL)	1-1	4.41	14	4	0	0	0	32.2	39	19	16	3	2	16-1	21	0	0	.298
1996	Louisville (AmAs)	6-13	5.18	36	21	3	0	0	156.1	180	106	90	22	7	42-2	95	5	0	.286
1997	ST. LOUIS (NL)	5-2	2.48	59	0	0	0	0	80.0	74	25	22	5	6	33-5	58	4	0	.247
1998	ST. LOUIS (NL)	3-4	4.14	69	0	0	0	0	95.2	95	48	44	11	3	36-3	49	2	0	.256
1999	ARIZONA (NL)	1-4	4.09	26	0	0	0	0	33.0	31	16	15	6	1	12-4	15	0	0	.256
1999	TORONTO (AL)	7-1	3.41	33	0	0	0	1	37.0	42	16	14	5	1	9-4	22	5	0	.292
2000	TORONTO (AL)	2-4	5.42	60	0	0	0	0	73.0	87	51	44	14	7	33-2	30	3	0	.301
Minor Totals		37-53	4.26	196	82	12	3	29	648.0	677	385	307	46	23	208-10	471	22	10	.266
TORONTO TOTALS		9-5	4.25	93	0	0	0	1	110.0	129	67	58	19	8	42-6	52	8	0	.298
NL TOTALS		10-12	3.78	169	5	0	0	0	244.2	246	114	103	27	12	99-19	145	7	0	.262
MAJOR TOTALS		19-17	4.09	262	5	0	0	1	354.2	375	181	161	46	20	141-19	197	15	0	.274

FRASCATORE — TRANSACTIONS

- Selected by the St. Louis Cardinals organization in the 24th round in the June 1991 First Year Player Draft.
- Traded to Arizona Diamondbacks in exchange for RHP Clint Sodowsky, March 30, 1999.
- Traded to the Toronto Blue Jays along with IF Tony Batista in exchange for LHP Dan Plesac, June 12, 1999.

CAREER HIGHS — FRASCATORE, John

<table>
<tr><td colspan="2">SEASON:</td><td colspan="2">GAME:</td></tr>
<tr><td>Wins</td><td>8 - 1999</td><td>ML Debut</td><td>Apr. 21, 1994 vs. ATL</td></tr>
<tr><td>Losses</td><td>5 - 1999</td><td>Innings Pitched:</td><td></td></tr>
<tr><td>Saves</td><td>1 - 1999</td><td> Starter</td><td>6.0 - May 18, 1995 at SF</td></tr>
<tr><td>ERA</td><td>2.48 - 1997</td><td> Reliever</td><td>4.0 - Jun. 24, 1998 at CLE</td></tr>
<tr><td>Games</td><td>69 - 1998</td><td>Walks:</td><td></td></tr>
<tr><td>Starts</td><td>4 - 1995</td><td> Starter</td><td>3 - May 13, 1995 at LA</td></tr>
<tr><td>Complete Games</td><td>None</td><td> Reliever</td><td>3 - Apr. 12, 1998 at SF</td></tr>
<tr><td>Shutouts</td><td>None</td><td></td><td>3 - Jul. 30, 2000 at SEA</td></tr>
<tr><td>Innings Pitched</td><td>95.2 - 1998</td><td>Strikeouts:</td><td></td></tr>
<tr><td>Walks</td><td>36 - 1998</td><td> Starter</td><td>6 - May 13, 1995 at LA</td></tr>
<tr><td>Strikeouts</td><td>58 - 1997</td><td> Reliever</td><td>4 - Jun. 1, 1997 vs. LA</td></tr>
<tr><td>Longest Win Streak</td><td>7 - Jun. 29-Aug. 8, 1999</td><td>Hits Allowed</td><td>8 - May 24, 1995 vs. ATL</td></tr>
<tr><td>Longest Losing Streak</td><td>2 - Apr. 10-12, 1998</td><td>Runs Allowed</td><td>7 - May 24, 1995 vs. ATL</td></tr>
<tr><td></td><td>2 - Apr. 5-9, 1999</td><td>ER Allowed</td><td>6 - Jul. 21, 1994 vs. ATL</td></tr>
<tr><td></td><td>2 - May 21-Jun. 1, 1999</td><td></td><td>6 - May 24, 1995 vs. ATL</td></tr>
<tr><td></td><td>2 - Jun. 6-Jul. 4, 2000</td><td>HR Allowed</td><td>3 - Aug. 26, 1998 vs. FLA</td></tr>
<tr><td>Scoreless Innings Streak</td><td>15.2 - Aug. 5-Sep. 5, 1997</td><td>Low Hit CG</td><td>None</td></tr>
<tr><td></td><td></td><td>Last Win</td><td>Sep. 1, 2000 vs. OAK</td></tr>
<tr><td></td><td></td><td>Last Save</td><td>Sep. 4, 1999 at KC</td></tr>
<tr><td></td><td></td><td>Last CG</td><td>None</td></tr>
<tr><td></td><td></td><td>Last ShO</td><td>None</td></tr>
<tr><td></td><td></td><td>Last Start</td><td>May 29, 1995 vs. COL</td></tr>
<tr><td></td><td></td><td>Last Relief App.</td><td>Oct. 1, 2000 at CLE</td></tr>
</table>

FIELDING

FRASCATORE, John—P

Year	PCT	G	PO	A	E	TC	DP
1994 (NL)	1.000	1	0	1	0	1	0
1995 (NL)	1.000	14	3	2	0	5	0
1997 (NL)	1.000	59	5	5	0	10	0
1998 (NL)	.917	69	11	11	2	24	1
1999 (NL)	1.000	26	1	2	0	3	0
1999 (AL)	1.000	33	2	6	0	8	0
2000 (AL)	.923	60	7	5	1	13	2
Total	.953	262	29	32	3	64	3

JOHN FRASCATORE PITCHING AT ML PARKS

Park	ERA	W-L-Sv	SvO	G	GS	IP	H	R	ER	HR	BB	SO
Camden Yards	3.00	0-0-0	0	5	0	6.0	7	3	2	2	4	2
Fenway Park	11.25	0-1-0	0	4	0	4.0	8	5	5	1	1	2
Edison Field	5.79	0-0-0	0	4	0	4.2	9	3	3	2	0	3
Comiskey Park	3.12	1-0-0	0	7	0	8.2	13	3	3	3	5	5
Jacobs Field	3.60	1-1-0	1	6	0	10.0	13	6	4	2	3	8
Tiger Stadium	3.86	0-1-0	0	2	0	2.1	2	1	1	0	3	0
Kauffman Stadium	0.00	0-0-1	1	3	0	3.1	1	0	0	0	1	3
County Stadium	3.86	0-0-0	0	3	0	2.1	5	1	1	0	0	0
Metrodome	6.75	0-0-0	0	2	0	1.1	1	1	1	0	2	0
Yankee Stadium	0.00	0-0-0	0	4	0	3.0	4	1	0	0	0	2
Oakland-Alameda	0.00	0-0-0	0	2	0	2.2	2	0	0	0	0	1
Arlington	5.40	1-0-0	1	5	0	5.0	6	3	3	2	3	4
SkyDome	5.61	5-1-0	2	44	0	51.1	57	37	32	7	18	23
Wrigley Field	0.82	0-0-0	0	7	0	11.0	5	1	1	1	2	10
Cinergy Field	1.35	1-0-0	0	5	0	6.2	5	1	1	0	6	5
Astrodome	3.12	0-1-0	1	8	0	8.2	12	3	3	0	6	2
Dodger Stadium	2.70	2-1-0	1	7	1	16.2	15	6	5	1	9	14
Olympic Stadium	5.19	0-1-0	1	7	0	8.2	9	5	5	1	2	6
Shea Stadium	2.08	0-0-0	0	7	0	8.2	7	2	2	0	2	3
Veterans Stadium	3.55	1-0-0	0	7	0	12.2	13	7	5	1	5	9
Three Rivers	1.74	0-0-0	0	5	0	10.1	8	3	2	0	1	6
Busch Stadium	4.69	5-4-0	3	75	3	103.2	113	61	54	15	39	60
Qualcomm Park	4.26	0-0-0	0	5	0	6.1	6	3	3	2	2	4
3 Com Park	3.77	1-2-0	0	6	1	14.1	11	6	6	1	9	9
Coors Field	10.80	0-1-0	1	6	0	6.2	9	8	8	5	2	4
Pro Player Stadium	4.50	0-0-0	0	2	0	2.0	2	1	1	0	4	1
Turner Field	5.40	0-3-0	1	6	0	6.2	10	4	4	0	6	5
BankOne Ballpark	0.61	0-0-0	0	11	0	14.2	12	1	1	0	2	1
Tropicana Field	0.00	0-0-0	0	1	0	2.0	2	0	0	0	0	3
Aloha Stadium	0.00	0-0-0	0	1	0	1.1	0	0	0	0	1	1
SAFECO Field	2.45	0-0-0	1	3	0	3.2	2	1	1	0	3	1
Comerica Park	6.75	1-0-0	0	2	0	5.1	6	4	4	0	0	0

JOHN FRASCATORE DETAILED PITCHING

	2000								CAREER							
	ERA	W-L-Sv	G	IP	H	ER	BB	SO	ERA	W-L-Sv	G	IP	H	ER	BB	SO
Total	5.42	2-4-0	60	73.0	87	44	33	30	4.09	19-17-1	262	354.2	375	161	141	197
ST	–	–	–	–	–	–	–	–	8.10	1-2-0	5	20.0	32	18	10	16
REL	5.42	2-4-0	60	73.0	87	44	33	30	3.85	18-15-1	257	334.2	343	143	131	181
Home	6.09	1-1-0	27	34.0	39	23	14	13	4.63	10-5-0	129	169.0	181	87	59	84
Away	4.85	1-3-0	33	39.0	48	21	19	17	3.59	9-12-1	133	185.2	194	74	82	113
March	–	–	–	–	–	–	–	–	0.00	0-0-0	1	0.2	0	0	0	0
April	10.03	0-0-0	12	11.2	19	13	7	6	5.87	1-5-0	43	53.2	70	35	28	36
May	4.20	1-1-0	11	15.0	13	7	6	4	3.92	5-4-0	47	80.1	73	35	24	47
June	8.44	0-1-0	7	10.2	15	10	5	4	4.50	3-2-0	38	54.0	68	27	26	32
July	2.45	0-1-0	12	14.2	13	4	7	5	4.36	5-3-0	50	64.0	67	31	28	30
August	3.12	0-0-0	10	8.2	10	3	6	6	2.28	3-0-0	42	51.1	45	13	19	26
September	5.79	1-1-0	7	9.1	15	6	2	3	3.77	2-3-1	38	45.1	47	19	15	22
October	3.00	0-0-0	1	3.0	2	1	0	2	1.69	0-0-0	3	5.1	5	1	1	4
vs. Ana	9.00	0-0-0	6	6.0	12	6	2	4	9.00	0-0-0	8	8.0	15	8	2	4
vs. Bal	3.00	0-0-0	5	6.0	8	2	4	2	2.08	3-0-0	9	8.2	9	2	4	4
vs. Bos	5.63	0-1-0	6	8.0	8	5	2	4	10.24	0-1-0	8	9.2	15	11	2	4
vs. CWS	5.06	0-0-0	4	5.1	7	3	4	1	1.65	1-0-0	12	16.1	17	3	7	10
vs. Cle	3.18	0-1-0	5	5.2	6	2	0	3	3.95	1-1-0	12	13.2	19	6	5	11
vs. Det	11.37	1-0-0	3	6.1	9	8	1	0	9.35	1-1-0	5	8.2	11	9	4	0
vs. KC	0.00	0-0-0	3	3.0	3	0	0	1	0.87	0-0-1	8	10.1	9	1	4	5
vs. Mil	–	–	–	–	–	–	–	–	9.82	0-0-0	5	3.2	10	4	0	0
vs. Min	3.86	0-0-0	3	2.1	2	1	3	1	3.38	0-0-0	4	2.2	2	1	3	1
vs. NYY	0.00	0-0-0	3	1.2	3	0	0	1	0.00	0-0-0	4	3.0	4	0	0	2
vs. Oak	0.00	1-0-0	2	1.0	0	0	0	0	0.00	1-0-0	5	6.0	4	0	0	2
vs. Sea	9.00	0-0-0	6	8.0	9	8	7	3	8.68	0-0-0	7	9.1	11	9	8	4
vs. TB	6.23	0-1-0	3	4.1	4	3	1	1	4.26	0-1-0	4	6.1	6	3	1	4
vs. Tex	4.76	0-0-0	5	5.2	5	3	5	4	5.63	1-0-0	8	8.0	10	5	5	6
vs. Ari	–	–	–	–	–	–	–	–	2.25	0-0-0	4	4.0	5	1	2	5
vs. Atl	5.40	0-1-0	2	3.1	4	2	3	2	9.58	1-5-0	13	20.2	32	22	13	15
vs. ChC	–	–	–	–	–	–	–	–	0.40	0-0-0	14	22.1	12	1	5	13
vs. Cin	–	–	–	–	–	–	–	–	3.45	1-2-0	12	15.2	13	6	13	6
vs. Col	–	–	–	–	–	–	–	–	5.82	0-1-0	12	17.0	20	11	4	12
vs. Fla	–	–	–	–	–	–	–	–	6.00	0-0-0	5	6.0	5	4	4	1
vs. Hou	–	–	–	–	–	–	–	–	4.58	0-1-0	14	17.2	20	9	9	7
vs. LA	–	–	–	–	–	–	–	–	2.43	2-1-0	17	29.2	24	8	13	23
vs. Mon	0.00	0-0-0	1	1.0	0	0	0	0	3.00	2-1-0	11	15.0	13	5	2	9
vs. NYM	2.45	0-0-0	2	3.2	6	1	1	2	1.29	1-0-0	16	21.0	24	3	5	7
vs. Phi	0.00	0-0-0	1	1.2	1	0	0	1	2.95	2-0-0	11	18.1	16	6	5	15
vs. Pit	–	–	–	–	–	–	–	–	5.02	0-0-0	10	14.1	20	8	2	6
vs. SD	–	–	–	–	–	–	–	–	3.55	0-0-0	11	12.2	9	5	5	5
vs. SF	–	–	–	–	–	–	–	–	3.46	2-2-0	13	26.0	20	10	14	16
Pre-All Star	7.14	1-3-0	35	40.1	51	32	20	14	4.59	10-12-0	142	200.0	226	102	84	117
Post-All Star	3.31	1-1-0	25	32.2	36	12	13	16	3.43	9-5-1	120	154.2	149	59	57	80

Ryan
FREEL

INFIELDER/OUTFIELDER

14

BIRTHDATE	March 8, 1976
OPENING DAY AGE	25
BIRTHPLACE	Jacksonville, FL
RESIDENCE	Jacksonville, FL
BATS/THROWS	R/R
HEIGHT/WEIGHT	5-10/185
CONTRACT STATUS	signed thru 2001
M.L. SERVICE	0.000

PERSONAL: Ryan Paul Freel... Graduated from Englewood High School, Florida, in 1994... Attended Tallahasse Community College.

LAST SEASON: Combined to hit .299 with 13 home runs and 44 RBI for three clubs, Dunedin (A), Tennessee (AA) and Syracuse (AAA)... Was slowed in the spring with a hamstring pull and began his season in May with the Dunedin Blue Jays where he hit .500 in four games with three home runs and six RBI... On May 22 against Sarasota was 5-5 with two home runs and five RBI... Was promoted to Tennessee on May 24 where he hit .295 in 12 games with eight RBI... Was promoted to Syracuse on June 5 where he hit .286 in 80 games with 14 doubles, five triples, ten home runs and 30 RBI... Recorded 30 stolen bases and was caught seven times... While with Syracuse played second base, shortstop, left-field, center-field and DH... Hit .324 in June with two home runs an nine RBI in 22 games... After hitting only .188 in July he rebounded with a .371 average in 26 August games with six home runs, 13 RBI and 17 stolen bases... Was the SkyChiefs Player of the Month in August... On August 24 vs Rochester was 4-5 with a grand slam and five RBI... Twice stole three bases in game, on August 28 at Pawtucket and August 30 vs Buffalo... Hit .370 (20-54) against left-handed pitching with Syracuse and .266 (61-229) against right-handers... Played for Scottsdale in the Arizona Fall League and hit .341 in 27 games with eight doubles, three triples, nine RBI and ten stolen bases... Following that joined Lara in the Venezuelan Winter League.

PROFESSIONAL CAREER: 1995: Led St. Catharines club in sacrifice hits (7) and sacrifice flies (5)... Hit .292 (33-113) in 30 August games... On August 2 had four hits (6AB) with a triple and three RBI at New Jersey and came back three days later with three triples in a 4-for-7 doubleheader performance at Batavia... **1996:** Led Dunedin squad in sacrifice hits (14) and stolen bases (19)... Hit .255 with 23 doubles, three triples, four home runs and 41 RBI... Hit .322 (38-118) after July 1... Played 94 games at second and five games at shortstop... Led the organization with 14 sacrifice hits...

1997: Opened the season with Knoxville (AA) of the Southern League where he hit just .202 in 33 games, all at shortstop... On base average was .348 after recording 19 walks in 94 at bats with just 13 strikeouts... Stole five of eight bases attempted... May 21 was optioned to Dunedin of the Florida State League (A)... Hit just .235 in May and .231 in June after joining Dunedin but rebounded hitting .315 (34-108) the rest of the season... Hit three home runs which all came in August... Drew 46 walks in 61 games (181AB) to post a .447 on base percentage... Did not play from July 2 to 19 after being placed on the disabled list (right hamstring)... Returned to the DL from July 23 to 30... Hit in a season high eight straight from July 30 to August 8 (14-26)... Stole 24 bases and was caught just 5 times... At Dunedin played 27 games at short, 18 in the outfield, seven at second and four at third... Had 29 stolen bases on the season to rank fourth in the organization...**1998:** Spilt the season between Knoxville (AA) and Syracuse (AAA) and made the transition from infield to outfield... Opened the season in Knoxville hitting .310 in April... Hit in a season high nine straight games

from May 27 to June 5... June 16 collected a season high five RBI against Carolina, was 3-4 with a double and a home run... Finished June batting .323 (31-96) with eight extra base hits and 18 RBI... Had three outfield assists... Homered in his final game with Knoxville on July 16 before promotion to Syracuse... At AAA hit just .229 in 37 games with two home runs and 12 RBI but posted a .377 on-base percentage... Recorded 26 walks and 16 strikeouts... Reached base via a hit or walk in 15 straight games from July 27 to August 12... Recorded a walk in nine straight games from August 2 to 12, 12 in total... **1999:** Appeared in only 31 games after a right shoulder problems... Had season ending surgery performed by Dr. James Andrews in Birmingham, Alabama on June 17... Opened the season with Knoxville (AA) where he hit .283 in 11 games with five doubles, a triple, a home run and nine RBI... Was promoted to Syracuse on April 20 and hit .299 with three doubles, two triples, a home run, 11 RBI and 15 runs scored in 20 games... Was successful in ten of 13 stolen base attempts.

RYAN FREEL

Year	Club & League	AVG	G	AB	R	H	TB	2B	3B	HR	RBI	SH-SF	HP	BB-IBB	SO	SB-CS	GIDP	SLG	OBP
1995	St. Catharines (NYP)	.280	65	243	30	68	97	10	5	3	29	7-5	7	22-0	49	12-7	3	.399	.350
1996	Dunedin (FSL)	.255	104	381	64	97	138	23	3	4	41	14-2	5	33-0	76	19-15	4	.362	.321
1997	Knoxville (Sou)	.202	33	94	18	19	22	1	1	0	4	1-0	2	19-0	13	5-3	3	.234	.348
1997	Dunedin (FSL)	.282	61	181	42	51	72	8	2	3	17	6-1	9	46-2	28	24-5	3	.398	.447
1998	Knoxville (Sou)	.286	66	252	47	72	107	17	3	4	36	3-4	1	33-0	32	18-9	3	.425	.366
1998	Syracuse (Int)	.229	37	118	19	27	37	4	0	2	12	0-3	4	26-0	16	9-4	3	.314	.377
1999	Knoxville (Sou)	.283	11	46	9	13	23	5	1	1	9	0-1	0	8-0	4	4-2	0	.500	.382
1999	Syracuse (Int)	.299	20	77	15	23	33	3	2	1	11	1-0	4	8-0	13	10-3	3	.429	.393
2000	Dunedin (FSL)	.500	4	18	7	9	19	1	0	3	6	0-0	0	0-0	1	0-0	0	1.056	.500
2000	Tennessee (Sou)	.295	12	44	11	13	18	3	1	0	8	2-0	1	8-0	6	2-3	3	.409	.400
2000	Syracuse (Int)	.286	80	283	62	81	135	14	5	10	30	4-2	9	35-1	44	30-7	3	.477	.380
Minor Totals		.272	493	1737	324	473	701	89	23	31	203	36-20	42	238-3	282	133-58	28	.404	.370

FREEL — TRANSACTIONS

- Selected by the Toronto Blue Jays in the 10th round (272nd overall) of the June 1995 First Year Player Draft.
- On disabled list (right hamstring) July 2-18, 1997.
- On disabled list (right hamstring) July 23-30, 1997.
- On disabled list (hamstring pull) April 10-May 3, 2000.
- On disabled list May 10-21, 2000.

Jeff
FRYE

INFIELDER

BIRTHDATE	August 31, 1966
OPENING DAY AGE	34
BIRTHPLACE	Oakland, CA
RESIDENCE	Fort Worth, TX
BATS/THROWS	R/R
HEIGHT/WEIGHT	5-9/170
CONTRACT STATUS	signed thru 2001
M.L. SERVICE	8.015

2

PERSONAL: Jeffrey Dustin Frye... Married, wife's name is Stacey... Two children, Darian (9/15/90) and Canon (3/14/98)... Graduated from Panama High School in Oklahoma in 1984 where he lettered in baseball, football & basketball... In 1986 graduated from Carl Albert Junior College in Poteau, Oklahoma with an Associate of Science degree... Named all-region in baseball both years... Played baseball two years (1987-88) at Southeastern State University in Durant, where he was a 1st team NAIA All-American & Oklahoma Intercollegiate Conference Player of the Year as a senior... Was twice an All-Conference selection... Played Little League, Babe Ruth, & American Legion baseball... Enjoys fishing, golf and hunting.

LAST SEASON: Combined to hit .307 with 19 doubles, one homer and 16 RBI in 106 games while playing for Boston and Colorado... Opened the season with Boston where he hit .289 in 69 games with 13 doubles and 13 RBI... Started slowly, hitting .133 in his first ten games... Hit .352 in May in 15 games with four doubles and three RBI... Hit in 12 straight games from May 15 to June 2... Collected three straight 3-hit

games from May 24- 27... Then hit in 13 straight from June 4 to June 19... Overall hit in 25 of 26 games... In July was batting .302 in 17 games before a July 27 trade in which he joined RHP's Brian Rose, John Wasdin and Jeff Taglienti heading to Colorado in exchange for IF Mike Lansing, RHP Rolando Arrojo... With the Rockies was platooned at second-base with Todd Walker and hit .356 in 37 games... Matched his career best with a four-hit performance on September 12 at San Diego, fourth career four-hit game... Hit .441 (15-34) at Coors Field in Colorado and .302 (16-58) on the road... With runners in scoring position for Colorado, Frye batted .167 (3-for-18)... As a pinch hitter with the Rockies hit .467 (7-15).

PROFESSIONAL CAREER: 1988: Made his pro debut with Butte of the Pioneer League... Hit .286 in 55 games and stole 16 bases to rank third on the team... **1989:** Led the South Atlantic League with a .313 average... Finished second in the SAL with 145 hits was fifth in runs with 85... Led league second basemen with a .977 fielding percentage... Stole 33 bases for Gastonia and was a SAL post-season All-Star...

1990: Hit .272 for Port Charlotte of the Florida State League and was second in the league with 503 at bats, third with 137 hits, fourth in runs with 77 and fifth in walks with 80... Set club records in AB and walks... Stole 28 bases to lead the team... **1991:** Joined Tulsa of the Texas League (AA) and hit .302 in 131 games... Was third in the league with 503 at bats and 11 triples, was tied for third with 32 doubles while tying for fifth in the league with 152 hits and 71 walks... Selected to the Texas Leage All-Star team... Played winter ball in Venezuela and was fifth in the league with a .312 batting average in 54 games with Puerto La Cruz... **1992:** Hit .300 in 87 games with Oklahoma City in the American Association (AAA)... Led club with 87 games played, 337 at bats, 64 runs, 101 hits 26 doubles, 51 walks and 11 stolen bases... Was second in the league with a .409 on-base percentage and tenth in batting... Selected as the All-Star second baseman... Contract was purchased by Texas on July 9... Started 65 of the Rangers final 76 games at second base... Made his ML debut on July 9 vs. Cleveland and reached base safely in his first three plate appearances (BB, 1B, 3B)... First ML home run was a lead-off home run on July 24 vs Baltimore... Selected as the Rangers Rookie of the Year... Played winter ball in Venezuela with Oriente and led the league in batting at .385... **1993:** Sustained torn ACL and torn cartilage in his right knee while jogging on January 26... Underwent surgery on February 15 and spent the season on disabled list... Played 38 games for Oriente in Venezuela and hit .291... Broke hamate bone in left wrist when HBP... Had surgery on December 10 to repair the injury... **1994:** Opened the season in Oklahoma City where he hit .279 in 17 games... Was recalled to Texas on April 30... In 57 games with the Rangers hit .327 with 20 doubles... Hit safely in his first six games and in 20 of first 24... Appeared at third base on May 2 at Detroit... Was his first professional game at any position other than second base... Tied a club record with two triples on May 10 vs. California... Doubled in five straight games, May 30 to June 4... On the disabled list with a pulled left hamstring from June 9 to 24... Had first career four hit game on August 3 vs Chicago... Missed five games from July 6-10 and eight games July 24-31 due to sore hamstring... **1995:** Had his first full season in the majors and hit .278 in 90 games with 15 doubles, two triples, four home runs and 29 RBI... In his first 23 games of the season he hit .337 with a hit in 20 of the 23 games... Suffered a pulled right hamstring and was on the disabled list from June 3 to 18... Returned to the disabled list from June 21 to July 6... On July 28 vs Boston he hit his first HR since July 24, 1992 in Baltimore... That kicked off four home runs in a 13 game span from July 28 to August 12... **1996:** Opened the season in Oklahoma and hit .238 in 49 games... Played 39 games at second base, five at shortstop, four in the outfield and two at third base... Hit .303 in his last 25 games before being released on June 5... Was

signed that day by Boston and joined the Red Sox where he went on to appear in 105 games hitting .286 with 27 doubles and 41 RBI... Was 1-4 with a walk and an RBI in his Red Sox debut, June 6 vs Chicago... Matched his career high with four hits on June 13 vs Texas... Delivered an RBI single in the bottom of the ninth off Wetteland to defeat the Yankees, 12-11 on July 17... Scored four runs on July 19 vs Baltimore to tie the ML high for the season, one short of the ML record of six (Johnny Pesky-1946 & Spike Owen- 1986)... Hit in 12 straight from July 31 to August 11... Hit all four home runs in August, a month when he hit .333 with 12 RBI... Tied his career high with three RBI on September 19 in Detroit... Hit .323 (80-248) in his last 64 games to raise his average from .234... Successful in 18 of 22 stolen base attempts, the 81.8 success rate ranked fourth in the AL... Hit lead-off in 47 games, 52 hitting second, twice at eighth and one in ninth... 97 starts at 2B, two in left field, one in center, twice in right and three appearances at shortstop... Made 1st ML appearances at SS, LF, CF, RF... **1997:** Set career highs of 127 games played, 126 hits, 36 doubles, 51 RBI, 19 stolen bases and 175 total bases... Started 100 games, 79 at second base, 13 at third base, four in left field, twice in right, once in center and once as DH... Sox were 43-36 when he started at 2B... Hit .414 (12-29) in April in 16 games, five starts... On June 7 vs Cleveland hit his first career PH-HR against Alvin Morman... As a pinch-hitter was 4-9... Tied career high with three RBI on June 4 in Milwaukee and July 18 in Cleveland... Set career high with seven total bases on July 18 in Cleveland (3-4, 2B, HR)... In July hit .344 with a home run and 17 RBI in 26 games... Hit in a career high 15 straight games from July 27 to August 14... Also posted an 11 game hit streak, September 5- 16... Started at 2B in 70 of Sox last 73 G and hit .336 (89-265)... In September hit .382 with one home run and 11 RBI... Hit .326 at home with two homers and 21 RBI and .300 on the road with one HR and 30 RBI... After the All-Star break hit .335 with two home runs and 34 RBI... Started at every spot in batting order except cleanup... **1998:** Suffered a torn ACL in his left knee during spring training while fielding ground balls... Was placed on the 15-day disabled list on March 23 and transferred to the 60-day disabled list for the rest of the season on April 30... **1999:** Opened the season as the opening day second baseman... Appeared in only 41 games after returning to the disabled list... Stole home on June 4 in 5-1 win vs. Atlanta off LHP Tom Glavine who threw pitch over C Javier Lopez's head on suicide squeeze play... Hit a game-winning HR off Minnesota's Mike Trombley in the bottom of the ninth on June 14... Was placed on the 15 day disabled list on June 16 with a left knee strain... Did not appear in a game until September 1 vs Kansas City... Hit .379 in nine games on rehab assignments with the Gulf Coast Red Sox and Pawtucket Red Sox (AAA).

JEFF FRYE

Year	Club & League	AVG	G	AB	R	H	TB	2B	3B	HR	RBI	SH-SF	HP	BB-IBB	SO	SB-CS	GIDP	SLG	OBP
1988	Butte (Pio)	.286	55	185	47	53	62	7	1	0	14	1-1	1	35-0	24	16-1	2	.335	.401
1989	Gastonia (SAL)	.313	125	464	85	145	180	26	3	1	40	5-1	1	72-5	53	33-13	4	.388	.405
1990	Charlotte (FSL)	.272	131	503	77	137	167	16	7	0	50	7-4	2	80-5	66	29-6	5	.332	.372
1991	Tulsa (Tex)	.302	131	503	92	152	218	32	11	4	41	5-3	1	71-1	60	15-8	9	.433	.388
1992	Oklahoma City (AmAs)	.300	87	337	64	101	137	26	2	2	28	8-0	11	51-0	39	11-9	9	.407	.409
1992	TEXAS (AL)	.256	67	199	24	51	65	9	1	1	12	11-1	3	16-0	27	1-3	2	.327	.320
1993								Injured — DID NOT PLAY											
1994	Oklahoma City (AmAs)	.279	17	68	7	19	25	3	0	1	5	2-1	0	6-0	7	2-0	1	.368	.333
1994	TEXAS (AL)	.327	57	205	37	67	93	20	3	0	18	5-3	1	29-0	23	6-1	1	.454	.408
1995	TEXAS (AL)	.278	90	313	38	87	118	15	2	4	29	8-4	5	24-0	45	3-3	7	.377	.335
1996	Oklahoma City (AmAs)	.238	49	181	25	43	56	10	0	1	18	2-1	3	24-1	21	10-1	5	.309	.335
1996	BOSTON (AL)	.286	105	419	74	120	163	27	2	4	41	5-3	5	54-0	57	18-4	6	.389	.372
1997	BOSTON (AL)	.312	127	404	56	126	175	36	2	3	51	2-7	2	27-1	44	19-8	12	.433	.352
1998								Injured — DID NOT PLAY											
1999	Red Sox (Gulf)	.400	6	20	4	8	9	1	0	0	1	0-0	0	2-0	2	0-0	0	.450	.455
1999	Pawtucket (Int)	.333	3	9	0	3	3	0	0	0	2	0-0	0	2-0	1	0-0	0	.333	.455
1999	BOSTON (AL)	.281	41	114	14	32	38	3	0	1	12	1-1	1	14-1	11	2-2	2	.333	.362
2000	BOSTON (AL)	.289	69	239	35	69	85	13	0	1	13	4-1	1	28-0	38	1-3	5	.356	.364
2000	COLORADO (NL)	.356	37	87	14	31	37	6	0	0	3	1-1	1	8-0	16	4-0	3	.425	.412
Minor Totals		.291	604	2270	401	661	857	121	24	9	199	30-11	19	343-12	273	116-38	35	.378	.387
AL TOTALS		.295	556	1893	278	558	737	123	10	14	176	36-26	18	192-2	245	50-24	35	.389	.356
MAJOR TOTALS		.294	593	1980	292	583	774	129	10	14	179	37-21	19	200-2	261	54-24	38	.391	.361

HOME RUN BREAKDOWN

			MEN ON				ONE GAME								
Total	H	A	0	1	2	3	2	3	4	LO	XN	IP	PH	RHP	LHP
14	8	6	8	5	1	0	0	0	0	1	0	0	1	8	6

FRYE — TRANSACTIONS

- Selected by the Texas Rangers in 30th round of the June 1988 First Year Player Draft.
- On disabled list (torn ACL in right knee) March 27-October 4, 1993.
- On disabled list (pulled left hamstring) June 9-24, 1994.
- Signed by the Detroit Tigers on February 6, 1996.
- Released by the Detroit Tigers on March 24, 1996.
- Signed by the Texas Rangers on March 26, 1996.
- Released by the Texas Rangers on June 5, 1996.
- Signed by the Boston Red Sox on June 5, 1996.
- On disabled list (torn ACL in left knee) March 13-October 30, 1998.
- On disabled list (strained left knee) June 15-September 1, 1999.
- Traded to the Colorado Rockies along with RHP Brian Rose, RHP John Wasdin and RHP Jeff Taglienti in exchange for RHP Rolando Arrojo, 2B Mike Lansing and RHP Rick Croushore on July 27, 2000.
- Signed by the Toronto Blue Jays on December 14, 2000.

CAREER HIGHS — FRYE, Jeff

SEASON:

Games	127 - 1997
Avg.	.312 - 1997
Runs	74 - 1996
Hits	175 - 1997
Doubles	36 - 1997
Home Runs	4 - 1995, 1996
RBI	51 - 1997
Walks	54 - 1996
Strikeouts	57 - 1997
Stolen Bases	19 - 1997
Longest Hitting Streak	15 - July 27-Aug. 4, 1997
Multi HR Games	None

GAME:

ML Debut	July 9, 1992 vs. CLE
Runs	5 - July 19, 1996 vs. BAL
Hits	4 - Aug. 3, 1994 vs. CWS
	4 - June 13, 1996 vs. TEX
	4 - June 14, 1999 vs. MIN
	4 - Sept. 12, 2000 at SD
Doubles	2 - 7 times, last July 30, 1997 vs. SEA
Home Runs	1 - 14 time, last July 5, 2000 at MIN
RBI	3 - 6 times, last July 18, 1997 at CLE
Stolen Bases	2 - Sept. 14, 1996 vs. CWS
Last ML Home Run	July 5, 2000 at MIN

FIELDING

FRYE, Jeff—2B

Year	PCT	G	PO	A	E	TC	DP
1992 (AL)	.978	67	120	196	7	323	7
1994 (AL)	.983	54	90	136	4	230	29
1995 (AL)	.975	83	173	248	11	432	55
1996 (AL)	.983	100	200	317	9	526	70
1997 (AL)	.991	80	196	228	4	428	63
1999 (AL)	.980	26	41	56	2	99	9
2000 (AL)	.991	53	95	122	2	219	20
2000 (NL)	.989	27	37	56	1	94	15
Total	.983	490	952	1359	40	2351	304

FRYE, Jeff—3B

Year	PCT	G	PO	A	E	TC	DP
1994 (AL)	.000	1	0	0	0	0	0
1997 (AL)	.878	18	11	32	6	49	2
1999 (AL)	.882	7	5	10	2	17	0
2000 (AL)	1.000	3	1	2	0	3	0
2000 (NL)	1.000	1	0	2	0	2	1
Total	.887	30	17	46	8	71	3

FRYE, Jeff—SS

Year	PCT	G	PO	A	E	TC	DP
1996 (AL)	1.000	3	1	0	0	1	0
1997 (AL)	1.000	3	2	2	0	4	0
1999 (AL)	1.000	2	6	5	0	11	1
Total	1.000	8	9	7	0	16	1

FRYE, Jeff—OF

Year	PCT	G	PO	A	E	TC	DP
1996 (AL)	1.000	5	10	0	0	10	0
1997 (AL)	.900	13	16	2	2	20	0
2000 (AL)	1.000	15	20	0	0	20	0
Total	.960	33	46	2	2	50	0

HITTING FOR THE CYCLE

FOR TORONTO:

PLAYER	DATE	SITE
Kelly Gruber (vs KC)	April 16, 1989	Exhibition Stadium

FOR OPPONENTS:

PLAYER	DATE	SITE
Mike Cubbage (Twins)	July 27, 1978	Metropolitan Stadium
Rich Gedman (Boston)	September 18, 1985	Fenway Park
George Brett (Royals)	July 25, 1990	SkyDome

What Gruber Did: Went 4-4 with a career high 6 RBI... Homered in the first inning against Floyd Bannister, had a 2-run double in the second inning also against Bannister... In the seventh inning, he notched a two-run triple versus Tom Gordon... In the ninth, Gruber had an RBI single off Jerry Don Gleaton to complete the cycle.

JEFF FRYE DETAILED HITTING

	2000									CAREER								
	Avg	AB	H	HR	RBI	BB	SO	OBP	SLG	Avg	AB	H	HR	RBI	BB	SO	OBP	SLG
Total	.307	326	100	1	16	36	54	.377	.374	.294	1980	583	14	179	200	261	.361	.391
vs. Left	.359	117	42	1	5	10	23	.411	.462	.307	592	182	6	58	67	86	.376	.421
vs. Right	.278	209	58	0	11	26	31	.359	.325	.289	1388	401	8	121	133	175	.355	.378
Home	.329	164	54	0	7	18	25	.397	.396	.313	958	300	8	81	101	123	.381	.411
Away	.284	162	46	1	9	18	29	.357	.352	.277	1022	283	6	98	99	138	.343	.372
April	.200	20	4	0	2	1	3	.238	.250	.298	114	34	0	9	12	12	.364	.351
May	.352	54	19	0	3	8	7	.444	.426	.307	322	99	0	28	43	38	.391	.376
June	.265	102	27	0	6	13	18	.345	.314	.266	335	89	2	25	43	43	.350	.343
July	.299	67	20	1	2	6	11	.356	.388	.281	434	122	4	39	41	64	.344	.396
August	.278	54	15	0	2	5	11	.344	.315	.279	427	119	7	38	37	61	.343	.396
September	.519	27	14	0	1	3	4	.567	.667	.337	326	110	1	34	23	40	.381	.445
October	.500	2	1	0	0	0	0	.500	.500	.455	22	10	0	6	1	3	.458	.545
Scoring Posn	.277	65	18	0	14	13	12	.387	.308	.285	449	128	3	153	55	63	.353	.374
Bases Loaded	.000	5	0	0	3	1	1	.125	.000	.216	37	8	0	27	5	6	.280	.243
DH	.333	3	1	0	0	1	0	.600	.333	.211	19	4	1	2	2	1	.286	.383
PH	.474	19	9	0	0	0	4	.500	.579	.378	37	14	1	2	4	7	.439	.541
vs. Ana	.143	7	1	0	1	0	1	.143	.143	.266	128	34	1	12	19	14	.368	.367
vs. Bal	.059	17	1	0	1	3	6	.200	.059	.168	125	21	1	10	13	22	.248	.232
vs. Bos	–	–	–	–	–	–	–	–	–	.343	67	23	1	2	4	10	.380	.448
vs. CWS	.000	9	0	0	0	4	4	.308	.000	.323	158	51	0	19	12	13	.370	.399
vs. Cle	.500	4	2	0	0	0	1	.500	.500	.373	118	44	2	12	10	15	.423	.542
vs. Det	.286	14	4	0	1	0	2	.286	.357	.241	162	39	0	16	17	20	.320	.309
vs. KC	.455	11	5	0	1	5	2	.625	.545	.292	106	31	0	4	14	11	.372	.368
vs. Mil	.200	5	1	0	0	0	1	.200	.200	.379	116	44	2	12	13	11	.447	.517
vs. Min	.320	25	8	1	2	1	5	.346	.520	.325	154	50	3	18	9	20	.355	.435
vs. NYY	.343	35	12	0	2	4	4	.400	.457	.251	175	44	0	16	17	31	.318	.360
vs. Oak	.000	5	0	0	0	0	2	.000	.000	.288	125	36	1	13	10	19	.343	.392
vs. Sea	–	–	–	–	–	–	–	–	–	.299	117	35	2	16	20	15	.408	.462
vs. TB	–	–	–	–	–	–	–	–	–	.273	11	3	0	2	4	0	.438	.273
vs. Tex	.400	5	2	0	1	1	0	.500	.600	.328	61	20	0	3	9	8	.408	.443
vs. Tor	.341	41	14	0	3	4	4	.413	.366	.311	164	51	1	19	13	22	.370	.366
vs. Ari	.500	4	2	0	0	3	2	.714	1.000	.500	4	2	0	0	3	2	.714	1.000
vs. Atl	.333	30	10	0	0	2	5	.375	.333	.283	46	13	0	1	2	9	.313	.304
vs. ChC	.200	5	1	0	0	0	2	.200	.400	.200	5	1	0	0	0	2	.200	.400
vs. Fla	.429	21	9	0	0	2	2	.478	.571	.409	22	9	0	0	2	3	.458	.545
vs. LA	.286	7	2	0	1	0	0	.286	.286	.286	7	2	0	1	0	0	.286	.286
vs. Mon	.188	16	3	0	0	0	1	.188	.188	.143	35	5	0	0	1	3	.167	.171
vs. NYM	.261	23	6	0	0	1	4	.292	.304	.207	29	6	0	0	2	4	.258	.241
vs. Phi	.364	22	8	0	2	3	4	.462	.364	.400	25	10	0	2	3	5	.483	.440
vs. Pit	.308	13	4	0	1	3	2	.412	.385	.308	13	4	0	1	3	2	.412	.385
vs. StL	.000	1	0	0	0	0	0	.000	.000	.000	1	0	0	0	0	0	.000	.000
vs. SD	.833	6	5	0	0	0	0	.833	1.000	.833	6	5	0	0	0	0	.833	1.000
Pre-All Star	.287	209	60	1	13	27	34	.370	.349	.286	896	256	3	75	109	107	.365	.360
Post-All Star	.342	117	40	0	3	9	20	.391	.419	.302	1084	327	11	104	91	154	.358	.416

JEFF FRYE HITTING AT ML PARKS

Park	Avg	G	AB	R	H	2B	3B	HR	RBI	SB	CS	BB	SO	OBP	Slg
Camden Yards	.246	20	61	7	15	4	0	1	6	3	0	5	12	.303	.361
Fenway Park	.308	180	614	99	189	39	4	6	53	19	8	58	85	.367	.401
Edison Field	.260	22	77	9	20	3	0	1	8	2	0	5	8	.318	.338
Comiskey Park	.268	24	82	10	22	6	1	0	12	0	0	8	8	.333	.366
Jacobs Field	.375	12	40	10	15	5	0	1	4	0	0	5	3	.444	.575
Tiger Stadium	.238	19	63	7	15	6	0	0	9	3	0	8	8	.324	.333
Kauffman Stadium	.232	19	69	6	16	2	1	0	2	1	2	6	5	.289	.290
County Stadium	.450	15	60	9	27	8	0	1	11	8	3	4	6	.477	.633
Metrodome	.265	24	83	18	22	3	0	1	9	3	0	6	13	.304	.337
Yankee Stadium	.242	22	91	10	22	10	1	0	8	2	2	8	18	.307	.374
Oakland-Alameda	.276	25	87	9	24	4	1	1	10	1	1	7	13	.333	.379
Kingdome	.300	16	50	8	15	5	0	0	6	3	0	8	7	.410	.400
Arlington	.338	81	269	46	91	18	5	2	25	5	3	39	28	.425	.465
SkyDome	.253	22	79	12	20	1	0	0	5	0	1	7	10	.337	.266
Wrigley Field	.000	1	4	0	0	0	0	0	0	0	0	0	2	.000	.000
Dodger Stadium	.250	2	4	0	1	0	0	0	1	0	0	0	0	.250	.250
Olympic Stadium	.115	8	26	2	3	1	0	0	0	0	1	1	2	.148	.154
Shea Stadium	.059	6	17	1	1	0	0	0	0	1	0	1	3	.111	.059
Veterans Stadium	.357	5	14	3	5	0	0	0	1	0	1	3	2	.471	.357
Three Rivers	.375	3	8	1	3	0	0	0	1	0	0	2	2	.455	.375
Busch Stadium	.000	1	1	0	0	0	0	0	0	0	0	0	0	.000	.000
Qualcomm Park	1.000	1	4	3	4	1	0	0	0	0	0	0	0	1.000	1.250
Coors Field	.441	18	34	6	15	5	0	0	1	2	0	5	6	.525	.588
Pro Player Stadium	.308	3	13	2	4	2	0	0	1	0	1	1	1	.357	.462
Turner Field	.286	5	14	2	4	0	0	0	0	0	0	2	4	.375	.286
Tropicana Field	.200	2	5	1	1	0	0	0	1	0	0	4	0	.556	.200
Cleveland Stadium	.333	3	6	1	2	1	0	0	1	0	0	0	2	.333	.500
Arlington Stadium	.260	33	104	10	27	5	1	0	5	0	2	7	13	.310	.327
Comerica Park	.000	1	1	0	0	0	0	0	0	0	0	0	0	.000	.000

Brad
FULLMER
FIRST BASEMAN/DH

20

BIRTHDATE	January 17, 1975
OPENING DAY AGE	26
BIRTHPLACE	Chatsworth, CA
RESIDENCE	Henderson, NV
BATS/THROWS	L/R
HEIGHT/WEIGHT	6-0/215
CONTRACT STATUS	signed thru 2002
M.L. SERVICE	2.155

PERSONAL: Bradley Ryan Fullmer... Single... Graduated in 1993 from Montclair Prep High School in Van Nuys, CA... Batted .568 with 15 home runs and 62 RBI in his senior year of high school... Named to the Baseball America and USA Today All American teams... Also named Division III Player of the Year in California... Received an offer from Stanford University... Enjoys running and weight lifting.

LAST SEASON: In his first season with Toronto hit .295 with 29 doubles and career highs of 32 home runs and 104 RBI... Set new club record for home runs and RBI by a designated hitter... Previous marks were 25HR's by Canseco in 1998 and 91 RBI by Winfield in 1992... Was second in the AL to Edgar Martinez for HR's and RBI by a DH... Acquired by Toronto from Montreal on March 16 in a three way deal which saw Texas acquire David Segui from Toronto and Montreal acquire 1B Lee Stevens from Texas... Opened the season by tying for the club lead in RBI in April at 24 with Batista, in April 17 hit his third home run of the season and his second career grand slam against the Angels Lou Pote... Had six consecutive multi-hit games, April 18-23... Hit in seven straight from May 7 to 14... From May 14 to June 11 had just 8H in 46AB, average dropped from .344 to .297... Hit .241 in May with six doubles, two home runs and six RBI... After a 3R-HR on May 13 did not collect another HR or RBI until June 12... From June 12 to 29 hit seven home runs in 15 games and totaled 17 RBI... Hit in 12 of 13 games from June 11 to 25... Recorded RBI in five straight games from June 22 to 27... At the All-Star break was batting .305 with 14HR and 49RBI, after the break hit .282 with 52 RBI and a team high 18 HR... Left July 13 game vs Philadelphia after suffering leg cramps... Posted his first of two 2HR games on July 26 vs Cleveland and collected 4RBI with two 2R-HR's off Bartolo Colon... Hit .284 in July with eight home runs and 18 RBI... Had a season high four RBI, seven times, twice in August... Had four RBI on August 22 vs Kansas City and then again on August 30 in Anaheim when he had his second two-homer game of the season and third career... Homered in three straight games from September 8 to 10 and collected seven RBI... Reached 100 RBI's on September 15 in Chicago... Suffered from a hyper-extended right elbow and did not play after September 24... Had an MRI which revealed loose bodies in his right elbow which were removed October 10, by Dr. Lewis Yocum... Hit .322 (46-140) with RISP... Against RHP posted a .311 average with 27 home runs and 85 RBI and against LHP batted .226 with five HR's and 19 RBI... Was one of Toronto's four players to hit 30HR's in 2000 (Batista, Cruz, Delgado) — it marks just the second time in AL history this has been done (Anaheim- 2000)... Also one of Toronto's seven players to hit 20 home runs and become just the second such group in Major League history (Baltimore- 1996).

PROFESSIONAL CAREER: 1993: After signing late only saw action in the Expos fall instructional league program... **1994:** Missed the entire campaign after undergoing rotator cuff surgery to his right shoulder in April... **1995:** Made his professional debut with Albany in the South Atlantic League (A) where he finished second to teammate Vladimir Guerrero in the batting race... Co-led the league with Fernando Tatis in hits (151), third in doubles (38) and fifth in on-base percentage (.387)... Alternated between first and third base... Selected Expos' player development player of the month in June (.387, 2 HR, 15 RBI) and Topps Player of the

Month in August... **1996:** Continued his apprenticeship at West Palm Beach (A) and was selected the Expos player development Player of the Month in July after batting .370 with three HR, 17 RBI... Jumped to AA to end the season... Finished one homer shy of winning the first Triple Crown in the history of the Hawaii Winter Baseball League as he took home league MVP honors as a member of the Maui Stingrays... Batted .333, six HR, 41 RBI, a league record... **1997:** Played in 94 games with Harrisburg (AA) and struck out just 25 times in 357 at-bats... Collected 34 multi-hit games... Hit in 11 straight games from May 7-17, going 15-for-41, .366 with two doubles, four HR and eight RBI... Homered eight times and drove in 16 runs in May... Posted two 2-HR games in three days, July 26 and 28, driving in 10 runs... On July 26th vs Bowie hit two HR, four RBI and on the 28th vs Trenton, his last game at AA, hit two more HR (#18-19) with six RBI... Batted .359 in July (28-for-78)... Played 68 games at first base and 18 in the outfield... Graduated to Ottawa on July 30 and went 2-for-3, two doubles, three RBI vs Columbus in his AAA debut... In 24 games in the International League, started 19 games at first base and one in the outfield... Named the Expos' Minor League Player of the Year and was selected second-best prospect in the Eastern League (AA) by Baseball America... Hit a combined .308 between AA and AAA, with 31 doubles, 22 home runs and 79 RBI... Led the organization in batting (.308), 3rd in HR and 4th in RBI... Graduated to the Ottawa Lynx (AAA) on July 30 and to the Expos on September 2... Became just second Expo to homer in his first ML plate appearance when he took the Red Sox' Bret Saberhagen deep in the 4th inning on September 2... Became the 73rd player all-time and just the 12th pinch-hitter to accomplish the feat... Collected 12 hits in his first 40 ML at-bats with two doubles and three HR, batting .300 with the Expos in September... Went 0-3 with an RBI in his first start at first base for the injured David Segui on September 6 vs the Phillies... Started five of the last six games at first base, going 7-for-20, with a 2B, HR, 4 RBI... Hit an inside-the-park home run as a pinch hitter on September 16 at Pittsburgh off Jon Lieber... Played for Peoria of the Arizona Fall League and hit .414 in 31 games with a league-leading 15 doubles, four homers and 29 RBI, missing by only nine at-bats to qualify for the batting title... Was selected by AFL managers as a top prospect at first base... Participated in the Rookie Career Development Program in January... **1998:** In his rookie season finished 7th in the league with 44 doubles which tied him with Barry Bonds and was seven shy of leader Craig Biggio... The 44 doubles set the club rookie record surpassing the 41 by Warren Cromartie in 1977... Was the was fourth-highest single season total in franchise history... Fullmer was among the elite group of NL rookie first basemen in 1998 with Colorado's Todd Helton, Arizona's Travis Lee, Florida's Derek Lee and Cincinnati's Sean Casey... Finished second on the team in RBI with 73... Batted .331 with runners in scoring position... First Expos' rookie in club history to bat clean-up on Opening Day, a role he would fill on 60 occasions... Among rookies was first in the NL for doubles, second to Helton for multi-hit games (41), extra base hits (59) and slugging percentage (.446); third in batting average (.273), RBI (73) and on base percentage (.327); fourth in hits (138), home runs (13), total bases (225) and fourth in runs (58) and walks (39)... On April 12 collected four hits and four RBI with two doubles against the Cubs... First career grand slam came on May 30 at Pittsburgh against Jose Silva and give him a career high five RBI... Hit safely in then career-best nine straight games twice, from May 22-31, (16-37/.432) and June 17-26 (14-36/.389)... Registered first career 2-HR game vs Brian Anderson on August 18 at Arizona, going 3-for-4 with 3 RBI... Lead the majors in doubles until June 28 with 34... Did not hit a double in next 24 games until August 9 vs Arizona... Made 135 starts at first base... In 137 games at first made 17 errors for a .985 fielding percentage... **1999:** Split the season between Montreal and Ottawa (AAA)... Opened the season hitting just .207 in the first 30 games before being optioned to Ottawa on May 16... Returned to Montreal and appeared in three games, going 4-for-13, but was returned to Ottawa as Rondell White came off the disabled list... With Ottawa hit .317 (45-142) with 11 homers and 32 RBI in 39 games... Was recalled to the Expos on July 15... Upon his return went 2-for-4 in Baltimore... Despite late recall in July he was named the Expos' Player of the Month for July after hitting .368 (21-57) with seven doubles, a triple, two home runs and ten RBI... Posted first career four hit game on July 19 at Yankee Stadium, was 4-4 with two doubles, a homer, three RBI vs Hideki Irabu... Hit

safely in a career-high 16 straight games from August 7-22... Hit a game-winning HR off San Francisco's John Johnstone in 12th inning on August 17 at 3-Com Park to break a 1-1 tie... Batted .219 with three homers and 11 RBI before the All-Star break and after the break hit .302 with 24 doubles, six homers and 36 RBI... Committed seven errors after posting 17 in 1998... Collected 34 doubles in 100 games... On April 23 vs Philadelphia tied a club record hitting three doubles... 35.4% of his hits were doubles.

CAREER NOTES: Now has three career two HR games... Was one of Toronto's four players to hit 30 HR's during the 2000 season, just the second time in the history of the AL (Anaheim- 2000), and the ninth time in ML history that four teammates each finished the season with 30 home runs... One of seven Toronto players to hit 20 home runs during the 2000 season to match the ML record done once previously (Baltimore-1996)... Holds the Blue Jays single season designated hitter records for home runs (32 in 2000) and RBI (104 in 2000).

BRAD FULLMER

Year	Club & League	AVG	G	AB	R	H	TB	2B	3B	HR	RBI	SH-SF	HP	BB-IBB	SO	SB-CS	GIDP	SLG	OBP
1994						INJURED — DID NOT PLAY													
1995	Albany (SAL)	.323	123	468	69	151	221	38	4	8	67	0-6	17	36-4	33	10-10	9	.472	.387
1996	West Palm Beach (FSL)	.303	102	380	52	115	161	29	1	5	63	0-8	11	32-2	43	4-6	9	.424	.367
1996	Harrisburg (East)	.276	24	98	11	27	45	4	1	4	14	0-0	2	3-0	8	0-0	3	.459	.311
1997	Harrisburg (East)	.311	94	357	60	111	196	24	2	19	62	0-4	7	30-5	25	6-4	11	.549	.372
1997	Ottawa (Int)	.297	24	91	13	27	43	7	0	3	17	0-5	2	3-0	10	1-1	3	.473	.317
1997	MONTREAL (NL)	.300	19	40	4	12	23	2	0	3	8	0-0	1	2-1	7	0-0	0	.575	.349
1998	MONTREAL (NL)	.273	140	505	58	138	225	44	2	13	73	0-1	2	39-4	70	6-6	12	.446	.321
1999	Ottawa (Int)	.317	39	142	31	45	87	9	0	11	32	0-1	3	12-1	16	2-2	5	.613	.380
1999	MONTREAL (NL)	.277	100	347	38	96	161	34	2	9	47	0-3	2	22-6	35	2-3	14	.464	.321
2000	TORONTO (AL)	.295	133	482	76	142	269	29	1	32	104	0-6	6	30-3	68	3-1	14	.558	.340
Minor Totals		.310	406	1536	236	476	753	111	8	50	255	0-24	42	116-12	135	23-23	40	.490	.369
NL TOTALS		.276	259	892	100	246	409	80	4	25	128	0-4	5	63-11	112	8-9	26	.459	.326
MAJOR TOTALS		.282	392	1374	176	388	678	109	5	57	232	0-10	11	93-14	180	11-10	40	.493	.331

HOME RUN BREAKDOWN

				MEN ON				ONE GAME								
Total	H	A	0	1	2	3	2	3	4	LO	XN	IP	PH	RHP	LHP
57	24	33	26	19	10	2	3	0	0	0	1	1	2	48	9

FULLMER — TRANSACTIONS

- Selected by the Montreal Expos in the 2nd round of the June 1993 First Year Player Draft.
- On disabled list (rotator cuff surgery on right shoulder) June 20-September 26, 1994.
- Traded to the Toronto Blue Jays in a three-way deal with 1B David Segui and cash going from Toronto to the Texas Rangers and 1B Lee Stevens going from Texas to Montreal on March 16, 2000.

CAREER HIGHS — FULLMER, Brad

SEASON:		GAME:	
Games	140 - 1998	ML Debut	Sep. 2, 1997 vs. BOS
Avg.	.295 - 2000	Runs	3 - Jun. 17, 2000 at BOS
Runs	76 - 2000		3 - Jun. 29, 2000 at TB
Hits	142 - 2000		3 - Sep. 19, 2000 vs. NYY
Doubles	44 - 1998	Hits	4 - Apr. 12, 1998 at CHI
Home Runs	32 - 2000		4 - Jul. 19, 1999 at NYY
RBI	104 - 2000		4 - Jun. 29, 2000 at TB
Walks	39 - 1998	Doubles	3 - Apr. 23, 1999 vs. PHI
Strikeouts	70 - 1998	Home Runs	2 - Aug. 18, 1998 at ARI
Stolen Bases	6 - 1998		2 - Jul. 26, 2000 vs. CLE
Longest Hitting Streak	16G - Aug. 7-22, 1999		2 - Aug. 30, 2000 at ANA
Multi HR Games	2 - 2000	RBI	5 - May 30, 1998 at PIT
		Stolen Bases	1 - 11 times, last Jun. 22, 2000 vs. DET
		Last ML Home Run	Sep. 17, 2000 at CWS

FIELDING

FULLMER, Brad—1B

Year	PCT	G	PO	A	E	TC	DP
1997	.982	8	49	7	1	57	6
1998	.985	137	1070	79	17	1166	81
1999	.991	94	700	41	7	748	48
2000	1.000	1	2	1	0	3	0
Total	.987	240	1821	128	25	1974	135

FULLMER, Brad—OF

Year	PCT	G	PO	A	E	TC	DP
1997	.500	2	1	0	1	2	0

BRAD FULLMER DETAILED HITTING

	2000									CAREER								
	Avg	AB	H	HR	RBI	BB	SO	OBP	SLG	Avg	AB	H	HR	RBI	BB	SO	OBP	SLG
Total	.295	482	142	32	104	30	68	.340	.558	.282	1374	388	57	232	93	180	.331	.493
vs. Left	.226	93	21	5	19	5	18	.279	.430	.234	244	57	9	43	16	41	.290	.422
vs. Right	.311	389	121	27	85	25	50	.355	.589	.293	1130	331	48	189	77	139	.340	.509
Home	.291	254	74	16	50	15	31	.337	.543	.271	711	193	24	108	42	91	.316	.466
Away	.298	228	68	16	54	15	37	.343	.575	.294	663	195	33	124	51	89	.346	.523
April	.363	80	29	5	24	9	12	.435	.663	.298	225	67	8	39	23	34	.372	.520
May	.241	79	19	2	9	9	13	.322	.392	.256	211	54	5	27	15	32	.306	.450
June	.333	81	27	7	16	3	9	.360	.667	.311	190	59	10	33	9	29	.343	.558
July	.284	81	23	8	18	3	12	.306	.605	.293	208	61	12	41	7	26	.313	.529
August	.273	88	24	6	23	4	17	.316	.523	.302	288	87	12	54	22	31	.354	.503
September	.274	73	20	4	14	2	5	.289	.493	.238	248	59	10	38	16	27	.288	.419
October	–	–	–	–	–	–	–	–	–	.250	4	1	0	0	1	1	.400	.250
Scoring Posn	.322	143	46	15	80	12	23	.376	.692	.311	380	118	24	182	41	51	.378	.579
Bases Loaded	.400	10	4	1	14	0	0	.333	.700	.367	30	11	2	30	0	3	.343	.633
DH	.295	478	141	32	104	30	68	.340	.561	.297	468	139	32	103	28	65	.341	.568
PH	.214	14	3	0	1	2	3	.294	.214	.208	24	5	2	6	0	4	.208	.542
vs. Ana	.342	38	13	4	16	4	8	.405	.711	.342	38	13	4	16	4	8	.405	.711
vs. Bal	.179	39	7	1	3	1	5	.200	.282	.222	63	14	1	4	3	8	.258	.317
vs. Bos	.286	42	12	4	6	1	6	.318	.595	.259	54	14	5	8	1	9	.286	.556
vs. CWS	.241	29	7	2	8	4	3	.324	.552	.241	29	7	2	8	4	3	.324	.552
vs. Cle	.323	31	10	2	9	2	4	.364	.548	.323	31	10	2	9	2	4	.364	.548
vs. Det	.381	42	16	5	12	3	8	.426	.857	.381	42	16	5	12	3	8	.426	.857
vs. KC	.351	37	13	4	15	5	5	.429	.730	.351	37	13	4	15	5	5	.429	.730
vs. Mil	–	–	–	–	–	–	–	–	–	.227	44	10	1	5	2	2	.277	.409
vs. Min	.190	21	4	1	4	0	4	.182	.429	.190	21	4	1	4	0	4	.182	.429
vs. NYY	.348	46	16	0	4	0	4	.354	.500	.328	64	21	1	9	1	11	.343	.531
vs. Oak	.261	23	6	2	4	2	1	.320	.565	.261	23	6	2	4	2	1	.320	.565
vs. Sea	.346	26	9	2	7	0	4	.346	.654	.346	26	9	2	7	0	4	.346	.654
vs. TB	.310	42	13	3	11	2	5	.326	.619	.315	54	17	4	14	2	7	.328	.648
vs. Tex	.222	36	8	0	3	2	8	.317	.222	.222	36	8	0	3	2	8	.317	.222
vs. Tor	–	–	–	–	–	–	–	–	–	.533	15	8	2	5	2	1	.588	1.133
vs. Ari	–	–	–	–	–	–	–	–	–	.256	43	11	2	6	2	1	.304	.488
vs. Atl	.000	1	0	0	0	0	0	.000	.000	.219	64	14	1	10	5	9	.286	.344
vs. ChC	–	–	–	–	–	–	–	–	–	.373	51	19	1	15	4	3	.404	.588
vs. Cin	–	–	–	–	–	–	–	–	–	.217	69	15	0	4	2	6	.247	.275
vs. Col	–	–	–	–	–	–	–	–	–	.258	66	17	2	7	5	7	.310	.424
vs. Fla	1.000	1	1	0	0	0	0	1.000	1.000	.265	68	18	2	7	8	8	.342	.426
vs. Hou	–	–	–	–	–	–	–	–	–	.234	47	11	1	5	2	13	.280	.340
vs. LA	–	–	–	–	–	–	–	–	–	.351	57	20	3	7	7	6	.422	.667
vs. Mon	.167	12	2	0	0	2	1	.286	.167	.167	12	2	0	0	2	1	.286	.167
vs. NYM	.250	8	2	1	1	2	0	.400	.625	.273	77	21	1	5	5	7	.317	.416
vs. Phi	.375	8	3	1	1	0	2	.375	.750	.281	64	18	2	8	2	14	.303	.516
vs. Pit	–	–	–	–	–	–	–	–	–	.320	50	16	2	13	4	5	.364	.540
vs. StL	–	–	–	–	–	–	–	–	–	.231	39	9	0	4	5	5	.318	.282
vs. SD	–	–	–	–	–	–	–	–	–	.239	46	11	2	6	4	5	.300	.413
vs. SF	–	–	–	–	–	–	–	–	–	.364	44	16	2	12	3	7	.404	.614
Pre-All Star	.305	266	81	14	53	22	37	.363	.541	.283	667	189	23	103	48	99	.335	.490
Post-All Star	.282	216	61	18	51	8	31	.310	.579	.281	707	199	34	129	45	81	.326	.496

BRAD FULLMER HITTING AT ML PARKS

Park	Avg	G	AB	R	H	2B	3B	HR	RBI	SB	CS	BB	SO	OBP	Slg
Camden Yards	.179	7	28	1	5	0	0	0	1	0	0	0	4	.179	.179
Fenway Park	.194	8	31	4	6	0	0	2	3	0	0	1	7	.219	.387
Edison Field	.222	4	18	3	4	2	0	2	6	0	0	1	5	.263	.667
Comiskey Park	.250	6	20	4	5	1	0	2	8	1	0	3	2	.333	.600
Jacobs Field	.308	3	13	0	4	0	0	0	3	0	0	1	1	.357	.308
Kauffman Stadium	.412	4	17	3	7	1	0	2	8	0	0	2	2	.474	.824
County Stadium	.320	6	25	5	8	3	1	0	3	0	1	1	0	.346	.520
Metrodome	.300	3	10	2	3	1	0	1	3	0	0	0	3	.300	.700
Yankee Stadium	.281	9	32	5	9	4	0	1	4	0	0	1	4	.294	.500
Oakland-Alameda	.400	6	15	4	6	1	0	2	4	0	0	2	1	.471	.867
Arlington	.263	5	19	0	5	0	0	0	2	0	0	1	4	.333	.263
SkyDome	.295	71	261	43	77	17	0	17	52	2	1	16	32	.342	.556
Wrigley Field	.286	8	28	2	8	4	0	0	5	0	0	4	3	.364	.429
Cinergy Field	.261	7	23	0	6	1	0	0	1	0	1	1	0	.292	.304
Astrodome	.300	5	20	2	6	1	0	1	4	0	1	0	7	.333	.500
Dodger Stadium	.361	9	36	8	13	4	0	2	5	0	0	2	1	.395	.694
Olympic Stadium	.260	133	458	40	119	46	2	8	58	5	3	27	60	.304	.421
Shea Stadium	.226	10	31	2	7	0	0	0	2	0	0	3	4	.294	.226
Veterans Stadium	.167	6	24	5	4	1	0	1	4	0	0	2	7	.231	.333
Three Rivers	.333	10	24	3	8	2	1	2	8	0	2	4	4	.414	.750
Busch Stadium	.182	5	11	2	2	0	0	0	0	0	0	2	2	.308	.182
Qualcomm Park	.238	6	21	3	5	1	0	1	3	0	0	3	3	.333	.429
3 Com Park	.435	8	23	5	10	2	0	1	7	0	0	2	2	.480	.652
Coors Field	.389	9	36	4	14	3	0	2	6	1	0	3	2	.436	.639
Pro Player Stadium	.200	8	25	6	5	1	0	1	1	0	0	4	4	.310	.360
Turner Field	.306	12	36	4	11	4	0	1	9	1	0	2	3	.342	.500
BankOne Ballpark	.273	6	22	3	6	2	0	2	4	0	0	1	0	.333	.636
Tropicana Field	.371	9	35	7	13	3	1	3	11	0	0	2	4	.395	.771
SAFECO Field	.385	4	13	1	5	1	0	1	3	0	0	0	4	.385	.692
Comerica Park	.368	5	19	5	7	3	0	2	4	0	1	2	5	.455	.842

BRAD FULLMER — MILESTONES

	DATE	OPP.	H/A	PITCHER	DESCRIPTION
HITS					
1	Sept. 2, 1997	MTL vs BOS	H	Bret Saberhagen	Home Run - PH
HR					
1	Sept. 2, 1997	MTL vs BOS	H	Bret Saberhagen	Home Run - PH
MULTI HR (3)					
1	August 18, 1998	MTL vs ARI	A	Brian Anderson	Solo, 2R
2	July 26, 2000	TOR vs CLE	H	Colon	2R, 2R
2	August 30, 2000	TOR vs ANA	H	Wise, Turnbow	3R, 1R
SLAMS (2)					
1	May 30, 1998	MTL vs PIT	A	Jose Silva	4th inn.
2	April 17, 2000	TOR vs ANA	H	Lou Pote	8th inn.

Alex
GONZALEZ
SHORTSTOP

8

BIRTHDATE	April 8, 1973
OPENING DAY AGE	27
BIRTHPLACE	Miami, FL
RESIDENCE	Coral Gables, FL
BATS/THROWS	R/R
HEIGHT/WEIGHT	6-0/195
CONTRACT STATUS	signed thru 2004
M.L. SERVICE	6.055

PERSONAL: Alexander Scott Gonzalez... Married, wife's name is Samantha... One son, Tyler William (8/25/99)... Graduated from Miami Killian High School in 1991... Played baseball earning All-State honours one season.

LAST SEASON: Set career bests with a .252 average, 31 doubles, 15 home runs and 69 RBI... Led the AL with 16 sacrifice hits which ties for the second highest single season total in club history (Gomez-19 in 1978)... Opened the season hitting in four straight... Hit .235 in April without a home run and six RBI... Hit his first home run on May 1 in Chicago... Homered again on May 5 vs Cleveland and then in two straight games, May 12 & 13 against TB for four home runs in 12 games... Had a season high three hits on six occasions, the first coming May 10 vs Baltimore... Collected hits and RBI in five straight games, June 5-9 (7-23, 8RBI)... On June 17 at Boston tied his career high with four RBI, both hits... Hit .276 (21-76) in June with three HR and 16RBI... On June 24 vs Boston hit HR #7 off Rose but then left the game with a right groin strain... Returned to the line-up after missing nine games to play on July 5 & 6 but aggravated his groin injury... Was placed on the 15-day disabled list from July 7 to 22... Appeared in one game on rehab stint with Syracuse on July 21... At the All-Star break was batting .240 with seven HR and 32 RBI... After the break and the DL hit .265 with eight home runs and 37 RBI... Hit in a career high 15 straight games from August 2 to 18 (25-69, 3-2B, 2-3B, 3HR, 12RBI)- previous high was 12 in 1998... Hit second in the batting order from August 2 to the end of the season, 53 games... On August 13 in Minnesota set a new career high with his first career five RBI game, was 3-5 with three run HR off Brad Radke... Would match that with five RBI on August 23 at Kansas City... In August hit .310 with five home runs and 19 RBI... Homered in two of the final three games to reach his career high 15 home runs... Hit .228 against LHP with two home runs and .259 against RHP with 13 home runs... Finished with a .975 fielding % to rank sixth in the AL... Was charged with 16 errors.

PROFESSIONAL CAREER: 1991: Led all Gulf Coast League shortstops in total chances (247) and assists (160)... Hit safely in 15 of 20 games in August... **1992:** Averaged better than a hit per game with Myrtle Beach (A) of the South Atlantic League... R. Howard Webster Award recipient as team MVP... Finished second in the loop in at-bats (535), tied for third in triples (9) and fifth in hits (145)... 26 steals placed him fourth in the Blue Jays minor league clubs... Led all South Atlantic League shortstops in games (134), putouts (248), assists (406) and total chances (702)... **1993:** Made the

move from single A to double A for 1993... Played all 142 games in the Knoxville (AA) schedule at shortstop... Led the Southern League in games (142) and total bases (253) while tying for top spot in runs (93)... Was second in hits (162) and at bats (561), tied for second in triples (7), third in stolen bases (38) and fourth in extra-base hits (52)... His 16 home runs were second on the club to teammate Carlos Delgado (25)... Played winter ball for Lara, Venezuela where he batted .277 and led the league in RBI (45) and tied for HR (7)... **1994:** Was youngest player in the AL to start the season and second youngest in the Majors (Ho Chan Park- Dodgers)... Started year 0-10 before collecting 2 doubles on his 21st birthday- April 8 vs Seattle... Is the 4th youngest player ever to play for Toronto... Suffered a strained hamstring on April 25... Was sent to AAA Syracuse of the International League for medical rehab beginning May 15... Was then recalled from rehab and optioned to Syracuse on May 27... Played in the IL All-Star Game and was chosen to the season end IL All-Star team... Stole 23 bases in 29 attempts for the Chiefs... 105 of 110 games at Syracuse came as SS... Hit .316 with runners on base for Syracuse... Voted by IL managers as the league's best defensive SS... **1995:** First full Major League season... Recorded career high 4 RBI on Opening Day against Oakland... Recorded first ML homer May 23 vs Kansas City... Was first of 2 HR's that game (both off Pittsley)... Was batting .216 through first 31 games... Picked average up to .269 on July 3... Batted .250 in August but just .220 after the All-Star break... Season high 6-game hit streak from June 27 to July 3... Started at 3B July 15 at Seattle... July 29 vs Oakland, registered second career 2-homer game... Recorded career high 4 hits in the second game of a doubleheader September 23 at Boston... Hit .316(18-57) with 2 HR and 6 RBI in the leadoff spot... His 4 sac flies tied the club record for rookies (Griffin, Myers, Kent, Olerud, Cedeno)... Struck out 2 or more times in a game 29 times and 3 or more 9 times... 114 strikeouts was 8th in AL while his 9 sac bunts tied for 9th... Ranked 13th in AL in fielding by SS (.957)... **1996:** Set career highs in home runs (14) and runs batted in (64)... Youngest player on opening day roster... Homered on opening day, April 1 at Las Vegas against Oakland's Carlos Reyes... April 26 vs Cleveland set the club mark and tied the AL record for assists by a shortstop in a nine inning game with 13... Now shares the AL mark with Bobby Reeves of the Washington Senators who set the mark at 13 on August 27, 1927... Played every inning of the season until May 5 when he was hit on the right wrist with Stan Belinda pitch in Boston- was the last Blue Jay to play every inning... Prior to hit by pitch had three doubles in the game... Stole 10 bases in a row from May 12 to July 16... Set season bests and tied career highs in hits and RBI on August 8 in Boston collecting four of each (4-5, 1-2B)... Sept 9 vs Texas hit homer #12 off Roger Pavlik (1R) to end an 0 for 33 skid... Twice homered in back to back games, August 24 & 25 in Chicago and September 21 & 22 in Baltimore... Collected career RBI's #100 & 101 on August 25 with a two run HR off Tony Castillo... Finished 7th among AL shortstops in fielding percentage at .973 (21E)... Struck out a career high 127 times... At home hit just .207, 3HR & 32 RBI versus a .265 road average with 11 HR's and 32 RBI... 14 HR's, 10-1R, 3-2R & 1-3R... Was 4-4 in steals of third... **1997:** Led AL shortstops with a .986 (8E/558TC) fielding percentage... Homered on opening day vs Chicago's Jaime Navarro, also homered on opening day of 1996... Eight errors on the season, three were committed in April... Hit .270 (2HR, 4RBI) in April... In May hit .247 with two home runs and 11 RBI, best RBI month of the season... Tied career high four RBI on June 14 in Philadelphia, was 3-5 with a solo HR... Hit second Inter-league HR on June 18 off Atlanta's John Smoltz... On June 25 scored four runs to match the club record... At the break was batting .241 with seven HR's and 24 RBI... Made six errors prior to the break and just two after... From July 12 made just one error through the remainder of the season... Opened August with a six game hit streak, started the streak with five multiple hit games... Homered in back to back games in Detroit on August 1 (Brocail-1R) and 2 (Jarvis-1R)... Suffered a fractured right index finger as he was hit by a LaTroy Hawkins pitch on August 13 forcing him to miss 30 games after being disabled... Prior to injury was hitting .429 (18-42, 2HR, 6RBI) in August... Activated from the DL on September 13... Hit .146 (6-41) after being activated... Had 11 sacrifice hits to tie for fourth in the AL... Was second on the club in stolen bases with 15... **1998:** Set career highs in games (158), at bats (568), hits (136), runs scored (70) and stolen bases (21) while matching his 1997 average of .239... Tied for the club lead in games played at 158 with Shawn Green, led the team in starts with 157... Hit just .200 in April with ten RBI... In his 29th at bat of the season he was struck out for the first time and finished April with 11 in 100 at bats - from May on he struck out 110 times in 468 at bats, once every 4.25 at bats... Third career four hit game on May 5 at Anaheim... Was the last player to start every game for the Blue Jays until sitting down on May 18... Homered in back to back games May 19 & 20 at Tampa Bay... June was the best offensive month hitting .293 (29-99) with five home runs and 13 RBI... Hit in eight straight from June 12 to 19 (15-31, 3HR, 6RBI)... July 1st collected 400th career hit, 3R-HR off Mel Rojas, the three RBI matched his season high, 2nd time... Played in his 500th career game on July 24 at Boston... August 9 was hit on the right hand by a pitch from Mike Oquist and missed two starts... Went 35 games between home runs from July 1 to August 15... Hit in a then career high 12 straight from August 19-29 (.405/17-42)... Recorded second four hit game of the season, fourth career on September 7 at Cleveland... On September 9 tied a ML record for strikeouts in an extra inning game at six, nine times... Struggled in September hitting just .172 (15-87) with three home runs, eight RBI and the most K's of any month of the season at 29... Delivered 13 sac hits to lead the team and tie for second in the AL... Posted a .976 fielding percentage to rank 7th in the AL, he committed 17 errors... Vs RHP posted a .229 average while hitting .272 against LHP... Seven of the 21 steals were of third base to tie for ninth in the AL... **1999:** Appeared in only 38 games before suffering a torn labrum of the right shoulder... Was disabled May 17 and had surgery performed by Dr. James Andrews on June 17... Was batting .292 with 13 doubles, two home runs and 12 RBI in 38 games... Entered 1999 with a career average of .236... Started the season by matching his career high with four hits on opening night at Minnesota... Hit in seven straight games from April 8 to 14 batting .429 (12-28) with a home run and seven RBI... Collected career hit number #500 on May 11 at KC (double)... Fielding percentage was .980 (201-205) with 34 double plays... In the spring hit .324 with 2 HR and 13 RBI.

CAREER NOTES: Tied the AL record and set a club mark for assists by a shortstop in a nine inning game with 13 on April 26, 1996 vs Cleveland... Now shares the AL mark with Bobby Reeves of the Washington Senators (August 27, 1927)... Was the second Blue Jays shortstop to lead the AL in fielding with a .986 mark in 1997, joins Tony Fernandez who led the league in 1986 at .983... With 57 sac hits he ranks second in club history to Alfredo Griffin at 74... Has played 720 games at shortstop for Toronto to rank third in club history, second is Alfredo Griffin at 907... Has the longest continuous service of the major league level on the team.

ALEX GONZALEZ

Year	Club & League	AVG	G	AB	R	H	TB	2B	3B	HR	RBI	SH-SF	HP	BB-IBB	SO	SB-CS	GIDP	SLG	OBP
1991	Blue Jays (Gulf)	.209	53	191	29	40	53	5	4	0	10	2-0	3	12-0	41	7-2	3	.277	.267
1992	Myrtle Beach (SAL)	.271	134	535	83	145	215	22	9	10	62	3-2	5	38-2	119	26-14	9	.402	.322
1993	Knoxville (Sou)	.289	142	561	93	162	253	29	7	16	69	0-4	6	39-2	110	38-13	9	.451	.339
1994	TORONTO (AL)	.151	15	53	7	8	13	3	1	0	1	1-0	1	4-0	17	3-0	2	.245	.224
1994	Syracuse (Int)	.284	110	437	69	124	190	22	4	12	57	4-2	1	53-1	92	23-6	9	.435	.361
1995	TORONTO (AL)	.243	111	367	51	89	146	19	4	10	42	9-4	1	44-1	114	4-4	7	.398	.322
1996	TORONTO (AL)	.235	147	527	64	124	206	30	5	14	64	7-3	5	45-0	127	16-6	12	.391	.300
1997	TORONTO (AL)	.239	126	426	46	102	165	23	2	12	35	11-2	5	34-1	94	15-6	9	.387	.302
1998	TORONTO (AL)	.239	158	568	70	136	205	28	2	13	51	13-3	6	28-1	121	21-6	13	.361	.281
1999	TORONTO (AL)	.292	38	154	22	45	64	13	0	2	12	0-0	3	16-0	23	4-2	4	.416	.370
2000	Syracuse (Int)	.000	1	5	0	0	0	0	0	0	0	0-0	1	0-0	2	0-0	0	.000	.000
2000	TORONTO (AL)	.252	141	527	68	133	213	31	2	15	69	16-1	4	43-0	113	4-4	14	.404	.313
Minor Totals		.272	440	1729	274	471	711	78	24	38	198	9-8	13	142-5	364	94-35	30	.411	.331
MAJOR TOTALS		.243	736	2622	328	637	1012	147	15	66	274	57-13	25	214-3	609	67-28	61	.386	.305

HOME RUN BREAKDOWN

			MEN ON				ONE GAME								
Total	H	A	0	1	2	3	2	3	4	LO	XN	IP	PH	RHP	LHP
66	28	38	42	19	5	0	2	0	0	1	1	0	0	50	16

GONZALEZ — TRANSACTIONS

- Selected by Toronto Blue Jays in 14th round (380th overall) in June 1991 First Year Draft.
- On disabled list (left hamstring) April 29-May 27, 1994 including rehabilitation assignment to Syracuse May 14-27, 1994.
- On disabled list (fracture of right index finger) August 13-September 13, 1997.
- On disabled list (torn labrum – right shoulder) May 17- remainder of season, 1999.
- On disabled list (right groin strain) July 7-22, 2000; including rehabilitation assignment to Syracuse July 21.

CAREER HIGHS — GONZALEZ, Alex

SEASON:

Games	158 - 1998
Avg.	.252 - 2000
Runs	70 - 1998
Hits	136 - 1998
Doubles	31 - 2000
Home Runs	15 - 2000
RBI	69 - 2000
Walks	45 - 1996
Strikeouts	127 - 1996
Stolen Bases	21 - 1998
Longest Hitting Streak	15G - Aug. 2-18, 2000
Longest Hitless Streak	33AB - Aug. 2-Sept 8, 1996
Multi HR Games	2 - 1995

GAME:

ML Debut	Apr. 4, 1994 at CWS
Runs	4 - Jun. 25, 1997 vs. BOS
Hits	4 - 5 times, last Apr. 6, 1999 at MIN
Doubles	3 - May 4, 1996 at BOS
Home Runs	2 - May 23, 1995 vs. KC
	2 - Jul. 29, 1995 vs. OAK
RBI	5 - Aug. 13, 2000 at MIN
	5 - Aug. 23, 2000 vs. KC
Stolen Bases	2 - 7 times, last Jun. 18, 2000 at BOS
Last ML Home Run	Oct. 1, 2000 at CLE

FIELDING

GONZALEZ, Alex—SS

Year	PCT	G	PO	A	E	TC	DP
1994	.918	15	18	49	6	73	6
1995	.957	97	158	216	17	391	46
1996	.973	147	279	465	21	765	122
1997	.986	125	209	341	8	558	77
1998	.976	158	259	427	17	703	98
1999	.980	37	69	132	4	205	34
2000	.975	141	213	407	16	636	100
Total	.973	720	1205	2037	89	3331	483

GONZALEZ, Alex—3B

Year	PCT	G	PO	A	E	TC	DP
1995	.895	9	6	11	2	19	1

ALEX GONZALEZ DETAILED HITTING

	2000									CAREER								
	Avg	AB	H	HR	RBI	BB	SO	OBP	SLG	Avg	AB	H	HR	RBI	BB	SO	OBP	SLG
Total	.252	527	133	15	69	43	113	.313	.404	.243	2622	637	66	274	214	609	.305	.386
vs. Left	.228	114	26	2	8	13	27	.305	.333	.255	705	180	16	63	63	146	.317	.406
vs. Right	.259	413	107	13	61	30	86	.315	.424	.238	1917	457	50	211	151	463	.300	.379
Home	.245	253	62	5	25	21	49	.313	.379	.238	1340	319	28	144	106	316	.301	.377
Away	.259	274	71	10	44	22	64	.313	.427	.248	1282	318	38	130	108	293	.309	.395
April	.235	85	20	0	6	8	15	.316	.294	.245	515	126	8	49	35	105	.304	.359
May	.224	98	22	4	8	9	18	.290	.378	.238	526	125	13	54	48	113	.302	.376
June	.276	76	21	3	16	5	19	.325	.500	.271	432	117	14	57	20	99	.307	.442
July	.256	43	11	0	6	2	12	.289	.302	.216	393	85	8	35	37	106	.285	.344
August	.310	113	35	5	19	6	25	.350	.522	.296	385	114	13	46	40	82	.369	.473
September	.204	108	22	2	12	13	24	.289	.324	.187	364	68	9	33	33	102	.258	.316
October	.500	4	2	1	2	0	0	.500	1.500	.286	7	2	1	2	1	2	.375	.857
Scoring Posn	.269	134	36	1	47	18	37	.357	.388	.230	677	156	12	194	67	181	.301	.353
Bases Loaded	.250	12	3	0	6	0	5	.250	.333	.197	61	12	0	32	2	19	.203	.295
DH	–	–	–	–	–	–	–	–	–	.273	11	3	1	1	2	3	.385	.545
PH	–	–	–	–	–	–	–	–	–	.000	2	0	0	0	0	1	.000	.000
vs. Ana	.190	42	8	0	0	6	7	.292	.190	.246	228	56	5	17	20	44	.311	.368
vs. Bal	.310	29	9	0	1	1	4	.333	.310	.260	215	56	6	22	15	51	.312	.409
vs. Bos	.184	38	7	2	6	2	11	.244	.368	.237	198	47	5	18	24	53	.333	.369
vs. CWS	.297	37	11	2	5	4	6	.366	.514	.260	146	38	5	16	15	34	.329	.404
vs. Cle	.295	44	13	3	9	3	12	.340	.614	.200	185	37	6	18	15	56	.260	.346
vs. Det	.220	41	9	1	5	5	9	.304	.415	.295	183	54	5	24	18	39	.358	.464
vs. KC	.381	42	16	1	9	0	9	.395	.619	.270	178	48	8	21	10	31	.312	.478
vs. Mil	–	–	–	–	–	–	–	–	–	.260	100	26	1	11	12	20	.342	.400
vs. Min	.212	33	7	1	7	2	10	.278	.303	.233	180	42	2	17	13	32	.298	.339
vs. NYY	.205	44	9	0	7	4	9	.271	.295	.194	227	44	2	21	17	55	.252	.278
vs. Oak	.189	37	7	1	2	2	5	.231	.270	.256	195	50	6	25	13	48	.305	.405
vs. Sea	.231	39	9	0	2	2	13	.286	.256	.215	191	41	1	11	17	54	.292	.298
vs. TB	.240	25	6	2	5	5	3	.367	.520	.264	87	23	6	15	6	23	.319	.529
vs. Tex	.308	39	12	2	3	5	7	.386	.590	.250	180	45	3	16	15	41	.308	.411
vs. Atl	.214	14	3	0	5	0	4	.200	.286	.171	35	6	2	7	0	10	.167	.371
vs. Fla	.333	12	4	0	1	0	4	.333	.500	.200	25	5	0	1	0	6	.231	.280
vs. Mon	.273	11	3	0	2	2	0	.385	.364	.237	38	9	0	5	2	5	.275	.289
vs. NYM	–	–	–	–	–	–	–	–	–	.300	10	3	2	5	1	3	.364	1.000
vs. Phi	–	–	–	–	–	–	–	–	–	.333	21	7	1	4	1	4	.364	.619
Pre-All Star	.240	267	64	7	32	23	55	.306	.378	.246	1574	387	36	171	112	349	.301	.384
Post-All Star	.265	260	69	8	37	20	58	.320	.431	.239	1048	250	30	103	102	260	.311	.388

ALEX GONZALEZ HITTING AT ML PARKS

Park	Avg	G	AB	R	H	2B	3B	HR	RBI	SB	CS	BB	SO	OBP	Slg
Camden Yards	.250	29	104	19	26	6	0	5	11	4	3	9	29	.316	.452
Fenway Park	.287	28	101	19	29	10	0	2	12	3	1	12	22	.368	.446
Edison Field	.258	34	120	19	31	5	0	4	10	2	2	12	23	.328	.400
Comiskey Park	.294	20	68	10	20	1	0	4	12	1	2	10	16	.375	.485
Jacobs Field	.207	23	87	8	18	3	0	3	9	1	1	5	22	.250	.345
Tiger Stadium	.313	19	67	9	21	5	1	2	8	5	1	5	13	.351	.507
Kauffman Stadium	.253	24	87	11	22	2	1	4	7	1	0	4	14	.286	.437
County Stadium	.154	14	39	3	6	2	0	0	2	1	0	7	7	.292	.205
Metrodome	.277	25	94	10	26	6	1	2	12	2	0	9	17	.346	.426
Yankee Stadium	.185	32	119	7	22	3	0	2	7	2	2	7	29	.236	.261
Oakland-Alameda	.317	23	82	15	26	5	0	3	10	0	1	6	18	.364	.488
Kingdome	.198	23	91	11	18	5	0	0	4	2	1	8	24	.270	.253
Arlington	.192	22	78	6	15	7	0	1	3	1	1	8	21	.267	.321
SkyDome	.238	382	1340	164	319	78	12	28	144	42	11	106	316	.301	.377
Olympic Stadium	.286	2	7	0	2	0	0	0	0	0	0	0	1	.286	.286
Veterans Stadium	.417	3	12	2	5	2	0	1	4	0	0	0	3	.417	.833
Pro Player Stadium	.200	6	25	3	5	2	0	0	1	0	0	0	6	.231	.280
Turner Field	.167	6	24	3	4	1	0	1	6	0	0	0	8	.160	.333
Tropicana Field	.281	9	32	5	9	1	0	3	6	0	1	3	8	.343	.594
Cashman Field	.429	2	7	1	3	0	0	1	2	0	1	1	2	.500	.857
SAFECO Field	.294	4	17	1	5	0	0	0	2	0	0	1	6	.333	.294
Comerica Park	.238	6	21	2	5	3	0	0	2	0	0	1	4	.273	.381

ALEX GONZALEZ — MILESTONES

	DATE	OPP.	H/A	PITCHER	DESCRIPTION
HITS					
1	April 8, 1994	TOR vs SEA	H	Dave Fleming	Double
500	May 11, 1999	TOR vs KC	A	Jim Pittsley	Double
HR					
1	May 23, 1995	TOR vs KC	H	Jim Pittsley	2R, 2HR game
RBI					
1	April 10, 1994	TOR vs SEA	H	Randy Johnson	Walk
SB					
1	April 16, 1994	TOR vs CAL	A	Mike Butcher	2nd
				Catcher-Greg Myers	
GM					
1	April 4, 1994	TOR vs CWS	H		0-3
500	July 24, 1998	TOR vs BOS	A		1-5
MULTI HR (2)					
2	May 23, 1995	TOR vs KC	H	Jim Pittsley 2R, 1R	1st, 3rd
2	July 29, 1995	TOR vs OAK	H	Ariel Prieto, 2R, Steve	2nd, 3rd
				Wojciechowski, 1R	

Todd
GREENE

OUTFIELDER/CATCHER

BIRTHDATE	May 8, 1971
OPENING DAY AGE	29
BIRTHPLACE	Augusta, GA
RESIDENCE	Alpharetta, GA
BATS/THROWS	R/R
HEIGHT/WEIGHT	5-10/208
CONTRACT STATUS	signed thru 2001
M.L. SERVICE	3.119

27

PERSONAL: Todd Anthony Greene... Married, wife's name Vanessa... Two children, Aryn (2/7/96) and Jacob (4/16/98)... Graduated Evans High School (GA) in 1989... Attended Georgia Southern (1990-93)... Played in 240 games during collegiate career and holds school career records in hits (311), home runs (88), RBI (257), total bases (640) and slugging percentage (.709)... HR total ranks third on all-time NCAA Division I list... Three-time All American... Four-time All Conference choice, two as Trans America Athletic Conference (TACC) and two as Southern Conference... Named conference Player of the Year twice: 1990 (TACC), marking only freshman so honored, and 1993 (Southern Conference)... Earned Bronze Medal at Pan American Games as member of 1991 USA Team... Signed by Angels' scout Bobby Myrick.

LAST SEASON: Hit .235 with five home runs and 10 RBI in 34 games... Was signed by the Toronto Blue Jays on April 10 after he was released by the Anaheim Angels following spring training... Joined Syracuse of the International League (AAA) and in 24 games hit .297 with seven HR's and 14 RBI prior to having his contract purchased by Toronto on May 19... Hit in three straight to begin his Blue Jays career, from May 22 to June 2... Hit his first HR in his second game on May 25 in Boston off Pete Schourek... Suffered a right knee strain while catching in place of Alberto Castillo on June 6 in Atlanta... Was on the disabled list from June 7 to 21... Appeared in 11 games, two starts, prior to All-Star break and hit .353 (6-17) with one HR and two RBI... Delivered a pinch hit, two run single on July 27 in Seattle to give Toronto the lead... Hit in four straight games from August 20 to September 1... Homered in two of three games September 25 to 29... Hit .260 against LHP with two HR's and .200 against RHP with three home runs... Started 20 games, all at DH.

PROFESSIONAL CAREER: 1993: Spent first professional season leading Boise (short-A) to Northwest League Championship with circuit-leading 15 HRs, 71 RBI and 76 games... Connected for three 2-HR games... Honored as league's "Player of the Week," June 20-26... Batted .409 (9-22) with two HRs and eight RBI during span... Selected to Northwest League All-Star team as outfielder and named league's MVP... **1994:** Spent entire season with single-A Lake Elsinore... Batted .302 (158-524) with 98 runs scored, 39 doubles, 35 HRs and 124 RBI in 133 games... Named to California League All-Star team as designated hitter... Selected as league's MVP and Rookie of the Year... Doubles, HRs and RBI led league... Also ranked first in total bases (306), extra base hits (76), HR/AB ratio (1:14.97) and slugging percentage (.584)... Named California League "Player of the Week" four times... Connected for a grand slam on July 24 at High Desert... Tied league record with three HRs, August 20 at Bakersfield... **1995:** Named Baseball Weekly's Minor League Player of the Year and Baseball America's Organizational Player of the Year in third professional season... Began campaign at double-A Midland, batting .327 (104-318) with 59 runs scored, 19 doubles, a triple, 26 home runs and 57 RBI in 82 games... Named Batter of the Week, May 8-14 and Topps Minor League Player of the Month, Texas League in May (.379, 21R, 6-2B, 13HR, 23RBI)... Selected Baseball America Classification All-Star, Texas-Mexican League All-Star and Texas League All-Star... Posted four two-home run games, May 8 & 9 in Tulsa, July 8 vs. San Antonio and July 12 vs. Shreveport... All eight HRs were solo... Promoted to Vancouver, July 13... Hit .250 (42-168) with 14 HRs and 35 RBI in 43 games... Overall on season, batted .300 (146-486) with 22 doubles, two triples, 40 home runs and 92 RBI in 125 games... Became first player to hit 40 home runs in one minor league season since Danny Tartabull in 1985... With Canadians, notched two multiple-HR games, including three-HR performance, August 7, in Salt Lake City (all solo)... Hit grand slam, August 13, at Albuquerque (Shawn Holman)... Played in 30 games for Tempe Rafters of Arizona Fall League during off-season... Had contract purchased by Angels from Vancouver, September 30... Did not appear in Angels' three remaining games... **1996:** Split season between triple-A Vancouver and California... Started with Canadians, posting .305 (68-223) average with 27 runs scored, 18 doubles, five home runs and 33 RBI in 60 games... Missed 42 games from April 10-May 25 due to surgery to remove hook of hamate of left wrist... Began rehab in Mesa, AZ, May 1... Homered in consecutive games, June 23-24... Recalled by Angels, July 29... Hit .190 (15-79) with nine runs scored, a double, two home runs and nine RBI in 29 games... Made major league debut, July 30 at Detroit, finishing 1-for-2 with a run scored and two RBI... Entered contest as pinch-hitter (fly out) in sixth inning and remained in game behind plate... Posted first ML hit and RBI in the eighth inning, a two-run single off Richie Lewis... First major league start was August 1 at Detroit where he collected his first ML home run off Brian Williams... Also homered on September 20 vs Texas (Darren Oliver)... First multiple-hit game came, August 22 at New York (2)... Posted 1.000 fielding percentage behind plate (26 games, 138 total chances)... **1997:** Began season with Angels, batting .111 (1-9) with one run scored, a double and RBI in four games... Optioned to triple-A Vancouver, April 15... Batted .354 (92-260) with 51 runs scored, 22 doubles, 25 home runs and 75 RBI in 64 games with the Canadians... Led team in home runs (club record), RBI and multiple-HR games (4)... Voted catcher for Pacific Coast League All-Star Team... Voted to AL Triple-A All-Star Team, a career first... Did not play due to recall by Angels... Named Topps "PCL Player of the Month" and Howe Sportsdata "Minor League Player of the Month" for May... Hit .429 (45-105) with 12 doubles, 16 home runs and 44 RBI in the month... Collected three home runs and five RBI, May 8 at Tucson... Marked first three homer game since August 7, 1995 at Salt Lake... Longest streak without home run was seven games, April 22-29... Twice totaled team-high 12 total bases, May 8 at Tucson (3 HR, 5 RBI) and May 14 vs. Phoenix (5-5, 2B, 2 HR) when he collected eight RBI... Eight RBI was tops in minor leagues in 1997, one shy of club mark he set in 1996... Named PCL "Player of the Week" for May 11-17... Hit .517 (15-29) with 11 runs scored, three doubles, seven home runs and 22 RBI in

seven games... Homered in five consecutive games (7 HR), May 13-17... Hit second PCL grand slam, June 3 at Salt Lake... Caught Darrell May's 4-0, no-hitter, June 27 vs. Salt Lake (2 G)... Broke Canadians' single-season home run record, June 30 at Edmonton (off Jimmy Haynes), his 25th of season... Recalled by Anaheim, July 3... Overall, batted .290 (36-124) with 24 runs scored, six doubles, nine home runs and 24 RBI in 34 games with Angels... Hit .304 (34-115) in 30 games after recall... Connected for first two-HR game of major league career, July 16 vs. Detroit (Mike Moehler)... Collected career-best four hits and six RBI, July 31 against Chicago... Three runs scored in same game equaled career high (July 17 vs. Detroit)... Six RBI that contest was most by Angel since Garret Anderson collected seven RBI, August 29, 1995 vs. New York... Homered in three straight games, July 28-31, marking second Angel to do so in 1997 (Tim Salmon; July 4-6)... Season ended August 20 vs. New York (1st game) after suffering a non-displaced fracture of distal ulnar bone in right wrist... Injury occurred on foul ball while catching... ... Posted 1.000 fielding percentage (160 TC) in 26 games (25 starts)... Posted seven assists and five passed balls... Threw out 4 of 19 base stealers (21%)... Had arthroscopic surgery on right shoulder, October 28... **1998:** Began season on 15-day disabled list as he was recovering from off-season arthroscopic right shoulder surgery... Marked second career DL stint... Transferred to 60-day DL on July 30... Appeared in 30 rehab games at triple-A Vancouver, batting .278 with 16 runs scored, 12 doubles, seven home runs and 20 RBI... In nine rehab games at single-A Lake Elsinore, batted .227 (10-44) with nine runs scored, two doubles, one home run and nine RBI... Recalled from rehabilitation and activated from 60-day disabled list on August 7... Batted .254 (18-71) with three runs scored, four doubles, one home run and seven RBI in 29 games with Anaheim... Season debut came August 8 at Chicago, in first game of doubleheader, collecting season-high three hits... Collected first major league pinch-hit on August 13 in Toronto, delivered a two-run double... Lone home run came on September 24 at Oakland, a two-run HR in the 1st inning against Jimmy Haynes... Made major league debut (start) at first base on August 11 at Detroit... Made three appearances (two starts) at position... Made ML debut in outfield (left field) in first game of doubleheader, August 8 at Chicago... Made 12 appearances (11 starts) at position... **1999:** Hit .243 with Anaheim with 36 runs scored, 20 doubles, 14 home runs and 42 RBI in 97 games... Hit in a career high eight straight games from April 9 to 17... Then matched that streak hitting in eight straight from May 9 to 22... Hit safely in 55 games, with 19 multiple-hit contests... 34 of 78 hits were for extra-bases... Registered an RBI in 30 games with ten multi-RBI games... Posted season-high four RBI on April 16 vs. Seattle... Had two RBI nine times... Homered in consecutive games three times, twice hitting in two straight (May 16 & 18, May 29 & 31) and once in three consecutive games (April 15-17)... Three straight equalled career-best set July 28-31, 1997... Hit his first career grand slam, April 16 vs. Seattle against Jamie Moyer... Hit a pinch-hit home run on August 11 vs. Cleveland's Mike Jackson in the 9th inning... Was the first Angel PH-HR since July 30, 1996 at Detroit (Jack Howell)... Hit .279 (50-179) in 53 road games and .197 (28-142) in 44 home games... Hit .293 (12-41) with RISP and two outs... Equalled club record for most strikeouts in game (4), June 30 vs. Texas... Was Angels' starting designated hitter in season opener, April 6 vs. Cleveland... Marked first such start of career... Made first start and appearance at catcher, April 12 at Texas, since August 20, 1997 vs. New York (first game)... Made first career start in right field, May 18 at Baltimore... Served three-game suspension, May 12-14, following ejection from game on April 18 vs. Seattle after charging the mound and pitcher Brett Hinchliffe... Marked first career ejection... Also fined an undisclosed amount by the AL... Posted .984 fielding percentage (1-63) with 55 putouts and seven assists in 12 games (11 starts) behind the plate... Allowed five passed balls... Threw out five-of-12 basestealers (42%)... Optioned to Edmonton (AAA) on July 7 and recalled on July 30... In 19 games in triple-A hit .243 with 10 runs scored, six doubles, five home runs and 14 RBI... Had two home runs and four RBI on July 24 vs. Vancouver.

TODD GREENE

Year	Club & League	AVG	G	AB	R	H	TB	2B	3B	HR	RBI	SH-SF	HP	BB-IBB	SO	SB-CS	GIDP	SLG	OBP
1993	Boise (NWST)	.269	76	305	55	82	148	15	3	15	71	0-3	9	34-6	44	4-3	3	.485	.356
1994	Lake Elsinor (Cal)	.302	133	524	98	158	306	39	2	35	124	0-6	4	64-12	96	10-3	12	.584	.378
1995	Midland (Tex)	.327	82	318	59	104	203	19	1	26	57	1-5	5	17-4	55	3-5	6	.638	.365
1995	Vancouver (PCL)	.250	43	168	28	42	89	3	1	14	35	0-2	4	11-2	36	1-0	3	.530	.308
1996	Vancouver (PCL)	.305	60	223	27	68	101	18	0	5	33	0-5	1	16-0	36	0-2	6	.453	.347
1996	CALIFORNIA (AL)	.190	29	79	9	15	22	1	0	2	9	0-0	1	4-0	11	2-0	4	.278	.238
1997	ANAHEIM (AL)	.290	34	124	24	36	69	6	0	9	24	0-0	0	7-1	25	2-0	1	.556	.328
1997	Vancouver (PCL)	.354	64	260	51	92	189	22	0	25	75	0-2	5	20-8	31	5-1	6	.727	.408
1998	Lake Elsinor (Cal)	.227	12	44	9	10	15	2	0	1	6	0-1	0	4-0	7	1-0	1	.341	.286
1998	Vancouver (PCL)	.278	30	108	16	30	63	12	0	7	20	0-2	3	12-0	17	1-0	2	.583	.360
1998	ANAHEIM (AL)	.254	29	71	3	18	25	4	0	1	7	0-0	0	2-0	20	0-0	0	.352	.274
1999	ANAHEIM (AL)	.243	97	321	36	78	140	20	0	14	42	0-2	3	12-0	63	1-4	8	.436	.275
1999	Edmonton (PCL)	.243	19	74	10	18	39	6	0	5	14	0-0	1	0-0	12	0-0	4	.527	.253
2000	Dunedin (FSL)	.200	5	20	2	4	8	1	0	1	4	0-0	1	2-1	4	0-0	0	.400	.304
2000	Syracuse (Int)	.297	24	91	14	27	51	3	0	7	14	0-1	0	6-0	16	1-0	3	.560	.337
2000	TORONTO (AL)	.235	34	85	11	20	37	2	0	5	10	0-0	0	5-0	18	0-0	4	.435	.278
Minor Totals		.295	548	2135	369	635	1212	140	7	141	453	1-27	33	186-33	354	26-14	46	.568	.359
MAJOR TOTALS		.246	223	680	83	167	293	33	0	31	92	0-2	4	30-1	137	5-4	17	.431	.281

HOME RUN BREAKDOWN

Total	H	A	0	MEN ON			ONE GAME			LO	XN	IP	PH	RHP	LHP
				1	2	3	2	3	4						
31	15	16	22	6	2	1	1	0	0	0	0	0	1	23	8

GREENE — TRANSACTIONS

- Selected by the California Angels organization in the 12th round (327th overall) in the June 1993 First Year Draft.
- On disabled list (hook of hamate left wrist) April 10-May 25, 1996.
- On disabled list (fractured right wrist) August 20 through remainder of the season, 1997.
- On disabled list (right shoulder surgery) March 19-August 5, 1998.
- Released by the Anaheim Angels on March 29, 2000.
- Signed by the Toronto Blue Jays organization, April 10, 2000.
- On disabled list (strained right knee) June 7-21, 2000; included rehabilitation assignment at Dunedin June 20.

CAREER HIGHS — GREENE, Todd

SEASON:		GAME:	
Games	97 - 1999	ML Debut	Jul. 30, 1996 at DET
Avg.	.243 - 1999	Runs	3 - Jul. 17, 1997 vs. DET
Runs	36 - 1999		3 - Jul. 31, 1997 vs. CWS
Hits	78 - 1999	Hits	4 - Jul. 31, 1997 vs. CWS
Doubles	20 - 1999	Doubles	2 - Jul. 31, 1997 vs. CWS
Home Runs	14 - 1999		2 - Sep. 3, 1999 vs. NYY
RBI	42 - 1999	Home Runs	2 - Jul. 16, 1997 vs. DET
Walks	12 - 1999	RBI	6 - Jul. 31, 1997 vs. CWS
Strikeouts	63 - 1999	Stolen Bases	1 - 5 times, last May 5, 1999 at DET
Stolen Bases	2 - 1996, 1997	Last ML Home Run	Sep. 29, 2000 at CLE
Longest Hitting Streak	8G - Apr. 7-17, 1999		
	8G - May 9-22, 1999		
Multi HR Games	1 - 1997		

FIELDING

GREENE, Todd—C

Year	PCT	G	PO	A	E	TC	DP
1996	1.000	26	119	19	0	138	1
1997	1.000	26	153	7	0	160	2
1999	.984	12	55	7	1	63	0
2000	1.000	2	2	0	0	2	0
Total	.997	66	329	33	1	363	3

GREENE, Todd—1B

Year	PCT	G	PO	A	E	TC	DP
1999	1.000	3	16	1	0	17	2

GREENE, Todd—OF

Year	PCT	G	PO	A	E	TC	DP
1998	1.000	12	12	0	0	12	0
1999	.974	30	36	1	1	37	0
2000	.000	1	0	0	0	0	0
Total	.980	43	48	1	1	50	0

TODD GREENE DETAILED HITTING

	2000									CAREER								
	Avg	AB	H	HR	RBI	BB	SO	OBP	SLG	Avg	AB	H	HR	RBI	BB	SO	OBP	SLG
Total	.235	85	20	5	10	5	18	.278	.435	.246	680	167	31	92	30	137	.281	.431
vs. Left	.260	50	13	2	6	5	8	.327	.420	.226	266	60	8	34	13	46	.262	.380
vs. Right	.200	35	7	3	4	0	10	.200	.457	.258	414	107	23	58	17	91	.293	.464
Home	.161	31	5	2	2	4	7	.257	.387	.222	302	67	15	35	19	65	.272	.414
Away	.278	54	15	3	8	1	11	.291	.463	.265	378	100	16	57	11	72	.288	.444
April	–	–	–	–	–	–	–	–	–	.205	73	15	4	16	5	14	.266	.411
May	.250	8	2	1	1	0	1	.250	.625	.316	79	25	7	10	4	18	.353	.671
June	.500	4	2	0	0	0	0	.500	.500	.222	90	20	2	6	2	13	.247	.322
July	.222	18	4	1	4	2	5	.300	.444	.289	90	26	6	21	4	20	.319	.533
August	.292	24	7	1	2	1	2	.320	.417	.250	216	54	8	25	9	38	.279	.407
September	.185	27	5	2	3	2	8	.241	.444	.211	128	27	4	14	6	32	.252	.352
October	.000	4	0	0	0	0	2	.000	.000	.000	4	0	0	0	0	2	.000	.000
Scoring Posn	.182	22	4	0	5	1	7	.217	.227	.228	189	43	6	52	10	49	.267	.376
Bases Loaded	.500	2	1	0	2	0	1	.500	.500	.158	19	3	1	8	0	8	.158	.316
DH	.216	74	16	5	9	5	18	.266	.432	.226	271	62	12	36	16	61	.261	.405
PH	.400	10	4	0	3	0	0	.400	.500	.250	36	9	1	9	5	8	.293	.361
vs. Ana	.125	8	1	0	1	0	2	.125	.125	.125	8	1	0	1	0	2	.125	.125
vs. Bal	.143	7	1	0	0	0	1	.143	.143	.259	58	15	4	6	1	13	.283	.483
vs. Bos	.200	5	1	1	1	0	1	.200	.800	.222	45	10	1	7	1	12	.239	.378
vs. CWS	.333	3	1	0	0	0	0	.333	.333	.261	46	12	1	9	2	4	.292	.413
vs. Cle	.200	15	3	1	2	1	5	.250	.400	.269	52	14	4	7	6	14	.345	.519
vs. Det	–	–	–	–	–	–	–	–	–	.362	47	17	5	10	3	8	.392	.745
vs. KC	.000	1	0	0	0	0	0	.000	.000	.182	33	6	1	2	1	8	.206	.273
vs. Mil	–	–	–	–	–	–	–	–	–	.353	17	6	1	3	0	3	.353	.588
vs. Min	.500	6	3	1	1	1	0	.571	1.000	.226	31	7	2	5	2	6	.273	.484
vs. NYY	.000	3	0	0	0	0	3	.000	.000	.224	67	15	2	7	3	14	.264	.388
vs. Oak	.250	12	3	0	0	2	1	.357	.333	.197	66	13	2	9	4	9	.243	.318
vs. Sea	.222	9	2	1	3	1	3	.300	.556	.180	50	9	3	9	2	13	.241	.400
vs. TB	.500	4	2	1	1	0	1	.500	1.250	.346	26	9	2	5	0	5	.346	.692
vs. Tex	.333	3	1	0	0	0	0	.333	.333	.217	46	10	3	7	1	15	.234	.435
vs. Tor	–	–	–	–	–	–	–	–	–	.231	52	12	0	2	3	7	.273	.250
vs. Ari	–	–	–	–	–	–	–	–	–	.364	11	4	0	1	0	1	.364	.455
vs. Atl	.000	1	0	0	0	0	0	.000	.000	.000	1	0	0	0	0	0	.000	.000
vs. Fla	.500	2	1	0	0	0	0	.500	.500	.500	2	1	0	0	0	0	.500	.500
vs. LA	–	–	–	–	–	–	–	–	–	.273	11	3	0	1	1	2	.333	.273
vs. Mon	.500	2	1	0	1	0	0	.500	1.000	.500	2	1	0	1	0	0	.500	1.000
vs. Phi	.000	4	0	0	0	0	1	.000	.000	.000	4	0	0	0	0	1	.000	.000
vs. SF	–	–	–	–	–	–	–	–	–	.400	5	2	0	0	0	0	.400	.600
Pre-All Star	.353	17	6	1	2	0	1	.353	.588	.244	271	66	13	34	11	51	.280	.443
Post-All Star	.206	68	14	4	8	5	17	.260	.397	.247	409	101	18	58	19	86	.281	.423

TODD GREENE HITTING AT ML PARKS

Park	Avg	G	AB	R	H	2B	3B	HR	RBI	SB	CS	BB	SO	OBP	Slg
Camden Yards	.300	11	30	4	9	1	0	3	3	0	0	0	6	.323	.633
Fenway Park	.229	10	35	4	8	3	0	1	7	0	0	1	11	.250	.400
Edison Field	.229	91	275	37	63	12	0	13	34	2	1	15	59	.273	.415
Comiskey Park	.286	5	21	3	6	2	0	0	3	0	0	0	2	.286	.381
Jacobs Field	.314	13	35	4	11	1	0	3	5	0	0	3	9	.368	.600
Tiger Stadium	.357	8	28	4	10	2	0	3	6	1	0	2	5	.400	.750
Kauffman Stadium	.231	6	13	0	3	0	0	0	1	1	0	0	3	.231	.231
County Stadium	.222	2	9	1	2	0	0	1	3	0	0	0	1	.222	.556
Metrodome	.200	4	10	0	2	1	0	0	2	0	0	0	1	.200	.300
Yankee Stadium	.171	11	35	4	6	1	0	1	3	1	1	1	6	.211	.286
Oakland-Alameda	.229	12	48	6	11	1	0	2	8	0	0	0	7	.229	.375
Kingdome	.100	2	10	1	1	1	0	0	0	0	0	0	3	.100	.200
Arlington	.261	8	23	2	6	1	0	1	5	0	0	1	6	.292	.435
SkyDome	.206	22	63	7	13	2	0	2	4	0	1	5	11	.265	.333
Dodger Stadium	.273	3	11	2	3	0	0	0	1	0	1	1	2	.333	.273
Olympic Stadium	.500	2	2	0	1	1	0	0	1	0	0	0	0	.500	1.000
3 Com Park	.400	2	5	0	2	1	0	0	0	0	0	0	0	.400	.600
Pro Player Stadium	.500	2	2	1	1	0	0	0	0	0	0	0	0	.500	.500
Turner Field	.000	1	1	0	0	0	0	0	0	0	0	0	0	.000	.000
Tropicana Field	.389	5	18	1	7	3	0	0	3	0	0	0	2	.389	.556
SAFECO Field	.333	3	6	2	2	0	0	1	3	0	0	1	3	.429	.833

Players

Roy
HALLADAY
PITCHER

BIRTHDATE	May 14, 1977
OPENING DAY AGE	23
BIRTHPLACE	Denver, CO
RESIDENCE	Arvada, CO
BATS/THROWS	R/R
HEIGHT/WEIGHT	6-6/230
CONTRACT STATUS	signed thru 2002
M.L. SERVICE	1.127

32

PERSONAL: Harry Leroy Halladay III... Married, wife's name is Brandy... One child, son Braden (8/14/00)... Graduated from Arvada (CO) West High School in 1995 where he competed in baseball and basketball... Was a first team All-Conference and All-State selection for three years and named League and State MVP two years... Also claimed second team All-State accolades in basketball... Played American Legion, Babe Ruth and Little League ball... Signed by Blue Jays scouts Bus Campbell and Chris Bourjos.

LAST SEASON: Split the season between Toronto and Syracuse of the International League (AAA)... With the Blue Jays was 4-7 with a 10.64 ERA in 19 games, 13 starts... At Syracuse was 2-3 with a 5.50 ERA in 11 starts with three complete games... Opened the season in Toronto's starting rotation... Won his season debut on April 4 vs KC... Lost his next two starts prior to winning 12-11 over Anaheim on April 20 to even his record at 2-2 with a 9.00ERA... Finished April 2-4 in six starts with an ERA of 10.57 with 48 hits and 16 walks in 30.2 innings... After a no-decision on May 5 was moved to the bullpen... Allowed three earned runs in his first relief appearance on May 15 vs Boston and was optioned to Syracuse on May 16... Made five starts with the SkyChiefs and was 1-1 with a 4.84 ERA... Tossed a complete game six-hitter on June 19 for the win in Indianapolis... Was re-called to Toronto on June 24... Inserted back into the starting rotation and won his first start, 6-4 vs Boston on June 24... At the All-Star break was 3-5 with an ERA of 11.86... Fell to 4-6 after losing start on July 21 vs the Orioles... Returned to the bullpen where he made three appearances and was 0-1 with a 4.50 ERA before he was optioned to Syracuse (AAA)... Started six games from August 5 to September 3 and was 1-2 with two complete games and an ERA of 6.10... Win came in his final start on September 3 with a complete game win in Ottawa in game one of a doubleheader... Recalled to Toronto on September 5... Appeared in three September games with Toronto, one start... As a starter with Toronto was 4-6 with an 11.13 ERA in 13 starts... Made six relief appearances and was 0-1 with a 6.43 ERA... Opponents hit .357 with left-handed hitters at .364 and right-handers at .350... Was 0-5 on grass with a 12.30 ERA and 4-2 on turf with a 9.58 ERA... Had two quality starts with Toronto.

PROFESSIONAL CAREER: 1995: Struck out nine batters on July 22 vs. the Gulf Coast Tigers and fanned eight batters in a game twice... Won back-to-back starts August 4-9 (14 IP, 8 H, 1 ER, 2 BB, 12 SO)... Combined on a shutout of the Gulf Coast Astros in his last start on August 25 (8 IP, 1 H, 3 BB, 3 SO) to earn Gulf Coast League Pitcher-of-the-Week honours... **1996:** Led the Blue Jays minor leagues in wins as he was 15-7 and captured the R. Howard Webster Award (MVP) in Dunedin... Tied for second in the Florida State League in wins and shutouts (2) and was fifth in the loop in ERA at 2.73... Won five straight games from May 2 to June 12 going 5-0 with a 1.91 ERA... From July 5 to August 11 allowed no more than two runs in eight straight starts... Named Dunedin Pitcher of the Month in June and July... In July was the organizational Pitcher of the Month, 4-1 with a 1.29 ERA... Won six of his last seven decisions... Pitched at least 6.0 innings in 22 of 27 starts... Did not allow an earned run in seven of the 27 starts... Named to both the All-Star Game and the All-Star Team... Selected to the Howe Sportsdata All-Teen Team... Rated the top prospect in the organization by Baseball America and the third best in the Florida State League... **1997:** Started the season with

Knoxville where in seven starts was 2-3 with a 5.40 ERA... Was 2-2 with a 4.50 ERA in April... Set season high of seven strikeouts in first start, April 3, over 5.0 innings at Birmingham... In two May starts was 0-1 with an 8.31 ERA... Promoted to Syracuse where he became the youngest pitcher in the league... Was 7-10 with a 4.58 ERA but tied for the club lead in wins... Lost AAA debut on May 14 to Columbus... Started 0-5 and was 7-5 the rest of the season... Won back to back games on June 25 and June 30 as he pitched a combined 14.0 shutout innings allowing just eight hits... June 30 was a seven inning complete game shutout (DH)... Finished June 2-2 with a 2.04ERA... Lost three straight starts in July, but from July 31 to September 1, was 5-2 in seven starts... August 5 at Scranton tossed second shutout of the season allowing five hits in a seven inning doubleheader game... Rated top prospect in the International League by Baseball America, who also recognized him for having the best fastball in the IL and the top prospect in the organization... **1998:** Pitched for the Syracuse SkyChiefs of the International League (AAA) and was then a September call-up to Toronto... At Syracuse was 9-5 with a 3.79 ERA in 21 starts and collected 71 strikeouts in 116.1 innings... The 3.79 ERA was sixth in the IL... Was 4-1 at home with a 2.86 ERA in nine starts and on the road was 5-4 with a 4.50 ERA in 12 starts... Went 2-0 in May with an ERA of 1.06 in three starts... Disabled from May 15 to June 17 with a right shoulder strain... Won five consecutive starts from July 9 to August 6 posting an ERA of 2.53... Struck out a season high nine on July 9 in 6.2 innings at home against Buffalo... July 20 at Charlotte he tossed a one hit shutout in a seven inning game with one walk, one hit batter and four strikeouts... In 21 starts pitched at least 7.0 innings on eight occasions including six of his last eight starts... Was recalled to Toronto on September 14... Made his ML debut as a starter in Tampa Bay on Sept. 20, ND in a 7-5 win (5.0IP, 8H, 3R, 2ER, 1HR, 2BB, 5K)... Struck out the first batter he faced, Randy Winn... At 21 years, 130 days he became the third youngest pitcher to ever start for the Blue Jays and became the 15th pitcher to make his ML debut as starter for Toronto... First ML win and complete game on September 27 starting the final game of the season at home against Detroit - took a no-hitter into the ninth inning before a two out pinch hit solo HR by Bobby Higginson... Pitched 9.0 innings allowing one hit, the homerun, with eight strikeouts, walked none and threw just 94 pitches, 73 strikes... Rated by Baseball America as the top prospect in the organization for the third straight season and the third best prospect in the International League... **1999:** Was 8-7 with one save and an ERA of 3.92 in 36 games, 18 starts... As a starter was 5-6 with a 3.97 ERA and one complete game shutout, while in relief was 3-1 with one save and an ERA of 3.80... Earned first professional save in season debut on April 7 at Minnesota (90th pro game)... Opened the season 2-0 with a save after not allowing an earned run in his first 20.0 innings over five games, two starts... In his sixth game, third start, allowed a career high 11 earned runs in 2.1 innings in Anaheim... Started eight straight games from April 18 to May 25... On May 20 vs Detroit became the third youngest pitcher in club history, at 22 years- six days, to throw a shutout, was his second career complete game... Youngest was Phil Huffman at 21 yrs, two months and seven days on August 27, 1979... Had four consecutive scoreless outings from June 19 to 30, tossing 15.2 scoreless innings - June 19 & 24 were consecutive scoreless starts in which he allowed only five hits in 12.2

innings but walked 12... Pitched 4.1 scoreless innings in relief on July 7... Through July was 8-4 with a 3.54 ERA... In August was 0-2 with a 6.93 ERA in six games, four starts... Season ERA excluding August was 3.32... Struck out a season high eight batters on August 13 in a loss to Oakland...

In September was 0-1 in four starts despite posting an ERA of 1.98... Last six starts of the season were all quality starts but was 0-2... Finished with 11 quality starts... Started four of Toronto's nine shutouts.

ROY HALLADAY

Year	Club & League	W-L	ERA	G	GS	CG	ShO	SV	IP	H	R	ER	HR	HB	BB-IBB	SO	WP	BK	OBA
1995	Blue Jays (Gulf)	3-5	3.40	10	8	0	0	0	50.1	35	25	19	4	1	16-0	48	9	2	.190
1996	Dunedin (FSL)	15-7	2.73	27	27	2	2	0	164.2	158	75	50	7	6	46-0	109	1	2	.251
1997	Knoxville (Sou)	2-3	5.40	7	7	0	0	0	36.2	46	26	22	4	0	11-0	30	4	0	.305
1997	Syracuse (Int)	7-10	4.58	22	22	2	2	0	125.2	132	74	64	13	1	53-1	64	8	3	.276
1998	Syracuse (Int)	9-5	3.79	21	21	1	1	0	116.1	107	52	49	11	8	53-3	71	9	0	.246
1998	TORONTO (AL)	1-0	1.93	2	2	1	0	0	14.0	9	4	3	2	0	2-0	13	0	0	.176
1999	TORONTO (AL)	8-7	3.92	36	18	1	1	1	149.1	156	76	65	19	4	79-1	82	6	0	.270
2000	Syracuse (Int)	2-3	5.50	11	11	3	0	0	73.2	85	46	45	10	2	21-0	38	4	0	.290
2000	TORONTO (AL)	4-7	10.64	19	13	0	0	0	67.2	107	87	80	14	2	42-0	44	6	1	.357
Minor Totals		38-33	3.95	98	96	8	5	0	567.1	563	298	249	49	18	200-4	360	35	7	.259
MAJOR TOTALS		13-14	5.77	57	33	2	1	1	231.0	272	167	148	35	6	123-1	139	12	1	.293

HALLADAY — TRANSACTIONS

- Selected by the Toronto Blue Jays organization in the 1st round (17th overall) in the June 1995 First Year Draft.
- On disabled list May 15-June 17, 1998 (right shoulder strain).

CAREER HIGHS — HALLADAY, Roy

SEASON:

Wins	8 - 1999
Losses	7 - 1999, 2000
Saves	1 - 1999
ERA	3.92 - 1999
Games	36 - 1999
Starts	18 - 1999
Complete Games	1 - 1998, 1999
Shutouts	1 - 1998
Innings Pitched	149.1 - 1999
Walks	79 - 1999
Strikeouts	82 - 1999
Longest Win Streak	3 - Jun. 19-Jul. 20, 1999
Longest Losing Streak	3 - Aug. 13-Sep. 19, 1999
Scoreless Innings Streak	19.0 - Apr. 7-24, 1999

GAME:

ML Debut	Sep. 20, 1998 at TB
Innings Pitched:	
Starter	9.0 - Sep. 27, 1998 vs. DET
	9.0 - May 20, 1999 vs. DET
Reliever	4.1 - Apr. 13, 1999 vs. TB
	4.1 - Jul. 7, 1999 at BAL
Walks:	
Starter	6 - Jun. 19, 1999 vs. KC
	6 - Jun. 24, 1999 vs. CLE
	6 - May 5, 2000 vs. CLE
Reliever	3 - Apr. 11, 1999 at BAL
	3 - Jul. 28, 2000 at SEA
Strikeouts:	
Starter	8 - Sep. 27, 1998 vs. DET
	8 - Aug. 13, 1998 vs. CLE
Reliever	3 - Apr. 7, 1999 at MIN
	3 - Aug. 7, 1999 at TEX
Hits Allowed	11 - Jun. 7, 1999 at NYM
	11 - Apr. 20, 2000 vs. ANA
Runs Allowed	11 - Apr. 29, 1999 at ANA
ER Allowed	11 - Apr. 29, 1999 at ANA
HR Allowed	3 - Jun. 7, 1999 at NYM
Low Hit CG	1 - Sep. 27, 1998 vs. DET
Last Win	Jul. 16, 2000 vs. NYM
Last Save	Apr. 7, 1999 at MIN
Last CG	May 20, 1999 vs. DET
Last ShO	May 20, 1999 vs. DET
Last Start	Sep. 23, 2000 vs. TB
Last Relief App.	Sep. 28, 2000 at BAL

FIELDING

HALLADAY, Roy—P

Year	PCT	G	PO	A	E	TC	DP
1998	1.000	2	1	2	0	3	0
1999	1.000	36	8	16	0	24	3
2000	1.000	19	4	7	0	11	0
Total	1.000	57	13	25	0	38	3

NEAR NO-HITTERS SPOILED IN THE 9TH INNING

Pitcher	Date	Opposition	Outs	Final	Details
Jim Clancy	Sept. 28/82 (G#1)	Minnesota (H)	0	3-0 win	Bush single
Dave Stieb	Sept. 24/88	Cleveland (A)	2	1-0 win	Franco single
Dave Stieb	Sept. 30/88	Baltimore (H)	2	4-0 win	Traber single
Dave Stieb	Aug. 4/89	New York (H)	2	2-1 win	Kelly double, Sax single
David Cone	June 17/95	Texas (H)	1	4-3 win	Gil single
Roy Halladay	Sept. 27/98	Detroit (H)	2	2-1 win	Higginson home run

ROY HALLADAY DETAILED PITCHING

	2000 ERA	W-L-Sv	G	IP	H	ER	BB	SO	CAREER ERA	W-L-Sv	G	IP	H	ER	BB	SO
Total	10.64	4-7-0	19	67.2	107	80	42	44	5.77	13-14-1	57	231.0	272	148	123	139
ST	11.13	4-6-0	13	60.2	92	75	36	42	6.23	10-12-0	33	179.0	215	124	95	116
REL	6.43	0-1-0	6	7.0	15	5	6	2	4.15	3-2-1	24	52.0	57	24	28	23
Home	9.58	4-2-0	10	41.1	64	44	20	28	4.81	11-7-0	30	140.1	151	75	67	87
Away	12.30	0-5-0	9	26.1	43	36	22	16	7.25	2-7-1	27	90.2	121	73	56	52
April	10.57	2-4-0	6	30.2	48	36	16	16	7.98	4-5-1	12	53.0	71	47	30	24
May	21.21	0-0-0	2	4.2	13	11	6	4	6.21	2-1-0	7	33.1	51	23	17	19
June	10.24	1-1-0	2	9.2	10	11	6	6	5.05	3-2-0	10	35.2	35	20	24	16
July	8.15	1-2-0	6	17.2	24	16	12	14	5.68	3-3-0	13	38.0	41	24	21	24
August	–	–	–	–	–	–	–	–	6.93	0-2-0	6	24.2	31	19	15	21
September	10.80	0-0-0	3	5.0	12	6	2	4	2.91	1-1-0	9	46.1	43	15	16	35
vs. Ana	11.81	1-0-0	1	5.1	11	7	2	4	21.13	1-1-0	2	7.2	20	18	5	5
vs. Bal	16.20	0-2-0	3	6.2	17	12	6	3	4.98	2-2-0	7	21.2	25	12	13	6
vs. Bos	7.88	1-0-0	2	8.0	10	7	2	5	5.63	1-1-0	4	16.0	22	10	5	10
vs. CWS	–	–	–	–	–	–	–	–	5.11	0-1-0	4	12.1	11	7	8	5
vs. Cle	14.00	0-0-0	3	9.0	16	14	11	9	8.40	1-0-0	4	15.0	19	14	17	11
vs. Det	–	–	–	–	–	–	–	–	1.05	4-0-0	4	25.2	17	3	2	18
vs. KC	3.86	1-0-0	1	7.0	5	3	1	3	1.83	2-0-0	3	19.2	15	4	10	10
vs. Min	–	–	–	–	–	–	–	–	5.79	0-0-1	2	4.2	4	3	2	4
vs. NYY	7.71	0-1-0	2	7.0	9	6	3	4	4.29	0-1-0	5	21.0	20	10	10	14
vs. Oak	20.25	0-1-0	1	4.0	8	9	5	2	9.58	0-3-0	4	20.2	28	22	18	14
vs. Sea	9.00	0-2-0	3	7.0	13	7	5	2	4.50	0-2-0	4	14.0	17	7	7	7
vs. TB	18.00	0-0-0	1	3.0	6	6	1	3	5.29	0-0-0	5	17.0	25	10	8	10
vs. Tex	11.57	0-1-0	1	4.2	7	6	3	3	8.64	0-2-0	4	16.2	28	16	11	12
vs. Atl	–	–	–	–	–	–	–	–	2.45	1-0-0	1	3.2	2	1	1	2
vs. Mon	–	–	–	–	–	–	–	–	3.00	0-0-0	1	3.0	2	1	1	2
vs. NYM	4.50	1-0-0	1	6.0	5	3	3	6	7.36	1-1-0	2	11.0	16	9	4	8
vs. Phi	–	–	–	–	–	–	–	–	6.75	0-0-0	1	1.1	1	1	1	1
Pre-All Star	11.68	3-5-0	11	49.1	77	64	31	31	6.49	9-8-1	33	137.1	172	99	79	68
Post-All Star	7.85	1-2-0	8	18.1	30	16	11	13	4.71	4-6-0	24	93.2	100	49	44	71

ROY HALLADAY PITCHING AT ML PARKS

Park	ERA	W-L-Sv	SvO	G	GS	IP	H	R	ER	HR	BB	SO
Camden Yards	6.75	1-1-0	0	4	1	9.1	12	14	7	1	10	1
Edison Field	42.43	0-1-0	0	1	1	2.1	9	11	11	2	3	1
Comiskey Park	10.80	0-0-0	0	1	0	1.2	1	2	2	1	1	1
Jacobs Field	12.46	0-0-0	0	1	1	4.1	6	6	6	0	3	5
Tiger Stadium	3.18	1-0-0	0	1	1	5.2	8	3	2	2	2	3
Kauffman Stadium	1.50	0-0-0	0	1	1	6.0	8	1	1	1	3	3
Metrodome	5.79	0-0-1	1	2	0	4.2	4	3	3	0	2	4
Yankee Stadium	5.40	0-1-0	0	4	2	13.1	15	12	8	2	8	8
Oakland-Alameda	10.80	0-1-0	0	2	2	10.0	15	12	12	3	10	4
Arlington	10.13	0-1-0	0	2	1	8.0	12	9	9	2	3	6
SkyDome	4.81	11-7-0	0	30	20	140.1	151	81	75	16	67	87
Olympic Stadium	3.00	0-0-0	0	1	0	3.0	2	1	1	1	1	2
Shea Stadium	10.80	0-1-0	0	1	1	5.0	11	6	6	3	1	2
Veterans Stadium	6.75	0-0-0	0	1	0	1.1	1	1	1	0	1	1
Tropicana Field	3.00	0-0-0	0	2	1	6.0	9	3	2	1	3	5
SAFECO Field	1.80	0-1-0	0	3	1	10.0	8	2	2	0	5	6

Joey *HAMILTON*

PITCHER

50

BIRTHDATE . . . . September 9, 1970
OPENING DAY AGE 30
BIRTHPLACE . . . . Statesboro, GA
RESIDENCE . . . . Norcross, GA
BATS/THROWS . . . . R/R
HEIGHT/WEIGHT 6-4/240
CONTRACT STATUS . . . . signed thru 2001
M.L. SERVICE 6.132

PERSONAL: Johns Joseph Hamilton... Married, wife's name is Angie... One son, Johns (August 4, 1998)... Attended Statesboro High School in Georgia and was drafted by Baltimore in the 28th round of the 1988 draft... Opted to attend Georgia Southern University... In three seasons was 35-19 with a 3.67 ERA and 353 strikeouts in 377.2 innings... Led Division I pitchers in wins with 18 in 1990 and was named MVP of the NCAA Midwest Regional Tournament... Led the Eagles into the College World Series... In 1991 was ranked by Baseball America as the No. 1 College pitching prospect.

LAST SEASON: Was 2-1 for Toronto in six starts with a 3.55 ERA... Spent most of the season recovering from right shoul-der surgery performed on September 9, 1999... Attended spring training with the major league team but did not see game action... On March 21 was placed on the 15-day disabled list... Remained in Florida and attended the extended spring program... Was transferred to the 60-day disabled list on April 28... Started rehabilitation assignment with Syracuse on July 17... Made six starts for the SkyChiefs posting a 3-2 record with a 3.66ERA... Lost his first two starts but then won three of the last four starts... Returned from Syracuse and was activated from the DL to start against Minnesota on August 19, had a no-decision after tossing 6.0 shutout innings and allowing just three hits... Was his first appearance since August 31, 1999 when he defeated Minnesota... First win of the season came in his second start on

August 26 vs Texas in a 9-3 win, allowed two runs on four hits in 6.0 innings... Was 2-0 in his first four starts, all four were quality starts... Lost 10-2 in New York on September 12 lasting just 4.0 innings... On September 17 at Chicago pitched 3.0 shutout innings allowing just two hits before leaving the game with right shoulder tightness... Did not pitch the rest of the season... Held opponents to a .233 batting average with right-handers at .213 and left-handers at .247.

PROFESSIONAL CAREER: 1991: Selected in the eighth round of the June First Year Draft... Signed late and did not see any action during the season... **1992:** Led the Padres farm system with a 2.97 ERA in 22 games (21 starts) between Charleston (A), High Desert (A) and Wichita (AA)... Combined was 9-5 with 104 strikeouts and 33 walks in 118.2 innings pitched... Was named by Baseball America as the California League's 6th best prospect despite appearing in only nine games for High Desert... **1993:** Was disabled to start the season with right shoulder tendinitis... Activated on April 20 and made two starts with Rancho Cucamonga (A) before promotion to Wichita (AA)... Was 4-9 in 15 starts with a 3.97 ERA... Promoted to Las Vegas (AAA) after going 3-0 with a 1.63 ERA in his last five starts... Made AAA debut on July 27 at Portland... Finished 3-2 in eight starts with a 4.40 ERA... **1994:** Started the season with Las Vegas (AAA) and was 3-5 with a 2.73 ERA in nine starts... Ranked third in the Pacific Coast League in ERA when his contract was purchased by San Diego on May 24... Won his ML debut 6-3 over the Giants that night (6.0IP, 5H, 3ER, 3BB, 3K)... Won first two starts, first Padre rookie to do so since Dave Freisleben in 1974... Led the Padres with nine wins which tied the Cubs' Steve Trachsel for most rookie wins in 1994... Started 3-0 with a 2.36 ERA in first four starts... Tossed a six hit shutout on June 25 at Cincinnati... Surrendered one earned or less in seven of 16 starts... Named to Topps Rookie All-Star Team... Was fifth in Baseball America's Top 20 Rookies list... **1995:** Was 6-9 with a 3.08 ERA in 31 games, 30 starts... Ranked fifth in the NL in ERA and fourth in innings pitched (204.1)... Was the first NL pitcher since 1988 (Joe Magrane) to rank in the top 5 in ERA with less than eight wins... Held opponents to a .246 batting average, 10th in the NL... Had a no-decision on June 3 despite pitching a three hit shutout over nine innings in a 1-0, 10 inning loss to Montreal and Pedro Martinez who had a perfect game until the tenth... From June 3 on was 3-0 with a 1.92 ERA in his next eight games, seven starts... Tossed two shutouts, June 14 at St. Louis and June 24 at Colorado, both games were completed in less than two hours... June 14 was a two hitter in a 3-0 win... Had two three game win streaks and a three and a four game losing streak... Doubled to center field off the Mets Pete Harnisch on June 9 to snap a career opening 0-57 stretch at the plate... Finished the season batting .108 (7-65)... Collected two hits on July 5 at Florida... Set a then career high with eight strikeouts on July 23 in Atlanta... Lost last four decisions despite posting a 3.21 ERA over the nine starts... Left-hand hitters hit just .229, 5th in NL, while right handers hit .260... **1996:** Led the Padres with career highs of 15 wins, 33 starts, 211.2 innings pitched, 184 strikeouts and three complete games... Was 8th in the NL with a .625 (15-9) winning percentage and strikeouts per nine innings (7.8), was ninth in strikeouts... Opened the season going 5-1 in April with a 3.40 ERA, the first pitcher in Padre history to record five wins in April... Tossed a two hit shutout of Houston on April 29, fourth career complete game shutout... Started the season 8-3 picking up decisions in each of his first 11 starts... Set a career high with 10 strikeouts on May 22 vs Philadelphia... Padres lost three of his starts by 1-0 scores giving him two losses - lost May 11 to Cincinnati and July 22 at Houston and received a no-decision on August 7 at St. Louis... In June and July was 2-3 with a 5.91 ERA after suffering from a right shoulder soreness... Lone relief appearance was July 6 vs San Francisco, a scoreless seventh inning in which the scoreboard radar gun registered 99 m.p.h... In August rebounded and was 3-1 with a 1.76 ERA in six starts despite allowing six earned runs in one of the starts... Held opponents scoreless in three of the six starts... Tossed 7.0 shutout innings and hit his first ML home run on August 18 against the Mets Paul Wilson in Monterrey, Mexico... Won his final two home starts as the Padres clinched

post-season birth... At home was 12-2 with a 3.03 ERA and on the road was 3-7 with a 5.47 ERA... **1997:** Led the Padres in wins with 12 and was second in starts (29), innings pitched (192.2) and strikeouts (124)... Finished the season 12-7 with a 4.25 ERA... Made his first career opening day start and won 12-5 over the Mets despite walking a career high six batters... Was on the DL from April 24 to May 17 with right shoulder tendinitis... Homered on May 22 against the Dodgers Hideo Nomo and again on June 27 at LA... Lost only four times in his last 22 outings (20 starts)... At the plate led the staff with seven hits, two home runs and six RBI... Won a career high six straight from June 27 to August 6, in 12 games (11 starts) posted a 3.30 ERA... On August 1 recorded his 7th career complete game with a first relief, 8-2 win in Montreal... Appeared twice in relief matching his career total heading into 1997... Worked 3.0 innings in relief on July 6 in Los Angeles and won in relief in the final game of the season, September 28 at San Francisco... Struck out a season high nine on September 7 vs Atlanta in a 4-0 loss... Was 9-1 on the road with a 3.90 ERA while at home was 3-6 with a 4.56 ERA... Worked 8.0 innings at least three times, 7.0 innings in 16 of 29 starts and at least 6.0 innings in 22 starts... Right-hand hitters posted a .238 average with 8 home runs while left-handers posted a .306 mark with 14 homers... **1998:** Was 13-13 with a 4.27 ERA in a career high 34 starts... Set a career high with 217.1 innings pitched... Received second lowest run support in the NL at 3.4 runs per starts (Willie Blair 3.29)... Padres scored three runs or less in 22 of his 34 starts and totaled 34 runs in his 13 losses (2.61 avg.)... Posted a 5.82 first inning ERA allowing 23 runs, 22 earned, in the first innings of his 34 starts... Lost a career high six consecutive starts from May 7 to June 3... On May 29 vs St. Louis struck out a career high 11 batters but took the loss in an 8-3 game... Won four starts in a row from July 3 to 23 with a 1.67 ERA... Was 5-0 from July 3 to August 11 with a 2.70 ERA in eight starts... Prior to the break was 6-9 with 5.15 ERA in 19 starts and following the break was 7-4 with a 3.13 ERA in 15 starts... Hit his fourth career home run on July 12 against the Dodgers Brian Bohanon, three of his four career homers have come against the Dodgers... Led the NL with 106 walks... On July 23 in a 3-0 combined shutout vs Arizona did not walk a batter for the first time in 31 starts (August 11, 1997 at MON)... Pitched eight innings of three hit ball and struck out ten batters... August 26 in Philadelphia pitched five hit ball over seven shutout innings in a 2-0 victory... Combined on a 1-0 shutout of September 11 vs. LA with eight innings of six hit ball... In the post season made five appearances, one start and was 0-1 with a 3.09 ERA... **1999:** In his first AL season was 7-8 with a 6.52 ERA in 22 games, 18 starts... Started the season 0-2 with an ERA of 19.29 in his first two starts and was placed on the disabled list on April 16 with right shoulder impingement... On May 10 was assigned to Syracuse on a medical rehabilitation assignment... Was 0-1 in three starts with a 5.11 ERA with Syracuse... Activated from the DL on May 24... Upon return made four appearances in relief before returning to the rotation on June 5... Fell to 0-4 on the season before capturing his first win on June 21 vs KC... After 0-4 start was 7-4 the rest of the season... Was 1-5 at the All-Star break with an 8.57 ERA... Following the break was 6-3 with a 4.44 ERA... Won his first two starts of the second half after winning 3-2 over Atlanta on July 18 and 2-1 over the White Sox on July 23... Longest start of the season was 8.0 innings in a 8-0 loss to Boston on July 28... Was 4-2 in August with a 6.15 ERA in six starts... August 20 vs Oakland had his shortest career start allowing seven ER in 0.1 innings... Season ending surgery on September 9 by Dr. James Andrews who mended some fraying of the rotator cuff and the labrum of his right shoulder... Opponents hit .337 (30-89) in the first inning, scoring runs in nine of 18 starts... 21 of 71 earned runs were scored in the first... Opponents hit .298, LH hitters posted a .348 average and right handers a .243 average... At SkyDome was 2-5 with an 8.27 ERA and on the Road was 5-3 with a 4.78 ERA... As a starter was 7-8 with a 6.37 ERA and in four relief appearances was 0-0 with a hold and a 10.80 ERA.

CAREER NOTES: Owns five 10K games... Through 2000 remained seventh on the Padres All-Time win list with 55... Was the eighth Padre pitcher to record 500 career strikeouts and through 2000 remains 8th with 639... Has a career batting average of .117 (35-300) with four home runs.

POST SEASON EXPERIENCE: 1996: Lost only start of the Division Series against St. Louis (6.0IP, 5H, 3R/ER, 6K)... **1998:** In the Division Series against Houston made two scoreless relief appearances covering 3.1 innings... Pitched in games two and four of the Padres 3-1 series victory... Made two appearances in the NLCS... Started and lost game #4, 8-3 in San Diego... Pitched in relief in game #6, a 5-0 series winning shutout of the Braves... In the World Series against the Yankees made one appearance, in relief in game three pitching a scoreless seventh inning (1BB, 1K).

JOEY HAMILTON

Year	Club & League	W-L	ERA	G	GS	CG	ShO	SV	IP	H	R	ER	HR	HB	BB-IBB	SO	WP	BK	OBA
1992	Charlestn-SC (SAL)	2-2	3.38	7	7	0	0	0	34.2	37	24	13	2	0	4-0f	35	6	4	.261
1992	High Desert (Cal)	4-3	2.74	9	8	0	0	0	49.1	46	20	15	0	4	18-0	43	2	2	.245
1992	Wichita (Tex)	3-0	2.86	6	6	0	0	0	34.2	33	12	11	2	1	11-1	26	1	0	.258
1993	Rancho Cucamonga (Cal)	1-0	4.09	2	2	0	0	0	11.0	11	5	5	0	1	2-0	6	0	0	.244
1993	Wichita (Tex)	4-9	3.97	15	15	0	0	0	90.2	101	55	40	3	5	36-2	50	2	1	.277
1993	Las Vegas (PCL)	3-2	4.40	8	8	0	0	0	47.0	49	25	23	0	4	22-1	33	6	0	.266
1994	Las Vegas (PCL)	3-5	2.73	9	9	1	1	0	59.1	69	25	18	2	1	22-0	32	3	0	.297
1994	SAN DIEGO (NL)	9-6	2.98	16	16	1	1	0	108.2	98	40	36	7	6	29-3	61	6	0	.241
1995	SAN DIEGO (NL)	6-9	3.08	31	30	2	2	0	204.1	189	89	70	17	11	56-5	123	2	0	.246
1996	SAN DIEGO (NL)	15-9	4.17	34	33	3	1	0	211.2	206	100	98	19	9	83-3	184	14	1	.256
1997	SAN DIEGO (NL)	12-7	4.25	31	29	1	0	0	192.2	199	100	91	22	12	69-2	124	7	0	.271
1998	SAN DIEGO (NL)	13-13	4.27	34	34	0	0	0	217.1	220	113	103	15	8	106-10	147	4	0	.267
1999	Syracuse (Int)	0-1	5.11	3	3	0	0	0	12.1	15	8	7	2	2	5-0	9	0	0	.313
1999	TORONTO (AL)	7-8	6.52	22	18	0	0	0	98.0	118	73	71	13	3	39-0	56	4	1	.298
2000	Syracuse (Int)	3-2	3.66	6	6	1	0	0	39.1	44	18	16	1	4	12-0	17	0	0	.281
2000	TORONTO (AL)	2-1	3.55	6	6	0	0	0	33.0	28	13	13	3	2	12-0	15	0	0	.233
Minor Totals		23-24	3.52	65	64	2	1	0	378.1	402	192	148	12	22	132-4	251	20	7	.272
TORONTO TOTALS		9-9	5.77	28	24	0	0	0	131.0	146	86	84	16	5	51-0	71	4	0	.283
NL TOTALS		55-44	3.83	146	142	7	4	0	934.2	912	442	398	80	46	343-23	639	33	2	.258
MAJOR TOTALS		64-53	4.07	174	166	7	4	0	1065.2	1058	528	482	96	51	394-23	710	37	2	.261

DIVISION SERIES RECORD

Year	Club & League	W-L	ERA	G	GS	CG	ShO	SV	IP	H	R	ER	HR	HB	BB-IBB	SO	WP	BK	OBA
1996	SAN DIEGO (NL)	0-1	4.50	1	1	0	0	0	6.0	5	3	3	1	1	0-0	6	0	0	.217
1998	SAN DIEGO (NL)	0-0	0.00	2	0	0	0	0	3.1	1	0	0	0	0	2-0	3	0	0	.100
DIVISION TOTALS		0-1	2.89	3	1	0	0	0	9.1	6	3	3	1	1	2-0	9	0	0	.182

CHAMPIONSHIP SERIES RECORD

Year	Club & League	W-L	ERA	G	GS	CG	ShO	SV	IP	H	R	ER	HR	HB	BB-IBB	SO	WP	BK	OBA
1998	SAN DIEGO (NL)	0-1	4.91	2	1	0	0	0	7.1	7	4	4	1	0	3-0	6	0	0	.241

WORLD SERIES RECORD

Year	Club & League	W-L	ERA	G	GS	CG	ShO	SV	IP	H	R	ER	HR	HB	BB-IBB	SO	WP	BK	OBA
1998	SAN DIEGO (NL)	0-0	0.00	1	0	0	0	0	1.0	0	0	0	0	0	1-0	1	0	0	.000

HAMILTON — TRANSACTIONS

- Selected by the San Diego Padres in first round (eighth overall) of the June 1991 First Year Player Draft.
- On disabled list August 7-17, 1992.
- On disabled list September 6-30, 1992.
- On disabled list April 8-20, 1993.
- On disabled list (right shoulder tendinitis) April 24 to May 17, 1997.
- Traded to the Toronto Blue Jays in exchange for RHP Woody Williams, RHP Carlos Almanzar and OF Peter Tucci on December 13, 1998.
- On disabled list (right shoulder impingement) April 16-May 24, 1999; including rehabilitation assignment at Syracuse.
- On disabled list (right shoulder surgery) March 21-August 19, 2000; including rehabilitation assignment at Syracuse July 17-August 14.

FIELDING

HAMILTON, Joey—P

Year	PCT	G	PO	A	E	TC	DP
1994 (NL)	.958	16	7	16	1	24	3
1995 (NL)	.875	31	12	30	6	48	1
1996 (NL)	.978	34	17	27	1	45	2
1997 (NL)	.967	31	10	19	1	30	0
1998 (NL)	.938	34	15	30	3	48	3
1999 (AL)	1.000	22	4	10	0	14	0
2000 (AL)	1.000	6	2	2	0	4	1
Total	.944	174	67	134	12	213	10

CAREER HIGHS — HAMILTON, Joey

SEASON:

Wins	15 - 1996
Losses	13 - 1998
Saves	None
ERA	3.08 - 1995
Games	34 - 1996, 1998
Starts	34 - 1998
Complete Games	3 - 1996
Shutouts	2 - 1995
Innings Pitched	217.1 - 1998
Walks	106 - 1998
Strikeouts	184 - 1996
Longest Win Streak	6 - Jun. 27-Aug. 6, 1997
Longest Losing Streak	6 - May 7-Jun. 3, 1998
Scoreless Innings Streak	15.0 - Aug. 2-7, 1996

GAME:

ML Debut	May 24, 1994 vs. SF
Innings Pitched:	
Starter	9.0 - 6 times, last Aug. 1, 1997 at MON
Reliever	3.0 - Jul. 6, 1997 vs. LA
Walks:	
Starter	7 - Jun. 3 1998 vs. HOU
Reliever	1 - 5 times, last Jun. 1, 1999 vs. CWS
Strikeouts:	
Starter	11 - May 29, 1998 at STL
Reliever	3 - Jul. 9, 1995 at HOU
Hits Allowed	13 - Jul. 12, 1997 at COL
Runs Allowed	8 - May 3, 1995 at COL
	8 - Apr. 13, 1999 vs. TB
	8 - Aug. 14, 1999 vs. OAK
ER Allowed	8 - Apr. 13, 1999 vs. TB
HR Allowed	3 - Apr. 6, 1997 vs. PHI
	3 - Aug. 11, 1997 vs. MON
Low Hit CG	2 - Jun. 14, 1995 at STL
Last Win	Sep. 6, 2000 vs. SEA
Last Save	None
Last CG	Aug. 1, 1997 at MON
Last ShO	Apr. 29, 1996 vs. HOU
Last Start	Sep. 17, 2000 at CWS
Last Relief App.	Jun. 1, 1999 vs. CWS

JOEY HAMILTON DETAILED PITCHING

	2000									CAREER						
	ERA	W-L-Sv	G	IP	H	ER	BB	SO	ERA	W-L-Sv	G	IP	H	ER	BB	SO
Total	3.55	2-1-0	6	33.0	28	13	12	15	4.07	64-53-0	174	1065.2	1058	482	394	710
ST	3.55	2-1-0	6	33.0	28	13	12	15	4.07	63-53-0	166	1054.2	1050	477	390	702
REL	–	–	–	–	–	–	–	–	4.09	1-0-0	8	11.0	8	5	4	8
Home	2.25	1-0-0	3	20.0	17	5	7	10	3.75	33-29-0	91	564.1	535	235	206	414
Away	5.54	1-1-0	3	13.0	11	8	5	5	4.43	31-24-0	83	501.1	523	247	188	296
April	–	–	–	–	–	–	–	–	4.94	8-5-0	19	114.2	121	63	47	81
May	–	–	–	–	–	–	–	–	4.72	8-10-0	25	139.1	147	73	49	104
June	–	–	–	–	–	–	–	–	3.99	11-11-0	36	234.1	221	104	96	129
July	–	–	–	–	–	–	–	–	3.85	14-8-0	33	203.1	205	87	74	150
August	1.50	1-0-0	2	12.0	7	2	4	9	3.63	17-8-0	35	223.0	209	90	66	151
September	4.71	1-1-0	4	21.0	21	11	8	6	3.87	6-11-0	26	151.0	155	65	62	95
vs. Ana	–	–	–	–	–	–	–	–	3.48	1-1-0	3	20.2	18	8	7	15
vs. Bal	–	–	–	–	–	–	–	–	11.57	0-0-0	2	9.1	17	12	5	7
vs. Bos	–	–	–	–	–	–	–	–	4.50	0-1-0	1	8.0	7	4	1	5
vs. CWS	0.00	0-0-0	1	3.0	2	0	0	1	0.84	1-0-0	3	10.2	6	1	3	4
vs. Det	–	–	–	–	–	–	–	–	0.00	0-0-0	1	0.2	0	0	0	1
vs. KC	–	–	–	–	–	–	–	–	6.75	1-0-0	1	5.1	9	4	1	3
vs. Mil	–	–	–	–	–	–	–	–	5.14	0-1-0	1	7.0	6	4	0	6
vs. Min	0.00	0-0-0	1	6.0	3	0	3	6	10.45	0-2-0	3	10.1	19	12	7	8
vs. NYY	13.50	0-1-0	1	4.0	5	6	4	1	8.49	1-1-0	4	11.2	13	11	6	5
vs. Oak	3.86	0-0-0	1	7.0	10	3	0	3	6.38	1-1-0	4	18.1	21	13	8	11
vs. Sea	2.57	1-0-0	1	7.0	4	2	4	1	5.70	2-2-0	4	23.2	31	15	11	7
vs. TB	–	–	–	–	–	–	–	–	8.49	0-2-0	2	11.2	18	11	4	6
vs. Tex	3.00	1-0-0	1	6.0	4	2	1	3	4.09	2-0-0	2	11.0	9	5	3	7
vs. Ari	–	–	–	–	–	–	–	–	1.35	2-0-0	3	20.0	12	3	3	23
vs. Atl	–	–	–	–	–	–	–	–	5.20	3-8-0	11	71.0	79	41	23	43
vs. ChC	–	–	–	–	–	–	–	–	3.19	4-3-0	13	84.2	78	30	31	59
vs. Cin	–	–	–	–	–	–	–	–	2.99	2-4-0	12	78.1	68	26	22	42
vs. Col	–	–	–	–	–	–	–	–	4.50	4-4-0	10	60.0	65	30	31	49
vs. Fla	–	–	–	–	–	–	–	–	4.82	2-1-0	6	37.1	46	20	19	32
vs. Hou	–	–	–	–	–	–	–	–	4.12	4-4-0	10	59.0	59	27	33	39
vs. LA	–	–	–	–	–	–	–	–	2.48	8-2-0	15	101.2	84	28	33	69
vs. Mon	–	–	–	–	–	–	–	–	3.79	4-4-0	10	71.1	64	30	17	41
vs. NYM	–	–	–	–	–	–	–	–	4.07	5-3-0	13	86.1	87	39	32	66
vs. Phi	–	–	–	–	–	–	–	–	3.80	4-5-0	13	85.1	87	36	27	72
vs. Pit	–	–	–	–	–	–	–	–	5.36	3-8-0	8	47.0	52	28	20	30
vs. StL	–	–	–	–	–	–	–	–	2.42	4-2-0	9	63.1	45	17	24	35
vs. SF	–	–	–	–	–	–	–	–	4.67	4-1-0	10	52.0	58	27	23	25
Pre-All Star	–	–	–	–	–	–	–	–	4.49	31-27-0	91	543.0	550	271	214	350
Post-All Star	3.55	2-1-0	6	33.0	28	13	12	15	3.63	33-26-0	83	522.2	508	211	180	360

JOEY HAMILTON PITCHING AT ML PARKS

Park	ERA	W-L-Sv	SvO	G	GS	IP	H	R	ER	HR	BB	SO
Camden Yards	16.20	0-0-0	0	1	1	3.1	10	6	6	2	1	1
Edison Field	2.57	1-0-0	0	1	1	7.0	4	2	2	0	3	5
Comiskey Park	0.93	1-0-0	0	2	2	9.2	5	1	1	1	2	4
Tiger Stadium	0.00	0-0-0	0	1	0	0.2	0	0	0	0	0	1
Metrodome	27.00	0-1-0	0	1	1	2.1	9	7	7	0	3	1
Yankee Stadium	6.30	1-1-0	0	2	2	10.0	9	7	7	2	4	4
Oakland-Alameda	0.00	1-0-0	0	1	1	6.0	3	0	0	0	3	3
Kingdome	9.31	0-2-0	0	2	2	9.2	18	11	10	3	4	3
Arlington	4.09	2-0-0	0	2	2	11.0	9	5	5	3	3	7
SkyDome	6.52	3-5-0	0	15	12	69.0	84	52	50	7	29	38
Atlanta-Fulton	6.63	0-3-0	0	3	3	19.0	24	14	14	4	5	13
Wrigley Field	4.38	2-1-0	0	6	6	37.0	35	20	18	4	16	22
Cinergy Field	3.65	5-2-0	0	7	7	44.1	39	18	18	1	14	21
Astrodome	2.79	2-2-0	0	5	4	29.0	22	12	9	0	18	25
Dodger Stadium	2.81	4-1-0	0	7	7	48.0	43	17	15	4	14	31
Olympic Stadium	2.51	3-0-0	0	4	4	32.1	25	11	9	1	5	18
Shea Stadium	3.43	2-0-0	0	6	6	42.0	37	17	16	3	9	26
Veterans Stadium	5.06	1-3-0	0	7	7	42.2	52	25	24	2	15	34
Three Rivers	5.82	0-1-0	0	3	3	17.0	23	11	11	2	11	6
Busch Stadium	1.22	2-1-0	0	5	5	37.0	23	8	5	2	12	12
Qualcomm Park	3.41	29-24-0	0	75	73	488.1	445	207	185	44	176	366
3 Com Park	6.49	2-0-0	0	5	4	26.1	33	20	19	2	13	12
Coors Field	7.71	1-2-0	0	4	4	21.0	36	24	18	2	12	14
Pro Player Stadium	6.94	1-1-0	0	4	4	23.1	35	18	18	3	12	19
Turner Field	8.49	0-2-0	0	2	2	11.2	17	11	11	2	6	5
BankOne Ballpark	2.25	0-0-0	0	1	1	4.0	4	1	1	1	2	6
Tropicana Field	3.86	0-1-0	0	1	1	7.0	8	3	3	1	1	3
Monterrey Stadium	0.00	1-0-0	0	1	1	7.0	6	0	0	0	1	10

JOEY HAMILTON — MILESTONES

	DATE	OPP.	H/A	W/L (IP)	AGAINST/NOTES
WIN					
1	May 24, 1994	SD vs SF	H	W6-3 (6.0)	Bryan Hickerson/(Debut)
10 Ks					
10	May 22, 1996	SD vs PHI	H	W5-2 (6.1)	Mike Grace
10	July 28, 1996	SD at FLA	A	L8-2 (5+)	Al Leiter
10	Aug. 18, 1996	SD vs NY (N)	H	W8-0 (7.0)	Paul Wilson
11	May 29, 1998	SD vs STL	H	L8-3 (7.1)	Mark Petkovsek
10	July 23, 1998	SD vs ARI	H	W3-0 (8.0)	Brian Anderson
SHO					
1	June 25, 1994	SD at CIN	A	W6-0	6 Hits, 1K
2	June 14, 1995	SD at STL	A	W3-0	2 Hits, 3K
3	June 24, 1995	SD vs COL	H	W2-0	4 Hits, 5K
4	April 29, 1997	SD vs HOU	H	W2-0	4 Hits, 2K
LOW HIT (2 or less)					
2	June 14, 1995	SD at STL	H	W3-0	3K

Mark HENDRICKSON

PITCHER

37

BIRTHDATE	June 23, 1974
OPENING DAY AGE	26
BIRTHPLACE	Mt. Vernon, WA
RESIDENCE	Mt. Vernon, WA
BATS/THROWS	L/L
HEIGHT/WEIGHT	6-9/230
CONTRACT STATUS	signed thru 2001
M.L. SERVICE	0.000

PERSONAL: Attended Mount Vernon High School in Washington State where he played baseball, basketball and tennis...Led baseball team to the State championship in his senior year and in the State semi-final tossed a four-hitter with 12 strikeouts...Was 10-1 with 0.84 ERA and posted 115 strikeouts while batting .315...Led basketball team to State title after averaging 20 points and 13 rebounds...Selected by the Atlanta Braves in the 12th round of the 1992 draft following High School...Attended Washington State University where he continues to play baseball and basketball...Was a two-time basketball selection to the All-Pac 10 Conference first team... Drafted by the San Diego Padres in the 21st round in 1993, by the Atlanta Braves in the 32nd round in 1994, by Detroit in the 16th round in 1995 and the Texas Rangers in 1996 in the 19th round...Selected and signed by the Philadelphia 76'ers in the second round of the 1996 NBA draft...Selected by the Toronto Blue Jays in the 1997 draft (20th round)...Was his sixth time being selected in baseball's June draft.

LAST SEASON: Started 18 games and was 5-3 between the Dunedin Blue Jays (A) and the Tennessee Smokies (AA)... Opened the season in Dunedin of the Florida State League where he was 2-2 in 12 starts with a 5.61 ERA... Held opponents scoreless in his first two starts, May 30 & June 3, but pitched only 7.0 innings combined... First decision was a victory on June 20 at Clearwater after holding the Phillies to one run over 5.0 innings... Twice had starts of 6.0 innings, July 21 and 31... On July 31 suffered his second loss after a complete game effort (6.0IP) in game one of a doubleheader... Following that start was promoted to Tennessee where he made six starts and was 3-1 with a 3.63 ERA... Won first two starts with the Smokies... On August 13 vs Mobile tossed a season high 8.0 shutout innings allowing just three hits... On August 19 at West Tenn struck out a season high seven batters in 5.2 innings... Pitched 6.0 innings in four of his six starts and the last three of the season... At Tennessee held left-handed hitters to a .171 average while right-handers hit only .234... Combined between the two clubs recorded 67 strikeouts in 91.0 innings with 41 walks... Pitched for Scottsdale in the Arizona Fall League and was 2-3 with a 2.67 ERA in seven starts... In his first four starts, did not allow a run in 16.0 innings.

PROFESSIONAL CAREER: 1998: Made pro baseball debut with Dunedin of the Florida State League (A) and posted a 4-3 record in 16 games, five starts...Posted one save...Left handed batters hit .226 (7-31) with two doubles and nine strikeouts... **1999:** Joined Knoxville of the Southern League (AA) and was 2-7 in 12 games, 11 starts...Started the season 0-4 before first win on August 8 vs Carolina - tossed one hit ball over 7.0 innings allowing a solo HR... Earned second win on a combined shutout on August 23 (7.0IP, 4H)...Struckout a season high seven in final start of the season, September 3 at Carolina...Allowed four home runs in 55.2 innings...Lasted 6.0 innings in his last three starts of the season after doing once in the eight previous starts.

PRO BASKETBALL CAREER: 1996-1997: Appeared in 29 games with Philadelphia 76'ers averaging 2.9 points and 3.2 rebounds in 10.4 minutes per game...Played the final 13 games of the season and averaged 4.5 points and 5.2 rebounds...Sat out 34 games with a lumbar spine strain and sprain which he suffered in November and twice re-aggravated...Scored a season high 12 points on two occasions...**1997-1998:** Opened the season in the CBA with the LaCrosse Catbirds...Signed with the Sacramento Kings on December 23...Player in 48 games with the Kings averaging 3.4 points and 3.0 rebounds in 15.4 minutes per game...**1998-1999:** Again began the season with LaCrosse in the CBA until signing with the New Jersey Nets...Signed two 10-day contracts and then for the remainder of the season on April 14...In 22 games, six starts, averaged 5.3 points and 3.1 rebounds in 18.1 minutes per game...Shot .443 from the field and .840 from the foul line...Scored a career high 19 points on May 5 in season finale against Milwaukee...Posted only double - double (14 points, 10 rebounds) on May 1 against Washington when he played a career high 46 minutes...**1999-2000:** Signed as a free agent by the Cleveland Cavaliers on December 27...Was waived by Cleveland on January 5...Signed by Cleveland to a ten day contract on January 8 and again on January 18...Was released by Cleveland on January 27.

MARK HENDRICKSON

Year	Club & League	W-L	ERA	G	GS	CG	ShO	SV	IP	H	R	ER	HR	HB	BB-IBB	SO	WP	BK	OBA
1998	Dunedin (FSL)	4-3	2.37	16	5	0	0	1	49.1	44	16	13	2	0	26-1	38	2	0	.249
1999	Knoxville (Sou)	2-7	6.63	12	11	0	0	0	55.2	73	46	41	4	2	21-0	39	2	1	.319
2000	Dunedin (FSL)	2-2	5.61	12	12	1	0	0	51.1	63	34	32	7	0	29-0	38	1	0	.315
2000	Tennessee (Sou)	3-1	3.63	6	6	0	0	0	39.2	32	17	16	5	0	12-0	29	4	0	.216
Minor Totals		**11-13**	**4.68**	**46**	**34**	**1**	**0**	**1**	**196.0**	**212**	**113**	**102**	**18**	**2**	**88-1**	**144**	**9**	**1**	**.281**

HENDRICKSON — TRANSACTIONS

- Selected by the Atlanta Braves in the 12th round of the June 1992 First Year Player Draft.
- Selected by the San Diego Padres in the 21st round of the June 1993 First Year Player Draft.
- Selected by the Atlanta Braves in the 32nd round of the June 1994 First Year Players Draft.
- Selected by the Detroit Tigers in the 16th round of the June 1995 First Year Player Draft.
- Selected by the Texas Rangers in the 19th round of the June 1996 First Year Player Draft.
- Selected by the Toronto Blue Jays in the 20th round (599th overall) of the June 1997 First Year Player Draft.

Aaron
HOLBERT

INFIELDER

61

BIRTHDATE	January 9, 1973
OPENING DAY AGE	28
BIRTHPLACE	Torrance, CA
RESIDENCE	Fontana, CA
BATS/THROWS	R/R
HEIGHT/WEIGHT	6-0/160
CONTRACT STATUS	signed thru 2001
M.L. SERVICE	0.005

PERSONAL: Aaron Keith Holbert... Married, wife's name Jacqueline... Graduated from Long Beach-Jordan High School in 1990 where was named to All-California High School All-Star team for baseball... His brother Ray played in the Detroit Tigers organization.

LAST SEASON: Split the season between Red Sox and Marlins organizations and combined to hit .259 with 18 doubles, seven home runs and 41 RBI... Opened the season with Pawtucket of the International League (AAA) where he hit .252 in 80 games with 13 doubles, three home runs and 23 RBI... Best month was May where he hit .297 in 19 games with three doubles, two triples, a home run and eight RBI... Hit in 12 of 13 games from May 19 to June 4... Hit only .248 in June and then in 17 games in July hit just .196... Traded to the Florida Marlins organization on August 2 for a player to be named later and assigned to Calgary of the Pacific Coast League (AAA) where he hit .279 in 29 games with five doubles, four home runs and 18 RBI... Hit in a season high eight straight games from August 14 to 21.

PROFESSIONAL CAREER: 1990: Began his professional career with Johnson City (Rookie)... Hit his first professional home run on July 1 vs. Martinsville... Stayed in extended spring training until assigned to Springfield (A) May 14... Spent six weeks on the DL with a broken right ankle... **1992:** Ranked second in the Southern League (AA) in steals (62) while with Savannah... Registered 12 multi-steal games... Stole 11 bases in 30 games for the Cardinals instructional team... **1993:** Finished second in the Florida State League with 45 stolen bases... Participated in the Hawaiian Winter League... **1993:** Sidelined May through late July with a knee injury while at Arkansas (AA)... Played only 59 games, but tied a league high with six triples... Hit .375 in August to finish the season at .296... **1995:** Belted nine HR and 40 RBI with Louisville, his first season in AAA... Batted .367 in 29 games for Peoria of the Arizona Fall League before a wrist injury in the final week ended his career... **1996:** Opened the season at Louisville, going 8 for 19 (.421) in his first five games... Was re-called to St. Louis on April 11 after Ozzie Smith was placed on the disabled list... Made his major league debut April 14 vs. Philadelphia at second base after spending his career at shortstop, was 0 for 3... Optioned back to AAA the next day... Missed 15 games in June with a bruised left heel... **1997:** Played the entire year at Louisville, his third year at the Triple-A level with St. Louis... Hit .255 (4th highest on club) in 93 games... Appeared in 81 games at shortstop and four at second base... Stole nine bases, his fewest total since 1991... **1998:** Split the season between AA Orlando and AAA Tacoma of the Seattle Mariners organization... Saw time with both clubs at second base, but primarily played shortstop... Hit nearly 85 points better when playing second base (.373) as opposed to shortstop (.289)... Hit .287 for the O-Rays with 34 RBI and 10 stolen bases... Promoted to Tacoma June 29 and immediately hit in 11 straight games (19-43), longest streak of the year... Hit safely in 46 of 56 games with the Rainiers and batted predominantly in the leadoff spot including 21 of final 24 games of the season... On September 1 was 3-4 with two

doubles and a season-high 5 RBI against Fresno... His .314 average with Tacoma was his highest to-date at the AAA level... Between the two clubs had career-bests of 124 games played, 480 at-bats, 84 runs, 144 hits, 25 doubles, 12 home runs and 65 RBI... **1999:** Joined the Devil Rays organization and spent the season with Durham (AAA)... Hit .311 in 100 games with 18 doubles, four triples and 12 home runs... Stole 14 bases in 19 attempts... Opened the season with a .333 average in April, his best month of the season... Has a two homer game on June 27 at Pawtucket... Posted two four-hit games, May 30 at Ottawa and July 27 vs Scranton... Hit in 15 straight games from July 31 to August 15... In August hit .306 in 27 games and his highest RBI total of any month at 18... Appeared in 53 games at second base, 22 at shortstop, 10 as the designated hitter, seven in left field, five as a pinch-runner, four at third base, three as a pinch-hitter and he pitched twice.

AARON HOLBERT

Year	Club & League	AVG	G	AB	R	H	TB	2B	3B	HR	RBI	SH-SF	HP	BB-IBB	SO	SB-CS	GIDP	SLG	OBP
1990	Johnson City (Appy)	.172	54	174	27	30	39	4	1	1	18	1-1	3	24-1	31	4-5	2	.224	.282
1991	Springfield (Mid)	.223	59	215	22	48	58	5	1	1	24	1-2	6	15-0	28	5-8	3	.270	.290
1992	Savannah (SAL)	.267	119	438	53	117	145	17	4	1	34	6-3	8	40-0	57	62-25	4	.331	.337
1993	St. Petersburg (FSL)	.265	121	457	60	121	151	18	3	2	31	15-1	4	28-2	61	45-22	6	.330	.312
1994	Arkansas (Tex)	.296	59	233	41	69	97	10	6	2	19	4-1	2	14-0	25	9-7	5	.416	.340
1994	Cardinals (Ariz)	.167	5	12	3	2	2	0	0	0	0	0-0	0	2-0	2	2-0	0	.167	.286
1995	Louisville (AmAs)	.257	112	401	57	103	154	16	4	9	40	3-5	5	20-1	60	14-6	10	.384	.297
1996	Louisville (AmAs)	.264	112	436	54	115	155	16	6	4	32	5-4	2	21-0	61	20-14	8	.356	.298
1996	ST. LOUIS (NL)	.000	1	3	0	0	0	0	0	0	0	0-0	0	0-0	0	0-0	0	.000	.000
1997	Louisville (AmAs)	.255	93	314	32	80	112	14	3	4	32	3-4	2	15-1	56	9-5	9	.357	.290
1998	Orlando (Sou)	.287	68	251	46	72	104	13	5	3	34	4-1	5	22-0	41	10-14	3	.414	.355
1998	Tacoma (PCL)	.314	56	229	38	72	111	12	0	9	31	2-1	3	12-0	40	6-6	3	.485	.355
1999	Durham (Int)	.311	100	347	77	108	170	18	4	12	56	8-5	5	25-0	56	14-5	4	.490	.361
2000	Pawtucket (Int)	.252	80	294	38	74	100	13	2	3	23	1-0	4	15-0	54	8-6	4	.340	.297
2000	Calgary (PCL)	.279	29	104	18	29	48	5	1	4	18	0-0	1	10-0	12	3-4	2	.462	.348
Minor Totals		.266	1067	3905	566	1040	1446	161	40	55	392	53-28	50	263-5	584	211-127	63	.370	.319

HOLBERT — TRANSACTIONS

- Selected by the St. Louis Cardinals in the 1st round (18th overall) of the June 1990 First Year Player Draft.
- On disabled list (broken right ankle) June 5-July 17, 1991.
- On disabled list (knee injury) May 1-July 30, 1994.
- On disabled list May 15-22, 1995.
- On disabled list July 28-August 4, 1995.
- On disabled list June 5-20, 1996.
- On disabled list April 16-May 1, 1997.
- Signed by the Seattle Mariners on April 7, 1998.
- Signed by the Tampa Bay Devil Rays on November 24, 1998.
- Signed by the Boston Red Sox on December 16, 1999.
- On disabled list June 30-July 7, 2000.
- Traded to the Florida Marlins for a player to be named on August 2, 2000.
- Signed by the Toronto Blue Jays on November 5, 2000.

FIELDING

HOLBERT, Aaron—IF

Year	PCT	G	PO	A	E	TC	DP
1996	1.000	1	0	1	0	0	0

SHORT TERM BLUE JAYS (Maximum 2 games)

PLAYER	POSITION	GAME(S)	YEAR	PLAYER	POSITION	GAME(S)	YEAR
Mike Darr	RHP	1	1977	Jose Silva	RHP	2	1996
Steve Luebber	RHP	1	1979	Aaron Small	RHP	1	1994
Steve Grilli	RHP	1	1979	Randy St. Claire	RHP	2	1994
Nino Espinosa	RHP	1	1981	Shannon Withem	RHP	1	1998
Rick Luecken	RHP	1	1990	Eric Ludwick	RHP	1	1999
Mark Wiley	RHP	2	1978	Curtis Goodwin	OF	2	1999
Brian Milner	C	2	1978	Gary Glover	RHP	1	1999
Mickey Mahler	LHP	2	1986	Pasqual Coco	RHP	1	2000
Tom Gilles	RHP	2	1990	Leoncio Estrella	RHP	2	2000
Mickey Weston	RHP	2	1991	Josh Phelps	C	1	2000
Ricky Trlicek	RHP	2	1992	Andy Thompson	OF	2	2000

Trenidad
HUBBARD
OUTFIELDER

BIRTHDATE	May 11, 1966
OPENING DAY AGE	34
BIRTHPLACE	Chicago, IL
RESIDENCE	Missouri City, TX
BATS/THROWS	R/R
HEIGHT/WEIGHT	5-9/203
CONTRACT STATUS	signed thru 2001
M.L. SERVICE	4.066

68

PERSONAL: Trenidad Aviel Hubbard... Married, wife's name is Angela... Has one son, Jaylen (3) and one daughter, Jasmine (1)... Graduated from South Shore High School in Chicago, IL... Majored in Business Management at Southern University... Played baseball... Turned a 9th-inning, conference-clinching triple play against rival Grambling University... Cousin of former Buffalo Bills All-Pro running back Joe Cribbs... Co-owns Game Face, with former Brave teammate Brian Jordan and ex-Blue Jays pitcher Danny Cox, a sports apparel clothing company.

LAST SEASON: Split the season between Atlanta and Baltimore combining to hit .185 in 92 games... Opened the season with Atlanta appearing in 61 games and batting .185... Lone home run came on April 30 in San Diego when he posted a season high three RBI... Was traded to Baltimore along with catcher Fernando Lunar and RHP Luis Rivera on July 31 in exchange for OF B.J. Surhoff and RHP Gabe Molina... Tripled in his Oriole debut on August 2 vs Minnesota... Appeared in 31 games for Baltimore, making three starts... Hit .244 against left-handers and .149 against right-handers.

PROFESSIONAL CAREER: 1986: After being selected by Houston in the draft he started his pro career with Auburn and was named as the team MVP... Hit .310 in 70 games with 35 stolen bases... **1987:** Named team MVP for Asheville... **1988:** Named team MVP for Osceola... Stole 44 bases and had 15 doubles, 11 triples, 68 runs with a career high 65 RBI... **1989:** Hit .264 with eight triples and 28 stolen bases for Columbus... Appeared in 21 games with Tucson and hit .220... **1990:** Posted a career high four home runs while at Columbus in 95 games... **1991:** Spent most of the season at Double-A Jackson before a late season call-up to Tucson... Ranked third among Astros' farmhands with 39 steals and fourth with 135 hits... Led Texas League second basemen with 81 double plays, 296 assists and 653 total chances... Also pitched, facing four batters in an inning at Jackson, walked two and did not allow a hit... **1992:** Ended the season as the starting second baseman with a .310 average at Triple-A Tucson with the Houston organization... Stole 34 bases in 44 attempts (77 percent)... **1993:** Went to spring training as an invitee in his first Rockies' camp and wound up at Colorado Springs (AAA)... Batted .314 with seven home runs and 56 RBI in 117 games for the Sky Sox... **1994:** Made his Major League debut with Colorado on July 6 after spending 8-plus seasons in the minor leagues... Hit .280 (7-for-25) in 18 games for the Rockies, including .417 (5-for-12) in a pinch-hitting role... Collected his first ML hit on July 15 vs. St. Louis, an infield single off Rich Rodriguez... Connected for his first ML home run on July 20 vs. Chicago off Willie Banks... Opened the season at Colorado Springs and hit .363 in 79 games... Was named to the Triple-A All-Star Team, but did not appear in the game at Nashville because of his promotion to the big leagues... **1995:** Spent most of the season with Colorado Springs of the Pacific Coast League... Led the Pacific Coast League with a .340 average, 102 runs, 163 hits, 37 stolen bases and a .416 on-base percentage at the time of the call-up... Was named the Sky Sox's MVP despite not finishing the season at Colorado Springs... Hit .424 (56x132) during a career high 30-game hitting streak from July 5-August 7... The streak included 11 consecutive games in which he scored at least one run... Contract purchased by Colorado on August 23 and batted .310 with three home runs and nine RBI in 24 games with the Rockies... Appeared in three post-season games and was

hitless in two at bats... **1996:** Split most of the season with Colorado and Triple-A Colorado Springs before being claimed off outright waivers by San Francisco on August 21, spending the remainder of the season with the Giants... Overall, batted .213 (19-for-89) with five doubles, two triples, two home runs and 14 RBI in 55 games... Opened the season with the Rockies but was optioned to Colorado Springs on May 12... Appeared in 24 games for the Rockies with three starts in center field and hit .192 (5-for-26) with four RBI... Was recalled by Colorado on June 7... Homered off the Braves' John Smoltz in his first game back on June 9 vs. Atlanta as a defensive replacement... Was optioned back to Colorado Springs on July 14 and was with the Sky Sox until being claimed off waivers by San Francisco on August 21... Batted .217 with one home run and 12 RBI in 45 games with the Rockies... Made his debut on August 21 vs New York, entered as a defensive replacement for Barry Bonds... Started six consecutive games in left field due to Bonds' sore left hamstring in late August... Missed the remainder of the season after fracturing the hamate bone in his left hand on September 1 at New York attempting to check his swing... Was placed on the 15-day disabled list on September 2 and had surgery to remove the bone on September 3... Was transferred to the 60-day disabled list on September 13... On November 13 was sent to the Cleveland Indians as a player to be named later in the trade for Matt Williams... **1997:** Spent most of the season with Buffalo but appeared in seven games with Cleveland... Had a .312 average with 16 home runs, 60 RBI and 26 stolen bases in 103 games with Buffalo who captured the American Association title (AAA)... The 16 home runs were the most of his professional career... Led the league with a .401 on-base percentage and was 3rd in batting... Started the season at Buffalo after being optioned from Cleveland on March 31... Batted .400 (40-for-100) with five home runs and 23 RBI during a 21-game hit streak from May 2 to June 1... Drove in at least one run in eight consecutive games from May 2-9... Had a .316 average at Buffalo when he was recalled by the Indians on June 17... Was optioned back to Buffalo on June 20... With Cleveland hit .250 with one double and two stolen bases... Made only one error in 89 games in the outfield at Buffalo... **1998:** After signing as a free agent with the Dodgers he hit .298 for Los Angeles in 94 games with nine doubles, a triple, seven home runs, 18 RBI and 29 runs scored... Ranked 2nd on the Dodgers in batting average and set career highs in nearly every offensive category, including games, at-bats (208), runs, hits (62), doubles, home runs, RBI, walks (18), strikeouts (46) and stolen bases (9)... Saw outfield action in 81 games, including 26 starts in center field and 22 starts in left field... Committed one error in 114 total chances for a .991 fielding percentage, tying Gary Sheffield for the club lead among outfielders... Was the Dodgers' Opening Day starter in center field... As a starter, batted .286 (48-for-168) with five doubles, seven home runs, 16 RBI and 23 runs scored... Collected a hit in 37 of his 48 starts, including a 19-game hitting streak as a starter from May 11-August 29... Missed 34 games on the 15-day disabled list from May 16 to June 21 with a left knee sprain... Tied his career high with three hits on July 9 vs. San Diego... Was optioned to Triple-A Albuquerque on July 12 but did not need to report... Was recalled two days later to Los Angeles... Had his best stretch of the season from August 5-29, going 18-for-50 (.360) with two doubles, a home run, four RBI and six runs scored in 16 games... Collected a hit in a career-best seven consecutive games for the 2nd time in his career from August 22-29... In his last 61 games, batted .310 with seven doubles, four homers and 13 RBI... As a pinch-hitter was 6-for-23 (.261) with two doubles and two RBI... Hit .366 against left-handed pitching with four home runs and eight RBI... **1999:** Batted .314 in 82 games for the Dodgers with one home run and 13 RBI... Began season at Triple-A Albuquerque where he hit .333 in 32 games with five home runs and 24 RBI... Stole four bases in one game for the Dukes against Memphis on May 11... Was recalled by Dodgers on May 18 after pitcher Antonio Osuna was placed on the disabled list... Made his ML debut at second base July 29 vs. Cincinnati and at catcher July 11 vs. Seattle after

Todd Hundley was ejected in a bench-clearing brawl with the Mariners... Played five positions (LF, CF, RF, C, 2B)... Only Tripp Cromer (6) played more positions... Drove in career-high five runs on July 11 vs Seattle... Went 6-for-27 as a pinch hitter... Only home run came on August 24 at Milwaukee off Scott Karl, a 2-run shot in the 7th inning as Los Angeles won 5-2 and completed a 3-game sweep at County Stadium... Hit a team-high .444 (12-for-27) with runners in scoring position... Batted .375 prior to the All-Star break and .220 in the 2nd half... Hit .310 in his last 48 games with nine RBI and 12 runs scored... Started four games in left field, 10 in center field and two in right field.

TRENIDAD HUBBARD

Year	Club & League	AVG	G	AB	R	H	TB	2B	3B	HR	RBI	SH-SF	HP	BB-IBB	SO	SB-CS	GIDP	SLG	OBP
1986	Auburn (NYP)	.310	70	242	42	75	92	12	1	1	32	2-2	1	28-0	42	35-5	2	.380	.381
1987	Asheville (SAL)	.236	101	284	39	67	80	8	1	1	35	0-7	0	28-1	42	28-13	4	.282	.298
1988	Osceola (FSL)	.260	130	446	68	116	162	15	11	3	65	1-3	3	61-0	72	44-18	10	.363	.351
1989	Columbus (Sou)	.264	104	348	55	92	124	7	8	3	37	4-2	2	43-3	53	28-6	8	.356	.347
1989	Tucson (PCL)	.220	21	50	3	11	13	2	0	0	2	0-0	1	1-0	10	3-3	2	.260	.250
1990	Tucson (PCL)	.222	12	27	5	6	12	2	2	0	2	0-0	0	3-0	6	1-1	1	.444	.300
1990	Columbus (Sou)	.251	95	335	39	84	118	14	4	4	35	8-2	3	37-0	51	17-8	7	.352	.329
1991	Jackson (Tex)	.297	126	455	78	135	168	21	3	2	41	6-2	9	65-2	81	39-20	4	.369	.394
1991	Tucson (PCL)	.000	2	4	0	0	0	0	0	0	0	0-0	0	0-0	0	0-0	1	.000	.000
1992	Tucson (PCL)	.310	115	420	69	130	160	16	4	2	33	9-2	4	45-1	68	34-10	7	.381	.380
1993	Colorado Springs (PCL)	.314	117	439	83	138	199	24	8	7	56	5-1	6	47-3	57	33-18	4	.453	.387
1994	Colorado Springs (PCL)	.363	79	320	78	116	172	22	5	8	38	2-1	2	44-1	40	28-10	7	.538	.441
1994	COLORADO (NL)	.280	18	25	3	7	13	1	1	1	3	0-0	0	3-0	4	0-0	1	.520	.357
1995	Colorado Springs (PCL)	.340	123	480	102	163	242	29	7	12	66	2-5	5	61-5	59	37-14	2	.504	.416
1995	COLORADO (NL)	.310	24	58	13	18	31	4	0	3	9	1-0	0	8-0	6	2-1	2	.534	.394
1996	COLORADO (NL)	.217	45	60	12	13	23	5	1	1	12	0-0	1	9-0	22	2-0	1	.383	.329
1996	Colorado Springs (PCL)	.314	50	188	41	59	102	15	5	6	16	0-1	2	28-0	14	6-8	4	.543	.406
1996	SAN FRANCISCO (NL)	.207	10	29	3	6	11	0	1	1	2	0-0	0	2-0	5	0-0	2	.379	.258
1997	Buffalo (AmAs)	.312	103	375	71	117	189	22	1	16	60	0-6	3	57-0	52	26-10	10	.504	.401
1997	CLEVELAND (AL)	.250	7	12	3	3	4	1	0	0	0	0-0	0	1-0	3	2-0	0	.333	.308
1998	Albuquerque (PCL)	.300	11	30	6	9	18	0	0	3	5	0-0	1	5-0	5	2-1	1	.600	.417
1998	LOS ANGELES (NL)	.298	94	208	29	62	94	9	1	7	18	3-3	3	18-0	46	9-5	5	.452	.358
1999	Albuquerque (PCL)	.333	32	123	24	41	68	8	2	5	24	0-3	0	16-1	27	16-4	4	.553	.401
1999	LOS ANGELES (NL)	.314	82	105	23	33	41	5	0	1	13	1-1	0	13-1	24	4-3	2	.390	.387
2000	ATLANTA (NL)	.185	61	81	15	15	22	2	1	1	6	3-0	1	11-0	20	2-1	1	.272	.290
2000	BALTIMORE (AL)	.185	31	27	3	5	7	0	1	0	0	0-0	0	0-0	3	2-1	2	.259	.185
Minor Totals		.298	1291	4566	803	1359	1919	217	62	73	547	36-37	42	569-17	679	377-149	77	.420	.378
AL TOTALS		.205	38	39	6	8	11	1	1	0	0	0-0	0	1-0	6	4-1	2	.282	.225
NL TOTALS		.272	334	566	98	154	235	26	5	15	63	8-4	5	64-1	127	19-10	14	.415	.356
MAJOR TOTALS		.268	372	605	104	162	246	27	6	15	63	8-4	5	65-1	133	23-11	16	.407	.342

DIVISION SERIES RECORD

Year	Club & League	AVG	G	AB	R	H	TB	2B	3B	HR	RBI	SH-SF	HP	BB-IBB	SO	SB-CS	GIDP	SLG	OBP
1995	COLORADO (NL)	.000	3	2	0	0	0	0	0	0	0	0-0	0	0-0	0	0-0	0	.000	.000

HOME RUN BREAKDOWN

			MEN ON			ONE GAME								
Total	H	A	0	1	2	3	2	3	4	LO	XN	IP	PH	RHP	LHP
15	7	8	9	5	1	0	0	0	0	1	0	0	0	9	6

HUBBARD — TRANSACTIONS

- Selected by the Houston Astros in the 12th round of the June 1986 First Year Player Draft.
- Signed by the Colorado Rockies on November 3, 1992.
- Claimed on waivers by the San Francisco Giants from the Colorado Rockies on August 21, 1996.
- On disabled list (broken hamate bone in left hand) September 13 through remainder of the season, 1996.
- Traded to the Cleveland Indians in exchange for RHP Joe Roa on December 16, 1996, completing trade in which the San Francisco Giants sent 3B Matt Williams and a player to be named to the Cleveland Indians in exchange for IF Jeff Kent, IF Jose Vizcaino, RHP Julian Tavarez and a player to be named (Nov. 13, 1996).
- Signed by the Los Angeles Dodgers on December 3, 1997.
- On disabled list (left knee sprain) May 16-June 21, 1998.
- Signed by the Atlanta Braves on January 24, 2000.
- Traded to the Baltimore Orioles along with C Fernando Lunar and RHP Luis Rivera in exchange for OF B.J. Surhoff and RHP Gabe Molina on July 31, 2000.
- Signed by the Toronto Blue Jays on December 15, 2000.

CAREER HIGHS — HUBBARD, Trenidad

SEASON:		GAME:	
Games	94 - 1998	ML Debut	Jul. 7, 1994 at FLA
Avg.	.304 - 1999	Runs	3 - Jul. 4, 1999 vs. SF
Runs	29 - 1998	Hits	3 - 6 times, last Jul. 4, 1999 vs. SF
Hits	62 - 1998	Doubles	2 - Jul. 6, 1996 at LA
Doubles	9 - 1998	Home Runs	1 - 15 times, last Apr. 30, 2000 at SD
Home Runs	7 - 1998	RBI	5 - Jul. 11, 1999 vs. SEA
RBI	18 - 1998	Stolen Bases	1 - 23 times, last Sep. 17, 2000 vs. SEA
Walks	18 - 1998	Last ML Home Run	Apr. 30, 2000 at SD
Strikeouts	46 - 1998		
Stolen Bases	9 - 1998		
Longest Hitting Streak	7G - Aug. 23-Sep. 2, 1995		
	7G - Aug. 22-29, 1998		
Multi HR Games	None		

FIELDING

HUBBARD, Trenidad—OF

Year	PCT	G	PO	A	E	TC	DP
1994 (NL)	1.000	5	4	0	0	4	0
1995 (NL)	1.000	16	16	1	0	17	0
1996 (NL)	1.000	28	51	1	0	52	0
1997 (AL)	1.000	6	3	0	0	3	0
1998 (NL)	.991	81	110	3	1	114	0
1999 (NL)	.980	51	49	1	1	51	0
2000 (NL)	1.000	44	40	1	0	41	0
2000 (AL)	.929	24	12	1	1	14	0
Total	.990	255	285	8	3	296	0

HUBBARD, Trenidad—2B

Year	PCT	G	PO	A	E	TC	DP
1999 (NL)	.000	1	0	0	0	0	0

HUBBARD, Trenidad—3B

Year	PCT	G	PO	A	E	TC	DP
1998 (NL)	.000	1	0	0	0	0	0

HUBBARD, Trenidad—C

Year	PCT	G	PO	A	E	TC	DP
1999 (NL)	1.000	1	1	0	0	1	0

TRENIDAD HUBBARD HITTING AT ML PARKS

Park	Avg	G	AB	R	H	2B	3B	HR	RBI	SB	CS	BB	SO	OBP	Slg
Camden Yards	.278	19	18	3	5	0	1	0	0	3	1	0	2	.278	.389
Fenway Park	.000	1	2	0	0	0	0	0	0	0	0	0	1	.000	.000
Edison Field	.600	4	5	2	3	0	0	0	0	1	1	1	1	.667	.600
Comiskey Park	.500	2	2	0	1	0	0	0	0	0	0	0	0	.500	.500
Jacobs Field	.200	3	5	2	1	0	0	0	0	0	0	0	2	.200	.200
Kauffman Stadium	.000	2	4	0	0	0	0	0	0	0	0	0	0	.000	.000
County Stadium	.200	7	5	3	1	0	0	1	1	2	0	1	2	.429	.800
Metrodome	.000	2	1	0	0	0	0	0	0	0	0	0	0	.000	.000
Yankee Stadium	.200	3	5	2	1	1	0	0	0	2	0	1	1	.333	.400
Oakland-Alameda	.000	3	3	2	0	0	0	0	0	0	0	1	1	.250	.000
Arlington	.000	1	0	0	0	0	0	0	0	0	0	0	0	.000	.000
Atlanta-Fulton	.200	2	5	0	1	0	0	0	0	0	0	0	4	.200	.200
Wrigley Field	.176	10	17	3	3	0	0	2	2	0	0	2	2	.263	.529
Cinergy Field	.167	4	6	0	1	0	0	0	0	0	0	1	3	.286	.167
Astrodome	.000	6	8	1	0	0	0	0	0	0	0	1	4	.111	.000
Dodger Stadium	.313	96	176	27	55	10	0	2	17	5	5	10	39	.346	.403
Olympic Stadium	.364	7	11	2	4	1	0	0	1	1	1	2	4	.533	.455
Shea Stadium	.276	18	29	4	8	2	1	0	0	3	0	5	7	.382	.414
Veterans Stadium	.176	12	17	1	3	1	0	0	3	0	0	1	4	.211	.235
Three Rivers	.300	15	20	1	6	2	0	0	1	0	0	3	3	.391	.400
Busch Stadium	.167	8	18	4	3	1	0	1	2	1	0	3	3	.286	.389
Qualcomm Park	.240	10	25	4	6	0	0	1	3	0	2	3	8	.321	.360
3 Com Park	.205	22	39	4	8	1	1	2	4	1	0	5	5	.295	.436
Coors Field	.342	43	79	23	27	6	1	3	18	3	1	13	16	.441	.557
Pro Player Stadium	.200	10	15	1	3	0	0	1	1	0	0	2	4	.294	.400
Turner Field	.241	37	54	9	13	2	1	0	3	1	0	7	11	.339	.315
BankOne Ballpark	.154	5	13	1	2	0	0	1	3	1	0	1	2	.200	.385
Tropicana Field	.333	4	3	2	1	0	0	1	0	0	0	0	0	.333	.333
Mile High Stadium	.294	11	17	3	5	0	1	1	2	0	0	2	3	.368	.588
Enron Field	.500	2	2	0	1	0	0	0	1	0	0	0	1	.500	.500
Comerica Park	.000	3	1	0	0	0	0	0	0	0	0	0	0	.000	.000

Players

TRENIDAD HUBBARD DETAILED HITTING

	2000									CAREER								
	Avg	AB	H	HR	RBI	BB	SO	OBP	SLG	Avg	AB	H	HR	RBI	BB	SO	OBP	SLG
Total	.185	108	20	1	6	11	23	.267	.269	.268	605	162	15	63	65	133	.342	.407
vs. Left	.244	41	10	0	3	4	11	.326	.341	.282	255	72	6	26	27	58	.351	.420
vs. Right	.149	67	10	1	3	7	12	.230	.224	.257	350	90	9	37	38	75	.335	.397
Home	.233	60	14	0	1	6	9	.313	.333	.287	335	96	7	37	32	66	.350	.421
Away	.125	48	6	1	5	5	14	.208	.188	.244	270	66	8	26	33	67	.331	.389
March	–	–	–	–	–	–	–	–	–	.000	2	0	0	0	0	1	.000	.000
April	.200	20	4	1	4	4	4	.333	.400	.235	68	16	3	12	9	17	.329	.441
May	.212	33	7	0	1	4	7	.316	.303	.225	71	16	1	3	9	19	.321	.324
June	.133	15	2	0	0	1	6	.188	.133	.276	87	24	1	10	12	25	.370	.368
July	.154	13	2	0	1	2	3	.267	.154	.321	109	35	2	15	9	20	.367	.459
August	.214	14	3	0	0	0	0	.214	.357	.290	138	40	5	12	15	24	.368	.493
September	.167	12	2	0	0	0	0	.167	.167	.250	124	31	3	11	10	24	.304	.347
October	.000	1	0	0	0	0	0	.000	.000	.000	6	0	0	0	1	3	.143	.000
Scoring Posn	.185	27	5	1	6	5	5	.313	.296	.255	153	39	2	43	23	39	.344	.340
Bases Loaded	.000	1	0	0	1	1	0	.500	.000	.182	11	2	0	8	3	2	.357	.273
DH	.000	2	0	0	0	0	1	.000	.000	.000	2	0	0	0	0	1	.000	.000
PH	.308	13	4	0	1	0	5	.308	.308	.255	111	28	0	10	14	38	.344	.327
vs. Ana	.000	0	0	0	0	0	0	.000	.000	.500	8	4	0	1	1	2	.556	.500
vs. Bal	.000	0	0	0	0	0	0	.000	.000	.000	0	0	0	0	0	0	.000	.000
vs. Bos	.000	2	0	0	0	0	1	.000	.000	.000	2	0	0	0	0	1	.000	.000
vs. CWS	1.000	1	1	0	0	0	0	1.000	1.000	.667	3	2	0	0	0	0	.667	.667
vs. Cle	.000	0	0	0	0	0	0	.000	.000	.000	0	0	0	0	0	0	.000	.000
vs. Det	.333	3	1	0	0	0	0	.333	.333	.333	3	1	0	0	0	0	.333	.333
vs. KC	.000	4	0	0	0	0	0	.000	.000	.000	4	0	0	0	0	0	.000	.000
vs. Mil	.000	1	0	0	0	1	1	.500	.000	.235	17	4	1	2	2	3	.350	.471
vs. Min	.167	6	1	0	0	0	0	.167	.500	.167	6	1	0	0	0	0	.167	.500
vs. NYY	.000	3	0	0	0	0	1	.000	.000	.125	8	1	0	0	1	2	.222	.250
vs. Oak	.000	5	0	0	0	0	1	.000	.000	.000	8	0	0	0	1	2	.111	.000
vs. Sea	.500	2	1	0	0	0	0	.500	.500	.429	7	3	0	5	0	0	.375	.571
vs. TB	.333	3	1	0	1	0	0	.333	.333	.333	3	1	0	1	0	0	.333	.333
vs. Tex	.000	0	0	0	0	0	0	.000	.000	.545	11	6	0	0	0	2	.545	.727
vs. Tor	1.000	2	2	0	0	0	0	1.000	1.000	1.000	2	2	0	0	0	0	1.000	1.000
vs. Ari	–	–	–	–	–	–	–	–	–	.115	26	3	1	3	1	8	.143	.231
vs. Atl	–	–	–	–	–	–	–	–	–	.256	39	10	1	5	2	15	.293	.359
vs. ChC	.000	4	0	0	0	0	2	.000	.000	.185	27	5	3	4	5	4	.313	.593
vs. Cin	–	–	–	–	–	–	–	–	–	.304	23	7	0	1	3	7	.385	.304
vs. Col	.400	5	2	0	1	1	0	.500	.600	.400	25	10	0	3	1	7	.423	.560
vs. Fla	.333	6	2	0	0	1	1	.429	.333	.192	26	5	1	1	5	7	.323	.308
vs. Hou	.500	2	1	0	1	0	1	.500	.500	.261	23	6	0	4	2	6	.333	.261
vs. LA	.250	4	1	0	0	1	0	.400	.250	.250	16	4	0	2	2	3	.333	.375
vs. Mon	.000	4	0	0	0	1	2	.200	.000	.213	47	10	1	4	4	11	.302	.340
vs. NYM	.000	8	0	0	0	1	3	.111	.000	.255	47	12	1	1	5	12	.327	.426
vs. Phi	.100	20	2	0	0	2	4	.182	.100	.182	66	12	0	6	10	14	.286	.227
vs. Pit	.167	6	1	0	0	1	2	.286	.167	.343	35	12	0	2	5	7	.425	.457
vs. StL	–	–	–	–	–	–	–	–	–	.343	35	12	3	7	6	3	.439	.629
vs. SD	.333	12	4	1	3	2	3	.467	.833	.341	44	15	2	8	5	11	.420	.591
vs. SF	.000	5	0	0	0	0	1	.000	.000	.318	44	14	1	3	4	6	.375	.432
Pre-All Star	.178	73	13	1	5	10	20	.286	.274	.262	267	70	5	33	31	70	.343	.390
Post-All Star	.200	35	7	0	1	1	3	.222	.257	.272	338	92	10	30	34	63	.340	.420

Cesar
IZTURIS

INFIELDER

3

BIRTHDATE . . . . February 10, 1980
OPENING DAY AGE 21
BIRTHPLACE . . . . Barquisimeto, VZ
RESIDENCE . . . . Lara, VZ
BATS/THROWS . . . . S/R
HEIGHT/WEIGHT 5-9/175
CONTRACT STATUS . . . . signed thru 2001
M.L. SERVICE 0.000

PERSONAL: Cesar D. Izturis... Signed by Emilio Carrasquel and Mike Russell... Married, wife's name is Liliana Parra... One son, Cesar Daniel (11/11/99).

LAST SEASON: Jumped from A-ball in 1999 to AAA with Syracuse in the International League... Hit .218 in 132 games with 16 doubles, five triples and 27 RBI... Stolen 21 bases... Hit .204 in April with six extra-base hits and three RBI... In May hit .235 and scored 12 runs, most of any month... Collected a season high four hits on May 3 at Richmond, was 4-4 with two doubles and an RBI... Scored runs in seven straight games from May 16 to 27... Posted best month average in June when he hit .241 with six RBI... Collected ten RBI over 13 games from July 23 to August 5... Hit in a season high six straight games from August 7 to 12... Hit .208 at home and .338 on the road... Posted a .194 average against left-hand pitching and .226 with 24 of his 27 RBI against right-hand pitching... Baseball America rated as having the best infield arm in the International League and the third best prospect in the Blue Jays organization... Played winter ball with Lara in Venezuela.

PROFESSIONAL CAREER: 1997: Made professional debut with St. Catharines and hit just .190 in 70 games... Led club with eight sacrifice bunts... Posted a seven game hit streak from July 19-25 in which he hit .360 (9-25)... **1998:** With Hagerstown of the South Atlantic League (A) hit .262 with one home run and 38 RBI... Was second in the SAL with just one strikeout every 10.40 plate appearances... Led club with 20 stolen bases... Hit in nine straight from April 15 to 24... Hit .348 in August with five doubles, 15 runs scored and 18 RBI... In five SAL play-off games he hit .319 (6-19) with a double, a home run and 2 RBI... Appeared in 18 games for Lara in the Venezuelan Winter League... **1999:** Hit .308 in 131 games with Dunedin of the Florida State League (A) and was selected as the R. Howard Webster award winner as team MVP... Was second in the league with 165 hits, third in triples with 12 and sixth in average... The 165 hits were a club record and eighth in class-A baseball... In class-A baseball overall he was fourth in batting average by a switch-hitter and average by a shortstop... Opened the season earning organizational Player of the Month honours

in April after hitting .354 with five doubles, five triples and 21 RBI... Posted a 21 game hit streak from April 17 to May 7... Hit three home runs on the season, all in May including two in three days, May 1 & 3... For May hit .323 with six doubles, three triples, the three home runs and 21 RBI... Average did not fall below .300 after April 13... Had a five-hit game on August 24 at Clearwater... Posted monthly highs in August with a .370 average, 22 runs scored and eight doubles... Hit .358 (53-148) against left hand pitching and .289 (112-388) against right-handers... Hit .319 (92-288) on the road and .294 (73-248) at home... With runners in scoring position hit .340 (49-144)... Rated by Baseball America at the third best prospect in the organization and the fifth best in the Florida State League.

CESAR IZTURIS

Year	Club & League	AVG	G	AB	R	H	TB	2B	3B	HR	RBI	SH-SF	HP	BB-IBB	SO	SB-CS	GIDP	SLG	OBP
1997	St. Catharines (NYP)	.190	70	231	32	44	50	3	0	1	11	8-2		15-0	27	6-3	3	.216	.241
1998	Hagerstown (SAL)	.262	130	413	56	108	126	13	1	1	38	9-2	2	20-0	43	20-9	5	.305	.297
1999	Dunedin (FSL)	.308	131	536	77	165	226	28	12	3	77	17-9	6	22-4	58	32-16	9	.422	.337
2000	Syracuse (Int)	.218	132	435	54	95	121	16	5	0	27	13-2	1	20-0	44	21-11	5	.278	.253
Minor Totals		.255	463	1615	219	412	523	60	18	5	153	47-15	10	77-4	172	79-39	22	.324	.291

IZTURIS — TRANSACTIONS
- Signed as a non-drafted free agent by the Toronto Blue Jays on July 3, 1996.

Billy
KOCH
PITCHER

44

BIRTHDATE	December 14, 1974
OPENING DAY AGE	26
BIRTHPLACE	Rockville Center, NY
RESIDENCE	Clearwater, FL
BATS/THROWS	R/R
HEIGHT/WEIGHT	6-3/215
CONTRACT STATUS	signed thru 2002
M.L. SERVICE	1.152

PERSONAL: William Christopher Koch... Pronounced "Kotch"... Married, wife's name is Brandi... Three children, Amanda, Joseph and Madyson... Graduated from West Babylon High Scool in New York... Attended Clemson University... In 1996 was selected as a Second-team All-American... Is the second highest drafted baseball player in Clemson history (Kris Benson- 1996)... Member of 1996 U.S. Olympic Baseball Team... Brother Eric pitches for Charleston Southern College.

LAST SEASON: In his first full season was 9-3 with a 2.63 ERA in 68 games with 33 saves... The 33 saves were a career high and tied for seventh in the AL... Was the fourth highest single season total in club history... Finished 62 games which was second in the AL and tied for second in club history (Henke- 1987)... Was tied for third in the AL with nine wins in relief and fourth in relief ERA at 2.63... Converted 33 of 38 save opportunities to rank sixth in the AL at 86.8 save percentage... Pitched more than one inning 17 times... Of his 33 saves, 12 were of more than 1.0IP... Had seven saves in which he pitched 2.0 innings... Finished tied for fourth in the AL for the Rolaids Relief Man of the Year... Earned his first ML win on opening day, April 3 vs Kansas City... In April was 1-0 with five saves and a 3.97 ERA... Recorded saves in six consecutive outings from April 24 to May 2... In May was 2-0 with six saves and an ERA of 3.52... Suffered a blown save on May 22 vs Chicago after allowing his first home run of the season (Perry-2R) in his 20th appearance... Did not allow a run in nine games from June 7 to 25 spanning 12.0 innings and striking out 15... In July was 1-0 with seven saves and an ERA of 0.00 over 14.2 innings (allowed runs in his last June and first August games)... Converted 21 straight save opportunities from June 7 to August 28... At the All-Star break was 4-1 with 20 saves and an ERA of 2.74... Following the break was 5-2 with 13 saves and a 2.48 ERA... Recorded saves in three consecutive games against Texas, August 3, 4, 5... In August was 1-2 with eight saves and a 4.26 ERA... In September

had just two save opportunities and was 1-2 while posting a 3-0 record with a 2.53 ERA... Pitched 2.0 innings only one time from July 23 through the end of the season... The 33 saves made winners of Wells- 8 times, Castillo- 6, Escobar- 5, Carpenter- 4, Halladay- 4, Loaiza- 2, Quantrill- 2, Cubillan- 1 and Trachsel- 1... Opponents hit .258 with six home runs, left-handed batters hit .255 with two home runs and right-handed batters hit .261 with four home runs.

COLLEGE NOTES: 1996: Pitched for Clemson University where he posted a 10-5 record with one save and a 3.14 ERA... Appeared in 19 games and struckout 152 batters in 112 innings... Was fifth in strikeouts (152) among NCAA Division I pitchers and ranked third in strikeouts per nine innings at 12.3... Struck out 16 batters on May 5 against Florida State... In College World Series was 0-0 in two games with one save... Was third in ERA at 2.45 among pitchers with 7.0 IP... Struckout nine in seven innings... Was fourth in Clemson history with 337 strikeouts... Rated fourth best College prospect by Baseball America... Member of the 1996 Bronze Medal winning U.S. Olympic Team... For Team USA was 5-2 with a 4.25 ERA in nine games... Struckout 45 batters in 42 innings... In the Olympics appeared in three games and was 0-1 with a 6.23 ERA.

PROFESSIONAL CAREER: 1996: Rated sixth best prospect in the Blue Jays organization by Baseball America... **1997:** Attended ML spring training and saw action in three games, was 0-0 with a 9.82ERA (4ER, 3.2IP)... Opened the season with Dunedin (A)... Pitched in three games before season ending surgery on his right elbow... Was 0-1 with a 2.08 ERA in three starts and in 21.2IP has just three walks and 20 strikeouts... April 23 had re-constructive ulnar collateral ligament surgery performed on his right elbow by Dr. James Andrews in Birmingham Alabama... **1998:** Rebounded successfully to earn Howe Sportsdata's Comeback Player of the Year... Spent most of the season with Dunedin where he was 14-7 with a 3.75 ERA and was named to the Florida State League All-Star team... The 14 wins tied for the league lead in wins... Started the season slow going 1-2 in four April starts with a 5.06 ERA... Was 5-6 through his start on June 12, from that point on was 9-1 to finish 14-7... Combined on three shutouts pitching six innings in each of the three games... On July 17 received a no-decision set a season high with 10 K in five innings and a season low in walks with none... Finished August 4-0 for Dunedin with a 2.35 ERA in four starts with 28 strikeouts in 23.0 innings and just five walks... Held opponents to four or fewer hits in 13 of his 25 starts... Joined Syracuse (AAA) for two starts to end the season and was 0-1 with a 14.29 ERA... In the IL playoffs pitched 1.1 scoreless innings in one relief appearance... Rated the second best prospect in the organization by Baseball America... **1999:** Set what was then an American League record for saves by a rookie with 31 to surpass the 24 by Gregg Olson in 1989 with Baltimore... Was 0-5 with an ERA of 3.39... Along with the club rookie save record appeared in 56 games which is the fifth most by a Blue Jay rookie... Named the Topps Major League Rookie Right-handed Pitcher of the Year... Selected by the Toronto chapter of the BBWAA as the Blue Jays' Rookie of the Year and Pitcher of the Year... Opened the season with Syracuse of the International League (AAA) and was 3-0 in five starts with a 3.86 ERA... Contract was purchased from Syracuse on May 5... Made his ML debut on May 5 tossing 2.2 scoreless innings and retiring the first six Oakland A's he faced - only other career relief came in the 1998 International League

Play-offs on September 11 (1.1IP)... In his second appearance earned his first save with 2.0 hitless innings for Pat Hentgen... Converted his first four save opportunities... In 11 games in June was 0-0 with six saves and an ERA of 0.61 (2ER/14.2IP)... Captured the AL Rolaids Relief Award in July after setting a club record for saves in a month with 11... First Blue Jay winner since Duane Ward in August of 1993... Had saves in ten consecutive appearances from July 18 to August 8 to tie the club record set by Duane Ward (1991) and Darren Hall (1994)... Converted 14 straight save opportunities from July 18 to September 12... Had a stretch of 20 straight games which were save opportunities and was 18-20... At the All-Star break was 0-0 with 14 saves and a 1.34 ERA... In the second half was 0-5 with 17 saves and a 5.70 ERA... Posted saves on three consecutive days, July 21-23... Retired 36 of 56 first batters faced and stranded five of 12 inherited runners... Opponents hit .235 (55-235), left-hand hitters posted a .209 mark and right-handers a .261 average... Saved 31 wins, Hentgen- 7, Frascatore- 4, Hamilton- 4, Carpenter- 3, Escobar- 3, Halladay- 3, Quantrill- 3, Wells- 2, Lloyd- 1 & Spoljaric- 1.

CAREER NOTES: Now has 64 career saves to rank 3rd in club history... Is 64-73 in career save opportunities (87.7%)... In 1999 set a then AL record for saves by a rookie with 31... Recorded saves in ten consecutive appearances in 1999 to tie the club record... Owns the club record for saves in a month with 11 in July of 1999.

BILLY KOCH

Year	Club & League	W-L	ERA	G	GS	CG	ShO	SV	IP	H	R	ER	HR	HB	BB-IBB	SO	WP	BK	OBA
1997	Dunedin (FSL)	0-1	2.08	3	3	0	0	0	21.2	27	10	5	1	0	3-0	20	1	1	.325
1998	Dunedin (FSL)	14-7	3.75	25	25	0	0	0	124.2	120	65	52	8	7	41-0	108	4	3	.252
1998	Syracuse (Int)	0-1	14.29	2	2	0	0	0	5.2	9	9	9	1	0	5-0	9	0	1	.360
1999	Syracuse (Int)	3-0	3.86	5	5	0	0	0	25.2	27	11	11	3	2	10-0	22	0	2	.276
1999	TORONTO (AL)	0-5	3.39	56	0	0	0	31	63.2	55	26	24	5	3	30-5	57	0	0	.235
2000	TORONTO (AL)	9-3	2.63	68	0	0	0	33	78.2	78	28	23	6	2	18-4	60	1	0	.258
Minor Totals		17-9	3.90	35	35	0	0	0	177.2	183	95	77	13	9	59-0	159	5	7	.268
MAJOR TOTALS		9-8	2.97	124	0	0	0	64	142.1	133	54	47	11	5	48-9	117	1	0	.248

KOCH — TRANSACTIONS

- Selected by the Toronto Blue Jays organization in the 1st round (4th overall) in the June 1996 First Year Draft.
- On disabled list (right elbow-acute ulnar collateral ligament tear) April 14 to end of season 1997.

CAREER HIGHS — KOCH, Billy

SEASON:		GAME:	
Wins	9 - 2000	ML Debut	May 5, 1999 vs. OAK
Losses	5 - 1999	Innings Pitched:	
Saves	33 - 2000	Starter	None
ERA	2.63 - 2000	Reliever	2.2 - May 5, 1999 vs. OAK
Games	68 - 2000	Walks:	
Starts	None	Starter	None
Complete Games	None	Reliever	3 - Sep. 26, 1999 vs. CLE
Shutouts	None	Strikeouts:	
Innings Pitched	78.2 - 2000	Starter	None
Walks	30 - 1999	Reliever	4 - Jun. 11, 2000 vs. MON
Strikeouts	60 - 2000		4 - Jun. 17, 2000 at BOS
Longest Win Streak	4 - Aug. 16-Sep. 23, 2000	Hits Allowed	5 - Jun. 15, 1999 vs. FLA
Longest Losing Streak	5 - Jul. 15-Sep. 26, 1999	Runs Allowed	4 - Jun. 15, 1999 vs. FLA
Scoreless Innings Streak	15.2 - Jul. 3-Aug. 1, 2000		4 - Sep. 9, 1999 vs. NYY
Consec. Saves Converted	21 - Jun. 7-Aug. 28, 2000		4 - Sep. 26, 1999 vs. CLE
			4 - Sep. 7, 2000 vs. SEA
		ER Allowed	4 - Jun. 15, 1999 vs. FLA
			4 - Sep. 26, 1999 vs. CLE
		HR Allowed	2 - Jun. 3, 2000 at FLA
		Low Hit CG	None
		Last Win	Sep. 23, 2000 vs. TB
		Last Save	Sep. 15, 2000 at CWS
		Last CG	None
		Last ShO	None
		Last Start	None
		Last Relief App.	Sep. 30, 2000 at CLE

FIELDING

KOCH, Billy—P

Year	PCT	G	PO	A	E	TC	DP
1999	1.000	56	3	12	0	15	0
2000	1.000	68	5	8	0	13	2
Total	1.000	124	8	20	0	28	2

BILLY KOCH DETAILED PITCHING

	2000								CAREER							
	ERA	W-L-Sv	G	IP	H	ER	BB	SO	ERA	W-L-Sv	G	IP	H	ER	BB	SO
Total	2.63	9-3-33	68	78.2	78	23	18	60	2.97	9-8-64	124	142.1	133	47	48	117
REL	2.63	9-3-33	68	78.2	78	23	18	60	2.97	9-8-64	124	142.1	133	47	48	117
Home	2.70	8-0-17	36	40.0	38	12	10	31	3.73	8-3-30	64	72.1	71	30	26	60
Away	2.56	1-3-16	32	38.2	40	11	8	29	2.19	1-5-34	60	70.0	62	17	22	57
April	3.97	1-0-5	10	11.1	15	5	2	6	3.97	1-0-5	10	11.1	15	5	2	6
May	3.52	2-0-6	13	15.1	18	6	6	12	3.07	2-0-9	22	29.1	29	10	10	24
June	1.93	1-1-6	11	14.0	13	3	4	17	1.26	1-1-12	22	28.2	21	4	13	31
July	0.00	1-0-7	11	14.2	7	0	3	9	2.08	1-1-18	23	26.0	22	6	8	18
August	4.26	1-2-8	13	12.2	12	6	0	11	3.04	1-3-14	24	23.2	21	8	4	21
September	2.53	3-0-1	10	10.2	13	3	3	5	5.82	3-3-4	21	21.2	25	14	11	15
October	–	–	–	–	–	–	–	–	0.00	0-0-2	2	1.2	0	0	0	2
vs. Ana	1.50	1-0-2	5	6.0	4	1	0	3	0.96	1-0-5	8	9.1	5	1	2	7
vs. Bal	1.23	0-0-4	6	7.1	5	1	2	4	0.73	0-0-7	10	12.1	8	1	4	11
vs. Bos	0.00	0-0-5	7	7.2	7	0	3	10	3.00	0-0-6	11	12.0	14	4	6	12
vs. CWS	4.50	1-0-3	5	6.0	5	3	4	6	2.61	1-0-6	9	10.1	9	3	7	8
vs. Cle	3.38	1-0-1	4	5.1	7	2	2	2	5.25	1-1-7	11	12.0	13	7	8	8
vs. Det	3.38	1-0-1	4	5.1	8	2	0	3	2.57	1-0-6	10	14.0	15	4	2	10
vs. KC	3.60	1-0-3	5	5.0	5	2	1	4	4.50	1-0-4	8	8.0	10	4	1	7
vs. Min	8.10	0-0-2	3	3.1	7	3	0	3	4.26	0-0-3	6	6.1	9	3	1	6
vs. NYY	2.70	1-0-1	3	3.1	4	1	1	2	6.00	1-1-2	6	6.0	7	4	3	5
vs. Oak	4.76	0-1-2	4	5.2	6	3	0	6	4.50	0-2-2	7	10.0	9	5	2	9
vs. Sea	2.45	0-0-0	4	3.2	4	1	2	1	5.06	0-1-0	6	5.1	6	3	4	3
vs. TB	0.00	1-0-2	5	5.0	2	0	1	2	0.00	1-0-4	9	9.0	4	0	2	6
vs. Tex	3.86	0-1-4	6	4.2	6	2	1	3	1.86	0-1-7	10	9.2	8	2	1	7
vs. Atl	0.00	0-0-1	1	2.0	1	0	1	3	0.00	0-0-2	2	3.0	1	0	1	4
vs. Fla	18.00	0-1-0	1	1.0	2	2	0	2	40.50	0-2-0	2	1.1	7	6	0	2
vs. Mon	0.00	1-0-1	2	4.0	2	0	0	5	0.00	1-0-2	4	6.0	2	0	0	8
vs. NYM	0.00	0-0-1	2	2.1	2	0	0	1	0.00	0-0-1	3	4.2	4	0	2	2
vs. Phi	0.00	1-0-0	1	1.0	1	0	0	0	0.00	1-0-0	2	3.0	2	0	2	2
Pre-All Star	2.74	4-1-20	37	46.0	48	14	13	40	2.15	4-1-34	62	79.2	70	19	26	72
Post-All Star	2.48	5-2-13	31	32.2	30	9	5	20	4.02	5-7-30	62	62.2	63	28	22	45

BILLY KOCH PITCHING AT ML PARKS

Park	ERA	W-L-Sv	SvO	G	GS	IP	H	R	ER	HR	BB	SO
Camden Yards	1.69	0-0-3	3	5	0	5.1	4	1	1	0	1	6
Fenway Park	1.69	0-0-4	4	5	0	5.1	6	1	1	0	1	6
Edison Field	0.00	0-0-2	2	4	0	4.1	1	0	0	0	1	2
Comiskey Park	1.69	0-0-5	5	5	0	5.1	6	1	1	0	4	2
Jacobs Field	0.00	0-0-5	5	6	0	6.2	3	0	0	0	3	6
Tiger Stadium	0.00	0-0-2	2	3	0	4.2	1	0	0	0	1	3
Kauffman Stadium	6.00	0-0-1	1	3	0	3.0	6	2	2	0	0	3
Metrodome	4.50	0-0-0	0	2	0	2.0	4	1	1	0	0	4
Yankee Stadium	0.00	1-0-2	2	3	0	3.1	2	0	0	0	1	0
Oakland-Alameda	6.75	0-2-2	2	4	0	5.1	7	4	4	1	1	5
Arlington	4.15	0-1-3	3	5	0	4.1	6	2	2	0	1	2
SkyDome	3.73	8-3-30	37	64	0	72.1	71	37	30	6	26	60
Olympic Stadium	0.00	0-0-2	2	2	0	3.0	1	0	0	0	0	3
Shea Stadium	0.00	0-0-0	1	1	0	2.1	2	0	0	0	2	1
Veterans Stadium	0.00	0-0-0	0	1	0	2.0	1	0	0	0	2	2
Pro Player Stadium	18.00	0-1-0	1	1	0	1.0	2	2	2	2	0	2
Turner Field	0.00	0-0-1	1	1	0	2.0	1	0	0	0	1	3
Tropicana Field	0.00	0-0-1	1	4	0	4.0	2	0	0	0	1	4
SAFECO Field	6.75	0-1-0	0	3	0	2.2	2	2	2	1	2	0
Comerica Park	2.70	0-0-1	1	2	0	3.1	5	1	1	1	0	3

MOST SAVES FIRST TWO SEASONS IN THE LEAGUE

PLAYER	ROOKIE YEAR	TEAM	SAVES (Yr. 1)	SAVES (Yr. 2)	TOTAL
TODD WORRELL	1986	STL	36	33	69
GREGG OLSON	1989	BAL	27	37	64
BILLY KOCH	1999	TOR	31	33	64

Chris
LATHAM
OUTFIELDER

BIRTHDATE	May 26, 1973
OPENING DAY AGE	27
BIRTHPLACE	Coeur D'Alene, ID
RESIDENCE	Las Vegas, NV
BATS/THROWS	S/R
HEIGHT/WEIGHT	6-0/198
CONTRACT STATUS	signed thru 2001
M.L. SERVICE	0.155

62

PERSONAL: Christopher Joseph Latham... Married, wife's name is Sarah... Two children, Christopher (5) and Alexis (2)... Graduated from Basic Tech High School in Nevada in 1991 where he played baseball and football... Earned Most Valuable Player honors in his sophomore and junior seasons... His father, William Sledge, played in the Phillies system during the 1960's.

LAST SEASON: Hit .245 with Colorado Springs in the Pacific Coast League (AAA) with seven home runs, 49 RBI and 29 stolen bases... Struggled in April hitting just .206... After a season best .279 average in June posted just a .192 average in July... Went 22 games without an extra base hit from June 27 to July 21... Finished the season strong hitting .325 (25-77) in his final 25 games with eight doubles, two triples and two home runs... Hit .290 with runners in scoring position... Hit .275 on the road with five home runs while at home hit .211 with two home runs... Against left-handed pitching posted a .288 average with four home runs and against right-handed pitching only .224 with three home runs.

PROFESSIONAL CAREER: 1991: Began his pro career as a second baseman with the Gulf Coast League Dodgers hitting .239 with 14 stolen bases... **1992:** Opened the season with Great Falls in the Pioneer League (A) and hit .324 in 17 games... Joined the Gulf Coast League Dodgers on August 5 and hit .229 in 14 games... **1993:** Converted from second base to the outfield with Yakima (A) and hit .260 in 54 games with four home runs and 17 RBI... Led the league with six triples and stole 25 bases... Was promoted to Bakersfield (A) on August 27 and appeared in six games... **1994:** Opened the season with Bakersfield and was named the fastest baserunner in the California League by Baseball America... Hit .215 in 52 games with two home runs, 15 RBI and 28 stolen bases... Joined Yakima in the Northwest League and captured the league batting title hitting .340... Led the league in runs (69), hits (98), total bases (148) and triples (8), was second in at bats (288), stolen bases (33) and extra base hits (32) and tied for second in doubles (19)... Was the All-Star Game MVP... Combined stole 61 bases on the season which was sixth in the minor leagues... Named as a Baseball America Short-Season All-Star... **1995:** Saw action in A, AA and AAA... Opened the season with Vero Beach in the Florida State League (A) where he hit .286 in 71 games with six home runs and 42 stolen bases... Earned the Topps Florida State League Player of the Month after stealing 19 bases in May... Was an All-Star selection and was second in stolen bases and stolen-base percentage (.792)... Baseball America tabbed him the best and fastest baserunner & the most exciting player in the FSL... Joined San Antonio (AA) on June 26 and appeared in 58 games batting .299 with nine home runs and 37 RBI... Spent the final week of the season with Albuquerque (AAA)... Combined to

draw 90 walks which was sixth in all of the minors... The 54 combined steals ranked ninth... Was the player to be named in the trading-deadline deal that sent Kevin Tapani to the Dodgers... Played in the Arizona Fall League following the season... Had arthroscopic surgery performed on his right shoulder by Dr. John Steubs on November 8... **1996:** Opened the season with Minnesota's AAA affiliate in Salt Lake where he hit .274 in 115 games with nine homers, 50 RBI and 26 stolen bases which was fifth in the league... Stole three bases on June 9 vs. Colorado Springs... Suffered a broken left wrist on August 30 to end his season... Hit .318 in the leadoff spot and was successful in 76 percent of his stolen-base attempts (26-for-35)... **1997:** Opened the season in Salt Lake (AAA) but joined Minnesota on April 11... Made his debut at Kansas City on April 12... On April 16 vs. Anaheim, he collected his first major league hit, a double off Alan Watson... Was optioned back to Salt Lake on May 1... Reached base safely in 21 straight games from May 8 to 28... Drove in five runs on August 14 at Albuquerque... Twice posted 11-game hitting streaks... In the leadoff role, he batted .352 (62-176)... Recalled to Minnesota on September 1... Made four starts for the Twins in center... **1998:** Opened the season with Salt Lake and hit safely in 11 of the first 13 games... Was recalled on April 29 for a one-month stay, until May 30... Was also with the Twins from August 1 to 8 appearing in fine games... Hit a grand slam on August 22 vs. Tucson... Overall at Salt Lake he hit .312 with two homers vs. LHP and .328 with nine homers vs. RHP... Hit .418 with runners in scoring position and .455 with the bases loaded... Was successful on 85 percent of his steal attempts (29-for-34)... Was tied for third in the Pacific Coast League with 29 steals and eighth in batting at .324... Was recalled to Minnesota on September 8... Hit safely in four of five big-league games from September 23 to 27... On September 23 vs. the White Sox delivered the game winning RBI with a 12th-inning single... Hit his first ML home run on September 26 at home against Cleveland's Dave Burba... **1999:** Made his first career Opening Day roster and made 12 appearances, four starts, before being outrighted on May 21 to Salt Lake (AAA)... Spent the remainder of the year with Salt Lake and hit .322 with 93 runs scored, 15 home runs and 51 RBI... June 11 at Oklahoma City, he recorded a season-high five hits... Hit in 15 straight games from July 24 to August 8... Finished the season hitting safely in 16 of his last 17 games... Homered in three straight games, September 1, 2 & 3... Was fourth in the league with eight triples and was tenth in batting... Traded to the Colorado Rockies on December 7 in exchange for RHP Scott Randall.

CAREER NOTES: Has made 374 stolen-base attempts in his professional career, an average of 42 per season... Has been successful in 68.7 of those attempts, has 257 career steals.

CHRIS LATHAM

Year	Club & League	AVG	G	AB	R	H	TB	2B	3B	HR	RBI	SH-SF	HP	BB-IBB	SO	SB-CS	GIDP	SLG	OBP
1991	Dodgers (Gulf)	.239	43	109	17	26	30	2	1	0	11	0-1	0	16-0	45	14-5	0	.275	.333
1992	Great Falls (Pio)	.324	17	37	8	12	14	2	0	0	3	0-0	0	8-0	8	1-1	0	.378	.444
1992	Dodgers (Gulf)	.229	14	48	4	11	13	2	0	0	2	1-1	0	5-1	17	2-3	0	.271	.296
1993	Yakima (NWST)	.260	54	192	46	50	76	2	6	4	17	0-0	1	39-0	53	25-9	2	.396	.388
1993	Bakersfield (Cal)	.185	6	27	1	5	6	1	0	0	3	0-0	0	4-0	5	2-2	2	.222	.290
1994	Bakersfield (Cal)	.215	52	191	29	41	56	5	2	2	15	4-0	2	28-1	49	28-7	2	.293	.321
1994	Yakima (NWST)	.340	71	288	69	98	148	19	8	5	32	3-0	2	55-7	66	33-20	1	.514	.449
1995	Vero Beach (FSL)	.286	71	259	53	74	113	13	4	6	39	2-3	2	56-4	54	42-11	2	.436	.413
1995	San Antonio (Tex)	.299	58	214	38	64	115	14	5	9	37	1-1	2	33-0	59	11-11	2	.537	.396
1995	Albuquerque (PCL)	.167	5	18	2	3	5	0	1	0	3	0-1	0	1-0	4	1-0	0	.278	.200
1996	Salt Lake (PCL)	.274	115	376	59	103	158	16	6	9	50	4-3	2	36-1	91	26-9	5	.420	.338
1997	Salt Lake (PCL)	.309	118	492	78	152	208	22	5	8	58	4-1	4	58-0	110	21-19	8	.423	.386
1997	MINNESOTA (AL)	.182	15	22	4	4	5	1	0	0	1	0-0	0	0-0	8	0-0	0	.227	.182
1998	Salt Lake (PCL)	.324	97	377	81	122	184	21	4	11	51	4-0	1	56-4	99	29-5	5	.488	.412
1998	MINNESOTA (AL)	.160	34	94	14	15	19	1	0	1	5	1-0	0	13-0	36	4-2	0	.202	.262
1999	Salt Lake (PCL)	.322	94	382	93	123	208	24	8	15	51	4-2	1	54-2	95	18-13	5	.545	.405
1999	MINNESOTA (AL)	.091	14	22	1	2	2	0	0	0	3	0-2	0	0-0	13	0-0	0	.091	.083
2000	Colorado Springs (PCL)	.245	126	339	76	83	132	16	6	7	49	3-6	2	71-3	105	29-7	8	.389	.373
Minor Totals		.289	941	3349	654	967	1466	159	56	76	421	30-19	19	520-23	860	282-122	42	.438	.385
MAJOR TOTALS		.152	63	138	19	21	26	2	0	1	9	1-2	0	13-0	57	4-2	0	.188	.222

HOME RUN BREAKDOWN

Total	H	A		MEN ON				ONE GAME			LO	XN	IP	PH	RHP	LHP
			0	1	2	3	2	3	4							
1	1	0	1	0	0	0	0	0	0	0	0	0	0	0	1	0

LATHAM — TRANSACTIONS

- Selected by the Los Angeles Dodgers in the 11th round of the June 1991 First Year Player Draft.
- Traded to the Minnesota Twins on October 30, 1995, completing trade in which the Minnesota Twins sent RHP Kevin Tapani and LHP Mark Guthrie to the Los Angeles Dodgers in exchange for IF Ron Coomer, RHP Greg Hansell, RHP Jose Parra and a player to be named (July 31, 1995).
- On disabled list (broken left wrist) August 30 through remainder of the season, 1996.
- Traded to the Colorado Rockies in exchange for RHP Scott Randall on December 7, 1999.
- Signed by the Toronto Blue Jays on December 2, 2000.

CAREER HIGHS — LATHAM, Chris

GAME:

ML Debut	Apr. 12, 1997 at KC
Runs	2 - May 2, 1998 at BAL
Hits	2 - May 2, 1998 at BAL
	2 - Sep. 16, 1998 at CLE
	2 - Sep. 25, 1998 vs. CLE
	2 - Sep. 26, 1998 vs. CLE
Doubles	1 - Apr. 16, 1997 vs. ANA
	1 - Sep. 25, 1998 vs. CLE
Home Runs	1 - Sep. 26, 1998 vs. CLE
RBI	1 - 9 times, last Apr. 22, 1999 vs. TEX
Stolen Bases	1 - Apr. 13, 1998 vs. OAK
	1 - Apr. 14, 1998 vs. SEA
	1 - Sep. 19, 1998 at DET
	1 - Sep. 22, 1998 vs. CWS
Last ML Home Run	Sep. 26, 1998 vs. CLE
Longest Hitting Streak	3G - Sep. 25-27, 1998

FIELDING

LATHAM, Chris—OF

Year	PCT	G	PO	A	E	TC	DP
1997	.917	10	11	0	1	12	0
1998	.972	32	69	1	2	72	0
1999	1.000	14	13	0	0	13	0
Total	.969	56	93	1	3	97	0

CHRIS LATHAM HITTING AT ML PARKS

Park	Avg	G	AB	R	H	2B	3B	HR	RBI	SB	CS	BB	SO	OBP	Slg
Camden Yards	.286	5	7	2	2	0	0	0	1	0	0	1	4	.375	.286
Fenway Park	.250	1	4	1	1	0	0	0	1	0	0	0	1	.250	.250
Edison Field	.333	4	6	3	2	0	0	0	0	0	0	2	2	.500	.333
Jacobs Field	.133	5	15	1	2	0	0	0	0	0	0	1	6	.188	.133
Tiger Stadium	.000	5	10	1	0	0	0	0	0	1	1	1	5	.091	.000
Kauffman Stadium	.000	3	5	2	0	0	0	0	0	1	0	0	1	.000	.000
Metrodome	.138	33	80	8	11	2	0	1	6	3	1	8	35	.213	.200
Yankee Stadium	.000	1	3	0	0	0	0	0	0	0	0	0	1	.000	.000
Kingdome	1.000	3	2	0	2	0	0	0	0	0	0	0	0	1.000	1.000
Arlington	.200	2	5	1	1	0	0	0	0	0	0	0	2	.200	.200
Wrigley Field	.000	1	1	0	0	0	0	0	0	0	0	0	0	.000	.000

CHRIS LATHAM DETAILED HITTING

	2000									CAREER								
	Avg	AB	H	HR	RBI	BB	SO	OBP	SLG	Avg	AB	H	HR	RBI	BB	SO	OBP	SLG
Total	–	–	–	–	–	–	–	–	–	.152	138	21	1	9	13	57	.222	.188
vs. Left	–	–	–	–	–	–	–	–	–	.107	28	3	0	2	1	14	.138	.143
vs. Right	–	–	–	–	–	–	–	–	–	.164	110	18	1	7	12	43	.242	.200
Home	–	–	–	–	–	–	–	–	–	.138	80	11	1	6	8	35	.213	.200
Away	–	–	–	–	–	–	–	–	–	.172	58	10	0	3	5	22	.234	.172
April	–	–	–	–	–	–	–	–	–	.107	28	3	0	4	0	11	.100	.143
May	–	–	–	–	–	–	–	–	–	.161	31	5	0	2	4	12	.257	.161
August	–	–	–	–	–	–	–	–	–	.000	6	0	0	0	3	2	.333	.000
September	–	–	–	–	–	–	–	–	–	.178	73	13	1	3	6	32	.241	.233
Scoring Posn	–	–	–	–	–	–	–	–	–	.176	34	6	0	8	2	13	.211	.206
Bases Loaded	–	–	–	–	–	–	–	–	–	.000	4	0	0	1	0	2	.000	.000
PH	–	–	–	–	–	–	–	–	–	.000	7	0	0	0	1	4	.125	.000
vs. Ana	–	–	–	–	–	–	–	–	–	.333	9	3	0	1	2	2	.455	.444
vs. Bal	–	–	–	–	–	–	–	–	–	.200	10	2	0	1	2	5	.333	.200
vs. Bos	–	–	–	–	–	–	–	–	–	.250	4	1	0	1	0	1	.250	.250
vs. CWS	–	–	–	–	–	–	–	–	–	.125	8	1	0	1	1	3	.222	.125
vs. Cle	–	–	–	–	–	–	–	–	–	.250	32	8	1	3	1	13	.273	.375
vs. Det	–	–	–	–	–	–	–	–	–	.000	12	0	0	0	3	6	.200	.000
vs. KC	–	–	–	–	–	–	–	–	–	.000	10	0	0	1	2	3	.154	.000
vs. NYY	–	–	–	–	–	–	–	–	–	.000	12	0	0	0	0	5	.000	.000
vs. Oak	–	–	–	–	–	–	–	–	–	.111	9	1	0	0	1	7	.200	.111
vs. Sea	–	–	–	–	–	–	–	–	–	.267	15	4	0	0	1	6	.313	.267
vs. TB	–	–	–	–	–	–	–	–	–	.000	3	0	0	0	0	0	.000	.000
vs. Tex	–	–	–	–	–	–	–	–	–	.083	12	1	0	1	0	6	.077	.083
vs. Tor	–	–	–	–	–	–	–	–	–	.000	1	0	0	0	0	0	.000	.000
vs. ChC	–	–	–	–	–	–	–	–	–	.000	1	0	0	0	0	0	.000	.000
Pre-All Star	–	–	–	–	–	–	–	–	–	.136	59	8	0	6	4	23	.185	.153
Post-All Star	–	–	–	–	–	–	–	–	–	.165	79	13	1	3	9	34	.250	.215

Joe LAWRENCE

CATCHER

BIRTHDATE	February 13, 1977
OPENING DAY AGE	24
BIRTHPLACE	Lake Charles, LA
RESIDENCE	Lake Charles, LA
BATS/THROWS	R/R
HEIGHT/WEIGHT	6-2/190
CONTRACT STATUS	signed thru 2001
M.L. SERVICE	0.000

6

PERSONAL: Joseph Dudley Lawrence... 1996 graduate of Barbe High School in Lake Charles, LA where he was All-State in baseball and football... Was named 1996 Coca-Cola Player of the Year in football, as well as earning Parade Magazine's pre-season All-American honours... Named 1996 Gatorade Baseball Player of the Year (Louisiana and Region), Mizuno and Baseball America pre-season and post-season All-American and Mr. Baseball for the state of Louisiana... Selected 16th overall by Toronto with the pick they received as compensation for Roberto Alomar... Turned down a chance to attend Louisiana State University.

LAST SEASON: In his first full season as a catcher had an All-Star season with Dunedin in the Florida State League (A) hitting .301 in 101 games with 32 doubles, 13 home runs and 67 RBI... Was selected as the team MVP and was ninth in the league in batting and third in on-base percentage at .414 — posted 69 walks... Stole 21 bases and was caught seven times... Opened the season hitting .333 in April with seven doubles, eight home runs, 20 RBI and was named the Organizational Player of the Month... Scored a run in 12 straight games from April 16 to 27... Reached base safely in 28 consecutive games from May 10 through June 6... Hit .327 in May with 17 RBI... Named as the catcher on the Baseball America Class A All-Star Team... Hit .317 in 68 games at catcher and just .267 as the designated hitter... Was promoted to Tennessee of the Southern League (AA) on July 26 where he appeared in 39 games and hit .263 with nine doubles, nine RBI, stole seven bases and posted a .407 on-base percentage... Finished the season hitting in 13 of the last 15 games... Named as Mr. Baseball for the State of Louisiana... Played in the Arizona Fall League with Scottsdale... Selected by Baseball America as the fourth best prospect in the organization.

PROFESSIONAL CAREER: 1996: Hit .224 in his pro debut with St. Catharines... Collected 11 RBI in 29 games and had 14 walks... **1997:** Hit .229 with Hagerstown of the South Atlantic League (A)... Collected 24 doubles with eight home runs and 38 RBI... April 27 turned in a 4-4 performance with two doubles vs. Augusta... Hit two home runs, including a grand slam, and drove in five runs on July 19... Was named tenth best prospect in the organization by Baseball America... **1998:** Hit .309 for Dunedin of the Florida State League (A) with 31 doubles, six triples, 11 home runs and 44 RBI... Led the FSL in walks with 105 and finished second in the league in both runs scored with 102 and on-base percentage at .441... Also ranked ninth in batting average... Reached base safely in 67 straight games to begin the season... Hit .307 in April... Hit three doubles on April 12 vs St. Petersburg (3-4)... May was his top month for average as he hit .384 with 23 runs scored and was named the organizational Player of the Month... Hit in a season high ten straight games from May 7 to 16... Made up for a poor July (.208) with an August which saw him hit .368 with 14 RBI, 21 walks and seven stolen bases... In six September games hit .421... Selected by Baseball America as the organizations eighth best prospect... Worked in the Instructional League as a catcher... **1999:** Hit .264 in 70 games for the Knoxville Smokies of the Southern League (AA)... Posted a .402 on-base average after collecting 56 walks and striking out just 48... Hit .307 in April... In the first 14 games with two home runs and five RBI... Through May had three home runs and then hit four in June with 10 RBI... Was selected to play in MLB Futures Game in Boston as part of the All-Star festivities... Season was cut short after suffering a sprained right ankle... Despite injury was selected as the 13th best prospect in the organization by Baseball America... Attended instructional league to work on catching.

JOE LAWRENCE

Year Club & League	AVG	G	AB	R	H	TB	2B	3B	HR	RBI	SH-SF	HP	BB-IBB	SO	SB-CS	GIDP	SLG	OBP
1996 St. Catharines (NYP)	.224	29	98	23	22	33	7	2	0	11	1-3	2	14-1	17	1-1	1	.337	.325
1997 Hagerstown (SAL)	.229	116	446	63	102	152	24	1	8	38	3-2	5	49-0	107	10-12	3	.341	.311
1998 Dunedin (FSL)	.308	125	454	102	140	216	31	6	11	44	5-1	4	105-2	88	15-12	11	.476	.441
1999 Knoxville (Sou)	.264	70	250	52	66	107	16	2	7	24	0-2	3	56-0	48	7-6	10	.428	.402
2000 Dunedin (FSL)	.301	101	375	69	113	186	32	1	13	67	0-3	5	69-6	74	21-7	9	.496	.414
2000 Tennessee (Sou)	.263	39	133	22	35	44	9	0	0	9	1-1	3	30-0	27	7-1	2	.331	.407
Minor Totals	.272	480	1756	331	478	738	119	12	39	193	10-12	22	323-9	361	61-39	36	.420	.389

LAWRENCE — TRANSACTIONS

- Selected by the Toronto Blue Jays in the 1st round (16th overall) of the June 1996 First Year Player Draft.
- On disabled list (sprained right ankle) June 30 through the remainder of the season, 1999.

Cole
LINIAK

INFIELDER

BIRTHDATE	August 23, 1976
OPENING DAY AGE	24
BIRTHPLACE	Encinitas, CA
RESIDENCE	Rancho La Costa, CA
BATS/THROWS	R/R
HEIGHT/WEIGHT	6-1/190
CONTRACT STATUS	signed thru 2001
M.L. SERVICE	0.042

31

PERSONAL: Cole Edward Liniak... Name pronounced lin-ee-AK... Graduated from San Dieguito High School in Encinitas, California, in 1995.

LAST SEASON: Was on the Cubs' Opening Day roster and made three pinch-hitting appearances (0-3) prior to being optioned to Iowa (AAA) on April 7... With Iowa of the Pacific Coast League hit .236 in 123 games with 24 doubles, a triple, 19 home runs and 58 RBI... After hitting .208 in April with a home run and four RBI, rebounded in May to post best month for average (.279), home runs (7) and RBI (22)... Had a season high four hits on May 5 at Oklahoma... Had five games with four or more RBI, three of which came in May... On May 21 drove in seven runs after going 3-4 with two home runs against Memphis' Alan Benes... With the bases loaded hit .308 (4-13) with two grand slams and 16 RBI... Hit .250 with four HR's and 13 RBI against left-handed pitching and against right-handed pitching hit .232 with 15 HR's and 45 RBI... Appeared in 116 games at third, one at second and one as the DH... Made seven pinch-hit appearances (0-5, 2BB)... Contract was outrighted to Iowa on September 12.

PROFESSIONAL CAREER: 1995: Began his professional career with the Red Sox's Gulf Coast (Rookie) club and batted .266 with 1 homer and 8 RBI in 23 games... **1996:** Spent the campaign at Michigan (A), playing in 121 games and hitting .263 with 65 runs scored, 26 doubles, three homers and 46 RBI... Led Midwest League third basemen with a .967 fielding percentage (11 E/338 TC)...

1997: Split the campaign between Sarasota (A) and Trenton (AA), batting .309 in a combined 117 games... Was selected to the Florida State League mid-season All-Star team at Sarasota... With Sarasota hit .336 in 64 games... Had a three-homer game on April 17 at West Palm Beach... Received a second-half promotion to Trenton, where he batted .280 in 53 games... **1998:** Had best offensive season of his pro career, hitting .261 with 31 doubles, 17 homers and 59 RBI for Pawtucket... During the month of June, hit .360 (36-100) with 15 multi-hit games, 26 runs scored, nine homers and 21 RBI... Was on the disabled list August 10-August 31 due to a sprained left ankle... **1999:** Split the season between the Cubs and Red Sox organizations... Opened the season as on of Boston's Top 10 prospects as selected by Baseball America... With Pawtucket of the International League (AAA) hit .264 in 95 games with 12 home runs and 42 RBI... Had a 2-homer contest May 7 at Durham, going 4-for-4 with four runs scored and three RBI... Was on the disabled list from May 24 to June 17 with a right wrist contusion... Was traded to the Chicago Cubs along with LHP Mark Guthrie in exchange for RHP Rod Beck on September 1... Appeared in 12 games for the Cubs, including nine starts at third base, and went 7-for-29 with two RBI... Made his ML debut on September 3 vs. Los Angeles, going 1-for-3... Singled in his first ML at bat against Chan Ho Park... Had back-to-back multi-hit games on September 8 against Cincinnati (3-3) and September 10 at Houston (2-3, RBI double).

COLE LINIAK

Year Club & League	AVG	G	AB	R	H	TB	2B	3B	HR	RBI	SH-SF	HP	BB-IBB	SO	SB-CS	GIDP	SLG	OBP
1995 Red Sox (Gulf)	.266	23	79	9	21	31	7	0	1	8	2-0	1	4-0	8	2-0	2	.392	.310
1996 Michigan (Mid)	.263	121	437	65	115	154	26	2	3	46	3-8	10	59-1	59	7-6	12	.352	.358
1997 Sarasota (FSL)	.336	64	217	32	73	107	16	0	6	42	3-2	3	22-1	31	1-2	2	.493	.402
1997 Trenton (East)	.280	53	200	20	56	73	11	0	2	18	3-1	1	17-0	29	0-1	6	.365	.338
1998 Pawtucket (Int)	.261	112	429	65	112	196	31	1	17	59	4-3	5	39-1	71	4-4	11	.457	.328
1998 Red Sox (Gulf)	.000	2	8	1	0	0	0	0	0	0	0-0	1	0-0	0	0-0	0	.000	.111
1999 Pawtucket (Int)	.264	95	348	55	92	153	25	0	12	42	3-1	1	40-1	57	0-5	7	.440	.341
1999 CHICAGO (NL)	.241	12	29	3	7	9	2	0	0	2	0-0	0	1-0	4	0-1	2	.310	.267
2000 Iowa (PCL)	.236	123	411	63	97	180	24	1	19	58	4-4	3	39-0	77	5-3	16	.438	.304
2000 CHICAGO (NL)	.000	3	3	0	0	0	0	0	0	0	0-0	0	0-0	2	0-0	0	.000	.000
Minor Totals	.266	593	2129	310	566	894	140	4	60	273	22-19	25	220-4	333	19-21	56	.420	.339
MAJOR TOTALS	.219	15	32	3	7	9	2	0	0	2	0-0	0	1-0	6	0-1	2	.281	.242

LINIAK — TRANSACTIONS

- Selected by the Boston Red Sox in the 7th round of the June 1995 First year Player Draft.
- On disabled list (sprained left ankle) August 10-31, 1998.
- On disabled list (contusion right wrist) May 24-June 17, 1999.
- Traded to the Chicago Cubs on September 1, 1999, completing deal in which the Chicago Cubs sent RHP Rod Beck to the Boston Red Sox in exchange for LHP Mark Guthrie and a player to be named (Aug. 31, 1999).
- Traded to the Toronto Blue Jays in exchange for a player to be named later on December 11, 2000.

CAREER HIGHS — LINIAK, Cole
GAME:

ML Debut	Sep. 3, 1999 vs. LA
Runs	1 - Sep. 3, 1999 vs. LA
	1 - Sep. 8, 1999 vs. CIN
	1 - Sep. 10, 1999 at HOU
Hits	3 - Sep. 8, 1999 vs. CIN
Doubles	1 - Sep. 8, 1999 vs. CIN
	1 - Sep. 10, 1999 at HOU
Home Runs	None
RBI	1 - Sep. 10, 1999 at HOU
	1 - Sep. 16, 1999 at CIN
Stolen Bases	None
Last ML Home Run	None
Longest Hitting Streak	2G - Sep. 8-9, 1999

FIELDING
LINIAK, Cole—IF

Year	PCT	G	PO	A	E	TC	DP
1999	1.000	10	8	8	0	16	1

COLE LINIAK DETAILED HITTING

	2000									CAREER								
	Avg	AB	H	HR	RBI	BB	SO	OBP	SLG	Avg	AB	H	HR	RBI	BB	SO	OBP	SLG
Total	.000	3	0	0	0	0	2	.000	.000	.219	32	7	0	2	1	6	.242	.281
vs. Left	.000	3	0	0	0	0	2	.000	.000	.200	5	1	0	0	0	3	.200	.200
vs. Right	–	–	–	–	–	–	–	–	–	.222	27	6	0	2	1	3	.250	.296
Home	.000	1	0	0	0	0	1	.000	.000	.250	20	5	0	0	0	4	.250	.300
Away	.000	2	0	0	0	0	1	.000	.000	.167	12	2	0	2	1	2	.231	.250
March	.000	2	0	0	0	0	1	.000	.000	.000	2	0	0	0	0	1	.000	.000
April	.000	1	0	0	0	0	1	.000	.000	.000	1	0	0	0	0	1	.000	.000
September	–	–	–	–	–	–	–	–	–	.241	29	7	0	2	1	4	.267	.310
Scoring Posn	.000	1	0	0	0	0	1	.000	.000	.000	6	0	0	1	1	1	.143	.000
Bases Loaded	–	–	–	–	–	–	–	–	–	.000	2	0	0	0	0	0	.000	.000
PH	.000	3	0	0	0	0	2	.000	.000	.200	5	1	0	0	0	3	.200	.200
vs. Mil	–	–	–	–	–	–	–	–	–	.000	1	0	0	0	0	0	.000	.000
vs. Cin	–	–	–	–	–	–	–	–	–	.273	11	3	0	1	0	2	.273	.364
vs. Hou	–	–	–	–	–	–	–	–	–	.333	6	2	0	1	1	0	.429	.500
vs. LA	–	–	–	–	–	–	–	–	–	.111	9	1	0	0	0	1	.111	.111
vs. NYM	.000	2	0	0	0	0	1	.000	.000	.000	2	0	0	0	0	1	.000	.000
vs. Phi	–	–	–	–	–	–	–	–	–	.000	1	0	0	0	0	1	.000	.000
vs. StL	.000	1	0	0	0	0	1	.000	.000	.500	2	1	0	0	0	1	.500	.500
Pre-All Star	.000	3	0	0	0	0	2	.000	.000	.000	3	0	0	0	0	2	.000	.000
Post-All Star	–	–	–	–	–	–	–	–	–	.241	29	7	0	2	1	4	.267	.310

COLE LINIAK HITTING AT ML PARKS

Park	Avg	G	AB	R	H	2B	3B	HR	RBI	SB	CS	BB	SO	OBP	Slg
Wrigley Field	.263	8	19	2	5	1	0	0	0	0	0	0	3	.263	.316
Cinergy Field	.000	1	3	0	0	0	0	0	1	0	0	0	0	.000	.000
Astrodome	.333	2	6	1	2	1	0	0	1	0	1	1	0	.429	.500
Veterans Stadium	.000	1	1	0	0	0	0	0	0	0	0	0	1	.000	.000
Busch Stadium	.000	1	1	0	0	0	0	0	0	0	0	0	1	.000	.000

Esteban
LOAIZA
PITCHER

BIRTHDATE	December 31, 1971
OPENING DAY AGE	29
BIRTHPLACE	Tijuana, MX
RESIDENCE	South Lake, TX
BATS/THROWS	R/R
HEIGHT/WEIGHT	6-3/215
CONTRACT STATUS	signed thru 2002
M.L. SERVICE	5.052

21

PERSONAL: Esteban (s-TAY-bahn) Antonio Veyna Loaiza (low-EYE-zah)... Favorite major league players while growing up were Roger Clemens, Tony Gwynn, and Fernando Valenzuela... Favorite team was the San Diego Padres... Was born on New Year's Eve in 1971... Played baseball at Mar Vista High School in Imperial Beach, CA, graduating in 1991... Also participated in several amateur programs.

LAST SEASON: Finished the season with a 10-13 record and a 4.56 ERA while pitching for Texas and Toronto... Had a career high 137 strikeouts... Appeared in 34 games making 31 starts and posted one shutout and a save... Opened the season with Texas and was 5-6 with a 5.37 ERA in 20 games, 17 starts... Was traded to Toronto on July 19 in exchange for RHP Darwin Cubillan and minor league 2B Mike Young... Opened the season with 1-1 record in April in four starts and a 2.90 ERA... Pitched 7.0 plus innings in each of his first four starts... On April 16 vs Cleveland had a no-decision while striking out a career high ten batters, allowed two hits over 7.1 shutout innings... In May was 2-2 with a 6.88 ERA in six starts... Won back-to-back starts on May 20 and 25 against Baltimore and at Kansas City... Lost his next three decisions to fall to 3-5 on June 15... Won start on June 21 vs Minnesota... Three of his next five appearances were in relief... On June 25 recorded his first career save with 2.0 shutout innings vs Tampa Bay... Was 5-5 at the All-Star break with a save and a 4.56 ERA... Following the break was 5-8 in 15 starts with a 3.90 ERA... Made his Blue Jays debut July 22 vs Baltimore and suffered a loss... Captured his first win with Toronto on July 27 at Seattle in his second start... In August was 2-2 with a 4.34 ERA, four of his six starts were quality starts... From August 28 to September 20 posted five consecutive quality starts and was 3-2... On September 8 vs Detroit tossed his second career shutout, a five-hitter in a 3-0 win with a career high 11 strikeouts... In three starts, September 8-20, was 1-2 with a 1.17 ERA... Lost final two starts of the season to finish 10-13... In September was 2-4 despite posting a 2.53 ERA in six starts... Was 6-5 in home games with a 4.42 ERA and on the road was 4-8 with a 4.68 ERA... Opponents hit .288 with 29 home runs which was tied for ninth in the AL.

PROFESSIONAL CAREER: 1991: Had staff's lowest ERA (2.26) and tied for lead in wins (5) and starts (11) at Bradenton (Gulf)... **1992:** Led Augusta (A- SAL) in wins (10), starts (25), and complete games (3)... Was on disabled list from July 17-27 with right elbow trouble... **1993:** Was 9-8, 3.73 in 28 games with three clubs... Was 6-7, 3.39 in 17 starts at Salem and was selected to play in Carolina League All-Star game... Promoted to Mexico City on May 7 and then assigned to Carolina on August 7... Fanned 40 batters in 43.0 innings... **1994:** Was 5th in the Southern League (AA) in strikeouts (115) and topped Carolina in wins (10)... Started the season on disabled list recovering from surgery to remove loose bodies from right elbow in November... Was activated on April 28 before returning to the disabled list from July 7-14 with a blister on right little finger... **1995:** Tied for NL lead in starts (31) and tied for 4th among league rookies in wins (8)... Topped NL in runs (115) and earned runs (99) allowed and led staff in home runs issued (21)... Won his ML debut, starting on April 29 at Philadelphia... Had a four game winning streak, June 20 to July 9... Combined on 1-0 shutout victory at Montreal on June 25... First career complete game was on July 9 against New York... Singled off the Phillies Tyler Green in first major league at bat on April 29... **1996:** Began the year at Calgary (AAA)... Was Pacific Coast

League co-Pitcher of the Week, June 2-8... Was recalled by Pittsburgh on June 7 but allowed nine runs in 7.0 innings in two relief appearances and returned to Calgary on June 19... Was assigned to Class AAA Mexico City on July 23 and went 2-0 in five starts to earn promotion back to Pittsburgh on August 22... Was 0-2, 10.31 in his first five starts but 2-0, 2.10 in final five outings, allowing two or fewer ER four times in that span... Tossed first major league CG shutout on September 13 at San Francisco... Win snapped a six-game losing streak dating back to August 22, 1995... **1997:** Topped the Pirates in innings (196.1) and tied for team lead in wins (11)... Set career bests for wins, starts (32), innings, and strikeouts (122)... Was 4-0, 2.44 in season's first seven starts, the first Pirate to win first four decisions in a year since Randy Tomlin in 1992... Was 7-11, 4.67 the rest of the season... In five September outings posted a 2.88 ERA... Became first native of Tijuana, Mexico to ever start a game on April 9 at San Diego in a 4-2 victory... Tied for 3rd in NL in hit batters (12)... Topped Pirate pitchers with .167 (10-60) average and had five RBI... Underwent arthroscopic surgery on October 15 to repair tendon damage in right ankle... **1998:** Was 9-11, 5.16 ERA in 35 games, 28 starts with the Pirates and Rangers, establishing a career high for appearances and second highest total in strikeouts (108)... With Pittsburgh was 4-5, 4.94 ERA in 14 starts and in seven relief appearances was 2-0 with a 2.03 ERA... Began the year in the rotation, going 2-3, 5.40 ERA in 10 starts... Worked first 7.2 innings of a combined 8-0 shutout, May 12 vs. Colorado... Was moved to the bullpen after losing at Florida on May 22... Allowed a run in three of seven relief appearances... Failed in only save opportunity, June 10 at Cleveland... Returned to the rotation with a win on June 21 at Milwaukee and was 2-2, 3.96 ERA in his final four starts before the trade... At the time of the trade, was tied for 3rd on the Pittsburgh staff in wins and was 4th in innings (91.2)... Acquired by the Texas Rangers on July 17... Was 0-3, 3.12 ERA in his first five starts with Texas... Allowed a career low four hits and struck out a then career high nine in an 8.0 inning complete game, 1-0 loss at Toronto on July 30... Took shutouts into the 8th inning on August 11 at Cleveland and August 31 in Detroit... Recorded first AL win in game against the Indians, allowing one run in 7.1 frames... From September 13 on, was 0-3, with a 14.21 ERA in his last four contests, working more than 3.0 innings only once... Allowed 11 runs in 4.1 innings over two starts in a three-day span, September 13 at Tampa Bay and September 15 at Baltimore... Became the first Ranger to start on one day rest since Roger Pavlik, June 29 and July 1, 1995... Tied for 3rd on the Rangers staff for most homers allowed (15), including a career high four homers on August 21 vs. New York... **1999:** Was 9-5 with a 4.56 ERA in 30 games, 15 starts for Texas... Tied for 4th on the staff in wins (9), ranked 5th in strikeouts (77) and was 6th in innings (120.1) while his 4.56 ERA was lowest among the starters... He also issued just 40 walks, the 2nd lowest total among Rangers starters... All nine of his wins came after the All-Star break, which was second to Aaron Sele for the most on the club over the last half of the season... As a reliever finished 1-1, 6.91 (22 ER/28.2 IP) in 15 appearances... Allowed a run in 11 of 15 outings... Permitted six of 18 inherited runners to score while first batters faced were 1-15 (.067)... Was beaten out by Mike Morgan as the 5th starter in spring training and made first 10 outings out of the bullpen... Allowed six ER in his first two outings, April 5-9 (6.1IP)... Then gave up just five ER (4.09 ERA) over next six outings, April 15-May 1... Had no-decision in a spot start at

Chicago on May 11... Broke right hand after slamming it in a car door on May 15 and was placed on the disabled list the following day... Was assigned to Oklahoma (AAA) on rehab assignment on June 28 and pitched 4.1 scoreless innings in two starts before being activated on July 5... Returned to the bullpen for five more outings, July 5-19... Suffered first loss on July 11, allowing two ER in 1.1 innings... Pitched a season high 4.2 innings in relief on July 19 vs. San Francisco for his first victory since August 31, 1998 at Detroit... As a starter was 8-4, 3.83 ERA as Texas went 10-5 in his 15 starts... Allowed three or fewer runs in 11 of 15 starts while issuing a home run in just six of 15 efforts... Pitched at least 6.0 innings in 12 of last 13 starts... From July 24 on remained in the rotation making 14 starts and posted an 8-4 record with a 3.53 ERA... Had a career-high seven game win streak from July 19 to August 25 — was 6-0, 2.82 ERA over seven starts... Threw 8.0 shutout innings on August 15 at Chicago, combining on a 10-0 win... Had a streak of 13.2 scoreless innings, August 15-20... Fanned 20 batters in 27.1 innings over four starts from August 15 to 30... Lost three straight, August 30 to September 10, allowing 10 ER in 13.2 innings... Gave up five hits and five ER in one inning on September 10 at Kansas City, the 2nd shortest start of

career... Went 2-1, 3.18 (10 ER/28.1 IP) in last four games of the regular season... Had a season-high seven strikeouts on September 26 at Oakland, allowed one ER in 7.0 innings for the win to clinch the AL West title for the Rangers... Was 6-2, 4.54 ERA (36 ER/71.1 IP) at home and 3-3, 4.59 ERA (25 ER/49.0 IP) on the road... Opponents batted .275 (128-466) against him, .290 (73-252) by right handers and .257 (55-214) by lefties... In the post season started Game 3 of the AL Division Series vs. the Yankees on October 9 in Arlington... Allowed a three-run homer to Darryl Strawberry in the 1st inning, then shut out New York over the next six frames in a 3-0 loss... Overall, allowed three ER on five hits with four strikeouts in 7.0 innings of work.

POST SEASON EXPERIENCE: 1998: Was moved to the bullpen for the Division Series vs. the Yankees, but did not see any post-season action... **1999:** Started Game 3 of the AL Division Series vs. the Yankees on October 9 in Arlington... Allowed a three-run homer to Darryl Strawberry in the 1st inning, then shut out New York over the next six frames in a 3-0 loss... Overall, allowed three ER on five hits with four strikeouts in 7.0 innings of work.

ESTEBAN LOAIZA

Year	Club & League	W-L	ERA	G	GS	CG	ShO	SV	IP	H	R	ER	HR	HB	BB-IBB	SO	WP	BK	OBA
1991	Bradenton (Gulf)	5-1	2.26	11	11	1	1	0	51.2	48	17	13	0	5	14-0	41	2	1	.241
1992	Augusta (SAL)	10-8	3.89	26	25	3	0	0	143.1	134	72	62	7	10	60-0	123	7	4	.249
1993	Salem (Caro)	6-7	3.39	17	17	3	0	0	109.0	113	53	41	7	4	30-0	61	8	0	.268
1993	Mexico City (Mex)	1-1	5.18	4	3	0	0	0	24.1	32	18	14	0	0	4-0	15	0	0	.305
1993	Carolina (Sou)	2-1	3.77	7	7	1	0	0	43.0	39	18	18	5	0	12-0	40	3	0	.241
1994	Carolina (Sou)	10-5	3.79	24	24	3	0	0	154.1	169	69	65	15	5	30-0	115	1	1	.280
1995	PITTSBURGH (NL)	8-9	5.16	32	31	1	0	0	172.2	205	115	99	21	5	55-3	85	6	1	.300
1996	Calgary (PCL)	3-4	4.02	12	11	1	1	0	69.1	61	34	31	5	3	25-2	38	0	0	.243
1996	Mexico City (Mex)	2-0	2.43	5	5	0	0	0	33.1	28	12	9	1	2	14-0	16	1	0	.228
1996	PITTSBURGH (NL)	2-3	4.96	10	10	1	1	0	52.2	65	32	29	11	2	19-0	32	0	0	.308
1997	PITTSBURGH (NL)	11-11	4.13	33	32	1	0	0	196.1	214	99	90	17	12	56-9	122	2	3	.279
1998	PITTSBURGH (NL)	6-5	4.52	21	14	0	0	0	91.2	96	50	46	13	3	30-1	53	1	2	.275
1998	TEXAS (AL)	3-6	5.90	14	14	1	0	0	79.1	103	57	52	15	2	22-3	55	3	0	.316
1999	TEXAS (AL)	9-5	4.56	30	15	0	0	0	120.1	128	65	61	10	0	40-2	77	2	0	.275
1999	Oklahoma (PCL)	0-0	0.00	2	2	0	0	0	4.1	3	0	0	0	0	3-0	6	0	0	.188
2000	TEXAS (AL)	5-6	5.37	20	17	0	0	1	107.1	133	67	64	21	3	31-1	75	1	0	.302
2000	TORONTO (AL)	5-7	3.62	14	14	1	1	0	92.0	95	45	37	8	10	26-0	62	0	0	.270
Minor Totals		38-26	3.54	104	102	12	2	0	608.1	595	275	239	40	29	188-2	440	22	6	.257
AL TOTALS		22-24	4.83	78	60	2	1	1	399.0	459	234	214	54	15	119-6	269	6	0	.290
NL TOTALS		27-28	4.63	96	87	3	1	0	513.1	580	296	264	62	22	160-13	292	9	6	.289
MAJOR TOTALS		49-52	4.72	174	147	5	2	1	912.1	1039	530	478	116	37	279-19	561	15	6	.289

DIVISION SERIES RECORD

Year	Club & League	W-L	ERA	G	GS	CG	ShO	SV	IP	H	R	ER	HR	HB	BB-IBB	SO	WP	BK	OBA
1998	TEXAS (AL)								DID NOT PLAY										
1999	TEXAS (AL)	0-1	3.86	1	1	0	0	0	7.0	5	3	3	1	0	1-0	4	0	0	.192

LOAIZA — TRANSACTIONS

- Signed as a non-drafted free agent by the Pittsburgh organization on March 21, 1991...Signed by Angel Figueroa (Pirates).
- On disabled list, July 17-27, 1992.
- Loaned by Pirates to Mexico City of the Mexican League, May 7-28, 1993.
- On disabled list (shoulder surgery recovery to remove loose bodies in the right elbow) April 7-28, 1994.
- On disabled list (blister on right little finger) July 7-14, 1994.
- Loaned by Pirates to Mexico City of the Mexican League, June 19-August 13, 1996.
- Acquired by the Texas Rangers in exchange for RHP Todd Van Poppel and IF Warren Morris on July 17, 1998.
- On disabled list (broken right hand) May 12-July 5, 1999; included rehabilitation assignment to Oklahoma, June 28-July 5.
- Traded to the Toronto Blue Jays in exchange for RHP Darwin Cubillan and IF Mike Young on July 19, 2000.

FIELDING
LOAIZA, Esteban—P

Year	PCT	G	PO	A	E	TC	DP
1995 (NL)	1.000	32	13	27	0	40	3
1996 (NL)	.947	10	6	12	1	19	0
1997 (NL)	.949	33	11	26	2	39	1
1998 (NL)	1.000	21	10	18	0	28	3
1998 (AL)	1.000	14	11	6	0	17	0
1999 (AL)	1.000	30	8	17	0	25	0
2000 (AL)	.932	34	12	29	3	44	4
Total	.972	174	71	135	6	212	11

CAREER HIGHS — LOAIZA, Esteban

SEASON:

Wins	11 - 1997
Losses	13 - 2000
Saves	1 - 2000
ERA	4.13 - 1997
Games	35 - 1998
Starts	32 - 1997
Complete Games	1 - 1995, 96, 97, 98, 2000
Shutouts	1 - 1996, 2000
Innings Pitched	199.1 - 2000
Walks	57 - 2000
Strikeouts	137 - 2000
Longest Win Streak	7 - Jul. 19-Aug. 25, 1999
Longest Losing Streak	4 - Aug. 27-Sep. 18, 1995
Scoreless Innings Streak	13.2 - Aug. 10-20, 1999

GAME:

ML Debut	Apr. 29, 1995 at PHI
Innings Pitched:	
Starter	9.0 - Jul. 9, 1995 vs. NYM
	9.0 - Sep. 13, 1996 at SF
	9.0 - Sep. 20, 1997 vs. STL
	9.0 - Sep. 8, 2000 vs. DET
Reliever	5.0 - Jun. 16, 1998 at PHI
Walks:	
Starter	4 - Apr. 23, 1997 vs. PHI
Reliever	3 - Jun. 16, 1998 vs. PHI
Strikeouts:	
Starter	11 - Sep. 8, 2000 vs. DET
Reliever	4 - Apr. 20, 1999 at NYY
Hits Allowed	12 - Aug. 16, 1998 at NYY
Runs Allowed	8 - May 3, 1995 at STL
	8 - Jun. 16, 1995 vs. SD
	8 - May 9, 2000 vs. SEA
	8 - Jun. 10, 2000 at COL
ER Allowed	8 - May 3, 1995 at STL
	8 - May 9, 2000 vs. SEA
	8 - Jun. 10, 2000 at COL
HR Allowed	4 - Aug. 21, 1998 at NYY
Low Hit CG	4 - Jul. 30, 1998 at TOR
Last Win	Sep. 20, 2000 vs. NYY
Last Save	Jun. 25, 2000 vs. TB
Last CG	Sep. 8, 2000 vs. DET
Last ShO	Sep. 8, 2000 vs. DET
Last Start	Sep. 30, 2000 at CLE
Last Relief App.	Jul. 9, 2000 at SD

ESTEBAN LOAIZA DETAILED PITCHING

	2000								CAREER						
	ERA	W-L-Sv	G	IP	H	ER	BB	SO	ERA	W-L-Sv	G	IP	H	ER	BB	SO
Total	4.56	10-13-1	34	199.1	228	101	57	137	4.72	49-52-1	174	912.1	1039	478	279	561
ST	4.71	10-13-0	31	193.0	225	101	56	132	4.75	46-51-0	147	858.0	987	453	262	522
REL	0.00	0-0-1	3	6.1	3	0	1	5	4.14	3-1-1	27	54.1	52	25	17	39
Home	4.42	6-5-1	17	93.2	105	46	24	64	4.90	24-26-1	88	448.0	503	244	135	285
Away	4.68	4-8-0	17	105.2	123	55	33	73	4.54	25-26-0	86	464.1	536	234	144	276
April	2.90	1-1-0	4	31.0	27	10	9	24	3.40	5-2-0	22	111.1	110	42	30	68
May	6.88	2-2-0	6	34.0	49	26	7	22	6.46	5-8-0	29	138.0	183	99	41	84
June	5.65	2-2-1	6	28.2	41	18	8	18	5.43	10-7-1	27	126.0	157	76	36	78
July	5.96	1-2-0	6	25.2	31	17	10	20	4.87	9-10-0	29	138.2	150	75	47	92
August	4.34	2-2-0	6	37.1	42	18	14	28	4.21	13-8-0	33	194.1	234	91	64	112
September	2.53	2-4-0	6	42.2	38	12	9	25	4.20	7-17-0	33	197.0	199	92	60	122
October	–	–	–	–	–	–	–	–	3.86	0-0-0	1	7.0	6	3	1	5
vs. Ana	3.95	1-0-0	2	13.2	13	6	2	10	4.33	1-0-0	5	27.0	26	13	3	21
vs. Bal	4.26	1-2-0	4	25.1	27	12	7	13	5.25	1-3-0	6	36.0	40	21	9	17
vs. Bos	–	–	–	–	–	–	–	–	4.50	1-0-0	1	6.0	5	3	3	5
vs. CWS	6.48	0-1-0	1	8.1	10	6	1	5	4.88	1-2-0	4	27.2	30	15	6	14
vs. Cle	1.42	0-1-0	2	12.2	9	2	5	12	4.22	2-2-0	7	32.0	31	15	9	27
vs. Det	3.21	1-1-0	2	14.0	15	5	2	14	3.62	4-2-0	8	49.2	58	20	11	35
vs. KC	9.39	1-1-0	3	15.1	26	16	4	9	9.27	2-2-0	5	22.1	37	23	6	11
vs. Mil	–	–	–	–	–	–	–	–	3.77	1-1-0	3	14.1	11	6	3	10
vs. Min	2.33	3-1-0	4	27.0	31	7	11	19	3.41	6-3-0	12	60.2	71	23	21	40
vs. NYY	1.93	1-1-0	2	14.0	12	3	4	5	4.34	2-2-0	7	37.1	44	18	10	25
vs. Oak	3.25	1-1-0	4	27.2	26	10	8	21	3.16	2-2-0	9	42.2	39	15	16	36
vs. Sea	9.31	1-1-0	2	9.2	15	10	2	9	11.37	1-2-0	3	12.2	21	16	3	11
vs. TB	5.02	0-1-1	3	14.1	16	8	4	8	7.09	1-2-1	6	26.2	35	21	12	17
vs. Tor	–	–	–	–	–	–	–	–	2.55	0-1-0	3	17.2	13	5	4	16
vs. Ari	5.06	0-0-0	1	5.1	10	3	1	3	6.97	0-1-0	3	10.1	19	8	5	8
vs. Atl	–	–	–	–	–	–	–	–	3.79	2-2-0	6	38.0	33	16	14	22
vs. ChC	–	–	–	–	–	–	–	–	2.75	0-0-0	3	19.2	23	6	6	9
vs. Cin	–	–	–	–	–	–	–	–	4.66	1-4-0	8	48.1	55	25	16	34
vs. Col	27.00	0-1-0	1	2.2	8	8	3	2	6.27	3-2-0	9	47.1	62	33	15	17
vs. Fla	–	–	–	–	–	–	–	–	6.54	2-4-0	8	31.2	44	23	11	16
vs. Hou	–	–	–	–	–	–	–	–	4.30	2-2-0	6	37.2	42	18	9	20
vs. LA	–	–	–	–	–	–	–	–	6.11	0-2-0	7	35.1	45	24	11	17
vs. Mon	–	–	–	–	–	–	–	–	2.55	1-1-0	7	35.1	33	10	9	16
vs. NYM	–	–	–	–	–	–	–	–	7.07	1-1-0	6	28.0	37	22	10	17
vs. Phi	–	–	–	–	–	–	–	–	2.36	2-1-0	7	42.0	40	11	18	20
vs. StL	–	–	–	–	–	–	–	–	4.02	3-5-0	9	53.2	55	24	14	36
vs. SD	0.00	0-0-0	2	4.1	2	0	1	3	5.40	1-2-0	8	30.0	37	18	10	16
vs. SF	9.00	0-1-0	1	5.0	8	5	2	4	5.53	5-1-0	8	42.1	53	26	15	28
Pre-All Star	5.19	5-5-1	19	102.1	125	59	29	71	4.96	23-18-1	88	415.1	482	229	119	255
Post-All Star	3.90	5-8-0	15	97.0	103	42	28	66	4.51	26-34-0	86	497.0	557	249	160	306

ESTEBAN LOAIZA PITCHING AT ML PARKS

Park	ERA	W-L-Sv	SvO	G	GS	IP	H	R	ER	HR	BB	SO
Camden Yards	6.19	0-1-0	0	3	3	16.0	18	11	11	4	5	7
Edison Field	3.92	1-0-0	0	3	3	20.2	19	10	9	5	3	15
Comiskey Park	3.46	1-0-0	0	2	2	13.0	14	5	5	0	3	7
Jacobs Field	2.05	2-1-0	1	4	3	22.0	19	7	5	1	7	16
Tiger Stadium	1.88	1-1-0	0	2	2	14.1	14	3	3	3	6	7
Kauffman Stadium	9.69	1-2-0	0	3	3	13.0	24	14	14	0	4	7
County Stadium	3.86	1-1-0	0	2	2	14.0	11	6	6	1	3	10
Metrodome	6.08	1-3-0	0	5	4	23.2	37	19	16	2	7	17
Yankee Stadium	4.96	0-1-0	0	3	2	16.1	23	9	9	3	1	12
Oakland-Alameda	1.50	1-0-0	0	5	2	18.0	16	3	3	1	4	15
Kingdome	18.00	0-1-0	0	1	1	3.0	6	6	6	0	1	2
Arlington	4.90	10-6-1	1	32	21	156.0	178	95	85	24	50	107
SkyDome	3.54	3-4-0	0	9	8	56.0	52	25	22	5	12	43
Atlanta-Fulton	3.86	0-1-0	0	1	1	7.0	4	3	3	2	2	5
Wrigley Field	2.84	1-0-0	0	2	2	12.2	14	7	4	1	5	7
Cinergy Field	1.77	0-2-0	0	3	3	20.1	13	7	4	1	8	12
Astrodome	4.58	1-1-0	0	3	3	17.2	22	10	9	3	7	8
Dodger Stadium	5.00	0-1-0	0	5	5	27.0	29	16	15	4	8	14
Olympic Stadium	2.37	1-0-0	0	3	3	19.0	18	5	5	1	4	7
Shea Stadium	9.82	0-0-0	0	3	3	11.0	19	12	12	2	4	6
Veterans Stadium	2.01	2-0-0	0	4	3	22.1	24	7	5	1	7	10
Three Rivers	5.13	11-17-0	0	49	42	245.2	281	160	140	37	75	146
Busch Stadium	5.48	1-2-0	0	4	4	21.1	25	13	13	2	8	14
Qualcomm Park	3.95	1-1-0	0	3	2	13.2	14	7	6	1	4	6
3 Com Park	4.79	2-0-0	0	4	4	20.2	26	11	11	2	9	15
Coors Field	7.77	2-1-0	0	4	4	22.0	36	19	19	2	8	8
Pro Player Stadium	3.12	2-1-0	0	3	3	17.1	20	7	6	2	2	6
Turner Field	1.23	1-0-0	0	2	2	14.2	12	2	2	0	4	10
BankOne Ballpark	10.38	0-1-0	0	1	1	4.1	8	6	5	1	3	4
Tropicana Field	9.24	1-1-0	0	3	3	12.2	19	13	13	3	10	5
SAFECO Field	2.57	1-0-0	0	1	1	7.0	6	2	2	0	2	6
Pacific Bell	9.00	0-1-0	0	1	1	5.0	8	5	5	1	2	4
Comerica Park	9.00	0-1-0	0	1	1	5.0	10	5	5	1	1	3

Dustin
McGOWAN

PITCHER

59

BIRTHDATE	March 24, 1982
OPENING DAY AGE	19
BIRTHPLACE	Savannah, GA
RESIDENCE	Ludowici, GA
BATS/THROWS	R/R
HEIGHT/WEIGHT	6-3/190
CONTRACT STATUS	signed thru 2001
M.L. SERVICE	0.000

PERSONAL: Dustin Micheal McGowan... Graduated from Long County High School in Ludowici, Georgia where he played baseball, basketball and ran cross country... Was selected as the MVP of both the baseball and basketball teams, was an All-Region selection in basketball and an All-State selection in baseball.

LAST SEASON: Made his professional debut with Medicine Hat of the Pioneer League (A) and was 0-3 with a 6.48 ERA in eight starts... Allowed 18 earned runs in 25.0 innings with seven of those runs coming in his professional debut over 1.1 innings in Ogden... Season ERA without that outing would have been 4.18... In his final three starts was 0-1 with a 1.38 ERA and allowed just five hits in 13.0 innings... In his final outing pitched a season high five innings.

DUSTIN McGOWAN

Year Club & League	W-L	ERA	G	GS	CG	ShO	SV	IP	H	R	ER	HR	HB	BB-IBB	SO	WP	BK	OBA
2000 Medicine Hat (Pio)	0-3	6.48	8	8	0	0	0	25.0	26	21	18	2	3	25-0	19	8	0	.274

McGOWAN — TRANSACTIONS

- Selected by the Toronto Blue Jays in the 1st round (33rd overall) of the June 2000 First Year Player Draft.

Chris
MICHALAK
PITCHER

BIRTHDATE	January 4, 1971
OPENING DAY AGE	30
BIRTHPLACE	Joliet, IL
RESIDENCE	Lemont, IL
BATS/THROWS	L/L
HEIGHT/WEIGHT	6-2/195
CONTRACT STATUS	signed thru 2001
M.L. SERVICE	0.038

60

PERSONAL: Christian Matthew Michalak... Name pronounced mah-HALL-ick... Married, wife's name is Shannon... Two children, Madison and Tyler... Graduated in 1989 from Joliet Catholic High School in Illinois where he quarterbacked the football team to the state championship his junior year (threw the football right-handed).

LAST SEASON: Opened the season with Durham of the International League (AAA) where he made six appearances and was 0-0 with a 5.68 ERA... First four outings of the season were scoreless... Had seven K's in 6.1IP... Was released on April 25 and then signed by the Dodgers organization on May 6... Joined Albuquerque of the Pacific Coast League (AAA) was 11-3 in 23 games, 21 starts, with a 4.26 ERA... The 11 wins are a career high... Entering the season had started only six games in the past five years... Had an eight game win streak from May 26 to July 31... Made two relief appearances with Albuquerque, June 23 and September 4 and was 0-0 with a 5.40 ERA... As a starter was 11-3 with a 4.22 ERA... Tossed a complete game on August 17 at Memphis, was the second of his pro career... Held left-handed batters to a .286 average and right-handed batters to a .331 average.

PROFESSIONAL CAREER: 1993: Spent his first professional season at Southern Oregon of the Northwest League-A... Was 7-3 with a 2.85 ERA for the Oakland affiliate... **1994:** Set a then career highs of 10 wins and 144.1 innings pitched for West Michigan (A) and Modesto combined... Between the two clubs posted an ERA of 3.37 ERA... **1995:** Pitched at Huntsville (AA) and Modesto (A) combining for a career high 51 games... 44 of those appearances came with Modesto... **1996:** Again split the season between Modesto (A) and Huntsville (AA), his final campaign in the

Oakland system... Combined went 6-2 with a 4.79 ERA (62.0-IP/33-ER) in 42 relief outings... **1997:** Signed with Arizona after he was released by Oakland on the final day of spring training... Made his season debut for High Desert against the Athletics' Visalia affiliate, striking out six in 3.0 innings... His 2.65 season ERA was a career low... **1998:** Joined the Arizona organization and pitched for three different clubs on the season, was on loan with Tulsa, the AA affiliate of Texas Rangers, Tucson, the AAA affiliate for Arizona and finished with his first taste of big league action, appearing in five games for the Diamondbacks... Opened the season with Tulsa where he was 1-2 with a 1.83 ERA in 10 games... Surrendered only one earned run in his first nine appearances, spanning 17.2 innings, including a scoreless inning streak of 13.1 innings... Was promoted to Tucson (AAA) in May where he made 29 appearances, nine starts, with an ERA of 5.03... Had his contract purchased from AAA on August 21 and debuted that afternoon at Shea Stadium, throwing 2.0 innings allowing one run... Struck out the first two big league hitters he faced (Todd Hundley & Brian McRae)... Appeared in five games in the majors, posting a 11.81 ERA... **1999:** Pitched for a pair of AAA clubs, the Edmonton Trappers (Oakland Athletics) and Tucson Sidewinders (Arizona Diamondbacks) of the Pacific Coast League... Began with Edmonton and made 24 appearances before receiving his release on June 19... Signed four days later with Arizona and finished the season with 21 outings (6 starts) for Tucson... Combined on the season was 6-0 in 45 games with an ERA of 4.29... His start July 9 at Salt Lake in game two of a doubleheader was his first start since 1994 for Modesto... Was 4-0 as a starter with a 2.88 ERA... Did not allow an earned run in three of his six starts.

CHRIS MICHALAK

Year	Club & League	W-L	ERA	G	GS	CG	ShO	SV	IP	H	R	ER	HR	HB	BB-IBB	SO	WP	BK	OBA
1993	South Oregon (NWST)	7-3	2.85	16	15	0	0	0	79.0	77	41	25	2	6	36-0	57	4	3	.259
1994	West Michigan (Mid)	5-3	3.90	15	10	0	0	0	67.0	66	32	29	3	8	28-0	38	2	3	.265
1994	Modesto (Cal)	5-3	2.91	17	10	1	0	2	77.1	67	28	25	13	3	20-1	46	4	3	.238
1995	Huntsville (Sou)	1-1	11.12	7	0	0	0	1	5.2	10	7	7	1	1	5-0	4	2	0	.400
1995	Modesto (Cal)	3-2	2.62	44	0	0	0	2	65.1	56	26	19	3	4	27-1	49	2	1	.246
1996	Modesto (Cal)	2-2	3.03	21	0	0	0	4	38.2	37	21	13	4	2	17-0	39	0	2	.243
1996	Huntsville (Sou)	4-0	7.71	21	0	0	0	0	23.1	32	29	20	2	1	26-4	15	4	0	.340
1997	High Desert (Cal)	3-7	2.65	49	0	0	0	4	85.0	76	36	25	4	9	31-1	74	6	1	.238
1998	Tulsa (Tex)	1-2	1.83	10	0	0	0	0	19.2	10	4	4	2	2	2-0	15	0	2	.149
1998	Tucson (PCL)	3-8	5.03	29	9	0	0	0	73.1	91	47	41	11	4	29-3	50	4	3	.318
1998	ARIZONA (NL)	0-0	11.81	5	0	0	0	0	5.1	9	7	7	1	0	4-0	5	0	0	.375
1999	Edmonton (PCL)	1-0	5.72	24	0	0	0	0	28.1	28	20	18	3	1	14-0	25	1	0	.259
1999	Tucson (PCL)	5-0	3.66	21	6	0	0	3	64.0	64	30	26	6	6	26-2	41	1	1	.268
2000	Durham (Int)	0-0	5.68	6	0	0	0	0	6.1	6	4	4	1	0	1-0	7	1	0	.240
2000	Albuquerque (PCL)	11-3	4.26	23	21	1	0	0	133.0	166	72	63	18	4	55-0	83	4	3	.320
Minor Totals		51-34	3.75	303	71	2	0	16	766.0	786	397	319	73	51	317-12	543	35	22	.272

MICHALAK — TRANSACTIONS

- Selected by the Oakland Athletics in 12th round of the June 1993 First Year Player Draft.
- Signed by the Arizona Diamondbacks on April 8, 1997.
- Loaned by the Arizona Diamondbacks to the Texas Rangers from March 24-May 6, 1998.
- Signed by the Anaheim Angels on January 25, 1999.
- Signed by the Arizona Diamondbacks on June 23, 1999.
- Signed by the Tampa Bay Devil Rays on January 9, 2000.
- Signed by the Los Angeles Dodgers on May 6, 2000.
- Signed by the Toronto Blue Jays on November 10, 2000.

Players

CAREER HIGHS — MICHALAK, Chris
GAME:

ML Debut	Aug. 22, 1998 at NYM
Innings Pitched:	
Starter	None
Reliever	2.0 - Aug. 22, 1998 at NYM
Walks:	
Starter	None
Reliever	2 - Sep. 6, 1998 vs. HOU
Strikeouts:	
Starter	None
Reliever	Aug. 22, 1998 at NYM
	Sep. 23, 1998 at COL
Hits Allowed	3 - Aug. 25, 1998 vs. PIT
	3 - Sep. 11, 1998 at CIN
Runs Allowed	4 - Sep. 11, 1998 at CIN
ER Allowed	4 - Sep. 11, 1998 at CIN
HR Allowed	1 - Sep. 11, 1998 at CIN
Low Hit CG	None
Last Win	None
Last Save	None
Last CG	None
Last ShO	None
Last Start	None
Last Relief App.	None

FIELDING
MICHALAK, Chris—P

Year	PCT	G	PO	A	E	TC	DP
1998	.000	5	0	0	0	0	0

CHRIS MICHALAK DETAILED PITCHING

	2000								CAREER						
	ERA	W-L-Sv	G	IP	H	ER	BB	SO	ERA	W-L-Sv	G	IP	H	ER	BB	SO
Total	–	–	–	–	–	–	–	–	11.81	0-0-0	5	5.1	9	7	4	5
REL	–	–	–	–	–	–	–	–	11.81	0-0-0	5	5.1	9	7	4	5
Home	–	–	–	–	–	–	–	–	10.80	0-0-0	2	1.2	4	2	3	1
Away	–	–	–	–	–	–	–	–	12.27	0-0-0	3	3.2	5	5	1	4
August	–	–	–	–	–	–	–	–	10.13	0-0-0	2	2.2	4	3	1	3
September	–	–	–	–	–	–	–	–	13.50	0-0-0	3	2.2	5	4	3	2
vs. Cin	–	–	–	–	–	–	–	–	36.00	0-0-0	1	1.0	3	4	1	0
vs. Col	–	–	–	–	–	–	–	–	0.00	0-0-0	1	0.2	1	0	0	2
vs. Hou	–	–	–	–	–	–	–	–	0.00	0-0-0	1	1.0	1	0	2	0
vs. NYM	–	–	–	–	–	–	–	–	4.50	0-0-0	1	2.0	1	1	0	2
vs. Pit	–	–	–	–	–	–	–	–	27.00	0-0-0	1	0.2	3	2	1	1
Post-All Star	–	–	–	–	–	–	–	–	11.81	0-0-0	5	5.1	9	7	4	5

CHRIS MICHALAK PITCHING AT ML PARKS

Park	ERA	W-L-Sv	SvO	G	GS	IP	H	R	ER	HR	BB	SO
Cinergy Field	36.00	0-0-0	0	1	0	1.0	3	4	4	1	1	0
Shea Stadium	4.50	0-0-0	0	1	0	2.0	1	1	1	0	0	2
Coors Field	0.00	0-0-0	0	1	0	0.2	1	0	0	0	0	2
BankOne Ballpark	10.80	0-0-0	0	2	0	1.2	4	2	2	0	3	1

Izzy
MOLINA
CATCHER

57

BIRTHDATE	June 3, 1971
OPENING DAY AGE	29
BIRTHPLACE	New York, NY
RESIDENCE	Miami, FL
BATS/THROWS	R/R
HEIGHT/WEIGHT	6-1/200
CONTRACT STATUS	signed thru 2001
M.L. SERVICE	0.170

PERSONAL: Islay Molina... Married, wife's name is Kristen... One daughter, Sydney (5)... Graduated from Columbus High School in Miami... Turned down a scholarship offer from the University of Miami... Signed by Tony Arias.

LAST SEASON: Appeared in 90 games with Omaha, the triple-A affiliate of the Kansas City Royals... Hit .235 with ten home runs and 36 RBI... June was his top month hitting .354 in 19 games with two home runs and nine RBI... Hit in a season high nine straight games from June 22 to July 4... Hit .269 at home with five home runs and on the road hit .205 with five home runs... Hit .237 against left-handed pitching and .234 against right-handed pitching.

PROFESSIONAL CAREER: 1990: Hit .339 in 39 games with Scottsdale of the Arizona League... **1991:** Moved up to Madison where he hit .282 in 95 games with three home runs and 45 RBI... Named Madison's franchise winner of the 1991 Dave Stewart Community Service Award for his commitment to the community and his efforts to be a socially responsible athlete... **1992:** Named to the post-season California League All-Star team after driving in a career-high 75 runs for Reno and throwing out 40 percent (84-of-211) of potential base stealers... With Tacoma appeared in ten games, making nine starts... **1993:** Named the catcher on the California League post-season All-Star team for the second straight season... Hit for the cycle vs. Stockton on April 25, driving in eight runs... Threw out 42% (77 of 181) of would be base stealers... **1994:** Hit .216 in 116 games with Huntsville... Had eight home runs and 50 RBI... **1995:** Hit .259 with eight home runs and 26 RBI in 83 games with Huntsville... Fractured hit right thumb and was on the disabled list for the month of June... Led Southern League catchers in assists (74) and double plays (11)... Threw out 39.4% of base-runners (39 of 99)... Was promoted to Edmonton (AAA) where he played in two games (1-6)... **1996:** Spent his first full season in triple-A and made his ML debut with Oakland in August... Played in 98 games with Edmonton and hit .263 with 12 home runs and 56 RBI... Threw out 30 of 85 attempted base-stealers (35.3%)... Was promoted to Oakland on August 15 and made his ML debut that night against Baltimore, was 0-1 as a pinch-hitter... Made his first start on August 16 against the Orioles and collected his first ML hit against Rick Krivda... First RBI came on September 14 at Cleveland (gm #2)... **1997:** Split the season between Oakland and Edmonton (AAA)... Made the A's Opening Day roster and started 17 of the club's first 29 games behind the plate... Had three separate stints with Oakland... Struggled at the plate, hitting just .158, when he was optioned to Edmonton on May 5... Was re-called to Oakland on July 22 where he appeared in 14 games, seven starts, and hit .200 prior to returning to Edmonton on August 22... Returned on September 1 and that month hit .265 with three home runs and six RBI in 13 games... Hit his first ML HR on September 5, a game winning shot in the bottom of the 13th against Kansas City... **1998:** Made the Oakland A's Opening Day roster but appeared in just one game as a defensive replacement before being designated for assignment on April 8... Was outrighted to Triple-A Edmonton... Returned to Oakland on June 17 and appeared in five games before being designated for assignment again on June 27... Only big league hit of the season was a pinch-hit single against San Francisco on June 22... With Edmonton hit .241 in 86 games with eight home runs and 38 RBI... **1999:** Attended spring training with the Arizona Diamondbacks but spent the entire season with the World Champion New York Yankees Triple-A affiliate in Columbus... Was traded on March 30 in a deal that sent RHP Darren Holmes to Arizona... With Columbus hit .246 clip with four home runs and 51 RBI in 97 games for the Clippers in the International League.

IZZY MOLINA

Year	Club & League	AVG	G	AB	R	H	TB	2B	3B	HR	RBI	SH-SF	HP	BB-IBB	SO	SB-CS	GIDP	SLG	OBP
1990	Athletics (Ariz)	.339	39	127	20	43	59	12	2	0	18	1-3	2	9-1	22	5-0	0	.465	.383
1991	Madison (Mid)	.282	95	316	35	89	116	16	1	3	45	1-4	6	15-1	38	6-4	9	.367	.323
1992	Reno (Cal)	.259	116	436	71	113	164	17	2	10	75	7-6	7	39-0	57	8-7	20	.376	.326
1992	Tacoma (PCL)	.194	10	36	3	7	9	0	1	0	5	0-0	0	2-0	6	1-0	1	.250	.237
1993	Modesto (Cal)	.261	125	444	61	116	170	26	5	6	69	4-11	3	44-0	85	2-8	11	.383	.325
1994	Huntsville (Sou)	.216	116	388	31	84	129	17	2	8	50	7-7	5	16-0	47	5-1	10	.332	.252
1995	Edmonton (PCL)	.167	2	6	0	1	1	0	0	0	0	0-0	0	0-0	2	0-0	0	.167	.167
1995	Huntsville (Sou)	.259	83	301	38	78	120	16	1	8	26	0-2	8	26-0	62	3-4	6	.399	.332
1996	Edmonton (PCL)	.263	98	342	45	90	144	12	3	12	56	5-2	3	25-4	55	2-5	9	.421	.317
1996	OAKLAND (AL)	.200	14	25	0	5	7	2	0	0	1	0-0	0	1-0	3	0-0	0	.280	.231
1997	OAKLAND (AL)	.198	48	111	6	22	36	3	1	3	7	1-0	0	3-0	17	0-0	1	.324	.219
1997	Edmonton (PCL)	.261	61	218	33	57	92	11	3	6	34	1-0	0	12-0	27	2-0	4	.422	.300
1998	Edmonton (PCL)	.241	86	303	29	73	116	15	2	8	38	1-3	4	17-0	60	3-0	16	.383	.287
1998	OAKLAND (AL)	.500	6	2	1	1	1	0	0	0	0	0-0	0	0-0	0	0-0	0	.500	.500
1999	Columbus (Int)	.246	97	338	44	83	113	16	1	4	51	2-6	1	18-0	47	4-2	9	.334	.281
2000	Omaha (PCL)	.235	90	311	39	73	114	9	1	10	36	0-5	2	14-0	55	5-4	6	.367	.268
Minor Totals		.254	1018	3566	449	907	1347	167	24	75	503	29-49	41	237-6	563	46-35	101	.378	.304
MAJOR TOTALS		.203	68	138	7	28	44	5	1	3	8	1-0	0	4-0	20	0-0	1	.319	.225

HOME RUN BREAKDOWN

			MEN ON				ONE GAME							
Total	H	A	0	1	2	3	2	3	4	LO	XN	IP	PH	RHP	LHP
3	1	2	3	0	0	0	0	0	0	0	1	0	0	2	1

MOLINA — TRANSACTIONS

- Selected by the Oakland Athletics in 22nd round of the June 1990 First Year Player Draft.
- On disabled list June 1-30, 1995.
- Signed by the Arizona Diamondbacks on October 26, 1998.
- Traded to the New York Yankees along with RHP Ben Ford in exchange for RHP Darren Holmes on March 30, 1999.
- Signed by the Kansas City Royals on November 16, 1999.
- On disabled list April 6-13, 2000.
- Signed by the Toronto Blue Jays, December 13, 2000.

CAREER HIGHS — MOLINA, Izzy

GAME:

ML Debut	Aug. 15, 1996 at BAL
Runs	1 - 7 times, last Jun. 22, 1998 vs. SF
Hits	3 - Sep. 5, 1997 at KC
Doubles	1 - 5 times, last Sep. 22, 1997 vs. SEA
Home Runs	1 - Sep. 5, 1997 at KC
	1 - Sep. 20, 1997 vs. SEA
	1 - Sep. 28, 1997 at SEA
RBI	2 - Sep. 5, 1997 at KC
	2 - Sep. 7, 1997 at KC
Stolen Bases	None
Last ML Home Run	Sep. 28, 1997 at SEA
Longest Hitting Streak	4 - Aug. 16-25, 1996
	4 - Aug. 20-Sep. 7, 1997

FIELDING

MOLINA, Izzy—C

Year	PCT	G	PO	A	E	TC	DP
1996	1.000	12	31	1	0	32	1
1997	.992	48	218	17	2	237	1
1998	1.000	5	8	1	0	9	0
Total	.993	65	257	19	2	278	2

IZZY MOLINA DETAILED HITTING

	2000									CAREER								
	Avg	AB	H	HR	RBI	BB	SO	OBP	SLG	Avg	AB	H	HR	RBI	BB	SO	OBP	SLG
Total	–	–	–	–	–	–	–	–	–	.203	138	28	3	8	4	20	.225	.319
vs. Left	–	–	–	–	–	–	–	–	–	.194	67	13	1	2	1	6	.206	.284
vs. Right	–	–	–	–	–	–	–	–	–	.211	71	15	2	6	3	14	.243	.352
Home	–	–	–	–	–	–	–	–	–	.175	63	11	1	2	2	11	.200	.286
Away	–	–	–	–	–	–	–	–	–	.227	75	17	2	6	2	9	.247	.347
April	–	–	–	–	–	–	–	–	–	.160	50	8	0	1	1	6	.176	.180
May	–	–	–	–	–	–	–	–	–	.143	7	1	0	0	0	1	.143	.143
June	–	–	–	–	–	–	–	–	–	.500	2	1	0	0	0	0	.500	.500
July	–	–	–	–	–	–	–	–	–	.200	10	2	0	0	1	2	.273	.200
August	–	–	–	–	–	–	–	–	–	.231	26	6	0	0	1	5	.259	.346
September	–	–	–	–	–	–	–	–	–	.233	43	10	3	7	1	6	.250	.512
Scoring Posn	–	–	–	–	–	–	–	–	–	.240	25	6	0	5	2	5	.296	.320
DH	–	–	–	–	–	–	–	–	–	.000	3	0	0	0	0	0	.000	.000
PH	–	–	–	–	–	–	–	–	–	.400	5	2	0	0	0	0	.400	.400
vs. Ana	–	–	–	–	–	–	–	–	–	.000	2	0	0	0	0	0	.000	.000
vs. Bal	–	–	–	–	–	–	–	–	–	.130	23	3	0	0	1	4	.167	.217
vs. Bos	–	–	–	–	–	–	–	–	–	.182	22	4	0	0	1	2	.217	.227
vs. CWS	–	–	–	–	–	–	–	–	–	.000	0	0	0	0	0	0	.000	.000
vs. Cle	–	–	–	–	–	–	–	–	–	.111	9	1	0	1	0	1	.111	.222
vs. Det	–	–	–	–	–	–	–	–	–	.111	9	1	0	0	1	1	.200	.111
vs. KC	–	–	–	–	–	–	–	–	–	.400	15	6	1	4	0	4	.400	.667
vs. Mil	–	–	–	–	–	–	–	–	–	.000	2	0	0	0	0	1	.000	.000
vs. Min	–	–	–	–	–	–	–	–	–	.077	13	1	0	0	0	2	.077	.154
vs. NYY	–	–	–	–	–	–	–	–	–	.250	20	5	0	1	0	2	.250	.250
vs. Sea	–	–	–	–	–	–	–	–	–	.375	8	3	2	2	1	0	.444	1.250
vs. Tex	–	–	–	–	–	–	–	–	–	.000	3	0	0	0	0	0	.000	.000
vs. Tor	–	–	–	–	–	–	–	–	–	.286	7	2	0	0	0	2	.286	.286
vs. SF	–	–	–	–	–	–	–	–	–	.400	5	2	0	0	0	1	.400	.400
Pre-All Star	–	–	–	–	–	–	–	–	–	.169	59	10	0	1	1	7	.183	.186
Post-All Star	–	–	–	–	–	–	–	–	–	.228	79	18	3	7	3	13	.256	.418

IZZY MOLINA HITTING AT ML PARKS

Park	Avg	G	AB	R	H	2B	3B	HR	RBI	SB	CS	BB	SO	OBP	Slg
Camden Yards	.100	6	10	0	1	0	0	0	0	0	0	0	1	.100	.100
Fenway Park	.200	4	10	0	2	1	0	0	0	0	0	1	0	.273	.300
Edison Field	.000	2	2	0	0	0	0	0	0	0	0	0	0	.000	.000
Jacobs Field	.111	4	9	0	1	1	0	0	1	0	0	0	1	.111	.222
Tiger Stadium	.167	2	6	1	1	0	0	0	0	0	0	1	1	.286	.167
Kauffman Stadium	.556	2	9	1	5	1	0	1	4	0	0	0	2	.556	1.000
County Stadium	.000	1	0	0	0	0	0	0	0	0	0	0	0	.000	.000
Metrodome	.000	2	7	0	0	0	0	0	0	0	0	0	1	.000	.000
Yankee Stadium	.308	6	13	0	4	0	0	0	0	0	0	0	1	.308	.308
Oakland-Alameda	.175	33	63	2	11	2	1	1	2	0	0	2	11	.200	.286
Kingdome	.500	2	2	1	1	0	0	1	1	0	0	0	0	.500	2.000
Arlington	.000	1	0	0	0	0	0	0	0	0	0	0	0	.000	.000
SkyDome	.286	2	7	2	2	0	0	0	0	0	0	0	2	.286	.286
3 Com Park	.000	1	0	0	0	0	0	0	0	0	0	0	0	.000	.000

Raul
MONDESI
OUTFIELDER

43

BIRTHDATE	March 2, 1971
OPENING DAY AGE	30
BIRTHPLACE	San Cristobal, DR
RESIDENCE	San Cristobal, DR
BATS/THROWS	R/R
HEIGHT/WEIGHT	5-11/230
CONTRACT STATUS	signed thru 2003
M.L. SERVICE	7.055

PERSONAL: Raul Mondesi (MON-de-see)... Married, he and wife Ada have three children, Raul Jr. (9/28/92), Raul Adalberto (8/12/96) and Kisha Rauleiny (12/15/97)... Played baseball and basketball at Liceo Manual Maria Valencia High School in the Dominican Republic... Lists former major league player George Bell as his boyhood idol... Supplies uniforms and baseball equipment for the Raul Mondesi League in the Dominican Republic for approximately 500 children from the ages of six to 14... Also is a sponsor of softball and basketball leagues... Signed by the Dodgers Ralph Avila.

LAST SEASON: In his first season with Toronto hit .271 with 22 doubles, two triples, 24 home runs and 67 RBI in 96 games despite being placed on the 60-day disabled list...

Had right elbow surgery on August 14 performed in Coral Gables, Florida by Dr John Uribe, consulting orthopedic surgeon to the Miami Dolphins... Appeared in 95 games and scored 78 runs before being placed on the disabled list on July 22... Was on pace to score a career high 129 runs — career high is 98 in 1996 & 1999 and the Blue Jay club record for a season is 134... Led the club in spring training with 16 RBI while batting .236 with six home runs and seven stolen bases... Had a season high ten game hit streak from April 11 to 21... Scored a run in 11 straight games from April 11 to April 22... Was ejected on April 18 by HP umpire Al Clark... Posted two multi-HR games, May 9 vs Baltimore, June 18 at Boston, and now has 16 career multi-HR games... In May led the club with a 12 stolen bases... Stole 22 bases with only six caught stealing, had four steals of third base...

Stole two bases in a game on three occasions to match his career high, now accomplished 15 times... June was his top month for average (.280), home runs (8) and RBI (22)... Had 10 putouts on July 8 at Montreal to tie the club mark for most putouts by an outfielder in a nine inning game, first done by Jose Cruz on October 1, 1999... In a three game series at Montreal from July 7-9 he homered and drove in three runs in each game... Was activated from the disabled list on September 21... First action came on September 23, was 1-5 but suffered a sprained right ankle which kept him out of action the rest of the season... Was 0-9 with the bases loaded... Favorite opponent was Boston as he hit .356 with four home runs, 11 RBI and four stolen bases in 11 games... Hit .311 against LHP and .261 against RHP... 24HR's — 20 vs RHP, 4 vs LHP, 10 at Home, 14 on Road... With an 0-0 count hit .352 (25-71)... After 1-0 count was a .272 hitter while after a 0-1 count hit only .236... Had a .967 fielding percentage with five outfield assists.

PROFESSIONAL CAREER: 1988: Made his professional debut with Santo Domingo and hit .222 with two home runs and 44 RBI... **1989:** Led the Dominican Summer League Champion Santo Dominican Dodgers with 15 doubles and was third with 32 runs scored... **1990:** Selected to the Pioneer League (A) All-Star Team after batting .303 with eight home runs and 31 RBI to lead Great Falls to the league championship... Stole a team high 30 bases in 44 games... **1991:** Hit a combined .277 with eight home runs and 39 RBI in 83 games at three different levels... Named as the outfielder with the best arm in the California League and the fifth best prospect in the league by Baseball America... Selected as one of the top 50 minor league players by the Sporting News... Was on the disabled list for nearly two months with a knee injury... **1992:** Split the season between Albuquerque- AAA and San Antonio- AA... Opened the season in AAA and hit .312 in 35 games with four home runs and 15 RBI... Appeared in 18 games with San Antonio and hit .265 with two home runs and 14 RBI before being sidelined with a wrist injury... Had surgery performed by Dr. Norm Zemel on his fractured left wrist on July 1 at Centinela Hospital Medical Center in Los Angeles... Returned to play seven games in July and August before having surgery on his left knee by Dr. Ralph Gambardella on August 25 at the Centinela Hospital Medical Center to repair a medial meniscus tear... Had a combined 14 outfield assists and eight errors in 142 total chances... Named the Top Prospect in the Texas League by Baseball America, who also tabbed him as the 21st best overall prospect and the 7th best outfielder in the minor leagues... **1993:** Split the season between the Los Angeles Dodgers and Albuquerque... Opened the season in AAA and was recalled to Los Angeles on July 18... Made his ML debut on July 19 vs Philadelphia and singled as a pinch-hitter in the seventh inning against the Phillies David West... Made first ML start on July 20 vs Philadelphia and was 0-3... Delivered his first multi-hit game on July 23 vs New York, was 2-4 with two runs scored and his first ML stolen base... First ML home run came on July 31 against the Cubs Bob Scanlon to cap a five run 13th inning in a 7-2 victory... Started 20 games for the Dodgers... Threw out two runners on September 15 at San Diego... Joined Dodgers Friendship Series and traveled to Taipei, Taiwan and Fukuoka, Japan... In 110 games with Albuquerque hit .280 with 22 doubles, seven triples, 12 home runs and 65 RBI... **1994:** Named the NL Rookie of the Year after hitting .306 with 16 home runs, 56 RBI, 63 runs, 27 doubles and eight triples in the strike shortened season... Was the third straight Dodger to win the award... Was the 11th unanimous selection, seventh in the NL and second consecutive, in the 45 year history of Rookie of the Year Award... Was the first player from the Dominican Republic to win the award in the NL... Also named NL Rookie of the Year by Baseball Weekly & Baseball America... Led the Dodgers in hits (133), doubles and at bats (434)... Led the majors with 16 outfield assists... Started the season hitless in four games and then did not go more than two games without a hit the rest of the season... Was tied for third in the NL with eight triples, had two on August 5 at Colorado... Played winter ball in the Dominican Republic with Escogido and hit .317 with seven HR and 14 RBI in 31 games including his first two at bats when he received standing ovations and doubled and homered... **1995:** Hit .285 with 26 home runs,

88 RBI and 27 stolen bases... Was the first Dodger since Kirk Gibson in 1988 to post 20 HR and 20 SB in the same season... Earned his first Rawlings Gold Glove Award... Led the majors for the second straight season with 16 outfield assists... Selected to his first All-Star Game in Texas where he played right field but did not have an at bat... Was the NL Player of the Week from May 12-19 after hitting .361 (13-36) with four home runs, 10 RBI and seven runs scored... Stole 17 consecutive bases to start the season until being thrown out on July 16 by Florida's Charles Johnson... First career ejection came on August 10 vs St. Louis for arguing a called third strike... Hit his first career grand slam on August 15 vs. Chicago against Steve Trachsel in 7-5 win... Left game on September 29 with a sprained right knee... September 30 hit a game winning two-run home run off Doug Bochtler in San Francisco to clinch the NL Western Division for the Dodgers... **1996:** Set a then Dodger record (which he broke in 1997) of 71 extra base hits surpassing the old mark of 66 held by Steve Garvey (1978) and Pedro Guerrero (1983)... Was tied for fifth in the NL with 11 outfield assists, tied for sixth with 40 doubles, tied for eighth with seven triples and 10th with 188 hits... Reached the Loge Level with a home run on April 12 against the Marlins John Burkett, was the fifth player ever to do so joining Frank Howard, Dave Kingman, Dave Parker and Nick Esasky... Missed four games from June 21- 25 with a contusion to his left heel, had started first 73 games of the season... On June 30 at Colorado was 4-6 with two home runs, six RBI, three runs scored and a triple... July 14 broke up San Francisco Will VanLandingham's no-hitter with an eighth inning single... Hit safely in seven straight at bats on two occasions, June 5-6 and September 9-10... Named as having the best outfield arm in the majors in Baseball America's annual Best Tools survey of league managers... **1997:** Set career highs in batting .310, hits (191) and doubles (42) and then career highs of 30 home runs, 32 stolen bases... Became the first Dodger player in both Brooklyn and Los Angeles history to hit 30 home runs and steal 30 bases in the same season... Only three other players posted 30/30 season that season; Larry Walker, Barry Bonds and Jeff Bagwell... Collected his second Rawlings Gold Glove Award after committing four errors in 352 total chances for a .989 fielding percentage... Was tied for seventh in the NL with 10 outfield assists... Was the first outfielder from the Dominican Republic to win a Gold Glove since Cincinnati's Cesar Geronimo in 1977... Became just the second Dodger along with Pedro Guerrero to post two 20/20 seasons... Joined Mike Piazza (40), Todd Zeile (31) and Eric Karros (31) to become the second foursome in club history and the fifth in major league history to hit 30 or more home runs in a season... Was the second time for the Dodgers, the other three times were all by Colorado... Was third in NL with 77 extra-base hits, tied for fourth with 191 hits, fifth in doubles, sixth with 333 total bases... Seventh with 53 multi-hit games, ninth in batting, tied for ninth in stolen bases and was tenth in slugging percentage at .541... The 77 extra-base hits were a career high and a Dodger club record... Had a 14 game hit streak from July 12- 25... Also posted two 11 game hit streaks... On June 2 at Houston left the game after spraining his left shoulder and left pinky finger when he slid head first back into third base... Wore a brace on his left hand the rest of the season and was removed from the game on June 28 with shoulder pain... Stole 15 straight bases from June 12 to August 12... In the second half of the season hit .326 (95-291) with 13 home runs and 39 RBI in 74 games... In his final 57 games of the season hit .344 (76-221)... **1998:** Hit .279 in 148 games with 26 doubles, five triples, 30 home runs, 90 RBI and 16 stolen bases... His 90 RBI were a then career high as were his 30 home runs (also in 1997)... Led the Dodgers in games, at-bats (590), runs (85), hits (162), total bases (288), multi-hit games (41), doubles, triples, home runs and RBI... Was the third straight season to lead the Dodgers in extra-base hits... Started 147 games in the outfield and saw 94 starts in center field after a seven player trade with the Florida Marlins on May 15... Was tied for the team lead with six outfield assists, four as a center fielder... On April 12 hit a game-winning two run, two out home run against the Astro's Billy Wagner... Collected first career five hit game on April 27 vs Milwaukee, was 5-6 with a double, home run and an RBI in a 12 inning game... From June 27 to July 23 hit .375 (36-96) in 23 games

which included a season high 11 game hit streak from June 27 to July 11... Was the NL Player of the Week for the week ending July 5, hit .462 (12-26) in six games with two home runs, seven RBI, eight runs and 26 total bases... Missed all or parts of six games from July 30 to August 7 with lower back stiffness... Also missed three games from September 5- 7 with the same injury... Hit .385 (5-13) with 12RBI when the bases were loaded including his second career grand slam on May 31 vs. Cincinnati's Mike Remlinger... 15 of 30 home runs tied the game or gave the Dodgers the lead... Posted two multi-HR games, hit two on May 13 vs Philadelphia & August 3 at New York Mets... Hit .289 vs RHP with 24 HR & .241 vs LHP with six HR... Hit .253 at home with 13 home runs but on the road hit .304 with 17 home runs... **1999:** Hit only .253 but posted career highs with 33 home runs, 99 RBI, 71 walks and 36 stolen bases... Was his second career 30/30 season making him one of eight ML players to post multiple 30/30 seasons (list in career notes)... He and Jeff Bagwell were the only 30/30 players in the majors in 1999... Made his sixth straight opening day start for the Dodgers, hit two home runs and tied career high with six RBI in a 8-6 win over Arizona... His second homer was only the 26th Opening Day extra inning home run in baseball history... Was the NL Player of the Week from April 5 to 11 after hitting .381 (8-21) with four HR and 10 RBI... Led the majors

with 18 home runs through May 28... Hit one homerun over 39 games from May 29 to July 16 (152 at bats)... Hit just .211 in June and .198 in July as the Dodgers posted a 19-35 record during those two months... Hit the final home run in the history of Candlestick/3 Com Park on September 30 against the Giants Mark Gardner - was also his 1,000 career hit... Had five multiple home run games... Was the toughest player in the NL to get to hit in to a double play, done three times in 601 at bats... Collected seven outfield assists.

POST SEASON EXPERIENCE: 1995: Hit .222 with an RBI in three games against the Cincinnati Reds in the Division Series... **1996:** Faced the Atlanta Braves in the Division Series and hit .182 (2-11) with an RBI.

CAREER NOTES: Is one of only eight players in ML history to record multiple 30/30 seasons along with Willie Mays (1956-57), Bobby Bonds (1969, 1973, 1975, 1977-78), Howard Johnson (1987, 1989, 1991), Ron Gant (1990-91), Barry Bonds (1990, 1992, 1995-97), Sammy Sosa (1993, 1995) and Jeff Bagwell (1997, 1999)... Has one sacrifice in 3,789 at bats since 1994... Among Dodgers All-Time lists in slugging % (.504), home runs (163), extra-base hits (390), stolen bases (140), triples (37), doubles (190), total bases (1,757) and RBI (518)... Has hit 20 or more home runs in six straight seasons and now has 187 for his career.

RAUL MONDESI

Year	Club & League	AVG	G	AB	R	H	TB	2B	3B	HR	RBI	SH-SF	HP	BB-IBB	SO	SB-CS	GIDP	SLG	OBP
1988	Dodgers (DSL)	.222	36	117	21	26	47	10	1	2	44	0-0	0	23-0	36	4-0	0	.000	.000
1989	Dodgers (DSL)	.276	46	156	32	43	0	15	3	2	27	0-0	0	16-0	26	8-0	0	.000	.000
1990	Great Falls (Pio)	.303	44	175	35	53	95	10	4	8	31	0-1	2	11-1	30	30-7	0	.543	.349
1991	Bakersfield (Cal)	.283	28	106	23	30	50	7	2	3	13	0-1	3	5-1	21	9-4	1	.472	.330
1991	San Antonio (Tex)	.272	53	213	32	58	94	11	5	5	26	0-3	4	8-0	47	8-3	1	.441	.307
1991	Albuquerque (PCL)	.333	2	9	3	3	5	0	1	0	0	0-0	0	0-0	1	1-0	0	.556	.333
1992	Albuquerque (PCL)	.312	35	138	23	43	73	4	7	4	15	0-0	1	9-4	35	2-3	0	.529	.358
1992	San Antonio (Tex)	.265	18	68	8	18	30	2	2	2	14	0-3	0	1-0	24	3-2	1	.441	.264
1993	Albuquerque (PCL)	.280	110	425	65	119	191	22	7	12	65	0-5	2	18-4	85	13-10	4	.449	.309
1993	LOS ANGELES (NL)	.291	42	86	13	25	42	3	1	4	10	1-0	0	4-0	16	4-1	1	.488	.322
1994	LOS ANGELES (NL)	.306	112	434	63	133	224	27	8	16	56	0-2	2	16-5	78	11-8	9	.516	.333
1995	LOS ANGELES (NL)	.285	139	536	91	153	266	23	6	26	88	0-7	4	33-4	96	27-4	7	.496	.328
1996	LOS ANGELES (NL)	.297	157	634	98	188	314	40	7	24	88	0-2	5	32-9	122	14-7	6	.495	.334
1997	LOS ANGELES (NL)	.310	159	616	95	191	333	42	5	30	87	1-3	6	44-7	105	32-15	11	.541	.360
1998	LOS ANGELES (NL)	.279	148	580	85	162	288	26	5	30	90	0-4	3	30-4	112	16-10	8	.497	.316
1999	LOS ANGELES (NL)	.253	159	601	98	152	290	29	5	33	99	0-5	3	71-6	134	36-9	3	.483	.332
2000	TORONTO (AL)	.271	96	388	78	105	203	22	2	24	67	0-3	3	32-0	73	22-6	8	.523	.329
Minor Totals		.279	372	1407	242	393	585	81	32	38	235	0-13	12	91-10	305	78-29	7	.416	.326
NL TOTALS		.288	916	3487	543	1004	1757	190	37	163	518	2-23	23	230-35	663	140-54	45	.504	.334
MAJOR TOTALS		.286	1012	3875	621	1109	1960	212	39	187	585	2-26	26	262-35	736	162-60	53	.506	.333

DIVISION SERIES RECORD

Year	Club & League	AVG	G	AB	R	H	TB	2B	3B	HR	RBI	SH-SF	HP	BB-IBB	SO	SB-CS	GIDP	SLG	OBP
1995	LOS ANGELES (NL)	.222	3	9	0	2	2	0	0	0	1	0-0	1	0-0	2	0-0	0	.222	.300
1996	LOS ANGELES (NL)	.182	3	11	0	2	4	2	0	0	1	0-0	0	0-0	4	0-0	0	.364	.182
DIVISION TOTALS		.200	6	20	0	4	6	2	0	0	2	0-0	1	0-0	6	0-0	0	.300	.238

ALL-STAR GAME RECORD

Year	Club & League	AVG	G	AB	R	H	TB	2B	3B	HR	RBI	SH-SF	HP	BB-IBB	SO	SB-CS	GIDP	SLG	OBP
1995	NL at TEX	.000	1	0	0	0	0	0	0	0	0	0-0	0	0-0	0	0-0	0	.000	.000

HOME RUN BREAKDOWN

Total	H	A		MEN ON				ONE GAME			LO	XN	IP	PH	RHP	LHP
			0	1	2	3	2	3	4						
187	93	94	93	63	29	2	16	0	0	0	5	0	0	149	38

MONDESI — TRANSACTIONS

- Signed as non-drafted free agent by the Los Angeles Dodgers on June 6, 1988.
- On disabled list (knee) May 8-July 5, 1991.
- On disabled list (wrist injury) May 8-16, 1992.
- On disabled list June 2-16, 1992.
- On disabled list (fractured left wrist) June 24-August 10, 1992.
- Traded to the Toronto Blue Jays along with LHP Pedro Borbon in exchange for OF Shawn Green and IF Jorge Nunez on November 8, 1999.
- On disabled list (bone chips, right elbow) July 22-September 19, 2000.

CAREER HIGHS — MONDESI, Raul

SEASON:		GAME:	
Games	159 - 1997, 1999	ML Debut	Jul. 19, 1993 vs. PHI
Avg.	.310 - 1997	Runs	4 - Apr. 17, 1994 at PIT
Runs	98 - 1996, 1999		4 - Jul. 9, 2000 at MON
Hits	191 - 1997	Hits	5 - Apr. 27, 1998 vs. MIL
Doubles	42 - 1997	Doubles	2 - 14 times, last Apr. 20, 2000 at ANA
Home Runs	33 - 1999	Home Runs	2 - 16 times, last Jun. 18, 2000 at BOS
RBI	99 - 1999	RBI	6 - Aug. 1, 1995 at COL
Walks	71 - 1999		6 - Jun. 29, 1996 at COL
Strikeouts	134 - 1999		6 - Apr. 5, 1999 vs. ARI
Stolen Bases	36 - 1999	Stolen Bases	2 - 15 times, last Jun. 16, 2000 at BOS
Longest Hitting Streak	15G - Jun. 13-27, 1995	Last ML Home Run	Jul. 18, 2000 vs. NYM
Longest Hitless Streak	25AB - Apr. 21-29, 2000		
Multi HR Games	5 - 1999		

FIELDING
MONDESI, Raul—OF

Year	PCT	G	PO	A	E	TC	DP
1993 (NL)	.951	40	55	3	3	61	1
1994 (NL)	.965	112	206	16	8	230	1
1995 (NL)	.980	138	282	16	6	304	3
1996 (NL)	.967	157	337	11	12	360	4
1997 (NL)	.989	159	338	10	4	352	0
1998 (NL)	.980	148	284	6	6	296	1
1999 (NL)	.982	158	315	7	6	328	5
2000 (AL)	.967	96	203	5	7	215	3
Total	.976	1008	2020	74	52	2146	18

RAUL MONDESI DETAILED HITTING

	2000									CAREER								
	Avg	AB	H	HR	RBI	BB	SO	OBP	SLG	Avg	AB	H	HR	RBI	BB	SO	OBP	SLG
Total	.271	388	105	24	67	32	73	.329	.523	.286	3875	1109	187	585	262	736	.333	.506
vs. Left	.311	74	23	4	11	7	13	.386	.541	.272	878	239	38	121	79	155	.334	.469
vs. Right	.261	314	82	20	56	25	60	.315	.519	.290	2997	870	149	464	183	581	.333	.517
Home	.252	202	51	10	28	15	35	.301	.485	.283	1881	532	93	276	125	352	.327	.498
Away	.290	186	54	14	39	17	38	.357	.565	.289	1994	577	94	309	137	384	.339	.513
March	–	–	–	–	–	–	–	–	–	.000	4	0	0	0	0	2	.000	.000
April	.272	103	28	4	13	5	24	.309	.485	.272	596	162	31	92	43	113	.324	.490
May	.276	116	32	6	14	9	22	.333	.500	.286	787	225	50	138	46	149	.328	.560
June	.280	93	26	8	22	9	16	.343	.581	.298	678	202	31	87	42	113	.342	.510
July	.254	71	18	6	18	9	9	.338	.563	.287	711	204	28	94	42	131	.327	.474
August	–	–	–	–	–	–	–	–	–	.274	584	160	23	88	48	129	.329	.467
September	.200	5	1	0	0	0	2	.200	.200	.306	497	152	23	82	41	97	.363	.529
October	–	–	–	–	–	–	–	–	–	.222	18	4	1	4	0	2	.222	.444
Scoring Posn	.229	96	22	8	43	10	17	.294	.521	.267	951	254	50	393	113	205	.339	.501
Bases Loaded	.000	9	0	0	3	0	1	.000	.000	.264	72	19	2	58	3	13	.268	.444
PH	.000	1	0	0	0	0	0	.000	.000	.385	13	5	0	0	0	2	.385	.538
vs. Ana	.387	31	12	3	7	1	5	.406	.806	.352	91	32	6	13	3	10	.372	.648
vs. Bal	.286	28	8	4	6	3	0	.355	.714	.286	28	8	4	6	3	0	.355	.714
vs. Bos	.356	45	16	4	11	3	5	.396	.667	.356	45	16	4	11	3	5	.396	.667
vs. CWS	.267	30	8	1	1	1	6	.290	.500	.267	30	8	1	1	1	6	.290	.500
vs. Cle	.226	31	7	2	7	4	9	.314	.484	.226	31	7	2	7	4	9	.314	.484
vs. Det	.273	33	9	1	6	2	5	.297	.455	.273	33	9	1	6	2	5	.297	.455
vs. KC	.200	15	3	0	0	1	3	.250	.333	.200	15	3	0	0	1	3	.250	.333
vs. Mil	–	–	–	–	–	–	–	–	–	.339	56	19	2	8	5	6	.387	.518
vs. Min	.000	12	0	0	0	0	2	.000	.000	.000	12	0	0	0	0	2	.000	.000
vs. NYY	.167	18	3	0	2	1	6	.238	.278	.167	18	3	0	2	1	6	.238	.278
vs. Oak	.000	12	0	0	0	1	5	.077	.000	.313	48	15	0	5	5	11	.389	.375
vs. Sea	.357	14	5	1	3	1	2	.400	.643	.137	51	7	1	4	6	12	.224	.235
vs. TB	.241	29	7	2	4	6	8	.389	.483	.241	29	7	2	4	6	8	.389	.483
vs. Tex	.385	13	5	0	1	0	3	.385	.462	.375	56	21	4	12	2	9	.397	.804
vs. Ari	–	–	–	–	–	–	–	–	–	.269	93	25	6	19	10	18	.340	.495
vs. Atl	.333	12	4	1	3	2	1	.467	.667	.335	230	77	12	31	17	49	.385	.561
vs. ChC	–	–	–	–	–	–	–	–	–	.298	235	70	17	43	12	47	.331	.570
vs. Cin	–	–	–	–	–	–	–	–	–	.255	216	55	6	26	11	46	.290	.417
vs. Col	–	–	–	–	–	–	–	–	–	.320	281	90	14	51	21	53	.365	.577
vs. Fla	.133	15	2	1	4	0	5	.133	.333	.262	244	64	12	31	21	37	.326	.480
vs. Hou	–	–	–	–	–	–	–	–	–	.272	213	58	11	27	8	42	.302	.512
vs. Mon	.333	24	8	3	9	4	5	.429	.708	.302	268	81	11	50	17	51	.345	.511
vs. NYM	.214	14	3	1	2	1	3	.267	.429	.262	260	68	16	38	13	55	.302	.512
vs. Phi	.417	12	5	0	1	1	0	.462	.667	.250	280	70	14	46	17	51	.294	.454
vs. Pit	–	–	–	–	–	–	–	–	–	.298	238	71	14	47	17	40	.342	.538
vs. StL	–	–	–	–	–	–	–	–	–	.310	232	72	8	34	15	36	.365	.509
vs. SD	–	–	–	–	–	–	–	–	–	.255	267	68	9	33	19	53	.306	.423
vs. SF	–	–	–	–	–	–	–	–	–	.309	275	85	10	30	22	66	.365	.491
Pre-All Star	.278	345	96	23	63	29	67	.337	.545	.287	2280	655	122	356	144	417	.333	.522
Post-All Star	.209	43	9	1	4	3	6	.261	.349	.285	1595	454	65	229	118	319	.335	.483

RAUL MONDESI HITTING AT ML PARKS

Park	Avg	G	AB	R	H	2B	3B	HR	RBI	SB	CS	BB	SO	OBP	Slg
Camden Yards	.333	4	12	3	4	0	0	2	3	0	0	2	0	.429	.833
Fenway Park	.385	6	26	7	10	1	0	3	7	2	1	1	4	.407	.769
Edison Field	.348	10	46	8	16	2	0	2	5	0	0	0	7	.348	.522
Comiskey Park	.308	3	13	2	4	0	1	1	1	2	0	1	3	.357	.692
Jacobs Field	.231	3	13	3	3	1	0	0	2	0	1	1	4	.286	.308
County Stadium	.306	9	36	5	11	2	0	1	6	2	0	3	4	.350	.444
Yankee Stadium	.167	2	6	1	1	0	0	0	0	2	0	0	0	.286	.167
Oakland-Alameda	.290	8	31	4	9	0	1	0	1	2	1	3	9	.371	.355
Kingdome	.100	5	20	2	2	1	0	0	0	1	0	3	4	.217	.150
Arlington	.400	8	35	7	14	4	2	1	7	3	0	1	6	.417	.714
SkyDome	.252	49	202	36	51	15	1	10	28	8	4	15	35	.301	.485
Atlanta-Fulton	.271	13	48	3	13	0	1	2	5	2	0	1	10	.294	.438
Wrigley Field	.295	33	129	19	38	4	1	9	18	3	2	4	28	.313	.550
Cinergy Field	.209	31	110	12	23	4	2	2	10	3	1	4	29	.239	.336
Astrodome	.229	26	105	9	24	7	1	2	5	4	2	2	24	.243	.371
Dodger Stadium	.286	454	1679	250	481	89	10	83	248	76	33	110	317	.331	.500
Olympic Stadium	.248	34	133	24	33	8	3	5	26	4	0	8	27	.299	.466
Shea Stadium	.306	28	108	22	33	10	1	7	19	6	0	7	22	.361	.611
Veterans Stadium	.259	33	135	20	35	7	0	6	18	6	3	10	26	.315	.444
Three Rivers	.304	32	125	31	38	5	2	9	31	4	1	11	18	.357	.592
Busch Stadium	.314	30	121	23	38	11	2	4	17	4	1	7	21	.366	.537
Qualcomm Park	.280	36	132	18	37	5	0	6	21	6	3	13	23	.349	.455
3 Com Park	.288	40	153	28	44	8	2	4	19	5	1	15	34	.351	.444
Coors Field	.297	29	128	23	38	5	3	8	30	1	1	7	23	.333	.570
Pro Player Stadium	.279	35	136	26	38	6	2	9	21	4	0	10	23	.338	.551
Turner Field	.375	18	72	15	27	7	0	5	14	6	2	7	12	.438	.681
BankOne Ballpark	.255	12	47	6	12	2	0	3	9	1	0	8	9	.364	.489
Tropicana Field	.353	5	17	4	6	1	0	2	4	3	0	5	5	.522	.765
Mile High Stadium	.571	10	35	6	20	5	4	1	8	0	3	2	6	.595	1.029
Comerica Park	.273	6	22	4	6	2	0	0	2	2	0	1	3	.292	.364

RAUL MONDESI — MILESTONES

	DATE	OPP.	H/A	PITCHER	DESCRIPTION
HITS					
1	July 19, 1993	LA vs PHI	H	David West	Single - PH
1000	Sept. 30, 1999	LA vs SF	A	Mark Gardner	2R-HR
HR					
1	July 31, 1993	LA vs CHI	A	Bob Scanlon	2R-13th inn.
100	Sept. 28, 1997	LA vs COL	A	Jeff McCurry	Solo, 30HR/30SB
RBI					
1	July 31, 1993	LA vs CHI	A	Bob Scanlan	2R-13th inn.
SB					
1	July 23, 1991	LA vs NY	H	Frank Tanana	2nd
				Catcher-Todd Hundley	
GM					
1	July 19, 1993	LA vs PHI	H		1-2, PH-RF
500	May 29, 1997	LA vs STL	A		3-4, Starting RF
MULTI HR (16)					
2	April 25, 1995	LA vs FLA	A	John Burkett	2R
				John Johnstone	2R
2	August 1, 1995	LA vs COL	A	Mark Thompson	2R, 2R
2	Sept. 2, 1995	LA vs MON	H	Kirk Rueter	2R
				Jose DeLeon	2R
2	June 30, 1996	LA vs COL	A	Mark Thompson	Solo
				Bruce Ruffin	2R
2	June 11, 1997	LA vs HOU	H	Mike Hampton	3R
				Ramon Garcia	2R
2	August 3, 1997	LA vs CHI	A	Steve Trachsel	Solo, Solo
2	Sept. 26, 1997	LA vs COL	A	Jamey Wright	Solo
				Jeff McCurry	Solo
2	May 13, 1998	LA vs PHI	H	Tyler Green	Solo
				Ryan Nye	3R
2	August 3, 1998	LA vs NY	A	Hideo Nomo	Solo
				Greg McMichael	2R
2	April 5, 1999	LA vs ARI	H	Greg Olson	3R
				John Frascatore	2R
2	May 10, 1999	LA vs CHI	H	Steve Trachsel	2R, 2R
2	May 11, 1999	LA vs CHI	H	Kyle Farnsworth	2R
				Terry Adams	Solo
2	August 8, 1999	LA vs NY	A	Pat Mahomes	3R, 2R
2	Sept. 6, 1999	LA vs FLA	A	Brian Meadows	Solo
				Dennis Springer	2R
2	May 9, 2000	TOR vs BAL	H	Mike Mussina	1R, 1R
2	June 18, 2000	TOR vs BOS	A	Fassero, Cormier	3R, 1R
GRAND SLAMS (2)					
1	August 15, 1995	LA vs CHI	H	Steve Trachsel	
2	May 31, 1998	LA vs CIN	H	Mike Remlinger	

Mickey
MORANDINI
INFIELDER

BIRTHDATE	April 22, 1966
OPENING DAY AGE	34
BIRTHPLACE	Leechburg, PA
RESIDENCE	Chesterton, IN
BATS/THROWS	L/R
HEIGHT/WEIGHT	5-11/180
CONTRACT STATUS	signed thru 2001
M.L. SERVICE	10.034

12

PERSONAL: Micheal Robert Morandini... Mickey and his wife, Peg, have three children, Jordan (11/15/94), Griffin (5/18/97) and Braydon (12/01/00)... Graduated from Leechburg Area High School in 1984... Played college baseball at Indiana University... Won a gold medal as a member of the United States Olympic Team at the Seoul Games in 1988.

LAST SEASON: Hit .258 in 126 games between the Philadelphia Phillies and the Toronto Blue Jays... With Philadelphia hit .252 in 91 games with 22 RBI... Was ranked fourth in NL among second basemen in fielding percentage at .987 (5E/378TC)... Reported to spring training as a member of the Montreal Expos... On March 28 was sent to Philadelphia for cash... Opened the season hitting .266 in April with seven RBI... Hit .256 in May but in June hit just .213 in 21 games... With Philly had four 3-hit games including June 23 at Montreal when he was 3-4 with a double, a triple and a season high four RBI... Played in his 900th game as a Phillie on June 25 at Montreal... Committed only two errors in his last 64 games with Philadelphia... Was traded to Toronto on August 6 for a player to be named later which on August 7, was OF Rob Ducey... In his second game with Toronto matched his season high with three hits on August 8... Hit .354 in this first 16 games with Toronto... Hit in 11 of 12 from August 26 to September 13... Started 31 games at second base for Toronto and posted a .993 fielding percentage with one error in 151 total chances... Hit in 21 of his 34 Blue Jays starts... On the season hit .266 against right-handed pitching with 27 RBI and against left-handed pitching hit .196 with two RBI... Hit .245 prior to the All-Star break with 17 RBI and .274 after the break with 12 RBI.

PROFESSIONAL CAREER: 1989: Played for three Phillies farm teams during his first pro season... Was a South Atlantic League mid-season All-Star after hitting .338 in 63 games for Spartanburg (A)... Was promoted to Clearwater (A) on June 29... Received another promotion on July 21, this time to Reading (AA)... In 48 double-A contests, he batted .351... Combined average was .338... Paul Owens Award winner for best player in the Phillies minor league system... **1990:** Saw action in 139 games for Scranton and batted .260 with 24 doubles and an International League-high 10 triples... Became Phils starting 2nd baseman when called up from AAA on August 31, after Tom Herr was dealt to the Mets... Collected 1st ML hit in his first game on September 1 vs San Diego, a single off Greg Harris... Hit his first HR (solo) on September 22 vs Montreal's Scott Anderson... **1991:** Opened the year with Scranton/Wilkes-Barre (AAA), was recalled on April 23 when Jim Fregosi took over as manager... Had .986 fielding % in 95 games at 2nd base... Had a then career high nine-game hit streak from May 25 to June 9... Had four 3-hit games... Stole 13 bases in 15 attempts... **1992:** Committed only five errors at second base... His .991 fielding percentage ranked 2nd in the NL while the five errors were a league low among NL 2nd basemen... Played in 124 games at second base and three at shortstop... Started at shortstop July 8 at San Francisco, his only ML start at a position other than second base... On September 20 at Pittsburgh, turned an unassisted triple play in the sixth inning — was the ninth player ever — and the first second baseman to do so in a regular-season game... Runners were on first and second, he caught Jeff King's liner, stepped on second base to retire Andy Van Slyke, then tagged Barry Bonds coming from first... Was the first NL player to record an unassisted triple play since Cubs shortstop Jimmy Cooney turned the feat on May 30, 1927... Had

a 59-game errorless streak from July 9 to September 29... First career inside-the-park home run on May 26 against Mike Stanton of the Braves... Recorded hits in seven consecutive at-bats September 6 to September 8... Had eight triples to lead the club and tie for sixth in the NL... **1993:** Member of the NL champion Phillies... Posted a .990 (5E/501TC) fielding percentage, the second-best average among NL second basemen... Had a 66-game errorless stretch from June 1 to September 22... Hit his first ML grand slam July 10 off San Francisco's Dave Righetti — had a career-high 5 RBI in the game... Hit his first career pinch-hit homer on July 30 off Pittsburgh's Bob Walk... Had a then career-high 12-game hit streak from August 27 to September 29... Had 13 stolen bases in 15 attempts... Saw his first career post-season action... Appeared in four games of the NL Championship Series against Atlanta and in three World Series contests vs Toronto... Had five hits in 21 at-bats... In Game #6 of the NLCS had a triple and two RBI as the Phillies won the pennant... **1994:** Hit a then career-best .292 in 87 games, 70 starts... Hit .220 before May 14 and then .312 the rest of the way... Had team-best 10-game hit streak from May 15 to 29... Did not strikeout until 51st plate appearance, May 6 at FLA... Committed just one error in the first 32 games, made just two errors from June 1, 1993 to June 1, 1994, a span of 103 games... Five triples were tied for club lead and tied for 9th in NL... Tied a then career-high four hits on July 31 at Atlanta... Hit .313 with runners in scoring position... His .985 fielding % ranked 4th among NL second basemen... Struck out only 33 times in 274 at-bats... **1995:** Had his first career All-Star season... Went 0-for-1 during the mid-summer Classic in Arlington, TX... The NL team was managed by Expos' Felipe Alou... Finished the season with a .283 average, 34 doubles and 49 RBI... Finishing 5th in NL with .346 average with runners in scoring position (min 100 AB), behind Gwynn, Bichette, Piazza and Larkin... Also led the team and finished among leaders in doubles and triples... Was the 4th straight season led Phils in triples... Reached career-highs in AB, runs, hits, 2B, 3B, homers, RBI, walks and strikeouts and tied his best with 127 games... His six home runs doubled his previous high of three... Hit a game-winning, 2-run pinch-hit HR in 13th inning on May 17 at Florida against Richie Lewis... Had a career-high five hits on June 24 at St. Louis... Had surgery performed by Dr. Lewis Yocum on October 6 to remove a bone spur and loose bodies from his right elbow... **1996:** Stole a career high 26 bases in 140 games for the Phillies... Recorded his first career steal of home May 12 vs Atlanta (front half of a double steal)... Had two triples in that contest — his third career two-triple affair... Was successful in his first 19 SB attempts until being thrown out on July 7 by Florida's Bob Natal... Had an 11-game hit streak from May 23 to June 4... Also reached base safely via hit or walk in 27 straight games from May 8 to June 8... Had his first career stint on the DL from June 15 to 29 after suffering a first degree acromiclavicular sprain of his right shoulder after a collision with teammate Glenn Murray on June 14 in Colorado... Collected a season-high four twice in one week, September 11 at Houston and September 17 vs Florida... Finished 7th among NL 2nd basemen in fielding %, .982... **1997:** Appeared in a career-high 150 games with 142 starts at second base... Also set career highs in batting (.295), AB (553), runs (83), hits (163), 2B (40), and BB (62)... Had slow start, hitting just .215 through May 5... After that hit .314 in last 121 games... Raised average to .299 on May 26 and kept it at .291 or above for rest of season... The 40 doubles were tied for 7th in NL... Doubled in five straight games, May 24 to 28... Finished 2nd among NL 2nd basemen & third in the majors in fielding % at .990 (6E/610 TC)... Was error-free in first 39 games of season, giving him a 52-game errorless streak dating back to September 10, 1996... Made just one error in final 42 games... Appeared at shortstop for 4th time in career on May 24 vs NY... Traded to Cubs for Doug Glanville on December 23... **1998:** Posted careeer highs in batting (.296), games (154), runs (93), home runs (8) and RBI (53)... Led NL 2nd basemen with a .993 fielding percentage, committed five errors in 676 total chances... Singled in his first at-bat as a Cub on opening day, March 31, off Florida's Livan Hernandez... Opened the season playing errorless ball in his first 24 games... Had a 59-game errorless streak from May 6 to July18 and a 45-game errorless stretch July 20-September 9... Collected two hits in 1st inning of an April 18 game vs LA... Recorded his 1,000th career hit September 19 — a single off Cincinnati's Danny Graves... Had a career-high 14-game hitting streak from May 19 to June 3... Over a 69-game span from May 19 to August 8, hit .349 (94-269)... Had a trio of four-hit efforts... Went 2-for-9 in the Division Series against Atlanta... **1999:** Hit .241 in 144 games, the third-highest total of his nine-year major league career... Over a 26-game stretch from May 14 to June 14, batted

.359... Hit in 11 straight from May 14 to 25... Struggled in the second half hitting .211... Had a .991 fielding percentage at second base, made only five errors in 563 total chances... Had a 44-game errorless streak snapped July 2 at Philadelphia, a throwing error ended his seventh career errorless stretch of at least 40 games... Committed a fielding error on May 5 vs Colorado to snap a 39-game errorless stretch dating back to 1998... Recorded his first career two-homer game on July 1 vs Milwaukee, hitting solo shots off Hideo Nomo and Cal Eldred... The homer off Nomo was his first career opposite-field roundtripper... Served a National League-imposed two-game suspension September 23 & 24 after a September 17 argument with an umpire.

CAREER NOTES: Presented 1995 Media Good Guy Award by the Philadelphia chapter of the BBWAA... Has had seven errorless streaks of 40 or more games in his career... Career fielding percentage at second base of .989 (64E/5649TC).

POST SEASON EXPERIENCE: 1993: Was a combined 5-21 in seven games of the NLCS and World Series for Philadelphia... In Game #6 of the NLCS had a triple and two RBI as the Phillies won the pennant that night... **1998:** Was 2-9 in three games of the Division Series for the Chicago Cubs.

MICKEY MORANDINI

Year	Club & League	AVG	G	AB	R	H	TB	2B	3B	HR	RBI	SH-SF	HP	BB-IBB	SO	SB-CS	GIDP	SLG	OBP
1989	Spartanburg (SAL)	.338	63	231	43	78	102	19	1	1	30	4-2	3	35-0	45	18-9	3	.442	.428
1989	Clearwater (FSL)	.302	17	63	14	19	25	4	1	0	4	0-1	1	7-1	8	3-1	0	.397	.375
1989	Reading (East)	.351	48	188	39	66	95	12	1	5	29	1-0	1	23-4	32	5-5	2	.505	.425
1990	Scranton-WB (Int)	.260	139	503	76	131	178	24	10	1	31	10-0	5	60-0	90	16-6	10	.354	.345
1990	PHILADELPHIA (NL)	.241	25	79	9	19	26	4	0	1	3	2-0	0	6-0	19	3-0	1	.329	.294
1991	Scranton-WB (Int)	.261	12	46	7	12	19	4	0	1	9	0-1	0	5-0	6	2-0	0	.413	.327
1991	PHILADELPHIA (NL)	.249	98	325	38	81	103	11	4	1	20	6-2	2	29-0	45	13-2	7	.317	.313
1992	PHILADELPHIA (NL)	.265	127	422	47	112	145	8	8	3	30	6-2	0	25-2	64	8-3	4	.344	.305
1993	PHILADELPHIA (NL)	.247	120	425	57	105	151	19	9	3	33	4-2	5	34-2	73	13-2	7	.355	.309
1994	PHILADELPHIA (NL)	.292	87	274	40	80	112	16	5	2	26	4-0	4	34-5	33	10-5	4	.409	.378
1995	PHILADELPHIA (NL)	.283	127	494	65	140	206	34	7	6	49	4-1	9	42-3	80	9-6	11	.417	.350
1996	PHILADELPHIA (NL)	.250	140	539	64	135	180	24	6	3	32	5-4	9	49-0	87	26-5	15	.334	.321
1997	PHILADELPHIA (NL)	.295	150	553	83	163	210	40	2	1	39	12-5	8	62-0	91	16-13	8	.380	.371
1998	CHICAGO (NL)	.296	154	582	93	172	224	20	4	8	53	4-2	9	72-4	84	13-1	14	.385	.380
1999	CHICAGO (NL)	.241	144	456	60	110	150	18	5	4	37	7-4	6	48-2	61	6-6	10	.329	.319
2000	PHILADELPHIA (NL)	.252	91	302	31	76	95	13	3	0	22	5-1	4	29-1	54	5-2	11	.315	.324
2000	TORONTO (AL)	.271	35	107	10	29	33	2	1	0	7	2-0	0	7-0	23	1-0	2	.308	.316
Minor Totals		.297	279	1031	179	306	419	63	13	8	103	15-4	10	130-5	181	44-21	15	.406	.380
NL TOTALS		.268	1263	4451	587	1193	1602	207	53	32	344	59-23	56	430-19	691	122-45	92	.360	.335
MAJOR TOTALS		.268	1298	4558	597	1222	1635	209	54	32	351	61-23	56	437-19	714	123-45	94	.359	.338

DIVISION SERIES RECORD

Year	Club & League	AVG	G	AB	R	H	TB	2B	3B	HR	RBI	SH-SF	HP	BB-IBB	SO	SB-CS	GIDP	SLG	OBP
1998	CHICAGO (NL)	.222	3	9	1	2	2	0	0	0	1	0-1	0	2—	2	0-1	–	.222	.333

CHAMPIONSHIP SERIES RECORD

Year	Club & League	AVG	G	AB	R	H	TB	2B	3B	HR	RBI	SH-SF	HP	BB-IBB	SO	SB-CS	GIDP	SLG	OBP
1993	PHILADELPHIA (NL)	.250	4	16	1	4	6	0	1	0	2	0-0	0	0-0	3	1-0	–	.375	.250

WORLD SERIES RECORD

Year	Club & League	AVG	G	AB	R	H	TB	2B	3B	HR	RBI	SH-SF	HP	BB-IBB	SO	SB-CS	GIDP	SLG	OBP
1993	PHILADELPHIA (NL)	.200	3	5	1	1	1	0	0	0	0	0-0	0	1—	2	0-0	–	.200	.333

ALL-STAR GAME RECORD

Year	Club & League	AVG	G	AB	R	H	TB	2B	3B	HR	RBI	SH-SF	HP	BB-IBB	SO	SB-CS	GIDP	SLG	OBP
1995	NL at TEX	.000	1	1	0	0	0	0	0	0	0	0-0	0	0-0	1	0-0	0	.000	.000

HOME RUN BREAKDOWN

Total	H	A	MEN ON 0	1	2	3	ONE GAME 2	3	4	LO	XN	IP	PH	RHP	LHP
32	20	12	19	10	2	1	1	0	0	1	1	1	2	29	3

MORANDINI — TRANSACTIONS

- Selected by the Philadelphia Phillies in fifth round of the June 1988 First Year Draft.
- On disabled list (sprained right shoulder) June 15-30, 1996.
- Traded to the Chicago Cubs in exchange for OF Doug Glanville December 23, 1997.
- On suspended list September 23-25, 1999.
- Signed by the Montreal Expos on January 17, 2000.
- Contract purchased by the Philadelphia Phillies on March 28, 2000.
- Traded to the Toronto Blue Jays in exchange for a player to be named later (OF Rob Ducey) on August 6, 2000.

CAREER HIGHS — MORANDINI, Mickey

SEASON:

Games	154 - 1998
Avg	.296 - 1998
Runs	93 - 1998
Hits	172 - 1998
Doubles	40 - 1997
Home Runs	8 - 1998
RBI	53 - 1998
Walks	72 - 1998
Strikeouts	91 - 1997
Stolen Bases	26 - 1996
Longest Hitting Streak	14G - May 19-Jun. 3, 1998
Multi HR Games	1 - 1999

GAME:

ML Debut	Sep. 1, 1990 vs. SD
Runs	4 - Jun. 13, 1998 at PHI
Hits	5 - Jun. 24, 1995 at STL
Doubles	2 - 15 times, last May 18, 2000 vs. STL
Home Runs	2 - Jul. 1, 1999 vs. MIL
RBI	5 - Jul. 10, 1993 vs. SF
Stolen Bases	2 - 7 times, last Apr. 19, 1997 vs. MON
Last ML Home Run	Sep. 7, 1999 vs. CIN

FIELDING

MORANDINI, Mickey—2B

Year	PCT	G	PO	A	E	TC	DP
1990 (NL)	.990	25	37	61	1	99	10
1991 (NL)	.986	97	183	254	6	443	45
1992 (NL)	.991	124	236	333	5	574	64
1993 (NL)	.990	111	208	288	5	501	48
1994 (NL)	.985	79	167	216	6	389	39
1995 (NL)	.989	122	269	337	7	613	74
1996 (NL)	.982	137	286	352	12	650	87
1997 (NL)	.990	146	254	350	6	610	87
1998 (NL)	.983	152	267	404	5	676	70
1999 (NL)	.991	132	239	319	5	563	72
2000 (NL)	.987	85	179	196	5	380	45
2000 (AL)	.993	35	58	92	1	151	28
Total	.989	1245	2383	3202	64	5649	669

MORANDINI, Mickey—SS

Year	PCT	G	PO	A	E	TC	DP
1992 (NL)	.857	3	3	3	1	7	1
1997 (NL)	.000	1	0	0	0	0	0
Total	.857	4	3	3	1	7	1

MICKEY MORANDINI HITTING AT ML PARKS

Park	Avg	G	AB	R	H	2B	3B	HR	RBI	SB	CS	BB	SO	OBP	Slg
Camden Yards	.182	6	22	2	4	1	0	0	1	1	0	2	2	.240	.227
Fenway Park	.083	3	12	2	1	1	0	0	0	0	0	2	3	.214	.167
Edison Field	.500	2	8	0	4	0	0	0	2	0	0	0	1	.500	.500
Comiskey Park	.167	4	18	3	3	0	0	0	1	0	1	1	6	.211	.167
Jacobs Field	.333	5	18	3	6	1	1	0	0	0	0	2	1	.400	.500
Tiger Stadium	.333	4	15	4	5	2	0	2	2	0	0	2	1	.412	.867
Kauffman Stadium	.304	6	23	4	7	0	0	0	0	1	0	0	3	.304	.304
County Stadium	.254	15	63	8	16	3	0	1	5	1	0	5	8	.314	.349
Metrodome	.167	4	18	1	3	1	0	0	2	0	0	0	6	.167	.222
Yankee Stadium	.250	4	12	0	3	1	0	0	1	0	0	1	4	.308	.333
Arlington	.286	3	7	2	2	0	0	0	0	0	0	2	1	.444	.286
SkyDome	.267	21	60	5	16	3	1	0	5	1	0	4	14	.313	.350
Atlanta-Fulton	.299	28	97	12	29	6	0	0	14	3	0	7	18	.349	.361
Wrigley Field	.301	183	634	101	191	34	7	7	59	10	5	82	79	.389	.410
Cinergy Field	.236	40	127	16	30	7	2	0	4	7	2	19	24	.342	.323
Astrodome	.248	42	145	18	36	7	1	1	11	7	2	15	26	.327	.331
Dodger Stadium	.223	48	179	14	40	7	1	0	12	5	3	15	32	.287	.274
Olympic Stadium	.279	50	172	28	48	9	6	1	17	4	2	17	26	.347	.419
Shea Stadium	.250	41	160	16	40	5	4	0	9	1	1	7	33	.292	.331
Veterans Stadium	.266	500	1734	214	461	86	21	13	132	56	19	161	289	.333	.362
Three Rivers	.257	51	179	28	46	8	3	1	4	7	3	26	29	.364	.352
Busch Stadium	.230	42	148	19	34	7	0	0	10	2	1	15	16	.309	.277
Qualcomm Park	.186	47	161	17	30	1	1	3	10	5	0	10	22	.237	.261
3 Com Park	.267	39	146	18	39	6	0	1	14	5	1	11	17	.323	.329
Coors Field	.333	22	90	16	30	5	1	1	9	3	1	5	11	.371	.444
Pro Player Stadium	.258	43	155	20	40	5	2	1	15	3	1	12	27	.320	.335
Turner Field	.431	18	72	11	31	3	1	0	5	0	3	5	9	.474	.500
BankOne Ballpark	.302	13	43	7	13	0	1	0	3	0	0	4	4	.362	.349
Mile High Stadium	.500	5	12	3	6	0	1	0	1	0	0	0	1	.500	.667
Pacific Bell	.200	3	10	0	2	0	0	0	0	1	0	0	1	1	.273
Enron Field	.333	6	18	5	6	0	0	0	2	1	0	4	0	.458	.333

				2000										CAREER					
	Avg	AB	H	HR	RBI	BB	SO	OBP	SLG	Avg	AB	H	HR	RBI	BB	SO	OBP	SLG
Total	.257	409	105	0	29	36	77	.322	.313	.268	4558	1222	32	351	437	714	.338	.359
vs. Left	.196	56	11	0	2	2	18	.237	.214	.220	994	219	3	74	106	167	.304	.283
vs. Right	.266	353	94	0	27	34	59	.335	.329	.281	3564	1003	29	277	331	547	.348	.380
Home	.252	206	52	0	10	20	45	.328	.330	.273	2253	616	20	188	230	353	.347	.372
Away	.261	203	53	0	19	16	32	.317	.296	.263	2305	606	12	163	207	361	.329	.345
March	–	–	–	–	–	–	–	–	–	.400	5	2	0	0	0	0	.400	.400
April	.266	64	17	0	7	7	10	.342	.297	.265	608	161	6	55	76	101	.350	.362
May	.256	78	20	0	4	7	10	.326	.321	.286	825	236	3	55	78	117	.353	.371
June	.213	75	16	0	6	8	22	.289	.293	.266	794	211	7	62	75	125	.335	.389
July	.267	75	20	0	4	7	11	.345	.347	.281	877	246	9	84	82	119	.349	.379
August	.333	54	18	0	4	5	10	.390	.333	.256	677	173	2	44	67	120	.330	.310
September	.233	60	14	0	4	2	14	.258	.300	.252	723	182	5	50	55	127	.310	.337
October	.000	3	0	0	0	0	0	.000	.000	.224	49	11	0	1	4	5	.283	.245
Scoring Posn	.318	88	28	0	26	9	14	.384	.409	.286	958	274	9	303	134	168	.377	.390
Bases Loaded	.222	9	2	0	4	0	2	.222	.222	.263	76	20	1	52	8	14	.333	.368
PH	.429	7	3	0	0	0	1	.429	.429	.254	71	18	2	8	16	18	.404	.380
vs. Ana	.500	12	6	0	2	0	1	.500	.500	.500	12	6	0	2	0	1	.500	.500
vs. Bal	.190	21	4	0	0	0	2	.190	.238	.194	31	6	0	1	2	3	.235	.258
vs. Bos	.000	9	0	0	0	1	1	.000	.000	.048	21	1	0	0	3	4	.167	.095
vs. CWS	.222	9	2	0	0	0	4	.222	.222	.229	35	8	0	1	3	6	.289	.229
vs. Cle	.000	6	0	0	0	0	1	.000	.000	.292	24	7	0	1	4	1	.414	.417
vs. Det	.300	10	3	0	0	0	1	.300	.500	.320	25	8	2	2	2	2	.370	.720
vs. KC	.429	14	6	0	0	3	2	.529	.429	.359	39	14	0	3	5	4	.432	.385
vs. Mil	.250	20	5	0	0	3	5	.348	.350	.255	110	28	3	12	11	18	.331	.400
vs. Min	.091	11	1	0	1	0	5	.091	.091	.200	30	6	0	3	2	8	.242	.233
vs. NYY	.263	19	5	0	2	1	6	.300	.316	.313	32	10	0	2	1	10	.333	.344
vs. Oak	.286	7	2	0	0	0	3	.286	.571	.286	7	2	0	0	0	3	.286	.571
vs. Sea	.333	6	2	0	2	1	2	.429	.333	.333	6	2	0	2	1	2	.429	.333
vs. TB	.125	24	3	0	1	1	7	.160	.125	.125	24	3	0	1	1	7	.160	.125
vs. Tex	.286	7	2	0	0	2	1	.444	.286	.286	7	2	0	0	2	1	.444	.286
vs. Tor	.167	6	1	0	2	0	3	.167	.333	.154	13	2	0	2	2	4	.267	.231
vs. Ari	.250	12	3	0	1	0	1	.250	.250	.312	77	24	0	5	12	7	.411	.338
vs. Atl	.286	35	10	0	2	1	8	.306	.286	.331	326	108	2	33	23	66	.380	.429
vs. ChC	.308	13	4	0	1	4	1	.500	.385	.298	292	87	1	14	35	39	.383	.404
vs. Cin	.000	7	0	0	0	0	2	.000	.000	.226	252	57	2	18	29	41	.309	.333
vs. Col	.200	15	3	0	0	1	5	.250	.200	.294	204	60	1	16	15	30	.342	.397
vs. Fla	.100	20	2	0	0	2	4	.182	.150	.272	283	77	2	25	34	44	.356	.350
vs. Hou	.333	18	6	0	2	4	0	.458	.333	.240	312	75	3	27	29	54	.316	.311
vs. LA	.429	21	9	0	1	2	0	.500	.524	.264	371	98	1	33	34	58	.328	.348
vs. Mon	.333	24	8	0	6	4	5	.429	.542	.256	347	89	3	28	32	49	.326	.378
vs. NYM	.200	5	1	0	0	2	1	.429	.200	.273	337	92	2	29	26	63	.332	.377
vs. Phi	–	–	–	–	–	–	–	–	–	.250	56	14	0	1	5	7	.323	.339
vs. Pit	.250	16	4	0	0	2	2	.333	.250	.266	346	92	3	15	39	57	.350	.355
vs. StL	.455	22	10	0	4	1	3	.500	.682	.272	320	87	0	28	27	39	.337	.347
vs. SD	.100	10	1	0	1	0	0	.100	.100	.243	313	76	4	20	26	49	.304	.323
vs. SF	.200	10	2	0	1	1	1	.273	.200	.265	306	81	3	27	32	37	.338	.340
Pre-All Star	.245	245	60	0	17	25	45	.319	.302	.275	2540	699	22	202	265	382	.349	.375
Post-All Star	.274	164	45	0	12	11	32	.328	.329	.259	2018	523	10	149	172	332	.324	.338

Jaime NAVARRO

PITCHER

71

BIRTHDATE .... March 27, 1968
OPENING DAY AGE 33
BIRTHPLACE .... Bayamon, PR
RESIDENCE .... Mukwonago, WI
BATS/THROWS .... R/R
HEIGHT/WEIGHT 6-4/250
CONTRACT STATUS .... signed thru 2001
M.L. SERVICE 10.138

PERSONAL: Jaime Navarro... Married, wife's name is Tamara... Two children, Jaime Jr. and Jaycee Lynn... His father, Julio, pitched in the Majors with the Los Angeles Dodgers (1962-64), Detroit Tigers (1964-66) and Atlanta Braves (1970)... In 1997 named Outstanding Alumni by the American Association of Community Colleges... Graduated from Luis Pales Matos High School in Bayamon, Puerto Rico in 1985... Graduated from Miami-Dade Community College-New World Center in 1987... Has continued to support Miami-Dade-Wolfson's athletic programs and holds an annual Jaime Navarro Celebrity Golf Classic as a fund raiser for the school.

LAST SEASON: In 12 games, seven starts was 0-6 with a 10.53 ERA... Opened the season with Milwaukee after a

January 12 deal in which he and RHP John Snyder were acquired in exchange for RHP Cal Eldred and IF Jose Valentin... Made five starts for the Brewers and was 0-5 with a 12.54 ERA... Did not pitch 5.0 innings in any of the starts... Was released by the Brewers on April 30... Signed a minor league deal with the Rockies and made five starts with Colorado Springs (AAA)... Was 3-2 with a 5.30 ERA and averaged over 7.0 innings pitched per start (35.2IP)... Signed a major league contract with the Cleveland Indians on June 16... Made two starts with the Indians and was 0-1 after allowing nine earned runs in 8.0 innings... Was designated for assignment on June 24 and then outrighted to Buffalo of the International League (AAA) on June 28... Appeared in five games, all in relief from June 28 to July 13, and was 1-0 with a 0.00 ERA... Pitched at least 2.0 innings in all five outings... Contract was purchased from Buffalo on July 15... Made five relief appearances in July, three of which were scoreless... In relief was 0-0 with a 5.40 ERA (4ER/6.2IP)... Was designated for assignment again on July 29 and outrighted to Buffalo on August 2... Finished the season in Buffalo, making seven more appearances and two starts... In his two starts allowed 10 ER in 6.1 innings pitched... Finished the season with a 1-2 record and a 4.44 ERA with Buffalo.

PROFESSIONAL CAREER: 1987: Made his professional debut at Rookie Helena of the Pioneer League... Named to the All-Star team... Struck out 95 batters in 85.2 innings... **1988:** Spent the season at Class A Stockton leading Milwaukee's Minor League system in victories (15) and innings pitched (174.2)... Posted a 15-5 record with a 3.09 ERA... Rated the league's second best pitcher in a poll of California League managers... **1989:** Opened the season at Double A El Paso going 5-2 with a 2.47 ERA in 11 starts... Was promoted to Denver (AAA) on May 31 making three starts before being promoted to Milwaukee... Made his Major League debut on June 20 vs Kansas City allowing one earned run over 6.2 innings and received a no-decision... First Major League win came against the Chicago White Sox on June 25... Pitched his first career complete game on September 26 vs Baltimore... **1990:** Had three stints with the Brewers and two with Triple A Denver... Opened the season with Milwaukee before being optioned on May 15... Was recalled by the Brewers on May 27... Went back to Denver from June 11 to July 4 and was 2-3 in six starts... Was recalled and remained in Milwaukee the rest of the season... Piched up first career save on June 19 vs Seattle... **1991:** Spent his first full season in the Major Leagues... Threw a career-high 10 complete games in his 34 starts... Tied for third in baseball in complete games and ranked ninth in the American League in innings pitched (234.0)... Led the Brewers in starts, complete games and innings pitched... **1992:** Set career highs in wins (17), shutouts (3) and innings pitched (246.0)... Was the first Brewers pitcher to top 15 wins in consecutive seasons since Ted Higuera in 1987-88... Also was the first to throw three shutouts in a season since Higuera (1987)... Pitched a career-high 9.2 innings on May 17 in a 2-1, 10-inning loss to Texas... Pitched a two-hitter against the Rangers in a 4-1 victory on July 22... **1993:** Recorded five complete games for the Brewers... Surpassed the 200.0 IP mark for the third consecutive season... Won five straight decisions from May 16-June 16... **1994:** Made 10 starts in addition to 19 appearances out of the bullpen... Was 2-6 with a 7.96 ERA in his starts... Worked a career-high 5.0 innings out of the bullpen on June 12 vs Cleveland... **1995:** Ranked 10th in the National League in ERA (3.28) and tied for fifth in wins (14)... Was ranked fifth in the NL in innings pitched (200.1)... His .700 winning percentage ranked sixth in the league... Averaged just 2.2 walks per nine innings... Began the season 5-0, the best start for a Cubs pitcher since Steve Wilson won his first five decisions in 1989... First Major League hit came on May 6 at Pittsburgh off Jeff McCurry... **1996:** Led the Cubs staff in victories (15),

starts (35), complete games (4), innings pitched (236.2) and strikeouts (158)... Strikeout total was a career-high eclipsing his previous high by 30... Posted a career-best eight-game win streak from July 26-September 8... Posted a monthly career-high with five wins in August... Only three Major League pitchers owned longer streaks during the season... Was the longest streak by a Cubs pitcher since Greg Maddux won nine in 1988... Was 8-0 with a 2.78 ERA over nine starts during the streak... Tied for second in the National League in starts and fourth in innings pitched... Tied for ninth in wins and seven in complete games... Pitched at least 7.0 innings in 15 starts and 8.0 or more 10 times... Averaged just 2.7 walks per nine innings... Made his first career Opening Day start on April 1 vs San Diego receiving a no-decision... Tossed a five-hit shutout on July 11 vs St. Louis... Tied a ML record for pitchers after committing three errors in one inning on August 18 vs Houston... **1997:** Led the White Sox in starts (33), innings pitched (209.2) and strikeouts (142)... Topped 200.0 IP for the fifth time in six seasons, with the 1994 strike-shortened season being the exception... The 142 strikeouts was the second highest total of his career... Threw 3,525 pitches, ninth in the AL... Threw 120 pitches or more, 10 times... Recorded his 100th career victory on August 12 vs Anaheim... Made 16 quality starts and lasted 7.0 or more innings 19 times... Pitched 8.0 or more innings in eight starts... White Sox were 15-18 in his starts... Posted second complete game on July 20 at Baltimore... Recorded a career monthly best with 34 strikeouts in April... Tossed 7.0 scoreless innings striking out a career-high 11 for his first victory with the White Sox... Was his first AL win since July 31, 1994 at Boston... Struck out a career high 19 in consecutive starts on April 1-6... Struck out eight in 6.0 innings in second career Opening Day start on April 1 at Toronto — first Opening Day start in the American League... **1998:** Was 8-15 with a 6.21 ERA in 27 starts and 0-1 with a 7.58 ERA in 10 relief appearances... Made his third career Opening Day start on March 31 at Texas, pitched 6.0 scoreless innings in a 9-2 White Sox victory... Won three straight decisions from April 29-May 15, his longest streak since winning a career-high eight in a row from July 26-September 8, 1996... Recorded his 32nd career complete game vs Kansas City on June 4... Suffered his 100th career loss on June 19 vs Minnesota... Recorded his 1,000th career strikeout during his 300th career game on July 20 vs Cleveland... Moved to the bullpen following loss on August 15 vs Seattle... Made first relief appearance on August 19 at Oakland, his first since August 9, 1994 while pitching for Milwaukee... Converted his only save opportunity on September 1 at Baltimore for his second career save... **1999:** Held right-handed hitters to a .265 batting average... Was 7-12 with a 6.24 ERA in 27 starts and 1-1 with a 3.24 ERA in five relief appearances... Was 2-0 with a 3.68 ERA on turf... Won three straight decisions from May 28 to June 8 for the first time since winning three straight from April 29-May 15, 1998... Moved to the bullpen on September 4 to close out the season... Pitched 2.0 perfect innings on September 18 at Toronto for his first relief victory since July 31, 1994 at Boston while with Milwaukee.

FIELDING
NAVARRO, Jaime—P

Year	PCT	G	PO	A	E	TC	DP
1989 (AL)	.917	19	6	16	2	24	0
1990 (AL)	.967	32	10	19	1	30	2
1991 (AL)	.936	34	16	28	3	47	3
1992 (AL)	.897	34	17	18	4	39	1
1993 (AL)	.946	35	14	21	2	37	2
1994 (AL)	1.000	29	4	7	0	11	1
1995 (NL)	.964	29	14	13	1	28	1
1996 (NL)	.868	35	8	25	5	38	1
1997 (AL)	.909	33	15	15	3	33	0
1998 (AL)	.966	37	8	20	1	29	1
1999 (AL)	.923	32	9	15	2	26	2
2000 (NL)	1.000	5	1	0	0	1	0
2000 (AL)	.000	7	0	0	0	0	0
Total	.930	361	122	197	24	343	14

JAIME NAVARRO

Year	Club & League	W-L	ERA	G	GS	CG	ShO	SV	IP	H	R	ER	HR	HB	BB-IBB	SO	WP	BK	OBA
1987	Helena (Pio)	4-3	3.57	13	13	3	0	0	85.2	87	37	34	5	1	18-1	95	5	1	.261
1988	Stockton (Cal)	15-5	3.09	26	26	4	1	0	174.2	148	70	60	6	6	74-1	151	22	2	.231
1989	El Paso (Tex)	5-2	2.47	11	11	1	0	0	76.2	61	29	21	3	1	35-1	78	5	1	.219
1989	Denver (AmAs)	1-1	3.60	3	3	1	0	0	20.0	24	8	8	0	0	7-2	17	0	0	.308
1989	MILWAUKEE (AL)	7-8	3.12	19	17	1	0	0	109.2	119	47	38	6	1	32-3	56	3	0	.277
1990	MILWAUKEE (AL)	8-7	4.46	32	22	3	0	1	149.1	176	83	74	11	4	41-3	75	6	5	.293
1990	Denver (AmAs)	2-3	4.20	6	6	1	0	0	40.2	41	27	19	1	0	14-0	28	2	1	.255
1991	MILWAUKEE (AL)	15-12	3.92	34	34	10	2	0	234.0	237	117	102	18	6	73-3	114	10	0	.261
1992	MILWAUKEE (AL)	17-11	3.33	34	34	5	3	0	246.0	224	98	91	14	6	64-4	100	6	0	.246
1993	MILWAUKEE (AL)	11-12	5.33	35	34	5	1	0	214.1	250	135	127	21	11	73-4	114	11	0	.295
1994	MILWAUKEE (AL)	4-9	6.62	29	10	0	0	0	89.2	115	71	66	10	4	35-4	65	3	0	.314
1995	CHICAGO (NL)	14-6	3.28	29	29	1	1	0	200.1	194	79	73	19	3	56-7	128	1	0	.251
1996	CHICAGO (NL)	15-12	3.92	35	35	4	1	0	236.2	244	116	103	25	10	72-5	158	10	0	.269
1997	CHICAGO (AL)	9-14	5.79	33	33	2	0	0	209.2	267	155	135	22	3	73-6	142	14	1	.309
1998	CHICAGO (AL)	8-16	6.36	37	27	1	0	1	172.2	223	135	122	30	7	77-1	71	18	0	.315
1999	CHICAGO (AL)	8-13	6.09	32	27	0	0	0	159.2	206	126	108	29	11	71-1	74	9	0	.313
2000	MILWAUKEE (NL)	0-5	12.54	5	5	0	0	0	18.2	34	31	26	6	0	18-3	7	1	0	.410
2000	Colorado Springs (PCL)	3-2	5.30	5	5	0	0	0	35.2	48	26	21	8	0	6-0	20	2	0	.320
2000	Buffalo (Int)	1-2	4.44	12	2	0	0	0	26.1	36	16	13	1	0	10-2	13	0	0	.324
2000	CLEVELAND (AL)	0-1	7.98	7	2	0	0	0	14.2	20	13	13	3	1	5-0	9	0	0	.328
Minor Totals		**31-18**	**3.45**	**76**	**66**	**10**	**1**	**0**	**459.2**	**445**	**213**	**176**	**24**	**8**	**164-7**	**402**	**36**	**5**	**.254**
AL TOTALS		**87-103**	**4.93**	**292**	**240**	**27**	**6**	**2**	**1599.2**	**1841**	**980**	**876**	**164**	**54**	**544-29**	**820**	**80**	**6**	**.290**
NL TOTALS		**29-23**	**3.98**	**69**	**69**	**5**	**2**	**0**	**455.2**	**472**	**226**	**202**	**50**	**13**	**146-15**	**293**	**12**	**0**	**.267**
MAJOR TOTALS		**116-126**	**4.72**	**361**	**309**	**32**	**8**	**2**	**2055.1**	**2313**	**1206**	**1078**	**214**	**67**	**690-44**	**1113**	**92**	**6**	**.285**

NAVARRO — TRANSACTIONS

- Selected by the Milwaukee Brewers in 3rd round of the June 1987 First Year Player Draft.
- Signed by the Chicago Cubs on April 9, 1995.
- Signed by the Chicago White Sox on December 12, 1996.
- Traded to the Milwaukee Brewers along with RHP John Snyder in exchange for SS Jose Valentin and RHP Cal Eldred on January 12, 2000.
- Released by the Milwaukee Brewers on April 30, 2000.
- Signed by the Colorado Rockies on May 19, 2000.
- Released by the Colorado Rockies on June 15, 2000.
- Signed by the Cleveland Indians on June 16, 2000.
- On disabled list August 20-September 1, 2000.
- Signed by the Toronto Blue Jays on December 13, 2000.

CAREER HIGHS — NAVARRO, Jaime

SEASON:

Wins	17 - 1992
Losses	16 - 1998
Saves	1 - 1990, 1998
ERA	3.28 - 1995
Games	37 - 1998
Starts	35 - 1996
Complete Games	10 - 1991
Shutouts	3 - 1992
Innings Pitched	246.0 - 1992
Walks	77 - 1998
Strikeouts	158 - 1996
Longest Win Streak	8 - Jul. 26-Sep. 8, 1996
Longest Losing Streak	6 - Jul. 20-Sep. 24, 1998
	6 - Apr. 6-Jun. 23, 2000
Scoreless Innings Streak	19.0 - Jul. 22-Aug. 1, 1992

GAME:

ML Debut	Jun. 20, 1989 vs. KC
Innings Pitched:	
Starter	9.2 - May 17, 1992 vs. TEX
Reliever	5.0 - Jun. 12, 1994 vs. CLE
Walks:	
Starter	6 - 5 times, Last Apr. 12, 2000 vs. FLA
Reliever	3 - Jun. 12, 1994 vs. CLE
	3 - Aug. 8, 1998 at SEA
	3 - Aug. 28, 1998 vs. TEX
	3 - Sep 22, 1999 at NYY
Strikeouts:	
Starter	11 - Apr. 6, 1997 vs. DET
Reliever	5 - Jul. 31, 1994 at BOS
Hits Allowed	14 - Jul. 15, 1997 at MIN
Runs Allowed	11 - Jul. 31, 1997 at ANA
	11 - Aug. 22, 1997 at TEX
ER Allowed	11 - Jul. 31, 1997 at ANA
	11 - Aug. 22, 1997 at TEX
HR Allowed	3 - 5 times, Last Apr. 28, 2000 vs. HOU
Low Hit CG	2 - Jul. 22, 1992 vs. TEX
Last Win	Sep. 18, 1999 at TOR
Last Save	Sep. 1, 1998 at BAL
Last CG	Jun. 4, 1998 at KC
Last ShO	Jul. 11, 1996 vs. STL
Last Start	Jun. 23, 2000 vs. DET
Last Relief App.	Jul. 26, 2000 at TOR

JAIME NAVARRO DETAILED PITCHING

	2000								CAREER							
	ERA	W-L-Sv	G	IP	H	ER	BB	SO	ERA	W-L-Sv	G	IP	H	ER	BB	SO
Total	10.53	0-6-0	12	33.1	54	39	23	16	4.72	116-126-2	361	2055.1	2313	1078	690	1113
ST	11.81	0-6-0	7	26.2	51	35	21	12	4.73	112-121-0	309	1956.1	2216	1029	652	1051
REL	5.40	0-0-0	5	6.2	3	4	2	4	4.45	4-5-2	52	99.0	97	49	38	62
Home	9.22	0-3-0	6	13.2	21	14	12	4	4.44	59-58-1	174	1005.0	1088	496	345	564
Away	11.44	0-3-0	6	19.2	33	25	11	12	4.99	57-68-1	187	1050.1	1225	582	345	549
March	–	–	–	–	–	–	–	–	0.00	1-0-0	1	6.0	5	0	1	2
April	12.54	0-5-0	5	18.2	34	26	18	7	5.79	9-20-0	48	276.2	323	178	120	164
May	–	–	–	–	–	–	–	–	4.65	23-20-0	56	344.2	408	178	98	177
June	10.13	0-1-0	2	8.0	17	9	3	5	4.33	22-19-0	60	361.1	379	174	126	192
July	5.40	0-0-0	5	6.2	3	4	2	4	4.58	17-23-1	70	355.1	393	181	114	170
August	–	–	–	–	–	–	–	–	5.20	24-25-0	66	363.1	421	210	119	210
September	–	–	–	–	–	–	–	–	4.15	18-18-1	56	319.0	355	147	103	186
October	–	–	–	–	–	–	–	–	3.10	2-1-0	4	29.0	29	10	9	12
vs. Ana	–	–	–	–	–	–	–	–	3.86	5-5-0	19	114.1	120	49	37	51
vs. Bal	–	–	–	–	–	–	–	–	4.02	11-6-1	23	136.2	136	61	49	59
vs. Bos	–	–	–	–	–	–	–	–	4.32	11-5-0	23	123.0	137	59	44	59
vs. CWS	–	–	–	–	–	–	–	–	3.32	2-5-0	15	81.1	87	30	19	44
vs. Cle	–	–	–	–	–	–	–	–	4.68	5-9-0	21	127.0	129	66	41	59
vs. Det	10.13	0-1-0	2	8.0	17	9	3	5	4.66	8-4-0	24	123.2	154	64	28	73
vs. KC	13.50	0-0-0	1	2.0	1	3	2	1	6.12	8-8-0	24	122.0	163	83	45	61
vs. Mil	–	–	–	–	–	–	–	–	5.56	0-1-0	2	11.1	13	7	2	9
vs. Min	0.00	0-0-0	1	1.0	0	0	0	1	5.49	7-12-0	24	132.2	173	81	32	55
vs. NYY	–	–	–	–	–	–	–	–	6.97	3-11-0	21	102.0	136	79	51	51
vs. Oak	–	–	–	–	–	–	–	–	3.55	5-6-0	17	99.0	93	39	51	66
vs. Sea	–	–	–	–	–	–	–	–	6.08	5-12-1	23	117.0	155	79	43	56
vs. TB	–	–	–	–	–	–	–	–	6.00	0-1-0	1	6.0	9	4	2	3
vs. Tex	–	–	–	–	–	–	–	–	5.47	7-7-0	22	126.2	144	77	44	70
vs. Tor	5.40	0-0-0	1	1.2	2	1	0	1	4.44	7-5-0	21	117.2	121	58	41	67
vs. Atl	–	–	–	–	–	–	–	–	2.60	2-0-0	4	27.2	26	8	6	19
vs. ChC	–	–	–	–	–	–	–	–	7.47	0-2-0	3	15.2	19	13	5	15
vs. Cin	11.25	0-1-0	1	4.0	6	5	2	3	4.46	1-3-0	6	38.1	42	19	16	23
vs. Col	–	–	–	–	–	–	–	–	6.53	2-2-0	5	30.1	42	22	7	26
vs. Fla	1.93	0-1-0	1	4.2	5	1	6	0	2.60	4-1-0	7	45.0	42	13	19	28
vs. Hou	13.50	0-1-0	2	3.1	6	5	3	1	5.40	4-4-0	11	61.2	78	37	18	38
vs. LA	–	–	–	–	–	–	–	–	3.89	2-2-0	5	34.2	31	15	15	21
vs. Mon	14.73	0-1-0	1	3.2	8	6	4	0	5.22	2-3-0	5	29.1	38	17	11	15
vs. NYM	20.25	0-1-0	1	4.0	9	9	3	3	3.25	4-1-0	5	36.0	34	13	10	25
vs. Pit	0.00	0-0-0	1	1.0	0	0	0	1	3.21	3-1-0	5	33.2	31	12	11	22
vs. Pit	–	–	–	–	–	–	–	–	5.07	2-4-0	9	49.2	56	28	14	31
vs. StL	–	–	–	–	–	–	–	–	5.23	2-2-0	7	43.0	54	25	14	19
vs. SD	–	–	–	–	–	–	–	–	2.35	2-1-0	4	30.2	17	8	5	19
vs. SF	–	–	–	–	–	–	–	–	2.75	2-3-0	5	39.1	33	12	10	29
Pre-All Star	11.81	0-6-0	7	26.2	51	35	21	12	4.81	58-68-0	185	1090.2	1231	583	376	581
Post-All Star	5.40	0-0-0	5	6.2	3	4	2	4	4.62	58-58-2	176	964.2	1082	495	314	532

JAIME NAVARRO PITCHING AT ML PARKS

Park	ERA	W-L-Sv	SvO	G	GS	IP	H	R	ER	HR	BB	SO
Camden Yards	4.41	3-2-1	1	8	6	49.0	49	32	24	7	11	22
Fenway Park	5.66	5-3-0	0	13	11	68.1	94	51	43	9	26	33
Edison Field	5.82	0-4-0	0	7	6	38.2	46	27	25	2	15	15
Comiskey Park	5.17	15-21-0	0	53	45	301.0	344	187	173	34	120	161
Jacobs Field	7.64	0-1-0	0	6	3	17.2	24	20	15	5	7	10
Tiger Stadium	7.11	1-3-0	0	9	7	44.1	66	39	35	9	12	26
Kauffman Stadium	5.06	6-5-0	0	14	13	80.0	102	51	45	5	27	38
County Stadium	4.17	34-28-1	1	91	74	515.2	544	273	239	32	167	265
Metrodome	5.23	4-7-0	0	15	13	82.2	103	51	48	9	19	30
Yankee Stadium	5.65	2-5-0	0	11	9	57.1	70	38	36	8	27	21
Oakland-Alameda	3.39	3-4-0	0	12	9	66.1	59	28	25	3	35	40
Kingdome	7.03	2-7-0	0	11	8	48.2	71	38	38	9	16	27
Arlington	8.14	2-2-0	0	5	5	24.1	35	24	22	6	12	11
SkyDome	4.21	5-2-0	0	13	10	72.2	81	41	34	9	17	50
Atlanta-Fulton	2.66	1-0-0	0	3	3	20.1	20	7	6	3	5	10
Wrigley Field	3.81	10-11-0	0	32	32	215.0	215	103	91	20	66	158
Cinergy Field	8.10	0-2-0	0	2	2	10.0	13	9	9	5	6	8
Astrodome	5.16	2-2-0	0	5	5	29.2	38	18	17	5	10	19
Dodger Stadium	3.52	2-0-0	0	2	2	15.1	13	6	6	1	4	8
Olympic Stadium	7.47	0-3-0	0	3	3	15.2	23	14	13	2	8	3
Shea Stadium	5.68	2-1-0	0	3	3	19.0	20	12	12	3	5	11
Veterans Stadium	0.77	3-0-0	0	3	3	23.1	12	4	2	1	8	12
Three Rivers	4.28	2-2-0	0	4	4	27.1	31	14	13	1	5	17
Busch Stadium	7.27	1-1-0	0	5	5	26.0	39	22	21	4	11	12
Qualcomm Park	1.17	1-0-0	0	1	1	7.2	4	2	1	1	0	6
3 Com Park	1.08	2-1-0	0	3	3	25.0	17	4	3	1	5	20
Coors Field	9.56	1-1-0	0	3	3	16.0	29	17	17	5	4	12
Pro Player Stadium	2.21	3-0-0	0	3	3	20.1	18	5	5	2	6	14
Cleveland Stadium	3.83	2-6-0	0	8	8	56.1	58	28	24	6	17	20
Arlington Stadium	5.28	1-0-0	0	5	5	29.0	33	17	17	4	7	18
Memorial Stadium	3.97	1-0-0	0	2	2	11.1	13	5	5	0	3	3
Comiskey Park	2.25	0-1-0	1	4	4	12.0	13	6	3	0	3	8
SAFECO Field	15.75	0-1-0	0	1	1	4.0	8	9	7	2	4	1
Comerica Park	6.75	0-0-0	0	1	1	5.1	8	4	4	1	2	4

Players

Lance PAINTER

PITCHER

BIRTHDATE	July 21, 1967
OPENING DAY AGE	33
BIRTHPLACE	Bedford, England
RESIDENCE	Gilbert, AZ
BATS/THROWS	L/L
HEIGHT/WEIGHT	6-1/200
CONTRACT STATUS	signed thru 2001
M.L. SERVICE	6.150

28

PERSONAL: Lance Telford Painter... Married, wife's name is Kelly... One daughter, Jordan Anne (5/15/98)... Born in England, became a naturalized U.S. citizen prior to the start of the 1994 season... Graduated from Nicolet High School in Glendale, WI, where he hurled a perfect game in his senior season... Pitched for the University of Wisconsin.

LAST SEASON: Was 2-0 with a 4.72 ERA in 42 games, two starts, in his first season in the AL... In 40 games in relief was 1-0 with a 4.68 ERA with five holds... Started two games for Toronto... Was 1-0 with a 5.00 ERA... Started the season slowly allowing five earned runs and three home runs in his first two outings over 3.2 innings... In his next seven outings, from April 11 to May 3 allowed one earned run over 13.1 innings... Finished April with a 3.45 ERA in eight games... After ten relief appearance made two starts for Toronto... Won his first start on May 10 vs Baltimore as he allowed one run on two hits in 5.0 innings while setting a career high with eight strikeouts... Had a no-decision in his second start on May 16 , a 7-6 win over Boston... Returned to the bullpen where he allowed runs in four straight outings... Was then placed on the 15-day disabled list from May 17 to June 6 after suffering from a tender left elbow... Had six consecutive outings without an earned run from June 25 to July 7... At the All-Star break was 1-0 with a 4.42 ERA in 23 games... Following the break was 1-0 with a 5.14 ERA in 19 games... July was his top month posting an ERA of 2.38 in ten games... Appeared in seven August games and was 0-0 with a 4.70 ERA... Earned his second win of the season on September 17 with 3.0 innings of work against the White Sox... Pitched three or more innings in relief on four occasions... Pitched a season high 3.2 innings on September 23 vs Tampa Bay... Lowered his ERA to 3.70 for the season before being roughed up for a career high eight earned runs in his final outing of the season on September 28 in a 23-1 loss in Baltimore... ERA in the second half excluding that outing would have been 2.67 (8ER/27.0IP)... Opponents hit .271 with nine home runs... Held left-handed batters to a .291 average with four homers while right-handed batters hit .257 with five homers... Was 1-0 at home with a 3.75 ERA and 1-0 on the road with a 5.87 ERA.

PROFESSIONAL CAREER: 1990: Selected by San Diego in the 25th round of the June draft... Made pro debut with Spokane where he held Northwest League (A) batters to a .174 batting average... Was 7-3 with a 1.51 ERA in 23 games, 1 start and averaged 13.06 strikeouts per nine innings pitched. (104K/71.2IP)... **1991:** Used as a starter by Waterloo of the Midwest League and was 14-8 with a 2.30 ERA in 28 starts... Led all Class A with four shutouts... Finished as league runner up with seven complete games, 200 innings and 201 strikeouts, was fourth in wins at 14... Named team MVP and earned spot on Midwest League All-Star team... **1992:** Won five of first seven starts en route to a 10-5 season with Wichita- AA... Led the Texas league with a .667 winning percentage and tied for the lead in starts... Struck out a season high 11 on July 30 at Arkansas... Tossed one shutout in the regular season and then matched that with a shutout in the post-season against Shreveport... Selected by the Colorado Rockies in the expansion draft in November... **1993:** Opened the season in AAA with Colorado Springs... Was promoted to Colorado and made his ML debut, starting on May 19 at San Diego where he collected a hit but took the loss... Made two more starts before being optioned to Colorado Springs on June 2... Was 9-7 in 23 games, 22 starts and tied for the Pacific Coast League lead with four complete games... Recalled to Colorado on August 27 and won his first two starts... First ML victory came on August 29 at New York Mets allowing just five hits in a complete game 6-1 win in which he drove in a run... Hit .300 (3-10) with three sac bunts and a walk... Made first of four relief appearance on September 18 at Los Angeles... **1994:** Split the season between Colorado and Colorado Springs... Was the Rockies Rookie-of-the-Year as voted by the Colorado BBWAA... Was 4-6 in 15 games, 14 starts with a 6.11 ERA... Won consecutive starts June 17 at LA and June 22 at Houston... On June 22 held Astros to two runs over eight innings and drove in two runs with a sac fly and a double... Posted a career high six strikeouts in six innings against Florida on July 8... Only relief appearance came August 4 at Houston, three days after capturing his fourth win of the season in Houston... **1995:** Opened the season on the disabled list after spraining his left ankle early in spring training... Activated from the disabled list on May 6 and joined the bullpen... Made two appearances before he was optioned to Colorado Springs after expanded rosters were reduced... Was recalled on June 5 and made three more appearances before being optioned... Recalled for the remainder of the season on July 12... Would finish the season 28-for-33 in first batter efficiency and permitted only six of 27 inherited runners to score... Allowed two earned runs in his first 15 games upon return on a HR by Ryan Thompson on July 14 at NY... Had tossed 16.2 scoreless innings from July 14 to August 11... July 25 at Philadelphia retired 10 batters in order with four strikeouts... On the season walked 10 batters in 45.1 innings but none in his final 14 games (19.2IP)... First ML save was August 15 at Cincinnati retiring the only batter he faced, first pro save since 1990 in his pro debut with Spokane... Made one start on September 12 vs Atlanta and allowed two ER over five innings... In the post-season made two appearances in the Division Series against Atlanta... In Game One appeared as a pinch-hitter and started in game two and allowed three runs over five innings and finished with a no-decision in the Braves 7-4 win... **1996:** First entire season in the majors and finished with a 5.86 ERA in 34 games, one start... Lone start was April 7 at Montreal where he took the loss and matched his career high with six strikeouts... April 10 recorded his 100th career strikeout vs the Cubs... Won career high four straight decisions over 15 games from April 27 to June 14... Had eight consecutive scoreless outings from April 30 to June 1 (6.1IP)... July 4 at LA allowed one hit over four shutout innings with four strikeouts... Walked only batter faced on August 3 at Chicago and was placed on the disabled list the next day... Had arthroscopic surgery on September 13 to repair a torn labrum in his left shoulder... Was claimed on waivers by the St. Louis Cardinals on December 2... **1997:** Was limited to 14 appearances with the Cardinals due to a right hamstring strain which disabled him April 5 to 13 and May 20 to September 1... Earned lone victory in the season finale on September 28 vs Chicago, pitched final 1.2 innings in a 2-1 win... Allowed one hit in his 7.1 shutout innings at Busch Stadium... Retired 11 of 14 first batters faced... Appeared in 18 games, two starts with Louisville and was 1-0 with a 5.23 ERA and had 22 strikeouts in 20.2 innings... **1998:** Appeared in a career high 65 games and led the team with 21 holds which was tied for third most in the NL... Matched career high with four wins and a career best ERA of 3.99... Was fourth among NL relievers allowing only 19% of inherited runners to score... Left-handed batters hit just .205... Earned first win of the season on May 23 vs San Francisco in an 11-10 win...

Earned second career save, first as a Cardinal, on July 31 at Atlanta striking out the final two batters of the game with the bases loaded... Posted a season best ERA of 1.42 in September... **1999:** Was 4-5 with a save and a 4.83 ERA in 56 games, four starts for the Cardinals... Ranked second among NL pitchers in first batter efficiency allowing only a .140 batting average (6-43)... Allowed seven of 40 inherited runners to score to rank fifth in the league... Posted ten holds... Was on the disabled list from June 14 to 29 with a strained left shoulder... Lost his first four decisions before capturing a win on July 3 at Arizona... Tossed 13.0 scoreless innings over 19 games from July 3 to August 22... Earned only save on September 29 vs San Diego in a 4-3 win (1.0IP)... Had stretch of 38 games without allowing a home run until his final appearance of the season on October 2 when Jeff Reed of the Chicago Cubs homered... Had not allowed a HR since May 28 when Henry Rodriguez of the Cubs homered... In the second half of the season was 3-1 with a 3.04 ERA and 26 strikeouts in 23.2 innings... Opponents hit .308 before the break and only .183 following.

CAREER NOTES: Is 3-8 in save situations... Has a career batting average of .156 (10-64) with two doubles, a triple and five RBI.

POST SEASON EXPERIENCE: 1995: Appeared in two games for the Colorado Rockies in the Division Series against Atlanta... Used as a pinch-hitter in Game One and started Game Two, a no-decision after allowing three earned runs over 5.0 innings on five hits.

LANCE PAINTER

Year	Club & League	W-L	ERA	G	GS	CG	ShO	SV	IP	H	R	ER	HR	HB	BB-IBB	SO	WP	BK	OBA
1990	Spokane (NWST)	7-3	1.51	23	1	0	0	3	71.2	45	18	12	4	2	15-0	104	3	3	.174
1991	Waterloo (Mid)	14-8	2.30	28	28	7	4	0	200.0	162	64	51	14	2	57-7	201	3	1	.225
1992	Wichita (Tex)	10-5	3.53	27	27	1	1	0	163.1	138	74	64	11	10	55-1	137	6	3	.228
1993	Colo Springs (PCL)	9-7	4.30	23	22	4	1	0	138.0	165	90	66	10	5	44-2	91	6	2	.302
1993	COLORADO (NL)	2-2	6.00	10	6	1	0	0	39.0	52	26	26	5	0	9-0	16	2	0	.321
1994	Colo Springs (PCL)	4-3	4.79	13	13	1	0	0	71.1	83	42	38	5	5	28-2	59	3	0	.291
1994	COLORADO (NL)	4-6	6.11	15	14	0	0	0	73.2	91	51	50	9	1	26-2	41	3	1	.302
1995	COLORADO (NL)	3-0	4.37	33	1	0	0	1	45.1	55	23	22	9	2	10-0	36	4	1	.296
1995	Colo Springs (PCL)	0-3	5.96	11	4	0	0	0	25.2	32	20	17	3	1	11-1	12	0	1	.305
1996	COLORADO (NL)	4-2	5.86	34	1	0	0	0	50.2	56	37	33	12	3	25-3	48	1	0	.280
1997	ST. LOUIS (NL)	1-1	4.76	14	0	0	0	0	17.0	13	9	9	1	0	8-2	11	0	0	.213
1997	Louisville (AmAs)	1-0	5.23	18	2	0	0	0	20.2	18	14	12	2	1	4-0	22	0	1	.234
1998	ST. LOUIS (NL)	4-0	3.99	65	0	0	0	1	47.1	42	24	21	5	4	28-3	39	2	0	.249
1999	Arkansas (Tex)	0-0	0.00	1	1	0	0	0	2.0	1	0	0	0	0	0-0	4	0	0	.143
1999	ST. LOUIS (NL)	4-5	4.83	56	4	0	0	1	63.1	63	37	34	6	2	25-1	56	4	0	.265
2000	Dunedin (FSL)	0-0	0.00	1	1	0	0	0	1.0	0	0	0	0	0	0-0	0	0	0	.000
2000	TORONTO (AL)	2-0	4.73	42	2	0	0	0	66.2	69	37	35	9	2	22-1	53	4	0	.271
Minor Totals		45-29	3.37	145	99	13	6	3	693.2	644	322	260	49	26	214-13	630	21	11	.247
NL TOTALS		22-16	5.22	227	26	1	0	3	336.1	372	207	195	47	12	131-11	247	16	2	.282
MAJOR TOTALS		24-16	5.14	269	28	1	0	3	403.0	441	244	230	56	14	153-12	300	20	2	.280

DIVISION SERIES RECORD

Year	Club & League	W-L	ERA	G	GS	CG	ShO	SV	IP	H	R	ER	HR	HB	BB-IBB	SO	WP	BK	OBA
1995	COLORADO (NL)	0-0	5.40	2	1	0	0	0	5.0	5	3	3	2	0	2-0	4	0	0	.250

PAINTER — TRANSACTIONS

- Selected by the San Diego Padres in 25th round (681 overall) of the June 1990 First Year Draft.
- Selected by the Colorado Rockies in the second round of the Expansion Draft on November 17, 1992.
- On disabled list (sprained ankle) April 17-May 6, 1995.
- On disabled list (torn Labrum left shoulder) August 6, 1996 to end of the season.
- Claimed on waivers by the St. Louis Cardinals from the Colorado Rockies on December 2, 1996.
- On disabled list (right hamstring) April 5-May 12, 1997.
- On disabled list (right hamstring) May 20-September 1, 1997.
- On disabled list (strained left shoulder) June 14-29, 1999; included rehabilitation assignment at Arkansas, June 28-29.
- Traded to the Toronto Blue Jays along with C Alberto Castillo and RHP Matt DeWitt in exchange for RHP Pat Hentgen and LHP Paul Spoljaric on November 11, 1999.
- On disabled list (tender left elbow) May 17-June 6, 2000; included rehabilitation assignment at Dunedin June 4.

FIELDING

PAINTER, Lance—P

Year	PCT	G	PO	A	E	TC	DP
1993 (NL)	1.000	10	1	9	0	10	0
1994 (NL)	1.000	15	5	11	0	16	1
1995 (NL)	1.000	33	3	6	0	9	0
1996 (NL)	.750	34	2	7	3	12	0
1997 (NL)	1.000	14	4	3	0	7	1
1998 (NL)	1.000	65	6	12	0	18	1
1999 (NL)	.938	56	3	12	1	16	1
2000 (AL)	1.000	42	4	17	0	21	2
Total	.963	269	28	77	4	109	6

CAREER HIGHS — PAINTER, Lance

SEASON:

Wins	4 - 1994, 96, 98, 99
Losses	6 - 1994
Saves	1 - 1995, 98, 99
ERA	3.99 - 1998
Games	65 - 1998
Starts	73.2 - 1994
Complete Games	1 - 1993
Shutouts	None
Innings Pitched	73.2 - 1994
Walks	28 - 1999
Strikeouts	56 - 1999
Longest Win Streak	4 - Apr. 27-Jun. 14, 1996
	4 - May 23-Aug. 15, 1998
Longest Losing Streak	4 - Apr. 18-Jun 2, 1999
Scoreless Innings Streak	14.0 - Jul. 22-Aug. 12, 1995

GAME:

ML Debut	May 19, 1993 at SD
Innings Pitched:	
Starter	9.0 - Aug. 29, 1993 at NYM
Reliever	4.0 - Jul. 14, 1995 at NYM
	4.0 - Jul. 4, 1996 at LA
Walks:	
Starter	3 - 6 times, last Jun. 7, 1999 at KC
Reliever	3 - 8 times, last Aug. 23, 2000 vs. KC
Strikeouts:	
Starter	8 - May 10, 2000 vs. BAL
Reliever	5 - Jul. 14, 1995 at NYM
	5 - Apr. 28, 1996 vs. MON
Hits Allowed	12 - May 19, 1993 at SD
	12 - Sep. 4, 1993 vs. PIT
Runs Allowed	8 - Sep. 28, 2000 at BAL
ER Allowed	8 - Sep. 28, 2000 at BAL
HR Allowed	3 - May 30, 1993 vs. PHI
	3 - Apr. 7, 2000 at TEX
Low Hit CG	5 - Aug. 29, 1993 at NYM
Last Win	Sep. 17, 2000 at CWS
Last Save	Sep. 29, 2000 vs. SD
Last CG	Aug. 29, 1993 at NYM
Last ShO	None
Last Start	May 16, 2000 vs. BOS
Last Relief App.	Sep. 28, 2000 at BAL

LANCE PAINTER DETAILED PITCHING

	2000								CAREER						
	ERA	W-L-Sv	G	IP	H	ER	BB	SO	ERA	W-L-Sv	G	IP	H	ER	BB	SO
Total	4.72	2-0-0	42	66.2	69	35	22	53	5.14	24-16-3	269	403.0	441	230	153	300
ST	5.00	1-0-0	2	9.0	10	5	2	11	5.78	8-11-0	28	143.1	177	92	45	84
REL	4.68	1-0-0	40	57.2	59	30	20	42	4.78	16-5-3	241	259.2	264	138	108	216
Home	3.75	1-0-0	21	36.0	30	15	13	29	5.38	16-5-1	136	204.0	226	122	85	146
Away	5.87	1-0-0	21	30.2	39	20	9	24	4.88	8-11-2	133	199.0	215	108	68	154
March	–	–	–	–	–	–	–	–	0.00	0-0-0	1	0.1	0	0	0	0
April	3.45	0-0-0	8	15.2	9	6	5	12	4.98	1-3-0	40	56.0	51	31	19	48
May	5.25	1-0-0	4	12.0	11	7	4	11	8.22	3-5-0	38	65.2	84	60	34	48
June	5.40	0-0-0	7	8.1	12	5	0	7	6.50	5-1-0	39	70.2	95	51	35	48
July	2.38	0-0-0	10	11.1	9	3	6	7	3.06	5-4-1	58	88.1	81	30	33	73
August	4.70	0-0-0	7	7.2	10	4	4	7	4.23	4-2-1	43	55.1	56	26	11	33
September	7.71	1-0-0	6	11.2	18	10	3	9	4.22	5-1-1	46	64.0	71	30	21	48
October	–	–	–	–	–	–	–	–	6.75	1-0-0	4	2.2	3	2	0	2
vs. Ana	2.70	0-0-0	3	6.2	5	2	2	5	2.70	0-0-0	3	6.2	5	2	2	5
vs. Bal	7.30	1-0-0	6	12.1	15	10	2	12	7.30	1-0-0	6	12.1	15	10	2	12
vs. Bos	7.94	0-0-0	3	5.2	10	5	1	4	7.94	0-0-0	3	5.2	10	5	1	4
vs. CWS	1.93	1-0-0	2	4.2	2	1	1	2	2.00	2-0-0	5	9.0	5	2	2	5
vs. Cle	7.71	0-0-0	2	2.1	2	2	3	2	10.13	0-0-0	3	2.2	2	3	6	2
vs. Det	9.00	0-0-0	1	1.0	3	1	0	1	3.00	0-0-0	2	6.0	7	2	1	5
vs. KC	3.38	0-0-0	3	2.2	2	1	3	2	3.24	0-0-0	6	8.1	6	3	6	5
vs. Mil	–	–	–	–	–	–	–	–	4.05	1-1-0	14	13.1	11	6	4	11
vs. Min	13.50	0-0-0	2	0.2	3	1	1	0	4.50	0-0-0	4	2.0	5	1	1	3
vs. NYY	1.69	0-0-0	3	5.1	5	1	1	6	1.69	0-0-0	3	5.1	5	1	1	6
vs. Oak	0.00	0-0-0	2	5.1	3	0	1	6	0.00	0-0-0	2	5.1	3	0	1	6
vs. Sea	0.00	0-0-0	3	6.0	1	0	4	5	0.00	0-0-0	3	6.0	1	0	4	5
vs. TB	0.00	0-0-0	3	6.0	4	0	1	5	0.00	0-0-0	3	6.0	4	0	1	5
vs. Tex	16.20	0-0-0	2	3.1	6	6	1	1	16.20	0-0-0	2	3.1	6	6	1	1
vs. Ari	–	–	–	–	–	–	–	–	5.40	1-0-0	7	5.0	7	3	4	4
vs. Atl	27.00	0-0-0	1	0.1	1	1	0	0	6.32	2-3-1	19	31.1	43	22	7	20
vs. ChC	–	–	–	–	–	–	–	–	3.90	1-1-0	21	30.0	29	13	7	25
vs. Cin	–	–	–	–	–	–	–	–	2.95	1-0-1	16	18.1	11	6	10	14
vs. Col	–	–	–	–	–	–	–	–	0.00	1-0-0	9	5.0	5	0	4	3
vs. Fla	–	–	–	–	–	–	–	–	4.57	0-3-0	8	21.2	20	11	7	18
vs. Hou	–	–	–	–	–	–	–	–	7.33	3-1-0	13	23.1	33	19	10	7
vs. LA	–	–	–	–	–	–	–	–	7.88	1-0-0	15	24.0	36	21	9	21
vs. Mon	11.57	0-0-0	3	2.1	6	3	0	2	5.55	1-2-0	16	24.1	29	15	8	25
vs. NYM	0.00	0-0-0	2	1.2	0	0	0	0	4.25	1-0-0	15	29.2	30	14	8	20
vs. Phi	27.00	0-0-0	1	0.1	1	1	1	0	6.33	1-1-0	16	21.1	21	15	12	15
vs. Pit	–	–	–	–	–	–	–	–	5.01	3-0-0	15	23.1	26	13	13	12
vs. StL	–	–	–	–	–	–	–	–	2.84	2-0-0	9	19.0	18	6	5	13
vs. SD	–	–	–	–	–	–	–	–	9.82	0-2-1	19	22.0	37	24	6	15
vs. SF	–	–	–	–	–	–	–	–	4.97	2-2-0	12	12.2	11	7	10	13
Pre-All Star	4.42	1-0-0	23	38.2	36	19	11	33	6.26	10-11-0	134	220.0	258	153	102	168
Post-All Star	5.14	1-0-0	19	28.0	33	16	11	20	3.79	14-5-3	135	183.0	183	77	51	132

LANCE PAINTER PITCHING AT ML PARKS

Park	ERA	W-L-Sv	SvO	G	GS	IP	H	R	ER	HR	BB	SO
Camden Yards	19.64	0-0-0	0	3	0	3.2	10	8	8	1	1	3
Fenway Park	99.00	0-0-0	0	1	0	0.0	1	1	1	0	0	0
Edison Field	1.93	0-0-0	0	2	0	4.2	3	1	1	0	0	3
Comiskey Park	2.35	2-0-0	0	3	0	7.2	4	2	2	1	1	5
Jacobs Field	6.75	0-0-0	0	2	0	1.1	1	4	1	0	5	2
Kauffman Stadium	3.60	0-0-0	1	2	1	5.0	5	2	2	0	3	3
County Stadium	1.13	1-1-0	0	7	0	8.0	4	1	1	1	1	7
Metrodome	27.00	0-0-0	0	2	0	0.1	3	1	1	0	1	0
Yankee Stadium	3.00	0-0-0	0	2	0	3.0	5	1	1	0	0	3
Oakland-Alameda	0.00	0-0-0	0	1	0	2.2	1	0	0	0	0	3
Arlington	12.00	0-0-0	0	1	0	3.0	4	4	4	3	1	1
SkyDome	3.75	1-0-0	0	21	2	36.0	30	16	15	4	13	29
Atlanta-Fulton	2.84	0-0-0	0	5	0	6.1	6	2	2	1	0	5
Wrigley Field	2.84	0-1-0	0	9	1	12.2	10	4	4	1	4	13
Cinergy Field	2.16	1-0-1	1	8	1	8.1	6	2	2	1	3	7
Astrodome	10.93	1-1-0	1	8	2	14.0	22	17	17	5	5	3
Dodger Stadium	4.11	1-0-0	0	6	1	15.1	18	7	7	1	4	13
Olympic Stadium	5.40	0-2-0	0	9	2	16.2	19	10	10	3	5	17
Shea Stadium	3.94	1-0-0	0	7	1	16.0	14	7	7	1	1	12
Veterans Stadium	4.76	0-0-0	2	7	0	5.2	3	5	3	0	5	6
Three Rivers	1.86	0-0-0	0	8	1	9.2	6	2	2	1	5	4
Busch Stadium	4.16	7-1-1	2	69	2	67.0	62	32	31	4	37	57
Qualcomm Park	10.22	0-2-0	0	9	2	12.1	24	14	14	2	3	8
3 Com Park	4.91	0-2-0	0	6	0	7.1	8	4	4	2	4	6
Coors Field	5.43	6-0-0	0	45	1	61.1	75	41	37	14	23	45
Pro Player Stadium	4.50	0-2-0	0	4	2	12.0	13	9	6	2	4	11
Turner Field	8.44	0-0-1	1	6	0	5.1	8	5	5	1	3	3
BankOne Ballpark	9.00	0-0-0	0	2	0	1.0	1	1	1	0	1	1
Tropicana Field	0.00	0-0-0	0	1	0	2.0	1	0	0	0	0	2
Mile High Stadium	7.11	3-4-0	0	11	9	50.2	70	40	40	7	17	24
SAFECO Field	0.00	0-0-0	0	1	0	3.0	1	0	0	0	3	3
Comerica Park	9.00	0-0-0	0	1	0	1.0	3	1	1	0	0	1

Steve
PARRIS
PITCHER

39

BIRTHDATE	December 17, 1967
OPENING DAY AGE	33
BIRTHPLACE	Joliet, IL
RESIDENCE	Plainfield, IL
BATS/THROWS	R/R
HEIGHT/WEIGHT	6-0/195
CONTRACT STATUS	signed thru 2002
M.L. SERVICE	4.016

PERSONAL: Steven Micheal Parris... Married, wife's name is Gina (2/23/91)... Two children, son Cole (12/15/93) and daughter Ciara (9/14/97)... Graduated from Joliet (IL) West High School, the same school attended by Major Leaguer Jeff Reed... Went 7-2 his senior year and earned SICA West Conference MVP and All-Area honours... Attended the College of St. Francis in Joliet, IL, where he went 25-10, 3.07 in 51 games over three seasons... Made 37 career starts for the Saints and threw 23 complete games.

LAST SEASON: In his third season with the Reds was 12-17 with a 4.81 ERA in 33 starts... Set career highs in wins, losses, starts, innings pitched (192.2) and strikeouts (117)... Led the club in wins, losses, starts and innings pitched while ranking second with 117 strikeouts to Williamson... The 17 losses were the second-highest total in the Majors behind Philadelphia's Omar Daal who had 19... Were the most by a Reds pitcher since RHP Jeff Russell had 18 in 1984... In his first 23 starts was 5-14 with a 5.22 ERA through August 7, then from August 13 on was 7-3 in ten starts with a 3.94 ERA to finish the season... Won seven consecutive starts from August 13 to September 15 before finishing the season 0-3 in his final three starts with a 8.63 ERA... Was his longest career win streak... Lost 4-2 on September 20 at San Francisco to snap his win streak, in the fifth inning of that game allowed Barry Bonds' 493rd career HR, a solo shot into McCovey Cove that tied Bonds with Lou Gehrig for 17th on the all-time list... First Reds pitcher to win seven consecutive starts since LHP Tom Browning won 8 straight from 7/29-9/2, 1989 and the first Reds right-hander to do it since Tom Seaver won 7 straight from 5/16-6/16, 1978... In his 33 starts

allowed 22 runs in the first inning... Club was 15-18 in his 33 starts and averaged 4.3 runs per game scored... Lost six straight from May 14 to June 16 to set a career high... Started a pair of shutouts, threw 6.0 scoreless innings in the 2-0 win on May 9 vs SD and 7.2 scoreless innings in the 3-0 victory on 8/13 at Cubs... In a 9-2 loss on April 21 vs LA, he drove in the only runs with a bases-loaded double in the second inning... Was his first hit of the season, his third career double and his first double since 1995... Allowed a career high four home runs in a 6-5 loss to Cleveland on June 10, solo HR's by Fryman with two, Branyan and Lofton... Tossed a season high 8.0 innings on August 7 vs Atlanta and received a no-decision in a 10-inning, 4-3 victory (9H, 2ER)... Pitched 14.2 consecutive scoreless innings from August 13 (2.2IP) to August 19 (7.0)... In his final start of the season, threw a season-high 133 pitches and suffered the 6-2 loss at St. Louis... Twice allowed back-to-back homers, on June 10 at Cleveland (Fryman, Branyan) and July 26 vs Houston (Lugo, Bagwell)... Twice allowed 3 homers in an inning, on June 10 at Cleveland (Fryman, Branyan, Lofton) and July 26 vs Houston (Lugo, Bagwell, Alou)... Selected by the Cincinnati BBWAA as the Good Guy Award winner.

PROFESSIONAL CAREER: 1989: Made his professional debut with Batavia (A) and was 3-5 with a 3.92 ERA in 13 games, ten starts... **1990:** Went 7-1 for Batavia (A) and posted a 2.64 ERA in 14 starts... Led the New York-Penn League in winning percentage (.875) and the club in wins... **1991:** Spent the entire season at Class A Clearwater and made just six starts and 37 relief appearances... **1992:** Combined to post an 8-10 record with a 4.41 ERA in 29 games,

20 starts, for Reading (AA) and Scranton/Wilkes-Barre (AAA)... **1993:** Began the season with the Phillies' Class AAA affiliate in Scranton/Wilkes-Barre and appeared in three games in relief... April 19 was claimed on waivers by the Los Angeles Dodgers and was optioned to Class AA San Antonio... Did not pitch for San Antonio because of a right shoulder injury... Without pitching in the Dodgers organization was claimed off waivers by Seattle on April 27 and appeared in seven games, one start, for Jacksonville (AA) and was 0-1 with a 5.93 ERA... Was released by Seattle on August 3 and later that month had re-constructive surgery on his right shoulder performed by Dr. Frank Jobe... **1994:** Recovered from shoulder surgery and signed with the Pirates organization on June 24... Posted a 3-3 record in 17 games, seven starts with a 3.63 ERA for Salem (A)... **1995:** Began the season with Carolina (AA) and went 8-0 to equal the best start in club history... Allowed just one earned run in his first three starts (17.0 IP)... In April was 3-0 in five starts with a 2.48 ERA... Threw a pair of shutouts, a three-hitter on May 20 vs Greenville and a two-hitter on June 4 at Knoxville... Was the Pirate organization's Pitcher of the Month in April and May and twice was named Southern League Pitcher of the Week (April 8-14 & May 19-25)... Allowed just two home runs in 89.2IP... Was 9-1 in 14 starts with a 2.51 ERA when he was promoted to Pittsburgh on June 18... Made his ML debut on June 21 vs San Francisco... First ML victory came in his second start on June 26 at Chicago... On July 12 vs Atlanta set a career high with nine strikeouts and recorded his first Major League hit, a single off John Smoltz... Posted his first career shutout on August 15 at San Diego, a seven-hitter in a 6-0 win... Finished 6-6 in 15 starts with a 5.38 ERA... **1996:** Started the season on the DL after arthroscopic surgery on his right shoulder, performed March 6... Made six starts on a rehab assignment with Augusta (A) and Carolina (AA) and combined to go 2-0 with a 2.56 ERA... Was recalled and activated from the DL on July 11... Made four appearances in relief before joining the starting rotation on July 27... Made four starts and was 0-3 with a 5.32ERA before suffering a strained oblique muscle warming up prior to his start on August 17 at Atlanta... Placed on the DL the next day and did not pitch again the rest of the season... **1997:** Attended spring training with the Pirates but was released after three exhibition appearances... Signed with the Reds to a minor league contract on May 6... Combined to go 8-5 with a 3.96ERA and a shutout in 19 starts with Chattanooga (AA) and Indianapolis (AAA)... Started his season with Chattanooga, where he went 6-2 with a 4.13 ERA in 14 starts... Was on the Lookouts' disabled list from June 12- 26 with tendinitis in his right shoulder... On August 3 was promoted to Indianapolis on August 3 where he made five starts and was 2-3 with a 3.57 ERA, and a shutout... Was named American Association Pitcher of the Week after tossing a 1-hit shutout vs Louisville on August 23 with 11 strikeouts... Became a free agent following the season but re-signed with the Reds on October 27... **1998:** Began the season at Indianapolis (AAA)and went 6-1 in 13 starts with a 3.84 ERA before the Reds purchased his contract on June 19... At the time led the International

League with 102 strikeouts (84.1 IP) and was 6-1 with a 3.84 ERA... Was the IL Pitcher of the Week from May 25 to 31 after going 2-0 in two starts with a 0.00 ERA (17IP, 21K)... With the Reds was 6-5 in 18 games, 16 starts with a 3.73 ERA... Made his first two appearances in relief, tossing four shutout innings, and then finished the season making 16 consecutive starts... In his first six starts was 1-2 with a 6.12 ERA and then from August 4 on, was 5-3 in his last ten starts with a 2.73 ERA... In August was 3-1 with a 2.62 ERA in five starts... Finished the season 5-2 with a 2.61 ERA in his last eight starts, including a three-game winning streak from August 15 to 27... Reds were 9-7 in his 16 starts with 74 runs scored, 4.6 runs per games... Tossed a three-hit shutout, the second of his career, on August 22 in a 3-0 victory at Montreal... Made two starts in which the Reds were shutout, a 2-0 loss on July 20 at Los Angeles and a 1-0 loss on September 7 at Houston... **1999:** Was 11-4 with a 3.50 ERA, two complete games and a shutout in 22 games, 21 starts... Set then career highs in every major statistical category... Ranked second in the NL with a .733 winning percentage... Began the season with Indianapolis (AAA) where he was 0-1 with a 3.28 in four starts before he was recalled on May 3... Made his season debut that night vs Arizona and earned a no-decision in a 4-3 win... Won his second start on May 15, a 6-2 victory vs San Diego... In a 3-2 win on May 25 vs Los Angeles he tied his career high with 9 strikeouts and outdueled Kevin Brown for the victory... Started the season on a four game win streak, the first of his career... On May 9 at Colorado earned the win in a 24-12 victory, was his only relief appearance of the season and the longest of his career (3.1IP)... Suffered first loss on June 16, 5-2 to the New York Mets... On June 5 at KC, started Game 1 of the doubleheader and threw his third career complete game in the 9-4 victory... Was scheduled to start on June 4, but that game was postponed by a power failure, he spent the 1-hour, 50-minute delay signing autographs while sitting on top of the dugout... Was 7-1 when he was sidelined with a strained right triceps muscle and was placed on the DL on July 26... In his last six starts prior to the DL was 3-0 with a 1.95 ERA... The 7-1 start was the best by a Reds pitcher since 1995, when John Smiley began 11-1 and Xavier Hernandez started out 7-1... After two rehab starts with Indianapolis (0-1, 5.73) was activated from the DL on September 1... Returned to the rotation and went 4-2 with a 3.12 ERA with one shutout in 6 starts during September... Won four consecutive starts from September 8 to 24 and posted a 2.57 ERA as the Reds pulled within 2.5 games of division leading Houston and one game of wild card... On September 18 at Pittsburgh, in his first career appearance against his former team, threw his fourth career complete game and third career shutout in the 3-0 win - did not allow a runner to reach third base... Started the Reds' one-game playoff vs the Mets and suffered the 5-0 loss (2.2IP, 3H, 3ER, 3BB, 1K), Edgardo Alfonzo hit a 2-run HR in the first inning and Al Leiter threw a 2-hitter... Prior to Alfonzo's homer he had allowed just two home runs in his previous 42.2 IP... Reds were 14-7 in his 21 starts, including 7-3 in his last 10, and scored 101 runs in those 21 starts - 4.8 runs per game.

FIELDING
PARRIS, Steve—P

Year	PCT	G	PO	A	E	TC	DP
1995	1.000	15	4	10	0	14	0
1996	.857	8	2	4	1	7	1
1998	1.000	18	5	21	0	26	0
1999	.962	22	8	17	1	26	6
2000	.974	33	15	22	1	38	4
Total	.973	96	34	74	3	111	11

STEVE PARRIS

Year	Club & League	W-L	ERA	G	GS	CG	ShO	SV	IP	H	R	ER	HR	HB	BB-IBB	SO	WP	BK	OBA
1989	Batavia (NYP)	3-5	3.92	13	10	1	0	0	66.2	69	38	29	6	4	20-1	46	4	0	.263
1990	Batavia (NYP)	7-1	2.64	14	14	0	0	0	81.2	70	34	24	1	3	22-2	50	7	3	.233
1991	Clearwater (FSL)	7-5	3.39	43	6	0	0	0	93.0	101	43	35	1	9	25-4	59	3	4	.285
1992	Reading (East)	5-7	4.64	18	14	0	0	0	85.1	94	55	44	9	3	21-1	60	2	0	.277
1992	Scranton-WB (Int)	3-3	4.03	11	6	0	0	0	51.1	57	25	23	1	4	17-1	29	6	1	.285
1993	Scranton-WB (Int)	0-0	12.71	3	0	0	0	0	5.2	9	9	8	3	1	3-0	4	1	0	.346
1993	Jacksnville (Sou)	0-1	5.93	7	1	0	0	0	13.2	15	9	9	3	2	6-0	5	0	0	.273
1994	Salem (Caro)	3-3	3.63	17	7	0	0	0	57.0	58	24	23	7	6	21-1	48	1	0	.266
1995	Carolina (Sou)	9-1	2.51	14	14	2	2	0	89.2	61	25	25	2	4	16-1	86	3	0	.191
1995	PITTSBURGH (NL)	6-6	5.38	15	15	1	1	0	82.0	89	49	49	12	7	33-1	61	4	0	.283
1996	Augusta (SAL)	0-0	0.00	1	1	0	0	0	5.0	1	0	0	0	0	1-0	6	0	0	.067
1996	Carolina (Sou)	2-0	3.04	5	5	0	0	0	26.2	24	11	9	1	0	6-0	22	2	0	.235
1996	PITTSBURGH (NL)	0-3	7.18	8	4	0	0	0	26.1	35	22	21	4	1	11-0	27	2	0	.321
1997	Chattanooga (Sou)	6-2	4.13	14	14	0	0	0	80.2	78	44	37	9	1	29-0	68	2	0	.249
1997	Indianapolis (AmAs)	2-3	3.57	5	5	1	1	0	35.1	26	15	14	4	2	11-1	27	0	0	.203
1998	Indianapolis (Int)	6-1	3.84	13	13	1	1	0	84.1	74	38	36	8	1	26-1	102	6	0	.235
1998	CINCINNATI (NL)	6-5	3.73	18	16	1	1	0	99.0	89	44	41	9	4	32-3	77	1	1	.236
1999	Indianapolis (Int)	0-2	4.04	6	6	0	0	0	35.2	39	16	16	5	1	9-1	31	0	0	.291
1999	CINCINNATI (NL)	11-4	3.50	22	21	2	1	0	128.2	124	59	50	16	6	52-4	86	3	0	.260
2000	CINCINNATI (NL)	12-17	4.81	33	33	0	0	0	192.2	227	109	103	30	4	71-5	117	9	1	.294
Minor Totals		53-34	3.68	184	116	5	4	2	811.2	776	386	332	60	41	233-14	643	37	8	.252
MAJOR TOTALS		35-35	4.49	96	89	4	3	0	528.2	564	283	264	71	22	199-13	368	19	2	.275

PARRIS — TRANSACTIONS

- Selected by the Philadelphia Phillies in the 5th round of the June 1989 First Year Player Draft.
- Claimed on waivers by the Los Angeles Dodgers on April 19, 1993.
- Claimed on waivers by the Seattle Mariners on April 27, 1993.
- Released by the Seattle Mariners on August 2, 1993.
- Signed by the Pittsburgh Pirates on June 24, 1994.
- Released by Pittsburgh Pirates on March 13, 1997.
- Signed by the Cincinnati Reds on May 6, 1997.
- Traded to the Toronto Blue Jays in exchange for LHP Clayton Andrews and RHP Leo Estrella on November 22, 2000.

CAREER HIGHS — PARRIS, Steve

SEASON:

Wins	12 - 2000
Losses	17 - 2000
Saves	None
ERA	3.50 - 1999
Games	33 - 2000
Starts	33 - 2000
Complete Games	2 - 1999
Shutouts	1 - 1995, 1998, 1999
Innings Pitched	192.2 - 2000
Walks	71 - 2000
Strikeouts	117 - 2000
Longest Win Streak	7 - Aug. 13-Sept. 15, 2000
Longest Losing Streak	6 - May 14-June 16, 2000
Scoreless Innings Streak	16.0 - July 12-22, 1995

GAME:

ML Debut	June 21, 1995 vs. SF
Innings Pitched:	
Starter	9.0 - Aug. 15, 1995 at SD
	9.0 - Aug. 22, 1998 at MON
	9.0 - June 5, 1999 at KC
	9.0 - Sept. 18, 1999 at PIT
Reliever	3.1 - May 19, 1999 at COL
Walks:	
Starter	5 - July 29, 1998 vs. ATL
	5 - June 26, 1999 at HOU
	5 - Sept. 9, 2000 at PIT
Reliever	2 - July 15, 1996 vs. CHI
	2 - May 19, 1999 at COL
Strikeouts:	
Starter	9 - July 12, 1995 vs. ATL
	9 - May 25, 1999 vs. LA
Reliever	2 - July 14, 1996 at CIN
	2 - July 19, 1996 vs. CIN
Hits Allowed	10 - May 14, 2000 at HOU
	10 - June 10, 2000 at CLE
	10 - Sept. 26, 2000 at MIL
Runs Allowed	9 - Aug. 25, 1995 vs. CIN
ER Allowed	9 - Aug. 25, 1995 vs. CIN
HR Allowed	4 - June 10, 2000 at CLE
Low Hit CG	3 - Aug. 22, 1998 at MON
Last Win	Sept. 15, 2000 vs. MIL
Last Save	None
Last CG	Sept. 18, 1999 at PIT
Last ShO	Sept. 18, 1999 at PIT
Last Start	Oct. 1, 2000 at STL
Last Relief App.	May 19, 1999 at COL

STEVE PARRIS DETAILED PITCHING

	2000								CAREER							
	ERA	W-L-Sv	G	IP	H	ER	BB	SO	ERA	W-L-Sv	G	IP	H	ER	BB	SO
Total	4.81	12-17-0	33	192.2	227	103	71	117	4.49	35-35-0	96	528.2	564	264	199	368
ST	4.81	12-17-0	33	192.2	227	103	71	117	4.40	34-35-0	89	517.0	550	253	193	360
REL	—	—	—	—	—	—	—	—	8.49	1-0-0	7	11.2	14	11	6	8
Home	4.07	7-6-0	15	90.2	102	41	27	56	4.35	20-17-0	46	262.2	281	127	94	180
Away	5.47	5-11-0	18	102.0	125	62	44	61	4.64	15-18-0	50	266.0	283	137	105	188
April	6.38	1-3-0	5	24.0	27	17	12	12	6.38	1-3-0	5	24.0	27	17	12	12
May	4.46	1-4-0	6	34.1	39	17	10	20	4.40	4-4-0	11	61.1	66	30	20	40
June	6.59	1-4-0	5	27.1	32	20	11	19	4.44	5-5-0	15	81.0	81	40	35	58
July	4.88	2-2-0	5	31.1	37	17	8	21	4.89	7-8-0	27	138.0	151	75	50	105
August	2.21	4-1-0	6	40.2	47	10	12	23	3.66	9-6-0	19	123.0	129	50	40	78
September	4.97	3-2-0	5	29.0	37	16	14	19	4.18	9-7-0	17	92.2	99	43	35	71
October	9.00	0-1-0	1	6.0	8	6	4	3	9.35	0-2-0	2	8.2	11	9	7	4
vs. CWS	3.00	0-1-0	1	6.0	3	2	2	3	3.00	0-1-0	1	6.0	3	2	2	3
vs. Cle	6.23	1-1-0	2	13.0	15	9	1	9	7.00	1-1-0	3	18.0	20	14	5	12
vs. Det	11.57	0-1-0	1	4.2	7	6	2	4	4.58	2-1-0	3	17.2	22	9	5	12
vs. KC	—	—	—	—	—	—	—	—	3.27	1-0-0	2	11.0	11	4	3	8
vs. Mil	6.89	1-2-0	3	15.2	20	12	5	10	6.10	1-3-0	4	20.2	24	14	6	16
vs. Ari	3.55	1-0-0	2	12.2	16	5	5	8	2.78	2-0-0	5	32.1	30	10	13	17
vs. Atl	2.57	1-0-0	2	14.0	17	4	1	8	3.86	2-1-0	5	32.2	38	14	10	24
vs. ChC	2.45	1-1-0	2	14.2	13	4	5	6	4.12	4-1-0	7	39.1	39	18	14	30
vs. Cin	—	—	—	—	—	—	—	—	11.70	0-1-0	4	10.0	15	13	4	7
vs. Col	6.35	1-1-0	2	11.1	13	8	5	9	4.98	3-1-0	4	21.2	25	12	7	16
vs. Fla	—	—	—	—	—	—	—	—	6.93	3-1-0	5	24.2	32	19	8	16
vs. Hou	6.23	0-2-0	2	13.0	19	9	5	8	4.17	1-6-0	9	49.2	52	23	20	38
vs. LA	4.15	1-1-0	3	13.0	14	6	7	6	3.24	2-3-0	6	33.1	31	12	12	22
vs. Mon	3.65	1-1-0	2	12.1	15	5	3	7	2.27	4-1-0	5	35.2	32	9	9	21
vs. NYM	2.77	0-1-0	2	13.0	11	4	6	6	4.96	0-4-0	6	32.2	33	18	17	20
vs. Phi	3.86	1-1-0	2	11.2	16	5	4	9	6.32	1-5-0	7	31.1	43	22	17	21
vs. Pit	3.55	2-0-0	2	12.2	16	5	7	9	2.08	3-0-0	3	21.2	22	5	8	17
vs. StL	8.18	0-2-0	2	11.0	16	10	7	8	4.62	2-2-0	7	39.0	42	20	18	32
vs. SD	5.00	1-1-0	2	9.0	11	5	3	5	2.93	3-2-0	5	30.2	32	10	9	19
vs. SF	7.20	0-1-0	1	5.0	5	4	3	2	6.97	0-1-0	5	20.2	18	16	12	17
Pre-All Star	5.26	5-11-0	18	99.1	110	58	35	61	4.85	12-14-0	38	204.1	216	110	84	138
Post-All Star	4.34	7-6-0	15	93.1	117	45	36	56	4.27	23-21-0	58	324.1	348	154	115	230

STEVE PARRIS PITCHING AT ML PARKS

Park	ERA	W-L-Sv	SvO	G	GS	IP	H	R	ER	HR	BB	SO
Jacobs Field	9.00	0-1-0	0	1	1	6.0	10	6	6	4	1	5
Tiger Stadium	1.50	1-0-0	0	1	1	6.0	9	1	1	1	2	5
Kauffman Stadium	4.00	1-0-0	0	1	1	9.0	9	4	4	2	2	8
County Stadium	9.64	0-1-0	0	1	1	4.2	10	5	5	1	0	1
Wrigley Field	4.12	4-1-0	0	7	6	39.1	39	20	18	3	14	30
Cinergy Field	4.31	16-11-0	0	36	33	198.1	212	101	95	32	72	131
Astrodome	2.45	1-3-0	0	5	4	25.2	17	11	7	2	10	23
Dodger Stadium	1.53	1-1-0	0	3	3	17.2	12	6	3	1	6	6
Olympic Stadium	0.00	1-0-0	0	1	1	9.0	3	0	0	0	1	4
Shea Stadium	4.63	0-2-0	0	4	4	23.1	23	12	12	2	11	14
Veterans Stadium	5.93	0-2-0	0	3	3	13.2	19	10	9	0	7	9
Three Rivers	4.22	6-6-0	0	14	13	81.0	85	39	38	7	29	66
Busch Stadium	5.29	0-1-0	0	3	3	17.0	20	10	10	4	9	12
Qualcomm Park	3.75	1-1-0	0	2	2	12.0	13	7	5	2	4	7
3 Com Park	7.50	0-0-0	0	3	3	12.0	9	10	10	3	8	11
Coors Field	9.82	1-1-0	0	2	1	7.1	11	8	8	2	4	6
Pro Player Stadium	15.88	0-1-0	0	2	2	5.2	12	10	10	1	2	5
Turner Field	3.00	1-0-0	0	2	2	12.0	16	4	4	1	2	8
BankOne Ballpark	2.03	1-0-0	0	2	2	13.1	13	3	3	0	6	8
Pacific Bell	7.20	0-1-0	0	1	1	5.0	5	4	4	1	3	2
Enron Field	9.00	0-1-0	0	1	1	6.0	10	6	6	1	4	3
Comerica Park	11.57	0-1-0	0	1	1	4.2	7	6	6	1	2	4

George
PEREZ

PITCHER

54

BIRTHDATE	March 20, 1979
OPENING DAY AGE	22
BIRTHPLACE	San Pedro de Macoris, DR
RESIDENCE	San Pedro de Macoris, DR
BATS/THROWS	R/R
HEIGHT/WEIGHT	6-4/220
CONTRACT STATUS	signed thru 2001
M.L. SERVICE	0.000

PERSONAL: George Alonso Perez... Signed by Blue Jays Herb Rayburn as a non-drafted free agent on February 5, 1997.

LAST SEASON: Posted a 5-1 record with 12 saves and a 0.78 ERA for the Queens Kings of the New York-Penn League (A)... His 29 appearances were a team high as were his 12 saves were third in the league and fifth in the Blue Jays organization... Allowed runs in only two of his 29 outings... Was selection as the organization Player of the Month in July when he was 0-0 with six saves and a 1.29 ERA in ten games and again in August when he was 3-1 with five saves with a 0.66 ERA in 13 games... Recorded 35 strikeouts in his 34.2 innings while allowing 21 hits and 15 walks... Allowed only one HR on the season, on July 21 when he recorded a save against Jamestown despite allowing two earned runs... Held opponents hitless in 13 of 29 games... Played winter ball with Licey in the Dominican Republic.

PROFESSIONAL CAREER: 1998: Made his professional debut with the Blue Jays in the Dominican Summer League and was 0-0 in 12 games, two starts, with an ERA of 7.16 ERA... **1999:** Was 2-2 with a save for Medicine Hat of the Pioneer League (A) with an ERA of 5.79 in 15 games, eight starts... Only once did he make consecutive appearances as a starter... First win came as a starter on June 29 at Great Falls... Struckout a season high seven batters over a season high 6.1 innings pitched on July 31... Pitched four shutout innings in relief allowing only one hit for his second victory on September 1, his final outing of the season.

GEORGE PEREZ

Year	Club & League	W-L	ERA	G	GS	CG	ShO	SV	IP	H	R	ER	HR	HB	BB-IBB	SO	WP	BK	OBA
1997	Blue Jays (DSL)	1-3	3.97	20	4	0	1	1	47.2	35	24	21	1	2	29-0	34	3	2	.212
1998	Blue Jays (DSL)	0-0	7.16	12	2	0	0	2	16.1	17	17	13	0	0	17-0	12	8	0	.266
1999	Medicine Hat (Pio)	2-2	5.79	15	8	0	0	1	56.0	65	46	36	9	4	26-0	41	8	0	.289
2000	Queens (NYP)	5-1	0.78	29	0	0	0	12	34.2	21	3	3	1	3	15-2	35	3	0	.181
Minor Totals		8-6	4.25	76	14	0	1	16	154.2	138	90	73	11	9	87-2	122	22	2	.242

PEREZ — TRANSACTIONS

- Signed by the Toronto Blue Jays as a non-drafted free agent on February 5, 1997.

Josh
PHELPS

CATCHER

17

BIRTHDATE	May 12, 1978
OPENING DAY AGE	22
BIRTHPLACE	Anchorage, AK
RESIDENCE	Rathdrum, ID
BATS/THROWS	R/R
HEIGHT/WEIGHT	6-3/215
CONTRACT STATUS	signed thru 2001
M.L. SERVICE	0.016

PERSONAL: Joshua Lee Phelps... Graduated from Lakeland High School in Indiana where he received many awards for excellence in education and athletics... Named MVP in Baseball and graduated 4th in his class.

LAST SEASON: Played for three clubs, Dunedin (A), Tennessee (AA) and Toronto... Hit 21 home runs to rank fourth in the organization... Attended extended spring training after suffering from an inflamed right elbow... Opened the season with Tennessee where he hit .228 in 56 games with nine doubles, 12 home runs and 28 RBI in 56 games... Of those games 39 were as catcher, 14 at DH and three times as a pinch-hitter... On June 7 was recalled to Toronto until being optioned back on June 22... Appeared in only one game, making his ML debut as a defensive replacement on June 13 at Detroit, was 0-1 at the plate... Upon return hit just .194 in 21 July games... Hit five home runs over nine games from July 3 to July 14... Joined Dunedin of the Florida State League (A) on July 26... In 30 games in Dunedin hit .319 with seven doubles, 12 home runs and 34 RBI... On August 7 vs Lakeland was 3-5 with three home runs and five RBI... Named the FSL Hitter of the Week from August 7 to 13, hit .478 with four home runs and nine RBI... In 23 August games hit .341 with 11 home runs and 29 RBI... With Dunedin hit .329 against right-handed pitching with seven home runs and against left-handed pitching, average was .294 with five home runs... In the FSL playoffs hit .450 (9-20) with a home run and four RBI... Rated the 12th best prospect in the organization by Baseball America.

PROFESSIONAL CAREER: 1996: Made pro debut in Medicine Hat and hit .241 with five home runs and 29 RBI... Stole five bases... Led the team in being hit by pitch with six... **1997:** Hit .210 on the season at Hagerstown with seven home runs and 24 RBI... Hit .364 with three homers in August... Hit .239 at home with all seven home runs and .181 on the road... Hit in seven straight games from June 4 to 15... Posted five home runs in his last 17 games... Struck out 80 times in 233 at bats... **1998:** Hit .265 with Hagerstown of the South Atlantic League (A)... Started the season slow hitting only .244 in April and .200 in May... Season high hit streak was six games from April 10 to 16... May 15 had a season high four hits at Delmarva... June was his best month with a .377 (26-69) average, three home runs and 12 RBI... Had a season high four RBI on June 12 vs Ashville... Hit .315 (58-184) with seven of his eight home runs in Hagerstown and on the road was a .219 hitter with one HR and 12 RBI... In five SAL Playoff games hit .278 with a home run and three RBI... **1999:** Led the Florida State League (A) in slugging percentage (.562) and was second in batting (.328)... Led Dunedin with 88 RBI and was tied for the club lead in home runs with 20... Opened the season by batting .436 (17-39) in April with two home runs and 10 RBI... Homered in consecutive games April 16 & 17 and then again June 2 & 3... On May 24 had a season high four RBI... Was selected to the FSL All-Star game... In July hit .308 with five home runs

and 21 RBI... Hit in a season high nine straight games from July 16 to 25... In August was selected as the Topps Florida State League Player of the Month after hitting .393 with 20 runs scored, seven doubles, seven home runs and 27 RBI... Named league Batter of the Week for August 2-8... Hit two home runs on August 5 at Clearwater... Matched season high hit streak with nine straight from August 17 to 27... Selected to the end of season FSL All-Star team... Rated as the fifth best prospect in the organization by Baseball America.

JOSH PHELPS

Year	Club & League	AVG	G	AB	R	H	TB	2B	3B	HR	RBI	SH-SF	HP	BB-IBB	SO	SB-CS	GIDP	SLG	OBP
1996	Medicine Hat (Pio)	.241	59	191	28	46	64	3	0	5	29	2-1	6	27-0	65	5-3	5	.335	.351
1997	Hagerstown (SAL)	.210	68	233	26	49	81	9	1	7	24	0-2	8	15-0	72	3-2	6	.348	.279
1998	Hagerstown (SAL)	.265	117	385	48	102	152	24	1	8	44	1-5	8	40-1	80	2-0	12	.395	.342
1999	Dunedin (FSL)	.328	110	406	72	133	228	27	4	20	88	2-4	8	28-0	104	6-3	13	.562	.379
2000	Tennessee (Sou)	.228	56	184	23	42	80	9	1	9	28	1-2	7	15-0	66	1-0	6	.435	.308
2000	Dunedin (FSL)	.319	30	113	26	36	79	7	0	12	34	0-1	1	12-0	34	0-0	2	.699	.386
2000	TORONTO (AL)	.000	1	1	0	0	0	0	0	0	0	0-0	0	0-0	1	0-0	0	.000	.000
Minor Totals		.270	440	1512	223	408	684	79	7	61	247	6-15	38	137-1	421	17-8	44	.452	.343

PHELPS — TRANSACTIONS

- Selected by the Toronto Blue Jays in 10th round (279th overall) of the June 1996 First Year Player Draft.
- On disabled list (right elbow surgery) April 6-May 1, 2000.

FIELDING

PHELPS, Josh—C

Year	PCT	G	PO	A	E	TC	DP
2000	1.000	1	1	0	0	1	0

Dan
PLESAC

PITCHER

BIRTHDATE	February 4, 1962
OPENING DAY AGE	39
BIRTHPLACE	Gary IN
RESIDENCE	Valparaiso, IN
BATS/THROWS	L/L
HEIGHT/WEIGHT	6-5/217
CONTRACT STATUS	signed thru 2002
M.L. SERVICE	15.000

19

PERSONAL: Daniel Thomas Plesac (PLEE-sack)... Nickname: Sac or Sac-Man... Married, wife's name Leslie... Two daughters, Madeline (7/30/92) and Natalie (11/10/95)... Graduated from Crown Point High School (IN) where he earned All-State honours in baseball and basketball... Earned All-American honours in basketball... Attended North Carolina State University and was a two time All-Atlantic Conference selection in baseball and an All-American in 1983... Is the proprietor of the 'Three Up-Three Down Farm', Dan and his family breed harness racing horses and he is the President of DTP Standardbreds, Inc.

LAST SEASON: Was 5-1 with a 3.15 ERA in 62 games... Ranked second on the Diamondbacks in games, was his lowest games total since appearing in 58 games with the Pirates in 1995... Opposing hitters posted an overall .228 average, with right-handed hitters posting a .194 (14-72) and left-handers to a .260 (20-77) average... Three of his four home runs he surrendered were hit by lefties... Inherited 55 runners on the year with 14 scoring, including only nine of the last 41... Did not allow an inherited runner to score from May 4 to July 8 when Jeremy Giambi hit a grand slam — left 16 runners on base until then... In June was 1-0 with a 1.23 ERA in nine games... Picked up his first win on June 11 in his 23rd appearance, fanning Anaheim's Darin Erstad to end the seventh inning... Next decision was August 14 when he pitched a shutout inning in Philadelphia for his second win... That win started a streak in which he won four games over a 14 appearance stretch to run his record to 5-0... In August was 3-0 with a 1.08 ERA in 11 games... Allowed an earned run in only one of his last 22 appearances, was tagged for

three runs in Colorado on September 27... From August 12 to September 26 he appeared in 20 games without allowing an earned run, gave up seven hits in 13.0 innings with 15 strikeouts... Lone loss came in next-to-last appearance of the year on September 27 in Colorado when he was charged with his fourth blown save... Recorded nine holds and was 0-4 in save situations... Post All-Star was 4-1 with a 2.41 ERA in 31 games... Was his fourth straight season with more strikeouts that innings pitched (45 in 40.0IP).

PROFESSIONAL CAREER: 1983: Made professional debut with Paintsville where he led the Appalachian League (Rookie) in wins (9) and strikeouts (85)... Named to the league All-Rookie team... **1984:** Split the season between Stockton (A) and El Paso (AA)... Was a combined 8-8 with a 3.36 ERA in 23 starts... **1985:** Spent the entire season with El Paso of the Texas League (AA)... Started 24 of 25 games... Was first professional relief appearance... Led the team in wins (12)... Named to the Texas League All-Star team... **1986:** Spent entire season with Milwaukee and made his major league debut on April 11 at New York... Posted a 10-7 record with 14 saves and a 2.97 ERA in 51 games... First major league win came April 18 vs. New York and first save May 2 vs. California... Was second on the team with 51 games and 14 saves... **1987:** Finished fourth in the AL with 23 saves while posting a 5-6 record with a 2.61 ERA... Set a career high in strikeouts with 89 in just 79.1 innings pitched (1.21K/IP)... Made first career appearance in the All-Star Game working a perfect inning in relief... Was 23-34 in save situations... Injured left elbow on August 19 while fielding balls during batting practice but was not disabled... **1988:**

Appeared in 50 games with a 1-2 record along with a 2.41 ERA and a then career high 30 saves... Finished fourth in the AL in saves converting 30 of 35 opportunities... Pitched 1/3 of an inning in the All-Star Game (1K)... Suffered from left shoulder tendinitis limiting him to just three appearances after August 19... **1989:** Set a Milwaukee club record with a career high 33 saves... Was fifth in the AL in saves converting 33-40 opportunities... Posted a career low 2.35 ERA and limited opponents to a .213 batting average... Named to the AL All-Star team for the third straight season becoming the first Brewer pitcher ever named three consecutive seasons... Saved 14 games from June 15 to August 11... **1990:** Finished seventh in the league in games with a then career high of 66... Posted fourth straight 20 save season with 24, ranking tenth in the AL... **1991:** Was 2-7 with a 4.29 ERA in 45 games including ten starts... Started the season in the bullpen... From April 9 to May 23 allowed just one earned run over 17 games (18.2IP)... Won his first major league start on August 10 at Texas after 311 consecutive relief appearances... Remained in the rotation to finish the season and in 10 starts was 2-3 with a 4.69 ERA... Tossed a career high 8.0 innings on September 14 vs. Detroit... **1992:** Made four relief appearances before returning to the rotation on April 24... Started four games, 1-1 with a 5.14 ERA, before returning to the bullpen for the remainder of the season... In relief was 4-3 in 40 games with a 2.17 ERA and one save... In final 27 games posted a 1.23 ERA (5ER/36.2IP)... Lone save came September 4 at Detroit... **1993:** Spent first season in the NL with the Chicago Cubs posting a 2-1 record with a 4.74 ERA... Charged with an error on July 27 vs San Diego to end a streak of 310 consecutive errorless games... First fielding miscue since July 8, 1987... Recorded first NL win on August 24 at Montreal... Surrendered one HR in the second half (31G, 23.0IP)... **1994:** Finished eighth in the NL with 54 appearances... Earned first save since September 4, 1992 on July 20 at Colorado... Stranded 26 of 33 inherited runners... Held left-handed batters to a .186 average (13-70)... **1995:** Began Pittsburgh career with 16.0 scoreless innings and 13 straight scoreless appearances... Opponents hit .149 (10-67) in the first 18 games... ERA stood at 0.90 on June 7... Pitched in 500th career game on June 27 at Chicago... Pre All-Star was 3-0-1 with a 2.08 ERA and 1-4-2 with a 5.10 ERA in the second half... Did not allow a home run until July 13 after 28 games (30.1IP) without a HR... First ML hit on August 12 at Dodger Stadium off John Cummings... Was 3-4 in save situations and stranded 29 of 40 inherited runners to score... **1996:** Appeared in a career high 73 games which ranked eighth in the NL and second amongst left-handers... Saved 11 games which is the most since 1990 with Milwaukee... Struck out 76 batters in 70.1 innings - the most strikeouts since recording 89 in 1987 with Milwaukee... Opened in April with scoreless outings (6.2IP)... Opened May with seven consecutive scoreless outings (7.1IP) and earned his first save of the year on May 1 at Cincinnati... From May 1 to June 23 was 3-0 with three saves and a 1.33 ERA (3ER/20.1IP) and saw his ERA drop from 6.92 to 3.51... July 12 agreed to a contract extension... From July 7 to 30 did not allow an earned run in 14.0 innings and finished with a 1.47 ERA for the month (18.1IP)... Pitched in career game 600 on September 11 at San Diego... Was 11-17 in save situations and allowed 10 of 37 inherited runners to score... Prior to the All-Star break was 3-4 with six saves and a 3.94 ERA, post All-Star was 3-4 with six saves and a 3.94 ERA... In 24 day games was 3-1 with a 1.19 ERA... At the plate was 0-5... **1997:** Set then Blue Jays all-time record for appearances in a season by a left hand pitcher at 73 which ranked ninth in the AL and matched his career high... Was 2-4 with one save, a 3.58 ERA and a team high 27 holds which was 2nd in the AL and third in the majors... Recorded only save on April 22 at Anaheim, the 149th of his career... Allowed two ER in first 10 games (8.2IP) before allowing four on April 25 vs Seattle to see ERA jump from 2.08 to 6.00... Recorded four holds in eight games in May but was 0-0 with a 6.23 ERA (3ER, 4.1IP)... From June 1 to the end of the season allowed runs in just eight of 51 games... Fell to 0-3 on June 21 vs Baltimore to match his career high losing streak... Did not allow a run in nine games

from June 26 to July 14... Pitched a season high 2.0 innings on July 19 at Anaheim... Went a season high ten straight scoreless games, with five holds, from July 19 to August 10 (6.2IP)... Recorded first win on September 8 vs Anaheim... Last 11 games of the season recorded six holds and his second win of the season on September 28 vs Boston... Was 1-4 in save situations... Held left handed batters to a .200 (19-95) average and right handers hit .286 (28-98)... Prior to the All-Star break was 0-3 with one save and a 4.44ERA and following the break was 2-1 with a 2.77ERA... **1998:** Appeared in a career high 78 games and was 4-3 with four saves, an ERA of 3.78 and tied for the AL lead in holds at 27 with teammate Paul Quantrill... The 78 games are the most ever for Blue Jay left-hand pitcher breaking his own record of 77 set in 1997... Allowed just 15 of 80 inherited runners to score... Appeared in 16 of the 29 games in April and was 0-2 with a 4.35 ERA after allowing runs in four of the 16 games... Recorded five holds in April... In May made his 700th career appearance on the 9th in Seattle earning his eighth hold... Made ten appearances from May 12 to 30 without allowing a run (8.0IP, 2H, 11K)... Finished May 2-0 with a 1.69 ERA (2ER, 10.2IP) with seven holds... Appeared in four consecutive games June 7-10 (2.0IP)... Only Blown save of the season came on July 5 vs Tampa Bay, entered with bases loaded and surrendered a sac fly to McGriff, was his longest outing of the season pitching 1.2 hitless innings... At the All-star break was 3-2 with a 2.93 ERA... Recorded career save #150 on August 13 vs the Anaheim Angels (0.1IP, 1HB, 1K)... Converted final four save opportunities, first three saves came between August 13 to 28... Pitched in his 74th game on September 11 to break the club mark for games by a LHP which he set at 73 in 1997... Last seven games were scoreless (5.2IP)... Opponents hit .224, just .198 by left-handed batters and .264 by right-handers... With runners in scoring position held opponents to a .205 batting average... Pitched for the Major League Baseball All-Star team which played in Japan in November... **1999:** Split the season between Toronto and Arizona combining to post a 2-4 record with one save, 15 holds and a 5.89 ERA... Opened the season with Toronto appearing in 30 games posting an 0-3 record with an 8.34 ERA... Made 14 appearances in April and was 0-1 with five holds and a 6.55 ERA — allowed runs in four of the 14 games... Struggled in May posting an 0-2 record with an ERA of 8.64... Appeared in five June games prior to a June 12 trade in which he was sent to Arizona in exchange for IF Tony Batista and RHP John Frascatore... After an 8.34 ERA with the Blue Jays, he posted a 3.32 mark in 34 outings for Arizona... Was scored upon in only five of the 34 games he appeared... Down the stretch he threw 10.0 consecutive scoreless innings over an 11-appearance span... Streak was ended on October 1 by a Tony Gwynn homer — was the first surrendered to a left-handed batter since September 5, 1998 (Troy O'Leary)... Worked a 1-2-3 inning in the regular season finale to finish the year with one earned run allowed over 12.0 innings, a 0.75 ERA... Both of his wins with Arizona came in extra-innings — July 17 in Texas in a ten inning game and August 11 at Wrigley Field with 1.1 innings pitched... Held left-handed batters to a composite average of .198 (19-for-96).

CAREER NOTES: Reached the post-season in 1999 with Arizona, was his first appearance in the post-season snapping the second longest dry spell among active players who had not reached the post-season... The longest streak was also snapped as John Franco of the Mets reached the post-season in 1999... Finished the 2000 season tied with LHP Paul Assenmacher for 14th on the All-Time games pitched list at 884... Has never been on the disabled list... In save situations has a career mark of 154-224 and ranks 45th on the all-time save list, tied with Stu Miller... Despite not working for the Brewers since 1992, he remains their all-time leader in appearances (365) and saves (133)... Was a three-time All-Star in the American League, each time with Milwaukee (1987-89)... Has committed only three errors in 822 major league games, spanning 917.0 innings, and none since July 27, 1993, vs. San Diego.

DAN PLESAC

Year	Club & League	W-L	ERA	G	GS	CG	ShO	SV	IP	H	R	ER	HR	HB	BB-IBB	SO	WP	BK	OBA
1983	Paintsville (Appy)	9-1	3.50	14	14	2	0	0	82.1	76	44	32	6	1	57-0	85	11	0	–
1984	Stockton (Cal)	6-6	3.32	16	16	2	0	0	108.1	106	51	40	7	2	50-0	101	3	2	–
1984	El Paso (Tex)	2-2	3.46	7	7	0	0	0	39.0	43	19	15	2	0	16-0	24	0	0	.285
1985	El Paso (Tex)	12-5	4.97	25	24	2	0	0	150.1	171	91	83	12	0	68-1	128	13	1	.295
1986	MILWAUKEE (AL)	10-7	2.97	51	0	0	0	14	91.0	81	34	30	5	0	29-1	75	4	0	–
1987	MILWAUKEE (AL)	5-6	2.61	57	0	0	0	23	79.1	63	30	23	8	3	23-1	89	6	0	.213
1988	MILWAUKEE (AL)	1-2	2.41	50	0	0	0	30	52.1	46	14	14	2	0	12-2	52	4	6	–
1989	MILWAUKEE (AL)	3-4	2.35	52	0	0	0	33	61.1	47	16	16	6	0	17-1	52	0	0	.213
1990	MILWAUKEE (AL)	3-7	4.43	66	0	0	0	24	69.0	67	36	34	5	3	31-6	65	2	0	.257
1991	MILWAUKEE (AL)	2-7	4.29	45	10	0	0	8	92.1	92	49	44	12	3	39-1	61	2	1	.263
1992	MILWAUKEE (AL)	5-4	2.96	44	4	0	0	1	79.0	64	28	26	5	3	35-5	54	3	1	.229
1993	CHICAGO (NL)	2-1	4.74	57	0	0	0	0	62.2	74	37	33	10	0	21-6	47	5	2	.282
1994	CHICAGO (NL)	2-3	4.61	54	0	0	0	1	54.2	61	30	28	9	1	13-0	53	0	0	.279
1995	PITTSBURGH (NL)	4-4	3.58	58	0	0	0	3	60.1	53	26	24	3	1	27-7	57	1	0	.237
1996	PITTSBURGH (NL)	6-5	4.09	73	0	0	0	11	70.1	67	35	32	4	0	24-6	76	4	0	.247
1997	TORONTO (AL)	2-4	3.58	73	0	0	0	1	50.1	47	22	20	8	0	19-4	61	2	0	.244
1998	TORONTO (AL)	4-3	3.78	78	0	0	0	4	50.0	41	23	21	4	1	16-1	55	0	0	.224
1999	TORONTO (AL)	0-3	8.34	30	0	0	0	0	22.2	28	21	21	4	0	9-1	26	2	0	.308
1999	ARIZONA (NL)	2-1	3.32	34	0	0	0	1	21.2	22	9	8	3	0	8-1	27	1	0	.259
2000	ARIZONA (NL)	5-1	3.15	62	0	0	0	0	40.0	34	21	14	4	0	26-2	45	3	0	.228
Minor Totals		29-14	4.03	62	61	6	0	0	380.0	396	205	170	21	2	191-1	338	16	3	–
TORONTO TOTALS		6-10	4.54	181	0	0	0	5	123.0	116	66	62	16	1	44-6	142	4	0	.248
AL TOTALS		35-47	3.46	546	14	0	0	138	647.1	576	273	249	59	13	230-23	590	25	8	.239
NL TOTALS		21-15	4.04	338	0	0	0	16	309.2	311	158	139	33	2	119-22	305	14	2	.260
MAJOR TOTALS		56-62	3.65	884	14	0	0	154	957.0	887	431	388	92	15	349-45	895	39	10	.246

DIVISION SERIES RECORD

Year	Club & League	W-L	ERA	G	GS	CG	ShO	SV	IP	H	R	ER	HR	HB	BB-IBB	SO	WP	BK	OBA
1999	ARIZONA (NL)	0-0	54.00	1	0	0	0	0	0.1	3	2	2	0	0	0-0	0	0	0	.750

ALL-STAR GAME RECORD

Year	Club & League	W-L	ERA	G	GS	CG	ShO	SV	IP	H	R	ER	HR	HB	BB-IBB	SO	WP	BK	OBA
1987	AL at OAK	0-0	0.00	1	0	0	0	0	1.0	0	0	0	0	0	0-0	1	0	0	.000
1988	AL at CIN	0-0	0.00	1	0	0	0	0	0.1	0	0	0	0	0	0-0	1	0	0	.000
1989	AL at CAL	0-0	0.00	1	0	0	0	0	0.0	1	0	0	0	0	0-0	0	0	0	1.000
ALL-STAR TOTALS		0-0	0.00	3	0	0	0	0	1.1	1	0	0	0	0	0-0	2	0	0	.200

PLESAC — TRANSACTIONS

- Selected by St. Louis Cardinals organization in 2nd round of June, 1980, Free Agent Draft; did not sign.
- Selected by Milwaukee Brewers organization in 1st round (26th overall) of June, 1983, Free Agent Draft.
- Granted free agency, October 27, 1992.
- Signed by Chicago Cubs, December 8, 1992.
- Granted free agency, October 25, 1994.
- Signed by the Pittsburgh Pirates, November 9, 1994.
- Traded to the Toronto Blue Jays along with OF Orlando Merced and IF Carlos Garcia in exchange for RHP Jose Silva, RHP Jose Pett, LHP Mike Halperin, C Craig Wilson, IF Abraham Nunez and IF Brandon Cromer, November 14, 1996.
- Traded to the Arizona Diamondbacks in exchange for IF Tony Batista and RHP John Frascatore, June 12, 1999.
- Signed by the Toronto Blue Jays on December 8, 2000.

CAREER HIGHS — PLESAC, Dan

SEASON:

Wins	10 - 1986
Losses	7 - 1986, 1990, 1991
Saves	33 - 1989
ERA	2.35 - 1989
Games	78 - 1998
Starts	10 - 1991
Complete Games	None
Shutouts	None
Innings Pitched	92.1 - 1991
Walks	39 - 1991
Strikeouts	89 - 1987
Longest Win Streak	5 - Jun. 11-Sep. 13, 2000
Longest Losing Streak	4 - Jul. 8-27, 1987
	4 - Apr. 12-Jul. 20, 1991
	4 - Jul. 31-Aug. 13, 1996
	4 - Apr. 24-Jul. 1, 1999
Scoreless Innings Streak	17.1 - Jun. 14-Jul. 8, 1987

GAME:

ML Debut	Apr. 11, 1986 at NYY
Innings Pitched:	
Starter	8.0 - Sep. 14, 1991 vs. DET
Reliever	4.1 - May 14, 1986 at SEA
	4.1 - Jul. 9, 1986 vs. CAL
	4.1 - Aug. 19, 1989 vs. BOS
Walks:	
Starter	5 - Aug. 15, 1991 vs. TOR
Reliever	4 - Jun. 30, 1992 at BAL
Strikeouts:	
Starter	7 - Apr. 24, 1992 at CAL
Reliever	5 - Jun. 2, 1987 at CAL
	5 - Jul. 29, 1987 at TEX
	5 - Jul. 11, 1990 at CWS
	5 - Aug. 26, 1990 at NYY
Hits Allowed	8 - Oct. 5, 1991 at BOS
Runs Allowed	7 - May 21, 1990 vs. SEA
ER Allowed	7 - May 21, 1990 vs. SEA
HR Allowed	2 - 6 times, last Jul. 3, 1994 at HOU
Low Hit CG	None
Last Win	Sep. 13, 2000 vs. LA
Last Save	Jul. 28, 1999 at SD
Last CG	None
Last ShO	None
Last Start	May 21, 1992 at DET
Last Relief App.	Sep. 30, 2000 vs. SF

FIELDING
PLESAC, Dan—P

Year	PCT	G	PO	A	E	TC	DP
1986 (AL)	1.000	51	1	11	0	12	0
1987 (AL)	.857	57	0	12	2	14	1
1988 (AL)	1.000	50	0	6	0	6	0
1989 (AL)	1.000	52	2	8	0	10	0
1990 (AL)	1.000	66	1	7	0	8	1
1991 (AL)	1.000	45	2	5	0	7	0
1992 (AL)	1.000	44	1	8	0	9	1
1993 (NL)	.900	57	0	9	1	10	2
1994 (NL)	1.000	54	0	3	0	3	0
1995 (NL)	1.000	58	1	8	0	9	1
1996 (NL)	1.000	73	0	1	0	1	0
1997 (AL)	1.000	73	0	1	0	1	0
1998 (AL)	1.000	78	0	1	0	1	0
1999 (AL)	1.000	30	0	2	0	2	0
1999 (NL)	1.000	34	1	4	0	5	0
2000 (NL)	1.000	62	0	2	0	2	0
Total	.970	884	9	88	3	100	6

ALL-TIME GAMES PITCHED LEADERS

1.	Jesse Orosco	1096
2.	Dennis Eckersley	1071
3.	Hoyt Wilhelm	1070
4.	Kent Tekulve	1050
5.	Lee Smith	1022
6.	Rich Gossage	1002
7.	Lindy McDaniel	987
8.	Rollie Fingers	944
9.	John Franco	940
10.	Gene Garber	931
11.	Cy Young	906
12.	Sparky Lyle	899
13.	Jim Kaat	898
14.	Paul Assenmacher	884
	Dan Plesac	**884**

DAN PLESAC DETAILED PITCHING

	2000								CAREER							
	ERA	W-L-Sv	G	IP	H	ER	BB	SO	ERA	W-L-Sv	G	IP	H	ER	BB	SO
Total	3.15	5-1-0	62	40.0	34	14	26	45	3.65	56-62-154	884	957.0	887	388	349	895
ST	–	–	–	–	–	–	–	–	4.83	3-4-0	14	69.0	70	37	32	51
REL	3.15	5-1-0	62	40.0	34	14	26	45	3.56	53-58-154	870	888.0	820	351	317	844
Home	2.50	2-0-0	28	18.0	15	5	13	17	3.93	26-26-74	421	465.1	439	203	169	449
Away	3.68	3-1-0	34	22.0	19	9	13	28	3.39	30-36-80	463	491.2	448	185	180	446
April	5.06	0-0-0	8	5.1	8	3	4	5	4.05	5-12-18	134	144.1	130	65	56	144
May	2.70	0-0-0	10	6.2	5	2	5	5	3.42	8-8-32	146	166.0	149	63	59	162
June	1.23	1-0-0	9	7.1	4	1	3	12	3.65	11-7-32	167	172.2	161	70	62	152
July	9.82	0-0-0	10	3.2	4	4	9	3	3.76	8-15-33	160	167.2	168	70	64	158
August	1.08	3-0-0	11	8.1	5	1	3	9	3.00	15-9-20	139	156.0	131	52	57	133
September	3.12	1-1-0	14	8.2	9	3	2	11	4.12	9-11-17	129	137.2	136	63	51	135
October	–	–	–	–	–	–	–	–	3.55	0-0-2	9	12.2	12	5	6	11
vs. Ana	0.00	1-0-0	2	1.1	0	0	0	2	2.13	5-3-15	45	67.2	41	16	20	61
vs. Bal	–	–	–	–	–	–	–	–	3.02	2-3-12	38	47.2	39	16	18	56
vs. Bos	–	–	–	–	–	–	–	–	5.21	2-2-7	44	46.2	54	27	20	39
vs. CWS	–	–	–	–	–	–	–	–	2.70	3-7-4	41	40.0	34	12	24	36
vs. Cle	–	–	–	–	–	–	–	–	3.59	5-1-11	37	42.2	40	17	14	36
vs. Det	–	–	–	–	–	–	–	–	2.37	2-4-14	42	57.0	41	15	19	52
vs. KC	–	–	–	–	–	–	–	–	2.03	2-3-15	40	53.1	40	12	22	46
vs. Mil	0.00	0-0-0	6	4.0	2	0	4	2	0.90	0-0-0	14	10.0	6	1	4	11
vs. Min	–	–	–	–	–	–	–	–	6.32	1-3-12	33	31.1	39	22	13	23
vs. NYY	–	–	–	–	–	–	–	–	4.64	4-5-7	51	54.1	61	28	21	58
vs. Oak	81.00	0-0-0	2	0.1	3	3	1	1	3.61	2-4-9	41	42.1	49	17	18	48
vs. Sea	0.00	0-0-0	2	0.1	0	0	2	1	4.69	3-5-11	42	42.1	46	22	11	35
vs. TB	–	–	–	–	–	–	–	–	3.86	0-0-0	6	4.2	2	2	1	6
vs. Tex	0.00	0-0-0	1	0.1	0	0	0	0	3.83	4-2-9	43	51.2	42	22	17	43
vs. Tor	–	–	–	–	–	–	–	–	2.96	1-5-12	35	54.2	45	18	17	49
vs. Atl	0.00	0-0-0	1	1.0	2	0	0	1	3.98	0-3-1	24	20.1	21	9	7	17
vs. ChC	0.00	0-0-0	3	2.2	2	0	0	4	4.02	3-0-3	17	15.2	13	7	3	19
vs. Cin	0.00	0-0-0	3	2.0	0	0	2	1	3.03	1-1-5	31	35.2	32	12	11	32
vs. Col	9.64	0-1-0	5	4.2	9	5	1	6	7.59	0-1-2	23	21.1	28	18	6	25
vs. Fla	0.00	0-0-0	5	2.1	1	0	1	3	2.01	3-0-0	24	22.1	17	5	5	23
vs. Hou	–	–	–	–	–	–	–	–	2.79	0-0-1	22	19.1	19	6	5	18
vs. LA	0.00	1-0-0	5	4.0	2	0	2	3	3.44	3-1-1	23	18.1	18	7	12	16
vs. Mon	9.00	1-0-0	3	2.0	3	2	3	2	3.50	3-1-0	20	18.0	12	7	11	20
vs. NYM	0.00	0-0-0	6	4.1	2	0	0	6	2.67	3-2-0	29	30.1	28	9	7	28
vs. Phi	0.00	1-0-0	4	1.2	2	0	1	1	4.45	3-2-1	30	28.1	26	14	8	22
vs. Pit	0.00	0-0-0	3	1.1	0	0	0	2	3.55	0-0-0	15	12.2	12	5	3	15
vs. StL	10.80	0-0-0	3	1.2	2	2	4	1	6.75	0-0-0	25	22.2	32	17	8	25
vs. SD	0.00	0-0-0	2	1.1	0	0	2	3	4.19	0-2-1	24	19.1	28	9	10	20
vs. SF	3.86	0-0-0	6	4.2	4	2	3	6	5.47	1-2-1	25	26.1	29	16	14	24
Pre-All Star	3.80	1-0-0	31	21.1	20	9	15	24	3.69	27-31-98	505	548.1	506	225	194	518
Post-All Star	2.41	4-1-0	31	18.2	14	5	11	21	3.59	29-31-56	379	408.1	381	163	155	377

Players

DAN PLESAC PITCHING AT ML PARKS

Park	ERA	W-L-Sv	G	GS	IP	H	R	ER	HR	BB	SO
Camden Yards	5.00	0-0-0	9	0	9.0	10	6	5	2	5	12
Fenway Park	4.62	0-0-4	23	1	25.1	31	13	13	3	12	21
Edison Field	1.08	2-1-8	25	1	41.2	22	7	5	0	11	37
Comiskey Park-Old	3.24	2-2-0	10	0	8.1	9	3	3	1	5	4
Jacobs Field	4.50	0-0-0	7	0	4.0	5	2	2	1	3	4
Tiger Stadium	3.03	2-2-9	26	2	32.2	23	11	11	6	13	33
Kauffman Stadium	2.79	1-3-6	21	1	29.0	24	11	9	0	16	23
County Stadium	3.63	14-15-62	182	6	257.2	233	115	104	21	87	236
Metrodome	4.26	0-2-8	21	0	19.0	20	10	9	1	7	12
Yankee Stadium	4.44	2-3-2	26	0	24.1	21	12	11	4	10	30
Oakland-Alameda	5.89	0-4-5	19	0	18.1	20	12	12	5	13	22
Kingdome	1.99	1-2-5	20	0	22.2	24	6	5	2	4	14
Arlington-New	5.40	1-1-0	8	0	5.0	4	4	3	1	6	5
SkyDome	4.21	5-6-5	90	1	68.1	61	34	32	9	20	67
Atlanta-Fulton	3.52	0-1-0	9	0	7.2	9	4	3	0	5	3
Wrigley Field	4.56	4-2-1	67	0	71.0	68	41	36	11	20	72
Cinergy Field	2.16	1-1-3	16	0	16.2	12	5	4	1	3	14
Astrodome	4.76	0-0-1	13	0	11.1	13	6	6	2	1	10
Dodger Stadium	3.27	2-1-0	13	0	11.0	9	4	4	0	7	12
Olympic Stadium	3.38	3-1-0	8	0	8.0	7	5	3	2	4	7
Shea Stadium	3.86	1-2-0	17	0	16.1	18	9	7	2	2	16
Veterans Stadium	5.79	1-2-0	17	0	14.0	16	9	9	0	5	7
Three Rivers	3.32	4-4-9	72	0	76.0	73	31	28	5	30	82
Busch Stadium	11.00	0-0-0	12	0	9.0	16	11	11	0	7	7
Qualcomm Park	3.24	0-0-1	12	0	8.1	11	3	3	0	5	6
3 Com Park	4.15	1-0-0	9	0	13.0	15	6	6	1	4	13
Coors Field	7.04	0-1-0	10	0	7.2	9	6	6	1	3	9
Pro Player Stadium	2.35	1-0-0	10	0	7.2	7	2	2	0	1	8
Turner Field	0.00	0-0-0	2	0	2.0	2	0	0	0	0	3
BankOne Ballpark	3.03	2-0-0	46	0	29.2	28	15	10	3	18	32
Tropicana Field	18.00	0-0-0	2	0	1.0	1	2	2	0	1	2
Mile High Stadium	11.57	0-0-1	3	0	2.1	3	3	3	3	0	3
Cleveland Stadium	3.26	2-1-6	13	1	19.1	18	7	7	1	6	17
Arlington Stadium-Old	1.56	2-1-5	15	1	23.0	16	6	4	2	5	21
Memorial Stadium	3.45	1-2-5	11	0	15.2	10	6	6	2	4	10
Comiskey Park	4.00	1-2-2	9	0	9.0	12	4	4	0	5	12
Exhibition Stadium	0.00	0-0-6	8	0	9.2	6	0	0	0	1	6
Pacific Bell	0.00	0-0-0	3	0	1.1	1	0	0	0	0	3

DAN PLESAC — MILESTONES

	DATE	OPP.	H/A	W/L (IP)	AGAINST/NOTES
GAMES					
1	April 11, 1986	MIL vs NYY	A		
500	June 27, 1995	PIT vs CHI (NL)	A		
WIN					
1	April 18, 1986	MIL vs NYY	H		4.0 perfect inn
SV					
1	May 2, 1986	MIL vs CAL	H	Juan Nieves	1st ML win
100	Sept. 30, 1989	MIL vs BOS	A	0.2IP	

Paul
QUANTRILL

PITCHER

BIRTHDATE	November 3, 1968
OPENING DAY AGE	32
BIRTHPLACE	London, ON
RESIDENCE	Tarpon Springs, FL
BATS/THROWS	L/R
HEIGHT/WEIGHT	6-1/195
CONTRACT STATUS	signed thru 2001
M.L. SERVICE	8.018

48

PERSONAL: Paul John Quantrill... Name pronounced KWON-trill... Married the former Alyson Atwood (10/30/93); two children, son Cal (2/10/95), and daughter Reese Jayne (10/12/97)... Graduated in 1986 from Okemos High School in Michigan... Attended the University of Wisconsin where he was named 1987 Rookie of the Year and in 1989 the Top Pitcher and team MVP... Hobbies include hunting, fishing and golf.

LAST SEASON: Was 2-5 with a save and a 4.52 ERA in 68 games in his fifth season with Toronto... Was tied for the team lead in appearances with Billy Koch... It is the third time he has led the Blue Jays in games... Recorded the first of a team

leading 13 holds in his season debut with 2.0 scoreless innings on April 3 vs KC... Struggled in April posting a 5.68 ERA in ten games... In May was 0-2 with a save and a 3.00 ERA... On May 10 vs Baltimore pitched 3.2 scoreless innings to earn his first save since September 25, 1998 vs Boston... The 3.2 innings pitched was a season high... In June posted a season best ERA of 1.80 in 13 games... From June 7 to June 29 he allowed one earned run in 11.2 innings... Recorded five holds in June with three in four outings from June 6 to 12... Opened July by losing three straight appearances, July 2 at Baltimore, July 4 at Cleveland and July 7 in Montreal... On July 4 at Cleveland was tagged for seven earned runs to match his career high done once previously on September 16, 1996 in a start vs New York... Was the fourth time to allow seven runs... Following the three losses, allowed only two earned runs over the next ten outings, 11.0 innings... Collected his first win of the season on July 20 vs Tampa Bay with a scoreless inning... Win #2 came on August 4 in a 10-8 victory over Texas... In August was 1-0 with an ERA of 8.10... On September 7 made his 300th Blue Jays appearance and tossed a scoreless inning against Seattle... In September allowed runs in three of nine games and posted an ERA of 3.55... Opponents hit .298 with seven home runs, right-handed batters hit .296 with one home run while lefties hit .299... At home was 2-1 with a save and an ERA of 3.14 in 34 games... On the road was 0-4 with a 5.98 ERA... Had the steel rod removed from his right leg in January 2001, rod was inserted during surgery to repair a fractured femur suffered January 6, 1999.

PROFESSIONAL CAREER: 1989: Appeared in two games with the Gulf Coast Red Sox before joining the Elmira Pioneers of the New York Penn League... Pitched in Red Sox Hall of Fame Game at Cooperstown (6.0IP, 5H, 1R)... Threw five complete games in just seven starts... Co-winner of the Tony Latham Memorial Award presented for enthusiasm during the Red Sox Florida Instructional League... **1990:** Opened the season with Winter Haven but was promoted to New Britain of the Eastern League (AA)... Finished 3rd in the EL allowing starters allowing just 1.42 walks per 9 IP... **1991:** Was promoted from New Britain to Pawtucket of the International League (AAA) on May 8... Threw a 5-0, 3 hit shutout in his AAA debut May 11 at Richmond... Led Pawtucket in wins with 10 and was tied for the IL lead with six complete games... Named team most valuable pitcher... **1992:** At Pawtucket appeared in 19 games making 18 starts with four complete games... Promoted to Boston July 19 for the remainder of the season... Won ML debut on July 20 at KC entering a 3-3 tie (2.2 IP, 2 H, 3 SO)... Only HR allowed in 27 games (49.1 IP) was by Juan Gonzalez in the 10th inning in Texas, July 28... Earned 1st ML save on October 4 vs. New York... **1993:** First full ML season... Made 1st ML start on May 8 at Milwaukee in a 6-3 loss... 14 of 49 games were starts... First win as a starter came June 22 vs Min., 4-2... Threw only ML complete game to date, a two hit shutout at Seattle on July 4... Run support of 2.71 was lowest among Red Sox starters... Prevented team best 31 of 36 inherited runners to score (.861)... **1994:** Only Red Sox victory came April 11 at KC in relief... Used exclusively in relief (17 games) for Sox... Injured right index finger in a May 3 brawl vs. Seattle... Traded to the Phillies on May 31... Made NL debut on June 3 for the Phillies in Houston but left after 1.2 innings with a contusion to the right thigh... Earned 1st NL win on June 7 vs the Cubs and his 1st save on June 9 vs. St. Louis... Made one start replacing Shawn Boskie on July 2- first start since Oct. 1, 1993 vs. Milwaukee... Optioned to AAA Scranton on July 23 where he made 8 starts... Threw a 6 hit shutout August 27 vs Pawtucket... **1995:** Led the Phillies with a career high 11 wins, 29 starts and 179.1 innings pitched; 2nd on club with career high 103 strikeouts... Finished 7th in the NL with 2.2 walks per inning IP... Had 7 starts without a walk and nine with just one... Started and won home opener April 28 vs Pittsburgh tossing 6.0 shutout innings... Collected 1st ML hit on May 29 vs LA off Pedro Astacio... Combined with Heathcliff Slocumb on a 6 hit shutout at LA on June 9... Lasted 0.2 innings on June 29 vs Cincinnati after being hit above left knee with a line drive (Thomas Howard)... Won career best three straight, twice: April 28 to May 14 and June 9 to 24... Made 1st relief appearance on July 23 versus St. Louis... In four games in relief (7.0IP) was 1-0, 0.00 ERA... Threw a season high 8.0 innings 3 times- June 9 at LA, July 26 vs PIT, Sept. 20 vs FLA... Set career high for strikeouts on Sept 20 vs Florida with eight... **1996:** Was 5-14 with a 5.43 ERA in first season with Toronto... Started the season 0-4 after six starts... In April was 0-3 with an 8.17 ERA after allowing nine HR's in 25.1 innings... April 15 walked a career high five batters in a 5-1 loss in Anaheim... Won first game on May 9 at Texas retiring nine batters in order (5.1IP, 5H, 1R/ER/HR, 3K)... Was one of two Toronto wins vs Texas all season... Won his next outing on May 11 pitching a scoreless inning in relief vs Boston- 1st relief appearance of '96 after seven straight starts... Started next nine games going 2-4... Missed start on May 21 at Chicago- stomach flu... July 2

moved to bullpen with a record of 3-9, 6.27 ERA... Pitched a season high 5.2IP in relief on August 20 at KC (2H, 1HB, 1BB, 3K)... Made 17 relief appearances before serving as an emergency starter for Juan Guzman (appendectomy) on September 3... Earned 5th win in that start with 6.0 shutout innings at NY... The win ended a career high six game losing streak... Finished the season in the starting rotation going 1-1 in four starts... Finished 4-10, 6.29 ERA as a starter and 1-4, 2.76 ERA in relief... Was 4-9, 6.13 ERA pre All-Star and 1-4, 4.15 ERA after... **1997:** Set what was an all-time record for single season appearances by a Canadian born pitcher at 77 games, record had been held by John Hiller with 65 appearances for the Detroit Tigers in 1973... The 77 games were tied for the third most in the AL... Finished fourth among AL relief pitchers in ERA at 1.94... Was 6-7 with a then career high five saves... From April 15 to 26 was 3-0 in six games with a 0.00ERA (10.2IP)... Finished April 3-2 with a 2.09 ERA and was 9-9 in first batter efficiency and stranded all five inherited runners... Won fourth game on May 3 vs Minnesota despite being charged with a blown save... Converted next four save opportunities from May 8 to June 14... Threw a season high 3.2 innings on May 18 vs Cleveland... Did not allow an earned run from May 26 to June 25, a stretch of 14.2 innings over 14 games as ERA fell to a season low 1.43... In nine games against Boston was 0-1 with a 5.79 ERA (6ER, 9.1IP), against all other opponents was 6-6 with five saves and a 1.47ERA... In June was 0-0 with a 1.32 ERA... Suffered third loss of the season on July 27 against Kansas City... Was also the third loss against KC... Allowed earned runs in one of 16 games in August and posted a 1.37ERA (3ER, 1.2IP)... In September recorded five holds to finish the year with 16... Finished the season with seven straight scoreless outings (6.0IP)... With runners in scoring position opponents hit just .176 (19-108)... Prior to the All-Star break was 4-2 with four saves and a 1.64 ERA, post All-Star was 2-5 with one save and a 2.25ERA... **1998:** Was 3-7 with a career high seven saves and a 2.59 ERA... Was second in the AL with a career high 82 appearances and posted 27 holds to tie for the league lead with teammate Dan Plesac... His 82 appearances are the most ever by a Canadian born pitcher in a single season, surpassing his own record of 77 games set in 1997... The 2.59 ERA was fourth among AL relievers... Opened the season going 0-1 with one save and a 2.60 ERA in April... First save of the season came on April 14 at Texas, 2.0 scoreless innings (3K)... Did not record a decision or save in May after posting a 2.63 ERA and striking out 15 batters in 13.2 innings... Next two decisions were losses... First win of the season on July 5 vs Tampa Bay in Toronto (0.1IP)... From July 19 to August 23 did not allowed an earned run in 19 consecutive outings covering a span of 16.0 innings... Over the scoreless streak his ERA went from 3.04 to 2.34... During the stretch was 1-0 with three saves and three holds... After starting the season 1-6 in save opportunities he converted six of the last eight... Collected third win on Sept 6 vs Boston but was ejected by home plate umpire Dale Scott, was the first ejection of the season for a Blue Jay... Recorded five holds in his final eight outings... Was ninth in the AL in relief innings (80.0)... First batter efficiency was 52-82... At home was 3-0 with three saves and a 3.27ERA (15ER/41.1IP) and on the road was 0-4 with four saves with an ERA of 1.86 (8ER/38.2IP)... Held left-hand batters to .258 average while right-hand hitters posted a .305 average... Stranded 44 of 70 inherited runners... Made nine outings of at least 2.0 innings... **1999:** Was 3-2 in 41 games with an ERA of 3.33... Did not pitch with Toronto until June 15 as he recovered from a fractured right femur suffered January 6 in a snow-mobile accident... Was on the 15 day disabled list to start the season and transferred to the 60 day disabled list on May 7... Joined Dunedin on a medical rehabilitation assignment on June 4... Appeared in five games and was 0-1 with a 4.50 ERA in 6.0 innings... Then joined Syracuse (AAA) where he had two scoreless outings (2.0)... Returned from rehab assignment on June 13 and was activated on June 15... Appeared in nine June games and was 0-1 with a 2.53 ERA... In July was 1-0 with a 1.46 ERA in 11 games... First win of the season came July 10 in Montreal... Appeared in ten August games and posted an ERA of 3.65... Had eight holds three of which came in September... Was 2-1 in September/October and posted an ERA of 5.40... Had ten outings of 2.0 innings or more...

Worked a season high 2.1 innings on September 25 vs Cleveland... Was 0-4 in save situations... Stranded 17 of 30 inherited runners and retired 25 of 41 first batters faced.

CAREER NOTES: Is now tied for sixth with David Wells on the Blue Jays games pitched list at 306 games... Has finished 105 games for Toronto to tie for sixth all-time with Mark Eichhorn... Is 16-44 in saves situations... In 1996 became the eighth Canadian to play for the Toronto Blue Jays... Holds the record for most appearances by a Canadian born pitcher with 82 in 1998, first became the record holder in 1997 when he appeared in 77 games... Has a career batting average of .100 (6-60, 0RBI, 7SH, 3BB, 25K).

POST SEASON EXPERIENCE: Has not been involved in post season play.

PAUL QUANTRILL

Year	Club & League	W-L	ERA	G	GS	CG	ShO	SV	IP	H	R	ER	HR	HB	BB-IBB	SO	WP	BK	OBA
1989	Red Sox (Gulf)	0-0	0.00	2	0	0	0	2	5.0	2	0	0	0	0	0-0	5	0	0	.111
1989	Elmira (NYP)	5-4	3.43	20	7	5	0	2	76.0	90	37	29	5	6	12-2	57	1	2	.299
1990	Winter Haven (FSL)	2-5	4.14	7	7	1	0	0	45.2	46	24	21	3	0	6-0	14	3	0	.264
1990	New Britain (East)	7-11	3.53	22	22	1	1	0	132.2	148	65	52	3	4	23-2	53	3	2	.290
1991	New Britain (East)	2-1	2.06	5	5	1	0	0	35.0	32	14	8	2	1	8-0	18	0	0	.248
1991	Pawtucket (Int)	10-7	4.45	25	23	6	2	0	155.2	169	81	77	14	4	30-1	75	2	2	.282
1992	Pawtucket (Int)	6-8	4.46	19	18	4	1	0	119.0	143	63	59	16	4	20-1	56	1	1	.300
1992	BOSTON (AL)	2-3	2.19	27	0	0	0	0	49.1	55	18	12	1	1	15-5	24	1	0	.288
1993	BOSTON (AL)	6-12	3.91	49	14	1	1	1	138.0	151	73	60	13	2	44-14	66	0	1	.279
1994	BOSTON (AL)	1-1	3.52	17	0	0	0	0	23.0	25	10	9	4	2	5-1	15	0	0	.278
1994	PHILADELPHIA (NL)	2-2	6.00	18	1	0	0	1	30.0	39	21	20	3	3	10-3	13	0	2	.331
1994	Scranton-WB (Int)	3-3	3.47	8	8	1	1	0	57.0	55	25	22	5	2	6-0	36	1	0	.253
1995	PHILADELPHIA (NL)	11-12	4.67	33	29	0	0	0	179.1	212	102	93	20	6	44-3	103	0	3	.295
1996	TORONTO (AL)	5-14	5.43	38	20	0	0	0	134.1	172	90	81	27	2	51-3	86	1	1	.316
1997	TORONTO (AL)	6-7	1.94	77	0	0	0	5	88.0	103	25	19	5	1	17-3	56	1	0	.297
1998	TORONTO (AL)	3-4	2.59	82	0	0	0	7	80.0	88	26	23	5	3	22-6	59	1	0	.285
1999	Dunedin (FSL)	0-1	4.50	5	4	0	0	0	6.0	5	3	3	1	0	1-0	2	0	0	.238
1999	Syracuse (Int)	0-0	0.00	2	0	0	0	0	2.0	1	0	0	0	0	0-0	1	0	0	.167
1999	TORONTO (AL)	3-2	3.33	41	0	0	0	0	48.2	53	19	18	5	4	17-1	28	0	0	.282
2000	TORONTO (AL)	2-5	4.52	68	0	0	0	1	83.2	100	45	42	7	2	25-1	47	1	0	.298
Minor Totals		35-40	3.85	115	94	19	5	4	634.0	691	312	271	49	21	106-6	317	11	7	.282
TORONTO TOTALS		19-32	3.79	306	20	0	0	13	434.2	516	205	183	49	12	132-14	276	4	1	.299
AL TOTALS		28-48	3.68	399	34	1	1	15	645.0	747	306	264	67	17	196-34	381	5	2	.293
NL TOTALS		13-14	4.86	51	30	0	0	1	209.1	251	123	113	23	9	54-6	116	0	5	.300
MAJOR TOTALS		41-62	3.97	450	64	1	1	16	854.1	998	429	377	90	26	250-40	497	5	7	.295

QUANTRILL — TRANSACTIONS

- Selected by the Boston Red Sox organization in the 6th round of the June 1989 First Year player Draft.
- Acquired by the Philadelphia Phillies along with OF Billy Hatcher in exchange for OF Wes Chamberlin and RHP Mike Sullivan, May 31, 1994.
- Acquired by the Toronto Blue Jays in exchange for 3B Howard Battle and LHP Ricardo Jordan, December 6, 1995.
- On disabled list (fractured right femur) March 27-June 15, 1999; included rehabilitation assignment at Dunedin and Syracuse, June 4-13, 1999.

CAREER HIGHS — QUANTRILL, Paul

SEASON:

Wins	11 - 1995
Losses	12 - 1995
Saves	7 - 1998
ERA	1.94 - 1997
Games	82 - 1998
Starts	29 - 1995
Complete Games	1 - 1993
Shutouts	1 - 1993
Innings Pitched	179.1 - 1995
Walks	51 - 1996
Strikeouts	103 - 1995
Longest Win Streak	3 - Apr. 25-May 14, 1995
	3 - Jun. 9-Jun. 24, 1995
Longest Losing Streak	6 - Jun. 27-Aug. 27, 1996
Scoreless Innings Streak	14.2 - May 26-Jun. 23, 1997

GAME:

ML Debut	Jul. 20, 1992 at KC
Innings Pitched:	
Starter	9.0 - Jul. 4, 1993 at SEA
Reliever	5.2 - Aug. 20, 1996 at KC
Walks:	
Starter	5 - Apr. 17, 1996 at CAL
Reliever	3 - 6 times, last Apr. 5, 2000 vs. KC
Strikeouts:	
Starter	8 - Sep. 29, 1995 vs. FLA
Reliever	5 - Apr. 27, 1993 at OAK
	5 - Jul. 28, 1997 at MIL
	5 - Apr. 5, 1998 vs. TEX
Hits Allowed	12 - Jul. 26, 1995 vs. PIT
Runs Allowed	7 - Jun. 24, 1995 at STL
	7 - Apr. 7, 1996 at CLE
	7 - Sep. 16, 1996 vs. NYY
	7 - Jul. 5, 2000 at CLE
ER Allowed	7 - Sep. 16, 1996 vs. NYY
	7 - Jul. 5, 2000 at CLE
HR Allowed	3 - Jul. 9, 1993 at OAK
	3 - Apr. 7, 1996 at CLE
	3 - Apr. 22, 1996 at SEA
Low Hit CG	2 - Jul. 4, 1993 at SEA
Last Win	Aug. 4, 2000 vs. TEX
Last Save	May 10, 2000 vs. BAL
Last CG	Jul. 4, 1993 at SEA
Last ShO	Jul. 4, 1993 at SEA
Last Start	Sep. 27, 1996 vs. BAL
Last Relief App.	Sep. 29, 2000 at CLE

FIELDING
QUANTRILL, Paul—P

Year	PCT	G	PO	A	E	TC	DP
1992 (AL)	.833	27	4	6	2	12	0
1993 (AL)	.957	49	4	18	1	23	3
1994 (AL)	1.000	17	1	2	0	3	0
1994 (NL)	.875	18	1	6	1	8	1
1995 (NL)	.976	33	9	32	1	42	2
1996 (AL)	1.000	38	4	23	0	27	1
1997 (AL)	.857	77	1	17	3	21	3
1998 (AL)	1.000	82	4	14	0	18	2
1999 (AL)	1.000	41	2	9	0	11	1
2000 (AL)	1.000	68	3	9	0	12	0
Total	.955	450	33	136	8	177	13

PAUL QUANTRILL DETAILED PITCHING

	2000								CAREER							
	ERA	W-L-Sv	G	IP	H	ER	BB	SO	ERA	W-L-Sv	G	IP	H	ER	BB	SO
Total	4.52	2-5-1	68	83.2	100	42	25	47	3.97	41-62-16	450	854.1	998	377	250	497
ST	–	–	–	–	–	–	–	–	5.03	16-30-0	64	359.1	439	201	96	203
REL	4.52	2-5-1	68	83.2	100	42	25	47	3.20	25-32-16	386	495.0	559	176	154	294
Home	3.14	2-1-1	34	43.0	46	15	16	19	3.94	22-27-9	228	455.0	532	199	147	263
Away	5.98	0-4-0	34	40.2	54	27	9	28	4.01	19-35-7	222	399.1	466	178	103	234
April	5.68	0-0-0	10	12.2	16	8	5	9	4.02	6-6-1	55	100.2	113	45	33	70
May	3.00	0-2-1	13	18.0	15	6	5	5	3.61	7-9-2	65	142.0	151	57	29	88
June	1.80	0-0-0	13	15.0	16	3	3	10	3.92	8-11-4	78	172.1	203	75	42	100
July	6.46	1-3-0	13	15.1	20	11	8	8	4.20	8-13-2	85	143.2	187	67	47	86
August	8.10	1-0-0	10	10.0	18	9	2	5	3.81	5-11-3	83	149.0	164	63	59	75
September	3.55	0-0-0	9	12.2	15	5	2	10	4.08	6-10-3	78	128.0	157	58	36	72
October	–	–	–	–	–	–	–	–	5.79	1-2-1	6	18.2	23	12	4	6
vs. Ana	11.25	0-0-0	5	4.0	9	5	0	0	4.93	2-1-1	26	34.2	47	19	10	16
vs. Bal	1.42	0-1-1	4	6.1	4	1	0	2	3.10	2-3-1	29	49.1	51	17	10	27
vs. Bos	4.09	0-0-0	8	11.0	14	5	3	8	5.85	2-2-2	28	32.1	50	21	13	19
vs. CWS	2.70	0-0-0	4	6.2	5	2	0	6	3.69	1-1-0	22	31.2	32	13	10	26
vs. Cle	11.25	0-2-0	6	8.0	17	10	4	4	5.64	2-8-1	36	60.2	80	38	19	31
vs. Det	2.45	0-1-0	4	3.2	2	1	2	1	3.97	0-4-0	28	34.0	43	15	15	23
vs. KC	2.70	0-0-0	4	6.2	7	2	3	6	2.18	3-4-4	34	57.2	53	14	15	37
vs. Mil	–	–	–	–	–	–	–	–	4.13	0-2-0	13	32.2	38	15	9	12
vs. Min	6.75	0-0-0	4	5.1	7	4	2	3	3.79	3-4-0	25	54.2	80	23	14	21
vs. NYY	1.59	0-0-0	4	5.2	6	1	1	4	3.55	1-4-1	29	63.1	67	25	12	44
vs. Oak	4.91	0-0-0	3	3.2	6	2	1	2	2.39	5-2-3	30	52.2	52	14	14	37
vs. Sea	5.68	0-0-0	6	6.1	7	4	3	4	3.70	2-2-1	30	56.0	63	23	22	41
vs. TB	0.00	1-0-0	4	3.1	1	0	1	1	2.79	2-1-0	13	9.2	7	3	4	7
vs. Tex	6.75	1-0-0	3	1.1	2	1	1	0	3.06	2-5-0	23	35.1	34	12	12	22
vs. Tor	–	–	–	–	–	–	–	–	4.05	0-2-0	6	13.1	16	6	8	8
vs. Atl	3.86	0-0-0	3	2.1	3	1	1	1	5.71	0-1-0	11	17.1	19	11	7	7
vs. ChC	–	–	–	–	–	–	–	–	2.70	1-0-0	3	10.0	10	3	3	5
vs. Cin	–	–	–	–	–	–	–	–	7.04	0-1-0	3	7.2	10	6	1	6
vs. Col	–	–	–	–	–	–	–	–	7.20	0-1-0	1	5.0	6	4	1	4
vs. Fla	6.75	0-0-0	1	1.1	2	1	0	2	5.51	0-4-0	8	16.1	22	10	4	12
vs. Hou	–	–	–	–	–	–	–	–	4.87	1-0-0	5	20.1	28	11	5	14
vs. LA	–	–	–	–	–	–	–	–	6.00	2-1-0	6	24.0	32	16	7	13
vs. Mon	3.00	0-1-0	2	3.0	3	1	0	0	3.77	3-3-0	11	28.2	35	12	4	9
vs. NYM	0.00	0-0-0	1	2.0	1	0	1	1	4.50	1-3-0	8	26.0	31	13	8	15
vs. Phi	3.00	0-0-0	2	3.0	4	1	2	2	2.70	0-0-1	5	6.2	8	2	3	4
vs. Pit	–	–	–	–	–	–	–	–	4.13	3-1-0	6	28.1	38	13	6	12
vs. StL	–	–	–	–	–	–	–	–	3.86	2-0-1	4	11.2	9	5	0	4
vs. SD	–	–	–	–	–	–	–	–	2.35	1-0-0	2	7.2	10	2	4	3
vs. SF	–	–	–	–	–	–	–	–	3.71	0-2-0	5	26.2	27	11	10	18
Pre-All Star	4.68	0-5-1	39	50.0	57	26	15	25	3.96	24-33-7	219	466.0	526	205	120	286
Post-All Star	4.28	2-0-0	29	33.2	43	16	10	22	3.99	17-29-9	231	388.1	472	172	130	211

PAUL QUANTRILL — MILESTONES

	DATE	OPP.	H/A	W/L (IP)	AGAINST/NOTES
G					
1	July 20, 1992	BOS vs KC	A	W5-3 (2.2)	2H, 3K
WIN					
1	July 20, 1992	BOS vs KC	A	W5-3 (2.2)	ML Debut, 2H, 3K
SV					
1	October 4, 1992	BOS vs NYY	H	W8-2 (4.0)	1H, 2SO
SHO					
1	July 4, 1993	BOS vs SEA	A	W6-0	vs Bosio, 2H, 3BB, 6K, 118P
Low Hit CG (2 or less)					
2	July 4, 1993	BOS vs SEA	A	W6-0	vs Bosio, 3BB, 6K, 118P

PAUL QUANTRILL PITCHING AT ML PARKS

Park	ERA	W-L-Sv	SvO	G	GS	IP	H	R	ER	HR	BB	SO
Camden Yards	3.63	1-2-0	1	11	1	17.1	18	7	7	2	4	9
Fenway Park	3.62	5-9-3	5	64	9	141.2	162	65	57	10	44	69
Edison Field	4.98	2-1-0	1	13	2	21.2	28	12	12	3	7	14
Comiskey Park	4.60	0-0-0	2	12	0	15.2	18	9	8	3	2	13
Jacobs Field	6.66	1-3-1	2	15	1	24.1	32	19	18	8	4	11
Tiger Stadium	5.06	0-2-0	1	13	0	16.0	22	11	9	1	10	11
Kauffman Stadium	1.07	3-1-4	6	16	0	25.1	19	3	3	1	5	15
County Stadium	3.86	0-1-0	1	5	1	11.2	15	8	5	1	5	7
Metrodome	3.27	0-2-0	0	13	2	22.0	35	15	8	0	3	12
Yankee Stadium	2.03	1-2-0	1	14	2	26.2	26	6	6	2	3	17
Oakland-Alameda	2.73	1-2-0	0	14	2	26.1	26	10	8	5	4	20
Kingdome	2.59	1-0-0	1	10	2	24.1	21	8	7	3	7	16
Arlington	2.84	1-1-0	1	9	1	12.2	12	5	4	2	4	5
SkyDome	3.89	11-14-6	16	155	10	224.2	272	108	97	25	81	143
Atlanta-Fulton	0.00	0-0-0	0	1	0	1.2	0	0	0	0	0	2
Wrigley Field	0.00	0-0-0	0	1	0	2.2	3	0	0	0	0	1
Cinergy Field	5.14	0-0-0	0	2	1	7.0	5	4	4	1	0	5
Astrodome	3.27	1-0-0	0	3	1	11.0	11	5	4	0	1	5
Dodger Stadium	1.50	1-1-0	0	2	2	12.0	10	2	2	0	3	8
Olympic Stadium	4.97	2-2-0	0	6	1	12.2	16	7	7	0	0	4
Shea Stadium	3.48	1-1-0	1	4	1	10.1	11	5	4	1	3	6
Veterans Stadium	5.03	6-7-2	2	28	16	111.0	134	66	62	15	36	63
Three Rivers	5.65	1-1-0	1	4	2	14.1	21	9	9	1	3	5
Busch Stadium	9.00	1-0-0	0	1	1	5.0	7	7	5	2	0	1
Qualcomm Park	2.57	1-0-0	0	1	1	7.0	9	2	2	0	3	3
3 Com Park	3.95	0-2-0	0	3	2	13.2	15	8	6	1	5	9
Coors Field	7.20	0-1-0	0	1	1	5.0	6	4	4	1	1	4
Pro Player Stadium	11.12	0-2-0	0	4	1	5.2	15	8	7	1	1	4
Turner Field	3.38	0-0-0	0	4	0	2.2	4	1	1	0	1	1
Tropicana Field	4.26	0-1-0	1	8	0	6.1	6	3	3	0	3	4
Cleveland Stadium	9.00	0-2-0	1	3	0	2.0	5	5	2	0	2	1
Arlington Stadium	6.43	0-1-0	0	3	1	7.0	9	6	5	1	2	5
SAFECO Field	0.00	0-0-0	0	4	0	4.0	3	0	0	0	1	3
Comerica Park	3.00	0-1-0	0	3	0	3.0	2	1	1	0	2	1

Dominic
RICH

INFIELDER

56

BIRTHDATE	August 22, 1979
OPENING DAY AGE	21
BIRTHPLACE	Sunbury, PA
RESIDENCE	Herndon, PA
BATS/THROWS	L/R
HEIGHT/WEIGHT	5-10/190
CONTRACT STATUS	signed thru 2001
M.L. SERVICE	0.000

PERSONAL: Dominic Joseph Rich... Graduated from Line Mountain High School in Herndon, PA, where he lettered four years in baseball... Also played football and was an All-State tailback... In his senior season only played baseball and was an All-State selection and the league Most Valuable Player... Attended Auburn University where in his last year he hit .340 in 59 games with seven home runs, 55 RBI and 21 stolen bases.

LAST SEASON: Debuted with the Queens Kings of the New York-Penn League (A) where he hit .263 in 67 games with 11 doubles, four triples and 25 RBI... Was selected to the New York-Penn League All-Star team... Collected 38 walks while striking out only 33... Started slow hitting just .145 in his first 16 games... In the next 51 games he hit .298 (54-181)... On June 28 at Pittsfield was 4-4 with four doubles and two RBI... Hit in a season high nine straight from August 2 to 10... Hit .204 at home for the Kings while on the road posted a .313 average.

DOMINIC RICH

Year Club & League	AVG	G	AB	R	H	TB	2B	3B	HR	RBI	SH-SF	HP	BB-IBB	SO	SB-CS	GIDP	SLG	OBP
2000 Queens (NYP)	.263	67	236	37	62	81	11	4	0	25	4-3	5	38-0	33	10-4	8	.343	.372

RICH — TRANSACTIONS

- Selected by the Toronto Blue Jays in the 2nd round (58th overall) of the June 2000 First Year Player Draft.

Brian
SIMMONS
OUTFIELDER

22

BIRTHDATE . . . . September 4, 1973
OPENING DAY AGE 27
BIRTHPLACE . . . . Lebanon, PA
RESIDENCE . . . . McMurray, PA
BATS/THROWS . . . . S/R
HEIGHT/WEIGHT 6-2/190
CONTRACT STATUS . . . . signed thru 2001
M.L. SERVICE 1.114

PERSONAL: Brian Lee Simmons... Attended Peters Township High School in McMurray, Pennsylvania where he hit .542 as a senior... Led University of Michigan in home runs (13) and RBI (45) as a junior in 1995... Played in all of Michigan's 166 games from 1993-95, making 165 starts... Earned GTE CoSIDA District IV Academic All-America honors and Academic All-Big Ten honors... Academic All-Big Ten as a sophomore... Played for Cotuit in Cape Cod League in summer of 1994... Hit for cycle as a freshman vs. Northwestern... Selected by Baltimore in 35th round of the June 1992 free agent draft but did not sign.

LAST SEASON: Missed the entire season after rupturing his left Achilles tendon on March 30 vs. Colorado in the White Sox final spring training game... Marked the second straight season he suffered an injury late in spring training... Was placed on the 60-day disabled list on March 31... Spent part of the season at the Sox training complex in Tucson rehabilitating the injury... Played for Santurce in the Puerto Rico Winter League, batting .265 with a home run and five RBI in their regular season.

PROFESSIONAL CAREER: 1995: Split his first professional season between Rookie Sarasota and Class A Hickory... Hit his first career home run on August 7 vs. Macon... Attended the Fall Instructional League... **1996:** Spent majority of the season at Class A South Bend before being promoted to Class A Prince William at the end of July... Combined to hit .271 (132-487) with 21 home runs and 72 RBI... The 21 homers tied for second in the organization while his 72 RBI were fourth... Ranked second in runs scored with 90... Finished tied for third in the Midwest League with a .556 slugging percentage and tied for fourth with 52 extra-base hits... **1997:** Led the Southern League in triples (12) and walks (88), and ranked second in runs scored (108), games (138) and at-bats (546) at Class AA Birmingham... Topped the White Sox organization in runs scored, tied for the lead in triples (12), was third in walks (88) and fourth in extra-base hits (55)... Led the Barons in games, at-bats, walks and stolen bases (15)... Reached double figures in doubles (28), triples and home runs (15), the first Sox minor leaguer to accomplish that feat since Ray Durham at Class AAA Nash-

ville in 1994... Named Best Hustler in the SL by Baseball America... Hit two home runs and recorded five RBI on July 14 at Memphis... Homered twice on August 13 at Jacksonville... Played for the Mesa Saguaros in the Arizona Fall League where he hit .284 (42-148) with four home runs and 19 RBI, five triples, 23 runs scored and 11 stolen bases in 41 games... **1998:** Spent the season with Calgary (AAA) and following their playoffs joined the White Sox in late September... Was on the Cannons disabled list from June 21 to August 10 with a strained groin... After hitting .238 (20-84) in April, batted .306 (83-271) the rest of the season... Drove in a season high five runs on August 26 at Vancouver... Named Best Hustler on the team... Was recalled to Chicago on September 20... Made his major-league debut on September 21 at Minnesota... Collected hit first career hit in his first plate appearance on September 23 at Minnesota against LaTroy Hawkins... Became just the third player in White Sox history to homer from both sides of the plate on September 26 at Kansas City... Hit a two-run home run left-handed off Brian Barber in the fourth inning and a two-run homer right-handed off Allen McDill in the seventh... At five days within his major-league debut, also became the fastest player in history to accomplish the feat... Drove in a career-high five runs with nine total bases in the game... Posted two three-hit games, September 23 at Minnesota and September 26 at Kansas City... **1999:** Opened the season on the 15-day disabled list with a lacerated left palm suffered during a spring training game on March 22 at Seattle... Began play with Charlotte (AAA) where he hit .270 with 14 doubles, 10 home runs, 44 RBI and 53 runs scored in 78 games... Was thrown out once in nine stolen-base attempts... Was recalled on July 14 and appeared in 54 games, 29 starts, with the White Sox... Hit in five straight from July 23 to 29 (.375)... Hit a two-run homer on September 25 at Minnesota and a three-run HR on September 19 at Toronto... Recorded an outfield assist and two highlight style catches on July 26 vs Toronto... Cited by Baseball America as having the Best Outfield Arm in the White Sox organization... Played in 34 games for Santurce in the Puerto Rican Winter League, hitting .266 (33-124) with eight home runs and 16 RBI.

BRIAN SIMMONS

Year	Club & League	AVG	G	AB	R	H	TB	2B	3B	HR	RBI	SH-SF	HP	BB-IBB	SO	SB-CS	GIDP	SLG	OBP
1995	White Sox (Gulf)	.176	5	17	5	3	7	1	0	1	5	0-0	0	6-0	1	0-0	1	.412	.391
1995	Hickory (SAL)	.190	41	163	13	31	45	6	1	2	11	0-0	2	19-0	44	4-4	2	.276	.283
1996	South Bend (Mid)	.298	92	356	73	106	198	29	6	17	58	1-4	2	48-2	69	14-9	3	.556	.380
1996	Prince William (Caro)	.198	33	131	17	26	48	4	3	4	14	1-0	0	9-1	39	2-0	3	.366	.250
1997	Birmingham (Sou)	.262	138	546	108	143	240	28	12	15	72	2-3	2	88-5	124	15-12	10	.440	.365
1998	Calgary (PCL)	.290	94	355	72	103	171	21	4	13	51	3-3	1	41-1	82	10-6	6	.482	.363
1998	White Sox (Ariz)	.167	5	12	1	2	2	0	0	0	0	0-0	0	1-0	1	0-0	0	.167	.231
1998	CHICAGO (AL)	.368	5	19	4	7	13	0	0	2	6	0-0	0	0-0	2	0-1	0	.684	.368
1999	Charlotte (Int)	.270	78	285	53	77	121	14	0	10	44	1-1	5	37-1	60	8-2	5	.425	.363
1999	CHICAGO (AL)	.230	54	126	14	29	50	3	3	4	17	0-0	0	9-0	30	4-0	3	.397	.281
2000								Injured—DID NOT PLAY											
Minor Totals		.263	486	1865	342	491	832	103	26	62	255	8-11	12	249-10	420	53-33	30	.446	.352
MAJOR TOTALS		.248	59	145	18	36	63	3	3	6	23	0-0	0	9-0	32	4-1	3	.434	.292

HOME RUN BREAKDOWN

			MEN ON				ONE GAME								
Total	H	A	0	1	2	3	2	3	4	LO	XN	IP	PH	RHP	LHP
6	0	6	2	2	2	0	1	0	0	0	0	0	0	5	1

SIMMONS — TRANSACTIONS

- Selected by the Chicago White Sox in the 2nd round of the June 1995 First Year Player Draft.
- On disabled list July 6-14, 1995.
- On disabled list April 5-17, 1996.
- On disabled list (strained groin) June 22-August 10, 1998.
- On disabled list (lacerated left palm) March 26-April 28, 1999.
- On disabled list (torn left achilles tendon) March 31-November 8, 2000.
- Traded to the Toronto Blue Jays along with RHP Kevin Beirne, LHP Mike Sirotka and RHP Mike Williams in exchange for RHP Matt DeWitt and LHP David Wells on January 14, 2001.

CAREER HIGHS — SIMMONS, Brian
GAME:

ML Debut	Sep. 21, 1998 at MIN
Runs	2 - Sep. 26, 1998 at KC
	2 - Sep. 25, 1999 at MIN
Hits	3 - Sep. 23, 1998 at MIN
	3 - Sep. 26, 1998 at KC
Doubles	1 - Jul. 25, 1999 vs. TOR
	1 - Aug. 28, 1999 at OAK
	1 - Sep. 26, 1999 at MIN
Home Runs	2 - Sep. 26, 1998 at KC
RBI	5 - Sep. 26, 1998 at KC
Stolen Bases	1 - Jul. 29, 1999 vs. NYY
	1 - Jul. 31, 1999 at CLE
	1 - Sep. 1, 1999 vs. SEA
	1 - Sep. 25, 1999 at MIN
Last ML Home Run	Sep. 25, 1999 at MIN
Longest Hitting Streak	5G - Jul. 23-29, 1999

FIELDING
SIMMONS, Brian—OF

Year	PCT	G	PO	A	E	TC	DP
1998	1.000	5	13	0	0	13	0
1999	.976	46	79	2	2	83	1
Total	.979	51	92	2	2	96	1

BRIAN SIMMONS DETAILED HITTING

	2000										CAREER								
	Avg	AB	H	HR	RBI	BB	SO	OBP	SLG	Avg	AB	H	HR	RBI	BB	SO	OBP	SLG
Total	–	–	–	–	–	–	–	–	–	.248	145	36	6	23	9	32	.292	.434
vs. Left	–	–	–	–	–	–	–	–	–	.179	28	5	1	4	1	6	.207	.321
vs. Right	–	–	–	–	–	–	–	–	–	.265	117	31	5	19	8	26	.312	.462
Home	–	–	–	–	–	–	–	–	–	.224	67	15	0	5	5	13	.278	.299
Away	–	–	–	–	–	–	–	–	–	.269	78	21	6	18	4	19	.305	.551
July	–	–	–	–	–	–	–	–	–	.320	25	8	0	2	2	6	.370	.520
August	–	–	–	–	–	–	–	–	–	.182	33	6	1	3	1	7	.206	.303
September	–	–	–	–	–	–	–	–	–	.257	74	19	5	18	6	17	.313	.500
October	–	–	–	–	–	–	–	–	–	.231	13	3	0	0	0	2	.231	.231
Scoring Posn	–	–	–	–	–	–	–	–	–	.344	32	11	4	19	6	4	.447	.750
Bases Loaded	–	–	–	–	–	–	–	–	–	.000	2	0	0	0	0	1	.000	.000
DH	–	–	–	–	–	–	–	–	–	.500	4	2	0	1	0	2	.500	.750
PH	–	–	–	–	–	–	–	–	–	.400	5	2	0	1	0	1	.400	.600
vs. Ana	–	–	–	–	–	–	–	–	–	.400	5	2	0	2	0	2	.400	.400
vs. Bal	–	–	–	–	–	–	–	–	–	.000	0	0	0	0	0	0	.000	.000
vs. Bos	–	–	–	–	–	–	–	–	–	.125	8	1	0	0	0	1	.125	.125
vs. Cle	–	–	–	–	–	–	–	–	–	.250	12	3	1	1	0	2	.250	.500
vs. Det	–	–	–	–	–	–	–	–	–	.222	9	2	0	1	1	3	.300	.222
vs. KC	–	–	–	–	–	–	–	–	–	.308	13	4	2	5	0	1	.308	.769
vs. Mil	–	–	–	–	–	–	–	–	–	.000	1	0	0	0	0	1	.000	.000
vs. Min	–	–	–	–	–	–	–	–	–	.294	34	10	1	4	1	9	.314	.471
vs. NYY	–	–	–	–	–	–	–	–	–	.250	12	3	0	1	2	4	.357	.417
vs. Oak	–	–	–	–	–	–	–	–	–	.200	10	2	0	0	0	0	.200	.300
vs. Sea	–	–	–	–	–	–	–	–	–	.167	6	1	0	0	2	2	.375	.167
vs. TB	–	–	–	–	–	–	–	–	–	1.000	1	1	0	0	0	0	1.000	1.000
vs. Tex	–	–	–	–	–	–	–	–	–	.059	17	1	0	1	0	4	.059	.059
vs. Tor	–	–	–	–	–	–	–	–	–	.375	16	6	2	8	3	2	.474	.938
vs. StL	–	–	–	–	–	–	–	–	–	.000	1	0	0	0	0	1	.000	.000
Pre-All Star	–	–	–	–	–	–	–	–	–	.000	0	0	0	0	0	0	.000	.000
Post-All Star	–	–	–	–	–	–	–	–	–	.248	145	36	6	23	9	32	.292	.434

BRIAN SIMMONS HITTING AT ML PARKS

Park	Avg	G	AB	R	H	2B	3B	HR	RBI	SB	CS	BB	SO	OBP	Slg
Camden Yards	.000	2	0	1	0	0	0	0	0	0	0	0	0	.000	.000
Edison Field	.000	1	1	0	0	0	0	0	0	0	0	0	1	.000	.000
Comiskey Park	.224	26	67	9	15	1	2	0	5	2	0	5	13	.278	.299
Jacobs Field	.273	3	11	2	3	0	0	1	1	1	0	0	2	.273	.545
Tiger Stadium	.000	2	1	1	0	0	0	0	0	0	0	0	1	.000	.000
Kauffman Stadium	.308	3	13	3	4	0	0	2	5	0	0	0	1	.308	.769
County Stadium	.000	2	1	0	0	0	0	0	0	0	0	0	1	.000	.000
Metrodome	.333	7	21	3	7	1	1	1	4	1	1	1	7	.364	.619
Yankee Stadium	.200	2	5	1	1	0	0	0	1	0	0	1	2	.333	.200
Oakland-Alameda	.222	3	9	0	2	1	0	0	0	0	0	0	0	.222	.333
Arlington	.143	3	7	0	1	0	0	0	1	0	0	0	2	.143	.143
SkyDome	.286	2	7	2	2	0	0	2	6	0	0	2	1	.444	1.143
Busch Stadium	.000	1	1	0	0	0	0	0	0	0	0	0	1	.000	.000
Tropicana Field	1.000	1	1	0	1	0	0	0	0	0	0	0	0	1.000	1.000
SAFECO Field	.000	1	0	0	0	0	0	0	0	0	0	0	0	.000	.000

Mike
SIROTKA
PITCHER

33

BIRTHDATE	May 13, 1971
OPENING DAY AGE	29
BIRTHPLACE	Chicago, IL
RESIDENCE	Heathrow, FL
BATS/THROWS	L/L
HEIGHT/WEIGHT	6-1/200
CONTRACT STATUS	signed thru 2002
M.L. SERVICE	3.131

PERSONAL: Michael Robert Sirotka... Married, wife's name Linda... Graduated in 1993 from Louisiana State University with a degree in psychology... Went 12-6 in 1993 to help lead LSU to the national championship... Led the team in IP (145.0) and strikeouts (105) in 1993... Was 2-1 with a 2.37 ERA during the College World Series.

LAST SEASON: Won a career-high 15 games and matched his career best of 128 strikeouts (1998)... The 15 wins were the most by a White Sox lefty since Wilson Alvarez won 15 in 1996... Ranked third in the American League with a 3.79 ERA and was tied for eighth in wins... ERA was first among AL left-handers... 21 of his 32 starts were quality starts... ERA was below 4.00 every start after July 1... Was the Opening Day starter on April 3 in Texas, lost after allowing a career high four home runs, two each to Ivan Rodriguez and Gabe Kapler... Started the Sox home opener for the second straight season... Missed scheduled start on 4/20 vs. Seattle due to stiffness between his left forearm and elbow... In his first six starts of the season posted a 6.18 ERA... The rest of the season, 26 starts, was 13-7 with a 3.40 ERA... Struck out a career-high 10 in a victory on July 18 vs. Milwaukee (1 ER/8.0 IP), was the most strikeouts by a Sox left-hander since Wilson Alvarez fanned 12 on May 11, 1997 vs. Oakland... Was outdueled by Pedro Martinez, 1-0, on July 23 at Fenway Park... At the All-Star break was 8-6 with a 3.73 ERA and following the break was 7-4 with a 3.86 ERA... In July was 2-2 with a 3.92 ERA in six starts... From August 1 on was 6-2 with a 3.42 ERA and in 11 outings had nine quality starts... Was 5-0 with a 2.84 ERA (16 ER/50.2 IP) over his final eight starts from August 19 to September 28 - career-high five game win streak... Left his last start on September 28 vs. Boston after 3.0 IP for precautionary reasons with what was diagnosed as a hyperextension of his left elbow... Combined to go 6-3 with a 3.08 ERA (17 ER/49.2 IP) in nine starts against New York, Oakland and Seattle... Sox were 18-14 in his starts... Made 21 quality starts, including seven in his final eight starts... Opponents batted .269 with left-handers at .311 and right-handers .256... Won 12 of his last 17 decisions after June 1, posting a 3.52 ERA... Allowed three earned runs or less in 26 of his 32 starts, including 22 of his last 26... Lasted at least 8.0 innings in six starts... Ranked fourth in the AL with an average of 1.14 double plays induced per 9.0 IP... Made one start in the post-season and was 0-1 with a 4.76 ERA.

PROFESSIONAL CAREER: 1993: Appeared at Rookie Sarasota and made seven appearances at South Bend... Was recommended/signed by Doug Laumann/Ken Stauffer... **1994:** Selected as the left-handed pitcher on the Topps National Association Class A All-Star Team while at South Bend... Led the Midwest League in innings pitched (196.2) and complete games (eight)... Was second in strikeouts (173) and ninth in ERA (3.07)... Among all minor league pitchers was fourth in innings and tied for third in complete games... Named to the MWL mid-season and post-season All-Star teams... Set a South Bend record for complete games and strikeouts and tied the club mark for shutouts (two)... Led the Sox organization in strikeouts and IP while ranking fifth in ERA... Struck out eight or more in eight starts... Posted a season-high 15 strikeouts on July 31 at Beloit in a complete-game victory, had a no-hitter through 6.0 IP and had allowed just one hit through 7.0 IP... Tossed a four-hit shutout on May 27 at Western Michigan, striking out 10... Attended the Florida Instructional League... **1995:** Played for three clubs, Birmingham (AA), Nashville (AAA) and Chi-

cago, combining to post a 9-13 record... Opened the season with Birmingham and was 7-6 in 16 starts with a complete game and a 3.20 ERA... Won his last four decisions (five starts) with the Barons, posting a 1.29 ERA... Had his contract purchased by Chicago on July 19 and made his major-league debut that night vs. Boston... Suffered the loss despite making a quality start, allowing three earned runs over 6.2 IP... Was the first left-handed starting pitcher to make his major-league debut with the Sox since Greg Hibbard on May 31, 1989 vs. Detroit... Was optioned to Class AAA Nashville the next day, July 20... Posted a 1-5 record in eight starts with the Sounds, despite a 2.83 ERA... Was recalled to Chicago on September 3... Started on September 6 earning a no-decision and recording his first strikeout, fanned Texas' Juan Gonzalez... Earned first ML victory on September 27 at Kansas City, tossing 8.0 scoreless innings, allowed a season-low three hits while striking out a then career-high eight batters... In his six starts the Sox were 4-2... Allowed only five earned runs and struck out 17 batters over his final 22.2 IP (1.99 ERA)... **1996:** Split the season between Nashville (AAA) and Chicago... Made 15 appearances, four starts, with the White Sox and was 1-2 with a 7.18 ERA... Opened the season in Nashville but was recalled to Chicago on June 12... Made four appearances in relief before his first start on June 24 vs California (game two)... After three starts, 0-1, was optioned back to AAA on August 5... Overall started 15 games with Nashville, going 7-5 with a 3.60 ERA... Won five of his last six decisions from May 22 to August 29, going 5-1 with a 2.94 ERA... Tossed a complete-game three-hitter on June 8 at New Orleans with a season-high nine strikeouts... Was recalled To Chicago on September 16 and appeared in four games, making one start... Won start on September 19 vs. Minnesota, allowing two runs over 5.0 IP... **1997:** Was 7-5 for Nashville (AAA) with a 3.60 ERA in 19 starts and was 3-0 for the White Sox with an ERA of 2.25 in seven games, four starts... Opened the season in Nashville were his 3.28 ERA was second in the organization, fell 2.2IP short of ranking sixth in ERA for the American Association... Ranked third among AAA starters in walks per 9.0 IP (1.76) and fifth in runners per 9.0 IP (11.06)... Walked two or fewer batters in 18 of 19 starts... Was on the disabled list from May 23 to June 15 with soreness in his left shoulder... Upon return tossed 12.0 scoreless innings... Won six of his final decisions... Was 3-1 with a 2.10 ERA (7 ER/30.0 IP) over his final four starts... Was recalled to Chicago on August 14 and optioned on August 19... Won on August 17 vs Seattle (Gm #2)... Was recalled a second time to Chicago on August 29... Was 3-0 with a 2.45 ERA (7 ER/25.2 IP) in four starts with the White Sox and 0-0 with a 1.42 ERA (1 ER/6.1 IP) in three relief outings... Averaged 6.8 strikeouts and 1.4 walks per 9.0 IP... Tossed 4.1 IP in relief on September 2 at St. Louis... Posted his only hold with a scoreless inning on September 9 vs. Milwaukee... **1998:** Led the White Sox with 14 victories, five complete games, 33 starts and 128 strikeouts... His 15 defeats tied for fourth in the AL... Five complete games were tied for seventh in the league... Allowed an average of 2.0 walks per nine innings, the sixth-best total in the AL... Walked two or fewer batters in 30 of his 33 starts and did not walk more than three in a game... In April was 4-1 with a 3.60 ERA... Won a career-high four consecutive starts from April 10 to 27, posting a 2.87 ERA... Posted first win on April 10 vs. Tampa Bay, throwing 8.0 scoreless IP and matched his then career high with eight strikeouts... Tossed two complete-game four hitters, May 23 vs. Detroit and July 19 vs.

Cleveland... Was 6-4 in his first ten starts before his first no-decision on May 28 at Detroit... Induced 28 double play ground balls, tied for third in the league... Allowed 30 home runs, tied fifth in the AL... Made 16 quality starts, going 11-2 in those contests, team was 13-3... Was 8-8 with a 5.06 ERA before the All-Star Break... Earned his team-leading 10th victory on July 25 at New York before a Yankees Old Timer's Day crowd of 55,638... Lost five straight decisions from August 19 to September 15... Entered the streak with a 12-10 record... Won his final start on 9/25 at Kansas City with 8.1 scoreless IP... **1999:** Was 11-13 with a 4.00 ERA which ranked eighth in the AL... Was third among lefties, trailing Seattle's Jamie Moyer (3.85) and Kansas City's Jose Rosado (3.87)... Ranked among the league leaders in ERA at home (7th, 3.60), fewest walks per 9.0 IP (8th, 2.45) and strikeouts per walk ratio (10th, 2.19)... The 13 losses were tied for ninth in the league... Was 7-7 with a 3.60 ERA (44 ER/110.0 IP) at Comiskey Park... Compiled a 1.69 ERA (14 ER/71.2 IP) over a 10-start stretch from 4/23-6/12... Was 7-8 with a 3.20 ERA

before the All-Star Break, including a 2.43 ERA (9 ER/33.1 IP) in May... Recorded his first career shutout on April 23 vs. Detroit... In back to back start against the Yankees, May 16 & 22, allow just three runs over 16.0 IP (1.69 ERA)... Issued 14 of his 57 walks over a four-start span from July 20 to August 5, including a career-high six on August 5 at Oakland... Was 3-0 with a 2.67 ERA (8 ER/27.0 IP) over his final four starts... In his last 30 starts posted a 3.80 ERA... Made 19 quality starts... Tossed three complete games to raise his career total to eight... Sox scored two runs or less in 10 of his starts... Was 2-0 with a 2.12 ERA (8 ER/34.0 IP) during inter-league play... Allowed more than three earned runs just nine times in 32 starts... Sox were 14-18 in his starts... Tied an AL record for pitchers when he committed three errors in one inning (fifth) on 4/9 vs. Kansas City (Tommy John, Yankees on 7/27/88).

POST SEASON EXPERIENCE: 2000: Started game two of the division series for Chicago and lost to the Seattle Mariners by a score of 5-2 (5.2IP, 7H, 3ER, 2BB).

MIKE SIROTKA

Year	Club & League	W-L	ERA	G	GS	CG	ShO	SV	IP	H	R	ER	HR	HB	BB-IBB	SO	WP	BK	OBA
1993	White Sox (Gulf)	0-0	0.00	3	0	0	0	0	5.0	4	1	0	0	0	2-0	8	0	0	.211
1993	South Bend (Mid)	0-1	6.10	7	1	0	0	0	10.1	12	8	7	3	0	6-0	12	0	1	.273
1994	South Bend (Mid)	12-9	3.07	27	27	8	2	0	196.2	183	99	67	11	3	58-1	173	7	2	.245
1995	Birmingham (Sou)	7-6	3.20	16	16	1	0	0	101.1	95	42	36	11	2	22-0	79	4	1	.249
1995	CHICAGO (AL)	1-2	4.19	6	6	0	0	0	34.1	39	16	16	2	0	17-0	19	2	0	.298
1995	Nashville (AmAs)	1-5	2.83	8	8	0	0	0	54.0	51	21	17	4	1	13-1	34	1	0	.258
1996	Nashville (AmAs)	7-5	3.60	15	15	1	1	0	90.0	90	44	36	10	1	24-0	58	0	1	.255
1996	Chicago (AL)	1-2	7.18	15	4	0	0	0	26.1	34	27	21	3	0	12-0	11	1	0	.315
1997	Nashville (AmAs)	7-5	3.28	19	19	1	0	0	112.1	115	49	41	13	1	22-0	92	2	1	.261
1997	CHICAGO (AL)	3-0	2.25	7	4	0	0	0	32.0	36	9	8	4	1	5-1	24	0	0	.290
1998	CHICAGO (AL)	14-15	5.06	33	33	5	0	0	211.2	255	137	119	30	2	47-0	128	3	1	.300
1999	CHICAGO (AL)	11-13	4.00	32	32	3	1	0	209.0	236	108	93	24	3	57-2	125	4	0	.283
2000	CHICAGO (AL)	15-10	3.79	32	32	1	0	0	197.0	203	101	83	23	1	69-1	128	8	2	.269
Minor Totals		34-31	3.22	95	86	11	3	0	569.2	550	264	204	52	8	147-2	456	14	6	.252
MAJOR TOTALS		45-42	4.31	125	111	9	1	0	710.1	803	398	340	86	7	207-4	435	18	3	.286

DIVISION SERIES RECORD

Year	Club & League	W-L	ERA	G	GS	CG	ShO	SV	IP	H	R	ER	HR	HB	BB-IBB	SO	WP	BK	OBA
2000	CHICAGO (AL)	0-1	4.76	1	1	0	0	0	5.2	7	4	3	1	1	2-0	0	0	0	.350

SIROTKA — TRANSACTIONS

- Selected by the Chicago White Sox in the 15th round of the June 1993 First Year Player Draft.
- On disabled list July 1-28, 1993.
- On disabled list (soreness left shoulder) May 23-June 15, 1997.
- Traded to the Toronto Blue Jays along with RHP Kevin Beirne, OF Brian Simmons and RHP Mike Williams in exchange for RHP Matt DeWitt and LHP David Wells on January 14, 2001.

CAREER HIGHS — SIROTKA, Mike

SEASON:

Wins	15 - 2000
Losses	15 - 1998
Saves	None
ERA	3.79 - 2000
Games	33 - 1998
Starts	33 - 1998
Complete Games	5 - 1998
Shutouts	1 - 1999
Innings Pitched	211.2 - 1998
Walks	69 - 2000
Strikeouts	128 - 1998, 2000
Longest Win Streak	5 - Aug. 19-Sept. 21, 2000
Longest Losing Streak	5 - Aug. 19-Sep. 15, 1998
Scoreless Innings Streak	15.1 - Jun. 6-17, 1999

GAME:

ML Debut	July 19, 1995 vs. BOS
Innings Pitched:	
Starter	9.0 - 6 times, last Aug. 16, 1999 vs. ANA
Reliever	4.1 - Sep. 2, 1997 at STL
Walks:	
Starter	6 - Aug. 5, 1999 at OAK
Reliever	2 - Jun. 19, 1996 at CAL
	2 - Jul. 15, 1996 at MIN
	2 - Aug. 4, 1996 at TEX
	2 - Sep. 2, 1997 at STL
Strikeouts:	
Starter	10 - Jul. 18, 2000 vs. MIL
Reliever	4 - Sep. 2, 1997 at STL
Hits Allowed	12 - Jun. 28, 1998 vs. MIL
Runs Allowed	9 - Apr. 9, 1999 vs. KC
ER Allowed	8 - Jun. 7, 1998 at CHC
HR Allowed	4 - Apr. 3, 2000 at SEA
Low Hit CG	4 - May 23, 1998 vs. DET
Last Win	Sep. 21, 2000 at MIN
Last Save	None
Last CG	Jul. 18, 2000 vs. MIL (8.0IP)
Last ShO	Apr. 23, 1999 vs. DET
Last Start	Sep. 21, 2000 vs. BOS
Last Relief App.	Sep. 9, 1997 vs. MIL

FIELDING
SIROTKA, Mike—P

Year	PCT	G	PO	A	E	TC	DP
1995	1.000	6	1	5	0	6	0
1996	.750	15	0	3	1	4	0
1997	.800	7	1	3	1	5	0
1998	.977	33	9	34	1	44	1
1999	.879	32	5	24	4	33	0
2000	.958	32	5	18	1	24	2
Total	.931	125	21	87	8	116	3

MIKE SIROTKA DETAILED PITCHING

	2000								CAREER							
	ERA	W-L-Sv	G	IP	H	ER	BB	SO	ERA	W-L-Sv	G	IP	H	ER	BB	SO
Total	3.79	15-10-0	32	197.0	203	83	69	128	4.31	45-42-0	125	710.1	803	340	207	435
ST	3.79	15-10-0	32	197.0	203	83	69	128	4.28	45-42-0	111	692.1	781	329	199	422
REL	–	–	–	–	–	–	–	–	5.50	0-0-0	14	18.0	22	11	8	13
Home	3.56	8-5-0	17	108.2	104	43	35	77	4.02	26-21-0	64	371.1	411	166	95	231
Away	4.08	7-5-0	15	88.1	99	40	34	51	4.62	19-21-0	61	339.0	392	174	112	204
April	4.44	2-2-0	5	24.1	32	12	11	12	3.89	7-6-0	14	85.2	95	37	25	48
May	4.55	1-3-0	5	29.2	33	15	10	22	4.03	4-9-0	16	105.0	107	47	27	68
June	3.28	4-1-0	5	35.2	35	13	6	25	4.72	10-7-0	22	118.1	147	62	24	72
July	3.92	2-2-0	6	39.0	35	17	17	28	4.71	5-8-0	23	126.0	151	66	42	74
August	3.11	4-2-0	6	37.2	33	13	19	22	4.74	8-7-0	20	114.0	132	60	45	71
September	3.82	2-0-0	5	30.2	35	13	6	19	3.79	11-5-0	30	161.1	171	68	44	102
vs. Ana	5.91	1-0-0	2	10.2	15	7	4	6	6.92	3-5-0	11	53.1	69	41	24	34
vs. Bal	12.00	0-2-0	2	6.0	13	8	10	4	5.03	2-2-0	6	34.0	46	19	17	14
vs. Bos	1.89	1-1-0	3	19.0	11	4	7	11	3.64	3-4-0	10	64.1	72	26	23	35
vs. Cle	3.38	0-1-0	1	8.0	9	3	1	6	4.53	5-3-0	10	53.2	67	27	12	33
vs. Det	1.93	1-0-0	2	14.0	14	3	3	7	2.68	3-2-0	7	50.1	47	15	8	29
vs. KC	18.90	0-1-0	1	3.1	9	7	0	0	4.96	3-4-0	9	45.1	52	25	13	33
vs. Mil	1.13	1-0-0	1	8.0	6	1	3	10	4.71	1-0-0	4	21.0	27	11	8	16
vs. Min	3.60	1-0-0	2	15.0	17	6	3	7	4.71	4-3-0	12	63.0	75	33	16	25
vs. NYY	3.20	2-1-0	3	19.2	21	7	4	14	2.95	4-3-0	8	55.0	56	18	9	38
vs. Oak	2.79	2-1-0	3	19.1	17	6	7	14	4.97	3-5-0	9	58.0	62	32	20	36
vs. Sea	1.89	2-1-0	3	19.0	15	4	8	12	3.23	4-3-0	11	55.2	59	20	16	37
vs. TB	0.00	1-0-0	1	6.0	3	0	5	2	1.29	2-1-0	3	21.0	15	3	9	15
vs. Tex	5.56	0-1-0	2	11.1	14	7	3	9	7.31	0-4-0	8	32.0	50	26	10	18
vs. Tor	3.21	1-0-0	2	14.0	16	5	2	10	3.50	3-1-0	5	36.0	37	14	6	23
vs. ChC	3.46	1-0-0	2	13.0	10	5	2	7	4.50	2-1-0	5	30.0	33	15	4	21
vs. Hou	3.86	1-0-0	1	7.0	5	3	3	6	3.38	1-0-0	2	8.0	6	3	3	7
vs. Pit	–	–	–	–	–	–	–	–	1.84	2-0-0	2	14.2	13	3	3	9
vs. StL	17.18	0-1-0	1	3.2	8	7	4	3	5.40	0-1-0	3	15.0	17	9	6	12
Pre-All Star	3.73	8-6-0	17	103.2	108	43	32	66	4.18	23-24-0	59	344.2	386	160	86	206
Post-All Star	3.86	7-4-0	15	93.1	95	40	37	62	4.43	22-18-0	66	365.2	417	180	121	229

MIKE SIROTKA PITCHING AT ML PARKS

Park	ERA	W-L-Sv	SvO	G	GS	IP	H	R	ER	HR	BB	SO
Camden Yards	4.32	1-1-0	0	4	4	25.0	31	15	12	6	11	12
Fenway Park	3.86	0-3-0	0	4	4	25.2	33	15	11	2	7	14
Edison Field	10.41	0-3-0	0	6	4	23.1	38	30	27	4	14	15
Comiskey Park	4.02	26-21-0	0	64	58	371.1	411	187	166	38	95	231
Jacobs Field	8.82	1-2-0	0	4	3	16.1	28	18	16	4	7	10
Tiger Stadium	2.35	0-1-0	0	2	2	15.1	15	6	4	0	1	12
Kauffman Stadium	4.32	2-2-0	0	4	4	25.0	21	12	12	5	7	21
County Stadium	6.00	0-0-0	0	1	1	6.0	8	4	4	1	4	2
Metrodome	3.69	3-0-0	0	6	4	31.2	30	16	13	2	10	15
Yankee Stadium	3.46	2-2-0	0	4	4	26.0	37	13	10	3	2	15
Oakland-Alameda	3.69	3-1-0	0	5	5	31.2	30	17	13	4	13	16
Kingdome	15.75	0-1-0	0	2	1	4.0	8	8	7	2	3	2
Arlington	9.82	0-3-0	0	5	4	18.1	32	24	20	7	9	8
SkyDome	2.05	3-0-0	0	3	3	22.0	18	6	5	0	4	12
Wrigley Field	5.51	1-1-0	0	3	3	16.1	20	10	10	2	3	11
Three Rivers	2.25	1-0-0	0	1	1	8.0	7	4	2	0	2	6
Busch Stadium	1.59	0-0-0	0	2	1	11.1	9	2	2	2	2	9
SAFECO Field	1.42	1-1-0	0	3	3	19.0	14	7	3	2	9	16
Enron Field	3.86	1-0-0	0	1	1	7.0	5	3	3	0	2	6
Comerica Park	0.00	0-0-0	0	1	1	7.0	8	1	0	0	1	2

Players

Shannon
STEWART
OUTFIELDER

BIRTHDATE .... February 25, 1974
OPENING DAY AGE 27
BIRTHPLACE .... Cincinnati, OH
RESIDENCE .... Miami, FL
BATS/THROWS .... R/R
HEIGHT/WEIGHT 6-1/205
CONTRACT STATUS .... signed thru 2001
M.L. SERVICE 3.121

24

PERSONAL: Shannon Harold Stewart... Graduated from Southridge Senior High School in 1992 where he starred in baseball, football and track... Named to the All-Dade county baseball team in his senior year... Also earned Rookie of the Year honours and Outstanding Player Honours... Also named All-Dade county in football earning MVP honours on the junior varsity club... Played American Legion and Little League ball.

LAST SEASON: Set career highs in batting (.319), hits (186), doubles (43), home runs (21) and RBI (69) despite spending time on the disabled list... He placed fourth in the AL with 59 multi-hit games and was tied for eighth in doubles... The 43 doubles are tied for the fourth highest single season total in club history while ranking tenth in both hits and batting average... Opened the season with the first season lead-off home run in club history... Has now been accomplished 23 times since 1901 in the majors... On the season would hit .381/48-126 when leading off the first inning with nine doubles, two triples, five home runs, two hit by pitch and eight walks... Hit a second HR on opening day for his first career multi-HR game, he is now one of five players in club history to hit two or more home runs on opening day... April 5 vs KC stole the first of 20 bases on the season, was career steal #102 to pass Otis Nixon for sixth on Blue Jays All-Time list... On April 15 suffered a slight pull of his right hamstring which saw him sit out the next 11 games... In the first 12 games was batting .356... He played again on April 28 before being placed on the 15-day disabled list from April 29 until May 14 due to the hamstring... Returned from the disabled list and hit in 12 straight from May 16 to 28... In May hit .361 in 16 games... On June 8 vs Montreal matched the club record with four extra-base hits in one game, he had three doubles and a home run... Third Blue Jay to do so along with Damaso Garcia and Roy Howell... Would also have four extra-base hits on July 18 vs the Mets when he tied a ML record with four doubles in one game — now done 41 times, 21 times in the AL... Only other Blue Jay with four doubles in a game was Damaso Garcia in 1986... On June 25 hit his third lead-off home run of the season against Pedro Martinez, first off Martinez since 1996 (257 games)... In June hit .319 with five home runs and 20 RBI... At the All-Star break was batting .339 with 11 home runs and 36 RBI... On July 29 suffered a contusion to the soft tissue above his left eye after being hit by fly ball... In August hit .381 with 30 runs scored, 10 doubles, six home runs and 19 RBI... Had RBI in six consecutive games from August 9 to 15, nine total... Homered in three consecutive games August 9 & 10 against KC and August 11 against Minnesota... Hit in 13 straight from August 3 to 16... Struggled in September batting .233 in 28 games, was 1-4 in October... Had hit over .300 in every month prior... On September 19 vs New York was ejected by homeplate umpire Mark Carlson... Finished the season on a five-game hit streak which included his fifth lead-off HR on September 27 in Baltimore... Hit .322 against right-handed pitching with 30 doubles, 18 home runs and 60 RBI and against left-handed pitching hit .309 with 13 doubles, three home runs and nine RBI... At SkyDome hit .286 with 12 home runs while on the road hit .349 with nine home runs... Hit .271 with runners in scoring position... Recorded seven outfield assists and posted a .993 (2E/305TC) fielding percentage which led AL left-fielders... Finished the season with six four-hit games to match his career high... Was successful in 20 of 25 stolen base attempts.

PROFESSIONAL CAREER: 1992: Led the Gulf Coast in stolen bases with 32 and was second in runs scored with 44... **1993:** With St. Catharines led the New York Penn League in at bats (301), tied for the lead in runs (53), tied second in games (75), tied fourth in hits (84) and was fifth in stolen bases (25)... Scored 24 runs in his first 26 games... Collected seven consecutive hits at Welland, September 2-4, including a 5-5 outing on the second... **1994:** Was having an All Star season with Hagerstown of the South Atlantic League until suffering a season ending dislocated left shoulder in homeplate collision in June... Posted a 13 game hit streak April 15 to 28... Was 5-6 on April 26 in Macon... Selected to appear in the All Star game but was unable... Selected by Baseball America as the Best Defensive Outfielder in the South Atlantic League... **1995:** R. Howard Webster Award winner for Knoxville (AA) of the Southern League as club's MVP... Played 132 of 138 games in OF committing just 6 errors... Led the Southern League with 89 walks and was fourth in stolen bases with 42... His 89 runs scored were tops on the club and tied for 2nd in the league... Contract was purchased by Toronto from Knoxville on September 1... Notched first ML hit in his first ML appearance- September 2 at Chicago (single off Alvarez)... Hit in the head by a Mark Gubicza pitch on September 1 (Game 1) and had to leave the game... Hit in 5 straight from September 11-23 (6-22/.273)... Started 9 games in CF... Batted .240 vs RHP and .154 vs LHP... **1996:** Selected as the R. Howard Webster Award winner (MVP) for the Syracuse Chiefs... Led the International League in stolen bases with 35... Hit .298 with a club high 77 runs, 40 extra-base hits (26, 8, 6) and 42 RBI... Started slow batting .215 in April and .255 in May... Was disabled from May 13 to 31 with left oblique muscle pull... In June was the Chiefs Player of the Month batting .322 with 13 stolen bases... On June 29 collected the first of three 4-hit games... In July hit just .237 but after the first game of two on July 27 hit .388 the remainder of the season (57-147)... In game two on July 27 began a season high 13 game hit streak (.370/14-46)... Named IL Player of the Week for August 12 to 18 after batting .567 (3-2B, 2HR)... In August hit .388 (45-116, 9-2B, 4-3B, 4-HR, 13RBI)... Collected seven outfield assists and a .983 fielding percentage... Was selected by Baseball America as the fifth best prospect in the IL... Recalled to Toronto on September 3... Appeared in seven games making three starts... Selected as the second best prospect in the organization by Baseball America... Hit .391 with 21 RBI and 13 SB in 31 games with Lara in Venezuelan Winter League... **1997:** Opened the season with Toronto appearing in two games prior to being optioned to Syracuse (AAA) on April 16... In 58 games with Syracuse hit .346 (72-208, 13-2B, 1-3B, 5HR, 24RBI)... Against right hand pitchers hit .313 (56-179) and against left handers hit .552 (16-29)... Hit .310 (13-42) in August before being recalled to Toronto on August 12 after Otis Nixon was traded to the Los Angeles Dodgers... Syracuse was 30-24 with Stewart in the lineup and 15-47 without... With Toronto hit .286 (48-168) with 22 RBI and seven triples which was tied for fifth in the AL, second among rookies... Also ranked fourth among rookies with 10 stolen bases in just 44 games... Ten game hit streak from August 19 to 29... Collected a four-hit game with two doubles and three RBI on August 21 at Chicago... Led the Blue Jays in RBI in September with 14 and hit .283 (30-106) with ten doubles and five triples... On September 20 in New York became the eighth Blue Jay in club history to hit two triples in a game, was the tenth time it has been done... Hit .350

(14-40) with runners in scoring position... Was 10-3 in stolen base attempts... Appeared in 41 games for Toronto making 41 starts, 39 starts in center, one in left and one at DH... Started on August 13 at Cleveland but did not take the field after being hit on left ear flap in the top of the first (Juden)... **1998:** Hit .279 in his first full season in the majors with 12 home runs and 55 RBI... In the spring hit .364 (24-66) and set a club record with 12 stolen bases, then went on to swipe 51 bases in the regular season to rank third in the AL... Is the fifth player in franchise history to reach 50 stolen bases... Attempted to steal a league high 37.9% of the time he reached base... Stole third base seven times to tie for ninth in the AL... Hit leadoff in 117 games and finished second in the AL with a lead-off on-base average of .379... Suffered a mild strain of the left hamstring in the Opening Game on April 1st - missed four games... In April hit .277 with three RBI and stole five bases... Hit in ten straight games to match his then career high from April 15 to 27... On May 5 hit his first ML home run in Anaheim off Ken Hill... In July hit .329, scored 23 runs and stole 12 bases... On July 1 scored four runs vs. the Mets to tie a then club record (25th time, 16th player)... On July 3 matched his career high with a four hit game versus Tampa Bay... July 28 vs Texas hit his first career inside-the-park home run, a 2R-HR against Eric Gunderson... Did it again on September 7 against Cleveland's Chad Ogea to become the only Blue Jay to ever hit two inside the park home runs in the same season... On September 1 at KC hit his first career lead-off home run against Tim Belcher... Hit in ten straight games from Sept. 7-17 to match his season high, 2nd time, and his career high, 3rd time... Sept. 23 stole 50th base of the season... In September hit .308 (33-107) with five doubles, seven home runs, 18 RBI and 25 runs scored... Against LHP posted a .418 on-base average which ranked eighth in the AL... Started 125 games, 89 in left field, 36 in center field and hit first 117 times... **1999:** Hit .304 with 102 runs scorerd and 67RBI... In 145 games had

28 doubles, two triples and 11 home runs... Finished fourth in the AL in singles with 144, was tied for fourth with 37 stolen bases & 58 multi-hit games, fifth in lead-off on base percentage .377 (248-658) and ninth in batting with runners in scoring position at .350 (43-123)... Matched his career high with four RBI on April 7 at Minnesota... April 9 hit first of three lead-off HR against Baltimore's Sidney Ponson... Also hit lead off HR's on July 9 at Montreal (Powell) and August 10 in Minnesota (Radke)... Hit .352 in April with four home runs, 15 RBI and scored 24 runs... Named AL Player of the Week from April 26 to May 2 (.471/16-34, 5R, 3-2B, 1HR, 5RBI, 3SB)... In June hit .324 with ten RBI... June 21 matched career high with four hits vs KC - posted three four hit games in 1999 and now has nine career... Hit in 16 straight games from June 15 to June 30... At the All-Star break was batting .303 with eight home runs and 43 RBI with 29 stolen bases... After the break appeared in just 57 games and hit .306 with three home runs, 24 RBI and eight stolen bases... From August 1 to 29 hit in 26 straight games to tie the second longest hit streak in club history with Olerud (1993)... During the streak hit .342 (39-114)... On September 12 in Detroit suffered a jammed right ankle and was removed from the game... Appeared in three more games before aggravating the ankle and did not play again after September 21... Started 144 games, 135 in left field, six in center field, two at DH and September 12 when he did not take the field... Vs LHP hit .396 & vs. RHP hit .291.

CAREER NOTES: In the 2000 season had 20 stolen bases and 20 home runs, has now been done 11 times in club history and by nine different players... Is sixth in club history with 102 steals... Is one of 23 major league players to hit a lead-off home run on opening day... Recorded four doubles in one game on July 18, 2000 vs the Mets to tie the ML record, now done 44 times, 21 times in the AL... Has ten career lead-off home runs, club record is 22 by Devon White... Has 15 four-hit games.

SHANNON STEWART

Year	Club & League	AVG	G	AB	R	H	TB	2B	3B	HR	RBI	SH-SF	HP	BB-IBB	SO	SB-CS	GIDP	SLG	OBP
1992	Blue Jays (Gulf)	.233	50	172	44	40	44	1	0	1	11	4-2	3	24-0	27	32-5	3	.256	.333
1993	St. Catharines (NYP)	.279	75	301	53	84	112	15	2	3	29	3-3	2	33-1	43	25-11	7	.372	.351
1994	Hagerstown (SAL)	.324	56	225	39	73	105	10	5	4	25	2-2	1	23-1	39	15-11	3	.467	.386
1995	Knoxville (SAL)	.287	138	498	89	143	194	24	6	5	55	3-5	6	89-3	61	42-16	13	.390	.398
1995	TORONTO (AL)	.211	12	38	2	8	8	0	0	1	0-0	1	5-0	5	2-0	0	.211	.318
1996	Syracuse (Int)	.298	112	420	77	125	185	26	8	6	42	5-4	2	54-0	61	35-8	6	.440	.377
1996	TORONTO (AL)	.176	7	17	2	3	4	1	0	0	2	0-0	0	1-0	4	1-0	1	.235	.222
1997	Syracuse (Int)	.346	58	208	41	72	102	13	1	5	24	1-0	4	36-3	26	9-6	1	.490	.452
1997	TORONTO (AL)	.286	44	168	25	48	75	13	7	0	22	0-2	4	19-1	24	10-3	3	.446	.368
1998	TORONTO (AL)	.279	144	516	90	144	215	29	3	12	55	6-1	15	67-1	77	51-18	5	.417	.377
1999	TORONTO (AL)	.304	145	608	102	185	250	28	2	11	67	3-4	8	59-0	83	37-14	12	.411	.371
2000	Dunedin (FSL)	1.000	1	3	2	3	4	1	0	0	1	0-0	0	2-1	0	0-1	0	1.333	1.000
2000	TORONTO (AL)	.319	136	583	107	186	302	43	5	21	69	1-4	6	37-1	79	20-5	12	.518	.363
	Minor Totals	.296	490	1827	345	540	746	90	22	24	187	18-16	18	261-9	257	158-58	33	.408	.386
	MAJOR TOTALS	.297	488	1930	328	574	854	114	17	44	216	10-11	34	188-3	272	121-40	33	.442	.368

HOME RUN BREAKDOWN

			MEN ON			ONE GAME							
Total	H	A	0	1	2	3	2	3	4	LO	XN	IP	PH	RHP	LHP
44	12	22	27	12	5	0	1	0	0	10	0	2	0	38	6

STEWART — TRANSACTIONS

- Selected by the Toronto Blue Jays organization in the 1st round (19th overall) in June 1992 First Year Player Draft.
- On disabled list (dislocated left shoulder) June 13 through remainder of season, 1994.
- On disabled list (left oblique muscle) May 13 to May 31, 1996.
- On disabled list (right hamstring strain) April 29-May 13, 2000; included rehabilitation assignment at Dunedin May 12.

Lead Off Homers on Opening Day (since 1901)

04/17/1903	George Browne	NY (NL)	vs BRO	04/07/1986	Dwight Evans	BOS (AL)	@ DET
04/14/1925	Charlie Jamieson	CLE (AL)	@ SLA	04/08/1986	Bobby Grich	CAL (AL)	@ SEA
04/13/1932	Roy Johnson	DET (AL)	vs CLE	04/08/1986	R.J. Reynolds	PIT (NL)	vs NYN
04/19/1938	Heinie Mueller	PHI (NL)	vs BRO	04/06/1987	Oddibe McDowell	TEX (AL)	@ BAL
04/19/1949	Bill Rigney	NY (NL)	@ BRO	04/04/1988	Julio Franco	CLE (AL)	@ TEX
04/07/1969	Pete Rose	CIN (NL)	vs LAN	04/04/1988	Steve Sax	LAN (NL)	vs SFN
04/07/1977	Gary Thomasson	SF (NL)	@ LAN	04/03/1994	Ray Lankford	STL (NL)	@ CIN
04/06/1978	Terry Puhl	HOU (NL)	@ CIN	04/04/1994	Karl Rhodes	CHN (NL)	vs NYN
04/10/1980	Terry Puhl	HOU (NL)	vs LAN	04/05/1999	Juan Encarnacion	DET (AL)	@ TEX
04/05/1982	Bump Wills	CHN (NL)	@ CIN	04/03/2000	Gerald Williams	TB (AL)	@ MIN
04/05/1983	Lee Lacy	PIT (NL)	@ SLN	04/03/2000	Shannon Stewart	TOR (AL)	vs KCA
04/03/1984	Onix Concepcion	KC (AL)	vs NYA				

CAREER HIGHS — STEWART, Shannon

FIELDING
STEWART, Shannon—OF

Year	PCT	G	PO	A	E	TC	DP
1995	.955	12	20	1	1	22	0
1996	.800	6	4	0	1	5	0
1997	.980	41	97	1	2	100	0
1998	.980	144	295	4	6	305	1
1999	.981	142	256	4	5	265	1
2000	.993	136	298	5	2	305	2
Total	.983	481	970	15	17	1002	4

SHANNON STEWART DETAILED HITTING

	2000									CAREER							
	Avg	AB	H	HR	RBI	BB	SO	OBP	SLG	Avg	AB	H	HR	RBI	BB	SO	OBP	SLG
Total	.319	583	186	21	69	37	79	.363	.518	.297	1930	574	44	216	188	272	.368	.442
vs. Left	.309	139	43	3	9	6	20	.340	.468	.318	431	137	6	41	54	66	.400	.439
vs. Right	.322	444	143	18	60	31	59	.371	.534	.292	1499	437	38	175	134	206	.359	.444
Home	.286	276	79	12	32	14	37	.332	.518	.284	918	261	22	105	101	131	.366	.430
Away	.349	307	107	9	37	23	42	.391	.518	.309	1012	313	22	111	87	141	.370	.454
April	.347	49	17	3	5	4	5	.418	.633	.321	224	72	7	23	30	28	.412	.473
May	.361	72	26	2	7	1	8	.365	.542	.280	268	75	5	27	22	34	.337	.392
June	.319	113	36	5	20	7	23	.366	.558	.303	294	89	6	32	24	50	.361	.442
July	.308	107	33	3	11	11	15	.370	.486	.306	291	89	8	35	32	39	.385	.467
August	.381	118	45	6	19	9	13	.426	.619	.321	411	132	9	51	42	51	.393	.474
September	.233	120	28	2	7	5	14	.270	.358	.265	438	116	9	48	38	69	.333	.413
October	.250	4	1	0	0	0	1	.250	.250	.250	4	1	0	0	0	1	.250	.250
Scoring Posn	.271	129	35	5	50	9	19	.310	.450	.307	423	130	11	169	40	61	.367	.454
Bases Loaded	.333	9	3	0	7	0	1	.300	.444	.304	23	7	0	21	3	4	.360	.348
DH	–	–	–	–	–	–	–	–	–	.222	9	2	0	1	0	2	.200	.222
PH	–	–	–	–	–	–	–	–	–	.333	3	1	0	0	1	1	.500	.667
vs. Ana	.286	35	10	1	3	4	3	.359	.400	.333	141	47	3	12	14	22	.401	.475
vs. Bal	.333	42	14	2	4	1	3	.349	.619	.321	140	45	5	20	14	18	.382	.521
vs. Bos	.288	52	15	2	3	5	4	.362	.500	.243	148	36	2	13	15	14	.333	.331
vs. CWS	.281	32	9	1	3	1	6	.303	.469	.309	139	43	1	12	18	16	.400	.446
vs. Cle	.382	34	13	2	7	3	5	.421	.647	.278	90	25	4	16	7	17	.327	.478
vs. Det	.373	51	19	2	11	0	9	.365	.608	.338	145	49	4	26	18	20	.409	.497
vs. KC	.366	41	15	6	8	1	5	.422	.829	.299	137	41	7	16	9	15	.364	.504
vs. Mil	–	–	–	–	–	–	–	–	–	.143	14	2	0	0	1	1	.200	.143
vs. Min	.333	39	13	1	5	3	6	.381	.487	.317	126	40	4	19	11	17	.370	.460
vs. NYY	.276	29	8	0	1	2	4	.344	.345	.287	122	35	2	8	16	27	.389	.418
vs. Oak	.167	30	5	0	1	1	2	.194	.200	.241	133	32	3	16	9	16	.299	.406
vs. Sea	.345	29	10	0	1	3	4	.406	.448	.310	126	39	0	11	16	13	.393	.413
vs. TB	.178	45	8	1	2	1	8	.196	.244	.260	123	32	3	10	8	19	.316	.366
vs. Tex	.467	45	21	1	8	5	4	.510	.711	.356	135	48	2	18	11	17	.409	.474
vs. Atl	.385	13	5	0	2	1	5	.400	.462	.371	35	13	0	3	3	11	.410	.514
vs. Fla	.583	12	7	1	5	2	1	.667	1.000	.318	44	14	2	8	7	11	.423	.523
vs. Mon	.286	28	8	1	4	2	4	.333	.536	.262	65	17	2	7	4	8	.324	.446
vs. NYM	.308	13	4	0	1	2	2	.400	.615	.250	48	12	0	1	5	6	.333	.354
vs. Phi	.154	13	2	0	0	0	2	.154	.154	.211	19	4	0	0	2	4	.286	.316
Pre-All Star	.339	274	93	11	36	16	42	.380	.558	.305	893	272	21	94	83	124	.370	.441
Post-All Star	.301	309	93	10	33	21	37	.348	.482	.291	1037	302	23	122	105	148	.366	.444

SHANNON STEWART HITTING AT ML PARKS

Park	Avg	G	AB	R	H	2B	3B	HR	RBI	SB	CS	BB	SO	OBP	Slg
Camden Yards	.359	17	64	13	23	4	0	3	8	6	2	4	5	.391	.563
Fenway Park	.258	18	66	12	17	3	1	1	5	10	1	5	3	.329	.379
Edison Field	.342	17	76	12	26	2	0	2	9	3	2	7	14	.405	.447
Comiskey Park	.347	18	72	14	25	6	3	0	7	2	0	10	4	.440	.514
Jacobs Field	.255	15	51	10	13	2	1	1	7	4	0	1	9	.268	.392
Tiger Stadium	.316	15	57	12	18	3	0	2	11	4	1	6	6	.381	.474
Kauffman Stadium	.333	18	75	14	25	5	0	4	11	2	0	7	11	.398	.560
County Stadium	.000	1	4	0	0	0	0	0	0	0	0	0	0	.000	.000
Metrodome	.324	15	71	15	23	2	0	3	11	5	2	3	10	.347	.479
Yankee Stadium	.293	20	82	11	24	2	3	2	5	7	0	10	16	.383	.463
Oakland-Alameda	.239	15	71	9	17	4	2	0	7	4	1	2	7	.270	.352
Kingdome	.328	14	58	11	19	8	0	0	6	5	1	7	7	.409	.466
Arlington	.333	15	63	14	21	4	1	1	6	0	1	8	9	.419	.476
SkyDome	.284	238	918	153	261	58	5	22	105	59	23	101	131	.366	.430
Olympic Stadium	.300	8	30	6	9	3	0	1	2	1	1	2	6	.364	.500
Shea Stadium	.182	5	22	1	4	0	0	0	0	0	2	0	3	4	.280	.182
Veterans Stadium	.400	2	5	1	2	0	1	0	0	0	0	2	1	.571	.800
Pro Player Stadium	.381	6	21	7	8	3	0	1	5	5	0	3	4	.480	.667
Turner Field	.318	6	22	3	7	1	0	0	2	1	0	1	8	.333	.364
Tropicana Field	.271	14	59	5	16	2	0	1	3	1	4	3	10	.306	.356
SAFECO Field	.389	5	18	3	7	0	0	0	1	0	1	3	2	.476	.389
Comerica Park	.360	6	25	2	9	2	0	0	5	0	0	0	5	.346	.440

SHANNON STEWART — MILESTONES

	DATE	OPP.	H/A	PITCHER		DESCRIPTION
HITS						
1	Sept. 2, 1995	TOR vs CWS	A	Wilson Alvarez		Single
500	July 29, 2000	TOR vs SEA	A	Jamie Moyer		Single
HR						
1	May 5, 1998	TOR vs ANA	A	Ken Hill		2R
RBI						
1	Sept. 23, 1995	TOR vs BOS (G#2)	A	Tim Wakefield		Single
SB						
1	Sept. 23, 1995	TOR vs BOS (G#2)	A	Tim Wakefield Catcher-Mike McFarlane		2nd
100	Sept. 2, 1999	TOR vs MIN	H	Bob Wells Catcher-Terry Steinbach		2nd
GM						
1	Sept. 2, 1995	TOR vs CWS	A			1-3, Starting CF
INSIDE THE PARK HR						
1	July 28, 1998	TOR vs TEX	H	Eric Gunderson		2R
2	Sept. 7, 1998	TOR vs CLE	H	Steve Karsay		3R
LEAD OFF HR						
1	Sept. 1, 1998	TOR vs KC	A	Tim Belcher		
2	Sept. 13, 1998	TOR vs NYY	A	David Cone		
3	April 9, 1999	TOR vs BAL	A	Sidney Ponson		
4	July 9, 1999	TOR vs MTL	A	Jeremy Powell		
5	Aug. 10, 1999	TOR vs MIN	A	Brad Radke		
6	April 3, 2000	TOR vs KC	H	Jeff Suppan		
7	June 2, 2000	TOR vs FLA	A	Brad Penny		
8	June 25, 2000	TOR vs BOS	H	Pedro Martinez		
9	Aug. 7, 2000	TOR vs KC	A	Blake Stein		
10	Sept. 27, 2000	TOR vs BAL	A	Sidney Ponson		

BASE THEFTS ABOUND

On August 5, 1984 at Baltimore the Blue Jays set a club record with seven stolen bases. Dave Collins and Willie Upshaw each set personal highs with four and two respec- tively while Lloyd Moseby picked up one. Ironically, not one of the seven stolen bases figured in the scoring of a Blue Jays 4-3 win.

Raul
TABLADO

OUTFIELDER

67

BIRTHDATE	March 3, 1982
OPENING DAY AGE	19
BIRTHPLACE	North Bergen, NJ
RESIDENCE	Miami, FL
BATS/THROWS	R/R
HEIGHT/WEIGHT	6-2/175
CONTRACT STATUS	signed thru 2001
M.L. SERVICE	0.000

PERSONAL: Raul Manuel Tablado... Graduated from Miami Southridge High School... Played baseball and was the team MVP, an All-Dade selection and a state All-Star... Was signed by Tony Arias.

LAST SEASON: Hit .212 in 52 games with Queens of the New York Penn League... Improved each month hitting .141 in 18 games in July, .234 in 29 games in August and .350 in five games in September... Hit .256 in his first ten professional games before going hitless in nine straight games (34 AB)... Season average excluding the nine game slump at .256... Hit his first pro HR on August 12 vs Vermont... Had 19 of his 29 RBI in August... Played all 52 games at shortstop... Was third in the league with 76 strikeouts.

RAUL TABLADO

Year Club & League	AVG	G	AB	R	H	TB	2B	3B	HR	RBI	SH-SF	HP	BB-IBB	SO	SB-CS	GIDP	SLG	OBP
2000 Queens (NYP)	.212	52	198	27	42	63	8	2	3	29	1-3	1	31-0	76	1-1	6	.318	.318

TABLADO — TRANSACTIONS

- Selected by the Toronto Blue Jays in the 4th round (118th overall) of the June 2000 First year Player Draft.

Andy
THOMPSON

OUTFIELDER

15

BIRTHDATE	August 28, 1975
OPENING DAY AGE	25
BIRTHPLACE	Oconomowoc, WI
RESIDENCE	Cottage Grove, WI
BATS/THROWS	R/R
HEIGHT/WEIGHT	6-3/220
CONTRACT STATUS	signed thru 2001
M.L. SERVICE	0.014

PERSONAL: Andrew John Thompson... Married, wife's name is Christine... One child, Taylor (5/7/00)... 1994 graduate of Sun Prairie (WI) H.S. where he was a three-sport star... Won first team All-Conference and All-State honours in baseball, and was chosen Gatorade (Wisconsin) and Wisconsin Coaches Association Player-of-the-Year as a senior... Led his club that year to state championship and earned MVP honours in playoffs... Palyed in the Junior Olympic Festival for baseball in San Antonio in 1993 and for the Dayton Warhawks, a showcase team composed of outstanding players from across the nation in 1994... Was also an All-Conference and All-State selection as a quarterback and safety in football and earned Player-of-the-Year honours as a senior... Also an All-Conference selection in basketball.

LAST SEASON: Spent most of the season with Syracuse (AAA) but also had a stint with Toronto in May... Was third in the organization with 22 home runs with the SkyChiefs... 51 of his 105 hits were for extra bases... Hit only .241 in April but was recalled to Toronto on May 1 as Shannon Stewart was disabled... Made his ML debut on May 2, starting in LF in Chicago against the White Sox... Picked up his first ML hit and RBI on May 4 against Cleveland's Chuck Finley with a bases loaded single to right field... Appeared in just the two games before returning to Syracuse on May 14... In nine games from May 24 to June 1 hit .471 with four doubles, six home runs and 15 RBI... Two homer games came on May 30 vs Columbus and August 31 vs Buffalo... Overall hit .313 in 14 May games... Had two four-hit games, May 27 in Toledo and June 26 vs Durham... Was 2-6 with the bases loaded with a grand slam on August 21 vs Rochester... Hit .297 against left-handed pitching with four home runs in 101 at bats and .231 against right-handers with 18 home runs in 325 at bats.

PROFESSIONAL CAREER: 1995: Began pro career with Hagerstown of the South Atlantic League (A)... Was 2-5 with a homer and three RBI in his first pro game on April 6 vs Columbus... Hit .303 in June with two home runs and 12 RBI... Batted .281 at home and .195 on the road... **1996:** Led Dunedin of the Florida State League (A) in games (129) and tied for team lead in doubles (26)... Was fifth in organization in batting (.282)... Had a 12-game hit streak from May 31 to June 13, batting .395 (17-43) with three home runs and eight RBI... In June hit .337 (28-83)... Hit in 18 straight games from July 28 to August 16, hitting .444 (28-63) during the streak... Was the second-longest in the entire minor leagues... Hit .319 (29-91) in August... **1997:** Joined Knoxville of the Southern League (AA) and with .286 with 15 HR and 71 RBI... In May hit .287 with six homers, 20 runs scored and 19 RBI... Hit a grand slam on August 12 vs Memphis... In August hit .330 with six homers and 18 RBI... Homered in three consecutive games vs Memphis August 12-15 and won Southern League Player-of-the Week honours August 8-14... Committed 23 of his 31 errors before July 5... Batted .389 (7-18) in four playoff games... Hit .235 with eight homers and 15 RBI for Phoenix of the Arizona Fall League... Named sixth-best prospect in organization by Baseball America... **1998:** Led Knoxville in games (125), at-bats (481), runs (74), total bases (216), doubles (33) and RBI (88)... Hit a home run on Opening Day, April 2 vs Hudson Valley... Compiled 12-game hitting streak May 8-23 and had RBI's in each of the last six games of streak... Hit .372 with six homers and 16 RBI in June... Drove in 20 runs in both May and July... Hit .312 at home and .245 on the road... Hit .346 vs left-handers and .261 vs right-handers... With the bases loaded hit .636 (7-for-11) with two doubles and 18 RBI... **1999:** Split the season between Knoxville (AA) and Syracuse (AAA)... Hit a combined .267 with 31 home runs and 95 RBI... The 31 HR's led the Blue Jays system and the 95 RBI were third... Opened the season in Knoxville... Hit .244 in 67 games with 15 home runs and 53 RBI... Was a Southern League All-Star game selection and rated as the best power prospect in the league by Baseball America... Was the Southern League Player of the Week for April 16 to 22... In May hit .277 with 11 home runs and 24 RBI... Hit nine home runs in a span of 13 games from May 8 to May 23... Hit in 14 straight games from May 22 to June 4... Played 66 games in right field...

Joined Syracuse and hit .293 with 16 home runs and 42 RBI... In July hit .304 with five home runs and 16 RBI... On August 6 was 3-4 with five RBI against Pawtucket after hitting a grand slam... Named International League Player of the Week from August 16 to 22... Finished August hitting .330 for the month with nine home runs and 22 RBI... Rated as the 8th best prospect in the organization by Baseball America.

ANDY THOMPSON

Year	Club & League	AVG	G	AB	R	H	TB	2B	3B	HR	RBI	SH-SF	HP	BB-IBB	SO	SB-CS	GIDP	SLG	OBP
1995	Hagerstown (SAL)	.239	124	461	48	110	151	19	2	6	57	1-3	8	29-2	108	2-3	15	.328	.293
1996	Dunedin (FSL)	.282	129	425	64	120	189	26	5	11	50	1-3	1	60-1	108	16-4	5	.445	.370
1997	Knoxville (Sou)	.286	124	448	75	128	204	25	3	15	71	1-4	6	63-3	76	0-5	18	.455	.378
1998	Knoxville (Sou)	.285	125	481	74	137	216	33	2	14	88	0-5	3	54-2	69	8-3	10	.449	.357
1999	Knoxville (Sou)	.244	67	254	56	62	129	16	3	15	53	0-5	8	34-2	55	7-3	2	.508	.346
1999	Syracuse (Int)	.293	62	229	42	67	136	17	2	16	42	0-0	2	21-0	45	5-0	4	.594	.357
2000	Syracuse (Int)	.246	121	426	59	105	202	27	2	22	65	0-6	9	50-1	95	9-2	4	.474	.334
2000	TORONTO (AL)	.167	2	6	2	1	1	0	0	0	1	0-0	0	3-0	2	0-0	0	.167	.444
Minor Totals		.268	752	2724	418	729	1227	163	19	99	426	3-26	37	311-11	556	47-20	58	.450	.348

THOMPSON — TRANSACTIONS

• Selected by the Toronto Blue Jays in the 23rd round (651st overall) of the June 1994 First Year Player Draft.

FIELDING
THOMPSON, Andy—OF

Year	PCT	G	PO	A	E	TC	DP
2000	1.000	2	2	0	0	2	0

Ryan
THOMPSON

55

OUTFIELDER

BIRTHDATE.............................November 4, 1967
OPENING DAY AGE.......................33
BIRTHPLACE............................Chestertown, MD
RESIDENCE.............................Indianapolis, IN
BATS/THROWS...........................R/R
HEIGHT/WEIGHT.........................6-3/215
CONTRACT STATUS.......................signed thru 2001
M.L. SERVICE..........................3.081

PERSONAL: Ryan Orlando Thompson... Married, wife's name is Charon... Five children, Ryan Jr. (15), Cameron (12), Taylor (8), Trevor (6) and Brock (1)... Graduated from Kent County High School in Rock Hall, MD... Earned All-Conference honors in baseball, football and basketball... Played on championship teams in Little League, Pony League and American Legion football... Received the 1993 Walter Younce Maryland Star of the future Award from the Maryland Professional Baseball Association on January 8, 1993.

LAST SEASON: Attended spring training with the Yankees on a minor league contract but was released on March 2... Signed another minor league deal with the Yankees on May 1 and was assigned to Columbus (AAA)... Hit .285 in 86 games in Columbus with 23 home runs and 75 RBI... Hit .207 in May with seven home runs and 17 RBI in 25 games... In June hit .315 in 28 games with eight home runs and 23 RBI... His contract was purchased by New York on July 13 after hitting .408 with five home runs and 18 RBI in the first 12 games in July... Made his New York debut starting in LF on July 13 at Florida... In doing so became the 67th player to appear for both the Mets and Yankees... On July 14 vs Florida hit his first of three home runs for the Yankees... On August 8 was designated for assignment as Jose Canseco was added to the club... Joined Columbus and hit .253 with three home runs and 17 RBI in 23 August games before rejoining New York on September 1... Appeared in 16 games in September and hit .412 with one home run and eight RBI.

PROFESSIONAL CAREER: 1989: Led New York-Penn League (A) outfielders in assists (11) and fourth in the circuit in games played (117)... Topped St. Catharines in at-bats (278), runs (39), hits (76), doubles (14) and stolen bases (9)... **1990:** Batted .231 with six HR and 37 RBI in 117 games for Dunedin of the Florida State League (A)... **1991:** Played

his first full season in Double-A Knoxville... Batted .241 with eight HR and 40 RBI in 114 games... Had an 11-game hitting streak from May 6 to 16... Batted .281 in 25 games for Lara in the Venezuelan Winter League... **1992:** Opened the season in Syracuse (AAA) where he hit .282 with 20 doubles, seven triples, 14 home runs and 46 RBI in 112 games... On August 27 was sent to the Mets as the player to be named later in a trade in which Toronto acquired RHP David Cone and gave up IF Jeff Kent... Made 27 starts for the Mets, hitting .222 with three HR and 10 RBI in 30 games... Picked up his first ML hit, a double, against Chris Hammond in Cincinnati on September 3... Knocked in his first run with a sacrifice fly against the Reds' Tim Belcher the next day... Collected his first home run, a three-run shot, against the Cubs' Mike Morgan on September 22 at Shea... Had his first multi-home run game on September 28 with two against the Phillies, vs. Cliff Brantley in the fourth inning and Mike Hartley in the seventh... **1993:** Began the season with the Mets and was optioned to triple-A Norfolk of the International League on April 30... Hit .259 with 12 HR and 34 RBI for Norfolk... Was recalled on July 24... Combined with Jeremy Burnitz (13) to give the Mets two rookies with 10 or more homers for only the second time in club history... Ron Swoboda (19) and Johnny Lewis (15) accomplished the feat in 1965... Collected his second career two-homer game in a 9-8 loss at Chicago on September 4... In that game vs. the Cubs, he tied his then career best with three RBI... **1994:** Hit .225 for the Mets and set career highs with 18 HR and 59 runs scored... Batted .290 with runners in scoring position and two outs... Started 96 games in center field and made three errors in 282 chances for a fielding percentage of .989... Had five assists... Established a career best with three four-RBI games... Hit his first career grand slam on May 14 at Shea Stadium off the Braves' John Smoltz... Also drove in four runs at Pittsburgh on May 26 and at Colorado on June 8... Had a career-high seven game hitting streak from June 1 to 8... Second career four-hit game was on June 18 at Florida... On September 20 he underwent arthroscopic surgery on his right knee to repair a small cartilage tear at the Hospital for Special Surgery in Manhattan, New York... **1995:** Played only 75 games with the Mets after two stints on the disabled list... Was disabled from April 19 to May 30 with a medial collateral ligament tear in his right elbow and from July 18 to August 18 with a partial tear of his right hamstring... Batted .320 (31-for-97) with five HR and 14 RBI in June... Had 10 multi-hit games during the month, including three hits on three occasions... Had two seven-game hit streaks, June 7 to 14 and August 24 to 31... **1996:** Was traded to Cleveland on March 30 and played the majority of the season at Triple-A Buffalo before being called up to the parent club in September... Led the American Association with 540 at-bats and 317 putouts, while tying for first with 138 games played... Hit safely in 11 consecutive games from June 7 to 18... Hit .355 during a 17-game stretch from July 28 to August 12... Homered twice on August 11 against Nashville... Played in his first AL game on September 12 at California and collected his first AL hit on September 14 at

Oakland... Played eight games in center field for Cleveland after being called-up on September 11... Finished the season with a five-game hitting streak... **1997:** Began the season by playing 24 games for Triple-A Buffalo (Cleveland), before being traded to the Blue Jays on June 6 for IF Jeff Manto... Finished the season with Triple-A Syracuse, batting .288 with 23 doubles, 16 home runs and 58 RBI... Hit home runs in three consecutive games, June 12 to 14... Highlighted a nine-run fourth inning by hitting a grand slam on June 19 vs. Charlotte... **1998:** Spent the season playing for the Fukuoka Daiei Hawks of the Japanese League... Helped the Hawks to a third place finish by hitting .271 (29-for-107) with seven doubles, two homers and 16 RBI in 26 games... **1999:** Joined the Astros organization and hit .309 with 16 HR and 58 RBI in 104 games for Triple-A New Orleans... Ranked second on the team in home runs, RBI, runs (60), and third with 23 doubles... Named Astros' Organizational Player of the Week for the period of April 12 to 18... Missed a week and a half because of a pulled hamstring... Performed the National Anthem before a New Orleans home game in April... Made his first appearance in the majors since 1996, appearing in 12 games for the Astros... Hit .200 with one home run and drove in five runs.

RYAN THOMPSON

Year Club & League	AVG	G	AB	R	H	TB	2B	3B	HR	RBI	SH-SF	HP	BB-IBB	SO	SB-CS	GIDP	SLG	OBP
1987 Medicine Hat (PIO)	.245	40	110	13	27	35	3	1	1	9	0-0	0	6-0	34	1-2	1	.318	.284
1988 St. Catharines (NYP)	.175	23	57	13	10	14	4	0	0	2	1-0	4	24-0	21	2-2	0	.246	.447
1988 Dunedin (FSL)	.138	17	29	4	4	7	0	0	1	2	0-0	1	2-0	12	0-0	0	.241	.219
1989 St. Catharines (NYP)	.273	74	278	39	76	110	14	1	6	36	0-3	4	16-0	60	9-6	8	.396	.319
1990 Dunedin (FSL)	.231	117	438	56	101	144	15	5	6	37	3-4	2	20-1	100	18-5	5	.329	.265
1991 Knoxville (Sou)	.241	114	403	48	97	141	14	3	8	40	5-3	4	26-2	88	17-10	11	.350	.291
1992 Syracuse (Int)	.282	112	429	74	121	197	20	7	14	46	2-1	3	43-1	114	10-4	5	.459	.351
1992 NEW YORK (NL)	.222	30	108	15	24	42	7	1	3	10	0-1	0	8-0	24	2-2	2	.389	.274
1993 NEW YORK (NL)	.250	80	288	34	72	128	19	2	11	26	5-1	3	19-4	81	2-7	5	.444	.302
1993 Norfolk (Int)	.259	60	224	39	58	109	11	2	12	34	0-2	5	24-2	81	6-3	2	.487	.341
1994 NEW YORK (NL)	.225	98	334	39	75	145	14	1	18	59	3-4	10	28-7	94	1-1	8	.434	.301
1995 Norfolk (Int)	.340	15	53	7	18	27	3	0	2	11	0-4	0	4-0	15	4-1	0	.509	.361
1995 NEW YORK (NL)	.251	75	267	39	67	101	13	0	7	31	0-4	4	19-1	77	3-1	12	.378	.306
1995 Binghamton (East)	.500	2	8	2	4	7	0	0	1	4	0-0	0	1-0	2	0-0	0	.875	.556
1996 Buffalo (AmAs)	.259	138	540	79	140	237	26	4	21	83	2-4	7	21-1	119	12-5	14	.439	.294
1996 CLEVELAND (AL)	.318	8	22	2	7	10	0	0	1	5	0-0	0	1-0	6	0-0	0	.455	.348
1997 Buffalo (AmAs)	.242	24	66	10	16	19	0	0	1	6	0-0	0	5-1	16	2-0	1	.288	.296
1997 Syracuse (Int)	.288	83	330	37	95	168	23	1	16	58	0-3	3	21-1	59	4-3	10	.509	.333
1998 Fukuoka (PL-JPN)	.271	33	107	10	29	42	7	0	2	16	0-0	1	7-0	26	1-0	0	.393	.319
1999 New Orleans (PCL)	.309	112	404	60	125	200	23	2	16	58	0-2	2	37-0	78	4-9	17	.495	.369
1999 HOUSTON (NL)	.200	12	20	2	4	8	1	0	1	5	0-0	0	2-0	7	0-0	1	.400	.273
2000 Columbus (Int)	.285	86	326	45	93	191	23	3	23	75	0-2	2	27-0	72	10-3	8	.586	.342
2000 NEW YORK (AL)	.260	33	50	12	13	25	3	0	3	14	0-0	1	5-0	12	0-1	0	.500	.339
Minor Totals	.267	1017	3695	524	985	1606	179	29	128	501	13-28	37	277-9	871	99-53	82	.435	.322
AL TOTALS	.278	41	72	14	20	35	3	0	4	19	0-0	1	6-0	18	0-1	0	.486	.342
NL TOTALS	.238	295	1017	129	242	424	54	4	40	131	8-10	17	76-12	283	8-11	28	.417	.284
MAJOR TOTALS	.241	336	1089	143	262	459	57	4	44	150	8-10	18	82-12	301	8-12	28	.421	.302

HOME RUN BREAKDOWN

Total	H	A	MEN ON				ONE GAME			LO	XN	IP	PH	RHP	LHP
			0	1	2	3	2	3	4						
44	19	25	27	11		1	1	0	0	1	1	0	1	35	9

THOMPSON — TRANSACTIONS

- Selected by the Toronto Blue Jays in 13th round of the June 1987 First Year Player Draft.
- On disabled list May 29-June 7, 1991.
- Traded to the New York Mets on September 1, 1992, completing a trade in which the New York Mets sent RHP David Cone to the Toronto Blue Jays in exchange for IF Jeff Kent and a player to be named (August 27, 1992).
- On disabled list April 18-May 30, 1995; including rehabilitation assignment to Norfolk, May 13-30.
- On disabled list July 18-August 30, 1995; including rehabilitation assignment to Norfolk, August 16-30.
- Traded to the Cleveland Indians along with RHP Reid Cornelius in exchange for RHP Mark Clark on March 31, 1996.
- Signed by the Kansas City Royals on February 5, 1997.
- Released by the Kansas City Royals on March 26, 1997.
- Signed by the Cleveland Indians on April 21, 1997.
- Traded to the Toronto Blue Jays in exchange for IF Jeff Manto on June 6, 1997.
- Signed by the Fukuoka Hawks (Japan) in 1998.
- Signed by the Houston Astros on January 19, 1999.
- On disabled list August 5-13, 1999.
- Signed by the New York Yankees on December 15, 1999.
- Released by the New York Yankees on April 2, 2000.
- Signed by the New York Yankees on May 1, 2000.
- Released by the New York Yankees on November 15, 2000.
- Signed by the Toronto Blue Jays on December 13, 2000.

CAREER HIGHS — THOMPSON, Ryan

SEASON:		GAME:	
Games	98 - 1994	ML Debut	Sep. 1, 1992 vs. ATL
Avg.	.251 - 1995	Runs	3 - Sep. 28, 1992 vs. PHI
Runs	39 - 1994, 1995		3 - Sep. 30, 1992 vs. PHI
Hits	75 - 1994		3 - Aug. 1, 1993 at STL
Doubles	19 - 1993		3 - Sep. 4, 1993 at CHI
Home Runs	18 - 1994	Hits	4 - Aug. 1, 1993 at STL
RBI	59 - 1994		4 - Jun. 18, 1994 at FLA
Walks	28 - 1994	Doubles	2 - Sep. 9, 1993 at PIT
Strikeouts	94 - 1994		2 - Aug. 30, 1995 at LA
Stolen Bases	6 - 1993	Home Runs	2 - Sep. 28, 1992 vs. PHI
Longest Hitting Streak	7G - Jun. 1-9, 1994		2 - Sep. 4, 1993 at CHI
Multi HR Games	1 - 1992, 1993	RBI	4 - May 14, 1994 vs. ATL
			4 - May 26, 1994 at PIT
			4 - Jun. 6, 1994 at COL
		Stolen Bases	1 - 8 times, last Jul. 16, 1995 vs. COL
		Last ML Home Run	Sep. 14, 2000 vs. TOR

FIELDING

THOMPSON, Ryan—OF

Year	PCT	G	PO	A	E	TC	DP
1992 (NL)	.988	29	77	2	1	80	0
1993 (NL)	.987	76	228	4	3	235	0
1994 (NL)	.989	98	274	5	3	282	2
1995 (NL)	.985	74	193	4	3	200	2
1996 (AL)	1.000	8	5	0	0	5	0
1999 (NL)	.800	10	3	1	1	5	1
2000 (AL)	1.000	31	33	0	0	33	0
Total	.987	326	813	16	11	840	5

RYAN THOMPSON DETAILED HITTING

	2000									CAREER								
	Avg	AB	H	HR	RBI	BB	SO	OBP	SLG	Avg	AB	H	HR	RBI	BB	SO	OBP	SLG
Total	.260	50	13	3	14	5	12	.339	.500	.241	1089	262	44	150	82	301	.302	.421
vs. Left	.250	12	3	0	0	2	4	.357	.250	.245	322	79	9	29	22	79	.304	.385
vs. Right	.263	38	10	3	14	3	8	.333	.579	.239	767	183	35	121	60	222	.301	.437
Home	.258	31	8	2	11	2	8	.324	.548	.218	551	120	19	81	42	169	.281	.370
Away	.263	19	5	1	3	3	4	.364	.421	.264	538	142	25	69	40	132	.324	.474
April	–	–	–	–	–	–	–	–	–	.222	108	24	5	17	8	37	.294	.435
May	–	–	–	–	–	–	–	–	–	.169	77	13	5	21	6	25	.250	.403
June	–	–	–	–	–	–	–	–	–	.294	194	57	8	26	9	44	.335	.459
July	.200	30	6	2	6	4	7	.314	.433	.219	146	32	9	23	16	41	.305	.445
August	.000	1	0	0	0	1	0	.500	.000	.215	205	44	5	19	15	54	.274	.361
September	.412	17	7	1	8	0	4	.412	.706	.256	336	86	11	41	25	95	.311	.426
October	.000	2	0	0	0	0	1	.000	.000	.261	23	6	1	3	3	5	.346	.435
Scoring Posn	.294	17	5	1	12	2	3	.368	.588	.225	271	61	7	99	33	78	.310	.380
Bases Loaded	.500	2	1	0	4	1	1	.667	1.000	.261	23	6	1	19	2	4	.308	.565
PH	.333	3	1	0	0	0	1	.333	.667	.462	13	6	1	2	1	3	.500	.769
vs. Ana	–	–	–	–	–	–	–	–	–	.000	1	0	0	0	0	1	.000	.000
vs. Bal	.286	14	4	1	1	2	2	.375	.500	.286	14	4	1	1	2	2	.375	.500
vs. Bos	.000	1	0	0	0	0	0	.000	.000	.000	1	0	0	0	0	0	.000	.000
vs. CWS	–	–	–	–	–	–	–	–	–	.000	4	0	0	0	0	3	.000	.000
vs. Cle	.400	5	2	0	2	0	3	.400	.400	.400	5	2	0	2	0	3	.400	.400
vs. Det	1.000	1	1	0	0	0	0	1.000	2.000	1.000	1	1	0	0	0	0	1.000	2.000
vs. KC	.500	2	1	0	2	0	0	.500	.500	.444	9	4	1	5	0	1	.444	.778
vs. Mil	–	–	–	–	–	–	–	–	–	.000	0	0	0	0	0	0	.000	.000
vs. Min	.000	2	0	0	0	1	1	.333	.000	.273	11	3	0	1	2	2	.385	.273
vs. Oak	–	–	–	–	–	–	–	–	–	1.000	1	1	0	1	0	0	1.000	1.000
vs. Sea	.000	0	0	0	0	1	0	1.000	.000	.000	0	0	0	0	1	0	1.000	.000
vs. TB	.000	2	0	0	0	0	0	.000	.000	.000	2	0	0	0	0	0	.000	.000
vs. Tor	.429	7	3	1	4	0	1	.429	1.000	.429	7	3	1	4	0	1	.429	1.000
vs. Atl	–	–	–	–	–	–	–	–	–	.186	86	16	2	11	6	21	.239	.302
vs. ChC	–	–	–	–	–	–	–	–	–	.300	70	21	5	13	7	19	.380	.586
vs. Cin	–	–	–	–	–	–	–	–	–	.233	86	20	2	11	2	20	.269	.372
vs. Col	–	–	–	–	–	–	–	–	–	.243	74	18	5	15	5	18	.300	.486
vs. Fla	.250	8	2	1	5	1	3	.333	.750	.227	97	22	3	13	9	22	.299	.381
vs. Hou	–	–	–	–	–	–	–	–	–	.311	61	19	4	10	5	22	.364	.607
vs. LA	–	–	–	–	–	–	–	–	–	.262	61	16	2	11	6	21	.343	.443
vs. Mon	–	–	–	–	–	–	–	–	–	.160	75	12	1	6	7	24	.229	.213
vs. NYM	–	–	–	–	–	–	–	–	–	.167	6	1	0	1	0	3	.167	.333
vs. Phi	.000	8	0	0	0	0	2	.000	.000	.239	109	26	4	11	11	26	.309	.450
vs. Pit	–	–	–	–	–	–	–	–	–	.256	82	21	3	11	4	17	.295	.451
vs. StL	–	–	–	–	–	–	–	–	–	.286	63	18	4	7	4	22	.338	.540
vs. SD	–	–	–	–	–	–	–	–	–	.224	76	17	1	7	6	25	.302	.276
vs. SF	–	–	–	–	–	–	–	–	–	.195	87	17	5	9	5	28	.250	.402
Pre-All Star	–	–	–	–	–	–	–	–	–	.247	413	102	20	67	23	120	.301	.441
Post-All Star	.260	50	13	3	14	5	12	.339	.500	.237	676	160	24	83	59	181	.303	.410

Players

RYAN THOMPSON HITTING AT ML PARKS

Park	Avg	G	AB	R	H	2B	3B	HR	RBI	SB	CS	BB	SO	OBP	Slg
Camden Yards	.286	6	14	4	4	0	0	1	1	0	1	2	2	.375	.500
Fenway Park	.000	2	1	0	0	0	0	0	0	0	0	0	0	.000	.000
Comiskey Park	.000	1	4	0	0	0	0	0	0	0	0	0	3	.000	.000
Jacobs Field	.375	6	16	2	6	0	0	1	5	0	0	1	3	.412	.563
Kauffman Stadium	.667	4	3	2	2	0	0	0	2	0	0	0	0	.667	.667
County Stadium	.000	1	0	0	0	0	0	0	0	0	0	0	0	.000	.000
Metrodome	.000	2	2	1	0	0	0	0	0	0	0	1	1	.333	.000
Yankee Stadium	.258	19	31	5	8	3	0	2	11	0	0	0	8	.324	.548
SkyDome	.000	1	1	0	0	0	0	0	0	0	0	0	1	.000	.000
Atlanta-Fulton	.234	12	47	5	11	3	0	0	3	1	0	3	11	.280	.298
Wrigley Field	.250	10	36	7	9	2	1	3	6	0	0	4	8	.325	.611
Cinergy Field	.245	12	49	5	12	3	1	1	5	0	1	0	10	.255	.408
Astrodome	.242	13	33	4	8	4	0	2	7	0	0	3	12	.306	.545
Dodger Stadium	.333	10	30	6	10	3	0	2	7	0	0	2	11	.382	.633
Olympic Stadium	.195	12	41	5	8	1	0	1	5	1	1	5	9	.277	.293
Shea Stadium	.214	144	487	57	104	21	1	16	63	5	8	38	151	.277	.359
Veterans Stadium	.213	13	47	6	10	5	0	1	3	0	0	6	10	.309	.383
Three Rivers	.286	12	49	4	14	5	0	3	8	0	0	2	11	.308	.571
Busch Stadium	.333	9	33	5	11	3	0	3	5	1	0	3	9	.405	.697
Qualcomm Park	.256	13	39	4	10	0	0	1	2	0	0	4	11	.370	.333
3 Com Park	.275	14	51	10	14	1	0	4	6	0	1	1	17	.302	.529
Pro Player Stadium	.268	11	41	4	11	3	0	1	4	0	0	2	7	.318	.415
Mile High Stadium	.294	9	34	7	10	0	1	2	7	0	0	3	6	.368	.529

Vernon

WELLS

OUTFIELDER

10

BIRTHDATE	December 8, 1978
OPENING DAY AGE	22
BIRTHPLACE	Shreveport, LA
RESIDENCE	Arlington, TX
BATS/THROWS	R/R
HEIGHT/WEIGHT	6-1/210
CONTRACT STATUS	signed thru 2001
M.L. SERVICE	0.066

PERSONAL: Vernon Wells III... Attended Arlington (TX) Bowie HS where he was All-American in baseball and All-State in baseball and football... His father, Vernon, was a wide receiver who attended training camp with the NFL's Kansas City Chiefs and played in the Canadian Football League.

LAST SEASON: Spent the season with Syracuse of the International League (AAA) and was a September call-up with Toronto... With Syracuse hit .243 in 127 games with 31 doubles, seven triples, 16 home runs and 66 RBI... Opened the season batting .243 in April before struggling in May (.228) and June (.198)... Then rebounded the last two months hitting .260 in July and .286 in August... In May hit in a season high seven straight games from May 7 to 14... Had hit four home runs heading into July when he hit seven home runs and collected 16 RBI... Hit two home runs on July 2 in the second game of a doubleheader at Pawtucket... Participated in the MLB Futures game as part of the All-Star festivities... Also posted a two home run game on August 8 against Scranton, was 3-5 with a triple and a season high five RBI... From August 5 to 12, ten of his 12 hits were extra base hits (4-HR, 2-3B, 4-2B)... Hit .269 at home with eight home runs and 34 RBI and on the road hit .220 with eight home runs and 32 RBI... Stole 23 bases in 27 attempts... Was recalled to Toronto on September 1... Appeared in three games and was 0-2 at the plate... Was a defensive replacement in all three games... Was rated by Baseball America as the best prospect in the Blue Jays organization, the best defensive outfielder in the International League and the 7th best prospect in the league.

PROFESSIONAL CAREER: 1997: Made pro debut with St. Catharines and tied for third in New York-Penn League with 10 home runs and 31 extra-base hits, was tied for fourth with 20 doubles and fifth with 52 runs and a .504 slugging pct... Named second-best prospect in New York-Penn League by Baseball America... Named to league All-Star team... Collected four hits on June 29 vs. New Jersey (4-6, 2R, 2RBI)... Homered in three of four games July 1-4 vs. Vermont...

Named league Player-of-the-Week from July 21-27, hit .536 (15-28) with 7 runs, two homers and five RBI... Hit safely in 12 straight games July 16-27 (.549/28-51)... In July hit .378 with 12 doubles, six homers and 18 RBI... Hit .359 at home and .246 on the road... Named second-best prospect in organization by Baseball America... Played Winter ball for Sydney in Australia, hit .280 with five homers and 22 RBI... **1998:** Hit .285 in 134 games with Hagerstown of the South Atlantic League (A)... Finished fourth in the league with 35 doubles... Started slow hitting just .184 in April but drove in 12 runs and hit a monthly best four home runs... Rebounded in May hitting .340 with 20 runs, nine doubles, two home runs and 12 RBI... On June 8 hit a grand slam vs Charleston-WV... Hit .326 in July with a nine game hit streak to open the month... Hit in a season high 11 straight games from August 2 to 13... On August 9 was 3-3 with two home runs at Cape Fear... Excluding April hit .314 for the season... Then in the playoffs hit .476 (10-21) in five games with three doubles, four runs and two RBI... Rated fifth best prospect in the organization by Baseball America and ninth best in the South Atlantic League... **1999:** Played in four levels of baseball, including the major leagues, all in the same season... Started the season with Dunedin of the Florida State League (A) where he hit .343 with 16 doubles, two triples, 11 home runs and drove in 43 runs with 13 stolen bases... Was named the Florida State League MVP and was selected as the MVP of the the FSL All-Star game... Rated by Baseball America as the FSL's Most Exciting Player, Best Batting Prospect, and Best Defensive Outfielder... Was transferred to the Knoxville Smokies of the Southern League (AA) on June 23 where he hit .340 in 26 games with three home runs and 17 RBI... Participated in the Futures Game at Fenway Park as part of the All-Star Game festivities... Promoted to Syracuse of the International League (AAA) on July 26 and hit .310 with four home runs and 21 RBI... Combined, he led the Blue Jays minor league organization hitting .334 in 129 games with 18 home runs and 81 RBI... Contract was purchased by Toronto on August 30... Made his ML debut that day starting in center field and was 0-3 with an outfield assist... Collected his first hit in the majors on September 1, a double off Minnesota's Eric Milton... Hit just .132 in his first ten games... In the last 14 games he hit .360... On September 13 hit his first ML home run off the Yankees' Orlando Hernandez (1R)... Hit in six straight from September 12 to 22... Collected four hits on September 22 in Boston... Started 24 games in center field and had a 1.000 fielding percentage (55TC) with four assists... Hit .412 against LHP and .235 against RHP... Hit .353 at home and .204 on the road... Was selected to the Howe Sportsdata 1999 All-Prospect team... Named by Baseball America as the best prospect in the organization... Participated in the Arizona Fall League with Peoria.

VERNON WELLS

Year	Club & League	AVG	G	AB	R	H	TB	2B	3B	HR	RBI	SH-SF	HP	BB-IBB	SO	SB-CS	GIDP	SLG	OBP
1997	St. Catharines (NYP)	.307	66	264	52	81	133	20	1	10	31	0-2	1	30-1	44	8-6	2	.504	.377
1998	Hagerstown (SAL)	.285	134	509	86	145	217	35	2	11	65	1-2	1	49-1	84	13-8	8	.426	.348
1999	Dunedin (FSL)	.343	70	265	43	91	144	16	2	11	43	0-1	1	26-0	34	13-2	6	.543	.403
1999	Knoxville (Sou)	.340	26	106	18	36	55	6	2	3	17	0-2	0	12-1	15	6-2	6	.519	.400
1999	Syracuse (Int)	.310	33	129	20	40	62	8	1	4	21	0-3	1	10-0	22	5-1	3	.481	.357
1999	TORONTO (AL)	.261	24	88	8	23	31	5	0	1	8	0-0	0	4-0	18	1-1	6	.352	.293
2000	Syracuse (Int)	.243	127	493	76	120	213	31	7	16	66	1-5	4	48-1	88	23-4	8	.432	.313
2000	TORONTO (AL)	.000	3	2	0	0	0	0	0	0	0	0-0	0	0-0	0	0-0	0	.000	.000
Minor Totals		.290	456	1766	295	513	824	116	15	55	243	2-15	8	175-4	287	68-23	27	.467	.354
MAJOR TOTALS		.256	27	90	8	23	31	5	0	1	8	0-0	0	4-0	18	1-1	6	.344	.287

HOME RUN BREAKDOWN

				MEN ON				ONE GAME								
Total	H	A	0	1	2	3	2	3	4	LO	XN	IP	PH	RHP	LHP
1	1	0	1	0	0	0	0	0	0	0	0	0	0	1	0

WELLS — TRANSACTIONS

• Selected by the Toronto Blue Jays organization in the first round (fifth overall) of the June 1997 First Year Player Draft.

CAREER HIGHS — WELLS, Vernon
GAME:

ML Debut	Aug. 30, 1999 vs. MIN
Runs	2 - Sep. 18, 1999 vs. CWS
Hits	4 - Sep. 22, 1999 at BOS
Doubles	2 - Sep. 26, 1999 vs. CLE
Home Runs	1 - Sep. 13, 1999 vs. NYY
RBI	2 - Sep. 22, 1999 at BOS
	2 - Sep. 26, 1999 vs. CLE
Stolen Bases	1 - Sep. 24, 1999 vs. CLE
Longest Hitting Streak	6G - Sep. 12-22, 1999
Longest Hitless Streak	10AB - Sep. 2-4, 2000
Last ML Home Run	1 - Sep. 13, 1999 vs. NYY

FIELDING
WELLS, Vernon—OF

Year	PCT	G	PO	A	E	TC	DP
1999	1.000	24	51	4	0	55	1
2000	1.000	3	2	0	0	2	0
Total	1.000	27	53	4	0	57	1

VERNON WELLS DETAILED HITTING

	2000									CAREER							
	Avg	AB	H	HR	RBI	BB	SO	OBP	SLG	Avg	AB	H	HR	RBI	BB	SO	OBP	SLG
Total	.000	2	0	0	0	0	0	.000	.000	.256	90	23	1	8	4	18	.287	.344
vs. Left	—	—	—	—	—	—	—	—	—	.412	17	7	0	1	0	1	.412	.529
vs. Right	.000	2	0	0	0	0	0	.000	.000	.219	73	16	1	7	4	17	.260	.301
Home	.000	1	0	0	0	0	0	.000	.000	.343	35	12	1	4	0	11	.343	.543
Away	.000	1	0	0	0	0	0	.000	.000	.200	55	11	0	4	4	7	.254	.218
August	—	—	—	—	—	—	—	—	—	.000	7	0	0	0	0	3	.000	.000
September	.000	2	0	0	0	0	0	.000	.000	.278	72	20	1	7	2	15	.297	.389
October	—	—	—	—	—	—	—	—	—	.273	11	3	0	1	2	0	.385	.273
Scoring Posn	—	—	—	—	—	—	—	—	—	.368	19	7	0	7	3	5	.455	.474
Bases Loaded	—	—	—	—	—	—	—	—	—	.000	1	0	0	0	0	1	.000	.000
vs. Bal	.000	1	0	0	0	0	0	.000	.000	.000	1	0	0	0	0	0	.000	.000
vs. Bos	—	—	—	—	—	—	—	—	—	.500	8	4	0	2	0	2	.500	.500
vs. CWS	—	—	—	—	—	—	—	—	—	.600	5	3	0	1	0	1	.600	.800
vs. Cle	—	—	—	—	—	—	—	—	—	.304	23	7	0	3	2	3	.360	.391
vs. Det	—	—	—	—	—	—	—	—	—	.143	7	1	0	0	0	2	.143	.143
vs. KC	—	—	—	—	—	—	—	—	—	.071	14	1	0	1	1	2	.133	.071
vs. Min	—	—	—	—	—	—	—	—	—	.200	15	3	0	0	0	4	.200	.267
vs. NYY	.000	0	0	0	0	0	0	.000	.000	.333	6	2	1	1	0	3	.333	.833
vs. Oak	.000	1	0	0	0	0	0	.000	.000	.000	1	0	0	0	0	0	.000	.000
vs. Sea	—	—	—	—	—	—	—	—	—	.167	6	1	0	0	1	1	.286	.167
vs. TB	—	—	—	—	—	—	—	—	—	.250	4	1	0	0	0	0	.250	.500
Pre-All Star	—	—	—	—	—	—	—	—	—	.000	0	0	0	0	0	0	.000	.000
Post-All Star	.000	2	0	0	0	0	0	.000	.000	.256	90	23	1	8	4	18	.287	.344

VERNON WELLS HITTING AT ML PARKS

Park	Avg	G	AB	R	H	2B	3B	HR	RBI	SB	CS	BB	SO	OBP	Slg
Camden Yards	.000	1	1	0	0	0	0	0	0	0	0	0	0	.000	.000
Fenway Park	.500	2	8	1	4	0	0	0	2	0	0	0	2	.500	.500
Jacobs Field	.200	4	15	1	3	0	0	0	1	0	0	2	0	.294	.200
Tiger Stadium	.143	2	7	0	1	0	0	0	0	0	0	0	2	.143	.143
Kauffman Stadium	.071	3	14	0	1	0	0	0	1	0	0	0	1	.133	.071
SkyDome	.343	12	35	6	12	4	0	1	4	1	1	0	11	.343	.543
Tropicana Field	.250	1	4	0	1	1	0	0	0	0	0	0	0	.250	.500
SAFECO Field	.167	2	6	0	1	0	0	0	0	0	0	1	1	.286	.167

Players

Jayson WERTH

CATCHER

64

BIRTHDATE	May 20, 1979
OPENING DAY AGE	21
BIRTHPLACE	Springfield, IL
RESIDENCE	Chatham, IL
BATS/THROWS	R/R
HEIGHT/WEIGHT	6-5/215
CONTRACT STATUS	signed thru 2001
M.L. SERVICE	0.000

PERSONAL: Jayson Richard Gowan Werth... Married, wife's name Julia... His grandfather, Dick "Ducky" Schofield, was a 19-year major league infielder while his uncle, Dick Schofield, played 14 years in the majors ('93 & '94 with Toronto)... His stepfather, Dennis Werth, played in parts of four seasons (1979-82) with the New York Yankees and Kansas City Royals and his mother, Kim Schofield Werth, competed in the U.S. Olympic Trials in the long jump and 100 meters... Graduated from Glenwood High School where he hit .652 in his senior year with 15 home runs in 31 games... Signed a letter of intent with the University of Georgia before signing with the Orioles on June 13, 1997... Enjoys golf and fishing.

LAST SEASON: Spent most of the season with Bowie of the Eastern League (AA) where he hit .228 with five home runs and 26 RBI in 85 games with Bowie... Hit .254 in April with six RBI and stole seven bases — would finish the season with a total of 14... Had all seven stolen bases in his first six games and did not attempt to steal from April 14 until May 8 when he was caught... Next stolen base came June 4... Hit three homers in June while batting .250... After posting a .237 average in July he was sent to Frederick (A) where he hit .277 in 24 games with 18 RBI... Had a two-homer, five RBI game on August 4... Hit in eight of nine games before being re-called to Bowie on August 29... Played three more games for Bowie, including his only game of the season in the outfield on August 29.

PROFESSIONAL CAREER: 1997: Began his professional career with the Gulf Coast League Orioles where he appeared in 32 games, 21 behind the plate, eight at first base,

twice in the outfield and as the designated hitter once... Finished the season hitting .295 after maintaining his average at .300 or higher in 20 of the 32 games... Hit in six straight from July 11 to 18... **1998:** Spent most of the season with Delmarva in South Atlantic League (A)... Appeared in five games for AA Bowie in September after the Shorebirds completed their season... In 16 games from May 6 to 23 he hit .421 (24-57) with 12 RBI and 10 extra-base hits... Batted .311 (28-90) in month of May... Had pair of two-HR games, June 8 at Cape Fear and July 23 at Savannah... When promoted to Bowie, he caught the final five games as the club posted a 5-0 record... Hit safely in his first three games in the Eastern League... Was named to Howe SportsData's All-Teen Team... **1999:** Opened the season with Fredrick (A) before advancing to Bowie (AA) in June... Combined to hit .294 (105-357) which was the 3rd best average among Oriole minor leaguers, with four HR and 41 RBI... Ranked eighth among all full-season minor league catchers in batting average... Stole 23 bases in 27 attempts... Opened the season with a six game hit streak... Posted a season high nine game hit streak with 10 RBI from May 29 to June 5... Had two four-hit games, one for Frederick on June 1 at Lynchburg and one for Bowie on July 2 at Akron... Had hits in six straight at-bats July 1-2... Batted .347 (26-75) with 14 runs and 13 RBI in 20 games in June... Promoted to Bowie on June 29... Hit .388 in July but only .197 the remainder of the season after breaking a bone in his right wrist when hit by a throw on July 18 in Harrisburg... Was disabled from July 20 to August 16... Was successful in his first seven stolen base attempts with Bowie... Threw out 9 of 36 (25%) basestealers with Baysox.

JAYSON WERTH

Year	Club & League	AVG	G	AB	R	H	TB	2B	3B	HR	RBI	SH-SF	HP	BB-IBB	SO	SB-CS	GIDP	SLG	OBP
1997	Orioles (Gulf)	.295	32	88	16	26	35	6	0	1	8	0-1	0	22-0	22	7-1	0	.398	.432
1998	Delmarva (SAL)	.265	120	408	71	108	158	20	3	8	53	1-2	15	50-0	92	21-6	14	.387	.364
1998	Bowie (East)	.158	5	19	2	3	5	2	0	0	1	0-0	0	2-0	6	1-0	0	.263	.238
1999	Frederick (Caro)	.305	66	236	41	72	93	10	1	3	30	1-2	3	37-2	37	16-3	4	.394	.403
1999	Bowie (East)	.273	35	121	18	33	43	5	1	1	11	1-3	2	17-0	26	7-1	1	.355	.364
2000	Bowie (East)	.228	85	276	47	63	98	16	2	5	26	4-1	4	54-1	50	9-3	10	.355	.361
2000	Frederick (Caro)	.277	24	83	16	23	32	3	0	2	18	1-2	0	10-1	15	5-1	3	.386	.347
Minor Totals		.266	367	1231	211	328	464	62	7	20	147	8-11	24	192-4	248	66-15	32	.377	.373

WERTH — TRANSACTIONS

- Selected by the Baltimore Orioles in the 1st round (22nd overall) of the June 1997 First Year Player Draft.
- On disabled list July 21-August 17, 1999.
- Traded to the Toronto Blue Jays in exchange for LHP John Bale on December 11, 2000.

NAME THE TEAM CONTEST

The Blue Jays were named in a contest conducted in June and July of 1976. Over 30,000 individual entries were received, suggesting over 4,000 names for the new American League club. From the list of names submitted, specially-appointed panels of judges selected ten names to submit to the Board of Directors. The Directors chose the name "Blue Jays" from that list and announced their decision on August 12th, at which time the team officially became the Toronto Blue Jays Baseball Club.

A total of 154 people submitted the name "Blue Jays" and a drawing was held to select a grand prize winner from those who submitted the name. Dr. William Mills of Etobicoke, Ontario, won a pair of season tickets for 1977 and an all-expenses paid trip for himself and his family to watch the Blue Jays at spring training in Dunedin, Florida. Nine runners-up also won season tickets.

Dewayne WISE

OUTFIELDER

11

BIRTHDATE	February 24, 1978
OPENING DAY AGE	23
BIRTHPLACE	Columbia, SC
RESIDENCE	Chapin, SC
BATS/THROWS	L/L
HEIGHT/WEIGHT	6-1/180
CONTRACT STATUS	signed thru 2001
M.L. SERVICE	1.000

PERSONAL: Larry Dewayne Wise... Graduated from Chapin High School, South Carolina, in 1997 where he played baseball, football and basketball... Was an All-State selection in baseball and football for three consecutive seasons... Was selected as conference Player of the Year in football his senior year... Was an All-Conference selection in basketball.

LAST SEASON: Appeared in 28 games for Toronto and hit .136... The Rule 5 selection hit .162 in spring training with a double, three RBI and stole five bases in 22 games... Made his ML debut on April 6 vs KC as he entered defensively and was 0-1... On April 15 vs SEA replaced Stewart in LF and collected his first ML hit, a single off John Halama... Made hit first start on April 24 in Oakland and was 0-4... Started again on April 25 in Oakland and was 1-3... Finished April batting .118 in nine games... Stole first base of his career on June 5 at Atlanta... On June 6 was placed on the 15-day disabled list due to a sore right great toe... On June 16 was transferred to the 60-day disabled list... On June 19 had surgery to remove a pin from his right great toe which was inserted on November 4, 1998 when a bunionectomy was performed... Began a rehab assignment on August 11 with the Tennessee Smokies of the Southern League (AA)... In 15 games with the Smokies hit .250 with ten runs scored, five double, two triples, two home runs and eight RBI... Also stole five bases on rehab... Activated from the disabled list on September 1... Appeared in nine September games...

Started three games, two in left field and once in right field... Following the season played in the Arizona Fall League with the Scottsdale Scorpions.

PROFESSIONAL CAREER: 1997: Made pro debut with Billings of the Pioneer League and was named to the League All-Star Team and was rated by Baseball America as the No. 3 prospect in the league and the No. 4 prospect in the Reds organization... Hit .313 with seven home runs, 41 RBI and a league high nine triples... **1998:** Hit .224 with Burlington of the Midwest League A... Was third in the Reds farm system with 27 stolen bases... Had 15 doubles, nine triples and two home runs... In 124 games in the outfield posted a .972 fielding percentage with eight outfield assists... **1999:** Hit .253 for Rockford of the Midwest League with 20 doubles, 13 triples, 11 home runs, 63 RBI and 35 stolen bases... The 13 triples tied for fourth in Class-A ball and was tied for second in the Midwest League... Led Rockford in games (131), hits (127) & RBI (81) and was second in runs scored with 70... Posted a .975 fielding percentage with 16 outfield assists in 131 games, all in center field... Started the season swiping 11 straight bases without being caught... Hit five triples in May including four in 11 games from May 5 to 16... Best month was July when he posted a .311 average with three home runs and 23 RBI... Posted two four hit games, July 4 and July 17... Longest hit streak was seven games which he did four times... On August 19 vs South Bend was 3-3 with a double, two triples and six RBI.

DEWAYNE WISE

Year	Club & League	AVG	G	AB	R	H	TB	2B	3B	HR	RBI	SH-SF	HP	BB-IBB	SO	SB-CS	GIDP	SLG	OBP
1997	Billings (Pio)	.313	62	268	53	84	136	13	9	7	41	1-3	2	9-0	47	18-8	2	.507	.337
1998	Burlington (Mid)	.224	127	496	61	111	150	15	9	2	44	7-9	1	41-1	111	27-17	4	.302	.280
1999	Rockford (Mid)	.253	131	502	70	127	206	20	13	11	81	5-14	7	42-2	81	35-13	6	.410	.312
2000	Tennessee (Sou)	.250	15	56	10	14	29	5	2	2	8	0-0	0	7-0	13	3-2	2	.518	.333
2000	TORONTO (AL)	.136	28	22	3	3	3	0	0	0	0	0-0	1	1-0	5	1-0	0	.136	.208
Minor Totals		.254	335	1322	194	336	521	53	33	22	174	13-26	10	99-3	252	83-40	14	.394	.305

WISE — TRANSACTIONS

- Selected by the Cincinnati Reds in fifth round (158th overall) of the June 1997 First Year Player Draft.
- Selected by Toronto from Cincinnati in the Rule 5 Draft, December 13, 1999.
- On disabled list (left big toe) June 6-September 1, 2000; including rehabilitation assignment at Tennessee August 11-31.

CAREER HIGHS — WISE, Dewayne
GAME:

ML Debut	Apr. 6, 2000 vs. KC
Runs	1 - Apr. 9, 2000 at TEX
	1 - Apr. 15, 2000 vs. SEA
	1 - Sep. 14, 2000 at NYY
Hits	1 - Apr. 15, 2000 vs. SEA
	1 - Apr. 25, 2000 at OAK
	1 - Jun. 5, 2000 at ATL
Doubles	None
Home Runs	None
RBI	None
Stolen Bases	1 - Jun. 5, 2000 at ATL
Last ML Home Run	None

FIELDING
WISE, Dewayne—OF

Year	PCT	G	PO	A	E	TC	DP
2000	1.000	18	20	0	0	20	0

DEWAYNE WISE DETAILED HITTING

	2000									CAREER								
	Avg	AB	H	HR	RBI	BB	SO	OBP	SLG	Avg	AB	H	HR	RBI	BB	SO	OBP	SLG
Total	.136	22	3	0	0	1	5	.208	.136	.136	22	3	0	0	1	5	.208	.136
vs. Left	.333	3	1	0	0	1	0	.500	.333	.333	3	1	0	0	1	0	.500	.333
vs. Right	.105	19	2	0	0	0	5	.150	.105	.105	19	2	0	0	0	5	.150	.105
Home	.143	7	1	0	0	0	1	.250	.143	.143	7	1	0	0	0	1	.250	.143
Away	.133	15	2	0	0	1	4	.188	.133	.133	15	2	0	0	1	4	.188	.133
April	.118	17	2	0	0	1	5	.167	.118	.118	17	2	0	0	1	5	.167	.118
May	.000	2	0	0	0	0	0	.000	.000	.000	2	0	0	0	0	0	.000	.000
June	1.000	1	1	0	0	0	0	1.000	1.000	1.000	1	1	0	0	0	0	1.000	1.000
September	.000	2	0	0	0	0	0	.333	.000	.000	2	0	0	0	0	0	.333	.000
Scoring Posn	.000	4	0	0	0	1	1	.333	.000	.000	4	0	0	0	1	1	.333	.000
DH	.000	0	0	0	0	0	0	.000	.000	.000	0	0	0	0	0	0	.000	.000
PH	1.000	1	1	0	0	0	0	1.000	1.000	1.000	1	1	0	0	0	0	1.000	1.000
vs. Bal	.000	1	0	0	0	0	0	.000	.000	.000	1	0	0	0	0	0	.000	.000
vs. Bos	.000	1	0	0	0	0	0	.000	.000	.000	1	0	0	0	0	0	.000	.000
vs. CWS	.000	0	0	0	0	0	0	.000	.000	.000	0	0	0	0	0	0	.000	.000
vs. Cle	.000	1	0	0	0	0	0	.000	.000	.000	1	0	0	0	0	0	.000	.000
vs. Det	.000	0	0	0	0	0	0	.000	.000	.000	0	0	0	0	0	0	.000	.000
vs. KC	.000	1	0	0	0	0	0	.000	.000	.000	1	0	0	0	0	0	.000	.000
vs. NYY	.000	6	0	0	0	1	3	.143	.000	.000	6	0	0	0	1	3	.143	.000
vs. Oak	.143	7	1	0	0	0	1	.250	.143	.143	7	1	0	0	0	1	.250	.143
vs. Sea	.250	4	1	0	0	0	1	.250	.250	.250	4	1	0	0	0	1	.250	.250
vs. TB	.000	0	0	0	0	0	0	.000	.000	.000	0	0	0	0	0	0	.000	.000
vs. Tex	.000	0	0	0	0	0	0	.000	.000	.000	0	0	0	0	0	0	.000	.000
vs. Atl	1.000	1	1	0	0	0	0	1.000	1.000	1.000	1	1	0	0	0	0	1.000	1.000
vs. Fla	.000	0	0	0	0	0	0	.000	.000	.000	0	0	0	0	0	0	.000	.000
Pre-All Star	.150	20	3	0	0	1	5	.190	.150	.150	20	3	0	0	1	5	.190	.150
Post-All Star	.000	2	0	0	0	0	0	.333	.000	.000	2	0	0	0	0	0	.333	.000

DEWAYNE WISE HITTING AT ML PARKS

Park	Avg	G	AB	R	H	2B	3B	HR	RBI	SB	CS	BB	SO	OBP	Slg
Camden Yards	.000	1	1	0	0	0	0	0	0	0	0	0	0	.000	.000
Fenway Park	.000	1	1	0	0	0	0	0	0	0	0	0	0	.000	.000
Comiskey Park	.000	2	0	0	0	0	0	0	0	0	0	0	0	.000	.000
Jacobs Field	.000	1	0	0	0	0	0	0	0	0	0	0	0	.000	.000
Yankee Stadium	.000	4	5	1	0	0	0	0	0	0	0	1	3	.167	.000
Oakland-Alameda	.143	3	7	0	1	0	0	0	0	0	0	0	1	.143	.143
Arlington	.000	1	0	1	0	0	0	0	0	0	0	0	0	.000	.000
SkyDome	.143	12	7	1	1	0	0	0	0	0	0	0	1	.250	.143
Pro Player Stadium	.000	1	0	0	0	0	0	0	0	0	0	0	0	.000	.000
Turner Field	1.000	1	1	0	1	0	0	0	0	1	0	0	0	1.000	1.000
Tropicana Field	.000	1	0	0	0	0	0	0	0	0	0	0	0	.000	.000

Orlando WOODARDS

PITCHER

49

BIRTHDATE	January 2, 1978
OPENING DAY AGE	23
BIRTHPLACE	Stockton, CA
RESIDENCE	Stockton, CA
BATS/THROWS	R/R
HEIGHT/WEIGHT	6-2/200
CONTRACT STATUS	signed thru 2001
M.L. SERVICE	0.000

PERSONAL: Orlando Lee Woodards... Married, wife's name Karisa... One son, Orlando Jr. (11/8/98)... Graduated from Franklin High School in Sacramento, California before attending Sacramento City College... Signed by the Blue Jays' Dave Blume after being selected in the 40th round (1,179 overall) of the June 1996 draft.

LAST SEASON: Made 41 appearances, one start, for Dunedin of the Florida State League (A) and was 8-1 with seven saves and a 2.27 ERA... Opened the season with eight scoreless outings totaling 17.0 innings from April 6 to May 1... Was the Dunedin Pitcher of the Month in April with a 1-0 record with one save... Allowed 22 earned runs on the season, nine of which came in two games, four on May 5 in 1.0 inning against Kissimmee and five in 1.2 innings of work on July 10, his lone loss of the season... Lone start came May 26 vs Fort Myers, ND after one earned run over 3.0 innings... In June was the organizational Pitcher of the Month after posting a 2-0 record with a 1.80 ERA in nine games with 20 strikeouts in 15.0 innings with just three walks... Tossed a season high 4.0 innings on two occasions — earned a save with four scoreless innings and five strikeouts on August 3 in Clearwater & on August 27 when he allowed one run against Charlotte... Was 4-1 at home with four saves and a 3.24 ERA while on the road was 4-0 with three saves and a 0.96 ERA... Opponents hit just .207 with left-handed batters at .214 and right-handed batters at .204.

PROFESSIONAL CAREER: 1997: Made his professional debut with St. Catharines of the New York Penn League (A) and was 2-2 with two saves and a 5.15 ERA... Posted two saves and a 3.12 ERA after July 29... **1998:** Posted a 1-3 record with three saves and a 3.58 ERA in 26 games, one start, for Medicine Hat (A)... Ranked fifth among Pioneer League relievers in games (26), strikeouts per 9.0 innings pitched (10.99) and walks per 9.0 innings pitched (1.73)... In August was 1-1 with a 1.31 ERA and two saves while recording 30 strikeouts in 20.2 innings pitched... **1999:** Joined Hagerstown of the South Atlantic League (A) where he was 7-4 with two saves and a 4.15 ERA in 44 games, three starts... Ranked third on Hagerstown in games pitched and fourth in wins (7)... From April 18 to May 23 went

3-1 with a 1.03 ERA and two saves in a 19 game stretch with 28 strikeouts in 26.1 innings... In seven games between July 21 and August 8 was 2-0 with a 2.00 ERA in nine innings... In his three starts posted an 0-0 record with a 2.89 ERA.

ORLANDO WOODARDS

Year	Club & League	W-L	ERA	G	GS	CG	ShO	SV	IP	H	R	ER	HR	HB	BB-IBB	SO	WP	BK	OBA
1997	St. Catharines (NYP)	2-2	5.15	21	0	0	0	2	36.2	41	23	21	2	1	24-0	32	5	2	.281
1998	Medicine Hat (Pio)	1-3	3.58	26	1	0	0	3	50.1	48	27	20	4	2	11-0	58	5	2	.242
1999	Hagerstown (SAL)	7-4	4.15	44	3	0	0	2	80.1	66	45	37	5	7	43-3	79	7	1	.224
2000	Dunedin (FSL)	8-1	2.27	41	1	0	0	7	87.1	65	26	22	4	3	32-1	69	2	0	.207
Minor Totals		18-10	3.53	132	5	0	0	14	254.2	220	121	100	15	13	110-4	238	19	5	.231

WOODARDS — TRANSACTIONS

- Selected by the Toronto Blue Jays Blue Jays in 40th round (1179th overall) of the June 1996 First Year Player Draft.

Chris

WOODWARD

SHORTSTOP

BIRTHDATE	June 27, 1976
OPENING DAY AGE	24
BIRTHPLACE	Covina, CA
RESIDENCE	Chino, CA
BATS/THROWS	R/R
HEIGHT/WEIGHT	6-0/173
CONTRACT STATUS	signed thru 2001
M.L. SERVICE	1.020

5

PERSONAL: Christopher Michael Woodward... 1994 graduate of Northview H.S. in Covina, Cal. where he played football and baseball... Named All-League, All-Valley, second team All-CIF and team MVP in baseball and also grabbed Gold Glove honors... Attended Mt. Sacramento College in Walnut Creek, Cal. where he was All-Conference in baseball.

LAST SEASON: Split the season between Toronto where he hit .183 in 37 games and Syracuse of the International League (AAA) where he hit .322 in 37 games with 13 doubles, two triples, five home runs and 25 RBI... At Syracuse appeared in 20 games at second base, 12 at third base and six shortstop... In the spring hit .372 with five doubles and six RBI and saw action at 1B, 2B, 3B & SS... Opened the season with Toronto before being optioned to Syracuse on April 18 after appearing in one game without an at bat... Was then recalled on May 5 and did not appear in game before being optioned to Syracuse on May 19... Was recalled on May 26... On May 28 made his season debut at the plate against Detroit and was 2-4 with two doubles and set a career high with three RBI... Made first ML start at 3B on May 31 vs Minnesota and hit his first ML home run against Brad Radke... Would start eight straight games at third base from May 31 to June 7... Homered in back-to-back games in Atlanta, June 5 off Burkett to match career high with three RBI and June 6 off Glavine which was his first against LHP... On June 13 at Detroit entered defensively at 1B, his debut at that position... Hit .160 in nine starts with ten runs scored, two doubles, two home runs and six RBI in 21 games... Started 17 games at shortstop and was 9-60 while Alex Gonzalez was on the disabled list from July 7 to 22... Was optioned to Syracuse on August 7 and recalled on September 5... Appeared in two September games and was 0-1... Started 28 games for Toronto, 17 at SS, eight at third base and three at second base... Hit .235 against left-handed pitching with one home run and .172 against right-handed pitching with two home runs... With runners in scoring position hit .269... Played in the Arizona Fall League and hit .319 in 25 games with a home run and 18 RBI.

PROFESSIONAL CAREER: 1995: Led Pioneer League shortstops in games (72), total chances (338), putouts (106)

and assists (202)... Tied for team lead in hit-by-pitch (6) and led the squad in sacrifice hits (5)... Batted .311-3-13 in 28 games in August, including a 3-for-5 performance with a homer and four RBI on the 5th vs Billings... Hit .222 with two doubles in five playoff games... **1996:** Paced league shortstops in putouts (214)... Led Hagerstown team in sacrifice hits with seven... Compiled a 15-game hitting streak August 10-26 and batted .350 (21-60) during the streak... **1997:** Ranked third in Florida State League in on-base percentage (.397)... Placed eighth among full-season-A shortstops in range factor (4.63)... Led Dunedin team with four triples... Went 4-for-5 with a homer and two RBI on May 2 vs St. Petersburg... Went 5-for-5 on May 31 vs Tampa... Hit .333 in May and .348 in August... Hit .309 on the road... **1998:** Best month was June hitting .277 with a homer and ten RBI... Went 4-for-4 with a double, three runs and an RBI on July 5... Promoted to Syracuse in early August... Hit .267 in 31 games for Frederick of Maryland Fall Instructional Baseball League... **1999:** Split the season between Syracuse (AAA) and Toronto... Appeared in 14 games for Toronto and hit .231 with two RBI... In 75 games with Syracuse hit .292 with one home run and 20 RBI... Opened the season with Syracuse and hit .351 in 21 games with six RBI... Hit in 11 straight from April 9 to 20... Appeared in four May games and was placed on the disabled list from May 2 to 16 and again from May 21 to June 6 with a left groin strain... Returned from the DL and on June 7 his contract was purchased by Toronto... Made his ML debut that same night in New York starting at shortstop against the Mets... Delivered a sacrifice fly in his first plate appearance and an RBI single off Orel Hershiser in his first at bat... Started six straight games and hit .227 with one double and two RBI... Was optioned to Syracuse on June 14 after the Blue Jays acquired Tony Batista... Upon his return hit .281 in June for Syracuse... Hit .273 in July with 14 runs scored and seven RBI... Hit in a season high 14 straight games from July 23 to August 8... Was recalled to Toronto on August 9... Appeared in four games in August and four in September, was 1-4 at the plate... Appeared in 14 games overall with six starts at shortstop... Played in the Arizona Fall League with Peoria.

CHRIS WOODWARD

Year	Club & League	AVG	G	AB	R	H	TB	2B	3B	HR	RBI	SH-SF	HP	BB-IBB	SO	SB-CS	GIDP	SLG	OBP
1995	Medicine Hat (Pio)	.232	72	241	44	56	73	8	0	3	21	5-3	6	33-1	41	9-4	1	.303	.336
1996	Hagerstown (SAL)	.224	123	424	41	95	126	24	2	1	48	7-5	5	43-1	70	11-3	3	.297	.300
1997	Dunedin (FSL)	.293	91	314	38	92	116	13	4	1	38	3-4	5	52-0	52	4-8	3	.369	.397
1998	Knoxville (Sou)	.245	73	253	36	62	83	12	0	3	27	3-3	3	26-1	47	3-5	4	.328	.319
1998	Syracuse (Int)	.200	25	85	9	17	29	6	0	2	6	2-0	0	7-0	20	1-1	4	.341	.261
1999	Syracuse (Int)	.292	75	281	46	82	111	20	3	1	20	1-0	1	38-1	49	4-1	5	.395	.378
1999	TORONTO (AL)	.231	14	26	1	6	7	1	0	0	2	0-1	0	2-0	6	0-0	1	.269	.276
2000	Syracuse (Int)	.322	37	143	23	46	78	13	2	5	25	1-0	0	11-0	30	2-0	2	.545	.370
2000	TORONTO (AL)	.183	37	104	16	19	35	7	0	3	14	1-0	0	10-3	28	1-0	1	.337	.254
Minor Totals		.258	496	1741	237	450	616	96	11	16	185	22-15	20	210-4	309	34-22	22	.354	.342
MAJOR TOTALS		.192	51	130	17	25	42	8	0	3	16	1-1	0	12-3	34	1-0	2	.323	.259

WOODWARD — TRANSACTIONS

- Selected by the Toronto Blue Jays organization in the 54th round (1438th overall) in the June 1994 First Year Player Draft.
- On disabled list (left groin strain) May 2-16 and May 21-June 6, 1999.

CAREER HIGHS — WOODWARD, Chris
GAME:

ML Debut	Jun. 7, 1999 at NYM
Runs	2 - May 28, 2000 at DET
	2 - Jun. 5, 2000 at ATL
	2 - Jun. 6, 2000 at ATL
	2 - Jun. 25, 2000 vs. BOS
Hits	3 - Jun. 2, 2000 at FLA
Doubles	2 - May 28, 2000 at DET
Home Runs	1 - May 31, 2000 vs. MIN
	1 - Jun. 5, 2000 at ATL
	1 - Jun. 6, 2000 at ATL
RBI	3 - May 28, 2000 at DET
	3 - Jun. 5, 2000 at ATL
Stolen Bases	1 - Jun. 2, 2000 at FLA
Longest Hitting Streak	4G - Jul. 19-Aug. 3, 2000
Longest Hitless Streak	16AB - Jul. 7-19, 2000
Last ML Home Run	Jun. 6, 2000 at ATL

FIELDING
WOODWARD, Chris—SS

Year	PCT	G	PO	A	E	TC	DP
1999	.939	10	8	23	2	33	2
2000	.955	22	26	58	4	88	9
Total	.950	32	34	81	6	121	11

WOODWARD, Chris—3B

Year	PCT	G	PO	A	E	TC	DP
1999	1.000	2	0	3	0	3	0
2000	1.000	9	5	18	0	23	3
Total	1.000	11	5	21	0	26	3

WOODWARD, Chris—2B

Year	PCT	G	PO	A	E	TC	DP
2000	.941	3	5	11	1	17	1

WOODWARD, Chris—1B

Year	PCT	G	PO	A	E	TC	DP
2000	1.000	3	6	1	0	7	1

CHRIS WOODWARD DETAILED HITTING

	2000									CAREER								
	Avg	AB	H	HR	RBI	BB	SO	OBP	SLG	Avg	AB	H	HR	RBI	BB	SO	OBP	SLG
Total	.183	104	19	3	14	10	28	.254	.337	.192	130	25	3	16	12	34	.259	.323
vs. Left	.235	17	4	1	7	5	4	.409	.529	.192	26	5	1	7	6	6	.344	.385
vs. Right	.172	87	15	2	7	5	24	.217	.299	.192	104	20	2	9	6	28	.234	.308
Home	.200	35	7	1	3	1	10	.222	.314	.189	37	7	1	3	2	11	.231	.297
Away	.174	69	12	2	11	9	18	.269	.348	.194	93	18	2	13	10	23	.269	.333
April	.000	0	0	0	0	0	0	.000	.000	.000	0	0	0	0	0	0	.000	.000
May	.429	7	3	1	5	1	1	.500	1.143	.429	7	3	1	5	1	1	.500	1.143
June	.160	50	8	2	6	6	12	.250	.320	.181	72	13	2	8	7	16	.250	.306
July	.179	39	7	0	2	3	13	.238	.256	.179	39	7	0	2	3	13	.238	.256
August	.143	7	1	0	1	0	2	.143	.143	.222	9	2	0	1	1	3	.300	.222
September	.000	1	0	0	0	0	0	.000	.000	.000	3	0	0	0	0	1	.000	.000
Scoring Posn	.269	26	7	2	12	6	6	.406	.615	.267	30	8	2	14	7	8	.395	.567
Bases Loaded	.000	2	0	0	1	1	0	.333	.000	.000	4	0	0	1	1	2	.200	.000
PH	–	–	–	–	–	–	–	–	–	1.000	1	1	0	0	0	0	1.000	1.000
vs. Bal	.158	19	3	0	1	0	7	.158	.211	.158	19	3	0	1	0	7	.158	.211
vs. Bos	.125	8	1	0	0	0	4	.125	.125	.125	8	1	0	0	0	4	.125	.125
vs. CWS	.000	0	0	0	0	0	0	.000	.000	.000	0	0	0	0	0	0	.000	.000
vs. Cle	.250	4	1	0	0	0	2	.250	.250	.167	6	1	0	0	0	3	.167	.167
vs. Det	.400	5	2	0	3	2	2	.571	.800	.400	5	2	0	3	2	2	.571	.800
vs. KC	.000	0	0	0	0	0	0	.000	.000	.000	0	0	0	0	0	0	.000	.000
vs. Min	.167	6	1	1	2	0	2	.167	.667	.143	7	1	1	2	0	3	.143	.571
vs. NYY	.000	0	0	0	0	0	0	.000	.000	.000	0	0	0	0	0	0	.000	.000
vs. Oak	–	–	–	–	–	–	–	–	–	.000	0	0	0	0	1	0	1.000	.000
vs. TB	.176	17	3	0	0	1	4	.222	.294	.176	17	3	0	0	1	4	.222	.294
vs. Tex	.143	7	1	0	1	0	2	.143	.143	.250	8	2	0	1	0	2	.250	.250
vs. Atl	.273	11	3	2	5	3	1	.429	.909	.273	11	3	2	5	3	1	.429	.909
vs. Fla	.273	11	3	0	1	1	1	.333	.273	.273	11	3	0	1	1	1	.333	.273
vs. Mon	.100	10	1	0	1	3	3	.308	.200	.100	10	1	0	1	3	3	.308	.200
vs. NYM	.000	4	0	0	0	0	1	.000	.000	.188	16	3	0	2	0	4	.176	.188
vs. Phi	.000	2	0	0	0	0	0	.000	.000	.167	12	2	0	0	1	1	.231	.250
Pre-All Star	.171	82	14	3	13	10	24	.261	.354	.183	104	19	3	15	11	28	.259	.337
Post-All Star	.227	22	5	0	1	0	4	.227	.273	.231	26	6	0	1	1	6	.259	.269

CHRIS WOODWARD HITTING AT ML PARKS

Park	Avg	G	AB	R	H	2B	3B	HR	RBI	SB	CS	BB	SO	OBP	Slg
Camden Yards	.063	5	16	1	1	1	0	0	1	0	0	0	7	.063	.125
Fenway Park	.000	1	0	0	0	0	0	0	0	0	0	0	0	.000	.000
Comiskey Park	.000	1	0	0	0	0	0	0	0	0	0	0	0	.000	.000
Jacobs Field	.200	3	5	0	1	0	0	0	0	0	0	0	3	.200	.200
Kauffman Stadium	.000	1	0	0	0	0	0	0	0	0	0	0	0	.000	.000
Arlington	1.000	1	1	1	1	0	0	0	0	0	0	0	0	1.000	1.000
SkyDome	.189	19	37	6	7	1	0	1	3	0	0	2	11	.231	.297
Olympic Stadium	.100	3	10	0	1	1	0	0	1	0	0	3	3	.308	.200
Shea Stadium	.250	3	12	0	3	0	0	0	2	0	0	0	3	.231	.250
Veterans Stadium	.200	3	10	0	2	1	0	0	0	0	0	1	1	.273	.300
Pro Player Stadium	.273	3	11	1	3	0	0	0	1	1	0	1	1	.333	.273
Turner Field	.273	3	11	5	3	1	0	2	5	0	0	3	0	.429	.909
Tropicana Field	.083	3	12	1	1	1	0	0	0	0	0	1	3	.154	.167
Comerica Park	.400	2	5	2	2	2	0	0	3	0	0	1	2	.500	.800

PLAYERS WITH MOST SEASONS WITH BLUE JAYS

Seasons	Player	Years		Seasons	Player	Years
15	Dave Stieb	1979-92; 1998		8	Tom Henke	1985-92
12	Jim Clancy	1977-88		8	Manuel Lee	1985-92
12	Ernie Whitt	1977-78; 1980-89		8	Alfredo Griffin	1979-84; 1992-93
11	Rance Mulliniks	1982-92		8	John Olerud	1989-96
11	Tony Fernandez	1983-90; 1993; 1998-99		8	Juan Guzman	1991-98
10	Lloyd Moseby	1980-90		8	Ed Sprague	1991-98
10	Duane Ward	1986-95		8	David Wells	1987-98; 1999-00
9	Jesse Barfield	1981-89		7	Damaso Garcia	1980-86
9	George Bell	1981; 1983-90		7	Jim Acker	1983-86; 1989-91
9	Kelly Gruber	1984-92		7	Todd Stottlemyre	1988-94
9	Jimmy Key	1984-92		7	Joe Carter	1991-97
9	Garth Iorg	1978; 1980-1987		7	Mike Timlin	1991-97
9	Pat Hentgen	1991-99		7	Alex Gonzalez	1994-00
8	Pat Borders	1988-94; 1999		7	Shawn Green	1993-99
8	Carlos Delgado	1993-00				

2001 BIRTHDAYS

January
- 1- Kevin Beirne (27)
- 2- Orlando Woodards (23)
- 4- Chris Michalak (30)
- 9- Arron Holbert (28)
- 13- George Poulis (36)
- 14- Pat Daneker (25)
- 17- Brad Fullmer (26)
- 28- Bob File (24)

February
- 4- John Frascatore (31)
- 4- Dan Plesac (39)
- 10- Alberto Castillo (31)
- 10- Cesar Izturis (21)
- 13- Joe Lawrence (24)
- 24- Dewayne Wise (23)
- 25- Shannon Stewart (27)
- 26- Scott Shannon (37)

March
- 3- Raul Tablado (19)
- 6- Cookie Rojas (62)
- 8- Ryan Freel (25)
- 12- Raul Mondesi (30)
- 17- Cito Gaston (57)
- 20- George Perez (22)
- 24- Dustin McGowan (19)
- 27- Jaime Navarro (33)
- 30- Jason Dickson (28)

April
- 8- Alex Gonzalez (28)
- 11- Kelvim Escobar (25)
- 19- Jose Cruz (27)
- 22- Mickey Morandini (35)
- 27- Chris Carpenter (26)

May
- 8- Todd Greene (30)
- 11- Trenidad Hubbard (35)
- 12- Josh Phelps (23)
- 13- Mike Sirotka (30)
- 14- Roy Halladay (24)
- 20- Jayson Werth (22)
- 26- Chris Latham (28)
- 27- Mark Connor (52)
- 30- Scott Eyre (29)

June
- 3- Izzy Molina (30)
- 23- Mark Hendrickson (27)
- 25- Carlos Delgado (29)
- 27- Chris Woodward (25)

July
- 21- Lance Painter (34)
- 27- Terry Bevington (45)

August
- 22- Dominic Rich (22)
- 23- Cole Liniak (25)
- 28- Andy Thompson (26)
- 31- Jeff Frye (35)

September
- 4- Brian Simmons (28)
- 5- Gil Patterson (46)
- 8- Pasqual Coco (24)
- 9- Joey Hamilton (31)

October
- 3- Darrin Fletcher (35)
- 12- Garth Iorg (47)
- 21- Jeff Krushell (33)
- 22- Hector Carrasco (32)

November
- 3- Paul Quantrill (33)
- 4- Ryan Thompson (34)
- 6- Peter Bauer (23)
- 11- Ryan Balfe (26)
- 12- Homer Bush (29)
- 15- Pedro Borbon (34)

December
- 5- Andy Stewart (31)
- 8- Vernon Wells (23)
- 9- Tony Batista (28)
- 11- Morrin Davis (19)
- 14- Billy Koch (27)
- 17- Steve Parris (34)
- 31- Esteban Loaiza (30)

AMERICAN LEAGUE EAST

	WON	LOST	PCT.	GB	HOME	ROAD	vs EAST	vs CENT	vs WEST	vs NL
NEW YORK	87	74	.540	—	44-36	43-38	25-24	26-28	25-16	11-6
BOSTON	85	77	.525	2.5	42-39	43-38	23-26	32-24	21-18	9-9
TORONTO	83	79	.512	4.5	45-36	38-43	28-21	28-25	18-24	9-9
BALTIMORE	74	88	.457	13.5	44-37	30-51	25-25	24-24	18-28	7-11
TAMPA BAY	69	92	.429	18.0	36-44	33-48	22-27	22-27	16-29	9-9

AMERICAN LEAGUE CENTRAL

	WON	LOST	PCT.	GB	HOME	ROAD	vs EAST	vs CENT	vs WEST	vs NL
CHICAGO	95	67	.586	—	46-35	49-32	30-24	29-20	24-17	12-6
CLEVELAND	90	72	.556	5.0	48-33	42-39	31-22	21-30	25-15	13-5
DETROIT	79	83	.488	16.0	43-38	36-45	24-31	22-28	23-16	10-8
KANSAS CITY	77	85	.475	18.0	42-39	35-46	24-26	28-20	17-29	8-10
MINNESOTA	69	93	.426	26.0	36-45	33-48	19-29	24-26	19-27	7-11

AMERICAN LEAGUE WEST

	WON	LOST	PCT.	GB	HOME	ROAD	vs EAST	vs CENT	vs WEST	vs NL
OAKLAND	91	70	.565	—	47-34	44-36	30-20	28-27	22-16	11-7
SEATTLE	91	71	.562	.5	47-34	44-37	35-17	26-28	19-19	11-7
ANAHEIM	82	80	.506	9.5	46-35	36-45	28-27	25-26	17-21	12-6
TEXAS	71	91	.438	20.5	42-39	29-52	22-34	25-27	17-19	7-11

CLUB MISCELLANEOUS

CLUB	vs LHS	vs RHS	GRASS	ARTIF	DAY	NIGHT	1-RUN	X-INN	vs NL	DblHdrs W-L-S
ANAHEIM	21-25	61-55	73-71	9-9	18-24	64-56	32-23	9-7	12-6	0-0-0
BALTIMORE	23-24	51-64	63-74	11-14	25-30	49-58	29-25	4-7	7-11	0-1-0
BOSTON	20-22	65-55	77-66	8-11	22-24	63-53	20-23	5-8	9-9	0-0-0
CHICAGO	21-10	74-57	81-62	14-5	26-30	69-37	28-18	7-4	12-6	0-1-0
CLEVELAND	17-21	73-51	79-62	11-10	37-15	53-57	17-24	6-5	13-5	0-0-0
DETROIT	24-21	55-62	72-71	7-12	21-28	58-55	20-18	8-4	10-8	0-0-0
KANSAS CITY	18-24	59-61	68-75	9-10	29-19	48-66	21-26	7-8	8-10	0-0-0
MINNESOTA	11-29	58-64	28-37	41-56	22-27	47-66	22-26	7-9	7-11	0-0-0
NEW YORK	22-24	65-50	80-62	7-12	34-25	53-49	20-18	4-4	11-6	0-0-0
OAKLAND	21-26	70-44	79-67	12-3	35-25	56-45	21-19	8-5	11-7	0-0-0
SEATTLE	20-11	71-60	77-67	14-4	32-24	59-47	15-22	3-4	11-7	1-0-0
TAMPA BAY	11-25	58-67	25-41	44-51	22-30	47-62	26-26	9-5	9-9	0-0-0
TEXAS	19-15	52-76	66-80	5-11	16-23	55-68	27-25	5-5	7-11	1-0-0
TORONTO	19-24	64-55	31-38	52-41	28-28	55-51	21-19	2-6	9-9	0-0-0

CLUB BATTING

CLUB	AVG	G	AB	R	H	2B	3B	HR	RBI	SH-SF	BB	SO	SB	CS	SLG	OBP
CLEVELAND	.288	162	5683	950	1639	310	30	221	889	41-52	685	1057	113	34	.470	.367
KANSAS CITY	.288	162	5709	879	1644	281	27	150	831	56-70	511	840	121	35	.425	.348
CHICAGO	.286	162	5646	978	1615	325	33	216	926	55-61	591	960	119	42	.470	.356
TEXAS	.283	162	5648	848	1601	330	35	173	806	48-48	580	922	69	47	.446	.352
ANAHEIM	.280	162	5628	864	1574	309	34	236	837	47-43	608	1024	93	52	.472	.352
NEW YORK	.277	161	5556	871	1541	294	25	205	833	16-50	631	1007	99	48	.450	.354
DETROIT	.275	162	5644	823	1553	307	41	177	785	42-49	562	982	83	38	.438	.343
TORONTO	.275	162	5677	861	1562	328	21	244	826	29-34	526	1026	89	34	.469	.341
BALTIMORE	.272	162	5549	794	1508	310	22	184	750	27-54	558	900	126	65	.435	.341
MINNESOTA	.270	162	5615	748	1516	325	49	116	711	24-51	556	1021	90	45	.407	.337
OAKLAND	.270	161	5560	947	1501	281	23	239	908	26-44	750	1159	40	15	.458	.360
SEATTLE	.269	162	5497	907	1481	300	26	198	869	63-61	775	1073	122	56	.442	.361
BOSTON	.267	162	5630	792	1503	316	32	167	755	40-48	611	1019	43	30	.423	.341
TAMPA BAY	.257	161	5505	733	1414	253	22	162	692	52-40	559	1022	90	46	.399	.329
TOTALS	.276	1133	78547	11995	21652	4269	420	2688	11418	566-705	8503	14012	1297	587	.433	.349

CLUB PITCHING

CLUB	W	L	ERA	G	CG	SHO	SV	IP	H	R	ER	HR	HB	BB	IBB	SO	WP
BOSTON	85	77	4.23	162	7	12	46	1452.2	1433	745	683	173	57	499	40	1121	33
SEATTLE	91	71	4.49	162	4	10	44	1441.2	1442	780	720	167	38	634	37	998	43
OAKLAND	91	70	4.58	161	7	11	43	1435.1	1535	813	730	158	48	615	57	963	46
CHICAGO	95	67	4.66	162	5	7	43	1450.1	1509	839	751	195	54	614	27	1037	43
DETROIT	79	83	4.71	162	6	6	44	1443.1	1583	827	755	177	47	496	22	978	51
NEW YORK	87	74	4.76	161	9	6	40	1424.1	1458	814	753	177	52	577	23	1040	49
CLEVELAND	90	72	4.84	162	6	5	34	1442.1	1511	816	775	173	42	666	45	1213	50
TAMPA BAY	69	92	4.86	161	10	8	38	1431.1	1553	842	773	198	66	533	33	955	57
ANAHEIM	82	80	5.00	162	5	3	46	1448.0	1534	869	805	228	36	662	44	846	47
TORONTO	83	79	5.14	162	15	4	37	1437.1	1615	908	821	195	64	560	19	978	37
MINNESOTA	69	93	5.14	162	6	4	35	1432.2	1634	880	819	212	35	516	12	1042	68
BALTIMORE	74	88	5.37	162	14	6	33	1433.1	1547	913	855	202	36	665	32	1017	51
KANSAS CITY	77	85	5.48	162	10	6	29	1439.1	1585	930	876	239	42	693	35	927	77
TEXAS	71	91	5.52	162	3	4	39	1429.0	1683	974	876	202	63	661	40	918	40
TOTALS	1143	1122	4.91	1133	107	92	551	20141.0	21622	11950	10992	2696	680	8391	466	14033	692

CLUB FIELDING

CLUB	PCT	G	PO	A	E	TC	DP	TP	PB
CLEVELAND	.988	162	4327	1665	72	6064	147	0	10
SEATTLE	.984	162	4325	1629	99	6053	176	0	8
TORONTO	.984	162	4312	1679	100	6091	176	0	11
KANSAS CITY	.983	162	4318	1751	102	6171	185	0	7
DETROIT	.983	162	4330	1754	105	6189	172	0	7
MINNESOTA	.983	162	4298	1526	102	5926	155	0	13
BOSTON	.982	162	4358	1647	109	6114	120	0	26
NEW YORK	.981	161	4273	1487	109	5869	132	0	13
TAMPA BAY	.981	161	4294	1814	118	6226	169	0	14
BALTIMORE	.981	162	4300	1578	116	5994	151	1	6
ANAHEIM	.978	162	4344	1746	134	6224	182	0	6
CHICAGO	.978	162	4351	1686	133	6170	190	0	13
OAKLAND	.978	161	4306	1726	134	6166	164	1	8
TEXAS	.978	162	4287	1594	135	6016	162	0	8
TOTALS	.982	1133	60423	23282	1568	85273	2281	2	150

CLUB STARTING PITCHING

CLUB	W-L	PCT	ERA	G	GS	CG	ShO	IP	H	TBF	R	ER	HR	SH-SF	HB	BB-IBB	SO	WP	BK	OBA
BOSTON	56-54	.509	4.47	162	162	7	4	886.1	871	3800	472	440	113	19-22	40	306-14	696	20	1	.255
SEATTLE	71-47	.602	4.56	162	162	4	4	956.2	984	4143	526	485	107	28-30	19	383-18	592	23	4	.267
OAKLAND	71-53	.573	4.62	161	161	7	4	971.1	1007	4275	555	499	116	21-34	32	425-25	631	27	0	.268
NEW YORK	65-58	.528	4.87	161	161	9	2	964.2	1004	4226	561	522	133	28-27	39	366-10	685	20	5	.267
CHICAGO	65-46	.586	4.90	162	162	5	2	915.0	1002	4039	558	498	132	21-22	31	388-9	603	31	8	.280
DETROIT	54-65	.454	4.99	162	162	6	1	964.2	1106	4254	580	535	127	18-34	31	319-6	621	33	4	.287
CLEVELAND	65-50	.565	5.13	162	162	6	2	909.2	956	4027	543	519	121	19-22	21	319-22	790	30	0	.270
TAMPA BAY	43-57	.430	5.17	161	161	10	3	902.0	1041	3978	563	518	140	18-31	40	291-8	534	27	2	.290
TORONTO	59-59	.500	5.23	162	162	15	3	957.2	1053	4204	599	556	130	27-19	37	363-3	651	24	3	.280
BALTIMORE	52-67	.437	5.28	162	162	14	2	999.1	1077	4429	622	586	130	25-35	27	418-7	668	31	0	.275
KANSAS CITY	48-55	.466	5.43	162	162	10	3	943.2	1017	4208	605	569	156	20-26	25	456-13	579	49	5	.276
ANAHEIM	53-56	.486	5.54	162	162	5	2	896.0	978	3987	589	552	157	22-35	24	414-12	488	27	8	.280
TEXAS	50-67	.427	5.56	162	162	3	0	944.0	1111	4303	643	583	133	29-31	40	414-16	550	19	2	.293
MINNESOTA	51-71	.418	5.58	162	162	6	2	920.1	1085	4079	612	571	149	23-28	20	317-4	630	36	2	.294
TOTALS	803-805	.499	5.09	1133	2265	107	34	13131.1	14292	57952	8028	7433	1844	318-396	423	5286-159	8717	397	42	.277

CLUB RELIEF PITCHING

CLUB	W-L	PCT	ERA	RG	SV	IP	H	TBF	R	ER	HR	SH-SF	HB	BB-IBB	SO	WP	BK	OBA
BOSTON	29-23	.558	3.88	155	46	566.1	562	2425	273	244	60	27-27	18	192-26	425	13	1	.260
ANAHEIM	29-24	.547	4.16	157	46	552.0	556	2414	280	255	71	18-18	15	248-32	358	20	2	.263
DETROIT	25-18	.581	4.21	156	44	478.2	477	2041	247	224	50	15-29	16	177-16	357	18	1	.264
CHICAGO	30-21	.588	4.27	157	43	535.1	507	2298	281	254	63	18-27	23	226-18	434	12	0	.253
CLEVELAND	25-22	.532	4.33	156	34	532.2	555	2353	273	256	52	15-20	21	240-31	423	20	3	.270
TAMPA BAY	26-35	.426	4.34	151	38	529.1	512	2305	279	255	58	24-14	26	242-25	421	30	1	.256
MINNESOTA	18-22	.450	4.39	156	35	512.1	549	2257	268	250	63	18-18	15	199-8	412	32	2	.274
SEATTLE	20-24	.455	4.47	158	44	485.0	458	2126	254	241	60	11-25	19	251-19	406	20	2	.252
OAKLAND	20-17	.541	4.48	154	43	464.0	528	2080	258	231	42	14-17	16	190-32	332	19	1	.287
NEW YORK	22-16	.579	4.52	152	40	459.2	454	2030	253	231	44	17-21	13	211-13	355	29	1	.257
TORONTO	24-20	.545	5.07	147	37	479.2	562	2173	309	270	65	17-21	27	197-16	327	13	0	.294
TEXAS	21-24	.467	5.44	159	39	485.0	572	2256	331	293	69	13-31	23	247-24	368	21	4	.295
BALTIMORE	22-21	.512	5.58	148	33	434.0	470	2004	291	269	72	23-22	9	247-25	349	20	1	.276
KANSAS CITY	29-30	.492	5.59	152	29	495.2	568	2235	325	308	83	19-19	17	237-22	348	28	2	.292
TOTALS	340-317	.518	4.60	2158	551	7009.2	7330	30997	3922	3581	852	249-309	258	3104-307	5315	295	21	.271

2000 AL Statistics

CLUB DESIGNATED HITTING

CLUB	AVG	AB	R	H	TB	2B	3B	HR	RBI	SH-SF	HP	BB-IBB	SO	SB-CS	GIDP	SLG	OBP
SEATTLE	.324	577	110	187	333	32	0	38	149	0-7	5	101-8	101	5-1	13	.577	.425
CHICAGO	.296	581	99	172	311	43	0	32	117	0-6	4	104-16	101	1-2	12	.535	.403
DETROIT	.293	597	89	175	267	34	5	16	91	2-10	1	72-4	87	10-5	12	.447	.365
TEXAS	.288	608	92	175	275	33	2	21	88	2-5	3	64-5	86	4-1	13	.452	.356
TORONTO	.285	606	92	173	325	33	1	39	120	0-6	6	38-3	93	3-2	18	.536	.331
KANSAS CITY	.283	600	91	170	262	35	0	19	101	3-10	6	58-1	93	12-3	15	.437	.347
ANAHEIM	.275	578	93	159	264	27	0	26	81	1-1	7	86-3	96	8-5	11	.457	.375
NEW YORK	.275	557	88	153	248	23	3	22	71	1-8	6	79-1	132	10-5	9	.445	.366
MINNESOTA	.268	586	79	157	231	35	0	13	84	1-11	5	58-2	115	3-3	23	.394	.333
CLEVELAND	.266	579	103	154	313	30	0	43	117	1-2	5	88-4	153	0-1	11	.541	.366
BALTIMORE	.262	584	71	153	231	32	2	14	72	0-3	3	63-12	100	6-3	15	.396	.335
TAMPA BAY	.260	565	86	147	258	36	0	25	89	1-3	5	89-4	145	4-2	9	.457	.364
BOSTON	.242	591	71	143	260	28	1	29	94	2-8	6	64-3	151	0-1	11	.440	.318
OAKLAND	.242	563	94	136	213	23	3	16	67	3-3	10	103-3	153	5-2	12	.378	.367
TOTALS	.276	8172	1258	2254	3791	444	17	353	1341	17-83	72	1067-69	1606	71-36	184	.464	.361

CLUB PINCH HITTING

CLUB	AVG	AB	R	H	TB	2B	3B	HR	RBI	SH-SF	HP	BB-IBB	SO	SB-CS	GIDP	SLG	OBP
ANAHEIM	.232	82	12	19	28	3	0	2	11	2-2	1	22-0	19	1-1	1	.341	.393
BALTIMORE	.213	61	5	13	22	6	0	1	9	0-1	1	10-3	17	0-0	2	.361	.329
BOSTON	.256	133	10	34	47	4	0	3	19	1-1	0	20-2	32	0-2	3	.353	.351
CHICAGO	.192	73	7	14	26	1	1	3	16	0-0	0	9-1	19	0-0	0	.356	.280
CLEVELAND	.231	65	5	15	21	3	0	1	5	0-1	0	6-0	17	0-0	2	.323	.292
DETROIT	.299	107	15	32	46	3	1	3	19	2-1	1	14-0	22	1-1	1	.430	.382
KANSAS CITY	.250	120	13	30	33	0	0	1	18	0-3	0	11-0	26	2-0	1	.275	.306
MINNESOTA	.253	146	14	37	48	6	1	1	25	1-3	0	27-2	39	2-1	4	.329	.364
NEW YORK	.237	76	10	18	32	2	0	4	15	0-1	1	7-0	23	2-0	1	.421	.306
OAKLAND	.212	137	14	29	38	3	0	2	20	0-1	3	21-3	41	0-0	3	.277	.302
SEATTLE	.202	94	10	19	24	3	1	0	12	0-2	1	11-2	26	1-1	1	.255	.287
TAMPA BAY	.265	98	8	26	38	1	1	3	18	3-0	1	11-3	19	0-0	3	.388	.345
TEXAS	.340	103	13	35	59	8	2	4	22	1-0	1	16-1	16	1-0	1	.573	.433
TORONTO	.333	51	6	17	20	3	0	0	8	1-1	0	6-1	7	1-0	2	.392	.397
TOTALS	.251	1346	142	338	482	46	7	28	217	11-17	10	191-18	323	11-6	25	.358	.345

TOP 15 QUALIFIERS FOR BATTING CHAMPIONSHIP

(3.1 plate appearances per team games played)

BATTER	TEAM	B	AVG	G	AB	R	H	TB	2B	3B	HR	RBI	SH-SF	HB	BB-IBB	SO	SB-CS	GIDP	SLG	OBP	E
Garciaparra, N	BOS	R	.372	140	529	104	197	317	51	3	21	96	0-7	2	61-20	50	5-2	8	.599	.434	18
Erstad, D	ANA	L	.355	157	676	121	240	366	39	6	25	100	2-4	1	64-9	82	28-8	8	.541	.409	3
Ramirez, M	CLE	R	.351	118	439	92	154	306	34	2	38	122	0-4	3	86-9	117	1-1	9	.697	.457	2
Delgado, C	TOR	L	.344	162	569	115	196	378	57	1	41	137	0-4	15	123-18	104	0-1	12	.664	.470	13
Jeter, D	NYY	R	.339	148	593	119	201	285	31	4	15	73	3-3	12	68-4	99	22-4	14	.481	.416	24
Segui, D	CLE/TEX	S	.334	150	574	93	192	293	42	1	19	103	0-6	1	53-2	84	0-1	20	.510	.388	0
Sweeney, M	KC	R	.333	159	618	105	206	323	30	0	29	144	0-13	15	71-5	67	8-3	15	.523	.407	9
Giambi, Ja	OAK	L	.333	152	510	108	170	330	29	1	43	137	0-8	9	137-6	96	2-0	9	.647	.476	6
Thomas, F	CWS	R	.328	159	582	115	191	364	44	0	43	143	0-8	5	112-18	94	1-3	13	.625	.436	1
Damon, J	KC	L	.327	159	655	136	214	324	42	10	16	88	8-12	1	65-4	60	46-9	7	.495	.382	5
Martinez, E	SEA	R	.324	153	556	100	180	322	31	0	37	145	0-8	5	96-8	90	3-0	13	.579	.423	0
Dye, J	KC	R	.321	157	601	107	193	337	41	2	33	118	0-6	3	69-6	99	0-1	12	.561	.390	7
Fryman, T	CLE	R	.321	155	574	93	184	296	38	4	22	106	0-10	1	73-2	111	1-1	15	.516	.392	8
Stewart, S	TOR	L	.319	136	583	107	186	302	43	5	21	69	1-4	6	37-1	79	20-5	12	.518	.363	2
Rodriguez, A	SEA	R	.316	148	554	134	175	336	34	2	41	132	0-11	7	100-5	121	15-4	10	.606	.420	10

TOP 15 QUALIFIERS FOR EARNED-RUN CHAMPIONSHIP

(Minimum 1.0 IP per team games)

PITCHER	TEAM	T	W-L	ERA	G	GS	CG	ShO	GF	SV	IP	H	TBF	R	ER	HR	SH-SF	HB	BB-IBB	SO	WP	BK	OPP AVG
Martinez, P	BOS	R	18-6	1.74	29	29	7	4	0	0	217.0	128	817	44	42	17	2-1	14	32-0	284	1	0	.167
Clemens, R	NYY	R	13-8	3.70	32	32	1	0	0	0	204.1	184	878	96	84	26	1-2	10	84-0	188	2	1	.236
Mussina, M	BAL	R	11-15	3.79	34	34	6	1	0	0	237.2	236	987	105	100	28	8-6	3	46-0	210	3	0	.255
Sirotka, M	CWS	L	15-10	3.79	32	32	1	0	0	0	197.0	203	832	101	83	23	4-3	1	69-1	128	8	2	.269
Colon, B	CLE	R	15-8	3.88	30	30	2	1	0	0	188.0	163	807	86	81	21	2-4	4	98-4	212	4	0	.233
Wells, D	TOR	L	20-8	4.11	35	35	9	1	0	0	229.2	266	972	115	105	23	6-7	8	31-0	166	9	1	.289
Heredia, G	OAK	R	15-11	4.12	32	32	2	0	0	0	198.2	214	860	106	91	24	4-6	4	66-5	101	3	0	.274
Lopez, A	TB	R	11-13	4.13	45	24	4	1	10	2	185.1	199	798	95	85	24	6-3	1	70-3	96	4	1	.277
Hudson, T	OAK	R	20-6	4.14	32	32	2	2	0	0	202.1	169	847	100	93	24	5-7	7	82-5	169	7	0	.227
Finley, C	CLE	L	16-11	4.17	34	34	3	0	0	0	218.0	211	936	108	101	23	5-4	2	101-3	189	9	0	.256
Abbott, P	SEA	R	9-7	4.22	35	27	0	0	0	2	179.0	164	766	89	84	23	1-4	5	80-4	100	3	0	.243
Parque, J	CWS	L	13-6	4.28	33	32	0	0	0	0	187.0	208	828	105	89	21	5-5	11	71-1	111	2	5	.283
Weaver, J	DET	R	11-15	4.32	31	30	2	0	0	0	200.0	205	849	102	96	26	3-9	15	52-2	136	3	2	.271
Suzuki, M	KC	R	8-10	4.34	32	29	1	1	0	0	188.2	195	839	100	91	26	2-3	3	94-6	135	11	0	.265
Pettitte, A	NYY	L	19-9	4.35	32	32	3	1	0	0	204.2	219	903	111	99	17	7-4	4	80-4	125	2	3	.271

TOP DESIGNATED HITTERS

(Based on 100 AB minimum)

BATTER	TEAM	B	AVG	G	AB	R	H	TB	2B	3B	HR	RBI	SH-SF	HP	BB-IBB	SO	SB-CS	GI DP	SLG	OBP
Segui, D	CLE	S	.331	68	263	38	87	133	19	0	9	39	0-2	0	23-0	40	0-1	11	.506	.382
Damon, J	KC	L	.330	25	106	20	35	46	11	0	0	10	1-2	0	7-0	15	8-2	2	.434	.365
Martinez, E	SEA	R	.323	146	545	100	176	317	30	0	37	143	0-7	5	95-8	94	3-0	13	.582	.423
Thomas, F	CWS	R	.321	127	467	88	150	274	34	0	30	102	0-6	3	97-15	81	1-2	8	.587	.436
Gonzalez, J	DET	R	.305	48	200	26	61	91	13	1	5	26	0-1	0	15-2	37	1-1	5	.455	.352
Belle, A	BAL	R	.303	31	122	11	37	48	8	0	1	12	0-1	0	12-5	19	0-1	2	.393	.363
Ortiz, D	MIN	L	.303	88	310	50	94	148	27	0	9	50	0-6	0	38-1	62	1-0	13	.477	.373
Sweeney, M	KC	R	.301	45	183	37	55	93	11	0	9	41	0-2	6	18-0	25	3-0	4	.508	.378
Fullmer, B	TOR	L	.295	129	478	75	141	268	29	1	32	104	0-6	6	30-3	68	3-1	14	.561	.340
Justice, D	NYY	L	.291	37	141	22	41	82	11	0	10	32	0-0	0	22-1	24	0-0	6	.582	.387
Polonia, L	NYY	L	.290	51	193	25	56	81	8	4	3	19	1-4	0	12-0	17	8-3	3	.420	.325
Bichette, D	BOS	R	.289	30	114	13	33	59	5	0	7	14	0-0	0	8-0	22	0-0	3	.518	.336
Salmon, T	ANA	R	.287	33	115	23	33	55	7	0	5	15	0-0	2	28-0	18	0-0	3	.478	.434
Palmeiro, R	TEX	L	.266	46	173	28	46	85	8	2	9	34	0-2	1	27-5	20	0-0	3	.491	.365
Canseco, J	NYY	R	.258	86	306	46	79	139	18	0	14	46	0-4	4	60-2	93	2-0	6	.454	.382

DESIGNATED HITTING LEADERS (By Department)

BATTING AVG.	.331	Segui, D	CLE	HOME RUNS	37	Martinez, E	SEA
RUNS	100	Martinez, E	SEA	RBIS	143	Martinez, E	SEA
HITS	176	Martinez, E	SEA	BASE ON BALLS	97	Thomas, F	CWS
TOTAL BASES	317	Martinez, E	SEA	SLUGGING PCT.	.587	Thomas, F	CWS
DOUBLES	34	Thomas, F	CWS	ON-BASE PCT.	.436	Thomas, F	CWS
TRIPLES	4	Polonia, L	NYY				

TOP PINCH HITTERS

(Based on 20 AB minimum)

BATTER	TEAM	B	AVG	G	AB	R	H	TB	2B	3B	HR	RBI	SH-SF	HP	BB-IBB	SO	SB-CS	GI DP	SLG	OBP
Saenz, O	OAK	R	.400	24	20	2	8	12	1	0	1	4	0-0	1	3-1	4	0-0	1	.600	.500
McCarty, D	KC	R	.391	28	23	3	9	12	0	0	1	9	0-2	0	3-0	3	0-0	0	.522	.429
Magee, W	DET	R	.385	27	26	2	10	13	0	0	1	5	0-0	0	0-0	3	0-0	0	.500	.385
Catalanott, F	TEX	L	.357	32	28	4	10	13	1	1	0	4	0-0	1	3-0	5	1-0	0	.464	.438
Cox, S	TB	L	.333	25	21	1	7	8	1	0	0	2	0-0	0	4-0	2	0-0	2	.381	.440
Hocking, M	MIN	S	.333	33	24	3	8	8	0	0	0	3	1-1	0	7-0	9	1-0	0	.333	.469
Cummings, M	BOS	L	.319	54	47	2	15	18	3	0	0	12	0-0	0	5-0	5	0-0	1	.383	.385
Hatteberg, S	BOS	L	.292	28	24	2	7	13	0	0	2	5	0-0	0	4-0	3	0-0	1	.542	.393
Spiezio, S	ANA	S	.286	36	28	5	8	14	0	0	2	8	0-2	1	5-0	5	0-0	1	.500	.389
Becker, R	DET	L	.269	31	26	6	7	10	0	0	1	4	0-0	0	5-0	10	0-1	0	.385	.387
Giambi, Je	OAK	L	.250	26	24	1	6	6	0	0	0	3	0-1	0	1-0	11	0-0	0	.250	.269
Palmeiro, O	ANA	L	.250	31	20	4	5	6	1	0	0	1	2-0	0	8-0	4	1-0	0	.300	.464
Pose, S	KC	L	.222	30	27	4	6	6	0	0	0	1	0-0	0	3-0	7	0-0	1	.222	.300
Javier, S	SEA	S	.200	23	20	4	4	6	2	0	0	5	0-0	0	3-1	4	0-1	0	.300	.304

PINCH HITTING LEADERS (By Department)

BATTING AVG.	.400	Saenz, O	OAK	HOME RUNS	3	Trammell, T	NY
RUNS	6	Becker, R	DET	RBIS	12	Cummings, M	BOS
HITS	15	Cummings, M	BOS	BASE ON BALLS	8	Palmeiro, O	CAL
TOTAL BASES	18	Cummings, M	BOS	SLUGGING PCT.	.600	Saenz, O	OAK
DOUBLES	3	Cummings, M	BOS	ON-BASE PCT.	.500	Saenz, O	OAK
TRIPLES	1	7 PLAYERS TIED FOR FIRST PLACE					

FEWEST ERRORS IN A FULL SEASON, MAJOR LEAGUE HISTORY

	Team	Year	Errors		Team	Year	Errors
1.	New York Mets	1999	68	11.	Baltimore	1991	91
2.	Cleveland	2000	72	11.	New York	1996	91
3.	Baltimore	1998	81	11.	Kansas City	1997	91
4.	Minnesota	1988	84	11.	Atlanta	1998	91
5.	**Toronto**	**1990**	**86**	15.	Detroit	1997	92
6.	Baltimore	1989	87	15.	Minnesota	1999	92
6.	Oakland	1990	87	17.	Baltimore	1992	93
6.	Texas	1996	87	17.	Toronto	1992	93
9.	Milwaukee	1992	89	17.	Boston	1988	93
9.	Baltimore	1999	89	17.	San Francisco	2000	93

The 1999 New York Mets set a Major League record for Fewest Errors in a season by committing only 68. In 1995, a shortened 144 game season, both Baltimore (72 errors) and the New York Yankees (74 errors) were on pace to break the Twins' 1988 low mark. If the season had been the full 162 games and if Baltimore and New York Yankees had continued at their same 1995 pace, the Orioles would have committed just 81 errors and the Yankees 83 miscues.

TOP ROAD HITTERS

(3.1 plate appearances per team games played)

BATTER	TEAM	B	AVG	G	AB	R	H	TB	2B	3B	HR	RBI	SH-SF	HP	BB-IBB	SO	SB-CS	GI DP	SLG	OBP
Garciaparr, N	BOS	R	.370	68	270	49	100	169	25	1	14	45	0-2	1	23-7	23	2-2	3	.626	.419
Sweeney, M	KC	R	.359	78	309	52	111	164	17	0	12	71	0-6	9	33-4	37	5-1	5	.531	.429
Rodriguez, A	SEA	R	.356	73	289	82	103	203	16	0	28	81	0-8	2	43-2	56	5-3	4	.702	.433
Stewart, S	TOR	R	.349	70	307	59	107	159	19	3	9	37	0-4	1	23-0	42	14-4	6	.518	.391
Ramirez, M	CLE	R	.345	60	226	44	78	148	18	2	16	53	0-3	1	50-5	60	1-0	5	.655	.461
Martinez, E	SEA	R	.341	77	293	51	100	174	20	0	18	75	0-4	3	41-4	45	2-0	7	.594	.422
Jeter, D	NYY	R	.340	72	294	52	100	143	18	2	7	37	2-2	7	30-2	49	11-3	5	.486	.411
Fryman, T	CLE	R	.331	77	281	46	93	152	16	2	13	56	0-6	1	39-1	51	1-1	5	.541	.407
Segui, D	CLE	S	.331	68	260	38	86	139	18	1	11	54	0-2	1	23-1	45	0-0	7	.535	.385
Lee, C	CWS	R	.329	75	295	55	97	155	18	2	12	49	1-3	0	17-1	44	7-2	9	.525	.362
Delgado, C	TOR	L	.329	81	286	51	94	158	29	1	11	62	0-3	10	64-8	62	0-0	4	.552	.463
Olerud, J	SEA	L	.320	79	281	50	90	133	25	0	6	51	1-4	2	58-8	41	0-2	6	.473	.435
Erstad, D	ANA	L	.320	76	328	56	105	175	18	5	14	42	2-1	1	35-6	38	10-5	4	.534	.386
Everett, C	BOS	S	.320	65	244	41	78	151	16	3	17	57	0-3	3	24-1	55	5-3	1	.619	.383
Vizquel, O	CLE	S	.319	79	310	57	99	132	13	1	6	38	5-1	1	52-0	35	10-6	6	.426	.418

ROAD HITTING LEADERS (By Department)

BATTING AVG.	.370	Garciaparr, N	BOS	HOME RUNS	28	Rodriguez, A	SEA
RUNS	82	Rodriguez, A	SEA	RBIS	81	Rodriguez, A	SEA
HITS	111	Sweeney, M	KC	BASE ON BALLS	64	Delgado, C	TOR
TOTAL BASES	203	Rodriguez, A	SEA	SLUGGING PCT.	.702	Rodriguez, A	SEA
DOUBLES	29	Delgado, C	TOR	ON-BASE PCT.	.463	Delgado, C	TOR
TRIPLES	6	4 PLAYERS TIED FOR FIRST PLACE					

MAJOR LEAGUE LEADERS

AMERICAN LEAGUE		BATTING		NATIONAL LEAGUE
Nomar Garciaparra, BOS	.372	**Average**	.372	Todd Helton, COL
Jose Cruz, TOR	162	**Games**	162	Luis Gonzalez, ARI
Carlos Delgado, TOR	162		162	Shawn Green, LA
			162	Neifi Perez, COL
Darin Erstad	676	**At Bats**	656	Andruw Jones, ATL
Johnny Damon	136	**Runs**	152	Jeff Bagwell, HOU
Darin Erstad	240	**Hits**	216	Todd Helton, COL
Carlos Delgado, TOR	378	**Total Bases**	405	Todd Helton, COL
Carlos Delgado, TOR	99	**Extra Base Hits**	103	Todd Helton, COL
Darin Erstad	170	**Singles**	158	Luis Castillo, FLA
Carlos Delgado, TOR	57	**Doubles**	59	Todd Helton, COL
Cristian Guzman, MIN	20	**Triples**	14	Tony Womack, ARI
Troy Glaus, ANA	47	**Home Runs**	50	Sammy Sosa, CHI
Edgar Martinez, SEA	145	**Runs Batted In**	147	Todd Helton, COL
Johnny Damon	46	**Stolen Bases**	62	Luis Castillo, FLA
Gabe Kapler, TEX	28	**Longest Hitting Streak**	24	Tony Eusebio, HOU
Manny Ramirez, CLE	.697	**Slugging Percentage**	.698	Todd Helton, COL
Jason Giambi, OAK	.476	**On-Base Percentage**	.463	Todd Helton, COL
Alex Gonzalez, TOR	16	**Sacrifice Hits**	16	Rickey Gutierrez, CHI
Magglio Ordonez, CWS	15	**Sacrifice Flies**	14	J.T. Snow, SF
Jason Giambi, OAK	137	**Base on Balls**	117	Barry Bonds, SF
Nomar Garciaparra, BOS	20	**Intentional Walks**	23	Vladimir Guerrero, MTL
Carlos Delgado, TOR	15	**Hit by Pitch**	28	Fernando Vina, STL
Mike Sweeney, KC	15			
Mo Vaughn, ANA	181	**Strikeouts**	187	Preston Wilson, FLA
Ben Grieve, OAK	32	**GIDP Most**	21	Moises Alou, HOU

AMERICAN LEAGUE		PITCHING		NATIONAL LEAGUE
Pedro Martinez, BOS	1.74	**Earned Run Average**	2.58	Kevin Brown, LA
Tim Hudson, OAK	20	**Wins**	21	Tom Glavine, ATL
David Wells, TOR	20			
Brad Radke, MIN	16	**Losses**	19	Omar Daal, PHI
Todd Jones, DET	42	**Saves**	45	Antonio Alfonseca, FLA
Derek Lowe, BOS	42			
Kelly Wunsch, CWS	83	**Games**	83	Steve Kline, MON
Rick Helling, TEX	35	**Games Started**	35	Tom Glavine, ATL
David Wells, TOR	35		35	Randy Johnson, ARI
			35	Jon Lieber, CHI
			35	Greg Maddux, ATL
			35	Kevin Millwood, ATL
Pedro Martinez, BOS	4	**Shutouts**	3	Randy Johnson, ARI
			3	Greg Maddux, ATL
Mike Mussina, BAL	237.2	**Innings**	251.0	Jon Lieber, CHI
David Wells, TOR	266	**Hits**	254	Livan Hernandez, SF
Pedro Martinez, BOS	284	**Strikeouts**	347	Randy Johnson, ARI
Kevin Appier, OAK	102	**Base on Balls**	125	Matt Clement, SD
Jeff Suppan, KC	36	**Home Runs**	48	Jose Lima, HOU
Dan Reichert, KC	18	**Wild Pitches**	23	Matt Clement, SD
Jim Parque, CWS	5	**Balks**	5	Reid Cornelius, FLA

WINS AND LOSSES: The Blue Jays finished the 2000 season with a 83-79 record to place third in the American League East... Were 4.5 games back of New York in the East which is the closest Toronto has finished to first since winning the division in 1993... Was the 14th winning season in the clubs 24 year history and the third consecutive... Other clubs with current consecutive winning seasons are, in order, Atlanta (10), New York Yankees (8), Cleveland (7), New York Mets (4), San Francisco (4), Boston (3), Arizona (2), Cincinnati (2) and Oakland (2)... After losing records in 1999 the following clubs posted winning seasons: Anaheim, Chicago White Sox, Colorado, St. Louis and Seattle... The 83 wins were one fewer than 84 recorded in the 1999 season... Of the 83 wins, 41 of them saw the Blue Jays come from behind... In 1999 the Blue Jays had 39 come from behind wins... Toronto was 45-36 at home and 38-43 on the road... Were 2-6 in extra inning games with a 1-2 record at SkyDome and a 1-4 mark on the road... Preferred the night life with a 55-51 record in the pm and a 28-28 record in day games... Were 31-38 on grass and 52-41 on artificial turf... Played in 11 shutouts games and were 4-7 with a home mark of 2-4 and a 2-3 record on the road... Toronto had 30 of their games decided in the last at bat and were 17-13... Against LH starters were 19-24 with a home mark of 12-10 and 7-14 on the road... FRANCHISE RECORD now stands at 1867-1897-3... Against the AL East were 28-21, against the Central were 28-25 and against the West were 18-24... In Interleague play were 9-9... Toronto finished with a 17-1 record in games played prior to an off-day and following an off day were 5-13.

HOME IN THE SKYDOME: Toronto posted a 45-36 record at home... The 45 wins were an improvement of five over 1999 when the club posted a home record of 40-41... The 45 home wins were the most in the AL East... Tops in the AL was 48 by Cleveland... 2000 was the year of the HR at SkyDome as the Blue Jays hit a franchise and American League home record 134 HR's... The previous home mark was 112 in the 1998 season and the AL record had been 133 by the Cleveland Indians in 1970.

ON THE ROAD: Had record of 38-43... This was six wins fewer than the 1999 road total of 44 wins against 37 losses... Toronto has had one winning season on the road over the last seven seasons... Have 11 winning road seasons in club history.

CLOSE GAMES: Toronto played 62 games that were decided by two or fewer runs and were 35-27... In one runs games were 21-19 with a 15-5 mark at home and a 6-14 record on the road... In games decided by two runs the Blue Jays were 14-8, going 8-5 at home and 6-3 on the road.

AGAINST THE BIG BOYS: Against the four American League playoff teams Toronto posted a 17-25 record... Were 5-5 against the White Sox, 7-5 against the Yankees, 2-8 against the Mariners and 3-7 against Oakland... In 1999 Toronto was 16-30 against the four play-off teams... Against the National League playoff teams the Blue Jays was 2-1 against the Atlanta Braves and 1-2 against the New York Mets.

IN THE STANDINGS: Finished third in the AL East division trailing the division winning Yankees by 4.5 games and the second place Boston Red Sox by 2.0 games... On June 6 Toronto leaped from third to first with a victory against Boston... Was the first time Toronto had been in first, other than April, since winning the AL East in 1993... On the season spent a total of 17 days in first place... The last time Toronto was in first place was July 6 with a 46-40 record.

	1ST	2ND	3RD	4TH	5TH	POS. in Standings
APRIL: 26 games (28 days)	3		5	17	3	4th, 4.5 GB
MAY: 28 games (31 days)			22			3rd, 4.0 GB
JUNE: 25 games (30 days)	8		22			1st, 3.0 GA
JULY: 27 games (31 days)	6	15	10			3rd, 4.5 GB
AUGUST: 27 games (31 days)			31			3rd, 5.5 GB
SEPT/OCT: 29 games (31 days)		10	21			3rd, 4.5 GB

SWEEPS: In 2000 the Blue Jays swept a total of five series... Took 11 in 1999... Of the five sweeps, four were of three game series and one of a two game series... Opponents swept Toronto only three times, all in three game series and only once at home.

By Toronto – five

Dates	Opponent	# games
May 8-10	at Baltimore	3
June 23-25	Boston	3
Jul 19-20	Tampa Bay	2
Sept. 8-10	Detroit	3
Sept. 19-21	New York	3

Of Toronto – three

Dates	Opponent	# games
April 14-17	Seattle	3
July 31-Aug. 2	at Oakland	3
Sept. 29-Oct. 1	at Cleveland	3

BY THE CALENDER: APRIL: Were 12-14 with an April record 43 home runs... Were 7-7 at home and 5-7 on the road... One of three sub .500 months of the season... **MAY:** Were 16-12 with a May record 43 home runs... Were 8-8 at home and 8-4 on the road... In May 1999 were 11-17... **JUNE:** Posted a 16-10 record with 48 home runs which is a new club record for any month... Were 7-3 at home and 9-7 on the road... In June of 1999 were 15-13... **JULY:** Were 11-16 and set a new club HR record for the month with 42... Were 5-9 at home and 6-7 on the road... In 1999 July was the best month of the season posting a 19-7 record... **AUGUST:** Were 15-11 and set a new HR record for August with 43... Were 8-3 at home and 7-8 on the road... In August of 1999 were just 12-16... **SEPT./OCT.:** Were 13-16 to finish the season... Were 9-8 at home and 3-9 on the road... Finished the 1999 season with a 14-14 record in September/October... **DAYS of the WEEK:** Monday's were 10-8, Tuesday 8-17, Wednesday 17-7, Thursday 12-5, Friday 11-15, Saturday 11-15 and Sunday were 14-12.

STREAKS- WIN/LOSS: In 2000 the **LONGEST WINNING STREAK** was five straight from June 20 to 25 against Detroit (2) and Boston (3)... Longest winning streak at home was six games from September 8 to 21 against Detroit (3) and New York (3)... The longest win streak on the road was three games which was done three times, May 13 to 23 against Tampa Bay (2) and Boston (1), July 8 to 27 against Montreal (2) and Seattle (1) and August 26 to 28 against Texas (2) and Anaheim (1)... **LONGEST LOSING STREAK:** Dropped six straight from July 28 to August 2 at Seattle (3) and at Oakland (3)... The longest streak at home was five games from April 5 to 16 against Kansas City (2) and Seattle (3)... The longest losing steak on the road was seven games from July 28 to August 7 against Seattle (3), Oakland (3) and Kansas City (1).

THE MANAGER: Jim Fregosi finished with a 83-79 record, third in the AL East... In his two seasons as Blue Jays manager had a record of 167-157 with two third place finishes... Fregosi ranks fourth in Blue Jays wins with 167 after passing Tim Johnson (88), Bobby Mattick (104) and Roy Hartsfield (166)... On May 14 at Tampa Bay managed his 2000th regular season game and won 3-2... Captured his 1000th career managerial victory on July 27 in Seattle to become the 47th manager to post 1000 career wins... His career record is now 1028-1095 in 2,123 games... The 1,028 career wins rank 46th all-time and seventh among managers active during the 2000 season (LaRussa, Cox, Torre, Johnson, Pinella, Kelly)... Was ejected three times during the season, July 30 at Seattle, August 10 at KC and September 30 at CLE.

FIELDING: Were third in the AL in fielding percentage at .984 (100E/6,091TC)... In 1999 were ranked fifth after posting a .983 percentage... Made 100 errors which ranked third in the AL (made 106 last season)... Had 51 errors at the All-Star break and 49 after the break... Turned 176 double plays to tie for fourth in the AL... Had 11 passed balls... Longest errorless streak was seven games from September 21 to 27... Committed a season high five errors on May 21 at home against Chicago... Played 97 errorless games.

PITCHING: Posted an 83-79 record with 37 saves and an ERA of 5.14 which was tenth in the AL... Were 0.91 points behind the league leading mark of 4.23 by the Boston Red Sox... Was 0.22 points more than the 1999 mark of 4.92... Toronto led the AL in complete games with 15 which was second only to Arizona (16) in the majors... Toronto had 14 complete games in 1999... At home posted an ERA of 5.22 which was 12th in the AL... Leading the AL in home ERA was Seattle at 3.84... Had 19 saves at home which was third in the AL and eight complete games which led the AL... On the road Toronto posted the AL's fifth best ERA at 5.06 and were 38-43... Had 18 saves and seven complete games... Boston led the AL in road ERA at 4.29... At the All-Star break Toronto was 48-41 with a 5.47 ERA which was 12th in the AL... In the second half posted an ERA of 4.74 which was seventh in the AL and was 0.73 runs better than the first half... Opened the season with the AL worst ERA at 6.42 while posting a 12-14 record... Was the highest ERA for any month in club history, the previous mark was 6.04 in April of 1996... Rebounded in May from the worst ERA in April to fourth best in the AL at 4.39... In May tossed a season high 36.0 innings without allowing a home run, from May 14 to 19... Toronto then slipped back in June and July posting ERA's of 5.37 and

5.74 respectively... In August were fifth in the AL with a 4.66 ERA and allowed 26 home runs, the lowest total of any month... In September and October combined Toronto posted their second best ERA of the season at 4.41... On July 28 Dave Stewart took over for Rick Langford as the club's pitching coach... Under Langford the club was 53-47 with a 5.47 ERA and under Stewart were 30-32 with an ERA of 4.66... Recorded only four shutouts in 2000 after recording nine in 1999 and 11 in 1998... Of the four shutouts, three were complete games and one was combined... Toronto finished eighth in the league with 978 strikeouts, was the first time in the last five seasons not to reach 1,000 strikeouts... Toronto allowed the fifth fewest walks in the AL at 560... Allowed ten runs in 27 games with a 3-24 record in those contests... The ML mark for most ten run games allowed in a season is 45 by the 1930 Phillies... Toronto matched their club record of using 22 different pitchers in the 2000 season... The club mark was set in 1992... In the two seasons combined Toronto has used 33 different pitchers... Of the 22 pitchers this season, seven were left-handers and 15 were right-handers... Posted their best ERA of 3.68 ERA against the Chicago White Sox... Toronto also posted a sub 4.00 ERA against the New York Yankees at 3.99... Against Detroit had a season best nine wins despite allowing a season high 19 home runs... Held Boston, Kansas City and Minnesota to an opponent low eight home runs... For the second time in franchise history the staff allowed ten or more runs in three consecutive games from April 14-16 all against Seattle... In the three games the Mariners totaled 47 runs which is the most ever allowed in a three games span... Toronto pitchers totaled 23,549 pitches on the season.

STARTERS: Compiled a 59-59 record with AL high 15 complete games and an ERA of 5.23 (556ER/957.2IP) which ranked ninth in the AL... Boston starters led the AL with a 4.47 ERA... Mariners and A's starters tied with 71 wins... The staff averaged 5.91 innings pitched per start which ranked 5th in the AL... Last year averaged 6.19IP... Baltimore led the AL averaging 6.17 IP per start... Toronto starters pitched 6.0 innings in 99 games and posted a record of 65-34 in those games.

QUALITY STARTS: The Blue Jays turned in 74 quality starts in 2000 (6.0 innings pitched or more & three or fewer earned runs allowed)... Toronto had 71 in 1999, 94 in 1998, 85 in 1997 and 74 in 1996.

SUPPORT FOR STARTERS:

Pitcher	Starts	Runs	Runs/Start	Club Record	Quality Starts
ANDREWS	2	15	7.50	1-1	0
CARPENTER	27	136	5.04	10-17	11
CASTILLO	24	137	5.71	13-11	12
COCO	1	5	5.00	0-1	0
ESCOBAR	24	100	4.17	8-16	11
HALLADAY	13	77	5.92	6-7	2
HAMILTON	6	37	6.17	4-2	4
LOAIZA	14	57	4.07	6-8	9
MUNRO	3	17	5.67	1-2	2
PAINTER	2	14	7.00	2-0	0
TRACHSEL	11	63	5.73	6-5	4
WELLS	35	204	5.83	26-9	19

BULLPEN: Were 24-20 with 37 saves and a 4.97 ERA which ranked 11 in the AL... Dropped from their 1999 ERA of 4.49... Was the second consecutive season to post a winning record after not doing so since 1993... Were 37-52 in save situations and allowed 112 of 258 runners to score, stranding 146... The 37 saves were ninth in the AL... Totaled 479.2 innings pitched which was fifth lowest in the AL... Made 388 appearances was fourth lowest in the AL.

RELIEF PITCHERS FIRST BATTER EFFICIENCY

	IR	IS	Avg	AB	H	2B	3B	HR	RBI	BB	HBP	SO	GDP	OBP	SLG
Andrews	1	1	.333	6	2	0	0	0	1	0	0	0	0	.333	.333
Bale	3	3	.000	1	0	0	0	0	1	1	0	0	0	.500	.000
Borbon	41	20	.234	47	11	1	0	2	14	8	1	11	0	.339	.383
Carpenter	6	2	.333	6	2	0	0	0	0	1	0	2	0	.429	.333
Castillo	0	0	.000	1	0	0	0	0	0	0	0	0	0	.000	.000
Cubillan	7	2	.167	6	1	0	0	0	1	0	1	1	0	.286	.167
DeWitt	8	7	.500	8	4	0	0	2	7	0	0	2	0	.500	1.250
Escobar	9	5	.333	18	6	1	0	0	3	1	0	5	0	.368	.389
Estrella	1	1	1.000	2	2	0	0	0	0	0	0	0	0	1.000	1.000
Frascatore	39	14	.260	50	13	1	1	2	9	5	3	6	0	.356	.440
Gunderson	1	1	.667	6	4	1	1	0	1	0	0	1	0	.667	1.167
Guthrie	19	6	.333	18	6	0	0	1	6	5	0	3	0	.478	.500
Halladay	6	6	.750	4	3	1	0	0	4	2	0	0	0	.833	1.000
Koch	18	4	.212	66	14	4	0	0	2	2	0	14	0	.235	.273
Munro	6	3	.200	5	1	0	0	0	0	1	0	2	0	.333	.200
Painter	34	13	.333	39	13	3	0	1	10	1	0	5	3	.350	.487
Quantrill	59	24	.333	63	21	4	0	2	16	4	0	8	2	.368	.492

IR- Inherited runners **IS-** Inherited runners that Scored

CATCHERS PROFILES

Catcher	ERA	IP	H	R	ER	HR	BB	SO	SB	C-CS	P-CS	PKOF	C-CS%
Castillo, Alberto	4.77	501.2	561	304	266	63	192	364	25	16	1	3	39.0
Fletcher, Darrin	5.29	909.2	1022	584	535	127	354	598	73	20	1	0	21.5
Greene, Charlie	7.11	19.0	22	15	15	5	9	13	0	0	0	0	0.0
Greene, Todd	9.00	4.0	7	4	4	0	5	2	1	0	0	0	0.0
Phelps, Josh	3.00	3.0	3	1	1	0	0	1	0	0	0	0	0.0

PITCHING ANALYSIS:

	W-L-S	SV-OPP	ERA	GM	CG	IP	H	R	ER	HR	HB	BB	IBB	K	WP
STARTERS	59-59-0		5.23	162	15	957.2	1053	599	556	130	37	363	3	651	24
RELIEVERS	24-20-37	37-52	4.97	388		479.2	562	309	265	65	27	197	16	327	13
HOME	45-36-19	19-28	5.22	81	8	738.0	819	464	428	92	30	279	8	526	21
ROAD	38-43-18	18-24	5.06	81	7	699.1	796	444	393	103	34	281	11	452	16
PRE ASG	48-41-21	21-28	5.47	89	9	788.1	914	523	479	111	37	325	6	539	24
POST ASG	35-38-16	16-24	4.74	73	6	649.0	701	385	342	84	27	235	13	439	13

SHUTOUTS BY TORONTO – 4

Date	Opponent	Score	Pitcher(s)
April 8	at Texas	4-0	Wells (9.0)
June 21	Detroit	6-0	Escobar (9.0)
September 8	Detroit	3-0	Loaiza (9.0)
September 27	at Baltimore	4-0	Castillo (6.0), Escobar (2.0), Koch (1.0)

SHUTOUTS BY OPPONENTS – 7

Date	Opponent	Score	Pitcher(s)
April 10	at Anaheim	6-0	Schoeneweis (9.0)
April 28	at New York	6-0	Cone (7.0), Nelson (1.0), Stanton (1.0)
May 17	Boston	8-0	P.Martinez (7.0), Rose (1.0), Young (1.0)
August 25	at Texas (11)	1-0	Davis (8.0), Wetteland (2.0), Venafro (1.0)
September 2	Oakland	8-0	Heredia (7.1), Mecir (1.2)
September 4	Oakland	10-0	Zito (6.2), Tam (0.2), Belitz (– –), Matthews (0.2), Isringhausen (1.0)
September 24	Tampa Bay	6-0	Harper (9.0)

BLUE JAYS BULLPEN STATS

Pitcher	I.R.E.	1st Batter	Holds	Sv Sit'n	Longest Relief App.
ANDREWS	0-1	4-6	0	0-0	4.0, May 28 at Detroit
BALE	0-3	1-2	0	0-0	2.0, April 25 at Oakland
BORBON	21-41	39-59	12	1-1	2.0, twice, last on August 26 at Texas
CARPENTER	4-6	4-7	0	0	5.1, August 13 at Minnesota
CASTILLO	0-0	1-1	0	0	1.0, September 17 at Chicago
CUBILLAN	5-7	5-7	0	0	3.0, September 20 vs Detroit
DEWITT	1-8	4-8	0	0	3.0, June 20 vs Detroit
ESCOBAR	4-9	12-19	3	2-3	2.0, 7 times, last September 27 at Baltimore
ESTRELLA	0-1	0-2	0	0-0	3.0, July 18 vs New York Mets
FRASCATORE	25-39	39-60	13	0-4	3.1, September 28 at Baltimore
GUNDERSON	0-1	2-6	0	0-0	2.0, May 7 vs Cleveland
GUTHRIE	13-19	12-23	3	0-1	3.0, September 29 at Cleveland
HALLADAY	0-6	1-6	0	0-0	3.0, July 28 at Seattle
KOCH	14-18	52-68	0	33-38	2.0, 7 times, last July 23 vs BAL
MUNRO	3-6	4-6	0	0-0	4.0, April 14 vs Seattle
PAINTER	21-34	26-40	5	0-1	3.2, September 23 vs Tampa Bay
QUANTRILL	35-59	43-68	13	1-3	3.2, May 10 vs BAL

BATTING: Hit .275 and set club records in home runs (244), extra-base hits (593), total bases (2,664) and slugging percentage (.469)... The 244 home runs led the AL and surpassed the previous club mark of 221 which was set in 1998... It is the fourth time the Blue Jays have hit over 200 home runs in a season... The 593 extra base hits are 30 more than the previous club mark of 563 set in 1999... Toronto was first in the AL in extra base hits... The slugging percentage of .469 was third in the AL trailing only Cleveland and Chicago who both posted percentages of .470... Toronto's .275 average was eighth in the AL and was .005 points lower than the club record of .280 which was set in 1999... Toronto was second in the AL with 2,664 total bases to Cleveland who had had 2,672... Were second in doubles at 328 to Texas who had 330... It is the second highest double total in club history and the third straight season to hit 300 doubles... The Blue Jays opened the season hitting .281 in April with a club record 43 home runs... In May the club was fifth in the AL with a .280 average and a club record 41 home runs... In June were eighth in batting at .272 but again set a franchise mark for home runs in June at 48... The 48 home runs were a new club record for any month in franchise history... In July the Blue Jays hit .268 and hit a club record 44 home runs... In August the Blue Jays led the AL with a .314 average and again set a club mark with 43 homers... In September the Blue Jays were 13th in the AL with a .240 batting average and managed only 21 home runs... In the one October game the Blue Jays hit .229 with two home runs... At the All-Star break were sixth in the AL batting .278 and after the break hit .271 which was ninth in the AL... Toronto was fourth in the league with a .283 average with runners in scoring position... With the bases loaded the Blue Jays hit .281 which was 10th in the AL and hit a club record nine grand slams... Hit .275 against left-handed pitchers which was tenth in the AL... Against right-handers also hit .275 which ranked seventh in the AL... At home Toronto hit .278 which was ninth in the AL and on the road were sixth in the league with a .273 aver-age... Had 60 hit by pitch to lead the AL... Were walked intentionally 32 times which was seventh in the AL... Overall walked 526 times which was second lowest total in the AL which striking out 1,026 times which ranked fourth most in the AL... Were shutout seven times which tied for seventh in the league... Scored six or more runs in 11 straight games from April 12 to April 23, the feat had not been accomplished since 1979 when the Jim Fregosi managed California Angels did so... Had Toronto stretched it to 12 games it would have been the first time since the 1950 Boston Red Sox... For the second time in franchise history the Blue Jays scored ten runs in three straight games from April 18 to April 20 against Anaheim (2W-1L).

HOME RUNS: Hit a franchise record 244 home runs to lead the AL... Houston led the majors with 249 home runs... It was the fourth time Toronto has reached 200 home runs in a season and the third consecutive... Toronto hit 205 against right-handed pitching and 39 against left-handers... Hit an American League record 134 home runs at home which surpassed the previous franchise record of 112 in 1998... On the road totaled 110 home runs which was second in the AL... Hit 147 by the All-Star break and 97 following... Of the 244 home runs hit, 141 of them were solo shots, 67 were with one man on, 27 with two and a franchise record nine grand slams... The home runs accounted for 392 total runs which is 46% of the runs scored this season... Set club HR records in April, May, June, July and August... In June set the club record for any month in club history with 48... 74 home runs came in the seventh inning or later... Hit 55 with an 0-0 count, 74 after starting the count 0-1 and 115 after starting the count 1-0... Toronto homered in a club record 23 consecutive games from May 31 to June 25 to set a new franchise record... Entering this season the club record was 14 consecutive games with a home run set in 1996... Along with the 23 game streak Toronto also had consecutive home run streaks of 15 games (July 6-23) and two of 12 games (April 11-23, May 1-13).

RECORDS SET

	No	Dates	Previous mark
Most HR in a season	244	2000	221, 1998
Most HR at home	134	2000	112, 1998
AL record for HR's at Home	134	2000	133, Cleveland, 1970
Most consecutive games with a HR	23	May 31-June 25	14, 1996
Most consecutive games with a HR at home	22	June 1-July 23	21, April 3 to May 10, 2000
Club record for HR's in April	43	April	42, 1996
Club record for HR's in May	43	May	42, 1993
Club record for HR's in June	48	June	47, 1998
Club record for HR's in July	44	July	42, 1999
Club record for HR's in August	43	August	39, 1987
Club record for HR's in any Month	48	June	47, June 1998
Most lead-off HR's in a season	7	2000	6, 1991 & 1993
Club record for Grand Slams in a season	9	2000	8, 1989
ML- Most Players with 20HR by All-Star break	4	2000	3 many times
Most 20 HR players on Blue Jays	7	2000	4, 1987
AL- tied most 20 HR players on a team	7	2000	7, Baltimore, 1996
AL- tied 30 HR players on a team	4	2000	4, Anaheim 2000
ML- tied most 30 HR players on a team	4	2000	4, 7 other clubs

20 HOMERS AT BREAK: The 2000 Blue Jays set a Major League mark after becoming the only club to boast four players who had each hit 20 home runs by the All-Star break... They were Carlos Delgado with 28, Tony Batista with 24, Raul Mondesi with 22 and Jose Cruz with 20. The Blue Jays heading in to the to the 2000 season had never posted three 20HR men by the All-Star break... Only twice had Toronto even posted two 20-HR men at the All-Star break, they were Shawn Green (25) and Carlos Delgado (21) in 1999 and Ed Sprague (20) and Joe Carter (20) in 1996.

20 HR MEN: Seven players hit 20 home runs to tie the Major League record done once previously by the Baltimore Orioles in 1996... The seven players were Batista, Cruz, Delgado, Fletcher, Fullmer, Mondesi and Stewart... The most 20HR men Toronto had ever posted was four in the 1987 season — Barfield, Bell, McGriff and Moseby... NL record 6 by the 1965 Milwaukee Braves... FAST FIVE: Toronto had accomplished five — 20 HR players in just 102 games, making those the fastest group of five to that plateau in ML history — the players were Carlos Delgado, Tony Batista, Raul Mondesi, Jose Cruz and Brad Fullmer.

FOUR 30HR MEN – When Jose Cruz belted his 30th home run on September 15 in Yankee Stadium it gave the Blue Jays four players with 30 home runs (Batista, Cruz, Delgado and Fullmer)... This accomplishment has been done just twice in the history of the AL... Was also done by the 2000 Anaheim Angles (Anderson, Glaus, Salmon & Vaughn)... The NL had seen six teams post four 30 homer players in a season (Los Angeles- 1977 & 1997, Colorado- 1995, 1997 & 1999 and Atlanta, 1998).

DUO/TRIO – In 2000 Carlos Delgado and Tony Batista combined to hit 82 home runs, 41 each... This made them the third most prolific home run hitting pair in club history... The most productive pair was Carlos Delgado (44) and Shawn Green (42) who combined to hit 86 in the 1999 season... If you add Brad Fullmer's 32 home runs you get the second best trio of home run hitters in club history at 114... The top trio at 119 home runs was Jose Canseco (46), Carlos Delgado (38) and Shawn Green (35) in the 1998 season.

BLUE JAYS HOME RUNS

1R – 141 TOTAL: Delgado- 24, Batista- 23, Cruz- 21, Fletcher- 15, Stewart- 14, Fullmer- 13, Mondesi- 11, Gonzalez- 8, T. Greene- 5, Cordova- 3, Castillo- 1, Martinez- 1, Grebeck- 1, Bush- 1

2R – 67 TOTAL: Batista- 14, Delgado- 13, Fullmer- 11, Mondesi- 7, Cruz- 6, Gonzalez- 5, Stewart- 5, Grebeck- 2, Woodward- 2, Fletcher- 2

3R – 27 TOTAL: Fullmer- 8, Mondesi- 7, Cruz- 4, Delgado- 2, Batista- 2, Stewart- 1, Woodward- 1, Martinez- 1, Gonzalez- 1

SLAMS – 9 TOTAL: Fletcher- 3 (Apr 20 vs ANA-Mercker, May 8 vs BAL-Johnson, May 26 at DET-Brocail)... Batista- 2 (June 11 vs MON- Lira, July 3 at BAL-Johnson)... Delgado- 2 (June 7 at ATL- Millwood & Sept. 17 at CWS off Pena)... Cordova- 1 (July 16 vs NYM-Leiter)... Fullmer- 1 (Apr 17 vs ANA-Pote)

LEAD-OFF A GAME (8): Stewart- 5 (April 3 vs KC, June 2 at FLA, June 25 vs BOS, Aug 7 at KC, Sept 27 at BAL)... Cruz- 3 (April 19 vs ANA, April 22 & 23 vs NYY).

BACK-TO-BACK HR's (5): Fullmer-Batista, April 19 vs ANA... Fletcher-Cordova April 23 vs NYY... Fullmer-Batista, Aug 21 vs KC... Fletcher-Cruz, Aug. 27 at TEX... Fullmer-Batista, Aug. 30 at ANA

BK-TO-BK-TO-BK HR's (1): Grebeck-Mondesi-Delgado, April 18 vs ANA

HR IN GAME: FIVE (2)- May 5 vs Cleveland (Fletcher, Mondesi, Delgado, Cruz, Gonzalez) & Aug 27 at TEX (Fletcher- 3, Stewart, Cruz)

HR IN ONE INNING: 3- twice, April 18 vs ANA, 6th inning & Apr 23 vs NYY, 6th inning

GAME ENDING HRS (2): Batista, April 3 vs KC, Delgado, Aug 16 vs ANA

MULTI-HR GAMES (16): Delgado- 5, Batista- 4, Mondesi- 2, Fullmer- 2, Cruz- 1, Fletcher- 1, Stewart- 1

MULTI-HR INNINGS: Toronto- 19, Opponents- 14

MULTI-HR GAMES OPPONENTS (9): Clayton- 2, April 7 at TEX... Rodriguez- 3, April 16 vs SEA... Williams- 2 Apr 23 vs NYY (both sides)... Posada- 2, Apr 23 vs NYY (both sides)... Valentin- 2, May 3 at CWS... Higginson- June 13 at DET... Clark- 2, June 20 vs DET... Baines- 2, July 1 at BAL... Branyan- 2 July 4 at CLE

SLAMS OPPONENT (5): Martinez, SEA, April 15... Rodriguez, SEA, April 16... Kennedy, ANA, April 18... Cox, TB June 27... Piazza, NYM, July 18

PINCH HITTING: Toronto posted the second highest pinch-hitting average in the AL at .333 (17-51)... The Texas Rangers posted the highest average at .340 (35-103)... With only 51 at bats Toronto had the fewest in the AL... Brad Fullmer was the most used pinch-hitter with 14 at bats and hit .214 with one RBI... Also pinch-hitting, in order of at bats, were Fletcher (.308/4-13, 2RBI), T. Greene (.400/4-10, 3RBI), Cordova (.333/2-6, 1RBI), Grebeck (.500/1-2, 1RBI), Ducey (.000/0-2), Martinez (1-1), Morandini (1-1), Wise (1-1), Mondesi (0-1).

DESIGNATED HITTING: Toronto designated hitters hit .285 with 33 doubles, 39 home runs and 120 RBI... Was the fifth time that team DH's have amassed over 100RBI... The 120 this season is the most in club history surpassing the 112 set in 1992... The 39 home runs are the second most ever hit by Toronto DH's in a season, the club mark is 43 in 1998... In the AL, Toronto DH's ranked fifth in average, second in home runs and second in RBI... In 1999 were last in the AL in average at .250 and had 27 doubles, 24 home runs and 81 RBI... Brad Fullmer led the way hitting .295 with 29 doubles and set the Blue Jays club record for home runs and RBI by a DH with 32 and 104... He surpassed the previous club marks of 25 home runs by Canseco (1998) and 91 RBI by Dave Winfield (1992)... He was second in the AL in HR's and RBI by a DH to Seattle's Edgar Martinez (37, 143)... Also seeing time at DH, in order of at bats, were Todd Greene (23G, .216, 5HR, 9RBI), Marty Cordova (15G, .292, 1HR, 6RBI), Darrin Fletcher (2G, .333, 1HR, 1RBI) and Dewayne Wise (2G, -AB)... Starts at DH- 116 by Fullmer, Greene- 20, Cordova- 14, Fletcher- 2... In 1999 the Blue Jays saw 16 different players start at least one game at DH.

STOLEN BASES: Toronto stole just 89 bases in 2000 after swiping over 100 bases the previous four seasons... The 89 steals were 10th in the AL... Toronto was 89 for 123 to post a success percentage of 72.36%... In 1999 Toronto was successful in 71.26% of attempts... Toronto was led by Raul Mondesi who stole 22 and missed two months on the disabled list... Toronto had only three players swipe 10 bases, Mondesi, Shannon Stewart who had 20 and Jose Cruz who swiped a career high 15.

ALL-STARS: Toronto was represented at the 2000 All-Star game in Atlanta by David Wells, Carlos Delgado and Tony Batista... David Wells was selected to start the game and pitched two shutout innings... Was his second All-Star game start and the third All-Star game started by a Blue Jay (Dave Stieb in 1983 & 1984)... Carlos Delgado made his All-Star debut going 1-1 with a double... Tony Batista made his first All-Star appearance and was 0-1 in a pinch hit at bat.

AWARDS: Carlos Delgado was the 2000 recipient of the of the Hank Aaron Award (The annual award is bestowed on the player with the best offensive performance during the season)... As well, Delgado was named The Sporting News Player of the Year and won the Silver Slugger Award for firstbaseman in the American League... The American League Player of the Week Award was captured by the Blue Jays on three occasions... Carlos Delgado captured the honour twice during the season, April 17 to 23 and June 5 to 11... Jose Cruz was named Player of the Week from May 1 to 7.

THE ROSTER: In the 2000 season 45 different players appeared for the Blue Jays... In 1999 established a franchise high using 53 players... 45 players is tied for the second most matching the 1991 roster... This season the Blue Jays used 23 position players and 22 pitchers... The 22 pitchers matches the club record set in 1999... Toronto used 12 different starters and of the 12, five appeared as starters only

— Coco, Hamilton, Loaiza, Trachsel & Wells... Ten appeared exclusively in relief and seven pitchers saw dual roles... Toronto used five catchers, three first basemen, five second baseman, two third basemen, three shortstops and 11 outfielders... Toronto's lineup had only one switch-hitter (Cruz), seven left handed hitters and 15 right handed hitters... In 2000, eight players made their ML debut, Clayton Andrews, Pasqual Coco, Darwin Cubillan, Matt Dewitt, Leo Estrella, Josh Phelps, Andy Thompson, Dewayne Wise.

TIME OF GAME: In the 2000 season the average time of a Blue Jays game was 3:00... The average game time of a nine inning game was 2:56... At home the Blue Jays average game time for a nine inning game was 2:54... On the road the average for a nine inning game was 2:59... The average game time for a nine inning game in the American League was 3:00... Toronto played it's quickest game on May 31 vs Minnesota, game was 2:22 on April 10 in Anaheim... The longest nine inning game of the season was 3:51 on April 18 at home against Anaheim... The longest game overall was 13 inning game vs Seattle on July 29 which was 5 hours and four minutes.

EXTRA INNINGS: Were 2-6 in eight extra inning games... Were 1-2 at home and 1-4 on the road... Lost the first three extra innings games before winning 6-5 at home in 13 innings on June 25 over Boston... Then dropped the next four before posting a 3-2, 11 inning win on September 14 in New York... Were involved in two 13 inning games which were the most innings played this season, won 6-5 vs Boston on June 25 and lost 6-5 in Seattle on July 29.

ATTENDANCE: Toronto drew 1,819,886 fans to their 81 home games which is an average of 22,468 fans per game... Toronto ranked 10th in the AL in attendance average... Was the first time the Blue Jays have not drawn two million in a full season at SkyDome... Toronto was last under two million in 1983 when they drew 1,930,415... The largest single game crowd at SkyDome this season was 40,898 on Opening Day... The smallest crowd was 13,514 on April 4, the second game of the season.

EJECTIONS: The Toronto Blue Jays received nine ejections in the 2000 season after just two in 1999... Manager Jim Fregosi was ejected from three games, July 30 in Seattle by HP umpire Richard Reiker, August 10 at KC by Mike Everitt and September 30 at Cleveland by Jim Reynolds... Toronto had a season high three ejections on July 30, joining Fregosi were RHP John Frascatore by HP umpire Richard Reiker for an inside pitch to Alex Rodriguez and David Wells by crew chief Gerry Davis for comments from the dugout... Frascatore was only player ejected twice, he and OF Raul Mondesi were both sent to the showers by HP umpire Al Clark... Third base coach Terry Bevington was ejected on May 17 vs Boston Alberto Castillo on June 6 in Atlanta... Outfielder Shannon Stewart was ejected on September 19 by home plate umpire Mark Carlson.

BIG RBI GAMES (4 or More)

Player	# RBI	Date & Opponent
Batista	5	June 11 vs Montreal
	4	July 3 at Baltimore
Cordova	4	July 16 vs New York Mets
Cruz	4	April 22 at New York Yankees
Delgado	6	June 7 at Atlanta
	5	May 28 at Detroit
	4	July 6 at Cleveland
	4	August 16 vs Anaheim
	4	August 30 at Anaheim
	4	September 17 at Chicago
Fletcher	5	April 20 vs Anaheim
	4	May 8 vs Baltimore
	4	May 26 at Detroit

Player	# RBI	Date & Opponent
Fullmer	4	April 17 vs Anaheim
	4	April 19 vs Anaheim
	4	June 29 at Tampa Bay
	4	August 22 vs Kansas City
	4	August 30 at Anaheim
	4	September 9 vs Detroit
Gonzalez	5	August 13 at Minnesota
	5	August 23 vs Kansas City
	4	June 17 at Boston
Mondesi	4	June 2 at Florida
	4	June 18 at Boston
Stewart	4	June 2 at Florida
	4	June 9 vs Montreal

HITTING STREAKS

Player	Games	Dates
Batista	12	June 25 - July 7
Bush	9	July 3 - July 14
Castillo	4	May 28 - June 5 & June 7 - June 12
Cordova	5	April 29 - May 3 & May 7 - May 12
Cruz	8	April 18 - April 25
Delgado	22	June 4 - June 29
Fletcher	11	May 3 - May 16
Fullmer	11	April 16 - April 26
Gonzalez	15	August 2 - August 18
Grebeck	11	April 16 - May 25

Player	Games	Dates
Greene, C	1	July 1
Greene, T	4	August 20 - September 1
Martinez	21	August 6 - September 1
Mondesi	10	April 11 - April 21
Morandini	6	September 5 - September 13
Mottola	1	September 6
Stewart	13	August 3 - August 16
Thompson	1	May 4
Wise	1	Four times
Woodward	4	July 19 - August 3

10 RUN GAMES

Wins (16)	Score	Opponent
April 19	12-4	Anaheim
April 20	12-11	Anaheim
May 5	11-10	Cleveland
May 25	11-6	at Boston
May 28	12-7	at Detroit
June 7	12-8	at Atlanta
June 9	13-3	Montreal
June 17	11-10	at Boston
June 29	12-3	at Tampa Bay
July 9	13-3	at Montreal
August 4	10-8	Texas
August 10	15-7	at Kansas City
August 13	13-3	at Minnesota
August 30	11-2	at Anaheim
September 17	14-1	at Chicago
September 19	16-3	at New York

Losses (24)	Score	Opponent
April 7	11-5	at Texas
April 14	11-9	Seattle
April 15	17-6	Seattle
April 16	19-7	Seattle
April 18	16-10	Anaheim
April 23	10-7	New York
April 25	11-2	at Oakland
May 7	10-8 (12)	Cleveland
June 2	11-10	at Florida
June 10	11-2	Montreal
June 13	16-3	at Detroit
June 20	18-6	Detroit
June 27	11-1	at Tampa Bay
July 1	12-5	at Baltimore
July 5	15-7	at Cleveland
July 7	10-5	at Montreal
July 18	11-7	New York Mets
July 25	10-3	Cleveland
July 30	10-6	at Seattle
August 6	11-6	Texas
September 4	10-0	Oakland
September 12	10-2	at New York
September 28	23-1	at Baltimore
October 1	11-4	at Cleveland

INJURED PLAYERS & DISABLED LIST

Player	Injury	Dates	Games Missed
Joey Hamilton	Right shoulder	March 21-Aug 17	123
Shannon Stewart	Right hamstring	April 29-May 14	14
Lance Painter	Left elbow	May 17-June 5	19
Homer Bush	Right hip	May 22-June 5	14
Pete Munro	Right elbow	June 3-July 2	26
Dewayne Wise	Left great toe	June 6-Aug 31	72
Todd Greene	Right knee	June 7-June 21	12
Darrin Fletcher	Right shoulder	June 11-July 3	20
Alex Gonzalez	Right groin	July 7-July 21	12
Raul Mondesi	Right elbow	July 22-September 20	52
Homer Bush	Fracture in L hand	July 31- end of season	56
Frank Castillo	Sprained R forearm	August 14-September 15	27
Matt DeWitt	Broken R leg	August 23- end of season	35
13 stints on DL			**482**

SURGERIES IN 2000

Player	Date	Surgeon	Body part
Darrin Fletcher	February 28	Dr. Steve Mirabello	Right knee, frayed meniscus
Dewayne Wise	June 19	Dr. Allan Gross	Left great toe
Raul Mondesi	August 14	Dr. John Uribe	Right elbow
Homer Bush	September 6	Dr. Joe McCarthy	Right hip
Pedro Borbon	October 19	Dr. James Andrews	Left elbow
Brad Fullmer	October 10	Dr. Lewis Yokum	Right elbow

STARTS IN THE BATTING ORDER

Player	GS	GS Breakdown	1st	2nd	3rd	4th	5th	6th	7th	8th	9th
Batista	154	154-3B			10		46	98			
Bush	73	73-2B		52							21
Castillo	57	57-C								23	34
Cordova	52	14-DH/21-LF/17-RF					2	14	14	22	
Cruz	162	162-CF	25	6	7		3	21	50	50	
Delgado	162	162-1B				162					
Ducey	2	1-RF/1-LF	1							1	
Fletcher	105	103-C/2-DH					10	5	79	11	
Fullmer	116	116-DH			5		100	6	5		
Gonzalez	140	140-SS		61				3	5	32	39
Grebeck	60	55-2B/5-SS		39						9	12
Greene, C	2	2-C								2	
Greene, T	21	21-DH					1	14	2	4	
Martinez	46	46-RF			43			1	2		
Mondesi	95	95-RF			95						
Morandini	31	31-2B									31
Mottola	2	2-RF			2						
Stewart	136	136-LF	136								
Thompson	2	2-LF							2		
Wise	3	2-LF/1-RF									3
Woodward	28	17-SS/3-2B/8-3B		4					3	8	13
PITCHERS	9	9-P									9
TOTAL			162	162	162	162	162	162	162	162	162

	HITS by GAME						RBI by GAME						
	1	2	3	4	5	Total	1	2	3	4	5	6	Total
Batista	48	34	13	2		163	36	18	11	1	1		114
Bush	25	15	3			64	11	2	1				18
Castillo	25	4	2			39	10	3					16
Cordova	27	9		1		49	10	2		1			18
Cruz	57	31	9			146	38	11	4	1			76
Delgado	63	44	15			196	38	27	6	4	1	1	137
Ducey	2					2	1						1
Fletcher	47	22	10	3		133	19	10	2	2	1		58
Fullmer	47	32	9	1		142	27	14	7	7			104
Gonzalez	65	25	6			133	28	12	1	1	2		69
Grebeck	24	14	5	1		71	13	5					23
Greene, C	1					1							0
Greene, T	14	3				20	8	1					10
Martinez	18	13	4			56	9	2	3				22
Mondesi	36	24	7			105	17	12	6	2			67
Morandini	15	4	2			29	5	1					7
Mottola		1				2		1					2
Stewart	46	43	10	6		186	30	11	3	2			69
Thompson	1					1	1						1
Wise	3					3							0
Woodward	10	3	1			19	4	2	2				14

INNING SCORES:

	1st	2nd	3rd	4th	5th	6th	7th	8th	9th	10th	11th	12th	13th	Total
Blue Jays	118	83	112	97	99	96	95	90	68		2		1	861
Opponents	116	97	96	117	105	106	87	106	66	2	7	2	1	908

MULTIPLE RUN INNINGS:

	1R	2R	3R	4R	5R	6R	7R	8R	9R	10R	Total
Blue Jays	235	114	53	33	14	5	1				861
Opponents	247	108	49	31	18	6	3	1	1	1	908

GLANCING AT THE BLUE JAYS

Last Homestand	4-3
Last Roadtrip	1-5
Come From Behind Wins	41
Last Shutout by BJ	4-0, Sept. 27 at BAL
Last Shutout by Opp	6-0, Sept. 24 vs TB
April '00/ '99/ '98	12-14/ 13-11/ 10-16
May '00/ '99/ '98	16-12/ 11-17/ 18-11
June '00/ '99/ '98	16-10/ 15-13/ 14-14
July '00/'99/'98	11-16/ 19-7/ 12-15
August '00/'99/'98	15-11/ 12-16/ 17-10
Sept/Oct '00/'99/'98	13-16/ 14-14/ 17-8
At ASB	48-41
Since ASB	36-37
LONGEST WINNING STREAK	5, June 20-25
LONGEST LOSING STREAK	6, July 28-Aug. 2
FARTHEST FROM 1ST PLACE	10.0, Sept. 13
LARGEST 1ST PLACE LEAD	3.0, June 28-29-30
vs starting RHP/LHP	64-55/19-24
BJ's/OPP scoring first	51-27/32-52
GMS decided in final AB	17-13
1-Run/2-Run Games	21-19/14-8
Extra-Inning Games/Home/Road	2-6/1-2/1-4
Franchise record	1867-1897-3
Home/Road	45-36/38-43
Day/Night	28-27/55-51
vs EAST/CENTRAL/WEST/NL	28-21/28-25/18-24/9-9
Blue Jays HR Dome Open/Cld.	76/58
Opponents HR Dome Open/Cld.	44/48
2000 open/closed/other	26-12/16-21/3-3
1999 open/closed/other	17-34/18-6/4-2
All-time*/open/closed/other	237-226/237-168/34-30

*-includes post-season

When	Ahead	Tied	Trailing
After 6 innings	65-9	7-7	11-63
After 7 innings	69-6	6-7	8-66
After 8 innings	74-1	6-7	3-71
After 9 innings	—	2-6	—

OUTFIELD ASSISTS:

CORDOVA	1
CRUZ	8
DUCEY	1
MARTINEZ	8
MONDESI	7
STEWART	7

EXPANSION TEAMS WON-LOST RECORDS (BY PERCENTAGE)

TEAM	YEARS	WON	LOST	PCT
Arizona	1998-2000	250	236	.514
Kansas City	1969-2000	2548	2497	.505
Toronto	**1977-2000**	**1867**	**1897**	**.496**
Houston	1962-2000	3052	3138	.493
Montreal	1969-2000	2454	2596	.486
Anaheim	1991-2000	3069	3281	.483
Colorado	1993-2000	594	639	.482
Milwaukee*+	1969-2000	2421	2631	.479
New York Mets	1962-2000	2935	3244	.475
Texas**	1961-2000	2952	3381	.466
San Diego	1969-2000	2315	2742	.458
Seattle	1977-2000	1715	2048	.456
Florida	1993-2000	551	678	.448
Tampa Bay	1998-2000	201	284	.414

*- Franchise was located in Seattle in 1969.
**- Franchise was located in Washington DC from 1961-1971.
+- Franchise moved to the National League in 1998.

TEAM STATISTICS

+ = ROOKIE

PLAYER	AVG	G	AB	R	H	TB	2B	3B	HR	RBI	SH-SF	HP	BB-IBB	SO	SB-CS	GIDP	E	SLG	OBP
+Andrews, C	.000	8	3	0	0	0	0	0	0	0	0-0	0	0-0	2	0-0	0	0	.000	.000
Batista, T	.263	154	620	96	163	322	32	2	41	114	0-3	6	35-1	121	5-4	15	17	.519	.307
Bush, H	.215	76	297	38	64	75	8	0	1	18	4-1	5	18-0	60	9-4	10	6	.253	.271
Carpenter, C	.000	34	2	0	0	0	0	0	0	0	0-0	0	0-0	1	0-0	0	1	.000	.000
Castillo, A	.211	66	185	14	39	49	7	0	1	16	2-3	0	21-0	36	0-0	3	3	.265	.287
Castillo, F	.143	25	7	0	1	1	0	0	0	0	0-0	0	0-0	3	0-0	0	1	.143	.143
Cordova, M	.245	62	200	23	49	68	7	0	4	18	0-0	3	18-0	35	3-2	6	1	.340	.317
Cruz Jr, J	.242	162	603	91	146	281	32	5	31	76	2-3	2	71-3	129	15-5	11	3	.466	.323
RIGHT	.289	–	166	–	48	79	12	2	5	19	1-0	1	11-0	23	–	6	–	.476	.337
LEFT	.224	–	437	–	98	202	20	3	26	57	1-3	1	60-3	106	–	5	–	.462	.317
+Cubillan, D	.000	7	1	0	0	0	0	0	0	0	0-0	0	0-0	0	0-0	0	0	.000	.000
Delgado, C	.344	162	569	115	196	378	57	1	41	137	0-4	15	123-18	104	0-1	12	13	.664	.470
Ducey, R	.154	5	13	2	2	3	1	0	0	1	0-0	0	2-0	2	0-0	0	1	.231	.267
Escobar, K	.000	43	7	0	0	0	0	0	0	0	0-0	0	0-0	4	0-0	0	1	.000	.000
Fletcher, D	.320	122	416	43	133	214	19	1	20	58	0-4	5	20-3	45	1-0	8	4	.514	.355
Fullmer, B	.295	133	482	76	142	269	29	1	32	104	0-6	6	30-3	68	3-1	14	0	.558	.340
Gonzalez, A	.252	141	527	68	133	213	31	2	15	69	16-1	4	43-0	113	4-4	14	16	.404	.313
Grebeck, C	.295	66	241	38	71	99	19	0	3	23	1-1	2	25-0	33	0-0	7	9	.411	.364
+Greene, C	.111	3	9	0	1	1	0	0	0	0	0-0	0	0-0	5	0-0	0	0	.111	.111
Greene, T	.235	34	85	11	20	37	2	0	5	10	0-0	0	5-0	18	0-0	4	0	.435	.278
Koch, B	.000	68	1	0	0	0	0	0	0	0	0-0	0	0-0	1	0-0	0	0	.000	.000
Loaiza, E	.000	14	0	0	0	0	0	0	0	0	0-0	0	0-0	0	0-0	0	2	.000	.000
Martinez, D	.311	47	180	29	56	74	10	1	2	22	0-1	1	24-0	28	4-2	3	2	.411	.393
Mondesi, R	.271	96	388	78	105	203	22	2	24	67	0-3	3	32-0	73	22-6	8	7	.523	.329
Morandini, M	.271	35	107	10	29	33	2	1	0	7	2-0	0	7-0	23	1-0	2	1	.308	.316
+Mottola, C	.222	3	9	1	2	2	0	0	0	2	0-0	1	0-0	4	0-0	0	0	.222	.300
Munro, P	.000	9	1	0	0	0	0	0	0	0	0-0	0	0-0	1	0-0	0	0	.000	.000
+Phelps, J	.000	1	1	0	0	0	0	0	0	0	0-0	0	0-0	1	0-0	0	0	.000	.000
Quantrill, P	.000	68	0	0	0	0	0	0	0	0	0-0	0	1-0	0	0-0	0	0	.000	1.000
Stewart, S	.319	136	583	107	186	302	43	5	21	69	1-4	6	37-1	79	20-5	12	2	.518	.363
+Thompson, A	.167	2	6	2	1	1	0	0	0	1	0-0	0	3-0	2	0-0	0	0	.167	.444
Trachsel, S	.000	11	0	0	0	0	0	0	0	0	0-0	0	0-0	0	0-0	0	0	.000	.000
Wells, D	.167	35	6	0	1	1	0	0	0	0	0-0	0	0-0	2	0-0	0	3	.167	.167
+Wells, V	.000	3	2	0	0	0	0	0	0	0	0-0	0	0-0	0	0-0	0	0	.000	.000
+Wise, D	.136	28	22	3	3	3	0	0	0	0	0-0	1	1-0	5	1-0	0	0	.136	.208
+Woodward, C	.183	37	104	16	19	35	7	0	3	14	1-0	0	10-3	28	1-0	1	5	.337	.254
PITCHERS	.071	162	28	0	2	2	0	0	0	0	0-0	0	1-0	14	0-0	0	10	.071	.103
DH	.285	162	606	92	173	325	33	1	39	120	0-6	4	38-3	93	3-2	18	0	.536	.331
TORONTO	.275	162	5677	861	1562	2664	328	21	244	826	29-34	60	526-32	1026	89-34	130	100	.469	.341
OPPONENTS	.285	162	5669	908	1615	2584	338	23	195	862	44-40	64	560-19	978	99-38	142	103	.456	.354

PITCHER	R/L	W-L	ERA	G	GS	CG	SHO	SV	IP	H	R	ER	HR	HB	BB-IBB	SO	WP	BK	OPP AVG
+Andrews, C	L	1-2	10.02	8	2	0	0	0	20.2	34	23	23	6	0	9-0	12	0	1	.374
+Bale, J	L	0-0	14.73	2	0	0	0	0	3.2	5	7	6	1	2	3-0	6	0	0	.313
Borbon, P	L	1-1	6.48	59	0	0	0	1	41.2	45	37	30	5	5	38-5	29	0	0	.280
Carpenter, C	R	10-12	6.26	34	27	2	0	0	175.1	204	130	122	30	5	83-1	113	3	0	.290
Castillo, F	R	10-5	3.59	25	24	0	0	0	138.0	112	58	55	18	5	56-0	104	0	0	.220
+Coco (Reyn, P	R	0-0	9.00	1	1	0	0	0	4.0	5	4	4	1	1	5-0	2	1	0	.294
+Cubillan, D	R	1-0	8.04	7	0	0	0	0	15.2	20	14	14	5	1	11-0	14	0	0	.317
+Dewitt, M	R	1-0	8.56	8	0	0	0	0	13.2	20	13	13	4	2	9-0	6	1	0	.351
Escobar, K	R	10-15	5.35	43	24	3	1	2	180.0	186	118	107	26	3	85-3	142	4	0	.267
+Estrella, L	R	0-0	5.79	2	0	0	0	0	4.2	9	3	3	1	0	0-0	3	0	0	.450
Frascatore, J	R	2-4	5.42	60	0	0	0	0	73.0	87	51	44	14	7	33-2	30	3	0	.301
Gunderson, E	L	0-1	7.11	6	0	0	0	0	6.1	15	6	5	0	1	2-1	2	0	0	.455
Guthrie, M	L	0-2	4.79	23	0	0	0	0	20.2	20	12	11	3	1	9-0	20	2	0	.263
Halladay, R	R	4-7	10.64	19	13	0	0	0	67.2	107	87	80	14	2	42-0	44	6	1	.357
Hamilton, J	R	2-1	3.55	6	6	0	0	0	33.0	28	13	13	3	2	12-0	15	0	0	.233
Koch, B	R	9-3	2.63	68	0	0	0	33	78.2	78	28	23	6	2	18-4	60	1	0	.258
Loaiza, E	R	5-7	3.62	14	14	1	1	0	92.0	95	45	37	8	10	26-0	62	0	0	.270
Munro, P	R	1-1	5.96	9	3	0	0	0	25.2	38	22	17	1	3	16-0	16	1	0	.355
Painter, L	L	2-0	4.73	42	2	0	0	0	66.2	69	37	35	9	2	22-1	53	4	0	.271
Quantrill, P	R	2-5	4.52	68	0	0	0	1	83.2	100	45	42	7	2	25-1	47	1	0	.298
Trachsel, S	R	2-5	5.29	11	11	0	0	0	63.0	72	40	37	10	0	25-1	32	1	0	.293
Wells, D	L	20-8	4.11	35	35	9	1	0	229.2	266	115	105	23	8	31-0	166	9	1	.289
TORONTO		83-79	5.14	162	162	15	4	37	1437.1	1615	908	821	195	64	560-19	978	37	3	.285
OPPONENTS		79-83	5.03	162	162	9	7	35	1437.2	1562	861	804	244	60	526-32	1026	50	6	.275

INDIVIDUAL FIELDING

PITCHER	T	PCT	RANK	G	GS	PO	A	E	TC	DP	TP
+Andrews, C	L	1.000	0	8	2	0	1	0	1	0	0
+Bale, J	L	.000	0	2	0	0	0	0	0	0	0
Borbon, P	L	1.000	0	59	0	2	9	0	11	1	0
Carpenter, C	R	.950	25	34	27	7	12	1	20	2	0
Castillo, F	R	.964	0	25	24	8	19	1	28	4	0
+Coco (Reyn, P	R	.000	0	1	1	0	0	0	0	0	0
+Cubillan, D	R	1.000	0	7	0	1	2	0	3	1	0
+Dewitt, M	R	1.000	0	8	0	2	1	0	3	0	0
Escobar, K	R	.963	18	43	24	11	15	1	27	1	0
+Estrella, L	R	1.000	0	2	0	0	1	0	1	0	0
Frascatore, J	R	.923	0	60	0	7	5	1	13	2	0
Gunderson, E	L	.667	0	6	0	0	2	1	3	0	0
Guthrie, M	L	1.000	0	23	0	0	1	0	1	0	0
Halladay, R	R	1.000	0	19	13	4	7	0	11	0	0
Hamilton, J	R	1.000	0	6	6	2	2	0	4	1	0
Koch, B	R	1.000	0	68	0	5	8	0	13	2	0
Loaiza, E	R	.882	29	14	14	4	11	2	17	1	0
Painter, L	L	1.000	0	42	2	4	17	0	21	2	0
Quantrill, P	R	1.000	0	68	0	3	9	0	12	0	0
Trachsel, S	R	1.000	1	11	11	8	11	0	19	0	0
Wells, D	L	.897	35	35	35	8	18	3	29	1	0

CATCHER	T	PCT	RANK	G	GS	PO	A	E	TC	DP	TP	PB
Castillo, A	R	.993	0	66	57	372	31	3	406	2	0	5
Fletcher, D	R	.994	2	117	103	621	39	4	664	7	0	6
+Greene, C	R	1.000	0	3	2	13	0	0	13	0	0	0
Greene, T	R	1.000	0	2	0	2	0	0	2	0	0	0
+Phelps, J	R	1.000	0	1	0	1	0	0	1	0	0	0

FIRST BASE	T	PCT	RANK	G	GS	PO	A	E	TC	DP	TP
Delgado, C	R	.991	8	162	162	1416	82	13	1511	157	0
Fullmer, B	R	1.000	0	1	0	2	1	0	3	0	0
+Woodward, C	R	1.000	0	3	0	6	1	0	7	1	0

SECOND BASE	T	PCT	RANK	G	GS	PO	A	E	TC	DP	TP
Bush, H	R	.986	0	75	73	165	246	6	417	68	0
Grebeck, C	R	.968	0	56	55	100	174	9	283	34	0
Morandini, M	R	.993	0	35	31	58	92	1	151	28	0
+Woodward, C	R	.941	0	3	3	5	11	1	17	1	0

THIRD BASE	T	PCT	RANK	G	GS	PO	A	E	TC	DP	TP
Batista, T	R	.963	5	154	154	120	318	17	455	35	0
+Woodward, C	R	1.000	0	9	8	5	18	0	23	3	0

SHORTSTOP	T	PCT	RANK	G	GS	PO	A	E	TC	DP	TP
Gonzalez, A	R	.975	6	141	140	213	407	16	636	100	0
Grebeck, C	R	1.000	0	8	5	10	19	0	29	4	0
+Woodward, C	R	.955	0	22	17	26	58	4	88	9	0

OUTFIELDERS	T	PCT	RANK	G	GS	PO	A	E	TC	DP	TP
Cordova, M	R	.982	0	41	38	55	1	1	57	1	0
Cruz Jr, J	R	.993	6	162	162	405	9	3	417	1	0
Ducey, R	R	.889	0	3	2	8	0	1	9	0	0
Greene, T	R	.000	0	1	0	0	0	0	0	0	0
Martinez, D	L	.982	8	47	46	101	8	2	111	2	0
Mondesi, R	R	.967	0	96	95	203	5	7	215	3	0
+Mottola, C	R	1.000	0	3	2	5	0	0	5	0	0
Stewart, S	R	.993	4	136	136	298	5	2	305	2	0
+Thompson, A	R	1.000	0	2	2	2	0	0	2	0	0
+Wells, V	R	1.000	0	3	0	2	0	0	2	0	0
+Wise, D	L	1.000	0	18	3	20	0	0	20	0	0

BLUE JAYS SWITCH-HITTERS

Roberto Alomar	IF	Dave McKay	IF
Alan Ashby	C	Brian McRae	OF
Bobby Brown	OF	Otis Nixon	OF
Domingo Cedeno	IF	Tomas Perez	IF
Dave Collins	OF	Geno Petralli	C/IF
Felipe Crespo	IF	Tony Phillips	OF
Jose Cruz	OF	David Segui	IF/DH
Junior Felix	OF	Ruben Sierra	OF
Tony Fernandez	IF	Turner Ward	OF
Alfredo Griffin	IF	Mitch Webster	OF
Dave Hollins	DH	Devon White	OF
Manny Lee	IF	Mark Whiten	OF
Nelson Liriano	IF	Ted Wilborn	OF
Lee Mazzilli	OF/DH	Mookie Wilson	OF

Road Hitters

BATTER	AVG	G	AB	R	H	2B	3B	HR	RBI	SH-SF	HP	BB	SO	SB-CS	GIDP	E
Batista, T	.256	75	313	39	80	14	1	16	54	0-2	3	13	58	1-2	7	5
Bush, H	.217	35	138	23	30	4	0	0	2	4-0	3	11	28	6-1	9	1
Castillo, A	.189	36	106	8	20	4	0	0	10	1-2	0	12	22	0-0	3	3
Cordova, M	.235	29	85	8	20	3	0	1	3	0-0	0	8	15	0-1	1	1
Cruz Jr, J	.235	81	315	45	74	15	3	16	36	0-1	0	32	69	6-3	6	3
Delgado, C	.329	81	286	51	94	29	1	11	62	0-3	10	64	62	0-0	4	4
Ducey, R	.167	4	12	2	2	1	0	0	1	0-0	0	2	2	0-0	0	1
Fletcher, D	.306	58	196	19	60	8	1	10	24	0-3	3	10	24	1-0	6	1
Fullmer, B	.298	64	228	34	68	13	1	16	54	0-3	2	15	37	1-1	8	0
Gonzalez, A	.259	70	274	34	71	14	1	10	44	7-1	0	22	64	2-3	7	9
Grebeck, C	.293	35	133	24	39	10	0	1	11	0-1	2	13	22	0-0	3	9
Greene, C	.111	3	9	0	1	0	0	0	0	0-0	0	0	5	0-0	0	0
Greene, C	.278	23	54	6	15	1	0	3	8	0-0	0	1	11	0-0	1	0
Martinez, D	.312	23	93	14	29	2	0	1	11	0-1	0	12	17	3-1	1	1
Mondesi, R	.290	47	186	42	54	7	1	14	39	0-1	3	17	38	14-2	2	4
Morandini, M	.264	16	53	6	14	0	0	0	4	1-0	0	3	12	0-0	2	0
Mottola, C	.000	2	6	0	0	0	0	0	0	0-0	0	0	4	0-0	0	0
Phelps, J	.000	1	1	0	0	0	0	0	0	0-0	0	0	1	0-0	0	0
Stewart, S	.349	70	307	59	107	19	3	9	37	0-4	1	23	42	14-4	6	2
Thompson, A	.000	1	3	0	0	0	0	0	0	0-0	0	2	1	0-0	0	0
Wells, V	.000	1	1	0	0	0	0	0	0	0-0	0	0	0	0-0	0	0
Wise, D	.133	16	15	2	2	0	0	0	0	0-0	0	1	4	1-0	0	0
Woodward, C	.174	22	69	10	12	6	0	2	11	1-0	0	9	18	1-0	1	3
PITCHERS	.071	81	28	0	2	0	0	0	0	0-0	0	1	14	0-0	0	4
TOTALS	.273	81	2911	426	794	150	12	110	411	14-22	27	271	570	50-18	67	51

Designated Hitters

BATTER	B	AVG	G	AB	R	H	TB	2B	3B	HR	RBI	SH-SF	HP	BB-IBB	SO	SB-CS	DP	SLG	OBP
Cordova, M	R	.292	15	48	5	14	20	3	0	1	6	0-0	0	3-0	6	0-1	0	.417	.333
Fletcher, D	L	.333	2	6	2	2	5	0	0	1	1	0-0	0	0-0	1	0-0	0	.833	.333
Fullmer, B	L	.295	129	478	75	141	268	29	1	32	104	0-6	6	30-3	68	3-1	14	.561	.340
Greene, T	R	.216	23	74	10	16	32	1	0	5	9	0-0	0	5-0	18	0-0	4	.432	.266
Wise, D	L	.000	2	0	0	0	0	0	0	0	0	0-0	0	0-0	0	0-0	0	.000	.000
TOTALS		.285		606	92	173	325	33	1	39	120	0-6	6	38-3	93	3-2	18	.536	.331

Pinch Hitters

BATTER	B	AVG	G	AB	R	H	TB	2B	3B	HR	RBI	SH-SF	HP	BB-IBB	SO	SB-CS	DP	SLG	OBP
Cordova, M	R	.333	7	6	1	2	2	0	0	0	1	0-0	0	1-0	2	0-0	0	.333	.429
Ducey, R	L	.000	2	2	0	0	0	0	0	0	0	0-0	0	0-0	0	0-0	0	.000	.000
Fletcher, D	L	.308	14	13	1	4	5	1	0	0	2	0-0	0	1-0	2	0-0	0	.385	.357
Fullmer, B	L	.214	17	14	1	3	3	0	0	0	1	0-1	0	2-1	3	0-0	1	.214	.294
Grebeck, C	R	.500	4	2	1	1	2	1	0	0	1	0-0	0	0-0	0	0-0	0	1.000	.750
Greene, T	R	.400	10	10	2	4	5	1	0	0	3	0-0	0	0-0	0	0-0	1	.500	.400
Martinez, D	L	1.000	1	1	0	1	1	0	0	0	0	0-0	0	0-0	0	0-0	0	1.000	1.000
Mondesi, R	R	.000	1	1	0	0	0	0	0	0	0	0-0	0	0-0	0	0-0	0	.000	.000
Morandini, M	L	1.000	2	1	0	1	1	0	0	0	0	1-0	0	0-0	0	0-0	0	1.000	1.000
Wise, D	L	1.000	1	1	0	1	1	0	0	0	0	0-0	0	0-0	0	1-0	0	1.000	1.000
TOTALS		.333		51	6	17	20	3	0	0	8	1-1	0	6-1	7	1-0	2	.392	.397

TORONTO BLUE JAYS TEAM PINCH HITTING RECORDS

Season Records:

Most at-bats: 40, Rick Leach, 1987

Most Hits: 11, Wayne Nordhagen, 1982;
Cliff Johnson, 1984

Most Home Runs: 3, Willie Greene, 1999

Most RBI: 9, Garth Iorg, 1986

Most Walks: 12, Cliff Johnson, 1983

Most Strikeouts: 8, Cliff Johnson, 1984;
Cecil Fielder, 1987 & 1988; Shawn Green, 1995

Blue Jays' All Time Career Pinch Hit Leaders:

1. Rance Mulliniks - 59
2. Garth Iorg - 41
3. Rick Leach - 27
4. Ernie Whitt - 26
5. Cliff Johnson - 24
6. Pat Borders - 23
7. Jesse Barfield - 22
8. Buck Martinez - 14
9. Cecil Fielder - 11
9. Wayne Nordhagen - 11
9. Dave Collins - 11

Blue Jays Team Pinch Hitting Records, 1977-2000

		Year				Year
Most At Bats:	262	1982		Most Runs:	29	1984
Most Hits:	71	1982		Most Runs Batted In:	53	1982
Most Doubles:	14	1982		Most Walks:	39	1982
Most Triples:	2	1984		Most Strikeouts:	51	1984
Most Home Runs:	6	1984				

BATTING PROFILE

	AVG	AB	R	H	2B	3B	HR	RBI	SB	CS	TBB	SO	OBP	SLG
Total	.275	5677	861	1562	328	21	244	826	89	34	526	1026	.341	.469
vs. Left	.275	1428	–	392	90	6	39	184	13	10	135	256	.343	.428
vs. Right	.275	4249	–	1170	238	15	205	642	76	24	391	770	.341	.483
Home	.278	2766	435	768	178	9	134	415	39	16	255	456	.344	.494
Away	.273	2911	426	794	150	12	110	411	50	18	271	570	.338	.446
None on	.270	3169	–	857	178	16	141	141	0	0	273	572	.334	.470
Runners on	.281	2508	–	705	150	5	103	685	89	34	253	454	.350	.468
April	.281	896	143	252	57	3	43	137	13	7	73	153	.346	.496
May	.277	995	141	276	49	4	43	131	21	8	88	186	.337	.464
June	.272	934	161	254	51	4	48	157	24	3	82	174	.334	.489
July	.268	942	143	252	61	2	44	139	13	9	105	178	.344	.477
August	.314	947	155	297	52	4	43	152	12	3	85	156	.375	.513
September	.240	928	114	223	57	4	21	106	6	4	93	171	.314	.378
October	.229	35	4	8	1	0	2	4	0	0	0	8	.229	.429
None on/out	.288	1407	–	405	92	11	68	68	0	0	119	245	.349	.514
Scoring Posn	.283	1460	–	413	94	2	69	596	12	3	172	281	.358	.492
ScPos/2 Out	.240	647	–	155	41	0	32	227	9	1	91	140	.341	.451
Close & Late	.279	703	–	196	37	3	24	107	10	5	73	147	.349	.442
Bases Loaded	.281	128	–	36	5	0	9	111	0	0	2	21	.277	.531
Batting #1	.313	712	129	223	49	5	31	93	23	5	51	110	.363	.527
Batting #2	.244	685	96	167	33	2	12	64	8	4	51	136	.302	.350
Batting #3	.274	661	117	181	34	4	29	102	26	9	61	127	.341	.469
Batting #4	.345	571	116	197	58	1	41	138	0	1	123	105	.470	.665
Batting #5	.282	650	92	183	38	1	37	128	5	3	38	99	.326	.514
Batting #6	.263	642	94	169	29	3	39	108	5	3	41	120	.311	.500
Batting #7	.267	611	78	163	25	2	33	87	5	1	50	84	.324	.476
Batting #8	.252	571	79	144	40	2	15	55	11	7	66	129	.331	.408
Batting #9	.235	574	60	135	22	1	7	51	6	1	45	116	.294	.314
As ph for dh	.231	13	1	3	0	0	0	3	0	0	2	4	.313	.231
As p	.071	28	0	2	0	0	0	0	0	0	1	14	.103	.071
As c	.281	594	54	167	25	1	20	71	1	0	40	84	.328	.428
As 1b	.344	570	115	196	57	1	41	137	0	1	123	105	.469	.663
As 2b	.254	631	83	160	28	1	4	50	9	3	47	117	.311	.320
As 3b	.262	648	103	170	33	2	44	122	6	4	39	124	.309	.523
As ss	.240	613	76	147	37	2	15	72	4	4	50	136	.301	.380
As lf	.310	693	123	215	47	5	23	80	22	5	47	101	.360	.492
As cf	.240	609	91	146	32	5	31	76	15	5	71	129	.320	.461
As rf	.266	647	114	172	33	3	27	93	27	9	66	120	.337	.451
All OF	.273	1949	328	533	112	13	81	249	64	19	184	350	.340	.469
As dh (not ph)	.287	593	91	170	33	1	39	117	3	2	36	89	.331	.543
As ph (not dh	.368	38	5	14	3	0	0	5	1	0	4	3	.429	.447
As pr	.000	0	5	0	0	0	0	0	1	1	0	0	.000	.000
All DH	.285	606	92	173	33	1	39	120	3	2	38	93	.331	.536
All PH	.333	51	6	17	3	0	0	8	1	0	6	7	.397	.392
0-0 count	.347	848	–	294	63	2	55	178	–	–	20	0	.366	.620
After (0-1)	.242	2512	–	607	122	11	74	282	–	–	141	668	.288	.387
After (1-0)	.285	2317	–	661	143	8	115	366	–	–	365	358	.385	.503
Two strikes	.198	2576	–	511	99	5	67	259	–	–	233	1026	.271	.319
Grass	.268	2469	350	661	124	11	90	339	43	13	221	486	.331	.436
Turf	.281	3208	511	901	204	10	154	487	46	21	305	540	.349	.495
Day	.270	1991	314	537	120	7	92	304	28	13	171	387	.335	.476
Night	.278	3686	547	1025	208	14	152	522	61	21	355	639	.345	.466
Inning 1-6	.281	3856	605	1082	239	13	170	581	68	27	349	656	.345	.482
Inning 7+	.264	1821	256	480	89	8	74	245	21	7	177	370	.333	.443
vs. Ana	.319	429	82	137	23	1	24	79	3	3	45	59	.391	.545
vs. Bal	.245	436	52	107	16	3	22	52	7	2	27	72	.290	.447
vs. Bos	.273	440	62	120	16	2	21	57	16	2	30	77	.326	.461
vs. CWS	.252	349	45	88	22	1	16	44	6	3	34	72	.319	.458
vs. Cle	.291	433	77	126	28	2	21	76	5	4	52	100	.368	.510
vs. Det	.272	408	72	111	26	1	18	69	5	3	35	78	.331	.473
vs. KC	.295	353	64	104	20	2	21	63	8	1	27	57	.357	.541
vs. Min	.267	303	36	81	16	1	10	35	4	3	23	61	.320	.426
vs. NYY	.283	420	63	119	28	2	11	59	2	0	26	85	.333	.438
vs. Oak	.215	325	22	70	12	2	5	21	4	1	34	59	.299	.311
vs. Sea	.277	364	55	101	26	0	13	53	6	2	34	72	.347	.456
vs. TB	.259	410	53	106	22	1	17	48	5	4	42	62	.327	.441
vs. Tex	.308	364	56	112	25	2	14	52	3	2	36	61	.374	.503
vs. Atl	.284	109	27	31	9	0	5	27	3	0	17	27	.385	.505
vs. Fla	.283	113	18	32	7	0	4	18	4	0	7	25	.333	.451
vs. Mon	.308	214	47	66	18	0	10	44	5	1	32	29	.403	.533
vs. NYM	.243	107	19	26	9	1	6	18	3	2	19	19	.354	.514
vs. Phi	.250	100	11	25	5	0	6	11	0	1	6	11	.299	.480
Pre-All Star	.278	3146	502	875	179	11	147	481	65	20	285	575	.343	.482
Post-All Star	.271	2531	359	687	149	10	97	345	24	14	241	451	.339	.453

PITCHING PROFILE

	ERA	W-L	Sv	SvOp	GS	CG	IP	H	R	ER	HR	TBB	IBB	SO
Total	5.14	83-79	37	52	162	15	1437.1	1615	908	821	195	560	19	978
ST	5.23	59-59	0	0	162	15	957.2	1053	599	556	130	363	3	651
REL	4.97	24-20	37	52	0	0	479.2	562	309	265	65	197	16	327
Home	5.22	45-36	19	28	81	8	738.0	819	464	428	92	279	8	526
Away	5.06	38-43	18	24	81	7	699.1	796	444	393	103	281	11	452
April	6.42	12-14	5	6	26	4	227.0	285	175	162	36	94	2	143
May	4.39	16-12	7	10	28	2	254.0	258	132	124	27	102	1	169
June	5.37	16-10	6	8	26	3	231.1	274	151	138	34	93	2	177
July	5.74	11-16	7	10	27	2	240.0	265	170	153	34	122	7	169
August	4.66	15-11	9	12	26	1	230.0	260	130	119	26	75	3	163
September	4.23	13-15	3	6	28	3	247.0	261	139	116	34	73	4	150
October	10.13	0-1	0	0	1	0	8.0	12	11	9	4	1	0	7
Grass	5.13	31-38	17	23	69	4	596.1	688	384	340	90	257	10	389
Turf	5.15	52-41	20	29	93	11	841.0	927	524	481	105	303	9	589
Day	5.04	28-28	8	16	56	6	506.2	570	318	284	63	173	6	386
Night	5.19	55-51	29	36	106	9	930.2	1045	590	537	132	387	13	592
vs. Ana	5.91	7-5	2	2	12	1	105.0	129	72	69	17	43	2	70
vs. Bal	5.30	6-7	5	5	13	1	112.0	139	81	66	14	40	0	73
vs. Bos	4.55	8-4	5	5	12	0	112.2	130	67	57	8	39	1	87
vs. CWS	3.68	5-5	3	5	10	0	88.0	68	39	36	13	36	1	55
vs. Cle	7.13	4-8	1	4	12	1	106.0	139	95	84	18	58	3	85
vs. Det	4.82	9-3	2	3	12	2	106.1	116	61	57	19	39	0	74
vs. KC	4.70	6-4	3	5	10	0	88.0	104	54	46	8	26	1	49
vs. Min	4.10	4-5	2	3	9	1	79.0	84	39	36	8	33	0	68
vs. NYY	3.99	7-5	2	2	12	3	106.0	107	51	47	13	25	3	61
vs. Oak	5.34	3-7	2	2	10	1	87.2	103	54	52	16	28	0	63
vs. Sea	7.32	2-8	0	1	10	0	91.0	112	87	74	16	61	4	54
vs. TB	4.33	7-5	2	3	12	3	106.0	99	53	51	13	25	0	63
vs. Tex	4.84	6-4	5	6	10	1	89.1	97	51	48	11	34	1	54
vs. Atl	6.15	2-1	1	2	3	0	26.1	36	18	18	3	17	1	18
vs. Fla	4.32	1-2	0	1	3	1	25.0	30	15	12	3	11	0	25
vs. Mon	5.09	4-2	1	1	6	0	53.0	61	33	30	6	17	1	41
vs. NYM	6.52	1-2	1	2	3	0	29.0	33	21	21	5	19	0	19
vs. Phi	5.67	1-2	0	0	3	0	27.0	28	17	17	4	9	1	19
Pre-All Star	5.47	48-41	21	28	89	9	788.1	914	523	479	111	325	6	539
Post-All Star	4.74	35-38	16	24	73	6	649.0	701	385	342	84	235	13	439

BATTERS vs. PITCHER

	AVG	AB	R	H	2B	3B	HR	RBI	SB	CS	TBB	SO	OBP	SLG
Total	.285	5669	908	1615	338	23	195	862	99	38	560	978	.354	.456
vs. Left	.285	2405	–	686	163	10	86	389	41	16	285	429	.364	.469
vs. Right	.285	3264	–	929	175	13	109	473	58	22	275	549	.346	.446
ST	.280	3758	599	1053	234	15	130	514	66	32	363	651	.348	.454
REL	.294	1911	309	562	104	8	65	348	33	6	197	327	.365	.459
Home	.281	2910	464	819	182	11	92	440	58	20	279	526	.348	.446
Away	.289	2759	444	796	156	12	103	422	41	18	281	452	.359	.466
None on	.278	3091	–	860	180	14	109	109	0	0	294	527	.346	.451
Runners on	.293	2578	–	755	158	9	86	753	99	38	266	451	.362	.461
None on/out	.284	1378	–	391	86	6	44	44	0	0	117	208	.344	.451
Scoring Posn	.299	1482	–	443	92	4	51	648	22	9	190	271	.379	.470
1st IP	.287	1874	–	537	103	7	62	349	40	15	207	332	.361	.448
Inning 1-6	.287	3839	637	1102	227	16	144	604	72	34	384	666	.357	.467
Inning 7+	.280	1830	271	513	111	7	51	258	27	4	176	312	.347	.432
Close & Late	.267	761	–	203	37	1	18	97	17	3	76	138	.338	.389
Bases Loaded	.314	156	–	49	13	1	5	147	0	0	15	38	.361	.506
vs 1st Batr	.298	346	–	103	16	2	10	75	3	0	31	60	.359	.442
0-0 count	.324	822	–	266	51	3	31	142	–	–	17	0	.346	.506
After (0-1)	.243	2662	–	647	148	12	70	306	–	–	144	681	.289	.387
After (1-0)	.321	2185	–	702	139	8	94	414	–	–	399	297	.426	.521
Two strikes	.205	2568	–	526	104	12	51	241	–	–	248	978	.279	.314
Pitch 1-15	.298	1503	–	448	77	6	48	229	33	13	152	241	.368	.453
Pitch 16-30	.260	1186	–	308	73	7	48	192	24	5	109	248	.326	.454
Pitch 31-45	.291	807	–	235	44	2	29	118	12	4	85	126	.364	.458
Pitch 46-60	.298	597	–	178	45	1	21	114	6	4	63	100	.372	.482
Pitch 61-75	.289	567	–	164	36	2	19	79	13	5	50	98	.351	.460
Pitch 76-90	.282	485	–	137	31	1	11	61	7	2	46	81	.343	.419
Pitch 91-105	.294	340	–	100	17	4	11	46	3	3	35	50	.366	.465
Pitch 106-20	.247	158	–	39	13	0	6	18	1	1	14	25	.312	.443
Pitch 121-35	.231	26	–	6	2	0	2	5	0	1	6	9	.375	.538
Pre-All Star	.292	3135	523	914	194	16	111	498	56	24	325	539	.363	.470
Post-All Star	.277	2534	385	701	144	7	84	364	43	14	235	439	.342	.438

2000 CATCHER PROFILES

Statistics for team only

Catcher	ERA	IP	H	R	ER	HR	BB	SO	SB	C-CS	P-CS	PKOF	C-CS%
Castillo, Alber	4.77	501.2	561	304	266	63	192	364	25	16	1	3	39.0
Fletcher, Darri	5.29	909.2	1022	584	535	127	354	598	73	20	1	0	21.5
Greene, Charlie	7.11	19.0	22	15	15	5	9	13	0	0	0	0	0.0
Greene, Todd	9.00	4.0	7	4	4	0	5	2	1	0	0	0	0.0
Phelps, Josh	3.00	3.0	3	1	1	0	0	1	0	0	0	0	0.0

With Individual Pitchers, Minimum 20 Major League Appearances

Borbon, Pedro — 0 Pick-Offs, 0 as Pick-Off CS

Catcher	ERA	IP	H	R	ER	HR	BB	SO	SB	CS	CS%
Castillo, Alberto	5.14	14.0	16	11	8	2	8	9	1	0	0.0
Fletcher, Darrin	7.16	27.2	29	26	22	3	29	20	4	0	0.0
Greene, Todd	0.00	0.0	0	0	0	0	0	1	0	0	0.0

Carpenter, Chris — 0 Pick-Offs, 0 as Pick-Off CS

Catcher	ERA	IP	H	R	ER	HR	BB	SO	SB	CS	CS%
Castillo, Alberto	7.55	47.2	56	42	40	12	30	32	0	1	100.0
Fletcher, Darrin	5.34	123.0	141	79	73	15	50	78	4	6	60.0
Greene, Charlie	17.36	4.2	7	9	9	3	3	3	0	0	0.0

Castillo, Frank — 1 Pick-Off, 1 as Pick-Off CS

Catcher	ERA	IP	H	R	ER	HR	BB	SO	SB	CS	CS%
Castillo, Alberto	3.67	61.1	46	26	25	6	27	48	4	3	42.9
Fletcher, Darrin	3.49	67.0	55	28	26	11	26	47	10	3	23.1
Greene, Charlie	3.38	8.0	10	3	3	1	2	8	0	0	0.0
Greene, Todd	5.40	1.2	1	1	1	0	1	1	0	0	0.0

Cubillan, Darwin — 0 Pick-Offs, 0 as Pick-Off CS

Catcher	ERA	IP	H	R	ER	HR	BB	SO	SB	CS	CS%
Castillo, Alberto	9.26	11.2	16	12	12	4	7	10	0	1	100.0
Fletcher, Darrin	4.50	4.0	4	2	2	1	4	4	0	0	0.0

Escobar, Kelvim — 2 Pick-Offs, 0 as Pick-Off CS

Catcher	ERA	IP	H	R	ER	HR	BB	SO	SB	CS	CS%
Castillo, Alberto	4.14	63.0	55	31	29	5	28	54	3	1	25.0
Fletcher, Darrin	6.00	117.0	131	87	78	21	57	88	14	2	12.5

Frascatore, John — 0 Pick-Offs, 0 as Pick-Off CS

Catcher	ERA	IP	H	R	ER	HR	BB	SO	SB	CS	CS%
Castillo, Alberto	6.75	25.1	35	22	19	4	14	12	2	1	33.3
Fletcher, Darrin	5.00	45.0	52	29	25	10	17	18	3	0	0.0
Greene, Todd	0.00	0.2	0	0	0	0	2	0	0	0	0.0
Phelps, Josh	0.00	2.0	0	0	0	0	0	0	0	0	0.0

Guthrie, Mark — 0 Pick-Offs, 0 as Pick-Off CS

Catcher	ERA	IP	H	R	ER	HR	BB	SO	SB	CS	CS%
Castillo, Alberto	1.80	5.0	4	1	1	1	1	6	1	0	0.0
Fletcher, Darrin	5.74	15.2	16	11	10	2	8	14	2	1	33.3

Koch, Billy — 0 Pick-Offs, 0 as Pick-Off CS

Catcher	ERA	IP	H	R	ER	HR	BB	SO	SB	CS	CS%
Castillo, Alberto	2.03	31.0	29	9	7	2	11	29	2	1	33.3
Fletcher, Darrin	3.02	47.2	49	19	16	4	7	31	2	0	0.0

Loaiza, Esteban — 0 Pick-Offs, 0 as Pick-Off CS

Catcher	ERA	IP	H	R	ER	HR	BB	SO	SB	CS	CS%
Castillo, Alberto	3.73	31.1	37	18	13	1	12	24	1	2	66.7
Fletcher, Darrin	3.56	60.2	58	27	24	7	14	38	5	2	28.6

Painter, Lance — 0 Pick-Offs, 0 as Pick-Off CS

Catcher	ERA	IP	H	R	ER	HR	BB	SO	SB	CS	CS%
Castillo, Alberto	6.61	16.1	20	13	12	1	7	14	0	0	0.0
Fletcher, Darrin	4.21	47.0	45	23	22	8	15	36	3	0	0.0
Greene, Charlie	0.00	2.0	1	0	0	0	0	2	0	0	0.0
Greene, Todd	0.00	0.1	0	0	0	0	0	0	0	0	0.0
Phelps, Josh	9.00	1.0	3	1	1	0	0	1	0	0	0.0

Quantrill, Paul — 2 Pick-Offs, 0 as Pick-Off CS

Catcher	ERA	IP	H	R	ER	HR	BB	SO	SB	CS	CS%
Castillo, Alberto	4.62	25.1	32	16	13	3	6	11	1	0	0.0
Fletcher, Darrin	4.47	56.1	65	28	28	4	18	35	8	0	0.0
Greene, Charlie	0.00	1.0	0	0	0	0	0	0	0	0	0.0
Greene, Todd	9.00	1.0	3	1	1	0	1	1	1	0	0.0

Trachsel, Steve — 1 Pick-Off, 0 as Pick-Off CS

Catcher	ERA	IP	H	R	ER	HR	BB	SO	SB	CS	CS%
Castillo, Alberto	9.00	5.0	8	5	5	1	2	4	0	0	0.0
Fletcher, Darrin	4.97	58.0	64	35	32	9	23	28	3	0	0.0

Wells, David — 1 Pick-Off, 1 as Pick-Off CS

Catcher	ERA	IP	H	R	ER	HR	BB	SO	SB	CS	CS%
Castillo, Alberto	3.36	112.2	133	48	42	10	15	84	8	7	46.7
Fletcher, Darrin	4.85	117.0	133	67	63	13	16	82	6	0	0.0

MISCELLANEOUS STATS

	HOME W	HOME L	ROAD W	ROAD L	TOTALS W	TOTALS L
VS. BALTIMORE	4	2	2	5	6	7
VS. BOSTON	4	2	4	2	8	4
VS. NEW YORK	5	1	2	4	7	5
VS. TAMPA BAY	3	3	4	2	7	5
TOTALS VS. EAST	16	8	12	13	28	21
VS. CLEVELAND	3	3	1	5	4	8
VS. CHICAGO	1	3	4	2	5	5
VS. DETROIT	5	1	4	2	9	3
VS. KANSAS CITY	4	2	2	2	6	4
VS. MINNESOTA	3	3	1	2	4	5
TOTALS VS. CENTRAL	16	12	12	13	28	25
VS. ANAHEIM	4	2	3	3	7	5
VS. OAKLAND	1	3	2	4	3	7
VS. SEATTLE	1	5	1	3	2	8
VS. TEXAS	3	1	3	3	6	4
TOTALS VS. WEST	9	11	9	13	18	24
TOTALS VS. A.L.	41	31	33	39	74	70
VS. ATLANTA	0	0	2	1	2	1
VS. FLORIDA	0	0	1	2	1	2
VS. MONTREAL	2	1	2	1	4	2
VS. NEW YORK	1	2	0	0	1	2
VS. PHILADELPHIA	1	2	0	0	1	2
TOTALS VS. N.L.	4	5	5	4	9	9
OVERALL TOTALS	45	36	38	43	83	79

	HOME W	HOME L	ROAD W	ROAD L	TOTALS W	TOTALS L
SHUTOUTS	2	4	2	3	4	7
SHO-INDIVIDUAL	2	1	1	1	3	2
EXTRA INNINGS	1	2	1	4	2	6
ONE-RUN DECISIONS	15	5	6	14	21	19
TWO-RUN DECISIONS	8	5	6	3	14	8
VS. LH STARTERS	12	10	7	14	19	24
VS. RH STARTERS	33	26	31	29	64	55
GRASS FIELDS	0	0	31	38	31	38
ARTIFICIAL FIELDS	45	36	7	5	52	41
DAY GAMES	16	18	12	10	28	28
NIGHT GAMES	29	18	26	33	55	51

	TOR	OPP
DOUBLE PLAYS	176	154
TRIPLE PLAYS	0	0
LEFT ON BASE	1152	1157
GRAND SLAM HR	9	5
HOME RUNS-HOME	134	92
HOME RUNS-ROAD	110	103

	WON	LOST
STARTERS	59	59
RELIEVERS	24	20
STREAKS	5	6

DOUBLEHEADERS
HOME: WON 0   LOST 0   SPLIT 0
ROAD: WON 0   LOST 0   SPLIT 0

ATTENDANCE
HOME   1,819,886 (81 DATES) 22,468 AVG
ROAD   2,207,931 (81 DATES) 27,258 AVG

HOW LONG DID IT TAKE

LONGEST OFFICIAL GAME
HOME   5:20-May 17/88 vs Texas (14 innings)
ROAD   5:49-June 19/98 at Baltimore (15 innings)

SHORTEST OFFICIAL GAME
1:04-Sept. 15/77 vs Baltimore

(forfeit, 4.5 innings)

LONGEST NINE-INNING GAME
HOME   4:15-April 11/88 vs New York
ROAD   4:12-Sept. 15/93 at Detroit

SHORTEST NINE-INNING GAME
ROAD   1:39-June 16/77 vs Detroit
HOME   1:33-Sept. 28/82 (1st g) vs Minnesota

AVERAGE TIME OF NINE-INNING GAME

	Home	Away	AL		Home	Away	AL
1977	2:27	2:27	2:31	1989	2:43	2:51	2:48
1978	2:24	2:23	2:24	1990	2:51	2:52	2:49
1979	2:23	2:24	2:32	1991	2:50	2:50	2:50
1980	2:24	2:28	2:36	1992	2:55	3:01	2:53
1981	2:31	2:27	2:34	1993	2:51	2:53	2:52
1982	2:29	2:28	2:37	1994	2:51	2:54	2:59
1983	2:34	2:36	2:38	1995	2:53	2:54	2:56
1984	2:35	2:39	2:37	1996	2:45	2:47	2:53
1985	2:39	2:46	2:45	1997	2:46	2:49	2:57
1986	2:46	2:47	2:48	1998	2:48	2:53	2:52
1987	2:50	2:54	2:51	1999	2:55	2:55	2:56
1988	2:47	2:52	2:48	2000	2:54	2:59	3:00

Batting Profile

Category	AVG	G	AB	R	H	TB	2B	3B	HR	RBI	SH-SF	HP	BB-IBB	SO	SB-CS	GI DP	E	SLG	OBP
vs Left	.275	–	1428	192	392	611	90	6	39	184	9-8	17	135-8	256	13-10	33	–	.428	.343
vs Right	.275	–	4249	669	1170	2053	238	15	205	642	20-26	43	391-24	770	76-24	97	–	.483	.341
Home	.278	81	2766	435	768	1366	178	9	134	415	15-12	33	255-16	456	39-16	63	43	.494	.344
Road	.273	81	2911	426	794	1298	150	12	110	411	14-22	27	271-16	570	50-18	67	47	.446	.338
Day	.270	56	1991	314	537	947	120	7	92	304	10-7	27	171-11	387	28-13	34	36	.476	.335
Night	.278	106	3686	547	1025	1717	208	14	152	522	19-27	33	355-21	639	61-21	96	54	.466	.345
Grass	.268	69	2469	350	661	1077	124	11	90	339	14-20	24	221-12	486	43-13	54	40	.436	.331
Turf	.281	93	3208	511	901	1587	204	10	154	487	15-14	36	305-20	540	46-21	76	50	.495	.349
Runners on	.281	162	2508	720	705	1174	150	5	103	685	29-34	32	253-32	454	88-34	130	–	.468	.350
None on	.270	162	3169	441	857	1490	178	16	141	141	0-0	28	273-0	572	1-0	0	–	.470	.344
RISCP	.283	162	1460	624	413	718	94	2	69	596	15-34	19	172-32	281	13-3	52	–	.492	.358
RISCP 2OUT	.240	161	647	239	155	292	41	4	32	227	0-0	9	91-22	140	8-1	0	–	.451	.341
Innings 1-6	.281	162	3856	605	1082	1857	239	13	170	581	13-22	41	349-14	656	68-27	92	–	.482	.345
Innings 7+	.264	162	1821	356	480	807	89	8	74	245	16-12	19	177-18	370	21-7	38	–	.443	.333
DH	.285	153	606	92	173	325	33	1	39	120	0-6	6	38-3	93	3-2	18	–	.536	.331
vs A.L.	.275	144	5034	739	1382	2341	280	20	213	708	29-30	53	445-23	915	74-30	118	–	.465	.338
vs N.L.	.280	18	643	122	180	323	48	1	31	118	0-4	7	81-9	111	15-4	12	–	.502	.365
ANA	.319	12	429	82	137	234	23	1	24	79	3-1	6	45-1	59	3-3	16	4	.545	.391
ARI	.000	0	0	0	0	0	0	0	0	0	0-0	0	0-0	0	0-0	0	0	.000	.000
ATL	.284	3	109	27	31	55	9	0	5	27	0-2	2	17-2	27	3-0	2	0	.505	.385
BAL	.245	13	436	52	107	195	16	3	22	52	1-2	1	27-1	72	7-2	5	8	.447	.290
BOS	.273	12	440	62	120	203	16	2	21	57	1-2	6	30-3	77	16-2	7	6	.461	.326
CHI	.000	0	0	0	0	0	0	0	0	0	0-0	0	0-0	0	0-0	0	0	.000	.000
CWS	.252	10	349	45	88	160	22	1	16	44	1-1	1	34-4	72	6-3	7	9	.458	.319
CIN	.000	0	0	0	0	0	0	0	0	0	0-0	0	0-0	0	0-0	0	0	.000	.000
CLE	.291	12	433	77	126	221	28	2	21	76	2-2	2	52-3	100	5-4	11	9	.510	.368
COL	.000	0	0	0	0	0	0	0	0	0	0-0	0	0-0	0	0-0	0	0	.000	.000
DET	.272	12	408	72	111	193	26	1	18	69	3-6	4	35-0	78	5-3	7	8	.473	.331
FLA	.283	3	113	18	32	51	7	0	4	18	0-1	2	7-1	25	4-0	0	3	.451	.333
HOU	.000	0	0	0	0	0	0	0	0	0	0-0	0	0-0	0	0-0	0	0	.000	.000
KC	.295	10	353	64	104	191	20	2	21	63	2-0	7	27-0	57	8-1	10	8	.541	.357
LA	.000	0	0	0	0	0	0	0	0	0	0-0	0	0-0	0	0-0	0	0	.000	.000
MIL	.000	0	0	0	0	0	0	0	0	0	0-0	0	0-0	0	0-0	0	0	.000	.000
MIN	.267	9	303	36	81	129	16	1	10	35	3-1	1	23-1	61	4-3	6	6	.426	.320
MON	.308	6	214	47	66	114	18	0	10	44	0-0	2	32-3	29	5-1	7	4	.533	.403
NYM	.243	3	107	19	26	55	9	1	6	18	0-1	0	19-2	19	3-2	0	1	.514	.354
NYY	.283	12	420	63	119	184	28	2	11	59	4-5	8	26-1	85	2-0	13	6	.438	.333
OAK	.215	10	325	22	70	101	12	2	5	21	3-1	5	34-1	59	4-1	5	4	.311	.299
PHI	.250	3	100	11	25	48	5	0	6	11	0-0	1	6-1	11	0-1	3	0	.480	.299
PIT	.000	0	0	0	0	0	0	0	0	0	0-0	0	0-0	0	0-0	0	0	.000	.000
STL	.000	0	0	0	0	0	0	0	0	0	0-0	0	0-0	0	0-0	0	0	.000	.000
SD	.000	0	0	0	0	0	0	0	0	0	0-0	0	0-0	0	0-0	0	0	.000	.000
SF	.000	0	0	0	0	0	0	0	0	0	0-0	0	0-0	0	0-0	0	0	.000	.000
SEA	.277	10	364	55	101	166	26	0	13	53	0-2	6	34-4	72	6-2	12	8	.456	.347
TB	.259	12	410	53	106	181	22	1	17	48	1-3	1	42-1	62	5-4	11	1	.441	.327
TEX	.308	10	364	56	112	183	25	2	14	52	5-4	5	36-3	61	3-2	8	5	.503	.374

Pitching Profile

Category	W-L	ERA	G	GS	CG	SHO	GF	SV	IP	H	R	ER	HR	SH-SF	HB	BB-IBB	SO	WP	BK
vs L	–	–	–	–	–	–	–	–	–	686	–	–	86	20-15	22	286-10	430	14	3
vs R	–	–	–	–	–	–	–	–	–	929	–	–	109	24-25	42	274-9	548	23	3
Home	45-36	5.22	81	81	8	2	73	19	738.0	819	464	428	92	20-19	30	249-16	526	21	1
Road	38-43	5.12	81	81	7	1	74	18	699.1	796	444	398	103	24-21	34	281-11	452	16	2
Day	28-28	5.08	56	56	6	0	50	8	506.2	570	318	286	63	16-13	21	173-6	386	12	2
Night	55-51	5.22	106	106	9	3	97	29	930.2	1045	590	540	132	28-27	43	387-13	592	25	1
Grass	31-38	5.21	69	69	4	1	65	17	596.1	688	384	345	90	21-18	29	257-10	389	12	2
Turf	52-41	5.15	93	93	11	2	82	20	841.0	927	524	481	105	23-22	35	303-9	589	25	1
vs AL	74-70	5.13	144	144	14	3	130	34	1277.0	1427	804	728	174	37-35	59	487-16	856	33	1
vs NL	9-9	5.50	18	18	1	0	17	3	160.1	188	104	98	21	7-5	5	73-3	122	4	2
ANA	7-5	5.91	12	12	1	0	11	2	105.0	129	72	69	17	1-7	8	43-2	70	4	0
ARI	0-0	0.00	0	0	0	0	0	0	0.0	0	0	0	0	0-0	0	0-0	0	0	0
ATL	2-1	6.15	3	3	0	0	3	1	26.1	36	18	18	3	4-1	0	17-1	18	0	2
BAL	6-7	5.54	13	13	1	0	12	5	112.0	139	81	69	14	1-4	6	40-0	73	2	2
BOS	8-4	4.55	12	12	0	0	12	5	112.2	130	67	57	8	3-2	6	39-1	87	2	0
CHI	0-0	0.00	0	0	0	0	0	0	0.0	0	0	0	0	0-0	0	0-0	0	0	0
CIN	0-0	0.00	0	0	0	0	0	0	0.0	0	0	0	0	0-0	0	0-0	0	0	0
CLE	4-8	7.30	12	12	1	0	11	1	106.0	139	95	86	18	1-4	2	58-3	85	3	0
CWS	5-5	3.68	10	10	0	0	10	3	88.0	68	39	36	13	5-1	2	36-1	55	3	0
COL	0-0	0.00	0	0	0	0	0	0	0.0	0	0	0	0	0-0	0	0-0	0	0	0
DET	9-3	4.82	12	12	2	2	10	2	106.1	116	61	57	19	3-0	1	39-0	74	6	0
FLA	1-2	4.32	3	3	1	0	2	0	25.0	30	15	12	3	0-1	1	11-0	25	0	0
HOU	0-0	0.00	0	0	0	0	0	0	0.0	0	0	0	0	0-0	0	0-0	0	0	0
KC	6-4	4.70	10	10	0	0	10	3	88.0	104	54	46	8	1-3	4	26-1	49	1	0
LA	0-0	0.00	0	0	0	0	0	0	0.0	0	0	0	0	0-0	0	0-0	0	0	0
MIN	4-5	4.10	9	9	1	0	8	2	79.0	84	39	36	8	1-1	0	33-0	68	1	0
MIL	0-0	0.00	0	0	0	0	0	0	0.0	0	0	0	0	0-0	0	0-0	0	0	0
NYY	7-5	3.99	12	12	3	0	9	2	106.0	107	51	47	13	1-1	4	25-3	61	0	0
MON	4-2	5.09	6	6	0	0	6	1	53.0	61	33	30	6	1-2	2	17-1	41	2	0
OAK	3-7	5.34	10	10	1	0	9	2	87.2	103	54	52	16	3-2	5	28-0	63	3	0
NY	1-2	6.52	3	3	0	0	3	1	29.0	33	21	21	5	0-0	1	19-0	19	2	2
SEA	2-8	7.32	10	10	0	0	10	0	91.0	112	87	74	16	6-5	10	61-4	54	1	0
PHI	1-2	5.67	3	3	0	0	3	0	27.0	28	17	17	4	2-1	1	9-1	19	0	0
TB	7-5	4.33	12	12	3	0	9	2	106.0	99	53	51	13	7-2	5	25-0	63	4	0
PIT	0-0	0.00	0	0	0	0	0	0	0.0	0	0	0	0	0-0	0	0-0	0	0	0
TEX	6-4	4.84	10	10	1	1	9	5	89.1	97	51	48	11	4-3	2	34-1	54	3	0
SD	0-0	0.00	0	0	0	0	0	0	0.0	0	0	0	0	0-0	0	0-0	0	0	0
SF	0-0	0.00	0	0	0	0	0	0	0.0	0	0	0	0	0-0	0	0-0	0	0	0
STL	0-0	0.00	0	0	0	0	0	0	0.0	0	0	0	0	0-0	0	0-0	0	0	0

Season in Review

STARTING PITCHERS

PITCHER	W-L	PCT	ERA	G	GS	CG	IP	H	TBF	R	ER	HR	SH-SF	HB	BB-IBB	SO	WP	BK	AVG
Andrews, C	0-1	.000	19.80	2	2	0	5.0	18	34	11	11	3	1-0	0	3-0	2	0	1	.600
Carpenter, C	8-12	.400	6.55	27	27	2	156.2	182	716	120	114	28	2-1	5	81-1	95	3	0	.290
Castillo, F	10-5	.667	3.61	24	24	0	137.0	112	573	58	55	18	5-2	5	56-0	104	0	0	.222
Coco (Reyn, P	0-0	.000	9.00	1	1	0	4.0	5	23	4	4	1	0-0	1	5-0	2	1	0	.294
Escobar, K	7-13	.350	5.42	24	24	3	152.2	155	673	102	92	20	4-3	3	78-1	113	3	0	.265
Halladay, R	4-6	.400	11.13	13	13	0	60.2	92	304	75	75	14	1-3	1	36-0	42	6	1	.350
Hamilton, J	2-1	.667	3.55	6	6	0	33.0	28	135	13	13	3	0-1	2	12-0	15	0	0	.233
Loaiza, E	5-7	.417	3.62	14	14	1	92.0	95	391	45	37	8	2-1	10	26-0	62	0	0	.270
Munro, P	0-1	.000	4.80	3	3	0	15.0	18	68	11	8	1	1-0	2	8-0	7	1	0	.316
Painter, L	1-0	1.000	5.00	2	2	0	9.0	10	39	5	5	1	1-0	0	2-0	11	0	0	.278
Trachsel, S	2-5	.286	5.29	11	11	0	63.0	72	276	40	37	10	4-1	0	25-1	32	1	0	.293
Wells, D	20-8	.714	4.11	35	35	9	229.2	266	972	115	105	23	6-7	8	31-0	166	9	1	.289
TOTALS	59-59	.500	5.23	162	162	15	957.2	1053	4204	599	556	130	27-19	37	363-3	651	24	3	.280

RELIEF PITCHERS

PITCHER	W-L	PCT	ERA	APP	GF	SV	IP	H	TBF	R	ER	HR	SH-SF	HB	BB-IBB	SO	WP	BK	AVG
Andrews, C	1-1	.500	6.89	6	1	0	15.2	16	68	12	12	3	0-1	0	6-0	10	0	0	.262
Bale, J	0-0	.000	14.73	2	0	0	3.2	5	22	7	6	1	0-1	2	3-0	6	0	0	.313
Borbon, P	1-1	.500	6.48	59	6	1	41.2	45	213	37	30	5	2-7	5	38-5	29	0	0	.280
Carpenter, C	2-0	1.000	3.86	7	1	0	18.2	22	79	10	8	2	1-0	0	2-0	18	0	0	.289
Castillo, F	0-0	.000	0.00	1	1	0	1.0	0	3	0	0	0	0-0	0	0-0	0	0	0	.000
Cubillan, D	1-0	1.000	8.04	7	1	0	15.2	20	75	14	14	5	0-0	1	11-0	14	0	0	.317
Dewitt, M	1-0	1.000	8.44	7	4	0	10.2	20	58	10	10	4	0-0	2	9-0	6	1	0	.351
Escobar, K	3-2	.600	4.94	19	8	2	27.1	31	121	16	15	6	1-1	0	7-2	29	1	0	.277
Estrella, L	0-0	.000	5.79	2	1	0	4.2	9	21	3	3	1	0-1	0	0-0	3	0	0	.450
Frascatore, J	2-4	.333	5.42	60	15	0	73.0	87	335	51	44	14	2-4	7	33-2	30	3	0	.301
Gunderson, E	0-1	.000	7.11	6	1	0	6.1	15	37	6	5	0	0-1	1	2-1	2	0	0	.455
Guthrie, M	0-2	.000	4.79	23	5	0	20.2	20	88	12	11	3	1-1	1	9-0	20	2	0	.263
Halladay, R	0-1	.000	6.43	6	4	0	7.0	15	45	12	5	0	1-0	1	6-0	2	0	0	.405
Koch, B	9-3	.750	2.63	68	62	33	78.2	78	326	28	23	6	4-0	2	18-4	60	1	0	.258
Munro, P	1-0	1.000	7.59	6	2	0	10.2	20	59	11	9	0	0-0	1	8-0	9	0	0	.400
Painter, L	1-0	1.000	4.68	40	11	0	57.2	59	246	32	30	8	4-1	2	20-1	42	4	0	.269
Quantrill, P	2-5	.286	4.52	68	24	1	83.2	100	367	45	42	7	1-3	2	25-1	47	1	0	.298
TOTALS	24-20	.545	5.04	387	147	37	476.2	562	2173	306	267	65	17-21	27	197-16	327	13	0	.294

BLUE JAYS PLAYERS IN WINTER LEAGUES

* – Lefthanded # – Switch Hitter

INDIVIDUAL BATTING

PLAYER	AVG	G	AB	R	H	TB	2B	3B	HR	RBI	SH-SF	HP	BB-IB	SO	SB-CS	DP	SLG	OBP	Team	League
Castillo, Alberto	.205	42	117	11	24	34	1	0	3	11	0-0	0	20-0	14	1-0	0	.291	.321	Aguilas	DOMR
#Cosby, Robert	.000	2	2	0	0	0	0	0	0	0	0-0	0	1-0	0	0-0	0	.000	.333	Caguas	PR
Freel, Ryan	.341	27	91	18	31	45	8	3	0	9	1-0	0	10-0	11	10-1	0	.495	.406	Scottsdale	AFL
Freel, Ryan	.236	14	55	11	13	22	4	1	1	7	#-#	#	7-#	12	2-1	#	.400	.333	Lara	VENZ
#Izturis, Cesar	.154	16	65	9	10	12	2	0	0	3	2-0	3	9-0	9	3-0	0	.185	.286	Lara	VENZ
*Langaigne, Selwyn	.270	46	122	12	33	49	7	3	1	16	1-1	0	13-0	18	1-3	0	.402	.338	Lara	VENZ
Lawrence, Joe	.145	23	76	9	11	14	1	1	0	6	0-1	0	6-0	21	2-2	2	.184	.205	Scottsdale	AFL
#Lopez, Felipe	.310	45	155	32	48	78	10	1	6	23	1-1	1	21-0	37	7-3	1	.503	.393	Santurce	PR
Lopez, Luis	.304	49	158	19	48	75	9	0	6	24	1-1	1	24-0	13	0-3	6	.475	.397	Santurce	PR
Malpica, Martin	.167	4	6	0	1	1	0	0	0	0	#-#	#	1-#	2	0-0	#	.167	.286	Lara	VENZ
Mondesi, Raul	.000	2	6	1	0	0	0	0	0	0	0-0	0	2-0	2	0-0	0	.000	.250	Aguilas	DOMR
Negron, Miguel	.281	23	57	7	16	21	2	0	1	5	#-#	#	6-#	17	1-0	#	.368	.359	Caguas	PR
Rios, Alexis	.188	9	16	2	3	4	1	0	0	0	1-0	0	0-0	3	0-1	2	.250	.188	Caguas	PR
#Simmons, Brian	.265	23	83	10	22	29	4	0	1	5	2-1	1	8-0	14	2-0	0	.349	.333	Santurce	PR
Thompson, Ryan	.286	2	7	1	2	3	1	0	0	2	0-0	0	0-0	2	0-0	1	.429	.286	Mayaguez	PR
Umbria, Jose	.000	2	1	0	0	0	0	0	0	0	0-0	0	0-0	0	0-0	0	.000	.000	Lara	VENZ
*Wise, Dewayne	.217	20	69	9	15	31	2	1	4	14	0-0	0	4-0	15	1-2	1	.449	.260	Scottsdale	AFL
Woodward, Chris	.319	25	91	15	29	41	5	2	1	18	0-1	0	7-0	16	8-2	1	.451	.364	Scottsdale	AFL

INDIVIDUAL PITCHING

PITCHER	W-L	PCT	ERA	G	GS	CG	ShO	SV	IP	H	AB	TBF	R	ER	HR	HB	BB	SO	WP	BK	Team	League
Beirne, Kevin	0-1	.000	6.75	1	1	0	0	0	2.2	6	13	13	3	2	0	0	1	1	1	0	Bayamon	PR
Bowles, Brian	0-0	.000	2.35	3	2	0	0	0	7.2	5	0	0	2	2	0	0	4	9	1	0	Lara	VENZ
Carrasco, Hector	0-0	.000	1.38	8	0	0	0	0	13.0	11	#	#	3	2	0	0	2	13	0	#	Aguilas	DOMR
*Chacin, Gustavo	5-3	.625	2.98	14	13	0	0	0	60.1	63	0	0	29	20	1	1	22	43	3	0	Lara	VENZ
Coco, Pascual	1-1	.500	2.56	10	0	0	0	0	31.2	23	0	0	12	9	0	0	15	27	0	0	Escogido	DOMR
Cornett, Brad	1-4	.200	7.40	6	5	0	0	0	24.1	24	97	110	22	20	5	1	10	18	3	0	Santurce	PR
Cornett, Brad	1-8	.111	8.75	10	9	0	0	0	37.0	44	25	29	38	36	9	3	16	20	3	0	Bayamon	PR
Escobar, Kelvim	1-0	1.000	1.08	9	0	0	0	4	8.1	7	#	#	1	1	1	1	1	10	0	#	Lara	VENZ
File, Bob	2-1	.667	3.38	15	0	0	0	5	16.0	24	73	79	12	6	1	0	6	15	3	0	Scottsdale	AFL
Guzman, Alexis	0-1	.000	2.76	9	1	0	0	0	16.1	16	0	0	7	5	2	1	5	9	0	0	Lara	VENZ
*Hendrickson, Mark	2-3	.400	2.67	7	7	0	0	0	30.1	31	118	132	16	9	2	1	12	19	1	0	Scottsdale	AFL
McClellan, Matt	1-0	1.000	4.00	15	0	0	0	2	18.0	14	0	0	8	8	3	0	12	19	0	0	Lara	VENZ
Navarro, Alexis	0-0	.000	3.86	5	5	0	0	0	19.2	25	78	91	9	8	1	1	12	7	2	0	Caguas	PR
Perez, George	0-0	.000	7.88	7	0	0	0	0	8.0	6	0	0	7	7	0	0	6	9	0	0	Licey	DOMR
Sandoval, Marcos	0-1	.000	27.00	3	0	0	0	0	2.0	4	0	0	6	6	0	1	3	1	0	0	Lara	VENZ

RUNNERS IN SCORING POSITION

PLAYER	AVG	AB	H	2B	3B	HR	RBI-SP	MISP	MOB	BB	IBB	SO	SH	SF	GIDP
Andrews, C	.000	1	0	0	0	0	0	1	1	0	0	1	0	0	0
Batista, T	.287	181	52	11	0	13	55	225	326	12	1	26	0	3	8
Bush, H	.183	71	13	3	0	0	17	95	127	6	0	20	2	1	2
Castillo, A	.205	44	9	2	0	0	14	67	92	5	0	11	2	3	1
Castillo, F	.000	2	0	0	0	0	0	4	6	0	0	1	0	0	0
Cordova, M	.250	48	12	1	0	1	13	67	101	7	0	6	0	0	2
Cruz Jr., J	.271	133	36	7	1	7	36	183	273	24	3	33	1	3	4
Delgado, C	.384	172	66	18	0	13	78	247	342	38	18	34	0	4	4
Ducey, R	.333	3	1	1	0	0	1	4	7	0	0	0	0	0	0
Escobar, K	.000	4	0	0	0	0	0	5	7	0	0	2	0	0	0
Fletcher, D	.280	93	26	6	0	3	29	124	175	7	3	13	0	4	4
Fullmer, B	.322	143	46	8	0	15	57	189	274	12	3	23	0	6	4
Gonzalez, A	.269	134	36	13	0	1	40	188	272	18	0	37	9	1	5
Grebeck, C	.328	64	21	7	0	0	18	84	111	6	0	5	0	1	1
Greene, C	.000	1	0	0	0	0	0	1	2	0	0	0	0	0	0
Greene, T	.182	22	4	1	0	0	5	27	38	1	0	7	0	0	3
Koch, B	.000	1	0	0	0	0	0	1	2	0	0	1	0	0	0
Martinez, D	.311	61	19	1	1	1	18	82	114	8	0	12	0	1	2
Mondesi, R	.229	96	22	4	0	8	29	125	184	10	0	17	0	3	3
Morandini, M	.286	21	6	0	0	0	7	30	43	1	0	4	0	0	1
Mottola, C	.500	2	1	0	0	0	2	5	7	0	0	0	0	0	0
Stewart, S	.271	129	35	8	0	5	42	161	230	9	1	19	0	4	7
Thompson, A	.333	3	1	0	0	0	1	6	9	1	0	1	0	0	0
Wells, D	.000	1	0	0	0	0	0	1	2	0	0	1	0	0	0
Wise, D	.000	4	0	0	0	0	0	6	9	1	0	1	0	0	0
Woodward, C	.269	26	7	3	0	2	8	36	52	6	3	6	1	0	1
BLUE JAYS	.283	1460	413	94	2	69	470	1964	2806	172	32	281	15	34	52

BATTING WITH THE BASES LOADED

PLAYER	AVG	AB	H	2B	3B	HR	RBI-SP	MISP	MOB	BB	IBB	SO	SH	SF	GIDP
Batista, T	.400	15	6	1	0	2	13	32	48	0	0	1	0	1	2
Bush, H	.167	6	1	0	0	0	2	12	18	0	0	1	0	0	0
Castillo, A	.143	7	1	0	0	0	1	14	21	0	0	4	0	0	0
Castillo, F	.000	2	0	0	0	0	0	4	6	0	0	1	0	0	0
Cordova, M	.286	7	2	0	0	1	4	14	21	0	0	2	0	0	0
Cruz Jr., J	.444	9	4	1	0	0	8	22	33	1	0	1	0	1	0
Delgado, C	.333	12	4	1	0	2	12	30	45	0	0	1	0	3	1
Ducey, R	.000	1	0	0	0	0	0	2	3	0	0	0	0	0	0
Fletcher, D	.333	9	3	0	0	3	10	24	36	0	0	1	0	2	0
Fullmer, B	.400	10	4	0	0	1	12	30	45	0	0	0	0	4	1
Gonzalez, A	.250	12	3	1	0	0	5	24	36	0	0	5	0	0	1
Grebeck, C	.250	4	1	0	0	0	2	8	12	0	0	0	0	0	0
Greene, T	.500	2	1	0	0	0	2	4	6	0	0	1	0	0	0
Martinez, D	.000	5	0	0	0	0	2	12	18	0	0	1	0	1	1
Mondesi, R	.000	9	0	0	0	0	3	22	33	0	0	1	0	2	0
Morandini, M	.400	5	2	0	0	0	4	10	15	0	0	0	0	0	0
Mottola, C	.000	1	0	0	0	0	1	4	6	0	0	0	0	0	0
Stewart, S	.333	9	3	1	0	0	6	20	30	0	0	1	0	1	1
Thompson, A	1.000	1	1	0	0	0	1	2	3	0	0	0	0	0	0
Woodward, C	.000	2	0	0	0	0	1	6	9	1	0	0	0	0	0
BLUE JAYS	.281	128	36	5	0	9	89	296	444	2	0	21	0	15	7

MILEAGE

In the 2001 season the Blue Jays will travel 31,987 miles from the time they depart Dunedin (Tampa) on March 30 to the conclusion of the regular season. The Blue Jays will make 39 separate flights. Following are the miles traveled for the last four seasons: 1997 — 32,976 miles on 42 flights; 1998 — 35,829 miles on 44 flights; 1999 — 33,886 miles on 38 flights; 2000 — 34,543 miles on 36 flights. Below is the mileage for each flight for the 2001 season.

	Miles		Miles
Tampa to Puerto Rico	979	Tampa to Toronto	1,245
Puerto Rico to Tampa	979	Toronto to Philadelphia	375
Tampa to New York	1,002	Philadelphia to New York	95
New York to Toronto	366	New York to Toronto	366
Toronto to Kansas City	822	Toronto to New York	366
Kansas City to Toronto	822	New York to Boston	187
Toronto to Oakland	2,260	Boston to Toronto	446
Oakland to Seattle	671	Toronto to Seattle	2,060
Seattle to Toronto	2,060	Seattle to Anaheim	954
Toronto to Anaheim	2,176	Anaheim to Toronto	2,176
Anaheim to Texas	1,235	Toronto to Minnesota	679
Texas to Toronto	1,199	Minnesota to Baltimore	936
Toronto to Boston	446	Baltimore to New York	184
Boston to Chicago	867	New York to Toronto	366
Chicago to Toronto	436	Toronto to Detroit	214
Toronto to Montreal	315	Detroit to Baltimore	404
Montreal to Baltimore	466	Baltimore to Toronto	384
Baltimore to Boston	370	Toronto to Cleveland	193
Boston to Toronto	446	Cleveland to Tampa	1,195
Toronto to Tampa	1,245	**TOTAL**	**31,987**

BATTING, PRE ALL-STAR BREAK

PLAYER	AVG	G	AB	R	H	TB	2B	3B	HR	RBI	SH-SF	HP	BB-IBB	SO	SB-CS	GIDP	E	SLG	OBP
Batista, T	.289	81	329	56	95	188	19	1	24	72	0-2	5	15-0	59	3-3	8	11	.571	.328
Bush, H	.214	61	243	32	52	59	7	0	0	14	4-0	1	16-0	50	7-4	8	6	.243	.274
Castillo, A	.211	43	133	10	28	36	5	0	1	13	1-3	0	13-0	23	0-0	2	0	.271	.275
Cordova, M	.271	43	144	16	39	51	6	0	2	12	0-0	3	10-0	21	2-1	3	1	.354	.331
Cruz Jr., J	.240	89	346	52	83	165	16	3	20	47	1-2	0	42-2	73	9-2	4	3	.477	.321
RIGHT	.291	–	79	–	23	33	5	1	1	9	1-0	0	2-0	12	–	3	–	.418	.309
LEFT	.225	–	267	–	60	132	11	2	19	38	0-2	0	40-2	61	–	1	–	.494	.324
Delgado, C	.363	89	320	74	116	227	27	0	28	80	0-2	5	66-7	64	0-0	7	6	.709	.476
Fletcher, D	.349	56	189	20	66	108	10	1	10	33	0-2	4	9-2	14	1-0	6	3	.571	.387
Fullmer, B	.305	75	266	44	81	144	19	1	14	53	0-3	4	22-2	37	3-1	5	0	.541	.363
Gonzalez, A	.240	77	267	34	64	101	16	0	7	32	6-1	3	23-0	55	4-3	5	5	.378	.306
Grebeck, D	.276	30	127	21	35	51	7	0	3	10	0-1	1	9-0	18	0-0	4	2	.402	.326
Greene, C	.111	3	9	0	1	1	0	0	0	0	0-0	0	0-0	5	0-0	0	0	.111	.111
Greene, T	.353	11	17	3	6	10	1	0	1	2	0-0	0	0-0	1	0-0	0	0	.588	.353
Mondesi, R	.278	86	345	73	96	188	19	2	23	63	0-3	3	29-0	67	21-4	5	6	.545	.337
Phelps, J	.000	1	1	0	0	0	0	0	0	0	0-0	0	0-0	1	0-0	0	0	.000	.000
Stewart, S	.339	64	274	49	93	153	21	3	11	36	1-3	4	16-0	42	13-2	4	0	.558	.380
Thompson, A	.167	2	6	2	1	1	0	0	0	1	0-0	0	3-0	2	0-0	0	0	.167	.444
Wise, D	.150	19	20	2	3	3	0	0	0	0	0-0	0	1-0	5	1-0	0	0	.150	.190
Woodward, C	.171	27	82	14	14	29	6	0	3	13	1-0	0	10-3	24	1-0	1	3	.354	.261
Andrews, C	.000	8	3	0	0	0	0	0	0	0	0-0	0	0-0	2	0-0	0	0	.000	.000
Bale, J	.000	2	0	0	0	0	0	0	0	0	0-0	0	0-0	0	0-0	0	0	.000	.000
Borbon, P	.000	41	0	0	0	0	0	0	0	0	0-0	0	0-0	0	0-0	0	0	.000	.000
Carpenter,	.000	18	2	0	0	0	0	0	0	0	0-0	0	0-0	1	0-0	0	0	.000	.000
Castillo, F	.143	17	7	0	1	1	0	0	0	0	0-0	0	0-0	3	0-0	0	1	.143	.143
Cubillan, D	.000	7	1	0	0	0	0	0	0	0	0-0	0	0-0	0	0-0	0	0	.000	.000
Dewitt, M	.000	7	0	0	0	0	0	0	0	0	0-0	0	0-0	0	0-0	0	0	.000	.000
Escobar, K	.000	18	7	0	0	0	0	0	0	0	0-0	0	0-0	4	0-0	0	1	.000	.000
Frascatore,	.000	35	0	0	0	0	0	0	0	0	0-0	0	0-0	0	0-0	0	1	.000	.000
Gunderson,	.000	6	0	0	0	0	0	0	0	0	0-0	0	0-0	0	0-0	0	1	.000	.000
Halladay, R	.000	11	0	0	0	0	0	0	0	0	0-0	0	0-0	0	0-0	0	0	.000	.000
Koch, B	.000	37	1	0	0	0	0	0	0	0	0-0	0	0-0	1	0-0	0	0	.000	.000
Munro, P	.000	9	1	0	0	0	0	0	0	0	0-0	0	0-0	1	0-0	0	0	.000	.000
Painter, L	.000	23	0	0	0	0	0	0	0	0	0-0	0	0-0	0	0-0	0	0	.000	.000
Quantrill,	.000	39	0	0	0	0	0	0	0	0	0-0	0	1-0	0	0-0	0	0	.000	.000
Wells, D	.167	19	6	0	1	1	0	0	0	0	0-0	0	0-0	2	0-0	0	1	.167	.167
PITCHERS	.071	89	28	0	2	2	0	0	0	0	0-0	0	1-0	14	0-0	0	5	.071	.103
TORONTO	.278	89	3146	502	875	1517	179	11	147	481	14-22	36	285-16	575	65-20	62	51	.482	.343
OPPONENT	.292	89	3135	523	914	1473	194	16	111	498	20-22	37	325-6	539	56-24	87	62	.470	.363
DH	.303	89	314	48	95	164	22	1	15	56	0-3	4	24-2	42	3-2	5	0	.522	.357

BATTING, POST ALL-STAR BREAK

PLAYER	AVG	G	AB	R	H	TB	2B	3B	HR	RBI	SH-SF	HP	BB-IBB	SO	SB-CS	GIDP	E	SLG	OBP
Batista, T	.234	73	291	40	68	134	13	1	17	42	0-1	1	20-1	62	2-1	7	6	.460	.284
Bush, H	.222	15	54	6	12	16	1	0	1	4	0-1	1	2-0	10	2-0	2	0	.296	.259
Castillo, A	.212	23	52	4	11	13	2	0	0	3	1-0	0	8-0	13	0-0	1	3	.250	.317
Cordova, M	.179	19	56	7	10	17	1	0	2	6	0-0	0	8-0	14	1-1	3	0	.304	.281
Cruz Jr., J	.245	73	257	39	63	116	16	2	11	29	1-1	2	29-1	56	6-3	7	0	.451	.325
RIGHT	.287	–	87	–	25	46	7	1	4	10	0-0	1	9-0	11	–	3	–	.529	.361
LEFT	.224	–	170	–	38	70	9	1	7	19	1-1	1	20-1	45	–	4	–	.412	.307
Delgado, C	.321	73	249	41	80	151	30	1	13	57	0-2	10	57-11	40	0-1	5	7	.606	.462
Ducey, R	.154	5	13	2	2	3	1	0	0	1	0-0	0	2-0	2	0-0	0	1	.231	.267
Fletcher, D	.295	66	227	23	67	106	9	0	10	25	0-2	1	11-1	31	0-0	2	1	.467	.328
Fullmer, B	.282	58	216	32	61	125	10	0	18	51	0-3	2	8-1	31	0-0	9	0	.579	.310
Gonzalez, A	.265	64	260	34	69	112	15	2	8	37	10-0	1	20-0	58	0-1	9	11	.431	.320
Grebeck, D	.316	36	114	17	36	48	12	0	0	13	1-0	1	16-0	15	0-0	3	7	.421	.405
Greene, T	.206	23	68	8	14	27	1	0	4	8	0-0	0	5-0	17	0-0	4	0	.397	.260
Martinez, D	.311	47	180	29	56	74	10	1	2	22	0-1	1	24-0	28	4-2	3	2	.411	.393
Mondesi, R	.209	10	43	5	9	15	3	0	1	4	0-0	0	3-0	6	1-2	1	1	.349	.261
Morandini,	.271	35	107	10	29	33	2	1	0	7	2-0	0	7-0	23	1-0	2	1	.308	.316
Mottola, C	.222	3	9	1	2	2	0	0	0	2	0-0	1	0-0	4	0-0	0	0	.222	.300
Stewart, S	.301	72	309	58	93	149	22	2	10	33	0-1	2	21-1	37	7-3	8	2	.482	.348
Wells, V	.000	3	2	0	0	0	0	0	0	0	0-0	0	0-0	0	0-0	0	0	.000	.000
Wise, D	.000	9	2	1	0	0	0	0	0	0	0-0	1	0-0	0	0-0	0	0	.000	.333
Woodward, C	.227	10	22	2	5	6	1	0	0	1	0-0	0	0-0	4	0-0	0	2	.273	.227
Borbon, P	.000	18	0	0	0	0	0	0	0	0	0-0	0	0-0	0	0-0	0	0	.000	.000
Carpenter,	.000	16	0	0	0	0	0	0	0	0	0-0	0	0-0	0	0-0	0	1	.000	.000
Castillo, F	.000	8	0	0	0	0	0	0	0	0	0-0	0	0-0	0	0-0	0	0	.000	.000
Coco (Reyn	.000	1	0	0	0	0	0	0	0	0	0-0	0	0-0	0	0-0	0	0	.000	.000
Dewitt, M	.000	1	0	0	0	0	0	0	0	0	0-0	0	0-0	0	0-0	0	0	.000	.000
Escobar, K	.000	25	0	0	0	0	0	0	0	0	0-0	0	0-0	0	0-0	0	0	.000	.000
Estrella, L	.000	2	0	0	0	0	0	0	0	0	0-0	0	0-0	0	0-0	0	0	.000	.000
Frascatore,	.000	25	0	0	0	0	0	0	0	0	0-0	0	0-0	0	0-0	0	0	.000	.000
Guthrie, M	.000	23	0	0	0	0	0	0	0	0	0-0	0	0-0	0	0-0	0	0	.000	.000
Halladay, R	.000	8	0	0	0	0	0	0	0	0	0-0	0	0-0	0	0-0	0	0	.000	.000
Hamilton, J	.000	6	0	0	0	0	0	0	0	0	0-0	0	0-0	0	0-0	0	0	.000	.000
Koch, B	.000	31	0	0	0	0	0	0	0	0	0-0	0	0-0	0	0-0	0	0	.000	.000
Loaiza, E	.000	14	0	0	0	0	0	0	0	0	0-0	0	0-0	0	0-0	0	2	.000	.000
Painter, L	.000	19	0	0	0	0	0	0	0	0	0-0	0	0-0	0	0-0	0	0	.000	.000
Quantrill,	.000	29	0	0	0	0	0	0	0	0	0-0	0	0-0	0	0-0	0	0	.000	.000
Trachsel, S	.000	11	0	0	0	0	0	0	0	0	0-0	0	0-0	0	0-0	0	0	.000	.000
Wells, D	.000	16	0	0	0	0	0	0	0	0	0-0	0	0-0	0	0-0	0	2	.000	.000
PITCHERS	.000	73	0	0	0	0	0	0	0	0	0-0	0	0-0	0	0-0	0	5	.000	.000
TORONTO	.271	73	2531	359	687	1147	149	10	97	345	15-12	24	241-16	451	24-14	68	49	.453	.339
OPPONENT	.277	73	2534	385	701	1111	144	7	84	364	24-18	27	235-13	439	43-14	55	41	.438	.342
DH	.267	73	292	44	78	161	11	0	24	64	0-3	2	14-1	51	0-0	13	0	.551	.302

PITCHING, PRE ALL-STAR BREAK

PITCHER	R/L	W-L	ERA	G	GS	CG	GF	SHO	SV	IP	H	R	ER	HR	HB	BB-IBB	SO	WP	BK	OPP AVG
Andrews, C	L	1-2	10.02	8	2	0	1	0	0	20.2	34	23	23	6	0	9-0	12	0	1	.374
Bale, J	L	0-0	14.73	2	0	0	0	0	0	3.2	5	7	6	1	2	3-0	6	0	0	.313
Borbon, P	L	1-0	4.76	41	0	0	4	0	0	28.1	33	22	15	4	5	17-2	22	0	0	.295
Carpenter	R	7-7	6.13	18	18	2	0	0	0	108.2	124	76	74	20	4	50-0	63	2	0	.289
Castillo,	R	6-5	4.17	17	17	0	0	0	0	99.1	86	49	46	14	5	46-0	76	0	0	.232
Cubillan,	R	1-0	8.04	7	0	0	1	0	0	15.2	20	14	14	5	1	11-0	14	0	0	.317
Dewitt, M	R	1-0	7.11	7	0	0	4	0	0	12.2	18	10	10	3	2	8-0	5	1	0	.346
Escobar, K	R	6-9	5.26	18	18	3	0	1	0	114.2	127	72	67	14	2	55-0	80	1	0	.285
Frascator	R	1-3	7.14	35	0	0	9	0	0	40.1	51	37	32	9	5	20-1	14	3	0	.313
Gunderson	L	0-1	7.11	6	0	0	1	0	0	6.1	15	6	5	0	1	2-1	2	0	0	.455
Halladay,	R	3-5	11.68	11	10	0	1	0	0	49.1	77	64	64	9	1	31-0	31	5	0	.356
Koch, B	R	4-1	2.74	37	0	0	35	0	20	46.0	48	16	14	4	0	13-2	40	0	0	.271
Munro, P	R	1-1	5.96	9	3	0	2	0	0	25.2	38	22	17	1	3	16-0	16	1	0	.355
Painter, L	L	1-0	4.42	23	2	0	6	0	0	38.2	36	21	19	7	1	11-0	33	3	0	.247
Quantrill	R	0-5	4.68	39	0	0	16	0	1	50.0	57	29	26	4	2	15-0	25	0	0	.286
Wells, D	L	15-2	3.44	19	19	4	0	1	0	128.1	145	55	49	10	3	18-0	100	8	1	.282
TORONTO		48-41	5.47	89	89	9	80	2	21	788.1	914	523	479	111	37	325-6	539	24	2	.292
OPPONENTS		41-48	5.40	89	89	5	84	3	16	790.2	875	502	474	147	36	285-16	575	32	6	.278

PITCHING, POST ALL-STAR BREAK

PITCHER	R/L	W-L	ERA	G	GS	CG	GF	SHO	SV	IP	H	R	ER	HR	HB	BB-IBB	SO	WP	BK	OPP AVG
Borbon, P	L	0-1	10.13	18	0	0	2	0	1	13.1	12	15	15	1	0	21-3	7	0	0	.245
Carpenter	R	3-5	6.48	16	9	0	1	0	0	66.2	80	54	48	10	1	33-1	50	1	0	.292
Castillo,	R	4-0	2.09	8	7	0	1	0	0	38.2	26	9	9	4	0	10-0	28	0	0	.190
Coco (Rey	R	0-0	9.00	1	1	0	0	0	0	4.0	5	4	4	1	1	5-0	2	1	0	.294
Dewitt, M	R	0-0	27.00	1	0	0	0	0	0	1.0	2	3	3	1	0	1-0	1	0	0	.400
Escobar, K	R	4-6	5.51	25	6	0	8	0	2	65.1	59	46	40	12	1	30-3	62	3	0	.235
Estrella,	R	0-0	5.79	2	0	0	1	0	0	4.2	9	3	3	1	0	0-0	3	0	0	.450
Frascator	R	1-1	3.31	25	0	0	6	0	0	32.2	36	14	12	5	2	13-1	16	0	0	.286
Guthrie, M	L	0-2	4.79	23	0	0	5	0	0	20.2	20	12	11	3	1	9-0	20	2	0	.263
Halladay,	R	1-2	7.85	8	3	0	3	0	0	18.1	30	23	16	5	1	11-0	13	1	1	.357
Hamilton,	R	2-1	3.55	6	6	0	0	0	0	33.0	28	13	13	3	2	12-0	15	0	0	.233
Koch, B	R	5-2	2.48	31	0	0	27	0	13	32.2	30	12	9	2	2	5-2	20	1	0	.240
Loaiza, E	R	5-7	3.62	14	14	1	0	1	0	92.0	95	45	37	8	10	26-0	62	0	0	.270
Painter, L	L	1-0	5.14	19	0	0	5	0	0	28.0	33	16	16	2	1	11-1	20	1	0	.303
Quantrill	R	2-0	4.28	29	0	0	8	0	0	33.2	43	16	16	3	0	10-1	22	1	0	.314
Trachsel,	R	2-5	5.29	11	11	0	0	0	0	63.0	72	40	37	10	0	25-1	32	1	0	.293
Wells, D	L	5-6	4.97	16	16	5	0	0	0	101.1	121	60	56	13	5	13-0	66	1	0	.298
TORONTO		35-38	4.74	73	73	6	67	2	16	649.0	701	385	342	84	27	235-13	439	13	1	.277
OPPONENTS		38-35	4.59	73	73	4	69	4	19	647.0	687	359	330	97	24	241-16	451	18	0	.271

BASEBALL WRITER'S ASSOCIATION OF AMERICA

BBWAA TORONTO CHAPTER - 2001

EXECUTIVE
HONORARY CHAIRMAN - Neil MacCarl
CHAIRMAN - Bob Elliott, Toronto Sun
VICE-CHAIRMAN - Larry Millson, Globe and Mail
SECRETARY/TREASURER - Tom Maloney, National Post

DIRECTORS:
Geoff Baker, Toronto Star
Mike Ganter, Toronto Sun
Richard Griffin, Toronto Star
Tom Maloney, National Post

MEMBERS:
Geoff Baker, Toronto Star
Jeff Blair, Globe and Mail
Stephen Brunt, Globe and Mail
Neil Campbell, Globe and Mail*
Cam Cole, National Post
Neil Davidson, Canadian Press*
Rosie DiManno, Toronto Star
Bob Elliott, Toronto Sun
Ken Fidlin, Toronto Sun
Mike Ganter, Toronto Sun
Richard Griffin, Toronto Star
Chris Jones, National Post

Bill Lankhof, Toronto Sun
Tom Maloney, National Post
Tony Maraschiello, Toronto Sun
Larry Millson, Globe and Mail
Steve Milton, Hamilton Spectator
Scott Morrison, Toronto Sun*
Graham Parley, National Post*
Dave Perkins, Toronto Star
Mike Rutsey, Toronto Sun
Allan Ryan, Toronto Star
Steve Tustin, Toronto Star
Mark Zwolinski, Toronto Star

* - Denotes Sports Editor

Honorary Members:
Milt Dunnell
Trent Frayne
George Gross
Neil MacCarl

2000 TORONTO BLUE JAYS DAY-BY-DAY

Pitcher in Caps – Complete Game   r – Relief Pitcher

	W-L	HOME	ROAD	POS	GB	OPP	D/N	SCORE	WINNER	LOSER
APRIL										
3	1-0	1-0		T1	0	KC	D	W5-4	rKoch (1-0)	rSpradlin (0-1)
4	2-0	2-0		T1	0	KC	N	W6-3	Halladay (1-0)	Witasick (0-1)
5	2-1	2-1		T1	0	KC	N	L4-3	Rosado (1-0)	Carpenter (0-1)
6	2-2	2-2		T3	-0.5	KC	N	L9-3	Durbin (1-0)	Escobar (0-1)
7	2-3		0-1	T3	-1.5	@TEX	N	L11-5	Clark (1-0)	FCastillo (0-1)
8	3-3		1-1	3	-1.5	@TEX	N	W4-0	WELLS (1-0)	Rogers (0-1)
9	3-4		1-2	3	-2.5	@TEX	D	L7-5	Helling (1-0)	Halladay (1-1)
10	3-5		1-3	3	-3.0	@ANA	N	L6-0	SCHOENEWEIS (2-0)	Carpenter (0-2)
11	3-6		1-4	4	-3.0	@ANA	N	L5-4	Ortiz (1-0)	Escobar (0-2)
12	4-6		2-4	4	-2.0	@ANA	N	W6-2	rBorbon (1-0)	rPetkovsek (0-1)
13	4-6			4	-2.0	—OFF DAY—				
14	4-7	2-3		4	-3.0	SEA	D	L11-9	Moyer (2-1)	Wells (1-1)
15	4-8	2-4		4	-4.0	SEA	D	L17-6	rfRodriguez (1-0)	Halladay (1-2)
16	4-9	2-5		5	-5.0	SEA	D	L19-7	Garcia (2-1)	Carpenter (0-3)
17	5-9	3-5		5	-5.0	ANA	N	W7-1	Escobar (1-2)	Ortiz (1-2)
18	5-10	3-6		5	-6.0	ANA	N	L16-10	Dickson (2-0)	FCastillo (0-2)
19	6-10	4-6		5	-6.0	ANA	D	W12-4	WELLS (2-1)	Hill (1-3)
20	7-10	5-6		4	-5.5	ANA	N	W12-11	Halladay (2-2)	Bottenfield (1-2)
21	8-10	6-6		4	-4.5	NYY	D	W8-3	CARPENTER (1-3)	Mendoza (2-1)
22	9-10	7-6		4	-3.5	NYY	D	W8-2	ESCOBAR (2-2)	Cone (1-2)
23	9-11	7-7		4	-4.5	NYY	D	L10-7	Hernandez (4-0)	rAndrews (0-1)
24	10-11		3-4	4	-3.5	@OAK	N	W3-2	Wells (3-1)	Appier (3-2)
25	10-12		3-6	4	-3.5	@OAK	N	L11-2	Hudson (2-2)	Halladay (2-3)
26	11-12		4-5	4	-3.5	@OAK	N	W4-2	Carpenter (2-3)	Olivares (1-3)
27	11-12			4	-3.5	—OFF DAY—				
28	11-13		4-6	4	-4.5	@NYY	N	L6-0	Cone (1-2)	Escobar (2-3)
29	12-13		5-6	4	-3.5	@NYY	D	W6-2	Wells (4-1)	Hernandez (4-1)
30	12-14		5-7	4	-4.5	@NYY	D	L7-1	Clemens (2-2)	Halladay (2-4)
MAY										
1	13-14		6-7	4	-4.5	@CWS	N	W5-3	Carpenter (3-3)	Rwells (2-3)
2	14-14		7-7	4	-4.5	@CWS	N	W4-1	FCastillo (1-2)	rWunsch (0-1)
3	14-15		7-8	4	-5.5	@CWS	N	L7-3	Baldwin (5-0)	Escobar (2-4)
4	15-15	8-7		4	-5.0	CLE	N	W8-1	Wells (5-1)	Finley (1-3)
5	16-15	9-7		4	-5.0	CLE	N	W11-10	rKoch (2-0)	rShuey (1-1)
6	16-16	9-8		4	-6.0	CLE	N	L8-6	rRincon (1-0)	rQuantrill (0-3)
7	16-17	9-9		4	-6.0	CLE	D	L10-8 (12)	rShuey (2-1)	rGunderson (0-1)
8	17-17	10-9		4	-6.0	BAL	N	W6-5	Escobar (3-4)	Johnson (0-2)
9	18-17	11-9		3	-6.0	BAL	N	W6-4	Wells (6-1)	Mussina (1-4)
10	19-17	12-9		3	-5.5	BAL	N	W7-2	Painter (1-0)	Erickson (0-5)
11	19-17			3	-5.0	—OFF DAY—				
12	19-18		7-9	3	-5.0	@TB	N	L4-3	rWhite (1-2)	CARPENTER (3-4)
13	20-18		8-9	3	-4.0	@TB	D	W8-4	Escobar (4-4)	rLidle (0-1)
14	21-18		9-9	3	-3.5	@TB	D	W3-2	WELLS (7-1)	rLopez (2-3)
15	21-19	12-10		4	-4.5	BOS	N	L8-1	Schourek (2-3)	FCastillo (1-3)
16	22-19	13-10		3	-3.5	BOS	N	W7-6	rMunro (1-0)	rLowe (2-1)
17	22-20	13-11		4	-4.5	BOS	N	L8-0	PMartinez (7-1)	Carpenter (3-5)
18	22-20			4	-4.5	—OFF DAY—				
19	22-21	13-12		4	-4.5	CWS	N	L5-3	Sirotka (3-3)	Escobar (4-5)
20	22-22	13-13		4	-5.5	CWS	D	L6-2	BALDWIN (7-0)	Wells (7-2)
21	22-23	13-14		4	-5.5	CWS	D	L2-1	Eldred (4-2)	FCastillo (1-4)
22	23-23	14-14		3	-5.0	CWS	D	W4-3	rKoch (3-0)	rHowry (0-1)
23	24-23		10-9	3	-4.0	@BOS	N	W3-2	Carpenter (4-5)	PMartinez (7-2)
24	24-24		10-10	3	-5.0	@BOS	N	L6-3 (11)	rCormier (2-0)	rFrascatore (1-1)
25	25-24		11-10	3	-4.0	@BOS	N	W11-6	Wells (8-2)	Schourek (2-4)
26	26-24		12-10	3	-4.0	@DET	N	W8-2	rFrascatore (1-1)	rBrocail (1-3)
27	26-25		12-11	3	-4.0	@DET	D	L4-3	rBrocail (2-3)	rQuantrill (1-3)
28	27-25		13-11	3	-4.0	@DET	D	W12-7	rAndrews (1-1)	rBlair (2-1)
29	27-25			3	-4.0	—OFF DAY—				
30	27-26	14-15		3	-5.0	MIN	N	L4-1	Redman (4-0)	Escobar (4-6)
31	28-26	15-15		3	-4.0	MIN	N	W4-2	Wells (9-2)	RADKE (3-6)
JUNE										
1	28-27	15-16		3	-4.0	MIN	D	L5-1	Milton (5-1)	FCastillo (1-5)
2	28-28		13-12	3	-4.0	@FLA	N	L11-10	rBones (1-0)	Munro (1-1)
3	28-29		13-13	3	-4.0	@FLA	D	L2-1	rLooper (3-1)	rKoch (3-1)
4	29-29		14-13	3	-4.0	@FLA	D	W7-2	ESCOBAR (5-6)	Nunez (0-6)
5	30-29		15-13	3	-3.0	@ATL	N	W9-3	Wells (10-2)	Burkett (4-3)
6	30-30		15-14	3	-4.0	@ATL	N	L7-6	rRemlinger (2-1)	rFrascatore (1-2)
7	31-30		16-14	3	-4.0	@ATL	N	W12-8	rCubillan (1-0)	Millwood (4-5)
8	31-30			3	-4.0	—OFF DAY—				
9	32-30	16-16		3	-3.0	MTL	D	W13-3	Carpenter (5-5)	Tucker (5-5)
10	32-31	16-17		3	-4.0	MTL	D	L11-2	Armas (2-3)	Escobar (5-7)
11	33-31	17-17		3	-3.5	MTL	N	W8-3	rKoch (4-1)	rMota (0-1)
12	34-31		17-14	3	-3.0	@DET	N	W4-2	FCastillo (2-5)	Nomo (2-6)
13	34-32		17-15	3	-3.0	@DET	N	L16-3	Blair (3-1)	Andrews (1-2)
14	35-32		18-15	3	-3.0	@DET	N	W8-1	Carpenter (6-5)	Weaver (4-7)
15	35-32			3	-2.5	—OFF DAY—				
16	35-33		18-16	3	-3.0	@BOS	N	L7-4	rPichardo (2-0)	Escobar (5-8)
17	36-33		19-16	3	-2.0	@BOS	D	W11-10	Wells (11-2)	RMartinez (5-4)
18	37-33		20-16	3	-1.0	@BOS	D	W5-1	FCastillo (3-5)	Fassero (6-3)
19	37-33			3	-1.0	—OFF DAY—				
20	37-34	17-18		3	-2.0	DET	N	L18-6	Weaver (4-6)	Carpenter (6-6)
21	38-34	18-18		3	-1.0	DET	N	W6-0	ESCOBAR (6-8)	Moehler (4-4)
22	39-34	19-18		T2	0	DET	N	W7-4	Wells (12-2)	NOMO (2-7)
23	40-34	20-18		1	+0.5	BOS	N	W5-4	FCastillo (4-5)	Wasdin (0-3)
24	41-34	21-18		1	+1.0	BOS	N	W6-4	Halladay (3-4)	Rose (1-3)
25	42-34	22-18		1	+2.0	BOS	D	W6-5(13)	rDewitt (1-0)	rFlorie (0-2)
26	42-34			1	+2.0	—OFF DAY—				
27	42-35		20-17	1	+2.0	@TB	N	L11-1	Trachsel (6-7)	Escobar (6-9)
28	43-35		21-17	1	+3.0	@TB	N	W5-2	WELLS (13-2)	Yan (4-6)
29	44-35		22-17	1	+3.0	@TB	D	W12-3	FCastillo (5-5)	Lidle (1-3)
30	44-36		22-18	1	+3.0	@BAL	N	L8-3	Rapp (5-5)	Halladay (3-5)

	W-L	HOME	ROAD	POS	GB	OPP	D/N	SCORE	WINNER	LOSER
JULY										
1	44-37		22-19	1	+2.0	@BAL	N	L12-5	PONSON (5-4)	Carpenter (6-7)
2	44-38		22-20	1	+1.0	@BAL	D	L3-2	rTrombley (4-2)	rQuantrill (0-3)
3	45-38		23-20	1	+1.5	@BAL	D	W6-4	Wells (14-2)	Johnson (0-7)
4	45-39		23-21	1	+1.5	@CLE	D	L9-4	Colon (8-5)	rFrascatore (1-3)
5	45-40		23-22	1	+0.5	@CLE	N	L15-7	rBrewington (2-0)	rQuantrill (0-4)
6	46-40		24-22	1	+0.5	@CLE	N	W9-6	Carpenter (7-7)	Burba (8-4)
7	46-41		24-23	2	-0.5	@MON	N	L10-5	rLira (2-0)	rQuantrill (0-5)
8	47-41		25-23	2	-1.0	@MON	N	W6-3	Wells (15-2)	Armas (4-6)
9	48-41		26-23	2	+2.5	@MON	D	W13-3	FCastillo (6-5)	Hermanson (6-7)
10										
11						– ALL-STAR BREAK –				
12										
13	48-42	22-19		2	-	PHI	N	L8-5	Schilling (5-5)	Carpenter (7-8)
14	49-42	23-19		2		PHI	N	W3-2	rKoch (5-1)	rBrantley (1-3)
15	49-43	23-20		2	-0.5	PHI	D	L7-3	Chen (5-0)	Wells (15-3)
16	50-43	24-20		2	-0.5	NYM	N	W7-3	Halladay (4-5)	Leiter (10-3)
17	50-44	24-21		2	-0.5	NYM	N	L7-5(11)	rJFranco (4-3)	rBorbon (1-1)
18	50-45	24-22		3	-1.5	NYM	N	L11-7	Jones (4-4)	Carpenter (7-9)
19	51-45	25-22		3	-1.5	TB	N	W5-2	Escobar (7-9)	LOPEZ (6-7)
20	52-45	26-22		3	-0.5	TB	N	W6-5	rQuantrill (1-5)	rWhite (3-3)
21	52-46	26-23		3	-1.5	BAL	N	L9-5	Rapp (6-6)	Halladay (4-6)
22	52-47	26-24		3	-1.5	BAL	D	L8-2	Mercedes (5-4)	Loaiza (6-7)
23	53-47	27-24		3	-1.5	BAL	D	W4-1	FCastillo (7-5)	MUSSINA (6-10)
24	53-47			3	-2.0	–OFF DAY–				
25	53-48	27-25		3	-3.0	CLE	N	L10-3	Finley (9-7)	Escobar (7-10)
26	54-48	28-24		3	-3.0	CLE	D	W8-1	WELLS (16-3)	Colon (8-6)
27	55-48		27-23	2	-2.0	@SEA	N	W7-2	Loaiza (6-7)	rRhodes (3-5)
28	55-49		27-24	3	-3.0	@SEA	N	L7-4	Garcia (3-1)	Carpenter (7-10)
29	55-50		27-25	3	-4.0	@SEA	D	L6-5 (13)	rTomko (5-3)	rHalladay (4-7)
30	55-51		27-26	3	-4.0	@SEA	N	L10-6	Sele (12-6)	Escobar (7-11)
31	55-52		27-26	3	-4.5	@OAK	N	L6-1	Hudson (12-3)	WELLS (16-4)
AUGUST										
1	55-53		27-28	3	-5.5	@OAK	D	L3-1(10)	rIsringhausen (5-3)	rKoch (5-2)
2	55-54		27-29	3	-5.5	@OAK	D	L5-4	rMecir (8-2)	rGuthrie (1-2)
3	56-54	29-25		3	-5.5	TEX	N	W3-1	FCastillo (8-5)	Rogers (14-9)
4	57-54	30-25		3	-5.5	TEX	N	W10-8	rQuantrill (2-5)	rVenafro (1-1)
5	58-54	31-25		3	-4.5	TEX	D	W8-5	Wells (17-4)	Davis (4-3)
6	58-55	31-26		3	-4.5	TEX	D	L11-6	Glynn (3-1)	Escobar (7-12)
7	58-56		27-30	3	-4.5	@KC	N	L8-7	Stein (3-3)	Loaiza (6-8)
8	59-56		28-30	3	-4.5	@KC	N	W6-1	FCastillo (9-5)	Suzuki (5-7)
9	59-57		28-31	3	-5.5	@KC	N	L5-3	Suppan (6-6)	Trachsel (6-11)
10	60-57		29-31	3	-5.5	@KC	D	W15-7	rCarpenter (8-10)	rFussell (4-3)
11	60-58		29-32	3	-5.5	@MIN	N	L9-4	Romero (2-1)	Escobar (7-13)
12	60-59		29-33	3	-5.5	@MIN	N	L6-3	Redman (11-5)	Loaiza (6-9)
13	61-59		30-33	3	-5.5	@MIN	D	W13-3	rCarpenter (9-10)	Radke (8-13)
14	61-59			3	-6.0	–OFF DAY–				
15	61-60	31-27		3	-7.0	ANA	N	L8-4	MWise (1-1)	Wells (18-5)
16	62-60	32-27		3	-6.0	ANA	D	W8-6	rKoch (6-2)	rPote (1-1)
17	62-60			3	-6.5	–OFF DAY–				
18	63-60	33-27		3	-5.5	MIN	N	W3-2	Loaiza (7-9)	Kinney (0-1)
19	63-61	33-28		3	-6.5	MIN	N	L5-1	Radke (9-13)	rGuthrie (1-3)
20	64-61	34-28		3	-5.5	MIN	D	W6-3	DWELLS (18-5)	rCarrasco (3-3)
21	64-61			3	-6.0	–OFF DAY–				
22	65-61	35-28		3	-5.0	KC	N	W7-5	rEscobar (8-13)	rSantiago (6-4)
23	66-61	36-28		3	-5.0	KC	N	W9-8	rEscobar (9-13)	rLarkin (0-2)
24	66-61			3	-5.5	–OFF DAY–				
25	67-61		30-34	3	-5.5	@TEX	N	L1-0(11)	rVenafro (2-1)	rKoch (6-3)
26	67-62		31-34	3	-5.5	@TEX	N	W9-3	Hamilton (1-0)	Sikorski (1-2)
27	68-62		32-34	3	-5.5	@TEX	N	W6-4	Trachsel (7-11)	Helling (14-9)
28	69-62		33-34	3	-5.5	@ANA	N	W4-2	Loaiza (8-9)	Ortiz (4-5)
29	69-63		33-35	3	-5.5	@ANA	N	L9-4	rHoltz (2-2)	Carpenter (9-11)
30	70-63		34-35	3	-5.5	@ANA	N	W11-2	Wells (19-5)	Wise (3-2)
31	70-63			3	-5.5	–OFF DAY–				
SEPTEMBER										
1	71-63	37-28		3	-5.5	OAK	N	W4-3	rFrascatore (2-3)	rJones (3-2)
2	71-64	37-29		3	-6.5	OAK	D	L8-0	Heredia (14-9)	Trachsel (7-12)
3	71-65	37-30		3	-6.5	OAK	D	L4-3	Hudson (15-6)	Loaiza (8-10)
4	71-66	37-31		3	-7.5	OAK	D	L10-0	Zito (3-3)	Wells (19-6)
5	71-67	37-32		3	-8.5	SEA	N	L4-3	rRhodes (4-7)	rEscobar (9-14)
6	72-67	38-32		3	-7.5	SEA	N	W7-3	Hamilton (2-0)	Halama (11-8)
7	72-68	38-33		3	-8.5	SEA	D	L8-1	Garcia (6-4)	Trachsel (7-13)
8	73-68	39-33		3	-8.5	DET	N	W3-0	LOAIZA (9-10)	WEAVER (9-13)
9	74-68	40-33		3	-8.5	DET	N	W6-5	rKoch (7-3)	rNitowski (4-9)
10	75-68	41-33		2	-8.5	DET	D	W6-2	Carpenter (10-11)	Sparks (6-4)
11	75-68			3	-8.0	–OFF DAY–				
12	75-69		34-26	3	-9.0	@NYY	N	L10-2	Neagle (7-4)	Hamilton (2-1)
13	75-70		34-37	3	-10.0	@NYY	N	L3-2	Clemens (13-6)	Loaiza (9-11)
14	76-70		35-37	3	-9.0	@NYY	N	W3-2(11)	rKoch (8-3)	rChoate (0-1)
15	77-70		36-37	3	-8.0	@CWS	N	W6-5	rEscobar (10-14)	Garland (9-7)
16	77-71		36-38	3	-9.0	@CWS	N	L6-3	rWunsch (6-3)	rEscobar (10-15)
17	78-71		37-38	3	-8.0	@CWS	D	W14-1	rPainter (2-0)	Rwells (5-9)
18	78-71			3	-7.5	–OFF DAY–				
19	79-71	42-33		3	-6.5	NYY	N	W16-3	Trachsel (8-13)	Pettitte (18-8)
20	80-71	43-33		2	-5.5	NYY	D	W7-2	Loaiza (10-11)	Cone (4-13)
21	81-71	44-33		2	-4.5	NYY	N	W3-1	DWELLS (20-6)	Hernandez (12-12)
22	81-72	44-34		2	-4.5	TB	N	L3-2	Lidle (3-6)	rFrascatore (2-4)
23	82-72	45-34		2	-4.5	TB	D	W7-6	rKoch (9-3)	rEnders (0-1)
24	82-73	45-35		2	-5.5	TB	D	L6-0	HARPER (1-2)	Trachsel (8-14)
25	82-74	45-36		2	-5.5	TB	N	L5-1	Wilson (1-4)	Loaiza (10-13)
26	82-75		37-39	3	-5.5	@BAL	N	L2-1	Mercedes (13-7)	DWELLS (20-7)
27	83-75		38-39	3	-4.5	@BAL	N	W4-0	FCastillo (10-5)	Ponson (8-7)
28	83-76		38-40	3	-4.5	@BAL	N	L23-1	Rapp (9-12)	Carpenter (10-12)
29	83-77		38-41	3	-4.5	@CLE	N	L8-4	rSpeier(5-2)	Trachsel (8-15)
30	83-78		38-42	3	-4.5	@CLE	D	L6-5	Finley (16-11)	Loaiza (10-13)
OCTOBER										
1	83-79		38-43	3	-4.5	@CLE	D	L11-4	Woodard (3-3)	DWells (20-8)

Season in Review

2000

DATE	TRANSACTION
Feb. 16	LHP ERIC GUNDERSON signed a minor league contract with an invitation to the major league camp.
Mar. 6	C JOE LAWRENCE optioned to Syracuse (AAA). IF CESAR IZTURIS, LHP KURT BOGOTT and RHP MATT MCCLELLAN re-assigned to the minor league camp.
Mar. 9	IF LUIS LOPEZ and RHP MIKE ROMANO re-assigned to the minor league camp.
Mar. 12	RHP PASQUAL COCO, RHP LEO ESTRELLA and C JOSH PHELPS optioned to Tennessee (AA). RHP JOHN SNEED, RHP GARY GLOVER and IF MIKE YOUNG optioned to Syracuse (AAA). OF CHAD MOTTOLA returned to Syracuse (AAA).
Mar. 15	RHP MATT DEWITT, LHP JOHN BALE and 3B CASEY BLAKE optioned to Syracuse (AAA). IF FELIPE LOPEZ was re-assigned to minor league camp.
Mar. 16	IB/DH BRAD FULLMER acquired from the Montreal Expos in a three-way deal with Texas. IB/DH DAVID SEGUI and cash to TEXAS and 1B LEE STEVENS to Montreal.
Mar. 17	IB KEVIN WITT and OF ANDY THOMPSON optioned to Syracuse (AAA). C MARK DALESANDRO re-assigned to minor league camp.
Mar. 21	RHP JOEY HAMILTON placed on the 15-day disabled list.
Mar. 22	C KEVIN BROWN, C CHARLIE GREENE and IF WILLIS OTANEZ returned to minor league camp; OF VERNON WELLS optioned to Syracuse (AAA); Minor League IF JERSEN PEREZ acquired from the New York Mets in exchange for waiving the rights to RHP JIM MANN, who was a Rule V selection.
Mar. 27	Signed OF MARTY CORDOVA to a minor-league contract.
Mar. 28	RHP NERIO RODRIGUEZ claimed off waivers by the New York Mets.
Mar. 29	Designated OF ANTHONY SANDERS for assignment. Purchased contract of OF MARTY CORDOVA. Claimed LHP MIKE KUSIEWICZ off waivers from the Minnesota Twins.
Mar. 31	OF ANTHONY SANDERS claimed on waivers by the Seattle Mariners. Outrighted LHP MIKE KUSIEWICZ to Tennessee of the Double-A Southern League.
Apr. 1	Purchased the contract of RHP FRANK CASTILLO and added him to the 40-man roster. Returned LHP ERIC GUNDERSON to minor league camp. LHP CLAYTON ANDREWS optioned to Syracuse (AAA).
Apr. 2	LHP PEDRO BORBON signed to a two-year contract extension.

OPENING DAY ROSTER	
PITCHERS: (11 + 1DL)	Pedro Borbon, Chris Carpenter, Frank Castillo, Kelvim Escobar, John Frascatore, Roy Halladay, Billy Koch, Peter Munro, Lance Painter, Paul Quantrill, David Wells, DL – Joey Hamilton
CATCHERS: (2)	Alberto Castillo, Darrin Fletcher
INFIELDERS: (7)	Tony Batista, Homer Bush, Carlos Delgado, Brad Fullmer, Alex Gonzalez, Craig Grebeck, Chris Woodward
OUTFIELDERS: (5)	Marty Cordova, Jose Cruz, Raul Mondesi, Shannon Stewart, Dewayne Wise

Apr. 16	LHP CLAYTON ANDREWS recalled from Syracuse (AAA). IF CHRIS WOOWARD optioned to Syracuse (AAA).
Apr. 17	LHP JOHN BALE recalled from Syracuse (AAA). RHP PETE MUNRO optioned to Syracuse (AAA).
Apr. 28	LHP ERIC GUNDERSON purchased from Syracuse (AAA). LHP JOHN BALE optioned to Syracuse (AAA): RHP JOEY HAMILTON transferred to 60-day DL
May 1	OF SHANNON STEWART placed on 15-day DL (right hamstring pull). OF ANDY THOMPSON recalled from Syracuse (AAA).
May 5	IF CHRIS WOODWARD recalled from Syracuse (AAA). LHP CLAYTON ANDREWS optioned to Syracuse (AAA).
May 12	OF SHANNON STEWART assigned to Dunedin (A) for rehabilitation.
May 14	OF SHANNON STEWART recalled from rehabilitation assignment at Dunedin (A) and activated from 15-day DL. OF ANDY THOMPSON optioned to Syracuse (AAA)
May 16	RHP PETE MUNRO recalled from Syracuse (AAA). RHP ROY HALLADAY optioned to Syracuse (AAA).
May 19	IF CASEY BLAKE and LHP ERIC GUNDERSON designated for assignment. IF CHRIS WOODWARD optioned to Syracuse (AAA). C/OF TODD GREENE & RHP DARWIN CUBILLAN purchased from Syracuse (AAA).
May 23	LHP ERIC GUNDERSON outright to Syracuse (AAA).
May 25	LHP LANCE PAINTER placed on 15-day DL (left elbow tenderness) retroactive to May 17. IF CHRIS WOODWARD and LHP CLAYTON ANDREWS recalled from Syracuse (AAA).
May 26	2B HOMER BUSH placed on 15-day DL (right hip) retroactive to May 22.
June 4	RHP PETE MUNRO placed on 15-day DL (strained right elbow).
June 6	2B HOMER BUSH and LHP LANCE PAINTER activated from 15-day DL. OF DEWAYNWE WISE placed on 15-day DL (left foot-big toe).
June 7	C/OF TODD GREENE placed on 15-day DL (strained right knee). C JOSH PHELPS recalled from Tennessee (AA)
June 14	RHP MATT DEWITT recalled from Syracuse (AAA). LHP CLAYTON ANDREWS optioned to Syracuse (AAA).
June 17	C DARRIN FLETCHER placed on 15-day DL (right shoulder strain) retroactive to June 11. C CHARLIE GREENE purchased from Syracuse (AAA). Transferred OF DEWAYNE WISE from the 15-day to 60-day DL (left-foot big toe).
June 23	C/OF TODD GREENE activated from 15-day DL (strained right knee). Optioned C JOSH PHELPS to Tennessee (AA); RHP DARWIN CUBILLAN optioned to Syracuse (AAA).
June 24	RHP ROY HALLADAY recalled from Syracuse (AAA).
July 3	RHP PETE MUNRO activated from 15-day DL and optioned to Syracuse (AAA)

July 4	C DARRIN FLETCHER activated from 15-day DL. C CHARLIE GREENE designated for assignment.
July 10	C CHARLIE GREENE outrighted to Syracuse (AAA).
July 17	SS ALEX GONZALEZ placed on 15-day DL (right groin strain) retroactive to July 7. RHP PASQUAL COCO recalled from Syracuse (AAA). RHP JOEY HAMILTON assigned to Syracuse (AAA) on medical rehabilitation.
July 18	RHP PASQUAL COCO optioned to Tennessee (AA). RHP LEO ESTRELLA recalled from Syracuse (AAA).
July 19	RHP ESTEBAN LOAIZA acquired from the Texas Rangers in exchange for IF MIKE YOUNG and RHP DARWIN CUBILLAN.
July 21	RHP MATT DEWITT optioned to Syracuse (AAA).
July 22	SS ALEX GONZALEZ activated from 15-day DL. RHP LEO ESTRELLA optioned to Syracuse (AAA). OF RAUL MONDESI placed on 15-day DL (right elbow).
July 26	OF ROB DUCEY acquired from Philadelphia for a player to be named later.
July 31	RHP STEVE TRACHSEL and LHP MARK GUTHERIE acquired from Tampa Bay in exchange for 2B BRENT ABERNATHY and a player to be named later. IF HOMER BUSH placed on 15-day DL (left hand).
July 31	RHP JOHN SNEED assigned to Philadelphia (NL) to complete Rob Ducey trade.
Aug. 4	Acquired OF DAVE MARTINEZ from Texas for a player to be named later. RHP ROY HALLADAY optioned to Syracuse (AAA). OF ROB DUCEY designated for assignment.
Aug. 6	IF MICKEY MORANDINI acquired from Philadelphia for a player to be named later. IF CHRIS WOODWARD optioned to Syracuse (AAA). RHP PETE MUNRO designated for assignment.
Aug. 7	OF ROB DUCEY awarded to Philadelphia on a waiver claim to complete MICKEY MORANDINI trade.
Aug. 8	RHP PETE MUNRO awarded to Texas on a waiver claim to complete trade for OF DAVE MARTINEZ.
Aug. 11	OF DEWAYNE WISE assigned to Tennessee (AA) for rehabilitation.
Aug. 15	RHP JOEY HAMILTON recalled from rehabilitation assignment at Syracuse (AAA). RHP FRANK CASTILLO placed on 15-day DL (strained ligament in right forearm & elbow) retroactive to Aug 14.
Aug. 18	Transferred OF RAUL MONDESI from 15-day DL to 60-day DL.
Aug. 19	RHP JOEY HAMILTON activated off 60-day DL .
Aug. 23	RHP MATT DEWITT recalled from Syracuse (AAA) and placed on 60-day DL (broken right leg). Claimed RHP PAT DANEKER off waivers from the Chicago White Sox.
Aug. 30	OF DEWAYNE WISE recalled from rehabilitation assignment.
Sept. 1	OF VERNON WELLS recalled from Syracuse (AAA). OF DEWAYNE WISE reinstated from 60-day DL. IF HOMER BUSH transferred to 60-day DL (eligible Sept 29).
Sept. 5	IF CHRIS WOODWARD and RHP ROY HALLADAY recalled from Syracuse (AAA). OF CHAD MOTTOLA contract purchased from Syracuse. IB KEVIN WITT designated for assignment.
Sept. 11	IF KEVIN WITT outrighted to Syracuse (AAA).
Sept. 16	RHP FRANK CASTILLO activated from 15-day DL.
Sept. 20	OF RAUL MONDESI activated from the 60-day DL. RHP PAT DANEKER designated for assignment.
Sept. 25	RHP PAT DANEKER outrighted to Syracuse (AAA).
Oct. 2	RHP JOHN SNEED claimed on waivers from Philadelphia. OF MARTY CORDOVA designated for assignment.
Oct. 4	OF MARTY CORDOVA elected free agency.
Oct. 6	RHP JOHN SNEED awarded to Minnesota on a waiver claim.
Oct. 9	RHP MARK LUKASIEWICZ contract purchased from Syracuse (AAA).
Oct. 11	RHP MARK LUKASIEWICZ awarded to Anaheim on a waiver claim.
Oct. 30	IF ALEX GONZALEZ elected free agency.
Oct. 31	RHP FRANK CASTILLO, RHP STEVE TRACHSEL, LHP MARK GUTHRIE, IF MICKEY MORANDINI, IF CRAIG GREBECK and OF DAVE MARTINEZ elected free agency.
Nov. 3	IF HOMER BUSH and RHP MATT DEWITT reinstated from 60-day DL.
Nov. 7	LHP SCOTT EYRE acquired from the Chicago White Sox in exchange for RHP GARY GLOVER.
Nov. 13	Signed free agent RHP JASON DICKSON to a AAA contract.
Nov. 20	Added RHP BOB FILE, IF RYAN FREEL, IF CESAR IZTURIS, RHP GEORGE PEREZ and RHP ORLANDO WOODARDS to the 40-man roster.
Nov. 22	Acquired RHP STEVE PARRIS from the Cincinnati Reds in exchange for LHP CLAYTON ANDREWS and RHP LEO ESTRELLA.
Dec. 6	IF MICKEY MORANDINI signed to a AAA contract.
Dec. 8	Free Agent LHP DAN PLESAC signed.
Dec. 11	Acquired C JAYSON WERTH from Baltimore in exchange for LHP JOHN BALE. Acquired 3B COLE LINIAK from the Chicago Cubs in exchange for a player to be named later.
Dec. 12	Free agent SS ALEX GONZALEZ re-signed
Dec. 14	Signed free agent IF JEFF FRYE.
Dec. 20	RHP MATT DeWITT designated for assignment.

2001

Jan. 4	Assigned RHP MATT DEWITT outright to Syracuse (AAA).
Jan. 14	Acquired LHP MIKE SIROTKA, RHP KEVIN BEIRNE, RHP MIKE WILLIAMS and OF BRIAN SIMMONS in exchange for LHP DAVID WELLS and RHP MATT DEWITT. RHP JOHN FRASCATORE and OF CHAD MOTTOLA. designated for assignment.
Jan. 16	OF CHAD MOTTOLA traded to the Florida Marlins for a player to be named later or cash considerations.
Jan. 23	RHP JOHN FRASCATORE assigned outright to Syracuse (AAA).

Team Batting
Game - Blue Jays

Most At Bats	46	Aug. 13 at Minnesota
	50	May 7 vs. Cleveland (12.0 innings)
	50	June 25 vs. Boston (13.0 innings)
Most Runs	16	Sept. 19 vs. New York Yankees
Most Runs, Both Clubs	26	April 16 vs. Seattle (19), Toronto (7)
	26	April 18 vs. Anaheim (16), Toronto (10)
Most Hits	20	Aug. 13 at Minnesota
Most Hits, Both Clubs	36	April 18 vs. Anaheim (19), Toronto (17)
Most Singles	14	Aug. 30 at Anaheim
Most Extra Base Hits	11	July 18 vs. New York Mets (8-2B, 3B, 2-HR)
Most Doubles	8	July 18 vs. New York Mets
Most Triples	2	May 25 at Boston
Most Home Runs	5	May 5 vs. Cleveland
	5	Aug. 27 vs. Texas
Most Home Runs, Both Clubs	10	June 20 vs. Detroit (8), Toronto (2)
Most Total Bases	33	Aug. 13 at Minnesota
Most Stolen Bases	5	June 18 at Boston
Most Walks	10	July 5 at Cleveland
	10	July 17 vs. New York Mets (11.0 innings)
Most Strikeouts	14	July 26 vs. Cleveland
	15	July 29 at Seattle (13.0 innings)
Fewest Strikeouts	0	July 20 at Tampa Bay
Most Left on Base	15	Aug. 26 vs. Texas
Most Runs, Inning	7	May 26 at Detroit (8th inning)
Most Hits, Inning	7	April 18 vs. Anaheim (9th inning)
	7	May 10 vs. Anaheim (3rd inning)
	7	July 9 at Montreal (5th inning)
Most Hits, Consecutive At Bats, Inning	7	July 9 at Montreal (5th inning)
Most Consecutive Times Reaching Base, Inning	7	June 9 vs. Montreal (7th inning)
	7	July 9 at Montreal (5th inning)
	7	Sept. 19 vs. New York Yankees (8th inning)
Most Home Runs, Inning	3	April 18 vs. Anaheim (6th inning)
	3	April 23 vs. New York Yankees (6th inning)
Most Consecutive Games, Home Run	23	May 31-June 7, 9-14, 16-18, 20-25 (44 home runs)
Most Consecutive Games, No Home Runs	6	Sept. 1-6
Most Consecutive At Bats, No Home Runs	235	Aug. 31-Sept. 7

Team Fielding
Game - Blue Jays

Most Double Plays	4	May 20 vs. Chicago
	4	June 13 at Detroit
	4	June 20 vs. Detroit
Most Assists	19	May 1 at Chicago
Most Errors	5	May 21 vs. Chicago
Most Consecutive Games, Errorless	7	Sept. 21-27

Team Pitching
Game - Blue Jays

Most Strikeouts	15	June 11 vs. Montreal
Most Walks	11	July 30 at Seattle
Fewest Walks	0	18 times, last Sept. 26 at Baltimore
Most Pitchers Used	7	Aug. 4 vs. Texas
	7	June 25 vs. Boston (13.0 innings)
Fewest Hits Allowed	1	May 21 vs. Chicago
Most Consecutive Games, Allowing Home Run	10	May 24-28, 30-June 3 (13 home runs)
	10	June 27-July 6 (15 home runs)
Most Consecutive Games, Not Allowing Home Run	3	Five times, last Sept. 8-10

Team Batting
Game - Opponents

Most At Bats	54	Sept. 28 at Baltimore
Most Runs	23	Sept. 28 at Baltimore
Most Hits	23	Sept. 28 at Baltimore
Most Extra Base Hits	12	June 20 vs. Detroit (3-2B, 3B, 8-HR)
Most Singles	18	Sept. 28 at Baltimore
Most Doubles	7	May 5 vs. Cleveland
Most Triples	1	23 times, last Sept. 12 at New York Yankees
Most Home Runs	8	June 20 vs. Detroit
Most Home Runs, Inning	4	May 3 at Chicago
Most Total Bases	47	June 20 vs. Detroit
Most Stolen Bases	4	April 18 vs. Anaheim
Most Left on Base	15	May 5 vs. Cleveland
	15	Aug. 25 at Texas
	16	July 29 at Seattle (13.0 innings)
Most Runs, Inning	10	Sept. 28 at Baltimore (4th inning)
Most Hits, Inning	9	April 20 vs. Anaheim (6th inning)
Most Hits, Consecutive At Bats, Inning	9	April 20 vs. Anaheim (6th inning)

Team Fielding
Game - Opponents

Most Double Plays	4	Aug. 7 at Kansas City
Most Errors	5	May 12 at Tampa Bay

Team Pitching
Game - Opponents

Most Strikeouts	14	July 26 vs. Cleveland
Most Walks	10	July 5 at Cleveland
	10	July 17 vs. New York Mets (11.0 innings)
Fewest Hits Allowed, 9 Innings	2	Sept. 4 vs. Oakland
	2	Sept. 24 vs. Tampa Bay
	2	Sept. 28 at Baltimore

Individual Batting - Blue Jays
Game

Most Runs	4	Shannon Stewart, May 25 at Boston
	4	Homer Bush, July 9 at Montreal
	4	Raul Mondesi, July 9 at Montreal
Most Hits	4	14 times, last Darrin Fletcher , Sept. 22 vs. Tampa Bay
Most Doubles	4	Shannon Stewart, July 18 vs. New York Mets
Most Triples	1	20 times, last Jose Cruz, Sept. 30 at Cleveland
Most Home Runs	3	Darrin Fletcher, Aug. 27 at Texas
Most Total Bases	12	Darrin Fletcher, Aug. 27 at Texas
Most Runs Batted In	6	Carlos Delgado, June 7 at Atlanta
Most Extra Base Hits	4	Shannon Stewart, June 9 vs. Montreal (3-2B, HR)
	4	Shannon Stewart, July 18 vs. New York Mets (4-2B)
Most Stolen Bases	2	Six times, last Stewart & Gonzalez, June 18 at Boston
Longest Hitting Streak	22	Carlos Delgado, June 4-7, 9-14, 16-18, 20-25, 27-29
Most Consecutive Games Hitting Home Run	3	Carlos Delgado, May 4-6
	3	Jose Cruz, May 5-7
	3	Tony Batista, June 29-July 1
	3	Raul Mondesi, July 7-9
	3	Shannon Stewart, Aug. 9-11
	3	Jose Cruz, Aug. 26-28
	3	Brad Fullmer, Sept. 8-10
Most Walks	3	Nine times, last Carlos Delgado, Sept. 9 vs. Detroit
Most Strikeouts	3	24 times, last Tony Batista, Sept. 15 at Chicago
	3	Jose Cruz, May 7 vs. Cleveland (12.0 innings)
	3	Chris Woodward, June 25 vs. Boston (13.0 innings)
	3	Jose Cruz, July 29 at Seattle (13.0 innings)
	3	Carlos Delgado, Sept. 14 at New York Yankees
	3	Todd Greene, Sept. 14 at New York Yankees
	4	Tony Batista, July 29 at Seattle (13.0 innings)
Most HBP	2	Brad Fullmer, Aug. 5 vs. Texas

Individual Pitching - Blue Jays
Game

Most Strikeouts, Starter	11	David Wells, June 11 vs. Montreal
	11	David Wells, July 26 vs. Cleveland
	11	Esteban Loaiza, Sept. 8 vs. Detroit
Most Strikeouts, Reliever	7	Chris Carpenter, Aug. 13 at Minnesota
Most Walks, Starter	8	Chris Carpenter, April 10 at Anaheim
Most Walks, Reliever	4	Pete Munro, April 14 vs. Seattle
Most Home Runs Allowed	3	Eight times, last Esteban Loaiza, Sept. 3 vs. Oakland
Most Innings, Starter	9.0	12 times, last David Wells, Sept. 26 at Baltimore
Most Innings, Reliever	5.1	Chris Carpenter, Aug. 13 at Minnesota
Longest Winning Streak	8	David Wells, May 25-July 8
	8	Frank Castillo, June 12-Aug. 8
Longest Losing Streak	5	Paul Quantrill, May 6-July 7
Most Consecutive Scoreless Innings, Starter	19.0	David Wells, Aug. 20-30
Most Consecutive Scoreless Innings, Reliever	15.2	Billy Koch, June 30-Aug. 1
Fewest Hits, Complete Game	4	Kelvim Escobar, June 21 vs. Detroit
Most Consecutive Save Opportunities Converted	21	Billy Koch, June 7-Aug. 28

Team Miscellaneous

Longest Winning Streak	5	June 21-25
Longest Winning Streak, Home	6	Sept. 8-10, 19-21
Longest Winning Streak, Road	3	May 13-14, 23
	3	July 8-9, 27
	3	Aug. 25-28
Longest Losing Streak	6	July 28-Aug. 2
Longest Losing Streak, Home	5	April 5-6, 14-16
Longest Losing Streak, Road	7	July 28-Aug. 2, 7
Longest Game, Innings	13.0	June 25 vs. Boston
	13.0	July 29 at Seattle
Longest Game Time, 9 Innings	3:51	April 18 vs. Anaheim
Longest Game Time, Extra Innings	5:04	July 29 at Seattle (13.0 innings)
Shortest Game Time, 9 Innings	2:15	May 31 vs. Minnesota
Largest Margin of Victory	13	Sept. 17 at Chicago (14-1)
	13	Sept. 19 vs. New York Yankees (16-3)
Largest Margin of Defeat	22	Sept. 28 at Baltimore (23-1)
Largest Crowd, SkyDome	40,898	April 3 vs. Kansas City
Smallest Crowd, SkyDome	13,514	April 4 vs. Kansas City
Largest Crowd, Road	43,721	April 30 at New York Yankees
Smallest Crowd, Road	8,266	April 25 at Oakland
Largest First Place Lead	+3.0	June 28, 29
Furthest from First Place	−10.0	Sept. 13
Most Games +.500	10	Sept. 21 (81-71)
	10	Sept. 23 (82-72)
Most Games −.500	5	April 16 (4-9)
	5	April 18 (5-10)
Largest Lead Overcome	6	Aug. 23 vs. Kansas City (8-2), W
	6	Sept. 23 vs. Tampa Bay (6-0), W
Largest Lead Surrendered	6	May 7 vs. Cleveland (6-0), L

BLUE JAYS SCORE 11

July 20, 1984: Trailing 3-1 at Seattle's Kingdom going into the 9th inning on July 20, 1984 the Blue Jays erupted for 11 runs in the 9th to win the game 12-7... Blue Jay club marks for one inning were set for: MOST RUNS (11), MOST HITS (11), MOST PLATE APPEARANCES (16), MOST CONSECUTIVE BATTERS REACHED BASE (10)... Here is what happened... Lloyd Moseby led off with a triple... Willie Upshaw struck out... Willie Aikens singled scoring Moseby... Pitcher Mike Stanton was replaced by Paul Mirabella... Cliff Johnson had a PH single sending Alfredo Griffin, who had pinch run for Aikens to second... George Bell had a PH single sending Griffin to third and Garth Iorg who had pinch-run for Johnson to second. However, Seattle third baseman Jim Presley was called for obstruction and Alfredo Griffin was waved home... Jesse Barfield then singled to load the bases... Tony Fernandez then singled scoring Iorg and Bell... Mirabella was replaced by Edwin Nunez... Damaso Garcia singled to score Barfield... Dave Collins walked to re-load the bases... Dave Giesel then replaced Nunez on the mound for Seattle... Moseby up for the second time in the inning, singled (his 2nd hit in the inning) to drive in Fernandez and Garcia... Upshaw singled scoring Collins... Rick Leach ran for Upshaw... Griffin had a bloop single to score Moseby... Garth Iorg hit into a fielder's choice to erase Griffin... George Bell walked to load the bases... Barfield the 15th batter of the inning singled (his 2nd hit) to score Leach and Iorg... Fernandez struck out to end the inning... The line for the inning read 11 runs, 11 hits, one error, two walks, two left on base... The Mariners scored four times in the bottom of the ninth on a grand slam HR by Alvin Davis to help set an American League record for most runs in the 9th inning (15).

April 25, 1995: In the opening game of the season with David Cone facing Oakland's Dave Stewart at SkyDome the Blue Jays scored 11 runs in the second inning and went on to defeat the Athletics 13-1. With the score tied at 1, John Olerud led off the bottom of the second with a walk... Roberto Alomar then singled to left moving Olerud to second... Shawn Green was save on an error by second-baseman Mike Gallego and the bases were loaded... Ed Sprague walked to scored Olerud... Lance Parrish struck out for the Blue Jays first out... Devon White then doubled to right scoring Alomar and Green with Sprague moving to third... Alex Gonzalez doubled to left-centre scoring White... With Paul Molitor at the plate Stewart wild pitched Gonzalez to third... Molitor walked... Joe Carter then drove in Gonzalez with an infield single with Molitor stopping at second... Stewart was then replaced by LHP Chris Eddy on the mound... Olerud on his second at bat of the inning singled to left driving in Molitor and sending Carter to third with Olerud going to second on the throw... Alomar then grounded out to third with both runners holding... Shawn Green then singled to right to score Carter and send Olerud to third... Sprague singled to centre scoring Olerud with Green stopping at second... Parrish then walked to load the bases... White then singled to left for his second hit of the inning and drove in Green and Sprague for his third and fourth runs batted in of the inning... Gonzalez completed the inning as he grounded into a fielders choice with White out at second... The line for inning read 11 runs, 8 hits, one error, four walks, two left on base, 15 plate appearances.

10 CONSECUTIVE HITS

The Toronto Blue Jays tied an American League record September 4, 1992 at SkyDome by collecting 10 consecutive hits in an eight-run second inning against the Minnesota Twins.

The Blue Jays tied the mark set by the Boston Red Sox on June 2, 1901 and equalled by the Detroit Tigers on September 20, 1983.

The major league record of 12 straight hits was set by the St. Louis Cardinals in 1920 and equalled by the Brooklyn Dodgers in 1930.

With one out in the second, Toronto's Kelly Gruber reached on an infield single against Twins' starter Kevin Tapani.

Singles by Pat Borders and Manuel Lee scored Gruber to cut Minnesota's lead to 3-1.

Devon White doubled in a run and Roberto Alomar followed with a two-run single to give the Blue Jays a 4-3 lead. Joe Carter tripled home Alomar and scored on Dave Winfield's single off reliever Tom Edens. Winfield was thrown out at second for the inning's second out, but John Olerud singled and scored on Candy Maldonado's triple to open a 7-3 cushion. Gruber's bloop double to right-center scored Maldonado and ended the string of 10 straight hits.

Borders flied to center to end the inning.

Toronto's previous club record was nine consecutive hits, set against California on July 3, 1992.

BLUE JAYS HITS IN ONE GAME

HITS	DATE	OPPONENT	BLUE JAYS-OPP. SCORE
25	Aug. 9, 1999	at Texas	19-4
24	June 26, 1978	vs Baltimore	24-10
22	Sept. 29, 1985	at Milwaukee	13-5
22	Sept. 22, 1999	at Boston	14-9
21	June 26, 1983	at Seattle	19-7
21	Sept. 14, 1987	vs Baltimore	18-3
21	June 8, 1992	at New York	16-3
21	Sept. 4, 1992	vs Minnesota	16-5
21	July 19, 1993	at Chicago	15-7
21	Aug. 24, 1997	at Kansas City (13 Inn)	11-8
21	Aug. 19, 1998	at Seattle	16-2
20	July 9, 1985	at Seattle (13 Inn)	9-4
20	May 14, 1987	at Minnesota	16-4
20	April 11, 1988	vs New York	17-9
20	June 22, 1992	at Texas	16-7
20	Aug. 13, 2000	at Minnesota	13-3

2000 BLUE JAYS ATTENDANCE

AMERICAN LEAGUE CLUB	DATES	AT SKYDOME AVERAGE	TOTAL	DATES	ON THE ROAD AVERAGE	TOTAL
BALTIMORE	6	20,535	123,209	7	36,622	256,351
BOSTON	6	23,869	143,215	6	32,814	196,882
NEW YORK	6	27,336	164,018	6	35,497	212,984
TAMPA BAY	6	21,509	129,053	6	17,501	105,005
EAST	24	23,312	559,495	25	30,849	771,222
CHICAGO	4	18,948	75,790	6	19,882	119,293
CLEVELAND	6	23,096	138,577	6	42,940	257,638
DETROIT	6	20,274	121,644	6	27,388	164,329
KANSAS CITY	6	21,479	128,872	4	16,001	64,005
MINNESOTA	6	24,165	144,992	3	23,159	69,477
CENTRAL	28	21,781	609,875	25	26,990	674,742
TEXAS	4	25,817	103,266	6	34,267	205,582
OAKLAND	4	23,607	94,428	6	14,776	88,656
SEATTLE	6	18,357	110,139	4	41,609	166,436
ANAHEIM	6	19,035	114,207	6	16,828	100,970
WEST	20	21,102	422,040	22	25,529	561,644
AL TOTALS	72	22,103	1,591,410	72	27,883	2,007,608

NATIONAL LEAGUE CLUB	DATES	AT SKYDOME AVERAGE	TOTAL	DATES	ON THE ROAD AVERAGE	TOTAL
MONTREAL	3	27,400	82,199	3	17,742	53,226
FLORIDA	–	–	–	3	13,587	40,762
ATLANTA	–	–	–	3	35,445	106,335
NEW YORK METS	3	25,967	77,901	–	–	–
PHILADELPHIA	3	22,792	68,376	–	–	–
NL TOTALS	9	25,386	228,476	9	22,258	200,323
GRAND TOTALS	81	22,468	1,819,886	81	27,258	2,207,931

ATTENDANCE RECORDS

(REGULAR SEASON)

Largest Home	50,533	Fri., Apr. 9/93	Cleveland
Smallest Home	10,074	Tues., Apr. 17/79	Chicago
Smallest SkyDome	13,514	Tues., Apr. 4/00	Kansas City
Largest Opening Day	50,533	Fri., Apr. 9/93	Cleveland
Largest Day	50,533	Fri., Apr. 9/93	Cleveland
Smallest Day	10,074	Thurs., Apr. 17/79	Chicago
Largest Night	50,532	Wed., Sept. 22/93	Boston
Smallest Night	10,125	Tues., May 3/83	Texas
Doubleheader (Day)	48,641	Mon., July 17/89	California
Doubleheader (TN)	45,102	Tues., Aug. 2/83	New York
Series, Four Dates (Home)	202,093	July 29-Aug. 1/93 (4 Games)	Detroit
Series, Four Dates (Road)	214,510	Sept. 12-15/85 (4 Games)	New York
Series, Three Dates (Home)	151,584	Sept. 21-23/93 (3 Games)	Boston
Series, Three Dates (Road)	142,181	July 29-31/94 (3 Games)	Baltimore
Series, Two Dates (Home)	101,036	July 27,28/93 (2 Games)	Baltimore
Series, Two Dates (Road)	91,522	July 16, 17/97 (2 Games)	Texas
Largest Road	61,340	Fri., May 23/86	Cleveland
Smallest Road	746	April 9/97	Chicago
Season, Home	4,057,947	1993	
Season, Road	2,549,438	1993	
Season, Home & Road	6,607,385	1993	

OPPONENTS' RECORDS IN TORONTO

	LARGEST		SMALLEST	
BALTIMORE	50,528	June 25/94	11,080	Sept. 13/79
BOSTON	50,532	Sept. 22/93	10,428	Apr. 23/82
CALIFORNIA	50,529	Sept. 11/93	11,295	May 15/78
		May 29/94		
CHICAGO	50,518	Apr. 24/93	10,074	Apr. 17/79
CLEVELAND	50,533	Apr. 9/93	10,173	Apr. 20/83
DETROIT	50,532	July 31/93	10,087	Apr. 13/82
KANSAS CITY	50,531	July 16/93	10,169	Apr. 17/78
MILWAUKEE	50,517	Aug. 6/93	10,127	Apr. 14/83
MINNESOTA	50,530	Aug. 10/93	10,155	May 1/79
NEW YORK	50,530	June 11/94	13,306	Apr. 19/78
OAKLAND	50,529	Sept. 8/93	11,339	May 9/78
SEATTLE	50,527	Aug. 20/93	10,213	June 11/79
TEXAS	50,529	July 23/94	10,101	Apr. 27/82
ATLANTA	34,409	June 16/97	28,366	July 20/99
FLORIDA	35,229	Aug. 30/97	22,449	July 16/99
MONTREAL	50,436	July 1/97	24,147	June 4/99
PHILADELPHIA	31,176	June 5/98	21,385	July 14/00
TAMPA BAY	31,240	July 5/98	18,063	Sept. 22/00
NEW YORK (NL)	37,252	July 1/98	23,129	July 17/00

Attendance Data

BLUE JAYS ON THE ROAD

AT	LARGEST		SMALLEST	
ANAHEIM	61,292	July 4/95	10,239	June 7/77
BALTIMORE	47,900	June 27/97	7,053	Sept. 6/79
BOSTON	35,735	Sept. 28/90	7,542	April 16/82
CHICAGO	42,796	July 25/91	746	April 9/97
CLEVELAND	61,340	May 23/86	2,724	April 28/77
DETROIT	52,528	April 7/78	6,210	Sept. 22/80
KANSAS CITY	41,086	April 8/85	11,194	April 14/98
MILWAUKEE	53,852	May 6/79	5,298	April 21/82
MINNESOTA	53,067	April 8/88	2,830	Sept. 20/82
NEW YORK	55,367	May 27/78	9,685	April 18/77
OAKLAND	46,770	July 4/85	1,289	August 14/79
SEATTLE	56,120	April 6/93	4,113	June 1/79
TEXAS	46,511	July 15/94	6,819	May 13/82
TAMPA BAY	35,689	Sept. 19/98	12,549	Sept. 28/99

TWENTY LARGEST HOME CROWDS

ATTENDANCE	DATE	OPPONENT	EVENT
52,382	Tuesday, July 9, 1991	National League	All-Star Game
52,268	Thursday, October 22, 1992	Atlanta	Game #5-WS
52,195	Saturday, October 23, 1993	Philadelphia	Game #6-WS
52,090	Wednesday, October 21, 1992	Atlanta	Game #4-WS
52,062	Sunday, October 17, 1993	Philadelphia	Game #2-WS
52,011	Saturday, October 16, 1993	Philadelphia	Game #1-WS
51,889	Saturday, October 9, 1993	Chicago	Game #4-LCS
51,813	Tuesday, October 20, 1992	Atlanta	Game #3-WS
51,783	Friday, October 8, 1993	Chicago	Game #3-LCS
51,526	Saturday, October 12, 1991	Minnesota	Game #4-LCS
51,454	Friday, October 11, 1991	Minnesota	Game #3-LCS
51,425	Sunday, October 13, 1991	Minnesota	Game #5-LCS
51,375	Sunday, October 10, 1993	Chicago	Game #5-LCS
51,335	Wednesday, October 14, 1992	Oakland	Game #6-LCS
51,114	Thursday, October 8, 1992	Oakland	Game #2-LCS
51,039	Wednesday, October 7, 1992	Oakland	Game #1-LCS
50,533	Friday, April 9, 1993	Cleveland	Home Opener
50,532	Saturday, July 31, 1993	Detroit	Camera Day
50,532	Wednesday, September 22, 1993	Boston	Night-Game
50,531	Thursday, July 15, 1993	Kansas City	Night-Game

HOW THEY HAVE DRAWN

ATTENDANCE RE-CAP 1977–2000

AMERICAN LEAGUE

RANK	CLUB	DATES	ATTENDANCE	AVERAGE
1	NEW YORK	143	5,334,700	37,306
2	DETROIT	150	5,145,101	34,301
3	BOSTON	146	4,891,185	33,501
4	BALTIMORE	144	4,598,082	31,931
5	CLEVELAND	139	4,330,903	31,158
6	KANSAS	137	4,303,934	31,416
7	MILWAUKEE	132	4,287,401	32,480
8	OAKLAND	134	4,204,613	31,378
9	CHICAGO	131	4,161,702	31,769
10	ANAHEIM	135	4,158,373	30,803
11	TEXAS	134	4,134,872	30,857
12	MINNESOTA	131	4,147,690	31,662
13	SEATTLE	129	3,923,358	30,414
14	TAMPA BAY	19	478,567	25,188
AL TOTALS		**1,804**	**58,100,481**	**32,206**

NATIONAL LEAGUE

RANK	CLUB	DATES	ATTENDANCE	AVERAGE
1	MONTREAL	11	347,516	31,592
2	ATLANTA	6	188,049	31,342
3	NEW YORK	6	172,800	28,800
4	FLORIDA	6	170,248	28,375
5	PHILADELPHIA	6	155,890	25,982
NL TOTAL		**35**	**1,034,503**	**29,557**
GRAND TOTALS		**1,839**	**59,134,984**	**32,156**

2000 AMERICAN LEAGUE ATTENDANCE

CLUB	TOTAL	HOME AVERAGE	DATES	TOTAL	ROAD AVERAGE	DATES
CLEVELAND	3,456,278	42,670	81	2,377,993	29,358	81
BALTIMORE	3,295,128	40,681	81	2,014,809	25,185	80
NEW YORK	3,227,657	40,346	80	2,876,506	35,512	81
SEATTLE	3,148,317	38,868	81	2,208,974	27,612	80
TEXAS	2,800,147	35,002	80	2,406,986	29,716	81
BOSTON	2,586,032	31,926	81	2,524,776	31,170	81
DETROIT	2,533,752	31,281	81	2,110,536	26,056	81
ANAHEIM	2,066,977	25,518	81	2,272,015	28,050	81
CHICAGO	1,947,799	24,347	80	2,353,137	29,051	81
TORONTO	1,819,886	22,468	81	2,207,931	27,258	81
OAKLAND	1,728,888	21,344	81	2,466,594	30,832	80
KANSAS CITY	1,677,915	20,715	81	2,323,443	28,684	81
TAMPA BAY	1,549,052	19,363	80	2,223,268	27,448	81
MINNESOTA	1,059,715	13,083	81	2,332,786	28,800	81
TOTAL	**32,897,543**	**29,113**	**1130**	**32,699,754**	**28,912**	**1131**

ATTENDANCE YEAR-BY-YEAR

	HOME	DATES	AVG.	AWAY	DATES	AVG.	TOTAL
1977	1,701,052	72	23,626	1,035,344	73	14,183	2,736,396
1978	1,562,585	73	21,405	1,264,940	71	17,816	2,827,525
1979	1,431,651	77	18,593	1,261,000	75	16,813	2,692,651
1980	1,400,327	75	18,671	1,285,409	77	16,694	2,685,736
1981	755,083	51	14,806	814,365	50	16,287	1,569,448
1982	1,275,978	77	16,571	1,392,301	77	18,082	2,668,279
1983	1,930,415	77	25,070	1,713,302	81	21,152	3,643,717
1984	2,110,009	79	26,709	1,709,172	77	22,197	3,819,181
1985	2,468,925	78	31,653	1,842,278	81	22,744	4,311,203
1986	2,455,477	78	31,480	1,716,243	81	21,188	4,171,720
1987	2,778,429	81	34,302	1,959,280	81	24,189	4,737,709
1988	2,595,175	81	32,039	1,972,865	81	24,356	4,568,040
1989	3,375,883	80	42,199	1,970,711	81	24,330	5,346,594
1990	3,885,284	81	47,966	2,039,772	81	25,182	5,925,056
1991	4,001,527	81	49,402	2,243,335	81	27,695	6,244,862
1992	4,028,318	81	49,732	2,301,012	81	28,408	6,329,330
1993	4,057,947	81	50,098	2,549,898	81	31,480	6,607,845
1994	2,907,933	59	49,287	1,775,829	55	32,288	4,683,762
1995	2,826,483	72	39,257	1,770,541	70	25,293	4,597,024
1996	2,559,573	81	31,600	1,980,397	81	24,449	4,539,970
1997	2,589,297	81	31,967	2,118,030	81	26,149	4,707,327
1998	2,454,283	81	30,300	2,164,254	81	26,719	4,618,537
1999	2,163,464	81	26,709	2,161,286	81	26,683	4,324,750
2000	1,819,886	81	22,468	2,207,931	81	27,258	4,027,817
TOTAL	**59,134,984**	**1,839**	**32,156**	**43,249,495**	**1,840**	**23,505**	**102,384,479**

HOW TO GET BLUE JAYS TICKETS FOR THE 2001 SEASON

TICKET INFORMATION

PRICES:
- $44.00 Premium Dugout
- $35.00 Field Level – Bases
- $23.00 200 Level Outfield
- $23.00 100 Level Outfield
- $16.00 SkyDeck Bases
- $41.00 Field Level – Infield
- $29.00 Field Level – Baselines
- $23.00 Sky Deck Infield
- $7.00 SkyDeck Baselines

SEASON TICKETS

Are now available by calling 416-341-1280. Season ticket prices range from $2,150.00 to $3,108.00 for 80 games at SkyDome.

BOX OFFICE at SKYDOME (hours of operation are subject to change without notice)

Game Days

Monday to Friday:	9:00am to 9:00pm
Saturday:	9:00am to 6:00pm
Sunday:	9:00am to 5:00pm

Non-Game Days

Monday to Friday:	9:00am to 6:00pm
Saturday:	10:00am to 5:00pm
Sunday:	Closed

Call Centre

Monday to Friday:	8:00am to 8:00pm
Saturday:	9:00am to 5:00pm
Sunday:	9:00am to 5:00pm (Game days only)
Sunday:	Closed (Non-game days)

ORDERING by PHONE

Fans may purchase tickets for Blue Jays home games by calling the Blue Jays FAN FONE at 416-341-1234 or 1-888-OK-GO-JAYS and place your order via a major credit card (Visa, Master Card, American Express). The Call Centre hours for the 2001 season will be Monday to Friday: 8:00am to 8:00pm, Saturday: 9:00am to 5:00pm and Sunday's (game days only): 9:00am to 5:00pm. Sunday's on non-game days, the Call Centre will be closed. There will be a $2.75 service charge per ticket, with a maximum charge of $22.00.

ORDERING by MAIL

Fans can also order tickets through the mail by selecting the game date and preferred seat locations along with a cheque or money order made payable to the Toronto Blue Jays Baseball Club (plus $8.00 per order for postage and handling). Orders received five days or less prior to the game date cannot be mailed and must be picked up on the day of the game at the Blue Jays "Paid Reservations" Window beside Gate 9 at the Blue Jays box office.

ORDERING ON-LINE

Order tickets online by logging into www.bluejays.com. A real-time ticket interface with photos of sight lines will allow fans to find the perfect seat, purchase and pay for tickets all online.

GROUP TICKETS

If you're planning an activity for a group of 20 or more at a Blue Jays game, contact the Group Sales Department for more details at (416) 341-1122.

MAILING ADDRESS:

Toronto Blue Jays **Tickets**
1 Blue Jays Way, Suite 3200
SkyDome
Toronto, Ontario
M5V 1J1
Fax: (416) 341-1177

Attendance Data

2000 BLUE JAYS ATTENDANCE DAY BY DAY

NUM	M/D	OPP	H/R	D/N	TIME OF GAME	ATTENDANCE	YTD HOME	YTD ROAD	H/R DATE
1	04/03	KC	H	D	2:46	40,898	40,898		1
2	04/04	KC	H	N	2:33	13,514	54,412		2
3	04/05	KC	H	N	2:45	14,957	69,369		3
4	04/06	KC	H	D	3:00	14,336	83,705		4
5	04/07	@ TEX	R	N	2:49	31,619		31,619	1
6	04/08	@ TEX	R	N	2:52	37,128		68,747	2
7	04/09	@ TEX	R	D	3:01	40,186		108,933	3
8	04/10	@ ANA	R	N	2:22	14,338		123,271	4
9	04/11	@ ANA	R	N	3:13	15,229		138,500	5
10	04/12	@ ANA	R	N	2:57	16,494		154,994	6
	04/13	–OFF DAY–							
11	04/14	SEA	H	N	3:06	17,306	101,011		5
12	04/15	SEA	H	D	3:22	21,754	122,765		6
13	04/16	SEA	H	D	3:24	15,325	138,090		7
14	04/17	ANA	H	N	3:03	13,622	151,712		8
15	04/18	ANA	H	N	3:51	13,825	165,537		9
16	04/19	ANA	H	N	2:45	13,572	179,109		10
17	04/20	ANA	H	N	2:59	13,985	193,094		11
18	04/21	NYY	H	D	2:20	25,921	219,015		12
19	04/22	NYY	H	D	2:30	30,167	249,182		13
20	04/23	NYY	H	D	3:09	20,485	269,667		14
21	04/24	@ OAK	R	N	2:50	8,363		163,357	7
22	04/25	@ OAK	R	N	2:40	8,266		171,623	8
23	04/26	@ OAK	R	N	2:53	14,477		186,100	9
	04/27	–OFF DAY–							
24	04/28	@ NYY	R	N	2:47	35,987		222,087	10
25	04/29	@ NYY	R	D	3:23	38,783		260,870	11
26	04/30	@ NYY	R	D	2:57	43,721		304,591	12
27	05/01	@ CWS	R	N	2:58	14,448		319,039	13
28	05/02	@ CWS	R	N	3:06	10,397		329,436	14
29	05/03	@ CWS	R	N	2:39	12,026		341,462	15
30	05/04	CLE	H	N	3:06	16,637	286,304		15
31	05/05	CLE	H	N	3:42	19,194	305,498		16
32	05/06	CLE	H	D	3:06	23,730	329,228		17
33	05/07	CLE	H	D	4:22	19,161	348,389		18
34	05/08	BAL	H	N	2:56	15,103	363,492		19
35	05/09	BAL	H	N	2:30	15,177	378,669		20
36	05/10	BAL	H	D	2:23	15,598	394,267		21
	05/11	–OFF DAY–							
37	05/12	@ TB	R	N	2:32	17,532		358,994	16
38	05/13	@ TB	R	D	3:10	20,054		379,048	17
39	05/14	@ TB	R	D	2:42	15,788		394,836	18
40	05/15	BOS	H	N	2:38	16,124	410,391		22
41	05/16	BOS	H	N	3:18	17,663	428,054		23
42	05/17	BOS	H	N	2:38	20,078	448,132		24
	05/18	–OFF DAY–							
43	05/19	CWS	H	N	2:49	18,268	466,400		25
44	05/20	CWS	H	D	2:22	20,091	496,491		26
45	05/21	CWS	H	D	2:39	18,264	504,755		27
46	05/22	CWS	H	N	2:32	19,167	523,922		28
47	05/23	@ BOS	R	N	2:55	33,402		428,238	19
48	05/24	@ BOS	R	N	3:39	31,250		459,488	20
49	05/25	@ BOS	R	N	3:06	32,716		492,204	21
50	05/26	@ DET	R	N	3:07	33,068		525,272	22
51	05/27	@ DET	R	D	2:45	29,584		554,856	23
52	05/28	@ DET	R	D	3:00	29,105		583,961	24
	05/29	–OFF DAY–							
53	05/30	MIN	H	N	3:01	16,371	540,293		29
54	05/31	MIN	H	N	2:15	17,305	557,598		30
55	06/01	MIN	H	D	2:44	30,444	588,042		31
56	06/02	@ FLA	R	N	3:46	12,209		596,170	25
57	06/03	@ FLA	R	D	2:25	17,546		613,716	26
58	06/04	@ FLA	R	D	2:44	11,007		624,723	27
59	06/05	@ ATL	R	N	2:58	33,641		658,364	28
60	06/06	@ ATL	R	N	3:44	39,454		697,818	29
61	06/07	@ ATL	R	N	3:26	33,240		731,058	30
	06/08	–OFF DAY–							
62	06/09	MTL	H	N	3:08	26,122	614,164		32
63	06/10	MTL	H	D	2:47	30,239	644,403		33
64	06/11	MTL	H	D	3:06	25,838	670,241		34
65	06/12	@ DET	R	N	2:55	21,779		752,837	31
66	06/13	@ DET	R	N	2:41	23,314		776,151	32
67	06/14	@ DET	R	N	2:50	27,479		803,630	33
	06/15	–OFF DAY–							
68	06/16	@ BOS	R	N	3:09	33,638		837,268	34
69	06/17	@ BOS	R	D	3:12	32,951		870,219	35
70	06/18	@ BOS	R	D	2:59	32,925		903,144	36
	06/19	–OFF DAY–							
71	06/20	DET	H	N	3:03	18,850	689,091		35
72	06/21	DET	H	N	2:29	18,125	707,216		36
73	06/22	DET	H	N	2:47	20,259	727,475		37
74	06/23	BOS	H	N	2:33	28,198	755,673		38
75	06/24	BOS	H	D	2:35	30,130	785,803		39
76	06/25	BOS	H	D	4:25	31,022	816,825		40
	06/26	–OFF DAY–							
77	06/27	@ TB	R	N	2:58	14,657		917,801	37
78	06/28	@ TB	R	N	2:36	15,308		933,109	38
79	06/29	@ TB	R	D	3:02	21,666		954,775	39
80	06/30	@ BAL	R	N	2:58	40,412		995,187	40
81	07/01	@ BAL	R	N	2:30	40,876		1,036,063	41

| --- | --- | --- | --- | --- | --- | --- | --- | --- | --- |
82	07/02	@ BAL	R	D	3:05	41,267		1,077,330	42
83	07/03	@ BAL	R	D	3:08	39,617		1,116,947	43
84	07/04	@ CLE	R	D	3:19	43,222		1,160,169	44
85	07/05	@ CLE	R	N	3:32	43,141		1,203,310	45
86	07/06	@ CLE	R	N	3:47	43,237		1,246,547	46
87	07/07	@ MON	R	N	3:23	13,317		1,259,864	47
88	07/08	@ MON	R	N	2:51	17,420		1,277,284	48
89	07/09	@ MON	R	D	3:22	22,489		1,299,773	49
	07/10								
	07/11				– ALL STAR BREAK –				
	07/12								
90	07/13	PHI	H	N	2:35	22,163	838,988		41
91	07/14	PHI	H	N	2:40	21,385	860,373		42
92	07/15	PHI	H	D	3:07	24,828	885,201		43
93	07/16	NYM	H	D	3:01	30,139	915,340		44
94	07/17	NYM	H	N	4:12	23,129	938,469		45
95	07/18	NYM	H	N	3:27	24,633	963,102		46
96	07/19	TB	H	N	2:21	18,751	981,853		47
97	07/20	TB	H	N	3:03	18,915	1,000,768		48
98	07/21	BAL	H	N	3:02	23,470	1,024,238		49
99	07/22	BAL	H	D	2:39	27,585	1,051,823		50
100	07/23	BAL	H	D	2:33	26,276	1,078,099		51
	07/24	–OFF DAY–							
101	07/25	CLE	H	N	3:17	28,672	1,106,771		52
102	07/26	CLE	H	D	2:50	31,183	1,137,954		53
103	07/27	@ SEA	R	N	3:26	40,398		1,340,171	50
104	07/28	@ SEA	R	N	3:11	37,126		1,377,297	51
105	07/29	@ SEA	R	D	5:04	45,264		1,422,561	52
106	07/30	@ SEA	R	D	3:18	43,648		1,466,209	53
107	07/31	@ OAK	R	N	2:31	13,608		1,479,817	54
108	08/01	@ OAK	R	D	3:04	17,469		1,497,286	55
109	08/02	@ OAK	R	D	2:35	26,473		1,523,759	56
110	08/03	TEX	H	N	2:52	24,825	1,162,779		54
111	08/04	TEX	H	N	3:39	23,518	1,186,297		55
112	08/05	TEX	H	D	3:12	26,143	1,212,440		56
113	08/06	TEX	H	D	3:06	28,780	1,241,220		57
114	08/07	@ KC	R	N	2:57	17,533		1,541,292	57
115	08/08	@ KC	R	N	2:51	14,086		1,555,378	58
116	08/09	@ KC	R	N	2:54	14,198		1,569,576	59
117	08/10	@ KC	R	D	3:11	18,188		1,587,764	60
118	08/11	@ MIN	R	N	3:10	13,660		1,601,424	61
119	08/12	@ MIN	R	N	3:03	30,161		1,631,585	62
120	08/13	@ MIN	R	D	2:44	25,656		1,657,241	63
	08/14	–OFF DAY–							
121	08/15	ANA	H	N	3:19	26,706	1,267,926		58
122	08/16	ANA	H	D	3:09	32,497	1,300,423		59
	08/17	–OFF DAY–							
123	08/18	MIN	H	N	2:54	23,074	1,323,497		60
124	08/19	MIN	H	D	3:07	25,171	1,348,668		61
125	08/20	MIN	H	D	2:40	32,627	1,381,295		62
	08/21	–OFF DAY–							
126	08/22	KC	H	N	3:14	22,551	1,403,846		63
127	08/23	KC	H	N	3:14	22,616	1,426,462		64
	08/24	–OFF DAY–							
128	08/25	@ TEX	R	N	3:46	35,365		1,692,606	64
129	08/26	@ TEX	R	N	3:20	39,388		1,731,994	65
130	08/27	@ TEX	R	N	3:00	21,896		1,753,890	66
131	08/28	@ ANA	R	N	2:39	17,483		1,771,373	67
132	08/29	@ ANA	R	N	3:09	17,773		1,789,146	68
133	8/30	@ ANA	R	N	3:08	19,653		1,808,799	69
	8/31	–OFF DAY–							
134	09/01	OAK	H	N	3:03	22,187	1,448,649		65
135	09/02	OAK	H	D	3:04	26,261	1,474,910		66
136	09/03	OAK	H	D	2:39	24,156	1,499,066		67
137	09/04	OAK	H	D	3:08	21,824	1,520,890		68
138	09/05	SEA	H	N	2:52	21,128	1,542,018		69
139	09/06	SEA	H	N	2:33	17,055	1,559,073		70
140	09/07	SEA	H	N	3:08	17,571	1,576,644		71
141	09/08	DET	H	N	2:24	19,121	1,595,765		72
142	09/09	DET	H	D	3:25	23,623	1,619,388		73
143	09/10	DET	H	D	2:24	21,666	1,641,054		74
	09/11	–OFF DAY–							
144	09/12	@ NYY	R	N	2:55	30,370		1,839,169	70
145	09/13	@ NYY	R	N	2:52	29,083		1,868,252	71
146	09/14	@ NYY	R	N	3:54	35,040		1,903,292	72
147	09/15	@ CWS	R	N	3:18	23,105		1,926,397	73
148	09/16	@ CWS	R	N	2:43	33,204		1,959,601	74
149	09/17	@ CWS	R	D	3:06	26,113		1,985,714	75
	09/18	–OFF DAY–							
150	09/19	NYY	H	N	2:24	28,908	1,669,962		75
151	09/20	NYY	H	N	2:59	28,463	1,698,425		76
152	09/21	NYY	H	N	2:33	30,074	1,728,499		77
153	09/22	TB	H	N	2:47	18,063	1,746,562		78
154	09/23	TB	H	D	3:03	24,437	1,770,999		79
155	09/24	TB	H	D	2:44	28,172	1,799,171		80
156	09/25	TB	H	N	2:30	20,715	1,819,886		81
157	09/26	@ BAL	R	N	2:29	31,614		2,017,328	76
158	09/27	@ BAL	R	N	2:36	30,362		2,047,690	77
159	09/28	@ BAL	R	N	2:47	32,203		2,079,893	78
160	09/29	@ CLE	R	N	2:38	42,768		2,122,661	79
161	09/30	@ CLE	R	D	3:27	42,676		2,165,337	80
162	10/01	@ CLE	R	D	2:36	42,594		2,207,931	81

Attendance Data

TOP ALL-TIME ATTENDANCE MARKS
FOUR MILLION CLUB

1.	Colorado Rockies	4,483,350	1993	3.	Toronto Blue Jays	4,028,318	1992
2.	Toronto Blue Jays	4,057,947	1993	4.	Toronto Blue Jays	4,001,526	1991

THREE MILLION CLUB

1.	Colorado Rockies	3,891,014	1996	32.	Colorado Rockies	3,285,710	2000
2.	Colorado Rockies	3,888,453	1997	33.	Atlanta Braves	3,284,897	1999
3.	Toronto Blue Jays	3,885,284	1990	34.	Colorado Rockies	3,281,511	1994
4.	Atlanta Braves	3,884,725	1993	35.	Los Angeles Dodgers	3,264,593	1985
5.	Colorado Rockies	3,789,347	1998	36.	Los Angeles Dodgers	3,249,287	1980
6.	Baltimore Orioles	3,711,132	1997	37.	Atlanta Braves	3,234,301	2000
7.	Baltimore Orioles	3,685,194	1998	38.	New York Yankees	3,227,657	2000
8.	Baltimore Orioles	3,646,950	1996	39.	St. Louis Cardinals	3,225,334	1999
9.	Baltimore Orioles	3,644,965	1993	40.	St. Louis Cardinals	3,195,021	1998
10.	Los Angeles Dodgers	3,608,881	1982	41.	Seattle Mariners	3,192,237	1997
11.	Arizona Diamondbacks	3,602,856	1998	42.	Los Angeles Dodgers	3,188,454	1996
12.	Baltimore Orioles	3,567,819	1992	43.	Los Angeles Dodgers	3,170,392	1993
13.	Los Angeles Dodgers	3,510,313	1983	44.	Seattle Mariners	3,148,317	2000
14.	Colorado Rockies	3,481,065	1999	45.	Philadelphia Phillies	3,137,674	1993
15.	Cleveland Indians	3,468,456	1999	46.	Los Angeles Dodgers	3,134,824	1984
16.	Cleveland Indians	3,467,299	1998	47.	Baltimore Orioles	3,098,475	1995
17.	Atlanta Braves	3,464,488	1997	48.	Los Angeles Dodgers	3,095,346	1999
18.	Cleveland Indians	3,456,278	2000	49.	Los Angeles Dodgers	3,089,222	1998
19.	Baltimore Orioles	3,433,150	1999	50.	St. Louis Cardinals	3,082,980	1989
20.	Cleveland Indians	3,404,750	1997	51.	Atlanta Braves	3,077,400	1992
21.	Colorado Rockies	3,390,037	1995	52.	St. Louis Cardinals	3,072,122	1987
22.	Toronto Blue Jays	3,375,883	1989	53.	Florida Marlins	3,064,847	1993
23.	Atlanta Braves	3,361,350	1998	54.	Houston Astros	3,056,139	2000
24.	Los Angeles Dodgers	3,348,170	1991	55.	New York Mets	3,055,445	1988
25.	Los Angeles Dodgers	3,347,845	1978	56.	New York Mets	3,034,129	1987
26.	St. Louis Cardinals	3,336,493	2000	57.	Minnesota Twins	3,030,672	1988
27.	Los Angeles Dodgers	3,319,504	1997	58.	Los Angeles Dodgers	3,023,208	1986
28.	Cleveland Indians	3,318,174	1996	59.	Arizona Diamondbacks	3,019,654	1999
29.	San Francisco Giants	3,315,330	2000	60.	Los Angeles Dodgers	3,010,819	2000
30.	Baltimore Orioles	3,295,128	2000	61.	Los Angeles Dodgers	3,002,396	1990
31.	New York Yankees	3,292,736	1999				

MAJOR LEAGUE ATTENDANCE RECORD

From 1991-1993, the TORONTO BLUE JAYS attracted over FOUR MILLION fans each season. Below is a listing of the ALL-TIME attendance records for Major League Baseball. In 1993, Toronto managed to set an American League record for attendance with 4,057,947 fans. The Colorado Rockies surpassed that mark in 1993 as they set a Major League record with a home attendance of 4,483,350 fans.

ALL-TIME LIST

1993	Colorado Rockies	4,483,350	1946	New York Yankees	2,265,512
1992	Toronto Blue Jays	4,028,318	1929	Chicago Cubs	1,485,166
1991	Toronto Blue Jays	4,001,526	1920	New York Yankees	1,289,422
1990	Toronto Blue Jays	3,885,284	1908	New York Giants	910,000
1982	Los Angeles Dodgers	3,608,881	1905	Chicago White Sox	687,419
1978	Los Angeles Dodgers	3,347,845	1904	Boston Red Sox	623,295
1977	Los Angeles Dodgers	2,955,087	1903	New York Giants	579,530
1962	Los Angeles Dodgers	2,755,184	1902	Philadelphia A's	442,473
1948	Cleveland Indians	2,620,627	1901	St. Louis Cardinals	379,988

BLUE JAYS TICKET PRICES SINCE 1977

Year											
1977			6.50				5.00		4.00	3.00	2.00
1978			6.50				5.00		4.00	3.00	2.00
1979			7.00				5.50		4.25	3.00	2.00
1980			7.00				5.50		4.25	3.00	2.00
1981			8.00				6.50		5.00	3.00	2.00
1982			8.00				6.50		5.00	3.00	2.00
1983			8.50				7.00		5.50	3.00	2.00
1984			9.50				8.00		6.50	4.00	3.00
1985			10.50				9.00		7.50	5.00	4.00
1986			12.00				10.00		8.50	6.00	4.00
1987			13.00				11.00		9.00	6.00	4.00
1988			15.00				13.00		10.00	7.00	4.00
1989			15.00				12.00		9.00	4.00	
1990	18.00		15.00				12.00		9.00	4.00	
1991	21.00		17.50				13.50		10.00	4.00	
1992	21.00		17.50				13.50		10.00	4.00	
1993	23.00		19.50				15.00		11.00	5.00	
1994	27.00		23.00				18.00		13.00	6.00	
1995	27.00		23.00				18.00		13.00	6.00	
1996	27.00		23.00				18.00		13.00	6.00	
1997	30.00		25.00				20.00		13.00	4.00	
1998	35.00		27.50				20.00		13.00	4.00	
1999	38.00	36.00	40.00	37.00	32.00	29.50	22.00	15.00	6.00		
2000			42.00	39.00	33.50	30.75	23.00	16.00	7.00		
2001			44.00	41.00	35.00	29.00	23.00	16.00	7.00		

1976 . . . March 26, American League votes to expand to Toronto, awarding franchise to group consisting of Imperial Trust, Ltd., Labatt's Breweries, and the Canadian Imperial Bank of Commerce... June 18, Franchise fee of $7 million (US) determined and Metro Baseball, Ltd., appoints Peter Bavasi, Executive Vice-President and General Manager of new franchise... August 12, Directors select "Blue Jays" from over 4,000 names and 30,000 entries in a "Name the Team" contest... August 25, Blue Jays announce Dunedin, Florida as new spring training site... September 22, Roy Hartsfield appointed field manager for inaugural season... October 8, Club reveals distinctive "Blue Jays logo", as season ticket sales begin... October 22, Blue Jays acquire first player in purchase of catcher Phil Roof from the Chicago White Sox... November 5, Blue Jays announce first trade at conclusion of expansion draft, sending Al Fitzmorris to Cleveland for catcher Alan Ashby and infielder outfielder Doug Howard.

1977 . . . March 11, Blue Jays defeat New York Mets 3-1 at Dunedin, Florida, in first spring training game... April 7, 44,649 fans brave snow and freezing temperatures as Major League baseball makes a successful debut in Toronto. Doug Ault becomes an instant hero hitting two home runs in the Blue Jays 9-5 win over the Chicago White Sox... August 9, Blue Jays defeat Minnesota 6-2 in front of 23,450 fans, which pushes the home attendance to 1,219,551 and establishes a new attendance record for a first-year expansion club after only 50 home dates... September 10, Roy Howell drives in nine runs with five hits, including two home runs and two doubles as the Blue Jays inflict a 19-3 loss on the New York Yankees. Jays' total is most runs scored against the Yankees in New York in over a half century... September 15, Blue Jays awarded 9-0 forfeit win over Baltimore Orioles as Orioles' manager Earl Weaver removes team from field in fifth inning... October 2, Blue Jays complete their first year with a 54-107 record with 1,701,052 fans having made their way to Exhibition Stadium to see the team in their inaugural season... November 24, Board of Directors names Peter Bavasi, President and Chief Operating Officer of Toronto Blue Jays Baseball Club.

1978 . . . April 22, Jim Clancy gets the credit for a 4-2 Jacket Day win over the Chicago White Sox in front of 44,327 including Prime Minister Pierre Trudeau and in doing so helps his own cause by starting the Blue Jays first ever triple play... June 26, Blue Jays explode for 24 runs on 24 hits en route to a 24-10 shellacking of the Baltimore Orioles.

1979 . . . September 23, Blue Jays complete their home schedule and announce a expansion attendance record total of 4,695,288 fans have come to see Blue Jays baseball in their first 3 seasons... October 18, Bobby Mattick named Field Manager for the 1980 season... November 26, Alfredo Griffin named co-winner of the American League's Rookie of the Year Award... December 2-7, the Blue Jays play host to the first Winter Meetings held outside the United States since 1936.

1980 . . . September 12, Blue Jays defeat Baltimore 7-5 to win their 60th game of the season and in doing so set a new club record for victories in a single season... September 26, Continuing to break all records for expansion teams, the Blue Jays reach the 6 million mark in home attendance... October 5, Toronto defeats Boston 4-1 to chalk up their 67th win of the season, also more victories than ever before.

1981 . . . October 7, Bobby Mattick resigns as Field Manager to become Executive Co-Ordinator, Baseball Operations... October 15, Bobby Cox, former Atlanta Braves Manager (1978-81), named Blue Jays Manager for the 1982 season... November 24, Peter Bavasi, President & Chief Operating Officer resigns.

1982 . . . July 22, N.E. Hardy appointed Chief Executive Officer... September 11, Blue Jays set a new club mark for road attendance, surpassing the previous mark of 1,285,409... October 3, Blue Jays set new club marks for best home (44-37) and road (34-47) records... Club establishes an American League record for the fewest games behind an American league leader for a last place club (17)

since divisional play started in 1969... Toronto wins 78th game to tie Cleveland for sixth place, the first season that the club did not finish in 7th place.

1983 . . . May 23, Lloyd Moseby becomes third consecutive Blue Jays player to capture AL Player of the Week honours (others being Luis Leal and Dave Stieb) marking only the second time in league history that one club had captured the honour for three consecutive weeks... July 4, Blue Jays lead the AL East at the All-Star break, a club first... July 25, Blue Jays are tied for first place, setting a new mark for the latest date that the club was ever in first place... August 2, 45,102 fans (a new record) see Blue Jays sweep TN-DH from the Yankees... September 19, Lloyd Moseby becomes first Blue Jays player to score 100 runs... September 20, Willie Upshaw becomes first Blue Jay player to drive in 100 runs... October 2, Blue Jays finish season at 89-73, good for 4th place, 9 games back, and also the first time the franchise had finished with an above .500 record.

1984 . . . April 17, Blue Jays set a new team record with 9,104 season tickets sold... April 28, Blue Jays gain sole possession of second place, a position they would never relinquish... May 27, Alfredo Griffin has his major league leading consecutive game streak snapped at 392 games... June 2, Blue Jays win their 19th one-run game in a row... August 5, Blue Jays steal seven bases in a 5-3 win at Baltimore... August 5, Cliff Johnson sets a new major league record with his 19th career pinch hit home run... September 2, Blue Jays reach 22-games over .500 (79-57) for the first time in club history... September 19, Blue Jays become the 18th major league franchise to surpass the two million mark in home attendance... September 23, Blue Jays draw 2,110,009 at home, a new franchise mark... September 29, Blue Jays clinch second place, their highest standing ever.

1985 . . . April 16, Blue Jays place an 11,500 ceiling on season tickets... May 1, Jimmy Key becomes the club's first starting LHP to win a game since Oct. 4, 1980 (614-games)... May 20, Blue Jays gain sole possession of 1st place, a position they would not relinquish for the remainder of the season... June 8-9, Blue Jays draw back-to-back 40,000 fan crowds for the first time ever... June 27, Blue Jays surpass one million mark in home attendance, the earliest date ever... July 21, Blue Jays win their 10th straight home game and push their first place lead to a club record 9.5-games... July 27, Blue Jays average home attendance, surpasses the 30,000 mark for the first time ever... September 12-15, Blue Jays and Yankees set an AL record for a 4-game series with 214,510 fans in attendance... September 29, Blue Jays move to a club record 41-games over .500 (98-57)... October 4, 47,686 see the Blue Jays play New York - a new club attendance mark... October 5, Blue Jays captured first division title (American League East)... October 6, Blue Jays draw 2,468,925 fans at home - a new club mark... October 25, Jimy Williams succeeds Bobby Cox as manager.

1986 . . . Blue Jays place a ceiling of 14,000 on season tickets in celebrating their 10th anniversary season... April 15, Club's first home rainout since July 4, 1983. The game vs the Orioles was made up the next day ... May 6, Jesse Barfield cracks 2 home runs vs Oakland to become the club's all-time franchise leader at 93... June 20, Cliff Johnson homers vs Detroit for his major league leading 20th career pinch hit home run... June 27, Damaso Garcia ties a major league record with four doubles vs New York... July 10, Damaso Garcia becomes the first player to register 1000 hits in a Blue Jays uniform... July 28, Jim Clancy becomes the first pitcher to record 100 wins in a Blue Jays uniform... September 22, Tony Fernandez becomes the first Blue Jays player to reach the 200 hit mark in one season, while he and Jesse Barfield become the first Blue Jays to win a Rawlings Gold Glove for defensive excellence.

1987 . . . June 2, Blue Jays embark on a club record 11-game win streak... July 1, Blue Jays set a club record when a Canada Day crowd of 47,828 fans saw the Yankees... July 14, George Bell participates in the All-Star Game and is the first Blue Jay ever selected by the fans... September 14,

Ernie Whitt becomes the second Blue Jays player to have a 3 home run game as Blue Jays set a Major League Record with 10 home runs in a game vs the Orioles... September 30, Blue Jays final home attendance reached 2,778,429, the most ever for an AL East team and the club led the AL in attendance for first time ever... November 17th, George Bell named AL MVP... December 8th, George Bell is named the ML Player of the Year by The Sporting News.

1988 ... April 3, George Bell becomes the first major leaguer to hit 3 home runs on Opening Day... April 11, Blue Jays defeat the Yankees in their home opener before their largest Opening Day crowd (45,185)... May 31, Dave Stieb tosses his first career One Hitter, defeating Milwaukee 9-0... June 4, Blue Jays complete a 4-game sweep at Fenway Park, their first sweep ever in Boston... July 12, Dave Stieb makes his sixth career All-Star appearance, placing him tied/7th on the All-time pitchers list... September 5, George Bell is named AL Player of the Week for the period ending September 4 and in doing so was the only league player to be twice honoured in 1988... September 30, Dave Stieb became the sixth modern ML pitcher to toss consecutive one hitters... October 2, Blue Jays finish the season with a 22-7 September/October, a club record.

1989 ... January 10, Paul Beeston named President of the Blue Jays... April 16, Kelly Gruber becomes the first franchise player to hit for the cycle against Kansas City at Exhibition Stadium... May 15, Jimy Williams is dismissed as manager, replaced on an interim basis by Cito Gaston... It was the club's first managerial change in franchise history to take place during a season... May 28, Blue Jays play their final game at Exhibition Stadium, defeating Chicago 7-5... May 31, Cito Gaston is named as the fifth manager in franchise history... June 3, Blue Jays overcome a 10-0 seventh inning deficit to defeat Boston 13-11 in 12 innings... Blue Jays place a ceiling of 26,000 season tickets at Sky-Dome... June 5, Blue Jays lose 5-3 to Milwaukee in the club's first game at SkyDome... July 9, Blue Jays win 2-0 at Detroit for the club's first-ever sweep at Tiger Stadium... August 4, Dave Stieb loses a perfect game after 8.2 innings when New York's Roberto Kelly doubles... August 31, Blue Jays defeat Chicago 5-1 to move into a first place tie with Baltimore.They would remain in first place for the remainder of the season... September 4, George Bell is named American League Player of the Month for August... September 16, 49,501 watch the Blue Jays defeat the Indians as the Blue Jays set a new American League record for home attendance... September 30, Blue Jays defeat Baltimore 4-3 to capture their second divison title in five seasons... October 8, Blue Jays draw 50,024 for Game 5 of the ALCS marking the 41st consecutive sellout at SkyDome... December 17, an era ends as Ernie Whitt is traded to the Atlanta Braves.He was the club's final link with the 1976 Expansion Draft.

1990 ... April 10, the Blue Jays begin their first full season at SkyDome... June 29, Dave Stewart of Oakland pitches the first No-Hitter in Toronto and at the SkyDome... August 14, George Bell ties a Major League record with 3 Sacrifice Flies in a game vs the White Sox... August 18, Mr. R. Howard Webster, the Blue Jays' Honourary Chairman passes away at age 80... September 2, Dave Stieb pitches the club's first No-Hitter vs the Cleveland Indians at Cleveland—final score: Toronto 3, Cleveland 0... September 19, with a crowd of 49,902, the Blue Jays set a Major League season attendance record, breaking the old record set by the L.A. Dodgers in 1982.The new record stands at 3,885,284... October 3, Blue Jays set a team record along with the Oakland Athletics for club fielding with a .986 average ... December 5, the Blue Jays make a blockbuster trade with San Diego, trading Tony Fernandez and Fred McGriff for Roberto Alomar and Joe Carter... December 14, Mr. N.E. Hardy steps down as the Blue Jays' Chairman of the Board and CEO and is appointed Honourary Chairman as Mr. William R. Ferguson is named Chairman of the Board and Mr. P.N.T. Widdrington is appointed Vice-Chairman and Chief Executive Officer.

1991 ... April 8, Toronto opens the season with a 6-2 loss to the defending AL East Champion Boston Red Sox... May 1, Blue Jays extend radio contract with CJCL through 1994 and in Texas, Nolan Ryan tosses his seventh career No-Hitter (first vs Blue Jays)... It was the third No-Hitter vs the Blue

Jays... July 1, Joe Carter named American League Player of the Month for June (.352, 11 HR, 29 RBI)... July 9, 52,382 fans watch the 62nd All-Star Game in Toronto as the American League defeated the National League 4-2. Toronto pitcher Jimmy Key was credited with the win in the game... August 13, Tom Henke's streak of consecutive saves comes to an end with a Paul Molitor home run in the ninth. Henke still sets a Major League mark for consecutive saves with 25... October 1, Juan Guzman sets a club record for consecutive wins by a Blue Jay starter with his 10th vs California... October 2, Toronto clinches the AL East with a come-from-behind 6-5 win over the Angels at the SkyDome in the final game of the regular season... Toronto also surpasses 4-million mark in attendance, becoming the first club ever to break 4-million (4,001,526)... October 31, John Labatt Limited purchases portion of club owned by Imperial Trust and thus obtained a 90% ownership of the club (10% Canadian Imperial Bank of Commerce)... December 13, Mr. Peter N.T. Widdrington is appointed Chairman of the Board for the Blue Jays and Mr. Paul Beeston is appointed Chief Executive Officer... December 18, Toronto signs pitcher Jack Morris to the richest contract in Blue Jays history... December 19, outfielder Dave Winfield agrees to a one-year deal with Toronto.

1992 ... April 6, the Blue Jays open the season in Detroit with newly acquired pitcher, Jack Morris setting a Major League record with his 13th consecutive opening day start.He tosses a complete game as Toronto wins 4-2... April 13, Toronto's six game win streak to start the season comes to an end as the Yankees down the Blue Jays 5-2... May 1, Roberto Alomar named AL Player of the Month for April (.382, 34H, 19R, 3HR, 8SB)... September 24, Dave Winfield sets a Blue Jays record for homers by a DH with his 23rd and becomes the oldest man in ML history to register 100 or more RBI in a season... October 3, Juan Guzman gets the win as the Blue Jays clinch their fourth AL East Title... October 4, with a crowd of 50,421 the Blue Jays surpass the 4-million mark in home attendance for the second straight season and set a new ML attendance record with 4,028,318 fans... October 14, Toronto defeats the Athletics in six games earning their first ever World Series berth... October 17, Toronto plays their first ever World Series game, losing 3-1 to the Braves... October 24, the Blue Jays emerge victorious over Atlanta in 11 innings capturing the World Series and thus becoming the first Canadian team to win the Commissioner's Trophy.

1993 ... April 30, Joe Carter sets a club record for RBI in April with 25... June 11, shortstop Tony Fernandez is re-acquired in a trade with the New York Mets... July 13, at Baltimore, a record tying seven Blue Jays are selected to the All-Star team, managed by Cito Gaston (Alomar, Carter, Hentgen, Molitor, Olerud, Ward, White)... July 31, Blue Jays acquire leadoff man Rickey Henderson from the A's for the stretch run in return for minor leaguer's Steve Karsay and Jose Herrera... August 2, the last day that John Olerud would be batting .400- average dipped to a season ending .363, becoming the first ever Blue Jay to win a batting title... August 23, Joe Carter collects 3 home runs vs the Indians for his fifth career 3 homer game; an AL record... September 26, Blue Jays break their own American League attendance record with a crowd of 50,518 to push the year's home attendance to 4,057,947... September 27, Toronto clinches AL East title with a 2-0 win in Milwaukee as Pat Hentgen wins his 19th game... October 3, Roberto Alomar goes 3-5 to move into third place (.326) in the AL batting race to finish behind teammates John Olerud (.363) and Paul Molitor (.332). It is the first time in 100 years that teammates had finished 1-2-3 in the batting race... October 12, Toronto defeats the Chicago White Sox 6-3 in the sixth game of the ALCS to win their second straight AL pennant and advance to the World Series against Philadelphia... October 23, In Game Six of the World Series, the Blue Jays led by Joe Carter's 3-run home run in the bottom of the ninth, defeat the Phillies 8-6 at SkyDome to become the first team since 1977-78 Yankees to capture back-to-back World Series Championships.

1994 ... April 4, club defeats the 1993 AL West Champion Chicago White Sox 7-3 as Toronto opens their 18th season... May 1, Joe Carter named AL Player of the Month after setting

Major League record for RBI in April with 31... May 20, Toronto extends managerial contract of Cito Gaston through the 1996 season... Same day, team President and CEO Paul Beeston is named Canada's Baseball Man of the Year for 1993 by Toronto and Montreal BBWAA... June 7, Manager Cito Gaston receives Honourary Doctor of Laws Degree from University of Toronto... July 8, Duane Ward undergoes arthroscopic surgery on right shoulder... August 11, Toronto defeats the New York Yankees 8-7 in 13 innings, in what would be the final game of 1994... August 12, Major League players strike begins... September 14, Office of the Commissioner announces that the remainder of the 1994 season will not be completed... October 14, Gord Ash named Vice-President and General Manager effective October 31... October 31, Pat Gillick steps down as General Manager of the Toronto Blue Jays.

1995 ... April 6, David Cone, who pitched for the Blue Jays in the 1992 World Series, is re-acquired in a trade with Kansas City... April 26, The strike-delayed season begins at home with a 13-1 pounding of Oakland, in which the Blue Jays, in front of their only sell-out crowd of the season, set a new club record scoring 11 times in the second inning... July 4, Roberto Alomar saw his string of 484 errorless chances come to an end with an error in a game in California. The 484 chances without an error was a new Major League record and the string of 104 games without an error established a new American League standard... July 13, Seattle turns the third ever triple play against the Blue Jays, in the ninth inning of their game in the Kingdome... July 28, David Cone was traded to the New York Yankees in exchange for minor league pitchers Marty Janzen, Jason Jarvis and Mike Gordon... October 1, The Blue Jays lose their fifth straight game to close out the 1995 season with a 56-88 record and finish in last place for the first time since 1979.

1996 ... January 16, Blue Jays Howard Starkman awarded Robert O. Fishel Award for Public Relations excellence in Major League Baseball... April 1, Blue Jays begin 20th season of play with a 9-6 win over Oakland in Las Vegas... April 9, Blue Jays honour George Bell and Dave Stieb as the first two players enshrined on the "Level of Excellence" as part of 20th season home opening festivities... April 16, Blue Jays promote Moose Johnson and Gord Lakey to Special Assistants to the Vice-President and General Manager... May 1, Juan Guzman named the AL Pitcher of the Month for April... August 26, Vice President, Baseball Al LaMacchia resigns to accept a position with the Tampa Bay Devil Rays... September 14, Blue Jays present first annual Bobby Mattick and Al LaMacchia Awards for excellence in Player Development and Scouting respectively. Rocket Wheeler captured the inaugural Bobby Mattick Award while Duane Larson captured the Al LaMacchia Award... September 3, Pat Hentgen captures consecutive AL Pitcher of the Month Awards, winning in July and August... September 30, Juan Guzman becomes the third Blue Jay to lead the AL in ERA posting a 2.93 mark... November 14, Blue Jays complete largest trade in club history, a nine player deal with the Pittsburgh Pirates in which the club acquires IF Carlos Garcia, OF Orlando Merced and LHP Dan Plesac... November 12, Pat Hentgen is named the American League Cy Young Award winner... November 19, Toronto Blue Jays unveil their new logo and uniforms, the first logo change in club history... December 9, Signed free agent catcher Benito Santiago to a two year deal... December 13, Blue Jays sign free agent pitcher Roger Clemens to a three year deal.

1997 ... February 28, Bob Engle is promoted from Assistant GM to Senior Advisor, Baseball Operations... June 2, Roger Clemens named the AL Pitcher of the Month for May... June 13, Blue Jays play first inter-league game in Philadelphia, losing 4-3 to the Phillies... June 31, Blue Jays play first ever regular season game with the Montreal Expos, three game series in SkyDome highlighted by July 1, Canada Day match-up... July 22, Paul Beeston, President and Chief Executive Officer of the Toronto Blue Jays resigns from position and accepts post with Major League Baseball as President and Chief Operating Officer... July 31, Blue Jays acquire OF Jose Cruz Jr. in a trade with the Seattle Mariners in exchange for RHP Mike Timlin and LHP Paul Spoljaric... September 2, Roger Clemens named the AL Pitcher of the Month for August... September 24, Blue Jays manager Cito Gaston relieved of his duties, Mel Queen appointed interim manager for the rest of the season... September 27, Blue

Jays announce Omar Malave as the Bobby Mattick Award winner and Jim Hughes as the Al LaMacchia award winner... September 28, Blue Jays announce coaches Nick Leyva, Gene Tenace, Alfredo Griffin and Willie Upshaw will not retrun for the 1998 season... October 30, Interbrew S.A. announces that they are no longer trying to sell the Toronto Blue Jays Baseball Club, the Toronto Argonauts Football Team or their share in SkyDome... November 10, Roger Clemens named as the American League Cy Young Award winner, his fourth and the second straight by a Blue Jay... November 24, Tim Johnson appointed as Manager of the Toronto Blue Jays... November 26, Blue Jays sign free agent pitcher Randy Myers to a three year contract and catcher Darrin Fletcher to a two year deal... November 26, Blue Jays radio rights awarded to Headline Sports... December 8, Blue Jays sign free agent 1B/DH Mike Stanley and 2B Tony Fernandez.

1998 ... February 4, sign free agent outfielder Jose Canseco... March 2, Gord Ash is promoted from Vice-President to Executive Vice President, Baseball and General Manager, Bob Nicholson from Vice President, Business to Executive Vice-President, Business, Howard Starkman appointed Vice-President, Media Relations, George Holm appointed Vice President, Sales and Operations & Susan Quigley appointed to Vice President, Finance and Administration... June 17, Dave Stieb returns to Blue Jays from Syracuse and first pitches on June 18 in Baltimore... July 4, Tony Fernandez becomes the franchise leader in hits collecting his 1,320 hit as a Blue Jay off Dennis Springer of Tampa Bay... July 5, Roger Clemens becomes the 11th pitcher to record 3000 career strikeouts after fanning Tampa Bay's Randy Winn... July 26, Jose Canseco hit career HR #380 to become the All-Time HR leader for non-US born players... July 27, Toronto Blue Jays play the Baltimore Orioles in the Hall of Fame Game in Cooperstown New York... July 30, Blue Jays trade Mike Stanley to Boston for RHP's Peter Munro and Jay Yennaco... July 31, Blue Jays trade RHP Juan Guzman to Baltimore for RHP Nerio Rodriguez and OF Shannon Carter... August 6, Trade Randy Myers to San Diego for C Brian Loyd and cash considerations... September 1, Roger Clemens named the AL Pitcher of the Month in August... September 4, Shawn Green becomes just the ninth player in the history of the American League, and the first Blue Jay, to hit 30 home runs and steal 30 bases in the same season... September 23, Blue Jays reach a multi -year agreement with CTV Sportsnet to broadcast up 42 games... November 16, Roger Clemens named American League Cy Young Award winner for the second consecutive season, his fifth and the third in club history... November 3, Name Dave Stewart as Assistant General Manager... December 13, Acquired RHP Joey Hamilton from the San Diego Padres in exchange for RHP's Woody Williams, Carlos Almanzar and OF Peter Tucci... December 8, Wayne Morgan promoted to the position of Special Assistant to the General Manager and Director, International Scouting... December 13 Roger Clemens named the AL's Joe Cronin Award winner for significant achievement.

1999 ... January 29, Sam Pollack retires as Chairman and CEO of the Blue Jays but will continue to serve as Senior Chairman and Director of the Toronto Blue Jays... Allan Chapin appointed Chairman of the Board of Directors... Gord Ash appointed President of Baseball Operations... Bob Nicholson appointed Executive Vice President and Chief Operating Officer... Terry Zuk added in the position of Vice-President, Marketing... February 20, traded RHP Roger Clemens to the New York Yankees in exchange for LHP David Wells, 2B Homer Bush and LHP Graeme Lloyd... March 17, Jim Fregosi replaces Tim Johnson as manager... April 5, Canadian Baseball Hall of Fame announces that it will induct Blue Jays Bobby Mattick... April 30, Minor League Catching instructor Ernie Whitt announced as Manager of Canada's baseball team for the 1999 Pan-Am games... June 12, traded LHP Dan Plesac to Arizona in exchange for IF Tony Batista and RHP John Frascatore... June 16, Alex Gonzalez has arthroscopic surgery and is out for the rest of the season... July 1, John Frascatore wins his third consecutive game in relief in three days to tie a ML record... July 4, Pat Hentgen become's fourth Blue Jays pitcher to post 100 wins... July 30, Blue Jays honour Joe Carter and Cito Gaston with their appointments to the Level of Excellence... August

30, Vernon Wells called up to Toronto after starting the season with Dunedin (A)... September 17, Tony Fernandez becomes franchise leader in games after playing in his 1,393 game as a Blue Jay... October 2, Billy Koch records his 31st save which is an AL rookie record and second in the majors... October 3, Shawn Green finishes the season with a club record 87 extra-base hits and 134 runs scored... October 12, Bob Engle, Senior Advisor, Baseball Operations, announces his retirement... Cito Gaston named as hitting coach... November 8, acquired OF Raul Mondesi and LHP Pedro Borbon Jr. in exchange for OF Shawn Green and 2B Jorge Nunez... November 11, traded RHP Pat Hentgen and LHP Paul Spoljaric to St. Louis in exchange for LHP Lance Painter, RHP Matt DeWitt and C Alberto Castillo... December 10, Sign Carlos Delgado to a three year contract extension... December 20, Tim McCleary named Vice-President, Baseball Operations and Assistant General Manager.

2000 . . . February 10, unveil two new mascots and begin "Name the Mascots Contest"... March 4, name new mascots ACE and DIAMOND... April 22 & 23, Jose Cruz become just the second Blue Jay to hit leadoff home runs in consecutive games... April 23 Carlos Delgado ties a club record with an RBI in eight consecutive games... June 20 vs. Detroit allowed eight home runs to tie a franchise record... June 25 the set a new franchise record with home runs in 23 consecutive games... July 5, 1B Carlos Delgado and LHP David Wells named to the American League All-Star team... July 8, David Wells sets club record for most wins at the All-Star break with 15 and is named as the starting pitcher for the AL All-Star team... Blue Jays become the first team in Major League history to have four players with 20 or more home runs at the All-Star break (Delgado-28, Batista-24, Mondesi-22, Cruz-20)... July 24, Assistant General Manager Dave Stewart takes over as Pitching Coach for the balance of the season... August 14, Raul Mondesi has surgery on his right elbow to remove bone chips... August 27 at Texas Darrin Fletcher becomes the ninth AL catcher and the second Blue

Jays catcher to hit three home runs in a game... September 1, Rogers Communications Inc. purchases 80% of the Toronto Blue Jays Baseball Club with Labatt's maintaining 20% interest, while CIBC relinquishes it's 10% share... Paul Godrey is named President and CEO of the Toronto Blue Jays... September 18, Carlos Delgado sets new club record for RBI with 135... September 8 reached an agreement to remain in Dunedin for spring training for an additional 15 years beginning in 2002... September 12 signed a four-year player development contract with the Auburn Doubledays of the New York-Penn State League (A)... September 19 signed a two-year player development contract with the Charleston Ally Cats of the South Atlantic League (A)... September 21 vs. the New York Yankees, David Wells becomes the second oldest pitcher in ML history to win 20 games for the first time in his career... September 25, Todd Greene hit his 4th home run and the club's 134th at home to set a new AL club record for most home runs in one season at home... The Blue Jays finish the season with a franchise record and 2000 AL high 244 home runs... Tied Major League record with four players hitting 30 or more home runs in a season... Tied AL record with seven players hitting 20 or more home runs... October 10, Gord Ash, President, Baseball Operations and General Manager, signed a three-year contract... Manager, Jim Fregosi's contract was not renewed... October 20, Carlos Delgado signs a four-year contract, replacing the previous three-year deal... Carlos Delgado named as the AL Hank Aaron Award winner... Blue Jays launch 25th season logo... October 23, Carlos Delgado named as the "Sporting News Player of the Year"... October 31, Tim Wilken named Vice President, Baseball... November 1, Darrin Fletcher signs a three-year contract... November 3, Buck Martinez named Manager of the Blue Jays... December 8 announced Paul Allamby as Senior VP, Sales and Marketing and promoted Mark Lemmon to VP, Corporate Partnerships and Business Development... December 10, signed Alex Gonzalez to a four-year contract.

STIEB'S NO-HITTER
SEPTEMBER 2, 1990 at CLEVELAND — TORONTO 3, CLEVELAND 0

DAVE STIEB chalked up his first no-hitter and the first in BLUE JAYS history as he stopped the Cleveland Indians on a sunny Sunday afternoon at Cleveland Stadium before a crowd of 23,640.

The game ended as Cleveland's Jerry Browne whacked a fly to right field where JUNIOR FELIX put the squeeze on it.

Stieb had a season high nine strikeouts and walked four over his 122-pitch afternoon.

There were no tough plays and only a couple of well hit balls. Closest the Tribe came to a hit was KEN PHELPS pulling a liner about three feet foul to open the eighth inning.

The BLUE JAYS and STIEB got their offensive support from FRED McGRIFF who hit two solo home runs and from MANNY LEE who doubled home KENNY WILLIAMS in the fifth inning.

Stieb had previously gone 8.2 innings, three times, protecting no-hitters. He had back-to-back attempts in September 1988; on September 24, 1988 at Cleveland Stadium, JULIO FRANCO had a bad hop single over second baseman MANNY LEE's head. In his next start, against Baltimore at Exhibition Stadium, JIM TRABER looped a single over his first baseman FRED McGRIFF's outstretched glove hand. Both no-hit bids were lost on 2-2 pitches. STIEB also had a perfect game for 8.2 innings on August 4, 1989 vs the Yankees at SkyDome. ROBERTO KELLY doubled to left to break it up.

TORONTO	0	0	0		1	1	0		0	0	1	—	3 8 0
CLEVELAND	0	0	0		0	0	0		0	0	0	—	0 0 1

STIEB and BORDERS

BLACK, OROSCO (8), OLIN (9) and SKINNER

WP-STIEB (17-5)   LP-BLACK (10-9)

STIEB PITCHING LINE: 9 IP 0 H 0 R 0 ER 4 BB 9 SO

HOME SELLOUT STREAKS — REGULAR SEASON
DATES

60	—	May 18, 1990 to April 8, 1991 (Opening Day)
50	—	June 9, 1993 to April 4, 1994 (Opening Day)
46	—	May 27, 1992 to September 15, 1992
39	—	July 4, 1991 to April 11, 1992 (2nd game)
38	—	July 13, 1989 to April 10, 1990 (Opening Day)

ALL TIME BLUE JAYS ROSTER

MANAGERS, COACHES AND PLAYERS 1977 thru 2000
Total number of players — 379 + Interim Manager
(Includes all players who have participated in one or more official American League games.)

MANAGERS (10)
Cox, Bobby ('82–'85)
Fregosi, Jim ('99–00)
Gaston, Cito ('89–'97)
Hartsfield, Roy ('77–'79)
Johnson, Tim ('98)
Mattick, Bobby ('80–'81)
Queen, Mel ('97)+
Tenace, Gene ('91)+
Warner, Harry ('78)+
Williams, Jimy ('86–'89)

COACHES (41)
Bailor, Bob ('92–'95)
Bevington, Terry ('99–)
Butera, Sal ('98)
Cisco, Galen ('88; '90–'95)
de Armas, Roly ('00)
Doerr, Bobby ('77–'81)
Elia, Lee ('00)
Felske, John ('80–'81)
Gaston, Cito ('82–'89; '00–)
Griffin, Alfredo ('96–'97)
Guerrero, Epy ('81)
Hacker, Rich ('91–'94)
Hisle, Larry ('92–'95)
Holmberg, Dennis ('94–'95)
Hubbard, Jack ('98)
Iorg, Garth ('96)
Knoop, Bobby ('00)
Langford, Rick ('00)
Leppert, Don ('77–'79)
Lett, Jim ('97–'99)
Leyva, Nick ('93–'97)
Llenas, Winston ('89)
Matthews, Gary ('98–'99)
McLaren, John ('86–'90)
Menke, Denis ('80–'81)
Miller, Bob ('77–'79)
Moore, Jackie ('77–'79)
Moseby, Lloyd ('99)
Pevey, Marty ('99)
Queen, Mel ('96–'99)
Rodriguez, Eddie ('98)
Smith, Billy ('84–'88)
Squires, Mike ('89–'91)
Stewart, Dave ('00)
Sullivan, John ('82–'93)
Tenace, Gene ('90–'97)
Torres, Hector ('90–'91)
Upshaw, Willie ('96–'97)
Warner, Harry ('77–'80)
Widmar, Al ('80–'89)
Williams, Jimy ('80–'85)

PLAYERS

A (14)
Acker, Jim (rhp) ('83–'86; '89–'91)
Adams, Glenn (dh) ('82)
Ainge, Dan (if-of) ('79–'81)
Aikens, Willie (dh-1b) ('84–'85)
Alberts, Butch (dh) ('78)
Alexander, Doyle (rhp) ('83–'86)
Allenson, Gary (c) ('85)
Almanzar, Carlos (rhp) ('97–'98)
Alomar, Roberto (if) ('91–'95)
Andrews, Clayton (lhp) ('00)
Andujar, Luis (rhp) ('96–'98)
Aquino, Luis ('86)
Ashby, Alan (c) ('77–'78)
Ault, Doug (1b-of) ('77–'78; '80)

B (42)
Bailor, Bob (if-of-p) ('77–'80)
Bair, Doug (rhp) ('88)
Baker, Dave (if) ('82)
Bale, John (lhp) ('99–'00)
Barfield, Jesse (of) ('81–'89)
Barlow, Mike (rhp) ('80–'81)
Batista, Tony ('99–)
Batiste, Kevin (of) ('89)
Battle, Howard (3b) ('95)
Beamon, Charlie (1b-dh-of) ('81)
Bell, Derek (of) ('91–'92)
Bell, George (of) ('81; '83–'90)

Beniquez, Juan (of-dh) ('87–'88)
Berenguer, Juan (rhp) ('81)
Berroa, Geronimo (of) ('99)
Black, Bud (lhp) ('90)
Blair, Willie (rhp) ('90)
Blake, Casey (if) ('99)
Bohanon, Brian (lhp) ('96)
Bomback, Mark (rhp) ('81–'82)
Bonnell, Barry (of) ('80–'83)
Borbon, Pedro (lhp) ('00–)
Borders, Pat (c-if) ('88–'94; '99)
Bosetti, Rick (of) ('78–'81)
Boucher, Denis (lhp) ('91)
Bowling, Steve (of) ('77)
Braun, Steve (if-dh) ('80)
Brenly, Bob (c) ('89)
Brito, Tilson (if) ('95)
Brow, Scott (rhp) ('93–'96)
Brown, Bobby (of) ('79)
Brown, Kevin (c) ('98–'99)
Brumfield, Jacob (of) ('96–'97; '99)
Bruno, Tom (rhp) ('77)
Buice, DeWayne (rhp) ('89)
Burroughs, Jeff (dh) ('85)
Bush, Homer (if) ('99–)
Buskey, Tom (rhp) ('78–'80)
Butera, Sal (c) ('88)
Butler, Rich (of) ('97)
Butler, Rob (of) ('93–'94; '99)
Byrd, Jeff (rhp) ('77)

C (40)
Cabrera, Francisco (c) ('89)
Cadaret, Greg (rhp) ('94)
Cairo, Miguel (if) ('96)
Campusano, Sil (of) ('88)
Canate, Willie (of) ('93)
Candelaria, John (lhp) ('90)
Candiotti, Tom (rhp) ('91)
Cannon, J.J. (of) ('79)
Canseco, Jose (of-dh) ('98)
Carpenter, Chris (rhp) ('97–)
Carrara, Giovanni (rhp) ('95–'96)
Carter, Joe (of) ('91–'97)
Carty, Rico (dh) ('78–'79)
Castillo, Alberto (c) ('00)
Castillo, Frank (rhp) ('00)
Castillo, Tony (lhp) ('88–'89; '93–'96)
Caudill, Bill (rhp) ('85–'86)
Cedeno, Domingo (rf) ('93–'96)
Cerone, Rick (c) ('77–'79)
Cerutti, John (lhp) ('85–'90)
Clancy, Jim (rhp) ('77–'88)
Clark, Bryan (lhp) ('84)
Clarke, Stan (lhp) ('83; '85–'86)
Clemens, Roger (rhp) ('97–'98)
Coco, Pasqual (rhp) ('00–)
Coleman, Joe (rhp) ('78)
Coles, Darnell (of) ('93–'94)
Collins, Dave (of) ('83–'84)
Cone, David (rhp) ('92; '95)
Cooper, Don (rhp) ('83)
Cordova, Marty (of) ('00)
Cornett, Brad (rhp) ('94–'95)
Cox, Danny (rhp) ('93–'95)
Cox, Ted (if) ('81)
Crabtree, Tim (rhp) ('95–'97)
Crespo, Felipe (if) ('96–'98)
Cruz, Jose (of) ('97–)
Cruz, Victor (rhp) ('78)
Cubillan, Darwin (rhp) ('00)
Cummings, Steve (rhp) ('89–'90)

D (16)
Daal, Omar (lhp) ('97)
Dalesandro, Mark (c) ('98–'99)
Darr, Mike (rhp) ('77)
Darwin, Danny (rhp) ('95)
Davey, Tom (rhp) ('99)

Davis, Bob (c) ('80)
Davis, Dick (of) ('82)
Davis, Steve (lhp) ('85–'86)
Dayley, Ken (lhp) ('91–'92)
DeBarr, Dennis (lhp) ('77)
Delgado, Carlos (c-1b) ('93–)
DeWillis, Jeff (c) ('87)
Dewitt, Matt (rhp) ('00)
Diaz, Carlos (c) ('90)
Ducey, Rob (of) ('87–'92; '00)
Duncan, Mariano (if) ('97)

E (8)
Edge, Butch (rhp) ('79)
Eichhorn, Mark (rhp) ('82; '86–'88; '92–'93)
Eppard, Jim (ph) ('90)
Escobar, Kelvim (rhp) ('97–)
Espinosa, Nino (rhp) ('81)
Estrella, Leoncio (rhp) ('00)
Evans, Tom (if) ('97–'98)
Ewing, Sam (if-of-dh) ('77–'78)

F (12)
Fairly, Ron (if-of) ('77)
Felix, Junior (of) ('89–'90)
Fernandez, Tony (if) ('83–'90; '93; '98–'99)
Fielder, Cecil (dh-1b) ('85–'88)
Filer, Tom (rhp) ('85)
Flanagan, Mike (lhp) ('87–'90)
Flener, Huck (lhp) ('93; '96–'97)
Fletcher, Darrin (c) ('98–)
Frascatore, John (rhp) ('99–)
Fraser, Willie (rhp) ('91)
Freisleben, Dave (rhp) ('79)
Fullmer, Brad (dh) ('00–)

G (26)
Garcia, Carlos (if) ('97)
Garcia, Damaso (if) ('80–'86)
Garcia, Pedro (if) ('77)
Garvin, Jerry (lhp) ('77–'82)
Geisel, Dave (lhp) ('82–'83)
Giannelli, Ray (if) ('91)
Gilles, Tom (rhp) ('90)
Glover, Gary (rhp) ('99)
Gomez, Luis (if) ('78–'79)
Gonzales, Rene (if) ('91)
Gonzalez, Alex (if) ('94–)
Goodwin, Curtis (of) ('99)
Gordon, Don (rhp) ('86–'87)
Gott, Jim (rhp) ('82–'84)
Gozzo, Mauro (rhp) ('89)
Grebeck, Craig (inf) ('98–'00)
Green, Shawn (of) ('93–'99)
Greene, Charlie (c) ('00)
Greene, Todd (of-c) ('00–)
Greene, Willie (of) ('99)
Griffin, Alfredo (if) ('79–'84; '92–'93)
Grilli, Steve (rhp) ('79)
Gruber, Kelly (if-of) ('84–'92)
Gunderson, Eric (lhp) ('00)
Guthrie, Mark (lhp) ('00)
Guzman, Juan (rhp) ('91–'98)

H (24)
Hall, Darren (rhp) ('94–'95)
Halladay, Roy (rhp) ('98–)
Hamilton, Joey (rhp) ('99–)
Hanson, Erik (rhp) ('96–'98)
Hargan, Steve (rhp) ('77)
Hartenstein, Chuck (rhp) ('77)
Hearron, Jeff (c) ('85–'86)
Henderson, Rickey (of) ('93)
Henke, Tom (rhp) ('85–'92)
Hentgen, Pat (rhp) ('91–'99)
Hernandez, Pedro (if-of) ('79; '82)
Hernandez, Toby (c) ('84)
Hernandez, Xavier (rhp) ('89)
Hill, Glenallen (of) ('89–'91)
Hodgson, Paul (of) ('80)
Hollins, Dave (dh) ('99)
Horsman, Vince (lhp) ('91)
Horton, Willie (dh) ('78)
Howell, Roy (if) ('77–'80)
Huff, Michael (of) ('94–'96)

Hudek, John (rhp) ('99)
Huffman, Phil (rhp) ('79)
Hurtado, Edwin (rhp) ('95)
Hutton, Tommy (if-of) ('78)

I (2)
Infante, Alex (if) ('87–'89)
Iorg, Garth (if-of) ('78; '80–'87)

J (11)
Jackson, Darrin (of) ('93)
Jackson, Roy Lee (rhp) ('81–'84)
Janzen, Marty (rhp) ('96–'97)
Jefferson, Jesse (rhp) ('77–'80)
Johnson, Anthony (of) ('82)
Johnson, Cliff (dh) ('83–'86)
Johnson, Dane (rhp) ('96)
Johnson, Jerry (rhp) ('77)
Johnson, Joe (rhp) ('86–'87)
Johnson, Tim (if) ('78–'79)
Jordan, Ricardo (lhp) ('95)

K (11)
Kelly, Pat D. (c) ('80)
Kelly, Pat F. (if) ('99)
Kent, Jeff (if) ('92)
Key, Jimmy (lhp) ('84–'92)
Kilgus, Paul (lhp) ('90)
Kirkwood, Don (rhp) ('78)
Klutts, Mickey (if) ('83)
Knorr, Randy (c) ('91–'95)
Koch, Billy (rhp) ('99–)
Kucek, Jack (rhp) ('80)
Kusick, Craig (if-p-f) ('79)

L (17)
Lamp, Dennis (rhp) ('84–'86)
Lavelle, Gary (lhp) ('85–'87)
Lawless, Tom (if) ('89–'90)
Leach, Rick (1b-of-p) ('84–'88)
Leal, Luis (rhp) ('80–'85)
Lee, Manuel (if) ('85–'92)
Leiter, Al (lhp) ('89–'95)
Lemanczyk, Dave (rhp) ('77–'80)
Lemongello, Mark (rhp) ('79)
Lennon, Patrick (of) ('98–'99)
Linton, Doug (rhp) ('92–'93)
Liriano, Nelson (if) ('87–'90)
Lloyd, Graeme (lhp) ('99)
Loaiza, Esteban (rhp) ('00–)
Ludwick, Eric (rhp) ('99)
Luebber, Steve (rhp) ('79)
Luecken, Rick (rhp) ('90)

M (45)
MacDonald, Bob (lhp) ('90–'92)
Macha, Ken (if) ('81)
Macha, Mike (if) ('80)
Mahler, Mickey (lhp) ('86)
Maksudian, Mike (c) ('92)
Maldonado, Candy (of) ('91–'92; '95)
Manrique, Fred (if) ('81; '84)
Martin, Norberto (if) ('99)
Martinez, Buck (c) ('81–86)
Martinez, Dave (of) ('00)
Martinez, Domingo (1b) ('92–'93)
Martinez, Sandy (c) ('95–'97)
Mason, Jim (if) ('77)
Matheny, Mike (c) ('99)
Matuszek, Len (dh) ('85)
Mayberry, John (1b) ('78–'82)
Mazzilli, Lee (of-dh) ('89)
McGriff, Fred (1b) ('86–'90)
McKay, Dave (if) ('77–'79)
McLaughlin, Joey (rhp) ('80–'84)
McRae, Brian (of) ('99)
Menhart, Paul (rhp) ('95)
Merced, Orlando (of) ('97)
Miller, Dyar (rhp) ('79)
Milner, Brian (c) ('78)
Mirabella, Paul (lhp) ('80–'81)
Moffitt, Randy (rhp) ('83)
Molitor, Paul (dh) ('93–'95)

Mondesi, Raul (of) ('00–)
Moore, Balor (lhp) ('78–'80)
Moore, Charlie (c) ('87)
Morandini, Mickey (if) ('00–)
Morgan, Mike (rhp) ('83)
Morris, Jack (rhp) ('92–'93)
Moseby, Lloyd (of) ('80–'89)
Mosquera, Julio (c) ('96–'97)
Mottola, Chad (of) ('00)
Mulliniks, Rance (if) ('82–'92)
Munro, Peter (rhp) ('99–'00)
Murphy, Tom (rhp) ('77–'79)
Murray, Dale (rhp) ('81–'82)
Musselman, Jeff (lhp) ('86–'89)
Musselman, Ron (rhp) ('84–'85)
Myers, Greg (c) ('87; '89–'92)
Myers, Randy (lhp) ('98)

N (6)
Nicosia, Steve (c) ('85)
Niekro, Phil (rhp) ('87)
Nixon, Otis (of) ('96–'97)
Nordbrook, Tim (if) ('77)
Nordhagen, Wayne (of-dh) ('82)
Nunez, Jose (rhp) ('87–'89)

O (5)
O'Brien, Charlie (c) ('96–'97)
Olerud, John (1b-dh) ('89–'96)
Oliver, Al (dh) ('85)
Orta, Jorge (of-dh) ('83)
Otanez, Willis (if) ('99)

P (11)
Painter, Lance (lhp) ('00–)
Parker, Dave (dh) ('91)
Parrish, Lance (c) ('95)
Perez, Robert (of) ('94–'97)
Perez, Tomas (if) ('95–'98)

Person, Robert (rhp) ('97–'99)
Petralli, Geno (c) ('82–'84)
Phelps, Josh (c) ('00–)
Phillips, Tony (of) ('98)
Plesac, Dan (lhp) ('97–'99)
Powell, Hosken (of-dh) ('82–'83)

Q (2)
Quantrill, Paul (rhp) ('96–)
Quinlan, Tom (lf) ('90; '92)

R (13)
Rader, Doug (if) ('77)
Ramos, Domingo (if) ('80)
Revering, Dave (1b-dh) ('82)
Righetti, Dave (lhp) ('94)
Risley, Bill (rhp) ('96–'98)
Roberts, Leon (of-dh) ('82)
Robertson, Bob (1b-dh) ('79)
Robinson, Ken (rhp) ('95; '97)
Rodriguez, Nerio (rhp) ('98–'99)
Rogers, Jimmy (rhp) ('95)
Romano, Mike (rhp) ('99)
Roof, Phil (c) ('77)
Ross, Mark (rhp) ('88)

S (29)
Samuel, Juan (if-of) ('96–'98)
Sanchez, Alex (rhp) ('89)
Sanders, Anthony (of) ('99)
Santiago, Benito (c) ('97–'98)
Schofield, Dick (ss) ('93–'94)
Schrom, Ken (rhp) ('80; '82)
Scott, John (of) ('77)
Segui, David (if) ('99)
Senteney, Steve (rhp) ('82)
Sharperson, Mike (if) ('87)
Shepherd, Ron (of) ('84–'86)
Sierra, Ruben (of) ('97)
Silva, Jose (rhp) ('96)

Sinclair, Steve (lhp) ('98–'99)
Singer, Bill (rhp) ('77)
Small, Aaron (rhp) ('94)
Snyder, Cory (if-of) ('91)
Sojo, Luis (if) ('90; '93)
Solaita, Tony (1b-dh) ('79)
Spoljaric, Paul (lhp) ('94; '96–'97; '99)
Sprague, Ed (if-c) ('91–'98)
St. Claire, Randy (rhp) ('94)
Staggs, Steve (if) ('77)
Stanley, Mike (dh) ('98)
Stark, Matt (c) ('87)
Stewart, Dave (rhp) ('93–'94)
Stewart, Shannon (of) ('95–)
Stieb, Dave (rhp-of) ('79–'92; '98)
Stottlemyre, Todd (rhp) ('88–'94)

T (8)
Tabler, Pat (if) ('91–'92)
Thompson, Andy (of) ('00–)
Thornton, Lou (of) ('85; '87–'88)
Timlin, Mike (rhp) ('91–'97)
Todd, Jackson (rhp) ('79–'81)
Torres, Hector (if) ('77)
Trachsel, Steve (rhp) ('00)
Trlicek, Rick (rhp) ('92)

U (2)
Underwood, Tom (lhp) ('78–'79)
Upshaw, Willie (if-of) ('78; '80–'87)

V (5)
Van Ryn, Ben (lhp) ('98)
Velez, Otto (if-of-dh) ('77–'82)
Viola, Frank (lhp) ('96)
Virgil, Ozzie (c) ('89–'90)

Vuckovich, Pete (rhp) ('77)

W (29)
Wallace, Dave (rhp) ('78)
Ward, Duane (rhp) ('86–'95)
Ward, Turner (of) ('91–'93)
Ware, Jeff (rhp) ('95–'96)
Weathers, Dave (rhp) ('91–'92)
Webster, Mitch (of) ('83–'85)
Weston, Mickey (rhp) ('91)
Wells, David (lhp) ('87–'92; '99–'00)
Wells, Greg (1b-dh) ('81)
Wells, Vernon (of) ('99–)
White, Devon (of) ('91–'95)
Whiten, Mark (of) ('90–'91)
Whitmer, Dan (c) ('81)
Whitt, Ernie (c) ('77–'78; '80–'89)
Wilborn, Ted (of-pr) ('79)
Wiley, Mark (rhp) ('78)
Williams, Kenny (of) ('90–'91)
Williams, Matt (rhp) ('83)
Williams, Woody (rhp) ('93–'98)
Willis, Mike (lhp) ('77–'81)
Wills, Frank (rhp) ('88–'91)
Wilson, Mookie (of) ('89–'91)
Winfield, Dave (of) ('92)
Wise, Dewayne (of) ('00–)
Withem, Shannon (rhp) ('98)
Witt, Kevin (1b) ('98–'99)
Woods, Al (of) ('77–'82)
Woods, Gary (of) ('77–'78)
Woodward, Chris (if) ('99–)

Z (1)
Zosky, Eddie (if) ('91–'92)

BLUE JAYS WHO ALSO PLAYED FOR EXPOS (35)

	Blue Jays Years	Expos Years		Blue Jays Years	Expos Years
Luis Aquino	1986	1995	Dave Martinez	2000	1988-91
Denis Boucher	1991	1993-94	Jim Mason	1977	1979
Sal Butera	1988	1984-85	Orlando Merced	1997	1999
John Candelaria	1990	1989	Balor Moore	1978-80	1970; 1972-74
Rick Cerone	1977-79	1992	Dale Murray	1981-82	1974-76; 1979-80
Omar Daal	1997	1996-97			
Ron Fairly	1977	1969-74	Steve Nicosia	1985	1985
Darrin Fletcher	1998-	1992-97	Otis Nixon	1996-97	1988-90
Willie Fraser	1991	1995	Charlie O'Brien	1996-97	2000
Brad Fullmer	2000-	1997-99	Al Oliver	1985	1982-83
Damaso Garcia	1980-86	1989	Robert Perez	1994-97	1998
Rene Gonzales	1991	1984; 1986	Bill Risley	1996-98	1992-93
Tommy Hutton	1978	1978-81	Randy St. Claire	1994	1984-88
Anthony Johnson	1982	1981	David Segui	1999	1995-97
Tom Lawless	1989-90	1984	Tony Solaita	1979	1979
Ken Macha	1981	1979-80	Hector Torres	1977	1972
Mickey Mahler	1986	1985	Mitch Webster	1983-85	1985-88
Fred Manrique	1984	1985	Kenny Williams	1990-91	1991

OLDEST & YOUNGEST BLUE JAYS

Oldest Blue Jays

Player	D.O.B	Last Game	Age at last Game
Phil Niekro	4/1/39	Aug. 29, 1987	48 yrs, 4 mths, 28 days
Dave Stieb	7/22/57	Sept. 25, 1998	41 yrs, 2 mths, 3 days
Dave Winfield	10/3/51	Oct. 24, 1992	41 yrs, 0 mths, 21 days
Dave Parker	6/9/51	Oct. 2, 1991	40 yrs, 3 mths, 23 days
Danny Darwin	10/25/55	July 4, 1995	39 yrs, 8 mths, 10 days
Rico Carty	10/1/39	May 29, 1979	39 yrs, 7 mths, 28 days
Paul Molitor	8/22/56	Oct. 1, 1995	39 yrs, 1 mth, 10 days

Youngest Blue Jays

Player	D.O.B	1st Game	Age at 1st Game
Brian Milner	11/17/59	June 23, 1978	18 yrs, 7 mths, 6 days
Fred Manrique	11/5/61	August 23, 1981	19 yrs, 9 mths, 18 days
Manny Lee	6/17/65	April 10, 1985	19 yrs, 9 mths, 24 days

PITCHING STATISTICS AS BLUE JAYS

('77 thru '00)
* Left Handed

PITCHER	W-L	ERA	G	GS	CG	SHO	SV	IP	H	R	ER	HR	HB	BB	SO	WP
ACKER	26-22	4.07	281	17	0	0	14	524.1	535	269	237	49	25	206	273	23
ALEXANDER	46-26	3.56	106	103	25	3	0	750.0	752	315	297	81	14	172	392	16
ALMANZAR	2-3	5.06	29	0	0	0	0	32.0	35	19	18	5	1	9	24	0
ANDREWS	1-2	10.02	8	2	0	0	0	20.2	34	23	23	6	0	9	12	0
ANDUJAR	1-7	6.43	25	10	0	0	0	70.0	102	59	50	13	1	24	34	4
AQUINO	1-1	6.35	7	0	0	0	0	11.1	14	8	8	2	0	3	5	1
BAILOR	0-0	7.71	3	0	0	0	0	2.1	4	2	2	2	0	1	0	0
BAIR	0-0	4.05	10	0	0	0	0	13.1	14	6	6	2	0	3	8	1
BALE*	0-0	14.29	3	0	0	0	0	5.2	7	10	9	2	2	5	10	0
BARLOW	3-1	4.11	52	1	0	0	5	70.0	79	40	32	5	6	27	24	5
BERENGUER	2-9	4.31	12	11	1	0	0	71.0	62	41	34	7	3	35	29	1
BLACK*	2-1	4.02	3	2	0	0	0	15.2	10	7	7	2	1	3	3	0
BLAIR	3-5	4.06	27	6	0	0	0	68.2	66	33	31	4	1	28	43	3
BOHANON*	0-1	7.77	20	0	0	0	1	22.0	27	19	19	4	2	19	17	2
BOMBACK	6-10	4.74	36	19	0	0	0	150.0	171	86	79	16	4	60	55	9
BORBON	1-1	6.48	59	0	0	0	0	41.2	45	37	30	5	5	38	29	0
BOUCHER*	0-3	4.58	7	7	0	0	0	35.1	39	20	18	6	2	16	16	0
BROW	2-4	5.81	42	4	0	0	0	85.2	98	67	55	11	2	54	45	2
BRUNO	0-1	7.85	12	0	0	0	0	18.1	30	181	16	4	1	13	9	3
BUICE	1-0	5.82	7	0	0	0	0	17.0	13	12	11	2	0	13	10	1
BUSKEY	9-12	3.86	85	0	0	0	7	158.2	156	73	68	22	1	55	85	3
BYRD	2-13	6.18	17	17	1	0	0	87.1	98	68	60	5	0	68	40	3
CADARET*	0-1	5.85	21	0	0	0	0	20.0	24	15	13	4	0	17	15	6
CANDELARIA*	0-3	5.48	13	2	0	0	1	21.1	32	13	13	2	2	11	19	2
CANDIOTTI	6-7	2.98	19	19	3	9	0	129.2	114	47	43	6	4	45	81	5
CARPENTER	34-34	5.04	105	88	8	3	0	581.2	666	363	326	71	15	229	410	24
CARRARA	2-5	8.26	23	7	1	0	0	63.2	87	65	58	15	1	37	37	2
CASTILLO, F	10-5	3.59	25	24	0	0	0	138.0	112	58	55	18	5	56	104	0
CASTILLO, T*	13-13	3.49	218	0	0	0	16	296.1	279	125	115	29	9	106	181	6
CAUDILL	6-10	4.09	107	0	0	0	16	105.2	89	51	48	15	4	52	78	0
CERUTTI*	46-37	3.87	191	108	7	2	2	772.1	800	378	332	110	16	254	369	30
CLANCY	128-140	4.10	352	345	73	11	1	2204.2	2185	1104	1005	219	28	814	1237	82
CLARK*	1-2	5.91	20	3	0	0	0	45.2	66	33	30	6	1	22	21	7
CLARKE*	1-2	6.18	24	0	0	0	0	27.2	31	19	19	7	0	17	18	0
CLEMENS	41-13	2.33	67	67	14	6	0	498.2	373	143	129	20	19	156	563	10
COCO	0-0	9.00	1	1	0	0	0	4.0	5	4	4	1	1	5	2	1
COLEMAN	2-0	4.60	31	0	0	0	0	60.2	67	34	31	6	1	30	28	5
CONE	13-9	3.14	25	24	5	2	0	183.1	151	69	64	15	8	70	149	9
COOPER	0-0	6.75	4	0	0	0	0	5.0	8	4	4	3	0	0	5	0
CORNETT	1-3	7.00	14	4	0	0	0	36.0	49	31	28	14	4	14	26	2
COX	9-10	4.21	78	0	0	0	5	147.1	137	74	69	12	2	69	136	13
CRABTREE	8-8	3.99	121	0	0	0	3	140.0	154	74	62	12	7	52	104	9
CRUZ	7-3	1.71	32	0	0	0	0	47.1	28	10	9	0	1	36	51	3
CUBILLAN	1-0	8.04	7	0	0	0	0	15.2	20	14	14	5	1	11	14	0
CUMMINGS	2-0	3.78	11	4	0	0	0	33.1	40	16	14	5	2	16	12	1
DAAL*	1-1	4.00	9	3	0	0	0	27.0	34	13	12	3	0	6	28	1
DARR	0-1	33.75	1	1	0	0	0	1.1	3	5	5	1	1	4	1	0
DARWIN	1-8	7.62	13	11	1	0	0	65.0	91	60	55	13	3	24	26	1
DAVEY	1-1	4.70	29	0	0	0	1	44.0	40	28	23	5	3	26	42	6
DAVIS*	2-1	5.12	13	5	0	0	0	31.2	31	21	18	7	0	18	27	1
DAYLEY*	0-0	5.40	10	0	0	0	0	5.0	8	5	3	0	1	9	5	2
DEBARR*	0-1	5.91	14	0	0	0	0	21.1	29	14	14	1	0	8	10	2
DEWITT	1-0	8.56	8	0	0	0	0	13.2	20	13	13	4	2	9	6	1
EDGE	3-4	5.23	9	9	1	0	0	51.2	60	32	30	6	1	24	19	4
EICHHORN	29-19	3.03	279	7	0	0	15	493.0	445	180	166	33	24	167	372	19
ESCOBAR	34-31	5.04	125	64	4	1	16	464.2	489	285	260	51	13	220	379	10
ESPINOSA	0-0	9.00	1	0	0	0	0	1.0	4	1	1	0	0	0	0	0
ESTRELLA	0-0	5.79	2	0	0	0	0	4.2	9	3	3	1	0	0	3	0
FILER	7-0	3.88	11	9	0	0	0	48.2	38	21	21	6	0	18	24	0
FLANAGAN*	26-27	3.96	76	76	3	1	0	452.1	480	217	198	39	11	150	194	9
FLENER*	3-3	5.21	29	12	0	0	0	95.0	108	59	55	12	1	39	53	3
FRASCATORE	9-5	4.25	93	0	0	0	1	110.0	129	67	58	19	8	42	52	8
FRASER	0-2	6.15	13	1	0	0	0	26.1	33	20	18	4	3	11	12	2
FREISLEBEN	2-3	4.95	42	2	0	0	3	91.0	101	57	50	5	2	54	35	6
GARVIN*	20-41	4.46	196	65	15	1	8	606.0	648	318	300	74	13	219	320	17
GEISEL*	1-4	4.39	63	2	0	0	5	84.0	79	43	41	10	4	48	72	2
GILLES	1-0	6.75	2	0	0	0	0	1.1	2	1	1	0	0	1	0	0
GLOVER	0-0	0.00	1	0	0	0	0	1.0	0	0	0	0	0	1	0	0
GORDON	0-1	6.06	19	0	0	0	1	32.2	36	25	22	3	1	11	16	0
GOTT	21-30	4.25	99	65	8	3	2	442.1	422	233	209	37	11	183	276	11
GOZZO	4-1	4.83	9	3	0	0	0	31.2	35	19	17	1	1	9	10	0
GRILLI	0-0	0.00	1	0	0	0	0	2.1	1	0	0	0	0	0	1	0
GUNDERSON	0-1	7.11	6	0	0	0	0	6.1	15	6	5	0	1	2	2	0
GUTHRIE	0-2	4.79	23	0	0	0	0	20.2	20	12	11	3	1	9	20	2
GUZMAN	76-62	4.07	195	195	15	2	0	1215.2	1099	612	550	115	23	546	1030	88
HALL	2-5	3.75	47	0	0	0	20	48.0	47	21	20	5	1	23	39	1
HALLADAY	13-14	5.77	57	33	2	1	1	231.0	272	167	148	35	6	123	139	12
HAMILTON	9-9	5.77	28	24	0	0	0	131.0	146	86	84	16	5	51	71	4

PITCHER	W - L	ERA	G	GS	CG	SHO	SV	IP	H	R	ER	HR	HB	BB	SO	WP
HANSON	13 - 20	5.68	49	45	4	1	0	278.2	331	190	176	39	3	137	195	15
HARGAN	1 - 3	5.22	6	5	1	0	0	29.1	36	17	17	2	0	14	11	2
HARTENSTEIN	0 - 2	6.59	13	0	0	0	0	27.1	40	22	20	8	1	6	15	0
HENKE	29 - 29	2.48	446	0	0	0	217	563.0	411	171	155	48	6	166	644	21
HENTGEN	105 - 76	4.14	252	222	31	9	0	1555.2	1587	783	716	191	37	557	995	55
HERNANDEZ	1 - 0	4.76	7	0	0	0	0	22.2	25	15	12	2	1	8	7	1
HORSMAN*	0 - 0	0.00	4	0	0	0	0	4.0	2	0	0	0	0	3	2	0
HUDEK	0 - 0	12.27	3	0	0	0	0	3.2	8	5	5	1	0	1	2	0
HUFFMAN	6 - 18	5.77	31	31	2	1	0	173.0	220	130	111	25	0	68	56	5
HURTADO	5 - 2	5.45	14	10	1	0	0	77.2	81	50	47	11	5	40	33	11
JACKSON	24 - 21	3.50	190	2	0	0	30	337.0	307	148	131	30	7	128	204	10
JANZEN	6 - 7	6.39	27	11	0	0	0	98.2	118	76	70	20	2	51	64	7
JEFFERSON	22 - 56	4.75	127	37	21	4	1	666.1	718	385	352	82	8	266	307	9
JOHNSON, D	0 - 0	3.00	10	0	0	0	0	9.0	5	3	3	0	0	5	7	0
JOHNSON, Je	2 - 4	4.60	43	0	0	0	5	86.0	91	50	44	9	0	54	54	2
JOHNSON, Jo	10 - 7	4.42	30	29	0	0	0	154.2	171	83	76	13	5	40	66	5
JORDAN*	1 - 0	6.60	15	0	0	0	1	15.0	18	11	11	3	2	13	10	1
KEY*	116 - 81	3.42	317	250	26	8	10	1695.2	1624	710	645	165	24	404	944	31
KILGUS*	0 - 0	6.06	11	0	0	0	0	16.1	19	11	11	2	1	7	7	0
KIRKWOOD	4 - 5	4.24	16	9	3	0	0	68.0	76	36	32	6	0	25	29	3
KOCH	9 - 8	2.97	124	0	0	0	64	142.1	133	54	47	11	5	48	117	1
KUCEK	3 - 8	6.75	23	12	0	0	1	68.0	83	56	51	9	1	41	35	3
KUSICK	0 - 0	4.91	1	0	0	0	0	3.2	3	2	2	1	0	0	0	0
LAMP	21 - 14	4.20	149	7	0	0	13	263.2	286	145	123	21	1	88	143	9
LAVELLE*	7 - 10	3.77	92	0	0	0	9	100.1	90	50	42	7	0	55	67	1
LEACH*	0 - 0	27.00	1	0	0	0	0	1.0	2	3	3	1	0	2	0	0
LEAL	51 - 58	4.14	165	151	27	3	1	946.0	958	476	435	101	22	320	491	23
LEITER*	26 - 24	4.20	91	61	4	2	2	415.1	394	209	194	30	12	240	329	24
LEMANCZYK	27 - 45	4.68	95	82	25	3	0	575.0	632	334	299	52	13	212	240	36
LEMONGELLO	1 - 9	6.29	18	10	2	0	0	83.0	97	64	58	14	3	34	40	2
LINTON	1 - 4	7.97	12	4	0	0	0	35.0	42	31	31	5	1	26	20	2
LLOYD*	5 - 3	3.63	74	0	0	0	3	72.0	68	36	29	11	4	23	47	1
LOAIZA	5 - 7	3.62	14	14	1	1	0	92.0	95	45	37	8	10	26	62	0
LUDWICK	0 - 0	27.00	1	0	0	0	0	1.0	3	3	3	0	0	2	0	0
LUEBBER	0 - 0	INF	1	0	0	0	0	0.0	2	1	1	0	0	1	0	0
LUECKEN	0 - 0	9.00	1	0	0	0	0	1.0	2	1	1	1	0	1	0	0
MacDONALD*	4 - 3	3.48	76	0	0	0	0	103.1	101	43	40	9	1	43	50	1
MAHLER*	0 - 0	0.00	2	0	0	0	0	1.0	1	0	0	0	1	0	0	0
McLAUGHLIN	22 - 24	3.88	195	10	0	0	31	341.0	343	169	147	36	5	148	207	10
MENHART	1 - 4	4.92	21	9	1	0	0	78.2	72	49	43	9	6	47	50	6
MILLER	0 - 0	10.57	10	0	0	0	0	15.1	27	18	18	3	0	5	7	2
MIRABELLA*	5 - 12	4.64	41	23	3	1	0	145.1	171	89	75	13	4	73	62	4
MOFFITT	6 - 2	3.77	45	0	0	0	10	57.1	52	27	24	5	1	24	38	0
MOORE*	12 - 17	4.96	102	37	7	0	1	348.1	376	213	192	39	19	164	148	11
MORGAN	0 - 3	5.16	16	4	0	0	0	45.1	48	26	26	6	0	21	22	3
MORRIS	28 - 18	4.87	61	61	10	2	0	393.1	411	230	213	36	13	145	235	23
MUNRO	1 - 3	6.00	40	5	0	0	0	81.0	108	60	54	7	5	39	54	4
MURPHY	9 - 12	4.00	79	1	0	0	9	164.1	173	76	73	18	1	63	67	9
MURRAY	9 - 7	2.92	67	0	0	0	11	126.1	127	50	41	3	3	37	72	5
MUSSELMAN, J*	20 - 11	4.26	94	19	0	0	3	190.1	182	99	90	14	6	98	100	9
MUSSELMAN, R	5 - 2	3.79	36	4	0	0	1	73.2	77	35	31	4	0	34	38	3
MYERS	3 - 4	4.46	41	0	0	0	28	42.1	44	21	21	4	2	19	32	2
NIEKRO	0 - 2	8.25	3	3	0	0	0	12.0	15	11	11	4	0	7	7	1
NUNEZ	5 - 3	4.40	56	12	0	0	0	137.0	127	71	67	15	1	77	131	7
PAINTER*	2 - 0	4.73	42	2	0	0	0	66.2	69	37	35	9	2	22	53	4
PERSON	8 - 13	6.18	61	22	0	0	8	177.2	179	129	122	29	11	97	142	9
PLESAC*	6 - 10	4.53	181	0	0	0	5	123.0	116	66	62	16	1	44	142	4
QUANTRILL	19 - 32	3.79	306	20	0	0	13	434.2	516	205	183	49	12	132	276	4
RIGHETTI*	0 - 1	6.75	13	0	0	0	0	13.1	9	10	10	2	0	10	10	0
RISLEY	3 - 6	4.83	72	0	0	0	0	100.2	88	61	54	16	4	61	73	4
ROBINSON	1 - 2	3.61	24	0	0	0	0	42.1	26	22	17	8	2	23	35	1
RODRIGUEZ	1 - 1	10.45	9	0	0	0	0	10.1	12	12	12	3	1	10	5	0
ROGERS	2 - 4	5.70	19	0	0	0	0	23.2	21	15	15	4	0	18	13	0
ROMANO	0 - 0	11.81	3	0	0	0	0	5.1	8	8	7	1	0	5	3	1
ROSS	0 - 0	4.91	3	0	0	0	0	7.1	5	6	4	0	0	4	4	0
SANCHEZ	0 - 1	10.03	4	3	0	0	0	11.2	16	13	13	1	0	14	4	1
SCHROM	2 - 0	5.44	23	0	0	0	1	46.1	45	29	28	5	0	34	21	1
SENTENEY	0 - 0	4.91	11	0	0	0	0	22.0	23	16	12	5	0	6	20	1
SILVA	0 - 0	13.50	2	0	0	0	0	2.0	5	3	3	1	0	0	0	0
SINCLAIR*	0 - 2	6.10	27	0	0	0	0	20.2	20	15	14	4	1	9	11	0
SINGER	2 - 8	6.79	13	12	0	0	0	59.2	71	54	45	5	2	39	33	3
SMALL	0 - 0	9.00	1	0	0	0	0	2.0	5	2	2	1	0	2	0	0
SPOLJARIC*	4 - 8	4.31	104	3	0	0	4	150.1	134	85	72	21	6	81	146	6
ST. CLAIRE	0 - 0	9.00	2	0	0	0	0	2.0	4	4	2	0	0	2	2	0
STEWART	19 - 16	5.09	48	48	1	0	0	295.1	297	175	167	49	8	134	207	10
STIEB	175 - 134	3.42	439	408	103	30	3	2873.0	2545	1208	1091	224	129	1020	1658	51
STOTTLEMYRE	69 - 70	4.39	206	175	15	4	1	1139.0	1182	597	555	115	49	414	662	30
TIMLIN	23 - 22	3.62	305	3	0	0	52	393.1	369	178	158	29	10	167	331	16
TODD	7 - 10	4.27	45	26	7	0	0	215.0	224	117	102	31	7	68	99	9
TRACHSEL	2 - 5	5.29	11	11	0	0	0	63.0	72	40	37	10	0	25	32	1
TRLICEK	0 - 0	10.80	2	0	0	0	0	1.2	2	2	2	0	0	2	1	0
UNDERWOOD*	15 - 30	3.88	64	62	19	2	1	424.2	414	218	183	46	11	182	267	18
VAN RYN*	0 - 1	9.00	10	0	0	0	0	4.0	6	4	4	0	0	2	3	0

PITCHER	W-L	ERA	G	GS	CG	SHO	SV	IP	H	R	ER	HR	HB	BB	SO	WP
VIOLA*	1 - 3	7.71	6	6	0	0	0	30.1	43	28	26	6	2	21	18	1
VUCKOVICH	9 - 7	3.47	53	8	3	1	8	148.0	143	64	57	13	5	59	123	12
WALLACE	0 - 0	3.86	6	0	0	0	0	148.0	12	6	6	1	0	11	7	1
WARD	32 - 36	3.18	452	2	0	0	121	650.2	529	255	230	30	16	278	671	50
WARE	3 - 6	7.47	18	9	0	0	0	59.0	63	52	49	8	3	52	29	8
WEATHERS	1 - 0	5.50	17	0	0	0	0	18.0	20	12	11	2	2	19	16	0
WELLS*	84 - 55	4.06	306	138	18	2	13	1148.2	1171	566	518	126	28	294	784	46
WESTON	0 - 0	0.00	2	0	0	0	0	2.0	1	0	0	0	0	1	1	0
WILEY	0 - 0	6.75	2	0	0	0	0	2.2	3	2	2	0	0	1	2	0
WILLIAMS, M	1 - 1	14.63	4	3	0	0.0	0	8.0	13	13	13	5	1	7	5	0
WILLIAMS, W	28 - 34	4.30	166	76	2	1.0	0	613.1	589	308	293	88	13	251	439	17
WILLIS*	7 - 21	4.59	144	6	1	0	15	296.0	312	161	151	36	3	123	149	9
WILLS	9 - 6	4.65	82	8	0	0	0	195.1	196	105	101	21	3	79	134	6
WITHEM	0 - 0	3.00	1	0	0	0	0	3.0	3	1	1	0	0	2	2	0

BATTING STATISTICS AS BLUE JAYS

('77 thru '00)

BATTER	AVG	G	AB	R	H	2B	3B	HR	RBI	SH - SF	HP	BB	SO	SB - CS
ADAMS	.258	30	66	2	17	4	0	1	11	0 - 3	0	4	5	0 - 0
AIKENS	.205	105	254	23	52	8	0	12	31	0 - 1	2	32	62	0 - 0
AINGE	.220	211	665	57	146	19	4	2	37	12 - 3	4	37	128	12 - 5
ALBERTS	.278	6	18	1	5	1	0	0	0	0 - 0	0	0	2	0 - 0
ALLENSON	.118	14	34	2	4	1	0	0	3	0 - 0	0	0	10	0 - 0
ALOMAR	.307	703	2706	451	832	152	36	55	342	39 - 22	16	322	291	206 - 46
ANDREWS	.000	8	3	0	0	0	0	0	0	0 - 0	0	0	2	0 - 0
ASHBY	.230	205	660	52	152	31	3	11	58	14 - 2	3	78	82	1 - 3
AULT	.234	247	693	66	162	28	5	17	86	5 - 4	7	70	105	4 - 5
BAILOR	.264	523	1878	230	495	75	19	8	138	21 - 11	15	127	107	46 - 28
BAKER	.250	9	20	3	5	1	0	0	2	1 - 0	2	3	3	0 - 0
BARFIELD	.265	1032	3463	530	919	162	27	179	527	13 - 24	27	342	855	55 - 40
BATISTA	.271	252	995	157	270	57	3	67	193	3 - 8	10	57	200	7 - 4
BATISTE	.250	6	8	1	2	0	0	0	0	0 - 0	0	0	5	0 - 0
BATTLE	.200	9	15	3	3	0	0	0	0	0 - 0	0	4	8	1 - 0
BEAMON	.200	8	15	1	3	1	0	0	0	0 - 0	0	2	2	0 - 0
BELL, D	.228	79	189	28	43	6	3	2	16	2 - 1	6	21	39	10 - 4
BELL, G	.286	1181	4528	641	1294	237	32	202	740	0 - 59	35	255	563	59 - 27
BENIQUEZ	.284	39	81	6	23	5	1	5	21	0 - 1	1	5	13	0 - 0
BERROA	.194	22	62	11	12	3	0	1	6	0 - 0	2	9	15	0 - 0
BLAKE	.256	14	39	6	10	2	0	1	1	0 - 0	0	2	7	0 - 0
BONNELL	.281	457	1504	184	422	76	14	33	187	10 - 13	6	114	187	31 - 16
BORDERS	.256	747	2309	205	590	127	9	54	272	19 - 17	6	112	364	6 - 6
BOSETTI	.252	376	1422	149	359	69	8	17	129	13 - 10	8	69	170	23 - 30
BOWLING	.206	89	194	19	40	9	1	1	13	3 - 2	0	37	41	2 - 3
BRAUN	.273	37	55	4	15	2	0	1	9	0 - 0	0	8	5	0 - 0
BRENLY	.170	48	88	9	15	3	1	1	6	1 - 0	0	10	17	1 - 0
BRITO	.228	75	206	19	47	10	0	1	15	2 - 2	5	19	46	2 - 1
BROWN, B	.000	4	10	1	0	0	0	0	0	0 - 0	0	2	1	0 - 0
BROWN, K	.277	54	119	18	33	9	1	2	16	3 - 4	2	9	34	0 - 0
BRUMFIELD	.238	210	652	99	155	32	6	16	91	5 - 7	5	57	128	17 - 9
BURROUGHS	.257	86	191	19	49	9	3	6	28	0 - 2	0	34	36	0 - 1
BUSH	.289	204	782	107	219	34	4	6	73	12 - 4	11	39	142	41 - 12
BUTERA	.233	23	60	3	14	2	1	1	6	1 - 0	0	1	9	0 - 0
BUTLER, Ri	.286	7	14	3	4	1	0	0	2	0 - 0	0	2	3	0 - 1
BUTLER, Ro	.209	66	129	22	27	4	1	0	8	4 - 2	3	14	20	2 - 3
CABRERA	.167	3	12	1	2	1	0	0	0	0 - 0	0	1	3	0 - 0
CAIRO	.222	9	27	5	6	2	0	0	1	0 - 0	1	2	9	0 - 0
CAMPUSANO	.218	73	142	14	31	10	2	2	12	2 - 1	4	9	33	0 - 0
CANATE	.213	38	47	12	10	0	0	1	3	2 - 1	1	6	15	1 - 1
CANNON	.177	131	192	30	34	1	1	1	9	3 - 0	1	1	48	14 - 4
CANSECO	.237	151	583	98	138	26	0	46	107	0 - 4	6	65	159	29 - 17
CARPENTER	.000	105	4	0	0	0	0	0	0	0 - 0	0	1	2	0 - 0
CARTER	.257	1039	4093	578	1051	218	28	203	736	1 - 65	49	286	696	78 - 26
CARTY	.269	236	848	99	228	42	0	32	123	1 - 0	1	82	86	4 - 2
CASTILLO, A	.211	66	185	14	39	7	0	1	16	2 - 3	0	21	36	0 - 0
CASTILLO, F	.143	25	7	0	1	0	0	0	0	0 - 0	0	0	3	0 - 0
CEDENO	.246	190	586	81	144	18	5	6	48	13 - 6	4	36	56	7 - 6
CERONE	.229	255	851	79	195	39	6	11	91	8 - 4	2	66	84	1 - 7
CLEMENS	.167	67	6	1	1	1	0	0	0	1 - 0	0	2	0	0 - 0
COLES	.234	112	337	41	79	15	2	8	41	1 - 4	5	26	54	1 - 1
COLLINS	.291	246	843	114	245	36	19	3	78	8 - 5	11	76	108	91 - 21
CORDOVA	.245	62	200	23	49	7	0	4	18	0 - 0	3	18	35	3 - 2
COX, T	.300	16	50	6	15	4	0	2	9	0 - 0	0	5	10	0 - 1
CRESPO	.246	100	207	20	51	12	2	2	24	5 - 2	5	29	44	5 - 3
CRUZ JR.	.243	428	1516	240	368	72	11	70	197	3 - 11	2	220	391	46 - 15
CUBILLAN	.000	7	1	0	0	0	0	0	0	0 - 0	0	0	0	0 - 0
DALESANDRO	.266	48	94	11	25	5	0	2	15	0 - 2	1	1	8	1 - 0
DAVIS, B	.189	123	307	24	58	13	0	5	27	14 - 0	2	17	40	0 - 0
DAVIS, J	.286	3	7	0	2	0	0	0	2	0 - 1	0	0	1	0 - 0
DELGADO	.282	829	2901	493	818	214	7	190	604	0 - 32	61	436	728	5 - 6
DeWILLIS	.120	13	25	2	3	1	0	1	2	1 - 0	0	2	12	0 - 0
DIAZ	.333	9	3	1	1	0	0	0	0	1 - 0	0	0	2	0 - 0

BATTER	AVG	G	AB	R	H	2B	3B	HR	RBI	SH-SF	HP	BB	SO	SB-CS
DUCEY	.234	188	333	52	77	18	3	2	31	4-4	1	37	95	8-3
DUNCAN	.228	39	167	20	38	6	0	0	12	0-0	3	6	39	4-2
EPPARD	.200	6	5	0	1	0	0	0	0	0-0	1	0	2	0-0
ESCOBAR	.000	125	8	0	0	0	0	0	0	0-0	0	0	5	0-0
EVANS	.229	19	48	7	11	2	0	1	2	0-0	1	3	12	0-1
EWING	.267	137	300	27	80	8	2	6	43	3-1	0	24	51	1-1
FAIRLY	.279	132	458	60	128	24	2	19	64	8-2	2	58	58	0-4
FELIX	.261	237	878	135	229	37	15	24	111	2-8	5	78	200	31-20
FERNANDEZ	.297	1402	5276	699	1565	287	72	59	601	34-43	47	438	485	172-85
FIELDER	.243	220	506	67	123	19	2	31	84	0-3	3	46	144	0-2
FLETCHER	.298	361	1235	128	368	68	2	47	190	1-15	17	71	131	1-0
FULLMER	.295	133	482	76	142	29	1	32	104	0-6	6	30	68	3-1
GARCIA, C	.220	103	350	29	77	18	2	3	23	10-4	2	15	60	11-3
GARCIA, D	.288	902	3572	453	1028	172	26	32	296	27-20	27	110	284	194-86
GARCIA, P	.208	41	130	10	27	10	1	0	9	3-0	3	5	21	0-0
GIANELLI	.167	9	24	2	4	1	0	0	0	0-0	0	5	9	1-0
GOMEZ	.227	212	576	50	131	14	3	0	42	21-3	0	40	58	3-10
GONZALES	.195	71	118	16	23	3	0	1	6	6-1	4	12	22	0-0
GONZALEZ	.243	736	2622	328	637	147	15	66	274	57-13	25	214	609	67-28
GOODWIN	.000	2	8	0	0	0	0	0	0	0-0	0	0	3	0-0
GREBECK	.289	202	655	89	189	43	2	5	60	12-4	8	69	88	2-2
GREEN	.286	716	2513	402	718	164	15	119	376	2-17	28	206	510	76-25
GREENE, C	.111	3	9	0	1	0	0	0	0	0-0	0	0	5	0-0
GREENE, T	.235	34	85	11	20	2	0	5	10	0-0	0	5	18	0-0
GREENE, W	.204	81	226	22	46	7	0	12	41	0-2	0	20	56	0-0
GRIFFIN	.249	982	3396	382	844	127	50	13	231	74-24	14	146	313	79-73
GRUBER	.259	921	3094	421	800	145	24	114	434	13-35	35	195	493	80-33
GUZMAN	.000	195	2	0	0	0	0	0	0	0-0	0	0	0	0-0
HALLADAY	.000	57	2	0	0	0	0	0	0	1-0	0	0	2	0-0
HAMILTON	.000	28	2	0	0	0	0	0	0	0-0	0	0	1	0-0
HEARRON	.200	16	30	2	6	1	0	0	4	0-0	0	3	9	0-0
HENDERSON	.215	44	163	37	35	3	1	4	12	1-2	2	35	19	22-2
HENTGEN	.056	252	18	0	1	0	0	0	0	1-0	0	0	8	0-0
HERNANDEZ, P	.000	11	9	2	0	0	0	0	0	0-0	0	0	3	0-0
HERNANDEZ, T	.500	3	2	1	1	0	0	0	0	0-0	0	0	0	0-0
HILL	.243	138	411	65	100	16	5	16	50	0-2	0	28	98	12-6
HODGSON	.220	20	41	5	9	0	1	1	5	2-0	0	3	12	0-1
HOLLINS	.222	27	99	12	22	5	0	2	6	0-0	0	5	22	0-0
HORTON	.205	33	122	12	25	6	0	3	19	0-1	0	3	29	0-0
HOWELL	.272	516	1954	219	532	101	17	43	234	12-11	13	178	337	5-6
HUFF	.267	152	374	50	100	24	5	4	34	5-6	4	50	53	3-2
HUTTON	.254	64	173	19	44	9	0	2	9	5-0	0	19	12	1-2
INFANTE	.185	40	27	8	5	0	0	0	0	1-0	0	2	5	1-0
IORG	.258	931	2450	251	633	125	16	20	238	21-19	11	114	298	22-17
JACKSON	.216	46	176	15	38	8	0	5	19	5-0	0	8	53	0-2
JOHNSON, A	.235	70	98	17	23	2	1	3	14	1-1	0	11	26	3-13
JOHNSON, C	.273	400	1175	162	321	58	3	54	202	1-10	12	178	203	0-3
JOHNSON, T	.212	110	165	15	35	4	1	0	9	5-1	1	16	31	0-2
KELLY, Pat D	.286	3	7	0	2	0	0	0	0	0-0	0	0	4	0-0
KELLY, Pat F	.267	37	116	17	31	7	0	6	20	1-3	0	10	23	0-1
KENT	.240	65	192	36	46	13	1	8	35	0-4	6	20	47	2-1
KLUTTS	.256	22	43	3	11	0	0	3	5	0-0	1	1	11	0-1
KNORR	.281	135	377	50	88	13	2	15	57	3-1	1	32	98	0-0
KOCH	.000	124	2	0	0	0	0	0	0	0-0	0	0	2	0-0
KUSICK	.204	24	54	3	11	1	0	2	7	0-1	1	7	7	0-0
LAWLESS	.207	74	82	21	17	1	0	0	4	1-1	0	7	13	12-3
LEACH	.283	376	763	95	216	46	6	8	95	0-9	3	67	99	0-2
LEE	.254	753	2152	231	547	67	17	16	199	28-17	2	160	426	26-15
LENNON	.242	11	33	4	8	4	0	1	6	0-0	1	2	12	0-0
LIRIANO	.251	318	1022	132	257	45	9	11	101	18-7	5	96	133	44-19
MACHA, K	.200	37	85	4	17	2	0	0	6	0-1	0	8	15	1-1
MACHA, M	.000	5	8	0	0	0	0	0	0	0-0	0	0	1	0-0
MAKSUDIA	.000	3	3	0	0	0	0	0	0	0-0	0	0	0	0-0
MALDONADO	.272	250	826	112	225	47	4	34	119	2-8	15	107	210	6-3
MANRIQUE	.189	24	37	1	7	0	0	0	2	0-0	1	0	13	0-1
MARTIN	.222	9	27	3	6	2	0	0	0	0-0	2	4	4	0-0
MARTINEZ, B	.222	454	1100	114	244	63	2	35	154	11-23	4	123	175	2-5
MARTINEZ, Da	.311	47	180	29	56	10	1	2	22	0-1	1	24	28	4-2
MARTINEZ, Do	.409	15	22	4	9	0	0	2	6	0-0	0	1	8	0-0
MARTINEZ, S	.232	141	422	30	98	21	3	5	43	1-2	5	24	104	0-0
MASON	.165	22	79	10	13	3	0	0	2	2-0	0	7	10	1-1
MATHENY	.215	57	163	16	35	6	0	3	17	2-1	1	12	37	0-0
MATUSZEK	.212	62	151	23	32	6	2	2	15	0-4	0	11	24	2-1
MAYBERRY	.256	549	1803	215	461	62	6	92	272	5-16	21	258	248	3-4
MAZZILLI	.227	28	66	12	15	3	0	4	11	0-1	2	17	16	2-0
McGRIFF	.278	578	1944	348	540	99	8	125	305	2-13	11	352	495	21-10
McKAY	.223	287	934	96	208	33	11	10	79	24-3	4	34	160	7-6
McRAE	.195	31	82	11	16	3	1	3	11	1-0	2	16	22	0-1
MERCED	.266	98	368	45	98	23	2	9	40	0-2	3	47	62	7-3
MILNER	.444	2	9	3	4	0	1	0	2	0-0	0	0	1	0-0
MOLITOR	.315	405	1615	270	508	98	11	51	246	4-17	9	193	172	54-4
MONDESI	.271	96	388	78	105	22	2	24	67	0-3	3	32	73	22-6
MOORE	.215	51	107	15	23	10	1	1	7	4-0	1	13	12	0-0

BATTER	AVG	G	AB	R	H	2B	3B	HR	RBI	SH - SF	HP	BB	SO	SB - CS
MORANDINI	.271	35	107	10	29	2	1	0	7	2 - 0	0	7	23	1 - 0
MOSEBY	.257	1392	5124	768	1319	242	60	149	651	38 - 40	50	547	1015	255 - 86
MOSQUERA	.233	11	30	2	7	3	0	0	2	0 - 0	0	0	5	0 - 1
MOTTOLA	.222	3	9	1	2	0	0	0	2	0 - 0	1	0	4	0 - 0
MULLINIKS	.280	1115	3013	382	843	204	14	68	389	13 - 24	4	416	465	12 - 10
MUNRO	.000	40	1	0	0	0	0	0	0	0 - 0	0	0	1	0 - 0
MYERS, G	.238	240	673	63	160	37	1	14	72	1 - 9	0	50	95	0 - 2
MYERS, R	.000	41	1	0	0	0	0	0	0	0 - 0	0	0	1	0 - 0
NICOSIA	.267	6	15	0	4	0	0	0	1	0 - 0	0	0	0	0 - 0
NIXON	.275	226	897	141	247	27	2	2	55	13 - 5	1	123	122	101 - 23
NORDBROOK	.175	31	63	10	11	0	1	0	1	1 - 0	1	4	11	1 - 0
NORDHAGEN	.270	72	185	12	50	6	0	1	20	0 - 2	0	10	22	0 - 2
O'BRIEN	.230	178	549	55	126	32	1	17	71	6 - 8	28	51	113	0 - 3
OLERUD	.293	920	3103	464	910	213	6	109	468	5 - 35	32	514	430	3 - 8
OLIVER	.251	61	187	20	47	6	1	5	23	0 - 0	1	7	13	0 - 0
ORTA	.237	103	245	30	58	6	3	10	38	0 - 4	0	19	29	1 - 2
OTANEZ	.252	42	127	21	32	8	0	5	13	0 - 0	1	9	30	0 - 0
PARKER	.333	13	36	2	12	4	0	0	3	0 - 0	0	4	7	0 - 1
PARRISH	.202	70	178	15	36	9	0	4	22	6 - 2	1	15	52	0 - 0
PEREZ, R	.271	144	336	36	91	16	1	5	30	4 - 1	1	8	39	3 - 0
PEREZ, T	.234	178	525	46	123	19	7	2	36	10 - 2	2	44	78	2 - 4
PERSON	.000	61	4	0	0	0	0	0	0	0 - 0	0	1	1	0 - 0
PETRALLI	.314	25	51	3	16	2	0	0	1	1 - 0	0	5	7	0 - 0
PHELPS	.000	1	1	0	0	0	0	0	0	0 - 0	0	0	1	0 - 0
PHILLIPS	.354	13	48	9	17	5	0	1	7	0 - 1	2	9	6	0 - 0
POWELL	.250	152	348	49	87	13	4	4	33	0 - 4	0	17	31	6 - 4
QUANTRILL	.000	306	1	0	0	0	0	0	0	0 - 0	0	1	1	0 - 0
QUINLAN	.118	14	17	2	2	1	0	0	2	0 - 0	1	2	10	0 - 0
RADER	.240	96	313	47	75	18	2	13	40	4 - 5	3	38	67	2 - 1
RAMOS	.125	5	16	0	2	0	0	0	0	0 - 0	0	2	5	0 - 0
REVERING	.215	55	135	15	29	6	0	5	18	0 - 2	0	22	30	0 - 3
ROBERTS	.229	40	105	6	24	4	0	1	5	0 - 1	0	7	16	1 - 1
ROBERTSON	.103	15	29	1	3	0	0	1	1	0 - 0	0	3	9	0 - 0
ROOF	.000	3	5	0	0	0	0	0	0	0 - 0	0	0	1	0 - 0
SAMUEL	.252	157	333	61	84	15	7	12	43	2 - 1	6	32	106	27 - 12
SANDERS	.286	3	7	1	2	1	0	0	2	0 - 0	0	0	2	0 - 0
SANTIAGO	.249	112	370	34	92	15	0	13	46	1 - 5	2	18	86	1 - 0
SCHOFIELD	.239	131	435	49	104	15	3	4	37	10 - 2	4	50	87	10 - 7
SCOTT	.240	79	233	26	56	9	0	2	15	6 - 0	0	8	39	10 - 8
SEGUI	.316	31	95	14	30	5	0	5	13	0 - 1	0	8	17	0 - 0
SHARPERSON	.208	32	96	4	20	4	1	0	9	1 - 0	1	7	15	2 - 1
SHEPHERD	.167	115	108	23	18	6	0	2	5	1 - 0	0	5	37	3 - 1
SIERRA	.208	14	48	4	10	0	2	1	5	0 - 1	0	3	13	0 - 0
SNYDER	.143	21	49	4	7	0	1	0	6	1 - 1	0	3	19	0 - 0
SOJO	.205	52	127	19	26	5	0	1	15	2 - 1	0	4	2	0 - 0
SOLAITA	.265	36	102	14	27	8	1	2	13	0 - 2	0	17	16	0 - 0
SPOLJARIC	.000	104	1	0	0	0	0	0	0	0 - 0	0	0	0	0 - 0
SPRAGUE	.245	888	3156	388	773	170	10	113	418	5 - 28	68	270	647	2 - 13
STAGGS	.258	72	291	37	75	11	6	2	28	3 - 1	0	36	38	5 - 9
STANLEY	.240	98	341	49	82	13	0	22	47	0 - 3	5	56	86	2 - 1
STARK	.083	5	12	1	0	0	0	0	0	0 - 0	0	0	0	0 - 0
STEWART	.297	488	1930	328	574	114	17	44	216	10 - 11	34	188	272	121 - 40
STIEB	.000	439	2	2	0	0	0	0	0	0 - 0	0	0	0	0 - 0
TABLER	.231	131	320	31	74	10	1	1	37	2 - 6	1	41	35	0 - 0
THOMPSON	.167	2	6	2	1	0	0	0	1	0 - 0	1	3	2	0 - 0
THORNTON	.237	79	76	24	18	1	1	1	8	0 - 0	1	3	24	1 - 1
TORRES	.241	91	266	33	64	7	3	5	26	5 - 4	1	16	33	1 - 1
UPSHAW	.265	1115	3710	538	982	177	42	112	478	27 - 24	21	390	576	76 - 50
VELEZ	.257	522	1531	204	394	76	10	72	243	9 - 14	11	278	333	6 - 9
VIRGIL	.125	12	16	2	2	1	0	1	2	0 - 0	0	4	6	0 - 0
WARD	.220	98	209	28	46	7	2	5	33	3 - 4	1	28	32	3 - 4
WEBSTER	.206	41	34	11	7	2	1	0	4	0 - 0	0	2	8	0 - 1
WELLS, D	.083	306	12	0	1	0	0	0	0	1 - 0	0	0	2	0 - 0
WELLS, G	.247	32	73	7	18	5	0	0	5	0 - 0	0	5	12	0 - 2
WELLS, V	.261	27	90	8	23	5	0	1	8	0 - 0	0	4	18	1 - 1
WHITE	.270	656	2711	452	733	155	34	72	274	13 - 17	29	209	572	126 - 23
WHITEN	.241	79	237	24	57	5	4	4	26	0 - 4	1	18	49	2 - 1
WHITMER	.111	7	9	0	1	1	0	0	0	0 - 0	0	1	2	0 - 0
WHITT	.253	1218	3514	424	888	164	15	131	518	20 - 36	4	403	450	22 - 24
WILBORN	.000	22	12	3	0	0	0	0	0	1 - 0	0	2	7	0 - 1
WILLIAMS, K	.198	62	101	18	20	8	1	1	11	0 - 2	2	11	23	8 - 2
WILLIAMS, W	.375	166	8	0	3	0	0	0	0	0 - 0	0	0	2	0 - 0
WILSON	.267	287	1067	139	285	57	9	7	96	11 - 7	7	42	174	46 - 8
WINFIELD	.290	156	583	92	169	33	3	26	108	1 - 3	1	82	89	2 - 3
WISE	.136	28	22	3	3	0	0	0	0	0 - 0	1	1	5	1 - 1
WITT	.195	20	41	3	8	1	0	1	5	1 - 0	0	2	12	0 - 0
WOODS, A	.270	595	1958	228	529	97	14	33	188	31 - 15	3	164	176	23 - 24
WOODS, G	.211	68	246	22	52	10	1	0	17	3 - 0	2	8	39	6 - 4
WOODWARD	.192	51	130	17	25	8	0	3	16	1 - 1	0	12	34	1 - 0
ZOSKY	.176	26	34	3	6	1	2	0	3	1 - 1	0	0	10	0 - 0

BLUE JAYS CAREER GAMES BY POSITION

FIRST BASEMEN

Willie Upshaw	950
John Olerud	766
Carlos Delgado	600
John Mayberry	494
Fred McGriff	474
Doug Ault	179
Joe Carter	94
Cecil Fielder	65

SECOND BASEMEN

Damaso Garcia	869
Roberto Alomar	694
Manny Lee	344
Garth Iorg	338
Nelson Liriano	288
Dave McKay	226

THIRD BASEMEN

Kelly Gruber	829
Ed Sprague	814
Rance Mulliniks	725
Garth Iorg	556
Roy Howell	490

SHORTSTOP

Tony Fernandez	1104
Alfredo Griffin	907
Alex Gonzalez	720
Manuel Lee	365
Luis Gomez	168
Dick Schofield	131
Tony Batista	98
Tomas Perez	72
Bob Bailor	69
Hector Torres	68

OUTFIELDERS

Lloyd Moseby	1349
George Bell	1066
Jesse Barfield	996
Joe Carter	835
Shawn Green	652
Devon White	650
Al Woods	531
Barry Bonnell	530
Shannon Stewart	481
Jose Cruz	428
Bob Bailor	404

CATCHERS

Ernie Whitt	1159
Pat Borders	691
Buck Martinez	441
Darrin Fletcher	351
Rick Cerone	251
Greg Myers	209
Alan Ashby	205

PITCHERS

Duane Ward	452
Tom Henke	446
Dave Stieb	439
Jim Clancy	352
Paul Quantrill	320
Jimmy Key	317
David Wells	306
Mike Timlin	305
Jim Acker	281
Mark Eichhorn	279
Pat Hentgen	252
Tony Castillo	218
Todd Stottlemyre	206
Jerry Garvin	196
Juan Guzman	195
Joey McLaughlin	195
John Cerutti	191
Roy Lee Jackson	190

In the Blue Jays first twenty-four seasons, the following number of players have been utilized at each position:

Catcher	42	**Third Basemen**	60	**Pitchers**	166
First Basemen	55	**Shortstop**	31		
Second Basemen	42	**Outfielders**	98		

MULTIPLE STINTS WITH THE BLUE JAYS

PITCHERS

	1ST STINT			2ND STINT	
YEARS	**W-L-S**	**ERA**	**YEARS**	**W-L-S**	**ERA**
Jim Acker (RHP)					
1983	5-1-1	4.33	1989	2-1-0	1.59
1984	3-5-1	4.38	1990	4-4-1	3.83
1985	7-2-10	3.23	1991	3-5-1	5.20
1986 (split)	2-4-0	4.35	**TOTALS**	**9-10-2**	**4.10**
TOTALS	**17-12-12**	**4.04**			
Tony Castillo (LHP)					
1988	1-0-0	3.00	1993	3-2-0	3.38
1989	1-1-1	6.11	1994	5-2-1	2.51
TOTALS	**2-1-1**	**4.68**	1995	1-5-13	3.22
			1996	2-3-1	4.23
			TOTALS	**11-12-15**	**3.35**
David Cone (RHP)					
1992 (split)	4-3-0	2.55	1995 (split)	9-6-0	3.38
TOTALS	**4-3-0**	**2.55**			
Mark Eichhorn (RHP)					
1982	0-3-0	5.45	1992 (split)	2-0-0	4.35
1986	14-6-10	1.72	1993	3-1-0	2.72
1987	10-6-4	3.17	**TOTALS**	**5-1-0**	**3.21**
1988	0-3-1	4.18			
TOTALS	**24-18-15**	**2.98**			
Paul Spoljaric (RHP)					
1994	0-1-0	38.57	1999	2-2-0	4.65
1996	2-2-1	3.08			
1997	0-3-3	3.69			
TOTALS	**2-6-4**	**4.08**			
Dave Stieb (RHP)					
1979	8-8-0	4.31	1998	1-2-2	4.83
1980	12-15-0	3.71			
1981	11-10-0	3.19			
1982	17-14-0	3.25			
1983	17-12-0	3.04			
1984	16-8-0	2.83			
1985	14-13-0	2.48			
1986	7-12-1	4.74			
1987	13-9-0	4.09			
1988	16-8-0	3.04			
1989	17-8-0	3.35			
1990	18-6-0	2.93			
1991	4-3-0	3.17			
1992	4-6-0	5.04			
TOTALS	**174-132-1**	**3.39**			

	1ST STINT			2ND STINT		
YEARS		W-L-S	ERA	YEARS	W-L-S	ERA

David Wells (LHP)

YEARS	W-L-S	ERA	YEARS	W-L-S	ERA
1987	4-3-1	3.99	1999	17-10-0	4.82
1988	3-5-4	4.62	2000	20-8-0	4.11
1989	7-4-2	2.40	**TOTALS**	**37-18-0**	**4.47**
1990	11-6-3	3.14			
1991	15-10-1	3.72			
1992	7-9-2	5.40			
TOTALS	**47-37-13**	**3.78**			

PLAYERS

YEARS	G	AVG	HR	RBI	YEARS	G	AVG	HR	RBI

Pat Borders (C)

YEARS	G	AVG	HR	RBI	YEARS	G	AVG	HR	RBI
1988	56	.273	5	21	1999	6	.214	1	3
1989	94	.257	3	29					
1990	125	.286	15	49					
1991	105	.244	5	36					
1992	138	.242	13	53					
1993	138	.254	9	55					
1994	85	.247	3	26					
TOTALS	**741**	**.255**	**53**	**269**					

Jacob Brumfield (OF)

YEARS	G	AVG	HR	RBI	YEARS	G	AVG	HR	RBI
1996	90	.256	12	52	1999	62	.235	2	19
1997	58	.207	2	20					
TOTALS	**148**	**.239**	**14**	**72**					

Rob Butler (OF)

YEARS	G	AVG	HR	RBI	YEARS	G	AVG	HR	RBI
1993	17	.271	0	2	1999	8	.143	0	1
1994	41	.176	0	5					
TOTALS	**58**	**.213**	**0**	**7**					

Rico Carty (DH)

YEARS	G	AVG	HR	RBI	YEARS	G	AVG	HR	RBI
1978	104	.284	20	68	1979	132	.256	12	55
TOTALS	**104**	**.284**	**20**	**68**					

Rob Ducey (OF)

YEARS	G	AVG	HR	RBI	YEARS	G	AVG	HR	RBI
1987	34	.188	1	6	2000 (split)	5	.154	0	1
1988	27	.315	0	6					
1989	41	.211	0	7					
1990	19	.302	0	7					
1991	39	.235	1	4					
1992	23	.048	0	0					
TOTALS	**183**	**.234**	**2**	**30**					

Tony Fernandez (IF)

YEARS	G	AVG	HR	RBI	YEARS	G	AVG	HR	RBI
1983	15	.265	0	2	1993 (split)	94	.306	4	50
1984	88	.270	3	19					
1985	161	.289	2	51		**3RD STINT**			
1986	163	.310	10	65	1998	138	.321	9	72
1987	146	.322	5	67	1999	142	.328	6	75
1988	154	.287	5	70	**TOTALS**	**280**	**.324**	**15**	**147**
1989	140	.257	11	64					
1990	161	.276	4	66					
TOTALS	**1028**	**.289**	**40**	**404**					

Tony Fernandez is the only player in franchise history to play three different times.

Alfredo Griffin (IF)

YEARS	G	AVG	HR	RBI	YEARS	G	AVG	HR	RBI
1979	153	.287	2	31	1992	63	.233	0	10
1980	155	.254	2	41	1993	46	.211	0	3
1981	101	.209	0	21	**TOTALS**	**109**	**.224**	**0**	**13**
1982	162	.241	1	48					
1983	162	.250	4	47					
1984	140	.241	4	30					
TOTALS	**873**	**.250**	**13**	**218**					

Cliff Johnson (DH)

YEARS	G	AVG	HR	RBI	YEARS	G	AVG	HR	RBI
1983	142	.265	22	76	1985 (split)	24	.274	1	10
1984	127	.304	16	61	1986	107	.250	15	55
TOTALS	**269**	**.283**	**38**	**137**	**TOTALS**	**131**	**.254**	**16**	**65**

Candy Maldonado (OF)

YEARS	G	AVG	HR	RBI	YEARS	G	AVG	HR	RBI
1991 (split)	52	.277	7	28	1995	61	.269	7	25
1992	137	.272	20	66	**TOTALS**	**61**	**.269**	**7**	**25**
TOTALS	**189**	**.273**	**27**	**94**					

Luis Sojo (IF)

YEARS	G	AVG	HR	RBI	YEARS	G	AVG	HR	RBI
1990	33	.225	1	9	1993	19	.170	0	6
TOTALS	**33**	**.225**	**1**	**9**	**TOTALS**	**19**	**.170**	**0**	**6**

BLUE JAYS TRADES

DATE	CLUB	OBTAINED	FOR
11-5-76	Cleveland	Alan Ashby, c	Al Fitzmorris, rhp
		Doug Howard, 1b-of	
12-6-76	Cleveland	Rick Cerone, c	Rico Carty, 1b-of
		John Lowenstein, of	
2-17-77	San Diego	Jerry Johnson, rhp	Dave Roberts, c-if
2-24-77	Oakland	Ron Fairly, 1b-of	Mike Weathers, if
3-29-77	Cleveland	Hector Torres, if	John Lowenstein, of
5-9-77	Texas	Roy Howell, if	Steve Hargan, rhp
			Jim Mason, if
12-6-77	St. Louis	Tom Underwood, lhp	Peter Vuckovich, rhp
		Victor Cruz, rhp	John Scott, of
12-8-77	California	Pat Kelly, c	Ron Fairly, 1b-of
		Butch Alberts, 1b-of	
3-3-78	St. Louis	Rick Bosetti, of	Tom Bruno, rhp
3-3-78	Cleveland	Rico Carty, dh	Dennis DeBarr, lhp
4-28-78	Milwaukee	Tim Johnson, if	Tim Nordbrook, inf
8-15-78	Oakland	Willie Horton, dh	Rico Carty, dh
		Phil Huffman, rhp	
9-12-78	San Diego	Mark Wiley, rhp	Andrew Dyes, of
11-27-78	Houston	Mark Lemongello, rhp	Alan Ashby, c
		Joe Cannon, of	
		Pedro Hernandez, if	
12-5-78	Houston	Don Pisker, of	Gary Woods, of
12-6-78	Cleveland	Alfredo Griffin, if	Victor Cruz, rhp
		Phil Lansford, 3b	
11-1-79	New York (AL)	Chris Chambliss, 1b	Tom Underwood, lhp
		Paul Mirabella, lhp	Rick Cerone, c
		Damaso Garcia, if	Ted Wilborn, of
12-5-79	Atlanta	Barry Bonnell, of	Chris Chambliss, 1b
		Joey McLaughlin, rhp	Luis Gomez, ss
		Pat Rockett, inf	
12-12-80	New York (NL)	Roy Lee Jackson, rhp	Bob Bailor, if-of
4-6-81	New York (NL)	Mark Bomback, rhp	Charlie Puleo, rhp
5-11-81	Milwaukee	Buck Martinez, c	Gil Kubski, of
6-10-81	Oakland	Future considerations	Rick Bosetti, of
11-18-81	New York (AL)	Aurelio Rodriguez, if	Mike Lebo, c
12-28-81	Minnesota	Hosken Powell, of	Greg Wells, 1b
12-28-81	Chicago (NL)	Dave Geisel, lhp	Paul Mirabella, lhp
3-25-82	Kansas City	Rance Mulliniks, if	Phil Huffman, rhp
4-2-82	Chicago (AL)	Wayne Nordhagen, of-dh	Aurelio Rodriguez, 3b
5-5-82	New York (AL)	Dave Revering, 1b-dh	John Mayberry, 1b
		Jeff Reynolds, 3b	
6-15-82	Philadelphia	Dick Davis, of	Wayne Nordhagen, of
			(to Pittsburgh)
10-27-82	New York (AL)	Tucker Ashford, 3b	'conditional'
11-5-82	Oakland	Cliff Johnson, dh	Al Woods, of
12-9-82	New York (AL)	Dave Collins, of	Dale Murray, rhp
		Mike Morgan, rhp	Tom Dodd, of-c
		Fred McGriff, 1b	
2-4-83	Kansas City	Cecil Fielder, 1b	Leon Roberts, of
2-4-83	New York (NL)	Jorge Orta, dh-of	Steve Senteney, rhp
12-9-83	Seattle	Bryan Clark, lhp	Barry Bonnell, of
12-19-83	Kansas City	Willie Aikens, if-dh	Jorge Orta, dh-of
12-8-84	Oakland	Bill Caudill, rhp	Dave Collins, of
			Alfredo Griffin, ss
1-26-85	San Francisco	Gary Lavelle, lhp	Jim Gott, rhp
			Jack McKnight, rhp
			Augie Schmidt, if
4-1-85	Philadelphia	Len Matuszek, 1b-dh	Dave Shipanoff, rhp
			Jose Escobar, if
			Ken Kinnard, of
7-9-85	Los Angeles	Al Oliver, dh	Len Matuszek, 1b-dh
8-29-85	Texas	Cliff Johnson, dh	Matt Williams, rhp
			Greg Ferlenda, rhp
			Jeff Mays, rhp
7-5-86	Atlanta	Duane Ward, rhp	Doyle Alexander, rhp
7-6-86	Atlanta	Joe Johnson, rhp	Jim Acker, rhp
2-2-87	Atlanta	Craig McMurtry, rhp	Damaso Garcia, if
			Luis Leal, rhp
7-14-87	Kansas City	Juan Beniquez, of-dh	Luis Aquino, rhp
8-31-87	Baltimore	Mike Flanagan, lhp	Oswald Peraza, rhp
			Jose Mesa, rhp
4-30-89	New York (AL)	Al Leiter, lhp	Jesse Barfield, of
7-31-89	New York (NL)	Mookie Wilson, of	Jeff Musselman, lhp
			Mike Brady, rhp

DATE	CLUB	OBTAINED	FOR
8-24-89	Atlanta	Jim Acker, rhp	Tony Castillo, lhp
			Francisco Cabrera, c
12-17-89	Atlanta	Ricky Trlicek, rhp	Ernie Whitt, c
			Kevin Batiste, of
7-27-90	Minnesota	John Candelaria, lhp	Nelson Liriano, if
			Pedro Munoz, of
9-17-90	Cleveland	Bud Black, lhp	Mauro Gozzo, rhp
			Alex Sanchez, rhp
			Steve Cummings, rhp
11-6-90	Atlanta	Nate Cromwell, lhp	Earl Sanders, rhp
11-6-90	California	Devon White, of	Junior Felix, of
		Willie Fraser, rhp	Luis Sojo, if
		Marcus Moore, rhp	Ken Rivers, c
12-5-90	San Diego	Joe Carter, of	Tony Fernandez, ss
		Roberto Alomar, if	Fred McGriff, 1b
1-15-91	Baltimore	Rene Gonzales, if	Rob Blumberg, lhp
6-27-91	Cleveland	Tom Candiotti, rhp	Glenallen Hill, of
		Turner Ward, of	Mark Whiten, of
			Denis Boucher, lhp
7-14-91	Chicago (AL)	Cory Snyder, of	Shawn Jeter, of
			Steve Wapnick, rhp
8-9-91	Milwaukee	Candy Maldonado, of	Rob Wishnevski, rhp
			William Suero, 2b
7-30-92	California	Mark Eichhorn, rhp	Rob Ducey, of
			Greg Myers, C
8-28-92	New York (NL)	David Cone, rhp	Jeff Kent, if
			Ryan Thompson, of
12-8-92	California	Luis Sojo, if	Kelly Gruber, 3b
3-30-93	San Diego	Darrin Jackson, of	Derek Bell, of
			Stoney Briggs, of
6-11-93	New York (NL)	Tony Fernandez, ss	Darrin Jackson, of
7-31-93	Oakland	Rickey Henderson, of	Steve Karsay, rhp
			Jose Herrera, of
3-29-94	Chicago (AL)	Mike Huff, of	Domingo Martinez, if
11-18-94	Florida	Scott Pace, lhp	Eddie Zosky, if
12-5-94	Philadelphia	Monetary compensation	Rob Butler, of
4-6-95	Kansas City	David Cone, rhp	David Sinnes, rhp
			Anthony Medrano, if
			Chris Stynes, if
7-28-95	New York (AL)	Marty Janzen, rhp	David Cone, rhp
		Jason Jarvis, rhp	
		Mike Gordon, rhp	
8-31-95	Texas	Player to be named later	Candy Maldonado, of
12-7-95	Philadelphia	Paul Quantrill, rhp	Howard Battle, if
			Ricardo Jordan, lhp
12-18-95	Seattle	Bill Risley, rhp	Paul Menhart, rhp
		Miguel Cairo, if	Edwin Hurtado, rhp
5-15-96	Pittsburgh	Jacob Brumfield, of	D.J.Boston, 1b
8-22-96	Chicago (AL)	Luis Andujar, rhp	Domingo Cedeno, if
		Allen Halley, rhp	Tony Castillo, lhp
11-14-96	Pittsburgh	Carlos Garcia, if	Jose Silva, rhp
		Orlando Merced, of	Jose Pett, rhp
		Dan Plesac, lhp	Mike Halperin, lhp
			Abraham Nunez, if
			Craig Wilson, c
			Brandon Cromer, if
11-20-96	Texas	Player to be named later	Lonell Roberts, of
11-20-96	Chicago (NL)	Jason Stevenson, rhp	Miguel Cairo, if
12-11-96	Detroit	Anton French, of	Roberto Duran, lhp
12-20-96	New York (NL)	Robert Person, rhp	John Olerud, 1b
3-17-97	Texas	Lonell Roberts, of	Player to be named from 11-20-96 trade
7-31-97	Seattle	Jose Cruz Jr., of	Mike Timlin, rhp
			Paul Spoljaric, lhp
8-12-97	Los Angeles	Bobby Cripps, c	Otis Nixon, of
3-14-98	Texas	Kevin Brown, c	Tim Crabtree, rhp
7-30-98	Boston	Peter Munro, rhp	Mike Stanley, dh
		Jay Yanneco, rhp	
7-31-98	Baltimore	Nerio Rodriguez, rhp	Juan Guzman, rhp
		Shannon Carter, of	
7-31-98	New York (NL)	Leoncio Estrella, rhp	Tony Phillips, of
8-6-98	San Diego	Brian Loyd, c	Randy Myers, lhp
12-13-98	San Diego	Joey Hamilton, rhp	Woody Williams, rhp
			Carlos Almanzar, rhp
			Peter Tucci, of
12-14-98	Detroit	Eric Ludwick, rhp	Beiker Graterol, rhp
02-20-99	New York (AL)	Homer Bush, if	Roger Clemens, rhp
		Graeme Lloyd, lhp	
		David Wells, lhp	

DATE	CLUB	OBTAINED	FOR
03-30-99	Anaheim	Dave Hollins, if	Tomas Perez, if
05-05-99	Philadelphia	Paul Spoljaric, lhp	Robert Person, rhp
06-12-99	Arizona	Tony Batista, if	Dan Plesac, lhp
		John Frascatore, rhp	
07-28-99	Seattle	David Segui, if	Tom Davey, rhp
			Steve Sinclair, lhp
08-09-99	Colorado	Brian McRae, of	Player to be named later
			(Pat Lynch, rhp, 08-25-99)
09-03-99	Cincinnati	Player to be named later	Juan Melo, if
		(Jamie Goudie, if, 09-13-99)	
11-08-99	Los Angeles	Pedro Borbon, lhp	Shawn Green, of
		Raul Mondesi, of	Jorge Nunez, if
11-11-99	St. Louis	Carlos Castillo, c	Pat Hentgen, rhp
		Matt Dewitt, rhp	Paul Spoljaric, lhp
		Lance Painter, lhp	
03-16-00	Montreal/Texas	Brad Fullmer, if	David Segui, if (Texas)
			Lee Stevens, if (Montreal)
03-22-00	New York (NL)	Jersen Perez, if	Jim Mann, rhp
07-19-00	Texas	Esteban Loaiza, rhp	Mike Young, if
			Darwin Cubillan, rhp
07-26-00	Philadelphia	Rob Ducey, of	Player to be named later
			(John Sneed, rhp, 07-31-00)
07-31-00	Tampa Bay	Steve Trachsel, rhp	Brent Abernathy, if
		Mark Guthrie, lhp	
08-04-00	Texas	Dave Martinez, of	Player to be named later
			(Pete Munro, rhp, 08-08-00)
08-06-00	Philadelphia	Mickey Morandini, if	Player to be named later
			(Rob Ducey, of, 08-07-00)
11-07-00	Chicago (AL)	Scott Eyre, lhp	Gary Glover, rhp
11-22-00	Cincinnati	Steve Parris, rhp	Clayton Andrew, lhp
			Leo Estrella, rhp
12-11-00	Baltimore	Jayson Werth, c	John Bale, lhp
12-11-00	Chicago (NL)	Cole Liniak, if	Player to be named later
01-14-01	Chicago (AL)	Mike Sirotka, lhp	David Wells, lhp
		Kevin Beirne, rhp	Matt DeWitt, rhp
		Mike Williams, rhp	
		Brian Simmons, of	
01-16-01	Florida	Player to be named later	Chad Mottola, of

FREE AGENCY

Free agency came about in 1976 when 244 players refused to sign contracts and opted for, at season's end, the right to participate in a re-entry draft.

That draft took place in New York on November 4. Clubs were permitted to select players with whom they could negotiate. There was no compensationn for clubs who lost players in this draft.

In later years, the draft was abolished and compensation was required.

Other than signing their own players who had opted for free agency and free agent players signed after being released, the Blue Jays' involvement in the free agent market has been:

Signed for:

1978	Luis Gomez	from ATLANTA BRAVES
1984	Dennis Lamp	from CHICAGO WHITE SOX
1991	Ken Dayley	from ST. LOUIS CARDINALS
1991	Pat Tabler	from NEW YORK METS
1992	Jack Morris	from MINNESOTA TWINS
	Dave Winfield	from CALIFORNIA ANGELS
1993	Dick Schofield	from CALIFORNIA ANGELS
	Dave Stewart	from OAKLAND ATHLETICS
	Paul Molitor	from MILWAUKEE BREWERS
	Darnell Coles	from CINCINNATI REDS
1994	Greg Cadaret	from KANSAS CITY ROYALS
1996	Erik Hanson	from BOSTON RED SOX
	Otis Nixon	from TEXAS RANGERS
	Charlie O'Brien	from ATLANTA BRAVES
	Ruben Amaro	from CLEVELAND INDIANS
	Brian Bohanon	from DETROIT TIGERS
	Rich Rowland	from BOSTON RED SOX
	Juan Samuel	from KANSAS CITY ROYALS
1997	Benito Santiago	from PHILADELPHIA PHILLIES
	Roger Clemens	from BOSTON RED SOX
	Darrell Whitmore	from CHIBA LOTTE MARINES
	Mike Aldrete	from NEW YORK YANKEES
	Marvin Freeman	from CHICAGO WHITE SOX
1998	Darrin Fletcher	from MONTREAL EXPOS
	Randy Myers	from BALTIMORE ORIOLES
	Pat Kelly	from NEW YORK YANKEES
	Craig Grebeck	from ANAHEIM ANGELS
	Mike Stanley	from NEW YORK YANKEES
	Tony Fernandez	from CLEVELAND INDIANS
	Phil Plantier	from ST. LOUIS CARDINALS
	Jose Canseco	from OAKLAND ATHLETICS
1999	Joey Cora	from CLEVELAND INDIANS
	Mike Matheny	from MILWAUKEE BREWERS
	Willie Greene	from BALTIMORE ORIOLES
	Cecil Fielder	from CLEVELAND INDIANS
2000	Frank Castillo	from PITTSBURGH PIRATES
	Chad Mottola	from CHICAGO WHITE SOX
	Andy Stewart	from PHILADELPHIA PHILLIES
2001	Jason Dickson	from ANAHEIM ANGELS
	Jeff Frye	from COLORADO ROCKIES
	Trenidad Hubbard	from BALTIMORE ORIOLES
	Dan Plesac	from ARIZONA DIAMONDBACKS
	Ryan Thompson	from NEW YORK YANKEES

Major League Rule 5 Draft, 1977-2000

Toronto has selected 22 players in the Major League Baseball Draft, since their inaugural season in 1977. Players with at least three years of professional service who are not protected on a team's major league roster are eligible for selection by another club for $50,000 (prior to 1985 the draft price was $25,000). The drafted player must remain with his new club for the full season or be offered back to his original club for $25,000. The drafting is in reverse order of previous season records and alternating between leagues. Following this major league draft, a separate selection is held by National Association clubs from class AAA to A levels. An "AAA" selection price is $12,000. An "AA" selection is $4,000.

Toronto selections:

Year	Player	Original Club	Status with Toronto
1977	Willie Upshaw (1B)	AAA-Syracuse, (NYY)	Played nine seasons in Toronto
	Andy Dyes (OF)	AAA-Denver, (MTL)	Spent one season in Toronto organization
1978	Ted Wilborn (OF)	AAA-Tacoma, (NYY)	Spent one season in Toronto organization
	Bob Davis (C)	AAA-Hawaii, (SD)	Played two seasons in Toronto
1979	Mike Macha (IF)	AAA-Richmond, (ATL)	Played one season in Toronto
1980	George Bell (OF)	AAA-Okl.City, (PHI)	Played nine seasons in Toronto
	Dan Whitmer (C)	AAA-Salt Lake, (CAL)	Played one season in Toronto
1981	Jim Gott (RHP)	AAA-Springfield, (STL)	Played three seasons in Toronto
	Anthony Johnson (OF)	AAA-Denver, (MTL)	Played one season in Toronto
1982	Jim Acker (RHP)	AAA-Richmond, (ATL)	In 2 stints,played 7 seasons for Toronto
	Mercedes Esquer (LHP)	AAA-Portland, (PIT)	Remained in the Toronto organization
1983	Kelly Gruber (IF)	AAA-Charleston, (CLE)	Played nine seasons in Toronto
	Terry Cormack (C)	AAA-Richmond, (ATL)	Returned to Atlanta March 25, 1984
1984	Manuel Lee (IF)	AAA-Tuscon, (HOU)	Played eight seasons in Toronto
	Louis Thornton (OF)	AAA-Tidewater, (NYM)	Played three seasons in Toronto
1985	Jose DeJesus (RHP)	AAA-Omaha, (KC)	Returned to Kansas City April 3, 1986
1986	Jose Nunez (RHP)	AAA-Omaha, (KC)	Played three seasons in Toronto
1990	Ricky Rhodes (RHP)	AAA-Columbus, (NYY)	Returned to New York March 29, 1991
1992	Billy Taylor (RHP)	AAA-Richmond, (ATL)	Returned to Atlanta April 1, 1993
1995	Carey Paige (RHP)	AA-Greenville, (ATL)	Remained in Toronto organization for two seasons
1997	Luis Saturria (OF)	A-Peoria, (STL)	Returned to St. Louis March 20, 1998
1999	Dewayne Wise (OF)	A-Rockford, (CIN)	Currently on Blue Jays 40-man roster

Selected from Toronto:

Year	Player	Team	Status after draft
1981	Ramon Lora (C)	by Los Angeles	Returned to Toronto March 31, 1982
	Domingo Ramos (IF)	by Seattle	Played five seasons with Seattle
1983	Dave Geisel (LHP)	by Seattle	Played two seasons with Seattle
1984	Mike Morgan (RHP)	by Seattle	Played two seasons with Seattle
1986	Cliff Young (LHP)	by Oakland	Returned to Toronto April 6, 1987
	Stan Clarke (LHP)	by Seattle	Played one season with Seattle
1987	Joe Johnson (RHP)	by California	Played in California farm system
	Santiago Garcia (IF)	by Chicago (AL)	Played in Chicago farm system
1988	Colin McLaughlin (RHP)	by Seattle	Played in Seattle farm system
	Chris Jones (RHP)	by Los Angeles	Returned to Toronto March 31, 1989
	Geronimo Berroa (OF)	by Atlanta	Played two seasons with Atlanta
	Matt Stark (C)	by Atlanta	Returned to Toronto March 27, 1989
	Eric Yelding (IF)	by Chicago (NL)	Claimed on waivers by Houston April 3,1989
1989	Steve Wapnick (RHP)	by Detroit	Returned to Toronto May 1, 1990
	Sil Campusano (OF)	by Philadelphia	Played one season with Philadelphia
	Xavier Hernandez (RHP)	by Houston	Played four seasons with Houston
1991	Jesse Cross (RHP)	by Minnesota	Returned to Toronto April 3, 1992
1992	Graeme Lloyd (LHP)	by Philadelphia	Acquired by Milwaukee for P John Trisler
1993	Tim Hyers (1B)	by San Diego	Played two seasons with San Diego
1994	Todd Steverson (OF)	by Detroit	Played with Detroit in 1995
	Freddy Garcia (3B)	by Pittsburgh	Played with Pittsburgh in 1995
1996	Mike Johnson (RHP)	by San Francisco	Traded to Baltimore
	Tom Davey (RHP)	by Baltimore	Returned to Toronto
1999	Brian Smith (RHP)	by Pittsburgh	Non-tendered, signed by Pittsburgh
	Jim Mann (RHP)	by New York (NL)	Spent one season in New York organization
2000	Jay Gibbons (1B)	by Baltimore	
	Rendy Espina (LHP)	by Anaheim	

THE ORIGINAL BLUE JAYS

American League Expansion Draft Selections

November 5, 1976

1. Bob Bailor, if-of, Baltimore
2. Jerry Garvin, lhp, Minnesota
3. Jim Clancy, rhp, Texas
4. Gary Woods, of, Oakland
5. Rico Carty, if-dh, Cleveland
6. Butch Edge, rhp, Milwaukee
7. Al Fitzmorris, rhp, Kansas City
8. Al Woods, of, Minnesota
9. Mike Darr, rhp, Baltimore
10. Pete Vuckovich, rhp, Chicago
11. Jeff Byrd, rhp, Texas
12. Steve Bowling, of, Milwaukee
13. Dennis DeBarr, lhp, Detroit
14. Bill Singer, rhp, Minnesota
15. Jim Mason, if, New York
16. Doug Ault, if, Texas
17. Ernie Whitt, c, Boston
18. Mike Weathers, if, Oakland
19. Steve Staggs, if, Kansas City
20. Steve Hargan, rhp, Texas
21. Garth Iorg, if, New York
22. Dave Lemanczyk, rhp, Detroit
23. Larry Anderson, rhp, Milwaukee
24. Jesse Jefferson, rhp, Chicago
25. Dave McKay, if, Minnesota
26. Tom Bruno, rhp, Kansas City
27. Otto Velez, of, New York
28. Mike Willis, lhp, Baltimore
29. Sam Ewing, of, Chicago
30. Leon Hooten, rhp, Oakland

BLUE JAYS LEVEL OF EXCELLENCE

The "Level of Excellence" is the highest award bestowed by the Toronto Blue Jays honouring tremendous achievements. The inaugural members of the Level of Excellence were **OF George Bell** and **RHP Dave Stieb** who were honoured in 1996 after their tremendous careers as the cornerstones of the franchise for many seasons. **OF JOE CARTER** and **Manager CITO GASTON** were recognized in 1999.

Outfielder **GEORGE BELL** spent nine seasons with Toronto and is the franchise leader in home runs (202), total bases (2201), runs batted in (740), extra base hits (471) and sacrifice hits (59). In 1987 he was named the American League MVP as he set franchise marks in home runs (47), extra base hits (83), total bases (369), RBI (134) and slugging percentage (.605). **BELL** made his first of two all star appearances in 1987 when he became the first Blue Jay ever voted to the starting line-up. During his nine seasons **BELL** was a four time club MVP, the Sporting News AL and major league player of the year in 1987, a three time Sporting News Silver Slugger, a two time Sporting News All Star team selection and the American League Player of the Week eight times. The 6'1" right hand batter also set a major league record hitting three home runs on opening day, April 4, 1988 at Kansas City.

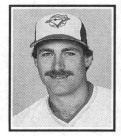

DAVE STIEB is the franchise leader in wins (175), innings pitched (2873.0), strikeouts (1658), starts (408), shutouts (30) and complete games (103). **STIEB** spent 15 seasons with Toronto, longer than any player in franchise history. **STIEB** appeared in an American League record seven All Star games and was the starting pitcher in both 1983 and 1984. **DAVE STIEB** also recorded the only no-hitter in Blue Jays history on September 2 1990 against the Indians in Cleveland. In 1982 he was named the Sporting News Pitcher of the Year after a 17-14 season with a 3.25 ERA and led the league in innings pitched (288) and complete games (20). **STIEB** was the Blue Jays pitcher of the year six times, a three time winner of the American League Pitcher of the Month and a three time winner of the American League Player of the Week.

Outfielder **JOE CARTER** is the franchise leader in home runs with 203 but will forever be remembered for just one, the ninth inning blast on October 23 to win the 1993 World Series. In 1,039 games from 1991 to 1997 with Toronto, **Carter** hit .257 with 578 runs scored, 218 doubles, 28 triples, 203 home runs with 736 RBI and 78 stolen bases. In his seven seasons he represented Toronto in five All-Star games including 1991 in Toronto, his first season with the Blue Jays after he was acquired from San Diego along with Roberto Alomar on December 5, 1990 in exchange for Tony Fernandez and Fred McGriff. Along with his tremendous on-field accomplishments Joe and his wife were active off the field as the Diana & Joe Carter Foundation operated the "Jumpin' with Joe" program which provided needy children throughout the Toronto area with at day a Teen-Ranch, Christian Youth Camp and tickets for a Toronto Blue Jay game where Joe would speak to all of the children. He worked with many other charities including Ronald McDonald House and also hosted an annual charity golf tournament. In his 16 year major league career Carter hit .259 with 432 doubles, 396 home runs and 1,445 RBI while playing for the Chicago Cubs (1983), the Cleveland Indians (1984-1989), the San Diego Padres (1990), the Toronto Blue Jays (1991-1997), the Baltimore Orioles (1998) and the San Francisco Giants (1998).

CITO GASTON led the Blue Jays to two World Championships, two American League Championships, four American League East titles and a franchise record 681 wins in his nine seasons as the Manager from 1989 to 1997. **Gaston** started as the Blue Jays hitting coach in 1981 where he groomed many young players including George Bell, Lloyd Moseby, Cecil Fielder, Jesse Barfield and Fred McGriff. In 1989 he served as the interim manager of the club before he was named the fifth manager in club history on May 31, 1989. He had the privilege of Managing in two All-Star games, 1993 and 1994. During his years as manager Cito gave much of his time to charity events throughout Toronto including the annual Cito Gaston Golf Classic.

ELEVEN STRAIGHT WINNING SEASONS

The Toronto Blue Jays had a string of eleven consecutive winning seasons from 1983-1993.

The current longest streak in the major leagues is held by the Atlanta Braves who have recorded 10 straight winning seasons from 1991 to 2000.

The New York Yankees' 39-year string (1926-1964) represents the Major League record.

The Baltimore Orioles have the second longest streak in baseball history with 18 consecutive winning seasons (1968-1985).

TORONTO CHAPTER BBWAA AWARD WINNERS

The NEIL MacCARL PLAYER OF THE YEAR AWARD is presented in honour of the long-time baseball writer for the Toronto Star.

YEAR	PLAYER OF THE YEAR	PITCHER OF THE YEAR	ROOKIE OF THE YEAR	GOOD GUY	MOST IMPROVED
1977	Bob Bailor	Dave Lemanczyk	Bob Bailor	Roy Hartsfield	—
1978	Bob Bailor	Jim Clancy	Victor Cruz	Mike Cannon	Alan Ashby
		Victor Cruz			
1979	Alfredo Griffin	Tom Underwood	Alfredo Griffin	John Silverman	Rick Cerone
1980	John Mayberry	Jim Clancy	Damaso Garcia	Howard Starkman	Al Woods
1981	Dave Stieb	Dave Stieb	—	Bob Mattick	Joey McLaughlin
1982	Damaso Garcia	Dave Stieb	Jesse Barfield	Buck Martinez	Jim Clancy
1983	Lloyd Moseby	Dave Stieb	Jim Acker	Ernie Whitt	Lloyd Moseby
1984	Dave Collins	Doyle Alexander	Tony Fernandez	Dave Collins	Dave Collins
1985	Jesse Barfield	Dennis Lamp		Rance Mulliniks	Dennis Lamp
1986	Jesse Barfield	Mark Eichhorn	Mark Eichhorn	Garth Iorg	Rick Leach
1987	George Bell	Jimmy Key	Jeff Musselman	Garth Iorg	Lloyd Moseby
1988	Fred McGriff	Dave Stieb	Pat Borders	John Cerutti	Kelly Gruber
1989	George Bell	Tom Henke	Junior Felix	Kelly Gruber	Todd Stottlemyre
1990	Kelly Gruber	Dave Steib	John Olerud	Jeff Ross	Pat Borders
				Tommy Craig	
1991	Roberto Alomar	Duane Ward	Juan Guzman	Joe Carter	Devon White
1992	Roberto Alomar	Jack Morris	Jeff Kent	John Brioux	Pat Borders
1993	Paul Molitor	Duane Ward	Randy Knorr	Bob Bailor	John Olerud
1994	Joe Carter	Pat Hentgen	Darren Hall	Rich Hacker	Randy Knorr
1995	Roberto Alomar	Al Leiter	Shawn Green	Galen Cisco	Ed Sprague
				Larry Hisle	
1996	Ed Sprague	Pat Hentgen	Paul Spoljaric	Howard Starkman	Juan Guzman
1997	Carlos Delgado	Roger Clemens	Jose Cruz	Brent Andrews	Paul Quantrill
1998	Carlos Delgado	Roger Clemens	Kevin Brown	Dan Plesac	Shawn Green
1999	Shawn Green	Billy Koch	Billy Koch	Pat Hentgen	Homer Bush
2000	Carlos Delgado	David Wells	—	Andy Stewart	Brad Fullmer

SCOUT OF THE YEAR AWARD

The Scout of the Year Award was first presented in 1985... The award and selection process was developed by three scouts; Tony Pacheo (Houston), Jim Russo (Baltimore) and Hugh Alexander (Philadelphia)... Each year, Scouting Directors from each Major League club submit the names of their scouting personnel who have accumulated 20 years of scouting experience in a full-time capacity... The Scouting Association conducts the voting... The awards are divided into three sections; one for each area of the United States (East, Mid-West, West)... The award recognizes the scout who has excelled in scouting, professionalism and performance on the job.

BLUE JAY SCOUT AWARD WINNERS

JOE FORD, a scouting supervisor who resides in Yukon, Oklahoma was chosen as Mid-West Scout of the Year in 1993... He is the first Blue Jays scout to garner the award.

JIM HUGHES, a scouting supervisor who resides in Prosper, Texas was chosen as Mid-West Scout of the Year in 1995. He has been scouting for Toronto since 1981.

BASEBALL WRITERS ASSOCIATION OF AMERICA AWARDS

Most Valuable Player (AL)	Rookie Of The Year (AL)	Cy Young Award (AL)	Manager Of The Year (AL)
1987 — George Bell	1979 — Alfredo Griffin	1996 — Pat Hentgen	1985 — Bobby Cox
		1997 — Roger Clemens	
		1998 — Roger Clemens	

ROLAIDS RELIEF MAN

The Rolaids Relief Man Award relies upon a unique scoring system:

- Four points for each "tough save"
- Three points for all other saves
- Two points for each win
- Two points deducted for each loss
- Two points deducted for each "blown save"

In the rare instance when a relief pitcher enters a game with a lead that is greater than what is allowed to qualify for a save — Scoring Rule 10.20 (3b) — and gives up the lead, he will be assessed a two — point penalty (as he would have had he blown a save opportunity. He will not be charged with a "blown save" since the opportunity for a save did not exist.

In case of ties (for monthly or annual awards), the relief pitcher with the better percentage of successful "save conversions" (saves divided by save opportunities) will be the winner. If a race is still tied, the pitcher with the lowest earned run average for relief appearances will be the winner.

"Tough Save"

The reliever comes into the game with the tying runs on base and saves the game. Example: Reliever comes in with a 5-3 lead, two outs and the bases loaded in the ninth inning.

"Blown Save"

When a relief pitcher enters a save situation and departs or the game ends with the save situation no longer in effect because he has given up the lead, he is charged with a "blown save". (If the save opportunity still exists when he leaves the game, he is not charged with a save opportunity. If the pitcher has not given up the lead when he leaves the game, though the save opportunity may no longer exist, he is not charged with a save opportunity.)

MLB-AL Hank Aaron Award

2000 — Carlos Delgado

The Sporting News Awards

PITCHER OF THE YEAR (AL)
1982 — Dave Stieb
1987 — Jimmy Key
1996 — Pat Hentgen
1997 — Roger Clemens
1998 — Roger Clemens

ROOKIE PITCHER OF THE YEAR (AL)
1986 — Mark Eichhorn
1991 — Juan Guzman

SILVER SLUGGER (AL)
1982 — Damaso Garcia, 2B
1983 — Lloyd Moseby, OF
1985 — George Bell, OF
1986 — George Bell, OF
1986 — Jesse Barfield, OF
1987 — George Bell, OF
1989 — Fred McGriff, 1B
1990 — Kelly Gruber, 3B
1991 — Joe Carter, OF
1992 — Roberto Alomar, 2B
1992 — Joe Carter, OF
1992 — Dave Winfield, DH
1993 — Paul Molitor, DH
1998 — Jose Canseco, DH
1999 — Shawn Green, OF
        Carlos Delgado, 1B
2000 — Carlos Delgado, 1B

MANAGER OF THE YEAR (ML)
1985 — Bobby Cox

MLB PLAYER OF THE YEAR
1987 — George Bell
2000 — Carlos Delgado

AL PLAYER OF THE YEAR
1987 — George Bell

SPORTSMEN OF THE YEAR
1993 — Pat Gillick/Cito Gaston

ALL-STAR TEAM (AL)
1982 — Damaso Garcia, 2B
1982 — Dave Stieb, P
1983 — Lloyd Moseby, OF
1985 — Damaso Garcia, 2B
1986 — Tony Fernandez, SS
1986 — George Bell, OF
1987 — George Bell, OF
1987 — Jimmy Key, LHP
1988 — Ernie Whitt, C
1989 — Fred McGriff, 1B
1990 — Kelly Gruber, 3B
1991 — Joe Carter, OF
1992 — Roberto Alomar, 2B
1992 — Joe Carter, OF
1992 — Dave Winfield, DH
1993 — Paul Molitor, DH
1996 — Pat Hentgen, RHP
1997 — Roger Clemens, RHP
1998 — Roger Clemens, RHP
1999 — Shawn Green, OF
2000 — Carlos Delgado, 1B
2000 — David Wells, LHP

Baseball Man of the Year in Canada

(Toronto—Montreal BBWAA)
Peter Bavasi, 1977
Pat Gillick, 1983
Jesse Barfield, 1986

Cito Gaston, 1989
Pat Gillick, 1991
Paul Beeston, 1993

American League All-Star Team (UPI)

1982 — Damaso Garcia, 2B
1983 — Lloyd Moseby, OF
1986 — Jesse Barfield, OF
1986 — Tony Fernandez, SS
1987 — George Bell, OF
1987 — Jimmy Key, LHP
1987 — Tom Henke, RP
1989 — Fred McGriff, 1B

1990 — Kelly Gruber, 3B
1991 — Joe Carter, OF
1992 — Roberto Alomar, 2B
1992 — Joe Carter, OF
1992 — Dave Winfield, DH
1993 — Roberto Alomar, 2B
1993 — Duane Ward, RHP
1996 — Pat Hentgen, RHP

Major League All-Star Team (AP)

1982 — Damaso Garcia, 2B
1986 — Tony Fernandez, SS
1986 — Jesse Barfield, RF
1987 — George Bell, OF
1987 — Jimmy Key, LHP

1992 — Roberto Alomar, 2B
1992 — Dave Winfield, DH
1993 — Roberto Alomar, 2B
1993 — Paul Molitor, DH
1998 — Roger Clemens, RHP

American League Executive of the Year (UPI)

1985 — Pat Gillick
1992 — Pat Gillick

1993 — Pat Gillick

American League Manager of the Year (UPI)

1985 — Bobby Cox

1993 — Cito Gaston

Leyland S. MacPhail Jr. Award (MVP of ALCS)

1992 — Roberto Alomar

1993 — Dave Stewart

World Series Most Valuable Player

1992—Pat Borders

1993—Paul Molitor

RAWLINGS GOLD GLOVE

Since 1957, the Rawlings Gold Glove Award has been presented annually to 18 of baseball's best fielders- one from each position in both the National and American Leagues. The winners are selected by Major League coaches and managers. Below are listed the Toronto Blue Jays players that have won Gold Gloves.

PLAYER	POSITION	YEAR	PLAYER	POSITION	YEAR
Tony Fernandez	SS	1986	Devon White	OF	1992
Jesse Barfield	OF	1986	Roberto Alomar	2B	1992
Tony Fernandez	SS	1987	Devon White	OF	1993
Jesse Barfield	OF	1987	Roberto Alomar	2B	1993
Tony Fernandez	SS	1988	Devon White	OF	1994
Tony Fernandez	SS	1989	Roberto Alomar	2B	1994
Kelly Gruber	3B	1990	Roberto Alomar	2B	1995
Devon White	OF	1991	Devon White	OF	1995
Roberto Alomar	2B	1991	Shawn Green	OF	1999

TORONTO BLUE JAYS ALL-STAR GAME SELECTIONS

ALL-STAR PLAYERS

YEAR	PLAYER	PERFORMANCE	VOTES	YEAR	PLAYER	PERFORMANCE	VOTES
1977	Ron Fairly OF	0-1		1992	**Roberto Alomar 2B**	1-3, 1R, 2 SB	1,868,247
1978	Roy Howell 3B	0-1			Joe Carter OF	2-3, 1 RBI	
1979	Dave Lemanczyk P	DID NOT PLAY			Juan Guzman P	1.0IP, 2H, 1BB, 2K	
1980	Dave Stieb P	1.0IP, 1H, 1R, 1BB		1993	**Roberto Alomar 2B**	1-3, HR, 1 RBI	1,852,280
1981	Dave Stieb P	1.2IP, 1H, 1BB, 1K			**Joe Carter OF**	1-3, 1K	1,407,179
1982	Jim Clancy P	1.0IP			Pat Hentgen P	DID NOT PLAY	
1983	Dave Stieb P	Starter (3.0IP, 1H, 1BB, 4K)			Paul Molitor DH	0-1, 1BB	
1984	Dave Stieb P	Starter (2.0IP, 2H, 2R, 1ER, 2K)			**John Olerud 1B**	0-2	1,285,280
					Duane Ward P	1.0IP, 2K, SAVE	
	Damaso Garcia 2B	0-1			Devon White OF	1-2, double, 1 RBI, 1 run, 1 SB	
	Alfredo Griffin SS	0-0					
1985	Dave Stieb P	1.0IP, 1BB, 1K		1994	**Roberto Alomar 2B**	1-3, 1 run	3,675,730
	Jimmy Key P	.1IP			**Joe Carter OF**	0-3, 1 run	3,683,682
	Damaso Garcia 2B	1-2			Pat Hentgen P	1.0IP, 1H	
	Ernie Whitt C	0-0			Paul Molitor IF	0-1	
1986	Jesse Barfield OF	0-3		1995	Roberto Alomar 2B	0-1, 1 SB (3rd)	
	Lloyd Moseby OF	0-0		1996	Joe Carter OF	1-1	
	Tony Fernandez SS	0-0		1997	Roger Clemens P	1.0IP, 1H	
1987	**George Bell OF**	0-3	1,144,575	1998	Roger Clemens P	1.0IP, 2H, 2R, 2ER, 1BB, 1K	
	Tony Fernandez SS	0-2					
	Tom Henke P	2.2IP, 2H					
1988	Dave Stieb P	1.0IP, 1H		1999	Tony Fernandez 3B	0-1	
1989	Kelly Gruber 3B	DID NOT PLAY			Shawn Green OF	0-1	
	Tony Fernandez SS	0-1		2000	Carlos Delgado 1B	1-1, 2B	
1990	George Bell OF	0-2			Tony Batista 3B	0-1, K	
	Kelly Gruber 3B	0-1, 2 SB			David Wells Starter	2.0IP, 2H, 2K	
	Dave Stieb P	2.0IP, 1BB, 1K					
1991	**Roberto Alomar 2B**	0-4	1,868,247				
	Joe Carter OF	1-1, 1BB, 1R					
	Jimmy Key P	Winning pitcher (1.0IP, 1H, 1K)					

NOTE: Bold name indicates this player was voted in as a starter.

ALL-STAR MANAGERS, COACHES, AND TRAINERS

1979	Roy Hartsfield, Coach	1993	John Sullivan, Coach
1980	Ken Carson, Trainer	1993	Galen Cisco, Coach
1985	Bobby Cox, Coach	1994	Cito Gaston, Manager
1991	Cito Gaston, Coach	1994	Galen Cisco, Coach
1991	Tommy Craig, Trainer	1994	Bob Bailor, Coach
1993	Cito Gaston, Manager	1994	Gene Tenace, Coach
1993	Gene Tenace, Coach		

BOBBY MATTICK AND AL LAMACCHIA AWARDS

In 1996 the Blue Jays organization established two awards: the **Bobby Mattick Player Development Award** and the **Al LaMacchia Scouting Award**. The awards were created to acknowledge the dedication, success and work ethics of Blue Jays baseball operations personnel, attributes so aptly displayed by the awards' namesakes.

The Bobby Mattick Award was named after the longtime baseball executive who has spent the last 21 years of his career with the Blue Jays. Mattick was responsible for the development of many of the young players who have gone through the Blue Jays system. As well as being Director of Player Development for many years he also managed the Major League Blue Jays for two seasons in 1980 and 1981.

The Al LaMacchia Award was named after the veteran scout who spent 20 seasons with the Blue Jays. The contributions of Al's scouting talents have been deeply etched in the Blue Jays short history.

	BOBBY MATTICK AWARD		AL LAMACCHIA AWARD
1996	Rockett Wheeler		Duane Larson
1997	Omar Malave		Jim Hughes
1998	Rolando Pino		Tom Hinkle
1999	Bruce Walton		Ellis Dungan
2000	Marty Pevey		Tim Wilken

Awards

AMERICAN LEAGUE PLAYER OF THE WEEK

- Otto Velez, July 23-29, 1979 (.500, 9 RBI, 5 runs scored, 1.050 slg. pct.)
- Dave Stieb, April 21-27, 1980 (2 complete game wins, 0.50 ERA)
- Jim Clancy, June 14-20, 1982 (1-0, 19.0 IP, 1 ER)
- Jim Clancy, September 27-October 3, 1982 (2 wins including 1-hitter vs Twins, Sept. 28)
- Luis Leal, May 9-15, 1983 (2-0, 0.64 ERA)
- Dave Stieb, May 16-22, 1983 (2-0, 0.50 ERA)
- Lloyd Moseby, May 23-29, 1983 (.556 BA, 3 HR, 2 doubles)
- Cliff Johnson, June 20-26, 1983 (.500 BA, 2 doubles, HR in consecutive at-bats)
- Jesse Barfield, August 29-September 4, 1983 (7 HR, 39 total bases, .424 BA)
- Willie Upshaw, April 21-28, 1985 (.409 BA, 3 HR, 2 doubles, 20 total bases, .909 slg. pct.)
- Lloyd Moseby, September 2-8, 1985 (.435 BA, 5 HR, 1.174 slg. pct.)
- Lloyd Moseby, August 18-24, 1986 (8 RBI, .435 BA, 3 HR, .870 slg. pct.)
- George Bell, September 1-7, 1986 (10 RBI, 9 runs, 433, BA, 2 doubles, 3 HR)
- Jim Clancy, May 19-24, 1987 (2 complete game wins, 1 shutout, 0.50 ERA, 18 strikeouts in 18.0 IP)
- George Bell, June 8-14, 1987 (.407 BA, 5 HR, 15 RBI, 1.037 slg. pct.)
- George Bell, July 27-August 3, 1987 (.500 BA, 3 HR, 7 RBI)
- George Bell, April 4-10, 1988 (.455 BA, 4 HR, 7 extra-base hits, 1.136 slg. pct.)
- George Bell, August 29-September 4, 1988 (3 HR, 12 RBI, .379 BA)
- Nelson Liriano, May 15-21, 1989 (3 doubles, 23 total bases, .600 BA, 7 RBI)
- Junior Felix, May 29-June 4, 1989 (11 RBI, 2 HR, .435 BA, 6 runs scored)
- George Bell, August 14-20, 1989 (12 RBI, .467 BA, 3 HR, 3 doubles)
- Lloyd Moseby, September 4-10, 1989 (.440 BA, 7 runs scored, 3 doubles, 4 stolen bases, .548 OBA)
- Kelly Gruber, April 23-29, 1990 (.414 BA, 4 HR, 9 RBI, 5 runs scored, .897 slg. pct.)
- George Bell, June 4-10, 1990 (3 HR, 11 RBI, .464 BA, 2 doubles, 7 runs scored)
- George Bell, June 18-24, 1990 (.500 BA, 5 HR, 11 RBI, 9 runs scored)
- Dave Stieb, August 27-September 2, 1990 (pitched no-hitter at Cleveland Sept. 2)
- Kelly Gruber, September 9-16, 1990 (14 RBI, .464 BA, 2 HR, 3 doubles)
- Joe Carter, June 17-23, 1991 (9 hits, 5 HR, 7 RBI, 7 runs scored, 26 total bases)
- Roberto Alomar, April 20-26, 1992 (.600 BA, 15 hits, 9 RBI, 7 consecutive hits)
- Joe Carter, August 10-16, 1992 (11 hits, 4 doubles, 24 total bases, 3 HR, .407 BA)
- John Olerud, June 1-6, 1993 (.445 BA, 10 hits, 5 HR, 11 RBI, 29 total bases)
- Joe Carter, April 4-10, 1994 (.333 BA, 4 HR, 12 RBI, 7 runs scored)
- Joe Carter, April 18-24, 1994 (9 hits, 4 doubles, 4 HR, 12 RBI)
- Pat Hentgen, May 1-7, 1994 (2-0, 0.51 ERA, 17.2IP, 8H, 23K)
- Paul Molitor, July 12-18, 1994 (.500 BA, 13 hits, 4 HR, 10 RBI, 10 runs scored)
- John Olerud, July 12-16, 1995 (.500 BA, 4 runs, 2 doubles, 18 total bases, .588 OBA, 1.286 slg. pct.)
- Roger Clemens, May 6-11, 1997 (2-0, 2.81 ERA, 2 GS, 16.0 IP, 24 K)
- Carlos Delgado, June 1-7, 1998 (.407 BA, 11-27, 4 HR, 9 RBI)
- Carlos Delgado, August 17-23, 1998 (.370 BA, 10-27, 4 HR, 10 RBI)
- Roger Clemens, August 24-30, 1998 (2-0, 0.00 ERA, 18.0 IP, 5 H, 25 K, 2 CG-SHO)
- Shannon Stewart, April 26-May 2, 1999 (.471 BA, 16H, 5R, 3-2B, 1HR, 5RBI, 3SB)
- Tony Fernandez, June 14-20, 1999 (.411 BA, 10H, 15TB, 2-2B, 1HR, .789 slg. pct., .571OBA)
- Homer Bush, Sept. 30-Oct. 3, 1999 (.452 BA, 14H, 6R, 2-2B, 2RBI)
- Carlos Delgado, April 17-23, 2000 (.480 BA, 12H, 11R, 4HR, 8RBI, 1.080 slg. pct.)
- Jose Cruz, May 1-7, 2000 (.387 BA, 9R, 3-2B, 4HR, 9RBI, 5BB)
- Carlos Delgado, June 5-11, 2000 (.556 BA, 10H, 4HR, 13RBI, 25TB, 9BB, 1.389 slg. pct.)

AMERICAN LEAGUE PLAYER OF THE MONTH

- Otto Velez, April 1977 (5 HR, 11 RBI, 11 runs scored, .865 slg. pct., .422 BA)
- Alredo Griffin, September 1979 (.407 BA, 4 triples, 62 total bases)
- Lloyd Moseby, August 1983 (.351 BA, 25 RBI, 15 extra-base hits)
- Fred McGriff, April 1989 (7 HR, 17 RBI, 28 hits, 21 runs scored)
- George Bell, August 1989 (22 game hitting streak, .370 BA)
- Kelly Gruber, September 1990 (.352 BA, 20 runs scored, 30 RBI)
- Joe Carter, June 1991 (11 HR, 36 hits, .352 BA, 11 doubles, 29 RBI, 21 runs scored)
- Roberto Alomar, April 1992 (.382 BA, 34 hits, 19 runs scored, 3 RH, 19 RBI, 8 stolen bases, .439 OBA)
- John Olerud, April 1993 (.450 BA, 36 hits, .650 slg. pct., .527 OBA, 18 RBI, 15 runs scored, 7 doubles, 3 HR)
- Paul Molitor, May 1993 (.374 BA, 43 hits, 5 HR, 22 RBI, 25 runs scored)
- John Olerud, June 1993 (.427 BA, 41 hits, 17 doubles, 5 HR, 30 RBI, 17 runs scored, 73 total bases, .525 OBA)
- Joe Carter, April 1994 (.312 BA, ML record for RBI in April with 31, 9 HR, 8 doubles, 64 total bases)

AMERICAN LEAGUE PITCHER OF THE MONTH

- Dave Stieb, April 1980 (3-0, 15 strikeouts, 1 shutout, 1.09 ERA)
- Dave Stieb, May 1983 (5 wins, 2 shutouts, 43 strikeouts)
- Doyle Alexander, September 1984 (2.23 ERA, 5-1, 6 complete games)
- Dave Stieb, May 1985 (4-1, 34 strikeouts, 1.69 ERA)
- Jim Clancy, May 1987 (5-1, 1.71 ERA, 40 strikeouts in 47.1 innings)
- Juan Guzman, April 1996 (3-1, 1.88 ERA, 39 strikeouts in 43.0 innings)
- Pat Hentgen, July 1996 (5-1, 2.72 ERA, 28 strikeouts in 46.1 innings)
- Pat Hentgen, August 1996 (5-1, 2.60 ERA, 33 strikeouts in 52.0 innings)
- Roger Clemens, May 1997 (6-0, 1.96 ERA, 46.0 IP, 51 K)
- Roger Clemens, August 1997 (4-0, 2.47 ERA, 2 CG, 47.1 IP, 54 K)
- Roger Clemens, August 1998 (4-0, 0.90 ERA, 3 CG, 50.0 IP, 68 K)

BASEBALL AMERICA

ALL-STAR TEAM (AL)

1983 — Dave Stieb, P
1983 — Lloyd Moseby, OF
1984 — Dave Stieb, P
1986 — Tony Fernandez, SS
1986 — Jesse Barfield, OF
1987 — George Bell, OF
1987 — Jimmy Key, SP
1987 — Tom Henke, RP
1989 — George Bell, OF(E)
1989 — Dave Stieb, P(E)

1990 — Kelly Gruber, 3B
1992 — Roberto Alomar, 2B
1992 — Dave Winfield, 2B
1993 — Roberto Alomar, 2B
1993 — John Olerud, 1B
1993 — Duane Ward, P
1996 — Pat Hentgen, P
1997 — Roger Clemens, P
1998 — Roger Clemens, P

PLAYER OF THE YEAR (AL)

1987 — George Bell

MAJOR LEAGUE PITCHER OF THE YEAR

1998 — Roger Clemens

Latin American All-Star Team-TSN

1985 — Damaso Garcia, 2B
1985 — George Bell, OF

All-Rookie Team — Topps

1977 — Bob Bailor, SS; Doug Ault, 1B; Jerry Garvin, LHP
1978 — Rick Bosetti, OF
1979 — Alfredo Griffin, SS; Dan Ainge, 2B
1980 — Damaso Garcia, 2B
1987 — Jeff Musselman, LHP
1995 — Shawn Green, OF
1997 — Jose Cruz, Jr., OF
1999 — Billy Koch, RHP

All-Rookie Team — Baseball Digest

1977 — Bob Bailor, CF; Jerry Garvin, LHP
1978 — Rick Bosetti, CF
1979 — Alfredo Griffin, SS; Dan Ainge, 2B
1980 — Damaso Garcia, 2B

Rolaids Relief Awards

1985, April — Bill Caudill
1985 — Toronto Blue Jays
1987, July — Tom Henke
1987, August — Tom Henke
1989, July — Tom Henke
1993, April — Duane Ward
1993, August — Duane Ward
1999, July — Billy Koch

R. HOWARD WEBSTER AWARDS

In 1982 the Blue Jays established a set of awards to be bestowed annually upon the 'Most Valuable Player' on each Blue Jay farm club.

The awards are named in honor of R. HOWARD WEBSTER, who was the first Chairman of the Board for the Toronto Blue Jays.

AAA-SYRACUSE CHIEFS: 1982-Tony Fernandez; 1983-Tony Fernandez; 1984-Fred Manrique; 1985-Rick Leach; 1986-Mike Sharperson; 1987-Todd Stottlemyre; 1988-Alexis Infante; 1989-Glenallen Hill; 1990-Mark Whiten; 1991-Derek Bell, 1992-Butch Davis, 1993-Robert Perez; 1994-Shawn Green; 1995-Robert Perez; 1996-Shannon Stewart; 1997-Rich Butler; 1998-Patrick Lennon; 1999-Luis Lopez; 2000-Chad Mottola

AA-KNOXVILLE BLUE JAYS: 1982-Tim Thompson; 1983-Dave Shipanoff; 1984-Mike Sharperson; 1985-Steve Davis; 1986-Glenallen Hill; 1987-Geronimo Berroa; 1988-Alex Sanchez; 1989-Derek Bell; 1990-Tom Quinlan; 1991-Jeff Kent, 1992-Juan De La Rosa, 1993-Carlos Delgado; 1994-Chris Stynes; 1995-Shannon Stewart; 1996-Ryan Jones; 1997-Kevin Witt; 1998-Luis Lopez; 1999-Tim Giles

AA-TENNESSEE SMOKIES: 2000-Jay Gibbons

A-KINSTON BLUE JAYS: 1982-Dave Shipanoff; 1983-Jose Escobar; 1984-Luis Aquino; 1985-Eric Yelding

A-VENTURA BLUE JAYS: 1986-Greg Myers

A-DUNEDIN BLUE JAYS: 1987-Steve Cummings; 1988-Pedro Munoz; 1989-Nate Cromwell; 1990-Jeff Kent; 1991-Nigel Wilson, 1992-Carlos Delgado; 1993-Chris Weinke; 1994-Kris Harmes; 1995-Jeff Patzke; 1996-Roy Halladay; 1997-Will Skett; 1998-Brent Abernathy; 1999-Cesar Izturis; 2000-Joe Lawrence

A-FLORENCE BLUE JAYS: 1982-Ken Kinnard; 1983-Cecil Fielder; 1984-Pat Borders; 1985-Sil Campusano; 1986-Pedro Munoz

A-MYRTLE BEACH BLUE JAYS: 1987-Doug Linton; 1988-Luis Sojo; 1989-Ray Giannelli; 1990-Mike Ogliaruso; 1991-Howard Battle, 1992-Alex Gonzalez

A-HAGERSTOWN SUNS: 1993-D.J. Boston; 1994-David Sinnes; 1995-Jeff Ladd; 1996-Mike Whitlock; 1997-Luis Lopez; 1998-John Sneed; 1999-Jorge Nunez; 2000-Reed Johnson

A-QUEENS KINGS: 2000-Martin Malpica

A-ST. CATHARINES BLUE JAYS: 1986-Willie Blair; 1987-Derek Bell; 1988-Woody Williams; 1989-Greg O'Halloran; 1990-Carlos Delgado; 1991-Robert Butler, 1992-Tim Crabtree, 1993-Alonso Beltran; 1994-Jeff Ladd; 1995-Joe Young; 1996-Will Skett; 1997-Selwyn Langaigne; 1998-Jarrod Kingery; 1999-Brandon Jackson

ROOKIE-MEDICINE HAT BLUE JAYS: 1982-Chris Johnston; 1983-Ronnie Robbins; 1984-Rob Ducey; 1985-Geronimo Berroa; 1986-Mark Whiten; 1987-Andy Dziadkoweic; 1988-Eddy Mendez; 1989-Shawn Holtzclaw; 1990-Brent Bowers; 1991-Felipe Crespo, 1992-Jose Herrera, 1993-Lorenzo de Iacruz; 1994-Julio Mosquera; 1995-Mike Peeples; 1996-Ryan Stromsborg; 1997-Greg Morrison; 1998-Jay Gibbons; 1999-Gustavo Chacin; 2000-Jeremy Johnson

ROOKIE-BRADENTON BLUE JAYS: 1982-Esteban Bolivar; 1983-Santiago Escobar; 1984-Santiago Garcia; 1985-Domingo Martinez; 1988-Wilberto Rojas **GULF COAST:** 1991-Christopher Stynes, 1992-Tilson Brito, 1993-Aaron Hightower; 1994-Kelvin Escobar; 1995-Mike Whitlock

DOMINICAN LEAGUE-SANTO DOMINGO: 1987-Marcos Taveras; 1988-Wilberto Rojas; 1989-Richard Orman; 1990-Mariano Dotel; 1991-Tilson Brito, 1992-Lorenzo De La Cruz, 1993-Fausto Solano; 1994-Jose Valdespino; 1995-Pablo Sencion **VILLA MELLA:** 1991-Diomedes Vasquez, 1992-Julio Mosquera, 1993-Irvin Abad; 1994-Pablo Sencion **BOCA CHICA:** 1996-Felipe Rodriguez; 1997-Isabel Giron; 1998-Victor Morales; 1999-Ubaldo Ramos; 2000-Maikel Jova

PLAYER AND PITCHER OF THE MONTH

Each month throughout the season, the Toronto Chapter of the Baseball Writers Association of America votes for the player and pitcher based on their appraisal of that player's or pitcher's performance during that particular month.

Year	April	May	June	July	August	Sept.	Most Valuable Player
1977	Velez	Fairly	Fairly	Rader	Bailor	Bowling	Bailor
1978	Howell	Bosetti	Howell	Mayberry	Bailor	Bailor & Bosetti	Howell
1979	Mayberry	Griffin	Underwood	Velez	Griffin	Griffin	Griffin
1980	Stieb	Woods	Mayberry	Woods	Garcia	Mayberry	Mayberry
1981	Todd	Bonnell	—	—	Moseby	Stieb	Stieb
1982	Barfield	Bonnell	Upshaw	Garcia	Garcia	Clancy	Garcia
1983	Barfield	Upshaw	Johnson	Moseby	Moseby	Upshaw	Moseby & Upshaw
1984	Upshaw	Collins	Upshaw	Mulliniks	Bell	Collins	Bell
1985	Upshaw	Garcia	Bell	Mulliniks	Barfield	Moseby	Barfield
1986	Bell	Barfield	Fernandez	Bell	Moseby	Barfield	Bell
1987	Bell	Bell	Moseby	Fernandez	Bell	Moseby	Bell
1988	Gruber	McGriff	Gruber	McGriff	Whitt	Fernandez	McGriff
1989	McGriff	Liriano	Gruber	McGriff	Bell	Bell	Bell
1990	Gruber	Gruber	Bell	McGriff	McGriff	Gruber	Gruber
1991	Carter	Alomar	Carter	Alomar	White	Alomar	Alomar
1992	Alomar	Alomar	Carter	Maldonado	Winfield	White	Alomar
1993	Olerud	Molitor	Olerud	Olerud	Molitor/Alomar	Alomar	Molitor
1994	Carter	Carter	Alomar	Molitor			Carter
1995		Alomar	Maldonado	Olerud	Molitor	Green	Alomar
1996	Carter	Olerud	Sprague	Carter	Brumfield	Sprague	Sprague
1997	Sprague	Carter	Merced	Green	Cruz	Stewart	Delgado
1998	Canseco	Delgado	Delgado	Stewart	Green	Fernandez	Delgado
1999	Green	Green	Fletcher	Green	Delgado	Bush	Green
2000	Fullmer	Delgado	Delgado	Delgado	Delgado	Fletcher	Delgado

PITCHER OF THE MONTH

Year	April	May	June	July	August	Sept.	Most Valuable Pitcher
1983	Stieb	Stieb	Gott	Clancy	Stieb	Alexander	Stieb
1984	Stieb	Alexander	Stieb	Stieb	Stieb & Clancy	Alexander	Stieb
1985	Caudill	Stieb	Stieb	Stieb	Henke	Alexander	Stieb
1986	Alexander	Eichhorn	Key	Clancy	Eichhorn	Stieb	Key
1987	Key	Key	Clancy	Key	Cerutti	Flanagan	Key
1988	Cerutti	Stieb	Ward	Key	Clancy	Stieb	Stieb
1989	Key	Key	Cerutti	Henke	Stieb	Stieb	Stieb
1990	Ward	Stieb	Henke	Stieb	Key	Key	Stieb
1991	Key	Wells	Key	Henke	Candiotti	Guzman	Ward
1992	Guzman	Guzman	Guzman	Ward	Morris	Key	Morris
1993	Hentgen	Cox	Hentgen	Ward	Ward	Stewart	Ward
1994	Castillo	Hentgen	Hentgen	Castillo			Hentgen
1995		Cone	Leiter	Castillo	Leiter	Timlin	Leiter
1996	Guzman	Timlin	Guzman	Hentgen	Hentgen	Hentgen	Hentgen
1997	Clemens	Clemens	Clemens	Clemens	Clemens	Clemens	Clemens
1998	Williams	Williams	Clemens	Clemens	Clemens	Escobar	Clemens
1999	Wells	Halladay	Wells	Koch	Hentgen	Wells	Koch
2000	Wells	Wells	Wells	Koch	Wells	Loaiza	Wells

Most Valuable Pitcher: 1978 - Clancy & Underwood 1979 - Underwood 1980 - Clancy
1981 - Stieb 1982 - Stieb

BLUE JAYS AND THE MVP VOTING

YEAR	WINNER	PTS	BLUE JAYS	RANK	PTS
1977	Rod Carew	273	--	--	--
1978	Jim Rice	352	--	--	--
1979	Don Baylor	347	--	--	--
1980	George Brett	335	--	--	--
1981	Rollie Fingers	319	Dave Stieb	T27	1
1982	Robin Yount	385	Damaso Garcia	T26	5
1983	Cal Ripken	322	Willie Upshaw	11	41.5
			Lloyd Moseby	14	21
1984	Willie Hernandez	306	Willie Upshaw	T16	8
			George Bell	T16	5
			Dave Stieb	T23	4
			Lloyd Moseby	T23	4
			Doyle Alexander	T27	1
1985	Don Mattingly	367	Jesse Barfield	7	88
			George Bell	8	84
			Tom Henke	20	5
			Dennis Lamp	T21	3
			Doyle Alexander	T21	3
			Damaso Garcia	24	2
1986	Roger Clemens	339	George Bell	4	125
			Jesse Barfield	5	107
			Tony Fernandez	14	17
1987	George Bell	332	George Bell	1	332
			Tony Fernandez	8	79
			Tom Henke	T13	14
1988	Jose Canseco	392	Fred McGriff	17	9
			Tony Fernandez	26	1
1989	Robin Yount	205	George Bell	4	205
			Fred McGriff	6	96
			Tony Fernandez	19	9
			Mookie Wilson	T25	1
1990	Rickey Henderson	317	Kelly Gruber	4	175
			Fred McGriff	10	30
			Dave Stieb	T25	1
1991	Cal Ripken	318	Joe Carter	5	136
			Roberto Alomar	6	128
			Devon White	16	15
1992	Dennis Eckersley	306	Joe Carter	3	201
			Dave Winfield	5	141
			Roberto Alomar	6	118
			Jack Morris	13	18
1993	Frank Thomas	392	Paul Molitor	2	209
			John Olerud	3	198
			Roberto Alomar	6	102
			Joe Carter	12	25
			Duane Ward	22	3
1994	Frank Thomas	372	Joe Carter	10	35
			Paul Molitor	T18	9
1995	Mo Vaughn	308	--	--	--
1996	Juan Gonzalez	290	--	--	--
1997	Ken Griffey Jr.	392	Roger Clemens	10	56
1998	Juan Gonzalez	357	Roger Clemens	11	49
1999	Ivan Rodriguez	252	Shawn Green	9	44
			Carlos Delgado	12	16
2000	Jason Giambi	317	Carlos Delgado	4	206
			David Wells	18	2

ROOKIE-OF-THE-YEAR

Thirteen Toronto Blue Jays have received votes in Rookie-of-the-Year balloting by the Baseball Writers Association of America. Alfredo Griffin, who shared the award in 1979 with John Castino of the Minnesota Twins, remains the only Toronto winner.

YEAR	PLAYER	FINISHED	WINNER
1979	Alfredo Griffin	Tied 1st	John Castino
1980	Damaso Garcia	4th	Joe Charboneau
1981	George Bell	8th	Dave Righetti
1982	Jesse Barfield	8th	Cal Ripken
1985	Tom Henke	7th	Ozzie Guillen
1986	Mark Eichhorn	3rd	Jose Canseco
1987	Nelson Liriano	7th	Mark McGwire
1990	John Olerud	4th	Sandy Alomar
1991	Juan Guzman	2nd	Chuck Knoblauch
	Mike Timlin	6th	—
1994	Darren Hall	4th	Bob Hamelin
1995	Shawn Green	5th	Marty Cordova
1996	Tim Crabtree	Tied 7th	Derek Jeter
1997	Jose Cruz	2nd	Nomar Garciaparra
1999	Billy Koch	Tied 7th	Carlos Beltran

BLUE JAYS & CY YOUNG VOTING

YEAR	WINNER	PTS	BLUE JAYS	RANK	PTS
1977	Sparky Lyle	56.5	–	–	–
1978	Ron Guidry	140	–	–	–
1979	Mike Flanagan	136	–	–	–
1980	Steve Stone	100	–	–	–
1981	Rollie Fingers	126	–	–	–
1982	Pete Vuckovich	87	Dave Stieb	4th	36
1983	Lamar Hoyt	116	–	–	–
1984	Willie Hernandez	88	Dave Stieb	8th	1
1985	Bret Saberhagen	127	Doyle Alexander	6th	5
			Dave Stieb	9th	2
1986	Roger Clemens	140	Mark Eichhorn	6th	2
1987	Roger Clemens	124	Jimmy Key	2nd	64
1988	Frank Viola	138	–	–	–
1989	Bret Saberhagen	138	–	–	–
1990	Bob Welch	107	Dave Stieb	6th	2
1991	Roger Clemens	119	Duane Ward	10th	3
1992	Dennis Eckersley	107	Jack Morris	5th	10
1993	Jack McDowell	124	Duane Ward	5th	5
			Pat Hentgen	6th	3
			Juan Guzman	7th	1
1994	David Cone	108			
1995	Randy Johnson	136	David Cone	4th	18
1996	**PAT HENTGEN**	**110**	**PAT HENTGEN**	**1st**	**110**
1997	**ROGER CLEMENS**	**134**	**ROGER CLEMENS**	**1st**	**134**
1998	**ROGER CLEMENS**	**140**	**ROGER CLEMENS**	**1st**	**140**
1999	Pedro Martinez	140	–	–	–
2000	Pedro Martinez	140	David Wells	3rd	46

BLUE JAYS IN FIRST PLACE
(before games on the 1st)

MAY 1st	JUNE 1st	JULY 1st	AUG. 1st	SEPT. 1st	OCT. 1st
1981	1983	1983	1985	1985	1987
1985	1985	1985	1991	1989	1989
1992	1991 (T)	1991	1992	1991	1991
	1992	1992	1993	1992	1992
		1993		1993	1993
		2000			

TRIPLE PLAYS

BY TORONTO

APR. 22/78 vs. Chicago at Toronto-With Jim Clancy pitching in the Chicago second, after Bobby Bonds homered Lamar Johnson doubled and stayed at second on an infield hit by Ron Blomberg. Junior Moore followed with an attempted bunt that was lined to Clancy who threw to John Mayberry at first to double Blomberg. Mayberry then fired the ball to Luis Gomez at second and Johnson was tripled up before he could return to the bag. Final Score-Toronto 4 Chicago 2.

SEPT. 7/79 at Cleveland-With Phil Huffman pitching in Cleveland's eighth and the bases loaded, Ted Cox grounded to third baseman, Roy Howell, who stepped on the bag forcing Mike Hargrove, threw to second baseman, Luis Gomez, who erased Rick Manning and then relayed to first baseman, John Mayberry to nip Cox. Final Score Cleveland 9 Toronto 8.

SEPT. 21/79 vs. New York at Toronto-With Tom Underwood pitching in New York's seventh, Chris Chambliss and Roy Staiger were at first and second on consecutive singles. Damaso Garcia, the batter, lined sharply to second baseman Dave McKay, who threw to Craig Kusick at first to double Staiger. Kusick relayed to shortstop Alfredo Griffin at second base to catch Chambliss off base for the third out. Final Score-Toronto 3 New York 2.

BY OPPOSITION

SEPT. 9/78 vs. Baltimore at Toronto-With Scott McGregor pitching in the Blue Jays' sixth Doug Ault and Dave McKay hit consecutive singles to put Toronto runners on first and second. Rick Cerone followed with a hard grounder to Doug DeCinces who stepped on third for the first out and then threw to Rick Dauer at second for a forceout. Dauer then fired the ball to first baseman Eddie Murray, beating Cerone to the bag. Final Score-Baltimore 4 Toronto 0.

SEPT. 10/91 vs. the Seattle Mariners at Toronto-With Brian Holman pitching for Seattle in the Blue Jays' fifth. Devon White and Roberto Alomar led off with consecutive singles to put men on first and second. Joe Carter stepped up to the plate and hit a grounder to third where Edgar Martinez threw to Harold Reynolds at second for the first out. Reynolds then relayed a throw to first to get Carter. Then, Mariner first baseman, Tino Martinez threw home where Seattle catcher David Valle put the tag on Devon White for the third out. Final Score-Seattle 5 Toronto 4.

JULY 13/95 at Seattle-With Jeff Nelson pitching for Seattle in the Blue Jays' ninth inning, Shawn Green led off with a single and moved to second on a hit by Alex Gonzalez. Sandy Martinez, the next batter, then attempted to bunt. Seattle pitcher Jeff Nelson let the ball drop in front of him and threw to second where shortstop Luis Sojo tagged out Green, stepped on second to force Gonzalez, and then threw to first (to second baseman Joey Cora covering) to get Martinez. Final Score-Toronto 4 Seattle 1.

JULY 28/97 (2nd game) at Milwaukee-With Joel Adamson pitching for Milwaukee in the Blue Jays' fourth inning, Ed Sprague led off with a single to left field. Benito Santiago singled to center and advanced Sprague to second. Alex Gonzalez hit a ground ball to third baseman Jeff Wills who touched third to force Sprague and then threw to Mark Loretta at second to force Santiago. Loretta then made the relay to first to Dave Nilsson to get Gonzalez. Final score-Toronto 3 at Milwaukee 9.

1985 AMERICAN LEAGUE CHAMPIONSHIP SERIES

TORONTO vs KANSAS CITY

As the Blue Jays entered post season play for the first time, they would face the Kansas City Royals in the first ever best-of-seven American League Championship Series. The Blue Jays, who finished nine games ahead of the Royals in the loss column, were the favourites and would enjoy the extra home game.

GAME #1: Dave Stieb lived up to superstar billing, shutting out the Royals on three hits through eight innings with no base runner advancing past second base. The Blue Jays struck quickly with two runs in the second, three in the third and one in the fourth. The Blue Jays offense was sparked by 2 RBI performances by Ernie Whitt and Tony Fernandez.

GAME #2: A much more even affair with the Blue Jays eeking out a 6-5, 10-inning win. The Royals jumped into a quick 3-0 lead after 3½ innings primarily on the strength of a 2 run HR by Willie Wilson in the 3rd inning. The Blue Jays rallied and took the lead on a George Bell sacrifice fly in the 8th. The Royals rallied, however, in the 9th on a pinch hit HR by Pat Sheridan with the go ahead run being delivered in the 10th on a Frank White single. The Blue Jays won it in the bottom of the 10th on a two-out 2 run single by Al Oliver. On to Kansas City, the Blue Jays were up 2 games to none.

GAME #3: George Brett put on a baseball clinic going 4-4, 2 HR's, 3 RBI with 4 runs scored enroute to a 6-5 Royals win. Leading 5-2 after 4½ innings the Blue Jays squandered the lead for good in the 8th when Brett led off the inning with a single and eventually scored.

GAME #4: The Blue Jays came within one win of a World Series berth with a 3-1 come-from-behind victory. The Blue Jays won the game dramatically with 3 runs in the top of the ninth inning, the big blow being a 2 run pinch hit double by Al Oliver.

GAME #5: LHP Danny Jackson went the distance checking Toronto on 8 hits and scoring a run in each of the first two innings. Blue Jays still led the series 3 games to 2.

GAME #6: The Blue Jays and Royals returned to Exhibition Stadium. Entering the 5th inning tied at 2-2 George Brett once again delivered the decisive blow with a solo HR. And, with 3.2 shutout innings of relief from Buddy Black and Dan Quisenberry, the Royals pulled even in the series for the first time at three games apiece.

GAME #7: Dave Stieb, the ace of the Toronto staff vs eventual Cy Young Award winner Bret Saberhagen. The Royals came out on top 6-2 shellacking Dave Stieb for six runs in 5.2 innings. The big blow being a wind-assisted bases clearing triple by Jim Sundberg to cap a four run 6th inning.

The Kansas City Royals became only the 5th club in major league history to trail a series 3 games to one and come back to win the series. The Blue Jays slumped immediately after scoring five runs in the 5th inning of Game 3 scoring only eight runs in the last 40 innings.

GAME 1
at TORONTO
Tuesday, October 8 (night)

											R	H	E
Kansas City	0	0	0	0	0	0	0	0	1		1	5	1
Toronto	0	2	3	1	0	0	0	X			6	11	0

LEIBRANDT, Farr (3), Gubicza (5), Jackson (8), and Sundberg
STIEB, Henke (9), and Whitt
HR: None
T: 2:24   A: 39,115

GAME 2
at TORONTO
Wednesday, October 9 (day)

											R	H	E
Kansas City	0	0	2	1	0	0	0	0	1	1	5	10	3
Toronto	0	0	0	1	0	2	0	1	0	2	6	10	0

Black, QUISENBERRY (8), and Sundberg
Key, Lamp (4), Lavelle (8), HENKE (8), and Whitt
HR: Kansas City (2) - Wilson, Sheridan
T: 3:39   A: 34,029

GAME 3
at KANSAS CITY
Friday, October 11 (night)

										R	H	E
Toronto	0	0	0	0	5	0	0	0		5	13	1
Kansas City	1	0	0	1	1	2	0	1	X	6	10	1

Alexander, Lamp (6), CLANCY (8), and Whitt
Saberhagen, Black (5), FARR (5), and Sundberg
HR: Toronto (2) - Barfield, Mulliniks;
  Kansas City (3) - Brett (2), Sundberg
T: 2:51   A: 40,224

GAME 4
at KANSAS CITY
Saturday, October 12 (night)

										R	H	E
Toronto	0	0	0	0	0	0	0	0	3	3	7	0
Kansas City	0	0	0	0	0	1	0	0	0	1	2	0

Stieb, HENKE (7), and Whitt, Hearron (9)
LIEBRANDT, Quisenberry (9), and Sundberg
HR: None
T: 3:02   A: 41,112

GAME 5
at KANSAS CITY
Sunday, October 13 (day)

										R	H	E
Toronto	0	0	0	0	0	0	0	0	0	0	8	0
Kansas City	1	1	0	0	0	0	0	0	X	2	8	0

KEY, Acker (6), and Whitt
JACKSON, and Sundberg
HR: None
T: 2:21   A: 40,046

GAME 6
at TORONTO
Tuesday, October 15 (night)

										R	H	E
Kansas City	1	0	1	0	1	2	0	0	0	5	8	1
Toronto	1	0	1	0	0	1	0	0	0	3	8	2

GUBICZA, Black (6), Quisenberry (9)(S), and Sundberg
ALEXANDER, Lamp (6), and Whitt, Hearron (8)
HR: Kansas City (1) - Brett
T: 3:12   A: 37,557

GAME 7
at TORONTO
Wednesday, October 16 (night)

										R	H	E
Kansas City	0	1	0	1	0	4	0	0	0	6	8	0
Toronto	0	0	0	0	1	0	0	0	1	2	8	1

Saberhagen, LEIBRANDT (4), Quisenberry (9), and Sundberg
STIEB, Acker (6), and Whitt
HR: Kansas City (1) - Sheridan
T: 2:49   A: 32,084

SCORE BY INNINGS

	1	2	3	4	5	6	7	8	9	R	H	E
Kansas City	3	2	3	3	2	9	0	1	2	26	51	6
Toronto	1	2	4	2	6	3	0	1	4	25	65	4

E-Balboni (2), Brett (2), Fernandez (2), Sundberg, Upshaw, Smith, Barfield
DP-Kansas City (7), Toronto (4)
LOP-Kansas City (44), Toronto (49)
SB-Barfield, Moseby, Wilson, Smith
S-Biancalana, McRae, Wilson, White
SF-Fernandez, Bell, White, Motley
WP-Black (2), Alexander, Gubicza
HBP-Bell (by Black), Oliver (by Saberhagen)
McRae (by Stieb)
ATT: 264,167

Post Season

BATTER	AVG	G	AB	R	H	2B	3B	HR	RBI	SH-SF	HB	BB	SO	SB-CS	E
BARFIELD	.280	7	25	3	7	1	0	1	4-0	0-0	0	3	7	1-1	1
BELL	.321	7	28	4	9	3	0	0	1-0	0-1	1	0	4	0-1	0
BURROUGHS	.000	1	1	0	0	0	0	0	0-0	0-0	0	0	0	0-0	0
FERNANDEZ (L)	.333	—	9	2	3	1	0	0	1-0	0-1	0	0	0	0-0	2
FERNANDEZ (R)	.333	—	15	0	5	1	0	0	1-0	0-0	0	1	2	0-0	0
FERNANDEZ (T)	.333	7	24	2	8	2	0	0	2-0	0-1	0	1	2	0-0	2
FIELDER	.333	3	3	0	1	1	0	0	0-0	0-0	0	0	1	0-0	0
GARCIA	.233	7	30	4	7	4	0	0	1-0	0-0	0	3	3	0-0	0
HEARRON	.000	2	0	0	0	0	0	0	0-0	0-0	0	0	0	0-0	0
IORG	.133	6	15	1	2	0	0	0	0-0	0-0	0	1	3	0-0	0
JOHNSON	.368	7	19	1	7	2	0	0	2-0	0-0	0	1	4	0-0	0
LEE (L)	.000	—	0	0	0	0	0	0	0-0	0-0	0	0	0	0-0	0
LEE (R)	.000	—	0	0	0	0	0	0	0-0	0-0	0	0	0	0-0	0
LEE (T)	.000	1	0	0	0	0	0	0	0-0	0-0	0	0	0	0-0	0
MOSEBY	.226	7	31	5	7	1	0	0	4-0	0-0	0	2	3	1-0	0
MULLINIKS	.364	5	11	1	4	1	0	1	3-0	0-0	0	2	2	0-0	0
OLIVER	.375	5	8	0	3	1	0	0	3-2	0-0	1	0	0	0-0	0
THORNTON	.000	2	0	1	0	0	0	0	0-0	0-0	0	0	0	0-0	0
UPSHAW	.231	7	26	2	6	2	0	0	1-0	0-0	1	1	4	0-0	1
WHITT	.190	7	21	1	4	1	0	0	2-1	0-0	0	2	4	0-0	0
DH	.370	7	27	2	10	3	0	0	5-2	0-0	1	1	4	0-0	0
PH	.462	7	13	0	6	2	0	0	4-1	0-0	0	0	2	0-0	0
BLUE JAYS	.269	7	242	25	65	19	0	2	23-3	0-2	3	16	37	2-2	4
ROYALS	.225	7	227	26	51	9	1	7	26-4	4-2	1	22	51	2-4	6

PITCHER	T	W-L	ERA	G	GS	CG	SHO	SV	IP	H	R	ER	HR	HB	BB	SO	WP
ACKER	R	0-0	0.00	2	0	0	0	0	6.0	2	0	0	0	0	0	5	0
ALEXANDER	R	0-1	8.71	2	2	0	0	0	10.1	14	10	10	4	0	3	9	1
CLANCY	R	0-1	9.00	1	0	0	0	0	1.0	2	1	1	0	0	1	0	0
HENKE	R	2-0	4.26	3	0	0	0	0	6.1	5	3	3	1	0	4	4	0
KEY	L	0-1	5.19	2	2	0	0	0	8.2	15	5	5	1	0	2	5	0
LAMP	R	0-0	0.00	3	0	0	0	0	9.1	2	0	0	0	0	1	10	0
LAVELLE	L	0-0	0.00	1	0	0	0	0	0.0	0	0	0	0	0	1	0	0
STIEB	R	1-1	3.10	3	3	0	0	0	20.1	11	7	7	1	1	10	18	0
BLUE JAYS		3-4	3.77	17	7	0	0	0	62.0	51	26	26	7	1	22	51	1
ROYALS		4-3	3.16	18	7	1	1	1	62.2	65	25	22	2	3	16	37	3

1989 AMERICAN LEAGUE CHAMPIONSHIP SERIES

TORONTO vs OAKLAND

For the second time in five seasons, the Blue Jays were American League East Division Champions. The Blue Jays would face the Oakland Athletics who had the best record in the Major Leagues in 1989.

GAME #1: The Blue Jays surrendered 2-0 and 3-1 leads as the Athletics scored three times in the sixth and twice in the eighth to win 7-3. In the sixth inning Mark McGwire cracked a lead off HR to tie the game and two runs scored when Carney Lansford's double play ball was botched. Dave Stewart allowed five hits over eight innings for the win.

GAME #2: The Athletics tallied twice in the fourth inning and three in the sixth en route to a 6-3 win. As outfielder Rickey Henderson was a one-man wrecking crew going 2-for-2 with two runs scored and four stolen bases. Athletics' righthander Mike Moore allowed just three hits and an unearned run in seven innings.

GAME #3: The Blue Jays snapped a five game post season losing streak dating back to 1985 with a convincing 7-3 win. The Blue Jays jumped on Athletics' starter Storm Davis for four runs on four hits in the fourth inning and salted the game away with another three runs in the seventh inning. The win ran the Blue Jays' record to 11-0 at SkyDome with the roof closed. Overcoming a 3-0 Athletics' lead Mookie Wilson and Tony Fernandez paced the Blue Jays with two hits apiece, the latter with two doubles.

GAME #4: The Athletics took a commanding 3-1 lead in games with a 6-6 win over the Blue Jays. Rickey Henderson was again a major catalyst with two HR's which accounted for four RBI. The Blue Jays collected 13 hits, 11 of which were singles and attempted to overcome a 5-2 deficit with one run in the sixth and seventh innings and two in the eighth.

GAME #5: The Blue Jays spotted the Athletics a 4-0 lead into the seventh inning before eventually losing the game 4-3 and the best-of-seven series in five games. Trailing 4-1 after eight innings the Blue Jays scored twice in the ninth inning on a leadoff HR by Geroge Bell and a sacrifice fly by Kelly Gruber.

Epilogue: In essence it was Rickey Henderson defeating the Blue Jays four games to one. Henderson batted .400, slugged 1.000, had a .609 on-base percentage and swiped a LCS record eight stolen bases. The Blue Jays hit .242 as a team (compared to Oakland's .272) with only eight of their hits being for extra bases. They were outscored 8-3 in the first three innings and 12-7 in the middle three before outscoring the Athletics 11-6 in the final three innings. Unfortunately it is virtually impossible to consistently battle back from an early inning deficit. Although anything can happen in a "short series" the best team of the regular season continued that charted course into post-season, winning eight of nine contests.

GAME 1
at OAKLAND
Tuesday, October 3 (night)

											R	H	E
Toronto	0	2	0	1	0	0	0	0	0		3	5	1
Oakland	0	1	0	0	1	3	0	2	X		7	11	0

STIEB, Acker (6), Ward (8), and Whitt
STEWART, Eckersley (9), and Steinbach
HR: Toronto (1) - Whitt;
   Oakland (2) - D. Henderson, McGwire
T: 2:52   1: 49,435

GAME 2
at OAKLAND
Wednesday, October 4 (day)

											R	H	E
Toronto	0	0	1	0	0	0	0	2	0		3	5	1
Oakland	0	0	0	2	0	3	1	0	X		6	9	1

STOTTLLEMYRE, Acker (6), Wells (7), Henke (7), Cerutti (8), and Whitt
MOORE, Honeycutt (8), Eckersley (8)(S), and Hassey
HR: Oakland (1) - Parker
T: 3:20   A: 49,444

GAME 3
at TORONTO
Friday, October 6 (night)

Oakland	1	0	1	1	0	0	0	0	0	3	8	1
Toronto	0	0	0	4	0	0	3	0	X	7	8	0

DAVIS, Honeycutt (7), Nelson (7), M.Young (8), and Steinbach
KEY, Acker (7), Henke (9), and Whitt
HR: Oakland (1) - Parker
T: 2:54 A: 50,268

GAME 4
at TORONTO
Saturday, October 7 (day)

Oakland	0	0	3	0	2	0	1	0	0	6	11	1
Toronto	0	0	0	1	0	1	1	2	0	5	13	0

WELCH, Honeycutt (6), Eckersley (8)(S), and Hassey
FLANAGAN, Ward (5), Cerutti (8), Acker (9), and Whitt, Borders (7)
HR: Oakland (3) - R. Henderson (2), Canseco
T: 3:29 A: 50,076

GAME 5
at TORONTO
Sunday, October 8 (day)

Oakland	1	0	1	0	0	0	2	0	0	4	4	0
Toronto	0	0	0	0	0	0	0	1	2	3	9	0

STEWART, Eckersley (9)(S), and Steinbach
STIEB, Acker (7), Henke (9), and Whitt
HR: Toronto (2) - Moseby, Bell
T: 2:52 A: 50,024

SCORE BY INNINGS

Oakland	2	1	5	3	3	6	4	2	0	26	43	3
Toronto	0	2	1	6	0	1	4	5	2	21	40	2

BATTER	AVG	G	AB	R	H	2B	3B	HR	RBI	SH-SF	HP	BB	SO	SB-CS	E
BELL	.200	5	20	2	4	0	0	1	2	0-1	0	0	3	0-0	0
BORDERS	1.000	1	1	0	1	0	0	0	1	0-0	0	0	0	0-0	0
FELIX (T)	.273	3	11	0	3	1	0	0	3	0-0	0	0	2	0-0	0
FELIX (R)	.500	–	2	–	1	0	0	0	1	0-0	0	0	0	–	–
FELIX (L)	.222	–	9	–	2	1	0	0	2	0-0	0	0	2	–	–
FERNANDEZ (T)	.350	5	20	6	7	3	0	0	1	0-0	0	1	2	5-0	0
FERNANDEZ (R)	1.000	–	1	–	1	1	0	0	0	0-0	0	0	0	–	–
FERNANDEZ (L)	.316	–	19	–	6	2	0	0	1	0-0	0	1	2	–	–
GRUBER	.294	5	17	2	5	1	0	0	1	0-1	0	3	2	1-0	0
LEE (T)	.250	2	8	2	2	0	0	0	0	0-0	0	0	1	0-0	0
LEE (R)	.667	–	3	–	2	0	0	0	0	0-0	0	0	0	–	–
LEE (L)	.000	–	5	–	0	0	0	0	0	0-0	0	0	1	–	–
LIRIANO (T)	.429	3	7	1	3	0	0	0	1	0-0	0	2	0	3-0	1
LIRIANO (R)	1.000	–	1	–	1	0	0	0	0	0-0	0	0	0	–	–
LIRIANO (L)	.333	–	6	–	2	0	0	0	1	0-0	0	2	0	–	–
MAZZILLI (T)	.000	–	3	8	0	0	0	0	0	0-0	0	0	2	0-0	0
MAZZILLI (R)	.000	–	0	–	0	0	0	0	0	0-0	0	0	0	–	–
MAZZILLI (L)	.000	–	8	–	0	0	0	0	0	0-0	0	0	2	–	–
McGRIFF	.143	5	21	1	3	0	0	0	3	0-0	0	4	4	0-0	1
MOSEBY	.313	5	16	4	5	0	0	1	2	0-0	0	5	2	1-0	0
MULLINIKS	.000	1	1	0	0	0	0	0	0	0-0	0	0	1	0-0	0
WHITT	.125	5	16	1	2	0	0	1	3	0-1	0	2	3	0-0	0
WILSON (T)	.263	5	19	2	5	0	0	0	2	0-0	0	2	2	1-0	0
WILSON (R)	.000	–	1	–	0	0	0	0	0	0-0	0	1	0	–	–
WILSON (L)	.278	–	18	–	5	0	0	0	2	0-0	0	1	2	–	–
PITCHERS	.000	18	0	0	0	0	0	0	0	0-0	0	0	0	0-0	0
BLUE JAYS	.242	5	165	21	40	5	0	3	19	0-3	0	15	24	11-0	2
ATHLETICS	.272	5	158	26	43	9	1	7	23	3-2	1	20	32	13-2	3

PITCHER	T	W-L	ERA	G	GS	CG	SHO	SV	IP	H	R	ER	HR	HB	BB	SO	WP
ACKER	R	0-0	1.42	5	0	0	0	0	6.1	4	2	1	0	1	1	4	0
CERUTTI	L	0-0	0.00	2	0	0	0	0	2.2	0	0	0	0	0	3	1	0
FLANAGAN	L	0-1	10.38	1	1	0	0	0	4.1	7	5	5	3	0	1	3	0
HENKE	R	0-0	0.00	3	0	0	0	0	2.2	0	0	0	0	0	0	3	0
KEY	L	1-0	4.50	1	1	0	0	0	6.0	7	3	3	1	0	2	2	0
STIEB	R	0-2	6.35	2	2	0	0	0	11.1	12	8	8	2	0	6	10	0
STOTTLEMYRE	R	0-1	7.20	1	1	0	0	0	5.0	7	4	4	1	0	2	3	0
WARD	R	0-0	7.36	2	0	0	0	0	3.2	6	3	3	0	0	3	5	1
WELLS	L	0-0	0.00	1	0	0	0	0	4.0	0	1	0	0	0	2	1	0
BLUE JAYS		1-4	5.02	5	5	0	0	0	43.0	43	26	24	7	1	20	32	1
ATHLETICS		4-1	3.89	5	5	0	0	3	44.0	40	21	19	3	0	15	24	1

1991 AMERICAN LEAGUE CHAMPIONSHIP SERIES

TORONTO vs MINNESOTA

In 1991, the Toronto Blue Jays won the American League East for the third time in the history of the organization. The Blue Jays faced the Western Division Champion Minnesota Twins in a series that would decide the American League Champion. The Minnesota Twins emerged victorious as they won the best of seven games series by a 4 games to 1 count. Below is a summary of the series.

GAME #1: Toronto starter Tom Candiotti lasted just 2.2 innings and allowed five earned runs before being lifted in favour of David Wells. The Twins would not need to score another run. The Blue Jays rallied for a run in the fourth and three runs in the sixth on five consecutive hits off Twins starter Jack Morris. Those four runs would be all Toronto could muster as they lost 5-4 at the Metrodome.

GAME #2: Toronto took an early lead as they jumped on Twins starter Kevin Tapani, scoring three times in the first three innings. Rookie Toronto starter Juan Guzman lasted 5.2 innings allowing four hits and just two earned runs before the ball was handed to the bullpen. Tom Henke and Duane Ward combined for 2.1 innings of shutout relief and six strikeouts. Devon White scored three of the five Toronto runs as the Blue Jays won their only 1991 ALCS game 5-2 in Minneapolis.

GAME #3: Joe Carter's first inning home run and a Candy Maldonado double put the Blue Jays ahead 2-0 until the sixth inning when the Twins were able to put their second run across the plate and tie the game at two apiece. Toronto starter Jimmy Key scattered five hits over six innings and allowed two earned runs. The game went into extra-innings

Post Season

and ended in dramatic fashion as Mike Pagliarulo, pinch hitting for Scott Leius, homered to right off of Blue Jays reliever Mike Timlin. Toronto was retired 1-2-3 in their half of the tenth as the Twins defeated Toronto 3-2 at SkyDome.

GAME #4: Blue Jays starter Todd Stottlemyre allowed seven hits in 3.2 innings before exiting with Toronto trailing 4-1. The Twins' Kirby Puckett hit his first home run of the series and Dan Gladden collected three RBI on three hits to pace Minnesota to a 9-3 win at SkyDome. It was Jack Morris' second win of the ALCS as he pitched eight innings allowing just two runs.

GAME #5: Kirby Puckett displayed his power once again as he homered in the first inning off Tom Candiotti to put the Twins ahead 1-0. Toronto put together three runs in the third and a pair in the fourth to go ahead 5-2. Minnesota was able to post three runs in their half of the sixth inning and tie the game at five. Duane Ward was handed the loss for Toronto as he allowed three runs in the eighth. Toronto was shutdown by five shutout innings of relief. Devon White, Roberto Alomar and Manuel Lee each collected a pair of hits in the losing effort as Minnesota took the American League crown with an 8-5 win.

GAME 1
at MINNESOTA
Tuesday, October 8 (night)

Toronto	0	0	0	1	0	3	0	0	0	4	9	3
Minnesota	2	2	1	0	0	0	0	0	X	5	11	3

CANDIOTTI, Wells (3), Timlin (6) and Borders
MORRIS, Wills (6), Aguilera (S)(8) and Harper, Ortiz (8)
T: 3:17 A: 54,766

GAME 2
at MINNESOTA
Wednesday, October 9 (day)

Toronto	1	0	2	0	0	0	2	0	0	5	9	0
Minnesota	0	0	1	0	0	1	0	0	0	2	5	1

GUZMAN, Henke (6), Ward (S)(8) and Borders
TAPANI, Bedrosian (7), Guthrie (7) and Harper
T: 3:02 A: 54,816

GAME 3
at TORONTO
Friday, October 11 (night)

Minnesota	0	0	0	0	1	1	0	0	0	1	3	7	0
Toronto	2	0	0	0	0	0	0	0	0		2	5	1

Erickson, West (5), Willis (7), GUTHRIE (9), Aguilera (S) and Ortiz, Harper (10)
Key, Wells (7), Henke (8), TIMLIN (10) and Borders
HR: Toronto (1) - Carter;
    Minnesota (1) - Pagliarulo
T: 3:36 A: 51,454

GAME 4
at TORONTO
Saturday, October 12 (night)

Minnesota	0	0	0	4	0	2	1	1	1	9	13	1
Toronto	0	1	0	0	0	1	0	0	1	3	11	2

MORRIS, Bedrosian (9) and Harper
STOTTLEMYRE, Wells (4), Acker (6), Timlin (7), MacDonald (9) and Borders
HR: Minnesota (1) - Puckett
T: 3:15 A: 51,526

GAME 5
at TORONTO
Sunday, October 13 (day)

Minnesota	1	1	0	0	0	3	0	3	0	8	14	2
Toronto	0	0	3	2	0	0	0	0	0	5	9	1

Tapani, WEST (5), Willis (8), Aguilera (S)(9) and Harper, Ortiz (9)
Candiotti, Timlin (6) WARD (6), Wells (8) and Borders
HR: Minnesota (1) - Puckett
T: 3:29 A: 51,425

SCORE BY INNINGS

Minnesota	3	3	2	4	1	7	1	4	1	1	27	50	4
Toronto	3	1	5	3	0	4	2	0	1	0	19	43	7

BATTER	AVG	G	AB	R	H	2B	3B	HR	RBI	SH-SF	HB	BB	SO	SB-CS	E
ALOMAR (T)	.474	5	19	3	9	0	0	0	4	2-0	0	2	3	2-0	0
ALOMAR (R)	.000	—	0	—	0	0	0	0	0	1-0	0	1	0	—	—
ALOMAR (L)	.474	—	19	—	9	0	0	0	4	1-0	0	1	3	—	—
BORDERS	.263	5	19	0	5	1	0	0	2	1-0	0	0	0	0-0	2
CARTER	.263	5	19	3	5	2	0	1	4	0-1	0	1	5	0-1	0
DUCEY	.000	1	1	0	0	0	0	0	0	0-0	0	0	0	0-0	0
GONZALES	.000	2	0	0	0	0	0	0	0	0-0	0	0	0	0-0	0
GRUBER	.286	5	21	1	6	1	0	0	4	0-0	0	0	4	1-0	3
LEE (T)	.125	5	16	3	2	0	0	0	0	0-0	0	1	5	0-0	1
LEE (R)	.000	—	3	—	0	0	0	0	0	0-0	0	0	0	—	—
LEE (L)	.154	—	13	—	2	0	0	0	0	0-0	0	1	5	—	—
MALDONADO	.100	5	20	1	2	1	0	0	1	0-0	0	1	6	0-0	0
MULLINIKS	.125	5	8	1	1	0	0	0	0	0-0	0	3	0	0-0	0
MYERS	.000	0	0	0	0	0	0	0	0	0-0	0	0	0	0-0	0
OLERUD	.158	5	19	1	3	0	0	0	3	0-0	0	3	1	0-0	0
SPRAGUE	.000	0	0	0	0	0	0	0	0	0-0	0	0	0	0-0	0
TABLER	.000	2	1	0	0	0	0	0	0	0-0	0	1	0	0-0	0
WHITE (T)	.364	5	22	5	8	1	0	0	0	0-0	0	2	3	3-0	0
WHITE (R)	.333	—	3	—	1	0	0	0	0	0-0	0	0	0	—	—
WHITE (L)	.368	—	19	—	7	1	0	0	0	0-0	0	0	0	—	—
WILSON (T)	.250	3	8	1	2	0	0	0	0	0-0	0	1	3	1-0	0
WILSON (R)	.000	—	1	—	0	0	0	0	0	0-0	0	1	1	—	—
WILSON (L)	.286	—	7	—	2	0	0	0	0	0-0	0	1	2	—	—
DH	.111	5	18	0	2	1	0	0	1	0-0	0	3	3	0-0	0
PITCHERS	.000	5	0	0	0	0	0	0	0	0-0	0	0	0	0-0	1
BLUE JAYS	.249	5	173	19	43	6	0	1	18	3-1	0	15	30	7-1	7
TWINS	.276	5	181	27	50	9	1	3	25	1-2	1	15	37	8-4	4

2-0 in WORLD SERIES PLAY

In 1992 the Toronto Blue Jays became the 10th franchise to win the World Series Championship in its 1st trip to the Fall Classic. Florida Marlins, in 1997, became the 11th.

In 1993 the Toronto Blue Jays won the World Series and became just the 4th team in history to go undefeated in their first two trips to the Fall Classic.

1903, 1912	Boston Red Sox
1906, 1917	Chicago White Sox
1920, 1948	Cleveland Indians
1992, 1993	Toronto Blue Jays

PITCHER	T	W-L	ERA	G	GS	CG	SHO	SV	IP	H	R	ER	HR	HB	BB	SO	WP
ACKER	R	0-0	0.00	1	0	0	0	0	0.2	1	0	0	0	0	0	1	0
CANDIOTTI	R	0-1	8.22	2	2	0	0	0	7.2	17	9	7	1	0	2	5	1
GUZMAN	R	1-0	3.18	1	1	0	0	0	5.2	4	2	2	0	0	4	2	1
HENKE	R	0-0	0.00	2	0	0	0	0	2.2	0	0	0	0	0	1	5	0
KEY	L	0-0	3.00	1	1	0	0	0	6.0	5	2	2	0	0	1	1	0
MacDONALD	L	0-0	9.00	1	0	0	0	0	1.0	1	1	1	0	0	1	0	0
STOTTLEMYRE	R	0-1	9.82	1	1	0	0	0	3.2	7	4	4	1	1	1	3	0
TIMLIN	R	0-1	3.18	4	0	0	0	0	5.2	5	4	2	1	0	2	5	0
WARD	R	0-1	6.23	2	0	0	0	1	4.1	4	3	3	0	0	1	6	0
WELLS	L	0-0	2.35	4	0	0	0	0	7.2	6	2	2	0	0	2	9	0
BLUE JAYS		1-4	4.60	5	5	0	0	1	45.0	50	27	23	3	1	15	37	2
TWINS		4-1	3.33	5	5	0	0	3	46.0	43	19	17	1	0	15	30	4

1992 AMERICAN LEAGUE CHAMPIONSHIP SERIES

TORONTO vs OAKLAND

GAME #1: Home runs were the story of the game as Oakland used three of them to beat the Blue Jays 4-3. The A's scored three runs in the second inning off Toronto starter Jack Morris on back-to-back homers by Mark McGwire and Terry Steinbach. The 3-0 lead stood until Pat Borders homered off Dave Stewart in the Blue Jays' fifth followed by a Dave Winfield homer in the sixth making the score 3-2. John Olerud tied the score at 3 in the bottom of the eighth with a two out single off reliever Jeff Russell scoring Winfield who had doubled in the previous at-bat. Harold Baines broke the tie with a solo shot to lead off the ninth and Dennis Eckersley shut down the Blue Jays in the home half of the ninth to seal the 4-3 Oakland victory.

GAME #2: The Blue Jays were able to rebound from a Game #1 loss as David Cone held the A's to just one run over 8.0 innings en route to a 3-1 win. Cone, the Major League's strikeout leader in 1992, fanned six as he collected his second career post-season victory. Mike Moore lasted seven innings in the losing effort for Oakland. Kelly Gruber doubled and hit a 2-run homer in the fifth which would prove to be the winning runs. Closer Tom Henke came on for the save in the ninth, his first ever post-season save.

GAME #3: For the first time since 1985 vs Kansas City, the Blue Jays put together a pair of wins in the post-season as they got past the A's 7-5. Toronto starter Juan Guzman notched his second career LCS win in 1992, lasting six inning before being lifted in favour of Duane Ward. Tom Henke earned his second save in as many games. Despite being out-hit 13-9 by the A's, 4 of Toronto's hits went for extra-bases including homers from Alomar (solo) and Maldonado (solo). The A's collected just 1 extra-base hit.

GAME #4: In what appeared at first to be a certain Oakland victory, the Toronto Blue Jays fought back to erase a five run deficit late in the game sending the game into extra-innings. Oakland batted around earning five runs in the third inning as they jumped on Toronto starter Jack Morris. The A's added another run in the sixth making the score 6-1. Toronto began their comeback in the top of the eighth as they strung together five consecutive hits. By the end of the inning, the score was 6-4. The A's were held off the board in the bottom of the eighth but in the top of the ninth, Devon White started off the inning with a single that was misplayed allowing White to get to third base. Roberto Alomar then homered off Dennis Eckersley to tie the game at 6-6. Toronto eventually won the game in the eleventh as they scored a run off Kelly Downs to win 7-6.

GAME #5: Oakland starter Dave Stewart held the Blue Jays in check for nine innings scattering seven hits, allowing just 2 runs as Oakland sent the series back to SkyDome. The complete game win was Stewart's first win of the 1992 post-season. The 6-2 loss for the Blue Jays ended their three game win streak. David Cone took the loss for Toronto. He lasted just 4.0 innings before Jimmy Key made his first appearance of the 1992 playoffs. Ruben Sierra homered and drove in 3 runs for the A's. Devon White notched 3 hits in the losing effort.

GAME #6: Toronto scored a pair of runs in the first on a Joe Carter homer off A's starter Mike Moore. The Blue Jays then added four more runs in the third including a Candy Maldonado 3-run homer to put Toronto ahead 6-0. Blue Jays' starter Juan Guzman went seven innings allowing just five hits and striking out eight before the ball was handed to Duane Ward in the eighth with the score Toronto 7, Oakland 1. The A's managed a run in the top of the ninth but the home town Blue Jays secured the win as Tom Henke tossed a perfect ninth sending Toronto to its first ever World Series with a 9-2 win over Oakland.

GAME 1
at TORONTO
Wednesday, October 7 (night)

											R	H	E
Oakland	0	3	0	0	0	0	0	1	4	6	1
Toronto	0	0	0	0	1	1	0	1	0	3	9	0

Stewart, RUSSELL (8), Eckersley (S)(9) and Steinbach
MORRIS and Borders
HR: Oakland (3) - McGwire, Steinbach, Baines;
    Toronto (2) - Borders, Winfield
T: 2:47   A: 51,039

GAME 2
at TORONTO
Thursday, October 8 (night)

											R	H	E
Oakland	0	0	0	0	0	0	0	1	1	6	0
Toronto	0	0	0	2	0	1	0	X	3	4	0

MOORE, Corsi (8), Parrett (8) and Steinbach
CONE, Henke (S)(9) and Borders
HR: Toronto (1) - Gruber
T: 2:58   A: 51,114

GAME 3
at OAKLAND
Saturday, October 10 (day)

											R	H	E
Toronto	0	1	0	1	1	0	2	1	1	7	9	1
Oakland	0	0	0	2	0	0	2	1	0	5	13	3

GUZMAN, Ward (7), Timlin (8), Henke (S)(9), and Borders
DARLING, Downs (7), Corsi (8), Russell (8), Honeycutt (9), Eckersley (9) and Steinbach
HR: Toronto (2) - Alomar, Maldonado
T: 3:40   A: 46,911

GAME 4
at OAKLAND
Sunday, October 11 (day)

											R	H	E
Toronto	0	1	0	0	0	0	3	2	0	1	7	17	4
Oakland	0	0	5	0	0	1	0	0	0	0	6	12	2

Morris, Stottlemyre (4), Timlin (8), WARD (9), Henke (S)(11) and Borders
Welch, Parrett (8), Eckersley (8), Corsi (9), DOWNS (10) and Steinbach
HR: Toronto (2) - Olerud, Alomar
T: 4:25   A: 47,732

```
Toronto    0 0 0  1 0 0  1 0 0   2 7 3          Oakland    0 0 0  0 0 1  0 1 0   2 7 1
Oakland    2 0 1  0 3 0  0 0 X   6 8 0          Toronto    2 0 4  0 1 0  0 2 X   9 13 0
```

CONE, Key (5), Eichhorn (8) and Borders
STEWART and Steinbach
HR: Oakland (1) - Sierra;
    Toronto (1) - Winfield
T: 2:51 A: 44,955

MOORE, Parrett (3), Honeycutt (5), Russell (7), Witt (8) and Steinbach
GUZMAN, Ward (8), Henke (9) and Borders
HR: Toronto (2) - Carter, Maldonado
T: 3:15 A: 51,335

SCORE BY INNINGS

Toronto	2 2 4	2 5 1	4 7 3	0 1	31	59	8
Oakland	2 3 6	2 3 2	2 2 2	0 0	24	52	7

BATTER	AVG	G	AB	R	H	2B	3B	HR	RBI	SH-SF	HB	BB	SO	SB-CS	E
ALOMAR (T)	.423	6	26	4	11	1	0	2	4	0-0	0	2	1	5-0	0
ALOMAR (R)	.000	–	2	–	0	0	0	0	0	0-0	0	0	0	–	–
ALOMAR (L)	.458	–	24	–	11	1	0	2	4	0-0	0	2	1	–	–
BELL	.000	2	0	1	0	0	0	0	0	0-0	0	1	0	0-0	0
BORDERS	.318	6	22	3	7	0	0	1	3	0-2	0	1	1	0-0	1
CARTER	.192	6	26	2	5	0	0	1	3	0-0	0	2	4	2-0	1
GRIFFIN (T)	.000	2	2	0	0	0	0	0	0	0-0	0	0	0	0-0	0
GRIFFIN (R)	.000	–	0	–	0	0	0	0	0	0-0	0	0	0	0-0	0
GRIFFIN (L)	.000	–	2	–	0	0	0	0	0	0-0	0	0	0	–	–
GRUBER	.091	6	22	3	2	1	0	1	2	1-0	0	2	3	0-0	1
LEE (T)	.278	6	18	2	5	1	1	0	3	0-1	0	1	2	0-0	3
LEE (R)	.000	–	1	–	0	0	0	0	0	0-0	0	0	0	–	–
LEE (L)	.294	–	17	–	5	1	1	0	3	0-1	0	1	2	–	–
MALDONADO	.273	6	22	3	6	0	0	2	6	0-0	0	3	4	0-1	0
OLERUD	.348	6	23	4	8	2	0	1	4	0-0	0	2	5	0-0	0
SPRAGUE	.500	2	2	0	1	0	0	0	0	0-0	0	0	1	0-0	0
WHITE (T)	.348	6	23	2	8	2	0	0	2	0-1	0	5	6	0-4	1
WHITE (R)	.000	–	2	–	0	0	0	0	0	0-0	0	0	1	–	–
WHITE (L)	.381	–	21	–	8	2	0	0	2	0-1	0	5	5	–	–
WINFIELD	.250	6	24	7	6	1	0	2	3	0-0	0	4	2	0-0	0
DH	.250	6	24	7	6	1	0	2	3	0-0	0	4	2	0-0	0
PITCHERS	.000	6	0	0	0	0	0	0	0	0-0	0	0	0	0-0	1
BLUE JAYS	.281	6	210	31	59	8	1	10	30	1-4	0	23	29	7-5	8
ATHLETICS	.251	6	207	24	52	5	1	4	23	3-2	0	24	33	16-2	7

PITCHER	T	W-L	ERA	G	GS	CG	SHO	SV	IP	H	R	ER	HR	HB	BB	SO	WP
CONE	R	1-1	3.00	2	2	0	0	0	12.0	11	7	4	1	0	5	9	0
EICHHORN	R	0-0	0.00	1	0	0	0	0	1.0	0	0	0	0	0	0	0	0
GUZMAN	R	2-0	2.08	2	2	0	0	0	13.0	12	3	3	0	1	5	11	0
HENKE	R	0-0	0.00	4	0	0	0	3	4.2	3	0	0	0	0	2	2	0
KEY	L	0-0	0.00	1	0	0	0	0	3.0	2	0	0	0	0	2	1	0
MORRIS	R	0-1	6.57	2	2	1	0	0	12.1	11	9	9	3	0	9	6	1
STOTTLEMYRE	R	0-0	2.45	1	0	0	0	0	3.2	3	1	1	0	0	1	1	0
TIMLIN	R	0-0	6.75	2	0	0	0	0	1.1	4	1	1	0	0	1	1	0
WARD	R	1-0	6.75	3	0	0	0	0	4.0	6	3	3	0	0	1	2	0
WELLS	L	0-0	–	1	0	0	0	0	0.0	0	0	0	0	0	0	0	0
BLUE JAYS		4-2	3.44	6	6	1	0	3	55.0	52	24	21	4	1	24	33	1
ATHLETICS		2-4	4.50	6	6	1	0	1	54.0	59	31	27	10	0	23	29	3

1992 WORLD SERIES

TORONTO vs ATLANTA

GAME #1: In the first game of the 89th World Series, the Blue Jays suffered a 3-1 loss to the Atlanta Braves. Home runs were the story of the game as Toronto took an early 1-0 lead in the fourth on a Joe Carter solo homer off starter Tom Glavine. It would be the only run Toronto would score. Jack Morris continued his shutout innings streak vs the Braves extending it to 18.0 innings until a 3-run homer by catcher Damon Berryhill in the sixth inning ended the streak. Glavine went the distance for the Braves becoming the first pitcher to toss a complete game in a World Series opener since Jack Morris accomplished the feat in 1984 vs San Diego.

GAME #2: Reserve catcher Ed Sprague proved to be the hero for the Blue Jays on this night at Fulton County Stadium. David Cone lasted just 4.1 innings allowing 4 runs over that span before exiting in favour of David Wells. Cone also contributed at the plate with a pair of hits and an RBI. His two hits marked the first two hit game by an AL pitcher in the World Series since Mickey Lolitch went 2-4 on October 3, 1968. Heading into the eighth inning, the Blue Jays trailed 4-2. After a run in the top of the eighth Toronto entered the ninth inning trailing by 1. After a Pat Borders fly out, rookie Derek Bell (pinch hitting for Lee) walked. Ed Sprague then pinch hitting for the pitcher Duane Ward knocked a first pitch offering from Jeff Reardon over the left field fence to put the

Blue Jays ahead 5-4. Tom Henke was able to retire the Braves in the bottom of the ninth for the save.

GAME #3: The game marked the first time the World Series had been played outside of the United States as the series moved to SkyDome. In another pitching duel, Steve Avery and Juan Guzman both went 8.0 innings. Atlanta was kept off the board in the fourth with a splendid defensive effort by Devon White. White ran down a deep drive off the bat of Dave Justice that sent Devon into the wall to make the catch. White returned the ball to the infield where Pendleton was doubled-up off first. The Blue Jays drew first blood in the fourth inning as Joe Carter connected for his second homer of the series, a solo shot putting Toronto ahead 1-0. In the sixth inning, the Braves rallied to tie things at 1-1. Each team traded runs in the eighth keeping the game knotted at 2-2. The Braves attempted a rally as Duane Ward came on to pitch the ninth. But after a key double play and a strikeout the inning was over. In the home half of the ninth, Roberto Alomar started the inning off with a leadoff single. After stealing second and a Dave Winfield sacrifice, Alomar stood at third with one out. Jeff Reardon came in to try to halt the Blue Jays' advance but Candy Maldonado with the bases loaded, hit a 2-strike pitch to right centre for a base hit allowing Alomar to score the winning run.

GAME #4: In what was the third consecutive 1-run game of the 1992 World Series, the Blue Jays posted a 2-1 win behind a strong pitching effort from starter Jimmy Key. Key went 7.2 innings allowing just 5 hits and 1 earned run while striking out six Braves batters. Toronto earned their first run in the third inning as catcher Pat Borders continued on his post season hit streak with a single homer to left. Toronto made the score 2-0 in the seventh when Devon White drove in Kelly Gruber from second base. Atlanta managed to score a run in their half of the eighth as Ron Gant led off with a double and eventually scored on a Mark Lemke groundout. Tom Henke came in to pitch the ninth for Toronto and tacked up a 1-2-3 inning for his second save of the series.

GAME #5: The game began in similar fashion as the previous four. Entering the fifth inning, the game was tied at 2-2. The Braves had collected a run in the first and fourth inning while the Blue Jays captured runs in the second and fourth. The fifth inning proved to be Atlanta's inning as they crossed the plate five times to seal the victory and send the series back to Atlanta for at least one more game. The fifth inning began for the Braves with 2 consecutive routine outs. An Otis Nixon single started the ball rolling and the Braves eventually loaded the bases on Toronto starter Jack Morris. Lonnie Smith stepped up to the plate and sent Morris' 1-2 offering over the right field wall for a grand slam making the score 7-2. The score remained the same over the final four innings making a winner out of John Smoltz.

GAME #6: The Toronto Blue Jays make history as they capture their first ever World Series and bring the Commissioner's Trophy outside of the United States for the first time. The 11-inning game began with the Blue Jays scoring in their first inning of the game. Devon White led off the game with a single off starter Steve Avery. After a stolen base and a ground out by Alomar, White stood on third. Carter then drove in White with a sacrifice fly. Atlanta answered the call in their half of the third as Deon Sanders scored Atlanta's fourth run of the series. Toronto returned the favour immediately as they regained the lead with a run in the top of the fourth on a Maldonado lead off homer. The score remained that way until the bottom of the ninth when Atlanta shortstop Jeff Blauser tied the game sending it into extra-innings. The tenth inning proved to be uneventful. In the eleventh, the Blue Jays led off with Jimmy Key popping out for out number 1. Devon White was hit by a Charlie Leibrandt offering. Alomar then singled to centre allowing White to move up to second. With two out, Dave Winfield stepped up to the plate and doubled down the left-field line allowing White and Alomar to score making it 4-2 Toronto. Atlanta was able to score once with Jimmy Key on the mound. Mike Timlin then came in to pitch for the Blue Jays with pinch runner Smoltz on third and two out... Otis Nixon attempted a drag bunt up the first base line, that was fielded by Timlin who threw to Carter at first in time for the final out.

GAME 1
at ATLANTA
Saturday, October 17 (night)

											R	H	E
Toronto	0	0	0		1	0	0		0	0	1	4	0
Atlanta	0	0	0		0	0	3		0	0	X	3	4	0

MORRIS, Stottlemyre (7), Wells (8) and Borders
GLAVINE and Berryhill
HR: Toronto (1) - Carter;
　　Atlanta (1) - Berryhill
T: 2:37　A: 51,763

GAME 2
at ATLANTA
Sunday, October 18 (night)

											R	H	E
Toronto	0	0	0		0	2	0		0	1	2	5	9	2
Atlanta	0	1	0		1	2	0		0	0	0	4	5	1

Cone, Wells (5), Stottlemyre (7), WARD (8), Henke (S)(9) and Borders
Smoltz, Stanton (8), REARDON (8) and Berryhill
HR: Toronto (1) - Sprague
T: 3:30　A: 51,763

GAME 3
at TORONTO
Tuesday, October 20 (night)

											R	H	E
Atlanta	0	0	0		0	0	1		0	1	0	2	9	0
Toronto	0	0	0		1	0	0		0	1	1	3	6	1

AVERY, Wholers (9), Stanton (9), Reardon (9) and Berryhill
Guzman, WARD (9) and Borders
HR: Toronto (2) - Carter, Gruber
T: 2:49　A: 51,813

GAME 4
at TORONTO
Wednesday, October 21 (night)

											R	H	E
Atlanta	0	0	0		0	0	0		1	0		1	5	0
Toronto	0	0	1		0	0	0		1	0	X	2	6	0

GLAVINE and Berryhill
KEY, Ward (8), Henke (S)(9) and Borders
HR: Toronto (1) - Borders
T: 2:21　A: 52,090

GAME 5
at TORONTO
Thursday, October 22 (night)

											R	H	E
Atlanta	1	0	0		1	5	0		0	0	0	7	13	0
Toronto	0	1	0		1	0	0		0	0	0	2	6	0

SMOLTZ, Stanton (S)(7) and Berryhill
MORRIS, Wells (5), Timlin (7), Eichhorn (8), Stottlemyre (9) and Borders
HR: Atlanta (2) - Justice, L. Smith
T: 3:05　A: 52,268

GAME 6
at ATLANTA
Saturday, October 24 (night)

												R	H	E
Toronto	1	0	0		1	0	0		0	0	0	2	4	14	1
Atlanta	0	0	1		0	0	0		0	0	1	0	1	3	8	1

Cone, Stottlemyre (7), Wells (7), Ward (8), Henke (9), KEY (10), Timlin (S)(11) and Borders
Avery, P.Smith (5), Stanton (8), Wholers (9), LEIBRANDT (10) and Berryhill
HR: Toronto (1) - Maldonado
T: 4:07　A: 51,763

SCORE BY INNINGS

												R	H	E
Toronto	1	1	1		4	2	0		1	2	3	0	2	17	45	4
Atlanta	1	1	1		2	7	4		0	2	1	0	1	20	44	2

BATTER	AVG	G	AB	R	H	2B	3B	HR	RBI	SH-SF	HB	BB	SO	SB-CS	E
ALOMAR (T)	.208	6	24	3	5	1	0	0	0	0-0	0	3	3	3-0	0
ALOMAR (R)	.188	–	16	–	3	0	0	0	0	0-0	0	1	3	–	–
ALOMAR (L)	.250	–	8	–	2	1	0	0	0	0-0	0	2	0	–	–
BELL	.000	2	1	1	0	0	0	0	0	0-0	0	1	0	0-0	0
BORDERS	.450	6	20	2	9	3	0	1	3	0-0	0	2	1	0-0	1
CARTER	.273	6	22	2	6	2	0	2	3	0-1	0	3	2	0-0	0
GRIFFIN	.000	2	0	0	0	0	0	0	0	0-0	0	0	0	0-0	1
GRUBER	.105	6	19	2	2	0	0	1	1	1-0	0	2	5	1-0	1
LEE (T)	.105	6	19	1	2	0	0	0	0	0-0	0	1	2	0-0	1
LEE (R)	.000	–	13	–	0	0	0	0	0	0-0	0	0	1	–	–
LEE (L)	.333	–	6	–	2	0	0	0	0	0-0	0	1	1	–	–
MALDONADO	.158	6	19	1	3	0	0	1	2	0-0	0	2	5	0-0	0
OLERUD	.308	4	13	2	4	0	0	0	0	0-0	0	4	0	0-0	0
SPRAGUE	.500	3	2	1	1	0	0	1	2	0-0	0	1	0	0-0	0
TABLER	.000	2	2	0	0	0	0	0	0	0-0	0	0	0	0-0	0
WHITE (T)	.231	6	26	2	6	1	0	0	2	0-0	1	0	6	1-0	0
WHITE (R)	.294	–	17	–	5	1	0	0	1	0-0	1	0	3	–	–
WHITE (L)	.111	–	9	–	1	0	0	0	1	0-0	0	0	3	–	–
WINFIELD	.227	6	22	0	5	1	0	0	3	1-0	0	2	3	0-0	0
CONE	.500	2	4	0	2	0	0	0	1	0-0	0	1	0	0-0	0
KEY	.000	2	1	0	0	0	0	0	0	0-0	0	0	0	0-0	0
MORRIS	.000	2	2	0	0	0	0	0	0	0-0	0	0	2	0-0	0
DH	.200	6	10	0	2	0	0	0	0	1-0	0	1	2	0-0	0
PITCHERS	.286	6	7	0	2	0	0	0	1	0-0	0	1	2	0-0	0
BLUE JAYS	.230	6	196	17	45	8	0	6	17	2-1	1	18	33	5-0	4
BRAVES	.220	6	200	20	44	6	0	3	19	2-2	1	20	48	15-3	2

PITCHER	T	W-L	ERA	G	GS	CG	SHO	SV	IP	H	R	ER	HR	HB	BB	SO	WP
CONE	R	0-0	3.48	2	2	0	0	0	10.1	9	5	4	0	0	8	8	1
EICHHORN	R	0-0	0.00	1	0	0	0	0	1.0	0	0	0	0	0	0	1	0
GUZMAN	R	0-0	1.13	1	1	0	0	0	8.0	8	2	1	0	0	1	7	0
HENKE	R	0-0	2.70	3	0	0	0	2	3.1	2	1	1	0	1	2	1	0
KEY	L	2-0	1.00	2	1	0	0	0	9.0	6	2	1	0	0	0	6	0
MORRIS	R	0-2	8.44	2	2	0	0	0	10.2	13	10	10	3	0	6	12	1
STOTTLEMYRE	R	0-0	0.00	4	0	0	0	0	3.2	4	0	0	0	0	0	4	0
TIMLIN	R	0-0	0.00	2	0	0	0	1	1.1	0	0	0	0	0	0	0	0
WARD	R	2-0	0.00	4	0	0	0	0	3.1	1	0	0	0	0	1	6	1
WELLS	L	0-0	0.00	4	0	0	0	0	4.1	1	0	0	0	0	2	3	0
BLUE JAYS		4-2	2.78	6	6	0	0	3	55.0	44	20	17	3	1	20	48	3
BRAVES		2-4	2.65	6	6	2	0	1	54.1	45	17	16	6	1	18	33	2

1993 AMERICAN LEAGUE CHAMPIONSHIP SERIES

TORONTO vs CHICAGO

GAME #1: The Blue Jays took a 2-0 lead in the fourth inning when third baseman Ed Sprague tripled to right field with Olerud and Molitor on base. Chicago then used their half of the fourth inning to produce three runs on two hits as they sent nine men to the plate. Toronto starting pitcher Juan Guzman managed to hold the White Sox in check for six innings but walked 8 batters and stranded 11 Chicago runners before exiting with a 5-3 lead. Jack McDowell lasted 6.2 innings allowing thirteen hits and all seven Toronto runs before the White Sox relief corps came on to hold Toronto for the remainder of the game. Danny Cox worked a shutout seventh and eighth allowing a single by Ozzie Guillen. Duane Ward came out for the ninth and walked the first two batters before striking out the side to end the Chicago threat.

GAME #2: Both clubs scored once in the first inning but it was the Blue Jays that would prevail as their two-run fourth inning provided the edge. The 3-1 win saw Toronto take a two games to none lead in the best of seven games series. The fourth inning started with a pair of outs by Carter and Olerud. Paul Molitor doubled off starter Alex Fernandez. Next, Tony Fernandez singled to score Molitor and moved to second on the throw home. After an intentional walk to Ed Sprague, Pat Borders singled to second base but Joey Cora threw the ball away allowing the third Toronto run to score. Dave Stewart worked six strong innings surrendering just four hits (all singles) and one run for his seventh career ALCS win against no losses. Al Leiter was credited with a hold as he pitched the seventh and eighth innings before closer Duane Ward came in to save the game in the ninth.

GAME #3: Nineteen game winner, Pat Hentgen started for Toronto but could not collect a win on this day as Toronto suffered their worst defeat of the series losing 6-1. The Blue Jays were able to hold off the White Sox attack until the third inning when they sent 10 players to the plate and combined for five runs on five singles. Hentgen lasted just three innings plus 2 batters before he was removed in favour of Danny Cox. Toronto scored their lone run in the bottom of the third as Rickey Henderson scored from third on a Devon White single. Wilson Alvarez, the Chicago starter pitched a complete game for his first career ALCS victory. He permitted just seven hits while issuing two walks and striking out six. Tim Raines provided most of the offensive support for Chicago going 4-5 with a run scored.

GAME #4: A two run home run by centre fielder Lance Johnson in the second inning gave the White Sox a 2-0 lead over Toronto. The light hitting Johnson had not hit a home run since the 1992 regular season. Todd Stottlemyre, making his first start of the 1993 ALCS lasted six innings for the home team but failed to hold onto a 3-2 lead that was handed to him in the third when Toronto batted around on rookie starter Jason Bere. The right hander lasted just 2.1 innings before being pulled in favour of Tim Belcher. Stottlemyre allowed three more Chicago runs in the sixth including a Frank Thomas solo homer and a Lance Johnson triple before departing. Roberto Alomar doubled home Henderson in the bottom of the sixth to cut the Chisox lead to one (5-4) but the visiting White Sox notched a single run off Al Leiter in the seventh and another run off Mike Timlin in the ninth to seal the win by a 7-4 margin.

GAME #5: As was the case with each of the previous four games, the team that scored first emerged victorious. This time, Toronto scored first when Rickey Henderson crossed the plate in the first inning after leading off the game with a double and a stolen base. Starting pitcher Jack McDowell allowed a Toronto run in the second and third before being lifted following just 2.1 innings. Meanwhile, Blue Jays starter Juan Guzman cruised through the first 4.1 innings without allowing a hit or a walk until Ellis Burks went deep to left field for what would be the only blemish on Guzman's slate that afternoon. He lasted seven innings permitting just two hits while walking one and striking out six. Roberto Alomar reached base in all five plate appearances (3 hits, 2 walks) to lead the Toronto attack. Tony Castillo worked a scoreless eighth allowing a single and a base on balls. Duane Ward had some difficulty in the ninth. He struck out Joey Cora and Frank Thomas following a single to lead off the inning by Raines. He then issued a two run homer to Robin Ventura that brought Chicago within two. With the tying run at the plate, Ward struck out Bo Jackson to end the game and preserve the 5-3 Toronto win.

GAME #6: With his 7-0 record in ALCS play on the line, Blue Jays' starter Dave Stewart provided the win which put Toronto into their second consecutive World Series as the Blue Jays won 6-3 over Chicago. Toronto scored first with a pair of runs in the second inning as a 2-out single by catcher Pat Borders off Alex Fernandez cashed in John Olerud and Paul Molitor. The White Sox tied the game in the third inning when a bases loaded walk by Frank Thomas and a fielder's choice by Robin Ventura scored two runs. Stewart managed to restrict the Chisox to just 4 hits and 2 earned runs before handing Duane Ward a 3-2 lead after 7.1 innings. Ward struck out the final two batters to end the eighth. Toronto added to their lead as Devon White homered off reliever Scott Radinsky to make the score 4-2. Toronto added two more runs before the inning was over as Paul Molitor tripled to centre. Duane Ward allowed his second home run of the series as Warren Newson hit a solo shot in the bottom of the ninth but that was all the scoring that the Pale Hose would achieve as the Blue Jays were crowned American League Champions for the second straight season.

GAME 1
at CHICAGO
Tuesday, October 5 (night)

Toronto	0	0	0	2	3	0	2	0	0	7	17	1
Chicago	0	0	0	3	0	0	0	0	0	3	6	1

GUZMAN, Cox (7), Ward (9) and Borders
McDOWELL, DeLeon (7), Radinsky (8), McCaskill (9) and Karkovice
HR: Toronto (1) - Molitor
T: 3:38 A: 46,246

GAME 2
at CHICAGO
Wednesday, October 6 (day)

Toronto	1	0	0	2	0	0	0	0	0	3	8	0
Chicago	1	0	0	0	0	0	0	0	0	1	7	2

STEWART, Leiter (7), Ward (S)(9) and Borders
A. FERNANDEZ, Hernandez (9), Karkovice and LaValliere (7)
T: 3:00 A: 46,101

GAME 3
at TORONTO
Friday, October 8 (night)

Chicago	0	0	5	1	0	0	0	0	0	6	12	0
Toronto	0	0	1	0	0	0	0	0	0	1	7	1

ALVAREZ and Karkovice
HENTGEN, Cox (4), Eichhorn (7), Castillo (9) and Borders
T: 2:56 A: 51,783

GAME 4
at TORONTO
Saturday, October 9 (night)

Chicago	0	2	0	0	0	3	1	0	1	7	11	0
Toronto	0	0	3	0	0	1	0	0	0	4	9	0

Bere, BELCHER (3), McKaskill (7), Radinsky (8), Hernandez (S)(9) and Karkovice
STOTTLEMYRE, Leiter (7), Timlin (7) and Borders
HR: Chicago (2) - Johnson, Thomas
T: 3:30 A: 51,889

GAME 5
at TORONTO
Sunday, October 10 (day)

Chicago	0	0	0	0	1	0	0	0	2	3	5	1
Toronto	1	1	1	0	0	1	0	1	X	5	14	0

McDOWELL, DeLeon (3), Radinsky (7), Hernandez (7) and Karkovice
GUZMAN, Castillo (8), Ward (9) and Borders
HR: Chicago (2) - Ventura, Burks
T: 3:09 A: 51,375

GAME 6
at CHICAGO
Tuesday, October 12 (night)

Toronto	0	2	0	1	0	0	0	0	3	6	10	0
Chicago	0	0	2	0	0	0	0	0	1	3	5	3

STEWART, Ward (S)(8), LaValliere and Karkovice (8)
A. FERNANDEZ, McCaskill (8), Radinsky (9), Hernandez (9) and Borders
HR: Toronto (1) - White; Chicago (1) - Newson
T: 3:31 A: 45,527

SCORE BY INNINGS

Toronto	2	3	5	6	3	1	3	0	3	26	65	2
Chicago	1	2	7	4	1	3	1	0	4	23	46	7

BATTER	AVG	G	AB	R	H	2B	3B	HR	RBI	SH-SF	HB	BB	SO	SB-CS	E
ALOMAR (T)	.292	6	24	3	7	1	0	0	4	0-0	0	4	3	4-0	0
ALOMAR (R)	.200	–	5	–	1	0	0	0	0	0-0	0	1	0	–	–
ALOMAR (L)	.316	–	19	–	6	1	0	0	4	0-0	0	3	3	–	–
BORDERS	.250	6	24	1	6	1	0	0	3	0-0	0	0	6	1-0	0
BUTLER	.000	0	0	0	0	0	0	0	0	0-0	0	0	0	0-0	0
CANATE	.000	0	0	0	0	0	0	0	0	0-0	0	0	0	0-0	0
CARTER	.259	6	27	2	7	0	0	0	2	0-0	0	1	5	0-0	0
COLES	.000	0	0	0	0	0	0	0	0	0-0	0	0	0	0-0	0
FERNANDEZ (T)	.318	6	22	1	7	0	0	0	1	1-0	0	2	4	0-0	0
FERNANDEZ (R)	.500	–	4	–	2	0	0	0	0	0-0	0	0	1	–	–
FERNANDEZ (L)	.278	–	18	–	5	0	0	0	1	1-0	0	2	3	–	–
GRIFFIN (T)	.000	0	0	0	0	0	0	0	0	0-0	0	0	0	0-0	0
GRIFFIN (R)	.000	–	0	–	0	0	0	0	0	0-0	0	0	0	–	–
GRIFFIN (L)	.000	–	0	–	0	0	0	0	0	0-0	0	0	0	–	–
HENDERSON	.120	6	25	4	3	2	0	0	0	0-0	0	4	5	2-1	1
KNORR	.000	0	0	0	0	0	0	0	0	0-0	0	0	0	0-0	0
MOLITOR	.391	6	23	7	9	2	1	1	5	0-0	1	3	3	0-0	0
OLERUD	.348	6	23	5	8	1	0	0	3	0-0	1	4	1	0-0	1
SCHOFIELD	.000	0	0	0	0	0	0	0	0	0-0	0	0	0	0-0	0
SPRAGUE	.286	6	21	0	6	0	1	0	5	0-1	0	2	4	0-0	0
WHITE (T)	.444	6	27	3	12	1	1	1	2	0-0	0	1	5	0-1	0
WHITE (R)	.333	–	6	–	2	0	0	1	2	0-0	0	0	0	–	–
WHITE (L)	.476	–	21	–	10	1	1	0	0	0-0	0	1	5	–	–
DH	.391	6	23	7	9	2	1	1	5	0-0	1	3	3	0-0	0
PITCHERS	.000	6	0	0	0	0	0	0	0	0-0	0	0	0	0-0	0
BLUE JAYS	.301	6	216	26	65	8	3	2	24	1-1	2	21	36	7-2	2
WHITE SOX	.237	6	194	23	46	5	1	5	22	5-1	3	32	43	3-2	7

Post Season

PITCHER	T	W-L	ERA	G	GS	CG	SHO	SV	IP	H	R	ER	HR	HB	BB	SO	WP
CASTILLO	L	0-0	0.00	2	0	0	0	0	2.0	0	0	0	0	0	1	1	0
COX	R	0-0	0.00	2	0	0	0	0	5.0	3	0	0	0	0	2	5	0
EICHHORN	R	0-0	0.00	1	0	0	0	0	2.0	1	0	0	0	0	1	1	0
GUZMAN	R	2-0	2.08	2	2	0	0	0	13.0	8	4	3	1	1	9	9	3
HENTGEN	R	0-1	18.00	1	1	0	0	0	3.0	9	6	6	0	0	2	3	0
LEITER	L	0-0	3.38	2	0	0	0	0	2.2	4	1	1	0	0	2	2	0
STEWART	R	2-0	2.03	2	2	0	0	0	13.1	8	3	3	0	1	8	8	2
STOTTLEMYRE	R	0-1	7.50	1	1	0	0	0	6.0	6	5	5	2	0	4	4	0
TIMLIN	R	0-0	3.86	1	0	0	0	0	2.1	3	1	1	0	0	0	2	0
WARD	R	0-0	5.79	4	0	0	0	2	4.2	4	3	3	2	1	3	8	0
BLUE JAYS		4-2	3.67	6	6	0	0	2	54.0	46	23	22	5	3	32	43	5
WHITE SOX		2-4	3.57	6	6	1	0	1	53.0	65	26	21	2	2	21	36	2

1993 WORLD SERIES

TORONTO vs PHILADELPHIA

GAME #1: For the first time in baseball annals, the World Series began on Canadian soil. The Blue Jays fell behind 2-0 in the first inning as the Phillies' catcher Darren Daulton singled home a pair of runs off starting pitcher Juan Guzman. After holding Philadelphia in check in the top of the second, Toronto rallied with two runs of their own on four singles off Curt Schilling. Both teams traded solo runs in the third and fifth to keep the score knotted at 4-4. With 1 out in the bottom of the sixth, John Olerud took a first pitch offering from Schilling over the right field fence for a solo home run putting Toronto ahead by one. Toronto scored what would prove to be the winning run in the bottom of the seventh as four consecutive hits by Borders, Henderson, White and Alomar produced an 8-4 lead heading into the eighth. Al Leiter, who would prove to be the winning pitcher, relieved Guzman to start the sixth and held the Phillies scoreless over 2.2 innings before turning the ball over to closer Duane Ward. Ward surrendered a run in the ninth inning as a Jim Eisenreich single scored John Kruk who had led off the frame with a single and moved to second on an error. Ricky Jordan flied out to Joe Carter for the last out to put Toronto ahead 1 game to 0 with the 8-5 win.

GAME #2: The big inning would prove to be the Philly advantage on this night as a Jim Eisenreich three run homer in the top of the third capped a five run inning that saw eight Philadelphia batters step up to the plate. Toronto starter and eventual loser, Dave Stewart lasted six innings with all five earned runs coming in that third frame. Toronto answered the Philly onslaught with a pair of runs in the bottom of the fourth as Joe Carter connected for his first of two World Series home runs. Philadelphia starter Terry Mulholland would allow just three runs over 5.2 innings before handing the ball to the bullpen. Lenny Dykstra led off the seventh inning with a solo homer off reliever Tony Castillo to stretch the Philly lead to 3 as the visitors were now ahead 6-3. Toronto scored one run in the eighth as Molitor led off with a double and eventually scored on an Olerud sac fly. Philly relievers Roger Mason (1.2 innings) and Mitch Williams (1 innings) closed out the game to preserve the 6-4 win and even the series.

GAME #3: The venue moved from SkyDome to Veteran's Stadium in Philadelphia for games three, four and five. This game featured solid pitching by the Blue Jays combined with a potent offence. The visiting Blue Jays jumped on Philly starter Danny Jackson in the top of the first as Paul Molitor drove home a pair of runs with a triple. He would also score as Carter lifted a sacrifice fly to right field. Molitor added a solo homer in the third to make it 4-0. Starting pitcher Pat Hentgen pitched six innings allowing just one run- that coming in the sixth as a two-out single by Eisenreich scored John Kruk who had reached base via a walk. Blue Jays added another run in the top of the sixth as Roberto Alomar scored on a sac fly after having reached base on a single and stealing second and third. Toronto continued to add to their lead as they scored three more runs in the seventh off reliever Ben Rivera. Roberto Alomar finished the night with a 4-hit game while Molitor had three hits, three runs and three RBI. Duane Ward surrendered a solo homer to Milt Thompson in the ninth to make the final score Toronto 10, Philadelphia 3.

GAME #4: In a slugfest, the Blue Jays put together one of the wildest comebacks in World Series history to beat the Phillies 15-14 and take a three games to one lead. Toronto

opened the scoring with three in the first off Philly starter Tommy Greene. But the home team would take advantage of four first inning walks by starter Todd Stottlemyre as they scored four runs in the first inning to move ahead 4-3. Philadelphia added two more runs to their tally as Lenny Dykstra connected for his second homer of the series, a 2-run shot in the second. The Blue Jays batted around in the third and collected four runs and sent Tommy Greene to the bench in favour of Roger Mason. Philadelphia then posted a five run fifth that included home runs from Dykstra and Daulton to extend their lead 12-7. Toronto countered with two runs in the top of the sixth as White and Alomar scored on a single and a ground out. The Phillies added a run in the sixth and one in the seventh to make the score 14-9. The Phillies relief corps could not hold Toronto from making a comeback. In the top of the eighth, the Blue Jays sent ten players to the plate. Devon White's triple with two out scored Pat Borders to tie the game and Rickey Henderson to put Toronto ahead 15-14. Mike Timlin, started the eighth and struck out the first two batters he faced before Duane Ward came on to strikeout Dykstra to end the inning. In the ninth Ward hurled a 1-2-3 inning for his second save of the series in a game that took 4 hours and 14 minutes to play and was the highest scoring game in World Series history. Tony Fernandez had five RBI in the game and White had four.

GAME #5: Curt Schilling shutout Toronto 2-0 in what was the second ever shutout of Toronto in the post season. Pitted against Blue Jays ace Juan Guzman, he allowed just five hits (all singles) and struck out six Toronto batters for his first World Series win. The Phillies scored the only run they would need in the first inning when Dykstra, who had walked to lead off the game, scored on a John Kruk groundout. They added a second run in the very next inning as a pair of doubles cashed in Daulton. In the eighth, the Blue Jays threatened with a pair of runners on base but a strikeout by White followed by an Alomar ground out ended their attempt. Guzman was equal to the challenge as he went seven innings allowing both Philly runs while fanning six. The win sent the series back to Toronto with the Blue Jays holding a 3-2 edge.

GAME #6: Toronto started their quest for a second straight World Series Championship early as they notched three runs off Philly starter Terry Mulholland in the bottom of the first. A run in the fourth and a solo home run by Molitor in the fifth put Toronto up 5-1. Dave Stewart, the Toronto starter held the Phillies to just one run over his first six innings. In the seventh he surrendered a three run homer to Lenny Dykstra- his fourth of the series. That led to Stewart being pulled from the game. Reliever Danny Cox came in with none out and surrendered two more runs before the Phillies were halted by Al Leiter. The damage had been done and Philadelphia was now leading 6-5. After leaving the bases loaded in the eighth, Toronto made World Series history by erasing a 1-run lead in the bottom of the ninth. Mitch Williams came in to start the inning and he walked Rickey Henderson who led off. After a Devon White fly out, Molitor singled to centre to put runners at first and second. Right fielder Joe Carter then stepped up to the plate. On a 2-2 offering from Williams, Carter homered over the left field wall for a three run home run and propelled Toronto to its second consecutive World Series Championship with an 8-6 win.

GAME 1
at TORONTO
Saturday, October 16 (night)

											R	H	E
Philadelphia	2	0	1	0	1	0	0	0	1	5	11	1
Toronto	0	2	1	0	1	1	3	0	X	8	10	3

SCHILLING, West (7), Andersen (7), Mason (8) and Daulton
Guzman, LEITER (6), Ward (S)(8) and Borders
HR: Toronto (2) - White, Olerud
T: 3:27   A: 52,011

GAME 2
at TORONTO
Sunday, October 17 (night)

											R	H	E
Philadelphia	0	0	5	0	0	0	1	0	0	6	12	0
Toronto	0	0	0	2	0	1	0	1	0	4	8	0

MULHOLLAND, Mason (6), Williams (S)(8) and Daulton
STEWART, Castillo (7), Eichhorn (8), Timlin (8) and Borders
HR: Philadelphia (2) - Dykstra, Eisenreich;
Toronto (1) - Carter
T: 3:35   A: 52,062

GAME 3
at PHILADELPHIA
Tuesday, October 19 (night)

											R	H	E
Toronto	3	0	1	0	0	1	3	0	2	10	13	1
Philadelphia	0	0	0	0	1	0	1	0	1	3	9	0

HENTGEN, Cox (7), Ward (9), and Borders
JACKSON, Rivera (6), Thigpen (7), Anderson (9) and Daulton
HR: Toronto (1) - Molitor;
Philadelphia (1) - Thompson
T: 3:16   A: 62,689

GAME 4
at PHILADELPHIA
Wednesday, October 20 (night)

											R	H	E
Toronto	3	0	4	0	0	2	0	6	0	15	18	0
Philadelphia	4	2	0	1	5	1	1	0	0	14	14	0

Stottlemyre, Leiter (3), CASTILLO (5), Timlin (8), Ward (S)(8) and Borders
Greene, Mason (3), West (6), Andersen (7), WILLIAMS (8), Thigpen (9)
and Daulton
HR: Philadelphia (3) - Dykstra (2), Daulton
T: 4:14   A: 62,731

GAME 5
at PHILADELPHIA
Thursday, October 21 (night)

											R	H	E
Toronto	0	0	0	0	0	0	0	0	0	0	5	1
Philadelphia	1	1	0	0	0	0	0	0	X	2	5	1

GUZMAN, Cox (8) and Borders, Knorr (8)
SCHILLING and Daulton
T: 2:53   A: 62,706

GAME 6
at TORONTO
Saturday, October 23 (night)

											R	H	E
Philadelphia	0	0	0	1	0	0	5	0	0	6	7	0
Toronto	3	0	0	1	1	0	0	0	3	8	10	2

Mulholland, Mason (6), West (8), Andersen (8), WILLIAMS (9) and Daulton
Stewart, Cox (7), Leiter (7), WARD (9) and Borders
HR: Philadelphia (1) - Dykstra;
Toronto (2) - Molitor, Carter
T: 3:27   A: 52,195

SCORE BY INNINGS

	1	2	3	4	5	6	7	8	9	R	H	E
Toronto	9	2	6	3	2	5	6	7	5	45	64	7
Philadelphia	7	3	6	2	6	2	8	0	2	36	58	2

BATTER	AVG	G	AB	R	H	2B	3B	HR	RBI	SH-SF	HB	BB	SO	SB-CS	E
ALOMAR (T)	.480	6	25	5	12	2	1	0	6	0-0	0	2	3	4-2	2
ALOMAR (R)	.600	–	10	–	6	2	0	0	4	0-0	0	1	1	–	–
ALOMAR (L)	.400	–	15	–	6	0	1	0	2	0-0	0	1	2	–	–
BORDERS	.304	6	23	2	7	0	0	0	1	0-0	0	2	1	0-0	1
BUTLER	.500	2	2	1	1	0	0	0	0	0-0	0	0	0	0-0	0
CANATE	.000	1	0	0	0	0	0	0	0	0-0	0	0	0	0-0	0
CARTER	.280	6	25	6	7	1	0	2	8	0-3	0	0	4	0-0	2
COLES	.000	0	0	0	0	0	0	0	0	0-0	0	0	0	0-0	0
FERNANDEZ (T)	.333	6	21	2	7	1	0	0	9	0-1	1	3	3	0-1	0
FERNANDEZ (R)	.444	–	9	–	4	1	0	0	3	0-0	0	1	0	–	–
FERNANDEZ (L)	.250	–	12	–	3	0	0	0	6	0-1	1	2	3	–	–
GRIFFIN (T)	.000	3	0	0	0	0	0	0	0	0-0	0	0	0	0-0	0
GRIFFIN (R)	.000	–	0	–	0	0	0	0	0	0-0	0	0	0	–	–
GRIFFIN (L)	.000	–	0	–	0	0	0	0	0	0-0	0	0	0	–	–
HENDERSON	.227	6	22	6	5	2	0	0	0	0-0	1	5	2	1-1	0
KNORR	.000	1	0	0	0	0	0	0	0	0-0	0	0	0	0-0	0
MOLITOR	.500	6	24	10	12	2	2	2	8	0-0	1	3	0	1-0	0
OLERUD	.235	5	17	5	4	1	0	1	2	0-1	0	4	1	0-0	0
SCHOFIELD	.000	0	0	0	0	0	0	0	0	0-0	0	0	0	0-0	0
SPRAGUE	.067	5	15	0	1	0	0	0	2	0-2	0	1	6	0-0	2
WHITE (T)	.292	6	24	8	7	3	2	1	7	0-0	0	4	7	1-0	0
WHITE (R)	.364	–	11	–	4	3	1	0	3	0-0	0	2	2	–	–
WHITE (L)	.231	–	13	–	3	0	1	1	4	0-0	0	2	5	–	–
CASTILLO	.000	2	1	0	0	0	0	0	0	0-0	0	0	1	0-0	0
COX	.000	3	1	0	0	0	0	0	0	0-0	0	0	0	0-0	0
GUZMAN	.000	2	2	0	0	0	0	0	0	0-0	0	0	1	0-0	0
HENTGEN	.000	1	3	0	0	0	0	0	0	0-0	0	0	1	0-0	0
LEITER	1.000	3	1	0	1	1	0	0	0	0-0	0	0	0	0-0	0
STOTTLEMYRE	.000	1	0	0	0	0	0	0	0	0-0	0	0	1	0-0	0
DH	.500	6	12	5	6	1	1	1	3	0-0	0	1	0	1-0	0
PITCHERS	.125	6	8	0	1	1	0	0	0	0-0	0	1	3	0-0	0
BLUE JAYS	.311	6	206	45	64	13	5	6	45	0-7	3	25	30	7-4	7
PHILLIES	.274	6	212	36	58	7	2	7	35	1-1	1	34	50	7-1	2

FIRST TRIP LUCKY

The Toronto Blue Jays became the 10th franchise in history to win the World Championship in its 1st trip to the fall classic. The Florida Marlins became the 11th franchise to accomplish the feat in 1997.

1903	Boston Red Sox	1924	Washington Senators
1905	New York Giants	1926	St. Louis Cardinals
1906	Chicago White Sox	1969	New York Mets
1914	Boston Braves	1992	Toronto Blue Jays
1919	Cincinnati Reds	1997	Florida Marlins
1920	Cleveland Indians		

PITCHER	T	W-L	ERA	G	GS	CG	SHO	SV	IP	H	R	ER	HR	HB	BB	SO	WP
CASTILLO	L	1-0	8.10	2	0	0	0	0	3.1	6	3	3	1	1	3	1	0
COX	R	0-0	8.10	3	0	0	0	0	3.1	6	3	3	0	0	5	6	0
EICHHORN	R	0-0	0.00	1	0	0	0	0	0.1	1	0	0	0	0	1	0	0
GUZMAN	R	0-1	3.75	2	2	0	0	0	12.0	10	6	5	0	0	8	12	1
HENTGEN	R	1-0	1.50	1	1	0	0	0	6.0	5	1	1	0	0	3	6	0
LEITER	L	1-0	7.71	3	0	0	0	0	7.0	12	6	6	2	0	2	5	0
STEWART	R	0-1	6.75	2	2	0	0	0	12.0	10	9	9	2	0	8	8	1
STOTTLEMYRE	R	0-0	27.00	1	1	0	0	0	2.0	3	6	6	1	0	4	1	0
TIMLIN	R	0-0	0.00	2	0	0	0	0	2.1	2	0	0	0	0	0	4	0
WARD	R	1-0	1.93	4	0	0	0	2	4.2	3	2	1	1	0	0	7	0
BLUE JAYS		4-2	5.77	6	6	0	0	2	53.0	58	36	34	7	1	34	50	2
PHILLIES		2-4	7.39	6	6	1	0	1	52.1	64	45	43	6	3	25	30	0

BLUE JAYS SINGLE GAME ALCS RECORDS

INDIVIDUAL BATTING:
AB:	6	Henderson, 10/5/93 at CWS, Gm #1
	6	White, Carter, Winfield, 10/11/92 at OAK, Gm #4, 11 inn
Runs:	3	White, 10/9/91 at MIN, Gm #2
		Olerud, 10/5/93 at CWS, Gm #1
Hits:	4	Gruber, 10/7/89 vs OAK, Gm #4
		Molitor, 10/5/93 at CWS, Gm #1
		Sprague, 10/5/93 at CWS, Gm #1
		Alomar, 10/11/92 at OAK, Gm #4, 11 inn
		Olerud, 10/11/92 at OAK, Gm #4, 11 inn
Hitting streak:	11	Alomar, Gm #1/91 – Gm #6/92
Doubles:	2	Garcia, 10/11/85 at KC, Gm #3
		Fernandez, 10/6/89 vs OAK, Gm #3
Triples:	1	Lee, 10/10/92 at OAK, Gm #3
		Sprague, 10/5/93 at CWS, Gm #1
		White, 10/9/93 vs CWS, Gm #4
		Molitor, 10/12/93 at CWS, Gm #6
Home Runs:	1	by several
Extra-base hits:	2	by several
Total bases:	7	Molitor, 10/5/93 at CWS, Gm #1
	8	Alomar, 10/11/92 at OAK, Gm #4, 11 inn
		Olerud, 10/11/92 at OAK, Gm #4, 11 inn
RBI:	3	Alomar, 10/13/91 vs MIN, Gm #5
		Maldonado, 10/14/92 vs OAK, Gm #6
		Molitor, 10/5/93 at CWS, Gm #1
		Borders, 10/12/93 vs CWS, Gm #6
SB:	3	Alomar, 10/10/93 vs CWS, Gm #5
CS:	1	several times
SH:	1	5 times
SF:	1	several times

INDIVIDUAL PITCHING:
Innings:	9.0	Morris, 10/7/92 vs OAK, Gm #1
Strikeouts:	8	Stieb, 10/8/85 vs KC, Gm #1
Walks:	8	Guzman, 10/5/93 at CWS, Gm #1
Hits:	9	Candiotti, 10/13/91 vs MIN, Gm #5
		Hentgen, 10/8/93 vs CWS, Gm #3
Runs:	6	Stieb, 10/16/85 vs KC, Gm #7
		Cone, 10/12/92 at OAK, Gm #5
		Hentgen, 10/8/93 vs CWS, Gm #3
Earned Runs:	6	Stieb, 10/16/85 vs KC, Gm #7
		Hentgen, 10/8/93 vs CWS, Gm #3
WP	3	Guzman, 10/5/93 at CWS, Gm #1
CG's:		Morris, 10/7/92 vs OAK, Gm #1
Low Hit CG:	6	Morris, 10/7/92 vs OAK, Gm #1
Low Run CG:	4	Morris, 10/7/92 vs OAK, Gm #1

RELIEF PITCHING:
Innings:	3.2	Lamp, 10/9/85 vs KC, Gm #2
		Lamp, 10/15/85 vs KC, Gm #6
		Stottlemyre, 10/11/92 vs OAK, Gm #4
Hits:	4	Ward, 10/7/89 vs OAK, Gm #5
Strikeouts:	5	Lamp, 10/15/85 vs KC, Gm #6
Walks:	2	Cox , 10/8/93 vs CWS, Gm #3
		Ward, 10/7/93 vs CWS, Gm #1
Runs:	3	Ward, 10/13/91 vs MIN, Gm #5
Earned Runs:	3	Ward, 10/13/91 vs MIN, Gm #5

INDIVIDUAL FIELDING:
Assists:	6	Lee, 10/13/91 vs MIN, Gm #5
Putouts:	14	Olerud, 10/8/93 vs CWS, Gm #3
	16	Olerud, 10/11/91 vs MIN, Gm #3, 10 inn
Total Chances:	15	Olerud, 10/8/93 vs CWS #3
	16	Olerud, 10/11/91 vs MIN, Gm #3, 10 inn
Errors:	2	Gruber, 10/9/91 at MIN, Gm #2
		Lee, 10/11/92 at OAK, Gm #4

CLUB BATTING:

AB:	44	at CWS, 10/5/93, Gm #1
	49	at OAK, 10/11/92, Gm #4, 11 inn
Runs:	9	vs OAK, 10/14/92, Gm #6
Runs, Inning:	5	at KC, 10/11/85, Gm #3
Hits:	17	at CWS, 10/5/93, Gm #1
	17	at OAK, 10/11/92, Gm #4, 11 inn
Doubles:	5	at KC, 10/12/85, Gm #4
Triples:	1	4 times
Home Runs:	2	6 times
Total Bases:	23	at CWS, 10/5/93, Gm #1
	25	at OAK, 10/11/93, Gm #4, 11 inn
Extra-Base hits:	5	at KC, 10/11/85, Gm #3
		at KC, 10/12/85, Gm #4
Strikeouts:	8	at CWS, 10/5/93, Gm #1
	8	at OAK, 10/11/92, Gm #4, 11 inn
Walks:	8	vs MIN, 10/11/91, Gm #3
Stolen Bases:	5	vs CWS, 10/10/93, Gm #1
Most Left on Base:	12	vs OAK, 10/7/89, Gm #4
		at CWS, 10/5/93, Gm #1
		vs CWS, 10/10/93, Gm #5
	14	at OAK, 10/11/92, Gm #4, 11 inn
Fewest Left on Base:	4	5 times

CLUB PITCHING:

Innings:	11.0	vs OAK, 10/11/92, Gm #4
Hits:	14	vs MIN, 10/13/91, Gm #5
Fewest Hits:	2	at KC, 10/12/85, Gm #4
Most Runs:	9	vs MIN, 10/12/91, Gm #4
Earned Runs:	9	vs MIN, 10/12/91, Gm #4
Shutouts:		never
Walks:	10	at CWS, 10/5/93, Gm #1
Fewest Walks:	1	vs KC, 10/8/85, Gm #1
Strikeouts:	11	vs KC, 10/15/85, Gm #6
Home Runs:	3	at KC, 10/11/85, Gm #3
		vs OAK, 10/7/89, Gm #4
		vs OAK, 10/7/92, Gm #1

MISCELLANEOUS CLUB:

Attendance- Home:		51,889 vs CWS, 10/9/93, Gm #4
Road:		54,816 at MIN, 10/9/91, Gm #2
Winning Streak:	3	1992 (3)
		1992, (1) – 1993 (2)
Losing Streak:	5	1985 (3 vs KC) – 1989 (2 vs OAK)
Longest Game, innings:	11	vs OAK, 10/11/92, Gm #4, 11 inn
Longest Game, time:	3:40	at OAK, 10/10/92, Gm #3
	4:25	at OAK, 10/11/92, Gm #4, 11 inn
Shortest Game, time:	2:21	at KC, 10/13/85, Gm #5
Home:	2:24	vs KC, 10/8/85, Gm #1
Largest Margin of Victory:	7	vs OAK, 10/14/92, Gm #6, 9-2
Largest Margin of Defeat:	6	vs MIN, 10/12/91, Gm #4, 9-3
Biggest Comeback win:	5	vs OAK, 10/11/92, Gm #4
Most Errors, game:	3	vs MIN, 10/8/91, Gm #1
		at OAK, 10/10/92, Gm #5
	4	at OAK, 10/11/92, Gm #4, 11 inn

BLUE JAYS SINGLE GAME WS RECORDS

INDIVIDUAL BATTING:

AB:	6	Alomar, 10/20/93 at PHI, Gm #4
		Carter, 10/20/93 at PHI, Gm #4
		Fernandez, 10/20/93 at PHI, Gm #4
	6	Alomar, 10/24/92 at ATL, Gm #6, 11 inn
		Maldonado, 10/24/92 at ATL, Gm #6, 11 inn
Runs:	3	White, 10/16/93 vs PHI, Gm #1
		Molitor, 10/19/93 at PHI, Gm #3
		Molitor, 10/23/93 vs PHI, Gm #6
Hits:	4	Alomar, 10/19/93 vs PHI, Gm #3
Hitting streak:	8	Borders, Gm #1/92 - Gm #2/92
Doubles:	1	by several
	2	Carter, 10/24/92 at ATL, Gm #6, 11 inn
Triples:	1	Alomar, 10/19/93 at PHI, Gm #3
		White, 10/19/93 at PHI, Gm #3
		Molitor, 10/19/93 at PHI, Gm #3
		White, 10/20/93 at PHI, Gm #4
		Molitor, 10/23/93 vs PHI, Gm #6
Home Runs:	1	12 times
Extra-base hits:	2	White, 10/16/93 vs PHI, Gm #1
		Molitor, 10/19/93 vs PHI, Gm #3
		White, 10/20/93 at PHI, Gm #4
		Molitor, 10/23/93 vs PHI, Gm #6
	2	Carter, 10/24/92 at ATL, Gm #6, 11 inn

Total bases:	8	Molitor, 10/19/93 at PHI, Gm #3
		Molitor, 10/23/93 vs PHI, Gm #6
RBI:	5	Fernandez, 10/20/93 at PHI, Gm #4
SB:	2	Alomar, 10/19/92 at PHI, Gm #3
CS:	1	Fernandez, 10/16/93 vs PHI, Gm #1
		Alomar, 10/21/93 at PHI, Gm #5
SH:	1	2 times
SF:	1	several times

INDIVIDUAL PITCHING:

Innings:	8.0	Guzman, 10/20/92 vs ATL, Gm #3
Strikeouts:	7	Morris, 10/17/92 at ATL, Gm #1
		Guzman, 10/20/92 vs ATL, Gm #3
Walks:	5	Morris, 10/17/92 at ATL, Gm #1
		Cone, 10/18/92 at ATL, Gm #2
Hits:	9	Morris, 10/22/92 vs ATL, Gm #5
Runs:	7	Morris, 10/22/92 vs ATL, Gm #5
Earned Runs:	7	Morris, 10/22/92 vs ATL, Gm #5
CG's:		none
Low Hit CG:		none
Low Run CG:		none

RELIEF PITCHING:

Innings:	2.2	Leiter, 10/16/93 vs PHI, Gm #1
		Leiter, 10/20/93 at PHI, Gm #4
Hits:	8	Leiter, 10/20/93 at PHI, Gm #4
Strikeouts:	3	Ward, 10/16/93 vs PHI, Gm #1
		Cox, 10/21/93 at PHI, Gm #5
Walks:	3	Castillo, 10/20/93 at PHI, Gm #4
Runs:	6	Leiter, 10/20/93 at PHI, Gm #4
Earned Runs:	6	Leiter, 10/20/93 at PHI, Gm #4

INDIVIDUAL FIELDING:

Assists:	5	Alomar, 10/17/93 vs PHI, Gm #2
		Alomar, 10/20/93 at PHI, Gm #4
Putouts:	12	Borders, 10/16/93 vs PHI, Gm #1
Total Chances:	12	Borders, 10/16/93 vs PHI, Gm #1
Errors:	1	11 times

CLUB BATTING:

AB:	44	10/20/93 at PHI, Gm #4
	44	10/24/92 at ATL, Gm #6, 11 inn
Runs:	15	10/20/93 at PHI, Gm #4
Runs, Inning:	6	10/20/93 at PHI, Gm #4
Hits:	18	10/20/93 at PHI, Gm #4
Doubles:	5	10/20/93 at PHI, Gm #4
Triples:	3	10/19/93 at PHI, Gm #3
Home Runs:	2	10/20/92 vs ATL, Gm #3
		10/16/93 vs PHI, Gm #1
		10/23/93 vs PHI, Gm #6
Total Bases:	25	10/20/93 at PHI, Gm #4
Extra-Base hits:	6	10/20/93 at PHI, Gm #4
Strikeouts:	9	10/18/92 at ATL, Gm #2
		10/20/93 vs ATL, Gm #3
Walks:	7	10/20/93 at PHI, Gm #4
Stolen Bases:	2	several times
Most Left on Base:	10	10/20/93 at PHI, Gm #4
	13	10/24/92 at ATL, Gm #6, 11 inn
Fewest Left on Base:	2	10/17/93 at ATL, Gm #1

CLUB PITCHING:

Innings:	11.0	10/24/92 at ATL, Gm #6
Hits:	14	10/20/93 at PHI, Gm #4
Fewest Hits:	4	10/17/93 at ATL, Gm #1
Most Runs:	14	10/20/93 at PHI, Gm #4
Earned Runs:	14	10/20/93 at PHI, Gm #4
Shutouts:		none
Walks:	7	10/18/93 at ATL, Gm #2
		10/20/93 at PHI, Gm #4
Fewest Walks:	0	10/21/93 vs ATL, Gm #4
Strikeouts:	11	10/16/93 vs PHI, Gm #1
Home Runs:	3	10/20/93 at PHI, Gm #4

MISCELLANEOUS CLUB:

Attendance- Home:		52,268, 10/22/92 vs ATL, Gm #5
Road:		62,731, 10/20/93 at PHI, Gm #4
Winning Streak:	3	1992
Losing Streak:	1	1992, 1993
Longest Game, innings:	11.0	10/24/92 at ATL, Gm #6
Longest Game, time:	4:14	10/20/93 vs PHI, Gm #4
Shortest Game, time:	2:21	10/21/92 vs ATL, Gm #4
Road:	2:37	10/17/92 at ATL, Gm #1
Largest Margin of Victory:	7	10/19/93 vs PHI, Gm #3, 10-3
Largest Margin of Defeat:	5	10/22/92 vs PHI, Gm #5, 7-2
Biggest Comeback win:	5	10/20/93 at PHI, Gm #4, 14-9
Most Errors, game:	3	10/16/93 vs PHI, Gm #1

LONGEST RAIN DELAYS

At Exhibition Stadium

- 3 hours, 34 minutes - vs Cleveland, August 2, 1987 (3 hours, 34 minutes to start. Game started at 5:09 P.M. and ended at 7:55 P.M. T-2:46)
- 3 hours, 18 minutes - vs Boston, September 26, 1985 (3 hours, 18 minutes delay to start. Game started at 10:53 P.M. and ended at 1:02 A.M. T-2:09)
- 3 hours, 16 minutes - vs Boston, June 22, 1985 (3 hours, 16 minutes delay bottom of 5th inning. Game started at 1:39 P.M. and ended at 7:47 P.M. T-2:25)
- 3 hours, 1 minute - vs Boston, June 17, 1984 (1 hour, 33 minutes delay to start and 1 hour, 28 minutes delay at start of bottom of the 5th inning. Game started at 3:08 P.M. and ended at 7:47 P.M. T-2:48)

LATEST ENDING GAMES

- 1:02 A.M. - at Baltimore (Memorial Stadium), August 3, 1984. T-2:45, rain delay 2 hours, 7 minutes in top of 4th. Blue Jays - 5, Orioles - 2.
- 1:02 A.M. - Boston (Exhibition Stadium), September 26, 1985. T-2:09. 3 hours, 18 minutes delay to start. Red Sox - 4, Blue Jays - 1.

- 2 hours, 47 minutes - vs Boston, June 11, 1986 (2 hours, 47 minutes delay to start. Game started at 10:22 P.M. and ended at 12:51 A.M. T 2:29)
- 2 hours, 13 minutes - vs Chicago, August 23, 1988 (2 hours, 13 minutes delay to start. Game started at 9:48 P.M. and ended at 12:28 A.M. T-2:40)

At Fenway Park, Boston

- 2 hours, 43 minutes - at Boston, May 3, 1996 (2 hours, 43 minutes to start of game)

At Jacobs Field, Cleveland

- 2 hours, 21 minutes - at Cleveland, July 31, 1996 (2 hours, 21 minutes rain delay)

- 1:06 A.M. - at Boston (Fenway Park), May 3, 1996. Suspended game after six innings, resumed next day.
- 1:25 A.M. - at Baltimore (Camden Yards), June 19, 1998. T-5:49. 15 innings. Orioles - 7, Blue Jays - 4.

SUSPENDED GAMES: The Blue Jays have played three suspended games in their history... The first game was August 28, 1980 in a 7-5, 15-inning loss to Minnesota... The game was suspended after 14 innings due to a 5 pm Canadian National Exhibition curfew... The second suspended game was an 8-7, 13-inning loss at New York on September 17, 1980 which was completed the next day... Play was halted with the Blue Jays batting in the 10th inning... The last suspended game was at Fenway Park, Boston on May 3, 1996. Play was stopped at 1:06 A.M. after 6.0 innings, due to the 1:00 A.M. curfew. The game was completed the next day with Boston winning 8-7.

BLUE JAYS HOME POSTPONEMENTS

1. April 22, 1977, vs. Boston (Friday—Day)
2. April 23, 1977, vs. Boston (Saturday—Day)
3. September 24, 1977, vs. New York (Saturday—Day)
4. September 30, 1977, vs. Cleveland (Friday—Night)
5. October 1, 1977, vs. Cleveland (Saturday—Day)

6. April 20, 1978, vs. New York (Thursday—Day)
7. May 8, 1978, vs. Oakland (Monday—Night)
8. May 14, 1978, vs. Seattle (Sunday—Day)
9. June 12, 1978, vs. Minnesota (Monday—Night)

10. May 25, 1979, vs. Boston (Friday—Night)

11. April 14, 1980, vs. Milwaukee (Monday—Opening Day)
12. April 28, 1980, vs. Kansas City (Monday—Night)
13. May 13, 1980, vs. Seattle (Tuesday—Night)
14. June 19, 1980, vs. Chicago (Thursday—Night)

15. May 5, 1981, vs. Cleveland (Tuesday—Night)—Fog
16. August 30, 1981, vs. Kansas City (Sunday—Day)
17. September 21, 1981, vs. Oakland (Monday—Night)

18. June 5, 1982, vs. Cleveland (Saturday—Day)
19. June 25, 1982, vs. Minnesota (Friday—Night)
20. September 14, 1982, vs. Oakland (Tuesday—Night)

21. April 30, 1983, vs. Chicago (Saturday—Day)
22. May 29, 1983, vs. Boston (Sunday—2nd g—DH)
23. July 4, 1983, vs. Seattle (Monday—Night)

24. April 30, 1984, vs. Texas (Monday—Night) (Winds)

25. April 16, 1986, vs. Baltimore (Wednesday—Day)
26. September 10, 1986, vs. New York (Wednesday—Night)
27. October 4, 1986, vs. Milwaukee (Saturday—Day)

28. April 15, 1988, vs. Minnesota (Friday—Night) (Cold)

29. May 17, 1989, vs. California (Sunday—Day)

SEASON OPENER

DATE	OPPONENT	W/L	SCORE	WP	LP	ATT
Apr. 7, 1977	Chicago	W	9-5	Johnson	Brett	44,649
Apr. 7, 1978	at Detroit	L	6-2	Fidrych	Lemanczyk	52,528
Apr. 5, 1979	at Kansas City	L	11-2	Leonard	Underwood	37,754
Apr. 9, 1980	at Seattle	L	8-6	Parrott	Lemanczyk	22,588
Apr. 9, 1981	at Detroit	L	6-2	Morris	McLaughlin	51,452
Apr. 9, 1982	Milwaukee	L	15-4	Vuckovich	Bomback	30,216
Apr. 5, 1983	at Boston	W	7-1	Stieb	Eckersley	33,842
Apr. 4, 1984	at Seattle	L	3-2	Stanton	Lamp	43,200
Apr. 8, 1985	at Kansas City	L	2-1	Black	Stieb	41,086
Apr. 8, 1986	at Texas	L	6-3	Guzman	Stieb	40,602
Apr. 6, 1987	Cleveland	W	7-3	Key	Candiotti	40,404
Apr. 4, 1988	at Kansas City	W	5-3	Key	Saberhagen	40,648
Apr. 3, 1989	at Kansas City	W	4-3	Key	Gubicza	38,595
Apr. 9, 1990	at Texas	L	4-2	Ryan	Stottlemyre	40,907
Apr. 8, 1991	Boston	L	6-2	Clemens	Stieb	50,114
Apr. 6, 1992	at Detroit	W	4-2	Morris	Gullickson	51,068
Apr. 6, 1993	at Seattle	L	8-1	Johnson	Morris	56,120
Apr. 4, 1994	Chicago	W	7-3	Guzman	McDowell	50,484
Apr. 26, 1995	Oakland	W	13-1	Cone	Stewart	50,426
Apr. 1, 1996	at Oakland (Las Vegas)	W	9-6	Hanson	Reyes	7,294
Apr. 1, 1997	Chicago	L	6-5(10)	Castillo	Plesac	40,299
Apr. 1, 1998	Minnesota	W	3-2	Clemens	Tewksbury	41,387
Apr. 6, 1999	at Minnesota	L	6-1	Radke	Hentgen	45,601
Apr. 3, 2000	Kansas City	W	5-4	Koch	Spradlin	40,898

HOME OPENER

DATE	OPPONENT	W/L	SCORE	WP	LP	ATT
Apr. 7, 1977	Chicago	W	9-5	Johnson	Brett	44,649
Apr. 14, 1978	Detroit	W	10-8	Kirkwood	Wilcox	35,761
Apr. 13, 1979	Kansas City	W	4-1	Clancy	Splittorf	40,035
Apr. 16, 1980	Milwaukee	W	11-2	Stieb	Slaton	12,688
Apr. 13, 1981	New York	W	5-1	Clancy	John	25,112
Apr. 9, 1982	Milwaukee	L	15-4	Vuckovich	Bomback	30,216
Apr. 9, 1983	New York	W	7-4	Jackson	Gossage	36,459
Apr. 17, 1984	Baltimore	W	3-2	Key	T.Martinez	35,602
Apr. 16, 1985	Texas	L	9-4	Mason	Leal	41,284
Apr. 14, 1986	Baltimore	L	2-1	Boddicker	Alexander	43,587
Apr. 6, 1987	Cleveland	W	7-3	Key	Candiotti	40,404
Apr. 11, 1988	New York	W	17-9	Wells	Rhoden	45,185
Apr. 14, 1989	Kansas City	W	3-0	Key	Leibrandt	46,028
Apr. 10, 1990	Texas	W	2-1	Stieb	Hough	49,673
Apr. 8, 1991	Boston	L	6-2	Clemens	Stieb	50,114
Apr. 10, 1992	Baltimore	W	4-3	Hentgen	Olson	50,424
Apr. 9, 1993	Cleveland	W	13-10	Eichhorn	Power	50,533
Apr. 4, 1994	Chicago	W	7-3	Guzman	McDowell	50,484
Apr. 26, 1995	Oakland	W	13-1	Cone	Stewart	50,426
Apr. 9, 1996	California	W	5-0	Hentgen	Langston	36,316
Apr. 1, 1997	Chicago	L	6-5(10)	Castillo	Plesac	40,299
Apr. 1, 1998	Minnesota	W	3-2	Clemens	Tewksbury	41,387
Apr. 12, 1999	Tampa Bay	W	7-1	Wells	Saunders	37,160
Apr. 3, 2000	Kansas City	W	5-4	Koch	Spradlin	40,898

SEASON OPENING DAY RECORDS

OVER ALL RECORD:	11-13
HOME OPENERS:	19-5
EXTRA INNINGS:	0-1
MOST RUNS:	13 vs Oakland, April 26, 1995
MOST HITS:	16 vs Chicago, April 7, 1977
FEWEST HITS:	3 at Texas, April 9, 1990
MOST RUNS, OPPONENT:	15 vs Milwaukee, April 9, 1982
MOST HITS, OPPONENT:	16 vs Milwaukee, April 9, 1982
FEWEST HITS, OPPONENT:	3 at Boston, April 5, 1983
EARLIEST OPENING DAY:	at Oakland (Las Vegas), April 1, 1996, Chicago, April 1, 1997, Minnesota, April 1, 1998
LATEST OPENING DAY:	April 26, 1995
RECORD VS OPPONENTS:	Boston, 1-1; Chicago, 2-1; Cleveland, 1-0; Detroit, 1-2; Kansas City, 3-2; Milwaukee, 0-1; Minnesota, 1-1; Seattle, 0-3; Texas, 0-2; Oakland, 2-0
MOST STARTS:	Dave Stieb (4), Jimmy Key (3)
MOST WINS:	Jimmy Key (3)
MOST LOSSES:	Dave Stieb (3)
LARGEST OPENING DAY CROWD:	56,120, April 6, 1993 at Seattle
SMALLEST OPENING DAY CROWD:	30,216, April 9, 1982 vs Milwaukee 7,294, April 1, 1996 at Oakland (Las Vegas)

SEASON OPENING DAY LINEUPS

1977
vs CHICAGO
John Scott	-LF
Hector Torres	-SS
Doug Ault	-1B
Otto Velez	-DH
Gary Woods	-CF
Steve Bowling	-RF
Pedro Garcia	-2B
Dave McKay	-3B
Rick Cerone	-C
Bill Singer	-P
Roy Hartsfield	-MGR

1978
at DETROIT
Rick Bosetti	-CF
Al Woods	-LF
Roy Howell	-3B
Rico Carty	-DH
John Mayberry	-1B
Tommy Hutton	-RF
Dave McKay	-2B
Luis Gomez	-SS
Alan Ashby	-C
Dave Lemanczyk	-P
Roy Hartsfield	-MGR

1979
at KANSAS CITY
Alfredo Griffin	-SS
Bob Bailor	-RF
Roy Howell	-3B
Rico Carty	-DH
John Mayberry	-1B
Rick Bosetti	-CF
Bobby Brown	-LF
Dave McKay	-2B
Rick Cerone	-C
Tom Underwood	-P
Roy Hartsfield	-MGR

1980
at SEATTLE
Alfredo Griffin	-SS
Bob Bailor	-RF
John Mayberry	-1B
Otto Velez	-DH
Roy Howell	-3B
Barry Bonnell	-LF
Rick Bosetti	-CF
Damaso Garcia	-2B
Ernie Whitt	-C
Dave Lemanczyk	-P
Bob Mattick	-MGR

1981
at DETROIT
Alfredo Griffin	-SS
Lloyd Moseby	-CF
Otto Velez	-DH
John Mayberry	-1B
Willie Upshaw	-LF
Damaso Garcia	-2B
Barry Bonnell	-RF
Danny Ainge	-3B
Ernie Whitt	-C
Jim Clancy	-P
Bob Mattick	-MGR

1982
vs MILWAUKEE
Alfredo Griffin	-SS
Al Woods	-LF
Lloyd Moseby	-CF
Willie Upshaw	-1B
John Mayberry	-DH
Jesse Barfield	-RF
Ernie Whitt	-C
Damaso Garcia	-2B
Rance Mulliniks	-3B
Mark Bomback	-P
Bobby Cox	-MGR

1983
at BOSTON
Damaso Garcia	-2B
Dave Collins	-LF
Willie Upshaw	-1B
Cliff Johnson	-DH
Jesse Barfield	-RF
Ernie Whitt	-C
Lloyd Moseby	-CF
Rance Mulliniks	-3B
Alfredo Griffin	-SS
Dave Stieb	-P
Bobby Cox	-MGR

1984
at SEATTLE
Damaso Garcia	-2B
Rance Mulliniks	-3B
Lloyd Moseby	-CF
Willie Upshaw	-1B
Cliff Johnson	-DH
George Bell	-LF
Jesse Barfield	-RF
Ernie Whitt	-C
Alfredo Griffin	-SS
Jim Clancy	-P
Bobby Cox	-MGR

1985
at KANSAS CITY
Damaso Garcia	-2B
Lloyd Moseby	-CF
George Bell	-LF
Jesse Barfield	-RF
Jeff Burroughs	-DH
Willie Upshaw	-1B
Buck Martinez	-C
Garth Iorg	-3B
Tony Fernandez	-SS
Dave Stieb	-P
Bobby Cox	-MGR

1986
at TEXAS
Lloyd Moseby	-CF
Tony Fernandez	-SS
Rance Mulliniks	-3B
Willie Upshaw	-1B
George Bell	-LF
Jesse Barfield	-RF
Ernie Whitt	-C
Cecil Fielder	-DH
Damaso Garcia	-2B
Dave Stieb	-P
Jimy Williams	-MGR

1987
vs CLEVELAND
Tony Fernandez	-SS
Rance Mulliniks	-3B
Lloyd Moseby	-CF
George Bell	-LF
Jesse Barfield	-RF
Willie Upshaw	-1B
Ernie Whitt	-C
Fred McGriff	-DH
Mike Sharperson	-2B
Jimmy Key	-P
Jimy Williams	-MGR

1988
at KANSAS CITY
Nelson Liriano	-2B
Lloyd Moseby	-LF
Tony Fernandez	-SS
George Bell	-DH
Rance Mulliniks	-3B
Ernie Whitt	-C
Jesse Barfield	-RF
Fred McGriff	-1B
Sil Campusano	-CF
Jimmy Key	-P
Jimy Williams	-MGR

1989
at KANSAS CITY
Lloyd Moseby	-CF
Rance Mulliniks	-3B
Tony Fernandez	-SS
George Bell	-LF
Fred McGriff	-1B
Jesse Barfield	-RF
Ernie Whitt	-C
Nelson Liriano	-DH
Manny Lee	2B
Jimmy Key	-P
Jimy Williams	-MGR

1990
at TEXAS
Tony Fernandez	-SS
Mookie Wilson	-CF
Kelly Gruber	-3B
George Bell	-LF
Fred McGriff	-1B
John Olerud	-DH
Greg Myers	-C
Nelson Liriano	-2B
Junior Felix	-RF
Todd Stottlemyre	-P
Cito Gaston	-MGR

1991
vs BOSTON
Devon White	-CF
Roberto Alomar	-2B
Kelly Gruber	-3B
Joe Carter	-RF
John Olerud	-1B
Rance Mulliniks	-DH
Greg Myers	-C
Manuel Lee	-SS
Mookie Wilson	-LF
Dave Stieb	-P
Cito Gaston	-MGR

1992
at DETROIT
Devon White	-CF
Roberto Alomar	-2B
Joe Carter	-RF
Dave Winfield	-DH
Kelly Gruber	-3B
John Olerud	-1B
Derek Bell	-LF
Pat Borders	-C
Manuel Lee	-SS
Jack Morris	-P
Cito Gaston	-MGR

1993
at SEATTLE
Devon White	-CF
Roberto Alomar	-2B
Paul Molitor	-DH
Joe Carter	-LF
Darrin Jackson	-RF
Domingo Martinez	-1B
Ed Sprague	-3B
Pat Borders	-C
Dick Schofield	-SS
Jack Morris	-P
Cito Gaston	-MGR

1994
vs CHICAGO
Devon White	-CF
Roberto Alomar	-2B
Paul Molitor	-DH
Joe Carter	-RF
John Olerud	-1B
Carlos Delgado	-LF
Ed Sprague	-3B
Pat Borders	-C
Alex Gonzalez	-SS
Juan Guzman	-P
Cito Gaston	-MGR

1995
vs OAKLAND
Devon White	-CF
Alex Gonzalez	-SS
Paul Molitor	-DH
Joe Carter	-LF
John Olerud	-1B
Roberto Alomar	-2B
Shawn Green	-RF
Ed Sprague	-3B
Lance Parrish	-C
David Cone	-P
Cito Gaston	-MGR

1996
at OAKLAND (Las Vegas)
Otis Nixon	-CF
Domingo Cedeno	-2B
Joe Carter	-LF
John Olerud	-DH
Ed Sprague	-3B
Carlos Delgado	-1B
Shawn Green	-RF
Sandy Martinez	-C
Alex Gonzalez	-SS
Erik Hanson	-P
Cito Gaston	-MGR

1997
vs Chicago
Otis Nixon	-CF
Carlos Garcia	-2B
Orlando Merced	-RF
Joe Carter	-1B
Ed Sprague	-3B
Carlos Delgado	-DH
Benito Santiago	-C
Shawn Green	-LF
Alex Gonzalez	-SS
Pat Hentgen	-P
Cito Gaston	-MGR

1998
vs Minnesota
Shannon Stewart	-LF
Tony Fernandez	-2B
Shawn Green	-RF
Jose Canseco	-DH
Mike Stanley	-1B
Darrin Fletcher	-C
Ed Sprague	-3B
Jose Cruz Jr.	-CF
Alex Gonzalez	-SS
Roger Clemens	-P
Tim Johnson	-MGR

1999
at Minnesota
Shannon Stewart	-LF
Homer Bush	-2B
Shawn Green	-RF
Dave Hollins	-DH
Carlos Delgado	-1B
Tony Fernandez	-3B
Jose Cruz Jr.	-CF
Darrin Fletcher	-C
Alex Gonzalez	-SS
Pat Hentgen	-P
Jim Fregosi	-MGR

2000
vs Kansas City
Shannon Stewart	-LF
Homer Bush	-2B
Raul Mondesi	-RF
Carlos Delgado	-1B
Brad Fullmer	-DH
Tony Batista	-3B
Darrin Fletcher	-C
Jose Cruz Jr.	-CF
Alex Gonzalez	-SS
David Wells	-P
Jim Fregosi	-MGR

openers

BLUE JAYS YEAR-BY-YEAR

WON-LOST

YEAR	WON-LOST		HOME	ROAD	PCT	POS	GB	MANAGER
1977	54-107		25-55	29-52	.335	7th	45.5	Roy Hartsfield
1978	59-102		37-44	22-58	.366	7th	50.0	Hartsfield/Warner
1979	53-109		32-49	21-60	.327	7th	50.5	Roy Hartsfield
1980	67-95		35-46	32-49	.414	7th	36.0	Bob Mattick
1981	16-42	(1st half)	17-36	20-33	.276	7th	19.0	Bob Mattick
	21-27	(2nd half)			.438	7th	7.5	Bob Mattick
1982	78-84		44-37	34-47	.481	T6th	17.0	Bobby Cox
1983	89-73		48-33	41-40	.549	4th	9.0	Bobby Cox
1984	89-73		49-32	40-41	.549	2nd	15.0	Bobby Cox
1985	99-62		54-26	45-36	.615	1st	+2.0	Bobby Cox
1986	86-76		42-39	44-37	.531	4th	9.5	Jimy Williams
1987	96-66		52-29	44-37	.593	2nd	2.0	Jimy Williams
1988	87-75		45-36	42-39	.537	T3rd	2.0	Jimy Williams
1989	89-73		46-35	43-38	.549	1st	+2.0	Williams/Gaston
1990	86-76		44-37	42-39	.531	2nd	2.0	Cito Gaston
1991	91-71		46-35	45-36	.562	1st	+7.0	Gaston/Tenace
1992	96-66		53-28	43-38	.593	1st	+4.0	Cito Gaston
1993	95-67		48-33	47-34	.586	1st	+7.0	Cito Gaston
1994	55-60		33-26	22-34	.478	3rd	16.0	Cito Gaston
1995	56-88		29-43	27-45	.389	5th	31.0	Cito Gaston
1996	74-88		35-46	39-42	.457	4th	18.0	Cito Gaston
1997	76-86		42-39	34-47	.469	5th	22.0	Gaston/Queen
1998	88-74		51-30	37-44	.543	3rd	26.0	Tim Johnson
1999	84-78		40-41	44-37	.519	3rd	14.0	Jim Fregosi
2000	83-79		45-36	38-43	.512	3rd	4.5	Jim Fregosi
TOTAL	1867-1897		992-891	875-1006	.496			

CLINCHING/ELIMINATION DATES

YEAR	DATE	GP		ELIMINATED BY	H/A	TOR-OPP	WINNER	GBL
*1977	Aug. 30	129		Did not play	−	−	New York	33.0
#1978	Aug. 29	133		Texas	A	4-1	New York	30.5
1979	Aug. 19	123		California	A	2-4	Baltimore	41.0
†1980	Sept. 7	137		Chicago	H	7-6	New York	27.0
‡1981	May 17	34	s	Cleveland	A	0-1	New York	10.0
	Sept. 22	39		Oakland	H	2-4	Milwaukee	5.5
1982	Sept. 14	143	a	Did not play	−	−	Milwaukee	19.0
1983	Sept. 21	153		Seattle	H	4-3	Baltimore	11.0
1984	Sept. 18	151		Boston	H	10-3	Detroit	13.0
1985	Oct. 5	160		New York	H	5-1	Toronto	+2.0
1986	Sept. 28	156		Boston	A	3-12	Boston	9.0
1987	Oct. 4	162		Detroit	A	0-1	Detroit	2.0
1988	Sept. 25	156		Cleveland	A	3-4	Boston	7.5
1989	Sept. 30	161		Baltimore	H	4-3	Toronto	+2.0
1990	Oct. 3	162		Baltimore	A	2-3	Boston	2.0
1991	Oct. 2	159		California	H	6-5	Toronto	+7.0
1992	Oct. 3	161		Detroit	H	3-1	Toronto	+3.0
1993	Sept. 27	156		Milwaukee	A	2-0	Toronto	+6.5
1994	SEASON ENDED DUE TO PLAYER STRIKE							
1995	Sept. 3	118		Chicago	A	5-6	Boston (AL East)	24.5
	Sept. 15	130		Milwaukee	H	5-1	Seattle (Wild Card)	16.0
1996	Sept. 13	147		New York	H	1-4	New York (AL East)	16.5
	Sept. 15	149	b	New York	H	3-1	Baltimore (Wild Card)	14.0
1997	Sept. 9	144	c	Anaheim	H	2-0	Baltimore (AL East)	20.0
	Sept. 15	150		Seattle	A	3-7	New York (Wild Card)	15.0
1998	Aug. 28	136	d	New York	H	7-6	New York (AL East)	29.0
	Sept. 24	160	e	Boston	H	6-3	Boston (Wild Card)	4.0
1999	Sept. 19	150		Chicago	H	2-3	New York (AL East)	13.5
	Sept. 24	154		Cleveland	H	4-18	Boston (Wildcard)	9.5
2000	Sept. 27	158	f	Oakland	A	4-0	Seattle (Wildcard)	8.0
	Sept. 28	159		Baltimore	A	1-23	New York (AL East)	4.5

* New York defeated Seattle, 6-5, to eliminate Blue Jays
\# Boston (leader on Aug. 29) defeated Seattle, 10-5, to eliminate Blue Jays
† New York defeated California, 4-1, to eliminate Blue Jays, 2nd game of DH
s 1st game of DH
‡ Split-Season
a Milwaukee defeated Detroit, 6-3, to eliminate Blue Jays
b Baltimore defeated Detroit, 16-6, to eliminate Blue Jays
c Baltimore defeated Cleveland, 9-3, to eliminate Blue Jays
d New York defeated Seattle, 10-3, to eliminate Blue Jays
e Boston defeated Baltimore, 9-6, to eliminate Blue Jays
f Oakland defeated Anaheim, 9-7, to eliminate Blue Jays

STANDING BY MONTH

	May 1st (GB)	June 1st (GB)	July 1st (GB)	Aug. 1st (GB)	Sept. 1st (GB)
1977	5(–3.0)	7(–9.0)	7(–13.5)	7(–23.0)	7(–32.5)
1978	7(–6.5)	7(–16.0)	7(–25.5)	7(–27.0)	7(–30.5)
1979	6(–7.0)	7(–19.0)	7(–30.5)	7(–39.5)	7(–45.0)
1980	1(+1.0)	3(–5.5)	7(–14.0)	7(–18.5)	7(–24.0)
*1981	7(–5.0)	7(–14.0)	—	—	6(–3.0)
1982	5(–5.0)	7(–9.0)	7(–11.0)	7(–10.0)	7(–17.5)
1983	6(–2.0)	1(+0.5)	1(+2.0)	4(–2.5)	5(–7.5)
1984	2(–6.0)	2(–5.5)	2(–10.0)	2(–12.0)	2(–9.5)
1985	1(+0.5)	1(+4.0)	1(+3.5)	1(+7.5)	1(+5.0)
1986	7(–5.0)	7(–10.0)	5(–10.5)	4(–5.5)	2(–1.0)
1987	3(5.5)	2(–2.0)	2(–2.0)	2(–2.5)	2(–1.0)
1988	6(–7.0)	6(–12.0)	T5(–9.0)	6(–11.5)	5(–10.5)
1989	7(–3.5)	7(–7.5)	4(–7.0)	2(–3.0)	T1
1990	3(–1.5)	1(+0.5)	2(–3.5)	T1	2(–5.5)
1991	2(–0.5)	T1	1(+4.5)	1(+6.0)	1(+3.5)
1992	1(+2.0)	1(+1.0)	1(+1.0)	1(+4.5)	1(+1.5)
1993	4(–2.5)	T2(–2.5)	1(+2.0)	T1	1(+1.5)
1994	4(–3.0)	4(–9.0)	5(–15.5)	4(–15.5)	—
1995	3(–0.5)	3(–6.5)	5(–10.0)	5(–10.0)	4(–21.5)
1996	3(–3.0)	3(–6.5)	3(–11.5)	3(–15.0)	4(–13.5)
1997	4(–5.0)	3(–10.0)	3(–13.5)	3(–17.0)	4(–21.0)
1998	5(–8.5)	3(–11.5)	3(–17.5)	4(–25.5)	3(–28.0)
1999	2(–2.5)	3(–8.0)	3(–9.5)	2(–6.0)	3(–12.5)
2000	4(–4.5)	3(–4.0)	1(+3.0)	3(–4.5)	3(–5.5)

* Split-Season

BATTING

YEAR	AVG.	G	AB	R	H	TB	2B	3B	HR T- H -A	RBI	BB	SO	SH-SF	HP	SB-CS	LOB	SLUG PCT	GIDP
1977	.252	161	5419	605	1367	2099	230	41	100- 45 - 55	552	499	819	81-34	23	65-55	1094	.365	156
1978	.250	161	5430	590	1358	1947	217	39	98- 50 - 48	550	448	645	77-37	23	28-52	1075	.359	124
1979	.251	162	5423	613	1362	1968	253	34	95- 50 - 45	562	448	663	65-38	36	75-56	1064	.363	131
1980	.251	162	5571	624	1398	2131	249	53	126- 56 - 70	580	448	813	63-34	33	67-72	1083	.383	119
1981	.226	106	3521	329	797	1163	137	23	61- 34 - 27	314	284	556	44-18	20	66-57	658	.330	72
1982	.262	162	5526	651	1447	2117	262	45	106- 62 - 44	605	415	749	48-50	28	118-81	1071	.383	107
1983	.277	162	5581	795	1546	2431	268	58	167- 101 - 66	748	510	810	36-54	32	131-71	1106	.436	117
1984	.273	163	5687	750	1555	2395	275	58	143- 59 - 84	702	460	816	35-49	52	193-67	1177	.421	90
1985	.269	161	5508	759	1482	2343	281	53	158- 75 - 83	714	503	807	21-44	30	143-77	1067	.425	121
1986	.269	163	5716	809	1540	2438	285	35	181- 87 - 94	767	496	848	24-49	33	110-59	1099	.427	122
1987	.269	162	5635	845	1514	2512	277	38	215- 101 - 114	790	555	970	30-35	38	126-50	1126	.446	136
1988	.268	162	5557	763	1491	2330	271	47	158- 78 - 80	706	521	935	34-50	31	107-36	1105	.419	145
1989	.260	162	5581	731	1449	2220	265	40	142- 64 - 78	685	521	923	30-53	31	144-58	1102	.398	124
1990	.265	162	5589	767	1479	2343	263	50	167- 93 - 74	729	526	970	18-62	28	111-52	1113	.419	125
1991	.257	162	5489	684	1412	2196	295	45	133- 75 - 58	649	499	1043	56-65	58	148-53	1134	.400	108
1992	.263	162	5536	780	1458	2292	265	40	163- 79 - 84	737	561	933	26-54	47	129-39	1159	.414	123
1993	.279	162	5579	847	1556	2434	317	42	159- 90 - 69	796	588	861	46-54	52	170-49	1187	.436	138
1994	.269	115	1064	566	1064	1679	210	30	115- 63 - 52	534	387	691	30-44	38	79-26	820	.424	96
1995	.260	144	5036	642	1309	1670	275	27	140- 67 - 73	613	492	960	33-45	44	75-16	1079	.409	119
1996	.259	162	5599	766	1451	2354	302	35	177- 87 - 90	712	529	1105	38-37	92	116-38	1169	.420	120
1997	.244	162	5473	654	1333	2131	275	41	147- 68 - 79	706	487	1138	38-52	59	134-50	1113	.389	102
1998	.266	163	5580	816	1482	2499	316	19	221- 112 - 109	776	564	1132	43-49	87	184-81	1133	.448	115
1999	.280	162	5642	883	1580	2581	337	14	212- 96 - 116	856	578	1077	28-45	76	119-48	1177	.457	129
2000	.275	162	5677	861	1562	2664	328	21	244- 134 - 110	826	526	1026	29-34	60	89-34	1152	.469	130

PITCHING

YEAR	W-L	ERA	G	RE	CG	SHO	SV	IP	H	R	ER	HR	BB	SO	HB	WP
1977	54-107	4.57	348	187	40	3	20	1428	1568	822	725	152	623	771	20	62
1978	59-102	4.55	374	213	35	5	23	1429	1529	775	723	149	614	758	22	47
1979	53-109	4.82	357	195	44	7	11	1417	1537	862	759	165	594	613	40	64
1980	67-95	4.19	448	286	39	9	23	1466	1523	762	683	135	635	705	28	41
1981	37-69	3.81	295	189	20	4	18	953	908	466	404	72	377	451	36	41
1982	78-84	3.95	382	220	41	13	25	1444	1428	701	633	147	493	776	25	38
1983	89-73	4.12	419	257	43	8	32	1445	1434	726	662	145	517	835	42	25
1984	89-73	3.86	420	257	34	10	33	1464	1433	696	628	140	528	875	34	42
1985	99-62	3.29	477	316	18	9	47	1448	1312	588	529	147	484	823	26	36
1986	86-76	4.08	453	290	16	12	44	1476	1467	733	669	164	487	1002	45	38
1987	96-66	3.74	—	—	18	8	43	1454	1323	655	605	158	567	1064	22	56
1988	87-75	3.80	455	293	16	17	47	1449	1404	680	611	143	528	904	59	48
1989	89-73	3.58	439	293	12	12	38	1467	1408	651	586	143	445	892	37	43
1990	86-76	3.84	479	317	6	9	48	1454	1434	661	620	143	445	892	37	43
1991	91-71	3.50	508	346	10	16	60	1462	1301	622	569	121	523	971	43	55
1992	96-66	3.91	446	284	18	14	49	1441	1346	682	624	124	541	954	45	66
1993	95-67	4.21	506	344	11	11	50	1441	1441	742	674	134	620	1023	32	83
1994	55-60	4.70	336	221	13	4	26	1025	1053	579	535	127	482	832	32	54
1995	56-88	4.88	409	265	16	8	22	1293	1336	777	701	145	654	894	44	73
1996	74-88	4.57	465	303	19	7	35	1446	1476	809	734	187	610	1033	36	61
1997	76-86	3.92	162	336	19	16	34	1443	1453	694	628	167	497	1150	39	54
1998	88-74	4.29	163	384	10	11	39	1465	1443	768	707	169	587	1154	45	34
1999	84-78	4.92	162	377	14	9	39	1439	1582	862	787	191	575	1009	53	55
2000	83-79	5.14	162	388	15	4	37	1437	1615	908	821	195	560	978	64	37

Blue Jays Records

FIELDING

YEAR	PCT	PO	A	E	TC	DP	TP	PB	RANK
1977	.974	4285	1798	164	6247	133	0	7	13
1978	.979	4288	1763	128	6179	163	1	16	5
1979	.975	4251	1878	158	6287	186	2	8	12
1980	.979	4398	1939	133	6470	206	0	8	3
1981	.975	2860	1164	105	4129	102	0	4	14
1982	.978	4331	1768	136	6235	146	0	7	11
1983	.981	4336	1637	115	6088	148	0	7	3
1984	.980	4392	1669	123	6184	166	0	9	4
1985	.980	4344	1729	125	6198	164	0	3	7
1986	.984	4428	1682	100	6210	150	0	9	1
1987	.982	4362	1700	111	6173	148	0	13	4
1988	.982	4347	1737	110	6194	170	0	12	4
1989	.980	4401	1864	127	6392	164	0	16	6
1990	.986	4362	1720	86	6168	144	0	14	1
1991	.980	4388	1686	127	6201	115	0	21	10
1992	.985	4322	1592	93	6007	109	0	15	4
1993	.982	4324	1583	107	6014	144	0	6	6
1994	.981	3075	1058	81	4214	105	0	14	9
1995	.982	3787	1399	97	5374	131	0	31	7
1996	.982	4337	1608	110	6055	187	0	16	8
1997	.984	4328	1536	94	5958	150	0	11	3
1998	.979	4395	1532	125	6052	131	0	9	11
1999	.983	4317	1664	106	6087	165	0	13	5
2000	.984	4312	1679	100	6091	176	0	11	3

DESIGNATED HITTING

YEAR	AVG	AB	R	H	2B	3B	HR	RBI	SH-SF	BB	SO	HP	SB-CS	SLG %	RANK
1977	.269	583	75	157	27	2	22	87	9-8	76	108	4	4-4	.436	5
1978	.250	621	75	155	25	0	25	96	1-8	52	83	1	2-3	.411	10
1979	.260	599	71	156	37	1	18	82	1-6	66	74	1	3-2	.416	8
1980	.229	599	73	137	21	4	22	84	1-5	75	129	1	1-0	.387	14
1981	.212	363	45	77	14	2	13	36	3-2	64	75	4	3-6	.369	13
1982	.238	596	52	142	18	3	8	58	1-8	60	91	0	7-16	.319	14
1983	.250	604	86	151	29	3	34	113	1-6	81	101	5	0-2	.477	12
1984	.270	612	91	165	32	1	27	93	0-4	79	121	5	4-4	.458	4
1985	.247	600	77	148	22	5	13	78	0-8	61	85	1	5-5	.365	6
1986	.242	616	86	149	26	3	20	83	0-2	67	119	5	2-4	.391	10
1987	.258	592	101	153	32	3	38	97	0-3	83	160	5	3-3	.515	7
1988	.288	612	90	176	33	3	25	95	3-5	81	126	1	3-1	.474	1
1989	.216	589	67	127	23	4	8	55	0-4	69	105	6	10-0	.309	14
1990	.220	604	65	133	28	4	14	68	1-11	69	132	3	4-4	.349	13
1991	.252	583	70	147	32	6	5	56	4-5	80	104	2	7-5	.353	7
1992	.267	619	95	165	32	2	29	112	1-5	78	101	6	2-3	.465	6
1993	.308	639	116	197	36	4	20	101	1-10	80	77	4	20-4	.471	1
1994	.333	457	84	152	30	3	14	75	0-4	53	53	1	17-0	.530	1
1995	.262	584	68	153	35	2	16	69	4-8	65	75	7	15-0	.411	9
1996	.260	628	95	163	28	4	32	109	0-9	72	161	9	5-0	.470	10
1997	.237	598	70	142	25	3	25	95	0-3	47	129	8	7-5	.415	13
1998	.228	597	94	136	22	0	43	101	1-6	68	170	8	14-13	.481	14
1999	.250	608	80	152	27	0	24	81	3-4	46	129	6	0-1	.413	14
2000	.285	606	92	173	33	1	39	120	0-6	38	93	6	3-2	.536	5

PINCH HITTING

YEAR	AVG	AB	R	H	2B	3B	HR	RBI	SH-SF	BB	SO	HP	OBP	SLG %
1977	.280	93	10	26	2	1	5	23	1-2	11	17	0	.349	.484
1978	.236	123	11	29	4	0	2	18	0-1	15	22	2	.326	.317
1979	.231	52	5	12	3	0	4	14	0-0	11	12	0	.365	.519
1980	.280	100	10	28	4	0	3	15	0-0	14	15	1	.374	.410
1981	.234	77	4	18	3	0	1	15	0-0	11	19	0	.330	.312
1982	.271	262	24	71	14	0	4	53	1-3	39	48	1	.364	.370
1983	.290	200	26	58	8	0	5	42	0-5	28	36	1	.372	.405
1984	.284	215	29	61	10	2	6	39	1-4	30	51	1	.368	.433
1985	.222	167	18	37	4	1	4	29	3-4	19	31	1	.319	.329
1986	.277	155	19	43	8	1	4	32	0-4	21	26	0	.356	.419
1987	.234	167	—	39	6	1	3	28	1-3	33	37	1	.358	.335
1988	.202	129	14	26	3	1	2	18	0-0	22	31	1	.322	.287
1989	.264	121	14	32	10	0	3	13	4-0	17	24	0	.355	.421
1990	.216	97	4	21	2	1	0	14	0-0	11	22	1	.303	.258
1991	.236	123	13	29	5	0	1	21	1-5	19	29	0	.327	.301
1992	.273	55	8	15	5	0	0	9	0-0	7	10	0	.355	.364
1993	.185	27	1	5	0	0	1	5	0-0	2	7	1	.267	.296
1994	.125	32	4	4	0	1	1	4	2-0	5	8	0	.243	.281
1995	.192	73	6	14	3	0	1	8	1-1	6	23	3	.277	.274
1996	.204	113	15	23	4	0	2	12	1-0	12	37	0	.280	.292
1997	.127	63	8	8	2	1	1	8	0-1	6	25	0	.200	.238
1998	.204	54	4	11	3	0	1	5	0-2	3	21	1	.250	.315
1999	.238	84	9	20	4	0	4	13	1-2	5	23	0	.275	.429
2000	.333	51	6	17	3	0	0	8	1-1	6	7	0	.397	.392

BLUE JAYS' LEAGUE LEADERS
BATTING LEADERS

Year	Category	Player	Totals
1980	Triples	Alfredo Griffin	15
1983	Hitting Streak	Damaso Garcia (tie)	21
		Lloyd Moseby (tie)	21
1984	Triples	Dave Collins (tie)	15
		Lloyd Moseby (tie)	15
1986	Home Runs	Jesse Barfield	40
	GWRBI	George Bell (tie)	15
1987	RBI	George Bell	134
	Total Bases	George Bell	369
1989	Home Runs	Fred McGriff	36
	Hitting Streak	George Bell	22
1990	Triples	Tony Fernandez	17
1993	Average	John Olerud	.363
	Hits	Paul Molitor	211
	Doubles	John Olerud	54
	OBP	John Olerud	.473
	Hitting Streak	John Olerud	26
1995	Hit by Pitch	Ed Sprague	15
1998	Strikeouts	Jose Canseco	159
1999	Total Bases	Shawn Green	361
	Doubles	Shawn Green	45
	Hitting Streak	Shawn Green	28
	Extra Base Hits	Shawn Green	87
2000	Doubles	Carlos Delgado	57
	Total Bases	Carlos Delgado	378
	Extra Base Hits	Carlos Delgado	99
	Sacrifice Hits	Alex Gonzalez	16
	Hit by Pitch	Carlos Delgado	15

PITCHING LEADERS

Year	Category	Player	Totals
1982	Games Started	Jim Clancy	40
	Complete Games	Dave Stieb	19
	Shutouts	Dave Stieb	5
	Innings Pitched	Dave Stieb	288.1
1984	Winning Percentage	Doyle Alexander	.739
	Innings Pitched	Dave Stieb	267.0
	Games Started	Jim Clancy (tie)	36
1985	ERA	Dave Stieb	2.48
1987	Winning Percentage	John Cerutti	.733
	ERA	Jimmy Key	2.76
	Games	Mark Eichhorn	89
	Games Finished	Tom Henke	62
1991	Games	Duane Ward	81
1992	Wins	Jack Morris (tie)	21
1993	Winning Percentage	Juan Guzman	.824
	Saves	Duane Ward (tie)	45
	Games Finished	Duane Ward	70
1995	Innings Pitched	David Cone	229.1
		(NYY-TOR)	
	Walks	Al Leiter	108
1996	ERA	Juan Guzman	2.93
	Complete Games	Pat Hentgen	10
	Shutouts	Pat Hentgen (tie)	3
	Innings Pitched	Pat Hentgen	265.2
	Batsmen Faced	Pat Hentgen	1100
1997	ERA	Roger Clemens	2.05
	Wins	Roger Clemens	21
	Games Started	Pat Hentgen (tie)	35
	Complete Games	Pat Hentgen	9
		Roger Clemens	9
	Innings Pitched	Pat Hentgen	264.0
		Roger Clemens	264.0
	Strikeouts	Roger Clemens	292
	Shutouts	Pat Hentgen	3
		Roger Clemens	3
1998	ERA	Roger Clemens	2.65
	Wins	Roger Clemens	20
	Strikeouts	Roger Clemens	271
1999	Complete Games	David Wells	7
	Innings Pitched	David Wells	231.2
2000	Wins	David Wells	20
	Complete Games	David Wells	9

DESIGNATED HITTERS

Year	Player	G	AB	H	HR	RBI	Avg.
1977	Ron Fairly	58	200	60	8	30	.300
	Doug Rader	34	119	24	5	16	.202
	Sam Ewing	27	86	25	3	14	.291
1978	Rico Carty	101	384	110	20	68	.286
1979	Rico Carty	129	458	117	12	53	.255
1980	Otto Velez	97	342	92	19	59	.269
1981	Otto Velez	74	233	48	10	25	.206
1982	Wayne Nordhagen	60	149	42	0	11	.282
	Dave Revering	49	116	24	4	11	.207
1983	Cliff Johnson	130	380	103	22	74	.271
1984	Cliff Johnson	109	337	102	16	60	.303
	Willie Aikens	81	222	43	9	21	.194
1985	Al Oliver	59	186	47	5	23	.253
	Jeff Burroughs	75	181	48	5	27	.265
1986	Cliff Johnson	95	326	81	15	51	.248
1987	Fred Mcgriff	90	256	65	18	39	.254
	Cecil Fielder	55	127	36	11	25	.283
1988	Rance Mulliniks	108	318	98	12	47	.308
	Cecil Fielder	50	120	30	8	19	.250
1989	Rance Mulliniks	73	186	45	0	14	.242
	George Bell	19	80	23	0	13	.288
1990	John Olerud	90	302	78	10	38	.258
	George Bell	36	138	32	3	17	.232
1991	Rance Mulliniks	81	217	56	2	20	.258
	Pat Tabler	57	116	29	0	12	.250
1992	Dave Winfield	130	490	136	23	91	.278
1993	Paul Molitor	137	543	169	17	90	.311
1994	Paul Molitor	110	436	148	13	70	.339
1995	Paul Molitor	129	525	142	15	60	.270
1996	Carlos Delgado	108	380	100	17	63	.263
	Juan Samuel	24	71	21	3	10	.296
	Joe Carter	15	59	12	2	7	.203
	John Olerud	15	58	17	5	14	.293
1997	Joe Carter	64	253	50	9	41	.198
	Shawn Green	35	124	44	9	30	.355
	Carlos Delgado	33	88	22	5	15	.250
1998	Jose Canseco	78	319	70	25	57	.219
	Mike Stanley	73	258	62	17	41	.240
1999	Willie Greene	50	183	39	9	33	.213
	David Segui	25	84	26	5	12	.310
	Dave Hollins	23	95	20	2	6	.211
2000	Brad Fullmer	129	478	141	32	104	.295
	Todd Greene	23	74	16	5	9	.216

BATTING LEADERS

* League Leader   #Based on 250 AB's

Year	AVG. (350 AB's)		AB		R		H		2B	
1977	B. Bailor	.310	B. Bailor	496	B. Bailor	62	B. Bailor	154	R. Fairly	24
	R. Howell	.316								
1978	R. Howell	.270	B. Bailor	621	B. Bailor	74	B. Bailor	164	B. Bailor	29
1979	A. Griffin	.287	A. Griffin	624	A. Griffin	81	A. Griffin	179	R. Bosetti	35
1980	Al Woods	.300	A. Griffin	653	A. Griffin	63	A. Griffin	166	D. Garcia	30
1981	D. Garcia	.252#	A. Griffin	388	L. Moseby	36	L. Moseby	88	A. Griffin	19
1982	D. Garcia	.310	W. Upshaw	580	D. Garcia	89	D. Garcia	185	D. Garcia	32
1983	B. Bonnell	.318	W. Upshaw	579	L. Moseby	104	W. Upshaw	177	R. Mulliniks	34
1984	D. Collins	.308	D. Garcia	633	L. Moseby	97	D. Garcia	180	G. Bell	39
1985	R. Mulliniks	.295	G. Bell	607	J. Barfield	94	G. Bell	167	J. Barfield	34
1986	T. Fernandez	.310	T. Fernandez	687	J. Barfield	107	T. Fernandez	213	G. Bell	38
1987	T. Fernandez	.322	G. Bell	610	G. Bell	111	G. Bell	188	G. Bell	32
1988	M. Lee	.291	T. Fernandez	648	F. McGriff	100	T. Fernandez	186	T. Fernandez	41
1989	G. Bell	.297	G. Bell	613	F. McGriff	98	G. Bell	182	G. Bell	41
1990	F. McGriff	.297	T. Fernandez	635	K. Gruber	92	T. Fernandez	175	K. Gruber	36
									M. Wilson	36
1991	R. Alomar	.295	D. White	642	D. White	110	R. Alomar	188	J. Carter	42
1992	R. Alomar	.310	D. White	641	R. Alomar	105	R. Alomar	177	D. Winfield	32
1993	J. Olerud	.363*	P. Molitor	636	P. Molitor	121	P. Molitor	211*	J. Olerud	54*
1994	P. Molitor	.341	P. Molitor	454	P. Molitor	115	P. Molitor	155	P. Molitor	40
1995	R. Alomar	.300	J. Carter	558	E. Sprague	77	R. Alomar	155	J. Olerud	32
1996	O. Nixon	.286	J. Carter	625	E. Sprague	88	J. Carter	158	J. Carter	35
									E. Sprague	35
1997	S. Green	.287	J. Carter	612	C. Delgado	79	J. Carter	143	C. Delgado	42
1998	T. Fernandez	.321	S. Green	630	S. Green	106	S. Green	175	C. Delgado	43
1999	T. Fernandez	.328	S. Green	614	S. Green	134	S. Green	190	S. Green	45*
2000	C. Delgado	.344	T. Batista	620	C. Delgado	115	C. Delgado	196	C. Delgado	57*

Year	3B		HR		RBI		BB		SO	
1977	S. Staggs	6	R. Fairly	19	R. Fairly	64	O. Velez	65	O. Velez	87
					D. Ault	64				
1978	D. McKay	8	J. Mayberry	22	J. Mayberry	70	J. Mayberry	61	D. McKay	90
1979	A. Griffin	10	J. Mayberry	21	J. Mayberry	74	J. Mayberry	69	R. Howell	91
1980	A. Griffin	15*	J. Mayberry	30	J. Mayberry	82	J. Mayberry	77	R. Howell	92
1981	A. Griffin	6	J. Mayberry	17	J. Mayberry	43	O. Velez	55	L. Moseby	86
					L. Moseby	43				
1982	L. Moseby	9	W. Upshaw	21	W. Upshaw	75	W. Upshaw	52	L. Moseby	106
1983	A. Griffin	9	J. Barfield	27	W. Upshaw	104	C. Johnson	67	J. Barfield	110
			W. Upshaw	27						
1984	D. Collins	15*	G. Bell	26	L. Moseby	92	L. Moseby	78	L. Moseby	122
	L. Moseby	15*								
1985	T. Fernandez	10	G. Bell	28	G. Bell	95	L. Moseby	76	J. Barfield	143
1986	T. Feranadez	9	J. Barfield	40*	J. Barfield	108	W. Upshaw	78	J. Barfield	146
					G. Bell	108				
1987	T. Fernandez	8	G. Bell	47	G. Bell	134*	L. Moseby	70	J. Barfield	141
1988	L. Moseby	7	F. McGriff	34	G. Bell	97	F. McGriff	79	F. McGriff	149
1989	T. Fernandez	9	F. McGriff	36	G. Bell	104	F. McGriff	119	F. McGriff	132
1990	T. Fernandez	17*	F. McGriff	35	K. Gruber	118	F. McGriff	94	F. McGriff	108
1991	R. Alomar	11	J. Carter	33	J. Carter	108	J. Olerud	68	D. White	135
1992	R. Alomar	8	J. Carter	34	J. Carter	119	R. Alomar	87	D. White	133
1993	T. Fernandez	9	J. Carter	33	J. Carter	121	J. Olerud	114	D. White	127
1994	D. White	6	J. Carter	27	J. Carter	103	J. Olerud	61	D. White	95
1995	R. Alomar	7	J. Carter	25	J. Carter	76	J. Olerud	84	A. Gonzalez	114
1996	J. Carter	7	E. Sprague	36	J. Carter	107	J. Olerud	60	C. Delgado	139
							E. Sprague	60		
1997	S. Stewart	7	C. Delgado	30	J. Carter	102	C. Delgado	64	C. Delgado	133
1998	S. Green	4	J. Canseco	46	C. Delgado	115	C. Delgado	73	J. Canseco	159*
1999	H. Bush	4	C. Delgado	44	C. Delgado	134	C. Delgado	86	C. Delgado	141
2000	J. Cruz	5	T. Batista	41	C. Delgado	137	C. Delgado	123	J. Cruz	129
	S. Stewart	5	C. Delgado	41						

BLUE JAYS "BIG" RBI GAMES

RBI	PLAYER	DATE	OPPONENT	RBI	PLAYER	DATE	OPPONENT
9	Roy Howell	Sept. 10, 1977	NYY (A)	6	Jesse Barfield	May 18, 1986	Cle (H)
7	John Mayberry	June 26, 1978	Bal (H)	6	George Bell	June 11, 1987	Bal (A)
7	Otto Velez	May 4, 1980	Cle (H) 1st gm	6	Ernie Whitt	Sept. 12, 1987	NYY (H)
7	George Bell	May 9, 1987	Tex (A)	6	Ernie Whitt	Sept. 27, 1988	Bal (A)
6	Roy Howell	July 3, 1979	Det (A)	6	Kelly Gruber	April 16, 1989	KC (H)
6	Barry Bonnell	May 3, 1980	Cle (H)	6	George Bell	June 8, 1990	Mil (A)
6	Lloyd Moseby	Aug. 19, 1981	KC (A)	6	Charlie O'Brien	May 14, 1997	Det (A)
6	Damaso Garcia	May 10, 1985	Sea (H)	6	Carlos Delgado	June 7, 2000	Atl (A)

Blue Jays Records

Year	SLUGGING %		ON BASE %		SB		SH		SF	
1977	R. Fairly	.465	R. Howell	.370	B. Bailor	15	A. Ashby	10	O. Velez	6
1978	J. Mayberry	.416	J. Mayberry	.330	R. Bosetti	6	L. Gomez	19	J. Mayberry	7
1979	J. Mayberry	.461	J. Mayberry	.374	A. Griffin	21	A. Griffin	16	R. Bosetti	7
1980	O. Velez	.487	O. Velez	.368	A. Griffin	18	A. Griffin	10	A. Griffin	5
							L. Moseby	10	R. Howell	5
1981	J. Mayberry	.452#	O. Velez	.366#	D. Garcia	13	A. Woods	8	L. Moseby	4
1982	W. Upshaw	.443	B. Bonnell	.345	D. Garcia	54	A. Griffin	11	G. Iorg	7
1983	W. Upshaw	.515	L. Moseby	.380	D. Collins	31	A. Griffin	11	W. Upshaw	7
					D. Garcia	31				
1984	C. Johnson	.507	C. Johnson	.393	D. Collins	60	A. Griffin	13	B. Martinez	9
1985	J. Barfield	.536	R. Mulliniks	.387	L. Moseby	37	T. Fernandez	7	G. Bell	8
1986	J. Barfield	.559	J. Barfield	.368	L. Moseby	32	T. Fernandez	5	R. Leach	7
									L. Moseby	7
1987	G. Bell	.605	T. Fernandez	.379	L. Moseby	39	G. Iorg	6	G. Bell	9
1988	F. McGriff	.552	F. McGriff	.376	L. Moseby	31	K. Gruber	5	G. Bell	8
							N. Liriano	5		
1989	F. McGriff	.525	F. McGriff	.399	L. Moseby	24	N. Liriano	10	G. Bell	14
1990	F. McGriff	.530	F. McGriff	.400	T. Fernandez	26	M. Wilson	6	K. Gruber	13
1991	J. Carter	.503	R. Alomar	.354	R. Alomar	53	R. Alomar	16	J. Olerud	10
1992	J. Carter	.498	R. Alomar	.405	R. Alomar	49	M. Lee	8	J. Carter	13
1993	J. Olerud	.599	J. Olerud	.473*	R. Alomar	55	P. Borders	7	J. Carter	10
1994	J. Carter	.524	P. Molitor	.410	P. Molitor	20	D. Schofield	7	J. Carter	13
1995	S. Green	.509	J. Olerud	.398	R. Alomar	30	A. Gonzalez	9	R. Alomar	7
									E. Sprague	7
1996	E. Sprague	.496	J. Olerud	.382	O. Nixon	54	D. Cedeno	7	C. Delgado	8
							A. Gonzalez	7		
							O. Nixon	7		
1997	C. Delgado	.528	O. Merced	.352	O. Nixon	47	A. Gonzalez	11	J. Carter	9
1998	C. Delgado	.592	T. Fernandez	.387	S. Stewart	51	A. Gonzalez	13	D. Fletcher	7
1999	S. Green	.588	T. Fernandez	.427	S. Stewart	37	H. Bush	8	C. Delgado	7
2000	C. Delgado	.664	C. Delgado	.470	R. Mondesi	22	A. Gonzalez	16*	B. Fullmer	6

Year	IBB		Pinch-Hits		Hitting Streaks	
1977	R. Fairly	11	Sam Ewing	9	Roy Howell (May 10-25)	15
1978	R. Carty	5	Otto Velez	8	Dave McKay (May 19-June 2)	16
1979	J. Mayberry	7	Otto Velez	5	Alfredo Griffin (Aug 28-Sept 12)	14
1980	J. Mayberry	9	Steve Braun	9	Alfredo Griffin (Aug 13-Sept 1)	19
					John Mayberry (May 31-June 18)	11
1981	A. Woods	5	Willie Upshaw	4	Damaso Garcia (May 29-June 9)	11
1982	W. Upshaw	8	Wayne Nordhagen	11	Damaso Garcia (Aug 4-21)	20
1983	C. Johnson	8	Rance Mulliniks	10	Damaso Garcia (June 21-July 16)	21*
	W. Upshaw	8			Lloyd Moseby (July 27-Aug 16)	21*
1984	W. Upshaw	9	Cliff Johnson	11	Damaso Garcia (April 15-May 1)	14
1985	E. Whitt	9	Rance Mulliniks	9	Jesse Barfield (May 8-26)	16
					Damaso Garcia (July 23-Aug 10)	16
1986	J. Barfield	5	Garth Iorg	10	Damaso Garcia (June 15-July 8)	8
			Rick Leach	10		
1987	G. Bell	7	Rance Mulliniks	8	Tony Fernandez (Aug 23-Sept 18)	18
1988	J. Barfield	6	Rance Mulliniks	6	Kelly Gruber (June 22-July 4)	12
	L. Moseby	6				
1989	F. McGriff	12	Bob Brenly	6	George Bell (Aug 8-31)	22*
1990	F. McGriff	12	Rance Mulliniks	8	Tony Fernandez (Apr 10-25)	15
					Kelly Gruber (Sept 10-25)	15
1991	J. Carter	12	Pat Tabler	9	Roberto Alomar (May 24-June 9)	15
1992	J. Olerud	11	John Olerud	4	Dave Winfield (April 22-May 9)	17
1993	J. Olerud	33	Turner Ward	2	John Olerud (May 26-June 22)	26*
1994	J. Olerud	12	Michael Huff	3	Joe Carter (April 12-28)	15
1995	J. Olerud	10	Michael Huff	4	Roberto Alomar (Aug 5-21)	19
1996	J. Olerud	6	Robert Perez	5	Otis Nixon (June 4-July 6)	13
1997	C. Delgado	9	Carlos Delgado	4	Carlos Delgado (Sept 11-28)	16
1998	C. Delgado	13	Felipe Crespo	2	Carlos Delgado (May 21-June 9)	19
			Darrin Fletcher	2		
			Juan Samuel	2		
1999	T. Fernandez	11	Willie Greene	6	Shawn Green (June 29-July 31)	28*
2000	C. Delgado	18	Darrin Fletcher	4	Carlos Delgado (June 4-29)	22
			Todd Greene	4		

PERFECT STARTS

Following is a list of Blue Jays pitchers starting the season perfectly

YEAR	PITCHER	RECORD	NOTES	YEAR	PITCHER	RECORD	NOTES
1997	Roger Clemens	11-0	RH starter	1992	Juan Guzman	6-0	RH starter
1985	Dennis Lamp	11-0	RH reliever	1977	Jerry Garvin	5-0	LH starter
1985	Tom Filer	7-0	RH starter	1992	Pat Hentgen	5-0	RH starter
1999	John Frascatore	7-0	RH reliever	1993	Juan Guzman	5-0	RH starter
1984	Luis Leal	6-0	RH starter	1989	Muaro Gozzo	4-0	RH starter
1988	Duane Ward	6-0	RH reliever	1993	Danny Cox	4-0	RH reliever

PITCHING LEADERS

Year	W		L		ERA (MIN 140 INN)		G		GS	
1977	D. Lemanczyk	13	J. Garvin	18	P. Vuckovich	3.47	P. Vuckovich	53	J. Garvin	34
									D. Lemanczyk	34
1978	J. Clancy	10	J. Jefferson	16	J. Clancy	4.09	T. Murphy	50	J. Clancy	30
									J. Jefferson	30
									T. Underwood	30
1979	T. Underwood	9	P. Huffman	18	T. Underwood	3.69	T. Buskey	44	T. Underwood	32
1980	J. Clancy	13	J. Clancy	16	J. Clancy	3.30	J. Garvin	61	J. Clancy	34
1981	D. Stieb	11	L. Leal	13	D. Stieb	3.19	J. McLaughlin	40	D. Stieb	25
1982	D. Stieb	17	L. Leal	15	D. Stieb	3.25	D. Murray	56	J. Clancy	40*
1983	D. Stieb	17	J. Gott	14	D. Stieb	3.04	J. McLaughlin	50	D. Stieb	36
1984	D. Alexander	17	J. Clancy	15	D. Stieb	2.83	J. Key	63	J. Clancy	36*
1985	D. Alexander	17	D. Stieb	13	D. Stieb	2.48*	G. Lavelle	69	D. Alexander	36
									D. Stieb	36
1986	J. Clancy	14	J. Clancy	14	M. Eichhorn	1.72	M. Eichhorn	69	J. Key	35
	J. Key	14								
	M. Eichhorn	14								
1987	J. Key	17	J. Clancy	11	J. Key	2.76*	M. Eichhorn	89	J. Key	36
1988	D. Stieb	16	J. Clancy	13	D. Stieb	3.04	D. Ward	64	M. Flanagan	34
			M. Flanagan	13						
1989	D. Stieb	17	J. Key	14	J. Cerutti	3.07	D. Ward	66	D. Stieb	33
									J. Key	33
1990	D. Stieb	18	T. Stottlemyre	17	D. Stieb	2.93	D. Ward	73	D. Stieb	33
									T. Stottlemyre	33
1991	J. Key	17	J. Key	12	J. Key	3.05	D. Ward	81	T. Stottlemyre	34
1992	J. Morris	21	J. Key	13	J. Guzman	2.64	D. Ward	79	J. Morris	34
1993	P. Hentgen	19	T. Stottlemyre	12	P. Hentgen	3.87	D. Ward	71	J. Guzman	33
			J. Morris	12						
1994	P. Hentgen	13	J. Guzman	11	P. Hentgen	3.40	T. Castillo	41	J. Guzman	25
1995	A. Leiter	11	J. Guzman	14	A. Leiter	3.64	T. Castillo	55	P. Hentgen	30
			P. Hentgen	14						
1996	P. Hentgen	20	E. Hanson	17	J. Guzman	2.93*	M. Timlin	59	E. Hanson	35
									P. Hentgen	35
1997	R. Clemens	21*	W. Williams	14	R. Clemens	2.05*	P. Quantrill	77	P. Hentgen	35
1998	R. Clemens	20*	J. Guzman	12	R. Clemens	2.65*	P. Quantrill	82	R. Clemens	33
1999	D. Wells	17	P. Hentgen	12	R. Halladay	3.92	G. Lloyd	74	P. Hentgen	34
									D. Wells	34
2000	D. Wells	20*	K. Escobar	15	D. Wells	4.11	B. Koch	68	D. Wells	35*
							P. Quantrill	68		

Year	CG		SV		ShO		IP		SO	
1977	J. Garvin	12	P. Vuckovich	8	J. Garvin	1	D. Lemanczyk	252.0	J. Garvin	127
					J. Clancy	1				
					P. Vuckovich	1				
1978	J. Jefferson	9	V. Cruz	9	J. Jefferson	2	J. Jefferson	211.2	T. Underwood	140
1979	T. Underwood	12	T. Buskey	7	D. Lemanczyk	3	T. Underwood	227.0	T. Underwood	127
1980	J. Clancy	15	J. Garvin	8	D. Stieb	4	J. Clancy	250.2	J. Clancy	152
1981	D. Stieb	11	J. McLaughlin	10	D. Stieb	2	D. Stieb	183.2	D. Stieb	89
1982	D. Stieb	19	D. Murray	11	D. Stieb	5	D. Stieb	288.1	D. Stieb	149
1983	D. Stieb	14	R. Moffitt	10	D. Stieb	4	D. Stieb	278.0	D. Stieb	187
1984	D. Alexander	11	R.L. Jackson	10	D. Alexander	2	D. Stieb	267.0	D. Stieb	198
	D. Stieb	11	J. Key	10	L. Leal	2				
					D. Stieb	2				
1985	D. Stieb	8	B. Caudill	14	D. Stieb	2	D. Stieb	265.0	D. Stieb	167
1986	J. Clancy	6	T. Henke	27	J. Clancy	3	J. Key	232.0	M. Eichhorn	166
1987	J. Key	8	T. Henke	34*	J. Clancy	1	J. Key	261.0	J. Clancy	180
					J. Key	1				
					D. Stieb	1				
1988	D. Stieb	8	T. Henke	25	D. Stieb	4	M. Flanagan	211.0	D. Stieb	147
1989	J. Key	5	T. Henke	20	D. Stieb	2	J. Key	216.0	D. Ward	122
1990	T. Stottlemyre	4	T. Henke	32	D. Stieb	2	D. Stieb	208.2	D. Stieb	125
1991	T. Candiotti	3	T. Henke	32	J. Key	2	T. Stottlemyre	219.0	D. Ward	132
1992	J. Morris	6	T. Henke	34	J. Key	2	J. Morris	240.2	J. Guzman	165
	T. Stottlemyre	6			T. Stottlemyre	2				
1993	J. Morris	4	D. Ward	45	J. Guzman	1	J. Guzman	221.0	J. Guzman	194
					A. Leiter	1				
					T. Stottlemyre	1				
1994	P. Hentgen	6	D. Hall	17	P. Hentgen	3	P. Hentgen	174.2	P. Hentgen	174
1995	D. Cone	5	T. Castillo	13	D. Cone	2	P. Hentgen	202.2	A. Leiter	153
1996	P. Hentgen	10	M. Timlin	31	P. Hentgen	3	P. Hentgen	265.2	P. Hentgen	177
1997	R. Clemens	9*	K. Escobar	14	R. Clemens	3*	R. Clemens	264.0	R. Clemens	292*
	P. Hentgen	9*			P. Hentgen	3*	P. Hentgen	264.0		
1998	R. Clemens	5	R. Myers	28	R. Clemens	3	R. Clemens	234.2	R. Clemens	271*
1999	D. Wells	7*	B. Koch	31	C. Carpenter	1	D. Wells	231.2	D. Wells	169
					R. Halladay	1				
					D. Wells	1				
2000	D. Wells	9*	B. Koch	33	K. Escobar	1	D. Wells	229.0	D. Wells	166
					E. Loaiza	1				
					D. Wells	1				

Year	BB	
1977	D. Lemanczyk	87
1978	J. Clancy	91
1979	T. Underwood	95
1980	J. Clancy	128
1981	J. Clancy	64
1982	L. Leal	79
1983	D. Steib	83
1984	J. Clancy	88
	D. Steib	88
1985	D. Steib	96
1986	D. Steib	87
1987	D. Steib	87
1988	M. Flanagan	80
1989	D. Steib	76
1990	T. Stottlemyre	69
1991	T. Stottlemyre	75
1992	J. Morris	80
1993	J. Guzman	110
1994	J. Guzman	76
1995	A. Leiter	108
1996	E. Hanson	102
1997	P. Hentgen	71
1998	R. Clemens	88
1999	K. Escobar	81
2000	K. Escobar	85

CONSECUTIVE WINS IN CONSECUTIVE GAME STARTS

Roger Clemens	8	April 30-June 6, 1997
Doyle Alexander	7	Aug. 27-Oct. 1, 1983
Dave Stewart	6	4GS in regular season plus 2GS in ALCS, 1993
Pat Hentgen	6	July 6-Aug. 6, 1996
David Wells	6	April 19-May 14, 2000
Jim Clancy	5	July 5-28, 1986
Dave Stieb	5	May 1-21, 1988
Dave Stieb	5	May 28-June 20, 1990
Jack Morris	5	May 31-June 22, 1992
Jimmy Key	5	Sept. 8-29, 1992
Roger Clemens	5	July 12-Aug. 2, 1998
David Wells	5	June 17-July 8, 2000

BLUE JAYS' CONSECUTIVE WINNING STREAKS BY PITCHERS (minimum 9 wins)

WINS	PITCHER	DATES
15	Roger Clemens	June 3- September 21, 1998
11	Dennis Lamp	April 26- September 23, 1985
11	Roger Clemens	April 2- June 6, 1997
10	Juan Guzman	June 22- October 1, 1991
9	Dave Stieb	May 1- June 20, 1988
9	Frank Castillo	June 12- September 27, 2000

SHUTOUTS AND ONE RUN GAMES

Shutouts

Year by Year	W	L
1977	3	15
1978	5	19
1979	7	15
1980	9	12
1981	4	20
1982	13	9
1983	8	8
1984	10	4
1985	9	4
1986	12	6
1987	8	10
1988	17	3
1989	12	7
1990	9	10
1991	16	9
1992	14	10
1993	11	1
1994	4	4
1995	8	10
1996	7	9
1997	16	11
1998	11	4
1999	9	8
2000	4	7
Total	**226**	**215**

1-Run Games

Year by Year	W	L
1977	17	27
1978	23	30
1979	19	28
1980	23	21
1981	10	17
1982	28	30
1983	25	20
1984	34	25
1985	26	21
1986	22	25
1987	27	24
1988	21	17
1989	25	22
1990	24	27
1991	28	20
1992	28	20
1993	23	22
1994	13	15
1995	16	23
1996	19	22
1997	29	30
1998	28	17
1999	26	18
2000	21	19
Total	**555**	**540**

Club by Club	W	L
Anaheim	17	15
Baltimore	17	24
Boston	12	25
Chicago	21	9
Cleveland	15	14
Detroit	16	12
Kansas City	25	15
Milwaukee	13	22
Minnesota	20	13
New York (A)	13	17
Oakland	19	15
Seattle	20	9
Tampa Bay	2	2
Texas	14	18
Atlanta	0	2
Florida	0	1
Montreal	2	1
New York (N)	0	1
Philadelphia	0	0
Total	**226**	**215**

Club by Club	W	L
Anaheim	39	40
Baltimore	46	32
Boston	47	52
Chicago	45	42
Cleveland	47	39
Detroit	42	46
Kansas City	43	41
Milwaukee	32	39
Minnesota	36	35
New York (A)	38	38
Oakland	44	43
Seattle	37	31
Tampa Bay	7	6
Texas	41	44
Atlanta	2	2
Florida	1	4
Montreal	6	3
New York (N)	0	1
Philadelphia	2	2
Total	**555**	**540**

Blue Jays Records

TORONTO'S BEST WON/LOST RECORDS

G	BEST W-L	BEST YR	WORST W-L	WORST YR
1	1-0	77/83/87/88/89/92/94/95/96/98/00	0-1	13 Times
2	2-0	87/88/92/94/95/96/00	0-2	79/81
3	3-0	92/96	0-3	79
4	4-0	92	1-3	78/79/80
5	5-0	92	1-4	78
6	6-0	92	2-4	78/81/98/00
7	6-1	92/94	2-5	78/81
8	7-1	92	2-6	78/81
9	8-1	92	2-7	78
10	9-1	92	2-8	78
11	9-2	92	3-8	78/81
12	10-2	92	3-9	78/81
13	10-3	92	3-10	81
14	11-3	92	4-10	81
15	12-3	92	5-10	78/79/81/82
16	12-4	92/99	5-11	78/81/82
17	13-4	92	6-11	78/79/81/82
18	14-4	92	6-12	79
19	15-4	92	6-13	79
20	15-5	92	6-14	79
21	15-6	92	7-14	79/81
22	16-6	92	7-15	79
23	16-7	92	7-16	79
24	16-8	92	7-17	79
25	16-9	92	7-18	79
26	17-9	92	8-18	78/79
27	18-9	92	8-19	79
28	19-9	92	8-20	79
29	20-9	92	8-21	79
30	21-9	92	8-22	79
31	21-10	92	8-23	79
32	21-11	87/92	8-24	79
33	22-11	92	9-24	79
34	23-11	92	9-25	79
35	24-11	92	9-26	79
36	25-11	92	9-27	79
37	25-12	92	10-27	79
38	25-13	92	10-28	79
39	25-14	84/85/92	10-29	79
40	26-14	84/85	10-30	79
41	27-14	84/85	10-31	79
42	28-14	84/85	11-31	79
43	29-14	84/85	11-32	79
44	30-14	84/85	11-33	79
45	31-14	84/85	12-33	79
46	31-15	84/85	12-34	79
47	32-15	84	12-35	79
48	33-15	84	12-36	79
49	34-15	84	12-37	79
50	34-16	84/85	12-38	79

G	BEST W-L	BEST YR	WORST W-L	WORST YR
51	35-16	85	12-39	79
52	36-16	85	13-39	79
53	36-17	84/85	13-40	79
54	36-18	84/85	13-41	79
55	36-19	84/85	13-42	79
56	37-19	85	14-42	79
57	38-19	85	15-42	79
58	38-20	85/87	16-42	79/81
59	39-20	87	16-43	79
60	39-21	87	17-43	79
61	39-22	84/85/87	17-44	79
62	40-22	84	18-44	79
63	41-22	84/87	18-45	79
64	41-23	84/87	18-46	79
65	41-24	84/87	19-46	79
66	42-24	84	20-46	79
67	42-25	84/87	21-46	78/79
68	43-25	84	22-46	78/79
69	43-26	84/85/87	22-47	78/79
70	44-26	87	23-47	78/79
71	44-27	85/87	23-48	79
72	45-27	85/87	23-49	79
73	45-28	85/87	23-50	79
74	46-28	85	23-51	79
75	46-29	85	24-51	79
76	46-30	85/93	24-52	79
77	47-30	85/93	24-53	79
78	48-30	93	24-54	79
79	48-31	85/92/93	24-55	79
80	49-31	92	24-56	79
81	50-31	92	24-57	79
82	51-31	92	25-57	79
83	52-31	92	26-57	79
84	53-31	92	26-58	79
85	53-32	85/92	27-58	79
86	53-33	85/92	27-59	79
87	53-34	85/92	27-60	79
88	54-34	92	28-60	79
89	54-35	92	28-61	79
90	55-35	92	28-62	79
91	56-35	92	28-63	79
92	56-36	92	29-63	79
93	57-36	92	29-64	79
94	57-37	85/92	29-65	79
95	58-37	85/92	29-66	79
96	59-37	85	29-67	79
97	60-37	85	29-68	79
98	61-37	85	29-69	79
99	62-37	85	29-70	79
100	63-37	85	30-70	79
101	63-38	85	31-70	79
102	64-38	85	31-71	79
103	65-38	85	32-71	79
104	66-38	85	32-72	79
105	67-38	85	32-73	79
106	67-39	85	32-74	79

G	BEST W-L	BEST YR	WORST W-L	WORST YR
107	68-39	85	32-75	79
108	69-39	85	32-76	79
109	69-40	85	33-76	79
110	69-41	85	33-77	79
111	70-41	85	33-78	79
112	70-42	85	34-78	79
113	71-42	85	34-79	79
114	72-42	85	34-80	79
115	72-43	85	35-80	79
116	72-44	85	35-81	79
117	73-44	85	36-81	79
118	73-45	85	37-81	79
119	74-45	85	38-81	79
120	74-46	85	38-82	79
121	75-46	85	39-82	79
122	76-46	85	39-83	79
123	77-46	85	39-84	79
124	77-47	85	39-85	79
125	78-47	85	39-86	79
126	79-47	85	39-87	79
127	79-48	85	40-87	79
128	80-48	85	40-88	79
129	81-48	85	41-88	79
130	81-49	85	42-88	79
131	82-49	85	42-89	79
132	82-50	85	42-90	79
133	83-50	85	42-91	79
134	84-50	85	43-91	79
135	84-51	85	43-92	79
136	85-51	85	44-92	79
137	86-51	85	44-93	79
138	87-51	85	44-94	79
139	88-51	85	44-95	79
140	88-52	85	44-96	79
141	89-52	85	44-97	79
142	90-52	85	44-98	79
143	91-52	85	45-98	79
144	91-53	85	46-98	79
145	91-54	85	46-99	79
146	92-54	85	47-99	79
147	93-54	85	48-99	79
148	93-55	85	49-99	79
149	94-55	85	50-99	79
150	95-55	85	50-100	79
151	95-56	85	50-101	79
152	95-57	85	50-102	79
153	96-57	85	51-102	79
154	97-57	85	52-102	77/79
155	98-57	85	52-103	77/79
156	98-58	85	52-104	77/79
157	98-59	85	52-105	77
158	98-60	85	53-105	77/79
159	98-61	85	53-106	77/79
160	99-61	85	53-107	79
161	99-62	85	53-108	79
162	96-66	87/92	53-109	79

PITCHERS BACK-TO-BACK SHUTOUTS

PITCHER	DATES	OPPONENT	SCORE
Dave Stieb	July 16, 1980	@ Seattle	W 5-0
	July 21, 1980	@ Oakland	W 1-0
Dave Stieb	Sept. 18, 1988	Cleveland	W 4-0
	Sept. 24, 1988	@ Cleveland	W 1-0
Dave Stieb	Sept. 24, 1988	@ Cleveland	W 1-0
	Sept. 30, 1988	Baltimore	W 4-0
Roger Clemens	Aug. 20, 1998	@ Seattle	W 7-0
	Aug. 25, 1998	Kansas City	W 3-0
	Aug. 30, 1998	Minnesota	W 6-0

BLUE JAYS MONTHLY RECORDS

Year		APR. W-L	MAY W-L	JUNE W-L	JULY W-L	AUG. W-L	SEPT./OCT. W-L	AT ALL-STAR W-L	POST ALL-STAR W-L	TOTAL W-L
1977	H	6-4	5-10	3-9	5-10	3-8	3-14	18-27	7-28	25-55
	A	4-7	3-7	7-8	2-11	7-10	6-9	16-31	13-21	29-52
	T	10-11	8-17	10-17	7-21	10-18	9-23	34-58	20-49	54-107
1978	H	4-7	7-7	6-8	7-7	10-3	3-12	19-23	18-21	37-44
	A	4-6	2-11	3-9	6-11	6-11	1-10	13-30	9-28	22-58
	T	8-13	9-18	9-17	13-18	16-14	4-22	32-53	27-49	59-102
1979	H	3-8	3-15	6-5	5-6	6-8	9-7	14-32	18-17	32-49
	A	4-7	2-8	6-14	3-11	5-9	1-11	15-32	6-28	21-60
	T	7-15	5-23	12-19	8-17	11-17	10-18	29-64	24-45	53-109
1980	H	3-1	8-9	7-7	5-10	6-8	6-11	18-19	17-27	35-46
	A	6-6	5-5	3-10	6-7	5-12	7-9	15-24	17-25	32-49
	T	9-7	13-14	10-17	11-17	11-20	13-20	33-43	34-52	67-95
1981	H	2-7	5-10	0-5	—	4-8	6-6	7-22	10-14	17-36
	A	5-5	4-10	0-5	—	5-2	6-11	9-20	11-13	20-33
	T	7-12	9-20	0-10	—	9-10	12-17	16-42	21-27	37-69
1982	H	5-6	6-5	7-10	9-4	7-8	10-4	19-24	25-13	44-37
	A	3-6	7-9	5-4	6-8	6-12	7-8	18-23	16-24	34-47
	T	8-12	13-14	12-14	15-12	13-20	17-12	37-47	41-37	78-84
1983	H	4-4	12-6	6-3	8-8	7-6	11-6	23-15	25-18	48-33
	A	4-6	6-3	10-9	7-4	8-13	6-5	20-18	21-22	41-40
	T	8-10	18-9	16-12	15-12	15-19	17-11	43-33	46-40	89-73
1984	H	5-5	15-2	9-5	7-6	6-5	7-9	34-15	15-17	49-32
	A	8-4	4-4	4-11	7-8	12-7	5-7	16-19	24-22	40-41
	T	13-9	19-6	13-16	14-14	18-12	12-16	50-34	39-39	89-73
1985	H	5-4	9-2	11-5	10-4	5-3	12-8	26-13	28-13	54-26
	A	8-3	8-6	5-8	8-6	12-7	6-6	27-22	18-24	45-36
	T	13-7	17-8	16-13	18-10	17-10	18-14	53-35	46-37	99-62
1986	H	4-7	7-5	10-8	5-5	11-5	5-9	26-25	16-14	42-39
	A	5-4	7-10	7-3	10-6	7-5	8-9	21-18	23-19	44-37
	T	9-11	14-15	17-11	15-11	18-10	13-18	47-43	39-33	86-76
1987	H	7-4	7-3	8-7	12-4	5-6	13-5	28-16	24-13	52-29
	A	5-4	9-8	9-4	3-8	12-6	6-7	23-20	21-17	44-37
	T	12-8	16-11	17-11	15-12	17-12	19-12	51-36	45-30	96-66
1988	H	4-9	6-5	10-4	4-8	7-7	14-3	23-24	22-12	45-36
	A	5-4	7-11	7-7	8-6	7-7	8-4	19-22	23-17	42-39
	T	9-13	13-16	17-11	12-14	14-14	22-7	42-46	45-29	87-75
1989	H	4-5	8-9	6-5	6-8	14-4	8-5	20-23	26-12	46-35
	A	5-11	3-6	11-5	9-4	6-5	9-6	22-22	21-16	43-38
	T	9-16	11-15	17-10	15-12	20-9	17-11	42-45	47-28	89-73
1990	H	9-4	5-9	6-8	9-5	5-8	10-3	26-23	18-14	44-37
	A	3-5	9-5	9-5	5-7	8-8	8-9	21-15	21-24	42-39
	T	12-9	14-14	15-13	14-12	13-16	18-12	47-38	39-38	86-76
1991	H	8-3	8-5	8-7	8-6	6-8	8-6	27-16	19-19	46-35
	A	4-6	7-7	8-5	7-5	9-6	10-7	22-18	23-18	45-36
	T	12-9	15-12	16-12	15-11	15-14	18-13	49-34	42-37	91-71
1992	H	11-4	8-6	4-5	11-4	7-4	12-5	31-18	22-10	53-28
	A	5-3	7-6	10-7	5-6	7-12	9-4	22-16	21-22	43-38
	T	16-7	15-12	14-12	16-10	14-16	21-9	53-34	43-32	96-66
1993	H	9-4	8-6	10-3	7-9	7-6	7-5	28-19	20-14	48-33
	A	4-6	8-6	9-6	5-5	10-6	11-5	21-21	26-13	47-34
	T	13-10	16-12	19-9	12-14	17-12	18-10	49-40	46-27	95-67
1994	H	9-2	10-8	3-8	9-4	2-4	—	24-19	9-7	33-26
	A	5-8	0-8	5-10	8-6	4-2	—	14-29	8-5	22-34
	T	14-10	10-16	8-18	17-10	6-6	—	38-48	17-12	55-60
1995	H	3-2	7-8	6-5	5-8	5-8	3-12	16-17	13-26	29-43
	A	—	4-8	3-11	10-6	6-10	4-10	11-23	16-22	27-45
	T	3-2	11-16	9-16	15-14	11-18	7-22	27-40	29-48	56-88
1996	H	5-9	8-5	5-6	7-7	5-9	5-10	19-22	16-24	35-46
	A	6-5	5-10	7-9	6-7	9-6	6-5	19-27	20-15	39-42
	T	11-14	13-15	12-15	13-14	14-15	11-15	38-49	36-39	74-88
1997	H	5-7	7-8	5-11	8-4	8-6	9-3	20-29	22-10	42-39
	A	6-5	8-5	6-4	5-11	7-9	2-13	20-14	14-33	34-47
	T	11-12	15-13	11-15	13-15	15-15	11-16	40-43	36-43	76-86
1998	H	5-8	8-6	8-5	9-4	11-5	10-2	25-20	26-10	51-30
	A	5-8	10-5	6-9	3-11	6-5	7-6	21-22	16-22	37-44
	T	10-16	18-11	14-14	12-15	17-10	17-8	46-42	42-32	88-74
1999	H	9-1	4-12	13-5	9-5	2-10	3-8	29-19	11-22	40-41
	A	4-10	7-5	2-8	10-2	10-6	11-6	18-24	26-13	44-37
	T	13-11	11-17	15-13	19-7	12-16	14-14	47-43	37-35	84-78
2000	H	7-7	8-8	7-3	6-7	8-3	9-8	22-18	23-18	45-36
	A	5-7	8-4	9-7	5-9	7-8	4-8	26-23	12-20	38-43
	T	12-14	16-12	16-10	11-16	15-11	13-16	48-41	35-38	83-79

Blue Jays Records

BEST/WORST HOMESTANDS AND ROADTRIPS
(Minimum 6 games)

PCT.	W-L	DATES	OPPONENTS
BEST HOMESTANDS			
.909	10-1	May 9-16, 1978	Oakland Seattle, California
.900	9-1	April 12-22, 1999	Tampa Bay, Baltimore, Anaheim
.857	6-1	April 10-16, 1992	Baltimore, New York
.857	6-1	August 7-13, 1978	Baltimore, Chicago, Kansas City
.857	6-1	Sept. 28-Oct. 3, 1982	Minnesota, Seattle
.857	6-1	July 6-12, 1987	Texas, Kansas City
.846	11-2	Aug. 22-Sept. 3, 1989	Detroit, Milwaukee, Chicago, Minnesota
.833	5-1	May 9-16, 1978	Oakland, Seattle, California
.833	5-1	July 22-27, 1997	Milwaukee, Kansas City
.833	5-1	Sept. 4-9, 1997	Texas, Anaheim
.833	5-1	June 29-July 5, 1998	New York (N), Tampa Bay
.833	5-1	Sept. 3-9, 1998	Boston, Cleveland
.833	5-1	Sept. 21-27, 1998	Baltimore, Detroit
.833	5-1	June 29-July 4, 1999	Baltimore, Tampa Bay
.833	5-1	June 20-25, 2000	Detroit, Boston
.818	9-2	July 28-28, 1985	Oakland, Seattle, California
BEST ROADTRIPS			
.900	9-1	June 8-17, 1990	Milwaukee, Minnesota, New York
.857	6-1	June 8-14, 1987	New York, Baltimore
.857	6-1	June 17-24, 1993	Boston/New York
.857	6-1	Aug. 26-Sept. 1, 1991	Baltimore, New York
.833	5-1	May 23-29, 1985	Cleveland, Chicago
.833	5-1	May 28-June 2, 1993	Oakland, California
.833	5-1	Aug. 13-18, 1993	Boston, Cleveland
.833	5-1	Sept. 23-28, 1988	Cleveland, Boston
.833	5-1	July 6-11, 1999	Baltimore, Montreal
.833	5-1	July 21-26, 1999	Cleveland, Chicago
.833	5-1	Sept. 28-Oct. 3, 1999	Tampa Bay, Cleveland
.714	5-2	June 23-30, 1983	Seattle, Minnesota
.700	7-3	April 26-May 5, 1985	Texas, Oakland, California, Seattle
.700	7-3	July 3-12, 1987	Chicago, Cleveland, Boston
.700	7-3	Aug. 16-25, 1996	Minnesota, Kansas City, Chicago
WORST HOMESTANDS			
.000	0-6	Sept. 26-Oct. 1, 1980	Boston, Detroit
.000	0-6	June 20-26, 1994	Boston, Baltimore
.000	0-6	Aug. 13-18, 1999	Oakland, Seattle
.111	1-8	Sept. 1-9, 1978	California, Cleveland, Milwaukee, Baltimore
.125	1-7	Sept. 2-8, 1977	Seattle, Boston
.125	1-7	May 15-22, 1990	Seattle, California, Oakland
.143	1-6	May 23-June 1, 1977	Oakland, California, Kansas City
.167	2-10	May 18-31, 1979	Baltimore, Cleveland, Boston, Detroit
.167	1-5	Aug. 30-Sept. 4, 1996	Chicago, Kansas City
.167	1-5	May 4-9, 1999	Oakland, Texas
.167	1-5	Sept. 13-19, 1999	New York (AL), Chicago
WORST ROADTRIPS			
.000	0-6	Sept. 3-9, 1979	Baltimore, Cleveland
.143	1-6	Aug. 20-26, 1982	New York, Baltimore
.143	1-6	April 24-30, 1989	Oakland, Seattle, California
.143	1-6	July 27-Aug. 2, 2000	Seattle, Oakland
.167	1-5	June 23-28, 1995	New York, Boston
.167	1-5	June 4-9, 1996	New York, Texas
.167	2-10	Sept. 10-22, 1997	Oakland, Seattle, Boston, New York (AL)
.167	1-5	June 7-13, 1999	New York (NL), Philadelphia
.167	1-5	Sept. 26-Oct. 1, 2000	Baltimore, Cleveland
.182	2-9	Aug. 28-Sept.6, 1995	Cleveland, Chicago, Kansas City
.200	2-8	July 4-14, 1977	Boston, Cleveland, Detroit, Chicago
.200	2-8	July 28-Aug. 5, 1997	Milwaukee, Detroit, Minnesota
.222	2-7	July 9-16, 1998	Detroit, Baltimore, Chicago
.250	2-6	June 21-27, 1984	Boston, Milwaukee
.250	2-6	June 2-11, 1995	Cleveland, Chicago, Kansas City
.273	3-8	April 23-May 3, 1999	New York (AL), Anaheim, Seattle
.285	2-5	Sept. 18-24, 1995	New York, Boston
.285	2-5	June 15-21, 1998	Tampa Bay, Baltimore
.300	3-7	June 10-19, 1985	New York, Boston, Milwaukee

NO SWEEPS

The 1992 Toronto Blue Jays became only the sixth team in Major League history to complete a season without being swept in a series. Following is a list of the other previous five teams:

1904 New York Giants
1905 Philadelphia Athletics
1910 Chicago Cubs
1921 Cleveland Indians
1943 St. Louis Cardinals

LONGEST WINNING STREAKS

11	1987	June 2-13	Sea 2, Bal 3, NYY 3, Bal 3
11	1998	Aug. 27-Sept. 7	KC 1, Min 3, KC 2, Bos 4, Cle 1
9	1993	Sept. 10-21	Cal 3, Det 2, Min 3, Bos 1
9	1986	Aug. 23-Sept. 1	Min. Cle 3, Min 3, Cle 1
9	1985	July 21-29	Oak 1, Sea 3, Cal 4, Bal 1
8	1985	May 20-28	CWS 3, Cle 4, CWS 1
8	1992	July 1-9	Tex 1, Cal 4, Sea 2, Oak 1
8	1994	July 17-24	Tex 1, Min 3, Tex 4
8	1999	April 14-22	TB 2, Bal 3, Ana 3

LONGEST LOSING STREAKS

12	1981	May 31-Aug. 10	Oak 1, Cal 3, Tex 3, CWS 2, KC 2, Det 1
11	1977	Aug. 26-Sept. 6	Oak 3, Min 2, Sea 3, Bos 3
10	1994	June 18-28	Det 2, Bos 3, Bal 3, Mil 2
9	1977	July 17-30	Det 1, CWS 2, Det 2, Tex 2, Mil 2
9	1978	June 4-14	Tex 1, Mil 4, Min 2, Mil 2

LONGEST HOME WINNING STREAKS

10	1985	July 21-Aug. 3	Oak 1, Sea 3, Cal 4, Tex 2
9	1984	May 21-June 2	Min 3, Cle 4, NYY 2
9	1994	July 9-24	KC 2, Min 3, Tex 4
9	1998	Aug. 27-Sept. 7	KC 1, Min 3, Bos 4, Cle 1
8	1992	July 1-9	Tex 1, Cal 4, Sea 2, Oak 1
8	1999	April 14-22	TB 2, Bal 3, Ana 3

LONGEST ROAD WINNING STREAKS

9	1993	Sept. 14-30	Det 2, Min 3, Mil 3, Bal 1
7	1985	April 14-May 1	Bal 1, Tex 3, Oak 2, Cal 1
7	1987	May 25-June 13	Sea 1, NYY 3, Bal 3
7	1996	Aug. 18-24	Min 1, KC 3, CWS 3

LONGEST HOME LOSING STREAKS

11	1977	Aug. 15-Sept. 6	Cal 2, Oak 3, Sea 3, Bos 3
9	1999	Aug. 13-29	Oak 3, Sea 3, Tex 3
7	1977	July 17-30	Det 1, CWS 2, Tex 2, Mil 2
7	1978	June 4-21	Tex 1, Min 2, Mil 2, Det 2
7	1978	Aug. 27-Sept. 6	Min 1, Cal 3, Cle 2, Mil 1
7	1979	April 15-29	KC 1, CWS 3, Mil 3
7	1994	June 20-July 8	Bos 3, Bal 3, KC 1
7	1995	Sept. 9-15	Det 3, Tex 3, Mil 1
7	1997	June 21-July 1	Bal 2, Bos 3, Mon 2

LONGEST ROAD LOSING STREAKS

12	1979	July 7-Aug. 11	Tex 2, Mil 2, Min 4, KC 3, CWS 1
10	1979	Aug. 19-Sept. 9	Cal 1, Sea 3, Bal 3, Cle 3
9	1978	Sept. 15-Oct. 1	Bal 3, NYY 3, Bos 3

PITCHERS AT THE PLATE

The Blue Jays never had a pitcher bat in a regular season game in their first twenty seasons.

DAVE STIEB batted against Minnesota Twins on August 29, 1980 at Exhibition Stadium but he was playing the outfield. Stieb had gone in to play left field in the 15th inning of a suspended game started on August 28th. In his only time at the plate he flied out to the center-fielder, Ken Landreaux in the bottom of the 15th. The pitcher was Al Williams. He played one inning and had no fielding opportunities as the Jays lost 7-5 in 15 innings.

In the 1992 World Series vs Atlanta, Blue Jays pitchers were 2-7 with DAVID CONE going 2-4, JIMMY KEY 0-1 and JACK MORRIS 0-2.

In the 1993 World Series vs Philadelphia, Blue Jays pitchers were 1-8. AL LEITER had the only hit, a double.

In 1997 with the introduction of INTER-LEAGUE PLAY, Blue Jays pitchers took their turn hitting. WOODY WILLIAMS became the first Blue Jays pitcher to come to bat and also had the first hit, a single, in his second at bat off Curt Schilling on June 13, 1997. ROGER CLEMENS had the other Blue Jays hit, a double off the right-field wall at Shea Stadium against the New York Mets on September 2, 1997. He came around to score the first run ever by a Blue Jays pitcher.

In 1998, Blue Jays pitchers combined to hit .100 (2-20). WOODY WILLIAMS had both Blue Jays hits, with two singles in six at bats.

In 1999 the Blue Jays pitchers batted .053 with one hit in 19 at-bats. PAT HENTGEN picked up the staffs' only hit, the first of his career, on June 8 at Shea Stadium vs. the New York Mets.

Blue Jays pitchers combined to hit .071 with two hits in 28 at-bats during the 2000 season. Frank Castillo and David Wells collected the two hits for the Jays staff with both being singles.

As a team Blue Jays pitchers have combined to hit .083 with seven hits in 84 at-bats, including a double, since INTER-LEAGUE play was introduced in 1997.

Blue Jays Records

SINGLE SEASON TOP TEN

AVERAGE (350 AB)

1.	Olerud	.363	1993
2.	Molitor	.341	1994
3.	Molitor	.332	1993
4.	Fernandez	.328	1999
5.	Alomar	.326	1993
6.	Fernandez	.322	1987
7.	Fernandez	.321	1998
8.	Bush	.320	1999
9.	Bonnell	.318	1983
10.	Howell	.316	1977

GAMES

1.	Fernandez	163	1986
2.	Bosetti	162	1979
	Carter	162	1991
	Griffin	162	1982
	Griffin	162	1983
6.	Alomar	161	1991
	Fernandez	161	1985
	Fernandez	161	1990
	McGriff	161	1989

HITS

1.	Fernandez	213	1986
2.	Molitor	211	1993
3.	Olerud	200	1993
4.	Bell	198	1986
5.	Alomar	192	1993
6.	Green	190	1999
7.	Alomar	188	1991
	Bell	188	1987
9.	Fernandez	186	1987
	Fernandez	186	1988

AT BATS

1.	Fernandez	687	1986
2.	Griffin	653	1980
3.	Fernandez	648	1988
4.	White	642	1991
5.	Bell	641	1986
	White	641	1992
7.	Alomar	638	1991
8.	Alomar	637	1991
9	Molitor	636	1993
10.	Fernandez	635	1990

RUNS

1.	Green	134	1999
2.	Molitor	121	1993
3.	White	116	1993
4.	Delgado	113	1999
5.	Bell	111	1987
6.	White	110	1991
7.	Alomar	109	1993
	Olerud	109	1993
9.	Barfield	107	1986
10.	Moseby	106	1987
	Green	106	1998

SINGLES

1.	Fernandez	161	1986
2.	Molitor	147	1993
3.	Griffin	145	1979
	D. Garcia	145	1982
5.	Fernandez	144	1987
	Stewart	144	1999
7.	D. Garcia	138	1984
8.	Fernandez	136	1988
9.	Alomar	134	1992
	Alomar	134	1993

DOUBLES

1.	Olerud	54	1993
2.	Green	45	1999
3.	Delgado	43	1998
4.	Carter	42	1991
	White	42	1993
	Delgado	42	1997
7.	Alomar	41	1991
	Fernandez	41	1988
	Bell	41	1989
	Fernandez	41	1999

TRIPLES

1.	Fernandez	17	1990
2.	Griffin	15	1980
	Collins	15	1984
	Moseby	15	1984
5.	Alomar	11	1991
6.	Griffin	10	1979
	Fernandez	10	1985
	White	10	1991
9.	8 players tied at 9		

HOME RUNS

1.	Bell	47	1987
2.	Canseco	46	1998
3.	Delgado	44	1999
4.	Green	42	1999
5.	Barfield	40	1986
6.	Delgado	38	1998
7.	McGriff	36	1989
	Sprague	36	1996
9.	McGriff	35	1990
	Green	35	1998

EXTRA BASE HITS

1.	Green	87	1999
2.	Bell	83	1987
	Delgado	83	1999
4.	Delgado	82	1998
5.	Olerud	80	1993
6.	Carter	78	1991
7.	Barfield	77	1986
8.	Bell	75	1986
	Delgado	75	1997
10.	McGriff	73	1988
	Gruber	73	1990
	Sprague	73	1996

TOTAL BASES

1.	Bell	369	1987
2.	Green	361	1999
3.	Bell	341	1986
4.	Olerud	330	1993
5.	Barfield	329	1986
6.	Delgado	327	1999
7.	Molitor	324	1993
8.	Carter	321	1991
	Green	321	1998
10.	Delgado	314	1998

RUNS BATTED IN

1.	Bell	134	1987
	Delgado	134	1999
3.	Green	123	1999
4.	Carter	121	1993
5.	Carter	119	1992
6.	Gruber	118	1990
7.	Delgado	115	1998
8.	Molitor	111	1993
9.	Barfield	108	1986
	Bell	108	1986
	Carter	108	1991
	Winfield	108	1992

SLUGGING (350 AB)

1.	Bell	.605	1987
2.	Olerud	.599	1993
3.	Delgado	.592	1998
4.	Green	.588	1999
5.	Delgado	.571	1999
6.	Batista	.565	1999
7.	Barfield	.559	1986
8.	McGriff	.552	1988
9.	Barfield	.536	1985
10.	Bell	.532	1986

ON-BASE

1.	Olerud	.473	1993
2.	Fernandez	.427	1999
3.	Molitor	.410	1994
4.	Alomar	.408	1993
5.	Alomar	.405	1992
6.	Molitor	.402	1993
7.	McGriff	.400	1990
8.	McGriff	.399	1989
9.	Olerud	.398	1995
10.	Johnson	.393	1984

STOLEN BASES

1.	Collins	60	1984
2.	Alomar	55	1993
3.	D. Garcia	54	1982
	Nixon	54	1996
5.	Alomar	53	1991
6.	Stewart	51	1998
7.	Alomar	49	1992
8.	Nixon	47	1997
9.	Moseby	39	1987
10.	Moseby	37	1985
	White	37	1992
	Stewart	37	1999

STRIKEOUTS (BATTER)

1.	Canseco	159	1998
2.	McGriff	149	1988
3.	Barfield	146	1986
	Sprague	146	1996
5.	Barfield	143	1985
6.	Green	142	1998
7.	Barfield	141	1987
	Delgado	141	1999
9.	Delgado	139	1996
	Delgado	139	1998

BASE ON BALLS

1.	McGriff	119	1989
2.	Olerud	114	1993
3.	McGriff	94	1990
4.	Alomar	87	1992
5.	Delgado	86	1999
6.	Olerud	84	1995
7.	Winfield	82	1992
8.	Alomar	80	1993
9.	McGriff	79	1988
10.	Moseby	78	1984
	Upshaw	78	1986

HITTING STREAKS

1.	Green	28	1999
2.	Olerud	26	1993
	Stewart	26	1999
4.	Bell	22	1989
5.	D. Garcia	21	1983
	Moseby	21	1983
7.	D. Garcia	20	1982
8.	Griffin	19	1980
	Fernandez	19	1992
	Alomar	19	1995
	Delgado	19	1998

PINCH-HITS

1.	Nordhagen	11	1982
	Johnson	11	1984
3.	Powell	10	1982
	Mulliniks	10	1983
	Iorg	10	1986
	Leach	10	1986
7.	Ewing	9	1977
	Braun	9	1980
	Iorg	9	1982
	Mulliniks	9	1985
	Tabler	9	1991

PINCH AT BATS

1.	Johnson	39	1983
2.	Johnson	34	1984
3.	Leach	31	1986
4.	Powell	30	1982
5.	Ewing	29	1978
	Orta	29	1983
	Burroughs	29	1985
8.	Iorg	28	1986
	Leach	28	1987
10.	Ewing	27	1977
	Mulliniks	27	1983
	Iorg	27	1985

ERA (162 INNINGS)

1.	Clemens	2.05	1997
2.	Stieb	2.48	1985
3.	Guzman	2.64	1992
4.	Clemens	2.65	1998
5.	Key	2.76	1987
6.	Stieb	2.83	1984
7.	Stieb	2.93	1990
	Guzman	2.93	1996
9.	Key	3.00	1985
10.	Stieb	3.04	1988

WINS

1.	Morris	21	1992
	Clemens	21	1997
3.	Hentgen	20	1996
	Clemens	20	1998
5.	Hentgen	19	1993
6.	Stieb	18	1990
7.	Stieb	17	1982
	Stieb	17	1983
	Stieb	17	1989
	Alexander	17	1984
	Alexander	17	1985
	Key	17	1987
	Wells	17	1999

LOSSES

1.	Garvin	18	1977
	Huffman	18	1979
3.	Jefferson	17	1977
	Stottlemyre	17	1990
	Hanson	17	1996
6.	Clancy	16	1980
	Underwood	16	1979
	Jefferson	16	1978
	Lemanczyk	16	1977
10.	Clancy	15	1984
	Leal	15	1982
	Stieb	15	1980

SAVES

1.	Ward	45	1993
2.	Henke	34	1987
	Henke	34	1992
4.	Henke	32	1990
	Henke	32	1991
6.	Timlin	31	1996
	Koch	31	1999
8.	Myers	28	1998
9.	Henke	27	1986
10.	Henke	25	1988

GAMES PITCHED

1.	Eichhorn	89	1987
2.	Quantrill	82	1998
3.	Ward	81	1991
4.	Ward	79	1992
5.	Plesac	78	1998
6.	Quantrill	77	1997
7.	Lloyd	74	1999
8.	Ward	73	1990
	Plesac	73	1997
10.	Henke	72	1987

GAMES STARTED

1.	Clancy	40	1982
2.	Leal	38	1982
	Stieb	38	1982
4.	Clancy	37	1987
5.	Clancy	36	1983
	Clancy	36	1984
	Alexander	36	1985
	Stieb	36	1986
	Key	36	1987
10.	Leal	35	1983
	Alexander	35	1984
	Leal	35	1984
	Stieb	35	1984
	Hanson	35	1996
	Hentgen	35	1996
	Hentgen	35	1997

COMPLETE GAMES

1.	Stieb	19	1982
2.	Clancy	15	1980
3.	Stieb	14	1980
	Stieb	14	1983
5.	Garvin	12	1977
	Underwood	12	1979
7.	Lemanczyk	11	1977
	Lemanczyk	11	1979
	Stieb	11	1981
	Clancy	11	1982
	Clancy	11	1983
	Alexander	11	1984
	Stieb	11	1984

INNINGS PITCHED

1.	Stieb	288.1	1982
2.	Stieb	278.0	1983
3.	Stieb	267.0	1984
4.	Clancy	266.2	1982
5.	Hentgen	265.2	1996
6.	Stieb	265.0	1985
7.	Clemens	264.0	1997
	Hentgen	264.0	1997
9.	Alexander	261.2	1984
10.	Key	261.0	1987

STRIKEOUTS (PITCHER)

1.	Clemens	292	1997
2.	Clemens	271	1998
3.	Stieb	198	1984
4.	Guzman	194	1993
5.	Stieb	187	1983
6.	Clancy	180	1987
7.	Hentgen	177	1996
8.	Wells	169	1999
9.	Stieb	167	1985
10.	Eichhorn	166	1986

SHUTOUTS

1.	Stieb	5	1982
2.	Stieb	4	1980
	Stieb	4	1983
	Stieb	4	1988
5.	Lemanczyk	3	1979
	Clancy	3	1982
	Clancy	3	1986
	Hentgen	3	1996
	Clemens	3	1997
	Hentgen	3	1997
	Clemens	3	1998

BLUE JAYS PITCHERS, TOP DUOS BY WINS

37-1992	Jack Morris (21) — Juan Guzman (16)
36-1997	Roger Clemens (21) — Pat Hentgen (15)
33-1993	Pat Hentgen (19) — Juan Guzman (14)
33-1984	Doyle Alexander (17) — Dave Stieb (16)
33-1982	Dave Stieb (17) — Jim Clancy (16)
33-1996	Pat Hentgen (20) — Erik Hanson (13)
32-1998	Roger Clemens (20) — Chris Carpenter (12) — Pat Hentgen (12)
32-1987	Jimmy Key (17) — Jim Clancy (15)
32-1983	Dave Stieb (17) — Jim Clancy (15)
31-1985	Doyle Alexander (17) — Jimmy Key (14) — Dave Stieb (14)
31-1991	Jimmy Key (16) — Todd Stottlemyre (15) — David Wells (15)
31-1990	Dave Stieb (18) — Jimmy Key (13) — Todd Stottlemyre (13)
31-1999	David Wells (17) — Kelvim Escobar (14)
30-1989	Dave Stieb (17) — Jimmy Key (13)
30-2000	David Wells (20) — Chris Carpenter (10) — Frank Castillo (10) — Kelvim Escobar (10)

BLUE JAYS PITCHERS — MOST WINS vs LOSSES

10 OR MORE

+15	Jack Morris	1992	21-6	+11	Doyle Alexander	1984	17-6
+14	Roger Clemens	1997	21-7		Dennis Lamp	1985	11-0
	Roger Clemens	1998	20-6		Juan Guzman	1992	16-5
+12	Dave Stieb	1990	18-6		Juan Guzman	1993	14-3
	David Wells	2000	20-8	+10	Pat Hentgen	1993	19-9
					Pat Hentgen	1996	20-10

ALL TIME TOP TEN

BATTING DEPARTMENTS

GAMES

1. Tony Fernandez	1402
2. Lloyd Moseby	1392
3. Ernie Whitt	1218
4. George Bell	1181
5. Rance Mulliniks	1115
Willie Upshaw	1115
7. Joe Carter	1039
8. Jesse Barfield	1032
9. Alfredo Griffin	982
10. Garth Iorg	931

AT BATS

1. Tony Fernandez	5276
2. Lloyd Moseby	5124
3. George Bell	4528
4. Joe Carter	4093
5. Willie Upshaw	3710
6. Damaso Garcia	3572
7. Ernie Whitt	3514
8. Jesse Barfield	3463
9. Alfredo Griffin	3396
10. Ed Sprague	3156

RUNS

1. Lloyd Moseby	768
2. Tony Fernandez	699
3. George Bell	641
4. Joe Carter	578
5. Willie Upshaw	538
6. Jesse Barfield	530
7. John Olerud	464
8. Damaso Garcia	453
9. Devon White	452
10. Roberto Alomar	451

HITS

1. Tony Fernandez	1565
2. Lloyd Moseby	1319
3. George Bell	1294
4. Joe Carter	1051
5. Damaso Garcia	1028
6. Willie Upshaw	982
7. Jesse Barfield	919
8. John Olerud	910
9. Ernie Whitt	888
10. Alfredo Griffin	844

DOUBLES

1. Tony Fernandez	287
2. Lloyd Moseby	242
3. George Bell	237
4. Joe Carter	218
5. John Olerud	213
6. Rance Mulliniks	204
7. Willie Upshaw	177
8. Damaso Garcia	172
9. Ed Sprague	170
10. Shawn Green	164
Ernie Whitt	164

TRIPLES

1. Tony Fernandez	72
2. Lloyd Moseby	60
3. Alfredo Griffin	50
4. Willie Upshaw	42
5. Roberto Alomar	36
6. Devon White	34
7. George Bell	32
8. Joe Carter	28
9. Jesse Barfield ·	27
10. Damaso Garcia	26

HOME RUNS

1. Joe Carter	203
2. George Bell	202
3. Jesse Barfield	179
4. Carlos Delgado	149
Lloyd Moseby	149
6. Ernie Whitt	131
7. Fred McGriff	125
8. Shawn Green	119
9. Kelly Gruber	114
10. Ed Sprague	113

EXTRA-BASE HITS

1. George Bell	471
2. Lloyd Moseby	451
3. Joe Carter	449
4. Tony Fernandez	420
5. Jesse Barfield	368
6. Willie Upshaw	331
7. John Olerud	328
8. Carlos Delgado	312
9. Ernie Whitt	310
10. Shawn Green	298

RUNS BATTED IN

1. George Bell	740
2. Joe Carter	736
3. Lloyd Moseby	651
4. Tony Fernandez	601
5. Jesse Barfield	527
6. Ernie Whitt	518
7. Willie Upshaw	478
8. John Olerud	471
9. Carlos Delgado	467
10. Kelly Gruber	434

SH

1. Alfredo Griffin	74
2. Alex Gonzalez	41
3. Roberto Alomar	39
4. Lloyd Moseby	38
5. Tony Fernandez	34
6. Al Woods	31
7. Manuel Lee	28
8. Damaso Garcia	27
Willie Upshaw	27
10. Dave McKay	24

SF

1. Joe Carter	65
2. George Bell	59
3. Tony Fernandez	43
4. Lloyd Moseby	40
5. Ernie Whitt	36
6. Kelly Gruber	35
John Olerud	35
8. Carlos Delgado	28
Ed Sprague	28
10. Jesse Barfield	24
Alfredo Griffin	24
Rance Mulliniks	24
Willie Upshaw	24

STOLEN BASES

1. Lloyd Moseby	255
2. Roberto Alomar	206
3. Damaso Garcia	194
4. Tony Fernandez	172
5. Devon White	126
6. Otis Nixon	101
Shannon Stewart	101
8. Dave Collins	91
9. Kelly Gruber	80
10. Alfredo Griffin	79

CAUGHT STEALING

1. Damaso Garcia	86
Lloyd Moseby	86
3. Tony Fernandez	85
4. Alfredo Griffin	74
5. Willie Upshaw	50
6. Roberto Alomar	46
7. Jesse Barfield	40
8. Shannon Stewart	35
9. Kelly Gruber	33
10. Rick Bosetti	30

BB

1. Lloyd Moseby	547
2. John Olerud	514
3. Tony Fernandez	438
4. Rance Mulliniks	416
5. Ernie Whitt	403
6. Willie Upshaw	390
7. Fred McGriff	352
8. Jesse Barfield	342
9. Roberto Alomar	322
10. Carlos Delgado	313

IBB

1. John Olerud	87
2. Willie Upshaw	46
3. Ernie Whitt	42
4. Lloyd Moseby	41
5. Joe Carter	39
6. George Bell	37
7. Carlos Delgado	35
8. Tony Fernandez	32
9. Jesse Barfield	31
Fred McGriff	31

HBP

1. Ed Sprague	68
2. Lloyd Moseby	50
3. Joe Carter	49
4. Tony Fernandez	47
5. Carlos Delgado	46
6. George Bell	35
Kelly Gruber	35
8. John Olerud	32
9. Devon White	29
10. Shawn Green	28
Charlie O'Brien	28
Shannon Stewart	28

STRIKEOUTS

1. Lloyd Moseby	1015
2. Jesse Barfield	855
3. Joe Carter	696
4. Ed Sprague	647
5. Carlos Delgado	624
6. Willie Upshaw	576
7. Devon White	572
8. George Bell	563
9. Shawn Green	510
10. Alex Gonzalez	496

GIDP

1. George Bell	112
2. Tony Fernandez	107
3. Rance Mulliniks	94
4. Lloyd Moseby	88
Ernie Whitt	88
6. Ed Sprague	87
7. Kelly Gruber	84
8. John Olerud	82
9. Pat Borders	73
10. Joe Carter	71

TOTAL BASES

1. George Bell	2201
2. Tony Fernandez	2173
3. Lloyd Moseby	2128
4. Joe Carter	1934
5. Jesse Barfield	1672
6. Willie Upshaw	1579
7. Ernie Whitt	1475
8. John Olerud	1462
9. Damaso Garcia	1348
10. Kelly Gruber	1335

BATTING AVERAGE
(Min. 2000 plate appearances)

1. Roberto Alomar	.307
2. Tony Fernandez	.297
3. John Olerud	.293
4. Damaso Garcia	.288
5. George Bell	.286
6. Shawn Green	.286
7. Rance Mulliniks	.280
8. Fred McGriff	.278
9. Roy Howell	.272
10. Devon White	.270

ON BASE PERCENTAGE
(Min. 2000 plate appearances)

1. John Olerud	.395
2. Fred McGriff	.389
3. Roberto Alomar	.382
4. Rance Mulliniks	.365
5. Carlos Delgado	.361
6. Tony Fernandez	.353
7. John Mayberry	.352
8. Shawn Green	.344
9. Willie Upshaw	.336
10. Roy Howell	.335

SLUGGING PCT
(Min. 2000 plate appearances)

1. Carlos Delgado	.531
2. Fred McGriff	.530
3. Shawn Green	.505
4. George Bell	.486
5. Jesse Barfield	.483
6. Joe Carter	.473
7. John Olerud	.471
8. Roberto Alomar	.451
9. John Mayberry	.450
10. Devon White	.432

PITCHING DEPARTMENTS

ERA (1000IP)
1. Dave Stieb 3.42
2. Jimmy Key 3.42
3. Juan Guzman 4.07
4. Jim Clancy 4.10
5. Pat Hentgen 4.14
6. Todd Stottlemyre 4.39

WINS
1. Dave Stieb 175
2. Jim Clancy 128
3. Jimmy Key 116
4. Pat Hentgen 105
5. Juan Guzman 76
6. Todd Stottlemyre 69
7. David Wells 64
8. Luis Leal 51
9. Doyle Alexander 46
   John Cerutti 46

LOSSES
1. Jim Clancy 140
2. Dave Stieb 134
3. Jimmy Key 81
4. Pat Hentgen 76
5. Todd Stottlemyre 70
6. Juan Guzman 62
7. Luis Leal 58
8. Jesse Jefferson 56
9. David Wells 47
10. Dave Lemanczyk 45

GAMES
1. Duane Ward 452
2. Tom Henke 446
3. Dave Stieb 439
4. Jim Clancy 352
5. Jimmy Key 317
6. Mike Timlin 305
7. Jim Acker 281
8. Mark Eichhorn 279
9. David Wells 271
10. Pat Hentgen 252

GAME STARTED
1. Dave Stieb 408
2. Jim Clancy 345
3. Jimmy Key 250
4. Pat Hentgen 222
5. Juan Guzman 195
6. Todd Stottlemyre 175
7. Luis Leal 151
8. John Cerutti 108
9. Doyle Alexander 103
   David Wells 103

COMPLETE GAMES
1. Dave Stieb 103
2. Jim Clancy 73
3. Pat Hentgen 31
4. Jimmy Key 28
5. Luis Leal 27
6. Doyle Alexander 25
   Dave Lemanczyk 25
8. Jesse Jefferson 21
9. Tom Underwood 19
10. Jerry Garvin 15
    Juan Guzman 15
    Todd Stottlemyre 15

SHUTOUTS
1. Dave Stieb 30
2. Jim Clancy 11
3. Jimmy Key 10
4. Pat Hentgen 9
5. Roger Clemens 6
6. Jesse Jefferson 4
   Todd Stottlemyre 4
8. Doyle Alexander 3
   Chris Carpenter 3
   Jim Gott 3
   Luis Leal 3
   Dave Lemanczyk 3

SAVES
1. Tom Henke 217
2. Duane Ward 121
3. Mike Timlin 52
4. Joey McLaughlin 31
   Billy Koch 31
6. Roy Lee Jackson 30
7. Randy Myers 28
8. Darren Hall 20
9. Tony Castillo 16
   Bill Caudill 16

GAMES FINISHED
1. Tom Henke 386
2. Duane Ward 266
3. Mike Timlin 175
4. Joey McLaughlin 123
5. Mark Eichhorn 105
6. Roy Lee Jackson 93
7. Jim Acker 82
8. Paul Quantrill 81
9. Bill Caudill 71
   Mike Willis 71

INNINGS PITCHED
1. Dave Stieb 2873.0
2. Jim Clancy 2205.2
3. Jimmy Key 1696.2
4. Pat Hentgen 1556.2
5. Juan Guzman 1216.2
6. Todd Stottlemyre 1139.0
7. Luis Leal 946.0
8. David Wells 919.0
9. John Cerutti 772.1
10. Doyle Alexander 750.0

HITS ALLOWED
1. Dave Stieb 2545
2. Jim Clancy 2185
3. Jimmy Key 1624
4. Pat Hentgen 1587
5. Todd Stottlemyre 1182
6. Juan Guzman 1099
7. Luis Leal 968
8. David Wells 905
9. John Cerutti 800
10. Doyle Alexander 752

BATTERS FACED
1. Dave Stieb 11965
2. Jim Clancy 9397
3. Jimmy Key 6983
4. Pat Hentgen 6675
5. Juan Guzman 5209
6. Todd Stottlemyre 4921
7. Luis Leal 4057
8. David Wells 3849
9. John Cerutti 3279
10. Doyle Alexander 3103

RUNS ALLOWED
1. Dave Stieb 1208
2. Jim Clancy 1104
3. Pat Hentgen 783
4. Jimmy Key 710
5. Juan Guzman 612
6. Todd Stottlemyre 597
7. Luis Leal 476
8. David Wells 451
9. Jesse Jefferson 385
10. John Cerutti 378

EARNED RUNS
1. Dave Stieb 1091
2. Jim Clancy 1005
3. Pat Hentgen 716
4. Jimmy Key 645
5. Todd Stottlemyre 555
6. Juan Guzman 550
7. Luis Leal 435
8. David Wells 413
9. Jesse Jefferson 352
10. John Cerutti 332

HOME RUNS ALLOWED
1. Dave Stieb 224
2. Jim Clancy 219
3. Pat Hentgen 191
4. Jimmy Key 165
5. Juan Guzman 115
   Todd Stottlemyre 115
7. John Cerutti 110
8. David Wells 103
9. Luis Leal 101
10. Woody Williams 88

BASES ON BALLS
1. Dave Stieb 1020
2. Jim Clancy 814
3. Pat Hentgen 557
4. Juan Guzman 546
5. Todd Stottlemyre 414
6. Jimmy Key 404
7. Luis Leal 320
8. Duane Ward 278
9. Jesse Jefferson 266
10. David Wells 263

INTENTIONAL BASE ON BALLS
1. Mark Eichhorn 39
   Duane Ward 39
3. Dave Stieb 36
4. Mike Timlin 32
5. David Wells 28
6. Todd Stottlemyre 27
7. Jimmy Key 25
8. Luis Leal 24
   Joey McLaughlin 24
10. Jerry Garvin 22
    Tom Henke 22

HIT BATSMEN
1. Dave Stieb 129
2. Todd Stottlemyre 49
3. Pat Hentgen 37
4. Juan Guzman 29
5. Jim Clancy 28
6. Jim Acker 25
7. Mark Eichhorn 24
   Jimmy Key 24
9. Luis Leal 22
10. David Wells 20

STRIKEOUTS
1. Dave Stieb 1658
2. Jim Clancy 1237
3. Juan Guzman 1030
4. Pat Hentgen 995
5. Jimmy Key 944
6. Duane Ward 671
7. Todd Stottlemyre 662
8. Tom Henke 644
9. David Wells 618
10. Roger Clemens 563

WILD PITCHES
1. Juan Guzman 88
2. Jim Clancy 82
3. Pat Hentgen 55
4. Dave Stieb 51
   Duane Ward 51
6. David Wells 37
7. Dave Lemanczyk 36
8. Jimmy Key 31
9. John Cerutti 30
   Todd Stottlemyre 30

BALKS
1. Dave Stieb 14
2. David Wells 10
3. Pat Hentgen 9
   Jimmy Key 9
5. Mark Eichhorn 8
6. John Cerutti 7
   Al Leiter 7
8. Luis Leal 6
   Todd Stottlemyre 6
10. Jeff Musselman 5

W-L PCT
(Min. 100 decisions)
1. Jimmy Key .589
2. Pat Hentgen .580
3. David Wells .577
4. Dave Stieb .566
5. Juan Guzman .551
6. Todd Stottlemyre .496
7. Jim Clancy .478
8. Luis Leal .468

LONGEST WINNING & LOSING STREAKS

YEAR	WON	LOST	YEAR	WON	LOST	YEAR	WON	LOST	YEAR	WON	LOST
1977	3	11	1983	5	6	1989	6	4	1995	4	8
1978	5	9	1984	7	6	1990	6	6	1996	7	6
1979	4	7	1985	9	6	1991	6	7	1997	5	7
1980	6	8	1986	9	5	1992	8	5	1998	11	4
1981	4	12	1987	11	7	1993	9	6	1999	8	7
1982	6	6	1988	6	6	1994	8	10	2000	5	6

.300 HITTERS
(350 or more At-Bats)

YEAR	PLAYER	AVG	YEAR	PLAYER	AVG	YEAR	PLAYER	AVG	YEAR	PLAYER	AVG
1977	Bob Bailor	.310	1984	Dave Collins	.308	1993	John Olerud	.363	1999	Homer Bush	.320
1977	Roy Howell	.316	1984	Cliff Johnson	.304	1993	Paul Molitor	.332	1999	Shawn Green	.309
1980	Al Woods	.300	1986	Tony Fernandez	.317	1993	Roberto Alomar	.326	1999	Shannon Stewart	.304
1982	Damaso Garcia	.310	1986	George Bell	.309	1993	Tony Fernandez	.306	2000	Carlos Delgado	.344
1983	Barry Bonnell	.318	1987	Tony Fernandez	.322	1994	Paul Molitor	.341	2000	Darrin Fletcher	.320
1983	Damaso Garcia	.307	1987	George Bell	.308	1994	Roberto Alomar	.306	2000	Shannon Stewart	.319
1983	Lloyd Moseby	.315	1987	George Bell	.308	1995	Roberto Alomar	.300			
1983	Willie Upshaw	.306	1990	Fred McGriff	.300	1998	Tony Fernandez	.321			
1984	Rance Mulliniks	.324	1992	Roberto Alomar	.310	1999	Tony Fernandez	.328			

80 RBI

YEAR	PLAYER	RBI	YEAR	PLAYER	RBI	YEAR	PLAYER	RBI	YEAR	PLAYER	RBI
1980	John Mayberry	82	1987	George Bell	134	1991	Joe Carter	108	1997	Joe Carter	102
1983	Willie Upshaw	104	1987	Lloyd Moseby	96	1992	Joe Carter	119	1997	Carlos Delgado	91
1983	Lloyd Moseby	81	1987	Jesse Barfield	89	1992	Dave Winfield	108	1998	Carlos Delgado	115
1984	Lloyd Moseby	92	1988	George Bell	97	1993	Joe Carter	121	1998	Jose Canseco	107
1984	George Bell	87	1988	Fred McGriff	82	1993	Paul Molitor	111	1998	Shawn Green	100
1984	Willie Upshaw	84	1988	Kelly Gruber	81	1993	John Olerud	107	1999	Carlos Delgado	134
1985	George Bell	95	1989	George Bell	104	1993	Roberto Alomar	93	1999	Shawn Green	123
1985	Jesse Barfield	84	1989	Fred McGriff	92	1994	Joe Carter	103	1999	Darrin Fletcher	80
1986	Jesse Barfield	108	1990	George Bell	86	1996	Joe Carter	107	2000	Carlos Delgado	137
1986	George Bell	108	1990	Kelly Gruber	118	1996	Ed Sprague	101	2000	Tony Batista	114
1986	Lloyd Moseby	86	1990	Fred McGriff	88	1996	Carlos Delgado	92	2000	Brad Fullmer	104

20 HOME RUNS

YEAR	PLAYER	HR's	YEAR	PLAYER	HR's	YEAR	PLAYER	HR's	YEAR	PLAYER	HR's
1978	Rico Carty	20	1986	Lloyd Moseby	21	1992	Candy Maldonaldo	20	1998	Shawn Green	35
1978	John Mayberry	22	1987	George Bell	47	1992	Dave Winfield	26	1998	Mike Stanley	22
1979	John Mayberry	21	1987	Jesse Barfield	28	1993	Joe Carter	33	1999	Carlos Delgado	44
1980	John Mayberry	30	1987	Lloyd Moseby	26	1993	John Olerud	24	1999	Shawn Green	42
1980	Otto Velez	20	1987	Fred McGriff	20	1993	Paul Molitor	22	1999	Tony Batista	26
1982	Willie Upshaw	21	1988	Fred McGriff	34	1994	Joe Carter	27	2000	Tony Batista	41
1983	Jesse Barfield	27	1988	George Bell	24	1995	Joe Carter	25	2000	Carlos Delgado	41
1983	Willie Upshaw	27	1989	Fred McGriff	36	1996	Ed Sprague	36	2000	Brad Fullmer	32
1983	Cliff Johnson	22	1990	Kelly Gruber	31	1996	Joe Carter	30	2000	Jose Cruz	31
1984	George Bell	26	1990	Fred McGriff	35	1996	Carlos Delgado	25	2000	Raul Mondesi	24
1985	George Bell	28	1990	George Bell	21	1997	Carlos Delgado	30	2000	Shannon Stewart	21
1985	Jesse Barfield	27	1991	Joe Carter	33	1997	Joe Carter	21	2000	Darrin Fletcher	20
1986	Jesse Barfield	40	1991	Kelly Gruber	20	1998	Jose Canseco	46			
1986	George Bell	31	1992	Joe Carter	34	1998	Carlos Delgado	38			

15-GAME WINNERS

YEAR	PITCHER	W	L	YEAR	PITCHER	W	L	YEAR	PITCHER	W	L	YEAR	PITCHER	W	L
1982	Dave Stieb	17	14	1985	Doyle Alexander	17	10	1991	Jimmy Key	16	12	1996	Pat Hentgen	20	10
1982	Jim Clancy	16	14	1987	Jimmy Key	17	8	1991	Todd Stottlemyre	16	8	1997	Roger Clemens	21	7
1983	Dave Stieb	17	12	1987	Jim Clancy	15	11	1991	David Wells	15	10	1997	Pat Hentgen	15	10
1983	Jim Clancy	15	11	1988	Dave Stieb	16	8	1992	Juan Guzman	16	5	1998	Roger Clemens	20	6
1984	Doyle Alexander	17	6	1989	Dave Stieb	17	8	1992	Jack Morris	21	6	1999	David Wells	17	10
1984	Dave Stieb	16	8	1990	Dave Stieb	18	6	1993	Pat Hentgen	19	9	2000	David Wells	20	8

YEARLY PINCH HITTING LEADER

YEAR	PLAYER	HITS	YEAR	PLAYER	HITS	YEAR	PLAYER	HITS	YEAR	PLAYER	HITS
1977	Sam Ewing	9	1984	Cliff Johnson	11	1990	Rance Mulliniks	8	1997	Carlos Delgado	4
1978	Otto Velez	8	1985	Rance Mulliniks	9	1991	Pat Tabler	9	1998	Felipe Crespo	2
1979	Otto Velez	5	1986	Rick Leach	10	1992	John Olerud	4	1998	Darrin Fletcher	2
1980	Steve Braun	9	1986	Garth Iorg	10	1993	Turner Ward	2	1998	Juan Samuel	2
1981	Willie Upshaw	4	1987	Rance Mulliniks	8	1994	Michael Huff	3	1999	Willie Greene	6
1982	Wayne Nordhagen	11	1988	Rance Mulliniks	6	1995	Michael Huff	4	2000	Darrin Fletcher	4
1983	Rance Mulliniks	10	1989	Bob Brenly	6	1996	Robert Perez	5	2000	Todd Greene	4

20 STOLEN BASES

YEAR	PLAYER	SB	YEAR	PLAYER	SB	YEAR	PLAYER	SB	YEAR	PLAYER	SB
1979	Alfredo Griffin	21	1986	Lloyd Moseby	32	1991	Devon White	33	1998	Shannon Stewart	51
1982	Damaso Garcia	54	1986	Tony Fernandez	25	1991	Joe Carter	20	1998	Shawn Green	35
1983	Dave Collins	31	1986	Willie Upshaw	23	1992	Roberto Alomar	49	1998	Jose Canseco	29
1983	Damaso Garcia	31	1987	Lloyd Moseby	39	1992	Devon White	37	1998	Alex Gonzalez	21
1983	Lloyd Moseby	27	1987	Tony Fernandez	32	1993	Roberto Alomar	55	1999	Shannon Stewart	37
1984	Dave Collins	60	1988	Lloyd Moseby	31	1993	Devon White	34	1999	Homer Bush	32
1984	Damaso Garcia	46	1988	Kelly Gruber	23	1993	Rickey Henderson	22	1999	Shawn Green	20
1984	Lloyd Moseby	39	1989	Lloyd Moseby	24	1993	Paul Molitor	22	2000	Raul Mondesi	22
1985	Lloyd Moseby	37	1989	Tony Fernandez	22	1994	Paul Molitor	20	2000	Shannon Stewart	20
1985	Damaso Garcia	28	1990	Tony Fernandez	26	1995	Roberto Alomar	30			
1985	George Bell	21	1990	Mookie Wilson	23	1996	Otis Nixon	54			
1985	Jesse Barfield	22	1991	Roberto Alomar	53	1997	Otis Nixon	47			

HOME/ROAD RBI LEADERS

YEAR	HOME		ROAD		YEAR	HOME		ROAD		YEAR	HOME		ROAD	
1977	33	Ron Fairly	33	Otto Velez	1985	49	Jesse Barfield	47	George Bell	1993	68	Paul Molitor	59	John Olerud
1978	40	John Mayberry	31	Roy Howell	1986	57	George Bell	57	Jesse Barfield	1994	70	Joe Carter	39	John Olerud
1979	41	Rick Bosetti	38	John Mayberry	1987	57	George Bell	78	George Bell	1995	39	Ed Sprague	42	Joe Carter
1980	40	Otto Velez	45	John Mayberry	1988	47	George Bell	50	George Bell	1996	52	Joe Carter	59	Ed Sprague
1981	22	John Mayberry	29	Lloyd Moseby	1989	57	George Bell	48	Fred McGriff	1997	59	Joe Carter	43	Joe Carter
1982	46	Willie Upshaw	29	Willie Upshaw	1990	62	Kelly Gruber	50	Fred McGriff	1998	61	Carlos Delgado	54	Carlos Delgado
1983	55	Willie Upshaw	49	Willie Upshaw	1991	64	Joe Carter	44	Joe Carter	1999	60	Shawn Green	76	Carlos Delgado
1984	52	Lloyd Moseby	42	Willie Upshaw	1992	65	Joe Carter	61	Dave Winfield	2000	75	Carlos Delgado	62	Carlos Delgado

PITCHERS WITH OVER 9 INNINGS IN ONE GAME

PITCHER	DATE	OPPONENT	INNINGS	W-L-S	SCORE
Jerry Garvin	May 25/77	Oak.	9.2	L	L5-6 (10)
Dave Lemanczyk	July 14/77	at CWS	11.0	W	W5-3 (11)
Dave Lemanczyk	July 17/77	at Det (2nd)	11.0	L	L6-7 (11)
Dave Lemanczyk	Oct. 2/77	Cle (1st)	11.0	W	W2-1 (11)
Jesse Jefferson	May 23/78	Bos	12.0	W	W2-1 (12)
Tom Underwood	Sept.3/79	at Bal (1st)	10.0	ND	L11-2 (11)
Jesse Jefferson	May 16/80	Oak	11.0	W	W1-0 (11)
Dave Stieb	May 17/80	Oak	12.0	ND	L2-4 (14)
Dave Stieb	Aug. 9/80	KC	10.0	ND	W4-3 (14)
Dave Stieb	Sept. 16/82	Cal	11.0	ND	W2-1 (12)
Dave Stieb	May 11/83	at CWS	10.0	W	W3-1 (10)
Dave Stieb	May 16/83	at Mil	10.0	W	W2-1 (10)
Jim Clancy	Sept. 24/83	at Oak	9.1	L	L1-2 (10)
Jimmy Key	June 6/85	Det	10.0	ND	W2-0 (12)
Jimmy Key	June 17/86	at Mil	10.0	ND	W2-1 (12)
Jimmy Key	July 27/86	at Oak	10.0	ND	L0-1 (15)
Mike Flanagan	Oct. 3/87	at Det	11.0	ND	L2-3 (12)
John Cerutti	Apr. 30/89	at Cal	10.0	ND	L0-1 (11)
Tom Candiotti	July 11/91	at KC	9.1	L	L2-1 (10)

MILESTONE VICTORIES

VICTORY #	DATE	OPPONENT	SCORE	WINNER	LOSER
1	Apr. 7/77	vs Chicago	9-5	Jerry Johnson	Ken Brett
100	Aug. 13/78	vs Kansas City	3-2(10)	Mike Willis	Al Hrabosky
200	July 11/80	vs Cleveland	6-3	Dave Stieb	Wayne Garland
300	June 19/82	at Oakland	3-1(12)	Joey McLaughlin	Bob Owchinko
400	July 18/83	vs Kansas City	8-2	Jim Clancy	Larry Gura
500	Aug. 5/84	at Baltimore	4-3	Jimmy Key	Tippy Martinez
600	Aug. 20/85	at Cleveland	3-2	Jimmy Key	Roy Smith
625	*Oct. 5/85	vs New York	5-1	Doyle Alexander	Joe Cowley
700	Sept. 3/86	vs Cleveland	3-1	Dave Stieb	Tom Candiotti
800	Sept. 18/87	at New York	6-3	Jim Clancy	Neil Allen
900	Apr. 16/89	vs Kansas City	2-1	David Wells	Bret Saberhagen
983	*Sept. 30/89	vs Baltimore	4-3	Frank Wills	Mark Williamson
1000	May 9/90	vs Chicago	4-3	Frank Wills	Wayne Edwards
1100	June 26/91	at Minnesota	5-2	David Wells	Mark Guthrie
1158	*Oct. 2/91	vs California	6-5	Mike Timlin	Bryan Harvey
1200	June 26/92	at Cleveland	6-1	Juan Guzman	Jack Armstrong
1256	*Oct. 3/92	vs Detroit	3-1	Juan Guzman	David Haas
ALCS	**Oct. 14/92	vs Oakland	9-2	Juan Guzman	Mike Moore
WS	#Oct. 24/92	at Atlanta	4-3	Jimmy Key	Charlie Leibrandt
1300	June 24/93	vs New York	7-2	Pat Hentgen	Scott Kamieniecki
1347	*Sept. 27/93	at Milwaukee	2-0	Pat Hentgen	Cal Eldred
ALCS	**Oct. 12/93	at Chicago	6-3	Dave Stewart	Alex Fernandez
WS	#Oct. 23/93	vs Philadelphia	8-6	Duane Ward	Mitch Williams
1400	Aug. 5/94	at Detroit	4-2	Juan Guzman	David Wells
1500	July 6/96	at Detroit	15-0	Pat Hentgen	Omar Olivares
1600	Aug. 27/97	at Chicago	13-2	Pat Hentgen	Doug Drabek
1700	Sept. 27/98	vs Detroit	2-1	Roy Halladay	Justin Thompson
1800	May 5/00	vs Cleveland	11-10	Billy Koch	Paul Shuey

* AL East Pennant Clincher   ** AL Pennant Clincher   # World Series Clincher

BLUE JAYS—10 WINS

AT HOME

PITCHER	HOME WINS	YEAR
DAVE STIEB	11	1983
DOYLE ALEXANDER	12	1984
DOYLE ALEXANDER	11	1985
JIMMY KEY	10	1985
JIMMY KEY	10	1987
JEFF MUSSELMAN	10	1987
DAVE STIEB	12	1988
JACK MORRIS	11	1992
ROGER CLEMENS	10	1997
ROGER CLEMENS	12	1998

ON ROAD

PITCHER	ROAD WINS	YEAR
DAVE STIEB	10	1989
JACK MORRIS	10	1992
PAT HENTGEN	12	1993
PAT HENTGEN	11	1996
ROGER CLEMENS	11	1997
DAVID WELLS	11	2000

BIGGEST INNINGS

BLUE JAYS

INN.	RUNS	H/A	DATE	OPP.	SCORE	WINNER	LOSER
1st	7	A	June 23, 1989	Oak	10-8	Buice	Young
	7	A	July 19, 1993	CWS	15-7	Stewart	Bolton
	7	H	Sept. 11, 1993	Cal	9-5	Hentgen	Hathaway
	7	A	June 4, 1995	Cle	8-9	Tavarez	Hall
2nd	11	H	April 26, 1995	Oak	13-1	Cone	Stewart
3rd	7	H	April 19, 1988	KC	12-3	Clancy	Saberhagen
	7	H	Aug. 21, 1988	Mil	8-4	Key	August
	7	H	July 3, 1992	Cal	10-1	Key	Langston
	7	A	Aug. 14, 1992	Cle	9-5	Wells	Nichols
4th	10	A	June 10, 1990	Mil	13-5	Wells	Navarro
5th	8	H	May 26, 1989	CWS	11-0	Key	Hillegas
6th	10	A	Aug. 3, 1987	CWS	14-5	Musselman	Bannister
7th	10	A	May 24, 1999	Det	12-6	Wells	Moehler
8th	8	A	May 28, 1986	Min	14-8	Clancy	Blyleven
	8	H	July 1, 1998	NYM	15-10	Plesac	Rojas
9th	11	A	July 20, 1984	Sea	12-7	Acker	Mirabella
10th	6	A	Aug. 3, 1995	Bal	8-2	Jordan	Clark
11th	5	A	July 22, 1983	Tex	10-5	Moffitt	Schmidt
12th	3	A	April 22, 1988	NYY	6-4	Wells	Stoddard
13th	5	A	July 9, 1985	Sea	9-4	Musselman	Vande Berg
14th	5	A	April 29, 1981	Mil	5-0	Leal	Easterly
	5	A	June 21, 1989	Cal	6-1	Henke	Minton
15th	3	A	June 12, 1983	Cal	6-5	Clarke	Brown
16th	2	A	Sept. 9, 1989	Cle	7-5	Wills	Kaiser
17th	1	A	Oct. 4, 1980	Bos	7-6	Leal	Stanley

OPPONENTS

INN.	RUNS	H/A	DATE	OPP.	SCORE	WINNER	LOSER
1st	10	H	June 21, 1994	Bos	1-13	Sele	Cornett
2nd	9	H	April 5, 1979	KC	2-11	Leonard	Underwood
3rd	9	H	May 17, 1990	Sea	6-14	Johnson	Key
	9	H	June 30, 1992	Tex	13-16	Brown	Wells
4th	10	A	Sept. 28, 2000	Bal	1-23	Rapp	Carpenter
5th	8	H	Sept. 17, 1988	Cle	3-12	Swindell	Key
6th	9	H	April 6, 2000	KC	3-9	Durbin	Escobar
7th	11	H	Aug. 6, 1979	KC	12-16	Mingori	Stieb
8th	8	H	June 30, 1977	NYY	5-11	Hunter	Garvin
9th	7	H	July 2, 1995	Bal	7-9	Benitez	Crabtree
10th	4	A	Sept. 17, 1980	NYY	7-8	T. Underwood	Kucek
10th	4	H	May 10, 1981	Bos	5-9	Burgmeier	Jackson
10th	4	A	Aug. 24, 1982	Bal	3-7	D. Martinez	McLaughlin
10th	4	A	Aug. 24, 1983	Bal	4-7	T. Martinez	McLaughlin
11th	5	H	Sept. 7, 1993	Oak	7-11	Honeycutt	Castillo
12th	5	H	July 1, 1987	NYY	1-6	Clements	Musselman
13th	6	H	June 2, 1982	NYY	6-12	Rawley	McLaughlin
14th	4	H	Aug. 8, 1991	Det	0-4	Gibson	Henke
15th	4	H	Sept. 15, 1995	Mil	1-5	Kiefer	Robinson
17th	1	A	June 8, 1998	Fla	3-4	Edmondson	Hanson

HIGHEST SCORING GAMES

BY BLUE JAYS (13 or More Runs Scored)

DATE	OPPONENT	SCORE	BLUE JAYS PITCHER OF RECORD
June 26, 1978	vs Baltimore	24-10	Tom Underwood
Sept. 10, 1977	at New York	19-3	Jim Clancy
June 26, 1983	at Seattle	19-7	Jim Acker
Aug. 9, 1999	at Texas	19-4	Joey Hamilton
Sept. 14, 1987	vs Baltimore	18-3	Jim Clancy
July 29, 1995	vs Oakland	18-11	Giovanni Carrara
April 11, 1988	vs New York	17-9	David Wells
April 20, 1990	vs Kansas City	17-6	Todd Stottlemyre
Sept. 11, 1983	vs Oakland	16-6	Jim Gott
May 14, 1987	at Minnesota	16-4	Dave Stieb
June 8, 1992	at New York	16-3	Todd Stottlemyre
June 22, 1992	at Texas	16-7	Jack Morris
Sept. 4, 1992	vs Minnesota	16-5	David Cone
April 22, 1996	at Seattle	16-7	Tony Castillo
Aug. 19, 1998	at Seattle	16-2	Pat Hentgen
May 3, 1999	at Seattle	16-10	David Wells
Sept. 19, 2000	vs New York	16-3	Steve Trachsel
June 22, 1986	vs New York	15-1	Jimmy Key
May 9, 1987	at Texas	15-4	Dave Stieb
June 19, 1987	vs Milwaukee	15-6	Jeff Musselman
June 15, 1988	vs Cleveland	15-3	Dave Stieb
Sept. 27, 1988	at Boston	15-9	Mike Flanagan
April 16, 1989	vs Kansas City	15-8	David Wells
Aug. 6, 1992	at Detroit	15-11	Jack Morris
July 19, 1993	at Chicago	15-7	Dave Stewart
June 30, 1996	vs Milwaukee	15-2	Erik Hanson
July 6, 1996	at Detroit	15-0	Pat Hentgen
July 13, 1996	at Milwaukee	15-7	Pat Hentgen
July 1, 1998	vs New York (N)	15-10	Dan Plesac
Sept. 7, 1998	vs Cleveland	15-1	Kelvim Escobar
Aug. 10, 2000	at Kansas City	15-7	Chris Carpenter
May 28, 1986	at Minnesota	14-8	Jim Clancy
June 27, 1986	at New York	14-7	Jim Acker
June 29, 1987	vs New York	14-15	Tom Henke
Aug. 3, 1987	at Chicago	14-5	Jeff Musselman
June 8, 1993	vs California	14-6	Woody Williams
Sept. 15, 1993	at Detroit	14-8	Todd Stottlemyre
April 11, 1994	at Oakland	14-5	Pat Hentgen
July 5, 1994	at Minnesota	14-3	Juan Guzman
Aug. 11, 1995	at Texas	14-5	Edwin Hurtado
June 22, 1998	vs Montreal	14-2	Juan Guzman
Aug. 29, 1998	vs Minnesota	14-7	Dave Stieb
Sept. 22, 1999	at Boston	14-9	Kelvim Escobar
Sept. 17, 2000	at Chicago	14-1	Lance Painter
July 18, 1978	at Seattle	13-12 (10)	Tom Murphy
June 14, 1983	vs Oakland	13-7	Roy Lee Jackson
Aug. 2, 1983 (gm 2)	vs New York	13-6	Matt Williams
Sept. 17, 1983	at Minnestoa	13-3	Luis Leal
April 5, 1984	at Seattle	13-5	Luis Leal
Sept. 29, 1985	at Milwaukee	13-5	Jim Acker
Aug. 16, 1986	vs Texas	13-1	Jimmy Key
Aug. 30, 1987	vs Oakland	13-3	Jim Clancy
Sept. 12, 1987	vs New York	13-1	Jimmy Key
June 16, 1988	at Detroit	13-5	Mike Flanagan
June 4, 1989	at Boston	13-11	Duane Ward
June 10, 1990	at Milwaukee	13-5	David Wells
Sept. 5, 1991	at Cleveland	13-1	Jimmy Key
April 23, 1992	at Cleveland	13-8	Todd Stottlemyre
June 30, 1992	vs Texas	13-16	David Wells
July 31, 1992	vs New York	13-2	Todd Stottlemyre
Sept. 18, 1992	vs Texas	13-0	Jimmy Key
April 9, 1993	vs Cleveland	13-10	Mark Eichhorn
May 30, 1993	at Oakland	13-11	Danny Cox
June 13, 1993	at Detroit	13-4	Pat Hentgen
April 15, 1994	at California	13-14	Todd Stottlemyre
April 19, 1994	vs Texas	13-3	Juan Guzman
April 26, 1995	vs Oakland	13-1	David Cone
Sept. 25, 1996	at Detroit	13-11	Scott Brow
May 31, 1997	at Oakland	13-3	Roger Clemens
Aug. 27, 1997	vs Chicago	13-2	Pat Hentgen
May 5, 1998	at Anaheim	13-11	Dan Plesac
June 18, 1998	at Baltimore	13-6	Chris Carpenter
June 15, 1999	vs Anaheim	13-2	David Wells
June 9, 2000	vs Montreal	13-3	Chris Carpenter
July 9, 2000	at Montreal	13-3	Frank Castillo
Aug. 13, 2000	at Minnesota	13-3	Chris Carpenter

BY OPPONENTS (13 or More Runs Scored)

DATE	OPPONENT	SCORE	BLUE JAYS PITCHER OF RECORD
Aug. 25, 1979	vs California	2-24	Balor Moore
Sept. 28, 2000	at Baltimore	1-23	Chris Carpenter
Aug. 28, 1992	vs Milwaukee	2-22	Jimmy Key
April 16, 2000	vs Seattle	7-19	Chris Carpenter
Sept. 24, 1999	vs Cleveland	4-18	Peter Munro
June 20, 2000	vs Detroit	6-18	Chris Carpenter
June 3, 1981	vs California	6-17	Jim Clancy
April 28, 1996	vs Cleveland	3-17	Frank Viola
April 17, 1999	at Anaheim	1-17	Roy Halladay
April 15, 2000	vs Seattle	6-17	Roy Halladay
May 8, 1979	at Minnesota	6-16	Mike Willis
Aug. 6, 1979	vs Kansas City	12-16	Dave Stieb
Aug. 31, 1983	vs Cleveland	11-16	Jim Acker
Aug. 15, 1984 (gm 1)	at Cleveland	1-16	Luis Leal
June 30, 1992	vs Texas	13-16	David Wells
Aug. 20, 1992	at Milwaukee	3-16	David Wells
April 18, 2000	at Anaheim	10-16	Frank Castillo
June 13, 2000	at Detroit	3-16	Clayton Andrews
Sept. 25, 1977 (gm 1)	vs New York	0-15	Jerry Garvin
April 9, 1982	vs Milwaukee	4-15	Mark Bomback
June 3, 1984	vs New York	2-15	Jim Clancy
June 29, 1987	vs New York	14-15	Tom Henke
July 5, 2000	at Cleveland	7-15	Paul Quantrill
July 26, 1977	vs Texas	0-14	Jim Clancy
Sept. 9, 1979	at Cleveland	10-14	Tom Buskey
July 20, 1983	vs Kansas City	8-14	Dave Stieb
Sept. 25, 1984	at Boston	6-14	Dave Stieb
April 9, 1987	vs Cleveland	3-14	Joe Johnson
Aug. 6, 1987	at Cleveland	5-14	Jim Clancy
May 17, 1990	vs Seattle	6-14	Jimmy Key
June 18, 1997	vs Detroit	10-14	Mike Timlin
April 15, 1994	at California	13-14	Todd Stottlemyre
May 12, 1995	at Milwaukee	5-14	Danny Darwin
July 4, 1995	at California	0-14	Juan Guzman
Aug. 31, 1999	vs Minnesota	3-14	Joey Hamilton
June 17, 1978	at Texas	2-13	Jim Clancy
July 22, 1979	at Minnesota	1-13	Dave Lemanczyk
Aug. 23, 1981	vs Chicago	2-13	Luis Leal
Aug. 22, 1984	vs Cleveland	3-13	Jim Clancy
Sept. 18, 1985	at Boston	1-13	Jim Clancy
May 9, 1986	at Seattle	3-13	Dave Stieb
July 25, 1987	vs Minnesota	9-13	Jeff Musselman
Sept. 20, 1988	vs Boston	2-13	Jeff Musselman
May 14, 1989	at Minnesota	1-13	Mike Flanagan
June 16, 1991	vs Baltimore	8-13	Duane Ward
May 12, 1993	vs Detroit	8-13	Pat Hentgen
May 17, 1994	vs Detroit	6-13	Todd Stottlemyre
June 21, 1994	vs Boston	1-13	Brad Cornett
April 16, 1996	vs Detroit	8-13	Erik Hanson
April 25, 1997	vs Seattle	8-13	Dan Plesac
June 25, 1997	vs Boston	12-13	Pat Hentgen
April 9, 1998	at Minnesota	2-13	Juan Guzman
May 4, 1999	vs Oakland	4-13	Roy Halladay
Aug. 14, 1999	vs Oakland	5-13	Joey Hamilton

Blue Jays Records

MARATHONS IN BLUE JAYS HISTORY

Date	Opponent	H/A	Inn	Score	Winner	Loser
Oct. 4/80	Boston	A	17	7-6	Leal	Stanley
	(1st)					
June 8/98	Florida	A	17	3-4	Edmondson	Hanson
July 3/88	Oakland	H	16	8-9	Burns	Cerutti
Sept. 9/89	Cleveland	A	16	7-5	Wills	Kaiser
*Aug. 28/80	Minnesota	H	15	5-7	Verhoeven	Jefferson
May 23/81	Oakland	A	15	2-3	Jones	Leal
June 12/83	California	A	15	6-5	Clarke	Brown
July 27/86	Oakland	A	15	0-1	Leiper	Clarke
June 22/90	New York	H	15	7-8	Cadaret	Blair
Sept. 15/95	Milwaukee	H	15	1-5	Kiefer	Robinson
June 19/98	Baltimore	A	15	4-7	Charlton	Risley
May 17/80	Oakland	H	14	2-4	Keough	McLaughlin
Aug. 9/80	Kansas City	A	14	4-3	Willis	Eastwick
July 31/78	Detroit	H	14	8-7	Coleman	Sykes
Sept. 24/78	Boston	H	14	6-7	Drago	Buskey
Apr. 29/81	Milwaukee	A	14	5-0	Leal	Easterley
Sept. 21/85	Milwaukee	H	14	2-1	Lamp	Darwin
May 17/88	Texas	H	14	6-7	Mohorcic	Eichhorn
June 21/89	California	A	14	6-1	Henke	Minton
Aug. 22/89	Boston	H	14	3-2	Gozzo	E. Nunez
Aug. 8/91	Detroit	H	14	0-4	Gibson	Henke
Aug. 30/95	Cleveland	A	14	3-4	Assenmacher	Castillo
Aug. 20/96	Kansas City	A	14	6-5	Timlin	Huisman
June 9/99	New York (N)	A	14	3-4	Mahones	Davey
June 8/77	California	A	13	1-2	LaRoche	Bruno
July 15/77	Detroit	H	13	8-6	Vuckovich	Crawford
May 28/78	New York	A	13	5-6	Gossage	Murphy
June 20/78	Detroit	H	13	3-4	Hiller	Willis
June 8/80	Minnesota	A	13	6-4	McLaughlin	Arroyo
	(2nd)					
Sept. 14/80	Baltimore	H	13	4-3	Barlow	D. Martinez
#Sept. 17/80	New York	A	13	7-8	T. Underwood	Kucek
Sept. 22/81	Oakland	H	13	2-3	Beard	Leal
	(1st)					
June 6/82	New York	H	13	6-12	Rawley	McLaughlin
June 30/83	Cleveland	H	13	6-5	McLaughlin	Anderson
Apr. 20/84	California	H	13	6-10	Sanchez	Acker
July 25/84	Kansas City	A	13	4-5	Quisenberry	Clark
Aug. 15/84	Cleveland	A	13	3-4	Jeffcoat	Key
	(2nd)					
July 9/85	Seattle	A	13	9-4	R. Musselman	Vande Berg
Aug. 13/86	Baltimore	A	13	6-7	Aase	Aquino
April 14/87	Chicago	H	13	4-3	Eichhorn	McKeon
Sept. 27/87	Detroit	H	13	2-3	Henneman	Nunez
June 22/89	Oakland	A	13	4-2	Hernandez	Corsi
Sept. 19/89	Boston	H	13	6-5	Henke	Harris
July 24/90	Kansas City	A	13	3-5	Farr	Ward
July 28/90	Texas	H	13	2-3	Arnsberg	Wills
Sept. 21/90	Cleveland	H	13	1-2	Valdez	Wills
Apr. 20/92	Boston	A	13	6-4	MacDonald	Bolton
June 2/92	Minnesota	A	13	7-5	Hentgen	Wayne
June 15/94	Cleveland	H	13	3-4	Mesa	Brow
Aug. 11/94	New York	A	13	8-7	Hall	Ausanio
Aug. 19/95	Kansas City	H	13	5-4	Rogers	Montgomery
April 21/97	Anaheim	A	13	4-5	DeLucia	Spoljaric
July 2/97	Montreal	H	13	7-6	Timlin	Telford
Aug. 24/97	Kansas City	A	13	11-8	Crabtree	Casian
Sept. 9/98	Cleveland	H	13	3-6	Jones	Almanzar
Sept. 26/98	Detroit	H	13	5-4	Risley	Sager
June 25/00	Boston	H	13	6-5	DeWitt	Florie
July 29/00	Seattle	A	13	5-6	Tomko	Halladay

* Suspended game, due to CNE curfew—completed on August 29th.
\# Suspended game, due to rain—completed on September 18th.

BLUE JAYS WITH 10 OR MORE STRIKEOUTS IN A GAME

SO	PITCHER	DATE & OPPONENT	SO	PITCHER	DATE & OPPONENT
18	Roger Clemens	Aug. 25, 1998 vs Kansas City	10	Jim Clancy	June 19, 1982 at Oakland (10 inn)
16	Roger Clemens	July 12, 1997 at Boston	10	Dave Stieb	May 6, 1983 vs Kansas City
15	Roger Clemens	Aug. 15, 1998 vs Anaheim	10	Dave Stieb	May 4, 1984 at Kansas City (10 inn)
15	Roger Clemens	Sept. 21, 1998 vs Baltimore	10	Luis Leal	Aug. 24, 1984 at Minnesota
14	Pat Hentgen	May 3, 1994 vs Kansas City	10	Dave Stieb	Aug. 26, 1984 at Minnesota
14	Roger Clemens	May 10, 1997 at Minnesota	10	Dave Stieb	Aug. 31, 1984 at Minnesota
14	Roger Clemens	Sept. 7, 1997 vs Texas	10	Jimmy Key	July 7, 1986 vs Seattle
14	Roger Clemens	Aug. 2, 1998 at Minnesota	10	Jim Clancy	Sept. 9, 1987 at Milwaukee
13	Roger Clemens	Aug. 12, 1997 vs Minnesota	10	Jimmy Key	April 24, 1989 at Oakland
12	Pete Vuckovich	June 26, 1977 at Baltimore	10	Juan Guzman	Sept. 13, 1991 vs Oakland
12	Jim Clancy	April 19, 1988 vs Kansas City	10	Juan Guzman	April 9, 1992 at Detroit
12	Dave Stieb	Aug. 22, 1988 vs Chicago	10	Juan Guzman	July 6, 1992 vs California
12	Tom Candiotti	Aug. 9, 1991 vs Detroit	10	Juan Guzman	Aug. 11, 1993 vs Minnesota
12	Roger Clemens	May 21, 1997 at New York (AL)	10	Juan Guzman	Aug. 27, 1993 at Seattle
12	Roger Clemens	June 16, 1997 vs Atlanta	10	Todd Stottlemyre	Sept. 21, 1993 vs Boston
11	Jim Clancy	Sept. 5, 1980 vs Chicago	10	Pat Hentgen	April 16, 1994 at California
11	Dave Stieb	Sept. 4, 1983 vs Detroit (10 inn)	10	Dave Stewart	April 25, 1994 at Kansas City
11	Doyle Alexander	July 23, 1985 vs Seattle	10	Pat Hentgen	July 21, 1994 vs Texas
11	Jose Nunez	July 9, 1987 vs Kansas City	10	David Cone	July 8, 1995 at Oakland
11	Jim Clancy	July 12, 1987 vs Kansas City	10	Juan Guzman	July 30, 1995 at Oakland
11	Dave Stieb	Aug. 4, 1989 vs New York (AL)	10	Al Leiter	Sept. 17, 1995 at Milwaukee
11	Juan Guzman	June 5, 1993 vs Oakland	10	Pat Hentgen	Sept. 9, 1996 vs Texas
11	Al Leiter	July 23, 1994 vs Texas	10	Pat Hentgen	Sept. 24, 1996 vs Detroit
11	David Cone	June 28, 1995 at Boston	10	Pat Hentgen	May 4, 1997 vs Minnesota
11	Juan Guzman	April 15, 1996 vs Detroit	10	Roger Clemens	May 5, 1997 vs Detroit
11	Juan Guzman	June 28, 1996 vs Milwaukee	10	Roger Clemens	July 6, 1997 vs New York (AL)
11	Roger Clemens	Aug. 17, 1997 at Cleveland	10	Roger Clemens	July 17, 1997 at Texas
11	Roger Clemens	Sept. 23, 1997 vs Baltimore	10	Roger Clemens	July 28, 1997 at Milwaukee (G#1)
11	Juan Guzman	May 10, 1998 at Seattle	10	Roger Clemens	Aug. 7, 1997 vs Cleveland
11	Roger Clemens	June 30, 1998 vs New York (NL)	10	Roger Clemens	Sept. 18, 1997 at Boston
11	Kelvim Escobar	Aug. 22, 1998 at Anaheim	10	Roger Clemens	June 3, 1998 vs Detroit
11	Roger Clemens	Sept. 5, 1998 vs Boston	10	Roger Clemens	July 12, 1998 at Detroit
11	Roger Clemens	Sept. 16, 1998 at Detroit	10	Chris Carpenter	July 16, 1998 at Chicago
11	Roger Clemens	Sept. 26, 1998 vs Detroit	10	Roger Clemens	July 17, 1998 vs New York (AL)
11	David Wells	June 11, 2000 vs Montreal	10	Kelvim Escobar	Sept. 7, 1998 vs Cleveland
11	David Wells	July 26, 2000 vs Cleveland	10	David Wells	April 19, 2000 vs Anaheim
11	Esteban Loaiza	Sept. 8, 2000 vs Detroit	10	Kelvim Escobar	June 4, 2000 at Florida
10	Jerry Garvin	April 14, 1977 vs Detroit			
10	Jim Clancy	Sept. 28, 1978 vs Boston			
10	Jesse Jefferson	May 16, 1980 vs Oakland			

1-0 GAMES (60)

DATE	OPP	RESULT	WP	LP
1978 (1)				
July 24	vs Oak	1-0 loss	Honeycutt	Lemanczyk
1979 (3)				
May 14	at Cle	1-0 loss	Waits	Underwood
May 27	vs Bos	1-0 loss	Rainey	Jefferson
May 31	vs Det	1-0 loss	P. Underwood	T. Underwood
1980 (6)				
April 17	vs Mil	1-0 win	Mirabella	Sorensen
May 15	vs Sea	1-0 win	Clancy	Bannister
May 16	vs Oak	1-0 win (11)	Jefferson	Norris
June 10	at CWS	1-0 win	Clancy	Baumgarten
June 24	at Bal	1-0 loss	McGregor	Stieb
July 21	at Oak	1-0 win	Stieb	Kingman
1981 (2)				
May 17	at Cle (G1)	1-0 loss	Walts	Stieb
Sept. 8	at Min	1-0 loss	Havens	Stieb
1982 (2)				
July 31	vs Det	1-0 win (10)	Gott	Rucker
Aug. 31	vs Bal	1-0 loss	Palmer	Leal
1984 (2)				
April 27	at KC	1-0 win	Alexander	Gubicza
May 19	vs CWS	1-0 win	Gott	Seaver
1985 (1)				
April 10	at KC	1-0 win (10)	Caudill	Beckwith
1986 (3)				
April 12	at KC	1-0 loss	Leonard	Acker
July 27	at Oak	1-0 loss (15)	Leiper	Clarke
Sept. 26	at Bos	1-0 win (12)	Eichorn	Schiraldi
1987 (2)				
Aug. 15	vs CWS	1-0 loss	Dotson	Clancy
Oct. 4	at Det	1-0 loss	Tanana	Key
1988 (3)				
Sept. 21	vs Bos	1-0 win	Flanagan	Gardner
Sept. 24	at Cle	1-0 win	Stieb	Nichols
Sept. 28	at Bos	1-0 win	Key	Hurst
1989 (2)				
April 30	at Cal	1-0 loss (11)	McClure	Henke
July 18	vs Cal	1-0 loss	Blyleven	Key
1990 (5)				
May 28	at Oak	1-0 win	Stieb	Moore
July 6	vs Sea	1-0 win	Wells	Holman
July 27	vs Tex	1-0 win	Stieb	Hough
Aug. 25	vs Bos	1-0 loss	Clemens	Wells
Aug. 26	vs Bos	1-0 loss	Harris	Stottlemyre
1991 (6)				
May 20	at Oak	1-0 win	Wells	Welch
June 3	vs Cle	1-0 win	MacDonald	Candiotti
June 12	at Cle	1-0 win	Timlin	Candiotti
June 13	at Cle	1-0 win	Key	Nagy
June 27	at Min	1-0 win	Guzman	Tapani
July 4	vs Min	1-0 loss	West	Key
1992 (6)				
April 17	at Bos	1-0 loss	Clemens	Wells
April 29	vs Cal	1-0 win	Stottlemyre	Abbott
June 5	at Bal	1-0 loss	Sutcliffe	Key
Sept. 9	at KC	1-0 win	Cone	Appier
Sept. 19	vs Tex	1-0 win	Cone	Chiamparino
Sept. 30	vs Bos	1-0 loss	Viola	Cone
1993 (1)				
April 24	vs CWS	1-0 win	Stottlemyre	Fernandez
1994 (2)				
April 28	at Tex	1-0 loss	Brown	Leiter
May 3	vs KC	1-0 loss	Hentgen	Appier
1995 (1)				
Aug. 2	at Bal	1-0 loss	Mussina	Menhart
1996 (3)				
June 20	at Oak	1-0 win	Hentgen	Wengert
July 28	vs Oak	1-0 win	Hentgen	Prieto
Aug. 22	at CWS	1-0 win (6)	Hanson	Fernandez
1997 (3)				
May 4	vs Min	1-0 win	Hentgen	Tewksbury
July 4	vs NYY	1-0 win	Escobar	Cone
July 28	at Mil (G1)	1-0 loss	Woodard	Clemens
1998 (3)				
April 27	at NYY	1-0 loss	Pettitte	Clemens
June 25	at Mon	1-0 loss	Williams	Perez
July 30	vs Tex	1-0 win	Guzman	Loaiza
1999 (2)				
April 10	at Bal	1-0 win	Mussina	Carpenter
July 11	at Mon	1-0 win	Wells	Pavano
2000 (1)				
Aug. 25	at Tex	1-0 loss (11)	Venafro	Koch

1-0 GAMES

The Blue Jays have played 60 games that have resulted in a 1-0 decision. In those 60 games, the club's record is 34-26.

YEAR	WON	LOST
1977	0	0
1978	0	1
1979	0	3
1980	5	1
1981	0	2
1982	1	1
1983	0	0
1984	2	0
1985	1	0
1986	1	2
1987	0	2
1988	3	0
1989	0	2
1990	3	2
1991	5	1
1992	3	3
1993	1	0
1994	1	1
1995	0	1
1996	3	0
1997	2	1
1998	2	1
1999	1	0
2000	0	1
TOTALS	**34**	**26**

VERSUS OPPONENTS

TEAM	WON	LOST
BALTIMORE	0	5
BOSTON	3	5
CALIFORNIA	1	2
CHICAGO	4	1
CLEVELAND	4	2
DETROIT	1	2
KANSAS CITY	4	1
MILWAUKEE	1	1
MINNESOTA	2	2
MONTREAL	2	0
NEW YORK (AL)	1	1
OAKLAND	6	2
SEATTLE	2	0
TEXAS	3	2
TOTALS	**34**	**26**

Toronto's last 1-0 victory was on July 11, 1999 at Montreal vs. the Expos. David Wells pitched a complete game two-hitter... The last 1-0 loss was at Texas vs. the Rangers on August 25, 2000 when Billy Koch was the losing pitcher for the Blue Jays in an 11.0 inning game.

LAST TIME

BLUE JAYS PITCHING – INDIVIDUAL

NO-HITTER: Dave Stieb, September 2, 1990 at Cleveland (Won 3-0).

ONE-HITTER: Roy Halladay, September 27, 1998 vs. Detroit (Won 2-1).

TWO-HITTER: David Wells, July 11, 1999 at Montreal (Won 1-0).

TEN OR MORE STRIKEOUTS: Esteban Loaiza (9.0, 11K), September 8, 2000 vs. Detroit (Won 3-0).

SHUTOUT: Esteban Loaiza (9.0), September 8, 2000 vs. Detroit (Won 3-0).

COMPLETE GAME, MAJOR LEAGUE DEBUT: None.

SHUTOUT, MAJOR LEAGUE DEBUT: None.

BACK-TO-BACK COMPLETE GAMES: David Wells, September 21, 2000 vs. New York (Won 3-1) and September 26, 2000 at Baltimore (Lost 2-1).

BACK-TO-BACK SHUTOUTS: Roger Clemens, August 20, 1998 at Seattle (Won 7-0), August 25, 1998 vs. Kansas City (Won 3-0), August 30, 1998 vs. Minnesota (Won 6-0).

10+ INNINGS PITCHED: John Cerutti (10.0), April 30, 1989 at California.

POSITION PLAYER PITCHING: Rick Leach, August 15, 1984 at Cleveland (Lost 16-1).

PITCHER PLAYING POSITION: Dave Stieb, August 29, 1980 vs. Minnesota (left field).

PITCHER SCORING A RUN: Roger Clemens, September 2, 1997 vs. New York Mets.

NON-PITCHER PITCHER: Rick Leach (1B/OF), August 15, 1984 vs. Cleveland (1.0).

HOME RUN BY PITCHER: None.

BLUE JAYS PITCHING – TEAM

NO-HITTER: Dave Stieb, September 2, 1990 at Cleveland (Won 3-0).

ONE-HITTER: Frank Castillo (7.0), Pedro Borbon (1.0), Billy Koch (1.0), May 21, 2000 vs. Chicago (Lost 2-1).

TWO-HITTER: Kelvim Escobar (8.0), Billy Koch (1.0), July 19, 2000 at Tampa Bay (Won 5-2).

SHUTOUT: Frank Castillo (6.0), Kelvim Escobar (2.0), Billy Koch (1.0), September 27, 2000 at Baltimore (Won, 4-0).

BACK-TO-BACK COMPLETE GAMES: Chris Carpenter, April 21, 2000 vs. New York Yankees (Won 8-3) and Kelvim Escobar, April 22, 2000 vs. New York Yankees (Won 8-2).

BACK-TO-BACK COMPLETE GAME WINS: Chris Carpenter, April 21, 2000 vs. New York Yankees (Won 8-3) and Kelvim Escobar, April 22, 2000 vs. New York Yankees (Won 8-2).

BACK-TO-BACK-TO-BACK COMPLETE GAMES: Juan Guzman, August 21,1996 at Kansas City (Won 6-2), Erik Hanson, August 22, 1996 at Chicago (Won 1-0) and Pat Hentgen, August 23, 1996 at Chicago (Won 4-2).

BACK-TO-BACK-TO-BACK COMPLETE GAME WINS: Juan Guzman, August 21,1996 at Kansas City (Won 6-2), Erik Hanson, August 22, 1996 at Chicago (Won 1-0) and Pat Hentgen, August 23, 1996 at Chicago (Won 4-2).

FOUR CONSECUTIVE COMPLETE GAMES: Dave Stieb, September 20, 1983 vs. Seattle (Won 7-3), Doyle Alexander, September 21, 1983 vs. Seattle (Won 4-3), Luis Leal, September 23, 1983 at Oakland (L 2-0) and Jim Clancy, September 24, 1983 at Oakland (L 2-1).

BACK-TO-BACK SHUTOUTS: Roger Clemens (5.2), Luis Andujar (1.1), Dan Plesac (1.0), Tim Crabtree (1.0), April 9, 1997 at Chicago (Won 5-0) and Juan Guzman (7.0), Dan Plesac (1.0), Mike Timlin (1.0), April 10, 1997 at Chicago (Won 4-0).

BACK-TO-BACK SHUTOUTS, COMPLETE GAME: Jimmy Key, September 28, 1988 at Boston (Won 1-0) and Dave Stieb, September 30, 1988 vs. Baltimore (Won 4-0).

BACK-TO-BACK 1-0 SHUTOUTS: Mike Timlin (6.0), Bob MacDonald (1.0), Jim Acker (0.2), Tom Henke (1.1), June 12, 1991 at Cleveland and Jimmy Key (9.0) June 13, 1991 at Cleveland.

1-0 GAME, WIN: July 11, 1999 at Montreal.

1-0 GAME, LOSS: August 25, 2000 at Texas (11.0 innings).

BLUE JAYS HITTING – INDIVIDUAL

LEADOFF HOME RUN: Shannon Stewart, September 27, 2000 at Baltimore.

INSIDE-THE-PARK HOME RUN: Tony Fernandez, September 22, 1998 vs. Baltimore.

GRAND SLAM HOME RUN: Carlos Delgado, September 17, 2000 at Chicago.

PINCH HIT HOME RUN: Willie Greene, September 5, 1999 at Kansas City (9th inning).

PINCH HIT GRAND SLAM: Jesse Barfield, April 24, 1982 vs. Boston.

WALK OFF HOME RUN: Carlos Delgado, August 16, 2000 vs. Anaheim.

TWO HOME RUNS, ONE GAME: Brad Fullmer, August 30, 2000 at Anaheim.

THREE HOME RUNS, ONE GAME: Darrin Fletcher, August 27, 2000 at Texas.

TWO HOME RUNS, SAME INNING: Joe Carter, Oct. 3, 1993 at Baltimore, 2nd inning.

HOME RUNS FROM BOTH SIDES OF THE PLATE, ONE GAME: Jose Cruz Jr., August 24, 1997 at Kansas City.

HOME RUN FIRST MAJOR LEAGUE AT-BAT: Junior Felix, May 4, 1989 vs. California.

HOME RUN FIRST MAJOR LEAGUE HIT: Junior Felix, May 4, 1989 vs. California.

HOME RUN INTO FIFTH DECK: Shawn Green (RF), April 22, 1999 vs. Anaheim, 449 feet.

FOUR HITS, ONE GAME: Darrin Fletcher, September 22, 2000 vs. Tampa Bay.

FIVE HITS, ONE GAME: Tony Fernandez, May 7, 1999 vs. Texas.

TWO HITS, SAME INNING: Marty Cordova, April 18, 2000 vs. Anaheim (9th inning, two singles).

FOUR OR MORE STEALS, ONE GAME: (4) Otis Nixon, August 14, 1996 vs. Boston.

STEALING HOME: Paul Molitor, Oct. 3, 1993 at Baltimore.

STOLEN BASE BY CATCHER: Darrin Fletcher, July 9, 2000 at Montreal (2nd base).

BATTING FOR THE CYCLE: Kelly Gruber, April 16, 1989 vs. Kansas City

BASES LOADED TRIPLE: Juan Samuel, June 10, 1997 vs. Seattle

BLUE JAYS HITTING – TEAM

BACK-TO-BACK HOME RUNS: Brad Fullmer (3R) and Tony Batista, August 30, 2000 at Anaheim.

BACK-TO-BACK-TO-BACK HOME RUNS: Craig Grebeck (2R), Raul Mondesi and Carlos Delgado, April 18, 2000 vs. Anaheim.

THREE HOME RUNS ONE INNING: April 23, 2000 vs. New York Yankees (6th inning, Carlos Delgado, Darrin Fletcher-2R, Marty Cordova).

FIVE HOME RUNS, ONE GAME: August 27, 2000 at Texas.

SIX HOME RUNS, ONE GAME: July 8, 1999 at Baltimore.

TWO GRAND SLAMS, ONE GAME: None.

HOME RUNS BY FIRST TWO BATTERS OF A GAME: Devon White and Roberto Alomar, August 18, 1991 at Detroit, (Bill Gullickson).

20 or MORE HITS ONE GAME: (20) August 13, 2000 at Minnesota.

THREE CONSECUTIVE 10 RUNS GAMES: April 18-20, 2000: April 18 vs. Anaheim (Lost 10-16), April 19 vs. Anaheim (Won 12-4), April 20 vs. Anaheim (Won 12-11).

5 or MORE STOLEN BASES: (5) June 18, 2000 at Boston.

NO STRIKEOUTS, BATTING: July 20, 2000 vs. Tampa Bay.

BLUE JAYS MISCELLANEOUS – TEAM

TRIPLE PLAY: September 21, 1979 vs. New York.

TURNED FIVE OR MORE DP'S: August 6, 1997 vs. Cleveland (5).

FOUR GAME SWEEP: September 3-6, 1998 vs. Boston.

TIE GAME: April 26, 1998 at Chicago (5-5).

THREE CONSECUTIVE EXTRA INNING GAMES: April 19-21, 1998: April 19 vs. Chicago (Won 5-4, 12.0), April 20 vs. New York (Lost 3-2, 11.0), April 21 vs. New York (Lost 5-3, 10.0).

SUSPENDED GAME: May 3, 1996 at Boston, (6th inning due to 1:00A.M. curfew), completed May 4, (Loss 8-7).

RAIN SHORTENED GAME: April 26, 1998 at Chicago (6th inning, 5-5 tie).

GAME POSTPONED: April 12, 1997 at Milwaukee (due to snow).

PLAYER EJECTION: Shannon Stewart, September 19, 2000 vs. New York Yankees.

MANAGER EJECTION: Jim Fregosi, August 10, 2000 at Kansas City.

BENCH BRAWL (Empty): July 30, 2000 at Seattle.

OPPONENTS PITCHING – INDIVIDUAL

PERFECT GAME: Len Barker at Cleveland, May 15, 1981 (Blue Jays lost 3-0).

NO-HITTER: Nolan Ryan at Texas, May 1, 1991 (Blue Jays lost 3-0).

ONE-HITTER: Frank Viola in Toronto September 30, 1992 (Blue Jays lost 1-0).

TWO-HITTER: Travis Harper, September 24, 2000 vs. Tampa Bay (Blue Jays lost 6-0).

TEN OR MORE STRIKEOUTS: Bartolo Colon (5.1, 10K), July 26, 2000 vs. Cleveland (Blue Jays won 8-1).

SHUTOUT: Travis Harper, (9.0), September 24, 2000 vs. Tampa Bay (Blue Jays lost 6-0).

BACK-TO-BACK SHUTOUTS: Mike Mussina (9.0), September 26, 1995 vs. Baltimore (5-0) and Scott Erickson (9.0), September 27, 1995 vs. Baltimore (7-0).

HOME RUN BY PITCHER: Felipe Lira, July 8, 2000 at Montreal

OPPONENTS PITCHING – TEAM

PERFECT GAME: Len Barker at Cleveland, May 15, 1981 (Blue Jays lost 3-0).

NO-HITTER: Nolan Ryan at Texas, May 1, 1991 (Blue Jays lost 3-0).

ONE-HITTER: Steve Woodard (8.0) and Mike Fetters (1.0), July 28, 1997 G1 at Milwaukee (Blue Jays lost 1-0).

TWO-HITTER: Patt Rapp (7.0), Jay Spurgeon (1.0), Buddy Groom (0.1) and Lesli Brea (0.2), September 28, 2000 at Baltimore (Blue Jays lost 23-1).

SHUTOUT: Travis Harper (9.0), September 24, 2000 vs. Tampa Bay (Blue Jays lost 6-0)

BACK-TO-BACK 1-0 SHUTOUTS: Roger Clemens (9.0), August 25, 1990 vs. Boston and Greg Harris (7.2), Jeff Gray (1.1), August 26, 1990 vs. Boston.

OPPONENTS HITTING – INDIVIDUAL

LEAD OFF HOME RUN: Brady Anderson, September 28, 2000 at Baltimore.

INSIDE-THE-PARK HOME RUN: Nomar Garciaparra, July 26, 1998 at Boston.

GRAND SLAM HOME RUN: Mike Piazza, July 18, 2000 vs. New York Mets.

PINCH HIT HOME RUN: Richie Sexson (1R), July 6, 2000 at Cleveland (7th inning).

PINCH HIT GRAND SLAM: Greg Colbrunn, August 4, 1997 at Minnesota (5th inning).

WALK OFF HOME RUN: Randy Velarde, August 1, 2000 at Oakland (Lost 3-1, 10th inning).

TWO HOME RUNS, ONE GAME: Russell Branyon, July 4, 2000 at Cleveland.

THREE HOME RUNS ONE GAME: Alex Rodriguez, April 16, 2000 vs. Seattle.

HOME RUNS FROM BOTH SIDES OF THE PLATE, ONE GAME: Jorge Posada and Bernie Williams, April 23, 2000 vs. New York Yankees.

HOME RUN INTO THE FIFTH DECK: Jose Canseco (LF), April 12, 1999 vs. Tampa Bay, 459 feet.

FOUR HITS, ONE GAME: Brook Fordyce, September 28, 2000 at Baltimore.

FIVE HITS, ONE GAME: Mike Stanley, September 4, 2000 vs. Toronto.

TWO HITS, SAME INNING: Mo Vaughn, April 20, 2000 vs. Anaheim (6th inning, two singles).

FOUR OR MORE STEALS, ONE GAME: (4) Lou Frazier, April 19, 1998 vs. Chicago.

STEALING HOME: Billy Hatcher at Boston, August 3, 1992.

BATTING FOR THE CYCLE: George Brett, vs. Kansas City, July 25, 1990

OPPONENTS HITTING – TEAM

BACK-TO-BACK HOME RUNS: Roberto Alomar (1R) and Manny Ramirez, September 30, 2000 at Cleveland.

BACK-TO-BACK-TO-BACK HOME RUNS: Jose Valentin (1R), Frank Thomas and Paul Konerko, May 3, 2000 at Chicago.

THREE HOME RUNS ONE INNING: (4) Mark Johnson (2R), Jose Valentin, Frank Thomas and Paul Konerko, May 3, 2000 at Chicago.

FIVE HOME RUNS ONE GAME: (8) June 20, 2000 vs. Detroit.

SIX HOME RUNS ONE GAME: (8) June 20, 2000 vs. Detroit.

TWO GRAND SLAMS, ONE GAME: Manny Ramirez and Dave Roberts, September 24, 1999 vs. Cleveland.

HOME RUNS BY FIRST TWO BATTERS OF A GAME: Tom Goodwin and Mark McLemore, May 7, 1999 vs. Texas (Pat Hentgen)

20 or MORE HITS, ONE GAMES: (23) September 28, 2000 at Baltimore.

THREE CONSECUTIVE 10 RUN GAMES: April 14-16, 2000: April 14 vs. Seattle (Lost 11-9), April 15 vs. Seattle (Lost 17-6), April 16 vs. Seattle (Lost 19-17).

NO STRIKEOUTS, BATTING: August 8, 2000 at Kansas City.

OPPONENTS MISCELLANEOUS – TEAM

TRIPLE PLAY: July 28, 1997 at Milwaukee G#2

TURNED FIVE OR MORE DP'S: July 6, 1999 at Baltimore (5, 10 innings) August 23, 1993 vs. Cleveland (5).

FOUR GAME SWEEP: July 28-29, 1997 at Milwaukee (swept in both double-headers).

AT THE ALL STAR BREAK

AVERAGE
Year	Player	AVG
1993	Olerud	.395
1999	Fernandez	.372
2000	Delgado	.363
1994	Molitor	.342
2000	Stewart	.339
1977	Bailor	.332
1999	Green	.327
1982	Bonnell	.325
1992	Alomar	.323
1986	Bell	.316
1995	Alomar	.316

HOME RUNS
Year	Player	HR
1987	Bell	29
2000	Delgado	28
1999	Green	25
1998	Canseco	24
2000	Batista	24
1996	Sprague	23
2000	Mondesi	23
1986	Barfield	21
1999	Delgado	21
1989	McGriff	20
1990	Gruber	20
1996	Carter	20
2000	Cruz	20

RBI
Year	Player	RBI
1994	Carter	80
2000	Delgado	80
1999	Delgado	77
1987	Bell	76
2000	Batista	72
1996	Carter	70
1999	Green	70
1993	Olerud	69
1990	Gruber	66
1986	Barfield	65
1986	Bell	65
1993	Carter	65
1992	Carter	63
2000	Mondesi	63
1990	Bell	60

STOLEN BASES
Year	Player	SB
1997	Nixon	37
1999	Stewart	29
1993	Alomar	28
1984	Garcia	27
1991	Alomar	27
1998	Stewart	26
1984	Collins	23
1985	Garcia	23
1985	Moseby	23
1987	Fernandez	23

WINS
Year	Player	W
2000	Wells	15
1997	Clemens	13
1990	Stieb	11
1992	Guzman	11
1993	Hentgen	11
1994	Hentgen	11
1987	Clancy	10
1988	Stieb	10
1991	Key	10
1992	Morris	10

LOSSES
Year	Player	L
1979	Underwood	12
1988	Clancy	11
	5 others at	10

SAVES
Year	Player	SV
1998	Myers	22
1993	Ward	22
2000	Koch	20
1987	Henke	17
1988	Henke	16
1990	Henke	16
1991	Henke	16
1992	Henke	15
1996	Timlin	15

STRIKEOUTS
Year	Player	SO
1997	Clemens	140
1992	Guzman	122
1998	Clemens	120
1994	Hentgen	112
1996	Guzman	105
1999	Wells	100
2000	Wells	100
1987	Key	98
1993	Guzman	98
1994	Guzman	98
1984	Stieb	95
1985	Stieb	95
1987	Clancy	94
1994	Stewart	90

YEAR	W-L	PCT.	POS.	GBL	HOME ATTENDANCE		YEAR	W-L	PCT.	POS.	GBL	HOME ATTENDANCE
1977	34-58	.370	7th	-19.0	1,020,152		1989	42-45	.483	T4th	-7.0	1,559,163
1978	32-53	.376	7th	-26.0	804,890		1990	47-38	.553	2nd	-0.5	2,288,900
1979	29-64	.312	7th	-31.5	785,030		1991	49-34	.590	1st	+5.5	2,090,001
1980	33-43	.434	7th	-17.0	675,556		1992	53-34	.609	1st	+4.0	2,416,036
1981*	16-42	.276	7th	-19.0	426,795		1993	49-40	.551	1st	+0.5	2,340,240
1982	37-47	.440	7th	-11.5	637,057		1994	38-48	.442	5th	-12.5	2,116,873
1983	43-33	.566	1st	+1.0	786,503		1995*	27-40	.403	5th	-11.5	1,295,643
1984	50-34	.595	2nd	-7.0	1,247,799		1996	38-49	.437	3rd	-15.0	1,289,964
1985	53-35	.602	1st	+2.5	1,123,502		1997	40-43	.482	T3rd	-14.0	1,547,513
1986	47-43	.522	5th	-10.5	1,442,158		1998	46-42	.523	3rd	-18.5	1,319,694
1987	51-36	.586	2nd	-3.0	1,413,455		1999	47-43	.522	3rd	-7.0	1,181,546
1988	42-46	.477	6th	-11.5	1,473,480		2000	48-41	.539	2nd	0.0	816,825

* Strike Season

BLUE JAYS COMEBACKS

Deficits Overcome:
10 runs - April 28, 1999 at Ana. (L 12-10)
10 runs - June 4, 1989 at Bos. (W 13-11, 11 inn.)
7 runs - Sept. 5, 1995 vs KC (L 9-8)
7 runs - April 14, 1993 vs Sea. (L 10-9)
7 runs - June 29, 1987 vs NYY (L 15-14)
6 runs - Sept. 23, 2000 vs TB (W 7-6)
6 runs - Aug. 23, 2000 vs KC (W 9-8)
6 runs - May 7, 1992 at Sea. (W 8-7)
6 runs - June 18, 1992 vs Det. (L 14-10)
6 runs - April 23, 1990 vs Cle. (W 12-9)
6 runs - May 16, 1989 vs Cle. (W 7-6)
6 runs - Sept. 4, 1988 vs Tex. (W 9-7)
6 runs - Aug. 31, 1987 vs Cal. (L 8-7, 11 inn.)
6 runs - June 20, 1986 vs NYY (L 10-8)
6 runs - July 2, 1983 vs Sea. (W 7-6)
6 runs - Aug. 19, 1983 vs Bos. (W 8-7)
6 runs - June 3, 1980 vs Cal. (W 7-6, 11 inn.)
6 runs - Aug. 1, 1980 vs Cal. (W 9-8)
6 runs - April 15, 1979 vs KC (L 12-10)

Leads Surrendered:
9 runs - Sept. 15, 1982 Gm 2 vs Oak. (W 12-11)
8 runs - June 4, 1995 at Cle. (L 9-8)
8 runs - Sept. 7, 1979 at Cle. (L 9-8)
7 runs - July 2, 1995 vs Bal. (L 9-7)
7 runs - April 15, 1994 at Cal. (L 14-13)
7 runs - June 13, 1979 Gm 1 vs Cal. (W 9-8)
6 runs - May 7, 2000 vs Cle (L 10-8)
6 runs - Sept. 6, 1998 vs Bos. (W 8-7)
6 runs - Aug. 27, 1993 at Sea. (L 7-6)
6 runs - July 22, 1988 vs Sea. (L 10-9, 11 inn.)
6 runs - May 17, 1985 at Min. (L 7-6, 11 inn.)
6 runs - July 12, 1983 at KC (W 9-6)
6 runs - July 28, 1982 at Bos. (L 9-7)
6 runs - Sept. 24, 1980 at Det. (L 9-8, 10 inn.)
6 runs - May 4, 1980 Gm 1 vs Cle. (W 9-8, 10 inn.)
6 runs - June 27, 1978 vs Bal. (W 9-8)

DOUBLEHEADER

Toronto last played a doubleheader on July 15, 1998 at Chicago, losing both games to the White Sox... Toronto has played 96 doubleheaders in club history and have a 19-37-40 record... Toronto last played back-to-back doubleheaders in 1997 at Milwaukee on July 28 & 29 and lost all four games... Toronto has played 10 back-to-back doubleheaders and are 2-6-2 including four straight DH's over six days in 1978 from June 11 to 16... Have played two split gate doubleheaders, September 23, 1995 in Boston and July 29, 1997 in Milwaukee... Toronto has had five seasons without playing a doubleheader, 1990, 1991, 1993, 1996 and 1999... In 1980 the Blue Jays posted their best doubleheader record at 5-1-4.

DOUBLEHEADER SHUTOUTS

Did you know that the Blue Jays have never shut out opponents in both ends of a doubleheader?... Conversely, the Blue Jays have been shut out in both ends of a doubleheader twice, losing 8-0 and 6-0 to Boston at Toronto on September 5, 1977 and 15-0 and 2-0 to New York at Toronto on September 25, 1977... The Blue Jays have been shut out in one end of a doubleheader on 14 occasions (ten DH losses and four splits)... The Blue Jays have also shut out the opposition in one end of a doubleheader on three occasions (two wins, one split).

DOUBLEHEADER vs. EACH CLUB

	DH		
TORONTO vs	**W**	**L**	**S**
Anaheim	1	0	1
Baltimore	2	7	2
Boston	1	2	6
Chicago	3	1	5
Cleveland	4	3	9
Detroit	2	1	2
Kansas City	0	3	0
Milwaukee	1	9	2
Minnesota	1	3	1
New York (A)	1	5	4
Oakland	1	2	3
Seattle	1	1	1
Tampa Bay	0	0	0
Texas	1	0	4
Atlanta	0	0	0
Florida	0	0	0
Montreal	0	0	0
New York (N)	0	0	0
Philadelphia	0	0	0
TOTALS	**19**	**37**	**40**

EXTRA INNING GAMES

Year by Year

				Home		Road	
	Games	W	L	W	L	W	L
1977	15	4	11	2	7	2	4
1978	15	7	8	4	3	3	5
1979	12	2	10	1	6	1	4
1980	18	10	8	5	3	5	5
1981	9	1	8	0	3	1	5
1982	15	10	5	7	1	3	4
1983	17	11	6	3	2	8	4
1984	18	6	12	4	2	2	10
1985	17	12	5	4	1	8	4
1986	23	10	13	3	4	7	9
1987	17	10	7	8	4	2	3
1988	12	6	6	3	4	3	2
1989	17	13	4	7	2	6	2
1990	12	4	8	1	5	3	3
1991	18	8	10	3	3	5	7
1992	9	7	2	4	1	3	1
1993	9	6	3	3	3	3	0
1994	9	3	6	1	1	2	5
1995	18	5	13	4	7	1	6
1996	17	7	10	5	7	2	3
1997	14	5	9	4	2	1	7
1998	16	8	8	6	4	2	4
1999	9	6	3	4	0	2	3
2000	8	2	6	1	2	1	4
Total	**344**	**163**	**181**	**87**	**77**	**76**	**104**

Club by Club

	W	L
Anaheim	12	16
Baltimore	11	10
Boston	14	17
Chicago	11	6
Cleveland	15	12
Detroit	17	17
Kansas City	13	13
Milwaukee	10	12
Minnesota	11	14
New York (A)	14	19
Oakland	7	17
Seattle	10	12
Tampa Bay	3	0
Texas	12	13
Atlanta	1	0
Florida	1	1
Montreal	1	0
New York (N)	0	2
Philadelphia	0	0
Total	**163**	**181**

THREE CONSECUTIVE EXTRA INNING GAMES

In 1998 the Blue Jays played three consecutive extra inning games from April 19 to 21 at the SkyDome... Toronto won 5-4 in 12 innings against the Chicago White Sox on April 19 and lost to the New York Yankees 3-2 in 11 innings on April 20 and 5-3 in ten innings on April 21... It was the fourth time Toronto had played three consecutive extra-inning games... The club record for consecutive extra-inning games is four from September 16 to 20, 1991. Played three straight extra inning games in Seattle and then in Oakland on the 20th.

TEAM RECORDS

GENERAL

Category	Record	Year
Doubleheaders, Most Played	17	1978
Doubleheaders, Fewest Played	0	1990, 1991, 1993, 1996
Doubleheaders, Best Record	5-1-4	1980
Doubleheaders, Most Wins	5	1980
Doubleheaders, Most Losses	8	1978
Doubleheaders, Most Split	8	1977
Extra Innings, Most Wins	13	1989
Extra Innings, Most Losses	13	1986
Extra Innings, Most Played	23	1986
Extra Innings, Fewest Played	8	2000
Games	163	1984, 1986, 1998
Games Won	99	1985
Games Lost	109	1979
Games Won, Consecutively	11	June 2-13, 1987,
	11	August 26-September 7, 1998
Games Lost, Consecutively	12	May 31-June 11 & Aug. 10, 1981
Home Wins, Consecutive	10	July 21-28, Aug. 2-3, 1985
Home Losses, Consecutive	11	Aug. 15-16, 26-28, Sept. 2-6 1977
Road Wins, Consecutive	9	Sept. 14-30, 1979
Road Losses, Consecutive	12	July 7-9, 19-23, 31-Aug. 1,
	12	Aug. 11, 1979
Games Won, Highest Percentage	.615	(99-62) 1985
Home Record, Best	54-26	(.675) 1985
Road Record, Best	47-34	(.580) 1993
Homestand, Best	10-1	May 17-27, 1984
Homestand, Worst	0-6	Sept. 26-Oct. 1, 1980;
	0-6	June 20-26, 1994;
	0-6	August 13-18, 1999
Home Wins, Fewest	25	1977
Road Wins, Fewest	21	1979
Home Losses, Most	55	1977
Road Losses, Most	60	1979
Road Trip, Best	9-1	June 8-17, 1990
Road Trip, Worst	0-6	Sept. 26-Oct. 1, 1978
	0-6	July 19-23, 1979
	0-6	Sept. 3-9, 1979
One Club, Most Wins vs	12	Baltimore, 1987, Cleveland, 1991
Consecutive Wins vs One Club	13	Cleveland, 12-1991, 1-1992
	13	Baltimore, 10-1999, 3-2000
One Club, Most Losses vs.	12	Boston (77) & Milwaukee, (78) &
	12	New York (95)
One Club, Most Home Wins	6	Bal., 1978, 1987, 1999; Tex., 1982, 1987; Min., 1984; Sea., 1985, Det., 1989; Cle., 1991; NYY, 1992; Bos., 1993; Tex., 1994; TB, 1998; Ana., 1999
One Club Home Losses	6	Bos. (1977); Cle. (1978); Det. (1979); Bal. (1982); Oak. (1999)
One Club, Most Road Wins	7	Boston, 1988
One Club, Most Road Losses	8	Milwaukee, 1978
One Run Games, Most	59	1984, 1997
One Run Games, Most Wins	34	1984
One Run Games, Most Losses	30	1978, 1982, 1997
One Run Games, Fewest Wins	17	1977
	16	(144 games) 1995
One Run Games, Fewest Losses	17	1998
Two Run Games, Most	41	1996
Two Run Games, Most Wins	20	1980, 1992, 1993
Two Run Games, Most Losses	23	1979, 1996
Two Run Games, Fewest Wins	7	1984
	6	(144 games) 1995
Two Run Games, Fewest Losses	8	1993, 2000
Day Games, Played	65	1979
Day Games, Most Won	38	1993
Day Games, Most Lost	44	1979
Night Games, Played	113	1998
Night Games, Most Won	67	1987, 1989
Night Games, Most Lost	68	1977, 1980
InterLeague, Most Wins	9	1998, 1999, 2000
InterLeague, Most Losses	11	1997
Players Used, Most	53	1999
Players Used, Fewest	33	1983, 1984
Pitchers Used, Most	22	1999, 2000
Pitchers Used, Fewest	13	1982, 1984
Righthanders, Most Wins vs	75	1985
Lefthanders, Most Wins vs	37	1990
Righthanders, Most Losses vs	75	1979
Lefthanders, Most Losses vs.	44	1982
Shutouts, Both Teams, Most	27	1997
Shutouts, Most Wins	16	1991, 1997
Shutouts, Most Losses	20	1981
Shutouts, Fewest Won	3	1977
Shutouts, Fewest Lost	2	1993

Category	Record	Year
Shutouts, Most vs One Team.	4 . . .	vs Detroit, 1989;
	4 . . .	vs New York (AL), 1997
Shutouts, Most By Opponent.	4 . . .	vs Milwaukee, 1978, vs Bos., 1990
Winning Margin, Highest	16 . . .	vs New York, Sept. 10, 1977
Winning Margin, Highest by Foe	22 . . .	vs California, Aug. 25, 1979
	22 . . .	at Baltimore, Sept. 28, 2000
Artificial Turf, Most Won	64 . . .	1985, 1992
Artificial Turf, Most Lost	60 . . .	1977 & 1978
Natural Turf, Most Won	39 . . .	1993
Natural Turf, Most Lost.	52 . . .	1978

BATTING

Category	Record	Year
At Bats, Most	5716 . . .	1986
Batting Average, Highest	.280 . . .	1999
Batting Average, Lowest	.244 . . .	1997
	.226 . . .	(106 games) 1981
Consecutive Games with At Least		
One Home Run	23 . . .	(44 Home Runs), 2000
Grounded Into Double Plays, Most	156 . . .	1977
Grounded Into Double Plays, Fewest	91 . . .	1984
Hit By Pitcher, Most	92 . . .	1996
Hit By Pitcher, Fewest	23 . . .	1977 & 1978
Hits, Most	1580 . . .	1999
Hits, Fewest	1333 . . .	1997
	1309 . . .	(144 games) 1995
Hits vs One Club, Most	152 . . .	vs Detroit, 1978
Hits vs One Club, Fewest (AL)	66 . . .	vs Milwaukee, 1997
Hits vs One Club, Fewest (NL)	14 . . .	vs New York Mets, 1997
Home Runs, Most	244 . . .	2000
Home Runs, Fewest.	95 . . .	1979
Home Runs, Home Most	134 . . .	2000
Home Runs, Home Fewest	45 . . .	1977
Home Runs, Road Most.	116 . . .	1999
Home Runs, Road Fewest.	44 . . .	1982
Home Runs vs One Club, Most	31 . . .	vs Baltimore, 1987
Home Runs vs One Club, Fewest (AL)	2 . . .	vs KC & Min, 1977
	2 . . .	vs Min & Oak, 1978
	2 . . .	vs Bos, 1995
Grand Slams, Most	9 . . .	2000
Inside The Park, Most	4 . . .	1983
Left On Base, Most	1187 . . .	1993
Left On Base, Fewest.	1064 . . .	1979
Singles, Most	1069 . . .	1984
Singles, Fewest	870 . . .	1997
Doubles, Most	337 . . .	1999
Doubles, Fewest	217 . . .	1978
Triples, Most.	68 . . .	1984
Triples, Fewest.	14 . . .	1999
Most Extra-Base Hits	593 . . .	2000
Pinch Hits, Most	71 . . .	1982
Pinch Hits, Fewest	5 . . .	1993
Pinch Hit Home Runs, Most.	6 . . .	1984
Pinch Hit Average, Highest	.341 . . .	2000
Runs Batted In, Most	856 . . .	1999
Runs Batted In, Fewest	550 . . .	1978
Runs Scored, Most	883 . . .	1999
Runs Scored, Fewest.	590 . . .	1978
Sacrifices, Most	81 . . .	1977
Sacrifices, Fewest	18 . . .	1990
Sacrifice Flies, Most	65 . . .	1991
Slugging Percentage, Highest	.469 . . .	2000
Slugging Percentage, Lowest	.358 . . .	1978
	.330 . . .	(106 games) 1981
Stolen Bases, Most Stolen	193 . . .	1984
Stolen Bases, Times Caught	81 . . .	1982, 1998
Stolen Bases, Fewest Stolen	28 . . .	1978
Strikeouts, Most	1138 . . .	1997
Strikeouts, Fewest	645 . . .	1978
Total Bases, Most.	2664 . . .	2000
Total Bases, Fewest.	1947 . . .	1978
Walks, Most	588 . . .	1993
Walks, Fewest	415 . . .	1982
On-Base Percentage, Highest.	.372 . . .	1983
Lowest	.293 . . .	1977
	.288 . . .	(106 games) 1981

FIELDING

Category	Record	Year
Assists, Most	1939	1980
Assists, Fewest	1532	1998
Chances Total, Most	6468	1980
Chances Total, Fewest	5958	1997
Double Plays, Most	206	1980
Double Plays, Fewest	109	1992
Errors, Most	164	1977
Errors, Fewest	86	1990
Fielding Average, Highest	.986	1990
Fielding Average, Lowest	.974	1977
Passed Balls, Most	31	1995
Passed Balls, Fewest	3	1985
Putouts, Most	4428	1986
Putouts, Fewest	4251	1979
Triple Plays	2	1979
Most Errorless Games	103	1990
Most Consecutive Errorless Games	11	1986

PITCHING

Category	Record	Year
Complete Games, Most	44	1979
Complete Games, Fewest	6	1990
Earned Run Average, Lowest	3.29	1985
Earned Run Average, Highest	5.14	2000
	4.88	(144 games) 1995
Hit Batsmen, Most	64	2000
Hit Batsmen, Fewest	20	1977
Hits, Most	1615	2000
Hits, Fewest	1301	1991
Home Runs, Most	195	2000
Home Runs, Fewest	99	1989
Home Runs, Home Most	102	1996
Home Runs, Home Fewest	50	1989
Home Runs, Road Most	103	2000
Home Runs, Road Fewest	49	1989, 1991
One Hit Games	3	1988
Runs, Most	908	2000
Runs, Fewest	588	1985
Earned Runs, Most	821	2000
Earned Runs, Fewest	529	1985
Relief Appearances, Most	388	2000
Relief Appearances, Fewest	187	1977
Saves, Most	60	1991
Saves, Fewest	11	1979
Strikeouts, Most	1154	1998
Strikeouts, Fewest	611	1979
Walks, Most	654	1995
Walks, Fewest	445	1990
Wild Pitches, Most	83	1993
Wild Pitches, Fewest	25	1983
Shutouts, Most	17	1988
Shutouts, Fewest	3	1977
1-0 Games, Won, Most	5	1980
1-0 Games, Lost, Most	3	1979, 1992

INDIVIDUAL SEASON RECORDS

R - Right hand batter   L - Left hand batter   B - Switch hitter   * - League Leader

BATTING

Highest Average (502 Plate App.)	(R)	.341	Paul Molitor-'94
	(L)	*.363	John Olerud-'93
	(B)	.328	Tony Fernandez-'99
Highest Average (100 games)	(R)	.341	Paul Molitor-'94
	(L)	*.363	John Olerud-'93
	(B)	.328	Tony Fernandez-'99
Most Games	(R)	162	Rick Bosetti-'79, Joe Carter-'91
	(L)	*162	Carlos Delgado-'00
	(B)	*163	Tony Fernandez-'86
Most at Bats	(R)	641	George Bell-'86
	(L)	630	Shawn Green-'98
	(B)	687	Tony Fernandez-'86
Most Runs	(R)	121	Paul Molitor-'93
	(L)	134	Shawn Green-'99
	(B)	109	Roberto Alomar-'93
Most Hits	(R)	*211	Paul Molitor-'93
	(L)	200	John Olerud-'93
	(B)	213	Tony Fernandez-'86
Most Total Bases	(R)	369	George Bell-'87
	(L)	*378	Carlos Delgado-'00
	(B)	294	Tony Fernandez-'86

BATTING

Highest Slugging Percentage	(R)	.605	George Bell-'87
	(L)	.664	Carlos Delgado-'00
	(B)	.492	Roberto Alomar-'93
Most Singles	(R)	147	Paul Molitor-'93
	(L)	120	John Olerud-'93
	(B)	*161	Tony Fernandez-'86
Most Extra Base Hits	(R)	83	George Bell-'87
	(L)	*99	Carlos Delgado-'00
	(B)	68	Jose Cruz-'00
Most Doubles	(R)	43	Shannon Stewart-'00
	(L)	*57	Carlos Delgado-'00
	(B)	42	Devon White-'93
Most Triples	(R)	9	Jesse Barfield-'85
	(L)	*15	Lloyd Moseby-'84
		15	Tony Fernandez-'90
		17	Tony Fernandez-'90
Most Home Runs	(R)	47	George Bell-'87
	(L)	44	Carlos Delgado-'99
	(B)	31	Jose Cruz-'00
Most Home Runs-Home	(R)	25	Jose Canseco-'98
		25	Tony Batista-'00
	(L)	30	Carlos Delgado-'00
	(B)	15	Jose Cruz-'00
Most Home Runs-Road	(R)	28	George Bell-'87
	(L)	27	Carlos Delgado-'99
	(B)	16	Jose Cruz-'00
Most Grand Slam Homers	(R)	2	George Bell-'85; '87
		2	Jesse Barfield-'88
		2	Ed Sprague-'95
		2	Joe Carter-'97
		2	Tony Batista-'00
	(L)	3	Carlos Delgado-'97
		3	Darrin Fletcher-'00
	(B)	1	Tony Fernandez-'89, '90
		1	Junior Felix-'89
		1	Roberto Alomar-'93
		1	Devon White-'95
Most Runs Batted In	(R)	*134	George Bell-'87
	(L)	137	Carlos Delgado-'00
	(B)	93	Roberto Alomar-'93
Most Base On Balls	(R)	82	Dave Winfield-'92
	(L)	123	Carlos Delgado-'00
	(B)	87	Roberto Alomar-'92
Most Intentional Base on Balls	(R)	12	Joe Carter-'91
	(L)	33	John Olerud-'93
	(B)	11	Tony Fernandez-'99
Most Times Striking Out	(R)	159	Jose Canseco-'98
	(L)	149	Fred McGriff-'88
	(B)	135	Devon White-'91
Most Sacrifice Bunts	(R)	19	Luis Gomez-'78
	(L)	12	Alfredo Griffin-'84
	(B)	16	Alfredo Griffin-'79, Roberto Alomar-'91
Most Sacrifice Flies	(R)	14	George Bell-'89
	(L)	10	John Olerud-'91
	(B)	10	Tony Fernandez-'89
Most Sacrifices Total	(R)	22	Luis Gomez-'78
	(L)	16	Alfredo Griffin-'84
	(B)	21	Roberto Alomar-'91
Most Times Hit by Pitch	(R)	17	Charlie O'Brien-'96
	(L)	15	Carlos Delgado-'99, '00
	(B)	11	Tony Fernandez-'98
Most Times GIDP	(R)	23	Ed Sprague-'93
	(L)	19	Darrin Fletcher-'98
	(B)	17	Tony Fernandez-'90
Fewest Times GIDP (100 games)	(R)	2	Buck Martinez-'84
	(L)	3	Fred McGriff-'87
	(B)	0	Dave Collins-'84, Jose Cruz Jr.-'98
Fewest Times Striking Out	(R)	21	Bob Bailor-'78
(502 Plate App.)	(L)	38	Al Woods-'77
	(B)	41	Tony Fernandez-'85
		41	Roberto Alomar-'94
Most Pinch-Hits	(R)	11	Wayne Nordhagen-'82
		11	Cliff Johnson-'84
	(L)	10	Hosken Powell-'82
		10	Rance Mulliniks-'83
		10	Rick Leach-'86
	(B)	6	Dave Collins-'84
Most Stolen Bases		60	Dave Collins-'84
Most Caught Stealing		23	Alfredo Griffin-'80

PITCHING

Most Wins	(R)	21	Jack Morris-'92
		*21	Roger Clemens-'97
	(L)	*20	David Wells-'00
Most Home Wins	(R)	12	Doyle Alexander-'84
		12	Dave Stieb-'88
		12	Roger Clemens-'98
	(L)	10	Jimmy Key-'85/'87
		10	Jeff Musselman-'87
Most Road Wins	(R)	12	Pat Hentgen-'93
	(L)	11	David Wells-'00
Most Losses	(R)	18	Phil Huffman-'79
	(L)	18	Jerry Garvin-'77
Most Home Losses	(R)	10	Jesse Jefferson-'77
		10	Dave Stieb-'80
	(L)	9	Jerry Garvin-'80
Most Road Losses	(R)	12	Luis Leal-'82
	(L)	9	Jerry Garvin-'77
		9	Jimmy Key-'91
Most Decisions	(R)	31	Dave Stieb-'82
	(L)	28	Jerry Garvin-'77
		28	Jimmy Key-'91
		28	David Wells-'00
Highest Winning Pct (10 decisions)	(R)	*1.000	Dennis Lamp-'85
		*.824	Juan Guzman-'93
	(L)	.733	John Cerutti-'87
Lowest ERA (162 IP)	(R)	*2.05	Roger Clemens-'97
	(L)	*2.76	Jimmy Key-'87
Lowest ERA (100 IP)	(R)	1.72	Mark Eichhorn-'86
	(L)	*2.76	Jimmy Key-'87
Most Appearances	(R)	89	Mark Eichhorn-'87
	(L)	78	Dan Plesac-'98
Most Games Started	(R)	40	Jim Clancy-'82
	(L)	36	Jimmy Key-'87
Most Complete Games	(R)	19	Dave Stieb-'82
	(L)	12	Jerry Garvin-'77
		12	Tom Underwood-'79
Most Shutouts	(R)	5	Dave Stieb-'82
	(L)	2	Jimmy Key-'86, '91, '92
Most Innings Pitched	(R)	288.1	Dave Stieb-'82
	(L)	261.0	Jimmy Key-'87
Most Hits Allowed	(R)	278	Dave Lemanczyk-'77
	(L)	266	David Wells-'00
Most Runs Allowed	(R)	143	Dave Lemanczyk-'77
		143	Erik Hanson-'96
	(L)	132	David Wells-'99
Most Earned Runs Allowed	(R)	129	Erik Hanson-'96
	(L)	124	David Wells-'99
Most Home Runs Allowed	(R)	36	Woody Williams-'98
	(L)	33	Jerry Garvin-'77
Most Bases on Balls	(R)	128	Jim Clancy-'80
	(L)	108	Al Leiter-'95
Most Strikeouts	(R)	*292	Roger Clemens-'97
	(L)	169	David Wells-'99
Most Hit Batsmen	(R)	*15	Dave Stieb-'86
	(L)	9	Tom Underwood-'79
Most Balks	(R)	6	Mark Eichhorn-'88
	(L)	5	Jimmy Key-'87
Most Wild Pitches	(R)	*26	Juan Guzman-'93
	(L)	14	Al Leiter-'95
Most Relief Appearances	(R)	89	Mark Eichhorn-'87
	(L)	78	Dan Plesac-'98
Most Relief Wins	(R)	14	Mark Eichhorn-'86
	(L)	12	Jeff Musselman-'87
Most Relief Losses	(R)	10	Tom Buskey-'79; Duane Ward-'89
	(L)	7	Mike Willis-'78
		7	Jerry Garvin-'80
		7	Gary Lavelle-'85
Most Saves	(R)	*45	Duane Ward-'93
	(L)	13	Tony Castillo-'95
Most Decisions in Relief	(R)	20	Mark Eichhorn-'86
	(L)	17	Jeff Musselman-'87
Highest Total of Wins & Saves	(R)	47	Duane Ward-'93
(Relief Only)	(L)	15	Jeff Musselman-'87
Innings Pitched In Relief	(R)	157.0	Mark Eichhorn-'86
	(L)	92.1	Mike Willis-'77
Most Games Finished	(R)	70	Duane Ward-'93
Most Consecutive Won, Season	(R)	15	Roger Clemens-'98
	(L)	8	David Wells-'00
Most Consecutive Lost, Season	(R)	9	Jeff Byrd-'77
		9	Juan Guzman-'95
	(L)	10	Jerry Garvin-'77
		10	Paul Mirabella-'80
Best Start (with no Losses)	(R)	11-0	Relief/Dennis Lamp-'85
	(R)	11-0	Starter/Roger Clemens-'97
	(L)	5-0	Jerry Garvin-'77

MISCELLANEOUS

Most Consecutive Wins	15	Roger Clemens	June 3-Sept. 21/98
Most Consecutive Wins (Starter)	15	Roger Clemens	June 3-Sept. 21/98
Most Consecutive Wins (Reliever)	11	Dennis Lamp	Apr. 6-Oct. 6/85
Most Consecutive Losses (Season)	10	Jerry Garvin	June 16-Aug. 7/77
	10	Jerry Garvin	May 21-July 23/78
	10	Paul Mirabella	May 23-Sept. 29/80
	9	Jeff Byrd	Aug. 11-Sept. 27/77
	9	Tom Underwood	Apr. 5-June 10/79
	9	Juan Berenguer	Aug. 24-Oct. 2/81
	9	Juan Guzman	July 19-Aug. 19/95
Most Consecutive Losses	13	Tom Underwood	Aug. 28-Sept. 26/78 (4) & Apr. 5-June 10/79 (9)
Most Consecutive Shutouts	3	Dave Stieb	Sept. 18-24-30/88
	3	Roger Clemens	Aug. 20-30/98
Most Consecutive Complete Games	7	Dave Stieb	June 18-July 21/80
Most Consecutive Scoreless Innings	33	Roger Clemens	Aug. 20-Sept. 5/98
Most Consecutive Games, one or more RBI's	8	Willie Upshaw	Sept. 11-20/83
	8	Carlos Delgado	April 16-23/00
Most Consecutive Games, Extra-base Hit	11	Jesse Barfield	Aug. 17-27/85
Most Consecutive Hits	8	Rance Mulliniks	Aug. 24-27/84
	8	Paul Molitor	Aug. 26-27/95
	8	Tony Fernandez	May 6-11/99
Most Consecutive Times Reached Base	11	Tony Fernandez	May 6-11/99
Most Consecutive Games Reached Base Safely	37	Joe Carter	1994
Most Consecutive Hits, Team	10	vs Minnesota (H) (2nd inning)	1992
Most Consecutive Innings, No Earned Runs	40	Pat Hentgen	1997
Most Saves, Consecutive Opportunities	25	Tom Henke	Apr. 9-Aug. 7/91
Most Saves, Consecutive Appearances	10	Dwane Ward	Apr. 25-May 13/91
		Darren Hall	July 15-Aug. 5/94
		Billy Koch	July 18-Aug. 8/99
Most Home Runs, One Inning	3	vs Baltimore (4th inning)	June 17/77
	3	at Seattle (9th inning)	June 23/82
	3	vs Detroit (4th inning)	May 23/83
	3	at Kansas City (4th inning)	July 12/83
	3	vs Oakland (6th inning) (Cons.)	Apr. 26/84
	3	at Detroit (4th inning)	June 5/84
	3	at Oakland (4th inning)	July 15/84
	3	vs Oakland (7th inning)	Aug. 30/87
	3	vs New York (A) (8th inning) (Cons.)	Sept. 12/87
	3	vs Baltimore (H) (2nd inning)	Sept. 14/87
	3	vs Detroit (4th inning)	May 6/90
	3	vs Oakland (6th inning)	May 22/90
	3	at Texas (2nd inning)	May 17/95
	3	vs Seattle (3rd inning)	Apr. 30/99
	3	vs Kansas City (3rd inning)	June 21/99
	3	vs Cleveland (3rd inning)	Oct. 2/99
	3	vs Anaheim (6th inning) (Cons.)	Apr. 18/00
	3	vs New York (A) (6th inning)	Apr. 23/00
Home Runs in Consecutive AB's	3	Cliff Johnson	June 20-21/83
	3	Joe Carter	Aug. 23-24/93
	3	Carlos Delgado	Aug. 4/98
Most Consecutive Stolen Bases	23	Joe Carter	1993-1995
	20	Paul Molitor	1994
Most Runs, One Inning	11	vs Seattle (A) (9th inning)	July 20/84
	11	vs Oakland (H) (2nd inning)	April 26/95
Most Hits, One Inning	11	vs Seattle (A) (9th inning)	July 20/84
	11	vs Oakland (H) (2nd inning)	April 26/96

MISCELLANEOUS

Most Batters, One Inning	16	vs Seattle (A)	
		(9th inning)	July 20/84
Most Consecutive Errorless Games	11		1986
Most Errorless Games	103		1990
Most Errors, Game	6	Texas (A)	May 13/82
Most Double Plays, Game	6	Detroit (H)	April 16/96
Most Innings, Home	15	vs Minnesota	Aug. 28/80
	15	vs Milwaukee	Sept. 15/95
Most Innings, Road	17	at Boston	Oct. 4/80 (1st game)
	17	at Florida	June 8/98
Hitting Streak	28	Shawn Green	June 29-July 31, 1999
Most Consecutive Times Shutout	3		May 13-15/81
Most Consecutive Scoreless Innings	33.0		May 12-16/81
Most Consecutive Complete Games	4		Sept. 20, 21, 23, 24/83
Most Consecutive Shutout Games	3		May 21, 22, 23/83
Most Consecutive Shutout			
Innings-Pitchers	28		June 4, 5, 6, 7/85
Most Consecutive Games Played	403	Tony Fernandez	Sept. 21/84-June 24/87
Most Years, Pitcher	15	Dave Stieb	1979-92, 1998
Most Years, Non-Pitcher	12	Ernie Whitt	1977-78, 1980-89
Longest Road Trip	15	Games	1978, 1984, 1995

FIELDING SEASON RECORDS

Based on 100 games

FIRST BASEMEN

Category	Record	Player, Year
Games, Most	162	Carlos Delgado, 2000
Putouts, Most	1460	Fred McGriff, 1989
Assists, Most	131	Willie Upshaw, 1986
Errors, Most	21	Willie Upshaw, 1983
Errors, Fewest	2	John Olerud, 1996 (101 games)
	4	John Olerud, 1995 (144 games)
	5	Fred McGriff, 1988
Total Chances, Most	1592	Fred McGriff, 1989
Double Plays, Most	157	Carlos Delgado, 2000
Best Percentage	.997	Fred McGriff, 1988
	.997	John Olerud, 1995 (144 games)
	.998	John Olerud, 1996 (101 games)

SECOND BASEMEN

Category	Record	Player, Year
Games, Most	160	Roberto Alomar, 1991
Putouts, Most	333	Roberto Alomar, 1991
Assists, Most	471	Damaso Garcia, 1980
Errors, Most	16	Damaso Garcia, 1980
Errors, Fewest	4	Manny Lee, 1990
	4	Roberto Alomar, 1995 (144 games)
Total Chances, Most	803	Damaso Garcia, 1980
Double Plays, Most	112	Damaso Garcia, 1980
Best Percentage	.994	Roberto Alomar
	.993	Roberto Alomar 1992/Manny Lee, 1990

THIRD BASEMEN

Category	Record	Player, Year
Games, Most	156	Kelly Gruber, 1988
Putouts, Most	133	Ed Sprague, 1995
Assists, Most	349	Kelly Gruber, 1988
Errors, Most	22	Roy Howell, 1978/Kelly Gruber, 1989
Errors, Fewest	6	Rance Mulliniks, 1986
Total Chances, Most	477	Kelly Gruber, 1988
Double Plays, Most	35	Tony Batista, 2000
Best Percentage	.975	Rance Mulliniks, 1986

SHORTSTOP

Category	Record	Player, Year
Games, Most	163	Tony Fernandez, 1986
Putouts, Most	319	Alfredo Griffin, 1982
Assists Most	501	Alfredo Griffin, 1979
Errors, Most	37	Alfredo Griffin, 1979
Errors, Fewest	6	Tony Fernandez, 1989
Total Chances, Most	824	Alfredo Griffin, 1982
Double Plays, Most	126	Alfredo Griffin, 1980
Best Percentage	.992	Tony Fernandez, 1989

CATCHERS

Category	Record	Player, Year
Games, Most	138 . .	Pat Borders, 1993
Putouts, Most	869 . .	Pat Borders, 1993
Assists, Most	88 . .	Pat Borders, 1992
Errors, Most	13 . .	Rick Cerone, 1979/Pat Borders, 1993
Errors, Fewest	2 . .	Darrin Fletcher, 1999
Passed Balls, Most	12 . .	Ernie Whitt, 1989/Pat Borders, 1991
Total Chances, Most	962 . .	Pat Borders, 1993
Double Plays, Most	12 . .	Pat Borders, 1993
Best Percentage	.997 . .	Darrin Fletcher, 1999

OUTFIELDERS

Category	Record	Player, Year
Games, Most	162 . .	Rick Bosetti, 1979
	162 . .	Jose Cruz, 2000
Putouts, Most	473 . .	Lloyd Moseby, 1984
Assists, Most	22 . .	Jesse Barfield, 1985
Errors, Most	15 . .	George Bell, 1988
Errors, Fewest	1 . .	Shawn Green (152g), 1999
Total Chances, Most	497 . .	Rick Bosetti, 1979
Double Plays, Most	8 . .	Jesse Barfield, 1985, 1986
Best Percentage	.998 . .	Devon White, 1991

PITCHERS

Category	Record	Player, Year
Games, Most	89 . .	Mark Eichhorn, 1987
Putouts, Most	34 . .	Dave Stieb, 1985
	34 . .	Jim Clancy, 1986
Assists, Most	66 . .	Jerry Garvin, 1977
Errors, Most	8 . .	Jesse Jefferson, 1977
Total Chances, Most	92 . .	Dave Stieb, 1985
Double Plays, Most	8 . .	Dave Stieb, 1980
Best Percentage (35 or more chances)	1.000 . .	Phil Huffman, 1979
		Jerry Garvin, 1978
		Luis Leal, 1982 & 1984
		Jimmy Key, 1986
		Mark Eichhorn, 1986
		Dave Stieb, 1988, 1989
		Mike Flanagan, 1988, 1989
		John Cerutti, 1988
		David Wells, 1990
		David Wells, 1999

ALL-TIME FIELDING BY POSITION

(100 Games)	Year	Pct	G	PO	A	E	TC	DP
John Olerud—1B	1996	.998	101	781	56	2	839	107
Fred McGriff—1B	1988	.997	153	1344	93	5	1442	143
Roberto Alomar—2B	1995	.994	128	272	367	4	643	84
Manny Lee—2B	1990	.993	112	259	286	4	549	65
Rance Mulliniks—3B	1986	.975	110	60	176	6	242	13
Tony Fernandez—SS	1989	.992	163	260	475	6	741	93
Devon White—OF	1991	.998	156	439	8	1	448	2
Darrin Fletcher—C	1999	.997	113	638	42	2	682	4
Jerry Garvin—P	1978	1.000	26	9	28	0	37	1
Phil Huffman—P	1979	1.000	31	7	30	0	37	0
Luis Leal—P	1982	1.000	38	17	31	0	48	2
Luis Leal—P	1984	1.000	35	12	30	0	42	3
Jimmy Key—P	1986	1.000	36	18	42	0	60	4
Mark Eichhorn—P	1986	1.000	69	16	21	0	37	1
Dave Stieb—P	1988	1.000	32	19	26	0	45	3
Mike Flanagan—P	1988	1.000	34	6	35	0	41	2
John Cerutti—P	1988	1.000	46	13	27	0	40	2
Mike Flanagan—P	1989	1.000	30	8	33	0	41	4
Dave Stieb—P	1989	1.000	33	18	29	0	47	1
David Wells—P	1990	1.000	43	7	32	0	39	1
David Wells—P	1999	1.000	34	7	30	0	37	2

(35 or more chances for pitchers)

BATTING

Category	Record	Opponent	Date
Runs	24	Baltimore (H)	June 26/78
Hits	25	Texas (A)	Aug. 9/99
Singles	17	Milwaukee (A)	Sept. 29/78
	17	Kansas City (A)	Aug. 24/97
	17	Boston (A)	Sept. 30/90
	15	Boston (H) (14 Inn)	Sept. 24/85
Doubles	9	Minnesota (A)	Sept. 19/93
Triples	4	Cleveland (H)	July 29/83
	4	Oakland (H)	Sept. 11/83
	4	Seattle (H)	July 5/84
Home Runs	10	Baltimore (H)	Sept. 14/87
Total Bases	53	Baltimore (H)	Sept. 24/87
Runs Batted in	24	Baltimore (H)	June 26/78
Extra Base Hits	12	Baltimore (H)	Sept. 14/87
	12	Seattle (A)	Aug. 19/98
Left On Base	17	Seattle (A)	July 17/92
	20	Cleveland (A) (13 Inn) (2nd g)	Aug. 15/84
Strikeouts	19	California (A) (13 Inn)	June 8/77
	18	California (A) (9 Inn)	June 8/77
	18	Texas (A) (9 Inn)	July 25/89
Base On Balls	13	Chicago (H)	April 16/79
	13	Texas (A)	June 29/92
	13	Milwaukee (A)	May 13/95
Stolen Bases	7	Baltimore (A)	Aug. 5/84
	7	Milwaukee (H)	April 14/83
Sacrifice Hits	4	Cleveland (A)	Sept. 17/77
	4	Chicago (A)	Aug. 14/90
Sacrifice Flies	3	9 Times: Last— Bal (H)	June 30/99
Hit by Pitch	3	12 Times: Last—Sea (A)	July 30/00
GIDP	6	Minnesota (A) (10 Inn)	Aug. 29/77 (1st g)
	5	Texas (A)	April 23/79
	5	Baltimore (A) (10 Inn)	July 6/99
Best Shutout Victory	15-0	Detroit (A)	July 6/96
Worst Shutout Defeat	0-15	New York (H)	Sept. 25/77 (1st g)
Best Winning Margin	16	New York (A) (Tor-19, NYY-3)	Sept. 10/77
Worst Losing Margin	22	California (H) (Tor-2, Cal-24)	Aug. 25/79
	22	Baltimore (A) (Tor-1, Bal-23)	Sept. 28/00
Most Consecutive Games, one or more HRs	23	(44 home runs)	May 31-June 25/00
Most Consecutive Games, one or more HRs at Home	22		June 1-July 23/00
Most Consecutive Games, one or more HRs at Home, 2 seasons	22		Sept. 4/98-May 4/99
Most Consecutive Games, No HRs	10		May 22-June 4/77
	10		May 14-May 23/79
	10		Sept 20-Oct. 1/95
Most Consecutive Strikeouts, Batters	6	California (Ryan)	June 8/77
Most Consecutive Strikeouts, Batters to Start a Game	6	Cleveland (Colon)	July 26/00
Most Consecutive Strikeouts, Outs	7	California (Ryan)	June 8/77

PITCHING

Category	Record	Opponent	Date
Most Runs	24	California (H)	Aug. 25/79
Most Earned Runs	22	Milwaukee (H)	Aug. 28/92
Most Unearned Runs	13	Baltimore (A)	Sept. 28/00
Most Hits	31	Milwaukee (H)	Aug. 28/92
Most Home Runs	8	Boston (A)	July 4/77
	8	Detroit (H)	June 20/00
Most Strikeouts	21	Detroit (H) (14 inn.)	Aug. 8/91
	18	Kansas City (H)	Aug. 25/98
Most Walks	14	Cleveland (A)	Sept. 9/79
Most Wild Pitches	4	Boston (A)	July 3/86
	4	Milwaukee (H)	Aug. 6/93
	4	Cleveland (R)	Aug. 31/95
	4	Boston (R)	Sept. 23/95
Most Hit Batsmen	3	7 Times: Last	Aug. 1/00
Longest 1-0 game, won	12 inn	Boston (A)	Sept. 26/86
Longest 1-0 game, lost	15 inn	Oakland (A)	July 27/86

FIELDING

Category	Record	Opponent	Date
Most Errors	6	Texas (A)	May 13/82
Most Doube Plays	6	Detroit (H)	April 16/96
	5	California (A)	May 7/80
	5	Chicago (A)	April 24/98

BLUE JAY GAME RECORDS—INDIVIDUAL

BATTING

Category	Record	Player	Opponent	Date
At Bats	9	Alfredo Griffin (17 inn.)	Boston (A), 1st g	Oct. 4/80
	8	Barry Bonnell & John Mayberry		
		(17 inn.)	Boston (A), 1st g	Oct. 4/80
		Shawn Green (17 inn.)	Florida (A)	June 8/98
Runs	5	Carlos Delgado	Seattle (A)	May 3/99
Hits	5	Roy Howell	New York (A)	Sept. 10/77
		Rick Bosetti	Milwaukee (H)	April 27/79
		Barry Bonnell	Milwaukee (H)	April 10/82
		Damaso Garcia	Oakland (A)	June 19/82
		George Bell	Kansas City (A)	April 6, /88
		Kelly Gruber	Kansas City (H)	April 16/89
		Fred McGriff	Cleveland (A)	Sept. 1/90
		George Bell	Milwaukee (A)	Sept. 24/90
		John Olerud	Kansas City (H)	April 29/93
		Paul Molitor	Kansas City (A)	Sept. 4/95
		Carlos Delgado	Seattle (A)	May 7/98
		Tony Fernandez	Texas (H)	May 7/99
Doubles	4	Damaso Garcia	New York (A)	June. 27/86
		Shannon Stewart	New York Mets (H)	July 18/00
Triples.	2	Alfredo Griffin	Minnesota (A)	May 8/79
		Alfredo Griffin	Milwaukee (A)	April 25/80
		Barry Bonnell	Oakland (H)	May 16/83
		Garth Iorg	Boston (H); 2nd g	Aug. 29/83
		Lloyd Moseby	New York (H)	June 1/84
		Dave Collins	Seattle (H)	July 5/84
		Tony Fernandez	Minnesota (H)	June 5/90
		Devon White	Seattle (H)	April 8/94
		Devon White	Kansas City (A) (12)	July 1/94
		Shannon Stewart	New York (A) (11)	Sept. 20/97
Home Runs	3	Otto Velez	Cleveland (H), 1st g	May 4/80
		Ernie Whitt	Baltimore (H)	Sept. 14/87
		George Bell	Kansas City (A)	April 4/88
		Joe Carter	Cleveland (H)	Aug. 23/93
		Darnell Coles	Minnesota (A)	July 5/94
		Carlos Delgado	Texas (A)	Aug. 4/98
		Carlos Delgado	Texas (A)	Aug. 6/99
		Darrin Fletcher	Texas (A)	Aug. 27/00
Total Bases	13	Roy Howell	New York (A)	Sept. 10/77
Extra-Base Hits	4	Roy Howell	New York (A)	Sept. 10/77
		Damaso Garcia	New York (A)	June 2/86
		Shannon Stewart	Montreal (H)	June 9/00
		Shannon Stewart	New York Mets (H)	July 18/00
RBI's	9	Roy Howell	New York (A)	Sept. 10/77
Sacrifice Bunts	2	Many Times		
Sacrifice Flies	3	George Bell	Chicago (A)	Aug. 14/90
Strikeouts	6	Alex Gonzalez (13 inn.)	Cleveland (H)	Sept. 9/98
	4	Many times		
Walks	4	Alfredo Griffin	Chicago (H)	April 16/79
		John Mayberry	Chicago (H)	April 16/79
		John Olerud	Detroit (A)	April 8/92
		Rickey Henderson	Cleveland (A)	Aug. 18/93
		John Olerud	Chicago (A)	June 7/94
		Felipe Crespo	Boston (A)	May 5/96
		Carlos Delgado	Chicago (A)	Sept. 18/99
Stolen Bases	4	Damaso Garcia	Oakland (H)	April 25/84
		Dave Collins	Baltimore (A)	Aug. 5/84
		Roberto Alomar	Baltimore (A)	June 8/91
		Otis Nixon	Boston (H)	Aug. 14/96
Hit By Pitch.	2	Jesse Barfield	Seattle (A)	May 11/86
		Joe Carter	Boston (H)	June 17/93
		Ed Sprague	Baltimore (A)	May 10/94
		Shannon Stewart	Boston (A)	Sept. 18/97
		Tony Fernandez	Montreal (A)	June 22/98
		Darrin Fletcher	Tampa Bay (H)	April 15/99
		Brad Fullmer	Texas (H)	Aug. 5/00

PITCHING

Category	Record	Player	Opponent	Date
Innings	12	Jesse Jefferson	Boston (H)	May 23/78
		Dave Stieb	Oakland (H)	May 17/80
Most Innings, Reliever	7.1	Mike Willis	Boston (H), 1st g	Sept. 27/77
Hits	13	Pete Vuckovich	Boston (A)	July 6/77
		Dave Lemanczyk	Detroit (H)	May 28/79
		Dave Stieb	Minnesota (H)	Aug. 29/80
		Jim Clancy	Seattle (A)	June 23/82
		Todd Stottlemyre	Cleveland (H)	April 23/92
		David Cone	Cleveland (A)	June 4/95
		Pat Hentgen	California (H)	July 20/95
		Pat Hentgen	Boston (H)	June 25/97
Runs	13	David Wells	Milwaukee (A)	Aug. 20/92

Category	Record		Player	Opponent	Date
Earned Runs	13		David Wells	Milwaukee (A)	Aug. 20/92
Unearned Runs	10		Dave Stewart	Boston (A)	May 19/93
Home Runs	5		Pat Hentgen	Cleveland (H)	May 26/95
			Pat Hentgen	Boston (H)	June 25/97
	4		Chuck Hartenstein	Boston (A)	July 4/77
			Jerry Garvin	Seattle (H)	Sept. 4/77
			Jesse Jefferson	Chicago (A)	April 11/78
			Dave Lemanczyk	Chicago (A)	April 12/78
			Balor Moore	Texas (H)	Aug. 21/78
			Jackson Todd	Detroit (H)	Sept. 30/80
			Jimmy Key	Oakland (A)	May 6/86
			Dave Stewart	Seattle (R)	Aug. 26/93
			Pat Hentgen	Detroit (H)	May 12/93
			Erik Hanson	Seattle (A)	April 21/96
			Juan Guzman	Texas (A)	April 20/97
			Woody Williams	Seattle (A)	June 3/97
			Juan Guzman	Baltimore (A)	July 15/97
			Woody Williams	Seattle (A)	Sept. 15/97
			Woody Williams	Oakland (A)	Aug. 18/98
Strikeouts	18		Roger Clemens	Kansas City (H)	Aug. 25/98
	16		Roger Clemens	Boston (A)	July 12/97
Walks	9		Jesse Jefferson	Baltimore (H)	June 18/77
			Jim Clancy	Chicago (A)	Aug. 30/84
			Tom Candiotti	Detroit (H)	Aug. 8/91
			Pat Hentgen	Seattle (A)	July 15/95
			Chris Carpenter	Seattle (H)	Aug. 16/99
Hit Batsmen	3		David Wells	Baltimore (H)	April 12/92
Wild Pitches	4		John Cerutti	Boston (A)	July 3/86

SINGLE GAME FIELDING RECORDS

PITCHERS

Category	Record		Player	Opponent	Date
Most Putouts	4		Dave Lemanczyk	Boston (H)	Sept. 7/77
			Jackson Todd	New York (A)	April 25/81
			Luis Leal	Chicago (A)	May 9/83
			Jim Clancy	California (H)	June 18/83
			Jim Clancy	Kansas City (A)	July 13/83
			Jimmy Key	Milwaukee (A)	May 1/92
Most Assists..........	8		Jim Clancy	Seattle (A)	April 4/84
Most Errors...........	3		Juan Guzman	Anaheim (H)	May 23/97
Most Double Plays......	3		Dave Lemanczyk	Boston (H)	Sept. 7/77
Most Total Chances.....	8		Jim Clancy	Seattle (A)	April 4/84

CATCHERS

Category	Record		Player	Opponent	Date
Most Putouts	18		Darrin Fletcher	Kansas City (H)	Aug. 25/98
	17		Darrin Fletcher (10 inn.)	Detroit (H)	Sept. 26/98
	16		Benito Santiago	Minnesota (A)	May 10/97
			Charlie O'Brien	Boston (A)	July 12/97
			Darrin Fletcher	Baltimore (H)	Sept. 21/98
Most Assists..........	4		Buck Martinez (12 inn.)	Oakland (A)	May 24/81
			Lance Parrish	Milwaukee (H)	Sept. 17/95
			Sandy Martinez	Kansas City (H)	Sept. 4/96
			Alberto Castillo	Montreal (H)	June 11/00
Most Errors...........	2		Ernie Whitt	California (A)	Sept. 28/83
			Darrin Fletcher (10 inn.)	Tampa Bay (H)	July 3/98
			Alberto Castillo	Cleveland (A)	Sept. 30/00
Most Passed Balls	2		Ernie Whitt	Texas (A)	April 14/84
			Charlie Moore	Milwaukee (H)	Sept. 30/87
			Pat Borders	Milwaukee (A)	Aug. 13/91
			Pat Borders	Minnesota (H)	May 22/93
			Pat Borders	Oakland (H)	June 5/93
			Pat Borders	Boston (H)	June 21/94
			Randy Knorr	Minnesota (H)	July 18/94
			Sandy Martinez	Cleveland (A)	Aug. 31/95
			Kevin Brown	Chicago (A)	April 25/98
Most Total Chances	18		Darrin Fletcher (15 inn.)	Baltimore (A)	June 19/98
			Darrin Fletcher	Kansas City (H)	Aug. 25/98
			Darrin Fletcher (10 inn.)	Detroit (H)	Sept. 26/98
			Alberto Castillo	Montreal (H)	June 11/00

BLUE JAYS WHO LED LEAGUE IN FIELDING

YEAR	PLAYER	POSITION	PERCENTAGE	YEAR	PLAYER	POSITION	PERCENTAGE
1984	Rance Mulliniks	3B	.968	1989	Tony Fernandez	SS	.992
1985	Rance Mulliniks	3B	.971	1990	Manuel Lee	2B	.993
1986	Rance Mulliniks	3B	.975	1991	Devon White	OF	.998
1986	Tony Fernandez	SS	.983	1995	Roberto Alomar	2B	.994
1986	Jimmy Key	P	1.000	1995	Al Leiter	P	1.000
1988	Fred McGriff	1B	1.000	1997	Alex Gonzalez	SS	.986

FIRST BASEMEN

Category	Record	Player	Opponent	Date
Most Putouts	21	Doug Ault (13 inn.)	Detroit (H)	July 15/77
	21	Rick Leach (14 inn.)	Milwaukee (H)	Sept. 21/85
	20	John Mayberry	Seattle (H)	Sept. 2/79
Most Assists	4	Doug Ault (3 times)	Detroit (H)	April 13/77
			Seattle (A)	June 11/77
			Boston (H)	Sept. 7/77
		John Mayberry	Chicago (H)	April 18/79
		John Olerud (6 times)	Last time,	
			Baltimore (A)	Aug. 1/95
		Willie Upshaw (6 times)	Last time,	
			Kansas City (A)	July 5/87
Most Errors	3	Willie Upshaw (1 inn.)	Boston (A)	July 1/86
		John Olerud	Texas (A)	May 5/93
Most Double Plays	5	John Mayberry	California (A)	May 7/80
		John Olerud	Detroit (H)	April 16/96
		Carlos Delgado	Oakland (A)	May 31/97
		Carlos Delgado	Chicago (A)	April 24/98
Most Total Chances	21	Doug Ault (13 inn.)	Detroit (H)	July 15/77
	21	Rick Leach (14 inn.)	Milwaukee (H)	Sept. 21/85
	20	John Mayberry	Seattle (H)	Sept. 2/79
	20	John Olerud	Kansas City (H)	Aug. 19/95

SECOND BASEMEN

Category	Record	Player	Opponent	Date
Most Putouts	12	Tomas Perez (14 inn.)	Kansas City (A)	Aug. 20/96
	8	Dave McKay	New York (A), 2nd g	May 28/78
		Damaso Garcia	Kansas City (H)	May 7/82
		Dan Ainge	Texas (A)	July 8/79
		Dan Ainge (11 inn.)	Milwaukee (A)	July 19/79
		Manny Lee	Minnesota (A)	Sept. 14/89
		Nelson Liriano (10 inn.)	California (A)	April 29/89
		Manny Lee	Boston (H)	Aug. 25/90
Most Assists	10	Dave McKay	Kansas City (H)	Aug. 12/78
Most Errors	3	Garth Iorg	California (A)	April 28/78
		Alfredo Griffin	Cleveland (H)	Aug. 22/84
Most Double Plays	5	Roberto Alomar (11 inn.)	New York (H)	May 10/95
		Tilson Brito	Detroit (H)	April 16/96
	4	Dan Ainge (10 inn.)	New York (H)	June 28/79
		Dan Ainge	Texas (A)	July 8/79
		Damaso Garcia	Seattle (A)	July 16/80
		Damaso Garcia	Milwaukee (H)	April 22/81
		Damaso Garcia	Boston (H)	Sept. 25/85
Most Total Chances	15	Dave McKay	New York (A), 2nd g	May 28/78
		Damaso Garcia	Kansas City (H)	May 7/82
		Nelson Liriano (10 inn.)	California (A)	April 29/89
		Tomas Perez (14 inn.)	Kansas City (A)	Aug. 20/96

THIRD BASEMEN

Category	Record	Player	Opponent	Date
Most Putouts	6	Dan Ainge (12 inn.)	Texas (A)	June 5/81
		Kelly Gruber	Milwaukee (H)	Aug. 27/92
Most Assists	9	Roy Howell	Milwaukee (H), 2nd g	June 14/78
Most Errors	3	Dave Baker	Oakland (H), 2nd g	Sept. 15/82
		Kelly Gruber	Baltimore (A)	June 27/89
		Kelly Gruber	Chicago (A)	May 23/92
Most Double Plays	3	Roy Howell	Texas (A)	July 8/79
		Roy Howell	Boston	Sept. 26/79
		Ed Sprague	Detroit (H)	April 16/96
Most Total Chances	11	Roy Howell	Milwaukee (H), 2nd g	June 14/78
			Milwaukee (H)	April 17/80

SHORTSTOPS

Category	Record	Player	Opponent	Date
Most Putouts	7	Alfredo Griffin	Texas (A)	Sept. 2/81
		Manuel Lee	Boston (H)	June 13/92
		Tony Fernandez	Milwaukee (H)	Aug. 8/93
		Tony Fernandez	Oakland (R)	Sept. 1/93
		Alex Gonzalez	Baltimore (H)	July 1/96
Most Assists	13	Alex Gonzalez	Cleveland (H)	April 26/96
Most Errors	3	Hector Torres	Baltimore (A)	June 24/77
		Alfredo Griffin	Texas (A)	May 13/82
		Luis Sojo	Cleveland (A)	Aug. 31/90
Most Double Plays	5	Alfredo Griffin	California (A)	May 7/80
		Alex Gonzalez	Chicago (A)	April 24/98
Most Total Chances	16	Alex Gonzalez	Cleveland (H)	April 26/96

OUTFIELDERS

Category	Record	Player	Opponent	Date
Most Putouts	10	Lloyd Moseby (10 inn.)	New York (H) 1st g	Aug. 2/83
		Shannon Stewart (11 inn.)	Boston (H)	Sept. 3/98
		Jose Cruz	Cleveland (A)	Oct. 1/99
		Raul Mondesi	Montreal (A)	July 8/00
Most Assists	3	Steve Bowling	Oakland (A)	Aug. 27/77
		Rick Bosetti	Detroit (H)	May 28/79
Most Errors	2	Al Woods	Seattle (A)	June 1/79
			New York (A)	June 21/79
		Otto Velez	Kansas City (H)	Aug. 9/79
		Bob Bailor	Baltimore (A)	Sept. 20/80
		George Bell (4 times)	California (A)	July 20/88
			Minnesota (A)	July 25/88
			Minnesota (H)	Aug. 3/88
			Detroit (A)	July 8/89
		Joe Carter	Chicago (A)	May 23/92
Most Double Plays	2	Rick Bosetti	Detroit (H)	May 28/79
		Bob Bailor	Boston (H)	May 20/80
		Jesse Barfield	Seattle (A)	July 9/85
Most Total Chances	10	Lloyd Moseby (10 inn.)	New York (H) 1st g	Aug. 2/83
		Shannon Stewart (11 inn.)	Boston (H)	Sept. 3/98
		Jose Cruz	Cleveland (A)	Oct. 1/99
		Raul Mondesi	Montreal (A)	July 8/00

MONTHLY RECORDS

TEAM

Category	Record	Year
Wins	20	Aug. '89
	22	Sept./Oct. '88
Losses	23	Sept./Oct. '77/May '79
Batting Average	.314	Aug. '00
Runs	170	Aug. '98
Hits	324	Aug. '83
2B	69	May '99
3B	16	June & July '84
HRs	48	June '00
RBIs	158	Aug. '98
SB	47	Aug. '84
Complete Games	11	June '79
Shutouts	6	Sept '88
Home Runs—Opponents	45	Aug. '99
ERA (Low)	2.62	Sept. '92
ERA (High)	6.42	April '00
Slugging Avg.	.513	Aug. '00
Best Record	22-7	Sept/Oct. '88
	19-6	May '84
Worst Record	4-22	Sept./Oct. '78

INDIVIDUAL PITCHING

Category	Record	Player	Date
Games	18	Mark Eichhorn	June '87
Wins	6	Roy Lee Jackson (Relief)	May '84
	6	Dave Stieb	May '88
	6	Roger Clemens	May '97
	5	Dave Lemanczyk	June '77
		Doyle Alexander	Sept. '83 & '84
		Dave Stieb	May '83
		Tom Filer	Aug. '85
		Jim Clancy	July '86
		Jim Clancy	May '87
		David Wells	May '91
		Jimmy Key	Sept. '92
		Jack Morris	Aug. '92
		Pat Hentgen	June '93
		Juan Guzman	July '94
		Pat Hentgen	July '96
		Pat Hentgen	Aug. '96
Losses	7	Jesse Jefferson	Aug. '80
IP	60.2	Doyle Alexander	Sept. '84
Saves	11	Billy Koch	July '99
ERA (Starters)	0.90	Roger Clemens	Aug. '98 (50.0IP)
	0.94	Dave Stieb	July '90 (28.2IP)
	1.09	Dave Stieb	April '80 (33.0IP)
ERA (Relievers)	0.00	Tom Henke	April '87 (12 app.)
	0.00	Tony Castillo	May '93 (9 app.)
	0.00	John Cerutti	Aug. '88 (8 app.)
	0.00	Tom Henke	June '92 (8 app.)
	0.00	Billy Koch	July '00 (11 app.)
	0.48	Tom Buskey	Aug. '79 (8 app.)
	0.48	Mark Eichhorn	April '86 (18.2IP)
	0.60	Paul Quantrill	Aug. '98 (15 app.)
	0.61	Billy Koch	June '99 (11 app.)
	0.92	Duane Ward	Sept. '92 (16 app.)

Category	Record	Player	Date
Complete Games	5	Tom Underwood	June '79
		Pat Hentgen	Aug. '96
Starts	8	Luis Leal	Aug. '82
	8	Jimmy Key	Sept./Oct. '87
SHO	3	Dave Stieb	Sept. '88
		Roger Clemens	Aug. '98

INDIVIDUAL BATTING

Category	Record	Player	Date
At Bats	134	Lloyd Moseby	Aug. '83
Hits	47	Lloyd Moseby	Aug. '83
Runs	31	Shawn Green	Aug. '98
2B	19	Carlos Delgado	July '00
3B	5	Alfredo Griffin	May '79
	5	Lloyd Moseby	June '84
HRs	12	Carlos Delgado	Aug. '99
RBIs	32	Dave Winfield	Aug. '92
	32	Carlos Delgado	Aug. '99
Total Bases	82	Joe Carter	June '91
	82	George Bell	May '87
Extra Base Hits	24	Carlos Delgado	July '00
Bases on Balls	30	Fred McGriff	Aug./Sept. '89
SH	6	Roberto Alomar	April '91
	6	Alex Gonzalez	June '98
SF	5	Lloyd Moseby	July '84
	5	George Bell	Sept. '89
	5	George Bell	Aug. '90
	5	Joe Carter	Sept. '92
	5	Joe Carter	May '94
SB	18	Dave Collins	Aug. '84
Avg	.450	John Olerud	April '93 (82 AB)
Slugging	.865	Otto Velez	April '77 (52 AB)
	.773	Carlos Delgado	July '00

BLUE JAYS WALK-OFF WINS

DATE	OPP	INN	RUNS	OUTS	FINAL	NOTES
July 15, 1977	DET	13	2	2	8-6	**Bailor two-run homer off Crawford**
October 2, 1977	CLE	11	1	2	2-1	G. Woods scored on wild pitch
April 19, 1978	NYY	9	1	0	4-3	Iorg scored on Gossage error
May 23, 1978	BOS	12	1	1	2-1	Bosetti singled home Johnson
June 27, 1978 (2)	BAL	9	1	1	9-8	Ewing singled home Velez
July 28, 1978	MIL	11	1	1	3-2	Bosetti singled home Upshaw
July 31, 1978	DET	14	1	1	8-7	**Velez solo home run off Sykes**
August 13, 1978	KC	10	1	2	3-2	Velez fielder's choice scored Bailor
August 26, 1978	MIN	10	1	0	4-3	**Mckay solo home run off Zahn**
September 22, 1978	BOS	9	2	1	5-4	Bosetti two-run single
May 26, 1979	BOS	9	3	2	7-6	**Howell three-run home run off Campbell**
June 17, 1979	OAK	9	2	1	10-9	Griffen single scored two
August 7, 1979	KC	9	1	2	3-2	Cerone single scored Cannon
August 31, 1979	SEA	11	1	1	5-4	**Kusick solo home run off McLaughlin**
September 17, 1979 (1)	BOS	9	3	1	5-4	Cerone doubled home two runs
April 17, 1980	MIL	9	1	1	1-0	**Bosetti solo homer off Sorenson**
May 4, 1980	CLE	10	1	0	9-8	**Velez solo home run off Monge**
May 16, 1980	OAK	11	1	2	1-0	Howell single scored Bailor
June 3, 1980	CAL	11	1	2	7-6	Mayberry single scored Griffin
June 14, 1980	TEX	9	2	2	7-6	Howell sacrifice fly scored Iorg
August 1, 1980	CAL	9	1	2	9-8	Davis double scored Moseby
August 9, 1980	KC	14	1	1	4-3	Braun single scored Griffin
August 30, 1980	MIN	9	3	2	3-2	Braun single scored Moseby
September 14, 1980	BAL	13	1	1	4-3	Bailor single scored Moseby
August 21, 1981	CWS	9	1	2	5-4	**Moseby solo homer off Farmer**
April 10, 1982	MIL	10	1	2	3-2	Bonnell single scored Garcia
April 14, 1982	DET	9	1	2	5-4	BMartinez single scored AJohnson
June 9, 1982	CAL	9	2	1	5-4	AWoods fielder's choice scores Moseby
June 27, 1982	MIN	9	1	0	3-2	**Garcia solo home run off Felton**
July 18, 1982	TEX	10	1	2	5-4	Griffin single scored AJohnson
July 30, 1982	DET	12	1	1	6-5	Mulliniks single scored Garcia
July 31, 1982	DET	10	1	2	10-9	Barfield single scored Garcia
August 28, 1982	NYY	11	1	2	3-2	Upshaw single scored Mulliniks
September 15, 1982 (2)	OAK	9	1	1	12-11	Baker single scored Iorg
September 16, 1982	CAL	12	1	1	2-1	Upshaw single scored Griffin
September 28, 1982	MIN	10	1	2	4-3	Petralli double scored Upshaw

DATE	OPP	INN	RUNS	OUTS	FINAL	NOTES
April 19, 1983	CLE	9	4	2	9-7	**Moseby two-run home run off Spillner**
June 30, 1983	MIN	9	1	2	2-1	Moseby single scored Whitt
July 2, 1983	SEA	9	1	2	7-6	Bonnell single scored Moseby
July 30, 1983	CLE	13	1	1	6-5	Whitt single scored Garcia
August 2, 1983	NYY	10	1	1	10-9	Collins single scored Iorg
September 4, 1983	DET	10	3	2	6-3	**Whitt three-run home run off Lopez**
April 19, 1984	BAL	9	1	1	2-1	Iorg triple scored Upshaw
May 4, 1984	KC	10	1	2	4-3	Griffin single scored Bell
May 6, 1984	KC	9	1	0	2-1	CJohnson single scored Barfield
June 2, 1984	NYY	10	1	1	9-8	Whitt single scored Griffin
June 15, 1984	BOS	11	2	2	4-3	Mulliniks single scored two runs
August 11, 1984	BAL	9	2	0	3-2	**Bell two-run home run off Davis**
August 28, 1984	CWS	11	1	1	7-6	Garcia double scored Fernandez
September 17, 1984	BOS	9	2	1	5-4	Iorg single scored two runs
September 22, 1984	MIL	9	1	2	2-1	Mulliniks single socred Moseby
April 17, 1985	TEX	10	3	0	3-1	**Barfield three-run home run off Stewart**
May 21, 1985	CWS	9	1	1	4-3	Burrough single scored Bell
June 6, 1985	DET	12	2	1	2-0	**BMartinez two-run homer off Lopez**
July 3, 1985	NYY	10	1	0	3-2	Error allows Moseby to score
September 21, 1985	MIL	11	1	1	2-1	Gruber single scored Bell
May 4, 1986	SEA	9	1	2	3-2	Upshaw single scored Garcia
May 31, 1986	CWS	11	1	2	4-3	Moseby double scored Iorg
June 14, 1986	DET	9	3	0	6-5	**BMartinez solo homer off Hernandez**
August 29, 1986	MIN	9	2	2	6-5	Barfield fielder's choice scored Fernandez
September 1, 1986	CLE	9	1	1	5-4	Moseby single scored Upshaw
April 14, 1987	CWS	13	1	0	4-3	Leach single scored Upshaw
May 1, 1987	TEX	10	1	0	3-2	**Barfield solo home run off Williams**
May 2, 1987	TEX	9	2	2	9-8	Fernandez double scored two
May 30, 1987	CAL	10	1	2	4-3	Ducey walked with bases loaded scoring Lee
June 6, 1987	BAL	11	3	2	8-5	**Barfield three-run home run off Dixon**
June 7, 1987	BAL	9	1	2	3-2	Iorg single scored Lee
July 23, 1987	MIN	9	1	2	4-3	Moseby single scored Iorg
September 1, 1987	CAL	10	1	1	4-3	Barfield double scored Ducey
September 4, 1987	SEA	10	1	0	6-5	**Feilder pinch hit solo homer off Powell**
September 6, 1987	SEA	11	1	2	3-2	Upshaw single scored Ducey
September 11, 1987	NYY	10	1	2	6-5	Whitt single scored Upshaw
September 25, 1987	DET	9	3	1	3-2	Moseby's fielder's choice scored Lee
September 26, 1987	DET	9	3	0	10-9	Beniquez triple scored three runs
May 27, 1988	CWS	9	2	1	4-3	Liriano single scored Beniquez
June 11, 1988	BOS	10	1	2	4-3	Campusano single scored Gruber
September 2, 1988	TEX	9	1	1	7-6	Bell single scored Fernandez
September 4, 1988	TEX	9	4	1	9-7	**Bell grand slam off Williams**
September 16, 1988	CLE	10	1	1	4-3	Gruber double scored Borders
May 10, 1989	SEA	9	3	2	3-2	Bell single scored Felix
May 23, 1989	MIN	9	1	2	2-1	Bell sacrifice fly scored Gruber
May 28, 1989	CWS	10	2	0	7-5	**Bell two-run home run off Thigpen**
June 12, 1989	DET	11	2	2	5-4	Gruber double scored two runs
June 16, 1989	SEA	9	2	0	4-3	Bell scored on a wild pitch
June 17, 1989	SEA	9	2	2	3-2	Gruber single scored Liriano
August 22, 1989	DET	14	1	2	3-2	Fernandez scored on throwing error
September 16, 1989	CLE	11	1	0	3-2	Bell scored on an error
September 19, 1989	BOS	13	2	2	6-5	Liriano double scored two runs
September 29, 1989	BAL	11	1	2	2-1	Moseby single scored Liriano
August 23, 1990	BOS	9	1	1	4-3	Gruber fielder's choice scored Wilson
September 14, 1990	BAL	9	3	2	8-7	Olerud single scores McGriff
September 15, 1990	BAL	9	3	0	4-3	**Gruber three-run home run off Schilling**
September 18, 1990	NYY	9	1	2	3-2	Mulliniks single scored Gruber
September 23, 1990	CLE	10	1	1	5-4	Wilson single scored KWilliams
April 12, 1991	MIL	11	1	0	5-4	**Whiten solo home run off Plesac**
July 1, 1991	SEA	9	3	0	4-3	Mulliniks fielder's choice scored Alomar
July 26, 1991	KC	11	1	1	6-5	Gruber fielder's choice scored White
August 23, 1991	NYY	9	2	1	6-5	Alomar single scored two runs
September 2, 1991	BAL	12	1	0	5-4	Snyder single scored Carter
October 2, 1991	CAL	9	2	0	6-5	Carter single scored Alomar

DATE	OPP	INN	RUNS	OUTS	FINAL	NOTES
April 10, 1992	BAL	9	2	2	4-3	Alomar single scored White
April 16, 1992	NYY	9	2	0	7-6	Carter single scored two runs
April 29, 1992	CAL	9	1	2	1-0	Tabler single scored Ducey
May 20, 1992	MIN	10	1	1	8-7	Borders single scored Gruber
May 30, 1992	CWS	11	1	2	2-1	Kent double scored Gruber
May 31, 1992	CWS	9	2	2	3-2	GMyers single scored Gruber
July 1, 1992	TEX	10	1	0	3-2	GMyers double scored Bell
July 7, 1992	SEA	9	1	1	4-3	White single scored Ducey
July 9, 1992	OAK	9	1	2	4-3	Maldanado single scored Alomar
September 17, 1992	CLE	10	2	1	7-5	**Olerud two-run home run off Plunk**
May 7, 1993	BAL	9	1	1	3-2	DJackson single scored Carter
May 13, 1993	DET	9	2	2	6-5	Molitor double scored two runs
June 4, 1993	OAK	12	1	0	4-3	Molitor double scored Alomar
June 20, 1993	BOS	12	1	1	3-2	Carter single scored Alomar
July 18, 1993	KC	9	1	0	4-3	**Canate solo home run off Pichardo**
July 28, 1993	BAL	10	1	1	5-4	Molitor scored on error
August 1, 1993	DET	9	2	2	2-1	Fernandez single scored Molitor
August 6, 1993	MIL	11	3	0	11-10	Olerud single scored White
April 9, 1994	SEA	9	2	1	8-6	**Carter two-run home run off Thigpen**
April 20, 1994	TEX	11	1	2	4-3	Borders single scored Olerud
May 7, 1994	MIL	9	2	2	3-2	Molitor single scored White
May 23, 1994	CLE	9	1	2	6-5	Carter single scored White
May 2, 1995	CWS	9	1	0	9-8	**Alomar solo home run off Marquez**
May 3, 1995	CWS	10	1	2	8-7	TPerez single in 1st ML AB to score Sprague
June 12, 1995	BOS	12	1	2	4-3	AGonzalez single scored Carter
June 30, 1995	BAL	9	1	1	6-5	AGonzalez single scored Cedeno
August 19, 1995	KC	13	1	2	5-4	Green single scored Carter
August 20, 1995	KC	9	1	2	4-3	Olerud single scored Huff
August 22, 1995	CLE	9	1	2	5-4	Throwing error allows Carter to score
August 26, 1995	CWS	9	2	2	3-2	Molitor single scored Gonzalez
September 16, 1995	MIL	11	1	1	5-4	Parrish single scored Huff
April 30, 1996	MIL	9	1	2	9-8	Delgado single scored Nixon
May 11, 1996	BOS	11	1	2	9-8	SMartinez single scored Samuel
May 12, 1996	BOS	10	1	1	8-7	RPerez single scored Delgado
May 23, 1996	MIN	10	1	1	5-4	O'Brien single scored Crespo
June 1, 1996	KC	10	2	2	5-3	**Carter two-run home run off Montgomery**
June 25, 1996	SEA	9	2	1	8-7	**Brumfield two-run homer off Charlton**
July 21, 1996	DET	12	1	2	5-4	AGonzalez single scored Brumfield
July 25, 1996	OAK	9	2	2	4-3	**Carter two-run home run off Witasick**
April 26, 1997	SEA	9	1	2	4-3	Carter single scored Nixon
May 3, 1997	MIN	9	1	2	6-5	Delgado walked with bases loaded
May 6, 1997	DET	10	1	2	2-1	Carter walked with bases loaded
May 25, 1997	ANA	11	1	0	4-3	Santiago walked with bases loaded
July 2, 1997	MON	13	1	2	7-6	Carter single scored Nixon
August 28, 1997	CWS	11	1	2	3-2	RPerez scored on wild pitch
September 28, 1997	BOS	9	2	1	3-2	Green double scored two runs
April 19, 1998	CWS	12	1	2	5-4	AGonzalez single scored Grebeck
May 12, 1998	OAK	10	1	0	4-3	**Canseco solo home run off Taylor**
May 14, 1998	ANA	9	1	2	5-4	**Stanley solo home run off Delucia**
May 17, 1998	SEA	9	1	2	4-3	Canseco single scored AGonzalez
July 3, 1998	TB	10	1	2	3-2	Stewart single scored Samuel
August 8, 1998	OAK	10	1	1	6-5	KBrown single scored Canseco
September 3, 1998	BOS	11	1	2	4-3	Stewart single scored Fernandez
September 26, 1998	DET	13	1	1	5-4	Stewart single scored Fletcher
April 14, 1999	TB	11	1	1	7-6	Cruz single scored Stewart
May 16, 1999	BOS	9	3	0	9-6	**Delgado three-run home run off Gross**
June 20, 1999	KC	9	1	2	2-1	Fernandez single scored Green
June 29, 1999	BAL	10	1	2	6-5	Stewart single scored Batista
June 30, 1999	BAL	10	3	1	10-9	**Fletcher three-run home run off Orosco**
July 19, 1999	ATL	10	1	0	8-7	**Batista solo home run off Hudek**
April 3, 2000	KC	9	1	2	5-4	**Batista solo home run off Spradlin**
May 5, 2000	CLE	9	1	2	11-10	Fletcher single scored Fullmer
May 22, 2000	CWS	9	1	1	4-3	Grebeck single scored Fletcher
June 25, 2000	BOS	13	1	2	6-4	Batista single scored Woodward
July 14, 2000	PHI	9	2	1	3-2	Mondesi fielder's choice scored Stewart
August 16, 2000	ANA	9	2	1	8-6	**Delgado two-run home run off Pote**
September 1, 2000	OAK	9	1	0	4-3	Batista single scored DMartinez
September 9, 2000	DET	9	1	2	3-2	Fullmer single scored Gonzalez
September 23, 2000	TB	9	1	2	7-6	Fletcher double scored Batista

LOW HIT GAMES BY BLUE JAYS

NO-HITTER
Sept. 2/90   –   Dave Stieb, Toronto-3 at Cleveland-0

ONE HIT GAMES
April 24/79   –   Dave Lemanczyk, Toronto-2 at Texas-0, Putnam single in third
Aug. 27/79   –   Phil Huffman, Oakland-0 at Toronto-7, Essian single in sixth
May 30/82   –   Jim Gott (6 innings), Roy Lee Jackson (3 innings) Toronto-6 at Baltimore-0, Dempsey single in the fifth
Sept. 28/82   –   Jim Clancy, Minnesota-0 at Toronto-3, Bush bloop single in ninth to break up perfect game
May 14/83   –   Luis Leal (5 innings), Roy Lee Jackson (4 innings) Toronto-8 at Cleveland-1, Bando single in eighth
May 22/86   –   Jimmy Key, Toronto-5 at Chicago-0, Guillen single in fifth
May 31/88   –   Dave Stieb, Milwaukee-0 at Toronto-9, Surhoff single in fourth
Sept. 24/88   –   Dave Stieb, Toronto-1 at Cleveland-0, Franco single in ninth with two out
Sept. 30/88   –   Dave Stieb, Baltimore-0 at Toronto-4, Traber single in ninth with two out
April 10/89   –   Dave Stieb, Toronto-8 at New York-0, Quirk single in fifth
Aug. 26/89   –   Dave Stieb, Milwaukee-0 at Toronto-7, Yount single in sixth
Aug. 26/92   –   Todd Stottlemyre, Toronto-9 at Chicago-0, Pasqua double with one out in the eighth
Aug. 2/95   –   Paul Menhart, Toronto-0 at Baltimore-1, Baines home run in second
May 2/98   –   Roger Clemens (7 innings), Paul Quantrill (2 innings), Toronto-7 at Oakland-0, Grieve single in seventh
Sept. 27/98   –   Roy Halladay, Detroit-1 at Toronto-2, Higginson homerun with two out in the ninth
May 21/00   –   Frank Castillo (7.0IP), Pedro Borbon (1.0IP), Billy Koch (1.0IP), Toronto-1 vs Chicago-2, Johnson single in the third

TWO HIT GAMES
Sept. 15/77   –   Jim Clancy, Baltimore-0 at Toronto-4, five innings forfeit, Bumbry double and Skaggs single in third
May 2/78   –   Tom Underwood, Toronto-1 at Oakland-2, North double and Alexander homer in fourth
April 13/79   –   Jim Clancy, Kansas City-1 at Toronto-4, 5;s1/;i2 innings - rain stopped - Otis single in first, Patek single in fifth
Aug. 7/79   –   Tom Underwood, Kansas City-2 at Toronto-3, Brett single in second, McRae homer in third
July 27/80   –   Jesse Jefferson, Seattle-0 at Toronto-5, Simpson single in fourth and Roberts single in eighth
Sept. 18/80   –   Luis Leal, Toronto-2 at New York-1, Jackson and Spencer, singles in fourth
Oct. 3/81   –   Dave Stieb (8.1 inn), Jerry Garvin (.1 inn), Joey McLaughlin (.1 inn), Toronto-4 at Seattle-1, Anderson homered in third, Zisk homered in ninth (both off Stieb)
Aug. 10/82   –   Dave Stieb, Boston-0 at Toronto-4, Lansford single in second, Allenson single in third
Sept. 6/82   –   Dave Stieb, Toronto-3 at Oakland-1, Armas homered in seventh, Burroughs single in eighth
July 14/83   –   Luis Leal, Toronto-8 at Chicago-0, Luzinski and Baines singles in fourth
June 16/84   –   Luis Leal, Boston at Toronto-7, Miller single in second, Rice double in seventh
July 3/84   –   Jim Gott, California-0 at Toronto-4, Carew single in fourth, Reggie Jackson single in fifth
Sept. 2/84   –   Doyle Alexander, Minnesota-0 at Toronto-6, Brunansky single in second, Putnam double in seventh
Sept. 5/85   –   Doyle Alexander, Minnesota-0 at Toronto-7, Hrbek double in fourth, Gagne single in sixth
May 25/86   –   John Cerutti (8IP), Bill Caudill (1IP), Toronto-8 at Cleveland-1, Carter single in the first, Tabler single in second
July 5/86   –   Jim Clancy (8IP), Tom Henke (1IP), California-3 at Toronto-7, Burleson single in fourth, Pettis single in eighth
May 3/87   –   Jim Clancy (8.1IP), Tom Henke (.2IP), Texas-1 at Toronto-3, O'Brien single in fifth, Petralli double in ninth
May 18/87   –   Jim Clancy, Toronto-12 at California-0, McLemore single in sixth, White single in seventh
Aug. 27/87   –   Jimmy Key (6IP), Mark Eichhorn (.2IP), Jeff Musselman (1.1IP), Tom Henke (1IP), Oakland-4 at Toronto-9, Canseco single in first, Lansford home run in first
July 15/88   –   Jimmy Key, Toronto-1 at Oakland-0, Baylor double and Gallego single in second
Aug. 13/88   –   Jeff Musselman (7IP), Duane Ward (2IP), Seattle-1 at Toronto-3, White single in second
April 14/89   –   Jimmy Key, Kansas City-0 at Toronto-3, Seitzer and Tartabull singles in seventh
Aug. 2/89   –   John Cerutti, Kansas City-0 at Toronto-8, Brett double in 7th, Wilson double in ninth
Aug. 4/89   –   Dave Stieb, New York-1 at Toronto-2, Kelly double with two out in ninth, followed by a single by Sax
April 14/91   –   Jimmy Key, Toronto-9 at Milwaukee-0, Molitor single with two out in third, Yount single in fourth
June 13/91   –   Jimmy Key, Toronto-1 at Cleveland-0, Skinner single in third, followed by single by Fermin
June 17/93   –   Al Leiter, Toronto-7 vs Boston-0, Greenwell single in third, Hatcher single in sixth
May 3/94   –   Pat Hentgen, Kansas City-0 at Toronto-1, Lind single in the third, Jose double in the fourth
May 21/96   –   Jeff Ware (6.1IP), Tony Castillo (1.2IP), Toronto-3 at Chicago-2, Frank Thomas double in the first, Darren Lewis double in the eighth
June 20/96   –   Pat Hentgen (8IP), Mike Timlin (1IP), Toronto-1 at Oakland-0, Ernie Young double in the sixth, Geronimo Berroa single in the seventh
Sept. 21/96   –   Woody Williams (5.2IP), Scott Brow (2.1IP), Toronto-3 at Baltimore-6, Chris Hoiles single in the sixth, Eddie Murray home run in the sixth
July 4/97   –   Juan Guzman (5.0IP), Kelvim Escobar (4.0IP), Kansas City-0 at Toronto-1, Derek Jeter leadoff double in first, Tino Martinez single in the seventh
Sept. 7/97   –   Roger Clemens (9.0IP), Texas-0 at Toronto-4, Juan Gonzalez single in the fourth, Rusty Greer single in the sixth
May 19/98   –   Woody Williams (8.0IP), Randy Myers (1.0IP), Tampa Bay-1 at Toronto-3, Stocker single in the eighth, Boggs single in the ninth
Aug. 30/98   –   Roger Clemens (9.0IP), Minnesota-6 at Toronto-0, Ochoa single in the first, Walker single in the seventh
April 15/99   –   Chris Carpenter (9.0IP), Tampa Bay-1 at Toronto-11, McGriff home run in the second, DeFelice double in the sixth
July 11/99   –   David Wells (9.0IP), Toronto -1 at Montreal-0, Mouton double in the first, Andrews single in the eighth
July 19/00   –   Kelvim Escobar (8.0IP), Billy Koch (1.0IP), Toronto-5 vs Tampa Bay-2, Cairo single in the third, Canseco home run in the fourth

BASEBALL RECORDS HELD OR TIED BY BLUE JAYS

MAJOR LEAGUE RECORDS SET

Most Home Runs, None on Base, Game, Club: 7, by Boston vs Toronto, July 4, 1977

Fewest Sacrifice Hits, Club, Season: 18, Toronto, 1990

Most Home Runs, Club, Game: 10, Toronto vs Baltimore, Sept. 14, 1987

Most Home Runs, opening day game: 3, George Bell, April 4, 1988

Highest Fielding Average, Shortstop, Season: .992, Tony Fernandez, 1989

Highest Home Attendance, Club, Season: 4,028,318, 1992

Longest nine inning night game: 4 hours, 12 minutes, Toronto vs Detroit, Sept. 15, 1993

Most Runs Batted In for Month of April: 31, Joe Carter, 1994

Most Consecutive Chances Accepted without an Error, Second Baseman, Lifetime: 484, Roberto Alomar, June 21, 1994 to July 4, 1995

Most Strikeouts, Game: 6, Alex Gonzalez, September 9, 1998 vs Cleveland (13 inn)

Most Seasons, 200-or-more strikeouts: 10, Roger Clemens, 1998

MAJOR LEAGUE RECORDS TIED

Home Run, First Time at Bat in Major Leagues: as Pinch Hitter: Al Woods, April 7, 1977, fifth inning

Home Run, First Time at Bat in Major Leagues: on first pitch: Junior Felix, May 4, 1989

Most Grounded into Double Play, Extra-Inning Game, Club: 6, by Toronto vs Minnesota, August 29, 1977, first game (10 innings)

Most Home Runs, Opening Game of Season: 2, Doug Ault, Toronto April 7, 1977, John Mayberry, Toronto, April 9, 1980

Highest Fielding Percentage, Club, Season: .976, Oakland, Toronto

Most Players, 100 or More Hits, Club, Season: 9, 1983

Most Doubles, Games: 4, Damasco Garcia, June 27, 1986 at New York

Most Pinch-Hit Home Runs, Club, Game: 2, Toronto, June 14, 1986 vs Detroit

Most Errors, First Baseman, Inning: 3, Willie Upshaw, Toronto, July 1, 1986 at Boston, fifth Inning

Most Players with two or more Home Runs, Club, Game: 3 Toronto vs Baltimore, Sept. 14, 1987 (Bell, Mulliniks, Whitt)

Most Home Runs, both Clubs, Game: 11, Toronto (10), Baltimore (1), Sept. 14, 1987

Most Players with 100 hits or more, Club, Season: 9, 1988, 1992

Most Consecutive One-Hit Games: 2, Dave Stieb, September 24, 30, 1988

Fewest Complete Games, Club, Season: 6

Fewest 1-0 Games Lost: 0, 1988

Fewest Doubleheaders, Club, Season: 0, 1990

Hitting Home Run, First Major League At-Bat: Al Woods, April 7, 1977, Junior Felix, May 4, 1989

Most Sacrifice Flies, Both Clubs, Game: 5, Toronto (4) vs Chicago (1), August 14, 1990

Most Consecutive Hits, Club, Inning: 10, Sept. 4, 1992 (2nd inning)

Most Home Runs, inning: 2, Joe Carter, Toronto, October 3, 1993, 2nd inning, at Baltimore

Most Seasons, 200-or-more Strikeouts: 10, Roger Clemens, 1998

Most Players, 30 or More Home Runs, Club, Season: 4, Carlos Delgado, Tony Batista, Jose Cruz, Brad Fullmer, 2000

AMERICAN LEAGUE RECORDS SET

Most Sacrifice Flies Allowed, Season: 70, 1977, Toronto

Most Long Hits, Game, Both Clubs: 19, Minnesota (12) vs Toronto (7), May 8, 1979

Most Consecutive Hits Allowed, Pitcher, Start of Game: 5, Luis Leal, June 2, 1980

Most Three-base Hits, Switch-hitter, Season: 15, Alfredo Griffin, 1980

Most Runs, Both Clubs-Ninth Inning: 15, Toronto (11), Seattle (4), July 20, 1984

Most Consecutive Games, One or More Extra-base Hits, Season: 11, Jesse Barfield, August 17-27, 1985

Largest attendance, 4-game series: Blue Jays at New York, September 12-15, 1985 (214,510)

Most Games Played, Shortstop, Season: 163, Tony Fernandez, 1986

Longest Nine Inning Night Game by Time: 3:59, Detroit vs Blue Jays, June 17, 1988

Highest Home Attendance, Club, Season: 4,028,318, 1992

Most Plate Appearances, Club, Nine inning game: 65, Milwaukee, August 28, 1992 vs Toronto

Most At-bats, Club, Nine inning game: 57, Milwaukee, August 28, 1992 vs Toronto

Most Hits, Club, Nine inning Game: 31, Milwaukee, August 28, 1992 vs Toronto

Most Singles, Club, Game: 26, Milwaukee, August 28, 1992 vs Toronto

Most times hitting three or more home runs in a game lifetime: 5, Joe Carter

Most Wild Pitches season: 26, Juan Guzman, 1993

Most Stolen Bases with no caught stealing, season: 20, Paul Molitor, 1994

Most Consecutive Errorless Games, Second Baseman, Lifetime: 104, Roberto Alomar, June 21, 1994 through July 3, 1995

Most times Hit by Pitch, Club, Season: 92, Toronto (set Major League record)

Most Saves, Rookie, Season: 31, Billy Koch, Toronto, 1999

Most Days Between Consecutive Pinch Hit Home Runs, Season: 10, Willie Greene, June 20-30, 1999

AMERICAN LEAGUE RECORDS TIED

Most Players 2 + Two-base Hits, Inning, Club: 2, vs Baltimore, June 26, 1978, 2nd inning

Most Home Runs, Doubleheader, Hitting Homers Each Game: 4, Otto Velez, May 4/80 (3, 1st game, 10 innings; 1, 2nd game)

Most Games, Switch-Hitter Season: 163, Tony Fernandez, 1986

Most Home Runs on Road, Righthanded Batter, Season: 28, George Bell, 1987

Most Games Pitched in Relief, Season: 89, Mark Eichhorn, 1987

Most Games allowing Zero Hits or One Hit, Season: 3, Dave Stieb, 1988

Most Players with four or more hits, Club, Game: 4, Milwaukee, August 28, 1992 vs Toronto

Most Assists, Shortstop, Nine inning Game: 13, Alex Gonzalez, April 26, 1996

Most Putouts, Second Baseman: 12, Tomas Perez, August 20, 1996 (14 innings)

Most Consecutive Seasons, 100-or-more Strikeouts: 13, Roger Clemens, 1998

Most Home Runs, Consecutive At-bats, Pinch Hitter, Season: 2, Willie Greene, June 20-30, 1999

Most Home Runs, Club, Home, Season: 134, 2000

FIVE HITS

Roy Howell
  Sept. 10/77 vs New York (A) (5 for 6;
  4 runs; 1-1B, 2-2B, 2-HR; 9-RBI)

Rick Bosetti
  Apr. 27/79 vs Milwaukee (H) (5 for 5;
  2 runs; 4-1B, 1-2B; 1-RBI)

Barry Bonnell
  Apr. 10/82 vs Milwaukee (H) (5 for 5;
  1 run; 4-1B, 1-2B)

Carlos Delgado
  May 7/98 vs Seattle (A) (5 for 5; 1
  run; 4-1B, 1-HR, 4-RBI)

Tony Fernandez
  May 7/99 vs Texas (H) (5 for 5; 3
  runs; 3-2B, 2-1B; 2-RBI)

Damaso Garcia
  June 19/82 vs Oakland (A) (5 for 5;
  1 run; 5-1B)

George Bell (2)
  April 6/88 vs Kansas City (A) (5 for
  5; 3 runs; 3-1B, 2-2B)
  Sept. 24/90 vs vs Milwaukee (A) (5
  for 5; 1 run; 3-1B, 2-2B)

Kelly Gruber
  June 12/89 vs Detroit (H) (5 for 6;
  4-1B, 1-2B; 3-RBI)

Fred McGriff
  Sept. 1/90 vs Cleveland (A) (5 for 5;
  1 run, 3-1B, 1-2B, 1-HR)

John Olerud
  April 29/93 vs Kansas City (H) (5 for
  5; 2 runs; 3-1B, 2-2B; 1-RBI)

Paul Molitor
  Sept. 4/95 (Game 1) vs Kansas City
  (A) (5 for 5; 1 run; 3-1B, 1-2B, 1-HR;
  3-RBI)

FOUR HITS

Roberto Alomar (8)

Alan Ashby (1)

Bob Bailor (6)

Jesse Barfield (11)

Tony Batista (2)
  April 19/00 vs Anaheim (H) 1-1B,
  2-2B, 1-HR
  Aug. 13/00 vs Minnesota (A) 4-1B,
  1-2B

George Bell (5)

Barry Bonnell (3)

Pat Borders (1)

Rick Bosetti (3)

Tilson Brito (1)

Jacob Brumfield (1)
  Aug. 9/99 vs Texas (A) 4-1B

Homer Bush (1)
  Aug. 9/99 vs Texas (A) 3-1B, 1-HR

Jose Canseco (1)

Joe Carter (6)

Rico Carty (1)

Dave Collins (4)

Marty Cordova (1)

Ted Cox (1)

Jose Cruz (1)
  August 24/97 vs Kansas City (A)
  2-1B, 2-HR

Carlos Delgado (5)
  April 30/96 vs Milwaukee (H) 3-1B,
  1-2B
  May 12/96 vs Boston (H) 3-1B, 1-2B
  June 7/96 vs Texas (A) 1-1B, 2-2B,
  1-HR
  May 13/99 vs Kansas City (A) 3-1B,
  1-2B
  Sept. 4/99 vs Kansas City (A) 3-1B,
  1-HR

Rob Ducey (1)

Ron Fairly (2)

Junior Felix (5)

Tony Fernandez (16)

Darrin Fletcher (4)
  June 22/98 vs Montreal (H) 4-1B
  April 30/00 vs New York (A) 4-1B
  July 9/00 vs Montreal (A) 3-1B, 1-2B
  Sept. 22/00 vs Tampa Bay (H) 3-1B,
  1-HR

Brad Fullmer (1)
  June 29/00 vs Tampa Bay (A) 2-1B,
  1-3B, 1-HR

Carlos Garcia (1)

Damaso Garcia (9)

Alex Gonzalez (5)
  September 23/95 (Game 2) vs Boston
  (A) 4-1B
  August 8/96 vs Chicago (A) 3-1B,
  1-2B
  May 5/98 vs Anaheim (A) 2-1B, 2-2B
  Sept. 7/98 vs Cleveland (H) 2-1B,
  2-2B
  April 6/99 vs Minnesota (A) 4-1B

Craig Grebeck (4)

Shawn Green (4)

Willie Greene (1)

Alfredo Griffin (5)

Kelly Gruber (6)

Roy Howell (9)

Garth Iorg (2)

Cliff Johnson (2)

Rick Leach (1)

Manuel Lee (2)

Nelson Liriano (3)

Candy Maldonado (1)

Buck Martinez (2)

Len Matuszek (1)

John Mayberry (2)

Paul Molitor (11)

Lloyd Moseby (7)

Julio Mosqueda (1)

Fred McGriff (6)

Dave McKay (1)

Rance Mulliniks (1)

Greg Myers (2)

Charlie O'Brien (1)

John Olerud (6)

Robert Perez (1)

Dick Schofield (1)

Ed Sprague (4)

Shannon Stewart (15)
  August 21/97 vs Chicago (A) 2-1B,
  2-2B
  May 5/98 vs Anaheim (A) 3-1B, 1-
  HR
  July 3/98 vs Tampa Bay (H) 3-1B,
  1-2B
  August 1/98 vs Minnesota (A) 3-1B,
  1-2B
  Sept. 3/98 vs Boston (H) 4-1B
  Sept. 7/98 vs Cleveland (H) 2-1B,
  1-2B, 1-HR
  April 26/99 vs Anaheim (A) 4-1B
  June 21/99 vs Kansas City (H) 4-1B
  Aug. 28/99 vs Texas (H) 4-1B
  June 2/00 vs Florida (A) 2-1B, 1-2B,
  1-HR
  June 9/00 vs Montreal (H) 3-2B, 1-
  HR
  July 6/00 vs Cleveland (A) 4-1B
  July 18/00 vs New York (N) 4-2B
  August 7/00 vs Kansas City (A) 2-
  1B, 1-2B, 1-HR
  Aug. 26/00 vs Texas (A) 3-1B, 1-2B

Willie Upshaw (5)

Otto Velez (2)

Vernon Wells (1)
  Sept. 22/99 vs Boston (A) 2-1B, 2-2B

Devon White (7)

Ernie Whitt (5)

Mookie Wilson (2)

Al Woods (6)

	Home	Road	Day	Night	vs East	vs Cent	vs West	vs NL	1-Run	Extra Inn's	DH's W-L-S
1977	25-55	29-52	27-39	27-68	31-58	–	23-49	–	17-27	4-11	1-7-8
1978	37-44	22-58	20-42	39-60	28-61	–	31-41	–	23-30	7-8	3-8-6
1979	32-49	21-60	21-44	32-65	22-56	–	31-53	–	19-28	2-10	0-3-7
1980	35-46	32-49	29-27	38-68	28-50	–	39-45	–	23-21	10-8	0-5-0
1981	17-36	20-33	16-27	21-42	15-27	–	22-42	–	10-17	1-8	0-10-0
1982	44-37	34-47	30-28	48-56	33-45	–	45-39	–	28-30	10-5	3-3-2
1983	48-33	41-40	35-23	54-50	39-39	–	50-34	–	25-20	11-6	1-1-4
1984	49-32	40-41	32-27	57-46	37-41	–	52-32	–	34-25	6-12	2-4-1
1985	54-26	45-36	34-24	65-38	44-33	–	55-29	–	26-21	12-5	2-0-1
1986	42-39	44-37	30-30	56-46	42-36	–	44-40	–	22-25	10-13	1-2-1
1987	52-29	44-37	29-28	67-38	44-34	–	52-32	–	27-24	10-7	0-1-0
1988	45-36	42-39	24-30	63-45	47-31	–	40-44	–	21-17	6-6	0-0-0
1989	46-35	43-38	22-29	67-44	46-32	–	43-41	–	25-22	13-4	1-0-0
1990	44-37	42-39	26-24	60-52	42-36	–	44-40	–	24-27	4-8	0-0-0
1991	46-35	45-36	28-24	63-47	46-32	–	45-39	–	28-20	8-10	0-0-0
1992	53-28	43-38	32-22	64-44	45-33	–	51-33	–	28-20	7-2	0-0-2
1993	48-33	47-34	38-16	57-51	50-28	–	45-39	–	23-22	6-3	0-0-0
1994	33-26	22-34	21-15	34-45	13-22	24-25	18-13	–	13-15	3-6	0-0-1
1995	29-43	27-45	23-27	33-61	18-34	22-31	16-23	–	16-23	5-13	0-0-2
1996	35-46	39-42	25-31	49-57	22-30	30-32	22-26	–	19-22	7-10	0-0-0
1997	42-39	34-47	23-34	53-52	23-25	29-26	20-24	4-11	29-30	5-9	0-1-1
1998	51-30	37-44	35-14	53-60	27-21	28-26	24-20	9-7	28-17	8-8	0-1-0
1999	40-41	44-37	26-26	58-52	24-25	34-20	17-24	9-9	26-18	6-3	0-0-0
2000	45-36	38-43	28-28	55-51	28-21	28-25	18-24	9-9	21-19	2-6	0-0-0

WINNING AND LOSING STREAKS — HOME and ROAD

	HOME		ROAD			HOME		ROAD	
	WIN	LOSS	WIN	LOSS		WIN	LOSS	WIN	LOSS
1977	3	11	6	5	1989	6	5	4	6
1978	5	7	3	9	1990	6	6	6	4
1979	4	7	3	12	1991	5	5	6	3
1980	3	6	6	6	1992	8	5	5	5
1981	3	6	4	7	1993	5	5	9	4
1982	6	4	4	7	1994	9	7	2	5
1983	5	3	4	6	1995	4	7	5	7
1984	9	4	3	6	1996	3	5	7	4
1985	10	3	7	6	1997	6	7	6	7
1986	7	4	5	4	1998	9	5	4	4
1987	7	4	7	5	1999	8	9	5	5
1988	4	5	5	5	2000	6	5	3	7

SWEEPS

BY TORONTO

	2-GM	3-GM	4-GM
Anaheim	6	9	2
Atlanta	0	1	0
Baltimore	3	13	2
Boston	2	7	3
Chicago	5	8	0
Cleveland	4	6	4
Detroit	2	9	0
Kansas City	4	4	0
Milwaukee	2	5	0
Minnesota	7	10	0
Montreal	2	0	0
New York	1	8	0
Oakland	8	4	0
Seattle	8	7	0
Tampa Bay	2	2	0
Texas	5	5	3
TOTAL	61	98	14

BY OPPONENT

	2-GM	3-GM	4-GM
Anaheim	4	6	0
Baltimore	4	10	2
Boston	5	8	5
Chicago	7	6	0
Cleveland	3	6	3
Detroit	3	6	1
Florida	0	1	0
Kansas City	8	4	2
Milwaukee	5	6	4
Minnesota	5	6	1
New York	2	14	1
NY Mets	0	2	0
Oakland	10	11	1
Seattle	3	9	1
Tampa Bay	0	1	0
Texas	7	5	1
TOTAL	66	101	22

QUICKEST TO 100 RBI

In 1994, Toronto outfielder Joe Carter reached the 100 RBI level on August 4 in his 104th game and the team's 108th game... It was the fastest ever to 100 RBI by a Blue Jays player... Prior to Carter, the fastest ever to 100 RBI was George Bell in 1987- he reached 100 RBI plateau in 112 games (118 team).

Blue Jays Records

MILESTONES

UPCOMING CAREER

TONY BATISTA
56 GAMES TO 600
21 RUNS TO 300
4 HITS TO 500
2 DOUBLES TO 100

PEDRO BORBON
36.2 INN. PITCHED TO 200
71 STRIKEOUTS TO 200

HOMER BUSH
41 GAMES TO 300
50 HITS TO 300
19 RBI TO 100
3 STOLEN BASES TO 50

CHRIS CARPENTER
12 STARTS TO 100
16 WINS TO 50
90 STRIKEOUTS 500

ALBERTO CASTILLO
49 GAMES TO 300
58 HITS TO 200
39 RBI TO 100

JOSE CRUZ
23 GAMES TO 500
32 RUNS TO 300
83 HITS TO 500
16 DOUBLES TO 100
18 HOME RUNS TO 100
69 RBI TO 300
3 STOLEN BASES TO 50

CARLOS DELGADO
71 GAMES TO 900
7 RUNS TO 500
182 HITS TO 1000
10 HOME RUNS TO 200
96 RBI TO 700
64 WALKS TO 500

JASON DICKSON
27 GAMES TO 100
103.0 INN. PITCHED TO 500
86 STRIKEOUTS TO 300

KELVIM ESCOBAR
16 WINS TO 50
35.1 INN. PITCHED TO 500
121 STRIKEOUTS 500

SCOTT EYRE
22 GAMES TO 100
58 STRIKEOUTS TO 200

DARRIN FLETCHER
67 RUNS TO 500
74 HITS TO 1000
12 DOUBLES TO 200

JOHN FRASCATORE
38 GAMES TO 300
3 STRIKEOUTS TO 200

JEFF FRYE
7 GAMES TO 600
8 RUNS TO 300
17 HITS TO 600
21 DOUBLES TO 150
21 RBI TO 200

BRAD FULLMER
8 GAMES TO 400
24 RUNS TO 200
112 HITS TO 500
41 DOUBLES TO 150
43 HOME RUNS TO 100
68 RBI TO 300

ALEX GONZALEZ
64 GAMES TO 800
63 HITS TO 700
3 DOUBLES TO 150
26 RBI TO 300
33 STOLEN BASES TO 100

TODD GREENE
17 RUNS TO 100
33 HITS TO 200
8 RBI TO 100

ROY HALLADAY
43 GAMES TO 100

JOEY HAMILTON
26 GAMES TO 200
34 STARTS TO 200
90 STRIKEOUTS TO 800

TRENIDAD HUBBARD
28 GAMES TO 400
38 HITS TO 200

BILLY KOCH
26 GAMES TO 150
36 SAVES TO 100
57.2 INN. PITCHED TO 200

ESTEBAN LOAIZA
26 GAMES TO 200
3 STARTS TO 150
1 WIN TO 50
87.2 INN. PITCHED TO 1000
39 STRIKEOUTS TO 600

RAUL MONDESI
79 RUNS TO 700
91 HITS TO 1200
13 HOME RUNS TO 200
15 RBI TO 600
38 STOLEN BASES TO 200

JAIME NAVARRO
39 GAMES TO 400
44.2 INN. PITCHED TO 2100
87 STRIKEOUTS TO 1200

LANCE PAINTER
31 GAMES TO 300

STEVE PARRIS
4 GAMES TO 100
11 STARTS TO 100
15 WINS TO 50
71.1 INN. PITCHED TO 600
132 STRIKEOUTS TO 500

DAN PLESAC
16 GAMES TO 900
3.0 INN. PITCHED TO 1000
5 STRIKEOUTS TO 900

PAUL QUANTRILL
50 GAMES TO 500
9 WINS TO 50
45.2 INN. PITCHED TO 900
3 STRIKEOUTS TO 500

MIKE SIROTKA
5 WINS TO 50
89.2 INN. PITCHED TO 800
65 STRIKEOUTS TO 500

BRIAN SIMMONS
41 GAMES TO 100
64 HITS TO 100

SHANNON STEWART
12 GAMES TO 500
72 RUNS TO 400
26 HITS TO 600
36 DOUBLES TO 150
6 HOME RUNS TO 50
84 RBI TO 300
29 STOLEN BASES TO 150

RYAN THOMPSON
64 GAMES TO 400
38 HITS TO 300
6 HOME RUNS TO 50
50 RBI TO 200

VERNON WELLS
73 GAMES TO 100
77 HITS TO 100

BLUE JAYS LONGEST HITTING STREAKS

28 games	**Shawn Green, 1999** (Club Record)	17 games	Tony Batista, 1999
26 games	John Olerud, 1993	16 games	Dave McKay, 1978
26 games	Shannon Stewart, 1999	16 games	Jesse Barfield, 1985
22 games	George Bell, 1989	16 games	Damaso Garcia, 1985
22 games	Carlos Delgado, 2000	16 games	Tony Fernandez, 1989
21 games	Damaso Garcia, 1983	16 games	Roberto Alomar, 1992
21 games	Lloyd Moseby, 1983	16 games	Joe Carter, 1992
21 games	Dave Martinez, 2000	16 games	Ed Sprague, 1995
20 games	Damaso Garcia, 1982	16 games	Carlos Delgado, 1997
19 games	Alfredo Griffin, 1980	16 games	Shannon Stewart, 1999
19 games	Roberto Alomar, 1995	15 games	Roy Howell, 1977
19 games	Carlos Delgado, 1998	15 games	George Bell, 1986
18 games	Damaso Garcia, 1986	15 games	Kelly Gruber, 1989
18 games	Tony Fernandez, 1987	15 games	Tony Fernandez, 1990
18 games	Jose Cruz Jr., 1998	15 games	Kelly Gruber, 1990
17 games	John Mayberry, 1980	15 games	Roberto Alomar, 1991
17 games	Damaso Garcia, 1982	15 games	Joe Carter, 1994
17 games	George Bell, 1987	15 games	Alex Gonzalez, 2000
17 games	Dave Winfield, 1992		

LONGEST HITLESS STREAKS (25 or more at-bats)

PLAYER	AT-BATS	DATES	PLAYER	AT-BATS	DATES
Ed Sprague	35	May 21-May 31, 1994	George Bell	26	May 8-14, 1986
Alex Gonzalez	33	August 28-September 8, 1996	Kelly Gruber	26	May 2-June 12, 1986
Buck Martinez	32	April 29-May 26, 1985	Kelly Gruber	26	August 17-27, 1990
Mike Stanley	30	April 22-May 3, 1998	Pat Tabler	26	September 6-October 6, 1991
Carlos Delgado	29	July 9-16, 1998	Carlos Delgado	25	June 16-23, 1999
Tomas Perez	28	September 7-25, 1997	Raul Mondesi	25	April 21-29, 2000
Tony Batista	27	July 25-August 1, 2000			

UPCOMING BLUE JAYS MILESTONES

HOMER BUSH
12 sacrifice hits from tying **DAVE McKAY** for 10th (24)
38 stolen bases from tying **ALFREDO GRIFFIN** for 10th (79)
39 stolen bases from tying **KELLY GRUBER** for 9th (80)
50 stolen bases from tying **DAVE COLLINS** for 8th (91)

CHRIS CARPENTER
12 wins from tying **DOYLE ALEXANDER** & **JOHN CERUTTI** for 9th (46)
17 wins from tying **LUIS LEAL** for 8th (51)
11 losses from tying **DAVE LEMANCZYK** for 10th (45)
15 starts from tying **DOYLE ALEXANDER** for 10th (103)
20 starts from tying **JOHN CERUTTI** for 9th (108)
1 shutout from tying **JESSE JEFFERSON** & **TODD STOTTLEMYRE** for 6th (4)
3 shutouts from tying **ROGER CLEMENS** for 5th (6)
168.1 innings pitched from tying **DOYLE ALEXANDER** for 10th (750.0)
190.2 innings pitched from tying **JOHN CERUTTI** for 9th (772.1)
86 hits allowed from tying **DOYLE ALEXANDER** for 10th (752)
134 hits allowed from tying **JOHN CERUTTI** for 9th (800)
15 runs allowed from tying **JOHN CERUTTI** for 10th (378)
22 runs allowed from tying **JESSE JEFFERSON** for 9th (385)
113 runs allowed from tying **LUIS LEAL** for 8th (476)
6 earned runs allowed from tying **JOHN CERUTTI** for 10th (332)
26 earned runs allowed from tying **JESSE JEFFERSON** for 9th (352)
109 earned runs allowed from tying **LUIS LEAL** for 8th (435)
17 home runs allowed from tying **WOODY WILLIAMS** for 10th (88)
30 home runs allowed from tying **LUIS LEAL** for 9th (101)
37 walks from tying **JESSE JEFFERSON** for 10th (266)
49 walks from tying **DUANE WARD** for 9th (278)
65 walks from tying **DAVID WELLS** for 8th (294)
7 HB from tying **LUIS LEAL** for 10th (22)
153 strikeouts from tying **ROGER CLEMENS** for 10th (563)
6 wild pitches from tying **JOHN CERUTTI** & **TODD STOTTLEMYRE** for 10th (30)

JOSE CRUZ
43 home runs from tying **ED SPRAGUE** for 10th (113)
33 stolen base from tying **ALFREDO GRIFFIN** for 10th (79)
74 strikeouts from tying **SHAWN GREEN** for 10th (510)

CARLOS DELGADO
102 games from tying **GARTH IORG** for 10th (931)
153 games from tying **ALFREDO GRIFFIN** for 9th (982)
255 at-bats from tying **ED SPRAGUE** for 10th (3156)
495 at-bats from tying **ALFREDO GRIFFIN** for 9th (3396)
562 at-bats from tying **JESSE BARFIELD** for 8th (3463)
37 runs from tying **JESSE BARFIELD** for 6th (530)
35 runs from tying **WILLIE UPSHAW** for 5th (538)
85 runs from tying **JOE CARTER** for 4th (578)
26 hits from tying **ALFREDO GRIFFIN** for 10th (844)
70 hits from tying **ERNIE WHITT** for 9th (888)
92 hits from tying **JOHN OLERUD** for 8th (910)
101 hits from tying **JESSE BARFIELD** for 7th (919)
164 hits from tying **WILLIE UPSHAW** for 6th (982)
210 hits from tying **DAMASO GARCIA** for 5th (1028)
4 doubles from tying **JOE CARTER** for 4th (218)
23 doubles from tying **GEORGE BELL** for 3rd (237)
28 doubles from tying **LLOYD MOSEBY** for 2nd (242)
12 home runs from tying **GEORGE BELL** for 2nd (202)
13 home runs from tying **JOE CARTER** for 1st (203)
9 extra-base hits from tying **TONY FERNANDEZ** for 4th (420)
38 extra-base hits from tying **JOE CARTER** for 3rd (449)
40 extra-base hits from tying **LLOYD MOSEBY** for 2nd (451)
60 extra-base hits from tying **GEORGE BELL** for 1st (471)
47 RBI from tying **LLOYD MOSEBY** for 3rd (651)
132 RBI from tying **JOE CARTER** for 2nd (736)
136 RBI from tying **GEORGE BELL** for 1st (740)
3 sacrifice flies from tying **KELLY GRUBER** & **JOHN OLERUD** for 6th (35)
4 sacrifice flies from tying **ERNIE WHITT** for 5th (36)
8 sacrifice flies from tying **LLOYD MOSEBY** for 4th (40)
2 walks from tying **TONY FERNANDEZ** for 3rd (438)
78 walks from tying **JOHN OLERUD** for 2nd (514)
111 walks from tying **LLOYD MOSEBY** for 1st (547)
7 HBP from tying **ED SPRAGUE** for 1st (68)
127 strikeouts from tying **JESSE BARFIELD** for 2nd (855)
56 total bases from tying **JESSE BARFIELD** for 5th (1672)
318 total bases from tying **JOE CARTER** for 4th (1934)

KELVIM ESCOBAR
12 wins from tying **DOYLE ALEXANDER** & **JOHN CERUTTI** for 9th (46)
17 wins from tying **LUIS LEAL** for 8th (51)
14 losses from tying **DAVE LEMANCZYK** for 10th (45)
4 saves from tying **DARREN HALL** for 8th (20)
12 saves from tying **RANDY MYERS** for 7th (28)
93 runs allowed from tying **JOHN CERUTTI** for 10th (378)
100 runs allowed from tying **JESSE JEFFERSON** for 9th (385)
46 walks from tying **JESSE JEFFERSON** for 10th (266)
58 walks from tying **DUANE WARD** for 9th (278)
74 walks from tying **DAVID WELLS** for 8th (294)
184 strikeouts from tying **ROGER CLEMENS** for 10th (563)

ALEX GONZALEZ
534 at-bats from tying **ED SPRAGUE** for 10th (3156)
23 doubles from tying **ED SPRAGUE** for 10th (170)
25 doubles from tying **DAMASO GARCIA** for 9th (172)
30 doubles from tying **WILLIE UPSHAW** for 8th (177)
16 sacrifice hits from tying **ALFREDO GRIFFIN** for 1st (74)
12 stolen bases from tying **ALFREDO GRIFFIN** for 10th (79)
13 stolen bases from tying **KELLY GRUBER** for 9th (80)
24 stolen bases from tying **DAVE COLLINS** for 8th (91)
2 caught stealing from tying **RICK BOSETTI** for 10th (30)
5 caught stealing from tying **KELLY GRUBER** for 9th (33)
4 HBP from tying **DEVON WHITE** for 10th (29)
7 HBP from tying **JOHN OLERUD** for 9th (32)
38 strikeouts from tying **ED SPRAGUE** for 5th (647)
87 strikeouts from tying **JOE CARTER** for 4th (696)

BILLY KOCH
57 saves from tying **DUANE WARD** for 2nd (121)
13 games finished from tying **JOEY McLAUGHLIN** for 4th (123)
65 games finished from tying **MIKE TIMLIN** for 3rd (175)

PAUL QUANTRILL
11 games from tying **JIMMY KEY** for 5th (317)
46 games finished from tying **JIM CLANCY** for 4th (352)
3 saves from tying **TONY CASTILLO**, **BILL CAUDILL** & **KELVIM ESCOBAR** for 10th (16)
18 games finished from tying **JOEY McLAUGHLIN** for 4th (123)

SHANNON STEWART
124 runs from tying **DEVON WHITE** for 10th (452)
125 runs from tying **DAMASO GARICA** for 9th (453)
136 runs from tying **JOHN OLERUD** for 8th (464)
9 triples from tying **DAMASO GARCIA** for 10th (26)
5 stolen bases from tying **DEVON WHITE** for 5th (126)
51 stolen bases from tying **TONY FERNANDEZ** for 4th (172)
6 caught stealing from tying **ROBERTO ALOMAR** for 6th (46)
10 caught stealing from tying **WILLIE UPSHAW** for 5th (50)
1 HBP from tying **GEORGE BELL** & **KELLY GRUBER** for 6th (35)

CONSECUTIVE GAMES WITH AT LEAST 1 RBI
(Minimum 7 games)

PLAYER	GAMES	RBI	DATES
Willie Upshaw	8	15	September 11-20, 1983
Carlos Delgado	8	11	April 16-23, 2000
Roberto Alomar	7	10	April 19-25, 1992
Devon White	7	9	May 9-15, 1995
Carlos Delgado	7	16	June 4-11, 2000

The Major League record is 17 games (Oscar Grimes of Chicago- June 27-July 23, 1922) and the AL record is 13 games (Taft S. Wright of Chicago- May 4-20, 1941; Mike Sweeney of Kansas City- June 23-July 4, 1999).

HIGHS & LOWS

TEAM

Category	Record	Year
Rookies on 25-man roster, opening day	9	1977
Rookies on opening day starting lineup	4	1977
Rookies to appear during season	16	1977
Major league debuts	12	1995
Greatest number of rookies on 25-man roster at one time	12	July 1-13, 23-27, 1977
Youngest rookie .... Brian Milner-		
18 yrs, 7 mos, 6 days		1978
Oldest rookie .... Dave Wallace-		
30 yrs, 8 mos, 26 days		1978
Total number of at bats by rookies	2,477	1977
Total number of hits by rookies	649	1977
Combined rookies' batting average	.262	1977
Total number of innings pitched by rookies	557	1977
Games started by rookies	68	1977
Games won by rookies	31	1986

BATTING

Category	Record	Year
Greatest number of rookies in starting lineup, game	7	(many times) 1977
Highest average (500 plate appearances)	310	Bob Bailor, 1977
Most games	153	Alfredo Griffin, 1979
Most at bats	624	Alfredo Griffin, 1979
Most hits	179	Alfredo Griffin, 1979
Most runs	81	Alfredo Griffin, 1979
Most total bases	227	Alfredo Griffin, 1979
Most extra-base hits	50	Shawn Green, 1995
Most doubles	31	Shawn Green, 1995
Most triples	10	Alfredo Griffin, 1979
Most home runs	20	Fred McGriff, 1987
Most runs batted in	64	Doug Ault, 1977
Most bases on balls	60	Fred McGriff, 1987
Most times striking out	104	Fred McGriff, 1987
Fewest times striking out (502 plate appearances)	26	Bob Bailor, 1977
Most sacrifice bunts	16	Alfredo Griffin, 1979
Most sacrifice flies	4	Alfredo Griffin, 1979
		John Olerud, 1990
		Alex Gonzalez, 1995
		Jose Cruz, 1997
		Kevin Brown, 1998
Highest slugging percentage	.509	Shawn Green, 1995
Most stolen bases	21	Alfredo Griffin, 1979
Most stolen base attempts	37	Alfredo Griffin, 1979
Most times caught stealing	16	Alfredo Griffin, 1979
Most times ground into double plays	20	Doug Ault, 1977
Fewest times grounded into double plays	5	Rick Bosetti, 1978
(502 plate appearances)		
Longest hitting streak	14	Alfredo Griffin, 1979
		Shawn Green, 1995
Longest hitting streak, start of career	8	Jesse Barfield, 1981

PITCHING

Category	Record	Year
Most wins	14	Mark Eichhorn, 1986
Most losses	18	Jerry Garvin, 1977;
		Phil Huffman, 1979
Most decisions	28	Jerry Garvin, 1977
Most games	69	Mark Eichhorn, 1986
Most games started	34	Jerry Garvin, 1977
Most relief appearances	69	Mark Eichhorn, 1986
Most games finished	48	Billy Koch, 1999
Most saves	31	Billy Koch, 1999
Lowest era (162 IP)	4.19	Jerry Garvin, 1977
Lowest era (100 IP)	1.72	Mark Eichhorn, 1986
Most innings pitched	244.2	Jerry Garvin, 1977
Most runs allowed	130	Phil Huffman, 1979
Most ER allowed	114	Jerry Garvin, 1977
Most home runs allowed	33	Jerry Garvin, 1977
Most bases on balls	85	Jerry Garvin, 1977
Most strikeouts	166	Mark Eichhorn, 1986
Most hit batsmen	7	Mark Eichhorn, 1986
Most wild pitches	11	Edwin Hurtado, 1995
Most balks	4	Denis Boucher, 1991
Most pickoffs	22	Jerry Garvin, 1977

ROOKIES—YEAR BY YEAR

1977 (16): Doug Ault, Bob Bailor, Steve Bowling, Tom Bruno, *Jeff Byrd, Rick Cerone, *Jim Clancy, *Mike Darr, *Dennis DeBarr, Sam Ewing, *Jerry Garvin, *Steve Staggs, Ernie Whitt, *Mike Willis, *Al Woods, Gary Woods, *Major League debut (8).

1978 (7): *Butch Alberts, Rick Bosetti, *Victor Cruz, *Garth Iorg, *Brian Milner, *Willie Upshaw, Dave Wallace, *Major Leage debut (5).

1979 (9): *Dan Ainge, *Bobby Brown, J.J. Cannon, *Butch Edge, Alfredo Griffin, *Pedro Hernandez, *Phil Huffman, *Dave Stieb, *Ted Wilborn, *Major League debut (7).

1980 (8): Damaso Garcia, *Paul Hodgson, *Pat Kelly, *Luis Leal, Mike Macha, *Lloyd Moseby, Domingo Ramos, *Ken Schrom, *Major League debut (5).

1981 (5): *Jesse Barfield, *George Bell, *Fred Manrique, *Greg Wells, Dan Whitmer, *Major League debut (4).

1982 (9): *Dave Baker, Jesse Barfield, *Mark Eichhorn, *Jim Gott, Pedro Hernandez, Anthony Johnson, *Geno Petralli, Ken Schrom, *Steve Senteney, *Major League debut (5).

1983 (6): *Jim Acker, *Stan Clarke, *Tony Fernandez, Geno Petralli, *Mitch Webster, *Matt Williams, *Major League debut (5).

1984 (7): Tony Fernandez, *Kelly Gruber, *Toby Hernandez, *Jimmy Key, Fred Manrique, *Ron Shepherd, Mitch Webster, *Major League debut (4).

1985 (10): *John Cerutti, Stan Clarke, *Steve Davis, *Cecil Fielder, Kelly Gruber, *Jeff Hearron, *Manny Lee, Ron Shepherd, *Lou Thorton, Mitch Webster, *Major League debut (6).

1986 (13): *Luis Aquino, John Cerutti, Stan Clarke, Steve Davis, Mark Eichhorn, Cecil Fielder, *Don Gordon, Kelly Gruber, Jeff Hearron, Joe Johnson, *Fred McGriff, *Jeff Musselman, Duane Ward, *Major League debut (4).

1987 (12): *Jeff DeWillis, *Rob Ducey, *Alexis Infante, *Nelson Liriano, Fred McGriff, Jeff Musselman, *Greg Myers, *Jose Nunez, *Mike Sharperson, *Matt Stark, Duane Ward, *David Wells, *Major League debut (9).

1988 (7): *Tony Castillo, David Wells, *Todd Stottlemyre, *Pat Borders, Alexis Infante, *Silvestre Campusano, Rob Ducey, *Major League debut (4).

1989 (12): *Kevin Batiste, *Francisco Cabrera, Tony Castillo, *Steve Cummings, *Junior Felix, *Mauro Gozzo, *Xavier Hernandez, *Glenallen Hill, Alexis Infante, Greg Myers, *John Olerud, *Alex Sanchez, *Major League debut (9).

1990 (11): *Willie Blair, Steve Cummings, *Carlos Diaz, Glenallen Hill, Rick Luecken, *Bob MacDonald, Greg Myers,

John Olerud, *Tom Quinlan, *Luis Sojo, *Mark Whiten, *Major League debut (6).

1991 (15): *Derek Bell, *Denis Boucher, *Ray Giannelli, *Juan Guzman, *Pat Hentgen, *Vince Horsman, *Randy Knorr, Bob MacDonald, *Ed Sprague, *Mike Timlin, Turner Ward, *David Weathers, Mickey Weston, Mark Whiten, *Eddie Zosky, *Major League debut (11).

1992 (11): Derek Bell, Pat Hentgen, *Jeff Kent, Randy Knorr, *Doug Linton, *Mike Maksudian, Domingo Martinez, Tom Quinlan, *Rick Trlicek, David Weathers, Eddie Zosky, *Major League debut (6).

1993 (11): *Scott Brow, *Rob Butler, *Willie Canate, *Domingo Cedeno, *Carlos Delgado, *Huck Flener, *Shawn Green, Randy Knorr, Doug Linton, Domingo Martinez, *Woody Williams, *Major League debut (8).

1994 (11): Scott Brow, Rob Butler, Domingo Cedeno, *Brad Cornett, Carlos Delgado, *Alex Gonzalez, Shawn Green, *Darren Hall, *Robert Perez, *Aaron Small, *Paul Spoljaric, *Major League debut (6).

1995 (15): *Howard Battle, Alex Gonzalez, Shawn Green, *Sandy Martinez, Robert Perez, *Tomas Perez, *Shannon Stewart, *Giovanni Carrara, *Tim Crabtree, *Edwin Hurtado, *Ricardo Jordan, *Paul Menhart, *Ken Robinson, *Jimmy Rogers, *Jeff Ware, *Major League debut (12).

1996 (13): Luis Andujar, *Tilson Brito, *Miguel Cairo, Giovanni Carrara, *Felipe Crespo, Huck Flener, *Marty Janzen, *Julio Mosquera, Robert Perez, *Jose Silva, Paul Spoljaric, Shannon Stewart, Jeff Ware, *Major League debut (6).

1997 (10): *Carlos Almanzar, *Rich Butler, *Chris Carpenter, Felipe Crespo, Jose Cruz, Jr., *Kelvim Escobar, *Tom Evans, Julio Mosquera, Ken Robinson, Shannon Stewart, *Major League debut (5).

1998 (9): Carlos Almanzar, Kevin Brown, Tom Evans, *Roy Halladay, Nerio Rodriguez, *Steve Sinclair, Ben Van Ryn, *Shannon Withem, *Kevin Witt, *Major League debut (4).

1999 (14): *John Bale, *Casey Blake, *Tom Davey, *Gary Glover, Roy Halladay, *Billy Koch, *Pete Munro, Willis Otanez, *Mike Romano, *Anthony Sanders, Steve Sinclair, *Vernon Wells, Kevin Witt, *Chris Woodward, *Major League debut (10).

2000 (13): *Clayton Andrews, John Bale, *Pasqual Coco, *Darwin Cubillan, *Matt DeWitt, *Leo Estrella, Charlie Greene, Chad Mottola, *Josh Phelps, *Andy Thompson, Vernon Wells, *Dewayne Wise, Chris Woodward, *Major League debut (8).

2001 ROOKIES

Pitchers (4): Pasqual Coco, Bob File, George Perez, Orlando Woodwards.

Catchers (3): Joe Lawrence, Josh Phelps, Jayson Werth.

Infielders (2): Ryan Freel, Cesar Izturis.

Outfielders (2): Andy Thompson, Vernon Wells.

BLUE JAYS PITCHERS WHOSE ML DEBUT CAME AS A STARTER

Jerry Garvin - April 10, 1977 vs Chicago: W 3-1
(8.0IP, 6H, 1R/ER, 4BB, 2K)

Jeff Byrd - June 20, 1977 vs Cleveland: ND in a 8-5 loss
(5.0IP, 5H, 3R/ER, 5BB, 4K)

Jim Clancy - July 26, 1977 vs Texas: L 14-0
(2.0IP, 5H, 5R/ER, 3BB, 1K)

Mike Darr - September 6, 1977 vs Boston: L 11-2
(1.1IP, 3H, 5R/ER, 1HR, 4BB, 1K, 1HB)

Dave Stieb - June 29, 1979 at Baltimore: L 6-1
(6.0IP, 6H, 6R, 5ER, 2BB, 5K, 2HR)

Butch Edge - August 13, 1979 at Oakland: W 4-2
(6.2IP, 6H, 1R/ER, 2BB, 5K)

Luis Leal - May 25, 1980 vs New York: W 9-6
(7.2IP, 12H, 3R/ER, 4BB)

Alex Sanchez - May 23, 1989 vs Minnesota: ND in a 2-1
win (6.0IP, 5H, 1R/ER, 5BB, 1K)

Mauro Gozzo - August 8, 1989 vs Texas: W 7-0
(8.0IP, 3H, 0R/ER, 3BB, 4K)

Juan Guzman - June 7, 1991 at Baltimore: L 5-3
(4.2IP, 6H, 4R/ER, 3BB, 4K)

Scott Brow - April 28, 1993 vs Kansas City: L 5-3
(6.0IP, 5H, 4R/ER, 2BB, 2K)

Giovanni Carrara - July 29, 1995 vs Oakland: W 18-11
(5.0IP, 7H, 5R/ER, 5BB, 2K)

Jeff Ware - September 2, 1995 at Chicago: L 10-4
(1.1IP, 7H, 7R, 6ER, 3BB, 1K)

Chris Carpenter - May 12, 1997 at Minnesota: L 12-2
(3.0IP, 8H, 7R, 5ER, 3BB, 5K)

Roy Halladay - September 20, 1998 at Tampa Bay: ND in
a 7-5 win (5.0IP, 8H, 3R, 2ER, 1HR, 2BB, 5K)

Pasqual Coco - July 17, 2000 vs New York Mets: ND in a
7-5 loss (4.0IP, 5H, 4R, 4ER, 1HR, 5BB, 2K, 1HB, 1WP)

ROOKIE TOP FIVE—thru 2000

BATTING AVERAGE
(350 plate appearnaces)

1	Bob Bailor	.310	1977
2	Shawn Green	.288	1995
3	Alfredo Griffin	.287	1979
4	Al Woods	.284	1977
5	Damaso Garcia	.278	1980

GAMES

1	Alfredo Griffin	153	1979
2	Damaso Garcia	140	1980
3	Jesse Barfield	139	1982
4	Rick Bosetti	136	1978
5	Doug Ault	129	1977

AT-BATS

1	Alfredo Griffin	624	1979
2	Rick Bosetti	568	1978
3	Damaso Garcia	543	1980
4	Bob Bailor	496	1977
5	Doug Ault	445	1977

MOST RUNS

1	Alfredo Griffin	81	1979
2	Bob Bailor	62	1977
	Junior Felix	62	1989
4	Rick Bosetti	61	1978
5	Al Woods	58	1977
	Fred McGriff	58	1987

MOST HITS

1	Alfredo Griffin	179	1979
2	Bob Bailor	154	1977
3	Damaso Garcia	151	1980
4	Rick Bosetti	147	1978
5	Al Woods	125	1977

DOUBLES

1	Shawn Green	31	1995
2	Damaso Garcia	30	1980
3	Rick Bosetti	25	1978
4	Lloyd Moseby	24	1980
5	Doug Ault	22	1977

TRIPLES

1	Alfredo Griffin	10	1979
2	Junior Felix	8	1989
3	Damaso Garcia	7	1980
	Shannon Stewart	7	1997
5	Steve Staggs	6	1977

HOME RUNS

1	Fred McGriff	20	1987
2	Jesse Barfield	18	1982
3	Shawn Green	15	1995
4	John Olerud	14	1990
4	Jose Cruz	14	1997

RUNS BATTED IN

1	Doug Ault	64	1977
2	Jesse Barfield	58	1982
3	Shawn Green	54	1995
4	John Olerud	48	1990
5	Damaso Garcia	46	1980

EXTRA BASE HITS

1	Shawn Green	50	1995
2	Damaso Garcia	41	1980
3	Doug Ault	36	1977
4	Rick Bosetti	35	1978
5	Alfredo Griffin	34	1979

TOTAL BASES

1	Alfredo Griffin	227	1979
2	Damaso Garcia	207	1980
3	Bob Bailor	200	1977
4	Shawn Green	193	1995
5	Rick Bosetti	197	1978

STOLEN BASES

1	Alfredo Griffin	21	1979
2	Junior Felix	18	1989
3	Bob Bailor	15	1977
4	Damaso Garcia	13	1980
	Nelson Liriano	13	1987

SACRIFICE HITS

1	Alfredo Griffin	16	1979
2	Lloyd Moseby	10	1980
3	Alex Gonzalez	9	1995
4	Dan Ainge	7	1979
5	Bob Bailor	6	1977
	Al Woods	6	1977
	Jesse Barfield	6	1982

SACRIFICE FLYS

1	Alfredo Griffin	4	1979
	John Olerud	4	1990
	Greg Myers	4	1990
	Jeff Kent	4	1992
	Domingo Cedeno	4	1994
	Alex Gonzalez	4	1995
	Jose Cruz	4	1997
	Kevin Brown	4	1998

HIT BY PITCH

1	Jeff Kent	6	1992
2	Alfredo Griffin	5	1979
	Derek Bell	5	1992
4	Doug Ault	4	1977
	Sil Campusano	4	1988

BASE ON BALLS

1	Fred McGriff	60	1987
2	John Olerud	57	1990
3	Alex Gonzalez	44	1995
4	Jesse Barfield	42	1982
5	Alfredo Griffin	40	1979

STRIKEOUTS

1	Alex Gonzalez	114	1995
2	Fred McGriff	104	1987
3	Junior Felix	101	1989
4	Lloyd Moseby	85	1980
5	Jesse Barfied	79	1982

WINS

1	Mark Eichhorn	14	1986
2	Jeff Musselman	12	1987
3	Mike Timlin	11	1991
4	Jerry Garvin	10	1977
	Juan Guzman	10	1991

LOSSES

1	Jerry Garvin	18	1977
	Phil Huffman	18	1978
3	Jeff Byrd	13	1977
4	Jim Gott	10	1982
5	Jim Clancy	9	1977

SAVES

1	Billy Koch	31	1999
2	Darren Hall	17	1994
3	Kelvim Escobar	14	1997
4	Mark Eichhorn	10	1986
	Jimmy Key	10	1984

ERA (100IP)

1	Mark Eichhorn	1.72	1986
2	Juan Guzman	2.99	1991
3	Mike Timlin	3.16	1991
4	Roy Halladay	3.92	1999
5	Mike Willis	3.95	1977

GAMES

1	Mark Eichhorn	69	1986
2	Jeff Musselman	68	1987
3	Jim Key	63	1984
	Mike Timlin	63	1991
5	Billy Koch	56	1999

STARTS

1	Jerry Garvin	34	1977
2	Phil Huffman	31	1978
3	Jim Gott	23	1982
4	Juan Guzman	23	1991
5	Dave Stieb	18	1978
	Roy Halladay	18	1999

INNINGS

1	Jerry Garvin	244.2	1977
2	Phil Huffman	173.0	1978
3	Mark Eichhorn	157.0	1986
4	Roy Halladay	149.1	1999
5	John Cerutti	145.1	1986

STRIKEOUTS

1	Mark Eichhorn	166	1986
2	Juan Guzman	123	1991
3	Jose Nunez	99	1987
4	John Cerutti	89	1986
5	Mike Timlin	85	1991

1991 ALL-STAR GAME

The 1991 All-Star Game was played at SkyDome in Toronto on Tuesday, July 9, 1991... It was the first time that the game had been held in Toronto and just the second time that it had been held outside of the United States (Montreal 1982)... Three Blue Jays players were selected to participate in the 63rd All-Star Game: second baseman Roberto Alomar, outfielder Joe Carter and pitcher Jimmy Key as well, manager Cito Gaston was a coach and Tommy Craig was named AL trainer... 52,382 fans came to SkyDome to watch the action unfold in person and millions more watched and listened to the mid-season classic on television and radio... 56 players from both the National and American Leagues came to Toronto to participate... Of those 56 players, 49 saw action as the American League defeated the National League by a 4-2 count... Toronto pitcher Jimmy Key was credited with the win in his second career All-Star Game appearance... Joe Carter was 1-1 with a run scored and Roberto Alomar went 0-4... It was the fourth consecutive win for the American League dating back to 1988.

HITTERS

Y	Tot	H	A	Consec			1-inn			One-game						Men on Base				Batters					Totals					vs	
				2	3	4	3	4	5	5	6	7	8	9	10	0	1	2	3	PH	LO	XN	IP	P	1	10	20	30	40	RHP	LHP
77	100	45	55	3	0	0	1	0	0	0	0	0	0	0	0	67	22	10	1	5	1	2	1	0	10	5	0	0	0	65	35
78	98	50	48	2	0	0	0	0	0	0	0	0	0	0	0	61	27	8	2	2	2	2	0	0	13	0	2	0	0	59	39
79	95	50	45	2	0	0	0	0	0	0	0	0	0	0	0	57	21	14	3	4	1	2	2	0	11	3	1	0	0	67	28
80	126	56	70	3	0	0	0	0	0	0	0	0	0	0	0	70	41	13	2	3	0	3	1	0	12	3	1	1	0	82	44
81	61	34	27	2	0	0	0	0	0	0	0	0	0	0	0	37	17	7	0	1	1	0	1	0	10	2	0	0	0	31	30
82	106	62	44	3	0	0	1	0	0	0	0	0	0	0	0	71	27	7	1	4	1	1	1	0	15	3	1	0	0	56	50
83	167	101	66	10	0	0	2	0	0	1	0	0	0	0	0	97	49	18	3	5	2	4	4	0	7	6	3	0	0	106	61
84	143	59	84	5	1	0	3	0	0	0	0	0	0	0	0	87	46	9	1	6	1	1	2	0	8	6	1	0	0	104	39
85	158	75	83	6	0	0	0	0	0	1	0	0	0	0	0	94	46	15	3	4	2	8	0	0	11	4	2	0	0	102	56
86	181	87	94	5	0	0	0	0	0	0	0	0	0	0	0	105	49	24	3	4	4	6	1	0	9	4	1	1	1	126	55
87	215	101	114	8	1	0	3	0	0	3	0	0	0	0	1	126	55	31	3	3	0	4	0	0	9	5	3	0	1	152	63
88	158	78	80	6	0	0	0	0	0	1	0	0	0	0	0	99	42	14	3	2	1	2	1	0	8	5	1	1	0	105	53
89	142	64	78	4	0	0	0	0	0	0	0	0	0	0	0	78	41	15	8	3	4	3	1	0	11	5	0	1	0	106	36
90	167	93	74	6	0	0	2	0	0	2	0	0	0	0	0	100	45	18	4	0	1	3	0	0	8	4	1	2	0	109	58
91	133	75	58	1	0	0	0	0	0	0	0	0	0	0	0	85	40	8	0	1	6	5	1	0	13	2	1	1	0	86	47
92	163	79	84	4	0	0	0	0	0	0	0	0	0	0	0	83	56	22	2	0	5	2	1	0	9	4	2	1	0	122	41
93	159	90	69	7	0	0	0	0	0	2	0	0	0	0	0	98	39	20	2	1	6	0	1	0	9	3	2	1	0	121	38
94	115	63	52	2	0	0	0	0	0	0	1	0	0	0	0	58	42	13	2	1	4	2	1	0	7	4	1	0	0	74	41
95	140	73	67	5	0	0	1	0	0	0	0	0	0	0	0	85	37	14	4	1	3	1	1	0	10	6	1	0	0	104	36
96	177	87	90	3	0	0	0	0	0	1	1	0	0	0	0	91	58	25	3	2	1	3	0	0	7	5	1	2	0	130	47
97	147	68	79	5	0	0	0	0	0	0	0	0	0	0	0	85	40	15	7	1	0	1	0	0	10	5	1	1	0	109	38
98	221	112	109	6	0	0	0	0	0	0	0	1	0	0	0	141	58	18	4	1	2	3	3	0	8	4	1	2	1	167	54
99	212	96	116	11	0	0	3	0	0	3	1	0	0	0	0	123	60	26	3	4	3	3	0	0	16	5	1	0	2	170	42
00	244	134	110	5	1	0	2	0	0	2	0	0	0	0	0	141	67	27	9	0	8	1	0	0	7	1	4	2	2	205	39

PITCHERS

Y	Tot	H	A	Consec			1-inn			One-game						Men on Base				Batters					Totals					vs	
				2	3	4	3	4	5	5	6	7	8	9	10	0	1	2	3	PH	LO	XN	IP	P	1	10	20	30	40	RHP	LHP
77	152	94	58	4	1	0	0	2	0	2	0	0	1	0	0	79	54	18	1	6	0	4	3	0	10	2	2	1	0	92	60
78	149	75	74	2	0	0	0	0	0	0	0	0	0	0	0	78	56	10	5	2	3	1	0	0	4	5	3	0	0	104	45
79	165	74	91	6	0	0	1	0	0	2	0	0	0	0	0	86	48	23	8	1	2	3	3	0	9	6	2	0	0	99	66
80	135	61	74	1	0	0	0	0	0	2	0	0	0	0	0	72	46	17	0	5	1	4	2	0	8	7	0	0	0	61	74
81	72	41	31	1	0	0	0	0	0	0	0	0	0	0	0	41	19	10	2	2	2	2	1	0	9	3	0	0	0	42	30
82	147	70	77	5	0	0	2	0	0	1	0	0	0	0	0	79	40	22	6	1	1	2	2	0	7	3	3	0	0	83	64
83	145	84	61	5	0	0	1	0	0	1	0	0	0	0	0	89	40	13	3	2	3	3	2	0	8	3	3	0	0	85	60
84	140	78	62	2	1	0	2	0	0	1	0	0	0	0	0	76	42	21	1	3	0	4	1	0	7	2	3	0	0	68	72
85	147	78	69	5	1	0	1	0	0	0	0	0	0	0	0	87	47	11	2	4	1	2	1	0	10	2	3	0	0	77	70
86	164	89	75	7	0	0	4	0	0	2	0	0	0	0	0	90	54	18	2	9	4	5	0	0	11	1	4	0	0	91	73
87	158	83	75	2	0	0	0	0	0	1	0	0	0	0	0	95	45	12	6	4	4	3	1	0	5	5	2	1	0	102	56
88	143	73	70	4	0	0	0	0	0	0	0	0	0	0	0	99	25	18	1	1	5	5	3	0	8	5	2	0	0	102	41
89	99	50	49	1	0	0	0	0	0	0	0	0	0	0	0	60	26	10	3	2	2	1	0	0	12	5	0	0	0	70	29
90	143	82	61	4	1	0	2	0	0	1	1	0	0	0	0	80	43	15	5	3	3	3	0	0	10	4	2	0	0	100	43
91	121	72	49	2	0	0	0	0	0	0	0	0	0	0	0	59	40	15	7	2	2	5	0	0	12	2	2	0	0	80	41
92	124	60	64	6	0	0	0	0	0	1	0	0	0	0	0	75	36	11	2	2	2	0	0	0	10	2	2	0	0	86	38
93	144	91	53	4	0	0	0	0	0	1	0	0	0	0	0	84	43	15	2	1	1	1	1	0	8	3	2	0	0	85	59
94	127	64	63	4	0	0	1	0	0	1	0	0	0	0	0	76	31	16	4	3	4	2	1	0	11	1	3	0	0	75	52
95	145	79	66	2	0	0	1	0	0	1	0	0	0	0	0	78	49	14	4	4	4	3	1	0	12	6	1	0	0	74	71
96	187	102	85	6	0	0	0	0	0	1	0	0	0	0	0	105	54	25	3	6	5	2	0	0	15	1	4	0	0	105	82
97	167	72	95	5	0	0	4	0	0	3	0	0	0	0	0	100	40	24	3	4	4	3	1	0	16	2	0	2	0	91	76
98	169	77	92	6	0	0	2	0	0	0	1	0	0	0	0	42	51	23	3	2	4	2	0	0	10	4	1	1	0	82	87
99	191	93	98	4	0	0	0	0	0	1	0	0	0	0	0	100	56	25	10	2	3	1	0	0	13	5	0	2	0	111	80
00	195	92	103	7	1	0	0	1	0	3	0	0	1	0	0	110	51	29	5	1	2	2	0	1	14	4	2	1	0	109	86

HOME RUNS (1977-2000)

TOTAL	3628
HOME	1832 (Exhibition Stadium-817, SkyDome-1015)
AWAY	1796
3 in inning	18
5 in game	16
6 in game	3 (July 5, 1994 at Minnesota; July 6, 1996 at Detroit; July 8, 1999 at Baltimore)
7 in game	1 (August 19, 1998 at Seattle)
10 in game	1 (September 14, 1987 vs Baltimore)
0 on base	2139
1 on base	1025
2 on base	391
3 on base	73
Inside-the-Park	23
Lead-off	59
Pinch-hit	58
Extra Innings	62
Off RH Pitcher	2558
Off LH Pitcher	1070

YEARLY HOME RUN LEADERS

AT HOME

YEAR	PLAYER	HR	YEAR	PLAYER	HR	YEAR	PLAYER	HR	YEAR	PLAYER	HR
1977	Ron Fairly	10	1983	Jesse Barfield	22	1990	Kelly Gruber	23	1997	Carlos Delgado	17
1978	John Mayberry	12	1984	George Bell	12	1991	Joe Carter	23	1998	Jose Canseco	25
1979	John Mayberry	13	1985	Jesse Barfield	15	1992	Joe Carter	21	1999	Shawn Green	20
1980	Otto Velez	12	1986	Jesse Barfield	16	1993	Joe Carter	21	2000	Carlos Delgado	30
1981	John Mayberry	10	1987	George Bell	19	1994	Joe Carter	18			
1982	Jesse Barfield	11	1988	Fred McGriff	18	1995	Joe Carter	13			
1982	Willie Upshaw	11	1989	Fred McGriff	18	1996	Ed Sprague	17			

ON THE ROAD

YEAR	PLAYER	HR	YEAR	PLAYER	HR	YEAR	PLAYER	HR	YEAR	PLAYER	HR
1977	Ron Fairly	9	1981	John Mayberry	7	1990	Fred McGriff	21	1997	Carlos Delgado	13
1977	Doug Rader	9	1982	Willie Upshaw	10	1991	Kelly Gruber	12	1998	Jose Canseco	21
1977	Otto Velez	9	1983	Cliff Johnson	12	1992	Joe Carter	13	1999	Carlos Delgado	27
1978	Rico Carty	10	1984	George Bell	14	1992	Dave Winfield	13	2000	Tony Batista	16
1978	John Mayberry	10	1985	George Bell	18	1993	John Olerud	15	2000	Jose Cruz	16
1979	John Mayberry	8	1986	Jesse Barfield	24	1994	Joe Carter	9	2000	Brad Fullmer	16
1979	Otto Velez	8	1987	George Bell	28	1995	Joe Carter	12			
1980	John Mayberry	20	1988	Fred McGriff	16	1996	Ed Sprague	19			

THREE HOME RUN GAMES

PLAYER	DATE	OPPONENT	PITCHERS
OTTO VELEZ	May 4, 1980	vs Cleveland (G#1)	Dan Spillner, Wayne Garland, Sid Monge
ERNIE WHITT	Sept. 14, 1987	vs Baltimore	Ken Dixon (2), Tony Arnold
GEORGE BELL	April 4, 1988	at Kansas City	Bret Saberhagen
JOE CARTER	Aug. 23, 1993	vs Cleveland	Albie Lopez (2), Jose Hernandez
DARNELL COLES	July 5, 1994	at Minnesota	Pat Mahomes, Larry Casian (2)
CARLOS DELGADO	Aug. 4, 1998	at Texas	Stottlemyre, Gunderson, Patterson
CARLOS DELGADO	Aug. 6, 1999	at Texas	Helling (2), Zimmerman
DARRIN FLETCHER	Aug. 27, 2000	at Texas	Helling (3)

TWO HOME RUN GAMES

PLAYER	DATE	OPPONENT	PITCHERS
DOUG AULT (1)	April 7, 1977	vs Chicago	Ken Brett
OTTO VELEZ	April 25, 1977	vs Boston	Luis Tiant, Bill Campbell
OTTO VELEZ	June 5, 1977	at Oakland	Vida Blue, Joe Coleman
ROY HOWELL (1)	Sept. 10, 1977	at New York	Catfish Hunter, Ken Clay
RICO CARTY (1)	April 27, 1978	at Kansas City	Larry Gura
JOHN MAYBERRY	May 22, 1978	vs Boston	Allen Ripley
JOHN MAYBERRY	May 26, 1978	at New York	Jim Beattie, Sparky Lyle
JOHN MAYBERRY	June 26, 1978	vs Baltimore	Joe Kerrigan, Larry Harlow
OTTO VELEZ	July 26, 1979	vs Texas	Doc Medich, Doyle Alexander
JOHN MAYBERRY	August 26, 1979	vs California	Nolan Ryan
JOHN MAYBERRY	April 9, 1980	at Seattle	Mike Parrott
JOHN MAYBERRY	June 1, 1980	at New York	Tom Underwood, Rich Gossage
JOHN MAYBERRY	August 14, 1980	at Milwaukee	Moose Haas
JOHN MAYBERRY	July 16, 1980	at Seattle	Glenn Abbott
JOHN MAYBERRY	May 30, 1981	vs Oakland	Mike Norris
OTTO VELEZ (4)	June 3, 1981	vs California	Geoff Zahn
JOHN MAYBERRY (10)	April 25, 1982	vs Boston	Bob Ojeda, Mark Clear
WILLIE UPSHAW	June 7, 1982	vs Cleveland	John Denny
WILLIE UPSHAW	August 17, 1982	vs Cleveland	Ed Whitson
LLOYD MOSEBY	April 19, 1983	vs Cleveland	Rick Sutcliffe, Dan Spillner
ERNIE WHITT	May 23, 1983	vs Detroit	Milt Wilcox
LLOYD MOSEBY	May 29, 1983	vs Boston	Dennis Eckersley
JESSE BARFIELD	June 14, 1983	vs Oakland	Tom Underwood
CLIFF JOHNSON	June 21, 1983	vs Minnesota	Bryan Oelkers, Jim Lewis
MICKEY KLUTTS (1)	June 26, 1983	at Seattle	Manny Castillo
LLOYD MOSEBY	August 2, 1983	vs New York (1stG)	Matt Keough
JESSE BARFIELD	August 29, 1983	vs Boston (1stG)	John Tudor
JESSE BARFIELD	Sept. 1, 1983	vs Baltimore	Jim Palmer
JESSE BARFIELD	Sept. 2, 1983	vs Detroit (1stG)	Juan Berenguer, Doug Bair
ERNIE WHITT	Sept. 4, 1983	vs Detroit	Glenn Abbot, Aurelio Lopez
CLIFF JOHNSON	April 6, 1984	at California	Jim Slaton
WILLIE UPSHAW	April 26, 1984	vs Oakland	Mike Warren
BUCK MARTINEZ (1)	June 23, 1984	at Boston	Rich Gale, Mike Brown
JESSE BARFIELD	July 1, 1984	vs Oakland	Curt Young, Keith Atherton
DAMASO GARCIA (1)	July 3, 1984	vs California	Tommy John
JESSE BARFIELD	July 6, 1984	vs Seattle	Edwin Nunez
CLIFF JOHNSON (3)	July 15, 1984	at Oakland	Keith Atherton, Chris Codiroli
WILLIE AIKENS (1)	Sept. 14, 1984	at Detroit	Jack Morris
WILLIE UPSHAW (4)	April 28, 1985	at Texas	Mike Mason, Greg Harris
JESSE BARFIELD	June 5, 1985	vs Minnesota	Mike Smithson
JESSE BARFIELD	July 31, 1985	at Baltimore	Dennis Martinez
JESSE BARFIELD	May 6, 1986	vs Oakland	Moose Haas, Steve Ontiveros
LLOYD MOSEBY	June 28, 1986	at New York	Joe Niekro, Alfonso Pulido
JESSE BARFIELD	July 3, 1986	at Boston	Oil Can Boyd, Mike Brown
RANCE MULLINIKS	July 3, 1986	at Boston	Oil Can Boyd, Mike Brown
GEORGE BELL	July 19, 1986	at California	John Candelaria, Donnie Moore

PLAYER	DATE	OPPONENT	PITCHERS
GEORGE BELL	July 21, 1986	at Seattle	Mark Huismann
JESSE BARFIELD	July 21, 1986	at Seattle	Mark Huismann, Karl Best
LLOYD MOSEBY	August 5, 1986	vs Kansas City	Scott Bankhead, Buddy Black
JESSE BARFIELD	Sept. 17, 1986	vs Detroit	Jack Morris
JESSE BARFIELD	October 1, 1986	at New York	Ron Guidry
GEORGE BELL	April 26, 1987	at Chicago	Jose DeLeon, Bobby Thigpen
JESSE BARFIELD	May 1, 1987	vs Texas	Jose Guzman, Mitch Williams
JESSE BARFIELD (15)	May 8, 1987	at Texas	Jose Guzman
GEORGE BELL	May 9, 1987	at Texas	Ed Correa, Dale Mohorcic
LLOYD MOSEBY	May 10, 1987	at Texas	Bobby Witt, Dale Mohorcic
GEORGE BELL	May 22, 1987	at Seattle	Scott Bankhead
KELLY GRUBER	May 22, 1987	at Seattle	Scott Bankhead, Jerry Reed
GEORGE BELL	May 25, 1987	at Seattle	Mike Morgan, Steve Shields
GEORGE BELL	June 8, 1987	at New York	Rick Rhoden, Rich Bordi
GEORGE BELL	June 11, 1987	at Baltimore	John Habyan
RANCE MULLINIKS	June 24, 1987	at Detroit	Jack Morris
GARTH IORG (1)	July 20, 1987	at Texas	Charlie Hough
GEORGE BELL	July 29, 1987	vs Boston	Bruce Hurst
FRED McGRIFF	August 4, 1987	at Chicago	Neil Allen
GEORGE BELL	August 30, 1987	vs Oakland	Jose Rijo, Dennis Lamp
ERNIE WHITT (3)	Sept. 12, 1987	vs New York	Rick Rhoden, Bill Fulton
GEORGE BELL	Sept. 14, 1987	vs Baltimore	Eric Bell, Mike Kinnunen
RANCE MULLINIKS (3)	Sept. 14, 1987	vs Baltimore	Ken Dixon, Eric Bell
LLOYD MOSEBY (7)	Sept. 29, 1987	vs Milwaukee	Chris Bosio
KELLY GRUBER	April 11, 1988	vs New York	Cecilio Guante, Charles Hudson
FRED McGRIFF	May 3, 1988	at Seattle	Mike Campbell
FRED McGRIFF	June 15, 1988	vs Cleveland	Greg Swindell, Dan Schatzeder
CECIL FIELDER	June 15, 1988	vs Cleveland	Greg Swindell, Dan Schatzeder
FRED McGRIFF	July 17, 1988	at Oakland	Curt Young, Gene Nelson
CECIL FIELDER (2)	July 24, 1988	at Seattle	Mark Langston, Rod Scurry
FRED McGRIFF	August 2, 1988	vs Minnesota	Charlie Lea, Jim Winn
FRED McGRIFF	April 11, 1989	at New York	Dave LaPoint
FRED McGRIFF	July 21, 1989	at Seattle	Gene Harris
FRED McGRIFF	August 23, 1989	vs Detroit	Jeff Robinson
KELLY GRUBER	April 24, 1990	vs Clevland	Greg Swindell
KELLY GRUBER	May 6, 1990	vs Detroit	Urbano Lugo
GLENALLEN HILL (1)	May 17, 1990	vs Seattle	Randy Johnson, Gene Harris
KELLY GRUBER	May 22, 1990	vs Oakland	Curt Young, Gene Nelson
GEORGE BELL	June 8, 1990	at Milwaukee	Mark Knudson
GEORGE BELL	June 21, 1990	vs New York	Andy Hawkins, Dave Righetti
JOHN OLERUD	June 21, 1990	vs New York	Andy Hawkins, Alan Mills
GEORGE BELL (14)	June 24, 1990	vs New York	Chuck Cary
FRED McGRIFF	June 28, 1990	at Boston	Roger Clemens
FRED McGRIFF	July 12, 1990	at California	Kirk McCaskill, Mike Fetters
FRED McGRIFF (11)	Sept. 2, 1990	at Cleveland	Bud Black, Jesse Orosco
KELLY GRUBER	Sept. 8, 1990	vs Chicago	Alex Fernandez
JOHN OLERUD	April 19, 1991	at Milwaukee	Don August
ROBERTO ALOMAR	May 10, 1991	vs Chicago	Bobby Thigpen, Scott Radinsky
JOE CARTER	June 20, 1991	vs New York	Tim Leary
JOE CARTER	July 3, 1991	vs Minnesota	Allan Anderson
JOE CARTER	July 14, 1991	vs Texas	John Barfield
JOE CARTER	August 9, 1991	at Boston	Joe Hesketh, Dennis Lamp
KELLY GRUBER (7)	April 23, 1992	at Cleveland	Dave Otto, Brad Arnsberg
DAVE WINFIELD (1)	April 28, 1992	vs California	Chuck Finley, Julio Valera
JOE CARTER	May 3, 1992	at Milwaukee	Bill Wegman
DEVON WHITE	June 1, 1992	at Minnesota	John Smiley, Carl Willis
JOHN OLERUD	June 26, 1992	at Cleveland	Jack Armstrong
PAUL MOLITOR	May 16, 1993	at New York	Mike Witt, Neal Heaton
DEVON WHITE (2)	May 24, 1993	vs Milwaukee	Mike Boddicker
JOHN OLERUD	May 31, 1993	at California	John Farrell
ROBBIE ALOMAR	June 2, 1993	at California	Julio Valera
JOE CARTER	October 4, 1993	at Baltimore	Ben McDonald
CARLOS DELGADO	April 11, 1994	at Oakland	Bobby Witt, Bill Taylor
JOHN OLERUD	April 11, 1994	at Oakland	Bobby Witt
PAUL MOLITOR	April 25, 1994	at Kansas City	David Cone
PAUL MOLITOR	May 21, 1994	vs Cleveland	Brian Barnes
PAUL MOLITOR (4)	July 21, 1994	vs Texas	Tim Leary, Matt Whiteside
RANDY KNORR (1)	July 23, 1994	vs Texas	Hector Fajardo, Rick Honeycutt
ROBERTO ALOMAR (3)	May 3, 1995	vs Chicago	Jim Abbott, Roberto Hernandez
ED SPRAGUE	May 19, 1995	vs New York	Melido Perez, John Wetteland
ALEX GONZALEZ	May 23, 1995	vs Kansas City	Jim Pittsley
LANCE PARRISH (1)	May 29, 1995	vs Detroit	Mike Moore, Joe Boever
JOE CARTER	June 2, 1995	at Cleveland	Charles Nagy
JOE CARTER	June 29, 1995	vs Baltimore	Sid Fernandez
JOHN OLERUD	July 16, 1995	at Seattle	Rafeal Carmona, Bill Risley
ALEX GONZALEZ (2)	July 29, 1995	vs Oakland	Arial Prieto, Steve Wojciechowski
JOE CARTER	August 20, 1995	vs Kansas City	Jason Jacome
JOE CARTER	September 11, 1995	vs Detroit	Ben Blomdahl, Joe Boever
JOE CARTER	April 19, 1996	at Seattle	Bob Wolcott
ED SPRAGUE	April 22, 1996	at Seattle	Edwin Hurtado, Sterling Hitchcock
ED SPRAGUE	April 30, 1996	vs Milwaukee	Ben McDonald
JOE CARTER (12)	May 3, 1996	at Boston	Aaron Sele, Stan Belinda
JOHN OLERUD (7)	July 1, 1996	vs Baltimore	Rocky Coppinger, Roger McDowell
CARLOS DELGADO	July 6, 1996	at Detroit	Omar Olivares, Greg Keagle

Home Runs

PLAYER	DATE	OPPONENT	PITCHERS
CHARLIE O'BRIEN (1)	July 11, 1996	at Milwaukee	Jeff D'Amico, Jose Mercedes
ROBERT PEREZ (1)	July 13, 1996	at Milwaukee	Scott Karl
JACOB BRUMFIELD (1)	August 14, 1996	vs Boston	Jeff Suppan
ED SPRAGUE	September 8, 1996	at New York	Andy Pettitte
SHAWN GREEN	April 25, 1997	vs Seattle	Dennis Martinez
ED SPRAGUE	April 29, 1997	at Kansas City	Glendon Rusch
BENITO SANTIAGO	May 10, 1997	at Minnesota	Greg Swindell
SHAWN GREEN	June 17, 1997	vs Atlanta	Greg Maddux, Mike Bielecki
CARLOS DELGADO	July 17, 1997	at Texas	John Burkett, Xavier Hernandez
BENITO SANTIAGO (2)	July 26, 1997	vs Kansas City	Kevin Appier, Hector Carrasco
CARLOS DELGADO	August 8, 1997	vs Detroit	Willie Blair, Mike Myers
JOSE CRUZ	August 24, 1997	at Kansas City	Ricky Bones, Larry Casian
CARLOS DELGADO	August 27, 1997	vs Chicago	Doug Drabek, Nelson Cruz
JOSE CRUZ	September 2, 1997	at New York (NL)	Turk Wendell
JOSE CANSECO	April 10, 1998	at Texas	Rick Helling, John Wetteland
JOSE CANSECO	May 21, 1998	vs Tampa Bay	Luis Arrojo, Jim Mecir
MIKE STANLEY	May 23, 1998	at Cleveland	Bartolo Colon
CARLOS DELGADO	June 1, 1998	vs Boston	Tim Wakefield, Jim Corsi
JOSE CANSECO	June 10, 1998	at Florida	Joe Fontenot, Jay Powell
MIKE STANLEY (2)	June 12, 1998	vs Baltimore	Jesse Orosco, Norm Charlton
ED SPRAGUE	June 21, 1998	at Baltimore	Sidney Ponson, Armando Benitez
SHAWN GREEN	June 28, 1998	at Atlanta	Tom Glavine, Rudy Seanez
CARLOS DELGADO	July 4, 1998	vs Tampa Bay	Matt Ruebel, Roberto Hernandez
ED SPRAGUE (7)	July 12, 1998	at Detroit	Brian Powell, Doug Bochtler
SHAWN GREEN	July 17, 1998	vs New York (AL)	Ramiro Mendoza, Mike Stanton
JOSE CANSECO	July 19, 1998	vs New York (AL)	Andy Pettitte
CARLOS DELGADO	August 19, 1998	at Seattle	Ken Cloude, Bobby Ayala
SHAWN GREEN	August 19, 1998	at Seattle	Ken Cloude, Bob Wells
CARLOS DELGADO	August 21, 1998	at Anaheim	Jeff Juden
SHAWN GREEN	August 28, 1998	vs Minnesota	LaTroy Hawkins, Mike Trombley
CARLOS DELGADO	September 17, 1998	at Detroit	Bryce Florie
JOSE CANSECO (5)	September 22, 1998	vs Baltimore	Mike Mussina
PAT KELLY (1)	April 22, 1999	vs Anaheim	Tim Belcher, Rich Levine
SHAWN GREEN	April 28, 1999	vs Anaheim	Tim Belcher, Scott Schoeneweis
CARLOS DELGADO	April 30, 1999	at Seattle	Jeff Fassero, John Halama
CARLOS DELGADO	May 3, 1999	at Seattle	Freddy Garcia, Jose Mesa
PAT KELLY (2)	May 9, 1999	vs Texas	John Burkett, Dan Patterson
DARRIN FLETCHER	June 2, 1999	vs Chicago	John Snyder, Bryan Ward
SHAWN GREEN	June 21, 1999	vs Kansas City	Chris Fussell, Tim Byrdak
SHAWN GREEN (9)	July 4, 1999	vs Tampa Bay	Dave Eiland, Rick White
TONY BATISTA	July 8, 1999	at Baltimore	Sidney Ponson, Rocky Coppinger
WILLIS OTANEZ (1)	July 8, 1999	at Baltimore	Sidney Ponson, Rocky Coppinger
CARLOS DELGADO	July 19, 1999	at Atlanta	Bruce Chen, Rudy Seanez
CARLOS DELGADO	August 10, 1999	at Minnesota	Brad Radke, Travis Miller
CARLOS DELGADO	September 8, 1999	at Seattle	Jamie Moyer, Jose Mesa
DARRIN FLETCHER (2)	September 10, 1999	at Detroit	Brian Moehler, Erik Hiljus
SHANNON STEWART (1)	April 3, 2000	vs Kansas City	Jeff Suppan
TONY BATISTA	April 3, 2000	vs Kansas City	Jeff Suppan, Jerry Spradlin
CARLOS DELGADO	April 16, 2000	vs Seattle	Freddy Garcia
JOSE CRUZ (3)	April 22, 2000	vs New York (AL)	David Cone
RAUL MONDESI	May 9, 2000	vs Baltimore	Mike Mussina
CARLOS DELGADO	May 28, 2000	at Detroit	Willie Blair
CARLOS DELGADO	June 7, 2000	at Atlanta	Kevin Millwood, Mike Remlinger
RAUL MONDESI (2)	June 18, 2000	at Boston	Jeff Fassero, Rheal Cormier
TONY BATISTA	June 22, 2000	vs Detroit	Hideo Nomo
TONY BATISTA	July 13, 2000	vs Philadelphia	Curt Schilling, Chris Brock
CARLOS DELGADO	July 20, 2000	vs Tampa Bay	Steve Trachsel
TONY BATISTA (5)	July 21, 2000	vs Baltimore	Pat Rapp, Buddy Groom
BRAD FULLMER	July 26, 2000	vs Cleveland	Bartolo Colon
CARLOS DELGADO (20)	August 23, 2000	vs Kansas City	Kris Wilson, Andy Larkin
BRAD FULLMER (2)	August 30, 2000	at Anaheim	Matt Wise, Derek Turnbow

LEAD OFF GAME HOME RUNS

#	DATE	D/N	BATTER	POS	PITCHER	OPP	SITE	#	DATE	D/N	BATTER	POS	PITCHER	OPP	SITE
1	Apr 27/77	N	Bob Bailor	CF	Wayne Garland	CLE	CLE	20	Sept 7/89	N	Lloyd Moseby	CF	Tom Candiotti	CLE	CLE
2	July 30/79	D	Rick Bosetti	CF	Eduardo Rodriguez	MIL	TOR	21	May 5/90	D	Tony Fernandez	SS	Jeff Robinson	DET	TOR
3	Sept 21/78	N	Rick Bosetti	CF	Catfish Hunter	NYY	TOR	22	July 21/91	N	Devon White	CF	Gerald Alexander	TEX	TEX
4	Aug 29/79	D	Alfredo Griffin	SS	Mike Norris	OAK	TOR	23	Aug 7/91	N	Devon White	CF	Frank Tanana	DET	TOR
5	Apr 28/81	N	Lloyd Moseby	CF	Mike Caldwell	MIL	MIL	24	Aug 18/91	D	Devon White	CF	Bill Gullickson	DET	DET
6	Sept 24/82	N	Damaso Garcia	2B	Ed Nunez	SEA	SEA	25	Aug 23/91	N	Devon White	CF	Wade Taylor	NYY	TOR
7	June 1/83	N	Damaso Garcia	2B	Dave Rozema	DET	DET	26	Sept 20/91	N	Devon White	CF	Bob Welch	OAK	OAK
8	June 2/83	D	Damaso Garcia	2B	Milt Wilcox	DET	DET	27	Oct 6/91	D	Devon White	CF	Tom Edens	MIN	MIN
9	July 3/84	N	Damaso Garcia	2B	Tommy John	CAL	TOR	28	June 1/92	N	Devon White	CF	John Smiley	MIN	MIN
10	Apr 21/85	D	Damaso Garcia	2B	Dennis Martinez	BAL	TOR	29	June 8/92	N	Devon White	CF	Greg Cadaret	NYY	NYY
11	June 30/85	D	Damaso Garcia	2B	Jack Morris	DET	DET	30	Aug 16/92	D	Devon White	CF	Dennis Cook	CLE	CLE
12	Apr 20/86	D	Lloyd Moseby	CF	Charlie Leibrandt	KC	TOR	31	Sept 11/92	D	Devon White	CF	Scott Chiamparino	TEX	TEX
13	May 25/86	D	Damaso Garcia	2B	Ken Schrow	CLE	CLE	32	Sept 22/92	N	Devon White	CF	Rick Sutcliffe	BAL	BAL
14	Aug 16/86	D	Tony Fernandez	SS	Charlie Hough	TEX	TOR	33	May 8/93	D	Devon White	CF	Rick Sutcliffe	BAL	TOR
15	Sept 24/86	N	Tony Fernandez	SS	Dan Petry	DET	DET	34	May 24/93	D	Devon White	CF	Mike Boddicker	MIL	TOR
16	May 23/88	N	Tony Fernandez	SS	Teddy Higuera	MIL	MIL	35	June 19/93	D	Devon White	CF	Daniel Darwin	BOS	TOR
17	Apr 25/89	N	Lloyd Moseby	CF	Storm Davis	OAK	OAK	36	June 24/93	N	Devon White	CF	Scott Kamieniecki	NYY	TOR
18	July 31/89	N	Tony Fernandez	SS	Andy Hawkins	NYY	NYY	37	Aug 14/93	D	Devon White	CF	John Dopson	BOS	BOS
19	Aug 15/89	N	Lloyd Moseby	DH	Mike Smithson	BOS	BOS	38	Sept 1/93	D	Rickey Henderson	LF	Mike Mahler	OAK	OAK

#	DATE	D/N	BATTER	POS	PITCHER	OPP	SITE	#	DATE	D/N	BATTER	POS	PITCHER	OPP	SITE
39	Apr. 17/94	D	Devon White	CF	Chuck Finley	CAL	CAL	50	July 9/99	N	Shannon Stewart	LF	Jeremy Powell	MON	MON
40	Apr. 22/94	N	Devon White	CF	Scott Erickson	MIN	TOR	51	Aug. 10/99	N	Shannon Stewart	LF	Brad Radke	MIN	MIN
41	May 14/94	D	Devon White	CF	Danny Darwin	BOS	BOS	52	Apr. 3/00	D	Shannon Stewart	LF	Jeff Suppan	KC	TOR
42	June 5/94	D	Devon White	CF	Dave Fleming	SEA	SEA	53	Apr. 19/00	N	Jose Cruz	CF	Ken Hill	ANA	TOR
43	May 12/95	N	Devon White	CF	Ricky Bones	MIL	MIL	54	Apr. 22/00	D	Jose Cruz	CF	David Cone	NYY	TOR
44	June 20/95	N	Devon White	CF	Sid Roberson	MIL	MIL	55	Apr. 23/00	D	Jose Cruz	CF	Orlando Hernandez	NYY	TOR
45	Sept. 19/95	N	Alex Gonzalez	SS	Andy Pettitte	NYY	NYY	56	June 2/00	N	Shannon Stewart	LF	Brad Penny	FLA	FLA
46	June 13/96	N	Jacob Brumfield	CF	Chuck Finley	CAL	CAL	57	June 25/00	D	Shannon Stewart	LF	Pedro Martinez	BOS	TOR
47	Sept. 1/98	N	Shannon Stewart	LF	Tim Belcher	KC	KC	58	Aug. 7/00	N	Shannon Stewart	LF	Blake Stein	KC	KC
48	Sept. 13/98	D	Shannon Stewart	LF	David Cone	NYY	NYY	59	Sept. 27/00	N	Shannon Stewart	LF	Sidney Ponson	BAL	BAL
49	Apr. 19/99	N	Shannon Stewart	LF	Sidney Ponson	BAL	BAL								

PINCH HIT HOME RUNS

DATE	PLAYER	H/A	OPPONENT
April 7, 1977	Al Woods	H	Off Francisco Barrios, Chicago, (5th inn., one on) (tied major league record as 11th player to homer as pinch-hitter in first major league at bat)
April 14, 1977	Otto Velez	H	Off John Hiller, Detroit (8th inn., two on)
April 21, 1977	Al Woods	A	Off Dick Tidrow, at New York (9th inn., none on)
August 9, 1977	Doug Ault	H	Off Tom Burgmeier, Minnesota (4th inn., none on)
August 24, 1977	Doug Rader	A	Off Mike Kekich, at Seattle (4th inn., none on)
June 26, 1978	John Mayberry	H	Off Joe Kerrigan, Baltimore (2nd inn., one on)
July 1, 1978	Sam Ewing	H	Off Sid Monge, Cleveland (8th inn., one on)
June 17, 1979	Otto Velez	H	Off Bob Lacey, Oakland (7th inn., two on)
July 4, 1979	Otto Velez	A	Off Dave Tobik , Detroit (11th inn., two on)
August 6, 1979	Rico Carty	H	Off Steve Mingori, Kansas City (8th inn., none on)
Sept. 22, 1979	Rico Carty	H	Off Jim Kaat, New York (4th inn., one on)
May 6, 1980	Roy Howell	A	Off Don Aase, California (7th inn., one on)
June 14, 1980	Bob Davis	H	Off Dave Rajsich, Texas (6th inn., none on)
August 7, 1980	Doug Ault	A	Off Rick Waits, Cleveland (7th inn., one on)
April 24, 1981	Willie Upshaw	A	Off Rich Gossage, New York (8th inn., none on)
April 24, 1982	Jesse Barfield	H	Off Tom Burgmeier, Boston (8th inn., three on)
June 23, 1982	Ernie Whitt	A	Off Mike Stanton, Seattle (9th inn., none on)
July 21, 1982	Ernie Whitt	H	Off Dan Quisenberry, Kansas City (9th inn., none on)
July 24, 1982	Jesse Barfield	A	Off Kevin Hickey, Chicago (8th inn., one on)
April 29, 1983	Mickey Klutts	H	Off Dick Tidrow, Chicago (7th inn., none on)
May 22, 1983	Cliff Johnson	H	Off Tippy Martinez, Baltimore (8th inn., none on)
June 25, 1983	Buck Martinez	A	Off Ed Vande Berg, Seattle (9th inn., none on)
July 14, 1983	Rance Mulliniks	A	Off Dennis Lamp, Chicago (7th inn., two on)
July 20, 1983	Ernie Whitt	H	Off Mike Armstrong, Kansas City (7th inn., two on)
August 1, 1984	Ernie Whitt	H	Off Bret Saberhagen, Kansas City (8th inn., one on)
August 3, 1984	Willie Aikens	A	Off Bill Swaggerty, Baltimore (6th inn., two on)
August 5, 1984	Cliff Johnson	A	Off Tippy Martinez, Baltimore (8th inn., none on)
August 14, 1984	George Bell	A	Off Tom Waddell, Cleveland (9th inn., none on)
August 28, 1984	Jesse Barfield	H	Off Bert Roberge, Cleveland (7th inn., one on)
Sept. 25, 1984	Kelly Gruber	A	Off Al Nipper, Boston (9th inn., one on)
April 24, 1985	Jeff Burroughs	H	Off Larry Gura, Kansas City (3rd inn., two on)
April 27, 1985	Willie Aikens	A	Off Tommy Boggs, Texas (9th inn., none on)
June 12, 1985	Rance Mulliniks	A	Off Rich Bordi, New York (10th inn., none on)
Sept. 25, 1985	Jeff Burroughs	H	Off Bruce Hurst, Boston (9th inn., none on)
June 13, 1986	Cliff Johnson	H	Off Willie Hernandez, Detroit (8th inn., lead off)
June 14, 1986	Rick Leach	H	Off Jack Morris, Detroit (7th inn., none on)
June 14, 1986	Buck Martinez	H	Off Willie Hernandez, Detroit (9th inn., one on)
June 15, 1986	Garth Iorg	H	Off Chuck Cary, Detroit (6th inn., two on)
June 28, 1987	Fred McGriff	A	Off Jay Aldrich, Milwaukee (8th inn., none on)
July 24, 1987	Juan Beniquez	H	Off Dan Schatzeder, Minnesota (7th inn., two on)
September 4, 1987	Cecil Fielder	H	Off Dennis Powell, Seattle (10th inn., none on)
May 23, 1988	Fred McGriff	A	Off Odell Jones, Milwaukee (8th inn., none on)
July 3, 1988	Jesse Barfield	H	Off Rick Honeycutt, Oakland (7th inn., none on)
May 5, 1989	Nelson Liriano	H	Off Brian Harvey, California, (9th inn., none on)
June 13, 1989	Kelly Gruber	A	Off Dan Plesac, Milwaukee, (9th inn., none on)
Sept. 9, 1989	Lee Mazzilli	A	Off Rich Yett, Cleveland, (6th inn., none on)
Sept. 20, 1991	Pat Borders	A	Off Gene Nelson, Oakland (6th inn., none on)
May 21, 1993	Darnell Coles	H	Off Mike Trombley, Minnesota (6th inn., two on)
May 30, 1994	Michael Huff	H	Off Vince Horsman, Oakland (9th inn., none on)
May 23, 1995	Carlos Delgado	H	Off Hipolito Pichardo, Kansas City (7th inn., lead off)
May 12, 1996	Charlie O'Brien	H	Off Heathcliff Slocumb, Boston (9th inn., none on)
June 1, 1996	John Olerud	H	Off Jeff Montgomery, Kansas City (9th inn., none on)
June 13, 1997	Robert Perez	A	Off Ricky Bottalico, Philadelphia (9th inn., none on)
June 22, 1998	Juan Samuel	H	Off Steve Kline, Montreal (8th inn., none on)
June 8, 1999	Jacob Brumfield	A	Off Dennis Cook, New York (NL) (6th inn., one on)
June 20, 1999	Willie Greene	H	Off Jeff Suppan, Kansas City (9th inn., none on)
June 30, 1999	Willie Greene	H	Off Mike Timlin, Baltimore (9th inn., none on)
September 5, 1999	Willie Greene	A	Off Jay Witasick, Kansas City (9th inn., none on)

PH HOME RUN LEADERS

The Blue Jays franchise has connected 58 times for pinch-hit home runs during regular season games... Jesse Barfield on April 24, 1982 vs Boston at Exhibition Stadium hit the Blue Jays only pinch-slam... Alvis Woods in the Blue Jays first ever game, April 7, 1977 vs the Chicago White Sox hit the first pitch of his first Major League career at bat for the Blue Jays first pinch-hit home run... Ed Sprague has the only pinch-hit home run in post-season for the Blue Jays which came on October 18 , 1992, Game #2 of the World Series vs Atlanta... On June 30, 1999 vs the Baltimore Orioles Willie Greene became the 16th player in AL history to hit home runs in consecutive pinch-hit at bats. Also holds the record for most days between consecutive pinch-hit home runs.

CAREER	NO
Ernie Whitt	4
Otto Velez	3
Cliff Johnson	3
Jesse Barfield	3
Willie Greene	3
Alvis Woods	2
Doug Ault	2
Rico Carty	2
Rance Mulliniks	2
Willie Aikens	2
Fred McGriff	2
Jeff Burroughs	2

SEASON	NO	YEAR
Willie Greene	3	1999
Alvis Woods	2	1977
Otto Velez	2	1979
Rico Carty	2	1979
Ernie Whitt	2	1982
Jeff Burroughs	2	1985

CLUB	SEASON
8	1986
6	1984
5	1977
5	1983

Home Runs

INSIDE-THE-PARK HOME RUNS

HR#	DATE	D/N	BATTER	POS	BAT ORD	PITCHER	OPP	H/A	IN	ON	OUT
1	Aug. 21/77	D	Doug Rader	DH	5	Frank Tanana	CAL	A	5	0	2
2	July 9/79	N	Al Woods	LF	6	Lary Sorensen	MIL	H	2	0	0
3	Aug. 28/79	D	Alfredo Griffin	SS	1	Rick Langford	OAK	H	5	1	2
4	Sept. 17/80	N	Roy Howell	3B	3	Tim Lollar	NYY	A	10	1	2
5	April 25/81	D	Lloyd Moseby	CF	1	Bill Castro	NYY	A	9	1	2
6	June 7/82	N	Willie Upshaw	1B	3	John Denny	CLE	H	3	1	2
7	April 14/83	D	Willie Upshaw	1B	7	Jerry Augustine	MIL	H	2	0	2
8	May 25/83	N	Jorge Orta	DH	4	Dan Petry	DET	H	4	0	0
9	May 30/83	N	Lloyd Moseby	CF	7	Dan Petry	DET	A	9	1	2
10	Sept. 14/83	N	Barry Bonnell	CF	5	Matt Young	SEA	A	2	0	0
11	June 6/84	N	George Bell	RF	6	Aurelio Lopez	DET	A	8	0	1
12	Aug. 10/84	N	Tony Fernandez	SS	9	Dennis Martinez	BAL	H	3	0	2
13	June 12/86	N	Kelly Gruber	2B	7	Bill Scherrer	DET	H	7	2	2
14	May 16/88	N	Kelly Gruber	3B	6	Jeff Bittiger	CWS	A	8	0	2
15	June 2/89	N	Junior Felix	RF	1	Bob Stanley	BOS	A	9	3	2
16	July 11/91	N	Rance Mulliniks	DH	5	Kevin Brown	TEX	H	8	0	2
17	June 1/92	N	Devon White	CF	1	Carl Willis	MIN	A	10	0	1
18	June 18/93	N	Roberto Alomar	2B	2	Tony Fossas	BOS	A	8	0	0
19	April 25/94	N	Paul Molitor	DH	3	David Cone	KC	A	1	0	2
20	June 17/95	D	Paul Molitor	DH	2	Kenny Rogers	TEX	H	5	0	2
21	July 28/98	N	Shannon Stewart	CF	3	Eric Gunderson	TEX	H	8	1	1
22	Sept. 7/98	D	Shannon Stewart	LF	1	Steve Karsay	CLE	H	3	2	2
23	Sept. 22/98	N	Tony Fernandez	3B	6	Mike Mussina	BAL	H	4	0	1

CONSECUTIVE GAME HOME RUNS

GEORGE BELL hit four home runs in four consecutive games (August 23, 24, 25, 26) in 1985 to set the club record. **JOE CARTER** hit five home runs in four consecutive games (June 20, 21, 22, 23) in 1991 to tie the record. **CARLOS DELGADO** hit four home runs in four consecutive games (June 3, 5, 6, 7) in 1997 to tie club record. In 1998 **SHAWN GREEN** hit four home runs in four consecutive games (April 5, 7, 8, 9) and **JOSE CANSECO** hit four home runs in four consecutive games (September 4, 5, 6, 7) to tie the club record. In 1999 **CARLOS DELGADO** hit five home runs in four consecutive games (August 8, 9, 10, 11) to tie the club mark and became the first Blue Jay to homer in four straight twice in his career.

The following players have hit home runs in three consecutive games.

Jesse Barfield	— May 19, 20, 21, 1985	Ron Fairly	— June 27, 28 (1st & 2nd game), 1977
	— April 30, May 1, 2, 1986	Brad Fullmer	— September 8, 9, 10, 2000
	— July 21, 22, 23, 1986	Shawn Green	— September 4, 5, 6, 1998
	— September 30, October 1, 3, 1986	Kelly Gruber	— July 13, 14, 15, 1989
	— August 21, 22, 23, 1988		— April 23, 24, 25, 1990
Tony Batista	— June 29, 30, July 1, 2000		— June 6, 7, 8, 1990
George Bell	— April 11, 12, 13, 1985	Cliff Johnson	— June 12, 13, 14, 1986
	— July 19, 20, 21, 1986	John Mayberry	— September 14, 16, 17, 1980
	— June 23, 24, 26, 1987	Fred McGriff	— August 22, 23, 24, 1988
	— July 21, 23, 24, 1988	Raul Mondesi	— July 7, 8, 9, 2000
Jacob Brumfield	— August 12, 13, 14, 1996	Lloyd Moseby	— July 2, 3, 4, 1982
Jose Canseco	— May 19, 20, 21, 1998		— July 29, 31, August 2, 1987
Joe Carter	— June 1, 2, 3, 1991	John Olerud	— May 30, 31, June 1, 1993
	— April 8, 9, 10, 1994	Doug Rader	— July 9, 10, 11, 1977
	— June 14, 15, 16, 1996	Ed Sprague	— May 30, 31, June 1 1993
Jose Cruz	— May 5, 6, 7, 2000		— June 21, 22, 26, 1996
	— August 26, 27, 28, 2000		— July 10, 11, 12, 1998
Carlos Delgado	— September 23, 25, 26, 1998	Shannon Stewart	— August 9, 10, 11, 2000
	— August 24, 25, 27, 1999	Ernie Whitt	— May 24, 25, 26, 1985
	— May 4, 5, 6, 2000		

BLUE JAYS ALL-TIME LONGEST HOMERLESS STRETCHES
ORGANIZED BY AT BATS:

ALFREDO GRIFFIN

DATES OF HOME RUNS	PITCHER	SPAN OF DROUGHT
July 30, 1980 vs. Oakland	Langford	255 Games, 956 At Bats
July 26, 1982 at Boston	Eckersly	

BOB BAILOR

DATES OF HOME RUNS	PITCHER	SPAN OF DROUGHT
May 7, 1978 at Seattle	Pole	228 Games, 845 At Bats
August 22, 1979 at Seattle	Honeycutt	

OTIS NIXON

DATES OF HOME RUNS	PITCHER	SPAN OF DROUGHT
April 16, 1996 vs. Detroit	Gohr	205 Games, 806 At Bats
August 1, 1997 at Detroit	Moehler	

MANNY LEE

DATES OF HOME RUNS	PITCHER	SPAN OF DROUGHT
June 17, 1990 at New York	Lapointe	245 Games, 804 At Bats
May 6, 1992 at Seattle	Acker	

GARTH IORG

DATES OF HOME RUNS	PITCHER	SPAN OF DROUGHT
August 2, 1980 vs. California	Laroche	240 Games, 771 At Bats
September 28, 1982 vs. Minnesota	Viola	

Extra-Inning Home Runs

HR #	DATE	D/N	BATTER	POS	BAT ORD	PITCHER	OPP	H/A	IN	ON	OUT
1	July 13/77	N	Doug Rader	3B	4	Jack Kucek	CWS	A	11	1	2
2	July 15/77	N	Bob Bailor	CF	3	Jim Crawford	DET	H	13	1	2
3	July 31/78	N	Otto Velez	RF	9	Bob Sykes	DET	H	14	0	1
4	Aug. 26/78	D	Dave McKay	2B	7	Geoff Zahn	MIN	H	10	0	0
5	July 4/79	N	Otto Velez	PH	9	Dave Tobik	DET	A	11	2	0
6	Aug. 31/79	D	Craig Kusick	1B	5	Byron McLaughlin	SEA	H	11	0	1
7	May 4/80	D	Otto Velez	DH	5	Sid Monge	CLE	H	10	0	0
8	Sept. 17/80	N	Roy Howell	3B	3	Tim Lollar	NYY	A	10	1	2
9	Sept. 19/80	N	Steve Braun	DH	5	Dennis Martinez	BAL	A	10	0	2
10	April 25/82	D	John Mayberry	1B	8	Mark Clear	BOS	H	12	0	2
11	Aug. 24/83	N	Cliff Johnson	DH	4	Tim Stoddard	BAL	A	10	0	0
12	Aug. 25/83	N	Barry Bonnell	RF	7	Tippy Martinez	BAL	A	10	0	2
13	Sept. 2/83	N	Ernie Whitt	C	6	Aurelio Lopez	DET	H	10	0	0
14	Sept. 4/83	D	Ernie Whitt	C	6	Aurelio Lopez	DET	H	10	2	2
15	May 10/84	N	Willie Upshaw	1B	6	Dennis Martinez	BAL	A	10	0	2
16	April 11/85	N	George Bell	LF	3	Dan Quisenberry	KC	A	10	0	0
17	April 11/85	N	Jesse Barfield	RF	5	Dave Stewart	TEX	H	10	2	0
18	June 6/85	N	Buck Martinez	C	7	Aurelio Lopez	DET	H	12	1	1
19	June 12/85	N	Rance Mulliniks	PH	8	Rich Bordi	NYY	A	10	0	0
20	July 9/85	N	George Bell	3B	4	Ed Vande Berg	SEA	A	13	3	1
21	July 29/85	N	Damaso Garcia	2B	1	Mike Boddicker	BAL	A	10	0	1
22	Aug. 11/85	D	Al Oliver	DH	3	Joe Beckwith	KC	A	10	0	0
23	Aug. 11/85	D	Garth Iorg	2B	6	Joe Beckwith	KC	A	10	0	2
24	May 10/86	N	Lloyd Moseby	CF	2	Peter Ladd	SEA	A	11	0	2
25	June 21/86	D	Cliff Johnson	DH	3	Alfonso Pulido	NYY	H	10	0	1
26	July 20/86	D	George Bell	LF	4	Donnie Moore	CAL	A	10	2	1
27	Aug. 17/86	D	Ernie Whitt	C	9	Jeff Russell	TEX	H	11	0	0
28	Aug. 27/86	N	Ernie Whitt	C	7	Bryan Oelkers	CLE	A	12	0	0
29	Sept. 26/86	N	Jesse Barfield	RF	5	Calvin Schiraldi	BOS	A	12	0	0
30	April 24/87	N	George Bell	LF	4	Bob James	CWS	A	10	1	1
31	May 1/87	N	Jesse Barfield	RF	5	Mitch Williams	TEX	H	10	0	0
32	June 6/87	D	Jesse Barfield	RF	3	Ken Dixon	BAL	H	11	2	2
33	Aug. 4/87	N	Cecil Fielder	PH	7	Dennis Powell	SEA	H	10	0	0
34	July 3/88	D	Tony Fernandez	SS	1	Greg Cadaret	OAK	H	12	1	0
35	Sept. 5/88	N	Ernie Whitt	C	5	G. Hernandez	DET	A	10	0	0
36	May 28/89	D	George Bell	LF	4	Bobby Thigpen	CWS	H	10	1	0
37	June 4/89	N	Junior Felix	RF	1	Dennis Lamp	BOS	A	12	1	1
38	June 22/89	N	Fred McGriff	1B	5	Brian Snyder	OAK	A	13	0	1
39	May 14/90	D	Fred McGriff	1B	5	Jerry Gleaton	DET	A	10	2	1
40	May 25/90	N	Fred McGriff	1B	5	Bill Swift	SEA	A	11	1	0
41	June 22/90	N	George Bell	LF	4	Dave Righetti	NYY	H	15	0	0
42	April 12/91	N	Mark Whiten	RF	8	Dan Plesac	MIL	H	11	0	0
43	May 10/91	N	Roberto Alomar	2B	2	Scott Radinsky	CWS	H	11	0	1
44	July 6/91	N	John Olerud	1B	5	Russ Swan	SEA	A	10	0	1
45	Sept.24/91	N	Pat Borders	C	8	Jim Abbott	CAL	A	10	2	1
46	Oct. 6/91	D	Rob Ducey	LF	6	Allan Anderson	MIN	A	10	0	1
47	June 1/92	N	Devon White	CF	1	Carl Willis	MIN	A	10	0	1
48	Sept. 17/92	N	John Olerud	1B	5	Eric Plunk	CLE	H	10	1	1
49	Aug. 11/94	D	Joe Carter	RF	4	Steve Howe	NYY	A	12	0	1
50	Aug. 11/94	D	Ed Sprague	3B	8	Joe Ausanio	NYY	A	13	0	0
51	Aug. 3/95	N	Ed Sprague	1B	5	Mike Oquist	BAL	A	10	1	2
52	June 1/96	D	Joe Carter	1B	3	Jeff Montgomery	KC	A	10	1	2
53	Aug. 20/96	N	Carlos Delgado	DH	8	Mark Huisman	KC	A	13	0	2
54	Aug. 20/96	N	Alex Gonzalez	SS	8	Mark Huisman	KC	A	14	0	0
55	Aug. 24/97	N	Jose Cruz	LF	3	Larry Casian	KC	A	13	1	1
56	May 12/98	N	Jose Canseco	DH	3	Billy Taylor	OAK	H	10	0	0
57	June 10/98	N	Jose Canseco	LF	3	Jay Powell	FLA	A	10	0	1
58	Aug. 15/98	N	Kevin Brown	C	7	Mike Fetters	ANA	H	11	0	2
59	June 30/99	N	Darrin Fletcher	C	6	Jesse Orosco	BAL	H	10	2	1
60	July 9/99	N	Tony Batista	SS	7	John Hudek	ATL	H	11	1	0
61	July 26/99	N	Tony Batista	SS	6	Bob Howry	CWS	A	11	0	2
62	Sept. 14/00	N	Jose Cruz	CF	7	Randy Choate	NYY	A	11	1	2

Most Home Runs in a Month

MONTH	TEAM HIGH	INDIVIDUAL HIGH
April	43-2000	Joe Carter, 9—1994
		Ed Sprague, 9—1996
		Shawn Green, 9—1999
May	43-2000	George Bell, 11—1987
June	48-2000	George Bell, 11—1987
		Joe Carter, 11—1991
July	44-2000	Shawn Green, 11—1999
August	43-2000	Carlos Delgado, 12—1999
Sept./Oct.	44-1998	Carlos Delgado, 11—1998

Home Run Trios, One Season

TOTAL	YEAR	PLAYERS
119	1998	Canseco-46, Delgado-38, Green-35
114	2000	Batista-41, Delgado-41, Fullmer-32
112	1999	Delgado-44, Green-42, Batista-26
101	1987	Bell-47, Barfield-28, Moseby-26
92	1986	Barfield-40, Bell-31, Moseby-21
91	1996	Sprague-36, Carter-30, Delgado-25
87	1990	McGriff-35, Gruber-31, Bell-21
80	1992	Carter-34, Winfield-26, Maldonado-20
79	1993	Carter-33, Olerud-24, Molitor-22

Home Run Duos, One Season

TOTAL	YEAR	PLAYERS
86	1999	Delgado-44, Green-42
84	1998	Canseco-46, Delgado-38
82	2000	Batista-41, Delgado-41
75	1987	Bell-47, Barfield-28
71	1986	Barfield-40, Bell-31
66	1990	McGriff-35, Gruber-31
66	1996	Sprague-36, Carter-30

Most Players 10 or More Home Runs

9—	1983-	Barfield, Bonnell, Johnson, Martinez, Moseby, Mulliniks, Orta, Upshaw, Whitt
	1987-	Barfield, Bell, Fielder, Gruber, McGriff, Moseby, Mulliniks, Upshaw, Whitt
8—	1996-	Brumfield, Carter, Delgado, Gonzalez, Green, O'Brien, Olerud, Sprague
	1998-	Canseco, Cruz, Delgado, Gonzalez, Green, Sprague, Stanley, Stewart
	2000-	Batista, Cruz, Delgado, Fletcher, Fullmer, Gonzalez, Mondesi, Stewart
7—	1984-	Aikens, Barfield, Bell, Johnson, Moseby, Upshaw, Whitt
	1985-	Barfield, Bell, Johnson, Moseby, Mulliniks, Upshaw, Whitt
	1986-	Barfield, Bell, Fernandez, Johnson, Moseby, Mulliniks, Whitt
	1988-	Barfield, Bell, Gruber, McGriff, Moseby, Mulliniks, White
	1990-	Bell, Borders, Felix, Gruber, Hill, McGriff, Olerud
	1992-	Borders, Carter, Gruber, Maldonado, Olerud, White, Winfield
	1995-	Alomar, Carter, Gonzalez, Green, Molitor, Sprague, White
	1999-	Batista, Cruz, Delgado, Fletcher, Green, Greene, Stewart

Grand Slam Home Runs

DATE	PLAYER	H/A	OPPONENT
June 27, 1977	Hector Torres	H	Off Ron Guidry, New York (5th inning)
May 7, 1978	Rick Bosetti	A	Off Enrique Romo, Seattle (8th inning)
July 31, 1978	Rico Carty	H	Off Jack Billingham, Detroit (1st inning)
July 3, 1979	Roy Howell	A	Off Jack Billingham, Detroit (1st inning)
August 27, 1979	Roy Howell	H	Off Craig Minetto, Oakland (6th inning)
Sept. 7, 1979	Rico Carty	A	Off Rick Waits, Cleveland (5th inning)
April 26, 1980	Barry Bonnell	A	Off Mike Caldwell, Milwaukee (9th inning)
May 4, 1980 (1st g.)	Otto Velez	H	Off Dan Spillner, Cleveland (1st inning)
April 24, 1982	Jesse Barfield	H	Off Tom Burgmeier, Boston (8th inning)
May 1, 1983	Barry Bonnell	H	Off Dick Tidrow, Chicago (7th inning)
June 5, 1983	Buck Martinez	A	Off Tim Stoddard, Baltimore (6th inning)
Sept. 11, 1983	Willie Upshaw	H	Off Chris Codiroli, Oakland (1st inning)
April 20, 1984	Lloyd Moseby	H	Off Mike Witt, California (6th inning)
June 23, 1985	Ernie Whitt	H	Off Bruce Kison, Boston (6th inning)
July 9, 1985	George Bell	A	Off Ed Vande Berg, Seattle (13th inning)
August 2, 1985	George Bell	H	Off Glen Cook, Texas (4th inning)
May 22, 1986	Ernie Whitt	A	Off Richard Dotson, Chicago (4th inning)
June 20, 1986	George Bell	H	Off Dave Righetti, New York (5th inning)
August 31, 1986	Lloyd Moseby	H	Off Mark Portugal, Minnesota (3rd inning)
June 11, 1987	George Bell	A	Off John Habyan, Baltimore (5th inning)
June 23, 1987	Willie Upshaw	A	Off Jeff Robinson, Detroit (4th inning)
August 27, 1987	George Bell	H	Off Greg Cadaret, Oakland (5th inning)
April 19, 1988	Jesse Barfield	H	Off Bret Saberhagen, Kansas City (3rd inning)
Sept. 4, 1988	George Bell	H	Off Mitch Williams, Texas (9th inning)
Sept. 13, 1988	Jesse Barfield	H	Off Paul Gibson, Detroit (7th inning)
April 7, 1989	Tony Fernandez	A	Off Bobby Witt, Texas, (2nd inning)
May 2, 1989	Rance Mulliniks	H	Off Bob Welch, Oakland, (1st inning)
June 2, 1989	Junior Felix	A	Off Bob Stanley, Boston, (9th inning)
June 4, 1989	Ernie Whitt	A	Off Lee Smith, Boston (9th inning)
July 7, 1989	Pat Borders	A	Off Guillermo Hernandez, Detroit, (8th inning)
July 21, 1989	Fred McGriff	A	Off Gene Harris, Seattle, (3rd inning)
July 22, 1989	Lloyd Moseby	A	Off Dennis Powell, Seattle, (9th inning)
Sept. 1, 1989	Glenallen Hill	H	Off Mark Guthrie, Minnesota, (4th inning)
April 11, 1990	George Bell	H	Off Kevin Brown, Texas (3rd inning)
August 14, 1990	Glenallen Hill	A	Off Adam Peterson, Chicago, (7th inning)
Sept. 11, 1990	Tony Fernandez	A	Off Mel Stottlemyre, Kansas City, (2nd inning)
Sept. 29, 1990	Kelly Gruber	A	Off Dennis Lamp, Boston, (9th inning)
May 7, 1992	Dave Winfield	A	Off Mike Schooler, Seattle (9th inning)
Sept. 1, 1992	Kelly Gruber	H	Off Don Pall, Chicago (7th inning)
June 8, 1993	Joe Carter	H	Off Darryl Scott, California (5th Inning)
August 29, 1993	Robbie Alomar	A	Off Erik Hanson, Seattle (3rd Inning)

DATE	PLAYER	H/A	OPPONENT
May 28, 1994	Dick Schofield	H	Off Mark Langston (2nd inning)
July 5, 1994	Paul Molitor	A	Off Dave Stevens, Minnesota(7th inning)
April 27, 1995	Ed Sprague	H	Off Ron Darling, Oakland (4th inning)
July 16, 1995	John Olerud	A	Off Rafael Carmona, Seattle (4th inning)
July 21, 1995	Ed Sprague	H	Off Salamon Torres, Seattle (3rd inning)
August 25, 1995	Devon White	H	Off Kirk McCaskill, Chicago (8th inning)
April 22, 1996	Joe Carter	A	Off Tim Davis, Seattle (5th inning)
May 27, 1996	John Olerud	H	Off Alex Fernandez, Chicago (3rd inning)
July 3, 1996	Ed Sprague	H	Off Rick Krivda, Baltimore (5th inning)
April 25, 1997	Carlos Delgado	H	Off Dennis Martinez, Seattle (1st inning)
May 14, 1997	Carlie O'Brien	A	Off Mike Myers, Detroit (8th inning)
June 6, 1997	Carlos Delgado	H	Off Mike Oquist, Oakland (1st inning)
July 10, 1997	Joe Carter	A	Off Tom Gordon, Boston (5th inning)
July 23, 1997	Joe Carter	H	Off Joel Adamson, Milwaukee (4th inning)
July 24, 1997	Carlos Delgado	H	Off Jose Mercedes, Milwaukee (1st inning)
August 11, 1997	Benito Santiago	H	Off Mike Myers, Detroit (8th inning)
May 7, 1998	Carlos Delgado	A	Off Jamie Moyer, Seattle (3rd inning)
July 17, 1998	Shawn Green	H	Off Mike Stanton, New York (A) (7th inning)
July 19, 1998	Jose Canseco	H	Off Andy Pettitte, New York (A) (3rd inning)
August 12, 1998	Carlos Delgado	H	Off Greg McCarthy, Seattle (7th inning)
July 19, 1999	Shawn Green	H	Off Bruce Chen, Atlanta (3rd inning)
July 20, 1999	Darrin Fletcher	H	Off Mike Remlinger, Atlanta (6th inning)
Oct. 3, 1999	Tony Batista	A	Off Mike Jackson, Cleveland (8th inning)
April 17, 2000	Brad Fullmer	H	Off Lou Pote, Anaheim (8th inning)
April 20, 2000	Darrin Fletcher	H	Off Kent Mercker, Anaheim (4th inning)
May 8, 2000	Darrin Fletcher	H	Off Jason Johnson, Baltimore (4th inning)
May 26, 2000	Darrin Fletcher	A	Off Doug Brocail, Detroit (8th inning)
June 7, 2000	Carlos Delgado	A	Off Kevin Millwood, Atlanta (5th inning)
June 11, 2000	Tony Batista	H	Off Felipe Lira, Montreal (8th inning)
July 3, 2000	Tony Batista	A	Off Jason Johnson, Baltimore (3rd inning)
July 16, 2000	Marty Cordova	H	Off Al Leiter, New York (N) (6th inning)
Sept. 17, 2000	Carlos Delgado	A	Off Jesus Pena, Chicago (6th inning)

GRAND SLAM LEADERS

The Blue Jays have hit 73 grand slams in franchise history... 17 were hit at Exhibition Stadium, 31 on the road, 25 at SkyDome... the club has never hit two slams in a game... there has been one pinch-slam in Blue Jays history, Jesse Barfield, April 24, 1982 vs Boston.

CAREER RECORD			SEASON RECORD				CLUB RECORD		
George Bell	7		Carlos Delgado	3	1997		9		2000
Carlos Delgado	7		Darrin Fletcher	3	2000		8		1989
Joe Carter	4		Joe Carter	2	1997		7		1997
Darrin Fletcher	4		Roy Howell	2	1979		4		1990
Jesse Barfield	3		George Bell	2	1985		4		1995
Lloyd Moseby	3		George Bell	2	1987		4		1998
Ernie Whitt	3		Jesse Barfield	2	1988				
Ed Sprague	3		Ed Sprague	2	1995				
Tony Batista	3		Carlos Delgado	2	1998				
Roy Howell	2		Tony Batista	2	2000				
Rico Carty	2		Carlos Delgado	2	2000				
Willie Upshaw	2								
Barry Bonnell	2								
Kelly Gruber	2								
Tony Fernandez	2								
John Olerud	2								
Shawn Green	2								

200 HOME RUNS

In the 2000 season, the Blue Jays hit a club record 244 home runs which led the AL league... It was the fourth time in franchise history to surpass the 200 mark and the third consecutive season to do so... Hit 215 home runs in 1987, 221 in 1998 and 212 in 1999... The Major League record for home runs in a season was set in 1997 when the Seattle Mariners hit 264, surpassing the previous mark of 257 set by the 1996 Baltimore Orioles... The National record for home runs was set by the 2000 Houston Astros after they hit 249 to surpass the previous mark of 239 set by the 1997 Colorado Rockies... When the Blue Jays hit 200 home runs for the first time in 1987, only the 1967 New York Yankees (240), 1987 Detroit Tigers (225), 1963 Minnesota Twins (225), 1964 Minnesota Twins (221) and the 1982 Milwaukee Brewers (216) had hit more home runs in the AL.

BLUE JAYS' HOME RUN RECORDS BY POSITION

POSITION	PLAYER	HR	YEAR	POSITION	PLAYER	HR	YEAR
1B	Carlos Delgado	41	2000	CF	Jose Cruz	31	2000
2B	Roberto Alomar	17	1993	RF	Shawn Green	42	1999
3B	Tony Batista	41	2000	C	Ernie Whitt	19	1985 & 1987
SS	Tony Batista	26	1999		Darrin Fletcher	19	2000
LF	George Bell	45	1987	DH	Brad Fullmer	32	2000

Home Runs

HOME RUNS SKYDOME

REGULAR SEASON

TEAM TOTALS

Blue Jays	1015
Opponents	913
Indians	87
Tigers	88
Orioles	76
Red Sox	73
Mariners	82
Athletics	77
Brewers	58
Yankees	64
Royals	58
White Sox	55
Rangers	52
Angels	55
Twins	38
Devil Rays	14
Expos	10
Mets	11
Marlins	4
Phillies	8
Braves	3
TOTAL	**1928**

LEADING BLUE JAYS

1.	Joe Carter	121
2.	Carlos Delgado	103
3.	Shawn Green	63
4.	Ed Sprague	58
5.	John Olerud	47
6.	Kelly Gruber	44
7.	Devon White	35
8.	Tony Batista	34
9.	Jose Cruz	31
10.	Roberto Alomar	30
	Pat Borders	30
12.	Alex Gonzalez	28
	Fred McGriff	28
13.	Paul Molitor	27
14.	Jose Canseco	25
15.	Darrin Fletcher	23

LEADING OPPONENTS

1.	Jose Canseco	18
2.	Cecil Fielder	16
3.	Albert Belle	14
	Ken Griffey Jr.	14
5.	Alex Rodriguez	13
6.	Juan Gonzalez	11
7.	Edgar Martinez	10
	Paul Sorrento	10
	Frank Thomas	10
10.	Brady Anderson	9
	Jay Buhner	9
	Tony Clark	9
	Mark McGwire	9
	Cal Ripken	9
	Mike Stanley	9
	Mo Vaughn	9

MOST ONE SEASON

	#	BLUE JAYS	#	OPPONENT
Club	134	2000	102	1996
Individual	30	Delgado, 2000	5	Canseco, 1991
				Anderson, 1996

OVERALL CAREER HOME RUNS AT SKYDOME

(At least one with Jays and one vs. Jays)

Carter	123	Molitor	32	Hill, G	17	Parrish	6	Segui	3
Olerud	48	McGriff	31	Henderson, R	7	Grebeck	5	Martinez, D	2
Gruber, K	45	Stanley	20	Kelly, P	7	Merced	4	Moseby	2
Canseco	43	Maldonado	19	Cordova, M	6	Sierra	4		
White	36	Winfield	18	Jackson, D	6	Whiten	4		
Alomar	33	Fullmer, B	17	McRae, B	6	Bell, De	3		

POST SEASON AT SKYDOME

BLUE JAYS

Bell	1	Gruber	2	Moseby	1	White	1
Borders	2	Maldonado	1	Olerud	1	Winfield	1
Carter	5	Molitor	1	Olerud	1		

FIVE OR MORE HOME RUN GAMES

DATE	OPP.	NO.	PITCHER	HITTER
Sept. 17, 1983 vs MINNESOTA		5	PETTIBONE	MULLINIKS
			PETTIBONE	WHITT
			O'CONNOR	BARFIELD
			WALTERS	UPSHAW
			WALTERS	JOHNSON
July 10, 1985 at SEATTLE		5	WILLIS	MULLINIKS
			WILLIS	MOSEBY
			WILLIS	BARFIELD
			SNYDER	OLIVER
			SNYDER	BELL
May 22, 1987 at SEATTLE		5	BANKHEAD	BELL
			BANKHEAD	BELL
			BANKHEAD	MOSEBY
			BANKHEAD	GRUBER
			REED	GRUBER
Aug. 30, 1987 vs OAKLAND		5	RIJO	BARFIELD
			RIJO	BELL
			RIJO	WHITT
			LEIPER	LIRIANO
			LAMP	BELL
Sept. 12, 1987 vs NEW YORK		5	RHODEN	MULLINIKS
			RHODEN	WHITT
			FULTON	WHITT
			FULTON	BARFIELD
			FULTON	GRUBER

DATE	OPP.	NO.	PITCHER	HITTER
Sept. 14, 1987 vs BALTIMORE		10	DIXON	WHITT
			DIXON	MULLINIKS
			DIXON	MOSEBY
			BELL	BELL
			BELL	MULLINIKS
			GRIFFIN	WHITT
			KINNUNEN	BELL
			KINNUNEN	MOSEBY
			ARNOLD	WHITT
			ARNOLD	McGRIFF
May 23, 1988 at MILWAUKEE		5	HIGUERA	FERNANDEZ
			JONES	McGRIFF
			CLEAR	BORDERS
			CLEAR	MULLINIKS
			CRIM	BELL
April 20, 1990 vs KANSAS CITY		5	SABERHAGEN	BELL
			McWILLIAMS	McGRIFF
			AQUINO	GRUBER
			AQUINO	MYERS
			CRAWFORD	LIRIANO
May 6, 1990 vs DETROIT		5	DUBOIS	BORDERS
			DUBOIS	LEE
			LUGO	GRUBER
			LUGO	McGRIFF
			LUGO	GRUBER

DATE	OPP.	NO.	PITCHER	HITTER
May 16, 1993 at NEW YORK		5	WITT	MOLITOR
			WITT	CARTER
			WITT	WHITE
			KAMIENIECKI	OLERUD
			HEATON	CARTER
May 31, 1993 at CALIFORNIA		5	FARRELL	OLERUD
			FARRELL	OLERUD
			FARRELL	BORDERS
			FARRELL	ALOMAR
			GRAHE	SPRAGUE
July 5, 1994 at MINNESOTA		6	MAHOMES	COLES
			STEVENS	MOLITOR
			STEVENS	CARTER
			CASIAN	COLES
			CASIAN	KNORR
			CASIAN	COLES
July 6, 1996 at DETROIT		6	OLIVARES	SPRAGUE
			OLIVARES	DELGADO
			OLIVARES	CARTER
			KEAGLE	GREEN
			KEAGLE	DELGADO
			WALKER	OLERUD
July 13, 1996 at MILWAUKEE		5	KARL	R. PEREZ
			KARL	SPRAGUE
			KARL	R. PEREZ
			SPARKS	CARTER
			SPARKS	O'BRIEN
Aug. 19, 1998 at SEATTLE		7	CLOUDE	CRUZ JR.
			CLOUDE	FLETCHER
			CLOUDE	GREEN
			CLOUDE	DELGADO
			WELLS	GREEN
			AYALA	DELGADO
			McCARTHY	CRESPO

DATE	OPP.	NO.	PITCHER	HITTER
April 30, 1999 at SEATTLE		5	FASSERO	GREEN
			FASSERO	DELGADO
			FASSERO	CRUZ
			FASSERO	BERROA
			HALAMA	DELGADO
June 21, 1999 vs KANSAS CITY		5	FUSSELL	BUSH
			FUSSELL	GREEN
			FUSSELL	FERNANDEZ
			BYRDAK	GREEN
			MONTGOMERY	BATISTA
July 8, 1999 at BALTIMORE		6	PONSON	OTANEZ
			PONSON	DELGADO
			PONSON	BATISTA
			COPPINGER	OTANEZ
			COPPINGER	BATISTA
			COPPINGER	STEWART
Aug. 10, 1999 at MINNESOTA		5	RADKE	STEWART
			RADKE	FLETCHER
			RADKE	DELGADO
			RADKE	BUSH
			MILLER	DELGADO
May 5, 2000 vs CLEVELAND		5	NAGY	FLETCHER
			NAGY	MONDESI
			NAGY	DELGADO
			MARTIN	CRUZ
			SHUEY	GONZALEZ
Aug. 27, 2000 at TEXAS		5	HELLING	FLETCHER
			HELLING	STEWART
			HELLING	FLETCHER
			HELLING	FLETCHER
			HELLING	CRUZ

MOST HOME RUNS IN A SEASON SERIES

(six or more)

YEAR	NAME	OPPOSING TEAM	HOMERS
1980	John Mayberry	New York	8
	John Mayberry	Seattle	6
	Otto Velez	Cleveland	7
1982	Willie Upshaw	Cleveland	6
1983	Willie Upshaw	Minnesota	6
	Ernie Whitt	Detroit	6
1986	Jessie Barfield	Detroit	7
	Jessie Barfield	New York	6
	Jessie Barfield	Seattle	6
1987	George Bell	Seattle	7
	George Bell	Baltimore	6
	George Bell	Oakland	6
	Ernie Whitt	Baltimore	6

YEAR	NAME	OPPOSING TEAM	HOMERS
1989	Fred McGriff	Seattle	6
	Fred McGriff	New York	6
1990	Kelly Gruber	Cleveland	7
1991	Joe Carter	Boston	6
1992	Joe Carter	Milwaukee	6
1993	Joe Carter	Cleveland	7
	Roberto Alomar	California	6
1998	Shawn Green	Minnesota	7
	Jose Canseco	Boston	6
	Jose Canseco	Tampa Bay	6
1999	Carlos Delgado	Texas	7
2000	Tony Batista	Baltimore	9
	Shannon Stewart	Kansas City	6

CONSECUTIVE GAMES WITH AT LEAST ONE HOME RUN–TEAM

(Minimum 10 games)

GAMES	DATE	NUMBER OF HOME RUNS
23	May 31-June 25, 2000	44
15	July 6-23, 2000	28
14	April 18-May 4, 1996	28
13	May 19-June 2, 1985	17
13	September 1-15, 1999	22
12	June 2-14, 1987	25
12	April 11-23, 2000	29
12	May 1-13, 2000	29

GAMES	DATE	NUMBER OF HOME RUNS
11	June 19-30, 1986	21
11	May 6-17, 1993	22
11	May 2-14, 1995	20
11	September 16-27, 1998	19
11	April 11-22, 1999	17
10	July 31-August 11, 1984	12
10	May 29-June 8, 1993	22
10	June 9-19, 1996	14

Home Runs

BLUE JAYS HOME RUN TRIVIA

PLAYER WHO HOMERED IN THEIR FINAL MAJOR LEAGUE AT BAT

WILLIE AIKENS, April 27, 1985... he came to bat for last time, pinch-hitting at Texas in the ninth inning. Batting for Tony Fernandez against Tommy Boggs, Aikens crashed a dramatic game-tying, two-run homer and Toronto went on to win 9-8. Three days later, Aikens was "designated for assignment" winding up in the minor leagues.

DESIGNATED HITTER

As a designated hitter, **BRAD FULLMER** hit 32 home runs in 2000 to surpass the club mark of 25 home runs by a DH set in 1998 by **JOSE CANSECO**. Prior to 1998 the most home runs hit by a Blue Jays DH was 23 set by **DAVE WINFIELD** in 1992.

MOST PLAYERS WITH 10 OR MORE HOME RUNS

Both the 1983 and 1987 Blue Jays tied the Major League record with nine players hitting 10 or more home runs.

TWO IN ONE INNING, BATTER

JOE CARTER is the only Blue Jay to hit two home runs in one inning. He had his two on October 3, 1993 at Baltimore in the 2nd inning.

SWITCH HITTING HOME RUNS IN ONE GAME, BATTER

ROBERTO ALOMAR hit home runs from the both sides of the plate in the same game twice. He accomplished the feat, both at SkyDome. May 10, 1991 vs Chicago White Sox and May 3, 1995 vs Chicago White Sox. **JOSE CRUZ** was the last Blue Jay to do it, August 24, 1997 at Kansas City.

40 HOME RUN SEASONS

In 1999 **CARLOS DELGADO** with 44 home runs and **SHAWN GREEN** with 42 home runs, became the first Blue Jays tandem to each hit 40 or more home runs in the same season. In 2000, the Blue Jays again had two players, **CARLOS DELGADO** and **TONY BATISTA** each hit 41, hit 40 plus homers in a season. Overall the Blue Jays have had six players, done seven times, hit 40 or more home runs in a season as **JESSE BARFIELD** hit 40 in 1986, **GEORGE BELL** hit 47 in 1987 and **JOSE CANSECO** hit 46 in 1998. **CARLOS DELGADO** is the only Blue Jay player to twice hit 40 or more home runs in a season.

100 or MORE HOME RUNS FOR TWO or MORE TEAMS

JOE CARTER and **FRED McGRIFF** are two of the 29 players who have hit 100 or more home runs for two or more clubs. **CARTER** hit 203 home runs for the Blue Jays and previously hit 151 for the Cleveland Indians. **McGRIFF** hit 125 with the Blue Jays before hitting 130 with the Atlanta Braves.

HOME RUNS BY THE FIRST TWO BATTERS OF GAME

DEVON WHITE and **ROBERTO ALOMAR** on August 18, 1991 at Detroit accomplished this feat for the only time in Blue Jays history.

HOME RUN IN FIRST MAJOR LEAGUE AT BAT

AL WOODS as a pinch-hitter, on April 7, 1977 vs the Chicago White Sox at Exhibition Stadium in Toronto's first game ever.

JUNIOR FELIX, May 4, 1989 vs the California Angels at Exhibition Stadium.

HOMERING AT HOME

The 2000 Toronto Blue Jays set an AL record with 134 home runs hit at home. The 1970 Cleveland Indians set the previous mark when they hit 133 home runs at home. **TODD GREENE** homered in the 2nd inning of the Blue Jays final home game of the 2000 season to set the record.

MOST PLAYERS WITH 20 OR MORE HOME RUNS

The 2000 Toronto Blue Jays tied an AL record with seven players hitting 20 or more home runs in a season. The Baltimore Orioles set the AL record with seven players hitting 20 or more homers in the 1996 season.

MOST PLAYERS WITH 30 OR MORE HOME RUNS

The 2000 Blue Jays had four players hit 30 or more home runs, which tied the ML record. It was just the second time the feat had been accomplished in the AL as the Anaheim Angels also had four players hit 30 plus homers earlier in the 2000 season.

20 HOME RUNS AT THE ALL-STAR BREAK

The 2000 Blue Jays became the first team in ML history to have four players hit 20 or more home runs at the All-Star Break. **CARLOS DELGADO** hit 28, **TONY BATISTA** hit 24, **RAUL MONDESI** hit 22 and **JOSE CRUZ** hit 20.

20-PLUS HOME RUN SEASONS

7 Joe Carter 1991 (33), 1992 (34), 1993 (33), 1994 (27), 1995 (25), 1996 (30), 1997 (21)	2 Willie Upshaw 1982 (21), 1983 (27)	John Olerud 1993 (24)
6 George Bell 1984 (26), 1985 (28), 1986 (31), 1987 (47), 1988 (24), 1990 (21)	Lloyd Moseby 1986 (21), 1987 (26)	Paul Molitor 1993 (22)
5 Carlos Delgado 1996 (25), 1997 (30), 1998 (38), 1999 (44), 2000 (41)	Kelly Gruber 1990 (31), 1991 (20)	Ed Sprague 1996 (36)
	Shawn Green 1998 (35), 1999 (42)	Jose Canseco 1998 (46)
	Tony Batista 1999 (26), 2000 (41)	Mike Stanley 1998 (22)
4 Jesse Barfield 1983 (27), 1985 (27), 1986 (40), 1987 (28)	1 Rico Carty 1978 (20)	Brad Fullmer 2000 (32)
Fred McGriff 1987 (20), 1988 (34), 1989 (36), 1990 (35)	Otto Velez 1980 (20)	Jose Cruz 2000 (31)
	Cliff Johnson 1983 (22)	Raul Mondesi 2000 (24)
3 John Mayberry 1978 (22), 1979 (21), 1980 (30)	Candy Maldonado 1992 (20)	Shannon Stewart 2000 (21)
	Dave Winfield 1992 (26)	Darrin Fletcher 2000 (20)

BLUE JAYS HOME RUNS, FIRST MAJOR LEAGUE APPEARANCE

When AL WOODS batted for Steve Bowling in the 5th inning on April 7, 1977 he became the 11th player in major league history to hit a home run as a pinch hitter in his first at bat.

JUNIOR FELIX on May 4, 1989 became the 11th major leaguer to homer on his first major league pitch vs California's Kirk McCaskill (solo).

TEN HOME RUN GAME

The BLUE JAYS etched a page in the record book with a 10 HR performance against the Baltimore Orioles on September 14th, 1987. Following is a list of highlights from that game: In the 18-3 victory the BLUE JAYS received HR's from ERNIE WHITT (3), GEORGE BELL (2), RANCE MULLINIKS (2), FRED McGRIFF (1), ROB DUCEY (1) and LLOYD MOSEBY (1)... WHITT became the second BLUE JAYS player since Otto Velez on May 10, 1980 to hit three HR's in one game ... The clubs combined to hit 11 HR's in the game, to tie the Major League mark... RANCE MULLINIKS hit his 10th and 11th of the season, enabling

the BLUE JAYS to become the 12th team in major league history to have at least nine players with at least 10 HR's... A club mark with 53 total bases in the game was set... The club hit three HR's in the second inning, marking the third time in 1987 and seventh time in franchise history that the club had a three HR inning... ROB DUCEY hit his first Major League HR... Most players with two or more home runs, club, game was tied as three BLUE JAYS, Bell, Mulliniks and Whitt had multiple home run games. The 10 home runs surpassed the previous record of eight.

HOME RUN BREAKDOWN vs EACH CLUB

	HRS	
TORONTO vs	F	A
Anaheim	265	271
Baltimore	307	316
Boston	263	320
Chicago	238	223
Cleveland	310	284
Detroit	337	344
Kansas City	228	197
Milwaukee	213	216
Minnesota	257	183
New York (A)	268	278
Oakland	257	259
Seattle	273	280
Tampa Bay	47	36
Texas	270	246
Atlanta	21	10
Florida	11	8
Montreal	27	17
New York (N)	20	19
Philadelphia	16	12
Total	**3628**	**3519**

BACK-TO-BACK-TO-BACK HOME RUNS

The Blue Jays have hit three consecutive home runs **THREE** times in their twenty-four year history. The first time it happened was **April 26, 1984** vs Oakland at Exhibition Stadium. In the bottom of the sixth inning with one out Willie Upshaw had a solo home run to left on the first pitch. George Bell followed with another home run to left on a 3-2 count. Jesse Barfield completed the trio of home runs with one to right field on a 0-1 pitch. All three home runs came off RHP Mike Warren. Final score of the game was Oakland 7, Toronto 4. The next time was **September 12, 1987** vs the Yankees at Exhibition Stadium. With two out in the eighth inning Ernie Whitt hit a three run home run against Tom Fulton. That was followed by solo shots by Jesse Barfield and Kelly Gruber also against Fulton. The final score was Toronto 13, New York 1. The last time was on **April 18, 2000** vs the Anaheim Angels at SkyDome in the bottom of the sixth inning. Craig Grebeck took Angels' starter Jason Dickson deep to left field on a 2-1 pitch with one on and no outs. Raul Mondesi followed with a blast off Dickson to left center on a 1-0 pitch before Carlos Delgado took Dickson deep to left center on a 2-0 count to complete the trio. The Blue Jays eventually lost the game to the Angels 16-10.

SKYDOME 500 LEVEL HOMERUNS

Player	Date	Visiting Team	Pitcher	
Jose Canseco	October 7, 1989*	Oakland	Mike Flanagan	480 (LF)
Mark McGwire	July 25, 1996	Oakland	Huck Flener	488 (LF)
Joe Carter	July 27, 1996	Oakland	John Wasdin	483 (LF)
Carlos Delgado	July 19, 1998	New York (A)	Andy Pettitte	467 (RF)
Jose Canseco	Sept. 5, 1998	Boston	Bret Saberhagen	451 (LF)
Jose Canseco	April 12, 1999	Tampa Bay	Graeme Lloyd	459 (LF)
Shawn Green	April 22, 1999	Anaheim	Tim Belcher	449 (RF)

* Game 4 of the ALCS

Home Runs

OPPONENTS

YEAR-BY-YEAR

BATTING

	AVG.	AB	R	H	TB	1B	2B	3B	HR H-A-T	RBI	BB	SO	SH-SF	HP	SB-CS	LOB	SLUG
1977	.278	5524	822	1568	2361	1074	241	55	94-58-152	762	623	771	64-70	20	84-75	1184	.427
1978	.279	5488	775	1529	2371	1037	291	52	75-74-149	730	614	758	79-51	22	101-66	1192	.432
1979	.281	5469	862	1537	2408	1042	284	46	91-74-165	809	594	613	67-50	40	85-56	1107	.440
1980	.274	5567	762	1523	2240	1105	254	29	75-60-135	720	635	705	92-47	28	115-53	1209	.402
1981	.252	3602	466	908	1348	640	168	28	41-31-72	435	377	451	38-36	36	55-35	763	.374
1982	.257	5546	701	1428	2275	1011	234	36	75-72-147	657	493	776	46-31	25	78-46	1109	.410
1983	.259	5531	726	1434	2254	947	299	43	84-61-145	689	517	835	34-50	42	83-46	1112	.408
1984	.257	5574	696	1433	2185	1009	236	48	78-62-140	662	528	875	54-45	34	75-40	1147	.392
1985	.243	5406	588	1312	2029	917	220	28	78-69-147	558	484	823	47-41	26	83-44	1072	.375
1986	.261	5621	733	1467	2283	1008	266	29	89-75-164	691	487	1002	59-51	45	95-46	1103	.406
1987	.244	5426	655	1323	2145	857	268	40	83-75-158	620	567	1064	56-32	22	123-59	1086	.395
1988	.251	5484	680	1404	2151	977	250	34	73-70-143	632	528	904	61-37	59	120-55	142	.392
1989	.255	5513	651	1408	2056	997	273	39	50-49-99	610	478	849	61-62	45	115-54	1107	.373
1990	.260	5524	661	1434	2198	994	259	38	82-61-143	610	478	849	61-62	45	115-54	1107	.373
1991	.238	5470	622	1301	1925	941	217	22	72-49-121	582	523	971	53-45	43	118-53	1126	.352
1992	.248	5432	682	1346	2014	944	260	18	60-64-124	642	541	954	32-55	45	144-62	1104	.371
1993	.261	5527	742	1441	2145	1036	240	31	81-53-134	694	620	1023	38-52	32	136-64	1203	.388
1994	.266	3954	579	1053	1665	716	189	21	64-63-127	547	482	832	29-38	32	101-43	882	.421
1995	.268	4994	777	1336	2094	901	257	33	79-66-145	723	654	894	36-37	51	98-50	1118	.419
1996	.266	5544	809	1476	2366	980	289	20	102-85-187	760	610	1033	31-48	36	74-41	1125	.427
1997	.263	5527	694	1453	2281	984	277	25	72-95-167	650	497	1150	49-37	39	77-64	1127	.413
1998	.256	5632	768	1443	2351	907	333	34	77-92-169	737	587	1154	42-44	45	149-47	1189	.417
1999	.280	5644	862	1582	2546	1033	325	33	93-98-191	824	575	1009	39-57	53	124-53	1189	.451
2000	.285	5669	908	1615	2584	1059	338	23	92-103-195	862	560	978	44-40	64	99-38	1157	.456

PITCHING

	W-L	ERA	AP	RA	CG	SV	SHO	IP	H	R	ER	HR	BB	SO	HB	WP
1977	107-54	3.25	345	184	52	43	15	1452.0	1367	822	525	100	499	819	23	35
1978	102-59	3.31	340	179	59	33	19	1450.0	1358	590	534	98	448	645	23	32
1979	109-53	3.32	347	185	53	41	15	1444.0	1362	613	533	95	448	663	36	37
1980	95-67	3.39	343	181	54	34	12	1481.0	1398	624	558	126	448	813	33	37
1981	69-37	2.76	239	133	30	21	20	967.0	797	329	297	61	284	556	20	25
1982	84-78	3.61	397	235	39	37	9	1448.0	1447	651	581	106	415	749	28	43
1983	73-89	4.48	413	251	26	33	8	1437.1	1546	795	716	167	510	810	32	45
1984	73-89	4.08	426	263	26	28	4	1453.0	1555	750	659	143	460	816	52	47
1985	62-99	4.28	427	266	24	23	4	1427.0	1482	759	679	158	503	807	30	8
1986	76-86	4.40	480	317	19	38	6	1470.0	1540	809	718	181	496	848	33	46
1987	66-96	4.72	—	—	26	33	10	1441.1	1514	845	756	215	555	970	38	64
1988	75-87	4.19	—	—	23	39	3	1442.0	1491	763	671	158	521	935	31	61
1989	73-89	4.02	—	—	17	38	7	1461.0	1449	731	653	142	521	923	31	52
1990	76-86	4.42	—	—	18	46	10	1447.2	1479	767	711	167	526	970	28	73
1991	71-91	3.93	—	—	22	43	9	1449.2	1412	684	633	133	499	1043	58	55
1992	66-96	4.40	—	—	13	36	10	1428.1	1458	780	699	163	561	933	47	51
1993	67-95	4.86	—	—	19	36	1	1428.1	1556	847	771	159	588	861	52	56
1994	60-55	4.27	—	—	13	27	4	1025.1	1064	566	486	115	387	691	38	40
1995	88-56	4.08	—	—	12	33	10	1309.2	1309	642	593	140	492	906	44	46
1996	88-74	4.38	—	—	13	43	9	1453.1	1451	766	707	177	529	1105	92	45
1997	86-76	3.61	—	—	12	40	11	1447.1	1333	654	580	147	487	1138	59	60
1998	74-88	4.69	—	—	14	33	4	1458.0	1482	816	759	221	564	1132	87	58
1999	78-84	5.08	—	—	10	34	8	1436.2	1580	883	811	212	578	1077	76	50
2000	79-83	5.03	—	—	9	35	7	1437.2	1562	861	804	244	526	1026	60	50

BATTING vs BLUE JAYS

CAREER LEADERS—75AB

AVG.		HITS		HR		RBI	
WOCKENFUSS	.376	YOUNT	263	CANSECO	41	BAINES	130
O. PALMEIRO	.369	RIPKEN	235	BAINES	37	YOUNT	129
RAY	.361	BOGGS	235	RICE	34	RIPKEN	126
CORDERO	.357	MOLITOR	228	GRIFFEY, Jr.	34	CANSECO	114
EASLER	.356	BAINES	223	FIELDER	30	BRETT	113
JAMES	.350	WHITAKER	216	MURRAY	29	MURRAY	110
HISLE	.349	TRAMMELL	205	RIPKEN	29	RICE	100
OLIVER	.349	R. HENDERSON	200	BELLE	29	WHITAKER	99
JOYNER	.348	BRETT	200	PARRISH	25	MOLITOR	98
C. JOHNSON	.342	MATTINGLY	196	YOUNT	25	SURHOFF	94
ALMON	.342	MURRAY	186	DAVIS	24	BELLE	94
R. KELLY	.333			PALMEIRO	24	Dw. EVANS	93
STOCKER	.333			GRICH	23	R. PALMEIRO	89
BOGGS	.327			WINFIELD	23	WINFIELD	88
				M. VAUGHN	23	MATTINGLY	87
						FIELDER	84

PITCHING vs BLUE JAYS

CAREER LEADERS—50IP

IP		AP		W		L	
MOORE	264.0	OROSCO	58	FLANAGAN	17	MOORE	19
CLEMENS	256.0	ECKERSLEY	57	CLEMENS	17	LANGSTON	14
MORRIS	239.0	STANLEY	56	MORRIS	14	HOUGH	13
TANANA	236.0	MONTGOMERY	52	STANLEY	14	VIOLA	13
FLANAGAN	218.1	HONEYCUTT	51	MOORE	14	ERICKSON	12
HOUGH	199.1	RIGHETTI	49	McGREGOR	13	BODDICKER	12
D. MARTINEZ	187.2	HENNEMAN	46	D. MARTINEZ	13	MORRIS	12
BODDICKER	187.1	PLUNK	44	ECKERSLEY	12	TANANA	12
FINLEY	186.1	GORDON	43	GORDON	12	GUBICZA	12
LANGSTON	186.1	ROGERS	42	R. JOHNSON	12	DARWIN	11
VIOLA	180.2	T. MARTINEZ	42	PETTITTE	12	TERRELL	11
ECKERSLEY	175.1	CLEAR	42	WITT	12		
STANLEY	175.1	QUISENBERRY	42				
BANNISTER	172.1	FETTERS	40				
		MOORE	40				

SV		ERA	
REARDON	23	FERNANDEZ	1.80
QUISENBERRY	22	NORRIS	2.09
R. HERNANDEZ	21	MATLACK	2.29
ECKERSLEY	20	C. ELDRED	2.31
RIGHETTI	18	D. MARTINEZ	2.35
HENNEMAN	18	HOYT	2.36
MONTGOMERY	18	QUISENBERRY	2.36
JONES	15	AASE	2.39
WETTELAND	15	OLIVER	2.39
GOSSAGE	14	NEIKRO	2.42
OLSON	14	HONEYCUTT	2.45
MESA	12		
PLESAC	12		
THIGPEN	12		

THREE HOME RUN GAMES (11)

PLAYER	DATE	OPPONENT	PITCHERS
John Mayberry	June 1, 1977	Kansas City	Johnson, Willis, Bruno
Cliff Johnson	June 30, 1977	New York	Jerry Garvin
Eddie Murray	Sept. 14, 1980	Baltimore	Jackson Todd (2),Barlow
Jim Rice	Aug. 29, 1983 (2nd g)	Boston	Acker (2), Moffitt
Jose Canseco	July 3, 1988	Oakland	Stottlemyre (2), Henke
Cecil Fielder	May 6, 1990	Detroit	Key (2), Wells
Tom Brunansky	Sept. 29, 1990	@ Boston	Stottlemyre, Ward, Leucken
Cecil Fielder	April 16, 1996	Detroit	Hanson, Carrara, Risley
Ken Griffey, Jr.	April 25, 1997	Seattle	Clemens (2), Timlin
Manny Ramirez	Sept. 15, 1998	@ Cleveland	Stieb (2), Quantrill
Alex Rodriguez	April 16, 2000	Seattle	Carpenter (2), Borbon

FIVE HIT GAMES BY OPPONENTS

June 1/77   Al Cowens, Kansas City (H) (5 for 5, 2 runs; 3-1B; 1-2B; 1-3B; 1RBI)
June 1/80   Eric Soderholm, New York (A) (5 for 5, 2 runs; 4-1B; 1-3B; 2RBI)
Sept. 29/80 Alan Trammell, Detroit (A) (5 for 6, 1 run; 3-1B; 2-2B; 1RBI)
Oct. 4/80   Dwight Evans, Boston (A) (5 for 7, 2 runs; 1-1B; 3-2B; 1-HR; 1RBI)
May 11/81   Rick Miller, Boston (H) (5 for 5, 3 runs; 1-1B; 4-2B; 1RBI)
June 3/81   Rick Burleson, California (H) (5 for 5, 2 runs; 4-1B; 1-2B, 3RBI)
July 31/83   Toby Harrah, Cleveland (H) (5 for 5, 1 run, 3-1B; 2-2B, 3RBI)
Sept. 16/83 Tim Teufel, Minnesota (A) (5 for 5 runs; 2-1B; 1-3B; 2-HR; 3RBI)
June 2/84   Don Mattingly, New York (H) (5 for 6, 1 run; 5-1B; 1RBI)
April 11/88 Rickey Henderson, New York (H) (5 for 5, 4 runs; 3-1B; 2-2B; 1RBI)
April 12/88 Don Mattingly, New York (H) (5 for 6, no runs; 5-1B; 2-2B; 1RBI)
June 12/89   Mike Heath, Detroit (H) (5 for 6, no runs; 5-1B; 2RBI)
July 2/89   Kevin Romine, Boston (H) (5 for 5, 2 runs; 3-1B; 2-2B)
June 6/90   Kirby Puckett, Minnesota (H) (5 for 5, 3 runs, 4-1B; 1-2B, 1RBI)
June 11/91   Luis Polonia, California (H) (5 for 6, 3 runs, 1-1B, 4-2B, 1RBI)
June 15/91   Bob Melvin, Baltimore (H) (5 for 5, 2 runs, 3-1B; 1-2B, 1-HR; 2RBI)
Aug. 28/92   Kevin Seitzer, Milwaukee (H) (5 for 7, 4 runs, 4-1B, 1-2B, 3RBI)
Aug. 28/92   Scott Fletcher, Milwaukee (H) (5 for 6, 3 runs, 5-1B, 5RBI)
Aug. 27/96   Paul Molitor, Minnesota (H) (5 for 5, 5-1B, 1RBI)
May 5/00   Einar Diaz, Cleveland (H) (5 for 5, 2-1B, 3-2B, 2RBI)
Sept. 4/00   Mike Stanley, Oakland (H) (5 for 5, 3-1B, 1-2B, 1-HR, 5RBI)

INSIDE-THE-PARK HOME RUNS (20)

DATE	PLAYER	H/A	OPPONENT
July 25, 1977	Ron Leflore	A	Detroit
April 2, 1979	Amos Otis	A	Kansas City
May 8, 1979	Ken Landreaux	A	Minnesota
June 10, 1979	Jim Essian	A	Oakland
July 23, 1979	Alan Bannister	H	Chicago
Aug. 15, 1980	George Brett	A	Kansas City
Aug. 20, 1980	Mike Cubbage	A	Minnesota
June 9, 1981	Wayne Nordhagen	A	Chicago
July 21, 1982	Willie Wilson	A	Kansas City
Sept. 30, 1982	Kent Hrbek	H	Minnesota

DATE	PLAYER	H/A	OPPONENT
May 25, 1983	Kirk Gibson	H	Detroit
Sept. 27, 1983	Gary Pettis	A	California
July 4, 1984	Rob Picciolo	H	California
Oct. 2, 1985	Kirk Gibson	A	Detroit
April 7, 1988	Kurt Stillwell	A	Kansas City
May 27, 1988	Ivan Calderon	H	Chicago
Sept. 4, 1988	Jim Sundberg	H	Texas
July 17, 1993	Brian McRae	H	Kansas City
May 24, 1997	Darrin Erstad	H	Anaheim
July 26, 1998	Nomar Garriaparra	A	Boston

FOUR HOME RUNS IN ONE INNING (3)

DATE	OPPONENT	INNING	HITTERS	PITCHER(S)
June 30, 1977	vs NYY	8th	C. Johnson	Garvin
			Pinella	Garvin
			Munson	J. Johnson
			C. Johnson	J. Johnson
July 4, 1977	at BOS	8th	Lynn	Hartenstein
			Rice	Hartenstein
			Yazstremski	Willis
			Scott	Willis

DATE	OPPONENT	INNING	HITTERS	PITCHER(S)
May 3, 2000	at CWS	6th	Johnson	Escobar
			Valentin	Escobar
			Thomas	Frascatore
			Konerko	Frascatore

THREE HOME RUNS IN ONE INNING (20)

DATE	OPPONENT	INNING	HITTERS	PITCHER(S)
May 8, 1979	at MIN	7th	Smalley	Moore
			Kusick	Moore
			Landreaux	Moore
May 5, 1982	at CWS	7th	Baines	Leal
			Morrison	Leal
			Almon	Jackson
June 22, 1982	at SEA	4th	Zisk	Garvin
			Henderson	Senteney
			Bulling	Senteney
Aug. 2, 1983	vs NYY	3rd, G1	Mattingly	Leal
			Nettles	Leal
			Kemp	Leal
June 3, 1984	vs NYY	4th	Gamble	Clancy
			Kemp	Clancy
			Harrah	Clancy
Sept. 18, 1984	vs BOS	6th	Evans	Gott
			Rice	Gott
			Armas	Gott
Aug. 24, 1985	at CWS	9th	Law	Stieb
			Little	Stieb
			Baines	Lavelle
May 6, 1986	vs OAK	3rd	Tettleton	Key
			Kingman	Key
			Lansford	Key
May 10, 1986	at SEA	4th	Phelps	Alexander
			Calderon	Alexander
			Presley	Alexander
May 14, 1986	at OAK	7th	Canseco	Stieb
			Kingman	Stieb
			Davis	Stieb

DATE	OPPONENT	INNING	HITTERS	PITCHER(S)
June 4, 1986	vs MIN	7th	Brunansky	Stieb
			Smalley	Stieb
			Reed	Acker
July 14, 1990	at CAL	7th	Winfield	Wills
			Downing	Ward
			Bichette	Ward
Aug. 7, 1990	vs DET	9th	Trammell	Key
			Fielder	Key
			Ward	Key
June 22, 1995	vs MIL	2nd	Valentin	Darwin
			Hamilton	Darwin
			Vaughn	Darwin
April 25, 1997	vs SEA	8th	Davis	Plesac
			Rodriguez	Timlin
			Griffey Jr.	Timlin
June 3, 1997	at SEA	6th	Buhner	Williams
			Sorrento	Williams
			Cruz Jr.	Williams
June 23, 1997	vs BOS	7th	Cordero	Williams
			Stanley	Williams
			Naehring	Williams
Sept. 15, 1997	at SEA	5th	Cora	Williams
			Griffey Jr.	Williams
			Sorrento	Janzen
July 14, 1998	at BAL	7th	Palmeiro	Person
			Surhoff	Person
			Carter	Person
Sept. 25, 1998	vs DET	3rd	Encarnacion	Williams
			Catalanotto	Williams
			Clark	Williams

OPPONENTS—GRAND SLAM HOME RUNS

DATE	PLAYER/CLUB	H/A	PITCHER
Sept. 6/77	Carlton Fisk, Boston	H	Mike Darr (1st inning)
April 18/78	Amos Otis, Kansas City	H	Dave Lemanczyk (1st inning)
April 25/78	Paul Dade, Cleveland	H	Jerry Garvin (4th inning)
May 26/78	Jim Spencer, New York – PH	A	Tom Murphy (7th inning)
June 24/78	Gary Alexander, Cleveland	A	Mike Willis (4th inning)
Aug. 6/78	Al Cowens, Kansas City	A	Balor Moore (1st inning)
May 22/79	Andre Thornton, Cleveland	H	Mark Lemongello (3rd inning)
June 3/79	Dan Meyer, Seattle	A	Mark Lemongello (3rd inning)
June 10/79	Jim Essian, Oakland – IP	A	Mike Willis (5th inning)
June 13/79 (1st)	Willie Aikens, California	H	Dyar Miller (3rd inning)
June 14/79	Willie Aikens, California	H	Phil Huffman (1st inning)
July 15/79	Dave Edwards, Minnesota	H	Jim Clancy (3rd inning)
Aug. 25/79	Don Baylor, California	H	Balor Moore (1st inning)
Sept. 9/79	Bobby Bonds, Cleveland	A	Tom Buskey (9th inning)
April 22/81	Paul Molitor, Milwaukee	H	Joey McLaughlin (5th inning)
June 7/81	Buddy Bell, Texas	A	Roy Lee Jackson (8th inning)
May 29/82 (2nd)	Benny Ayala, Baltimore – PH	A	Jerry Garvin (7th inning)
June 2/82	Bobby Murcer, New York	H	Mark Bomback (13th inning)
July 11/82	Harold Baines, Chicago	H	Jerry Garvin (2nd inning)
July 30/82	Alan Trammell, Detroit	H	Jim Clancy (4th inning)
Aug. 24/82	Joe Nolan, Baltimore	A	Joey McLaughlin (10th inning)
Aug. 26/82	Eddie Murray, Baltimore	A	Ken Schrom (3rd inning)
June 15/83	Dave Lopes, Oakland	H	Dave Geisel (5th inning)
Aug. 8/83 (2nd)	Ken Griffey, New York	A	Matt Williams (1st inning)
Aug. 20/83	Jim Rice, Boston	A	Dave Stieb (3rd inning)
July 20/84	Alvin Davis, Seattle	A	Roy Lee Jackson (7th inning)
April 19/85	Fritz Connally, Baltimore	H	Doyle Alexander (5th inning)
May 15/85	Jerry Narron, California – PH	H	Bill Caudill (9th inning)
May 8/86	Wally Joyner, California	A	Jim Acker (3rd inning)
May 9/86	Alvin Davis, Seattle	A	Don Gordon (7th inning)
April 9/87	Cory Snyder, Cleveland	H	Joe Johnson (1st inning)
June 29/87	Don Mattingly, New York	H	John Cerutti (2nd inning)
June 29/87	Dave Winfield, New York	H	Tom Henke (8th inning)
Aug. 6/87	Casey Parsons, Cleveland – PH	A	Mark Eichhorn (6th inning)
Aug. 10/87	Sam Horn, Boston	A	Jose Nunez (8th inning)
Sept. 26/87	Matt Nokes, Detroit	H	John Cerutti (3rd inning)
July 2/88	Terry Steinbach, Oakland	H	Mike Flanagan (3rd inning)
May 2/89	Mark McGwire, Oakland	H	Tom Henke (9th inning)
July 16/89	Terry Steinbach, Oakland	H	Duane Ward (7th inning)
Sept. 12/89	Kent Hrbek, Minnesota	A	Duane Ward (7th inning)
May 17/90	Brian Giles, Seattle	H	Frank Wills (5th inning)
May 22/90	Jose Canseco, Oakland	H	Frank Wills (4th inning)
July 17/90	Alvin Davis, Seattle	A	David Wells (6th inning)
Aug. 3/90	Steve Buechele, Texas	A	Jim Acker (7th inning)
Sept. 14/90	Sam Horn, Baltimore – PH	H	Duane Ward (6th inning)

DATE	PLAYER/CLUB	H/A	PITCHER
April 8/91	Jack Clark, Boston	H	Dave Stieb (3rd Inning)
June 1/91	Dave Winfield, California	H	Willie Fraser (2nd Inning)
June 16/91	Joe Orsulak, Baltimore – PH	H	Duane Ward (7th Inning)
Sept. 15/91	Jose Canseco, Oakland	H	Jim Acker (9th Inning)
June 3/92	Kirby Puckett, Minnesota	A	Juan Guzman (3rd Inning)
June 12/92	Wade Boggs, Boston	H	Dave Stieb (5th Inning)
April 13/93	Omar Vizquel, Seattle	H	Danny Cox (6th Inning)
April 30/93	Frank Thomas, Chicago	R	Todd Stottlemyre (3rd Inning)
April 6/94	Robin Ventura, Chicago	R	Paul Spoljaric (7th inning)
May 5/94	Brent Mayne, Kansas City	R	Juan Guzman (3rd inning)
June 7/94	Darrin Jackson, Chicago	H	Pat Hentgen (1st inning)
Aug. 2/94	Wes Chamberlin, Boston	H	Dave Stewart (4th inning)
June 21/95	Jose Valentin, Milwaukee	H	Mike Timlin (9th inning)
Aug. 1/95	Harold Baines, Baltimore	A	Edwin Hurtado (1st inning)
Aug. 18/95	Wally Joyner, Kansas City	H	Giovanni Carrara (3rd inning)
Aug. 25/95	Ray Durham, Chicago	H	Pat Hentgen (6th inning)
July 7/96	Cecil Fielder, Detroit	A	Jeff Ware (1st inning)
July 31/96	Albert Belle, Cleveland	A	Bill Risley (9th inning)
Sept. 21/96	Eddie Murray, Baltimore	A	Scott Brow (6th inning)
April 20/97	Dean Palmer, Texas	A	Juan Guzman (3rd inning)
May 17/97	Jim Thome, Cleveland	H	Woody Williams (3rd inning)
Aug. 4/97	Greg Colbrunn, Minnesota – PH	A	Omar Daal (5th inning)
July 19/98	Chris Hoiles, Baltimore	A	Woody Williams (1st inning)
July 18/98	Tim Raines, New York (AL)	H	Robert Person (8th inning)
July 23/98	Danon Buford, Boston	A	Dan Plesac (8th inning)
April 29/99	Andy Sheets, Anaheim	A	Roy Halladay (1st inning)
April 30/99	Ken Griffey, Seattle	A	Graeme Lloyd (8th inning)
May 22/99	John Valentin, Boston	A	Chris Carpenter (3rd inning)
July 28/99	Butch Huskey, Boston	A	Joey Hamilton (6th inning)
Aug. 13/99	Matt Stairs, Oakland	H	Paul Spoljaric (5th inning)
Aug. 14/99	A.J. Hinch, Oakland	H	Joey Hamilton (1st inning)
Sept. 14/99	Bernie Williams, New York (AL)	H	Billy Koch (8th inning)
Sept. 14/99	Paul O'Neill, New York (AL)	H	Paul Spoljaric (9th inning)
Sept. 24/99	Manny Ramirez, Cleveland	H	Mike Romano (5th inning)
Sept. 24/99	Dave Roberts, Cleveland	H	John Hudek (8th inning)
April 15/00	Edgar Martinez, Seattle	H	Pedro Borbon (6th inning)
April 16/00	Alex Rodriguez, Seattle	H	Pedro Borbon (8th inning)
April 18/00	Adam Kennedy, Anaheim	H	Frank Castillo (4th inning)
June 27/00	Steve Cox, Tampa Bay	A	Kelvim Escobar (4th inning)
July 18/00	Mike Piazza, New York (NL)	H	Chris Carpenter (5th inning)

LEADING OPPONENTS vs BLUE JAYS

	2000		Record	
Batting Average (30 AB's)	.426	Darin Erstad, Ana	.519	Don Mattingly, NYY-1986
Most at Bats	58	Ricky Ledee, NYY-Cle-Tex	70	Randy Velarde, Ana-Oak-1999
Most Runs	16	Alex Rodriguez, Sea	17	Ron LeFlore, Det-1977
				Ron LeFlore, Det-1978
Most Hits	20	Darin Erstad, Ana	27	Don Mattingly, NYY-1986
Most Total Bases	35	Bobby Higginson, Det	50	George Brett, KC-1983
Most Doubles	7	Deivi Cruz, Det	9	George Brett, KC-1979
Most Triples	2	Kenny Lofton, Cle	3	Ron LeFlore, Det-1977
		Derek Jeter, NYY		Rick Peters, Det-1981
				Julio Franco, Cle-1983
				Robin Yount, Mil-1987
				Devon White, Cal-1989
				George Brett, KC-1990
				Gary Pettis, Tex-1990
				Shane Mack, Min-1993
Most Home Runs	5	Alex Rodriguez, Sea	7	Bobby Grich, Cal-1979
		Bobby Higginson, Det		Jim Rice, Bos-1983
				Cecil Fielder, Det-1990
				Jose Canseco, Oak-1991
				Cecil Fielder, Det-NYY-1996
				Ken Griffey, Jr. Sea-1997
Most Runs Batted In	16	Alex Rodriguez, Sea	22	Carlton Fisk, Bos-1977
		Edgar Martinez, Sea		
Most Sacrifice Bunts	3	Jason Tyner, NYM-TB	4	Jim Sunberg, Tex-1977
				Roy Smalley, Min-1978
				Jim Morrison, CWS-1980
				Mike Gallego, Oak-1990
				Carlos Rodriguez, Bos-1994
Most Sacrifice Flies	3	Mike Cameron, Sea	4	Gary Gaetti, Min-1989
				Tino Martinez, NYY-1998
Most Times Striking Out	15	Brian Daubach, Bos	22	Bo Jackson, KC-1987
Most Walks	16	Jim Thome, Cle	19	Mickey Tettleton, Det-1992
Most Times Hit By Pitch	2	(14 Players)	4	Chet Lemon, CWS-1981
				Don Baylor, Bos-1986
Most Stolen Bases	5	Omar Vizquel, Cle	13	Rickey Henderson, NYY-1988
Most Times Caught Stealing	2	(4 Players)	5	Mike Caruso, CWS-1999
Most Times GIDP	4	Garret Anderson, Ana	6	Buddy Bell, Cle-1978
		Brad Ausmus, Det		Dave Engle, Min-1984
Most Wins	3	Freddy Garcia, Sea	4	Dennis Eckersley, Bos-1978
		Tim Hudson, Oak		Rick Waits, Cle-1978
				Dave Goltz, Min-1979
				Chuck Rainey, Bos-1979
				Luis Tiant, NYY-1979
				Steve Stone, Bal-1980
				Britt Burns, CWS-1982
				Dave Stewart, Oak-1987
				Mike Moore, Oak-1991
				Darren Oliver, Tex-1996
Most Losses	2	(12 Pitchers)	4	Mike Norris, Oak-1980
				Danny Darwin, Tex-1983
				Roger Clemens, Bos-1993
				Scott Erickson, Min-1993
Most Appearances	5	(7 Pitchers)	20	Keith Atherton, Oak-Min-1988
Most Complete Games	1	(9 Pitchers)	4	Mike Flanagan, Bal-1978
				Mike Norris, Oak-1980
Most Saves	4	Keith Foulke, CWS	6	Jeff Reardon, Bos-1991
				Mike Henneman, Tex-1996
Most Innings Pitched	27.0	Hideo Nomo, Det	40.0	Mike Flanagan, Bal-1978
Most Hits Allowed	25	Mike Mussina, Bal	43	Mike Flanagan, Bal-1978
		Hideo Nomo, Det		
Most Runs Allowed	18	Hideo Nomo, Det	23	Frank Viola, Min-1985
Most Earned Runs Allowed	18	Hideo Nomo, Det	21	Roger Clemens, Bos-1993
Most Home Runs Allowed	6	Bartolo Colon, Cle	7	Floyd Bannister, CWS-1987
		Mike Mussina, Bal		
		Jeff Weaver, Det		
Most Strikeouts	23	Pedro Martinez, Bos	44	Nolan Ryan, Cal-1977
		Hideo Nomo, Det		
Most Base on Balls	12	Hideo Nomo, Det	20	Nolan Ryan, Cal-1977
Most Hit Batsmen	4	Pedro Martinez, Bos	6	Tim Wakefield, Bos-1997
Most Wild Pitches	3	Mike Sirotka, CWS	6	Mike Moore, Oak-1992

AT SKYDOME—REGULAR SEASON

Name	HR	Name	HR	Name	HR	Name	HR	Name	HR
Abbott, K	2	Davis, G	3	Heep, D	1	McLemore, M	3	Sheets, L	1
Abreu, B	1	Davis, R	2	Henderson, D	3	McRae, B	5	Sheffield, G	1
Aldrete, M	2	Deer, R	7	Henderson, R	5	McReynolds, K	1	Sierra, R	3
Alexander, M	1	Dempsey, R	2	Hernandez, K	1	Meiske, M	3	Simmons, B	2
Alfonzo, E	2	DeShields, D	1	Higginson, B	4	Melvin, B	1	Smith, D	1
Alicea, L	1	Devereaux, M	2	Hill, D	1	Merced, O	1	Smith, M	1
Alomar, R	3	Diaz, E	1	Hill, G	7	Meulens, H	1	Snyder, C	1
Alomar, S	5	Disarcina, G	2	Hinch, AJ	1	Millar, K	1	Sorrento, P	10
Amaro, R	2	Duncan, M	1	Hocking, D	1	Miller, K	1	Sosa, S	1
Anderson, B	9	Durham, R	2	Hoiles, C	2	Milligan, R	2	Spencer, S	1
Anderson, G	4	Dye, J	1	Horn, S	1	Molitor, P	5	Spiers, B	2
Anthony, E	2	Easley, T	1	Houston, T	1	Morris, H	1	Spiezio, S	1
Ausmus, B	1	Edmonds, J	1	Howard, D	2	Moseby, L	1	Stairs, M	5
Baerga, C	5	Eisenreich, J	1	Howell, J	1	Naehring, T	2	Stanley, M	9
Baines, H	8	Encarnacion, J	3	Hrbek, K	1	Neel, T	2	Steinbach, T	3
Balboni, S	2	Erstad, D	6	Huskey, B	2	Neives, M	1	Stevens, L	3
Barfield, J	3	Esasky, N	2	Incaviglia, P	1	Nilsson, D	5	Strange, D	1
Bass, K	1	Espinoza, A	3	Jackson, B	1	Nixon, T	1	Surhoff, B	7
Becker, R	1	Evans, Dw	3	Jackson, D	2	Nokes, M	3	Sveum, D	1
Bell, D	2	Everett, C	1	Jaha, J	5	Nunally, J	2	Sweeney, M	1
Bell, J	2	Fasano, S	1	James, C	2	O'Brien, P	3	Tartabull, D	6
Belle, A	14	Fick, R	2	Jefferson, R	3	O'Leary, T	4	Tavarez, J	1
Benitez, Y	1	Fielder, C	16	Jeter, D	2	Olerud, J	1	Tejada, M	5
Berroa, G	4	Finley, S	1	Johnson, Ca	1	Oliver, J	1	Tettleton, M	4
Bichette, D	2	Flaherty, J	4	Johnson, L	1	O'Neill, P	4	Thon, D	1
Blowers, M	1	Fletcher, S	1	Jones, C	2	Ordonez, M	3	Thomas, F	10
Boggs, W	2	Fox, E	1	Jones, J	1	Orsulak, J	1	Thome, J	8
Bonilla, B	2	Franco, J	4	Jose, F	2	Palmeiro, R	7	Thurman, G	1
Bordick, M	1	Fryman, T	5	Joyner, W	7	Palmer, D	8	Timmons, O	1
Bradley, P	2	Fullmer, B	1	Justice, D	4	Paquette, C	1	Trammell, A	3
Bragg, D	3	Gaetti, G	4	Kapler, G	1	Parent, M	1	Trammell, B	1
Braggs, G	1	Gagne, G	6	Karkovice, R	5	Parker, D	5	Treadway, J	1
Brett, G	3	Gallego, M	1	Kelly, P	2	Parrish, L	2	Tucker, M	1
Briley, G	1	Gant, R	3	Kelly, R	2	Pasqua, D	2	Turner, C	1
Brock, G	1	Garcia, K	1	Kennedy, A	1	Pena, T	2	Valentin, John	8
Brogna, R	1	Garciaparra, N	6	King, J	2	Pendleton, T	1	Valentin, Jose	6
Brosius, S	3	Gates, B	1	Kirby, W	3	Perry, H	1	Valle, D	1
Buechele, S	3	Geren, B	1	Kittle, R	3	Phelps, K	1	Varitek, J	1
Buford, D	2	Giambi, Jason	5	Klesko, R	1	Phillips, T	7	Vaughn, G	8
Buhner, J	9	Giambi, Jeremy	1	Knoblauch, C	3	Piazza, M	2	Vaughn, M	9
Burks, E	2	Gibson, K	4	Lawton, M	1	Pirkl, G	1	Velarde, R	4
Burrell, P	1	Giles, B	2	Lee, C	1	Plantier, P	1	Ventura, R	6
Calderon, I	1	Gladden, D	1	Lemon, C	3	Posada, J	2	Vina, F	1
Cameron, M	1	Glanville, D	2	Leonard, J	2	Powell, A	1	Vitiello, J	1
Canseco, J	18	Glaus, T	3	Lewis, D	1	Pratt, T	2	Vizquel, O	6
Carter, J	2	Gomez, C	1	Leyritz, J	4	Pritchett, C	1	Walbeck, M	2
Castillo, C	1	Gomez, L	3	Listach, P	1	Puckett, K	3	Ward, G	2
Catalanotto, F	1	Gonzalez, J	11	Long, T	2	Quintana, C	3	Webster, M	2
Chavez, E	1	Goodwin, C	1	Lowell, M	1	Raines, T	3	Wedge, E	1
Cirillo, J	1	Goodwin, T	1	Lyons, S	1	Ramirez, M	8	Whitaker, L	3
Clark, D	1	Grebeck, C	1	Maas, K	2	Randa, J	4	White, D	1
Clark, J	2	Greenwell, M	7	Mabry, J	1	Reynolds, H	1	White, R	2
Clark, T	9	Greer, R	4	Macfarlane, M	5	Ready, R	1	Whiten, M	1
Clark, W	4	Grieve, B	4	Mack, S	3	Ripken, B	1	Widger, C	1
Codero, W	3	Griffey, K	14	Maldonado, C	2	Ripken, C	9	Williams, B	7
Cole, A	1	Gruber, K	1	Martin, A	1	Rivera, R	1	Williams, G	2
Conine, J	1	Guerrero, V	3	Martin, N	1	Roberts, D	1	Williams, K	1
Coomer, R	4	Guillen, O	1	Martinez, D	1	Rodriguez, A	13	Williams, M	3
Cora, J	2	Guzman, C	2	Martinez, E	10	Rodriguez, I	5	Wilson, D	2
Cordova, M	3	Hairston, J	1	Martinez, T	7	Rolen, S	1	Winfield, D	5
Cotto, H	3	Hall, M	4	Marzano, J	1	Sabo, C	1	Worthington, C	2
Cruz, D	1	Hamelin, B	5	Mattingly, D	3	Salas, M	1	Young, E	1
Cummings, M	1	Hamilton, D	2	Mayne, B	1	Salmon, T	4	Yount, R	3
Curtis, C	5	Hammonds, J	1	McDonald, J	1	Sax, S	1	Zaun, G	1
Damon, J	1	Harper, B	3	McEwing, J	1	Segui, D	2	Zeile, T	1
Daubach, B	1	Harris, L	1	McGriff, F	3	Seitzer, K	1		
Davis, C	7	Haselman, B	1	McGwire, M	9	Sexson, R	1		

AT SKYDOME—POST-SEASON

Name	HR	Name	HR	Name	HR	Name	HR
Baines, H	1	Eisenreich, J	1	McGwire	1	Smith, L	1
Burks, E	1	Henderson, R	2	Pagliarulo, M	1	Steinbach, T	1
Canseco, J	1	Johnson, L	1	Parker, D	1	Thomas, F	1
Dykstra, L	2	Justice, D	1	Puckett, K	2	Ventura, R	1

LOW HIT GAMES vs BLUE JAYS

NO HIT GAMES
May 15/81   —Len Barker, Toronto 0 at Cleveland 3, Perfect Game
June 29/90 —Dave Stewart, Oakland 5 at Toronto 0
May 1/91   —Nolan Ryan, Toronto 0 at Texas 3

ONE HIT GAMES
Sept. 3/78   —Chris Knapp, California 3 at Toronto 1, Horton homer in 2nd
July 7/79   —Doc Medich (6.2 IP), Jim Kern (2.1 IP), Toronto 0 at Texas 2, Mayberry single in 2nd
April 30/80   —Larry Gura, Kansas City 3 at Toronto 0, Garcia single in 6th
June 6/80   —Geoff Zahn, Toronto 0 at Minnesota 5, Mayberry single in 7th
Sept. 26/80   —Dennis Eckersley, Boston 3 at Toronto 1, Mayberry home run in 5th
May 27/83   —John Tudor, Boston 2 at Toronto 0, Collins single in 4th
Aug. 13/84   —Mike Boddicker, Baltimore 2 at Toronto 1, Mulliniks double in 3rd
April 23/89   —Nolan Ryan, Texas 4 at Toronto 1, Liriano triple in 9th
April 28/89   —Kirk McCaskill, Toronto 0 at California 9, Liriano double in 9th
Sept. 30/92   —Frank Viola, Boston 1 at Toronto 0, White single in 9th
July 28/97 (g.1) —Steve Woodard (8.0 IP), Mike Fetters (1.0 IP), Toronto 0 at Milwaukee 1, Otis Nixon single in in 1st

TWO HIT GAMES
July 24/77   —Bob Sykes, Toronto 2 at Detroit 6, Ashby single in 6th, Bailor homer in 9th
Oct. 2/77   —(1st game) Jim Bibby (6.0 IP), Don Hood (4.0 IP), Larry Andersen (0.2 IP),
                  Cleveland 1 at Toronto 2 (11 innings), G. Woods, singles in 6th and 11th
April 29/78   —Nolan Ryan, Toronto 0 at California 5, Upshaw triple in 3rd, Cerone single in 7th
Aug. 19/78   —Gary Serum, Toronto 0 at Minnesota 4, Ashby single in 3rd, A. Woods single in 5th
Oct. 1/78   —Luis Tiant, Toronto 0 at Boston 5, Howell single in 4th, Mayberry single in 7th
May 14/79   —Rick Waits, Toronto 0 at Cleveland 1, McKay single in 4th and double in 7th
Aug. 12/79   —(1st game) Ross Baumgarten, Toronto 2 at Chicago 7, Bailor single in 1st, A. Woods triple in 7th
May 2/80   —Len Barker (7.0 IP), Mike Stanton (2.0 IP), Cleveland 6 at Toronto 1, Garcia doubles in 3rd and 7th
July 30/80   —Rich Langford, Oakland 11 at Toronto 1, Griffin home run in 7th and Ault single in 8th
Sept. 5/80   —LaMarr Hoyt, Chicago 3 at Toronto 0, Woods single in 2nd and Iorg single in 6th
May 6/81   —Bert Blyleven, Cleveland 4 at Toronto 1, Moseby double in 9th, Bell single in 9th
April 18/83   —Ron Guidry, Toronto 0 at New York 3, Collins single in 1st, Martinez single in 6th
June 29/85   —Walt Terrell, Toronto 0 at Detroit 8, Moseby double in 1st, Upshaw single in 7th
May 23/86   —Don Schulze, Toronto 1 at Cleveland 3, Bell HR and Whitt single in the 2nd
July 26/86   —Eric Plunk (6.0 IP), Dave Leiper (0.1 IP), Dave Stewart (1.2 IP), Joaquin Andujar (1.0 IP),
                  Toronto 0 at Oakland 2, Moseby single in the 3rd, Leach double in the 4th
Aug. 11/86   —Mike Flanagan (8.1 IP), Don Aase (0.2 IP), Toronto 1 at Baltimore 3, Shepherd double in the 3rd, Fernandez double in the 9th
April 10/87   —Bruce Hurst, Toronto 0 at Boston 3, Iorg single in 3rd, Fernandez single in 6th
May 23/89   —Shane Rawley (8.0 IP), Juan Berenguer (0.2 IP), Minnesota 1 at Toronto 2, Liriano single in 6th, McGriff single in 7th
April 27/90   —Greg Hibbard (8.0 IP), Scott Radinsky (0.0 IP), Bobby Thigpen (1.0 IP), Toronto 1 at Chicago 6, Hill and Felix singles in 5th
July 18/90   —Matt Young, Toronto 2 at Seattle 5, Borders double in 4th, single in 6th
Aug. 26/90   —Greg Harris (7.2 IP), Jeff Gray (1.1 IP), Boston 1 at Toronto 0, McGriff single in 2nd, Myers single in 8th
Aug. 21/91   —Dan Plesac (4.0 IP), Julio Machado (4.0 IP), Edwin Nunez (1.0 IP), Toronto 0 at Milwaukee 3, Sprague single in 2nd, Carter single in 4th
July 12/92   —Ron Darling, Oakland 8 at Toronto 0, Maldonado single in the 8th, Lee single in the 9th
July 25/92   —Ron Darling, Toronto 0 at Oakland 6, Maldonado single in the 7th, White double in the 8th
May 22/95   —Kevin Appier (7.0 IP), Hipolito Pichardo (2.0 IP), Kansas City 7 at Toronto 0, Molitor single in the 4th, Sprague single in the 5th
Sept. 16/96   —Jimmy Key (8.0 IP), David Weathers (1.0 IP), Toronto 0 at New York 10, Tomas Perez single in the 6th, O'Brien single in the 8th
June 2/97   —Randy Johnson, Toronto 0 at Seattle 3, Alex Gonzalez single in 6th, Tilson Brito single in 6th
July 1/97   —Jeff Juden (8.1 IP), Ugueth Urbina (0.2 IP), Montreal 2 at Toronto 1, Shawn Green homerun in 8th, Orlando Merced single in 9th
July 27/97   —Jose Rosado (7.0 IP), Mike Perez (0.1 IP), Larry Casian (0.1 IP), Greg Olson (1.0 IP), Kansas City 3 at
                  Toronto 2, Benito Santiago single in 5th, Jacob Brumfield single in 6th
Sept. 1/97   —Jason Isringhausen (6.0 IP), Greg McMichael (1.0 IP), Mel Rojas (1.0 IP), John Franco (1.0 IP),
                  Toronto 0 at New York Mets 3, Tomas Perez single in 2nd, Benito Santiago single in 7th
Aug. 30/99   —Jay Ryan (8.0 IP), Minnesota 1 at Toronto 2, Tony Fernandez single in 1st, Tony Batista homer in 2nd
Sept. 4/00   —Barry Zito (6.2 IP), Jeff Tam (0.2 IP), Todd Belitz (0.0 IP), T.J. Mathews (0.2 IP), Jason Isringhausen (1.0 IP), Oakland 10 at Toronto 0,
                  Dave Martinez single in 4th, Craig Grebeck single in 7th
Sept. 24/00   —Travis Harper (9.0 IP), Tampa Bay 6 at Toronto 0, Darrin Fletcher single in 3rd, Tony Batista double in 7th
Sept. 28/00   —Pat Rapp (7.0 IP), Jay Spurgeon (1.0 IP), Buddy Groom (0.1 IP), Lesli Brea (0.2 IP), Toronto 1 at Baltimore 23, Shannon Stewart single in
                  4th, Darrin Fletcher home run in 5th

ANAHEIM ANGELS

SYNOPSIS: Toronto posted a 7-5 record against the Angels, third consecutive winning season... Over the last three seasons are 23-12... Were 4-2 at home and 3-3 on the road... Have five straight winning seasons at home with a 21-8 record over that time... Hit .319 with 82 runs and 24 home runs which were the best marks against any opponent in 2000... The Angels posted a .310 average with 17 home runs and 69 RBI... Leading the way for Toronto with four home runs and 16 RBI apiece were Carlos Delgado and Brad Fullmer... Also hitting four home runs were Tony Batista (11 RBI) and Jose Cruz (8 RBI)... Toronto scored 41 runs in a four game series from April 17-20 at home and were 3-1... Scored ten or more runs in three straight games, April 18-20... Toronto posted a 5.91 ERA with two saves while the Angels had a 6.99 ERA with one save... David Wells led the staff with two wins while five others each picked up a win... Billy Koch was 1-0 with two saves and an ERA of 1.50... Season series is now even at 10-10-4 while Toronto holds the edge in wins at 140-135... At the SkyDome have a lifetime record of 43-22.

	HOME W-L	AWAY W-L	TOTAL W-L		HOME W-L	AWAY W-L	TOTAL W-L		HOME W-L	AWAY W-L	TOTAL W-L
1977	1-4	3-2	4-6	1986	2-4	4-2	6-6	1995	1-5	1-3	2-8
1978	2-3	1-4	3-7	1987	5-1	2-4	7-5	1996	4-2	1-5	5-7
1979	3-3	2-4	5-7	1988	2-4	4-2	6-6	1997	3-2	2-4	5-6
1980	4-2	5-1	9-3	1989	2-4	3-3	5-7	1998	4-2	3-2	7-4
1981	3-3	3-3	6-6	1990	4-2	1-5	5-7	1999	6-0	3-3	9-3
1982	3-3	1-5	4-8	1991	3-3	3-3	6-6	2000	4-2	3-3	7-5
1983	4-2	4-2	8-4	1992	5-1	2-4	7-5	**TOTAL**	**79-59**	**61-76**	**140-135**
1984	2-4	3-3	5-7	1993	5-1	3-3	8-4				
1985	5-1	2-4	7-5	1994	2-1	2-2	4-3				

LAST SWEEP: BY TORONTO: At Toronto: June 15-17, 1999 (3 games);
   At Anaheim: August 24-25, 1999 (2 games).
LAST SWEEP: BY ANAHEIM: At Toronto: April 20-22, 1984 (3 games);
   At Anaheim: Sept. 3-5, 1993 (3 games).
SERIES SWEPT: BY TORONTO: 2-game (6), 3-game (9), 4-game (2).
   BY ANAHEIM: 2-game (4), 3-game (6).
LONGEST WIN STREAK: BY TORONTO: 7 games, Sept. 8, 1997-August 13, 1998.
   BY ANAHEIM: 7 games, July 13, 1978-June 5, 1979 and July 20, 1988-May 6, 1989.
MOST RUNS, GAME: BY TORONTO: 13 runs (three times), last 13-2, June 15, 1999 at Toronto.
   BY ANAHEIM: 24 runs, 24-2, August 25, 1979 at Toronto.
WIDEST MARGIN VICTORY: BY TORONTO: 12 runs, 12-0, May 18, 1997 at Anaheim.
   BY ANAHEIM: 22 runs, 24-2, August 25, 1979 at Toronto.

BALTIMORE ORIOLES

SYNOPSIS: After an 11-1 season in 1999 the Blue Jays were 6-7 in 2000 after posting winning records in the three seasons prior... Were 4-2 at home and 2-5 in Baltimore... Toronto won their first three games of the season against the O's to give them a franchise record 13 straight victories against Baltimore... Streak matches the club record done once previously against the Cleveland Indians from June 12, 1991 to April 21, 1992... Toronto lost at home on July 21 to end a 14-game win streak at home, the longest home winning streak against any opponent in club history... On September 28 in Baltimore suffered a 23-1 loss, the most runs ever allowed to the O's and the widest margin of defeat at 22 runs... The Blue Jays saw Baltimore hit .302 while hitting only .245 themselves, their second lowest mark against an AL opponent (Oakland- .215)... Toronto out-homered the O's 22 to 14... Leading the way was Tony Batista who hit .360 with nine home runs and 16 RBI... By hitting nine home runs he became the second player to ever hit nine in one season against the O's joining Frank Howard of the 1968 Washington Senators... They were the most by a Blue Jay against any one opponent in a season series... Toronto posted a 6-7 ERA as compared to a 3.98 ERA by the O's... Frank Castillo and David Wells each posted a pair of wins... For the O's RHP Pat Rapp was 3-0 with a 3.05 ERA... The season series now stands at 10-13-1... At SkyDome are 42-30 while in Camden Yards are 28-29.

	HOME W-L	AWAY W-L	TOTAL W-L		HOME W-L	AWAY W-L	TOTAL W-L		HOME W-L	AWAY W-L	TOTAL W-L
1977	2-5	3-5	5-10	1986	2-5	3-3	5-8	1995	2-4	4-3	6-7
1978	6-2	1-6	7-8	1987	6-0	6-1	12-1	1996	3-4	2-4	5-8
1979	2-4	0-7	2-11	1988	6-1	2-4	8-5	1997	2-4	4-2	6-6
1980	2-5	0-6	2-11	1989	3-3	3-4	6-7	1998	5-1	2-4	7-5
1981	1-2	1-3	2-5	1990	5-2	3-3	8-5	1999	6-0	5-1	11-1
1982	1-6	2-4	3-10	1991	3-3	5-2	8-5	2000	4-2	5-5	6-7
1983	4-2	2-5	6-7	1992	5-2	3-3	8-5	**TOTAL**	**83-65**	**67-87**	**150-152**
1984	5-2	4-2	9-4	1993	4-2	4-3	8-5				
1985	4-1	4-3	8-4	1994	0-3	2-4	2-7				

LAST SWEEP: BY TORONTO: At Toronto: May 8-10, 2000 (3 games);
   At Baltimore: July 6-8, 1999 (3 games).
LAST SWEEP: BY BALTIMORE: At Toronto: June 24-26, 1994 (3 games);
   At Baltimore: July 13-14, 1998 (2 games).
SERIES SWEPT: BY TORONTO: 2-game (3), 3-game (13), 4-game (2).
   BY BALTIMORE: 2-game (4), 3-game (10), 4-game (2).
LONGEST WIN STREAK: BY TORONTO: 13 games, April 11, 1999-May 10, 2000.
   BY BALTIMORE: 15 games, September 8, 1978-September 6, 1979.
MOST RUNS, GAME: BY TORONTO: 24 runs, 24-10, June 26, 1978 at Toronto.
   BY BALTIMORE: 23 runs, 23-1, Sept. 28, 2000 at Baltimore.
WIDEST MARGIN VICTORY: BY TORONTO: 15 runs, 18-3, September 14, 1987 at Toronto.
   BY BALTIMORE: 22 runs, 23-1, Sept. 28, 2000 at Baltimore.

BOSTON RED SOX

SYNOPSIS: Were 8-4 against the Red Sox, the most victories since winning ten in 1993... It marks the fifth time Toronto has posted eight or more wins in a season against Boston... Were 4-2 at home and 4-2 at Fenway Park... It was the first winning season in Boston since 1993 (4-2)... Toronto finished the season on a five game win streak which included a three game sweep at home from June 23-25... Toronto posted a 4.55 ERA and were led by David Wells (2-0) and Frank Castillo (2-1) who each posted two wins... RHP Billy Koch pitched 7.2 shutouts innings and earned five saves... Boston Pedro Martinez was 1-1 in three starts with a 2.91 ERA... At the plate Toronto hit .273 with 21 home runs and 16 stolen bases while Boston hit .286 with eight home runs and six stolen bases... Three Blue Jays posted ten or more RBI- Tony Batista (.302, 3, 12), Carlos Delgado (.326, 3, 10) & Raul Mondesi (.356, 4, 11)... Brad Fullmer matched Mondesi with a team high four home runs... Toronto was unable to contain Carl Everett who hit .421 with three home runs and ten RBI... The 16 stolen bases against Boston were the most against any opponent in 2000, Baltimore was second at seven... Toronto now has a 32-41 record at SkyDome.

	HOME W-L	AWAY W-L	TOTAL W-L		HOME W-L	AWAY W-L	TOTAL W-L		HOME W-L	AWAY W-L	TOTAL W-L
1977	2-6	1-6	3-12	1986	3-3	3-4	6-7	1995	2-5	3-3	5-8
1978	2-5	2-6	4-11	1987	4-3	3-3	7-6	1996	3-3	2-5	5-8
1979	3-4	1-5	4-9	1988	4-2	7-0	11-2	1997	3-3	3-3	6-6
1980	1-5	5-2	6-7	1989	2-5	6-0	8-5	1998	4-2	3-3	7-5
1981	0-4	0-0	0-4	1990	2-4	1-6	3-10	1999	1-5	2-4	3-9
1982	3-3	3-4	6-7	1991	2-5	2-4	4-9	2000	4-2	4-2	8-4
1983	3-4	3-3	6-7	1992	3-3	3-4	6-7	**TOTAL**	65-85	68-82	133-167
1984	4-2	4-3	8-5	1993	6-1	4-2	10-3				
1985	4-3	0-6	4-9	1994	0-3	3-4	3-7				

LAST SWEEP: BY TORONTO: At Toronto: June 23-25, 2000 (3 games);
At Boston: May 25-26, 1998 (2 games).
LAST SWEEP: BY BOSTON: At Toronto: July 27-28, 1999 (2 games);
At Boston: May 21-23, 1999 (3 games).
SERIES SWEPT: BY TORONTO: 2-game (2), 3-game (7), 4-game (3).
BY BOSTON: 2-game (5), 3-game (8), 4-game (5).
LONGEST WIN STREAK: BY TORONTO: 8 games; Aug. 11, 1987-June 11, 1988.
BY BOSTON: 7 games; September 26, 1980-May 11, 1981; April 25, 1977-Sept. 6, 1977
MOST RUNS, GAME: BY TORONTO: 15 runs, twice, last time 15-9 at Boston Sept. 27, 1988.
BY BOSTON: 14 runs, 14-6, at Boston, September 25, 1984.
WIDEST MARGIN VICTORY: BY TORONTO: 11 runs (twice), Last: 12-1, Sept. 4, 1998 at Toronto.
BY BOSTON: 12 runs, 13-1, September 18, 1985 at Boston.

CHICAGO WHITE SOX

SYNOPSIS: Toronto was 5-5 against the White Sox in 2000... Were 1-3 at home and 4-2 in Chicago... Have managed one win at home in each of the last two seasons... Have lost seven of the last nine at home... In the last five seasons have only once posted a losing record in Chicago (1998)... On September 17 the Blue Jays posted their widest margin of victory against Chicago with a 17-1 victory in the Windy City... Toronto hit only .252 with 16 home runs while the White Sox hit just .215 with 13 home runs... Jose Cruz and Carlos Delgado each hit three home runs to lead the club while Brad Fullmer collected a team high eight RBI... Toronto posted a 3.68 ERA while the White Sox had a 3.53 ERA... Frank Castillo was 1-1 with a 0.64 ERA in three games, two starts... Chris Carpenter was 1-0 in two starts with a 1.80 ERA... LHP Lance Painter was 1-0 with a 1.93 ERA... Also with wins were Kelvim Escobar and Billy Koch... Toronto now has a SkyDome record of 36-25 while in the New Comiskey Park are 24-19... Toronto holds the edge in the season series at 12-9-3.

	HOME W-L	AWAY W-L	TOTAL W-L		HOME W-L	AWAY W-L	TOTAL W-L		HOME W-L	AWAY W-L	TOTAL W-L
1977	2-3	1-5	3-8	1986	4-2	2-4	6-6	1995	4-1	1-5	5-6
1978	4-1	2-3	6-4	1987	3-3	5-1	8-4	1996	2-4	3-3	5-7
1979	1-5	4-2	5-7	1988	4-2	1-5	5-7	1997	3-2	3-3	6-5
1980	5-1	2-4	7-5	1989	5-1	6-0	11-1	1998	4-1	2-3	6-4
1981	2-4	3-3	5-7	1990	5-1	2-4	7-5	1999	1-5	3-1	4-6
1982	2-4	2-4	4-8	1991	3-3	2-4	5-7	2000	1-3	4-2	5-5
1983	2-4	5-1	7-5	1992	5-1	2-4	7-5	**TOTAL**	76-58	67-69	143-127
1984	4-2	4-2	8-4	1993	3-3	3-3	6-6				
1985	5-1	4-2	9-3	1994	2-1	1-1	3-2				

LAST SWEEP: BY TORONTO: At Toronto: April 17-19, 1998 (3 games);
At Chicago: April 9-10, 1997 (2 games).
LAST SWEEP: BY CHICAGO: At Toronto: Sept. 17-19, 1999 (3 games);
At Chicago: May 21-22, 1996 (2 games).
SERIES SWEPT: BY TORONTO: 2-game (5), 3-game (8).
BY CHICAGO: 2-game (7), 3-game (6).
LONGEST WIN STREAK: BY TORONTO: 7 games, May 28-April 27, 1990.
BY CHICAGO: 6 games, July 14, 1977-April 21, 1978.
MOST RUNS, GAME: BY TORONTO: 15 runs, 15-7, July 19, 1993 at Chicago.
BY CHICAGO: 16 runs, 16-7, July 11, 1982 at Toronto.
WIDEST MARGIN VICTORY: BY TORONTO: 13 runs, 14-1, Sept. 17, 2000 at Chicago.
BY CHICAGO: 11 runs, 13-2, August 23, 1981 at Toronto.

CLEVELAND INDIANS

SYNOPSIS: Toronto suffered their sixth losing season in the last seven years as they were 4-8 in 2000... Were 3-3 in Toronto and 1-5 at Jacobs Field... The Indians finished the season on a three game win streak after sweeping Toronto to close out the regular season in Cleveland, September 29 to October 1... With the win in 2000 the Indians have evened the season series record at 12-12-0... Cleveland won four straight, May 6 & 7 and July 4 & 5... Toronto hit .291 with 21 home runs while Cleveland hit .313 with 18 home runs... The Blue Jays were led by Carlos Delgado who hit .381 with three home runs and a team high 14 RBI... Jose Cruz hit .304 with four home runs and nine RBI... Also with nine RBI were Brad Fullmer and Alex Gonzalez... On the mound posted a 7.13 ERA which was bettered by Cleveland's 6.21... Toronto was led by David Wells who was 2-1 with a 2.79 ERA... Are now 14-24 at Jacobs Field and 39-32 at SkyDome... The only NO-HITTER in club history was thrown in Cleveland by Dave Stieb on September 2, 1990... Cleveland is the only club to throw a perfect game against Toronto (Len Barker, May 15, 1981).

	HOME W-L	AWAY W-L	TOTAL W-L		HOME W-L	AWAY W-L	TOTAL W-L		HOME W-L	AWAY W-L	TOTAL W-L
1977	1-5	4-4	5-9	1986	5-2	5-1	10-3	1995	2-4	1-6	3-10
1978	2-6	2-4	4-10	1987	4-2	4-3	8-5	1996	2-4	3-3	5-7
1979	4-2	1-6	5-8	1988	5-2	2-4	7-6	1997	3-2	2-4	5-6
1980	4-3	1-5	5-8	1989	5-1	3-4	8-5	1998	2-4	2-3	4-7
1981	1-1	1-3	2-4	1990	4-3	5-1	9-4	1999	2-4	5-1	7-5
1982	3-4	3-3	6-7	1991	6-0	6-1	12-1	2000	3-3	1-5	4-8
1983	4-2	5-2	9-4	1992	4-3	3-3	7-6	**TOTAL**	**83-66**	**71-77**	**154-143**
1984	5-2	2-4	7-6	1993	4-2	5-2	9-4				
1985	4-2	5-2	9-4	1994	4-3	0-3	4-6				

LAST SWEEP: BY TORONTO: At Toronto: August 6-7, 1997 (2 games);
At Cleveland: July 21-22, 1999 (2 games).
LAST SWEEP: BY CLEVELAND: At Toronto: Sept. 24-26, 1999 (3 games);
At Cleveland: Sept. 29-Oct. 1, 2000 (3 games).
SERIES SWEPT: BY TORONTO: 2-game (4), 3-game (6), 4-game (4).
BY CLEVELAND: 2-game (3), 3-game (6), 4-game (3).
LONGEST WIN STREAK: BY TORONTO: 13 games, June 12, 1991-April 21, 1992.
BY CLEVELAND: 7 games, April 26-July 9, 1977; July 10, 1980-May 6, 1981.
MOST RUNS, GAME: BY TORONTO: 15 runs (twice), Last: 15-1, Sept. 7, 1998 at Toronto.
BY CLEVELAND: 18 runs, 18-4, Sept. 24, 1999 at Toronto.
WIDEST MARGIN VICTORY: BY TORONTO: 14 runs, 15-1, Sept. 7, 1998 at Toronto.
BY CLEVELAND: 15 runs, 16-1, August 15, 1984 (1) at Cleveland.

DETROIT TIGERS

SYNOPSIS: Toronto continued to tame the Tigers posting a 9-3 record... Over the last two seasons are 19-5... Head into 2001 with more wins against Detroit than any other club at 162... Have not lost a season series since 1995 (6-7)... Were 5-1 at home and 4-2 in Detroit new Comerica Park... Over the last four seasons are18-5 at SkyDome... Finished the season on a five game win streak after sweeping a three game series in Toronto, September 8 to 10... Posted a 4.82 ERA with two shutouts while the Tigers ERA was 5.73... Kelvim Escobar was 1-0 in three games, one start, with a complete game shutout, a save and an ERA of 0.00... Also shutting out Detroit was Esteban Loiaza... Chris Carpenter was 2-1 despite a 7.65 ERA... Toronto hit .272 with 18 home runs while the Tigers hit .278 with 19 home runs... Brad Fullmer posted a team high five home runs while batting .381 with 12 RBI to tie for the club lead... Also with 12 RBI was Carlos Delgado who hit .357 with three home runs... Shannon Stewart hit .373 with two home runs and 11 RBI... Bobby Higginson hurt the Blue Jays hitting .378 with five HR's and 14 RBI... Toronto is now 50-35 at SkyDome... Toronto is now 14-9-1 in the season series.

	HOME W-L	AWAY W-L	TOTAL W-L		HOME W-L	AWAY W-L	TOTAL W-L		HOME W-L	AWAY W-L	TOTAL W-L
1977	5-3	0-7	5-10	1986	4-2	5-2	9-4	1995	3-4	3-3	6-7
1978	2-5	4-4	6-9	1987	4-3	2-4	6-7	1996	3-3	4-3	7-6
1979	1-6	3-3	4-9	1988	4-2	4-3	8-5	1997	4-2	2-4	6-6
1980	1-5	3-4	4-9	1989	6-1	5-1	11-2	1998	4-1	2-4	6-5
1981	1-3	3-3	4-6	1990	4-2	4-3	8-5	1999	5-1	5-1	10-2
1982	4-2	3-4	7-6	1991	5-2	3-3	8-5	2000	5-1	4-2	9-3
1983	4-3	3-3	7-6	1992	4-2	4-3	8-5	**TOTAL**	**87-65**	**75-77**	**162-142**
1984	2-4	3-4	5-8	1993	4-3	3-3	7-6				
1985	5-2	2-4	7-6	1994	3-3	1-2	4-5				

LAST SWEEP: BY TORONTO: At Toronto: Sept. 8-10, 2000 (3 games);
At Detroit: May 24-26, 1999 (3 games).
LAST SWEEP: BY DETROIT: At Toronto: September 7-9, 1984 (3 games);
At Detroit: October 1-3, 1987 (3 games).
SERIES SWEPT: BY TORONTO: 2-game (3), 3-game (9).
BY DETROIT: 2-game (3), 3-game (6), 4-game (1).
LONGEST WIN STREAK: BY TORONTO: 9 games, June 11, 1989-Sept. 25, 1989.
BY DETROIT: 6 games, Sept. 24-April 11, 1981.
MOST RUNS, GAME: BY TORONTO: 15 runs, 15-11, August 6, 1992 at Detroit; 15-0, July 6, 1996 at Detroit.
BY DETROIT: 16 runs, 16-3, June 13, 2000 at Detroit.
WIDEST MARGIN VICTORY: BY TORONTO: 15 runs, 15-0, July 6, 1996 at Detroit.
BY DETROIT: 13 runs, 16-3, June 13, 2000 at Detroit.

KANSAS CITY ROYALS

SYNOPSIS: Were 6-4 with a 4-2 record in Toronto and a 2-2 mark in Kansas City... Have won the season series four of the last five seasons... At home had not posted four wins since also going 4-2 in 1992... Opened the 2000 season at home against KC with a 5-4 victory... Six of the ten games were decided by two runs or less and four were one-run games... Toronto swept a two game series at home on August 22 and 23... Kelvim Escobar won both of the games in relief... Toronto posted a 4.70 ERA with three saves and the Royals had a 6.44 ERA with four saves... Toronto hit .295 with 21 home runs and eight stolen bases compared to the Royals who also hit .295 with eight home runs and nine stolen bases... Brad Fullmer hit .351 with four home runs and 15 RBI while Tony Batista hit .317 with five home runs and ten RBI... Shannon Stewart scored 12 runs in the ten games, batting .366 with six home runs and eight RBI... The season series now stands in Toronto's favour at 11-10-3... At SkyDome have a 34-32 record.

Year	HOME W-L	AWAY W-L	TOTAL W-L	Year	HOME W-L	AWAY W-L	TOTAL W-L	Year	HOME W-L	AWAY W-L	TOTAL W-L
1977	1-4	1-4	2-8	1986	3-3	4-2	7-5	1995	3-3	2-4	5-7
1978	2-3	3-2	5-5	1987	4-2	0-6	4-8	1996	3-3	5-2	8-5
1979	3-3	0-6	3-9	1988	4-2	4-2	8-4	1997	2-3	4-2	6-5
1980	2-4	1-5	3-9	1989	3-3	2-4	5-7	1998	2-4	3-2	5-6
1981	1-4	2-1	3-5	1990	3-3	4-2	7-5	1999	3-1	4-2	7-3
1982	5-1	3-3	8-4	1991	3-3	4-2	7-5	2000	4-2	2-2	6-4
1983	3-3	3-3	6-6	1992	4-2	3-3	7-5	**TOTAL**	**71-67**	**63-74**	**134-141**
1984	5-1	2-4	7-5	1993	3-3	1-5	4-8				
1985	2-4	3-3	5-7	1994	3-3	3-3	6-6				

LAST SWEEP: BY TORONTO: At Toronto: Aug. 22-23, 2000 (2 games);
At Kansas City: August 22-24, 1997 (3 games).

LAST SWEEP: BY KANSAS CITY: At Toronto: April 14-15, 1997 (2 games);
At Kansas City: April 29-30, 1998 (2 games).

SERIES SWEPT: BY TORONTO: 2-game (5), 3-game (5).
BY KANSAS CITY: 2-game (8), 3-game (4), 4-game (2).

LONGEST WIN STREAK: BY TORONTO: 5 games, (twice), Last: June 19-Sept. 4, 1999.
BY KANSAS CITY: 7 games, May 1-August 13, 1977; August 10, 1980-August 17, 1981.

MOST RUNS, GAME: BY TORONTO: 17 runs, 17-6, April 20, 1990 at Toronto.
BY KANSAS CITY: 16 runs, 16-12, August 12, 1979 at Toronto.

WIDEST MARGIN VICTORY: BY TORONTO: 11 runs, 17-6, April 20, 1990.
BY KANSAS CITY: 10 runs (twice), Last: 11-1, April 13, 1998 at Kansas City.

MINNESOTA TWINS

SYNOPSIS: Were 4-5 against the Twins, just the second losing season since 1989 (Were 5-8 in 1996)... Had 3-3 record in Toronto and a 1-2 mark at the Metrodome... Toronto was 1-4 in the first five games but took three of four to finish the season... Toronto hit .267 with ten home runs and only four stolen bases against the Twins, while they posted an average of .269 with eight home runs four stolen bases... Carlos Delgado had four of the clubs ten home runs, batted .385 with a team high eight RBI... In his five games Dave Martinez hit .381 with two doubles... Blue Jays posted a 4.10 ERA with a complete game and two saves... Minnesota had an ERA 3.92 with three save and one complete game... David Wells led the way for Toronto and was 2-0 in two starts with a complete game and an ERA of 2.12... Esteban Loaiza was 1-1 in two starts with a 1.98 ERA... Mark Redman shut down Toronto winning his two starts and posting an ERA of 1.38... The Blue Jays continue to lead the season series at 15-9-0... Have a 41-23 record at SkyDome and 59-48 at the Metrodome (were 5-20 at Metropolitan Stadium).

Year	HOME W-L	AWAY W-L	TOTAL W-L	Year	HOME W-L	AWAY W-L	TOTAL W-L	Year	HOME W-L	AWAY W-L	TOTAL W-L
1977	1-4	0-5	1-9	1986	5-1	3-3	8-4	1995	2-1	2-0	4-1
1978	2-3	2-3	4-6	1987	5-1	4-2	9-3	1996	3-4	2-4	5-8
1979	1-5	0-6	1-11	1988	3-3	2-4	5-7	1997	4-1	4-2	8-3
1980	2-4	3-3	5-7	1989	3-3	0-6	3-9	1998	4-1	3-3	7-4
1981	1-2	0-3	1-5	1990	3-3	6-0	9-3	1999	3-1	3-3	6-4
1982	4-2	3-3	7-5	1991	4-2	4-2	8-4	2000	3-3	1-2	4-5
1983	4-2	3-3	7-5	1992	4-2	3-3	7-5	**TOTAL**	**82-51**	**64-68**	**146-119**
1984	6-0	5-1	11-1	1993	5-1	5-1	10-2				
1985	5-1	3-3	8-4	1994	5-1	3-3	8-4				

LAST SWEEP: BY TORONTO: At Toronto: August 28-30, 1998 (3 games);
At Minnesota: July 17-18, 1995 (2 games).

LAST SWEEP: BY MINNESOTA: At Toronto: June 16-17, 1980 (2 games);
At Minnesota: September 12-14, 1989 (3 games).

SERIES SWEPT: BY TORONTO: 2-game (7), 3-game (10).
BY MINNESOTA: 2-game (5), 3-game (6), 4-game (1).

LONGEST WIN STREAK: BY TORONTO: 10 games, August 24, 1986-July 16, 1987.
BY MINNESOTA: 8 games, July 15, 1979-June 8, 1980.

MOST RUNS, GAME: BY TORONTO: 16 runs, 16-4, June 14, 1987 at Minnesota/16-5, September 4, 1992 at Toronto.
BY MINNESOTA: 16 runs, 16-8, May 8, 1979 at Minnesota.

WIDEST MARGIN VICTORY: BY TORONTO: 12 runs, 16-4, June 14, 1987 at Minnesota.
BY MINNESOTA: 12 runs twice, last time- 13-1, May 14, 1989 at Minnesota.

NEW YORK YANKEES

SYNOPSIS: Had their first winning season against the Yankees since 1994 (4-3) as Toronto posted a 7-5 record against the World Champions... Were 5-1 at home and 2-4 in New York... The five wins at home are the most since going 6-1 at home in 1992... Toronto finished the season on a four game win streak which included a three game sweep at home September 19 to 21 — was the first three game sweep in Toronto since July 31 to August 2, 1992... Won 16-3 on September 19, the third most runs ever scored against New York by Toronto... New York was one of two clubs that Toronto posted an ERA of under 4.00 against, was 3.99 with five saves... The Yankees posted an ERA of 4.79 with two saves... Toronto was led by David Wells who was 2-0 with a 1.23 ERA... Esteban Loaiza made two starts and was 1-1 with a 1.93 ERA... For New York Roger Clemens was 2-0 with a 1.29 ERA... At the plate Toronto hit .283 with 11 home runs while the Yankees hit .266 with 13 home runs... Jose Cruz posted team highs of four home runs and 12 RBI while hitting .255... Carlos Delgado hit .409 with three home runs and nine RBI... The season series remains in the Yankees favour at 9-14-1... At SkyDome are now 36-34.

	HOME W-L	AWAY W-L	TOTAL W-L		HOME W-L	AWAY W-L	TOTAL W-L		HOME W-L	AWAY W-L	TOTAL W-L
1977	2-5	4-4	6-9	1986	2-5	4-2	6-7	1995	1-5	0-7	1-12
1978	3-5	1-6	4-11	1987	2-4	5-2	7-6	1996	2-5	3-3	5-8
1979	2-4	2-5	4-9	1988	2-5	5-1	7-6	1997	2-4	3-3	5-7
1980	2-5	1-5	3-10	1989	2-4	4-3	6-7	1998	2-4	4-2	6-6
1981	1-1	2-1	3-2	1990	5-2	3-3	8-5	1999	1-5	1-5	2-10
1982	5-2	2-4	7-6	1991	3-3	4-3	7-6	2000	5-1	2-4	7-5
1983	4-2	2-5	6-7	1992	6-1	5-1	11-2	**TOTAL**	67-82	68-81	135-163
1984	4-3	1-5	5-8	1993	4-2	4-3	8-5				
1985	2-4	5-2	7-6	1994	3-1	1-2	4-3				

LAST SWEEP: BY TORONTO: At Toronto: July 31, Sept. 19-21, 2000 (3 games);
At New York: May 20-21, 1997 (2 games).

LAST SWEEP: BY NEW YORK: At Toronto: May 28-30, 1999 (3 games);
At New York: April 23-25, 1999 (3 games).

SERIES SWEPT: BY TORONTO: 2-game (1), 3-game (8).
BY NEW YORK: 2-game (2), 3-game (14), 4-game (1).

LONGEST WIN STREAK: BY TORONTO: 10 games, April 14-September 25, 1992.
BY NEW YORK: 13 games, May 10, 1995-June 4, 1996.

MOST RUNS, GAME: BY TORONTO: 19 runs, 19-3, September 10, 1977 at New York.
BY NEW YORK: 15 runs, 15-0, Sept. 27, 1977 at Toronto, (1st game).

WIDEST MARGIN VICTORY: BY TORONTO: 16 runs, 19-3, Sept. 10, 1977 at New York.
BY NEW YORK: 15 runs, 15-0, Sept. 27, 1977 at Toronto, (1st game).

OAKLAND ATHLETICS

SYNOPSIS: Toronto posted a 3-7 record against Oakland and are now 5-15 over the last two seasons... Were 1-3 in Toronto and 2-4 in Oakland... The one win at home halted a six game losing streak which dated back to 1999... Over the last two seasons are 1-9 at home against the A's... Opened the season winning two of three in Oakland and then were swept in Oakland, July 31 to August 2... Toronto then lost three of four at home September 1-4, enter 2001 on a three game losing streak... Were shut out on September 2 for the first time since July 25, 1992 at Oakland... Hit only .215 with five home runs which were lows against AL opponents... Tony Batista led the club with seven RBI but hit just .195... Carlos Delgado hit .300 with one home run and two RBI... The A's hit .294 with 16 home runs... Terrance Long hit .395 with five doubles, three home runs and six RBI... Toronto posted a 5.34 ERA while the A's had an ERA of 2.10... Toronto's three wins went to Carpenter, Wells and Frascatore... Lance Painter tossed 5.1 scoreless innings in relief... Tim Hudson was 3-0 against Toronto with an ERA of 1.59... At SkyDome are 26-37... The season series now stands at 8-13-3.

	HOME W-L	AWAY W-L	TOTAL W-L		HOME W-L	AWAY W-L	TOTAL W-L		HOME W-L	AWAY W-L	TOTAL W-L
1977	0-5	3-2	3-7	1986	3-3	1-5	4-8	1995	4-1	3-2	7-3
1978	4-2	0-5	4-7	1987	2-4	3-3	5-7	1996	3-3	5-1	8-4
1979	4-2	4-2	8-4	1988	0-6	3-3	3-9	1997	4-2	1-4	5-6
1980	2-4	2-4	4-8	1989	3-3	2-4	5-7	1998	3-2	3-3	6-5
1981	2-4	0-6	2-10	1990	1-5	4-2	5-7	1999	0-6	2-2	2-8
1982	3-3	6-0	9-3	1991	3-3	3-3	6-6	2000	1-3	2-4	3-7
1983	4-2	2-4	6-6	1992	3-3	3-3	6-6	**TOTAL**	58-78	66-69	124-147
1984	4-2	4-2	8-4	1993	2-4	5-1	7-5				
1985	3-3	4-2	7-5	1994	0-3	1-2	1-5				

LAST SWEEP: BY TORONTO: At Toronto: April 16-17, 1997 (2 games);
At Oakland: August 29-31, 1993 (3 games); At Las Vegas: April 1-3, 1996 (2 games).

LAST SWEEP: BY OAKLAND: At Toronto: August 13-15, 1999 (3 games);
At Oakland: July 31-Aug. 2, 2000 (3 games).

SERIES SWEPT: BY TORONTO: 2-game (8), 3-game (4).
BY OAKLAND: 2-game (10), 3-game (11), 4-game (1).

LONGEST WIN STREAK: BY TORONTO: 8 games, June 18-September 15, 1982.
BY OAKLAND: 9 games, July 22, 1980-May 24, 1981.

MOST RUNS, GAME: BY TORONTO: 18 runs, 18-11, July 29, 1995, at Toronto.
BY OAKLAND: 13 runs, (twice), Last: 13-5, August 14, 1999 at Toronto.

WIDEST MARGIN VICTORY: BY TORONTO: 11 runs, (twice), Last: 11-0, August 20, 1999 at Oakland.
BY OAKLAND: 11 runs, (twice), Last: 12-1, May 11, 1980 at Oakland.

SEATTLE MARINERS

SYNOPSIS: Continued to struggle against the Mariners posting only two wins for the second consecutive season... Were 2-8 with a 1-5 record at home and a 1-3 mark at Safeco Field... The 2-8 mark matches 1978 as the worst season record against the M's... Won on September 6 at home to end a seven game home losing streak... Were swept at home, April 14 to 16 as Seattle scored at least ten runs in three straight games, 47 overall in the three games... The 19-7 loss on April 16 was the widest margin of defeat to Seattle and the most runs ever allowed to the Mariners... Toronto hit .277 with 13 home runs while the Mariners hit .310 with 16 home runs... Carlos Delgado led the way hitting .405 with six doubles, three home runs and nine RBI... Brad Fullmer hit .346 with two home runs and seven RBI... On the mound Toronto posted their worst ERA against the Mariners at 7.32... Joey Hamilton and Esteban Loiaza earned the Blue Jays wins as they each made a start and both posted 2.57 ERA's... Freddy Garcia was 3-0 against Toronto with an ERA of 4.58... The season series now stands at 13-7-4... At SkyDome are 25-33 and at Safeco Field are 1-5.

	HOME W-L	AWAY W-L	TOTAL W-L		HOME W-L	AWAY W-L	TOTAL W-L		HOME W-L	AWAY W-L	TOTAL W-L
1977	2-3	4-1	6-4	1986	3-3	3-3	6-6	1995	1-2	3-1	4-3
1978	1-4	1-4	2-8	1987	5-1	5-1	10-2	1996	2-4	5-1	7-5
1979	3-3	1-5	4-8	1988	4-2	3-3	7-5	1997	2-3	1-5	3-8
1980	4-2	2-4	6-6	1989	4-2	3-3	7-5	1998	3-2	4-2	7-4
1981	2-1	1-2	3-3	1990	2-4	4-2	6-6	1999	0-3	2-4	2-7
1982	3-3	2-4	5-7	1991	3-3	4-2	7-5	2000	1-5	1-3	2-8
1983	3-3	5-1	8-4	1992	3-3	5-1	8-4	TOTAL	66-62	71-61	137-123
1984	3-3	4-2	7-5	1993	3-3	2-4	5-7				
1985	6-0	4-2	10-2	1994	3-0	2-1	5-1				

LAST SWEEP: BY TORONTO: At Toronto: August 11-12, 1998 (2 games);
At Seattle: August 19-20, 1998 (2 games).

LAST SWEEP: BY SEATTLE: At Toronto: April 14-16, 2000 (3 games);
At Seattle: Sept. 7-8, 1999 (2 games).

SERIES SWEPT: BY TORONTO: 2-game (8), 3-game (7).
BY SEATTLE: 2-game (3), 3-game (9), 4-game (1).

LONGEST WIN STREAK: BY TORONTO: 9 games, May 10-July 24, 1985.
BY SEATTLE: 8 games, Aug. 16, 1999-April 16, 2000.

MOST RUNS, GAME: BY TORONTO: 19 runs, 19-7, June 26, 1983 at Seattle.
BY SEATTLE: 19 runs, 19-7, April 16, 2000 at Toronto.

WIDEST MARGIN VICTORY: BY TORONTO: 14 runs, 16-2, August 19, 1998 at Seattle.
BY SEATTLE: 12 runs, 19-7, April 16, 2000 at Toronto.

TAMPA BAY DEVIL RAYS

SYNOPSIS: Were 7-5 for their third straight winning season against Tampa Bay... Were 3-3 in Toronto and 4-2 at Tropicana Field... Toronto is now 14-5 at home all time against Tampa Bay... Set a club mark with 12 runs scored against Tampa Bay in a 12-3 win on June 29... On June 27 had matched most runs allowed at 11 in an 11-1 loss which was the widest ever margin of defeat... Toronto hit .259 with 17 home runs while the Rays hit .250 with 13 home runs... Brad Fullmer had a team high 11 RBI while batting .310 with three home runs... Darrin Fletcher hit .410 with a home run and five RBI... Former Blue Jay Fred McGriff hit .341 with three home runs and 15 RBI... Toronto posted an ERA of 4.33 while the Devil Rays bettered that with a 4.09 ERA... David Wells led the way with a 2-0 record while posting a 3.63 ERA... Billy Koch appeared in five games and was 1-0 with two saves and did not allow a run... Travis Harper threw a complete game shutout on September 24, the second ever shutout at the hands of the Rays... The season series is 3-0 in Toronto's favour.

	HOME W-L	AWAY W-L	TOTAL W-L		HOME W-L	AWAY W-L	TOTAL W-L
1998	6-0	1-5	7-5	2000	3-3	4-2	7-5
1999	5-2	3-3	8-5	TOTAL	14-5	8-10	22-15

LAST SWEEP: BY TORONTO: At Toronto: July 19-20, 2000 (2 games);
At Tampa Bay: Sept. 28-29, 1999 (2 games).

LAST SWEEP: BY TAMPA BAY: At Toronto: none;
At Tampa Bay: June 15-17, 1998, (3 games).

SERIES SWEPT: BY TORONTO: 2-game (2), 3-game (2).
BY TAMPA BAY: 3-game (1).

LONGEST WIN STREAK: BY TORONTO: 4 games, (twice) Last: June 28-July 20, 2000.
BY TAMPA BAY: 3 games, (twice), Last: June 25-27, 1999.

MOST RUNS, GAME: BY TORONTO: 12 runs, 12-3, June 29, 2000 at Tampa Bay.
BY TAMPA BAY: 11 runs, (twice) Last: 11-1, June 27, 2000 at Tampa Bay.

WIDEST MARGIN VICTORY: BY TORONTO: 10 runs, 11-1, April 15, 1999 at Toronto.
BY TAMPA BAY: 10 runs, 11-1, June 27, 2000 at Tampa Bay.

TEXAS RANGERS

SYNOPSIS: Were 6-4 against the Rangers after losing seasons in 1998 and 1999... Were 3-1 at home and 3-3 in Arlington, Texas... Have had only one losing season in the past four in Texas... Five of the ten games were decided by two runs or less... On August 25 lost 1-0 in 11 innings at Texas — was the fifth 1-0 game against the Rangers in club history, are now 3-2 in those games... The Blue Jays hit .308 against the Rangers with 14 home runs which bettered the .276 average with 11 home runs posted by Texas... Carlos Delgado hit .289 with five doubles, a home run and a team high 11 RBI... Jose Cruz had a team high three homers... Shannon Stewart hit .467 with ten runs scored, six doubles, a triple, one home run and eight RBI... Were not able to out-pitch Texas as their 4.84 ERA was bettered by a 4.75 mark... David Wells was 2-0 in three starts with a 1.50 ERA and a complete game shutout on April 8 in Texas... Billy Koch made a team high six appearances and was 0-1 with four saves and a 3.86 ERA... At SkyDome the Blue Jays now have a 36-31 record... The season series is now in the Blue Jays favour at 11-10-3.

	HOME W-L	AWAY W-L	TOTAL W-L		HOME W-L	AWAY W-L	TOTAL W-L		HOME W-L	AWAY W-L	TOTAL W-L
1977	2-4	2-3	4-7	1986	4-2	3-3	7-5	1995	2-4	1-5	3-9
1978	4-1	3-3	7-4	1987	6-0	3-3	9-3	1996	1-5	1-5	2-10
1979	3-3	2-4	5-7	1988	4-2	2-4	6-6	1997	4-2	3-2	7-4
1980	3-3	2-4	5-7	1989	4-2	3-3	7-5	1998	3-3	1-4	4-7
1981	0-2	2-4	2-6	1990	4-2	1-5	5-7	1999	1-5	3-1	4-6
1982	6-0	2-4	8-4	1991	4-2	2-4	6-6	2000	3-1	3-3	6-4
1983	5-1	3-3	8-4	1992	4-2	5-1	9-3	**TOTAL**	82-55	60-79	142-134
1984	3-3	3-3	6-6	1993	2-4	3-3	5-7				
1985	4-2	5-1	9-3	1994	6-0	2-4	8-4				

LAST SWEEP: BY TORONTO: At Toronto: April 19-20, 1994 (2 games);
At Texas: June 22 and 24, 1992 (2 games).

LAST SWEEP: BY TEXAS: At Toronto: August 16-18, 1999 (3 games);
At Texas: August 4-5, 1998 (2 games).

SERIES SWEPT: BY TORONTO: 2-game (5), 3-game (5), 4-game (3).
BY TEXAS: 2-game (7), 3-game (5), 4-game (1).

LONGEST WIN STREAK: BY TORONTO: 9 games, August 10, 1986-May 9, 1987.
BY TEXAS: 8 games, June 7-September 10, 1996.

MOST RUNS, GAME: BY TORONTO: 19 runs, 19-4, August 9, 1999 at Texas.
BY TEXAS: 16 runs, 16-13, June 30, 1992 at Toronto.

WIDEST MARGIN VICTORY: BY TORONTO: 15 runs, 19-4, August 9, 1999 at Texas.
BY TEXAS: 14 runs, 14-0, July 26, 1977 at Toronto.

INTER-LEAGUE

SYNOPSIS: For the second straight season the Blue Jays posted a 9-9 record... The season inter-league record is now 1-1-2... The Blue Jays posted a 4-5 record in Toronto and 5-4 on the road... Began IL play with a six game road-trip to Florida and Atlanta... Were 1-2 in Florida with two one run losses... Shannon Stewart hit .583 with two doubles, a home run and five RBI... In Atlanta the Blue Jays took two of three with Delgado batting .556 with two home runs, including a grand slam, and had eight RBI... Against the Montreal Expos, won two of three at home from June 9-11 and two of three in Montreal, July 7-9... In the six games Toronto hit .308 with ten home runs... Tony Batista hit .370 with two home runs and 11 RBI... Raul Mondesi hit .333 with three home runs... Toronto finished their IL schedule with a six game homestand against the Phillies and the New York Mets... Lost two of three to Philadelphia and two of three to the Mets... In IL play Billy Koch was 2-1 with three saves and a 1.74 ERA and David Wells was 2-1 with a 4.67 ERA... In the 18 games Carlos Delgado hit .379 with nine doubles, seven home runs and 21 RBI... Tony Batista hit .320 with five homers and 17 RBI... Raul Mondesi had 19 RBI and hit .286 with six home runs... Darren Fletcher hit .326 with two home runs and six RBI while Shannon Stewart hit .329 with 17 runs, two home runs and 12 RBI.

ATLANTA BRAVES

	HOME W-L	AWAY W-L	TOTAL W-L
1997	1-2	0-0	1-2
1998	0-0	1-2	1-2
1999	3-0	0-0	3-0
2000	0-0	2-1	2-1
TOTAL	4-2	3-3	7-5

MONTREAL EXPOS

	HOME W-L	AWAY W-L	TOTAL W-L
1997	1-2	0-0	1-2
1998	2-0	2-0	4-0
1999	2-1	2-1	4-2
2000	2-1	2-1	4-2
TOTAL	7-4	6-2	13-6

PHILADELPHIA PHILLIES

	HOME W-L	AWAY W-L	TOTAL W-L
1997	0-0	2-1	2-1
1998	1-2	0-0	1-2
1999	0-0	1-2	1-2
2000	1-2	3-3	5-7
TOTAL	2-4	3-3	5-7

FLORIDA MARLINS

	HOME W-L	AWAY W-L	TOTAL W-L
1997	0-3	0-0	0-3
1998	0-0	1-2	1-2
1999	1-2	0-0	1-2
2000	0-0	1-2	1-2
TOTAL	1-5	2-4	3-9

NEW YORK METS

	HOME W-L	AWAY W-L	TOTAL W-L
1997	0-0	0-3	0-3
1998	2-1	0-0	2-1
1999	0-0	0-3	0-3
2000	1-2	0-0	1-2
TOTAL	3-3	0-6	3-9

CONSECUTIVE WINS AND LOSSES vs AMERICAN LEAGUE OPPONENTS

vs Anaheim

Most Consecutive Home Wins:	8	Aug. 16, 1998 - April 17, 2000
Most Consecutive Home Losses:	5	Sept. 5, 1983 - July 2, 1984
Most Consecutive Road Wins:	4	June 7, 1977 - Aug. 20, 1977
Most Consecutive Road Losses:	6	June 16, 1982 - June 10, 1983
Most Consecutive Wins:	7	Sept. 8, 1997 - Aug. 13, 1998
Most Consecutive Losses:	7	July 13, 1978 - June 5, 1979
	7	July 20, 1988 - May 6, 1989

vs Baltimore

Most Consecutive Home Wins:	14	June 13, 1998 - May 10, 2000
Most Consecutive Home Losses:	6	June 29, 1995 - July 21, 1996
Most Consecutive Road Wins:	5	June 8, 1991 - June 5, 1992
Most Consecutive Road Losses:	19	Sept. 15, 1978 - May 2, 1981
Most Consecutive Wins:	13	April 11, 1999 - May 10, 2000
Most Consecutive Losses:	15	Sept. 8, 1978 - Sept. 6, 1979

vs Boston

Most Consecutive Home Wins:	5	June 17, 1993 - Sept. 21, 1993
Most Consecutive Home Losses:	12	May 20, 1980 - May 11, 1981
Most Consecutive Road Wins:	15	Aug. 11, 1987 - Aug. 16, 1989
Most Consecutive Road Losses:	8	June 13, 1985 - July 1, 1986
Most Consecutive Wins:	8	Aug. 11, 1987 - June 11, 1988
Most Consecutive Losses:	7	April 25, 1977 - Sept. 6, 1977

vs Chicago

Most Consecutive Home Wins:	5	May 20, 1985 - Aug. 31, 1985
	5	May 28, 1989 - May 7, 1990
	5	May 9, 1990 - May 9, 1991
	5	May 29, 1992 - Sept. 1, 1992
	5	Aug. 5, 1997 - April 19, 1998
Most Consecutive Home Losses:	7	June 3, 1999 - May 21, 2000
Most Consecutive Road Wins:	6	May 19, 1989 - Sept. 6, 1989
Most Consecutive Road Losses:	5	Sept. 1, 1995 - May 22, 1996
Most Consecutive Wins:	7	May 28, 1989 - Sept. 6, 1989
Most Consecutive Losses:	6	July 14, 1977 - April 21, 1978

vs Cleveland

Most Consecutive Home Wins:	8	Sept. 23, 1990 - April 21, 1992
Most Consecutive Home Losses:	4	June 20, 1977 - June 23, 1977
	4	October 2, 1977 - June 30, 1978
Most Consecutive Road Wins:	7	June 12, 1991 - June 26, 1992
Most Consecutive Road Losses:	6	June 3, 1995 - Aug. 31, 1995
Most Consecutive Wins:	13	June 12, 1991 - April 21, 1992
Most Consecutive Losses:	7	April 28, 1977 - July 9, 1977
	7	July 10, 1980 - May 6, 1981

vs Detroit

Most Consecutive Home Wins:	5	June 11, 1989 - Aug. 24, 1989
	5	June 21, 2000 - Sept. 10, 2000
Most Consecutive Home Losses:	6	Aug. 1, 1978 - July 27, 1979
	6	Sept. 29, 1980 - April 18, 1981
Most Consecutive Road Wins:	6	Aug. 17, 1991 - Aug. 6, 1992
Most Consecutive Road Losses:	7	June 14, 1977 - April 7, 1978
Most Consecutive Wins:	9	June 11, 1989 - Sept. 25, 1989
Most Consecutive Losses:	6	Sept. 24, 1980 - April 11, 1981

vs Kansas City

Most Consecutive Home Wins:	5	May 7, 1982 - July 20, 1982
	5	June 19, 1999 - April 4, 2000
Most Consecutive Home Losses:	4	May 30, 1977 - Aug. 13, 1977
	4	Aug. 10, 1980 - Aug. 27, 1981
	4	July 27, 1997 - Aug. 24, 1998
Most Consecutive Road Wins:	3	April 26, 1978 - Aug 4, 1978
	3	Aug. 18, 1981 - April 29, 1982
	3	July 28, 1986 - July 30, 1986
	3	April 15, 1990 - Sept. 11, 1990
	3	Aug. 19, 1996 - Aug. 21, 1996
	3	Aug. 22, 1997 - Aug. 24, 1997
	3	Sept. 1, 1998 - May 11, 1999
	3	May 13, 1999 - Sept. 4, 1999
Most Consecutive Road Losses:	8	Aug. 5, 1978 - Aug. 1, 1979
Most Consecutive Wins:	5	April 27, 1984 - May 6, 1984
	5	June 19, 1999 - Sept. 4, 1999
Most Consecutive Losses:	7	May 1, 1977 - Aug. 13, 1977
	7	Aug. 10, 1980 - Aug. 17, 1981

vs Minnesota

Most Consecutive Home Wins:	10	May 21, 1984 - Sept. 6, 1985
Most Consecutive Home Losses:	5	Aug. 27, 1978 - July 13, 1979
	5	July 15, 1979 - Aug. 29, 1980
Most Consecutive Road Wins:	6	June 12, 1990 - Aug. 19, 1990
	6	June 15, 1993 - April 29, 1994
Most Consecutive Road Losses:	9	May 7, 1979 - June 8, 1980
Most Consecutive Wins:	10	Aug. 23, 1986 - July 16, 1987
Most Consecutive Losses:	8	July 15, 1979 - June 8, 1980

vs New York

Most Consecutive Home Wins:	7	April 14, 1992 - June 21, 1993
Most Consecutive Home Losses:	7	May 10, 1995 - June 11, 1996
Most Consecutive Road Wins:	6	Sept. 13, 1985 - June 29, 1986
Most Consecutive Road Losses:	9	June 21, 1979 - Sept. 17, 1980
Most Consecutive Wins:	10	April 14, 1992 - Sept. 25, 1992
Most Consecutive Losses:	13	May 10, 1995 - June 4, 1996

vs Oakland

Most Consecutive Home Wins:	4	June 15, 1979 - Aug. 27, 1979
	4	April 26, 1995 - July 29, 1995
	4	July 27, 1996 - April 17, 1997
Most Consecutive Home Losses:	7	April 26, 1988 - May 2, 1989
	7	June 6, 1993 - June 1, 1994
Most Consecutive Road Wins:	7	May 29, 1993 - April 11, 1994
Most Consecutive Road Losses:	8	July 22, 1980 - Sept. 30, 1981
Most Consecutive Wins:	8	June 18, 1982 - Sept. 15, 1982
Most Consecutive Losses:	9	July 22, 1980 - May 24, 1981

vs Seattle

Most Consecutive Home Wins:	6	May 10, 1985 - July 24, 1985
Most Consecutive Home Losses:	7	Aug. 16, 1999 - Sept. 5, 2000
Most Consecutive Road Wins:	4	May 25, 1990 - July 16, 1990
	4	Sept. 18, 1991 - July 16, 1992
Most Consecutive Road Losses:	5	June 3, 1979 - April 9, 1980
Most Consecutive Wins:	9	May 10, 1985 - July 24, 1985
Most Consecutive Losses:	8	Aug. 16, 1999 - April 16, 2000

vs Tampa Bay

Most Consecutive Home Wins:	7	May 19, 1999 - April 12, 1999
Most Consecutive Home Losses:	2	Sept. 24, 2000 - Sept. 25, 2000
Most Consecutive Road Wins:	3	June 28, 1999 - Sept. 29, 1999
Most Consecutive Road Losses:	5	June 15, 1998 - Sept. 19, 1998
Most Consecutive Wins:	4	July 3, 1999 - Sept. 29, 1999
	4	June 28, 2000 - July 20, 2000
Most Consecutive Losses:	3	June 15, 1998 - June 17, 1998
	3	June 25, 1999 - June 27, 1999

vs Texas

Most Consecutive Home Wins:	9	Aug. 15, 1986 - July 8, 1987
Most Consecutive Home Losses:	8	Sept. 12, 1995 - Sept. 10, 1996
Most Consecutive Road Wins:	4	Aug. 8, 1984 - April 28, 1985
Most Consecutive Road Losses:	5	July 26, 1989 - Aug. 4, 1990
Most Consecutive Wins:	9	Aug. 10, 1986 - May 9, 1987
Most Consecutive Losses:	8	June 7, 1996 - Sept. 10, 1996

HOMERUNS AT SKYDOME

Club	1989	1990	1991	1992	1993	1994	1995	1996	1997	1998	1999	2000	Total
Anaheim	1	6	5	3	7	0	5	4	7	3	5	9	55
Atlanta*	–	–	–	–	–	–	–	–	2	–	1	–	3
Baltimore	4	8	9	3	6	6	7	13	3	4	9	4	76
Boston	5	2	6	6	6	1	8	9	11	9	7	3	73
Chicago	0	4	9	3	1	7	4	10	3	6	5	3	55
Cleveland	3	8	1	9	10	9	12	7	6	10	8	4	87
Detroit	4	11	9	3	11	7	8	9	3	8	6	9	88
Florida*	–	–	–	–	–	–	–	–	2	–	2	–	4
Kansas City	0	6	4	4	6	8	7	6	4	6	2	5	58
Milwaukee***	5	6	7	5	10	3	8	8	6	–	–	–	58
Minnesota	3	6	1	3	3	5	3	4	1	2	3	4	38
Montreal*	–	–	–	–	–	–	–	–	4	1	2	2	9
New York	3	10	5	6	2	4	7	7	3	4	6	7	64
New York (N)**	–	–	–	–	–	–	–	–	–	6	–	6	12
Oakland	7	5	7	6	6	2	4	7	6	3	15	9	77
Philadelphia**	–	–	–	–	–	–	–	–	–	4	–	4	8
Seattle	2	6	6	7	4	7	4	9	9	10	5	13	82
Tampa Bay**	–	–	–	–	–	–	–	–	–	0	7	7	14
Texas	2	4	3	2	9	5	2	9	2	1	10	3	52
Toronto	45	93	75	79	90	63	73	87	68	112	96	134	1015
Opponents	39	82	72	60	81	64	79	102	72	77	93	92	913

*   Atlanta, Florida and Montreal did not play at Skydome until 1997.
**   Tampa Bay, New York (N) and Philadelphia did not play at Skydome until 1998.
*** Milwaukee moved to the National League in 1998.

OPPOSING BATTERS vs BLUE JAYS

Batter	2000 AVG.	AB	HITS	HR	RBI	CAREER AVG.	AB	HITS	HR	RBI
Abbott, Jeff	.214	14	3	1	1	.229	35	8	1	3
Abbott, Kurt	–	–	–	–	–	.182	22	4	1	5
Abreu, Bobby	.231	13	3	0	0	.342	38	13	2	5
Agbayani, Benny	.333	9	3	0	1	.313	16	5	2	3
Alcantara, Israel	.167	6	1	0	0	.167	6	1	0	0
Alexander, Manny	.250	24	6	0	0	.264	53	14	1	4
Alfonzo, Edgardo	.462	13	6	0	2	.353	51	18	3	8
Alicea, Luis	.290	31	9	0	2	.279	129	36	2	13
Allen, Chad	.000	0	0	0	0	.167	30	5	0	1
Alomar, Roberto	.269	52	14	2	7	.293	215	63	5	27
Alomar, Sandy	.355	31	11	1	6	.261	303	79	6	41
Alvarez, Gabe	–	–	–	–	–	.077	13	1	0	0
Alou, Moises	–	–	–	–	–	.200	10	2	0	2
Amaral, Rich	.000	4	0	0	0	.259	108	28	0	9
Anderson, Brady	.211	38	8	1	7	.241	473	114	15	43
Anderson, Garrett	.375	48	18	1	7	.298	262	78	5	36
Ardoin, Danny	.000	13	0	0	0	.130	23	3	1	2
Arias, Alex	.250	4	1	0	0	.348	23	8	0	3
Arias, George	–	–	–	–	–	.200	20	4	1	5
Armas, Tony	.000	1	0	0	0	.000	1	0	0	0
Ausmus, Brad	.278	36	10	1	3	.276	98	27	2	8
Baerga, Carlos	–	–	–	–	–	.283	336	95	7	50
Baines, Harold	.382	34	13	3	9	.295	757	223	37	130
Bako, Paul	.429	7	3	0	2	.296	27	8	0	3
Barrett, Michael	.000	7	0	0	0	.095	21	2	0	0
Bartee, Kimera	–	–	–	–	–	.071	28	2	0	0
Batista, Tony	–	–	–	–	–	.154	13	2	0	0
Becker, Rich	.250	20	5	1	2	.221	149	33	2	11
Bell, David	.160	25	4	0	3	.254	71	18	3	12
Bell, Derek	.357	14	5	1	3	.357	14	5	1	3
Bell, Jay	–	–	–	–	–	.292	89	26	3	14
Belle, Albert	.250	56	14	1	9	.309	460	142	29	94
Belliard, Rafael	–	–	–	–	–	.500	2	1	0	0
Bellinger, Clay	.133	15	2	0	0	.091	22	2	0	0
Beltran, Carlos	.235	17	4	0	0	.255	51	13	0	2
Beltre, Esteban	–	–	–	–	–	.250	28	7	0	0
Benitez, Yamil	–	–	–	–	–	.421	19	8	1	2
Berg, Dave	.143	7	1	0	0	.318	22	7	0	2
Bergeron, Peter	.167	12	2	0	1	.167	12	2	0	1
Berroa, Geronimo	–	–	–	–	–	.279	201	56	9	31
Bichette, Dante	–	–	–	–	–	.190	105	20	4	16
Blum, Geoff	.000	2	0	0	0	.000	2	0	0	0
Bones, Ricky	.000	0	0	0	1	.000	0	0	0	1
Bonilla, Bobby	.500	2	1	0	1	.272	81	22	5	17
Boone, Bret	–	–	–	–	–	.175	40	7	2	6
Borders, Pat	–	–	–	–	–	.225	40	9	1	5
Bordick, Mike	.308	39	12	0	3	.275	345	95	2	37
Bournigal, Rafael	–	–	–	–	–	.297	64	19	2	11
Bowers, Brent	–	–	–	–	–	.252	147	37	0	19
Bragg, Darren	–	–	–	–	–	.232	224	52	6	23
Branyan, Russell	.353	17	6	3	8	.353	17	6	3	8
Brogna, Rico	–	–	–	–	–	.231	39	9	1	5
Brosius, Scott	.242	33	8	0	0	.242	231	56	3	29
Brown, Brant	.000	3	0	0	0	.000	3	0	0	0
Buchanan, Brian	.143	7	1	0	0	.143	7	1	0	0
Buford, Damon	–	–	–	–	–	.221	86	19	5	19
Buhner, Jay	.400	25	10	3	10	.252	317	80	19	59
Burrell, Pat	.300	10	3	1	4	.300	10	3	1	4
Burks, Ellis	–	–	–	–	–	.253	257	65	6	24
Burnitz, Jeromy	–	–	–	–	–	.189	53	10	0	2
Bush, Homer	–	–	–	–	–	.600	5	3	0	0
Cabrera, Jolbert	.185	27	5	0	3	.200	30	6	0	3
Cabrera, Orlando	.261	23	6	0	1	.250	44	11	0	2
Caceres, Edgar	–	–	–	–	–	.286	7	2	0	1
Cairo, Miguel	.176	17	3	0	2	.200	90	18	0	9
Cameron, Mike	.200	35	7	1	6	.212	85	18	1	11
Canizaro, Jay	.176	17	3	0	1	.176	17	3	0	1
Canseco, Jose	.235	34	8	3	6	.279	484	135	41	114
Cardona, Javier	.333	3	1	0	0	.333	3	1	0	0
Carr, Chuck	–	–	–	–	–	.000	13	0	0	0
Castilla, Vinny	.050	20	1	0	1	.050	20	1	0	1
Castillo, Alberto	–	–	–	–	–	.000	1	0	0	0
Castillo, Luis	.429	7	3	0	0	.357	14	5	0	2
Catalanotto, Frank	.320	25	8	1	7	.262	65	17	2	9
Cedeno, Andujar	–	–	–	–	–	.182	22	4	0	3
Cedeno, Domingo	–	–	–	–	–	.000	3	0	0	0
Cedeno, Roger	–	–	–	–	–	.455	11	5	1	3
Chavez, Eric	.242	33	8	1	6	.250	48	12	2	9
Chen, Bruce	.000	1	0	0	0	.000	1	0	0	0
Christensen, McKay	.500	4	2	0	1	.500	4	2	0	1

Batter	2000					CAREER				
	AVG.	AB	HITS	HR	RBI	AVG.	AB	HITS	HR	RBI
Christenson, Ryan	.000	3	0	0	1	.231	26	6	1	5
Cirillo, Jeff	–	–	–	–	–	.289	114	33	3	16
Clark, Tony	.233	30	7	3	6	.274	201	55	14	32
Clark, Will	.458	24	11	4	5	.310	239	74	11	39
Clayton, Royce	.290	31	9	2	5	.259	58	15	2	9
Clemente, Edgard	.250	8	2	0	1	.250	8	2	0	1
Clyburn, Danny	–	–	–	–	–	.000	9	0	0	0
Coffie, Ivanon	.182	11	2	0	2	.182	11	2	0	2
Colbrunn, Greg	–	–	–	–	–	.350	20	7	1	8
Conine, Jeff	.435	23	10	0	1	.291	79	23	1	8
Cookson, Brent	–	–	–	–	–	.167	6	1	0	0
Coomer, Ron	.303	33	10	1	6	.288	132	38	4	20
Cooper, Scott	–	–	–	–	–	.279	111	31	0	10
Coquillette, Trace	.125	8	1	0	2	.125	8	1	0	2
Cordero, Wil	–	–	–	–	–	.357	115	41	5	23
Cordova, Marty	–	–	–	–	–	.311	148	46	4	20
Counsell, Craig	–	–	–	–	–	.250	20	5	1	3
Cox, Steve	.276	29	8	1	5	.273	33	9	1	5
Crede, Joe	.500	2	1	0	0	.500	2	1	0	0
Cruz, Deivi	.419	43	18	1	6	.270	141	38	4	18
Cruz, Fausto	–	–	–	–	–	.188	16	3	0	0
Cruz, Jose	–	–	–	–	–	.467	15	7	1	1
Cruz, Jacob	–	–	–	–	–	.167	6	1	0	1
Cummings, Midre	.154	13	2	1	2	.308	26	8	2	5
Curtis, Chad	.316	19	6	0	1	.254	268	68	9	37
Cuyler, Milt	–	–	–	–	–	.262	122	32	0	6
Dalesandro, Mark	–	–	–	–	–	.000	0	0	0	0
Damon, Johnny	.304	46	14	2	6	.260	254	66	5	20
Daubach, Brian	.211	38	8	2	6	.219	64	14	3	9
Davis, Eric	–	–	–	–	–	.265	49	13	1	8
Davis, Russ	–	–	–	–	–	.263	114	30	8	17
Dellucci, David	–	–	–	–	–	.125	8	1	0	0
Dempster, Ryan	.000	2	0	0	0	.000	2	0	0	0
DeShields, Delino	.277	47	13	2	11	.237	59	14	2	11
Devarez, Cesar	–	–	–	–	–	.222	36	8	2	5
Diaz, Einar	.429	21	9	0	6	.351	57	20	1	9
DiFelice, Mike	.455	11	5	1	1	.300	40	12	2	8
Disarcina, Gary	–	–	–	–	–	.283	258	73	4	28
Doster, David	–	–	–	–	–	.500	2	1	0	0
Ducey, Rob	.000	5	0	0	0	.186	43	8	0	2
Duncan, Mariano	–	–	–	–	–	.333	48	16	2	3
Dunston, Shawn	–	–	–	–	–	.000	4	0	0	0
Dunwoody, Todd	.400	15	6	0	5	.323	31	10	0	5
Durham, Ray	.111	36	4	0	3	.242	219	53	3	19
Dye, Jermaine	.297	37	11	1	7	.280	100	28	2	11
Easley, Damon	.273	33	9	0	5	.296	216	64	7	35
Edmonds, Jim	–	–	–	–	–	.301	166	50	4	22
Eisenreich, Jim	–	–	–	–	–	.224	152	34	1	15
Elster, Kevin	–	–	–	–	–	.169	65	11	1	7
Encarnacio, Angelo	–	–	–	–	–	.000	0	0	0	0
Encarnacio, Juan	.219	32	7	1	5	.284	88	25	3	14
Erstad, Darin	.426	47	20	3	11	.299	174	52	8	25
Evans, Tom	.000	5	0	0	1	.000	5	0	0	1
Everett, Carl	.421	38	16	3	10	.409	44	18	3	11
Fabregas, Jorge	–	–	–	–	–	.275	69	19	0	13
Fasano, Sal	.000	3	0	0	0	.150	20	3	1	2
Febles, Carlos	.143	28	4	0	2	.255	51	13	0	5
Fick, Rob	.600	5	3	1	5	.308	13	4	2	6
Finley, Steve	–	–	–	–	–	.217	46	10	1	7
Flaherty, John	.115	26	3	1	3	.182	132	24	5	15
Floyd, Cliff	.333	12	4	0	1	.333	24	8	0	2
Fordyce, Brook	.500	10	5	1	3	.259	27	7	1	3
Franco, Julio	–	–	–	–	–	.303	545	165	8	69
Franco, Matt	.000	3	0	0	0	.200	10	2	0	1
Frye, Jeff	.341	41	14	0	3	.311	164	51	1	19
Fryman, Travis	.184	49	9	0	7	.235	429	101	14	75
Fullmer, Brad	–	–	–	–	–	.533	15	8	2	5
Furcal, Rafael	.231	13	3	0	1	.231	13	3	0	1
Gagne, Greg	–	–	–	–	–	.253	368	93	10	53
Galarraga, Andres	.308	13	4	0	1	.308	13	4	0	1
Gant, Ron	.364	22	8	4	9	.382	34	13	4	13
Garica, Carlos	–	–	–	–	–	.333	3	1	0	0
Garcia, Jesse	.000	2	0	0	0	.250	4	1	0	0
Garcia, Karim	.000	1	0	0	0	.171	35	6	1	2
Garciaparra, Nomar	.308	26	8	1	9	.303	175	53	10	32
Gates, Brent	–	–	–	–	–	.235	153	36	1	27
Giambi, Jason	.300	30	9	2	4	.312	221	69	9	37
Giambi, Jeremy	.333	6	2	0	1	.231	26	6	1	4
Gil, Benji	.194	31	6	0	2	.227	97	22	1	11
Giles, Brian	–	–	–	–	–	.263	80	21	1	9
Gilkey, Bernard	–	–	–	–	–	.278	18	5	0	4
Gipson, Charles	.167	6	1	0	0	.111	9	1	0	0

Batter	2000 AVG.	AB	HITS	HR	RBI	CAREER AVG.	AB	HITS	HR	RBI
Girardi, Joe	–	–	–	–	–	.248	101	25	1	8
Glanville, Doug	.267	15	4	0	0	.341	44	15	2	4
Glaus, Troy	.333	48	16	4	12	.254	118	30	7	20
Glavine, Tom	.000	0	0	0	0	.667	3	2	0	3
Gonzalez, Alex	.250	8	2	0	1	.136	22	3	0	3
Gonzalez, Juan	.196	46	9	3	5	.267	375	100	20	60
Gonzalez, Luis	–	–	–	–	–	.179	39	7	3	4
Goodwin, Tom	–	–	–	–	–	.274	201	55	1	8
Graffanino, Tony	.000	3	0	0	0	.000	5	0	0	0
Grebeck, Craig	–	–	–	–	–	.303	89	27	1	8
Green, Scarborough	.000	0	0	0	0	.000	0	0	0	0
Greene, Charlie	–	–	–	–	–	.200	5	1	0	0
Greene, Todd	–	–	–	–	–	.231	52	12	0	2
Greene, Willie	–	–	–	–	–	.000	5	0	0	0
Greer, Rusty	.263	38	10	1	8	.262	244	64	7	46
Grieve, Ben	.250	36	9	2	7	.237	114	27	6	18
Griffey, Ken, Jr.	–	–	–	–	–	.317	385	122	34	75
Grissom, Marquis	–	–	–	–	–	.195	41	8	2	5
Grudzielanek, Mark	–	–	–	–	–	.222	27	6	0	3
Guerrero, Vladimir	.238	21	5	1	3	.310	71	22	4	11
Guerrero, Wilton	.273	22	6	0	3	.278	36	10	0	4
Guillen, Carlos	.125	8	1	0	0	.125	8	1	0	0
Guillen, Jose	.238	21	5	0	0	.222	27	6	0	0
Guillen, Ozzie	.231	13	3	0	2	.242	443	107	3	35
Guzman, Cristian	.324	37	12	2	5	.262	61	16	2	7
Gwynn, Chris	–	–	–	–	–	.370	46	17	0	6
Hairston Jr., Jerry	.231	13	3	0	2	.400	35	14	1	4
Hall, Toby	.286	7	2	1	1	.286	7	2	1	1
Halter, Shane	.333	21	7	0	1	.263	38	10	0	1
Hamilton, Darryl	–	–	–	–	–	.321	246	79	4	34
Hammonds, Jeffrey	–	–	–	–	–	.267	90	24	2	6
Harper, Brian	–	–	–	–	–	.239	188	45	6	24
Harris, Lenny	.625	8	5	1	2	.625	8	5	1	2
Haselman, Bill	.280	25	7	1	4	.256	90	23	3	12
Hatteberg, Scott	.276	29	8	0	8	.264	110	29	1	15
Hayes, Charlie	–	–	–	–	–	.235	81	19	0	3
Helfand, Eric	–	–	–	–	–	.000	7	0	0	0
Henderson, Rickey	.316	19	6	0	3	.288	695	200	20	78
Hermanson, Dustin	.000	1	0	0	0	.000	3	0	0	0
Hernandez, Livan	–	–	–	–	–	.250	4	1	0	1
Hernandez, Ramon	.200	25	5	0	2	.200	25	5	0	2
Herrera, Jose	–	–	–	–	–	.000	14	0	0	0
Higginson, Bobby	.378	45	17	5	14	.301	246	74	15	39
Hill, Glenallen	.100	10	1	1	1	.222	81	18	7	12
Hinch, A.J.	.400	5	2	0	0	.269	52	14	4	11
Hocking, Denny	.286	28	8	0	0	.216	102	22	1	8
Hollins, Dave	–	–	–	–	–	.227	88	20	2	8
Hubbard, Trenidad	1.000	2	2	0	0	1.000	2	2	0	0
Huff, Aubrey	.300	10	3	0	1	.300	10	3	0	1
Hulse, David	–	–	–	–	–	.245	143	35	0	6
Hundley, Todd	–	–	–	–	–	.455	11	5	0	1
Hunter, Brian	.000	4	0	0	0	.229	131	30	0	3
Hunter, Torii	.375	24	9	2	6	.298	57	17	2	7
Huskey, Butch	.273	11	3	0	1	.339	59	20	5	18
Huson, Jeff	–	–	–	–	–	.187	107	20	0	3
Ibanez, Raul	.571	7	4	0	0	.294	17	5	0	1
Ingram, Riccardo	–	–	–	–	–	.000	3	0	0	0
Isringhausen, Jason	–	–	–	–	–	.000	3	0	0	0
Jaha, John	–	–	–	–	–	.277	191	53	12	33
Javier, Stan	.455	22	10	0	5	.283	152	43	1	20
Jefferies, Gregg	.167	12	2	0	0	.324	105	34	1	13
Jefferson, Reggie	–	–	–	–	–	.308	172	53	6	23
Jensen, Marcus	.000	2	0	0	0	.000	2	0	0	0
Jeter, Derek	.348	46	16	1	5	.314	236	74	6	27
Jimenez, D'Angelo	–	–	–	–	–	.333	3	1	0	0
Johnson, Brian	.222	9	2	0	1	.118	17	2	0	1
Johnson, Charles	.415	41	17	3	12	.342	76	26	4	19
Johnson, Keith	.667	3	2	0	0	.667	3	2	0	0
Johnson, Lance	1.000	1	1	0	0	.285	239	68	2	22
Johnson, Mark	.429	14	6	1	3	.276	29	8	1	5
Johnson, Russ	.300	10	3	1	1	.300	10	3	1	1
Jones, Andruw	.500	12	6	0	2	.362	47	17	0	4
Jones, Chipper	.286	7	2	1	2	.190	42	8	3	4
Jones, Jacque	.323	31	10	1	3	.352	54	19	3	11
Jones, Terry	.417	12	5	0	4	.280	25	7	0	5
Jordan, Brian	.500	12	6	0	5	.500	24	12	0	8
Jordan, Kevin	.250	4	1	0	1	.217	23	5	0	2
Jordan, Ricky	–	–	–	–	–	.500	4	2	0	0
Jose, Felix	1.000	2	2	0	0	.223	121	27	2	12
Joyner, Wally	.500	2	1	0	0	.348	374	130	14	73
Justice, David	.303	33	10	2	10	.288	146	42	8	30
Kapler, Gabe	.270	37	10	1	4	.238	84	20	1	8

Batter	AVG.	AB	2000 HITS	HR	RBI	AVG.	AB	CAREER HITS	HR	RBI
Kelly, Roberto	–	–	–	–	–	.333	99	33	1	12
Kennedy, Adam	.283	46	13	1	11	.283	46	13	1	11
Kent, Jeff	–	–	–	–	–	.000	2	0	0	1
Kingsale, Gene	.273	11	3	0	2	.250	12	3	0	2
Klesko, Ryan	–	–	–	–	–	.318	22	7	2	7
Knoblauch, Chuck	.261	46	12	0	2	.286	412	118	4	31
Konerko, Paul	.107	28	3	2	3	.242	66	16	2	5
Koskie, Corey	.240	25	6	0	1	.349	43	15	0	7
Koslofski, Kevin	–	–	–	–	–	.200	10	2	0	3
Kotsay, Mark	.231	13	3	0	0	.235	34	8	0	0
Kreuter, Chad	–	–	–	–	–	.208	125	26	0	5
Lamb, David	.333	3	1	0	0	.200	5	1	0	0
Lamb, Mike	.304	23	7	0	0	.304	23	7	0	0
Lampkin, Tom	.000	3	0	0	0	.147	34	5	1	8
Lansing, Mike	–	–	–	–	–	.214	14	3	0	1
Latham, Chris	–	–	–	–	–	.000	6	0	0	0
La Croy, Matt	.000	7	0	0	0	.000	7	0	0	0
Lawton, Matt	.387	31	12	1	10	.278	162	45	3	27
Ledee, Ricky	.190	58	11	0	7	.200	90	18	0	11
Ledesma, Aaron	.000	0	0	0	0	.327	49	16	0	2
Lee, Carlos	.143	28	4	1	4	.257	70	18	3	13
Lee, Derek	.250	4	1	0	0	.412	17	7	0	0
Lennon, Patrick	–	–	–	–	–	.250	4	1	0	0
Lesher, Brian	.000	0	0	0	0	1.000	1	1	0	1
Levis, Jesse	–	–	–	–	–	.200	40	8	0	0
Lewis, Darrin	.400	30	12	0	5	.333	141	47	1	18
Lewis, Mark	.364	11	4	0	1	.252	115	29	0	11
Leyritz, Jim	.200	5	1	0	0	.223	179	40	7	25
Lieberthal, Mike	.200	10	2	0	2	.206	34	7	0	5
Liefer, Jeff	.000	4	0	0	0	.167	6	1	0	1
Lindsey, Rodney	.000	0	0	0	0	.000	0	0	0	0
Lira, Felipe	.500	2	1	1	1	.500	2	1	1	1
Lockhart, Keith	.143	7	1	0	0	.294	119	35	0	10
Lofton, Kenny	.367	30	11	1	8	.303	337	102	10	34
Long, Terrence	.395	43	17	3	6	.395	43	17	3	6
Lopez, Javy	.250	12	3	1	2	.316	38	12	3	7
Lopez, Luis	–	–	–	–	–	.200	20	4	0	0
Lowell, Mike	.500	12	6	1	4	.385	26	10	2	7
Lunar, Fernando	.000	2	0	0	1	.000	2	0	0	1
Mabry, John	.385	13	5	1	1	.280	25	7	2	2
Macfarlane, Mike	–	–	–	–	–	.238	256	61	9	28
Macias, Jose	.067	15	1	0	0	.063	16	1	0	0
Mack, Shane	–	–	–	–	–	.282	174	49	5	22
Maddux, Greg	–	–	–	–	–	.000	2	0	0	0
Magee, Wendell	.222	9	2	0	0	.222	9	2	0	0
Mahay, Rob	.000	1	0	0	0	.000	1	0	0	0
Martin, Al	.400	5	2	1	1	.400	5	2	1	1
Martinez, Dave	.000	4	0	0	0	.308	159	49	1	19
Martinez, Edgar	.310	42	13	2	16	.298	399	119	15	69
Martinez, Felix	.125	24	3	0	0	.135	37	5	0	1
Martinez, Tino	.205	44	9	1	4	.212	302	64	10	42
Mateo, Ruben	.385	13	5	1	1	.385	13	5	1	1
Matheny, Mike	–	–	–	–	–	.206	63	13	0	6
Matos, Luis	.154	13	2	0	0	.154	13	2	0	0
Maxwell, Jason	.000	4	0	0	0	.000	4	0	0	0
Mayne, Brent	–	–	–	–	–	.236	140	33	1	19
McCarty, Dave	.167	12	2	0	0	.169	59	10	0	3
McCracken, Quinton	–	–	–	–	–	.345	58	20	2	7
McDonald, Jason	–	–	–	–	–	.211	71	15	1	1
McDonald, John	–	–	–	–	–	.286	7	2	0	0
McEwing, Joe	.111	9	1	1	4	.111	9	1	1	4
McGinnis, Russ	–	–	–	–	–	.200	5	1	0	0
McGriff, Fred	.341	41	14	3	15	.298	121	36	9	27
McGwire, Mark	–	–	–	–	–	.207	305	63	20	54
McLemore, Mark	.206	34	7	1	5	.314	341	107	3	40
McMillon, Billy	.000	5	0	0	0	.000	5	0	0	0
Menechino, Frank	.333	9	3	0	1	.333	9	3	0	1
Merced, Orlando	–	–	–	–	–	.333	15	5	2	9
Merloni, Lou	–	–	–	–	–	.417	12	5	0	3
Merullo, Matt	–	–	–	–	–	.179	28	5	0	1
Mientkiewicz, Doug	–	–	–	–	–	.300	20	6	0	3
Mieske, Matt	–	–	–	–	–	.264	110	29	4	14
Millar, Kevin	.333	6	2	1	1	.278	18	5	2	2
Miller, Damian	–	–	–	–	–	.200	5	1	0	0
Miller, Orlando	–	–	–	–	–	.333	9	3	0	2
Millwood, Kevin	.000	1	0	0	0	.000	1	0	0	0
Minor, Ryan	.400	5	2	0	1	.500	6	3	0	2
Moeller, Chad	.000	0	0	0	0	.000	0	0	0	0
Molina, Ben	.222	36	8	0	3	.209	43	9	0	3
Molina, Izzy	–	–	–	–	–	.286	7	2	0	0
Monahan, Shane	–	–	–	–	–	.143	7	1	0	0
Mora, Melvin	.250	16	4	0	0	.222	18	4	0	0

Batter	AVG.	AB	2000 HITS	HR	RBI	AVG.	AB	CAREER HITS	HR	RBI
Morandini, Mickey	.167	6	1	0	2	.154	13	2	0	2
Mordecai, Mike	.111	9	1	1	3	.238	21	5	1	3
Morris, Hal	.500	4	2	0	0	.419	43	18	1	7
Mouton, Lyle	–	–	–	–	–	.283	46	13	1	9
Myers, Greg	.000	3	0	0	0	.274	106	29	2	14
Naehring, Tim	–	–	–	–	–	.250	132	33	3	15
Nagy, Charles	–	–	–	–	–	.000	2	0	0	0
Neel, Troy	–	–	–	–	–	.358	53	19	3	9
Nevin, Phil	–	–	–	–	–	.159	63	10	1	3
Newfield, Marc	–	–	–	–	–	.316	19	6	1	2
Newson, Warren	–	–	–	–	–	.140	57	8	1	4
Nieves, Melvin	–	–	–	–	–	.250	60	15	2	3
Nilsson, Dave	–	–	–	–	–	.252	147	37	7	17
Nixon, Otis	–	–	–	–	–	.276	152	42	1	13
Nixon, Trot	.270	37	10	1	7	.297	64	19	1	11
Nokes, Matt	–	–	–	–	–	.213	169	36	9	26
Norton, Greg	.053	19	1	0	0	.151	73	11	0	1
Nunez, Vladimir	.000	1	0	0	0	.000	1	0	0	0
Nunnally, Jon	–	–	–	–	–	.300	40	12	2	11
O'Brien, Charlie	–	–	–	–	–	.238	63	15	2	8
Ochoa, Alex	–	–	–	–	–	.211	19	4	0	1
Offerman, Jose	.195	41	8	0	1	.280	189	53	1	15
O'Leary, Troy	.130	23	3	0	1	.258	267	69	8	26
Olerud, John	.366	41	15	0	11	.324	74	24	2	16
Oliver, Joe	.286	14	4	1	2	.234	47	11	2	5
O'Neill, Paul	.258	31	8	0	9	.245	294	72	8	60
Ordaz, Luis	.000	5	0	0	0	.000	5	0	0	0
Ordonez, Magglio	.208	24	5	0	3	.219	96	21	3	12
Ordonez, Rey	–	–	–	–	–	.344	32	11	1	9
Ortiz, David	.348	23	8	0	2	.300	50	15	0	8
Ortiz, Hector	.500	4	2	0	1	.500	4	2	0	1
Otanez, Willis	–	–	–	–	–	.222	9	2	0	0
Palmeiro, Orlando	.263	19	5	0	2	.369	84	31	0	6
Palmeiro, Rafael	.227	44	10	3	6	.293	533	156	24	89
Palmer, Dean	.262	42	11	2	6	.281	366	103	20	68
Paul, Josh	.250	8	2	0	0	.250	8	2	0	0
Payton, Jay	.167	12	2	0	0	.167	12	2	0	0
Parent, Mark	–	–	–	–	–	.147	34	5	1	5
Pemberton, Ruby	–	–	–	–	–	.000	6	0	0	0
Penny, Brad	.000	2	0	0	0	.000	2	0	0	0
Perez, Eddie	–	–	–	–	–	.000	9	0	0	2
Perez, Eduardo	–	–	–	–	–	.267	45	12	2	8
Perry, Gerald	–	–	–	–	–	.314	35	11	1	2
Perry, Herbert	.357	14	5	1	2	.238	42	10	1	4
Piatt, Adam	.321	28	9	1	1	.321	28	9	1	1
Piazza, Mike	.267	15	4	1	5	.333	42	14	3	10
Pierzynski, A.J.	.000	6	0	0	0	.000	6	0	0	0
Polonia, Luis	.250	28	7	1	3	.310	355	110	6	28
Posada, Jorge	.351	37	13	3	4	.277	94	26	3	7
Pose, Scott	.333	3	1	0	0	.375	16	6	0	0
Pratt, Todd	.125	8	1	1	1	.158	19	3	2	4
Pride, Curtis	.375	8	3	0	0	.256	39	10	2	5
Pulliam, Harvey	–	–	–	–	–	.000	2	0	0	0
Quinn, Mark	.353	34	12	1	2	.353	34	12	1	2
Radmanovich, Ryan	–	–	–	–	–	.000	7	0	0	0
Raines, Tim	–	–	–	–	–	.261	245	64	4	34
Ramirez, Alex	.375	16	6	1	3	.455	22	10	2	6
Ramirez, Manny	.361	36	13	4	8	.248	318	79	19	53
Randa, Joe	.378	37	14	2	12	.322	121	39	4	21
Reboulet, Jeff	.125	8	1	0	1	0	100	20	1	8
Redmond, Mike	.333	3	1	0	0	.250	12	3	0	2
Relaford, Desi	.143	7	1	0	1	.176	17	3	0	1
Renteria, Edgar	–	–	–	–	–	.520	25	13	0	4
Richard, Chris	.250	12	3	0	1	.250	12	3	0	1
Ripken Jr., Cal	.364	22	8	0	3	.301	782	235	29	126
Rodriguez, Alex	.410	39	16	5	16	.332	193	64	15	48
Rodriguez, Henry	–	–	–	–	–	.000	13	0	0	0
Rodriguez, Ivan	.333	9	3	1	1	.303	346	105	10	51
Rolen, Scott	.400	10	4	1	2	.333	42	14	2	7
Sadler, Donnie	.292	24	7	0	2	.268	41	11	0	3
Saenz, Olmedo	.300	10	3	0	0	.276	29	8	1	5
Salmon, Tim	.167	36	6	1	4	.286	287	82	14	46
Sanchez, Rey	.219	32	7	0	1	.200	70	14	0	2
Sanders, Deion	–	–	–	–	–	.091	11	1	0	0
Sanders, Reggie	.400	10	4	1	3	.400	10	4	1	3
Santana, Julio	.000	1	0	0	0	.000	1	0	0	0
Santangelo, F.P.	–	–	–	–	–	.214	28	6	0	0
Schneider, Brian	.167	6	1	0	0	.167	6	1	0	0
Sefcik, Kevin	1.000	2	2	0	0	.500	10	5	0	0
Segui, David	.364	22	8	1	2	.282	174	49	4	20
Seguignol, Fernando	.500	6	3	1	1	.538	13	7	3	3
Sexson, Richie	.419	31	13	1	7	.299	87	26	4	18

Batter	2000 AVG.	AB	HITS	HR	RBI	CAREER AVG.	AB	HITS	HR	RBI
Sheets, Andy	1.000	1	1	0	0	.171	41	7	2	8
Sheffield, Gary	–	–	–	–	–	.200	90	18	1	9
Sheldon, Scott	.444	9	4	0	3	.357	14	5	0	3
Shipley, Craig	–	–	–	–	–	.600	5	3	0	1
Sierra, Ruben	–	–	–	–	–	.290	403	117	19	77
Simms, Mike	–	–	–	–	–	.300	10	3	1	2
Simmons, Brian	–	–	–	–	–	.375	16	6	2	8
Simon, Randall	–	–	–	–	–	.400	15	6	0	3
Singleton, Chris	.219	32	7	1	1	.271	70	19	1	7
Smith, Bobby	.185	27	5	0	2	.237	59	14	0	5
Smoltz, John	–	–	–	–	–	.000	1	0	0	0
Snopek, Chris	–	–	–	–	–	.125	32	4	0	3
Snow, J.T.	–	–	–	–	–	.302	116	35	1	19
Sojo, Luis	–	–	–	–	–	.250	112	28	2	13
Soriano, Alfonso	.000	3	0	0	0	.000	4	0	0	0
Sorrento, Paul	–	–	–	–	–	.256	285	73	21	52
Sosa, Sammy	–	–	–	–	–	.290	69	20	4	13
Spencer, Shane	.304	23	7	1	2	.306	36	11	2	3
Spiezio, Scott	.250	20	5	0	1	.209	110	23	5	16
Sprague, Ed	–	–	–	–	–	.211	19	4	0	1
Stairs, Matt	.286	28	8	1	5	.294	126	37	8	29
Stankiewicz, Andy	–	–	–	–	–	.292	24	7	0	1
Stanley, Mike	.310	29	9	1	9	.278	324	90	12	47
Stevens, Lee	.471	17	8	1	4	.320	122	39	4	24
Stinnett, Kelly	–	–	–	–	–	.000	0	0	0	0
Stocker, Kevin	.318	22	7	0	0	.333	78	26	1	11
Strange, Doug	–	–	–	–	–	.266	109	29	1	14
Stynes, Chris	–	–	–	–	–	.000	3	0	0	0
Surhoff, B.J.	.250	44	11	0	4	.292	538	157	15	94
Sutton, Larry	–	–	–	–	–	.362	47	17	2	12
Sweeney, Mike	.372	43	16	2	9	.266	143	38	3	18
Tatis, Fernando	–	–	–	–	–	.152	46	7	0	3
Taubensee, Ed	–	–	–	–	–	.000	7	0	0	0
Tejada, Miguel	.300	40	12	4	7	.248	101	25	7	19
Thomas, Frank	.281	32	9	2	7	.282	372	105	16	65
Thome, Jim	.353	34	12	3	11	.247	295	73	16	44
Thompson, Ryan	.429	7	3	1	4	.429	7	3	1	4
Timmons, Ozzie	.308	13	4	1	4	.286	14	4	1	4
Trammell, Bubba	.409	22	9	1	1	.340	53	18	3	7
Tucker, Michael	–	–	–	–	–	.246	69	17	2	8
Tyner, Jason	.313	16	5	0	1	.313	16	5	0	1
Valdez, Mario	.000	11	0	0	0	.129	31	4	0	2
Valentin, Javier	–	–	–	–	–	.316	19	6	0	5
Valentin, John	.111	9	1	0	0	.284	292	83	11	51
Valentin, Jose	.233	30	7	3	5	.272	169	46	10	28
Varitek, Jason	.333	27	9	1	7	.288	73	21	3	15
Vaughn, Greg	.273	22	6	0	3	.278	288	80	15	56
Vaughn, Mo	.415	41	17	4	10	.304	405	123	23	82
Velandia, Jorge	.000	1	0	0	0	.333	3	1	0	1
Velarde, Randy	.367	30	11	1	4	.294	306	90	8	42
Ventura, Robin	–	–	–	–	–	.257	323	83	11	48
Veras, Quilvio	.200	5	1	0	0	.200	5	1	0	0
Veras, Wilton	.367	30	11	0	1	.324	37	12	0	1
Vidro, Jose	.407	27	11	0	4	.348	46	16	0	6
Vina, Fernando	–	–	–	–	–	.252	115	29	1	7
Vitiello, Joe	–	–	–	–	–	.282	39	11	1	5
Vizcaino, Jose	.000	1	0	0	0	.308	13	4	0	0
Vizquel, Omar	.280	50	14	0	4	.292	435	127	8	36
Walbeck, Matt	.333	9	3	1	1	.236	127	30	2	11
Ward, Turner	–	–	–	–	–	.268	56	15	0	9
Waszgis, B.J.	.500	4	2	0	1	.500	4	2	0	1
Webster, Lenny	.000	1	0	0	0	.247	81	20	4	18
Weiss, Walt	.600	5	3	0	1	.234	145	34	0	19
Wendell, Turk	–	–	–	–	–	.000	3	0	0	0
White, Devon	–	–	–	–	–	.217	175	38	5	20
White, Rondell	.353	17	6	0	2	.309	55	17	2	6
Whiten, Mark	.000	2	0	0	0	.260	77	20	2	13
Widger, Chris	.313	16	5	1	2	.258	66	17	1	4
Williams, Bernie	.286	35	10	3	10	.263	391	103	9	54
Williams, George	–	–	–	–	–	.111	27	3	0	0
Williams, Gerald	.375	24	9	1	2	.321	106	34	4	9
Williams, Matt	–	–	–	–	–	.429	35	15	4	10
Wilson, Craig	.300	10	3	0	1	.235	17	4	0	1
Wilson, Dan	.304	23	7	1	5	.223	157	35	3	14
Wilson, Enrique	.125	8	1	0	0	.171	35	6	0	0
Wilson, Preston	.333	12	4	1	5	.364	22	8	1	5
Winn, Randy	.158	19	3	0	2	.226	84	19	0	4
Wolf, Randy	–	–	–	–	–	.000	2	0	0	0
Wooten, Shawn	1.000	1	1	0	0	1.000	1	1	0	0
Zeile, Todd	.286	14	4	0	2	.213	94	20	2	18

OPPOSING PITCHERS vs BLUE JAYS

Pitcher	ERA	W	L	S	G	IP	ER	ERA	W	L	S	G	IP	ER
Abbott, Paul	9.00	0	0	0	1	3.0	3	6.72	1	0	0	2	9.1	7
Acevedo, Juan	–	–	–	–	–	–	–	1.80	1	0	0	1	5.0	1
Adamson, Joel	–	–	–	–	–	–	–	2.33	1	0	0	2	7.2	2
Aguilera, Rick	–	–	–	–	–	–	–	2.56	1	4	10	30	45.2	13
Aldred, Scott	–	–	–	–	–	–	–	4.87	1	3	0	11	27.2	15
Anfonseca, Antonio	0.00	0	0	2	2	2.0	0	1.29	0	0	4	5	7.0	1
Almanza, Armando	0.00	0	0	0	1	1.1	0	0.00	0	0	0	1	1.1	0
Alvarez, Wilson	–	–	–	–	–	–	–	5.49	6	6	0	14	80.1	49
Anderson, Matt	10.80	0	0	0	2	1.2	2	8.38	1	0	0	11	9.2	9
Appier, Kevin	3.68	0	1	0	1	7.1	3	3.47	8	9	0	23	132.2	54
Armas Jr., Tony	4.35	1	1	0	2	10.1	5	4.35	1	1	0	2	10.1	5
Arrojo, Rolando Luis	–	–	–	–	–	–	–	5.88	1	1	0	4	18.1	12
Assenmacher, Paul	–	–	–	–	–	–	–	3.29	5	0	4	31	27.1	10
Avery, Steve	–	–	–	–	–	–	–	7.90	1	2	0	4	19.1	17
Baldwin, James	2.20	2	0	0	2	16.1	4	3.92	6	3	0	10	64.1	28
Banks, Willie	–	–	–	–	–	–	–	5.65	2	0	0	5	12.2	8
Barcelo, Lorenzo	0.00	0	0	0	1	1.0	0	0.00	0	0	0	1	1.0	0
Beck, Rod	0.00	0	0	0	4	4.0	0	4.50	0	1	0	6	6.0	3
Beirne, Kevin	0.00	0	0	0	1	1.0	0	0.00	0	0	0	1	1.0	0
Belcher, Tim	–	–	–	–	–	–	–	4.25	6	3	0	11	78.1	37
Belitz, Todd	0.00	0	0	0	1	0.0	0	0.00	0	0	0	1	0.0	0
Benitez, Armando	0.00	0	0	1	2	2.0	0	1.42	1	1	3	24	25.1	4
Bere, Jason	–	–	–	–	–	–	–	4.50	3	1	0	5	28.0	14
Blair, Willie	6.17	1	1	0	2	11.2	8	6.10	2	3	0	6	35.1	24
Boddicker, Mike	–	–	–	–	–	–	–	4.37	8	12	0	29	187.1	91
Boehringer, Brian	–	–	–	–	–	–	–	2.43	2	0	0	5	7.1	2
Bohanon, Brian	–	–	–	–	–	–	–	4.73	3	0	1	13	24.2	13
Bones, Ricky	0.00	1	0	0	1	2.1	0	4.55	4	4	0	17	77.0	39
Bottalico, Ricky	9.00	0	0	2	3	3.0	3	8.24	0	0	3	4	4.1	4
Bottenfield, Kent	22.09	0	1	0	1	3.2	9	22.09	0	1	0	1	3.2	9
Bradford, Chad	0.00	0	0	0	1	1.0	0	0.00	0	0	0	1	1.0	0
Brantley, Jeff	27.00	0	1	1	2	0.2	2	27.00	0	1	1	2	0.2	2
Brea, Lesli	0.00	0	0	0	1	0.2	0	0.00	0	0	0	1	0.2	0
Brewington, Jamie	2.45	1	0	0	2	3.2	1	2.45	1	0	0	2	3.2	1
Brocail, Doug	13.50	1	1	0	3	2.2	4	4.61	3	2	0	19	23.1	12
Brock, Chris	4.91	0	0	0	3	3.2	2	4.91	0	0	0	3	3.2	2
Brower, Jim	21.60	0	0	0	1	1.2	4	7.10	1	0	0	3	11.1	9
Brown, Kevin	–	–	–	–	–	–	–	5.06	6	5	0	16	101.1	57
Buehrle, Mark	0.00	0	0	0	1	3.1	0	0.00	0	0	0	1	3.1	0
Burba, Dave	12.27	0	1	0	2	7.1	10	5.44	2	3	0	9	46.1	28
Burkett, John	15.75	0	1	0	2	4.0	7	3.95	4	3	0	12	68.1	30
Byrdak, Tim	18.00	0	0	0	3	2.0	4	16.47	0	0	0	7	4.1	8
Cairncross, Cam	0.00	0	0	0	3	1.0	0	0.00	0	0	0	3	1.0	0
Carrasco, Hector	3.86	0	1	0	3	4.2	2	4.60	0	2	0	11	15.2	8
Castillo, Frank	–	–	–	–	–	–	–	0.00	0	0	0	1	2.0	0
Castillo, Tony	–	–	–	–	–	–	–	3.17	1	0	0	9	11.1	4
Chen, Bruce	0.00	1	0	0	2	9.0	0	3.60	1	0	0	3	15.0	6
Cho, Jin Ho	–	–	–	–	–	–	–	12.00	0	0	0	1	3.0	4
Choate, Randy	33.75	0	1	0	3	1.1	5	33.75	0	1	0	3	1.1	5
Clark, Mark	5.06	1	0	0	1	5.1	3	4.96	7	4	0	24	85.1	47
Clemens, Roger	1.29	2	0	0	2	14.0	2	3.06	17	10	0	37	256.0	87
Cloude, Ken	–	–	–	–	–	–	–	6.72	2	1	0	4	14.2	11
Colon, Bartolo	8.03	1	1	0	2	12.1	11	5.36	4	2	0	8	50.1	30
Cone, David	9.22	1	2	0	3	13.2	14	3.69	7	7	0	19	124.1	51
Cook, Dennis	0.00	0	0	0	2	2.2	0	3.77	1	1	0	18	33.1	14
Coppinger, Rocky	–	–	–	–	–	–	–	2.51	4	0	0	6	28.2	8
Corbin, Archie	–	–	–	–	–	–	–	24.30	0	0	0	1	0.1	1
Cordero, Francisco	6.75	0	0	0	4	4.0	3	10.80	0	1	0	5	5.0	6
Cormier, Rheal	6.14	1	0	0	6	7.1	5	6.20	2	0	0	15	20.1	14
Crabtree, Tim	6.00	0	0	0	4	3.0	2	3.47	0	0	0	12	10.1	4
Creek, Doug	5.40	0	0	0	3	5.0	3	5.40	0	0	0	3	5.0	3
Cruz, Nelson	0.00	0	0	0	1	1.2	0	7.65	0	1	0	5	9.1	8
Cubillan, Darwin	0.00	0	0	0	1	1.1	0	0.00	0	0	0	1	1.1	0
D'Amico, Jeff	–	–	–	–	–	–	–	3.17	1	1	0	2	11.1	4
Darensbourg, Vic	0.00	0	0	0	1	0.0	0	0.00	0	0	0	3	1.0	0
Darwin, Jeff	–	–	–	–	–	–	–	0.00	0	0	0	4	5.1	0
Davey, Tom	–	–	–	–	–	–	–	13.14	0	0	0	2	1.1	2
Davis, Doug	4.15	0	1	0	2	13.0	6	9.37	0	1	0	3	15.1	16
Dempster, Ryan	1.29	0	0	0	1	7.0	1	1.29	0	0	0	1	7.0	1
DePaula, Sean	0.00	0	0	0	2	3.0	0	1.22	0	0	0	6	7.1	1
Dickson, Jason	4.63	1	0	0	2	11.2	6	3.95	1	0	0	5	25.0	11
Dingman, Craig	18.00	0	0	0	1	1.0	2	18.00	0	0	0	1	1.0	2
DiPoto, Jerry	–	–	–	–	–	–	–	7.71	0	0	1	4	7.0	6
Dressendorfer, Kirk	–	–	–	–	–	–	–	7.59	0	1	0	1	4.2	4
Durbin, Chris	1.50	1	0	0	1	6.0	1	1.50	1	0	0	1	6.0	1
Einerston, Darrell	5.40	0	0	0	2	1.2	1	5.40	0	0	0	2	1.2	1
Eldred, Cal	0.00	1	0	0	1	6.2	0	2.31	4	4	0	10	74.0	19
Embree, Alan	–	–	–	–	–	–	–	3.76	0	1	1	8	14.1	6
Enders, Trevor	13.50	0	1	0	1	0.2	1	13.50	0	1	0	1	0.2	1
Erdos, Todd	3.00	0	0	0	2	3.0	1	3.00	0	0	0	2	3.0	1

Pitcher	ERA	W	L	S	G	IP	ER	ERA	W	L	S	G	IP	ER
Erickson, Scott	23.62	0	1	0	1	2.2	7	3.86	8	12	0	23	158.2	68
Eyre, Scott	0.00	0	0	0	1	0.2	0	2.99	2	0	0	7	15.0	5
Fassero, Jeff	7.88	0	1	0	2	8.0	7	5.36	3	2	0	9	45.1	27
Fernandez, Alex	–	–	–	–	–	–	–	1.79	5	5	0	18	130.1	26
Finley, Chuck	5.94	2	1	0	3	16.2	11	4.55	10	9	0	32	186.0	94
Florie, Bryce	0.00	0	1	0	2	1.2	0	4.75	0	1	0	9	17.0	9
Forster, Scott	0.00	0	0	0	3	2.0	0	0.00	0	0	0	3	2.0	0
Fossass, Tony	–	–	–	–	–	–	–	0.00	0	0	0	2	1.0	0
Foulke, Keith	1.42	0	0	4	5	6.1	1	1.17	0	0	4	17	23.0	3
Franco, John	0.00	1	0	0	2	1.2	0	0.00	1	0	2	7	6.2	0
Fussell, Chris	5.40	0	1	0	2	5.0	3	8.60	0	2	1	4	8.1	8
Garces, Rich	0.00	0	0	0	6	6.1	0	1.44	0	0	0	14	18.2	3
Garcia, Freddy	4.58	3	0	0	3	19.2	10	5.58	4	1	0	5	27.1	17
Garland, Jon	7.71	0	1	0	1	4.2	4	7.71	0	1	0	1	4.2	4
Ginter, Matt	27.00	0	0	0	1	1.0	3	27.00	0	0	0	1	1.0	3
Glavine, Tom	9.00	0	0	0	1	6.0	6	5.39	1	1	0	3	18.1	11
Glynn, Ryan	4.05	1	0	0	1	6.2	3	4.05	1	0	0	1	6.2	3
Gooden, Dwight	5.40	0	0	0	2	6.2	4	4.96	2	4	0	10	54.1	30
Gordon, Tom	–	–	–	–	–	–	–	3.62	12	7	5	43	154.0	62
Greisinger, Seth	–	–	–	–	–	–	–	4.26	0	1	0	3	19.0	9
Grimsley, Jason	1.42	0	0	0	4	6.1	1	5.56	3	1	3	27	43.2	27
Groom, Buddy	2.25	0	0	0	6	4.0	1	4.38	1	1	0	37	26.2	13
Guardado, Eddie	6.23	0	0	1	4	4.1	3	5.50	2	1	1	26	34.1	21
Gunderson, Eric	–	–	–	–	–	–	–	8.24	0	0	0	7	4.1	4
Guthrie, Mark	27.00	0	0	0	2	1.1	4	5.64	2	3	0	20	44.2	28
Guzman, Juan	–	–	–	–	–	–	–	6.60	0	2	0	3	16.1	12
Halama, John	6.17	0	1	0	3	11.2	8	5.67	1	1	0	5	19.0	12
Harper, Travis	0.00	1	0	0	1	9.0	0	0.00	1	0	0	1	9.0	0
Harris, Pep	–	–	–	–	–	–	–	5.49	0	0	0	11	14.2	9
Hasegawa, Shigetoshi	17.18	0	0	0	4	3.2	7	6.73	0	2	1	17	21.1	16
Hawkins, LaTroy	3.00	0	0	2	3	3.0	1	4.70	0	2	2	8	28.2	15
Haynes, Jimmy	–	–	–	–	–	–	–	4.34	4	0	0	7	29.0	14
Helling, Rick	5.40	1	1	0	2	13.1	8	2.77	5	1	0	8	61.2	19
Heredia, Felix	–	–	–	–	–	–	–	24.30	0	0	0	2	0.2	2
Heredia, Gil	0.00	1	0	0	1	7.1	0	3.19	2	1	6	22	42.1	15
Heredia, Wilson	–	–	–	–	–	–	–	0.00	0	0	0	2	2.0	0
Hermanson, Dustin	9.00	0	1	0	2	10.0	10	11.57	0	2	0	5	21.0	27
Hernandez, Livan	–	–	–	–	–	–	–	4.35	2	0	0	3	22.2	11
Hernandez, Orlando	6.41	1	2	0	3	19.2	14	4.07	3	3	0	6	42.0	19
Hernandez, Roberto	0.00	0	0	2	5	5.2	0	1.51	2	2	21	33	41.2	7
Hernandez, Xavier	–	–	–	–	–	–	–	5.65	0	0	0	6	6.1	4
Hill, Ken	27.00	0	1	0	1	3.1	10	6.82	1	6	0	9	54.0	41
Hitchcock, Sterling	–	–	–	–	–	–	–	4.64	4	0	0	6	33.0	17
Holman, Brian	–	–	–	–	–	–	–	4.29	2	4	0	9	63.0	30
Holmes, Darren	–	–	–	–	–	–	–	3.35	0	1	1	4	5.1	2
Holtz, Mike	3.38	1	0	0	3	2.2	1	2.45	1	0	0	17	11.0	3
Howry, Bob	3.38	0	1	0	4	2.2	1	2.24	0	2	3	12	12.0	3
Hudson, Tim	1.59	3	0	0	3	22.2	4	2.20	4	0	0	4	28.2	7
Hurtado, Edwin	–	–	–	–	–	–	–	12.02	0	1	0	2	6.2	9
Irabu, Hideki	–	–	–	–	–	–	–	5.11	2	1	0	4	19.1	11
Isringhausen, Jason	0.00	1	0	1	4	4.0	0	0.91	3	0	1	9	19.2	2
Jackson, Mike	–	–	–	–	–	–	–	2.89	1	3	7	30	37.1	12
James, Mike	–	–	–	–	–	–	–	4.68	1	2	1	13	15.1	8
Johns, Doug	–	–	–	–	–	–	–	7.38	0	2	0	7	20.2	17
Johnson, Jason	12.00	0	2	0	2	9.0	12	7.77	0	2	0	5	22.0	19
Johnson, Jonathan	6.00	0	0	0	1	3.0	2	6.00	0	0	0	1	3.0	2
Johnson, Mike	13.50	0	0	0	2	1.1	2	9.72	0	0	0	3	3.2	4
Johnson, Randy	–	–	–	–	–	–	–	2.82	12	4	0	20	143.1	45
Jones, Bobby J.	7.50	1	0	0	1	6.0	5	3.86	2	0	0	2	14.0	6
Jones, Bobby M.	9.00	0	0	0	1	1.0	1	9.00	0	0	0	1	1.0	1
Jones, Doug	3.86	0	1	0	2	2.1	1	2.28	3	3	15	28	43.1	11
Jones, Todd	3.38	0	0	0	4	2.2	1	2.44	2	1	6	20	18.1	5
Juden, Jeff	–	–	–	–	–	–	–	4.61	1	2	0	4	25.1	13
Kamieniecki, Scott	0.00	0	0	0	3	3.1	0	3.76	5	3	0	14	67.0	28
Karl, Scott	15.43	0	0	0	1	2.1	4	5.97	3	3	0	9	46.2	31
Karsay, Steve	1.23	0	0	3	6	7.1	1	4.85	1	2	3	14	29.2	16
Kinney, Matt	2.84	0	1	0	1	6.1	2	2.84	0	1	0	1	6.1	2
Kline, Steve	6.00	0	0	0	3	3.0	2	3.64	0	0	0	11	12.1	5
Kohlmeier, Ryan	0.00	0	0	1	1	1.0	0	0.00	0	0	1	1	1.0	0
Krivda, Rick	–	–	–	–	–	–	–	6.03	0	2	0	5	25.1	17
Lara, Yovanny	27.00	0	0	0	2	1.1	4	27.00	0	0	0	2	1.1	4
Larkin, Andy	3.38	0	1	1	3	2.2	1	3.38	0	1	1	3	2.2	1
Leiter, Al	9.53	0	1	0	1	5.2	6	4.77	2	2	0	4	26.1	14
Leiter, Mark	–	–	–	–	–	–	–	8.40	1	3	1	13	30.0	28
Levine, Al	0.00	0	0	0	3	3.2	0	4.08	0	0	0	11	11.0	5
Lidle, Cory	7.82	1	2	0	3	12.2	11	8.73	1	2	0	4	13.1	13
Ligtenberg, Kerry	0.00	0	0	0	2	2.0	0	3.00	0	0	0	3	3.0	1
Lilliquist, Derek	–	–	–	–	–	–	–	4.08	6	8	2	33	125.2	57
Lilly, Ted	99.00	0	0	0	1	0.0	4	99.00	0	0	0	1	0.0	4
Lima, Jose	–	–	–	–	–	–	–	3.51	2	2	1	7	15.1	6
Linton, Doug	–	–	–	–	–	–	–	4.77	0	1	0	5	20.2	11
Lira, Felipe	3.86	1	0	0	4	7.0	3	4.25	4	1	0	11	42.1	20

Pitcher	2000 ERA	W	L	S	G	IP	ER	CAREER ERA	W	L	S	G	IP	ER
Lloyd, Graeme	–	–	–	–	–	–	–	0.63	0	0	0	17	14.1	1
Loaiza, Estaban	–	–	–	–	–	–	–	2.54	0	1	0	3	17.2	5
Looper, Braden	16.20	1	0	0	2	1.2	3	11.22	2	0	0	4	2.1	3
Lopez, Albie	7.20	0	2	1	3	10.0	8	6.12	3	7	1	19	54.1	37
Lorraine, Andrew	0.00	0	0	0	2	1.1	0	13.32	0	0	0	3	2.2	4
Lowe, Derek	5.06	0	1	1	4	5.1	3	4.36	1	3	1	20	22.2	11
Lowe, Sean	0.00	0	0	0	1	1.0	0	3.28	0	0	0	5	2.2	1
Lundquist, David	–	–	–	–	–	–	–	0.00	0	0	0	1	1.0	0
Maddux, Greg	–	–	–	–	–	–	–	1.80	2	0	0	2	15.0	3
Maddux, Mike	–	–	–	–	–	–	–	3.43	2	0	0	8	21.0	8
Maduro, Calvin	0.00	0	0	0	1	1.0	0	0.00	0	0	0	1	1.0	0
Magnante, Mike	0.00	0	0	0	2	2.2	0	3.12	2	1	0	22	34.2	12
Mahay, Ron	3.60	0	0	0	2	5.0	2	2.88	1	0	0	7	9.1	3
Mahomes, Pat	0.00	0	0	0	2	2.1	0	3.25	2	1	0	12	44.1	16
Mantei, Matt	–	–	–	–	–	–	–	0.00	0	0	0	2	3.0	0
Marquis, Jason	0.00	0	0	0	1	1.0	0	0.00	0	0	0	1	1.0	0
Martin, Todd	5.40	0	0	0	3	5.0	3	5.40	0	0	0	3	5.0	3
Martinez, Pedro	2.91	1	1	0	3	21.2	7	2.67	5	2	0	9	67.1	20
Martinez, Ramon	21.00	0	1	0	1	3.0	7	21.00	0	1	0	1	3.0	7
Mathews, T.J.	2.45	0	0	0	3	3.2	1	2.90	2	2	0	12	12.1	4
Mays, Joe	4.50	0	0	0	2	2.0	1	5.18	1	1	0	6	17.1	10
McDill, Allen	10.80	0	0	0	2	1.2	2	10.80	0	0	0	2	1.2	2
McDonald, Ben	–	–	–	–	–	–	–	5.31	7	7	0	17	98.1	58
McElroy, Chuck	2.08	0	0	0	2	4.1	1	4.14	0	1	0	8	8.2	4
Meacham, Rusty	–	–	–	–	–	–	–	3.91	4	1	0	12	23.0	10
Meadows, Brian	17.18	0	0	0	1	3.2	7	6.75	0	0	0	2	10.2	8
Mecir, Jim	3.68	1	0	2	7	7.1	3	3.14	2	0	2	13	14.1	5
Mendoza, Ramiro	13.50	0	1	0	1	4.0	6	5.17	2	5	0	14	48.2	28
Menhart, Paul	–	–	–	–	–	–	–	4.50	0	1	0	1	6.0	3
Mercedes, Jose	0.84	2	0	0	4	21.1	2	2.41	3	1	0	11	41.0	11
Merker, Kent	5.79	0	0	0	4	4.2	3	9.43	0	0	0	6	12.1	13
Mesa, Jose	4.76	0	0	0	3	5.2	3	6.00	3	1	12	33	45.0	30
Miller, Travis	8.10	0	0	0	3	3.1	3	4.73	0	1	0	10	13.1	7
Mills, Alan	2.25	0	0	1	3	4.0	1	2.16	2	1	2	21	33.1	8
Millwood, Kevin	20.25	0	1	0	1	4.0	9	10.80	0	2	0	2	10.0	12
Milton, Eric	2.57	1	0	0	2	14.0	4	4.59	1	2	0	5	31.1	16
Mlicki, Dave	1.80	0	0	0	2	10.0	2	5.67	1	3	0	6	31.2	20
Moehler, Brian	7.11	0	1	0	1	6.1	5	6.13	3	4	0	9	54.1	37
Mohler, Mike	–	–	–	–	–	–	–	5.82	1	4	0	19	34.0	22
Morgan, Mike	–	–	–	–	–	–	–	5.73	1	4	0	2	11.0	7
Moraga, David	99.00	0	0	0	1	0.0	2	99.00	0	0	0	1	0.0	2
Morman, Alvin	–	–	–	–	–	–	–	4.01	0	1	0	8	6.2	3
Mota, Guillermo	13.50	0	1	0	1	1.1	2	8.10	0	1	0	3	3.1	3
Moyer, Jamie	7.36	1	0	0	2	11.0	9	4.63	7	5	0	22	130.1	67
Mulder, Mark	3.97	0	0	0	2	11.1	5	3.97	0	0	0	2	11.1	5
Mulholland, Terry	–	–	–	–	–	–	–	5.14	1	1	0	2	14.0	8
Munoz, Bobby	–	–	–	–	–	–	–	5.03	0	1	0	4	5.1	3
Munoz, Mike	–	–	–	–	–	–	–	2.44	1	0	0	8	7.1	2
Mussina, Mike	4.09	0	2	0	3	22.0	10	3.22	9	7	0	20	148.0	53
Myers, Mike	–	–	–	–	–	–	–	6.11	0	0	1	12	7.1	5
Myers, Randy	–	–	–	–	–	–	–	1.13	1	0	4	8	8.0	1
Nagy, Charles	15.75	0	0	0	1	4.0	7	4.38	8	5	0	22	143.2	70
Naulty, Dan	–	–	–	–	–	–	–	2.15	1	0	0	5	8.1	2
Navarro, Jaime	5.40	0	0	0	1	1.2	1	4.44	7	5	0	21	117.2	58
Neagle, Denny	2.35	1	0	0	1	7.2	2	1.66	2	1	0	3	21.2	4
Nelson, Jeff	0.00	0	0	0	5	4.0	0	2.11	1	1	1	37	38.1	9
Nitkowski, C.J.	9.00	0	1	0	5	7.0	7	8.87	1	2	0	15	25.1	25
Nomo, Hideo	6.00	0	2	0	4	27.0	18	6.30	0	2	0	5	30.0	21
Nunez, Vladimir	15.00	0	1	0	1	3.0	5	11.25	0	1	0	2	4.0	5
Ogea, Chad	–	–	–	–	–	–	–	5.36	3	3	0	9	42.0	25
Ohka, Tomokazu	–	–	–	–	–	–	–	0.00	0	0	0	1	0.1	0
Olivares, Omar	4.50	0	1	0	1	6.0	3	5.36	1	6	0	10	58.2	35
Oliver, Darren	–	–	–	–	–	–	–	2.39	6	3	0	13	64.0	17
Olson, Gregg	–	–	–	–	–	–	–	2.74	4	4	14	36	39.1	12
Oquist, Mike	–	–	–	–	–	–	–	4.35	4	3	0	16	72.1	35
Orosco, Jesse	–	–	–	–	–	–	–	5.36	1	3	0	58	47.0	28
Ortiz, Ramon	3.93	1	2	0	3	18.1	8	3.55	1	3	0	4	25.1	10
Paniaqua, Jose	2.25	0	0	2	5	8.0	2	1.80	0	0	3	11	15.0	3
Parque, Jim	1.38	0	0	0	2	13.0	2	3.12	0	2	0	5	31.2	11
Patterson, Danny	0.00	0	0	0	2	2.0	0	7.00	1	0	0	9	9.0	7
Pavano, Carl	–	–	–	–	–	–	–	5.00	0	2	0	2	9.0	5
Pena, Jesus	0.00	0	0	0	1	1.0	0	0.00	0	0	0	3	1.1	0
Penny, Brad	14.73	0	0	0	1	3.2	6	14.73	0	0	0	1	3.2	6
Percival, Troy	0.00	0	0	1	2	2.0	0	3.25	2	1	9	21	19.1	7
Perez, Carlos	–	–	–	–	–	–	–	1.00	0	1	0	1	9.0	1
Perez, Melido	–	–	–	–	–	–	–	3.41	5	7	0	16	110.2	42
Perisho, Matt	3.86	0	0	0	2	7.0	3	3.86	0	0	0	2	7.0	3
Person, Robert	–	–	–	–	–	–	–	0.00	0	0	0	1	1.0	0
Petkovsek, Mark	19.06	0	1	0	6	5.2	12	10.47	1	2	0	13	12.0	14
Pettitte, Andy	3.65	1	0	0	2	12.1	5	3.16	12	4	0	21	145.1	51
Pichardo, Hipolito	1.04	1	0	0	3	8.2	1	3.93	5	3	2	24	52.2	23
Plesac, Dan	–	–	–	–	–	–	–	2.96	1	5	12	35	54.2	18

Pitcher	2000 ERA	W	L	S	G	IP	ER	CAREER ERA	W	L	S	G	IP	ER
Plunk, Eric	–	–	–	–	–	–	–	2.65	4	5	2	44	85.0	25
Ponson, Sidney	4.86	1	1	0	2	16.2	9	7.59	1	4	0	6	34.1	29
Portugal, Mark	–	–	–	–	–	–	–	6.55	0	0	0	3	12.1	9
Pote, Lou	5.63	0	1	0	7	8.0	5	5.00	0	1	0	8	9.0	5
Prieto, Ariel	–	–	–	–	–	–	–	6.25	2	4	0	8	41.2	29
Pulsipher, Bill	–	–	–	–	–	–	–	5.17	0	0	0	2	1.2	1
Quantrill, Paul	–	–	–	–	–	–	–	4.04	0	2	0	6	13.1	6
Radinsky, Scott	–	–	–	–	–	–	–	1.59	2	0	0	24	17.0	3
Radke, Brad	6.23	1	2	0	3	17.1	12	4.51	8	6	0	16	103.2	52
Ramsay, Rob	5.40	0	0	0	2	1.2	1	5.40	0	0	0	2	1.2	1
Rapp, Pat	3.05	3	0	0	3	20.2	7	3.09	5	2	0	8	46.2	16
Redman, Mark	1.38	2	0	0	2	13.0	2	1.38	2	0	0	2	13.0	2
Reed, Rick	7.20	0	0	0	1	5.0	4	5.40	0	1	0	5	25.0	15
Reed, Steve	3.24	0	0	0	7	8.1	3	8.94	0	0	0	11	11.0	11
Reichert, Dan	4.00	0	0	0	2	9.0	4	4.00	0	0	0	2	9.0	4
Rekar, Bryan	1.64	0	0	0	2	11.0	2	1.42	1	0	0	3	19.0	3
Remlinger, Mike	9.00	1	0	0	2	2.0	2	13.35	1	0	0	4	3.1	5
Rhodes, Arthur	8.31	1	1	0	4	4.1	4	5.24	2	6	0	26	68.2	40
Rigby, Brad	6.00	0	0	1	1	3.0	2	4.81	0	0	1	2	3.2	2
Rincon, Ricky	6.75	1	0	0	5	2.2	2	4.98	1	0	0	11	9.0	5
Risley, Bill	–	–	–	–	–	–	–	6.57	0	0	0	3	2.2	2
Rivera, Mariano	2.45	0	0	2	3	3.2	1	2.16	1	0	9	21	25.0	6
Rocker, John	–	–	–	–	–	–	–	0.00	0	0	0	2	2.1	0
Rodriguez, Frank	1.69	1	0	0	2	5.1	1	3.05	4	2	0	12	53.0	18
Rodriguez, Nerio	–	–	–	–	–	–	–	1.52	2	1	0	4	17.2	3
Rodriguez, Rich	27.00	0	0	0	1	0.2	2	27.00	0	0	0	1	0.2	2
Rogers, Kenny	3.46	0	2	0	2	13.0	5	2.81	9	6	1	42	131.1	41
Rojas, Mel	–	–	–	–	–	–	–	22.50	0	1	0	3	2.0	5
Romero, J.C.	3.60	1	0	0	1	5.0	2	3.60	1	0	0	1	5.0	2
Rosado, Jose	3.00	1	0	0	1	6.0	2	3.23	3	6	0	12	72.1	26
Rose, Brian	9.82	0	1	0	2	3.2	4	7.71	0	1	0	3	4.2	4
Runyan, Sean	27.00	0	0	0	1	0.1	1	5.86	0	0	1	8	3.0	2
Rupe, Ryan	–	–	–	–	–	–	–	5.37	1	0	0	2	11.2	7
Rusch, Glendon	–	–	–	–	–	–	–	3.67	3	1	0	5	34.1	14
Russell, Jeff	–	–	–	–	–	–	–	4.92	2	6	11	35	49.1	27
Ryan, Jason	4.50	0	0	0	1	2.0	1	2.70	0	1	0	2	10.0	3
Saberhagen, Bret	–	–	–	–	–	–	–	4.59	6	9	1	24	131.1	67
Sager, A.J.	–	–	–	–	–	–	–	3.65	1	2	0	6	19.2	8
Salkeld, Roger	–	–	–	–	–	–	–	15.19	0	1	0	1	2.1	4
Santana, Julio	4.50	0	0	0	1	6.0	3	7.20	0	2	0	11	40.0	32
Santana, Marino	–	–	–	–	–	–	–	0.00	0	0	0	2	1.0	0
Santiago, Jose	6.00	0	1	0	2	3.0	2	7.20	0	1	0	4	5.0	4
Sasaki, Kazuhiro	4.50	0	0	2	4	4.0	2	4.50	0	0	2	4	4.0	2
Schilling, Curt	3.86	1	0	0	1	7.0	3	5.45	1	4	0	9	33.0	20
Schoeneweis, Scott	2.87	1	0	0	2	15.2	5	3.42	1	1	0	6	21.0	8
Schourek, Pete	4.60	1	1	0	3	15.2	8	5.23	1	1	0	4	20.2	12
Schrenk, Steve	40.50	0	0	0	1	0.2	3	40.50	0	0	0	1	0.2	3
Seanez, Rudy	0.00	0	0	0	1	1.0	0	10.46	0	0	0	7	7.2	9
Sele, Aaron	4.85	1	0	0	2	13.0	7	4.57	5	4	0	14	76.2	39
Shaw, Jeff	–	–	–	–	–	–	–	4.02	1	1	0	6	22.1	10
Shuey, Paul	3.86	1	1	0	5	7.0	3	1.64	3	1	1	23	33.0	6
Sikorski, Brian	6.35	0	0	0	1	5.2	4	6.35	0	1	0	1	5.2	4
Simas, Bill	4.50	0	0	0	2	2.0	1	3.09	1	0	2	19	20.1	7
Sinclair, Steve	–	–	–	–	–	–	–	0.00	0	0	0	1	0.1	0
Sirotka, Mike	3.21	1	0	0	2	14.0	5	3.50	3	1	0	5	36.0	14
Skrmetta, Matt	33.75	0	0	0	2	1.1	5	33.75	0	0	0	2	1.1	5
Slocumb, Heathcliff	–	–	–	–	–	–	–	5.32	1	2	10	22	22.0	13
Smoltz, John	–	–	–	–	–	–	–	6.43	0	2	0	2	14.0	10
Sodowsky, Clint	–	–	–	–	–	–	–	0.00	0	0	0	1	5.0	0
Sparks, Jeff	0.00	0	0	0	1	1.1	0	0.00	0	0	0	1	1.1	0
Sparks, Steve	3.12	0	1	0	2	8.2	3	4.09	2	2	0	7	37.1	17
Speier, Justin	3.38	1	0	0	3	5.1	2	3.38	1	0	0	3	5.1	2
Spoljaric, Paul	–	–	–	–	–	–	–	9.00	1	0	0	4	5.0	5
Spradlin, Jerry	6.75	0	1	0	3	4.0	3	4.01	0	1	0	6	6.2	3
Springer, Dennis	–	–	–	–	–	–	–	3.89	2	2	0	5	34.2	15
Springer, Russ	–	–	–	–	–	–	–	3.05	1	0	1	10	14.2	5
Spurgeon, Jay	0.00	0	0	0	1	1.0	0	0.00	0	0	0	1	1.0	0
Stanton, Mike	0.00	0	0	0	7	6.0	0	3.00	1	0	1	29	30.0	10
Stein, Blake	4.97	1	0	0	2	12.2	7	4.94	1	0	0	4	23.2	13
Stottlemyre, Todd	–	–	–	–	–	–	–	3.53	2	0	0	2	12.2	5
Strickland, Scott	6.75	0	0	0	2	1.1	1	6.75	0	0	0	2	1.1	1
Strong, Joe	4.50	0	0	0	1	2.0	1	4.50	0	0	0	1	2.0	1
Sturtze, Tanyon	1.93	0	0	0	2	4.2	1	2.43	0	0	0	3	7.1	2
Suppan, Jeff	4.85	1	0	0	2	13.0	7	5.35	1	1	0	9	43.2	26
Suzuki, Makoto	14.73	0	1	0	1	3.2	6	8.31	0	1	0	2	8.2	8
Swift, Bill	–	–	–	–	–	–	–	5.58	0	6	0	15	48.1	30
Tam, Jeff	0.00	0	0	0	4	2.1	0	0.00	0	0	0	6	4.1	0
Tapani, Kevin	–	–	–	–	–	–	–	5.08	6	10	0	19	117.0	66
Taverez, Julian	–	–	–	–	–	–	–	4.20	1	2	0	11	15.0	7
Taylor, Billy	–	–	–	–	–	–	–	6.22	0	3	5	18	17.1	12
Telford, Anthony	2.25	0	0	0	3	4.0	1	2.65	0	2	0	12	23.2	7
Tessmer, Jay	0.00	0	0	0	1	1.0	0	0.00	0	0	0	1	1.0	0

Pitcher	2000							CAREER						
	ERA	W	L	S	G	IP	ER	ERA	W	L	S	G	IP	ER
Thompson, Justin	–	–	–	–	–	–	–	3.45	2	2	1	6	47.0	18
Thurman, Mike	–	–	–	–	–	–	–	3.00	0	0	0	1	6.0	2
Timlin, Mike	0.00	0	0	0	3	2.0	0	2.81	1	2	1	17	16.0	5
Tomko, Brett	4.76	1	0	0	2	5.2	3	4.76	1	0	0	2	5.2	3
Torres, Dilson	–	–	–	–	–	–	–	5.00	0	0	0	3	9.0	5
Torres, Salomon	–	–	–	–	–	–	–	0.00	0	1	0	1	8.0	0
Trachsel, Steve	3.65	1	0	0	2	12.1	5	3.65	1	0	0	2	12.1	5
Trombley, Mike	0.00	1	0	0	4	2.2	0	4.91	3	5	1	29	47.2	26
Tucker, T.J.	15.00	0	1	0	1	3.0	5	15.00	0	1	0	1	3.0	5
Turnbow, Derek	2.16	0	0	0	3	8.1	2	2.16	0	0	0	3	8.1	2
Urbina, Ugueth	–	–	–	–	–	–	–	2.41	1	0	1	5	3.2	1
Van Poppel, Todd	–	–	–	–	–	–	–	3.57	0	1	0	7	27.2	11
Vazquez, Javier	–	–	–	–	–	–	–	1.50	0	0	0	1	6.0	1
Venafro, Mike	3.18	1	1	0	7	5.2	2	6.28	1	2	0	12	10.0	7
Villafuerte, Brandon	4.50	0	0	0	1	2.0	1	4.50	0	0	0	1	2.0	1
Vosberg, Ed	0.00	0	0	0	2	1.1	0	3.08	0	1	1	14	11.2	4
Wagner, Matt	–	–	–	–	–	–	–	7.50	0	0	0	1	6.0	5
Wakefield, Tim	6.43	0	0	0	4	14.0	10	4.34	3	5	1	20	103.2	50
Ward, Bryan	0.00	0	0	0	1	1.0	0	15.75	0	0	0	6	4.0	7
Wasdin, John	8.22	0	1	0	3	7.2	7	6.57	3	3	0	16	26.0	19
Watson, Allen	0.00	0	0	0	2	1.1	0	3.45	2	1	0	8	28.2	11
Weathers, David	–	–	–	–	–	–	–	0.00	0	0	0	1	1.0	0
Weaver, Jeff	6.87	1	2	0	3	18.1	14	7.12	1	4	0	5	30.1	24
Wells, Bob	3.00	0	0	0	4	3.0	1	1.55	2	0	0	16	29.0	5
Wells, David	–	–	–	–	–	–	–	3.77	3	3	0	8	57.1	24
Wells, Kip	8.49	0	2	0	2	11.2	11	6.72	1	2	0	3	17.1	13
Wendell, Turk	0.00	0	0	0	2	1.0	0	3.96	0	0	1	7	11.1	5
Wengert, Don	0.00	0	0	0	2	3.0	0	2.30	1	1	0	9	27.1	7
Wetteland, John	2.25	0	0	0	3	4.0	1	1.95	3	0	15	24	27.2	6
Wheeler, Dan	0.00	0	0	0	1	1.2	0	3.52	0	1	0	2	7.2	3
White, Rick	2.08	1	1	0	4	4.1	1	1.89	3	3	0	11	19.0	4
Wickman, Bob	0.00	0	0	1	1	1.0	0	3.17	2	0	2	21	39.2	14
Williams, Brian	6.75	0	0	0	1	2.2	2	5.06	0	0	0	3	10.2	6
Wilson, Kris	9.00	0	0	0	2	5.0	5	9.00	0	0	0	2	5.0	5
Wilson, Paul	0.00	1	0	0	1	7.0	0	0.00	1	0	0	1	7.0	0
Wilson, Trevor	–	–	–	–	–	–	–	0.00	0	0	0	3	1.1	0
Wise, Matt	7.59	1	1	0	2	10.2	9	7.59	1	1	0	2	10.2	9
Witasick, Jay	9.00	0	1	0	1	5.0	5	4.21	2	2	0	5	21.1	10
Witt, Bobby	32.40	0	0	0	1	1.2	6	4.85	12	7	0	27	159.2	86
Wohlers, Mark	–	–	–	–	–	–	–	0.00	0	0	1	1	1.0	0
Wolf, Randy	1.29	0	0	0	1	7.0	1	1.41	1	0	0	2	12.2	2
Woodard, Steve	4.76	1	0	0	1	5.2	3	1.98	2	0	0	2	13.2	3
Worrell, Tim	–	–	–	–	–	–	–	2.77	0	0	0	5	13.0	4
Wright, Jaret	7.50	0	0	0	1	6.0	5	10.00	0	2	0	4	18.0	20
Wunsch, Kelly	13.50	1	1	0	4	2.0	3	13.50	1	1	0	4	2.0	3
Yan, Esteban	4.20	0	1	0	5	15.0	7	3.79	0	2	0	13	23.2	10
Young, Tim	0.00	0	0	0	2	2.0	0	0.00	0	0	0	2	2.0	0
Zimmerman, Jeff	11.25	0	0	0	3	4.0	5	7.53	0	1	0	6	8.1	7
Zito, Barry	0.66	1	0	0	2	13.2	1	0.66	1	0	0	2	13.2	1

THREE HOME RUNS IN A GAME

BY TORONTO

PLAYER	DATE	OPPONENT	PITCHER(S)
Otto Velez	May 4, 1980 (1st gm)	vs Cleveland	Spillner, Garland, Monge
Ernie Whitt	Sept. 14, 1987	vs Baltimore	Dixon (2), Arnold
George Bell*	April 4, 1988	@ Kansas City	Saberhagen (3)
Joe Carter	Aug. 23, 1993	vs Cleveland	Lopez (2), Hernandez
Darnell Coles	July 5, 1994	@ Minnesota	Mahomes, Casian (2)
Carlos Delgado	Aug. 4, 1998	@ Texas	Stottlemyre, Gunderson, Patterson
Carlos Delgado	Aug. 6, 1999	@ Texas	Helling (2), Zimmerman
Darrin Fletcher	Aug. 27, 2000	@ Texas	Helling (3)

*: only American League player ever to hit 3 homers on Opening Day

BY OPPONENTS

PLAYER	DATE	SITE	PITCHER(S)
John Mayberry (KC)	June 1, 1977	Exhibition Stadium	Johnson, Willis, Bruno
Cliff Johnson (NYY)	June 30, 1977	Exhibition Stadium	Garvin (2), Johnson
Eddie Murray (Bal)	Sept. 14, 1980	Exhibition Stadium	Todd (2), Barlow (1)
Jim Rice (Bos)	Aug. 29, 1983	Exhibition Stadium	Acker (2), Moffit (1)- 2nd game
Jose Canseco (Oak)	July 3, 1988	Oakland	Stottlemyre (2), Henke
Cecil Fielder (Det)	May 6, 1990	SkyDome	Key (2), Wells (1)
Tom Brunansky (Bos)	Sept. 29, 1990	Fenway Park	Stottlemyre, Ward, Luecken
Cecil Fielder (Det)	April 16, 1996	SkyDome	Hanson, Carrara, Risley
Ken Griffey Jr. (Sea)	April 25, 1997	SkyDome	Clemens (2), Timlin
Manny Ramirez (Cle)	Sept. 15, 1998	Jacobs Field	Stieb (2), Quantrill
Alex Rodriguez (Sea)	April 16, 2000	SkyDome	Carpenter (2), Borbon

PLAYER DEVELOPMENT

Director, Minor League Operations	Bob Nelson
Field Coordinator	Jim Hoff
Roving Pitching Instructor	Bruce Walton
Roving Hitting Instructor	George Bell
Roving Hitting & Catching Instructor	Ernie Whitt
Roving Infield Instructor	Jerry Browne
Roving Outfield & Baserunning Instructor	Tack Wilson
Minor League Strength and Conditioning Coordinator	Paul Townsend
Minor League Training Coordinator	Jay Inouye
Minor League Equipment Coordinator	Bill Wardlow

SCOUTING

Director, Scouting	Chris Buckley
Assistant Director, Scouting	Mark Snipp
Special Assignment Scout/ National Cross Checker	Mike Mangan
Coordinator Scouting	Charlie Wilson
Coordinator Scouting	Jon Lalonde

SCOUTING – MAJOR LEAGUE

Advance Scout	Sal Butera
Special Assignment Scout	Chris Bourjos
Special Assignment Scout	Duane Larson
Special Assignment Scout	Ted Lekas
Special Assignment Scout	Mel Queen
Special Assignment Scout	Pat Kelly
Special Assistant to GM/ Director, International Scouting	Wayne Morgan

SCOUTING SUPERVISORS – NORTH AMERICA

Mike Cadahia – Southeastern Regional Supervisor	Miami Springs, FL
Jeff Cornell – Central Regional Supervisor	Lee's Summit, MO
Bill Moore –Western Regional Supervisor	Alta Loma, CA
Bill Byckowski – Northeastern Regional Supervisor	Georgetown, ON
Ron Tostenson – Northwest Regional Supervisor	Issaquah, WA
Charles Aliano	Columbia, SC
Tony Arias	Miami Lakes, FL
Jaymie Bane	Lexington, KY
Andy Beene	Center Point, TX
David Blume	Elk Grove, CA
Doug Boisvert	Edmonton, AL
Richard A. Cerrone	Henderson, NV
Jeff Cornell	Lee's Summit, MO
Joey Davis	Bridgeport, CT
Ellis Dungan	Pensacola, FL
Jim Fink	Regina, SK
Joe Ford	Yukon, OK
Ed Heather	Cambridge, ON
Tom Hinkle	Atascadero, CA
Steven Houle	Windsor, ON
Tim Huff	Cave Creek, AZ
Jim Hughes	Prosper,TX
Darrell Kemp	Niagara Falls, ON
Edwin Lawrence	Silver Springs, MD
Mike Lumley	London, ON
Duncan MacDonald	Dartmouth, NS
Marty Miller	Chicago, IL
Greg Miner	Pickering, On
Bill Moore	Atla Loma, CA
Ty Nichols	Broken Arrow, OK
Andy Pienovi	Portland, OR
Jack Pierce	Laredo, TX
Demerius Pittman	Chino, CA
Jorge Rivera	Puerto Nuevo, PR
Jim Rooney	St. Petersburg, FL
Lee Seras	Flanders, NJ
Joe Siers	Lexington, KY
Gerry Sobeck	Milpitas, CA

SCOUTS – ASSOCIATE – UNITED STATES

Dave Acton	Granbury,TX
Dan Bowers	Marshall, MO
Clyde Bone	La Mesa, CA
Dick Brammer	Huntington, WV
Sean Brinkley	Conyers, GA
Steve Chandler	Lexington, KY
Randolph DeWindt	St. Thomas, USVI
Dick Finn	Columbus, OH
James Graffam	Gorham, ME
Walter Guillory	Lafayette, LA
Dave Gutierrez	Felton, CA
Don Hara	Long Beach, CA
Kevin Hartigan	West Bolyston, MA
Jim Headley	South Gate, CA
Lance Hershberger	Fort Wayne, IN
Drew Hummel	N. Augusta, SC
Mike Huston	Greeley, CO
Terry Kieffer	Beaver Dam, WI
Denny McCrotty	Russellville, AR
Ron Mertus	Chatsworth, CA
Pete Ness	Portland, OR
Steve Partington	Troy, OH
Wayne Pechek	Pueblo, CO
Randall Phillips	Taylors, SC
Joe Platt	Arlington, TX
Vern Ramie	Ewa Beach, HI
Jon Richardson	Indianapolis, IN
John Smillie	Corinth, MS
Scott Sutherland	Spokane, WA
Brian Szakovits	Orangeburg, SC
Mark Tucker	Pilot Mtn., NC
Bob Warner	San Diego, CA
Frank Wills, Jr.	New Orleans, LA
Roger Wolf	Boise, ID
Andre Wood	Nassau, Bahamas

SCOUTS – INTERNATIONAL

Wayne Morgan	Director, International Scouting
Greg Wade	Coordinator, Pacific Rim
Wayne Durbidge	Adelaide, Australia
Paul Elliott	Sydney, Australia
Hans Frauenlob	Glenfield, New Zealand
Bob Goodin	Perth, Australia
Cees Herkemij	The Netherlands
Geoff Samuels	Czech Republic
Damian Shanahan	Victoria, Australia
Barry Sundstrom	NSW, Australia

SCOUTS – LATIN AMERICA

Tony Arias	Director, Latin America
Mike Cadahia	Special Assignment
Hilario Soriano, Scouting Supervisor	Santo Domingo, DR
Geovany Miranda, Scouting Supervisor	Chiriqui, Republic of Panama
Robinson Garces	Maracaibo, VZ
Boris Miranda	Republic of Panama
Rafael Moncada	Valencia, VZ
Juaan Salavarria	Caracas, VZ

SCOUTS – CANADA

Bill Byckowski	Director, Canadian Scouting & Northeastern Regional Supervisor
Jim Ridley . . .	Eastern Canadian, Scouting Supervisor
Don Cowan . .	Western Canadian, Scouting Supervisor
Doug Boisvert	Edmonton, AB
Jim Fink	Regina, SK

Ed Heather	Cambridge, ON
Darrell Kemp	Niagara Falls, ON
Mike Lumley	London, ON
Duncan MacDonald	Gloucester, ON
Grant MacDonald	Dartmouth, NS
Greg Miner	Pickering, ON

SCOUTS – ASSOCIATE – CANADA

Denny Berni	Toronto, ON
Greg Brons	Saskatoon, SK
Norm Caig	Kelowna, BC
Remo Cardinale	Mississauga, ON
Yen Chong	Toronto, ON
Brent Crowther . . . . North Vancouver, BC
George Gerlach	St. Albert, AB
Mike Lebel	Sault Ste. Marie, ON
Gerry LeBlanc	Dieppe, NB
Murray Marshall	Stoney Creek, ON
Kevin Matheson	Truro, NS

Rod Mackenzie	Listowel, ON
Sean McCann	Toronto, ON, ON
Schroeder Nichols	Hamilton, ON
Joe Pulia	Cornwall, ON
Jeff Sharpe	Ajax, ON
Bill Slack	Pierrefonds, PQ
Steve Terry	Peterborough, ON
Andrew Tinnish	Nepean, ON
Peter Topolie	North Bay, ON
Mike Zinyk	Tecumseh, ON

BLUE JAYS FARM CLUBS

SYRACUSE SKYCHIEFS   AAA – International

P & C Stadium
One Tex Simone Drive
Syracuse, NY 13208

Phone	(315) 474-7833
Press Box	(315) 476-5472
Fax:	(315) 474-2658
Website	www.skychiefs.com/skychiefs
E-mail	baseball@skychiefs.com
Executive Vice-President & CEO .	Anthony "Tex" Simone
General Manager	John Simone
Asst. GM, Director of Sales & Media Relations	Tom VanSchaack
Director of Group Sales	Vic Gallucci
Director of Operations	H.J. Refici
Accounting Manager	Don Lehtonen
Associate Director, Group/Corporate Sales . .	Andy Geo
Director of Merchandising	Wendy Shoen
Director of Ticket Sales	Mike Voutsinas
Sales, Accounting Associate	Kevin Stockwell
Head Groundkeeper	"Baseball" Jim Jacobson
Team Historian	Ron Gersbacher
Director, Concessions	Kyle Rogers
Club Physician	Dr. Bob Cupelo
Field Manager	Omar Malave
Coach	Ken Landreaux
Pitching Coach	Rick Langford
Trainer	Jon Woodworth
Stadium	P & C Stadium
Capacity	11,071
Outfield Distances	LF-328, CF-400, RF-328

TENNESSEE SMOKIES   AA – Southern

3450 Line Drive
Kodak, TN 37764

Phone	(865) 637-9494
Fax	(865) 523-9913
Website	www.smokiesbaseball.com
E-mail	info@smokiesbaseball.com
President/Owner	Donald C. Beaver
Vice President/General Manager	Dan Rajkowski
Assistant General Manager	Brian Cox
Executive Director of Marketing & Sales .	Mark Seaman
Director of Stadium Operations	Justin Ewart
Director of Community Relations	Jeff Shoaf
Director of Broadcasting/Media Relations . .	Tim Grubbs
Director of Field Maintenance	Bob Shoemaker
Field Manager	Rocket Wheeler
Coach	Hector Torres
Pitching Coach	Craig Lefferts
Trainer	Jeff Stay
Stadium	Smokies Park
Capacity	6,000
Outfield Distances	LF-330, CF-400, RF-330

DUNEDIN BLUE JAYS   A – Florida State (Advanced)

P.O. Box 957
Dunedin, FL 34697
Delivery Address
Grant Field
373 Douglas Avenue
Dunedin, Florida 34698

Phone	(727) 733-9302
Fax	(727) 734-7661
Website	www.dunedinbluejays.com
E-mail	dunedin@bluejays.ca
Director of Florida Operations & General Manager	Ken Carson
Administrative Assistant	Pat Smith
Assistant General Manager	Carrie Short
Manager Sales & Marketing	Bill Berger
Grounds Foreman	Steve Perry
Clubhouse Co-ordinator	Mickey McGee
Field Manager	Marty Pevey
Coach	Dennis Holmberg
Pitching Coach	Scott Breeden
Trainer	Mike Frostad
Stadium	Dunedin Stadium
Capacity	6,106
Outfield Distances	LF-335, CF-400, RF-315

CHARLESTON ALLEY CATS   A – South Atlantic

3403 MacCorkle Avenue, SE
Charleston, WV 25304

Phone	(304) 344-2287
Fax	(304) 344-0083
Website	www.charlestonalleycats.com
E-mail	team@charlestonalleycats.com
Owner	Wheelers Baseball LP
President	Andy Paterno
General Manager	Tim Bordner
Office Manager	Lisa Spoor
Broadcast/Media Relations Director	Dan Looney
Promotions Director	Shannon Hans
Stadium Operations Director	Patrick Day
Asst Merchandising Director	Kristie Mahoney
Concessions Director	Jamie Ball
Asst Concessions Director	Brian Ferek
Head Groundskeeper	Bob Hartman
Team Physician	Dr. Randy Swain
Field Manager	Rolando Pino
Coach	Geovany Miranda
Pitching Coach	Hector Berrios
Trainer	Schad Richea
Clubhouse Manager	Mike Spencer
Stadium	West Powell Park
Capacity	4,500
Outfield Distances	LF-340, CF-406, RF-330

AUBURN DOUBLEDAYS   A – New York Penn League (Short)

130 North Division Street
Auburn, New York 13201

Phone	(315) 255-2489
Fax	(315) 255-2675
Press Box	TBA
E-mail	TBA
Operated By	Auburn Community Baseball, Inc
CEO	Tom Ganey
President	Leo Pickney
General Manager	Dan Mahoney
Asst general Manager	David Hoffman
Head Groundskeeper	Rich Wild
Field Manager	Paul Elliott
Coach	Jorge Rivera
Pitching Coach	Dane Johnson
Trainer	Garrett DeGroot
Stadium	Falcon Park
Capacity	2,800
Outfield Distances	LF-330, CF-400, RF-330

MEDICINE HAT BLUE JAYS   Rookie Advanced – Pioneer

P.O. Box 465
Medicine Hat, AB
T1A 7G2

Phone	(403) 526-0404
Fax	(403) 504-2670
Operated by	Elmore Sports Group
Principal Owner	D.G. Elmore
President & General Manager	Paul Fetz
Assistant General Manager	Jason MacAskill
Administrative Assistants	TBA
Secretary	TBA
Field Manager	Tom Bradley
Coach	Jose Mendez
Pitching Coach	Jim Rooney
Trainer	Kevin Elliott
Stadium	Athletic Park
Capacity	3,000
Outfield Distances	LF-350, CF-380, RF-350

PRINGAMOSA BLUE JAYS   Rookie – Dominican Summer League

Administrator	Uridice Abreu de Acosta
Manager	Juan Bernhardt
Pitching Coach	Antonio Caceres
Coach	TBA
Trainer	Isidro Reyes

VENEZUELA SUMMER LEAGUE

Manager	TBA
Coach	Hedbertt Hurtado
Pitching Coach	TBA
Trainer	Enrique Vasquez

YUCATAN LIONS – Mexican League

(Leones de Yucatan)
Calle 50 No. 406-B entre 35 y 37
Col. Jesus Carranza
Merida, Yucatan
C.P. 97109, Mexico

Phone	(99) 26-30-22
Fax	(99) 26-36-31
Operated by	Prodebeis, S. A. de C. V.
Principal Owner & President	Gustavo Ricalde Duran
Vice-President	Ing. Wilbert Valle Acevedo
General Manager	C.P. Jose Rivero Ancona
Assistant GM	Juan Lopez Poveda
PR Dir	Ing. Alejandro Escalante C.
Stadium	Kukulcan
Capacity	13,600

BLUE JAYS MINOR LEAGUE MONTHLY AWARDS

2000	PLAYER	PITCHER
APRIL	Joe Lawrence - Dunedin	Darwin Cubillan - Syracuse
MAY	Reed Johnson - Hagerstown	Scott Cassidy - Dunedin
JUNE	Mike Peeples - Tennessee	Orlando Woodards - Dunedin
JULY	Jay Gibbons - Tennessee	Brandon Lyon - Queens
	Ron Davenport - Medicine Hat	
AUGUST	Ryan Freel - Syracuse	George Perez - Queens

MINOR LEAGUE PLAYER OF THE YEAR

The following is a list of Toronto minor league players that have been named Minor League Player of the Year:

PLAYER/POSITION	YEAR	PUBLICATION	CLUB	STATS
Carlos Delgado/C	1992	USA Today Baseball Wkly	Dunedin (A)	30HR, 100RBI, .324BA
Derek Bell/OF	1991	Baseball America	Syracuse (AAA)	13HR, 93RBI, .346BA

PLAYER DEVELOPMENT & SCOUTING

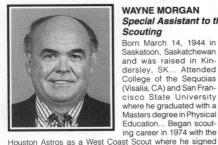

WAYNE MORGAN
Special Assistant to the General Manager/Director, International Scouting

Born March 14, 1944 in Saskatoon, Saskatchewan and was raised in Kindersley, SK... Attended College of the Sequoias (Visalia, CA) and San Francisco State University where he graduated with a Masters degree in Physical Education... Began scouting career in 1974 with the Houston Astros as a West Coast Scout where he signed Canadian outfielder Terry Puhl... Became West Coast Scout for the New York Yankees in 1975... Joined the Toronto Blue Jays in 1978 scouting the West Coast region... Named Regional Scouting Director on February 9, 1982... Promoted to Director, International Scouting on October 1st, 1990... Responsible for all scouting activities outside the United States and Canada... Named Special Assistant to the President, Baseball & GM and Director, International Scouting on December 8, 1998... Married, wife's name Karen... Two children, Jeffrey Wayne (1970) and Meri Anne (1973)... Resides in Morgan Hill, CA.

BOB NELSON
Director, Minor League Operations

Born February 3, 1951... Graduated from East York Collegiate in Toronto where he was All-City in Basketball and Football... Attended McMaster University in Hamilton, Ontario where he lettered in Basketball and Football... Hired by Toronto Blue Jays in 1985 as a scout responsible for Toronto and Southern Ontario... Joined the Blue Jays full-time January 1989 as Administrator of Player Personnel responsible for minor league contracts and overseeing the day to day operations of the Blue Jays' minor league teams... In 1996 had position title changed to Director, Baseball Administration... December 20, 1999 was named Director, Minor League Operations... Had been actively involved in amateur baseball in Ontario as both a player and coach for 16 years... Served as President of the Labatt Metro Major League Baseball League and Vice-President of the Metro Toronto Amateur Baseball Association... Bob resides in Toronto and has two daughters, Leah and Shannon.

CHRIS BUCKLEY
Director, Scouting

Born 12/31/58 in Summit, New Jersey... Graduated from Milburn High School where he played baseball, football and was a member of the track and field team... Attended Kean College in New Jersey and graduated with a degree in History... Played baseball professionally for two seasons in the Houston Astros organization... Following his playing career coached at the college level for Pace University (1983-85), Seton Hall University (1986-87) and Duke University (1986-1989)... Joined the Toronto Blue Jays in 1989 as an Area Scout working in Florida... Was promoted to National Cross Checker in 1996... On September 20, 2000 was named as the Director, Scouting... He and his wife, Ellen reside in Temple Terrace, Florida with their children Sean (11), Brianne (9) and Kevin (5).

BILL BYCKOWSKI
Director, Canadian Scouting & Northeastern Regional Supervisor

Born December 9, 1961 in Toronto, ON... Attended St. Clair Community College in Port Huron, Michigan, on a baseball scholarship from 1979-1981... Graduated from Wilfred Laurier University in 1983 with a B.A. in Physical Education... In 1983, Byckowski, a fullback, was drafted by British Columbia Lions of the Canadian Football League (3rd round)... From 1980-1990 was a member of the Toronto Maple Leafs of the Intercounty Baseball League where he was a nine time All-Star and three time batting champion... Member of Canadian National Baseball team participating in the 1987 Pan-Am Games and the 1988 Summer Olympics... Joined the Toronto Blue Jays in September, 1992 as Assistant Director, Canadian Scouting... Named Director, Canadian Scouting November 1, 1993... Responsible for scouting Canadian amateur talent as well as serving as liaison between professional and amateur baseball in Canada... Had Northeastern Regional Supervisor added to his title in November 2000... He and his wife Barb reside in Georgetown, Ontario with their three children, Jordan (13), Thomas (6) and Robert (4).

Player Development

TONY ARIAS
Director, Latin America Operations

Born April 3, 1962 in Hialeah, Florida... Entering his sixth season in the organization and his second as the Director, Latin America Operations after being named to the position on January 1, 2000... Joined Toronto as a scout in 1996 after scouting for the Oakland Athletics from 1989 to 1995... The former first baseman played up to AA in the Oakland organization from 1984 to 1988 after his 8th round selection in the 1984 draft... Had attended Miami-Dade Community College for two years prior to joining Oakland and then completed his Bachelors Degree in 1990 at Florida International University... Married, wife's name is Mary... Two children, Tony III and Nicholas.

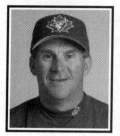

SAL BUTERA
Major League Advance Scout

The 48 year old former major league catcher is beginning his fourth season in the Blue Jays organization... Joined the organization in 1996 in the current position... Spent the 1998 season as the bullpen coach in Toronto before returning to scouting... Played parts of nine major league seasons with the Minnesota Twins (1980-82, 1987), Detroit Tigers (1983), Montreal Expos (1984-85), Cincinnati Reds (1986-87) and the Toronto Blue Jays (1988-89) before retiring from playing with a career .215 average with eight home runs and 76RBI... In 58 games with Toronto he hit .233, 1HR, 6RBI... In 1990 he joined the Houston Astros organization where he spent five seasons managing in their minor leagues... Was named the Texas League Manager of the Year in 1994 and selected as the Most Promising Manager in '94 — *Baseball America*... In 1995 he joined the Minnesota organization managing their AA Eastern League club in New Britain, CT.

MINOR LEAGUE COACHING STAFF & INSTRUCTORS

| Syracuse | Tennessee | Dunedin |

| **Omar Malave, Manager** | **Rocket Wheeler, Manager** | **Marty Pevey, Manager** |

| **Ken Landreaux, Coach** | **Hector Torres, Coach** | **Dennis Holmberg, Coach** |

| **Rick Langford, Pitching Coach** | **Craig Lefferts, Pitching Coach** | **Scott Breeden, Pitching Coach** |

Charleston

Ronaldo Pino, Manager

Geovany Miranda, Coach

Hector Berrios, Pitching Coach

Auburn

Paul Elliott, Manager

Jorge Rivera, Coach

Dane Johnson, Pitching Coach

Medicine Hat

Tom Bradley, Manager

Photo not available

Jose Mendez, Coach

Jim Rooney, Pitching Coach

Instructors

**Jim Hoff,
Field Coordinator**

**Ernie Whitt,
Roving Hitting &
Catching Instructor**

**Bruce Walton,
Roving Pitching Instructor**

**Jerry Browne,
Roving Infield Instructor**

**George Bell,
Roving Hitting Instructor**

**Tack Wilson,
Roving Outfield &
Baserunning Instructor**

2001 MINOR LEAGUE COACHES & FIELD STAFF

BELL, Jorge Antonio (George)   Roving Hitting Instructor

Former Outfielder ... HT: 6-01; **WT:** 210 ... **B-T:** R-R ... **BORN:** October 21, 1959, San Pedro de Mac., DR ... **RESIDES:** San Pedro de Macoris, Dom. Republic ... **RECOMMENDED/SIGNED BY:** (Phillies) ... **TRANSACTIONS:** Signed as a non-drafted free agent by Phillies on June 23, 1978. Selected by Blue Jays in Minor League Draft on December 8, 1980. Signed as a free agent by Cubs on December 24, 1990. Traded to White Sox for Ken Patterson and Sammy Sosa on March 30, 1992. ... **PRO CAREER:** 1979: Led Western Carolina League in total bases (270), triples (15), and RBI (102) and was third in batting (.305); 1980: Suffered a stress fracture in his shoulder on April 24 and shortly after returning to action in June, aggravated the injury sliding into home plate and missed the remainder of the season; 1981: Clubbed first major league home run on May 2 Baltimore's Scott McGregor; 1982: Sidelined with mononucleosis April 20-May 1 before suffering two serious injuries which landed him on the DL twice; did not play after July 8; 1983: Tied for lead among International League outfielders in double plays (4); 1984: Finished third in AL in doubles (39), fifth in extra-base hits (69) and eighth in total bases (302); hit 16 homers after the All-Star break; named Labatt's Blue Jays' MVP; 1985: Named to AL Silver Slugger team; hit grand slams at Seattle on July 9 and on August 2 vs. Texas; hit 18 homers on the road; hit .321 in ALCS vs. Kansas City (9-28) including three doubles; 1986: Finished fourth in AL MVP voting; tied for AL lead in game-winning RBI (15); finished third in total bases (341), third in extra-base hits (75), fourth in slugging (.532) and tied for fifth in RBI (108); was second among AL outfielders in assists (17); smacked a grand slam on June 20 off New York's Dave Righetti; compiled a 15-game hitting streak may 23-June 8 (.431); voted Labatt's Blue Player-of-the-Year; also earned spots on AL Silver Slugger team, AL UPI All-Star team and Sporting News All-Star team; 1987: Named AL MVP and AL Player-of-the-Year as voted by The Sporting News and Baseball America; named to AP and UPI All-Star teams; led AL in RBI (134) and total bases (369), finished second in slugging (.605) and tied for fifth in game-winning RBI (16); cracked a pair of grand slams, June 11 vs. Baltimore and August 27 vs. Oakland; 1988: Finished third in AL in game-winning RBI (17) and tenth in RBI (97); became first player in major league history to hit three home runs on opening day (April 4) when he stroked three off Kansas City's Bret Saberhagen; followed that up with a 5-for-5 performance against the Royals two days later; hit sixth career grand slam on September 4 off Texas' Mitch Williams in the bottom of the ninth to give the Jays a come-from-behind victory; 1989: Finished fourth in MVP balloting and earned a berth on Baseball America's All-Star team; led AL in sacrifice flies (14), finished fourth in doubles (41), sixth in RBI (104), tied for fifth in runs (88), eighth in total bases (281), tenth in hits (182) and tied for sixth in extra-base hits (61); had longest hitting streak in the league, when he hit safely in 22 straight games August 8-31, batting .368 during the streak; collected 1,000th major league hit on May 20 vs. Chicago and hit the last home run in Exhibition Stadium the following day to beat the White Sox; named Labatt's Blue Player-of-the-Year; hit .200 with a homer in the ALCS vs. Oakland; 1990: Named to AL All-Star team; won AL Player-of-the-Week honours twice in June; whacked a grand slam on April 11 off Texas's Kevin Brown; batted .394 (28-71) with eight homers and 24 RBI over a 17-games stretch June 7-24; tied a major league record with three sacrifice flies in a game August 4 against Chicago; 1991: Hit .294 with 16 homers and 50 RBI in the first half to make the All-Star team; had the tenth-best HR/AB ratio in the NL (1/22.3); 1992: Tied for fourth in AL with 112 RBI and led team with 25 homers; belted his eighth and ninth career grand slams on May 5 vs. Milwaukee and July 5 vs. Boston; twice was named AL Player-of-the-Week, once on June 29-July 5 (.414-3-14) and once on August 3-9 (.500, 13-26, 2 HR); hit .304 with nine homers and 25 RBI in August; registered an RBI in nine straight games June 24-July 3 (17 RBI); recorded third career five-hit game on April 30 vs. Texas. Rejoined Blue Jays organization as a roving hitting instructor in 1998 after attending the 1997 spring training camp as a guest instructor. Is one of only four men enshrined on the Blue Jays "Level of Excellence". Is the Blue Jays all-time RBI leader with 740 and is second with 202 home runs. Is the only AL MVP in club history setting club records with 47 home runs and 134 RBI in 1987.

PLAYING CAREER

Year	Club & League	AVG	G	AB	R	H	2B	3B	HR	RBI	BB	SO	SB
1978	Helena (Pio)	.311	33	106	20	33	6	1	0	14	9	18	3
1979	Spartanburg (SAL)	.305	130	491	78	150	24	15	22	102	26	98	10
1980	Reading (East)	.309	22	55	11	17	5	2	0	11	3	8	3
1981	TORONTO (AL)	.233	60	163	19	38	2	1	5	12	5	27	3
1982	Syracuse (Int)	.200	37	125	11	25	5	4	3	19	1	42	1
1983	Syracuse (Int)	.271	85	317	37	86	11	4	15	59	23	54	5
	TORONTO (AL)	.268	39	112	5	30	5	4	2	17	4	17	1
1984	TORONTO (AL)	.292	159	606	85	177	39	4	26	87	24	86	11
1985	TORONTO (AL)	.275	157	607	87	167	28	6	28	95	43	90	21
1986	TORONTO (AL)	.309	159	641	101	198	38	6	31	108	41	62	7
1987	TORONTO (AL)	.308	156	610	111	188	32	4	47	134	39	75	5
1988	TORONTO (AL)	.269	156	614	78	165	27	5	24	97	34	66	4
1989	TORONTO (AL)	.297	153	613	88	182	41	2	18	104	33	60	4
1990	TORONTO (AL)	.265	142	562	67	149	25	0	21	86	32	80	3
1991	CHICAGO (NL)	.285	149	558	63	159	27	0	25	86	32	62	2
1992	CHICAGO (AL)	.255	155	627	74	160	27	0	25	112	31	97	5
1993	CHICAGO (AL)	.217	102	410	36	89	17	2	13	64	13	49	1
	South Bend (Mid)	.125	2	8	1	1	0	0	0	0	1	0	0
MAJOR TOTALS		.278	1587	6123	814	1702	308	34	265	1002	331	771	67

MANAGERIAL/COACHING CAREER
(Rejoined Blue Jays Organization in 1998)

1998-2001   Roving hitting instructor, Minor Leagues

BERRIOS, Hector   Pitching Coach, CHARLESTON

Former Pitcher ... HT: 5-10; **WT:** 170 ... **B-T:** L-L ... **BORN:** November 1, 1965, Santurce, PR ... **RESIDES:** Bronx, New York ... **RECOMMENDED/SIGNED BY:** Ramon Pena (Royals) ... **TRANSACTIONS:** Signed as a non-drafted free agent by Royals on September 22, 1983. Signed as a free agent by Tigers on February 26, 1987. Signed as a free agent by Angels on April 5, 1991. Signed as a free agent by the Dodgers on February 19, 1992. Signed as a free agent by Cubs on May 29, 1992. ... **PRO CAREER:** 1994: Appeared in 22 games, 20 of which were in relief; struck out 70 batters in 57 innings; 1987: Appeared in a career-high 45 games, all in relief; finished 25 games; notched career-highs in wins (7) and saves (7) and fanned 93 batters in 87 innings; 1990: Posted a career-best 1.80 ERA in 21 relief outings; 1991: Pitched at three levels and reached Triple-A for the first time; 1992: Split season in Triple-A pitching for Albuquerque, then Iowa; 1997: Made his coaching debut as he assumed pitching coach duties for the Tigers' Gulf Coast League entry; 1998-2000: Joined Blue Jays organization as pitching coach for Hagerstown of the South Atlantic League (SAL). Is returning for his fourth year in the organization in the same capacity in 2001 with Charleston (SAL).

PLAYING RECORD

Year	Club & League	W-L	ERA	G	GS	CG	SHO	SV	IP	H	R	ER	BB	SO
1984	Eugene (NWST)	1-2	2.53	22	2	0	0	0	57	52	26	16	34	70
1985	Ft. Myers (FSL)	1-1	6.23	9	0	0	0	0	17	23	13	12	8	9
	Eugene (NWST)	6-4	5.33	13	13	1	0	0	76	85	60	45	30	65
1987	Fayetteville (SAL)	7-7	2.79	45	0	0	0	7	87	70	46	27	35	93
1988	Glens Falls (East)	3-0	3.55	25	8	0	0	1	51	51	25	20	28	36
1989	Fayetteville (SAL)	4-2	4.88	25	7	0	0	0	59	66	38	32	28	36
1990	Lakeland (FSL)	2-2	1.80	21	0	0	0	0	45	36	14	9	14	42
1991	Palm Springs (Cal)	0-2	4.94	10	0	0	0	0	24	23	16	13	11	29
	Edmonton (PCL)	3-1	3.86	17	0	0	0	1	16	15	7	7	8	12
	Midland (Tex)	2-1	2.81	18	0	0	0	2	16	13	5	5	3	17
1992	Albuquerque (PCL)	1-2	4.38	15	0	0	0	0	12	10	6	6	11	12
	Iowa (AmAs)	1-1	8.78	16	0	0	0	0	13	21	13	13	10	14

MANAGERIAL/COACHING CAREER
(Joined Blue Jays Organization in 1998)

1997	Pitching Coach, Tigers, Gulf Coast League
1998-2000	Pitching Coach, Hagerstown, South Atlantic League
2001	Pitching Coach, Charleston, South Atlantic League

BRADLEY, Tom   Manager, MEDICINE HAT

Former Pitcher ... **HT:** 6-02; **WT:** 180 ... **B-T:** R-R ... **BORN:** March 16, 1947, Asheville, North Carolina ... **RESIDES:** University, Maryland ... **RECOMMENDED/SIGNED BY:** (California Angels) ... **TRANSACTIONS:** Angels' fifth round selection in the 1968 draft. ... **PERSONAL BACKGROUND:** Married, wife is Kathy and has two children, son Andy and daughter Alix. Was a two-year letter winner on the Maryland baseball team ... Was an All-American selection in 1968 and was named as Maryland's Scholar-Athlete of the year. ... **PRO CAREER:** 1969-70: Began professional career in the California Angels organization in 1969. That same season made his major league debut with California. Spent two seasons with the Angels compiling a 2-6 mark in 20 games with a 5.90 ERA. Was traded to the Chicago White Sox following the 1970 season. 1971-72: In two seasons with Chicago was 28-26 in 85 games, posting a 2.97 ERA. Made 79 starts for Chicago and completed 18 games. Was traded to the San Francisco Giants following the 1972 season. 1973-75: Pitched three seasons with San Francisco and was 23-26 with a 4.56 ERA in 78 games for San Francisco. Was the opening day starter for San Francisco in 1974 at Candlestick Park. Finished his career with a 55-61 record and a 3.72 ERA. Retired from professional baseball following the 1977 season after rotator cuff surgery. 1979-90: Managed at Jacksonville University, NCAA Division I, where he compiled a 431-291 record over 12 seasons. Won the 1989 Sun Belt Conference championship and advanced to the 1989 NCAA Tournament. 1991-2000: Spent 10 years at his alma mater posting 243 wins and 306 losses. Led Maryland to school record 29 wins in first season at the helm in 1991. Coached 62 players who went onto play professional baseball. Joins the Blue Jays organization for the 2001 season where he will manage at Medicine Hat (Rookie) of the Pioneer League.

PLAYING RECORD

Year	Club & League	W-L	ERA	G	GS	CG	SHO	SV	IP	H	R	ER	BB	SO
1969	CALIFORNIA (AL)	0-1	27.00	3	0	0	0	0	2.0	9	6	1	0	2
1970	CALIFORNIA (AL)	2-5	4.13	17	11	1	1	0	69.7	71	32	3	33	53
1971	CHICAGO (AL)	15-15	2.96	45	39	7	6	2	285.7	273	94	16	74	206
1972	CHICAGO (AL)	15-14	2.98	40	40	11	2	0	260.0	225	86	19	65	209
1973	SAN FRANCISCO (NL)	13-12	3.90	35	34	6	1	0	224.0	212	97	26	69	136
1974	SAN FRANCISCO (NL)	8-11	5.16	30	21	2	0	0	134.3	152	77	15	52	72
1975	SAN FRANCISCO (NL)	2-3	6.21	13	6	0	0	0	42.0	57	29	6	18	13
MAJOR TOTALS		**55-61**	**3.72**	**183**	**151**	**27**	**10**	**2**	**1017.2**	**999**	**484**	**421**	**311**	**691**

MANAGERIAL/COACHING CAREER

1978	Pitching Coach, St Mary's College, California
1979-90	Head Coach, Jacksonville, NCAA Div I
1991-2000	Head Coach, Maryland, NCAA Div I
2001	Manager, Medicine Hat, Pioneer League

BREEDEN, Harold Scott (Scott)   Pitching Coach, DUNEDIN

Former Pitcher ... **HT:** 6-02; **WT:** 190 ... **B-T:** R-R ... **BORN:** Sept. 17, 1937, Charlottesville, VA ... **RESIDES:** Temple Terrace, Florida ... **RECOMMENDED/SIGNED BY:** (Dodgers) ... **PERSONAL BACKGROUND:** Graduated from Reily H.S. (Hamilton, Ohio), in 1956. Attended Miami University in Oxford, Ohio. ... **PRO CAREER:** Pitched a no-hit, no-run game in his first start for Kokomo in 1958 (May 19) against Keokuk. Led Midwest League in winning percentage (.773) in 1958 and had second lowest ERA (2.09). In 1963, he had ninth lowest ERA (3.48) in Pacific Coast League. Finished his playing career in Reds organization in 1967 and remained with the team in various capacities through the 1989 season with the exception of '82 and '83 when he was pitching coach for the Cubs' Triple-A affiliate at Iowa. Managed in Appalachian League in 1967 before becoming a minor league pitching instructor with the Reds, a position he held through 1981. Made major league debut as pitching coach for Reds in 1986 and held that position four years. Joined the Blue Jays organization as a roving minor league pitching instructor in 1990. Was the pitching coach at Dunedin of the Florida State League in 1996 and was Syracuse's pitching coach in 1997 and 1998. Returned to Dunedin as pitching coach in 1999 where he will return for his 12th season in the organization in 2001.

PLAYING RECORD

Year	Club & League	W-L	ERA	G	GS	CG	SHO	SV	IP	H	R	ER	BB	SO
1956	Kokomo (Mid)	0-2	10.59	6	4	0	–	–	17	22	0	20	14	12
	Hornell (Pony)	2-3	6.35	13	3	0	–	–	34	43	35	24	26	16
1957	Reno (Cal)	8-11	4.39	32	23	5	0	–	158	174	86	77	74	100
1958	Green Bay (III)	1-0	3.60	4	2	0	0	–	15	25	8	6	4	8
	Kokomo (Mid)	17-5	2.09	26	22	19	3	–	181	141	59	42	56	159
1959	Victoria (Tex)	11-6	3.53	38	20	11	0	–	163	159	76	64	49	69
1960	Spokane (PCL)	2-2	4.50	9	5	1	0	–	30	36	16	15	7	15
	Atlanta (Sou)	10-7	4.55	36	16	7	3	–	133	145	86	67	59	71
1961	Omaha (AmAs)	7-7	4.39	48	15	5	1	–	160	150	92	78	75	85
1962	Omaha (AmAs)	12-14	4.35	35	27	7	0	–	184	219	105	89	60	97
1963	San Diego (PCL)	9-10	3.48	34	23	11	3	–	186	161	78	72	37	120
1964	Dal/SD (PCL)	8-9	3.74	36	20	6	3	–	159	161	76	66	47	122
1965	SaltLakeCity (PCL)	8-11	5.28	30	30	4	0	–	174	191	111	102	54	102
1966	Buffalo (Int)	5-2	3.86	51	2	0	0	–	105	101	50	45	48	91
1967	Knoxville (Sou)	2-2	2.70	24	2	2	1	–	50	47	17	15	5	45

MANAGERIAL/COACHING CAREER
(Joined Blue Jays Organization in 1990).

1967	Manager, Wytheville, Appalachian League
1968-81	Instructor, Cincinnati Reds organization
1982-83	Pitching Coach, Iowa, American Association
1984-85	Instructor, Cincinnati Reds organization
1986-89	Pitching Coach, Cincinnati Reds
1990-95	Pitching Instructor, Toronto Blue Jays organization
1996	Pitching Coach, Dunedin, Florida State League
1997-98	Pitching Coach, Syracuse, International League
1999-2001	Pitching Coach, Dunedin, Florida State League

RECORD AS MANAGER

Year	Club & League	W-L	PCT	Finish
1967	Wytheville (Appy)	24-40	.375	(6th)

BROWNE, Jerome Austin (Jerry) — Roving Infield Instructor

Former Infielder ... **HT:** 5-10; **WT:** 170 ... **B-T:** S-R ... **BORN:** February 13, 1966, St. Croix, Virgin Islands ... **RESIDES:** Arlington, TX ... **RECOMMENDED/SIGNED BY:** Orlando Gomez (Rangers) ... **TRANSACTIONS:** Signed as non-drafted free agent by Rangers, March 3, 1983; Released by Indians, March 31, 1992; Signed by Athletics, April 11, 1992; On disabled list, April 19-July 18, 1993; Granted free agency, Oct. 26, 1993; Signed by Marlins, Jan. 5, 1994; Granted free agency, Oct. 20, 1994; Re-signed by Marlins, April 7, 1995; Granted free agency, Oct. 31, 1995; Signed by Mets, Feb. 11, 1996; On restricted list, April 4-Oct. 30, 1996; Released by Mets, Oct. 30, 1996; Signed by Rangers, Jan. 6, 1997; Released by Rangers, April 1, 1997. ... **PERSONAL BACKGROUND:** Graduated from Central High School in Killshill, Virgin Islands. Is single and is nicked named "Gov'nor". ... **PRO CAREER:** Began professional career in the Texas Rangers organization in 1984. Played in the Major Leagues for Texas (1986-88), Cleveland (1989-91), Oakland (1992-93) and Florida (1994-95). In 10 season batted .271 with 23 home runs, 288 RBI and 73 stolen bases in 982 Major League games. 1987 was the Rangers rookie of the year as voted by the Texas writers. 1989 was voted by the Cleveland chapter of BBWAA as Cleveland's "Man of the Year". During the 1990 season set an AL record for fewest double plays turned by a second baseman with 67 (150 or mores games). 1990 ranked second in the AL in runs scored with 92. 1991 tied for second in the AL with 11 pinch hits. Played in the post season in 1992 with Oakland vs. Toronto. In 10 post season games was 0-3 with four runs scored and two RBI.

PLAYING CAREER

Year	Club & League	AVG	G	AB	R	H	2B	3B	HR	RBI	SH-SF	HB	BB-IBB	SO	SB-CS	GDP	SLG	OBP
1984	Burlington (Mid)	.236	127	420	70	99	10	1	0	18	7-2	1	71-0	76	31-8	7	.264	.346
1985	Salem (CARO)	.267	122	460	69	123	18	4	3	58	1-1	1	82-2	62	24-16	8	.343	.379
1986	Tulsa (Tex)	.303	128	491	82	149	15	7	2	57	5-1	0	62-1	61	39-11	10	.375	.381
	TEXAS (AL)	.417	12	24	6	10	2	0	0	3	0-0	0	1-0	4	0-2	0	.500	.440
1987	TEXAS (AL)	.271	132	454	63	123	16	6	1	38	7-2	2	61-0	50	27-17	6	.339	.358
1988	TEXAS (AL)	.229	73	214	26	49	9	2	1	17	3-1	0	25-0	32	7-5	5	.304	.308
	Okla City (AMAS)	.252	76	286	45	72	15	2	5	34	4-2	0	37-2	29	14-5	9	.371	.335
1989	CLEVELAND (AL)	.299	153	598	83	179	31	4	5	45	14-4	1	68-10	64	14-6	9	.390	.370
1990	CLEVELAND (AL)	.267	140	513	92	137	26	5	6	50	12-11	2	72-1	46	12-7	12	.372	.353
1991	CLEVELAND (AL)	.228	107	290	28	66	5	2	1	29	12-4	1	27-0	29	2-4	5	.269	.292
1992	Tacoma (PCL)	.412	4	17	1	7	1	1	0	2	0-0	0	3-0	1	0-0	0	.588	.500
	OAKLAND (AL)	.287	111	324	43	93	12	2	3	40	16-6	4	40-0	40	3-3	7	.364	.366
1993	OAKLAND (AL)	.250	76	260	27	65	13	0	2	19	2-2	0	22-0	17	4-0	9	.323	.306
	Tacoma (PCL)	.240	6	25	3	6	0	0	0	2	0-0	0	0-0	4	1-0	1	.240	.240
1994	FLORIDA (NL)	.295	101	329	42	97	17	4	3	30	3-2	2	52-3	23	3-0	5	.398	.392
1995	FLORIDA (NL)	.255	77	184	21	47	4	0	1	17	9-1	1	25-0	20	1-1	7	.293	.346
	Brevard Cty (FSL)	.286	3	7	0	2	0	0	0	2	0-1	0	1-0	1	0-0	0	.286	.333
MAJOR TOTALS		.271	982	3190	431	866	135	25	23	288	78-33	13	393-14	325	73-45	65	.351	.351

MANAGERIAL/COACHING CAREER
(Joined Blue Jays Organization in 2001)

2001	Roving Infield Instructor, Minor League

ELLIOTT, Paul — Manager, AUBURN

HT: 6-02; **WT:** 205 ... **B-T:** R-R ... **BORN:** July 5, 1956, Sydney, Australia ... **RESIDES:** Sydney, Australia ... **PERSONAL BACKGROUND:** Played with the Australian Senior baseball team in Korea, Japan, the Phillipines, Taiwan and Holland from

1974 to 1987. Began his coaching career as the manager of the Parramatta Patriots in Australia in 1989-90. Served as coach from 1990 to 1995 with the Sydney Blues. Served his first season as a coach in the Blue Jays system in 1996 after scouting for the club in Australia. Served as a coach at Hagerstown in 1998 and will make his managerial debut for Medicine Hat of the Pioneer League in 1999.

MANAGERIAL/COACHING CAREER
(All in Blue Jays Organization)

1996	Coach, Medicine Hat, Pioneer League
1997	Coach, Knoxville, Southern League
1998	Coach, Hagerstown, South Atlantic League
1999-2000	Manager, Medicine Hat, Pioneer League
2001	Manager, Auburn, New York-Penn league

RECORD AS MANAGER

Year	Club & League	W-L	PCT	Finish
1999	Medicine Hat (Pio)	33-43	.434	(5th in Div.)
2000	Medicine Hat (Pio)	36-40	.473	(4th in Div.)
CAREER TOTALS (2years)		69-83	.454	

HOFF, James F. (Jim) — Field Coordinator

Former Infielder ... **HT:** 5-11; **WT:** 170 ... **B-T:** R-R ... **BORN:** April 16, 1945, Detroit, MI ... **RESIDES:** Tampa, Florida ... **RECOMMENDED/SIGNED BY:** (Reds) ... **TRANSACTIONS:** Signed as a non-drafted free agent by Reds. ... **PERSONAL BACKGROUND:** Graduated in 1963 from University of Detroit H.S. Attended Xavier University (Cincinnati, OH) and played varsity baseball. Batted .375 his senior year. Following his graduation, he walked into the Reds office and asked for a tryout. Played and managed in Cincinnati organization from 1967-83. Attended University of Notre Dame Law School. ... **PRO CAREER:** 1967: Led Northern League hit by pitch (6); 1969: Tied for Northern League lead in sacrifice hits (6); led league second basemen in fielding percentage (.959); 1970: Led Southern League second basemen in fielding percentage (.984). Spent 11 years managing in the Reds organization, receiving Manager-of-the-Year honours in 1978 at Billings, before becoming their minor league field coordinator in 1984, a position he held through the 1990 season. Spent seven years as the Blue Jays minor league infield instructor and in 1997 took over as Director of Development in 1998. Will return in the 2001 season as the minor league Field Coordinator, his ninth in the organization.

PLAYING CAREER

Year	Club & League	AVG	G	AB	R	H	2B	3B	HR	RBI	BB	SO	SB
1967	Sioux Falls (Nor)	.226	59	217	32	49	5	0	0	14	34	33	8
1968	Tampa (FSL)	.235	111	323	32	76	11	1	1	28	43	31	2
1969	Tampa (FSL)	.225	70	213	27	48	4	1	0	18	40	8	7
	Sioux Falls (Nor)	.289	55	194	31	56	10	1	2	20	37	23	6
1970	Asheville (Sou)	.229	126	398	41	91	12	2	1	23	31	17	11
1971	Three Rivers (East)	.288	96	281	25	81	7	1	0	18	28	17	2
1972	Indianapolis (AmAs)	.189	38	111	9	21	1	0	0	8	15	6	0
	Three Rivers (East)	.226	84	248	17	56	8	0	0	19	32	12	3

MANAGERIAL/COACHING CAREER
(Joined Blue Jays Organization in 1991)

1973	Manager, Seattle, Northwest League (Reds)
1974-76	Manager, Billings, Pioneer League (Reds)
1977	Manager, Tampa, Florida State League (Reds)
1978-81	Manager, Billings, Pioneer League (Reds)
1982-83	Manager, Tampa, Florida State League (Reds)
1984-90	Minor League Field Coordinator, Cincinnati Reds
1991-97	Infield Instructor, Toronto Blue Jays organization
1998-2000	Director of Minor League development, Toronto Blue Jays organization
2001	Field Coordinator, Toronto Blue Jays organization

RECORD AS MANAGER

Year	Club & League	W-L	PCT	Finish
1973	Seattle (NWST)	33-46	.418	(3rd in Div.)
1974	Billings (Pio)	35-37	.471	(2nd in Div.)
1975	Billings (Pio)	26-45	.366	(4th in Div.)
1976	Billings (Pio)	36-35	.507	(2nd in Div.)
1977	Tampa (FSL)	65-70	.481	(4th in Div.)
1978	Billings (Pio)	50-18	.735	(1st in Div.)
1979	Billings (Pio)	43-26	.623	(2nd in Div.)
1980	Billings (Pio)	44-26	.629	(1st in Div.)
1981	Billings (Pio)	30-40	.429	(2nd in Div.)
1982	Tampa (FSL)	71-59	.546	(1st in Div., 1st in Div.)
1983	Tampa (FSL)	56-72	.438	(T3rd in Div., 4th in Div.)
CAREER TOTALS (11 years)		489-474	.508	

POST-SEASON PLAY

Year	Club & League	W-L	PCT	Finish
1978	Billings (Pio)	2-0	1.000	(Def. Idaho Falls 2G to 0 to win league championship)
1980	Billings (Pio)	1-2	.333	(Lost to Lethbridge 2G to 1 in championship finals)
1982	Tampa (FSL)	2-3	.400	(Lost to Ft. Lauderdale 3G to 2 in championship finals)

HOLMBERG, Dennis

Coach, DUNEDIN

Former Third Baseman/Outfielder ... **HT:** 6-00; **WT:** 200 ... **B-T:** L-R ... **BORN:** August 2, 1951, Fremont, NE ... **RESIDES:** Palm Harbor, Florida ... **RECOMMENDED/SIGNED BY:** (Brewers) ... **TRANSACTIONS:** Brewers' fifth pick in 1970 January draft. ... **PERSONAL BACKGROUND:** Has two children, Brianne (10/20/79) and Kenny (02/21/83) ... **PRO CAREER:** Began as player in 1970 in the Brewers farm system where he remained for eight seasons, the last two as a player-coach with Burlington of the Midwest League and Holyoke of the Eastern League. Began his managerial career at Newark of the short-season New York Pennsylvania League in 1977. Joined the Blue Jays in 1978 as a full-time minor league instructor before joining Medicine Hat of the Pioneer League to manage the following season. Moved on to Kinston of the Carolina League in 1980 and then to Florence of the South Atlantic League where he piloted the club to within one game of the league championship in 1982, bowing to Greensboro in the deciding game. Dennis managed two more seasons with the same club before being named a coach with the Syracuse Chiefs in 1985, a post he held through 1986. Went back to managing later in '86 season as he guided Jays affiliate in Pioneer League at Medicine Hat, before assuming coaching duties again, this time at Dunedin in Florida State League from 1987-89. Guided Dunedin towards FSL record 53-14 in the first half of 1990 season (.791 winning percentage was also league record for a half season). Spent four years as manager of Dunedin club before making major league debut as coach with Toronto in 1994. Was Toronto's bullpen coach in 1994 and 1995. Became manager of the Dunedin team in the Florida State League in 1996 and returned to the same role in 1997. Has coached at Dunedin in since 1998 and will return in the same capacity in 2001, his 24th season in the Blue Jays organization.

PLAYING CAREER

Year	Club & League	AVG	G	AB	R	H	2B	3B	HR	RBI	BB	SO	SB
1970	Newark (NYP)	.262	67	214	35	56	1	0	6	25	45	53	3
1971	Danville (Mid)	.220	58	182	22	40	3	1	9	21	35	68	1
1972	San Antonio (Tex)	.203	76	177	18	35	9	0	3	15	28	51	0
1973	Danville (Mid)	.291	20	55	9	16	2	2	1	6	8	13	0
	Shreveport (Tex)	.162	48	117	12	19	3	0	1	13	14	21	0
1974	Danville (Mid)	.246	106	350	46	86	15	3	13	59	61	67	5
1975	Burlington (Mid)	.221	130	430	51	95	23	2	15	65	93	92	4
1976	Burlington (Mid)	.299	93	288	48	86	18	2	12	62	48	47	0
1977	Holyoke (East)	.186	16	43	4	8	0	0	1	4	2	7	0

MANAGERIAL/COACHING CAREER
(Joined Blue Jays Organization in 1978)

1977	Manager, Newark, New York-Penn League (Brewers)
1978	Minor League Instructor, Toronto Blue Jays
1979	Manager, Medicine Hat, Pioneer League
1980	Manager, Kinston, Carolina League
1981-84	Manager, Florence, South Atlantic League
1985-86	Coach, Syracuse, International League (until opening of Pioneer League season)
1986	Manager, Medicine Hat, Pioneer League
1987-89	Coach, Dunedin, Florida State League
1990-93	Manager, Dunedin, Florida State League
1994-95	Bullpen Coach, Toronto Blue Jays, American League
1996-97	Manager, Dunedin, Florida State League
1998-2001	Coach, Dunedin, Florida State League

RECORD AS MANAGER

Year	Club & League	W-L	PCT	Finish
1977	Newark (NYP)	43-29	.597	(2nd in Div.)
1979	Medicine Hat (Pio)	27-42	.391	(4th in Div.)
1980	Kinston (CARO)	67-69	.493	(2nd in Div., 3rd in Div.)
1981	Florence (SAL)	66-72	.478	(4th in Div., 2nd in Div.)
1982	Florence (SAL)	77-64	.546	(3rd in Div., 1st in Div.)
1983	Florence (SAL)	71-72	.497	(2nd in Div., 4th in Div.)
1984	Florence (SAL)	65-73	.471	(5th in Div., 3rd in Div.)
1986	Medicine Hat (Pio)	24-46	.343	(6th)
1990	Dunedin (FSL)	84-52	.618	(1st in Div; 3rd in Div.)
1991	Dunedin (FSL)	59-72	.450	(4th in Div., 3rd in Div.)
1992	Dunedin (FSL)	78-59	.569	(4th in Div., 1st in Div.)
1993	Dunedin (FSL)	68-64	.515	(5th in Div., 4th in Div.)
1996	Dunedin (FSL)	67-70	.489	(3rd in Div., 8th in Div.)
1997	Dunedin (FSL)	57-82	.410	(6th in Div., 8th in Div.)
CAREER TOTALS (14 years)		853-866	.496	

POST-SEASON PLAY

Year	Club & League	W-L	PCT	Finish
1982	Florence (SAL)	4-4	.500	(Def. Charleston 2G to 1 in semi-finals; lost to Greensboro 3G to 2 in championship finals)
1990	Dunedin (FSL)	0-2	.000	(Lost to Charlotte 2G to 0 in quarter-finals)
1992	Dunedin (FSL)	0-2	.000	(Lost to Clearwater 2G to 0 in quarter-finals)

JOHNSON, Dane Edward

Pitching Coach, AUBURN

Pitcher ... **HT:** 6-05; **WT:** 195 ... **B-T:** R-R ... **BORN:** February 10, 1963, Coral Gables, FL ... **RESIDES:** Miami, Florida ... **RECOMMENDED/SIGNED BY:** Tim Wilken (Blue Jays) ... **TRANSACTIONS:** Blue Jays' second round selection (No. 48 overall) in 1984 June draft. Signed by White Sox as a free agent on January 26, 1994. Signed by Brewers as a free agent on June 5, 1993. Signed by Blue Jays as a free agent on January 22, 1996. Claimed on waivers by Athletics on October 2, 1996. Signed as a free agent by Blue Jays on November 18, 1997. ... **PERSONAL BACKGROUND:** Graduated from Southwest Miami (Fla.) H.S. in 1981 where he played basketball and ran track and cross country. Was sixth in the National Junior Olympic Decathlon. Attended Biscayne College in Miami where he played baseball and basketball. Was an All-Conference selection in basketball. Played two years in the Chinese Professional Baseball League 1990-91 and spent two seasons in Taipei, Taiwan. Returned to the United States as an assistant coach at Lamar University in 1992. ... **PRO CAREER:** 1986:

Led all pitchers in South Atlantic League in putouts (23) and paced Florence pitching staff in games started (24); 1988: Won five in a row at one point (May 4 - June 1); 1994: Made major league debut on May 30 at New York and earned his first major league victory June 8 vs. Toronto; placed second in the American Association with 24 saves, finished third in relief points (64) and fourth in games finished (36); went 1-1 with a 0.66 ERA in May; allowed just two earned runs over his first 21 appearances (0.72 ERA, 25 IP); went 1-4 with a 1.88 ERA and 13 saves in 22 appearances on the road for Nashville; 1995: Tied for fourth in the American Association in saves (15) and ranked fifth in games finished (28) and relief points (45); yielded just one earned run over his last 23 games spanning 26 innings (0.35 ERA); saved nine games in 12 appearances in August; 1997: Did not give up an earned run until his fifth relief appearance on April 18. Began coaching career as Medicine Hat's pitching coach in 2000 and will perform the same duties with Auburn of the New York-Penn League in 2001.

PLAYING RECORD

Year	Club & League	W-L	ERA	G	GS	CG	SHO	SV	IP	H	R	ER	BB	SO
1984	Medicine Hat (Pio)	1-5	8.42	10	10	0	0	0	42	43	48	39	59	15
1985	Florence (SAL)	0-4	6.29	10	7	0	0	1	34	27	31	24	37	25
1986	Florence (SAL)	8-12	6.99	31	24	0	0	0	124	136	116	96	114	68
1987	Dunedin (FSL)	2-5	5.80	18	13	0	0	0	59	68	44	38	49	25
1988	Dunedin (FSL)	11-6	4.73	32	19	0	0	0	105	91	73	55	89	73
1989	Myrtle Beach (SAL)	0-0	1.59	4	0	0	0	0	6	5	1	1	4	5
1990-92							(Played in China and Taiwan)							
1993	El Paso (Tex)	2-2	3.91	15	1	0	0	1	25	23	12	11	10	26
	New Orleans (AmAs)	0-0	2.40	13	0	0	0	6	15	11	4	4	4	10
1994	Nashville (AmAs)	1-5	2.25	39	0	0	0	24	44	40	13	11	18	40
	CHICAGO (AL)	2-1	6.57	15	0	0	0	0	12	16	9	9	11	7
1995	Nashville (AmAs)	4-4	2.41	46	0	0	0	15	56	48	24	15	28	51
1996	Syracuse (Int)	3-2	2.45	43	0	0	0	22	51	37	14	14	17	51
	TORONTO (AL)	0-0	3.00	10	0	0	0	0	9	5	3	3	5	7
1997	Edmonton (PCL)	1-1	5.63	14	0	0	0	6	16	17	11	10	8	13
	OAKLAND (AL)	4-1	4.53	38	0	0	0	2	46	49	28	23	31	43
1998	Syracuse (Int)	1-0	3.18	7	0	0	0	3	6	5	2	2	5	4
	Charlotte (Int)	1-0	3.38	2	0	0	0	0	3	3	1	1	1	0
1999	Albany-Col (NorE)	0-0	2.38	9	0	0	0	3	11	8	3	3	4	12
MAJOR TOTALS		**6-2**	**4.70**	**63**	**0**	**0**	**0**	**2**	**67.0**	**70**	**40**	**35**	**47**	**57**

MANAGERIAL/COACHING CAREER

(Re-joins Blue Jays Organization in 2000)

2000	Pitching Coach, Medicine Hat, Pioneer League
2001	Pitching Coach, Auburn, New York-Penn League

KELLY, Dale Patrick (Pat)   Special Assignment Scout

Former Catcher ... **HT:** 6-03; **WT:** 210 ... **B-T:** R-R ... **BORN:** August 27, 1955 in Santa Maria, CA ... **RESIDES:** Sarasota, Florida ... **PERSONAL BACKGROUND:** 1973 graduate of Santa Maria (Calif.) HS, Alan Hancock College and Santa Barbara City College. ... **PRO CAREER:** 1979: Won Carolina League batting title with a .309 average. Played 11 seasons from 1973 to 1983. Began coaching career in the White Sox organization in 1983. Spent five years managing in the Padres organization, skippering Charleston of the South Atlantic League in 1986, Reno of the California League in 1987, Wichita of the Texas League in 1988 and 1989 and Las Vegas of the Pacific Coast League in 1990. Managed two years in the Expos system. Started 1991 with Rockford of the Midwest League where he compiled a record of 27-21 before taking over for Indianapolis of the International League on June 3, compiling a 46-46 mark. Stayed at Indianapolis in 1992 as manager. Spent 1993 and 1994 managing Chattanooga of the Southern League for the Reds. Back with the Expos, Kelly skippered Harrisburg of the Eastern League in 1995 and 1996 and won the league championship in 1996. Managed Ottawa of the International League for the Expos in 1997 and 1998. Joined the Blue Jays organization in 1999 and was slotted to be a major league advanced scout before being tabbed to manage Syracuse in the International League. Managed the Syracuse SkyChiefs in 2000 for 34 games. Has managed in the Puerto Rican Winter League each season since 1991. In 2001 will work in the Blue Jays scouting department as a Special Assignment Scout.

PLAYING CAREER

Year	Club & League	AVG	G	AB	R	H	2B	3B	HR	RBI	BB	SO	SB
1973	Idaho Falls (Pio)	.219	31	105	13	23	4	1	0	4	9	34	6
1974	Quad Cities (Mid)	.221	86	281	30	62	8	3	5	39	11	70	15
1975	Quad Cities (Mid)	.330	40	115	14	38	1	0	1	8	7	22	2
	Salinas (Cal)	.222	13	36	4	8	1	0	0	5	5	9	0
1976	Salinas (Cal)	.313	111	396	63	124	24	2	4	50	28	83	15
1977	El Paso (Tex)	.271	107	365	73	99	18	5	14	53	43	105	10
1978	Syracuse (Int)	.161	55	168	8	27	6	0	0	12	15	5	0
1979	Syracuse (Int)	.176	6	17	0	3	1	0	0	0	0	6	0
	Kinston (CARO)	.309	96	350	48	108	23	6	1	50	17	66	10
1980	Syracuse (Int)	.208	72	236	24	49	10	2	2	12	15	61	0
	TORONTO (AL)	.286	3	7	0	2	0	0	0	0	0	4	0
1981	Knoxville (Sou)	.274	30	106	7	29	7	0	0	10	7	31	1
	Florence (SAL)	.284	90	324	53	92	14	0	9	38	51	59	5
1982	Durham (CARO)	.231	7	13	1	3	1	0	0	1	1	4	0
	Savannah (Sou)	.234	18	64	6	15	1	2	2	11	4	15	1
1983	Glens Falls (East)	.180	21	61	4	11	3	0	0	4	7	1	0

MANAGERIAL/COACHING CAREER
(Joined Blue Jays Organization in 1999)

1983-85	Coach, Chicago White Sox Organization
1986	Manager, Charleston, South Atlantic League (Padres)
1987	Manager, Reno, California League (Padres)
1988	Manager, Wichita, Texas League (Padres)
1989	Manager, Wichita, Texas League (Padres)
1990	Manager, Las Vegas, Pacific Coast League (Padres)
1991	Manager, Rockford, Midwest League (Expos)
1991	Manager, Indianapolis, American Association (Expos)
1992	Manager, Indianapolis, American Association (Expos)
1993	Manager, Chattanooga, Southern League (Reds)
1994	Manager, Chattanooga, Southern League (Reds)
1995	Manager, Harrisburg, Eastern League (Expos)
1996	Manager, Harrisburg, Eastern League (Expos)
1997	Manager, Ottawa, International League (Expos)
1998	Manager, Ottawa, International League (Expos)
1999	Manager, Syracuse, International League
2000	Manager, Syracuse, International League

RECORD AS MANAGER

Year	Club & League	W-L	PCT	Finish
1986	Charleston (SAL)	63-69	.477	(3rd in Div., 4th in Div.)
1987	Reno (Cal)	76-66	.535	(4th in Div., 1st in Div.)
1988	Wichita (Tex)	60-76	.441	(3rd in Div., 4th in Div.)
1989	Wichita (Tex)	73-63	.537	(1st in Div., 1st in Div.)
1990	Las Vegas (PCL)	58-86	.493	(4th in Div., 4th in Div.)
1991	Rockford (Mid)	27-21	.563	(2nd in Div., 2nd in Div.)
1991	Indianapolis (AmAs)	46-46	.500	(2nd in Div.)
1992	Indianapolis (AmAs)	83-61	.576	(2nd in Div.)
1993	Chattanooga (Sou)	72-69	.511	(4th in Div., 2nd in Div.)
1994	Chattanooga (Sou)	67-73	.479	(5th in Div., 1st in Div.)
1995	Harrisburg (East)	61-80	.433	(5th in Div.)
1996	Harrisburg (East)	74-68	.521	(2nd in Div.)
1997	Ottawa (Int)	54-86	.386	(5th in Div.)
1998	Ottawa (Int)	69-74	.483	(5th in Div.)
1999	Syracuse (Int)	73-71	.507	(3rd in Div.)
2000	Syracuse (Int)	15-19	.441	(4th in Div.)
CAREER TOTALS (16 years)		971-1028	.486	

POST-SEASON PLAY

Year	Club & League	W-L	PCT	Finish
1987	Reno (Cal)	5-4	.556	(Def. Stockton 2G to 0; lost to Fresno 4G to 3 in finals)
1989	Wichita (Tex)	3-4	.429	(Lost to Arkansas 4G to 3 in finals)
1994	Chattanooga (Sou)	0-3	.000	(Lost to Huntsville 3G to 0 in semi-finals)
1996	Harrisburg (East)	6-3	.667	(Def. Trenton 3G to 2 in semi- finals; Def. Portland 3G to 1 in finals)

LANDREAUX, Kenneth Francis (Ken)   Coach, SYRACUSE

Former Outfielder ... **HT:** 5-11; **WT:** 184 ... **B-T:** L-R ... **BORN:** December 22, 1954, Los Angeles, CA ... **RESIDES:** Valinda, California ... **RECOMMENDED/SIGNED BY:** (California Angels) ... **TRANSACTIONS:** Angels' first selection in the June 1976 Free Agent Draft. ... **PERSONAL BACKGROUND:** Attended Arizona State Univ. where he was All-WAC selection in baseball and batted .413 to lead team to College World Series in his junior year. ... **PRO CAREER:** 1977: Selected Minor League Player-of-the-Year by The Sporting News; threw out three White Sox players, two trying to go to third and one attempting to score, in his first major league game on Sept. 11; 1979: Tied major league record on July 3 by smacking two doubles in the seventh inning vs. Seattle; led Twins in batting (.305); 1980: Fashioned a 31-game hitting streak, which was a club record, the longest in the majors and the longest in the American League since Dom DiMaggio hit in 34 straight in 1949; hit .392 during streak; added a 19-game hitting streak soon thereafter; tied a major league record with three triples in a game on July 3 vs. Texas; after regular season, hit .388 to capture MVP of Dominican Winter League; 1981: Tied for league lead with a perfect 1.000 fielding percentage (214 total chances); caught Bob Watson' fly ball to record final out of World Series; 1982: Had errorless streak snapped at 142 games; had career-high 31 stolen bases; suffered arm and shoulder injuries; 1983: hit career-high 17 homers, including first grand slam on July 23 of Cardinals' Bruce Sutter; finished second in league with 16 game-winning RBI; matched career-high with six RBI on season opener at Houston; collected five hits on July 20 vs. Pirates; 1984: hit in 13 of his first 15 games, but was hampered by partial tear in left middle finger; 1985: Collected RBI's in five straight games in August; had third career two-homer game on July 6 vs. Cardinals, including first Dodgers inside-the-park homer since Davey Lopes in 1979; 1986: Was hitting .301 at time of knee injury which forced arthroscopic surgery on July 29; went 4-for-4 on April 20 in Atlanta and collected 1,000th career hit. Began his coaching career and spent the 1999 and 2000 seasons with Hagerstown of the South Atlantic League. Will return for his third season in the organization in 2001 as a coach with Syracuse in the International League.

PLAYING CAREER

Year	Club & League	AVG	G	AB	R	H	2B	3B	HR	RBI	BB	SO	SB
1976	El Paso (Tex)	.220	21	59	15	13	3	1	2	11	8	9	0
1977	El Paso (Tex)	.354	57	209	57	74	17	4	16	59	36	28	12
	Salt Lake City (PCL)	.359	62	256	67	92	16	4	11	57	22	21	8
	CALIFORNIA (AL)	.250	23	76	6	19	5	1	0	5	5	15	1
1978	CALIFORNIA (AL)	.223	93	260	37	58	7	5	5	23	20	20	7
1979	MINNESOTA (AL)	.305	151	564	81	172	27	5	15	83	37	57	10
1980	MINNESOTA (AL)	.281	129	484	56	136	23	11	7	62	39	42	8
1981	LOS ANGELES (NL)	.251	99	390	48	98	16	4	7	41	25	42	18
1982	LOS ANGELES (NL)	.284	129	461	71	131	23	7	7	50	39	54	31
1983	LOS ANGELES (NL)	.281	141	481	63	135	25	3	17	66	34	52	30
1984	LOS ANGELES (NL)	.251	134	438	39	110	11	5	11	47	29	35	10
1985	LOS ANGELES (NL)	.268	147	482	70	129	26	2	12	50	33	37	15
1986	LOS ANGELES (NL)	.261	103	283	34	74	13	2	4	29	22	39	10
1987	LOS ANGELES (NL)	.203	115	182	17	37	4	0	6	23	16	28	5
1988	Rochester (Int)	.272	64	173	27	47	9	0	7	23	22	21	6
1989	Albuquerque (PCL)	.243	56	189	25	46	9	2	2	26	13	32	7
MAJOR TOTALS		**.268**	**1264**	**4101**	**522**	**1099**	**180**	**45**	**91**	**479**	**299**	**421**	**145**

MANAGERIAL/COACHING CAREER
(Joins Blue Jays Organization in 1999)

1999-2000	Coach, Hagerstown, South Atlantic League
2001	Coach, Syracuse, International League

LANGFORD, James Rick (Rick)   Pitching Coach, SYRACUSE

Former Pitcher ... **HT:** 6-00; **WT:** 185 ... **B-T:** R-R ... **BORN:** March 20, 1952, Farmville, VA ... **RESIDES:** Varina, Virginia ... **RECOMMENDED/SIGNED BY:** Harding Peterson (Pirates) ... **TRANSACTIONS:** Signed as a non-drafted free agent by Pirates in 1973. Traded with Doug Bair, Dave Giusti, Doc Medich, Tony Armas and Mitchell Page to Athletics for Chris Batton, Phil Garner and Tommy Helms on March 15, 1977. ... **PERSONAL BACKGROUND:** 1970 graduate of Varina H.S. in Richmond, Virginia where he lettered in baseball, basketball, football and track. Attended Manatee Junior College where he went 14-2 with a 1.84 ERA in 1972 and batted .318 when not pitching. Was the only junior college player chosen on the United States Collegiate All-Star team that toured Japan in 1972. Attended Florida State University where he played the outfield for one year, hitting .295 and leading the team in hits, RBI, homers, total bases and runs. ... **PRO CAREER:** 1974: Finished fourth in the Carolina League in ERA (2.69); 1976: Ranked eighth in the International League in ERA (3.20); tossed a no-hitter vs. Memphis on May 30; hit a double in his first major league at-bat; 1979: Named American League Pitcher-of-the-Month and Northern California Athlete-of-the-Month for August; led A's in innings (219) and complete games (14); 1980: Led the American League in complete games (28) and innings pitched (290), tied for sixth in wins (19) and was ninth in ERA (3.26); set the AL record for most consecutive chances accepted by a pitcher without an error (230 - April 13, 1977 to October 2, 1980); the streak-ending error was his first in the majors; set team record for most consecutive complete games (22) from May 23-September 12; 1981: Led the AL in complete games (18) and finished third in innings (195); 1982: Ranked third in the AL in complete games (15); led team in innings (237.1) and tied for the club lead in wins (11) and shutouts (2); 1983: Underwent elbow surgery late in the year; 1984: Pitched sparingly for Tacoma and Oakland as he rehabbed his elbow; 1985: Won three of his last four decisions; went 3-1 at home and 0-4 on the road. Served as pitching coach for Knoxville of the Southern League in 1996-97. Joined the Dunedin staff as a pitching coach in 1998 and became pitching coach of Syracuse of the International League in 1999. Earned a promotion to be the Blue Jays' pitching coach in 2000 and returns to Syracuse in the same capacity for the 2001 season.

PLAYING RECORD

Year	Club & League	W-L	ERA	G	GS	CG	SHO	SV	IP	H	R	ER	BB	SO
1973	Bradenton (Gulf)	1-0	0.00	3	2	0	0	0	10	5	3	0	7	10
1974	Salem (CARO)	11-7	2.69	26	23	7	0	0	174	143	63	52	74	125
1975	Shreveport (Tex)	5-2	3.61	16	5	1	0	0	42	40	25	17	22	39
	Charleston (Int)	7-2	3.34	13	8	3	0	0	65	55	26	24	20	41
1976	Charleston (Int)	9-5	3.19	16	16	9	0	0	121	106	51	43	48	95
	PITTSBURGH (NL)	0-1	6.08	12	1	0	0	0	24	27	17	16	14	17
1977	OAKLAND (AL)	8-19	4.02	37	31	6	1	0	208	223	107	93	73	141
1978	OAKLAND (AL)	7-13	3.43	37	24	4	2	0	176	169	77	67	56	92
1979	OAKLAND (AL)	12-16	4.27	34	29	14	1	0	219	233	114	104	57	101
1980	OAKLAND (AL)	19-12	3.26	35	33	28	2	0	291	276	119	105	64	102
1981	OAKLAND (AL)	12-10	3.00	24	24	18	2	0	195	190	81	65	58	84
1982	OAKLAND (AL)	11-16	4.21	32	31	15	2	0	237	265	121	111	49	79
1983	OAKLAND (AL)	0-4	12.15	7	7	0	0	0	20	43	28	27	10	2
	Modesto (Cal)	0-0	3.00	1	1	0	0	0	6	4	2	2	2	2
1984	Tacoma (PCL)	0-2	6.00	3	3	0	0	0	15	22	11	10	2	3
	OAKLAND (AL)	0-0	8.31	3	2	0	0	0	9	15	8	8	2	2
1985	Modesto (Cal)	0-0	6.00	1	1	0	0	0	6	10	5	4	2	3
	OAKLAND (AL)	3-5	3.51	23	3	0	0	0	59	60	24	23	15	21
1986	OAKLAND (AL)	1-10	7.36	16	11	0	0	1	55	69	49	45	18	30
1988	Columbus (Int)	9-6	3.13	21	21	1	0	0	127	109	47	44	28	84
MAJOR TOTALS		**73-106**	**4.01**	**260**	**196**	**85**	**10**	**0**	**1491**	**1570**	**745**	**664**	**416**	**671**

MANAGERIAL/COACHING CAREER
(Joined Blue Jays Organization in 1996)

1987	Roving Pitching Instructor, Expos and Pirates Rookie Teams
1995	Pitching Coach, Long Beach, Western League (Independent)
1996-97	Pitching Coach, Knoxville, Southern League
1998	Pitching Coach, Dunedin, Florida State League
1999	Pitching Coach, Syracuse, International League
2000	Pitching Coach, Toronto, American League
2001	Pitching Coach, Syracuse, International League

LEFFERTS, Craig Lindsay — Pitching Coach, TENNESSEE

Former Pitcher ... **HT:** 6-01; **WT:** 210 ... **B-T:** S-L ... **BORN:** September 29, 1957, Munich, Germany ... **RESIDES:** Knoxville, Tennessee ... **RECOMMENDED/SIGNED BY:** Gene Thompson (Cubs) ... **TRANSACTIONS:** Cubs' ninth round selection in 1980 June draft. Traded with Carmelo Martinez and Fritz Connally to Padres for Scott Sanderson on December 7, 1983. Traded with Dave Dravecky and Kevin Mitchell to Giants for Mark Davis, Mark Grant, Keith Comstock and Chris Brown on July 4, 1987. Signed as free agent by Padres on December 7, 1989. Traded to Orioles for Erik Schullstrom and a player to be named later (Ricky Gutierrez) on August 31, 1992. Signed as free agent by Rangers on January 13, 1993. Signed as free agent by Angels on January 13, 1994. ... **PERSONAL BACKGROUND:** 1975 graduate of Northeast H.S. in St. Petersburg, FL where he played baseball and basketball. Attended University of Arizona where he played baseball for four years. In 1979, he went 10-3, 3.68 ERA and helped Wildcats to Pac Ten and NCAA Division I Midwest Regional Tournament championships and to a fifth-place finish in College World Series. Participated in Pan-Am games and Intercontinental Cup in Cuba. Named to All College World Series team and was the starting and winning pitcher in the College World Series championship game vs Hawaii (6.2 IP, 1 ER). Originally drafted by Royals in 1979, but did not sign. ... **PRO CAREER:** 1980: Named to New York-Penn League All-Star team; led league in strikeouts (99), ranked third in wins (9), tied for fifth in innings (94) and was tenth in ERA (2.78); led league pitchers in fielding (.900); in first pro game, at Elmira on June 19, walked first three batters, then set down 19 in a row; allowed only one hit in seven scoreless innings; named Topps Player-of-the-Month for August; 1981: Tied for third in Texas League in complete games (11) and seventh in wins (12) and strikeouts (135); 1982: Hurled three-hit shutout on July 10 vs Oklahoma City; 1983: Made major league debut on April 7 vs Expos (2.0 IP, 1 H, 1 ER, 1 HR, 2 BB, 1 SO); earned first big league win on June 5 vs Pirates (7.1 IP, 6 H, 1 R, 1 ER, 1 SO); 1984: Posted career-best 2.13 ERA; tossed ten scoreless innings in six playoff games; was winning pitcher in final two NLCS games vs Cubs and earned the save in the Padres' only World Series victory vs Detroit; 1985: Led Padres staff with 60 appearances despite sore elbow; 1986: Set club record with 83 appearances, breaking Rollie Fingers' mark of 78 in 1977; hit first major league home run on April 25 vs. San Francisco's Greg Minton in the 12th inning for game-winning hit; 1987: Made three appearances in NLCS vs St. Louis (2.0 IP, 0 R) to run streak of post-season shutout innings to 12; 1988: Converted 11-of-14 save opportunities and stranded 35-of-45 inherited runners; did not allow a run in last 11.2 innings pitched, spanning nine games; 1989: Matched a Gary LaVelle's team record for saves by a southpaw (20); retired 29 consecutive batters April 9-22; successful on first 15 save opportunities; allowed just one run in first 25.1 innings; appeared in five post-season games, appearing twice in NLCS against Cubs (1 IP, 1 ER) and three times against A's in World Series (2.2 IP, 1 ER); 1990: Had career-high 23 saves, tying for fourth in National League; went 5-1, 1.36 ERA (39.2 IP, 6 ER) with ten saves in first 25 outings; named Rolaids Reliever-of-the-Month in August with eight saves and a 1.46 ERA; 1991: Finished sixth in Natinal League with 23 saves; posted 1.64 ERA over last 18 outings spanning 22 innings; 1992: First full season as starting pitcher in major leagues; tied for second in Padres' staff in wins (13) and placed third in starts (27) and innings (163.1); had 3.33 ERA after May 1; won five straight decisions April 26-May 25; hurled first complete game in first start after trade to Orioles, September 6, but lost to Angels; won first AL game on Sept. 26 (G2) vs Boston; set career-high with eight strikeouts on May 30 vs St. Louis and again on September 12 vs Milwaukee; 1993: Started on Opening Day and beat Baltimore 7-4; allowed just eight of 38 inherited runners to score (21%), ranking eighth best in American League; recorded 1.23 ERA June 26-August 5; retired 18 straight batters June 28-July 7. Joined Blue Jays organization as pitching coach for Medicine Hat in 1999. Jumped to AA in 2000 as Pitching Coach for Tennessee of the Southern League and will return to the Smokies in 2001.

PLAYING RECORD

Year	Club & League	W-L	ERA	G	GS	CG	SHO	SV	IP	H	R	ER	BB	SO
1980	Geneva (NYP)	9-1	2.78	12	12	5	1	0	94	74	35	29	24	99
1981	Midland (Tex)	12-12	4.14	26	25	11	3	0	185	203	95	85	36	135
1982	Iowa (AmAs)	8-5	3.05	18	14	3	0	0	97	97	50	33	25	71
1983	CHICAGO (NL)	3-4	3.13	56	5	0	0	1	89	80	35	31	29	60
1984	SAN DIEGO (NL)	3-4	2.13	62	0	0	0	10	106	88	29	25	24	56
1985	SAN DIEGO (NL)	7-6	3.35	60	0	0	0	2	83	75	34	31	30	48
1986	SAN DIEGO (NL)	9-8	3.09	83	0	0	0	4	108	98	41	37	44	72
1987	SAN DIEGO (NL)	2-2	4.38	33	0	0	0	2	51	56	29	25	15	39
	SAN FRANCISCO (NL)	3-3	3.23	44	0	0	0	4	47	36	18	17	18	18
1988	SAN FRANCISCO (NL)	3-8	2.92	64	0	0	0	11	92	74	33	30	23	58
1989	SAN FRANCISCO (NL)	2-4	2.69	70	0	0	0	20	107	93	38	32	22	71
1990	SAN DIEGO (NL)	7-5	2.52	56	0	0	0	23	79	68	26	22	22	60
1991	SAN DIEGO (NL)	1-6	3.91	54	0	0	0	23	69	74	35	30	14	60
1992	SAN DIEGO (NL)	13-9	3.69	27	27	0	0	0	163	180	76	67	35	81
	BALTIMORE (AL)	1-3	4.09	5	5	1	0	0	33	34	19	15	6	23
1993	TEXAS (AL)	3-9	6.05	52	8	0	0	0	83	102	57	56	28	58
	Oklahoma City	0-1	7.50	1	1	0	0	0	6	9	5	5	2	1
1994	California	1-1	4.67	30	0	0	0	1	35	50	20	18	12	27
MAJOR TOTALS		58-72	3.43	696	45	1	0	101	1146	1108	490	436	322	719

MANAGERIAL/COACHING CAREER

(Joins Blue Jays Organization in 1999)

1999	Pitching Coach, Medicine Hat, Pioneer League
2000-01	Pitching Coach, Tennessee, Southern League

MALAVE, Omar Antonio — Manager, SYRACUSE

Former Third Baseman/First Baseman ... **HT:** 6-01; **WT:** 178 ... **B-T:** R-R ... **BORN:** January 17, 1963, Cumana, Venez. ... **RESIDES:** Cumana, Venezuela ... **RECOMMENDED/SIGNED BY:** (Blue Jays) ... **TRANSACTIONS:** Signed as free agent by Blue Jays on August 23, 1980 (for 1981). ... **PRO CAREER:** 1984: Led all Carolina League third basemen in games (104), total chances (284), putouts (86) and tied for lead in doubleplays (19); 1985: Tied for fifth in Carolina League in batting (.288), tied for third in GWRBI (10) and was fourth in slugging percentage (.424); 1988: Began season with Myrtle Beach before being promoted to Knoxville. Started coaching career at Medicine Hat in 1990. Has had stints managing in Gulf Coast, Pioneer Leagues and South Atlantic Leagues. Was selected to coach in the SAL All-Star game at Hickory June 20, 1994. Managed Knoxville in the Southern League in 1996-99. Managed Lara in Venezuelan Winter League in 1996-97. Was the winner of the Bobby Mattick Award of Excellence in Player Development in 1997. Coached at Syracuse in 2000 and will return to the SkyChiefs in 2001 as Manager. Will be his tenth season as manager in the Blue Jays organization and has yet to post a losing record. Has spent his entire professional career as both a player and a coach in the Blue Jays organization.

PLAYING CAREER

Year	Club & League	AVG	G	AB	R	H	2B	3B	HR	RBI	BB	SO	SB
1981	Blue Jays (Gulf)	.253	53	158	17	40	1	3	0	16	9	23	6
1982	Florence (SAL)	.176	64	142	16	25	5	0	0	8	21	26	6
1983	Florence (SAL)	.250	88	232	41	58	8	4	3	27	35	34	2
	Kinston (CARO)	.239	14	46	4	11	1	0	1	10	7	8	0
1984	Kinston (CARO)	.265	109	404	56	107	11	1	5	52	33	44	3
1985	Kinston (CARO)	.288	105	354	42	102	16	1	10	55	32	57	9
1986	Ventura (Cal)	.234	70	201	29	47	8	1	4	30	31	33	2
1987	Dunedin (FSL)	.228	38	101	7	23	2	1	1	10	7	14	0
	Knoxville (Sou)	.200	2	5	1	1	0	0	0	1	1	0	0
1988	Myrtle Beach (SAL)	.450	8	20	3	9	3	0	0	1	2	3	0
	Knoxville (Sou)	.306	66	196	18	60	7	4	3	21	17	28	1
1989	Knoxville (Sou)	.222	29	72	7	16	4	0	0	8	7	10	1
	Syracuse (Int)	.217	8	23	1	5	1	0	0	1	2	5	0

MANAGERIAL/COACHING CAREER
(All in Blue Jays Organization)

1990-91	Coach, Medicine Hat, Pioneer League
1991-92	Manager, Blue Jays, Gulf Coast League
1993	Manager, Medicine Hat, Pioneer League
1994-95	Manager, Hagerstown, South Atlantic League
1996-99	Manager, Knoxville, Southern League
2000	Coach, Syracuse, International League
2001	Manager, Syracuse, International League

RECORD AS MANAGER

Year	Club & League	W-L	PCT	Finish
1991	Gulf Coast (Gulf)	31-28	.525	(2nd in Div.)
1992	Gulf Coast (Gulf)	35-24	.593	(1st in Div.)
1993	Medicine Hat (Pio)	39-34	.534	(2nd in Div.)
1994	Hagerstown (SAL)	80-56	.588	(1st in Div., 2nd in Div.)
1995	Hagerstown (SAL)	73-68	.518	(3rd in Div., 5th in Div.)
1996	Knoxville (Sou)	75-65	.536	(2nd in Div., 4th in Div.)
1997	Knoxville (Sou)	75-63	.543	(1st in Div., 3rd in Div.)
1998	Knoxville (Sou)	71-69	.507	(2nd in Div., 1st in Div.)
1999	Knoxville (Sou)	71-69	.507	(1st in Div., 3rd in Div.)
2000	Syracuse (Int)	1-0	1.000	(Interim)
CAREER TOTALS (10 years)		551-476	.537	

POST-SEASON PLAY

Year	Club & League	W-L	PCT	Finish
1992	Gulf Coast (Gulf)	0-1	.000	(Lost to Expos 1G to 0 in semi-finals)
1994	Hagerstown (SAL)	2-3	.400	(Def. Hickory 2G to 0 in semi-finals; lost to Savannah 3G to 0 in finals)
1997	Knoxville (Sou)	1-3	.250	(Lost to Greenville 3G to 1 in semi-finals)
1998	Knoxville (Sou)	0-3	.000	(Lost to Jacksonville 3G to 0 in semi-finals)
1999	Knoxville (Sou)	1-3	.333	(Lost to Orlando 3G to 1 in semi-finals)

MATTICK, Robert James (Bobby)   Vice President, Baseball

Former Infielder ... **HT:** 5-10; **WT:** 170 ... **B-T:** R-R ... **BORN:** December 5, 1915, Sioux City, IA ... **RESIDES:** Bellevue, Washington ... **RECOMMENDED/SIGNED BY:** (Los Angeles Angels, PCL) ... **TRANSACTIONS:** Contract purchased by Chicago Cubs following 1937 season. Traded by Chicago to Cincinnati with Jimmy Gleeson and cash for Billy Myers, December 4, 1940. ... **PERSONAL BACKGROUND:** Graduated Beaumont High (St. Louis, MO) 1933; lettered in baseball. Played American Legion ball. Signed by Los Angeles in the fall of 1933 after playing semi-pro ball in Missouri Illinois League. Father, Walter (Chick) Mattick, was an outfielder with Chicago White Sox, 1912-13, and St. Louis Cardinals, 1918, later a minor league manager and major league scout; in 1917-18 he was Dallas (Texas League) club's co-owner and center fielder. ... **PRO CAREER:** 1934: At age 18 he played on Los Angeles team which had best record (137-50 .733) in PCL history; 1935: Was on Disabled List most of season after fracturing his wrist; 1936: On April 24, during batting practice, he was struck over his left eye by a foul ball, suffering a fractured sinus bone and severe optical nerve damage; was disabled for three months; 1938: Placed on Voluntarily Retired List in May because of recurrence of vision problems.

PLAYING CAREER

Year	Club & League	AVG	G	AB	R	H	2B	3B	HR	RBI	BB	SO	SB
1934	Los Angeles (PCL)	.277	53	137	10	38	5	1	0	10	–	–	2
1935	Los Angeles (PCL)	.267	50	131	15	35	6	0	0	18	–	–	2
1936	Los Angeles (PCL)	.278	73	241	30	67	11	3	1	30	–	–	3
1937	Los Angeles (PCL)	.279	167	612	61	171	39	7	2	66	–	–	10
1938	CHICAGO (NL)	1.000	1	1	0	1	0	0	0	1	–	–	0
	Indianapolis (AA)	.119	29	67	6	8	3	0	0	6	4	7	1
	Syracuse (Int)	.063	5	16	1	1	1	0	0	0	–	–	0
1939	Milwaukee (AA)	.286	68	273	47	78	13	3	5	16	27	18	3
	CHICAGO (NL)	.287	51	178	16	51	12	1	0	23	6	19	1
1940	CHICAGO (NL)	.218	128	441	30	96	15	0	0	33	19	33	5
1941	CINCINNATI (NL)	.183	20	60	8	11	3	0	0	7	8	7	1
1942	CINCINNATI (NL)	.200	6	10	0	2	1	0	0	0	0	1	0
MAJOR TOTALS		.233	206	640	54	161	31	1	0	64	33	60	7

MANAGERIAL/COACHING CAREER
(Joined Blue Jays Organization in 1976)

1944	Coach, Birmingham, Southern Association
1945-47	Scout, New York Yankees
1948-51	Scout, Cincinnati Reds
1952	Scout, Chicago White Sox
1953-60	Scout, Cincinnati Reds
1961-63	Scout, Houston Colt .45s
1964-66	Scout, Cleveland Indians
1967	Scout, Baltimore Orioles
1968-70	Scout, Seattle Pilots
1972-75	Scout, Montreal Expos
1976-77	Scout, Toronto Blue Jays
1978-79	Director of Player Development, Toronto Blue Jays
1980-81	Manager, Toronto Blue Jays
1982-84	Executive Coordinator, Baseball Operations, Toronto Blue Jays
1984-2001	Vice President, Baseball Operations, Toronto Blue Jays

RECORD AS MANAGER

Year	Club & League	W-L	PCT	Finish
1948	Ogden* (Pio)	32-25	.561	4th
1980	TORONTO (AL)	67-95	.414	7th - Eastern Division
1981	TORONTO (AL)	16-42	.276	7th (1st half) - Eastern Div.
		21-27	.438	7th (2nd half) - Eastern Div.
CAREER TOTALS (3 years)		136-189	.418	

* Replaced Pip Koehler, July 18, with team in sixth place

POST-SEASON PLAY

Year	Club & League	W-L	PCT	Finish
1948	Ogden (Pio)	0-3	.000	(Lost first round of playoff to Twin Falls 3G to 0)

MIRANDA, Geovany Raul Gonzalez   Coach, CHARLESTON

Former Infielder ... **HT:** 5-11; **WT:** 170 ... **B-T:** R-R ... **BORN:** February 16, 1970, Chiriqui, PN ... **RESIDES:** David, Chiriqui, Panama ... **RECOMMENDED/SIGNED BY:** Herb Raybourn and Karl Heron (Royals) ... **TRANSACTIONS:** Signed as non-drafted free agent by Royals on February 16, 1988. Traded with Tony Gordon to White Sox for player to be named later on May 5, 1992. ... **PRO CAREER:** 1989: Led Baseball City in runs (38) and stolen bases (23); 1990: Named to Northwest League All-Star team; led Eugene squad with 16 steals; 1991: Had career-high 28 stolen bases. Managed Toronto's Dominican Summer League affiliate 1996-1998. Coached at Medicine Hat in 1999 and 2000 and will work in the same capacity with the Alley Cats in Charleston of the South Atlantic League.

PLAYING CAREER

Year	Club & League	AVG	G	AB	R	H	2B	3B	HR	RBI	BB	SO	SB
1988	Royals (Gulf)	.231	44	117	20	27	1	0	0	4	9	14	9
1989	Royals (Gulf)	.311	55	193	38	60	4	3	0	24	19	15	23
1990	Appleton (Mid)	.227	55	141	15	32	1	2	0	7	16	26	8
	Eugene (NWST)	.338	42	145	30	49	3	0	0	15	15	30	16
1991	Appleton (Mid)	.236	122	416	57	98	11	2	0	27	33	67	28
1992	Baseball Cty (FSL)	.167	7	24	4	4	0	0	0	1	2	6	1
	South Bend (Mid)	.000	2	3	0	0	0	0	0	0	0	1	0
	Sarasota (FSL)	.366	18	41	6	15	1	2	0	4	2	3	2
	Miracle (FSL)	.267	43	120	10	32	2	0	0	8	5	23	4
1993	Birmingham (Sou)	.094	12	32	2	3	0	0	0	0	1	6	0
	Sarasota (FSL)	.175	19	63	7	11	0	1	0	2	1	8	3
	Hickory (SAL)	.234	33	107	13	25	3	0	0	6	5	8	4
1994	Pr William (CARO)	.275	55	193	33	53	7	2	0	18	7	25	10
	Nashville (AmAs)	.333	16	42	7	14	3	0	0	8	1	3	0

MANAGERIAL/COACHING CAREER
(All in Blue Jays Organization)

1996-98	Manager, Boca Chica, Dominican Summer League
1999-2000	Coach, Medicine Hat, Pioneer League
2001	Coach, Charleston, South Atlantic League

RECORD AS MANAGER

Year	Club & League	W-L	PCT	Finish
1996	Boca Chica (DSL)	47-23	.671	(2nd in Div.)
1997	Boca Chica (DSL)	40-32	.556	(2nd in Div.)
1998	Boca Chica (DSL)	50-16	.758	(2nd in Div.)
CAREER TOTALS (3 years)		137-71	.659	

PEVEY, Marty A.   Manager, DUNEDIN

Former Catcher ... **HT:** 6-01; **WT:** 185 ... **B-T:** L-R ... **BORN:** September 18, 1961, Statesboro, GA ... **RESIDES:** Springfield, Georgia ... **RECOMMENDED/SIGNED BY:** Spud Chandler (Twins) ... **TRANSACTIONS:** Twins' 19th pick in 1982 June draft. Released by Twins in August, 1982. Signed by Cardinals as free agent on March 26, 1983. Acquired from St. Louis Cardinals in exchange for contract of Bob Sudo on February 11, 1988. Signed as free agent by Blue Jays Jan. 15, 1990. Signed by Tigers as free agent in November, 1991. Signed by Blue Jays as free agent January 19, 1994 (under six-year renewal plan).

... **PERSONAL BACKGROUND:** 1979 graduate of Windsor Forest H.S. in Savannah, Georgia. Was selected All-State in baseball. Attended Georgia Southern College for three years where he was selected All-Conference. ... **PRO CAREER:** 1983: Eighth in South Atlantic League in batting (.312); 1984: Fourth in Florida State League in batting (.308); selected to league All-Star game and received Howe Sportsdata's "Star of Stars" Award as Most Valuable Player in game; belted grand slam July 6 vs. Winter Haven and banged out five hits April 15 vs. West Palm Beach; selected to post-season All-Star team; 1985: Sixth in Florida State League in batting (.290); played in All-Star game; had five hits June 8 vs. Tampa; 1988: Named Most Valuable Player in the American Association Championship Series, hitting .545 (6-11) with one homer and three RBI; hit .185 in 27 games at Caracas in the Venezuelan Winter League; 1989: Called up to Expos in mid-May and made major league debut May 16 vs. Padres; had first big league hit in his next game at San Francisco May 24; went 3-for-3 with double vs. Phillies June 11; 1991: Banged out five hits September 3 vs. Rochester; 1993: Best offensive output of season came May 6 at Richmond as he went 4-for-5 with 2 RBI. Began his coaching career with Dunedin in 1996. In 1997, he became manager of Medicine Hat of the Pioneer League. He was named skipper at Hagerstown of the South Atlantic League in 1998 and was Toronto's bullpen coach in 1999. Returned to the managing ranks in 2000 with Dunedin where he was named as the Florida State League's Manager-of-the-Year. In 2001 will return for his seventh season in the Blue Jays organization as Manager with Dunedin.

PLAYING CAREER

Year	Club & League	AVG	G	AB	R	H	2B	3B	HR	RBI	BB	SO	SB
1982	Elizabethton (Appy)	.284	24	81	9	23	6	0	1	13	8	10	0
1983	Macon (SAL)	.312	122	436	74	136	23	2	7	77	45	70	8
1984	StPetersburg (FSL)	.308	128	441	53	136	16	4	2	60	48	47	7
1985	StPetersburg (FSL)	.290	104	393	48	114	12	4	3	41	28	56	5
1986	Louisville (AmAs)	.162	12	37	6	6	3	0	0	0	4	4	0
	Arkansas (Tex)	.326	55	172	28	56	11	2	2	20	16	18	6
1987	Arkansas (Tex)	.279	80	197	28	55	11	1	3	16	10	33	6
	Louisville (AmAs)	.237	16	38	5	9	2	0	1	5	0	10	0
1988	Jacksonville (Sou)	.261	31	111	21	29	11	0	4	17	8	13	3
	Indianapolis (AmAs)	.227	48	119	16	27	4	1	3	16	8	20	1
1989	Indianapolis (AmAs)	.259	34	108	12	28	4	2	1	14	8	20	3
	MONTREAL (NL)	.220	13	41	2	9	1	1	0	3	0	8	0
1990						(Did not play - Injured)							
1991	Syracuse (Int)	.280	55	193	24	54	8	2	3	23	20	41	1
1992	Toledo (Int)	.301	48	136	16	41	6	0	3	16	7	18	1
1993	Toledo (Int)	.274	62	175	11	48	8	1	2	18	16	36	3
1994	Syracuse (Int)	.270	96	259	29	70	13	2	6	31	20	55	2
1995	Tacoma (PCL)	.105	7	19	2	2	0	0	0	0	1	5	0
	Jacksonville (Sou)	.259	20	58	2	15	2	0	1	7	4	17	0

MANAGERIAL/COACHING CAREER
(All in Blue Jays Organization)

1996	Coach, Dunedin, Florida State League
1996-97	Manager, Medicine Hat, Pioneer League
1998	Manager, Hagerstown, South Atlantic League
1999	Coach, Toronto Blue Jays
2000-01	Manager, Dunedin, Florida State League

RECORD AS MANAGER

Year	Club & League	W-L	PCT	Finish
1996	Medicine Hat (Pio)	22-50	.306	(4th Div, 4th Div)
1997	Medicine Hat (Pio)	26-46	.361	(2nd Div, 4th Div)
1998	Hagerstown (SAL)	81-60	.574	(1st Div, 2nd Div)
2000	Dunedin (FSL)	84-54	.609	(1st Div, 2nd Div)
CAREER TOTAL (5 Years)		213-210	.504	

POST-SEASON PLAY

Year	Club & League	W-L	PCT	Finish
1998	Hagerstown (SAL)	3-2	.600	(defeated Delamarva 2G to 0 in the 1st round, Lost to Capital City 2G to 1 in the 2nd round.)
2000	Dunedin (FSL)	2-3	.400	(defeated Ft. Myers 2G to 1 in the 1st round, Lost to Daytona 3G to 0 in the finals)

PINO, Rolando James   Manager, CHARLESTON

Former Shortstop ... HT: 5-09; **WT:** 160 ... **B-T:** R-R ... **BORN:** January 20, 1964, Havana, Cuba ... **RESIDES:** Hialeah, Florida ... **RECOMMENDED/SIGNED BY:** Walt Widmayer (White Sox) ... **TRANSACTIONS:** White Sox' second selection in 1982 June draft. Released by White Sox and signed by Blue Jays as a free agent in May of '88. Signed by Twins as a free agent April 4, 1989. ... **PERSONAL BACKGROUND:** Graduated from Miami Springs (FL) Senior H.S. in 1982 where he starred for the 1982 district champions. Played in the Khoury League for five years and American Legion for three years. ... **PRO CAREER:** 1982: Fifth in Gulf Coast League in walks (36); tied for second in doubles (12); led league shortstops in total chances (278), putouts (75), assists (163) and doubleplays (26); 1984: Was fourth in Midwest League in walks (85); 1985: Led Eastern League second basemen in putouts (313) and was fourth in league in walks (83); 1986: Batted .413 (19-46) in June; saw some action at Triple-A Buffalo in mid-July; 1988: Cracked grand slam against Myrtle Beach June 11; 1989: Named to Midwest League All-Star team. Joined the Blue Jays organization as a coach in 1992. He began the '92 campaign with Knoxville (Class AA) of the Southern League until New York-Penn League started up in June. Joined Dunedin coaching staff in 1995 after three years at St. Catharines. Coached at Hagerstown in 1996 and at Medicine Hat in 1997. He took over managerial duties at Medicine Hat in 1998, and led the club to its best all-time record, 46-28. Was the recipient of the Bobby Mattick Player Development Award in 1998. Managed in the South Atlantic League for Hagerstown in 1999, 2000 and will do the same in 2001 for Charleston (SAL), his tenth season in the organization.

PLAYING CAREER

Year	Club & League	AVG	G	AB	R	H	2B	3B	HR	RBI	BB	SO	SB
1982	White Sox (Gulf)	.217	53	175	33	38	12	2	1	20	36	38	16
1983	Appleton (Mid)	.262	101	290	53	76	14	4	7	33	47	80	14
1984	Appleton (Mid)	.211	103	308	61	65	12	3	6	35	85	84	9
1985	Glens Falls (East)	.214	127	370	56	79	18	2	2	27	83	84	14
1986	Buffalo (AmAs)	.000	4	8	1	0	0	0	0	0	1	4	0
	Birmingham (Sou)	.256	105	308	50	79	17	0	6	45	65	74	16
1987	Birmingham (Sou)	.184	95	288	36	53	14	0	3	23	53	54	1
1988	Myrtle Beach (SAL)	.248	71	214	33	53	14	0	3	23	53	54	1
1989	Kenosha (Mid)	.217	81	244	42	53	13	3	6	36	74	45	17
	Portland (PCL)	.266	35	109	17	29	8	1	4	13	19	29	4
1990	Denver (AmAs)	.200	6	5	3	1	1	0	0	0	2	0	0
	Greenville (Sou)	.207	12	29	0	6	3	0	0	2	6	4	0

MANAGERIAL/COACHING CAREER
(All in Blue Jays Organization)

1992	Coach, Knoxville, Southern League
	Coach, St. Catharines, New York-Penn League
1993-94	Coach, St. Catharines, New York-Penn League
1995	Coach, Dunedin, Florida State League
1996	Coach, Hagerstown, South Atlantic League
1997	Coach, Medicine Hat, Pioneer League
1998	Manager, Medicine Hat, Pioneer League
1999-2000	Manager, Hagerstown, South Atlantic League
2001	Manager, Charleston, South Atlantic League

RECORD AS MANAGER

Year	Club & League	W-L	PCT	Finish
1998	Medicine Hat (Pio)	46-28	.621	(2nd in Div., 2nd in Div.)
1999	Hagerstown (SAL)	84-56	.600	(1st in Div., 2nd in Div.)
2000	Hagerstown (SAL)			
CAREER TOTALS (2 years)		130-84	.607	

POST-SEASON PLAY

Year	Club & League	W-L	PCT	Finish
1999	Hagerstown (SAL)	0-2	.000	(Lost to Cape Fear 2G to 0 in semi-finals)

QUEEN, Melvin Douglas (Mel) Special Assignment Scout

Former Infielder/Outfielder/Pitcher ... **HT:** 6-01; **WT:** 190 ... **B-T:** L-R ... **BORN:** March 26, 1942, Johnson City, NY ... **RESIDES:** San Luis Obispo, California ... **RECOMMENDED/SIGNED BY:** (Reds) ... **TRANSACTIONS:** Signed as a free agent by Reds in 1960. Sold to Angels on October 24, 1969. Deal was completed when Reds traded Alex Johnson and Chico Ruiz to Angels for Vern Geishert, Jim McGlothlin and Pedro Borbon on November 25, 1969. ... **PERSONAL BACKGROUND:** Son of Melvin Queen, Sr., pitcher with Yankees and Pirates, 1942-52. ... **PRO CAREER:** Made two position shifts during his 13 year professional career. Broke into Reds organization as a third baseman, moved to the outfield in 1963 before becoming a pitcher three years later. Enjoyed two good seasons in the minors when he finished third in III League in RBI (88) and in 1962 when he finished tied for second in South Atlantic League in doubles (35). Had his best season as a pitcher in 1967, his first full season as a hurler, when he finished 10th in NL in ERA (2.76). Had shoulder problems the following season and was able to compete in only five games. Became a relief pitcher for the most part, following his trade to the Angels. Coached in Indians organization four years beginning in 1979, including one year (1982) as pitching coach with the major league club. Joined the Blue Jays organization in 1986 as a minor league pitching instructor, a position he held for four years. Moved up to front office in 1990 as Blue Jays Director of Player Development, and became Toronto's pitching coach in 1996. Continued as the Blue Jays pitching coach through the 1999 season before becoming a Special Assistant to the GM in 2000. Took over as Manager for the Syracuse SkyChiefs of the International league midway through the 2000 season and posted a 58-47 record.

PLAYING CAREER — BATTING

Year	Club & League	AVG	G	AB	R	H	2B	3B	HR	RBI	BB	SO	SB
1960	Seattle (PCL)	.000	5	5	0	0	0	0	0	0	–	–	–
	Topeka (III)	.147	9	34	6	5	1	0	1	6	–	–	–
	Palatka (FSL)	.257	53	175	21	45	6	0	4	33	34	35	3
1961	Topeka (III)	.266	129	459	72	122	20	5	14	88	68	83	13
1962	Macon (SAL)	.275	137	524	96	144	35	3	11	93	58	72	11
1963	San Diego (PCL)	.260	134	504	70	131	26	3	25	78	35	72	0
1964	CINCINNATI (NL)	.200	48	95	7	19	2	0	2	12	4	19	0
1965	CINCINNATI (NL)	.000	5	3	0	0	0	0	0	0	0	1	0
	San Diego (PCL)	.275	139	491	60	135	15	2	14	49	43	68	3
1966	CINCINNATI (NL)	.127	56	55	4	7	1	0	0	5	10	12	0
MAJOR TOTALS		.179	269	274	20	49	7	0	2	25	21	50	2

PLAYING RECORD — PITCHING

Year	Club & League	W-L	ERA	G	GS	CG	SHO	SV	IP	H	R	ER	BB	SO
1966	CINCINNATI (NL)	0-0	6.43	7	0	0	0	0	7	11	5	5	6	9
1967	CINCINNATI (NL)	14-8	2.76	31	24	6	2	0	196	155	69	60	52	154
1968	CINCINNATI (NL)	0-1	6.00	5	4	0	0	0	18	25	15	12	6	20
1969	CINCINNATI (NL)	1-0	2.25	2	2	0	0	0	12	7	3	3	3	7
	Indianapolis (AmAs)	6-1	2.67	19	19	3	1	0	91	83	34	27	29	72
1970	CALIFORNIA (AL)	3-6	4.20	34	3	0	0	9	60	58	28	28	28	44
1971	CALIFORNIA (AL)	2-2	1.77	44	0	0	0	4	66	49	17	13	29	53
1972	CALIFORNIA (AL)	0-0	4.35	17	0	0	0	0	31	31	17	15	8	13
	Salt Lk City (PCL)	0-2	9.53	13	0	0	0	5	17	23	18	18	14	15
MAJOR TOTALS		**20-17**	**3.14**	**140**	**33**	**6**	**2**	**14**	**390**	**336**	**154**	**136**	**143**	**306**

MANAGERIAL/COACHING CAREER
(Joined Blue Jays Organization in 1986)

1979	Coach, Waterloo, Midwest League (Indians)
1980	Coach, Tacoma, Pacific Coast League (Indians)
1981	Coach, Charleston, International League (Indians)
1982	Pitching Coach, Cleveland Indians, American League
1986-89	Pitching Instructor, Toronto Blue Jays organization
1996-99	Pitching Coach, Toronto Blue Jays, American League
2000	Manager, Syracuse, International League

RECORD AS MANAGER

Year	Club & League	W-L	PCT	Finish
1997	TORONTO (AL)	4-1	.800	(Interim)
2000	Syracuse (Int)	58-47	.552	(4th Div)

RIVERA, Jorge Ahmed   Coach, AUBURN

Former Catcher ... **HT:** 5-11; **WT:** 161 ... **B-T:** R-R ... **BORN:** December 16, 1950 in Santurce, PR ... **RESIDES:** Puerto Nuevo, Puerto Rico ... **PERSONAL BACKGROUND:** Attended Padilla School in Puerto Nuevo, Puerto Rico. Following his playing career, attended two years of college and then worked for Puerto Rican government for the Department of National Parks and Services **PRO CAREER:** Played professional baseball from 1968 to 1983 in the Kansas City Royals and Pittsburgh Pirates organizations; played winter ball from 1969 to 1983 for Santurce, Arecibo and Bayamon of the Puerto Rican League. Joined Blue Jays as part-time scout in 1986. Added as a full-time scout in 1990 and continued to scout for Toronto while coaching during the summer. Named coach for Brooklyn of the New York-Penn League in 2000. Will remain in the New York-Penn League as a coach with Auburn in 2001.

PLAYING CAREER

Year	Club & League	AVG	G	AB	R	H	2B	3B	HR	RBI	BB	SO	SB
1969	Waterloo (Mid)	.250	10	24	5	6	2	1	0	1	2	4	2
	Kingsport (Appy)	.279	47	140	17	39	9	0	1	15	4	20	2
1970	San Jose (Cal)	.000	3	6	0	0	0	0	0	1	0	2	0
	Waterloo (Mid)	.273	95	355	40	97	15	4	1	16	12	44	3
1971	San Jose (Cal)	.223	61	193	21	43	6	2	3	27	14	32	0
1972	Jacksonville (Sou)	.192	C	9	26	2	5	0	0	0	1	0	6
1973	Salem (Caro)	.083	11	36	4	3	0	0	0	2	2	10	0
1979	Puerto Rico (Int-Am)	.209	16	43	4	9	2	0	0	5	–	–	0

MANAGERIAL/COACHING CAREER
(Joined Blue Jays Organization in 1986)

2000	Coach, Brooklyn, New York-Penn League
2001	Coach, Auburn, New York-Penn League

ROONEY, James Joseph (Jim)   Pitching Coach, MEDICINE HAT

Former Pitcher ... **HT:** 6-01; **WT:** 170 ... **B-T:** L-L ... **BORN:** January 1, 1961 in Bronx, NY ... **RECOMMENDED/SIGNED BY:** John Stokoe (Orioles) ... **TRANSACTIONS:** Selected by Orioles in first-round (No. 7 overall) of secondary phase of 1981 June draft. ... **PERSONAL BACKGROUND:** 1979 graduate of North Rockland HS in Stony Point, N.Y. where he was a two-time All-County selection in baseball. Was captain and MVP of baseball and basketball teams in his senior year. Pitched freshman year at Cornell University. Attended County College of Morris in Randolph, N.J. in 1980-81 where he won All-Region honors in 1981 and was MVP of the All-Star team. Had 7-1 record and 1.50 ERA at Morris, averaging 15 strikeouts per game. Pitched in Atlantic Collegiate Baseball League in summer. Began coaching career in 1987 at Pace University in New York. Moved to West Point Military Academy in 1988 before joining Rockland CC in New York where he coached from 1989 to 1995. Managed in France in 1996 and Italy in 1997 and 1998. ... **PRO CAREER:** 1981: Ranked second in Appalachian League in ERA (2.08) and won all six of his decisions; 1982: Finished third in Carolina League in games started (26); hurled two-hitter against Winston-Salem on June 21; 1983: Missed most of year due to shoulder surgery; 1984: Spent most of season on disabled list. Named coach for Somerset of the independent Atlantic League in 1999. Joined the Blue Jays as pitching coach for Queens of the New York-Penn League in 2000 and will assume the same responsibilities in 2001 with Medicine Hat of the Pioneer League.

PLAYING RECORD

Year	Club & League	W-L	ERA	G	GS	CG	SHO	SV	IP	H	R	ER	BB	SO
1981	Bluefield (Appy)	6-0	2.08	12	12	2	1	0	78	65	27	18	32	76
1982	Hagerstown (CARO)	8-8	3.51	26	26	5	1	0	156	152	70	61	51	108
1983	Charlotte (Sou)	0-4	9.20	4	4	0	0	0	15	25	16	15	7	6
1984	Newark (NYP)	0-0	13.50	5	0	0	0	0	9	12	13	13	11	8

MANAGERIAL/COACHING CAREER
(Joined Blue Jays Organization in 2000)

1999	Coach, Somerset, Independent Atlantic League
2000	Pitching Coach, Queens, New York-Penn League
2001	Pitching Coach, Medicine Hat, Pioneer League

TORRES, Hector Epitacio   Coach, TENNESSEE

Former Infielder ... HT: 6-00; **WT:** 178 ... **B-T:** R-R ... **BORN:** September 16, 1945, Monterrey, Mex. ... **RESIDES:** Dunedin, Florida ... **RECOMMENDED/SIGNED BY:** Dave Garcia (Giants) ... **TRANSACTIONS:** Signed as a free agent by Giants in 1962. Traded to Angels April 6, 1966 for Dave Marshall. Traded to Astros November 21, 1967 to complete deal August 7, 1967 which sent Jim Weaver to Angels. Traded to Cubs October 12, 1970 for Roger Metzger. Traded to Expos with Hal Breeden April 7, 1972 for Dan McGinn. Traded to White Sox October 23, 1973 for player to be named later (Dan Neumeier). Sold to Padres on April 3, 1975. Traded to Indians with John Grubb and Fred Kendall December 8, 1976 for George Hendrick. Traded to Blue Jays March 29, 1977 for John Lowenstein. Released by Blue Jays March 27, 1978. ... **PERSONAL BACKGROUND:** His father, Epitacio Torres, played pro ball in Mexico from 1938 to 1957. ... **PRO CAREER:** Led California League shortstops in fielding percentage in 1963 (.941) and 1964 (.942). Led in doubleplays participated in 1964 (72). Led Pacific Coast League shortstops in fielding percentage in 1974 (.960). Batted .216 in 622 big league games. Hit first grand slam in Blue Jays history in June 27, 1977 off Ron Guidry of the Yankees. After playing a final season in 1978, was a minor league instructor in the Blue Jays organization through 1984. Named manager at Florence in 1985 and promptly led Blue Jays to first place finish and the league championship, earning Manager-of-the-Year honours. Remained at the helm in Florence in 1986 before assuming coaching duties the next three years at Syracuse. Made debut as major league coach with Blue Jays in 1991 in between two stints as a Dunedin coach in Florida State League. Returned to managerial ranks with Jays affiliate in Gulf Coast League in 1993. Coached at Triple-A Syracuse in for three years. Coach at Dunedin of Florida State League in 1997. Split time as a roving infield instructor and as a coach for St. Catharines in 1998. Was a coach for Syracuse of the International League in 1999. Named coach at Tennessee of the Southern League in 2000 and will continue in the same role for the 2001 season. Is entering his 25th season in the Toronto organization, his 22nd in a coaching role.

PLAYING CAREER

Year	Club & League	AVG	G	AB	R	H	2B	3B	HR	RBI	BB	SO	SB
1962	Decatur (Mid)	.191	96	304	44	58	6	3	3	33	36	84	1
1963	Fresno (Cal)	.181	104	343	38	62	11	2	4	38	46	111	2
1964	Fresno (Cal)	.223	139	511	69	114	16	4	18	60	47	140	4
1965	Springfield (East)	.187	44	150	6	28	4	1	2	10	11	26	0
	Decatur (Mid)	.257	64	241	25	62	6	0	5	35	13	29	3
1966	Seattle (PCL)	.249	102	346	34	86	9	3	3	24	15	54	1
1967	Seattle (PCL)	.214	139	472	29	101	14	7	2	39	15	76	4
1968	HOUSTON (NL)	.223	128	466	44	104	11	1	1	24	18	64	2
1969	OklahomaCity (AmAs)	.238	29	105	13	25	3	0	0	5	6	9	2
	HOUSTON (NL)	.159	34	69	5	11	1	0	1	8	2	12	0
1970	OklahomaCity (AmAs)	.305	38	151	15	46	7	3	2	20	6	19	1
	HOUSTON (NL)	.246	31	65	6	16	1	2	0	5	6	8	0
1971	CHICAGO (NL)	.224	31	58	4	13	3	0	0	2	4	10	0
1972	MONTREAL (NL)	.155	83	181	14	28	4	1	2	7	13	26	1
1973	HOUSTON (NL)	.091	38	66	3	6	1	0	0	2	7	13	0
1974	Hawaii (PCL)	.259	123	425	41	110	14	1	7	47	23	42	2
1975	SAN DIEGO (NL)	.259	112	352	31	91	12	0	5	26	22	32	2
1976	SAN DIEGO (NL)	.195	74	215	8	42	6	0	4	15	16	31	2
1977	TORONTO (AL)	.241	91	266	33	64	7	3	5	26	16	33	1
1978	Syracuse (Int)	.206	111	344	37	71	10	2	7	41	16	54	1
MAJOR TOTALS		**.216**	**622**	**1738**	**148**	**375**	**46**	**7**	**18**	**115**	**104**	**229**	**7**

MANAGERIAL/COACHING CAREER
(All in Blue Jays Organization)

1979-84	Minor League Instructor, Toronto Blue Jays
1985-86	Manager, Florence, South Atlantic League
1987-89	Coach, Syracuse, International League
1990	Coach, Dunedin, Florida State League
1991	Coach, Toronto, American League
1992	Coach, Dunedin, Florida State League
1993	Manager, Blue Jays, Gulf Coast League
1994-96	Coach, Syracuse, International League
1997	Coach, Dunedin, Florida State League
1998	Coach, St. Catharines, New York-Penn League
	Roving Infield Instructor, Minor Leagues (Blue Jays)
1999	Coach, Syracuse, International League
2000-01	Coach, Tennessee, Southern League

RECORD AS MANAGER

Year	Club & League	W-L	PCT	Finish
1985	Florence (SAL)	82-55	.599	(2nd in Div., 1st in Div.)
1986	Florence (SAL)	56-76	.424	(5th in Div., 3rd in Div.)
1993	Blue Jays (Gulf)	22-38	.367	(4th in Div.)
CAREER TOTALS (3 years)		160-169	.486	

POST-SEASON PLAY

Year	Club & League	W-L	PCT	Finish
1985	Florence (SAL)	5-2	.714	(Def. Columbia 2G to 0 in semi-finals; def. Greens- boro 3G to 2 to win league championship)

WALTON, Bruce Kenneth

Pitching Coordinator

Former Pitcher ... **HT:** 6-02; **WT:** 195 ... **B-T:** R-R ... **BORN:** December 25, 1962, Bakersfield, California ... **RECOMMENDED/SIGNED BY:** (Athletics) ... **TRANSACTIONS:** Athletics' 16th pick in 1985 June draft. Signed as a free agent with Expos on December 7, 1992. Signed as a free agent by Astros on October 8, 1993. Signed as a free agent by Rockies on December 3, 1993. Signed as a free agent by St. Paul of the Northern League in June of 1995. ... **PERSONAL BACKGROUND:** 1981 graduate of North Bakersfield (CA) H.S. where he lettered in baseball and basketball. Attended University of Hawaii where he was named a College Freshman All-American. Married, wife's name Holly, and have two twin daughters Nicole and Mackenzie (11/05/91). ... **PRO CAREER:** 1986: Tied for California League lead in starts (27), placed second in innings pitched (176) and led the Modesto staff in wins (13) and strikeouts (107); 1991: Tied for second in the Pacific Coast League in saves (20) and placed third in games finished (38); made major league debut vs. the Yankees on May 11; won his first big league game on June 6 at Milwaukee; 1992: Finished third among Pacific Coast League relievers in baserunners/9 IP ratio (9.92) and fifth in BB/9 IP ratio (1.62); 1993: Led International League relievers in baserunners/9 IP ratio (8.44), finished third in opponents' batting average (.205) and third in BB/9 IP ratio (1.27); ranked fourth in the league in saves (16) and relief points (48) and tied for fifth in games finished (38); 1994: Tied for third in Pacific Coast League in saves (13), was fifth in games finished (33) and tied for fifth in relief points (37); 1995: Led the Northern League in saves (28) and games finished (38) and placed second in appearances (41); had a 1.82 ERA with 17 saves on the road; notched saves in 11 consecutive appearances July 8-August 4; appeared in three playoff games and hurled two scoreless innings for the Northern League champs. Began coaching career as the pitching coach for Medicine Hat in 1996. He became pitching coach at Hagerstown of the South Atlantic League in 1997 and became roving minor league pitching instructor in 1998.

PLAYING RECORD

Year	Club & League	W-L	ERA	G	GS	CG	SHO	SV	IP	H	R	ER	BB	SO
1985	Pocatello (Pio)	3-7	4.11	18	9	2	0	3	77	89	46	35	27	69
1986	Modesto (Cal)	13-7	4.09	27	27	4	0	0	176	204	96	80	41	107
	Madison (Mid)	0-0	5.40	1	1	0	0	0	5	5	3	3	1	1
1987	Modesto (Cal)	8-6	2.88	16	16	3	1	0	106	97	44	34	27	84
	Huntsville (Sou)	2-2	3.10	18	2	0	0	2	58	61	24	20	13	40
1988	Huntsville (Sou)	4-5	4.56	42	3	0	0	3	116	126	64	59	23	82
1989	Tacoma (PCL)	8-6	3.76	32	14	1	1	0	108	118	59	45	27	76
1990	Tacoma (PCL)	5-5	3.11	46	5	0	0	7	98	103	42	34	23	67
1991	Tacoma (PCL)	1-1	1.35	38	0	0	0	20	47	39	11	7	5	49
	OAKLAND (AL)	1-0	6.23	12	0	0	0	0	13	11	9	9	6	10
1992	OAKLAND (AL)	0-0	9.90	7	0	0	0	0	10	17	11	11	3	7
	Tacoma (PCL)	8-2	2.77	35	7	2	1	8	81	76	29	25	21	60
1993	MONTREAL (NL)	0-0	9.53	4	0	0	0	0	6	10	6	6	3	0
	Ottawa (Int)	4-4	1.05	40	0	0	0	16	43	32	12	5	8	40
	Tucson (PCL)	2-0	1.80	13	0	0	0	7	15	12	4	3	3	14
1994	Colo.Springs (PCL)	3-4	4.84	51	0	0	0	13	58	74	34	31	16	39
	COLORADO (NL)	1-0	8.44	4	0	0	0	0	5	6	5	5	3	1
1995	St. Paul (Nor)	2-2	4.37	41	0	0	0	28	45	53	23	22	10	44
MAJOR TOTALS		2-0	8.21	27	0	0	0	0	34	45	31	31	15	18

MANAGERIAL/COACHING CAREER
(All in Blue Jays Organization)

1996	Pitching Coach, Medicine Hat, Pioneer League
1997	Pitching Coach, Hagerstown, South Atlantic League
1998-2001	Roving Pitching Instructor, Minor Leagues (Blue Jays)

WHEELER, Ralph Norman (Rocket)

Manager, TENNESSEE

Former Infielder/Outfielder ... **HT:** 5-11; **WT:** 190 ... **B-T:** R-R ... **BORN:** January 11, 1955, Houston, TX ... **RESIDES:** Pawleys Island, So. Carolina ... **RECOMMENDED/SIGNED BY:** Al Lamacchia (Blue Jays) ... **TRANSACTIONS:** Blue Jays 13th selection in 1977 June draft. ... **PERSONAL BACKGROUND:** Graduated from Phyllis Wheatley H.S. in Houston, Texas. Attended University of Houston (Tex.) where he majored in Health and Physical Education and played baseball. ... **PRO CAREER:** Played six major league seasons. Began his coaching career in 1981 while also a full-time player at Florence. Spent more time coaching with Knoxville in 1982 under Manager Larry Hardy, before becoming full-time coach in organization in 1983 and made managerial debut at Medicine Hat the following year. Has managed or coached in Jays' minor league system for 15 seasons and took over the helm as skipper for St. Catharines in 1996 and remained manager of the Stompers until 1998, when he took the helm at Dunedin. Managed Dunedin in 1999 and was named FSL Manager-of-the-Year. In 1996 was the winner of the inaugural Boby Mattick Award for excellence in player development after being named Manager-of-the-Year in the New York-Penn League. 2001 will be his second season as skipper of Tennessee in the Southern League and his 21st season in the Toronto organization.

PLAYING CAREER

Year	Club & League	AVG	G	AB	R	H	2B	3B	HR	RBI	BB	SO	SB
1977	Utica (NYP)	.231	67	238	42	55	9	3	1	23	37	25	5
1978	Dunedin (FSL)	.271	126	465	66	126	9	2	3	25	41	49	3
1979	Kinston (CARO)	.294	132	493	69	145	24	5	5	69	48	43	6
1980	Knoxville (Sou)	.265	119	419	50	111	16	3	3	31	36	60	3
1981	Florence (SAL)	.277	133	523	89	145	20	9	7	67	58	57	11
1982	Florence (SAL)	.312	59	218	43	68	12	1	8	48	31	27	6
	Knoxville (Sou)	.276	12	29	9	8	2	0	1	4	3	4	2

MANAGERIAL/COACHING CAREER
(All in Blue Jays Organization)

1981	Player-Coach, Florence, South Atlantic League
1982	Player-Coach, Florence, South Atlantic League and Knoxville, Southern League
1983	Coach, Florence, South Atlantic League
1984	Coach, Florence, South Atlantic League and Manager, Medicine Hat, Pioneer League
1985	Manager, Blue Jays, Gulf Coast League
1986	Coach, Syracuse, International League
1987	Coach, Myrtle Beach, South Atlantic League
1988-89	Manager, Medicine Hat, Pioneer League
1990-93	Coach, Syracuse, International League
1994	Coach, Dunedin, Florida State League
1995	Manager, Blue Jays, Gulf Coast League
1996-97	Manager, St. Catharines, New York-Penn League
1998-99	Manager, Dunedin, Florida State League
2000-01	Manager, Tennessee, Southern League

RECORD AS MANAGER

Year	Club & League	W-L	PCT	Finish
1984	Medicine Hat (Pio)	32-38	.457	(3rd in Div.)
1985	Blue Jays (Gulf)	23-39	.371	(4th in Div.)
1988	Medicine Hat (Pio)	12-58	.171	(4th in Div.)
1989	Medicine Hat (Pio)	23-46	.333	(4th in Div.)
1995	Blue Jays (Gulf)	19-40	.322	(15th in Div.)
1996	St. Catharines (NYP)	44-32	.579	(1st in Div.)
1997	St. Catharines (NYP)	35-40	.467	(3rd in Div.)
1998	Dunedin (FSL)	82-58	.585	(2nd in Div., 4th in Div.)
1999	Dunedin (FSL)	85-51	.628	(2nd in Div., 1st in Div.)
2000	Tennessee (Sou)	71-69	.507	(4th in Div., 2nd in Div.)
CAREER TOTALS (10 years)		426-471	.475	

POST-SEASON PLAY

Year	Club & League	W-L	PCT	Finish
1996	St. Catharines (NYP)	3-2	.600	(Def. Watertown 2G to 0 in semis; Lost to Vermont 2G to 1 in finals)
1999	Dunedin (FSL)	3-4	.429	(Def. Clearwater 2G to 1 in semi-finals; Lost to Kissimmee 3G to 1 in finals)

WHITT, Leo Ernest (Ernie)   Roving Hitting & Catching Coordinator

Former Catcher ... **HT:** 6-02; **WT:** 205 ... **B-T:** L-R ... **BORN:** June 13, 1952, Detroit, Michigan ... **RESIDES:** Mt. Clemens, Michigan ... **RECOMMENDED/SIGNED BY:** (Boston Red Sox) ... **TRANSACTIONS:** Red Sox' 15th selection in 1972 June draft. Selected by Blue Jays in American League expansion draft on November 5, 1976. ... **PERSONAL BACK-GROUND:** Graduated from Brablec H.S. in Roseville, Mich. in 1970 and attended Macomb Community College in Warren, Mich. ... **PRO CAREER:** 1973: Sixth in the Carolina League in batting (.290); 1975: Was on the disabled list for two months; 1976: Hit first major league homer while with Red Sox on September 21 off Jim Colborn of Brewers; 1977: Second among International League catchers in fielding percentage (.992); 1979: Led Internationl League catchers in fielding percentage (.995); 1983: Enjoyed best major league season platooning with Buck Martinez for a second straight season, hit two homers in a game against Tigers on May 23 and September 4; had a four-hit game against Angels on June 12; 1984: Continued to platoon behind the plate with Buck Martinez. Injured his right achilles tendon in a game on June 15 against Boston, putting him on the disabled list for two weeks. Hit 10 of his home runs on the road and hit 11 from July 27 to the end of the season; 1985: Was third among American League catchers in home runs (19) behind Calton Fisk and Lance Parrish. Hit grand slam home run against Boston on June 23 (off Bruce Kison). Played in mid-season All-Star game at Minnesota, did not bat. Hit home run in division clinching game vs. New York on October 5 for the Jays' first run in the 5-1 victory. Saw much action due to injury to Buck Martinez in July. Batted .190 (4-for-21) in ALCS vs. Kansas City; 1986: Belted second career grand slam off Richard Dotson in Chicago May 22; 1987: Had fine season for 'Jays, setting career highs in batting average, at-bats, runs, hits, doubles and RBI; cracked two home runs September 12 vs. Yankees, the second being No. 100 in major league career; belted three more round-trippers just two days later in game vs. Orioles in which 'Jays established major league record by clubbing 10 home runs; 1988: Named top Sporting News All-Star team. Is the only player that has been with the Jays since the 1976 AL Expansion Draft. Was Labatts' "Blue" Player-of-the-Month in August (.318, 5 HR, 18 RBI). Hit 11 of his 16 HR from August 8 on. Hit 2 HRs and had 6 RBI at Boston on September 27. Has 121 HRs in his big league career, 120 with Blue Jays, placing him fourth on Blue Jays' All-Time list; 1989: Smashed third career grand slam off the Red Sox' Lee Smith on June 4th at Fenway Park; hammered 4 home runs in a 5 game stretch from May 20-May 27; 1997: Started his coaching career in 1997 as roving minor league catching instructor. Midway through the 1997 season took over as manager of Dunedin in the Florida State League. Returned to his current position as roving catching and hitting instructor in 1998.

PLAYING CAREER

Year	Club & League	AVG	G	AB	R	H	2B	3B	HR	RBI	BB	SO	SB
1972	Winter Haven (FSL)	.183	31	82	3	15	1	1	0	7	10	9	0
	Williamsport (NYP)	.500	1	4	1	2	1	0	0	0	0	0	0
1973	Winston-Sal (CARO)	.290	130	424	63	123	23	3	1	50	60	31	7
1974	Bristol (East)	.249	111	385	55	96	10	1	9	56	47	32	12
1975	Bristol (East)	.254	82	252	29	64	9	1	2	19	33	19	2
1976	Bristol (East)	.218	26	87	12	19	2	3	1	10	10	5	0
	Rhode Island (Int)	.266	90	304	33	81	16	2	7	42	39	32	1
	BOSTON (AL)	.222	8	18	4	4	2	0	1	3	2	2	0
1977	Charleston (Int)	.255	29	94	12	24	6	0	0	7	18	14	0
	TORONTO (AL)	.171	23	41	4	7	3	0	0	6	2	12	0
1978	Syracuse (Int)	.246	121	399	50	98	16	3	12	53	8	35	0
	TORONTO (AL)	.000	2	4	0	0	0	0	0	0	1	1	0
1979	Syracuse (Int)	.249	114	382	32	95	18	4	7	43	42	43	2
1980	TORONTO (AL)	.237	106	295	23	70	12	2	6	34	22	30	1
1981	TORONTO (AL)	.236	74	195	16	46	9	0	1	16	20	30	5
1982	TORONTO (AL)	.231	105	284	28	74	14	2	11	42	26	35	3
1983	TORONTO (AL)	.256	123	344	53	88	15	2	17	56	50	55	1
1984	TORONTO (AL)	.238	124	315	35	75	12	1	15	46	43	49	0
1985	TORONTO (AL)	.245	139	412	55	101	21	2	19	64	47	59	3
1986	TORONTO (AL)	.268	131	395	48	106	19	2	16	56	35	39	0
1987	TORONTO (AL)	.269	135	446	57	120	24	1	19	75	44	50	0
1988	TORONTO (AL)	.251	127	398	63	100	11	2	16	70	61	38	4
1989	TORONTO (AL)	.262	129	385	42	101	24	1	11	53	52	53	5
1990	ATLANTA (NL)	.172	67	180	14	31	8	0	2	10	23	27	0
	Greenville (Sou)	.333	4	12	1	4	1	0	0	0	2	1	0
1991	BALTIMORE (AL)	.242	35	62	5	15	2	0	0	3	8	12	0
MAJOR TOTALS		**.249**	**1328**	**3774**	**447**	**938**	**176**	**15**	**134**	**534**	**436**	**491**	**22**

MANAGERIAL/COACHING CAREER
(All in Blue Jays Organization)

1997-2001	Roving Catching Instructor, Minor Leagues
1997	Manager (Interim), Syracuse, International League
1997	Manager (Interim), Dunedin, Florida State League

RECORD AS MANAGER

Year	Club & League	W-L	PCT	Finish
1997	Syracuse (Int)	1-5	.167	(Interim)
1997	Dunedin (FSL)	15-21	.417	(Interim, 8th Div.)
CAREER TOTALS (Interim)		16-26	.381	

WILSON, Michael (Tack)   Outfield and Baserunning Instructor

Former Outfielder ... HT: 5-10; **WT:** 180 ... **B-T:** R-R ... **BORN:** May 16, 1956, SHREVEPORT, LA ... **RESIDES:** OAKLAND, CA ... **RECOMMENDED/SIGNED BY:** (Los Angeles Dodgers) ... **TRANSACTIONS:** Signed as a non-drafted free agent 1975. Signed by the Milwaukee Brewers as a six year minor league free agent 1990. ... **PERSONAL BACKGROUND:** Single ... **PRO CAREER:** Played professionally in seven different organizations from 1976-1990. Had two stints in the major leagues, with Minnesota in 1983 and with California in 1987. In 12 big league games was 2-6 with nine runs scored. Began coaching career in 1992 as a roving hitting instructor for the Atlanta Braves. Was the Braves single A affiliates hitting instructor in 1993 with Durham and in 1994 with Richmond (AAA) of the International League. Spent the last four seasons in the Chicago Cubs Organization and the last three as hitting coach for West Tennessee (AA) of the Southern League. Joins the Toronto organization in 2001 as the minor league Outfield and Baserunning Instructor.

PLAYING CAREER

Year	Club & League	AVG	G	AB	R	H	2B	3B	HR	RBI	SH-SF	HB	BB-IBB	SO	SB-CS	GDP	SLG	OBP
1976	Danville (Mid)	.500	2	2	1	1	0	0	0	0	0-0	0	1-0	1	2-0	0	.500	.667
	Bellingham (NWST)	.329	66	225	47	74	7	8	0	20	2-2	0	49-0	26	36-10	5	.431	.446
1977	Grays Harbor (NWST)	.333	40	144	29	48	9	2	3	17	5-0	1	26-0	8	15-8	2	.486	.439
	Clinton (Mid)	.270	44	148	46	40	5	5	1	14	2-0	1	34-0	20	25-6	3	.392	.410
1978	Visalia (Cal)	.349	134	525	126	183	24	4	5	79	12-4	11	119-2	50	63-25	8	.438	.475
1979	San Antonio (Tex)	.315	130	492	105	155	27	7	6	42	12-1	7	82-0	42	56-24	14	.435	.419
1980	Albuquerque (PCL)	.291	131	478	110	139	19	8	2	47	10-2	7	90-1	33	46-16	13	.377	.409
1981	Albuquerque (PCL)	.315	96	330	68	104	15	10	2	64	7-5	2	51-1	27	40-10	11	.439	.405
1982	Albuquerque (PCL)	.378	99	368	77	139	25	6	2	56	5-2	6	48-1	27	25-17	3	.495	.455
1983	Toledo (Int)	.325	109	416	71	135	20	3	3	33	6-0	2	55-3	36	53-26	8	.409	.406
	MINNESOTA (AL)	.250	5	4	4	1	1	0	0	1	0-0	0	0-0	0	0-0	0	.500	.250
1984	Toledo (Int)	.287	132	460	70	132	13	5	1	46	16-3	4	94-1	45	48-29	10	.343	.410
1985	Phoenix (PCL)	.319	140	518	109	165	20	4	3	45	9-4	2	93-2	38	56-22	23	.398	.421
1986	Phoenix (PCL)	.253	102	360	62	91	9	4	1	30	5-2	3	38-0	32	28-10	5	.308	.328
1987	CALIFORNIA (AL)	.500	7	2	5	1	0	0	0	0	1-0	0	1-0	0	0-0	0	.500	.667
	Edmonton (PCL)	.314	114	389	86	122	19	5	3	34	6-3	2	82-0	33	24-16	9	.411	.433
1988	Tulsa (Tex)	.279	19	61	7	17	2	0	0	3	0-0	0	8-0	8	0-1	3	.311	.279
1989	Okla City (AMAS)	.249	53	189	31	47	12	2	2	22	5-1	3	32-0	17	10-6	5	.365	.364
	Denver (AMAS)	.289	48	159	15	46	9	1	0	24	3-1	5	15-0	20	2-8	10	.358	.352
1990	Huntsville (Sou)	.220	83	255	34	56	9	1	0	16	11-0	1	39-0	30	9-6	11	.263	.323
MAJOR TOTALS		**.333**	**12**	**6**	**9**	**2**	**1**	**0**	**0**	**1**	**1-0**	**0**	**1-0**	**0**	**0-0**	**0**	**.500**	**.429**

MANAGERIAL/COACHING CAREER
(All in Blue Jays Organization)

1992	Roving Hitting Instructor, Atlanta, Minor leagues
1993	Hitting Coach, Durham, Atlanta
1994	Hitting Coach, Richmond, Atlanta
1997	Hitting Coach, Rockford, Chicago Cubs
1998-2000	Hitting Coach, West Tennessee, Chicago Cubs
2001	Roving Outfield and Baserunning Instructor, Toronto, Minor Leagues

Abbott, James D.

Pitcher ... **HT:** 6-4; **WT:** 230 ... **B-T:** R-R ... **BORN:** 19 OCT, 1977, Tucson, AZ **RESIDES:** Tucson, AZ ... **EDUCATION:** Arizona ... **TRANSACTIONS:** Selected by Blue Jays in eighth round of 2000 draft; signed June 16, 2000. **PRO CAREER:** 2000: Was 2-0 with 1.54 ERA in relief.

Year Club & League	W-L	ERA	G	GS	CG	ShO	SV	IP	H	R	ER	HR	HB	BB-IBB	SO	WP	BK	OBA
2000 Medcine Hat (PIO)	2-1	1.99	8	4	0	0	0	22.2	19	11	5	0	1	6-0	18	1	0	.226

Altuve, Juan J. Gutierrez

Pitcher ... **HT:** 6-3; **WT:** 195 ... **B-T:** R-R ... **BORN:** 22 FEB, 1983, Tovar Merida, VZ **RESIDES:** Tovar, Merida, VZ ... **TRANSACTIONS:** Signed as non-drafted free agent by Blue Jays, March 10, 2000

Year Club & League	W-L	ERA	G	GS	CG	ShO	SV	IP	H	R	ER	HR	HB	BB-IBB	SO	WP	BK	OBA
2000 Chino (VSL)	2-3	7.67	17	0	0	0	2	31.2	41	31	27	3	4	24-2	27	1	0	.331

Alvarez, Francis DeJesus (Jimmy)

Infielder ... **HT:** 5-10; **WT:** 168 ... **B-T:** S-R ... **BORN:** 04 OCT, 1979, Santo Domingo, DR **RESIDES:** Santo Domingo, DR ... **TRANSACTIONS:** Signed as non-drafted free agent by Twins, Nov. 12, 1996; Traded by Twins to Blue Jays for RHP Mike Romano, June 12, 2000. **PRO CAREER:** 1997: Tied for fifth in triples in Gulf Coast League with 4; 1998: Led team in triples with 4; 1999: Hit .298 with 40 RBI with runners in scoring position; had a pair of 5-RBI games May 26 vs. Wisconsin and May 30 against Beloit; was second on team in walks (81) and stolen bases (15); 2000: Hit .292 with runners on base while at Hagerstown; hit a career high (7) home runs.

Year Club & League	AVG	G	AB	R	H	TB	2B	3B	HR	RBI	SH-SF	HP	BB-IBB	SO	SB-CS	GIDP	SLG	OBP
1997 Twins (GULF)	.249	52	185	25	46	59	5	4	0	14	1-1	1	21-0	46	12-5	4	.319	.327
1998 Elizabethtn (APPY)	.219	46	155	32	34	50	8	4	0	14	2-2	3	33-0	37	6-2	4	.323	.363
1999 Quad City (MID)	.253	121	435	69	110	150	20	1	6	48	7-5	6	81-3	112	15-10	9	.345	.374
2000 Quad City (MID)	.224	43	134	14	30	53	7	2	4	21	3-0	2	19-1	38	3-1	0	.396	.329
Hagerstown (SAL)	.232	50	155	19	36	52	5	1	3	15	1-0	2	25-0	44	12-5	0	.335	.346
Minor Totals	.241	312	064	159	256	364	45	12	13	112	14-8	14	179-4	277	48-23	17	.342	.355

Arias, Jose L. Pinales

Shortstop ... **HT:** 6-0; **WT:** 162 ... **B-T:** S-R ... **BORN:** 20 MAY, 1981, Sabana grande de palenque, DR ... **RESIDES:** De Palenque, DR ... **TRANSACTIONS:** Signed as non-drafted free agent by Blue Jays, Jan. 5, 1999

Year Club & League	AVG	G	AB	R	H	TB	2B	3B	HR	RBI	SH-SF	HP	BB-IBB	SO	SB-CS	GIDP	SLG	OBP
1999 Sd Blue Jay (DSL)	.141	35	99	16	14	20	1	1	1	1	2-0	6	17-0	24	4-2	4	.202	.303
2000 Toronto (DSL)	.273	31	121	20	33	44	3	4	0	13	0-1	2	21-0	32	5-7	1	.364	.386
Minor Totals	.214	66	220	36	47	64	4	5	1	14	2-1	8	38-0	56	9-9	5	.291	.348

Arrieche, Gabriel A.

Third Baseman ... **HT:** 6-0; **WT:** 170 ... **B-T:** R-R ... **BORN:** 08 MAR, 1979, Barquisimeto, VZ **RESIDES:** Lara, VZ ... **TRANSACTIONS:** Signed as non-drafted free agent by Blue Jays, Sept. 27, 1997. **PRO CAREER:** - 1998: Led team in hit by pitches (13); 1999: Led Dominican Summer League club in games (67), doubles (9) and walks (47); had .391 on-base Percentage; 2000: Led Venezuelan Summer League in runs (53) and finished second in RBI (48) and hits (66); tied for second in stolen bases (19) and tied for fifth in batting (.353).

Year Club & League	AVG	G	AB	R	H	TB	2B	3B	HR	RBI	SH-SF	HP	BB-IBB	SO	SB-CS	GIDP	SLG	OBP
1998 Blue Jays (DSL)	.212	55	165	37	35	48	5	1	2	24	3-4	13	32-0	28	11-3	5	.291	.374
1999 Sd Blue Jay (DSL)	.244	67	217	31	53	67	9	1	1	20	1-1	6	47-2	24	19-6	6	.309	.391
2000 Chino (VSL)	.353	54	187	53	66	98	11	3	5	48	0-4	11	33-0	21	19-5	4	.524	.468
Minor Totals	.271	176	569	121	154	213	25	5	8	92	4-9	30	112-2	73	49-14	15	.374	.411

Baker, Christopher S. (Chris)

Pitcher ... **HT:** 6-1; **WT:** 194 ... **B-T:** R-R ... **BORN:** 24 AUG, 1977, Burbank, CA **RESIDES:** Valencia, CA ... **EDUCATION:** Oklahoma City ... **TRANSACTIONS:** Selected by Blue Jays in 29th round of 1999 draft; signed June 10, 1999. **PRO CAREER:** 1999: In three games with Medicine Hat had 3.12 ERA and struckout nine in 8.2 innings; tied for second on St. Catharines in games started (3), third in strikeouts (55); had 3.9-to-1 strikeout to walks ratio; on August 4, vs. Williamsport struck out nine batters in five innings, allowing two runs on four hits without decision; 2000: Was second in organization with 3.20 ERA; was 5-3 with 2.92 ERA and 5 saves in 35 appearances as reliever while fanning 72 in 74 innings.

Year Club & League	W-L	ERA	G	GS	CG	ShO	SV	IP	H	R	ER	HR	HB	BB-IBB	SO	WP	BK	OBA
1999 Medcine Hat (PIO)	0-1	3.12	3	1	0	0	0	8.2	8	4	3	0	1	2-0	9	1	1	.235
St.cathrnes (NYP)	2-4	6.20	12	10	0	0	0	49.1	61	37	34	6	1	14-1	55	7	2	.298
2000 Dunedin (FSL)	9-5	3.20	41	6	0	0	5	104.0	91	50	37	11	5	29-2	85	9	1	.226
Minor Totals	11-10	4.11	56	17	0	0	5	162.0	160	91	74	17	7	45-3	149	17	4	.249

Banks, Willie Anthony

Pitcher ... **HT:** 6-1; **WT:** 200 ... **B-T:** R-R ... **BORN:** 27 FEB, 1969, Jersey City, NJ **RESIDES:** Miami, FL ... **TRANSACTIONS:** Selected by Twins in first round (third overall) of 1987 draft; signed June 15, 1987; Traded by Twins to Cubs for RHP Dave Stevens and C Matt Walbeck, Nov. 24, 1993; Traded by Cubs to Dodgers for RHP Dax Winslett, June 19, 1995; Claimed on waivers from Dodgers, Aug. 10, 1995; Claimed on waivers by Phillies from Marlins, Oct. 4, 1995; Released by Phillies, March 8, 1996; Signed by Yankees, Dec. 21, 1996; Traded by Yankees to Diamondbacks for RHP Scott Brow and RHP Joe Lisio, June 3, 1998; Granted free agency, Dec. 19, 1998; Signed by Orix (Japan), 1999; Signed by Mets, July 10, 2000; Granted free agency, Oct. 15, 2000. **PRO CAREER:** 1987: Struck out 11 in game against Kingsport, July 29; 1989: Led California League in strikeouts (173) and tied for lead in shutouts (4); was fourth in wins (12), starts (27) and complete games (7); tossed no-hitter against Palm Springs, May 24; 1990: Tied for fifth in Southern League in starts (28); led team in strikeouts (114); was 2-0 in playoffs for Orlando; was 6-1 for Lara in Venezuelan Winter League; 1991: Compiled 7-0 record with 2.28 ERA during nine start stretch, June 13-July 27; won first Major League start against California, August 6; 1992: Won first five decisions with Portland; earned Pitcher of the Week honors in the PCL, May 3-9; 1993: Led Minnesota starters in ERA (4.04); was second on team in wins (11) and strikeouts (138); struck out 13 on August 14 against Oakland; 1994: Tossed shutout vs. Los Angeles, May 24; 1997: Tied for second in International League in wins with 14; 1998: (In Majors); 2000: Was 1-1 with 3.57 ERA in four starts at home.

Year	Club & League	W-L	ERA	G	GS	CG	ShO	SV	IP	H	R	ER	HR	HB	BB-IBB	SO	WP	BK	OBA
1987	Elizabethtn (APPY)	1-8	6.99	13	13	0	0	0	65.2	73	71	51	3	3	62-0	71	28	3	.281
1988	Kenosha (MID)	10-10	3.72	24	24	0	0	0	125.2	109	73	52	3	4	107-2	113	14	2	.236
1989	Visalia (CAL)	12-9	2.59	27	27	7	4	0	174.0	122	70	50	5	10	85-0	173	22	1	.197
	Orlando (SOU)	1-0	5.14	1	1	0	0	0	7.0	10	4	4	0	0	0-0	9	2	0	.333
1990	Orlando (SOU)	7-9	3.93	28	28	1	0	0	162.2	161	93	71	15	7	98-0	114	6	1	.259
1991	Portland (PCL)	9-8	4.55	25	24	1	1	0	146.1	156	81	74	6	6	76-1	63	14	1	.276
	MINNESOTA (AL)	1-1	5.71	5	3	0	0	0	17.1	21	15	11	1	0	12-0	16	3	0	.288
1992	Portland (PCL)	6-1	1.92	11	11	2	1	0	75.0	62	20	16	2	0	34-0	41	5	2	.228
	MINNESOTA (AL)	4-4	5.70	16	12	0	0	0	71.0	80	46	45	6	2	37-0	37	5	1	.288
1993	MINNESOTA (AL)	11-12	4.04	31	30	0	0	0	171.1	180	91	77	17	3	78-2	138	9	5	.271
1994	CHICAGO (NL)	8-12	5.40	23	23	1	1	0	138.1	139	88	83	16	2	56-3	91	8	1	.261
1995	CHICAGO (NL)	0-1	15.43	10	0	0	0	0	11.2	27	23	20	5	0	12-4	9	3	0	.458
	LOS ANGELES (NL)	0-2	4.03	6	6	0	0	0	29.0	36	21	13	2	1	16-2	23	4	1	.303
	FLORIDA (NL)	2-3	4.32	9	9	0	0	0	50.0	43	27	24	7	1	30-1	30	2	0	.235
1997	Columbus (INT)	14-5	4.27	33	24	1	0	3	154.0	164	87	73	18	4	45-0	130	7	0	.270
	NEW YORK (AL)	3-0	1.93	5	1	0	0	0	14.0	9	3	3	0	1	6-0	8	0	0	.188
1998	NEW YORK (AL)	1-1	10.05	9	0	0	0	0	14.1	20	16	16	4	1	12-2	8	1	0	.323
	ARIZONA (NL)	1-2	3.09	33	0	0	0	1	43.2	34	21	15	2	1	25-2	32	4	1	.217
1999	Orix (PL)	3-3	3.94	13	0	0	0	1	30.0	27	0	0	0	0	21-0	26	0	0	-
2000	Norfolk (INT)	2-4	5.08	9	9	0	0	0	51.1	56	32	29	5	2	25-2	20	5	1	.284
Minor Totals		62-54	3.93	171	161	12	6	3	961.2	913	531	420	57	36	532-5	734	103	11	–
MAJOR TOTALS		31-38	4.93	147	84	1	1	1	560.2	589	351	307	60	12	284-16	392	39	9	.271

Bell, Jason Andrew

Pitcher ... **HT:** 6-3; **WT:** 210 ... **B-T:** R-R ... **BORN:** 30 SEP, 1974, Ocala, FL **RESIDES:** Orlando, FL ... **EDUCATION:** Oklahoma St. ... **TRANSACTIONS:** Selected by Twins in second round of 1995 draft; signed July 10, 1995; Selected by Blue Jays from Twins in Rule 5 minor league draft, Dec. 13, 1999. **PRO CAREER:** 1995: Made his pro debut with Class-A Fort Wayne on July 25, tossing a perfect ninth inning against South Bend; went 3-1, 1.27 ERA in six starts and didn't give up more than one earned run in any of his outings; won three straight starts, August 15-26; owned a K/BB ratio of 6.67-to-1; 1996: Began the season at Class-A Fort Myers and ranked third best among Florida State League starters with a .193 average against over 13 starts; pitched seven innings of three-hit, scoreless ball but was not involved in the decision against Dunedin on April 10; struck out a season-high 12 batters and allowed just four hits over eight innings in a no-decision against St. Lucie on May 1 and followed up with 15 scoreless innings over his next two starts; was promoted to Double-A New Britain in June and went on to rank fourth among Eastern League starters with a ratio of 9.00 K/9 IP; struck out nine batters in back-to-back starts, June 24-29; tossed his first career complete game on August 5 against Bowie but was the losing pitcher; threw a one-hit shutout in his last start of the season, August 30 in the first game of a doubleheader against Binghamton; 1997: Spent the entire season at Double-A and ranked fourth in the Eastern League with 142 strikeouts and fifth in ERA (3.39); went 7-4, 2.45 ERA in 15 home starts; went 5-2, 1.90 ERA in August, including a one-hit shutout against Trenton on the 11th; held opponents to a .214 average with runners in scoring position; 1998: Spent a second full season at New Britain and led the Eastern League with 29 starts, tied for second with 166 strikeouts and ranked third anomg league starters with a .238 average against; pitched a complete game four-hitter with 10 strikeouts on June 3 to beat New Haven for his first victory of the season; went 3-1, 1.72 ERA with a .149 average against in five June starts; owned a 3-3 record, a 2.38 ERA and a .205 average against in seven August starts; 1999: Began the season with Triple-A Salt Lake and won his first two decisions; struck out a season-high nine batters over seven innings against Las Vegas on June 27 but went on the disabled list soon thereafter with a tender right shoulder; made three relief appearances with Salt Lake after being activated before being sent to Double-A New Britain; went 3-1, 2.73 ERA in four road starts and 0-2, 4.29 ERA at home with the Rock Cats; 2000: Was 3-0 with 1.65 ERA in May while at Tennessee; was 3-1 with 0.90 ERA in August with Syracuse.

Year	Club & League	W-L	ERA	G	GS	CG	ShO	SV	IP	H	R	ER	HR	HB	BB-IBB	SO	WP	BK	OBA
1995	Ft. Wayne (MID)	3-1	1.31	9	6	0	0	0	34.1	26	11	5	0	1	6-0	40	6	2	.203
1996	Ft. Myers (FSL)	6-3	1.69	13	13	0	0	0	90.1	61	20	17	1	6	22-0	83	3	0	.193
	New Britain (EAST)	2-6	4.40	16	16	2	1	0	94.0	93	54	46	13	5	38-1	94	6	1	.258
1997	New Britain (EAST)	11-9	3.39	28	28	3	1	0	164.2	163	71	62	19	5	64-0	142	13	2	.260
1998	New Britain (EAST)	8-11	4.67	29	29	2	0	0	169.2	148	90	88	21	5	61-1	166	4	2	.238
1999	Salt Lake (PCL)	5-5	6.37	18	15	0	0	0	76.1	96	58	54	12	3	35-0	72	4	1	.301
	New Britain (EAST)	3-3	3.42	7	7	0	0	0	47.1	46	21	18	4	2	11-0	34	0	1	.253
2000	Tennessee (SOU)	4-3	3.53	12	2	0	0	0	35.2	30	19	14	2	2	10-1	32	0	0	.233
	Syracuse (INT)	3-4	4.97	22	3	0	0	0	41.2	41	25	23	3	1	16-1	28	2	0	.272
Minor Totals		45-45	3.90	154	119	7	2	0	754.0	704	369	327	75	30	263-4	691	38	9	.248

Bernhardt, Jossephang Raymond

Shortstop ... **HT:** 6-1; **WT:** 185 ... **B-T:** R-R ... **BORN:** 22 SEP, 1980, San Pedro de Macoris, DR ... **RESIDES:** San Pedro de Macoris, DR ... **TRANSACTIONS:** Signed as non-drafted free agent by Blue Jays, July 18, 1996. **PRO CAREER:** 1997: Hit his first home run as a professional on August 21 vs. Great Falls; 1999: Led St. Catharines in at-bats (267) and sacrifice flies (7); from July 7-17 went on an 11-game hit streak, batting .367 (18-49) with seven runs and 10 RBI; had seven game hit streak from August 6-12, batted .375 (12-32); home batting average of .279 (38-136).

Year	Club & League	AVG	G	AB	R	H	TB	2B	3B	HR	RBI	SH-SF	HP	BB-IBB	SO	SB-CS	GIDP	SLG	OBP
1997	Medcine Hat (PIO)	.176	60	199	20	35	40	2	0	1	13	5-1	1	8-0	55	3-2	4	.201	.211
1998	St.cathrnes (NYP)	.182	59	181	18	33	52	11	1	2	19	1-2	0	17-1	61	0-0	4	.287	.250
1999	St.cathrnes (NYP)	.243	70	267	20	65	92	10	1	5	35	1-7	1	8-1	67	2-1	3	.345	.261
2000	Dunedin (FSL)	.250	3	4	0	1	2	1	0	0	3	0-0	0	1-0	1	0-0	0	.500	.400
	Hagerstown (SAL)	.125	2	8	1	1	2	1	0	0	0	0-0	0	0-0	3	0-0	0	.250	.125
	Queens (NYP)	.136	17	59	1	8	10	2	0	0	3	0-0	0	4-0	10	0-0	5	.169	.190
Minor Totals		.199	211	718	60	143	198	27	2	8	73	7-10	2	38-2	197	5-3	16	.276	.238

Berroa, Yesson D.

Pitcher ... **HT:** 6-3; **WT:** 182 ... **B-T:** R-R ... **BORN:** 20 JUL, 1983, San Pedro de Macoris, DR ... **RESIDES:** San Pedro de Macoris, DR ... **TRANSACTIONS:** Signed by Blue Jays, July 13, 2000 ... **PRO CAREER:** 2001 will be his first professional season.

Bimeal, Matthew T. (Matt)

Pitcher ... **HT:** 6-3; **WT:** 200 ... **B-T:** R-R ... **BORN:** 17 AUG, 1980, Johnstown, PA **RESIDES:** Davidsville, PA ... **TRANSACTIONS:** Selected by Blue Jays in 35th round of 1999 draft; signed Aug. 19, 1999. **PRO CAREER:** 2000: Averaged 10.39 SO/9 IP; surrendered only 3 walks in 24 innings at home.

Year	Club & League	W-L	ERA	G	GS	CG	ShO	SV	IP	H	R	ER	HR	HB	BB-IBB	SO	WP	BK	OBA
2000	Medcine Hat (PIO)	1-0	6.02	21	0	0	0	0	43.1	55	40	29	8	1	13-0	50	8	2	.304

Blackburn, John A.

Catcher ... **HT:** 6-1; **WT:** 200 ... **B-T:** R-R ... **BORN:** 30 DEC, 1982, London, ON, Canada **RESIDES:** London, ON, Canada ... **TRANSACTIONS:** Selected by Blue Jays in 19th round of 2000 draft; signed June 12, 2000; Selected by Blue Jays in 19th round of 2000 draft; signed June 12, 2000.

Year	Club & League	AVG	G	AB	R	H	TB	2B	3B	HR	RBI	SH-SF	HP	BB-IBB	SO	SB-CS	GIDP	SLG	OBP
2000	Medcine Hat (PIO)	.193	18	57	5	11	19	3	1	1	8	1-1	0	10-0	9	0-0	0	.333	.309

Bleazard, David Paul

Pitcher ... **HT:** 6-0; **WT:** 175 ... **B-T:** R-R ... **BORN:** 07 MAR, 1974, Salt Lake City, UT **RESIDES:** Tooele, UT ... **EDUCATION:** Oklahoma City ... **TRANSACTIONS:** Selected by Blue Jays in 22nd round of 1996 draft; signed June 15, 1996; On disabled list, April 6-Sept. 25, 2000. **PRO CAREER:** 1996: Led Pioneer League in saves (10) and relief points (30) and tied for second in games finished (14); named to Pioneer League post-season All-Star team; 1997: Won his first three starts and had a perfect 5-0 record when he went on the disabled list for good on June 9 with elbow tendinitis; named to South Atlantic League mid-season All-Star team; 1998: Returned from right elbow surgery on July 4 and allowed only one run in first five outings; struck out 20 batters in 19 innings; in August and September compiled ERA of 3.08; with runners on base and two out opposing batters hit .071 (1-14); with runners in scoring position and two out opposing batters hit .111 (1-9); 1999: tied for fourth in Southern League in shutouts (1);led entire organization in ERA (2.75); opened season with Dunedin and did not allow an earned run till fourth start; on May 31, vs. Sarasota tossed complete game three hit victory; made 10 quality starts of 13 outings; with Knoxville had rough first outing then settled down to make 10 quality starts in 15 outings; in next to last start of season on August 30, vs. Mobile threw complete game five hit shutout; at both stops catchers were able to throw out over 40% of would be base stealers; did not allow a base hit with bases loaded all season (0-8); started seven games for Lara, Venezuelan Winter League compiling 1-3, 4.00 ERA; 2000: On disabled list, April 6-Sept 25, with elbow surgery.

Year	Club & League	W-L	ERA	G	GS	CG	ShO	SV	IP	H	R	ER	HR	HB	BB-IBB	SO	WP	BK	OBA
1996	Medcine Hat (PIO)	0-0	4.56	20	0	0	0	10	23.2	29	16	12	0	2	14-0	31	1	0	.296
1997	Hagerstown (SAL)	5-0	3.32	10	10	0	0	0	59.2	52	25	22	1	5	20-0	58	5	4	.234
1998	Dunedin (FSL)	1-0	4.26	14	0	0	0	0	19.0	20	14	9	1	2	11-0	20	4	1	.270
1999	Dunedin (FSL)	6-6	2.28	14	13	1	0	0	90.2	73	36	23	1	2	30-1	58	5	1	.215
	Knoxville (SOU)	5-3	3.22	15	15	1	1	0	86.2	81	36	31	4	4	34-0	49	7	2	.257
2000									Injured — Did not play										
Minor Totals		17-9	3.12	73	38	2	1	10	279.2	255	127	97	7	15	109-1	216	22	8	.243

Bowles, Brian Christopher

Pitcher ... **HT:** 6-5; **WT:** 220 ... **B-T:** R-R ... **BORN:** 18 AUG, 1976, Harbor City, CA **RESIDES:** Manhattan Beach, CA ... **EDUCATION:** Cal-Santa Barbara ... **TRANSACTIONS:** Selected by Blue Jays in 50th round of 1994 draft; signed Aug. 23, 1994. **PRO CAREER:** 1995: Missed most of the season due to shoulder tendinitis; 1996: Led Medicine Hat staff in appearances (24); 1997: Tied for New York-Penn League lead in games started (16) and led St. Catharines staff in innings pitched (78.2); went 3-2, 2.18 ERA in July (33 IP, 27 H, 5 BB, 29 SO); 1998: Began season with Dunedin then moved to Hagerstown; in FSL, compiled 2.86 ERA in road appearances; with runners on base and two out, opponents batted .160 (4-25); with two out and runners in scoring position, opponents batted .071 (1-14); at Hagerstown in May, compiled 0.93 ERA in four appearances; from June 18-July 2 allowed only one earned run in six consecutive appearances; in SAL through August 4 (24 games) maintained ERA of 3.04; had road ERA of 2.48 in 14 games with Hagerstown; 1999: Second on Hagerstown in appearances (48) and games finished (22); in April compiled 1.50 ERA in eight outings; in only start of season on August 11, vs. Charleston-WV pitched five innings without allowing an earned run; from July 31-August 26 did not allow an earned run in nine games over 18.2 innings; for season averaged better than a strikeout per inning; leadoff hitters batted .194 (13-67) against him; with runners in scoring position and two out, opponents batted .152 (7-46). 2000: Tied for second on team in appearances (49); held left-hand batters to .168 average; fanned ten batters in 4 2/3 innings of relief against Jacksonville, August 2; was 3-1 in 11 appearances in August; played for Lara in the Venezuelan Winter League.

Year	Club & League	W-L	ERA	G	GS	CG	ShO	SV	IP	H	R	ER	HR	HB	BB-IBB	SO	WP	BK	OBA
1995	Blue Jays (GULF)	0-1	2.40	8	0	0	0	0	15.0	18	12	4	2	1	3-0	11	2	1	.277
1996	Medcine Hat (PIO)	2-2	6.35	24	0	0	0	1	39.2	53	35	28	5	5	21-1	29	9	0	.325
1997	Hagerstown (SAL)	1-0	6.97	4	0	0	0	0	10.1	14	10	8	2	1	5-0	9	1	0	.333
	Dunedin (FSL)	0-2	7.53	7	1	0	0	0	14.1	20	14	12	2	0	7-1	9	3	1	.333
	St.cathrnes (NYP)	5-8	5.03	16	16	0	0	0	78.2	76	53	44	6	11	35-0	64	4	1	.252
1998	Dunedin (FSL)	1-2	3.33	9	2	1	0	0	27.0	32	13	10	2	1	16-0	17	1	1	.299
	Hagerstown (SAL)	2-4	4.52	31	4	0	0	0	67.2	80	41	34	4	9	18-1	48	6	0	.292
1999	Hagerstown (SAL)	6-2	3.97	48	1	0	0	3	79.1	73	41	35	4	12	39-3	80	9	0	.246
2000	Tennessee (SOU)	4-4	2.98	49	0	0	0	0	81.2	64	31	27	1	8	36-1	72	11	0	.218
Minor Totals		21-25	4.39	196	24	1	0	4	413.2	430	250	202	28	48	180-7	339	46	4	.268

Brosseau, Richard F.

Shortstop ... **HT:** 5-11; **WT:** 180 ... **B-T:** L-R ... **BORN:** 22 SEP, 1978, Minneapolis, MN **RESIDES:** North Oaks, MN ... **EDUCATION:** Minnesota ... **TRANSACTIONS:** Selected by Blue Jays in 16th round of 2000 draft; signed June 15, 2000; Selected by Blue Jays in 16th round of 2000 draft; signed June 15, 2000.

Year	Club & League	AVG	G	AB	R	H	TB	2B	3B	HR	RBI	SH-SF	HP	BB-IBB	SO	SB-CS	GIDP	SLG	OBP
2000	Queens (NYP)	.164	15	55	9	9	15	0	3	0	2	1-0	0	4-0	15	2-0	0	.273	.220

Cabrera, Omar A. Lopez

Pitcher ... HT: 6-4; **WT:** 160 ... **B-T:** L-L **BORN:** 24 APR, 1983, San Pedro De Macoris, DR ... **RESIDES:** San Pedro de Macoris, DR ... **TRANSACTIONS:** Signed as a non-drafted free agent by Blue Jays, Nov. 29, 1999 ... **PRO CAREER:** 2001 will be his first professional season.

Caraballo, Angel Ramon

Pitcher ... HT: 6-0; **WT:** 180 ... **B-T:** R-R ... **BORN:** 20 JAN, 1980, Guanta, VZ **RESIDES:** Guanta, VZ ... **TRANSACTIONS:** Signed as non-drafted free agent by White Sox, May 5, 1997; Selected by Blue Jays from White Sox in Rule 5 minor league draft, Dec. 11, 2000. **PRO CAREER:** 1998: Led Arizona League in games started (13) and finished third in innings (63.2); struck out ten batters in four innings against Diamondbacks, July 26; 1999: Finished second in Appalachian League in wins (8), strikeouts (88) and innings (81); won eight straight starts, July 1-August 10; was 6-0 with 2.48 ERA in July; allowed two runs or less in first nine starts, June 20-August 5; fanned 13 batters vs. Johnson City, July 8; 2000: Tied for Appalachian League in wins (7) and games started (13), second in innings (77.1), seventh in ERA (3.14) and fifth in lowest batting average against (.230); was 5-0 with 1.72 ERA at home; pitched for Oriente of Venezuelan Winter League.

Year	Club & League	W-L	ERA	G	GS	CG	ShO	SV	IP	H	R	ER	HR	HB	BB-IBB	SO	WP	BK	OBA
1997	Guacara-1 (VSL)	5-4	3.78	13	0	0	0	0	64.1	63	38	27	0	0	32-0	42	0	0	—
1998	White Sox (ARIZ)	3-5	7.49	14	13	0	0	0	63.2	90	71	53	5	8	36-0	57	11	8	.326
1999	Bristol (APPY)	8-2	4.00	13	13	1	0	0	81.0	88	40	36	11	4	27-0	88	10	5	.276
2000	Bristol (APPY)	7-4	3.14	13	13	0	0	0	77.1	67	39	27	8	2	27-0	61	6	0	.235
Minor Totals		23-15	4.49	53	39	1	0	0	286.1	308	188	143	24	14	122-0	248	27	13	—

Cardwell, Brian Dean

Pitcher ... HT: 6-10; **WT:** 215 ... **B-T:** R-R ... **BORN:** 30 DEC, 1980, Marion, IN **RESIDES:** Kiefer, OK ... **TRANSACTIONS:** Selected by Blue Jays in fourth round of 1999 draft; signed June 8, 1999. **PRO CAREER:** 1999: At Medicine Hat split season between starting and relief; in four starts was 2-0 with 3.78 ERA; picked up only save of year on July 29, vs. Great Falls with four inning stint. 2000: Was 2-0 with 3.14 in six starts on road with Queens; fanned nine batters in a game twice, June 20 vs. Hudson Valley and August 14 against Vermont.

Year	Club & League	W-L	ERA	G	GS	CG	ShO	SV	IP	H	R	ER	HR	HB	BB-IBB	SO	WP	BK	OBA
1999	Medcine Hat (PIO)	2-1	5.16	10	4	0	0	1	29.2	34	22	17	5	4	8-0	26	3	1	.276
2000	Hagerstown (SAL)	0-5	9.09	11	6	0	0	0	31.2	41	38	32	7	1	21-0	29	2	1	.313
	Queens (NYP)	2-4	4.71	12	11	1	0	0	49.2	49	32	26	6	6	19-0	61	4	0	.268
Minor Totals		4-10	6.08	33	21	1	0	1	111.0	124	92	75	18	11	48-0	116	9	2	.284

Carter, Shannon Michael

Outfielder ... HT: 6-0; **WT:** 180 ... **B-T:** L-L ... **BORN:** 23 MAR, 1979, El Reno, OK **RESIDES:** El Reno, OK ... **EDUCATION:** HS ... **TRANSACTIONS:** Selected by Orioles in fourth round of 1997 draft; signed June 4, 1997; Traded by Orioles with RHP Nerio Rodriguez to Blue Jays for RHP Juan Guzman, July 31, 1998. **PRO CAREER:** 1997: Got off to a quick start by batting .345 (10-29) in the first eight games and was leading the Gulf Coast League in runs (12) and stolen bases (8) through July 1; 1998: Began season with Bluefield, where he batted .309 (17-55) in June; had back-to-back four-hit games against Johnson City on June 19-20 (8-10, 5 R, 2 SB); after aquisition by Blue Jays, played with St. Catharines from August 2, till end of season; home batting average of .414 (12-29); 1999: Led St. Catharines in triples (4) and stolen bases (15); second on team in runs (38) and average (.279), third in hits (60); had nine game hit streak from July 10-20, batted .385 (15-39) with nine runs scored; on July 26, vs. Mohawk Valley went 3-for-3 with four runs scored; finished New York-Penn season batting .400 (8-20) in last five games; had 19 multi-hit games in 55 opportunities; batted .444 (4-9) as pinch-hitter; called to Syracuse for two games at season's end; 2000: Tied for South Atlantic League lead in double plays for outfielders with 4; led team in games (123), runs (74) and stolen bases (33) and was second in hits (121) and triples (7); led organization in stolen bases; hit .343 against lefties and hit .312 with 39 RBI with runners on base; batted .306 with 13 RBI in June.

Year	Club & League	AVG	G	AB	R	H	TB	2B	3B	HR	RBI	SH-SF	HP	BB-IBB	SO	SB-CS	GIDP	SLG	OBP
1997	Orioles (GULF)	.195	50	159	22	31	38	3	2	0	11	0-0	4	12-0	45	13-5	1	.239	.269
1998	Bluefield (APPY)	.247	36	150	23	37	42	2	0	1	10	0-0	0	9-0	35	14-3	1	.280	.289
	St. Cathrnes (NYP)	.262	24	61	8	16	22	3	0	1	7	1-0	1	4-0	14	2-0	1	.361	.318
1999	St. Cathrnes (NYP)	.279	61	215	38	60	76	5	4	1	16	1-1	2	11-0	54	15-6	1	.353	.319
	Syracuse (INT)	.111	2	9	0	1	1	0	0	0	0	0-0	0	0-0	2	0-0	2	.111	.111
2000	Hagerstown (SAL)	.273	123	443	74	121	150	15	7	0	39	1-0	11	45-0	129	33-6	5	.339	.355
Minor Totals		.257	296	037	165	266	329	28	13	3	83	3-1	18	81-0	279	77-20	11	.317	.321

Casey, Joseph Lyle (Joe)

Pitcher ... HT: 6-0; **WT:** 192 ... **B-T:** R-R ... **BORN:** 25 JAN, 1979, Media, PA **RESIDES:** Honeybrook, PA ... **TRANSACTIONS:** Selected by Blue Jays in eighth round of 1997 draft; signed June 15, 1997. **PRO CAREER:** 1997: Tied for fourth in New York-Penn League with seven wins; won six out of seven starts July 20-August 22; went 3-1, 2.51 ERA in August; 1998: Only 11 of 24 would-be basestealers were successful against him, as his catchers threw out 54.2%; opened season with Hagerstown going 2-7 with a 4.66 ERA; in relief was 0-0 (2.25 ERA, 12 IP, 10 H, 14 SO), opponents batted .238 (10-42); pitched last month of season with St. Catharines; 1999: Led South Atlantic League in games started (28); third on Hagerstown in innings pitched (142); won back-to-back games on May 15-21, pitching 12 innings allowing just nine hits and three earned runs; on June 5, vs. Greensboro tossed eight shutout innings allowing just three hits en-route to victory; finished June 2-2 with a 2.43 ERA, allowing only 18 hits in 33.1 innings; on July 17, vs. Piedmont recorded win with seven, three-hit shutout innings; made 12 quality starts; opponents batted .152 (7-46) with runners in scoring position and two outs; 2000: Tied for fourth in Florida State League in games started (27) and fifth in innings (158.1); led team in starts, innings and strikeouts (96) and tied for team lead in wins (10); was 4-1 with 3.35 ERA in August.

Year	Club & League	W-L	ERA	G	GS	CG	ShO	SV	IP	H	R	ER	HR	HB	BB-IBB	SO	WP	BK	OBA
1997	St.cathrnes (NYP)	7-4	4.36	14	11	0	0	1	64.0	59	42	31	6	3	23-0	43	11	0	.234
1998	Hagerstown (SAL)	2-7	4.66	22	16	0	0	0	77.1	84	53	40	6	6	41-2	62	4	1	.290
	St.cathrnes (NYP)	1-2	12.27	4	3	0	0	0	11.0	18	19	15	1	2	11-0	9	2	0	.353
1999	Hagerstown (SAL)	7-14	4.69	28	28	0	0	0	142.0	150	99	74	10	10	64-0	79	25	3	.270
2000	Dunedin (FSL)	10-8	4.21	27	27	0	0	0	158.1	151	88	74	7	14	74-2	96	21	2	.259
Minor Totals		27-35	4.65	95	85	0	0	1	452.2	462	301	234	30	35	213-4	289	63	6	.267

Cash, Kevin F.

Catcher ... **HT:** 6-0; **WT:** 185 ... **B-T:** R-R ... **BORN:** 06 DEC, 1977, Tampa, FL **RESIDES:** Lutz, FL ... **EDUCATION:** Florida St. ... **TRANSACTIONS:** Signed as non-drafted free agent by Blue Jays, Aug. 7, 1999. **PRO CAREER:** 2000: Led South Atlantic League catchers by nailing 37 of 67 base stealers (.552); belted grand slam HR against Delmarva, July 12; led team in homers (10), all against right-hand pitching, despite playing in just 59 games; hit .291 at home; hit homers in three consecutive games, August 26-29.

Year	Club & League	AVG	G	AB	R	H	TB	2B	3B	HR	RBI	SH-SF	HP	BB-IBB	SO	SB-CS	GIDP	SLG	OBP
2000	Hagerstown (SAL)	.245	59	196	28	48	90	10	1	10	27	1-1	1	22-1	54	5-3	7	.459	.323

Cassidy, Scott Robert

Pitcher ... **HT:** 6-2; **WT:** 175 ... **B-T:** R-R ... **BORN:** 03 OCT, 1975, Syracuse, NY **RESIDES:** Clay, NY ... **EDUCATION:** Le Moyne (NY) ... **TRANSACTIONS:** Signed as non-drafted free agent by Blue Jays, May 21, 1998. **PRO CAREER:** 1998: Named to Pioneer League Post-Season All-Star team; tied for league lead in wins (8), ranked second in earned run average (2.43) and strikeouts (82), fourth in innings (81.1) and tied for fifth in starts (14); led league starting pitchers in BB/9 IP ratio (1.58), ranked second in baserunners/9 IP ratio (10.17) and fifth in batting average against (.240); led Medicine Hat staff in wins (8); named league Pitcher-of-the-Week July 20-26, when he went 1-0, 0.69 ERA (13 IP, 7 H, 1 ER, 3 BB, 12 SO); selected Organization Pitcher-of-the-Month for July when he went 5-0, 0.97 ERA (37 IP, 30 H, 6 BB, 36 SO); won last three starts of season going 3-0, 1.80 ERA (20 IP, 13 H, 5 BB, 17 SO); compiled home record of 3-1, 1.98 ERA (41 IP, 30 H, 5 BB, 35 SO), opponents batted .205 (30-146); 1999: Second in South Atlantic League in wins (13), strikeouts (178) and innings pitched (170.2); fourth in games started (27); fifth in BB/9 IP starters (1.58); led organization in strikeouts, third in ERA (3.27) and fourth in wins; Led Hagerstown in wins, ERA, strikeouts and complete games (1), second in innings pitched; on May 7, vs. Hickory pitched eight shutout innings striking out ten; from June 7-27 won four consecutive starts with an ERA of 2.87; on July 8, vs. Delmarva tossed six shutout innings, allowing three hits while striking out nine for the win; finished July 2-1, 1.98 ERA striking out 46 batters in 36.1 innings in six starts; pitched seven shutout innings allowing three hits striking out seven for victory on August 15, vs. Piedmont; finished season with 6-to-1 (178-30) strikeout to walk ratio; made 18 quality starts; took the loss in one playoff start, pitching eight innings allowing three runs while striking out seven; 2000: Was 8-3 with 1.20 ERA as starter in Dunedin; won eight consecutive decisions, April 17-May 28, including six straight starts, May 3-28; was 6-0 with 1.10 ERA in May; allowed two runs or fewer in 12 of his 13 starts; tossed 27 1/3 scoreless innings,May 8-28; pitched first six innings of combo no-hitter against Ft. Myers, April 22; was 4-1 with 0.78 ERA on road; held right-hand batters to .145 average; promoted to Tennessee in mid-June; led Blue Jays organization in ERA (2.82), tied for second in wins (11) and third in strikeouts (128).

Year	Club & League	W-L	ERA	G	GS	CG	ShO	SV	IP	H	R	ER	HR	HB	BB-IBB	SO	WP	BK	OBA
1998	Medcine Hat (PIO)	8-1	2.43	15	14	0	0	0	81.1	71	31	22	4	5	14-0	82	2	0	.236
1999	Hagerstown (SAL)	13-7	3.27	27	27	1	0	0	170.2	151	78	62	13	21	30-0	178	3	2	.236
2000	Dunedin (FSL)	9-3	1.33	14	13	1	0	0	88.0	53	15	13	4	3	34-2	89	4	0	.177
	Tennessee (SOU)	2-2	5.91	8	7	0	0	0	42.2	48	30	28	7	4	15-0	39	3	0	.289
Minor Totals		32-13	2.94	64	61	2	0	0	382.2	323	154	125	28	33	93-2	388	12	2	.230

Castellanos, Hugo P.

Pitcher ... **HT:** 6-4; **WT:** 204 **B-T:** R-R ... **BORN:** 30 JUN, 1980, Nuevo Laredo, Mexico **RESIDES:** Nuevo Laredo, Mexico ... **TRANSACTIONS:** Signed as non-drafted free agent by Devil Rays, Aug. 26, 1996; Released by Devil Rays, Feb. 3, 1998; Signed by Blue Jays, May 10, 2000. **PRO CAREER:** 2000: Led South Atlantic League relievers with lowest average against (.123); Tied for team lead in games finished (19) and was second in saves (7) at Hagerstown; had 0.64 ERA and four saves in 13 road road appearances; did not allow an earned run in 11 games in July; did not allow a hit in six consecutive appearances covering nine innings, June 27-July 16.

Year	Club & League	W-L	ERA	G	GS	CG	ShO	SV	IP	H	R	ER	HR	HB	BB-IBB	SO	WP	BK	OBA
1997							Injured — Did not play												
1998	Laredo (MEX)	0-2	11.74	8	2	0	0	0	7.2	11	11	10	0	0	15-0	8	4	0	.344
1999	Laredo (MEX)	0-0	6.94	24	1	0	0	0	36.1	44	32	28	6	1	24-1	22	3	0	.293
2000	Hagerstown (SAL)	0-3	1.64	29	0	0	0	0	38.1	16	11	7	1	5	18-1	30	5	0	.123
	Dunedin (FSL)	0-0	4.50	4	0	0	0	1	8.0	5	4	4	1	0	10-1	5	0	0	.200
Minor Totals		0-5	4.88	65	3	0	0	8	90.1	76	58	49	8	6	67-3	65	12	0	.226

Castro, Kendall

Pitcher ... **HT:** 6-4; **WT:** 180 ... **B-T:** R-R ... **BORN:** 09 AUG, 1983, La Romana, DR ... **RESIDES:** La Romana, DR ... **PRO CAREER:** 2001 will be his first professional season.

Ceballos, Carlos M. Taveras

Pitcher ... **HT:** 6-2; **WT:** 170 ... **B-T:** R-R ... **BORN:** 29 NOV, 1981, La Romana, DR **RESIDES:** La Romana, DR ... **TRANSACTIONS:** Signed as non-drafted free agent by Blue Jays, May 10, 1999. **PRO CAREER:** 1999: In Dominican Summer League split season between starting and relief; fifth on team in ERA (3.21), strikeouts (44) and innings pitched (56); 2000: Used as both starter and reliever; was 8-0 with 2.12 ERA and 62 strikeouts in 63.2 innings.

Year	Club & League	W-L	ERA	G	GS	CG	ShO	SV	IP	H	R	ER	HR	HB	BB-IBB	SO	WP	BK	OBA
1999	Sd Blue Jay (DSL)	2-4	3.21	16	6	1	0	0	56.0	45	25	20	1	4	16-0	44	3	1	.214
2000	Toronto (DSL)	8-0	2.12	14	6	0	0	2	63.2	50	20	15	4	1	21-0	62	5	2	.218
Minor Totals		10-4	2.63	30	12	1	0	2	119.2	95	45	35	5	5	37-0	106	8	3	.216

Chacin, Gustavo G. Adolfo

Pitcher ... HT: 5-11; **WT:** 185 ... **B-T:** L-L ... **BORN:** 04 DEC, 1980, Maracaibo, Zulia, VZ **RESIDES:** Maracaibo, Zulia, VZ ... **TRANSACTIONS:** Signed as non-drafted free agent by Blue Jays, July 3, 1998. **PRO CAREER:** 1998: Led Dominican Summer League Blue Jays in SO/9IP at 13.74; third-best ERA on staff among starters (2.70); pitched two shutouts in six starts; opponents batted .212 (28-132); did not give up a home run in 36.2 innings; pitched winter ball for Lara, Venezuelan League going 0-1, 3.68 ERA; 1999: Pioneer league all-star LHP; Third in League in ERA (3.09); Led Medicine Hat in ERA; second on team in wins (4), starts (9), innings pitched (64) and strikeouts (50); alternated between starting and relief; as starter was 3-3, 2.42 ERA with three quality starts; finished June 0-1, 1.10 ERA allowing just eight hits while striking out 15 in 16.1 innings; won two consecutive games on July 2-7; only save of year came on August 3, vs. Great Falls when he set down 11-of-12 batters in 3.1 innings, striking out three without allowing a hit; road ERA for season 1.97 in 32 innings; pitched for Lara, Venezuelan Winter League, posting 3.14 ERA in 53.2 innings in 14 games, 10 starts; 2000: Tied for third on team in wins (9) and second in innings (127.2); won five consecutive starts, May 10-31; was 5-0 with 3.44 ERA in May; was 7-3 with 3.77 ERA at home.

Year	Club & League	W-L	ERA	G	GS	CG	ShO	SV	IP	H	R	ER	HR	HB	BB-IBB	SO	WP	BK	OBA
1998	Blue Jays (DSL)	3-2	2.70	9	6	0	2	0	36.2	28	12	11	0	1	15-0	56	2	2	.212
1999	Medcine Hat (PIO)	4-3	3.09	15	9	0	0	1	64.0	68	33	22	6	7	23-0	50	4	3	.281
2000	Dunedin (FSL)	9-5	4.02	25	21	0	0	0	127.2	138	69	57	14	3	64-0	77	9	0	.269
	Tennessee (SOU)	0-2	12.60	2	2	0	0	0	5.0	10	7	7	1	1	6-0	5	0	1	.417
Minor Totals		16-12	3.74	51	38	0	2	1	233.1	244	121	97	21	12	108-0	188	15	6	.268

Chadwick, John T.

Pitcher ... HT: 6-4; **WT:** 225 ... **B-T:** L-R ... **BORN:** 03 MAY, 1978, Toronto, ON, Canada **RESIDES:** Brampton, ON, Canada ... **TRANSACTIONS:** Signed as a non-drafted free agent by the Blue Jays, July 20, 2000 ... **PRO CAREER:** 2001 will be his first professional season.

Chiaffredo, Paul Franklin

Catcher ... HT: 6-2; **WT:** 206 ... **B-T:** R-R ... **BORN:** 30 MAY, 1976, Atlanta, GA **RESIDES:** San Jose, CA ... **EDUCATION:** Santa Clara (CA) ... **TRANSACTIONS:** Selected by Blue Jays in sixth round of 1997 draft; signed June 12, 1997. **PRO CAREER:** 1997: Led St. Catharines squad in being hit by pitches (9); threw out 31.7% of would-be basestealers, nailing 19 runners in 60 attempts; 1998: Threw out 22.2% of would-be basestealers, nailing 30 out of 135; started slowly at plate; from July 23-August 3, hit in seven straight games, batting .360 (9-25); batted .319 (15-47) in August; with bases loaded, hit .500 (6-12, 9 RBI); 1999: Opened season with Knoxville but moved to Dunedin after 11 games; led Dunedin in hit-by-pitch (12); hit safely in first seven games with Dunedin, batting .417 (10-24) with five runs and four RBI; finished May batting .364 (28-77); from June 5-August 4 played 43 consecutive errorless games; batted .304 (21-69) against left-handers; cut down 35.4% (34-96) of would be base stealers; 2000: Hit grand slam against Lakeland, July 8 while at Dunedin; had four-hit game for Hagerstown vs. Hickory on May 24.

Year	Club & League	AVG	G	AB	R	H	TB	2B	3B	HR	RBI	SH-SF	HP	BB-IBB	SO	SB-CS	GIDP	SLG	OBP
1997	St.cathrnes (NYP)	.239	48	163	20	39	55	8	1	2	15	1-1	9	9-0	42	5-2	1	.337	.313
1998	Dunedin (FSL)	.234	89	290	34	68	99	19	0	4	41	6-3	6	16-0	68	1-3	8	.341	.286
1999	Knoxville (SOU)	.077	11	39	3	3	7	1	0	1	3	2-0	2	0-0	10	0-0	2	.179	.122
	Dunedin (FSL)	.253	88	261	39	66	101	22	2	3	21	4-4	12	17-0	44	1-4	12	.387	.323
2000	Tennessee (SOU)	.111	18	63	6	7	8	1	0	0	2	0-0	1	5-0	16	0-1	0	.127	.188
	Hagerstown (SAL)	.356	13	45	9	16	25	6	0	1	5	0-0	3	9-0	6	0-0	0	.556	.491
	Dunedin (FSL)	.289	11	38	7	11	18	1	0	2	6	0-0	1	5-0	9	0-0	0	.474	.386
Minor Totals		.234	278	899	118	210	313	58	3	13	93	13-8	34	61-0	195	7-10	23	.348	.304

Chourio, Junior J. Pirela

Second Baseman ... HT: 6-3; **WT:** 170 ... **B-T:** R-R ... **BORN:** 23 MAR, 1983, Maracaibo, VZ **RESIDES:** Maracaibo, VZ ... **TRANSACTIONS:** Signed as non-drafted free agent by Blue Jays, Sept. 5, 1999 ... **PRO CAREER:** 2001 will be his first professional season.

Chulk, Charles V.

Pitcher ... HT: 6-2; **WT:** 185 ... **B-T:** R-R ... **BORN:** 19 DEC, 1978, Miami, FL **RESIDES:** Miami, FL ... **EDUCATION:** St. Thomas (MN) ... **TRANSACTIONS:** Selected by Blue Jays in 12th round of 2000 draft; signed June 12, 2000. **PRO CAREER:** 2000: Finished sixth in Pioneer League in ERA (3.80); Was 1-0 with 1.80 ERA in four starts in July.

Year	Club & League	W-L	ERA	G	GS	CG	ShO	SV	IP	H	R	ER	HR	HB	BB-IBB	SO	WP	BK	OBA
2000	Medcine Hat (PIO)	2-4	3.80	14	13	0	0	0	68.2	75	36	29	5	2	20-0	51	3	0	.277

Clark, Chivas E.

Outfielder ... HT: 6-2; **WT:** 185 ... **B-T:** L-L ... **BORN:** 25 NOV, 1978, Macon, GA **RESIDES:** Macon, GA ... **TRANSACTIONS:** Selected by Blue Jays in 38th round of 1997 draft; signed Aug. 17, 1997; On disabled list, June 16-Sept. 14, 1998. **PRO CAREER:** 1998: On disabled list June 16-September 14, 1998; 1999: Fifth in Pioneer League in doubles (18); Led Medicine Hat in at-bats (267), runs (56), doubles, triples (3) and hit-by-pitch (6); hit home runs in back-to-back games on June 23-24 vs. Great Falls; from July 6-11 hit in five straight games, batting .636 (14-22) with four doubles; on July 15, vs. Ogden hit two home runs in two at-bats; from July 27-August 3 hit in eight straight games, batting .375 (12-32) with 11 runs and six RBI; had 10 game hit streak from August 16-26 batted .356 (16-45) with 10 runs; season home batting average .290 (38-131); 2000: Reached base safely in ten consecutive plate appearances (2 singles and 8 walks), July 9-14, while with Queens.

Year	Club & League	AVG	G	AB	R	H	TB	2B	3B	HR	RBI	SH-SF	HP	BB-IBB	SO	SB-CS	GIDP	SLG	OBP
1998	Injured	.000	0	0	0	0	0	0	0	0	0	0-0	0	0-0	0	0-0	0	.000	.000
1999	Medcine Hat (PIO)	.270	70	267	56	72	114	18	3	6	29	1-1	6	38-1	78	12-5	1	.427	.372
2000	Queens (NYP)	.220	15	41	9	9	12	1	1	0	5	2-1	0	17-0	9	2-1	0	.293	.441
	Hagerstown (SAL)	.159	37	113	15	18	24	6	0	0	10	2-0	1	15-1	27	1-2	0	.212	.264
Minor Totals		.235	122	421	80	99	150	25	4	6	44	5-2	7	70-2	114	15-8	1	.356	.352

Cordero, Dani Vasquez

Pitcher ... **HT:** 6-2; **WT:** 165 ... **B-T:** R-R ... **BORN:** 03 APR, 1984, Hato Mayor del Rey, DR **RESIDES:** Hato Mayor Del Rey, DR ... **TRANSACTIONS:** Signed as a non-drafted free agent by the Blue Jays, Nov. 13, 2000 ... **PRO CAREER:** 2001 will be his first professional season.

Cordero, Octavio

Outfielder ... **HT:** 5-9; **WT:** 150 ... **B-T:** L-L ... **BORN:** 19 OCT, 1983, La Romana, DR **RESIDES:** La Romana, DR ... **TRANSACTIONS:** Signed as a non-drafted free agent by the Blue Jays, July 12, 2000 ... **PRO CAREER:** 2001 will be his first professional season.

Cornett, Brad Byron

Pitcher ... **HT:** 6-3; **WT:** 6-3 ... **B-T:** R-R ... **BORN:** 04 FEB, 1969, Lamesa, TX ... **EDUCATION:** Lubbock Christn.(TX) **RESIDES:** Odessa, TX **TRANSACTIONS:** Signed as non-drafted free agent by Blue Jays, June 15, 1992; On disabled list, April 3-Sept. 10, 1997; Released by Blue Jays, Dec. 15, 1997; Signed by Diamondbacks, Jan. 23, 1998; Traded by Diamondbacks to Brewers for C Troy O'Neal, May 8, 1998; Granted free agency, Oct. 16, 1998; Signed by Devil Rays, May 28, 2000; Granted free agency, Oct. 15, 2000. **PRO CAREER:** 1992: Led team in appearances (25); averaged 9.6 SO/9 IP; 1993: Finished second in South Atlantic League in ERA (2.40), tied for third in strikeouts (161) and fourth in innings (172.1); was second among league starters in fewest walks per nine innings (1.58); was 3-1 with 2.30 ERA in six starts in July; pitched one inning in S.A.L. All-Star game; pitched for Sydney in Australian Baseball League and earned Pitcher of the Year award after going 10-4 with 2.45 ERA and nine complete games; 1994: Combined for 3-5 record and 2.08 ERA in ten starts at Knoxville and Syracuse; made Major League debut vs. Chicago, June 8; earned first M.L. victory against Texas, July 24, allowing no earned runs over six innings; had 3.18 ERA in day games over 17 IP; strained ligament in right elbow and did not pitch after August 1; 1995: On disabled list, July 21-September 3, with right elbow tendonitis; 1996: On disabled list, April 4-June 2, had right elbow UCL reconstruction surgery; 1997: On disabled list, April 3-September 10, right elbow UCL repair; 1998: On disabled list, July 19-September 12, with right shoulder tendonitis; 1999: Finished second in Atlantic League in strikeouts (118), third in innings (162.1), tied for fourth in games started (23), tied for fourth in complete games (3) and seventh in ERA (3.94); tossed first complete game since 1994 against Atlantic City, June 2; had CG, 11 strikeout performance vs. Bridgeport, August 1; fired two-hitter against Atlantic City, August 19; 2000: Won three straight starts, June 22-July 2; allowed only five runs over 25 innings in last six appearances (two starts and four relief outings) with 23 strikeouts.

Year	Club & League	W-L	ERA	G	GS	CG	ShO	SV	IP	H	R	ER	HR	HB	BB-IBB	SO	WP	BK	OBA
1992	St.cathrnes (NYP)	4-1	3.60	25	0	0	0	0	60.0	54	30	24	6	3	10-0	64	5	0	.238
1993	Hagerstown (SAL)	10-8	2.40	31	21	3	1	3	172.1	164	77	46	6	5	31-2	161	6	1	.247
1994	Knoxville (SOU)	2-3	2.41	7	7	1	0	0	37.1	34	18	10	2	1	6-0	26	3	0	.238
	Syracuse (INT)	1-2	1.42	3	3	0	0	0	19.0	18	8	3	0	0	9-1	12	0	0	.240
	TORONTO (AL)	1-3	6.68	9	4	0	0	0	31.0	40	25	23	1	3	11-2	22	2	0	.331
1995	TORONTO (AL)	0-0	9.00	5	0	0	0	0	5.0	9	6	5	1	1	3-0	4	1	0	.429
	Syracuse (INT)	0-1	4.91	3	3	0	0	0	11.0	13	6	6	1	0	4-0	3	0	0	.295
1996	Dunedin (FSL)	0-1	8.59	4	0	0	0	0	7.1	15	7	7	1	1	3-0	5	1	1	.405
1998	Tucson (PCL)	1-2	7.86	6	6	0	0	0	26.1	44	25	23	6	0	6-0	12	1	0	.373
	El Paso (TEX)	0-2	5.17	3	3	0	0	0	15.2	22	16	9	4	0	5-0	10	3	1	.319
	Louisville (INT)	3-3	3.65	12	8	0	0	0	61.2	64	30	25	9	2	14-0	34	1	0	.272
1999	Lehigh Val (ATL)	11-9	3.94	23	23	3	0	0	162.1	172	84	71	17	3	37-1	118	0	1	.272
2000	Lehigh Val (ATL)	2-1	4.78	5	4	0	0	0	26.1	33	15	14	0	0	10-0	20	2	0	.295
	Durham (INT)	4-5	4.26	19	12	0	0	0	88.2	100	46	42	7	2	24-1	72	1	1	.282
Minor Totals		25-28	3.51	113	63	4	1	4	499.1	528	263	195	42	14	112-4	399	21	4	.268
MAJOR TOTALS		1-3	7.00	14	4	0	0	0	36.0	49	31	28	2	4	14-2	26	3	0	.345

Cosby, Robert D. (Rob)

Third Baseman ... **HT:** 6-2; **WT:** 205 ... **B-T:** R-R ... **BORN:** 02 APR, 1981, San Juan, PR **RESIDES:** Rio Piedras, PR ... **TRANSACTIONS:** Selected by Blue Jays in 10th round of 1999 draft; signed June 30, 1999. **PRO CAREER:** 1999: Led Medicine Hat in sacrifice flies (4), third in stolen bases (10); began season with seven game hit streak, batting .321 (9-28) with 11 RBI; from July 28-August 6 hit in 10 straight games batting .439 (18-41) with eight runs; had nine game hit streak from August 13-25 driving in eight runs; appeared in nine games for Caguas, Puerto Rican League, batting .222; 2000: Reached base safely by hit or walk in twenty consecutive games, July 24-August 17 while at Queens; had nine-game hitting streak, July 24-August 2; played for Caguas in Puerto Rican Winter League.

Year	Club & League	AVG	G	AB	R	H	TB	2B	3B	HR	RBI	SH-SF	HP	BB-IBB	SO	SB-CS	GIDP	SLG	OBP
1999	Medcine Hat (PIO)	.270	46	178	22	48	68	9	1	3	25	0-4	0	12-0	29	10-3	3	.382	.309
2000	Hagerstown (SAL)	.237	77	291	31	69	90	9	0	4	29	0-2	0	16-0	37	2-3	7	.309	.275
	Queens (NYP)	.270	42	163	15	44	52	8	0	2	22	0-1	0	14-1	22	4-2	3	.319	.326
Minor Totals		.255	165	632	68	161	210	26	1	7	76	0-7	0	42-1	88	16-8	13	.332	.298

Davenport, Ulyses Ron (Ron)

Infielder ... **HT:** 6-2; **WT:** 190 ... **B-T:** L-R ... **BORN:** 16 OCT, 1981, Washington, NC **RESIDES:** Raleigh, NC ... **TRANSACTIONS:** Selected by Blue Jays in 22nd round of 2000 draft; signed June 14, 2000. **PRO CAREER:** 2000: Finished sixth in Pioneer League in batting (.345); had second-highest batting average among short-season first basemen; hit .363 with 32 RBI in July, which tied for the fourth highest RBI total in the month in all the minor leagues; ended season with 14-game hitting streak, August 17-September 3; was second on team in batting average, hits, doubles and total bases and third in RBI.

Year	Club & League	AVG	G	AB	R	H	TB	2B	3B	HR	RBI	SH-SF	HP	BB-IBB	SO	SB-CS	GIDP	SLG	OBP
2000	Medcine Hat (PIO)	.345	59	229	37	79	111	16	2	4	46	0-2	3	21-0	28	5-2	7	.485	.404

De Mota, Agustin Perez

Outfielder ... **HT:** 6-0; **WT:** 170 ... **B-T:** R-R ... **BORN:** 19 MAY, 1980, Higuey, DR **RESIDES:** La Romana, DR ... **TRANSACTIONS:** Signed as non-drafted free agent by Blue Jays, July 20, 1997. **PRO CAREER:** 1999: Third on Dominican Summer Blue Jays in stolen bases (9); 2000: Finished third in Dominican Summer League in triples (12) and extra-base hits (35) and fifth in RBI (60).

Year	Club & League	AVG	G	AB	R	H	TB	2B	3B	HR	RBI	SH-SF	HP	BB-IBB	SO	SB-CS	GIDP	SLG	OBP
1998	Blue Jays (DSL)	.197	46	71	16	14	21	3	2	0	9	3-1	3	15-0	29	1-2	1	.296	.356
1999	Sd Blue Jay (DSL)	.181	44	138	9	25	35	7	0	1	10	4-1	6	9-0	43	9-4	4	.254	.260
2000	Toronto (DSL)	.303	71	287	52	87	140	20	12	3	60	1-2	13	14-0	82	11-8	5	.488	.361
Minor Totals		.254	161	496	77	126	196	30	14	4	79	8-4	22	38-0	154	21-14	10	.395	.332

Dean, Aaron M.

Pitcher ... **HT:** 6-4; **WT:** 190 ... **B-T:** R-R ... **BORN:** 09 APR, 1979, Columbus, OH **RESIDES:** Pleasanton, CA ... **EDUCATION:** Canada (CA) JC ... **TRANSACTIONS:** Selected by Blue Jays in 38th round of June 1998 draft; signed May 30, 1999. **PRO CAREER:** 1999: Named New York-Penn League All-Star RHP; Led St. Catharines in wins (4), ERA (2.34) and strikeouts (68); second on team in game pitched (17) and innings pitched (61.2); began season in relief, last eight appearances were starts; did not allow a run until fourth relief outing; picked up only save of year on July 11, vs. Mohawk Valley with four shutout innings, allowing just one hit while striking out six; won two consecutive starts July 30-August 5; on July 30, vs. Batavia tossed six shutout innings allowing four hits, striking out eight; on August 26, vs. Mohawk Valley went six shutout innings, allowing three hits striking out six; as a starter compiled a 2-0, 1.99 ERA allowing just 34 hits in 40.2 innings striking out 42; participated in two combined shutouts; 2000: Started season at Hagerstown and was 3-0 with 2.45 ERA with 26 strikeouts in 22 innings in April; won six of his first seven decisions; named South Atlantic League Pitcher of the Week, April 14-20; tied for team lead in wins (8) despite moving to Dunedin in July; won first start at Dunedin, July 29 vs. Daytona, and was moved up to Double A; tossed a complete game in a 1-0 loss vs. Jacksonville on August 3, in his only start at Tennessee; finished fourth in organization in ERA (3.56).

Year	Club & League	W-L	ERA	G	GS	CG	ShO	SV	IP	H	R	ER	HR	HB	BB-IBB	SO	WP	BK	OBA
1999	St.cathrins (NYP)	4-0	2.34	17	8	0	0	1	61.2	50	18	16	3	5	13-0	68	7	2	.224
2000	Hagerstown (SAL)	8-3	3.28	19	19	0	0	0	112.2	99	55	41	8	6	38-0	89	4	0	.236
	Dunedin (FSL)	1-0	6.46	3	3	0	0	0	15.1	22	15	11	1	1	7-0	13	3	0	.324
	Tennessee (SOU)	0-1	1.50	1	1	1	0	0	6.0	5	1	1	1	1	5-0	4	2	0	.227
Minor Totals		13-4	3.17	40	31	1	0	1	195.2	176	89	69	13	13	63-0	174	16	2	.240

Delgado, Christopher Joseph (Chris)

First Baseman ... **HT:** 6-3; **WT:** 215 ... **B-T:** R-R ... **BORN:** 08 OCT, 1977, Hialeah, FL **RESIDES:** Pembroke Pines, Florida ... **EDUCATION:** Graduated in 1996 from St. Thomas Aquinas High School in Fort Lauderdale, Florida. Attended Okaloosa-Walton Junior College ... **TRANSACTIONS:** Selected by White Sox in 34th round of 1996 draft. Released by White Sox, March 28, 2000. Signed by Royals, April 1, 2000. Released by Royals, April 13, 2000. Signed by Rockies, April 24, 2000. Released by Rockies, June 25, 2000. Signed by Blue Jays Feb. 14, 2001 ... **PRO CAREER:** 1997: Made his pro debut at Rookie Sarasota; Led the team in doubles (12) and games played (51) and tied for the lead in runs scored (24); 1998: tied for the team lead at Rookie Tucson with five home runs, was second in doubles (12) and slugging percentage (.512) and fifth in average (.302); 1999: Spent the season at Bristol (Rookie Adv.); Led the team in total bases (119), home runs (14), RBI (54), slugging percentage (.548) and extra-base hits (25); Tied for third in the Appalachian League in home runs; Was named to the Appy All-Star Team; Hit .340 at home (34-100) and batted .404 (36-89) with eight home runs and 26 RBI in July; Was the league Player-of-the-Week for July 5-11 including two home runs on July 9 at Princeton and three the next night again at Princeton. 2000: Played in a combined 21 games in the Colorado organization, batting .181 (13-72) with one home run and five RBI.

Year	Club & League	AVG	G	AB	R	H	TB	2B	3B	HR	RBI	SH-SF	HP	BB-IBB	SO	SB-CS	GIDP	SLG	OBP
1997	White Sox (GULF)	.275	51	189	24	52	66	12	1	0	19	0-1	1	7-0	40	0-1	4	.349	.303
1998	White Sox (ARIZ)	.302	38	129	28	39	66	12	0	5	25	0-0	1	20-0	30	6-1	1	.512	.400
1999	Bristol (APPY)	.300	61	217	36	65	119	10	1	14	54	1-3	3	33-2	64	1-0	7	.548	.395
2000	Asheville (SAL)	.136	18	59	4	8	12	1	0	1	3	0-1	1	7-0	25	1-1	2	.203	.224
	Portland (NWST)	.385	3	13	2	5	5	0	0	0	2	0-0	1	0-0	2	0-0	0	.385	.429
Minor Totals		.278	171	607	94	169	268	35	2	20	103	1-5	6	67-2	161	8-3	14	.442	.353

Desouza, Adriano

Outfielder ... **HT:** 6-2; **WT:** 175 ... **B-T:** R-R ... **BORN:** 14 AUG, 1981, Havana, Cuba **RESIDES:** Marilia, Sao Paulo, Brazil ... **TRANSACTIONS:** Signed as non-drafted free agent by Blue Jays, Jan. 17, 2000.

Year	Club & League	AVG	G	AB	R	H	TB	2B	3B	HR	RBI	SH-SF	HP	BB-IBB	SO	SB-CS	GIDP	SLG	OBP
2000	Toronto (DSL)	.295	35	105	17	31	41	7	0	1	17	0-0	9	21-0	22	0-0	2	.390	.452

Diaz, Robinzon Henriquez

Catcher ... **HT:** 5-11; **WT:** 186 ... **B-T:** R-R ... **BORN:** 19 SEP, 1983, Monte Plata, DR **RESIDES:** Monte Plata, DR ... **TRANSACTIONS:** Signed as a non-drafted free agent by the Blue Jays, Nov. 19, 2000 ... **PRO CAREER:** 2001 will be his first professional season.

Dillinger, John William (John)

Pitcher ... **HT:** 6-5; **WT:** 240 ... **B-T:** R-R ... **BORN:** 28 AUG, 1973, Connellsville, PA **RESIDES:** Dawson, Pennsylvania ... **EDUCATION:** Manatee Community College ... **TRANSACTIONS:** Selected by Pirates in 20th round of 1992 draft. Loaned by Pirates to independent Lethbridge (Pioneer), June 14-Sept. 10, 1993. Released by Pirates, April 27, 1998. Signed by independent Allentown (Northeast), June 1998. Signed by Rangers, Dec. 5, 1998. Released by Rangers, April 15, 1999. Signed by Blue Jays, Feb. 14, 2001 ... **PRO CAREER:** Began professional career in the Gulf Coast League with Bradenton (Rookie); 1993: Led Pioneer league losses with 10 and tied for 2nd in games started with 15; 1994: Was named as the SAL Player-of-the-Week from April 23-30; 1997: Attended the Pirates' spring training camp on the 40-man roster. Played with Allentown of the Northeast League after being released by the Pirates.

Year	Club & League	W-L	ERA	G	GS	CG	ShO	SV	IP	H	R	ER	HR	HB	BB-IBB	SO	WP	BK	OBA
1992	Pirates (GULF)	3-3	3.44	13	10	0	0	1	52.1	43	37	20	1	6	42-0	45	6	2	.218
1993	Lethbridge (PIO)	3-10	3.92	15	15	3	0	0	80.1	65	51	35	2	5	60-1	94	9	3	.222
1994	Augusta (SAL)	5-9	4.29	23	22	1	0	0	119.2	107	77	57	5	3	54-1	118	8	5	.233
1995	Lynchburg (CARO)	6-6	4.02	27	22	0	0	0	123.0	111	62	55	10	7	67-4	97	9	7	.243
1996	Lynchburg (CARO)	10-5	3.74	33	15	2	0	0	132.1	101	65	55	11	4	58-0	113	11	1	.208
1997	Carolina (SOU)	6-4	6.00	23	11	0	0	0	81.0	88	66	54	8	5	52-0	64	7	1	.277
1998	Carolina (SOU)	0-1	14.29	4	0	0	0	0	5.2	11	9	9	4	2	4-0	4	0	0	.440
	Allentown (NEL)	7-3	3.57	14	14	0	0	0	88.1	96	46	35	7	3	47-0	66	5	0	.287
2000	Somerset (ATL)	0-1	10.13	3	0	0	0	0	5.1	9	8	6	0	0	5-1	4	1	0	.391
Minor Totals		33-38	4.32	138	95	6	0	1	594.1	526	367	285	32	32	337-6	535	50	19	.235

Dimma, Douglas F. (Doug)

Pitcher ... **HT:** 5-11; **WT:** 175 ... **B-T:** R-L ... **BORN:** 03 JUL, 1978, Richmond Hill, ON, Canada **RESIDES:** Richmond Hill, ON, Canada ... **EDUCATION:** Valdosta St. (GA) ... **TRANSACTIONS:** Selected by Blue Jays in 36th round of 1999 draft; signed June 4, 1999. **PRO CAREER:** 1999: Second on St. Catharines in wins (3) and games (17); pitched mainly in relief, making two starts; picked up save in first appearance of season with four shutout innings, completing a combined shutout; in last seven appearances, all in relief, compiled 1-0, 1.15 ERA allowing 10 hits while striking out 14 in 15.2 innings; 2000: Led team in games (43), was second in games finished (17) and in relief innings (79.2); earned only save on August 30 vs. Sarasota with three scoreless innings; posted 1.35 ERA in May (13.1 innings).

Year	Club & League	W-L	ERA	G	GS	CG	ShO	SV	IP	H	R	ER	HR	HB	BB-IBB	SO	WP	BK	OBA
1999	St.cathrnes (NYP)	3-1	3.78	17	2	0	0	1	47.2	48	29	20	1	3	28-1	42	4	2	.264
	Syracuse (INT)	0-0	9.00	1	0	0	0	0	1.0	2	1	1	1	0	0-0	1	0	0	.500
2000	Dunedin (FSL)	6-3	3.84	43	0	0	0	1	79.2	74	46	34	6	9	48-4	42	7	0	.247
Minor Totals		9-4	3.86	61	2	0	0	2	128.1	124	76	55	8	12	76-5	85	11	2	.285

Encarnacion, Victor A.

Catcher ... **HT:** 5-10; **WT:** 185 ... **B-T:** R-R ... **BORN:** 22 AUG, 1982, Santo Domingo, DR **RESIDES:** Santo Domingo, DR ... **TRANSACTIONS:** Signed as non-drafted free agent by TOR, Feb. 15, 2000

Year	Club & League	AVG	G	AB	R	H	TB	2B	3B	HR	RBI	SH-SF	HP	BB-IBB	SO	SB-CS	GIDP	SLG	OBP
2000	Toronto (DSL)	.302	56	179	40	54	76	7	3	3	29	2-2	2	21-1	26	1-0	14	.425	.377

Fagan, Shawn P.

Catcher ... **HT:** 5-11; **WT:** 200 ... **B-T:** R-R ... **BORN:** 02 MAR, 1978, Syosset, NY **RESIDES:** Levittown, NY ... **EDUCATION:** Penn St. ... **TRANSACTIONS:** Selected by Blue Jays in 13th round of 2000 draft; signed June 13, 2000. **PRO CAREER:** 2000: Started season at Queens with three straight mutiple-hit games, June 20-22; hit .333 in 14 games at home; sent to Hagerstown in mid-July; hit .314 in 28 games at both Queens and Hagerstown in July; had a four-hit, three RBI game vs. Delmarva, starting a run of five straight multiple-hits games, July 31-August 4; had season-high, eight-game hitting streak, August 6-15; hit .326 with 21 RBI with runners on base.

Year	Club & League	AVG	G	AB	R	H	TB	2B	3B	HR	RBI	SH-SF	HP	BB-IBB	SO	SB-CS	GIDP	SLG	OBP
2000	Queens (NYP)	.289	25	90	17	26	40	6	1	2	13	0-1	3	12-1	22	0-1	3	.444	.387
	Hagerstown (SAL)	.279	45	172	20	48	64	8	1	2	23	0-0	1	18-0	28	5-1	2	.372	.351
Minor Totals		.282	70	262	37	74	104	14	2	4	36	0-1	4	30-1	50	5-2	5	.397	.364

Fleming, Ryan Thomas

Outfielder ... **HT:** 5-11; **WT:** 180 ... **B-T:** L-L ... **BORN:** 11 FEB, 1976, Columbus, OH **RESIDES:** Grove City, OH ... **EDUCATION:** Dayton ... **TRANSACTIONS:** Selected by Blue Jays in 18th round of 1998 draft; signed June 5, 1998. **PRO CAREER:** 1998: Ranked fifth in Pioneer League in doubles (20) and SO/TPA ratio (1/10.41); finished second on Medicine Hat in stolen bases (17) and base on balls (37), third in runs (64) and hits (78); began season with six-game hit streak, batting .360 (9-25, 6 R); collected five hits against Butte on July 21 (5-6, 3 2B, 4 R, 2 RBI); hit in 11 straight games from July 24-August 6, batting .333 (15-45, 17 R, 11 RBI); scored four runs in two consecutive games on July 30-31; from August 24-August 30 hit in seven straight games, batting .370 (10-27, 6 R); compiled .333 (43-129) batting average on road; 1999: Opened season with Dunedin, batting .228 in 51 games; hit in four of five games between May 28-June 4, batting .368 (7-19); with Hagerstown hit home runs in three consecutive games on July 17-18-19, vs. Piedmont; from July 17-29 hit in 12 straight games, batting .364 (20-55) with nine runs and 10 RBI; hit safely in last seven games of season, batting .393 (11-28) scoring six runs; of 57 games with more than one at-bat in Dunedin 26 were multi-hit games; 2000: Started season at Dunedin; had eight-game hitting streak, June 2-9; had four-hit game vs. Ft. Myers, June 28; hit .372 with 10 RBI in June; batted .326 against right-handers; hit .369 with 25 RBI with runners in scoring position; promoted to Double A in July; hit home run vs. Carolina in second game at Tennessee.

Year	Club & League	AVG	G	AB	R	H	TB	2B	3B	HR	RBI	SH-SF	HP	BB-IBB	SO	SB-CS	GIDP	SLG	OBP
1998	Medcine Hat (PIO)	.306	70	255	64	78	106	20	1	2	41	2-4	4	37-0	29	17-3	0	.416	.397
1999	Dunedin (FSL)	.228	51	123	17	28	37	7	1	0	9	3-1	4	10-1	19	4-3	3	.301	.304
	Hagerstown (SAL)	.335	61	227	34	76	101	9	2	4	35	2-4	0	23-1	26	7-6	4	.445	.390
2000	Dunedin (FSL)	.304	90	309	40	94	126	18	1	4	32	6-5	1	28-1	38	6-8	1	.408	.359
	Syracuse (INT)	.182	3	11	1	2	2	0	0	0	1	0-0	0	0-0	0	0-0	0	.182	.182
	Tennessee (SOU)	.171	37	105	16	18	28	4	0	2	9	3-0	1	20-0	17	2-1	1	.267	.310
Minor Totals		.287	312	030	174	296	400	58	5	12	127	16-14	10	118-3	129	36-21	9	.388	.362

Flores, Neomar E.

Pitcher ... **HT:** 6-2; **WT:** 180 ... **B-T:** R-R ... **BORN:** 12 MAR, 1982, Guarenas, VZ **RESIDES:** Guarenas, VZ ... **TRANSACTIONS:** Signed as non-drafted free agent by Blue Jays, July 2, 1998. **PRO CAREER:** 1998: Appeared in three games for Lara of Venezuelan Winter League, hurling 3.2 scoreless innings; 1999: Second on Venezuelan Summer Blue Jays in starts (9), fourth in strikeouts (48) and fifth in innings pitched (50.1); pitched in just two games (2.1 innings) for Lara Venezuelan Winter League; 2000: Made only one start before being placed on disabled list, June 30-September 25, with right bicep tendonitis.

Year	Club & League	W-L	ERA	G	GS	CG	ShO	SV	IP	H	R	ER	HR	HB	BB-IBB	SO	WP	BK	OBA
1999	Chino (VSL)	4-4	3.58	16	9	0	0	2	50.1	50	25	20	1	6	17-0	48	8	2	.260
2000	Medcine Hat (PIO)	0-0	12.00	1	1	0	0	0	3.0	6	4	4	1	0	1-0	2	0	0	.462
Minor Totals		4-4	4.05	17	10	0	0	2	53.1	56	29	24	2	6	18-0	50	8	2	.273

Ford, Matthew Lee (Matt)

Pitcher ... **HT:** 6-1; **WT:** 175 ... **B-T:** S-L ... **BORN:** 08 APR, 1981, Plantation, FL **RESIDES:** Tamarac, FL ... **TRANSACTIONS:** Selected by Blue Jays in third round of 1999 draft; signed June 2, 1999. **PRO CAREER:** 1999: Led Pioneer League in AVG against relief (.176) and SO/9 IP relief (15.36); fifth in league in runners/9 IP relief (10.24); split season between starting and relief; led Medicine Hat in strikeouts (68); did not give up a run in first three appearances over nine innings allowing five hits, striking out ten; on July 27, vs. Helena pitched three hitless, shutout innings, striking out seven; in last six outings was 4-0, 1.11 ERA allowing 13 hits while striking out 36 in 24.1 innings; at home produced a 2-0, 1.37 ERA with 30 strikeouts in 19.2 innings; in relief was 3-0, 1.86 ERA with 33 strikeouts in 19.1 innings; named tenth best prospect in Pioneer League by Baseball America; 2000: Averaged 9.25 SO/IP; was 2-1 with 1.74 ERA in four starts in July; finished 2-1 with 2.40 ERA at home; placed on disabled list, July 25-September 25, with left elbow strain.

Year	Club & League	W-L	ERA	G	GS	CG	ShO	SV	IP	H	R	ER	HR	HB	BB-IBB	SO	WP	BK	OBA
1999	Medcine Hat (PIO)	4-0	2.05	13	7	0	0	0	48.1	31	11	11	0	0	23-0	68	1	0	.182
2000	Hagerstown (SAL)	5-3	3.87	18	14	1	0	0	83.2	81	42	36	5	3	36-0	86	5	0	.261
Minor Totals		9-3	3.20	31	21	1	0	0	132.0	112	53	47	5	3	59-0	154	6	0	.233

Garcia, Juan C.

Outfielder ... **HT:** 6-3; **WT:** 200 ... **B-T:** R-R ... **BORN:** 11 NOV, 1983, Santo Domingo, DR **RESIDES:** Santo Domingo, DR ... **TRANSACTIONS:** Signed as a non-drafted free agent by the Blue Jays, Aug. 26, 2000 ... **PRO CAREER:** 2001 will be his first professional season.

Gaud, Perfecto

Pitcher ... **HT:** 6-4; **WT:** 210 ... **B-T:** L-L ... **BORN:** 04 DEC, 1978, Hoboken, NJ **RESIDES:** Yauco, PR ... **EDUCATION:** HS ... **TRANSACTIONS:** Selected by Blue Jays in 25th round of 1997 draft; signed Jan. 12, 1998. **PRO CAREER:** 1998: Was second in games finished (9); from July 1-July 21, pitched in six straight games without allowing an earned run (7.2 IP, 4 GF, 2 H, 6 BB, 8 SO); finished season with home record of 0-0, 0.93 ERA (9.2 IP, 7 H, 6 BB, 10 SO, .184 OPP/BA); 1999: With Medicine Hat, started first two games, going 0-1, 4.91 ERA with 11 strikeouts in 7.1 innings; worked in relief rest of season; in last seven appearances, from July 27-August 31 compiled 3.60 ERA allowing nine hits while striking out 11 in 10 innings; 2000: Did not play, went back to school.

Year	Club & League	W-L	ERA	G	GS	CG	ShO	SV	IP	H	R	ER	HR	HB	BB-IBB	SO	WP	BK	OBA
1998	Medcine Hat (PIO)	0-1	4.91	17	0	0	0	0	18.1	19	16	10	0	1	19-0	15	3	0	.247
1999	Medcine Hat (PIO)	0-1	8.27	14	2	0	0	0	20.2	23	22	19	3	4	16-1	26	4	0	.280
2000										Did not play										
Minor Totals		0-2	6.69	31	2	0	0	0	39.0	42	38	29	3	5	35-1	41	7	0	.264

Goudie, Jaime Federico

Second Baseman ... **HT:** 5-10; **WT:** 180 ... **B-T:** R-R ... **BORN:** 08 MAR, 1979, Miami, FL **RESIDES:** Columbus, GA ... **TRANSACTIONS:** Selected by Dodgers in ninth round of 1997 draft; signed June 13, 1997; Released by Dodgers, March 29, 1999; Signed by Reds, April 12, 1999; Traded by Reds to Blue Jays, Sept. 13, 1999, completing trade in which Blue Jays sent SS Juan Melo to Reds for a player to be named (Sept. 3, 1999); Granted free agency, Oct. 15, 1999; Re-signed by Blue Jays, Oct. 22, 1999. **PRO CAREER:** 1997: Tied for second in the Northwest League with six triples; 1998: Split the season between San Bernardino, Yakima and Vero Beach; 1999: Went 4-for-6 with a bases-loaded triple and a two-run double in a 19-4 victory over Quad City on May 8; went 5-for-9 with a double and an RBI in a 21-inning, 3-2 win against Quad City on May 19; hit safely in 15 of 16 games from June 15 - July 10; was on the disabled list from July 14 - August 16; 2000: Led club in sacrifice hits (8); second in games (116), doubles (19) and stolen bases (26); third in hits (100) and RBI (51); hit .304 in June; batted .321 with 22 RBI with two outs and runners in scoring position; had five consecutive multiple hit games during eight-game hitting streak; hit .373 with 12 RBI in 19 games, May 25-June 12.

Year	Club & League	AVG	G	AB	R	H	TB	2B	3B	HR	RBI	SH-SF	HP	BB-IBB	SO	SB-CS	GIDP	SLG	OBP
1997	Yakima (NWST)	.239	56	230	33	55	77	10	6	0	16	1-0	2	16-0	38	21-5	2	.335	.294
1998	San Berndno (CAL)	.183	49	175	16	32	43	5	3	0	4	2-1	5	11-1	36	4-2	6	.246	.250
	Yakima (NWST)	.275	35	138	15	38	50	8	2	0	16	2-2	0	6-0	16	6-1	5	.362	.301
	Vero Beach (FSL)	.322	35	115	15	37	49	7	1	1	8	2-1	3	12-1	24	7-4	3	.426	.397
1999	Clinton (MID)	.321	84	340	56	109	146	20	4	3	50	0-2	2	21-2	46	16-6	8	.429	.362
	Reds (GULF)	.500	1	2	0	1	1	0	0	0	1	0-0	0	0-0	0	0-0	0	.500	.500
2000	Hagerstown (SAL)	.243	116	412	53	100	143	19	3	6	51	8-3	9	36-0	68	26-10	6	.347	.315
Minor Totals		.263	376	412	188	372	509	69	19	10	146	15-9	21	102-4	228	80-28	30	.360	.321

Gracesqui, Franklyn B.

Pitcher ... **HT:** 6-5; **WT:** 210 ... **B-T:** S-L ... **BORN:** 20 AUG, 1979, Santo Domingo, DR **RESIDES:** New York, NY ... **TRANSACTIONS:** Selected by Blue Jays in 21st round of 1998 draft; signed June 7, 1998. **PRO CAREER:** 1998: Struck out 19 batters in 16.1 IP while winning his only decision; 1999: Had 0.69 ERA in first six appearances, spanning 13 innings; nailed a season-high seven strikeouts over five shutout innings in winning his start vs. Mahoning Valley on August 11; did not throw a wild pitch or hit a batsman over his last five starts; was 1-0 with a 4.15 ERA at home; 2000: Had 1.29 ERA in four relief appearances at Medicine Hat; allowed one hit and no runs in five innings of relief following promotion to Hagerstown in August.

Year	Club & League	W-L	ERA	G	GS	CG	ShO	SV	IP	H	R	ER	HR	HB	BB-IBB	SO	WP	BK	OBA
1998	St.cathrnes (NYP)	1-0	6.61	11	0	0	0	0	16.1	16	12	12	2	3	12-0	19	5	2	.242
1999	St.cathrnes (NYP)	2-3	5.05	15	10	0	0	1	46.1	44	30	26	4	3	41-0	45	6	2	.253
2000	Medcine Hat (PIO)	0-1	2.63	8	4	0	0	0	24.0	15	11	7	1	2	21-0	20	5	0	.185
	Hagerstown (SAL)	0-1	4.91	3	1	0	0	0	7.1	4	4	4	1	1	9-0	6	0	0	.174
Minor Totals		3-5	4.69	37	15	0	0	1	94.0	79	57	49	8	9	83-0	90	16	4	.230

Guerrero, Aneudis Reyes

Pitcher ... **HT:** 6-2; **WT:** 160 ... **B-T:** R-R ... **BORN:** 04 JUL, 1982, San Pedro De Macoris, DR **RESIDES:** San Pedro de Macoris, DR ... **TRANSACTIONS:** Signed as non-drafted free agent by Blue Jays, Oct. 30, 1999.

Year	Club & League	W-L	ERA	G	GS	CG	ShO	SV	IP	H	R	ER	HR	HB	BB-IBB	SO	WP	BK	OBA
2000	Toronto (DSL)	0-0	7.45	7	0	0	0	0	9.2	16	8	8	0	2	3-0	4	1	0	.372

Gutierrez, Ricardo Said (Said)

Catcher ... **HT:** 5-10; **WT:** 196 ... **B-T:** R-R ... **BORN:** 26 MAR, 1980, Monterrey, Nuevo Leon, Mexico **RESIDES:** Merida Yucatan, Mexico ... **TRANSACTIONS:** Contract purchased by Yucatan (Mexican), March 18, 1998; Contract purchased by Yucatan (Mexican) from Padres, Dec. 13, 2000. **PRO CAREER:** 1998: Batted .317 (13-41) with 11 RBI in July; 1999: Combined to hit .311 in 33 games with Padres in Arizona League and Idaho Falls; hit in 11 of first 12 games with Idaho Falls; had 3-hit, 5-RBI game vs. Great Falls, July 22; 2000: On disabled list, May 7-June 9, with broken right hand.

Year	Club & League	AVG	G	AB	R	H	TB	2B	3B	HR	RBI	SH-SF	HP	BB-IBB	SO	SB-CS	GIDP	SLG	OBP
1997	Yucatan (MEX)	.000	1	0	0	0	0	0	0	0	0	0-0	0	0-0	0	0-0	0	.000	.000
1998	Padres (ARIZ)	.253	28	91	13	23	29	4	1	0	14	0-1	5	7-0	26	3-2	0	.319	.337
1999	Padres (ARIZ)	.316	7	19	2	6	9	0	0	1	6	0-1	0	2-0	0	0-0	0	.474	.364
	Idaho Falls (PIO)	.310	26	87	10	27	35	5	0	1	11	0-0	3	3-0	14	0-1	2	.402	.355
2000	Fort Wayne (MID)	.189	11	37	5	7	11	1	0	1	4	0-0	0	2-0	6	2-0	2	.297	.231
	Idaho Falls (PIO)	.220	17	50	4	11	12	1	0	0	5	0-2	0	9-0	10	1-0	3	.240	.328
Minor Totals		.261	90	284	34	74	96	11	1	3	40	0-4	8	23-0	56	6-3	7	.338	.329

Guzman, Alexis Ramon

Infielder ... **HT:** 6-0; **WT:** 175 ... **B-T:** S-R ... **BORN:** 23 APR, 1980, Cumana, Sucre, VZ **RESIDES:** Barcelona, Anzoategui, VZ ... **TRANSACTIONS:** Signed as non-drafted free agent by Blue Jays, March 8, 1997. **PRO CAREER:** 1998: From June 23-29 hit in four straight games batting .500 (4-8) while raising his average .190 to .333; batted .333 in June (5 H, 4 R, 4 BB). 1999: Improved his fielding percentage at SS to .931, from .846 in 1998; had .381 on-base percentage after August 3; 2000: Tied for second in Pioneer League in games (27) and was fifth in lowest BB/ 9 IP (2.06)for relievers; tied for team lead in games and was second in wins (6); led team in innings pitched for relievers (48); allowed only two earned runs over last nine appearances (17.1 IP), August 9-September 2; was 3-4 with 1.29 ERA in ten appearances in August; tossed five scoreless innings with five strikeouts in two playoff games.

Year	Club & League	AVG	G	AB	R	H	TB	2B	3B	HR	RBI	SH-SF	HP	BB-IBB	SO	SB-CS	GIDP	SLG	OBP
1997	S Joaquin-1 (VSL)	.244	34	86	10	21	24	3	0	0	3	0-2	0	12-0	25	1-0	2	.279	.330
1998	Medcine Hat (PIO)	.179	36	84	11	15	15	0	0	0	3	3-0	1	6-0	21	1-0	2	.179	.242
1999	Medcine Hat (PIO)	.215	47	149	28	32	42	8	1	0	10	1-3	1	18-0	39	3-1	3	.282	.298
Minor Totals		.213	117	319	49	68	81	11	1	0	16	4-5	2	36-0	85	5-1	7	.254	.293

Year	Club & League	W-L	ERA	G	GS	CG	ShO	SV	IP	H	R	ER	HR	HB	BB-IBB	SO	WP	BK	OBA
2000	Medicine Hat (PIO)	6-8	2.37	27	1	0	0	0	53.0	49	25	14	3	6	11-0	35	2	0	.241

Haltiwanger, Garrick Deseau

Outfielder ... **HT:** 6-0; **WT:** 195 ... **B-T:** R-L ... **BORN:** 03 MAR, 1975, Columbia, SC **RESIDES:** Irmo, SC ... **EDUCATION:** The Citadel (SC) ... **TRANSACTIONS:** Selected by Mets in 11th round of 1996 draft; signed June 15, 1996; Selected by Blue Jays from Mets in Rule 5 minor league draft, Dec. 13, 1999. **PRO CAREER:** 1996: Hit safely in 10 straight games (13-36, 1 2B, 1 3B, 3 HR, 9 RBI, 2 SB) July 15-23; 1997: Led club with 14 homers, 73 RBI and a .408 slugging percentage; homered May 15 & 16 against Hickory; finished fifth among New York farmhands in RBI and was sixth in HR; hit .320 with five homers in Australian Winter League; 1998: Homered in two straight games April 19 & 20 against Vero Beach and Tampa, respectively; 1999: Collected an RBI single and a two-run triple during a nine-run fifth inning for St. Lucie in a 12-1 win against Dunedin in the first game of a doubleheader on May 15; hit safely in 10 straight games (14-37, 1 2B, 1 3B, 1 HR, 6 RBI, 2 SB) May 9-18; collected a pair of hits during a six-run second inning and added a two-run single as part of a seven-run sixth as St. Lucie clobbered Vero Beach, 15-1, August 30; homered in first game for Binghamton on June 23 against Akron; 2000: Finished tied for seventh in organization in batting (.291); hit .311 with 32 RBI at home; batted .328 in April and .317 with 14 RBI in August; had ten-game hitting streak, May 27-June 5; batted .323 against lefties; had four-hit game vs. Jupiter, July 21; hit .295 with 43 RBI with runners in scoring position.

Year	Club & League	AVG	G	AB	R	H	TB	2B	3B	HR	RBI	SH-SF	HP	BB-IBB	SO	SB-CS	GIDP	SLG	OBP
1996	Pittsfield (NYP)	.256	60	203	36	52	92	9	2	9	37	1-2	4	24-3	55	9-4	3	.453	.343
1997	Columbia (SAL)	.261	125	441	59	115	180	19	2	14	73	1-2	10	45-0	107	20-7	4	.408	.341
1998	St. Lucie (FSL)	.186	108	344	35	64	110	11	1	11	42	5-3	7	34-0	69	7-6	5	.320	.271
1999	St. Lucie (FSL)	.265	111	423	67	112	172	18	6	10	71	0-5	13	31-3	77	20-12	6	.407	.331
	Norfolk (INT)	.000	6	13	0	0	0	0	0	0	0	0-0	0	0-0	8	0-0	1	.000	.000
	Binghamton (EAST)	.273	4	11	1	3	6	0	0	1	2	0-0	0	1-0	1	0-0	0	.545	.333
2000	Dunedin (FSL)	.291	100	354	57	103	166	27	3	10	56	0-1	3	37-1	67	18-4	10	.469	.362
Minor Totals		.251	514	789	257	449	726	84	14	55	281	7-13	37	172-7	384	74-33	29	.406	.327

Hamann, Robert Paul

Pitcher ... **HT:** 6-7; **WT:** 215 ... **B-T:** R-R ... **BORN:** 15 DEC, 1976, Franklin Park, IL **RESIDES:** Franklin Park, IL ... **EDUCATION:** Wheaton (IL) ... **TRANSACTIONS:** Selected by Blue Jays in 21st round of 1999 draft; signed June 3, 1999. **PRO CAREER:** 1999: Fourth in Pioneer League in BB/9 IP starters (2); ninth in league in ERA (3.93); led Medicine Hat in starts (13) and innings (75.2); 39% of his runs allowed were unearned (21 of 54); allowed three earned runs or less in nine of 13 starts and had a 3.75 ERA when starting; posted 2.83 ERA at home; 2000: Combined for 10-5 record with 11 saves and 2.52 ERA at Hagerstown and Dunedin; tied for team lead in wins (8) and games finished (19) at Hagerstown; allowed only one earned run in last nine appearances (14.2 IP, 3 wins, 3 saves) at Hagerstown; was 3-2 with 5 saves and 1.93 ERA in 19 appearances on road; sent to Dunedin in mid-July; did not allow more than one run in any of his 16 appearances; was 1-0 with 4 saves and 0.69 ERA in ninegames at home; held right-hand batters to .194 average.

Year	Club & League	W-L	ERA	G	GS	CG	ShO	SV	IP	H	R	ER	HR	HB	BB-IBB	SO	WP	BK	OBA
1999	Medcine Hat (PIO)	2-8	3.93	15	13	0	0	0	75.2	95	54	33	9	2	17-0	45	7	0	.305
2000	Hagerstown (SAL)	8-4	2.95	34	1	0	0	6	58.0	48	25	19	4	5	21-4	34	9	0	.225
	Dunedin (FSL)	2-1	1.50	16	0	0	0	5	24.0	16	5	4	2	0	7-3	14	2	1	.195
Minor Totals		12-13	3.20	65	14	0	0	11	157.2	159	84	56	15	7	45-7	93	18	1	.262

Hanson, David Houston

Pitcher ... **HT:** 5-11; **WT:** 175 ... **B-T:** R-R ... **BORN:** 07 AUG, 1980, Prosser, WA **RESIDES:** Richland, WA ... **TRANSACTIONS:** Selected by Blue Jays in sixth round of 1999 draft; signed June 14, 1999. **PRO CAREER:** 1999: Tied for fourth on Medicine Hat in games started (7) and innings pitched (45.2); on July 6 vs. Great Falls participated in combination shutout, allowing just two hits in six innings; went 1-1 with 3.95 ERA in 27.1 innings pitched in July; 2000: Tied for fourth in Pioneer League in wins (7), tied for second in games started (15) and was fourth in SO/9 IP (9.0); led team in wins, innings and strikeouts; won four straight decisions (five starts), July 19-August 9; was 4-1 with 4.43 ERA in seven starts on the road; finished 4-1 against Helena in five starts; fanned season-high ten batters in four innings vs. Great Falls, August 30; allowed one earned run and fanned seven in 7.1 innings in one playoff start.

Year	Club & League	W-L	ERA	G	GS	CG	ShO	SV	IP	H	R	ER	HR	HB	BB-IBB	SO	WP	BK	OBA
1999	Medcine Hat (PIO)	1-2	5.32	14	7	0	0	0	45.2	64	33	27	1	2	21-0	35	2	2	.335
2000	Medcine Hat (PIO)	7-3	5.81	15	15	0	0	0	79.0	82	55	51	6	5	29-0	79	12	1	.262
Minor Totals		8-5	5.63	29	22	0	0	0	124.2	146	88	78	7	7	50-0	114	14	3	.290

Harper, Jesse A.

Pitcher ... **HT:** 6-4; **B-T:** R-R ... **BORN:** 11 NOV. 80 ... **RESIDES:** Clute, TX ... **EDUCATION:** Galveston (TX) CC ... **TRANSACTIONS:** Selected by Blue Jays in 21st round of 2000 draft; signed Aug. 21, 2000. **PRO CAREER:** 2000: Pitched for Cotuit in Cape Cod League; was 1-0 with 3.18 ERA in seven relief appearances; struck out 18 batters in 17 innings as a reliever; was 1-0 with 0.87 ERA in four road games.

Hernandez, Alberto L.

Pitcher ... **HT:** 5-11; **WT:** 167 ... **B-T:** R-R ... **BORN:** 24 MAY, 1984, Santo Domingo, DR ... **RESIDES:** Santo Domingo, DR ... **TRANSACTIONS:** Signed as a non-drafted free agent by the Blue Jays, Nov. 17, 2000 ... **PRO CAREER:** 2001 will be his first professional season.

Hodge, Alvin A.

Outfielder ... **HT:** 6-1; **WT:** 155 ... **B-T:** R-R ... **BORN:** 09 JUL, 1983, San Pedro de Macoris, DR ... **RESIDES:** San Pedro de Macoris, DR ... **TRANSACTIONS:** Signed as non-drafted free agent by Blue Jays, Sept. 20, 1999.

Year	Club & League	AVG	G	AB	R	H	TB	2B	3B	HR	RBI	SH-SF	HP	BB-IBB	SO	SB-CS	GIDP	SLG	OBP
2000	Toronto (DSL)	.250	17	8	7	2	2	0	0	0	0	0-0	0	3-0	5	4-3	0	.250	.455

Holliday, Joshua S. (Josh)

Catcher ... **HT:** 5-10; **WT:** 190 ... **B-T:** S-R ... **BORN:** 14 SEP, 1976, Mesa, AZ **RESIDES:** Stillwater, OK ... **EDUCATION:** Oklahoma St. ... **TRANSACTIONS:** Selected by Blue Jays in ninth round of 1999 draft; signed June 18, 1999. **PRO CAREER:** 1999: Led New York-Penn League in walks (63); second in league in on-base percentage (.439); fifth in league in HR/AB (1/21.6); led St. Catharines in games (71), runs (50), total bases (100), home runs (10), RBI (37), sacrifice hits (5), hit by pitches (11), intentional walks (2), slugging percentage (.463) and on-base percentage (.439); on June 6-7 vs. Auburn smacked a homer in back-to-back games; from July 27-August 15 reached base by hit or walk in 20 consecutive games; from August 7-13 had seven-game hit streak, batting .577 (15-26) with nine runs, five doubles, three homers and seven RBI; on August 22, at Auburn, collected four hits, including a double, a home run and scored three runs; walked four times on August 25 vs. Williamsport; batted .293 (27-92) with 21 runs, six homers and 16 RBI in 32 games in month of August; hit .291 (32-110) on the road; hit .320 (41-128) when playing in the field and just .161 (14-87) as a designated hitter; 2000: Had four-hit game vs. Charleston-SC, May 4; belted pinch-hit grand slam against Charleston-SC, June 22; was second on team in walks (52).

Year	Club & League	AVG	G	AB	R	H	TB	2B	3B	HR	RBI	SH-SF	HP	BB-IBB	SO	SB-CS	GIDP	SLG	OBP
1999	St.cathrnes (NYP)	.255	71	216	50	55	100	13	1	10	37	5-4	11	63-2	57	1-2	2	.463	.439
2000	Hagerstown (SAL)	.220	74	218	46	48	81	13	1	6	29	3-4	7	52-1	64	2-0	2	.372	.381
Minor Totals		.237	145	434	96	103	181	26	2	16	66	8-8	18	115-3	121	3-2	4	.417	.410

Houston, Ryan K.

Pitcher ... **HT:** 6-4; **WT:** 192 ... **B-T:** R-R ... **BORN:** 22 SEP, 1979, Pensacola, FL **RESIDES:** Pensacola, FL ... **EDUCATION:** Pensacola (FL) JC ... **TRANSACTIONS:** Selected by Blue Jays in 31st round of June 1998 draft; signed April 22, 1999. **PRO CAREER:** 1999: Tied for fourth on Medicine Hat with seven starts and 45.2 innings pitched; on June 19 against Missoula allowed two runs in four innings of relief to earn the victory; from July 11-17 went 2-0 with 3.68 ERA in two games (7.1 innings); on July 22, vs. Butte tossed three scoreless innings to notch the save; went 2-1-1 with 3.98 ERA in six games at home (20.1 innings); 2000: Started season as reliever in Queens; was 1-1 with 1.74 ERA in nine appearances in July; finished season as starter in Hagerstown; held opponents scoreless in three of his six starts, including 15 innings over last two starts; was 4-1 with 2.73 ERA in five starts in August; held right-hand batters to .118 average.

Year	Club & League	W-L	ERA	G	GS	CG	ShO	SV	IP	H	R	ER	HR	HB	BB-IBB	SO	WP	BK	OBA
1999	Medcine Hat (PIO)	3-4	6.70	14	7	0	0	1	45.2	61	41	34	4	3	19-0	30	6	2	.321
2000	Queens (NYP)	1-2	2.83	12	0	0	0	0	28.2	23	11	9	1	3	8-0	29	1	0	.217
	Hagerstown (SAL)	5-1	2.21	6	6	0	0	0	36.2	17	9	9	2	4	13-0	27	1	0	.143
Minor Totals		9-7	4.22	32	13	0	0	1	111.0	101	61	52	7	10	40-0	86	8	2	.243

Hubbel, Travis Jay Roy

Pitcher ... **HT:** 6-0; **WT:** 190 ... **B-T:** R-R ... **BORN:** 27 JUN, 1979, Edmonton, AB, Canada ... **RESIDES:** Edmonton, AB, Canada ... **EDUCATION:** HS ... **TRANSACTIONS:** Selected by Blue Jays in 13th round of 1997 draft; signed June 5, 1997. **PRO CAREER:** 1999: switched from 3b to pitching after posting a career .186 batting average; did not allow a run in 7.2 innings of relief; picked up only save vs. Jamestown on June 26 with four shutout innings, allowing one hit while striking out five;

2000: Tied for team lead in wins (8)and was third in innings (113.1) and starts (19); was 5-2 in eight starts on the road; finished ninth in organization in ERA (3.87); held opposing batters to .182 average with runners in scoring position and less than two outs.

Year	Club & League	W-L	ERA	G	GS	CG	ShO	SV	IP	H	R	ER	HR	HB	BB-IBB	SO	WP	BK	OBA
1999	St.cathrnes (NYP)	0-0	1.80	5	3	0	0	1	20.0	16	5	4	1	1	7-0	19	0	0	.213
2000	Hagerstown (SAL)	8-6	3.89	19	19	0	0	0	113.1	103	62	49	7	10	55-0	75	13	0	.253
	Dunedin (FSL)	0-0	3.38	3	0	0	0	0	5.1	4	2	2	2	0	2-0	3	1	0	.235
Minor Totals		8-6	3.57	27	22	0	0	1	138.2	123	69	55	10	11	64-0	97	14	0	.246

Hudson, Orlando Thill

Second Baseman ... **HT:** 6-0; **WT:** 185 ... **B-T:** S-R ... **BORN:** 12 DEC, 1977, Darlington, SC **RESIDES:** Darlington, SC ... **TRANSACTIONS:** Selected by Blue Jays in 43rd round of 1997 draft; signed May 20, 1998. **PRO CAREER:** 1998: Began season hitting safely in 6-of-7 games batting .333 (9-27) with 2 doubles and 6 RBI, including a grand slam and 4 RBI on June 25; from July 28-August 13 hit in 11-out-of-13 games batting .340 (17-50) with 15 runs, 5 doubles, 4 home runs and 14 RBI, including scoring 5 runs on August 13; had a career-high 10 game hitting streak to end the season from August 25-September 3 batting .350 (14-40) with 8 runs and 5 doubles; was .310 (39-126) on the road with 10 doubles, 21 RBI and 29 runs; collected two or more hits in 21 games; 1999: South Atlantic League Player-of-the-Week April 30-May 6; Fifth in league in doubles (36); led Hagerstown in doubles and second on team in triples (6); third on team in games (132), at-bats (513) and RBI (74); batted .429 (12-28) with two home runs and 10 RBI during a seven-game hitting streak April 27-May 2; hit .304 (24-79) with two home runs in 20 games in month of May; on May 5 vs. Hickory knocked in four runs; on June 7 vs. Cape Fear went 2-for-5 with four RBI; from June 12-14 hit .750 (6-8) with three RBI in two games; from June 25-28 hit in four straight games and batted .471 (8-17) with five doubles and eight RBI; from July 10-14 had four-game hit streak, batting .500 (9-18) with three extra-base hits; on August 15 vs. Piedmont went 4-for-4; finished the season with a ten-game hit streak; batted .281 (73-260) at home; slugged six of his seven home runs against right-handed pitchers; hit .429 (6-14) and drove in 18 runs with the bases loaded; 2000: Opened season in Dunedin with eight-game hitting streak, April 6-16; batted .333 (28-84)with 12 RBI in April; hit .371 (43-116) against left-hand pitching; promoted to Tennessee at the end of July; hit .293 with 13 RBI with runners in scoring position; drove in runs in seven consecutive games, July 27-August 3.

Year	Club & League	AVG	G	AB	R	H	TB	2B	3B	HR	RBI	SH-SF	HP	BB-IBB	SO	SB-CS	GIDP	SLG	OBP
1998	Medcine Hat (PIO)	.293	65	242	50	71	115	18	1	8	42	0-2	7	22-0	36	6-5	3	.475	.366
1999	Hagerstown (SAL)	.267	132	513	66	137	206	36	6	7	74	1-5	2	42-3	85	8-6	10	.402	.322
2000	Dunedin (FSL)	.285	96	358	54	102	143	16	2	7	48	4-1	2	37-1	42	9-5	15	.399	.354
	Tennessee (SOU)	.239	39	134	17	32	48	4	3	2	15	1-2	2	15-1	18	3-2	3	.358	.320
Minor Totals		.274	332	247	187	342	512	74	12	24	179	6-10	13	116-5	181	26-18	31	.411	.340

Huesgen, Daniel J.

Pitcher ... **HT:** 6-0; **WT:** 195 ... **B-T:** R-R ... **BORN:** 08 OCT, 1977, St. Louis, MO **RESIDES:** Bridgeton, MO ... **EDUCATION:** Southeast Missouri ... **TRANSACTIONS:** Selected by Blue Jays in 38th round of 2000 draft; signed June 14, 2000. **PRO CAREER:** 2000: Was 2-0 with 1.65 ERA in appearances at home; did not give up an earned run in first six games; earned only save against Staten Island, August 15.

Year	Club & League	W-L	ERA	G	GS	CG	ShO	SV	IP	H	R	ER	HR	HB	BB-IBB	SO	WP	BK	OBA
2000	Queens (NYP)	2-1	2.42	16	0	0	0	1	26.0	27	9	7	2	0	10-0	17	1	0	.267

Hyde, Nathan D.

Outfielder ... **HT:** 6-6; **WT:** 210 ... **B-T:** R-R ... **BORN:** 01 MAR, 1979, Riverdale, CA **RESIDES:** Anderson, SC ... **TRANSACTIONS:** Signed as nondrafted free agent by Blue Jays, Sept. 5, 2000. **PRO CAREER:** 2001 will be first season in pro ball.

Jimenez, Richard A. Pimentel

Infielder ... **HT:** 6-1; **WT:** 175 ... **B-T:** S-R ... **BORN:** 03 JUL, 1981, Santo Domingo, DR **RESIDES:** Santo Domingo, DR ... **TRANSACTIONS:** Signed as non-drafted free agent by Blue Jays, Oct. 6, 1997. **PRO CAREER:** 1998: Tied for team lead with six sacrifice hits; 1999: Led Dominican Summer Blue Jays in batting average (.270), hits (66), sacrifice hits (5), hit by pitch (9) and stolen bases (35); Second on team in at-bats (244) and runs (33); 2000: Split season between Queens and Dominican Summer League.

Year	Club & League	AVG	G	AB	R	H	TB	2B	3B	HR	RBI	SH-SF	HP	BB-IBB	SO	SB-CS	GIDP	SLG	OBP
1998	Blue Jays (DSL)	.276	63	199	44	55	78	9	4	2	36	6-3	10	36-0	43	24-9	6	.392	.407
1999	Sd Blue Jay (DSL)	.270	63	244	33	66	74	6	1	0	18	5-0	9	17-0	39	35-14	2	.303	.341
2000	Queens (NYP)	.219	9	32	5	7	8	1	0	0	3	0-0	1	3-0	9	0-0	0	.250	.306
	Toronto (DSL)	.283	14	53	13	15	17	2	0	0	8	1-0	1	12-0	15	8-4	1	.321	.424
Minor Totals		.271	149	528	95	143	177	18	5	2	65	12-3	21	68-0	106	67-27	9	.335	.374

Johnson, Jeremiah D. (Jeremy)

Outfielder ... **HT:** 6-1; **WT:** 185 ... **B-T:** L-L ... **BORN:** 06 MAY, 1978, Mt. Vernon, IL **RESIDES:** Tamms, IL ... **EDUCATION:** Southeast Missouri ... **TRANSACTIONS:** Selected by Blue Jays in 26th round of 2000 draft; signed June 14, 2000. **PRO CAREER:** 2000: Led Pioneer League in on-base percentage (.498) and finished second in batting (.376), hits (92), doubles (24) and tied for second in extra-base hits (36); was third in total bases (149) and slugging percentage (.608); was fourth in loop in runs (66) and walks(55); fifth in RBI (58), SO/TPA (1/10.62) and slugging; led all short-season players in on-base pct. and finished tied for third among short-season players in doubles and extra-base hits; third in total bases, fourth in hits, fifth in runs and walks and seventh in RBI and batting average; named to Pioneer League All-Star team; had 14-game hitting streak, June 18-July 3; hit in 54 of 67 games; batted .396 with 19 RBI in June; hit .429 in playoffs; named Pioneer League Player of the Week, July 17-23; had two homers and 6 RBI,against Idaho Falls, July 19.

Year	Club & League	AVG	G	AB	R	H	TB	2B	3B	HR	RBI	SH-SF	HP	BB-IBB	SO	SB-CS	GIDP	SLG	OBP
2000	Medcine Hat (PIO)	.376	67	245	66	92	149	24	3	9	58	1-1	6	55-0	29	5-3	8	.608	.498

Johnson, Reed C.

Outfielder ... **HT:** 5-10; **WT:** 180 ... **B-T:** R-R ... **BORN:** 08 DEC, 1976, Riverside, CA **RESIDES:** Temecula, CA ... **EDUCATION:** California St. ... **TRANSACTIONS:** Selected by Blue Jays in 17th round of 1999 draft; signed June 19, 1999. **PRO CAREER:** 1999: from June 24-August 6 did not committ an error in 33 consecutive games; from August 4-10 hit in seven straight games; 2000: Started season at Hagerstown and finished second in South Atlantic League in on-base percentage (.422); led team in RBI (70), doubles (24) and walks (62) despite moving to Dunedin on July 26; led all Class A batters with 25 hit-by-pitch; had 11-game hitting streak, April 12-23; batted .323 with 37 RBI at home; hit .313 in May; batted .643 (9-14) with 19 RBI with bases loaded; hit game-winning home run in just second game with Dunedin, July 27 against Daytona; reached base seven times (3-H, 4-BB) in game vs. Lakeland, August 8; had eight-game hitting streak, August 21-28; batted .317 with 22 RBI in August; batted .459 (17-37) with 24 RBI with runners in scoring position.

Year	Club & League	AVG	G	AB	R	H	TB	2B	3B	HR	RBI	SH-SF	HP	BB-IBB	SO	SB-CS	GIDP	SLG	OBP
1999	St.cathrnes (NYP)	.241	60	191	24	46	64	8	2	2	23	4-4	2	24-1	31	5-5	4	.335	.326
2000	Hagerstown (SAL)	.290	95	324	66	94	152	24	5	8	70	2-3	14	62-1	49	14-2	9	.469	.422
	Dunedin (FSL)	.316	36	133	26	42	67	9	2	4	28	1-3	11	14-0	27	3-2	1	.504	.416
Minor Totals		.281	191	648	116	182	283	41	9	14	121	7-10	27	100-2	107	22-9	14	.437	.394

Jova, Maikel Lopez

Second Baseman ... **HT:** 6-0; **WT:** 195 ... **B-T:** R-R ... **BORN:** 05 MAR, 1981, Villa Clara, Cuba **RESIDES:** San Jose, Costa Rica ... **TRANSACTIONS:** Signed as non-drafted free agent by Blue Jays, Aug. 21, 1999. **PRO CAREER:** 2000: Finished third in Dominican Summer League in hits (93) and RBI (75), fourth in extra-base hits (34), tied for fourth in runs (69) and fifth in doubles (21); led team in runs, hits, doubles, home runs (10) and stolen bases (13).

Year	Club & League	AVG	G	AB	R	H	TB	2B	3B	HR	RBI	SH-SF	HP	BB-IBB	SO	SB-CS	GIDP	SLG	OBP
2000	Toronto (DSL)	.299	71	311	69	93	150	21	3	10	75	0-4	3	9-2	43	13-2	10	.482	.321

Keene, Kurt J.

Infielder ... **HT:** 6-0; **WT:** 190 ... **B-T:** R-R ... **BORN:** 22 AUG, 1977, Chattanooga, TN **RESIDES:** Chattanooga, TN ... **EDUCATION:** Florida ... **TRANSACTIONS:** Selected by Blue Jays in 24th round of 2000 draft; signed June 14, 2000. **PRO CAREER:** 2000: Started season at Queens and hit in first six games, including four consecutive mutiple hit games; promoted to Hagerstown on July 2; had eight-game hitting streak (15-35 with 12 RBI), July 31-August 7; batted .320 with 24 RBI with runners on base; had four-hit game against Cape Fear, August 6.

Year	Club & League	AVG	G	AB	R	H	TB	2B	3B	HR	RBI	SH-SF	HP	BB-IBB	SO	SB-CS	GIDP	SLG	OBP
2000	Queens (NYP)	.261	11	46	10	12	13	1	0	0	5	0-0	0	6-0	10	4-1	3	.283	.346
	Hagerstown (SAL)	.261	55	199	16	52	66	11	0	1	25	0-1	3	8-0	33	4-6	3	.332	.299
Minor Totals		.261	66	245	26	64	79	12	0	1	30	0-1	3	14-0	43	8-7	6	.322	.308

Kegley, Charles W.

Pitcher ... **HT:** 6-3; **WT:** 205 ... **B-T:** R-R ... **BORN:** 17 DEC, 1979, Jacksonville, FL ... **EDUCATION:** Okaloosa-Walton (FL) ... **RESIDES:** Orange Park, FL ... **TRANSACTIONS:** Selected by Blue Jays in 11th round of 1999 draft; signed July 20, 1999. **PRO CAREER:** 2000: Was tenth in organization in ERA (3.88); finished second on team in starts (23) and innings (111.1); held left-hand batters to .198 average; was 3-1 with 2.70 ERA in 11 home starts; fanned season-high eight batters in seven-inning, one run victory vs. Lakeland, August 7.

Year	Club & League	W-L	ERA	G	GS	CG	ShO	SV	IP	H	R	ER	HR	HB	BB-IBB	SO	WP	BK	OBA
2000	Dunedin (FSL)	3-9	3.88	23	23	0	0	0	111.1	96	60	48	6	8	74-1	66	11	5	.241

Kimberley, Glynn J.

Outfielder ... **HT:** 6-4; **WT:** 204 ... **B-T:** R-R ... **BORN:** 30 JUL, 1981, Sydney, Australia **RESIDES:** Bayswater, Victoria, Australia ... **TRANSACTIONS:** Signed as non-drafted free agent by Blue Jays, March 10, 2000. **PRO CAREER:** 2000: Had 3-hit and 3-RBI game vs. Helena, June 16.

Year	Club & League	AVG	G	AB	R	H	TB	2B	3B	HR	RBI	SH-SF	HP	BB-IBB	SO	SB-CS	GIDP	SLG	OBP
2000	Medcine Hat (PIO)	.229	26	83	13	19	26	4	0	1	13	0-1	3	9-0	32	0-0	2	.313	.323

Kingrey, Jarrod Ray

Pitcher ... **HT:** 6-1; **WT:** 200 ... **B-T:** R-R ... **BORN:** 23 AUG, 1976, Columbus, GA **RESIDES:** Forston, GA ... **EDUCATION:** Alabama ... **TRANSACTIONS:** Selected by Blue Jays in 10th round of 1998 draft; signed June 3, 1998. **PRO CAREER:** 1998: Named to Baseball America Short-Season All-Star team; named MVP of St. Catharines team; ranked fourth among short-season relief pitchers in SO/IP ratio (13.86); led New York-Penn League in relief points (48), finished second in saves (16) and tied for third in games finished (24); ranked second among league relievers in SO/9 IP ratio (13.86) and fifth in opponents' batting average (.162); tied for St. Catharines staff lead with 25 appearances; from June 16-July 5 in a span of eight games gave up no runs with five saves (13 IP, 6 H, 5 BB, 20 SO); in 11 appearances from July 28-August 27 gave up no runs and earned seven saves (12.2 IP, 8 H, 8 BB, 17 SO); gave up no earned runs and earned nine saves in 15 outings at home (21 IP, 9 H, 10 BB, 35 SO); named league Pitcher-of-the-Week July 13-19, when he went 0-0, 0.00 ERA and three saves (5.2 IP, 2 H, 2 BB, 11 SO); 1999: Led organization and South Atlantic League in saves (27); also led league in games (56), games finished (48) and relief points (83); led team in games, games finished and saves; finished first 10 games of the season, including seven saves, while posting 3.73 ERA; from May 18-June 7 did not allow a run in nine consecutive appearances, registering four saves; from June 12-27 saved six straight games with 0.00 ERA (6.2 innings); saved eight games with 0.79 ERA in 10 outings in month of June (11.1 innings); won last game of the season on September 6, vs. Delmarva, tossing one scoreless inning; went 1-1-13 with 2.31 ERA in 32 games (35 innings) at home; left handed opponents batted .217 (20-92) and right handed opponents hit .216 (29-134).

Year	Club & League	W-L	ERA	G	GS	CG	ShO	SV	IP	H	R	ER	HR	HB	BB-IBB	SO	WP	BK	OBA
1998	St.cathrnes (NYP)	0-0	0.48	25	0	0	0	16	37.2	21	7	2	1	0	17-0	58	5	1	.162
	Hagerstown (SAL)	0-1	3.86	1	0	0	0	0	2.1	3	2	1	0	0	0-0	3	0	0	.333
1999	Hagerstown (SAL)	3-2	3.10	56	0	0	0	27	61.0	49	24	21	5	6	26-0	69	1	4	.217
2000	Dunedin (FSL)	4-2	2.97	37	0	0	0	23	39.1	33	20	13	2	3	23-1	35	5	1	.224
	Tennessee (SOU)	2-0	2.12	16	0	0	0	7	17.0	11	6	4	0	1	15-2	16	1	0	.193
Minor Totals		9-5	2.35	135	0	0	0	73	157.1	117	59	41	8	10	81-3	181	11	6	.206

Kozlowski, Kristopher R.

Pitcher ... **HT:** 6-4; **WT:** 212 ... **B-T:** L-L ... **BORN:** 10 FEB, 1978, East Meadow, NY **RESIDES:** East Meadow, NY ... **EDUCATION:** Fordham (NY) ... **TRANSACTIONS:** Selected by Blue Jays in 32nd round of 2000 draft; signed June 13, 2000. **PRO CAREER:** 2000: Averaged 11.69 SO/9 IP; was 2-1 with 2.28 ERA and 30 strikeouts in 23.2 innings at home; allowed only two earned runs in eight August appearances (16 innings).

Year	Club & League	W-L	ERA	G	GS	CG	ShO	SV	IP	H	R	ER	HR	HB	BB-IBB	SO	WP	BK	OBA
2000	Queens (NYP)	4-1	2.82	21	0	0	0	0	44.2	38	21	14	2	0	20-0	58	3	2	.221

Kremblas, Michael Thomas (Mike)

Catcher ... **HT:** 6-0; **WT:** 180 ... **B-T:** R-R ... **BORN:** 01 OCT, 1975, Columbus, OH **RESIDES:** Carroll, OH ... **EDUCATION:** Ohio St. ... **TRANSACTIONS:** Selected by Blue Jays in eighth round of 1998 draft; signed June 9, 1998. **PRO CAREER:** 1998: Led Medicine Hat team in walks (40) and hit by pitches (9); threw out 40.7% of would-be basestealers, nailing 24 runners in 35 attempts; batted .476 (30-63, 8 2B, 4 HR, 19 R, 20 RBI) from August 13-September 3 a span of 21 games and raised his average .095 from .198; 1999: Led Hagerstown in hit by pitch (14); between May 21-June 7 hit in nine of 10 games with .343 average (11-32); batted .317 (13-41) in 14 games in month of June; hit .326 (14-43) as leadoff hitter; threw out 49% (31-63) of would be base stealers; 2000: Split season between Dunedin and Tennessee; batted .406 (13-32) with 10 RBI with runners on base at Dunedin; promoted to Tennessee on June 17.

Year	Club & League	AVG	G	AB	R	H	TB	2B	3B	HR	RBI	SH-SF	HP	BB-IBB	SO	SB-CS	GIDP	SLG	OBP
1998	Medcine Hat (PIO)	.293	59	184	40	54	81	15	0	4	36	1-2	9	40-1	30	5-4	4	.440	.438
1999	Hagerstown (SAL)	.206	58	165	22	34	41	7	0	0	7	1-1	14	15-0	28	2-0	5	.248	.323
2000	Dunedin (FSL)	.281	25	64	15	18	22	2	1	0	10	0-1	6	16-0	7	1-0	1	.344	.460
	Tennessee (SOU)	.275	30	69	16	19	26	4	0	1	6	5-2	10	9-0	14	1-1	2	.377	.422
Minor Totals		.259	172	482	93	125	170	28	1	5	59	7-6	39	80-1	79	9-5	12	.353	.402

Kusiewicz, Michael Edward (Mike)

Pitcher ... **HT:** 6-2; **WT:** 190 ... **B-T:** R-L ... **BORN:** 01 NOV, 1976, Montreal, PQ, Canada ... **RESIDES:** Nepean, ON, Canada ... **TRANSACTIONS:** Selected by Rockies in eighth round of 1994 draft; signed Aug. 18, 1994; Claimed on waivers by Twins from Rockies, Nov. 2, 2000; Claimed on waivers by Blue Jays from Twins, March 29, 2000. **PRO CAREER:** 1995: Led South Atlantic League in ERA (2.06) and was fourth in loop in runners/9 IP for starters(9.71); was 5-0 with 1.22 ERA in 11 starts at home; 1996: Fanned ten batters in a game twice, May 7 vs. Reading (6 IP) and July 30 against Canton(7 IP); on disabled list, May 25-June 26, with tendonitis in left shoulder; held left-hand batters to .186 average at New Haven; 1997: Finished third in Carolina League in ERA (2.52) and fifth in lowest batting average against starters (.233); tossed 32.1 consecutive scoreless innings (longest in minors)during five game winning streak, July 22-August 14; was 5-2 with 1.71 ERA in nine starts at home; garnered 4-1 record and 1.59 ERA in six starts in August; 1998: Led Eastern League in ERA (2.32) and lowest BB/9 IP (1.68); second in wins (14) and fewest runners/9 IP (10.49); third in innings (178.2); fourth in lowest batting average against starters (.238) and in strikeouts (151); named LHP on Eastern League All-Star team; named to Baseball America's Double A All-Star team; won six straight decisions (eight starts), June 10-July 16; was 4-2 with 1.95 ERA in seven starts in July; fanned season-high 11 batters vs. Bowie, July 16; 1999: On disabled list with left shoulder surgery; made six starts on rehab assignment in Arizona Rookie League; 2000: Finished second on team in wins (7), tied for second on team in starts (26) and third in innings (156); held opponents to .151 average with runners in scoring position and less than two outs; struck out ten batters vs. Chattanooga, July 5.

Year	Club & League	W-L	ERA	G	GS	CG	ShO	SV	IP	H	R	ER	HR	HB	BB-IBB	SO	WP	BK	OBA
1995	Asheville (SAL)	8-4	2.06	21	21	0	0	0	122.1	92	40	28	6	6	34-0	103	9	1	.208
	Salem (CARO)	0-0	1.50	1	1	0	0	0	6.0	7	1	1	0	2	0-0	7	0	1	.292
1996	New Haven (EAST)	2-4	3.30	14	14	0	0	0	76.1	83	38	28	4	2	27-2	64	0	1	.284
	Salem (CARO)	0-1	5.09	5	3	0	0	0	23.0	19	15	13	2	1	12-0	18	2	0	.224
1997	New Haven (EAST)	2-4	6.35	10	4	0	0	0	28.1	41	28	20	2	6	10-1	11	1	0	.347
	Salem (CARO)	8-6	2.52	19	18	1	1	0	117.2	99	44	33	5	9	32-0	107	7	1	.230
1998	New Haven (EAST)	14-7	2.32	27	26	2	0	0	178.2	161	59	46	4	16	35-0	151	9	1	.240
1999	Rockies (ARIZ)	1-3	5.47	6	6	0	0	0	24.2	26	16	15	0	2	9-0	27	1	1	.263
2000	Tennessee (SOU)	7-9	3.63	27	26	1	0	0	156.0	149	83	63	14	9	59-1	115	10	0	.247
Minor Totals		42-38	3.03	130	119	4	1	1	733.0	677	324	247	37	53	218-4	603	39	6	.245

LaChapelle, Yan Jean-Louis

Pitcher ... **HT:** 6-0; **WT:** 205 ... **B-T:** L-R ... **BORN:** 26 OCT, 1975, Hull, PQ, Canada ... **EDUCATION:** College-Cegep St.Laurent(PQ) ... **RESIDES:** Gatineau, PQ, Canada ... **TRANSACTIONS:** Selected by Blue Jays in third round of 1996 draft; signed June 5, 1996. **PRO CAREER:** 1996: Pitched only four innings, but they were perfect innings and he fanned 8 of the 12 batters he faced; 1997: Started season in the bullpen where he went 1-2, 2.73 ERA and three saves; moved into starting rotation on June 11 and went 6-5, 3.44 ERA in 15 starts; went 5-3, 2.71 ERA over the last two months; led the organization with a 3.26 earned run average and was fifth in the system in strikeouts (115); weaved a one-hitter on August 30 vs Cape Fear; went 7-2, 2.77 ERA at home and 0-5, 3.93 ERA on the road; named 12th-best prospect in Blue Jays' system by Baseball America; 1998: Ranked fifth among Florida State League pitchers in SO/9 IP ratio (8.98) and tied for fifth in organization with 126 strikeouts; led Dunedin staff in innings pitched (126.1); struck out 10 batters on June 26 in six innings against Tampa; from July 30-September 1 went 5-1, 1.05 ERA (43 IP, 32 H, 12 BB, 31 SO); lefty batters hit .205 (36-176); 1999: Split season as starter and reliever; posted 2-3 record with 5.06 ERA in seven starts (32 innings); on June 24-30 won back-to-back starts, allowing just one run and five hits in 10 innings; went 2-0 with 0.60 ERA in five games in month of June; limited opponents to .197 (13-66) with runners in scoring position; 2000: Used as both starter and reliever; was 2-1 with 2.92 ERA in 11 relief appearances and was 3-0 with 2.35 ERA in seven starts; was 2-0 with 1.45 ERA in nine appearances at home; held opponents to .163 average with runners in scoring position.

Year	Club & League	W-L	ERA	G	GS	CG	ShO	SV	IP	H	R	ER	HR	HB	BB-IBB	SO	WP	BK	OBA
1996	St.cathrnes (NYP)	0-0	0.00	3	0	0	0	0	4.0	0	0	0	0	0	0-0	8	0	0	.000
1997	Hagerstown (SAL)	7-7	3.26	26	15	1	1	3	118.2	73	54	43	7	6	74-0	115	12	1	.178
1998	Dunedin (FSL)	11-8	3.99	24	24	1	1	0	126.1	114	68	56	16	5	58-0	126	8	1	.240
1999	Dunedin (FSL)	2-3	5.24	15	7	0	0	1	44.2	46	28	26	3	7	22-0	36	5	0	.271
2000	Dunedin (FSL)	5-1	2.60	18	7	0	0	0	55.1	42	22	16	4	2	27-1	49	2	0	.209
Minor Totals		25-19	3.64	86	53	2	2	4	349.0	275	172	141	30	20	181-1	334	27	2	.217

Langaigne, Selwyn Alexis

Outfielder ... **HT:** 6-0; **WT:** 190 ... **B-T:** L-L ... **BORN:** 22 MAR, 1976, Caracas, VZ **RESIDES:** Las Acaias, VZ ... **TRANSACTIONS:** Signed as non-drafted free agent by Blue Jays, Dec. 15, 1993; Granted free agency, Oct. 15, 2000. **PRO CAREER:** 1996: Went 3-for-4 with a homer in his first game for Medicine Hat on June 19 vs Lethbridge; batted .316 (18-57) at Medicine Hat's Athletic Park; 1997: Struggled for a month and a half at Dunedin and was sent to St. Catharines when the New York-Penn League started in June; tied for second in New York-Penn League in walks (48), finished third in on-base percentage (.423), tied for third in games (74), tied for fourth in hits (85) and ranked sixth in batting (.320); led St. Catharines team with four triples and 19 stolen bases; hit .353 after July 1; hit safely in 30-of-33 games July 27-August 31; named New York-Penn League Player-of-the-Week July 28-August 3; batted .347 at St. Catharines' Community Park; winner of R. Howard Webster award as St. Catharines' team MVP; 1998: Led Dunedin team in games (128); went 4-for-5 with a run, a double and a RBI on April 11 vs Clearwater; collected four RBI and went 3-for-6 with a run and a double on July 16 against Tampa; from August 1-August 8 had a seven game hitting streak batting .333 (9-27); hit .283 wth 22 RBI for Lara of Venezuelan Winter League; 1999: Began season with Knoxville; on April 13 at Jacksonville collected four hits and knocked in five runs; hit .288 (15-52) in 18 games at home; went to Dunedin on June 24 and spent rest of the season there; from July 9-August 27 did not commit an error in 38 consecutive games; on July 31 at Tampa went 3-for-4, including an RBI triple; batted .341 (29-85) with 18 runs in 27 games in month of July; on August 17 vs. Kissimmee tallied three hits and three runs; hit .330 (35-106) with 16 RBI in 33 games on the road; batted .354 (28-79) and drove in 23 RBI with runners on base; had .303 average (50-165) against right-handed pitchers compared to .250 average (9-36) vs. left-handed pitchers; played winter ball with Lara, Venezuelan League, batting .259 in 41 games; 2000: Had nine-game hitting streak with Tennessee, May 13-25; promoted to Syracuse on August 12.

Year	Club & League	AVG	G	AB	R	H	TB	2B	3B	HR	RBI	SH-SF	HP	BB-IBB	SO	SB-CS	GIDP	SLG	OBP
1994	Toronto #1 (DSL)	.296	64	250	42	74	93	10	0	3	49	0-3	0	39-2	23	11-5	0	.372	.387
1995	Toronto (DSL)	.335	65	221	45	74	92	15	0	1	39	1-2	3	43-3	29	16-8	7	.416	.446
1996	Hagerstown (SAL)	.143	4	14	1	2	2	0	0	0	1	0-0	0	1-0	5	2-0	0	.143	.200
	Medcine Hat (PIO)	.260	32	100	19	26	38	4	1	2	11	2-0	1	17-0	20	8-2	4	.380	.373
	Dunedin (FSL)	.222	31	117	16	26	34	2	3	0	4	4-0	2	9-0	30	1-3	5	.291	.289
1997	Dunedin (FSL)	.189	42	90	9	17	23	3	0	1	7	4-0	0	10-0	26	4-1	4	.256	.270
	St.cathrnes (NYP)	.320	74	266	50	85	111	15	4	1	39	0-3	2	48-1	46	19-9	5	.417	.423
1998	Dunedin (FSL)	.261	128	475	52	124	131	7	0	0	38	7-2	2	37-0	73	21-17	12	.276	.316
1999	Knoxville (SOU)	.244	40	123	18	30	36	4	1	0	16	2-0	0	10-0	25	3-4	10	.293	.301
	Dunedin (FSL)	.294	62	201	35	59	76	9	1	2	25	3-3	0	16-0	29	5-5	2	.378	.341
2000	Dunedin (FSL)	.600	5	10	2	6	7	1	0	0	1	0-0	0	1-0	2	0-0	0	.700	.636
	Tennessee (SOU)	.244	76	213	26	52	58	4	1	0	22	2-1	1	21-1	43	1-5	7	.272	.314
	Syracuse (INT)	.239	16	46	3	11	16	5	0	0	0	1-0	0	1-0	8	0-1	1	.348	.255
Minor Totals		.276	639	126	318	586	717	79	11	10	246	26-14	11	253-8	359	91-60	57	.337	.354

Lizardo, Omar A.

Pitcher ... **HT:** 6-2; **WT:** 145 ... **B-T:** R-R ... **BORN:** 22 SEP, 1982, San Pedro De Macoris, DR ... **RESIDES:** San Pedro de Macoris, DR ... **PRO CAREER:** 2000: Held opponents to .179 average.

Year	Club & League	W-L	ERA	G	GS	CG	ShO	SV	IP	H	R	ER	HR	HB	BB-IBB	SO	WP	BK	OBA
2000	Toronto (DSL)	4-3	3.80	14	7	0	0	0	47.1	30	23	20	2	2	34-2	43	9	1	.179

Logan, Matthew Davidson (Matt)

First Baseman ... **HT:** 6-3; **WT:** 210 ... **B-T:** L-R ... **BORN:** 22 JUL, 1979, Cambridge, ON, Canada ... **RESIDES:** Brampton, ON, Canada ... **TRANSACTIONS:** Signed as non-drafted free agent by Blue Jays, Aug. 16, 1997. **PRO CAREER:** 1998: On July 9, drove in 5 runs against Ogden; from July 13-August 25 hit in 14 straight games batting .315 (17-54, 7 R, 5 2B, 2 HR, 13 RBI); 1999: Fourth on Hagerstown in at-bats (453), doubles (21) and home runs (9); hit a homer and drove in two runs on opening day at Columbia; on April 19 vs. Greensboro, smacked two home runs and had four RBI; from April 26-June 6 had 28-game errorless streak; knocked in four runs on May 4, vs. Hickory; from May 8-18 hit in 10 consecutive games, batting .378 (17-45) with eight RBI and two home runs; on May 10 at Cape Fear, went 4-for-4, including a homer, and also had four RBI; hit .298 (17-57) in 15 games in month of July; on August 5-6 hit four doubles and scored four runs in two games at Cape Fear; went 2-for-5 with two RBI as a pinch-hitter; against right-handed pitchers, batted .258 (98-380) with 16 doubles and eight homers and drove in 51 runs; 2000: Appeared in 124 games for Single-A Dunedin of the Flordia State League, collecting 104 hits for a .279 batting average in 373 at-bats. Smacked a three-run double in the top of the 10th inning as the Blue Jays topped Kissimmee, 7-4, on July 18, part of a season-high, five-RBI game. Homered in back-to-back games July 21-22 and had seven hits in 10 at-bats August 22-24.

Year	Club & League	AVG	G	AB	R	H	TB	2B	3B	HR	RBI	SH-SF	HP	BB-IBB	SO	SB-CS	GIDP	SLG	OBP
1998	Medcine Hat (PIO)	.266	47	173	29	46	69	12	1	3	30	0-1	4	23-0	41	1-1	5	.399	.363
1999	Hagerstown (SAL)	.243	119	453	55	110	160	21	1	9	57	2-4	2	32-1	130	3-2	6	.353	.293
2000	Dunedin (FSL)	.279	124	373	58	104	159	26	1	9	55	2-6	7	36-0	93	4-1	13	.426	.348
Minor Totals		.260	290	999	142	260	388	59	3	21	142	4-11	13	91-1	264	8-4	24	.388	.327

Lopez, Felipe

Shortstop ... **HT:** 6-0; **WT:** 175 ... **B-T:** S-R ... **BORN:** 12 MAY, 1980, Bayamon, PR **RESIDES:** Apopka, FL ... **TRANSACTIONS:** Selected by Blue Jays in first round (eighth overall) of 1998 draft; signed Aug. 11, 1998. **PRO CAREER:** 1998: After signing on August 11, hit safely in 17-out-of-19 games played with St. Catherines; had nine multiple-hit games, including a 4-for-8 performance on August 21 against Jamestown; was called up to Dunedin on September 3; ranked third-best prospect in organization and fourth-best prospect in New York-Penn League by Baseball America; 1999: Fifth in South Atlantic League in at-bats (537); led Hagerstown in batting average (.277), games (134) and sacrifice flies (6); second on team in at-bats (537), runs (87), hits (149), total bases (226), triples (4), and RBI (80); third on team in doubles (27) and also tied for third in home runs (14); on May 4, vs. Hickory went 3-for-4, including a triple and homer, with three runs and three RBI; from May 9-13 had two hits or more in four consecutive games; on May 16, at Macon, collected four hits and knocked in three runs; smacked two home runs on May 23 at Asheville; from May 25-June 3 had 10-game hitting streak and batted .432 (19-44) with 11 runs, three homers and nine RBI; hit .326 (42-129) with 15 extra-base hits, 29 runs and 24 RBI in 29 games in month of May; hit four home runs in month of June; hit home run in last game of the season vs. Delmarva; batted .429 (9-21) with four runs in five games in month of Septmber; hit .316 (36-114) against left-handed pitchers; nine of 14 homers were solo; batted .290 (73-252) with runners in scoring position; had 46 multi-hit games; chosen for Howe Sportsdata All-Teen team honorable mention; named second best prospect in organization and fourth best prospect in South Atlantic League by Baseball America; played winter ball for Santurce, Puerto Rican League, batting .261 in 20 games; 2000: Played in 127 games for Double-A Tennessee of the Southern League. Went 3-for-4 with a double, an RBI and a run scored in his first game of the season, April 6, and went 4-for-5 with a season-high three runs scored on May 19. Was suspended in late-May for violating team policy. Went 3-for-4 with a double and three stolen bases in a 5-4 victory over Orlando on June 17. Knocked home the eventual game-winning run with a sacrifice fly in the top of the 11th inning as the Smokies beat Greenville, 10-9, on July 19. Led off the bottom of the 13th inning with a solo home run to beat Greenville 10-9 on August 23.

Year	Club & League	AVG	G	AB	R	H	TB	2B	3B	HR	RBI	SH-SF	HP	BB-IBB	SO	SB-CS	GIDP	SLG	OBP
1998	St.cathrnes (NYP)	.373	19	83	14	31	43	5	2	1	11	0-0	0	3-0	14	4-2	1	.518	.395
	Dunedin (FSL)	.385	4	13	3	5	10	0	1	1	0-0	0	0-0	3	0-0	1	.769	.385
1999	Hagerstown (SAL)	.277	134	537	87	149	226	27	4	14	80	0-6	3	61-0	157	21-14	7	.421	.351
2000	Tennessee (SOU)	.257	127	463	52	119	172	18	4	9	41	8-3	1	31-0	110	12-11	6	.371	.303
Minor Totals		.277	284	096	156	304	451	50	11	25	133	8-9	4	95-0	284	37-27	15	.411	.335

Lopez, Luis

First Baseman ... **HT:** 6-0; **WT:** 205 ... **B-T:** R-R ... **BORN:** 05 OCT, 1973, Brooklyn, NY **RESIDES:** Corpus Christi, TX ... **TRANSACTIONS:** Signed by independent Ogden (Pioneer), July 8, 1995 ... Released by Ogden, Sept. 2, 1995; Signed by Blue Jays, June 15, 1996. **PRO CAREER:** 1995: Began pro career with St. Paul of the Northern League; finished fourth in Pioneer League batting race (.357) and placed fifth in slugging (.555); had the fifth-best HR/AB ratio in the league (1/26) and was also the fifth toughest batter to strike out (1/10.25 plate appearances); 1996: Tied for St. Catharines team lead with 17 doubles; hit .406 (26-64, 6 2B, 3 HR, 18 RBI) in 17 games July 19-August 6; hit safely in nine straight games August 5-13, batting .378 (14-37) during streak; 1997: Led South Atlantic League in batting (.358), hits (180) and on-base percentage (.430), finished second in doubles (47), tied for second in runs (96), ranked third in total bases (268) and extra-base hits (62) and fourth in RBI (99) and slugging (.533); finished second in SO/TPA ratio (1/12.82); led Hagerstown team in games (136), at-bats (503) and walks (60); winner of the R. Howard Webster award as team MVP; compiled a 15-game hitting streak May 1-16, hitting .523 (34-65) during the streak and earning the league's Player-of-the-Week honours; a week later, he embarked on an 11-game hitting streak, batting .400 (14-35) during the streak; clouted a grand slam on May 23 vs Delmarva; hit .455 (51-112) in May to lead the entire minor leagues; he also won the organization's Player-of-the-Month honours for May and August; winner of Howe Sportsdata's "Star of Stars" award as MVP of the All-Star game; went 5-for-5 with two doubles and three RBI on June 26 against Piedmont; hit safely in ten straight games July 25-August 4, batting .463 (19-41) during the streak; doubled in four consecutive games August 21-24; hit .371 at home and .344 on the road; played 87 games at first base without committing an error; 1998: Named MVP of Knoxville Smokies; finished fifth in Southern League in SO/TPA ratio (1/9.44) and eighth in batting (.313); led Knoxville squad in hits (141), sacrifice flies (8) and intentional walks (3) and tied for team lead in roundtrippers (15); began season with Knoxville and had a seven-game hitting streak April 4-9 batting .545 (12-22, 4 R, 4 RBI), including a 4-for-4 effort on April 7; from May 13-22 batted .300 (10-30, 6 R, 4 2B, 5 RBI) in an eight-game hitting streak; on June 12 went 4-for-4 with two runs and a double against Greenville; went 4-for-5 with three runs, two doubles and an RBI on June 21 against Mobile; batted .327 (107-327, 56 R, 19 2B, 1 3B, 13 HR, 69 RBI) vs right-handed pitchers; with runners in scoring position and two outs, batted .354 (17-48, 1 2B, 1 3B, 4 HR, 26 RBI); was called up to Syracuse on August 2 and proceeded to hit in first five games from August 2-6 batting .318 (7-22) with four runs; went 2-for-9 with 4 RBI in three playoff games for Knoxville; 1999: Third in International League and led organization in hits (171); fifth in league in SO/TPA (1/10.03); sixth in league and third in organization in average (.322); led Syracuse in batting, games (136), at-bats (531), runs (76), hits, total bases (222), doubles (35) and sacrifice hits (8); third on team in triples (2) and RBI (69); on May 6 at Durham went 4-for-5 with four runs and two RBI; from May 9-14 hit in six straight games, batting .400 (10-25) with five runs; between May 16-June 7 had at least one hit in 21 of 22 games and hit .352 (31-88) with 15 runs and 18 RBI; on May 18 against Durham smacked grand slam home run and finished with seven RBI; batted .347 (41-121) with 20 runs and 22 RBI in 30 games in month of May; from June 11-17 hit in seven consecutive games; batted .351 (40-114) in 28 games in month of June; hit grand slam homer on July 18 at Pawtucket; between July 20-August 7 hit in 22 of 24 games, batting .373 (25-67); hit .330 (30-91) with 15 runs in 25 games in month of July; had 13-game hit streak from August 12-24; on August 31 vs. Scranton-WB collected four hits; finished the season with seven-game hit streak and batted .500 (15-30) with eight runs in same span; hit .322 at home (82-255) and on the road (89-276); hit .360 (40-111) against left-handed pitchers; batted .346 (45-130) as a leadoff hitter; recorded 50 multi-hit games; 2000: Finished second in the International League with 161 hits and a .328 batting average for Triple-A Syracuse. Led the International League with one strikeout every 16.64 plate appearances. Drew 48 walks and had 35 extra-base hits in 130 games, spanning 491 at-bats, posting a .430 slugging percentage and a .384 batting average. Did not strike out in 14 consecutive games April 14-May 3, going 22-for-55 with 11 RBI. Had a season-high three doubles in a 15-7 loss against Buffalo on May 20 and did not strike out in 25 consecutive games May 12- June 13. Had a 12-game hitting streak July 4-16 and went 5-for-5 with a season-high five RBI in a 14-6 victory over Rochester on August 23.

Year	Club & League	AVG	G	AB	R	H	TB	2B	3B	HR	RBI	SH-SF	HP	BB-IBB	SO	SB-CS	GIDP	SLG	OBP
1995	St. Paul (NOR)	.111	13	27	43	3	3	0	0	0	0	0-0	0	7-0	3	0-0	0	.111	.294
	Ogden (PIO)	.357	46	182	36	65	101	15	0	7	39	3-2	2	16-0	20	1-1	5	.555	.411
1996	St.cathrnes (NYP)	.285	74	260	36	74	116	17	2	7	40	4-3	7	27-1	31	2-3	4	.446	.364
1997	Hagerstown (SAL)	.358	136	503	96	180	268	47	4	11	99	0-6	8	60-4	45	5-8	14	.533	.430
1998	Knoxville (SOU)	.313	119	450	70	141	215	27	1	15	85	0-8	3	58-3	55	0-2	18	.478	.389
	Syracuse (INT)	.220	11	41	6	9	12	0	0	1	3	0-1	0	6-0	6	0-0	2	.293	.313
1999	Syracuse (INT)	.322	136	531	76	171	222	35	2	4	69	2-8	1	40-2	58	1-0	22	.418	.366
2000	Syracuse (INT)	.328	130	491	64	161	211	27	1	7	79	0-8	2	48-1	33	3-1	10	.430	.384
Minor Totals		.326	652	458	384	801	145	168	10	52	414	9-36	23	255-11	248	12-15	75	.466	.389

Loyd, Brian Richard

Catcher ... **HT:** 6-2; **WT:** 205 ... **B-T:** R-R ... **BORN:** 03 DEC, 1973, Lynwood, CA **RESIDES:** Yorba Linda, CA ... **EDUCATION:** California St. ... **TRANSACTIONS:** Selected by Padres in fifth round of 1996 draft; signed Aug. 8, 1996; Traded by Padres with a player to be named to Blue Jays for LHP Randy Myers, Aug. 7, 1998. **PRO CAREER:** 1997: Hit safely in 13-of-18 games, including ten in a row, August 8-23, batting .377 (20-53); nailed 31% of would-be basestealers, throwing out 28 runners in 91 attempts; 1998: Hit safely in five straight games batting .526 (10-19, 2 R, 2 2B, 2 RBI) from April 22-26 for Rancho Cucamonga; went 4-for-5 with a double, two runs and two RBI on May 8 against Lake Elsinore; from June 5-13 had a nine-game hitting streak batting .350 (14-40, 7 R); went 4-for-5 with a run and two RBI on July 19 against Bakersfield; batted .411 (39-95, 24 R, 9 2B, 7 RBI) vs left-handed pitchers; threw out 30% of would-be basestealers, nabbing 24 runners in 80 attempts; 1999: Fourth on Knoxville in RBI (65), sacrifice flies (6) and stolen bases (9); hit three home runs in first nine games of the season; between May 8-20 had at least one hit in 11 of 12 games, batting .444 (16-36) with two home runs and nine RBI; on June 24 at Greenville, went 4-for-5 with three runs, including a solo homer; batted .302 (19-63) with three home runs and 12 RBI in 18 games in month of June; collected four hits and scored three runs on August 24 at Jacksonville; had 20 RBI in 26 games in month of August; launched a homer in final game of season at Carolina; hit .324 (60-185) with 34 runs and seven homers in 51 games on the road; slugged nine of 11 home runs against right-handed pitchers; batted .375 (6-16) and knocked in 17 runs with bases loaded; hit .317 (19-60) and drove in 23 runs with runners in scoring position and two outs; threw out 32 percent of runners attempting to steal (54-168); second on the team in postseason with a .471 batting average (8-17); had three doubles and four RBI in four playoff games; 2000: Began the season with Double-A Tennessee of the Southern League before being promoted to Triple-A Syracuse of the International League. Had 58 hits in 58 games for Tennessee, batting .299 in 194 at-bats. Delivered an RBI single in the bottom of the 13th inning to beat Chattanooga, 8-7, on April 21. Went 3-for-3 with a pair of RBI as the Smokies blanked Orlando, 3-0, May 27 and hit in 11 straight games from May 14-28, posting a .487 batting average. Smacked a pinch-hit, two-run double in the bottom of the 10th inning to beat Greenville, 8-7, July 15.

Year	Club & League	AVG	G	AB	R	H	TB	2B	3B	HR	RBI	SH-SF	HP	BB-IBB	SO	SB-CS	GIDP	SLG	OBP
1996	Clinton (MID)	.297	10	37	3	11	13	2	0	0	2	0-0	2	0-0	6	0-0	0	.351	.333
1997	Clinton (MID)	.274	73	259	35	71	87	10	0	2	33	4-5	8	25-2	41	6-4	12	.336	.350
1998	Rancho Cuca (CAL)	.305	87	318	55	97	130	19	1	4	35	2-2	10	42-1	45	1-4	8	.409	.401
	Dunedin (FSL)	.204	16	49	8	10	13	0	0	1	5	1-2	1	5-0	10	1-0	3	.265	.281
1999	Knoxville (SOU)	.280	104	364	53	102	155	18	1	11	65	4-6	4	46-3	57	9-2	11	.426	.362
2000	Tennessee (SOU)	.299	58	194	21	58	73	10	1	1	23	0-2	2	29-1	22	7-3	6	.376	.392
	Syracuse (INT)	.135	22	52	2	7	10	0	0	1	4	0-1	1	3-0	9	0-2	2	.192	.193
Minor Totals		.280	370	273	177	356	481	59	3	20	167	11-18	28	150-7	190	24-15	42	.378	.364

Lyon, Brandon J.

Pitcher ... **HT:** 6-1; **WT:** 175 ... **B-T:** R-R ... **BORN:** 10 AUG, 1979, Salt Lake City, UT **RESIDES:** Salt Lake City, UT ... **EDUCATION:** Dixie (UT) JC ... **TRANSACTIONS:** Selected by Blue Jays in 14th round of 1999 draft; signed May 31, 2000. **PRO CAREER:** 2000: Pitched in 15 games for the Queens Kings of the Single-A New York-Penn League, going 5-3 with a 2.39 ERA. Finished first in the league among starters with 0.95 walks per nine innings and allowing just under eight base runners per nine innings. He also finished fourth among starting pitchers with a .205 batting average against. Earned his first-career victory on June 26 versus Auburn, allowing a run and four hits over five innings, fanning four without issuing a walk. In his next start, he tossed five hitless innings against Staten Island, striking out seven and walking one, but he did not figure in the decision. Finished the year with 10-straight scoreless innings, posting a 2-0 record, scattering three hits, striking out 10 and walking none.

Year	Club & League	W-L	ERA	G	GS	CG	ShO	SV	IP	H	R	ER	HR	HB	BB-IBB	SO	WP	BK	OBA
2000	Queens (NYP)	5-3	2.39	15	13	0	0	0	60.1	43	20	16	1	2	6-0	55	1	1	.197

Malpica, Martin A. Moreno

Infielder ... **HT:** 6-2; **WT:** 208 ... **B-T:** R-R ... **BORN:** 21 SEP, 1979, Barquisimeto, VZ **RESIDES:** Lara, VZ ... **TRANSACTIONS:** Signed as non-drafted free agent by Blue Jays, May 6, 1997. **PRO CAREER:** 1999: Led Chino of Venezuela Summer Leauge in doubles (10) and hit by pitch (9); tied for first in sacrifice flies (3); second in batting average (.317); also third in home runs (4) and RBI (33); raised his career average .71 points; 2000: Had 60 hits in 55 games for Class-A Queens of the New York-Penn League. Began the season with seven hits and nine RBI in his first 14 at-bats, spanning four games, and went 3-for-5 with a pair of doubles and four RBI at Staten Island on July 1. Hit in 17 of 19 games July 20-August 10, for a .365 batting average. Had three, four-hit games during the season, including a 4-for-5 performance with two RBI and a season-high four runs scored against New Jersey on August 18.

Year	Club & League	AVG	G	AB	R	H	TB	2B	3B	HR	RBI	SH-SF	HP	BB-IBB	SO	SB-CS	GIDP	SLG	OBP
1997	S Joaquin-1 (VSL)	.236	35	89	10	21	32	5	0	2	10	0-2	0	7-0	17	0-0	1	.360	.286
1998	S Joaquin-2 (VSL)	.236	54	161	13	38	47	5	2	0	16	0-0	3	6-0	25	3-3	0	.292	.276
1999	Chino (VSL)	.317	48	142	24	45	67	10	0	4	33	1-3	9	16-1	16	0-2	0	.472	.412
2000	Queens (NYP)	.278	55	216	30	60	80	14	0	2	34	1-0	2	7-0	35	0-3	5	.370	.307
Minor Totals		.270	192	608	77	164	226	34	2	8	93	2-5	14	36-1	93	3-8	6	.372	.323

Markwell, Diegomar R.

Pitcher ... **HT:** 6-2; **WT:** 197 ... **B-T:** L-L ... **BORN:** 08 AUG, 1980, Curacao, Netherland Antilles ... **RESIDES:** Curacao, Netherland Antilles ... **TRANSACTIONS:** Signed as non-drafted free agent by Blue Jays, Aug. 8, 1996. **PRO CAREER:** 1997: Went 1-1, 2.29 ERA in July; 1998: Struck out seven batters in five innings on August 8 vs Oneonta; 1999: Led St. Catharines in games started (13); tied for second in wins (3); third in innings pitched (59.1); on June 29 vs. Williamsport allowed one earned run and struck out seven in five innings to earn the win; yielded just three hits and one unearned run and fanned six in six innings against Williamsport on August 24 to notch the victory; went 2-2 with 5.59 ERA in eight games (38.2 innings) at home; 2000: Began the season with Single-A Hagerstown of the South Atlantic League before being sent down to Class-A Queens of the New York-Penn League. Pitched just two innings, facing nine batters, while with Hagerstown. Tossed seven-scoreless innings in his first start with Queens June 23, scattering three hits while striking out eight and issuing a pair of walks to pick up the win. Matched his longest outing of the season with seven-scoreless innings of one-hit ball against Vermont on August 5, fanning seven and walking only one in the win.

Year	Club & League	W-L	ERA	G	GS	CG	ShO	SV	IP	H	R	ER	HR	HB	BB-IBB	SO	WP	BK	OBA
1997	St.cathrnes (NYP)	1-6	4.99	16	11	0	0	0	48.2	50	35	27	1	8	40-0	33	5	1	.265
1998	St.cathrnes (NYP)	3-3	5.54	17	5	0	0	0	52.0	61	39	32	2	3	35-0	40	7	1	.289
1999	St.cathrnes (NYP)	3-4	7.58	14	13	0	0	0	59.1	72	55	50	8	4	38-0	54	6	0	.287
2000	Hagerstown (SAL)	0-1	9.00	2	0	0	0	0	2.0	3	2	2	0	0	5-0	2	0	0	.333
	Queens (NYP)	4-3	3.05	14	13	0	0	0	73.2	59	29	25	2	3	31-0	66	2	0	.221
Minor Totals		11-17	5.19	63	42	0	0	0	235.2	245	160	136	13	18	149-0	195	20	2	.264

Marte, Leonardo R.

Catcher ... **HT:** 6-3; **WT:** 200 ... **B-T:** S-R ... **BORN:** 23 MAY, 1984, Santo Domingo, DR **RESIDES:** Santo Domingo, DR ... **TRANSACTIONS:** Signed as a non-drafted free agent by the Blue Jays, July 11, 2000 ... **PRO CAREER:** 2001 will be his first professional season.

Martin, Cesar A.

Infielder ... **HT:** 6-0; **WT:** 165 ... **B-T:** R-R ... **BORN:** 21 JUN, 1981, San Pedro de Macoris, DR ... **RESIDES:** San Pedro de Macoris, DR ... **TRANSACTIONS:** Signed as non-drafted free agent by Blue Jays, July 2, 1998. **PRO CAREER:** 1999: With Dominican Summer Blue Jays was second on team in batting average (.253), home runs (3) and slugging percentage (.347); third in total bases (74); 2000: Had 73 hits in 68 games for the Blue Jays of the Rookie Level Dominican Summer League, batting .274 with 43 RBI and 63 runs scored.

Year Club & League	AVG	G	AB	R	H	TB	2B	3B	HR	RBI	SH-SF	HP	BB-IBB	SO	SB-CS	GIDP	SLG	OBP
1999 Sd Blue Jay (DSL)	.253	58	190	23	48	66	7	1	3	19	1-1	5	30-2	36	5-3	4	.347	.367
2000 Toronto (DSL)	.274	68	266	64	73	97	15	0	3	52	0-7	9	42-0	36	7-1	6	.365	.383
Minor Totals	.265	126	456	87	121	163	22	1	6	71	1-8	14	72-2	72	12-4	10	.357	.376

Martinez, Casey J.

Catcher ... **HT:** 5-11; **WT:** 200 ... **B-T:** R-R ... **BORN:** 31 AUG, 1977, Kansas City, MO ... **EDUCATION:** Sacramento St. (CA) ... **RESIDES:** Holmdel, NJ ... **TRANSACTIONS:**Selected by Blue Jays in 47th round of 2000 draft; signed June 15, 2000. **PRO CAREER:** 2000: Played in nine games for Medicine Hat of the Rookie Level Pioneer League before being called up to Queens of the Single-A New York-Penn League, where he appeared in seven contests. Had a hit in five of his last six games for Medicine Hat before being promoted to Queens in the end of July. Son of Toronto Blue Jays Manager Buck Martinez.

Year Club & League	AVG	G	AB	R	H	TB	2B	3B	HR	RBI	SH-SF	HP	BB-IBB	SO	SB-CS	GIDP	SLG	OBP
2000 Medcine Hat (PIO)	.280	9	25	5	7	13	3	0	1	3	0-0	1	6-0	7	0-0	1	.520	.438
Queens (NYP)	.136	7	22	2	3	3	0	0	0	0	1-0	1	1-0	7	0-0	0	.136	.208
Minor Totals	.213	16	47	7	10	16	3	0	1	3	1-0	2	7-0	14	0-0	1	.340	.339

Mayorson, Manuel A. Hidalgo

Second Baseman ... **HT:** 5-10; **WT:** 167 ... **B-T:** R-R ... **BORN:** 10 MAR, 1983, Higuey, DR **RESIDES:** La Romana, DR ... **TRANSACTIONS:** Signed as non-drafted free agent by Blue Jays, July 5, 1999. **PRO CAREER:** 2000: Appeared in 56 games for Medicine Hat of the Rookie Level Pioneer League. Went 4-for-6 with a double, two RBI and a season-high four runs scored in his first game as a professional June 16. Had three hits and a run scored June 20 and went 3-for-6 with three runs scored on July 22. Reached base 81 times via a hit or a walk and scored 39 times, 48 percent of the time he was on base.

Year Club & League	AVG	G	AB	R	H	TB	2B	3B	HR	RBI	SH-SF	HP	BB-IBB	SO	SB-CS	GIDP	SLG	OBP
2000 Medcine Hat (PIO)	.220	56	218	39	48	52	2	1	0	12	2-0	1	33-0	27	3-2	6	.239	.325

McClellan, Matthew Brinton (Matt)

Pitcher ... **HT:** 6-7; **WT:** 220 ... **B-T:** R-R ... **BORN:** 13 AUG, 1976, Toledo, OH **RESIDES:** Toledo, OH ... **EDUCATION:** Oakland (MI) ... **TRANSACTIONS:** Selected by Blue Jays in seventh round of 1997 draft; signed June 5, 1997. **PRO CAREER:** 1998: Tied for fourth in organization in strikeouts (126) and ranked fifth in earned run average (3.09); from June 21-July 1 threw 15 scoreless innings going 1-1 (8 H, 7 BB, 15 SO), including a 10- strikeout performance on July 1 vs Greensboro; won back-to-back starts July 31 against Charleston-WV and August 6 against Augusta with a 0.60 ERA (15 IP, 6 H, 5 BB, 9 SO), incuding a three-hit complete game on August 6; did not earn decision in only playoff appearance (5.1 IP, 4 H, 2 R, 2 ER, 0 BB, 9 SO); 1999: Second in Florida State League and third in organization in strikeouts (146); fourth in league in SO/9 IP starter (8.85); fifth in league and fourth in organization in wins (13); fifth in league in games started (25) and Avg against starter (.213); seventh in organization in ERA (.379); Led Dunedin in games started and strikeouts; second on team in wins, innings pitched (147.1) and complete games (1); allowed just one hit and no runs while striking out 12 in first two starts of the season (9.0 innings); from April 28-May 3 won back-to-back games with 2.25 ERA and 11 strikeouts in 12 innings; on June 3 at Fort Myers tossed seven scoreless innings and fanned six to earn the victory; from June 28-July 27 posted 4-1 record with 2.79 ERA and 31 strikeouts in six starts (38.2 innings); fanned 36 batters in 30 innings in month of August; participated in combination shutout in his final game of season, striking out eight in seven innings; made 12 quality starts; fanned six or more batters in 13 of 25 starts; went 6-2 with 3.34 ERA in 11 games on the road (62 innings); right-handed opponents hit just .203 (64-316); limited opposing batters to .200 (12-60) with runners in scoring position and two outs; made two starts in the playoffs and posted 1-0 record with 1.64 ERA, while striking out 12 batters in 11 innings; 2000: Appeared in 28 games, making 27 starts, for Double-A Tennessee of the Southern League. Went 2-0 and allowed two earned runs or fewer in three consecutive starts, May 9-19, striking out 19 and walking just seven in 18 1/3 innings. Struck out a career-high 12 batters over eight innings, giving up a run and four hits, in a no-decision at Greenville on July 20. It was the third double-digit strikeout game of his four-year career.

Year Club & League	W-L	ERA	G	GS	CG	ShO	SV	IP	H	R	ER	HR	HB	BB-IBB	SO	WP	BK	OBA
1997 Medcine Hat (PIO)	2-5	6.92	14	6	0	0	0	39.0	50	36	30	7	3	24-0	43	2	0	.309
1998 Hagerstown (SAL)	8-7	3.09	25	25	1	0	0	139.2	109	65	48	8	14	58-3	126	6	5	.215
1999 Dunedin (FSL)	13-5	3.79	26	25	1	0	0	147.1	114	69	62	15	10	61-0	146	6	3	.213
2000 Tennessee (SOU)	6-12	4.80	28	27	0	0	0	168.2	174	100	90	16	11	69-1	140	11	3	.265
Minor Totals	29-29	4.18	93	83	2	0	0	494.2	447	270	230	46	38	212-4	455	25	11	.240

McCullem, Ryan Philip

Pitcher ... **HT:** 6-3; **WT:** 205 ... **B-T:** L-L ... **BORN:** 08 OCT, 1980, Columbia, MO **RESIDES:** Columbia, MO ... **TRANSACTIONS:** Selected by Blue Jays in eighth round of 1999 draft; signed June 4, 1999. **PRO CAREER:** 1999: Tied for fourth on Medicine Hat in victories (2); from August 16-21 won back-to-back games, allowing one unearned run in 6.1 innings; on August 21 vs. Ogden struck out six in five innings; 2000: Pitched in 16 games, making six starts, for Medicine Hat of the Rookie Level Pioneer League. Picked up victories in his first two starts of the season June 18-23, allowing five runs — four earned — and 11 hits over 10 1/3 innings, striking out 11 and walking only two.

Year Club & League	W-L	ERA	G	GS	CG	ShO	SV	IP	H	R	ER	HR	HB	BB-IBB	SO	WP	BK	OBA
1999 Medcine Hat (PIO)	2-1	6.08	9	5	0	0	0	23.2	34	17	16	1	0	11-0	19	3	1	.337
2000 Medcine Hat (PIO)	2-2	3.95	16	6	0	0	0	54.2	64	34	24	5	2	27-0	53	5	0	.291
Minor Totals	4-3	4.60	25	11	0	0	0	78.1	98	51	40	6	2	38-0	72	8	1	.305

McCulloch, Andrew B.

Pitcher ... **HT:** 6-1; **WT:** 205 ... **B-T:** R-R ... **BORN:** 26 FEB, 1978, Las Vegas, NV **RESIDES:** Las Vegas, NV ... **EDUCATION:** Nevada-Las Vegas ... **TRANSACTIONS:** Selected by Blue Jays in 20th round of 2000 draft; signed June 13, 2000. **PRO**

CAREER: 2000: Earned 15 saves in 27 games for Medicine Hat, which was tied for second most in the Rookie Level Pioneer League. Finished first in the league with 45 relief points and was second in the league with 24 games finished. Allowed 24 hits in 105 at-bats, spanning 27 innings while posting a 2.67 ERA. Allowed 10.33 baserunners per nine innings, finishing third among relievers in the league. Earned a save in six-straight appearances June 23-July 7, giving up just one run in 6 1/3 innings. Closed out the year with eight saves in 11 games, surrendering only two runs in 10 1/3 relief innings.

Year Club & League	W-L	ERA	G	GS	CG	ShO	SV	IP	H	R	ER	HR	HB	BB-IBB	SO	WP	BK	OBA
2000 Medcine Hat (PIO)	0-0	2.67	27	0	0	0	15	27.0	24	9	8	3	0	7-0	26	2	0	.229

McFarland, Stuart D.

Pitcher ... HT: 6-5; **WT:** 210 ... **B-T:** L-L ... **BORN:** 12 SEP, 1977, St. Louis, MN **RESIDES:** Arden Hills, MN ... **EDUCATION:** Florida ... **TRANSACTIONS:** Selected by Blue Jays in 50th round of 2000 draft; signed June 12, 2000. **PRO CAREER: 2000:** Made 19 appearances for Queens of the Single-A New York-Penn League, being used primarily out of the bullpen. Allowed just one run over his final 14 2/3 innings, spanning nine games.

Year Club & League	W-L	ERA	G	GS	CG	ShO	SV	IP	H	R	ER	HR	HB	BB-IBB	SO	WP	BK	OBA
2000 Queens (NYP)	2-2	2.08	19	0	0	0	2	26.0	12	9	6	0	8	22-1	21	1	0	.148

McKinney, Antonio DeVaughn

Outfielder ... HT: 5-10; **WT:** 175 ... **B-T:** R-R ... **BORN:** 02 JAN, 1978, Portland, OR **RESIDES:** Portland, OR ... **TRANSAC-TIONS:** Selected by Tigers in third round of 1996 draft; signed June 9, 1996; Selected by Blue Jays from Tigers in Rule 5 minor league draft, Dec. 11, 2000. **PRO CAREER: 1996:** Had 31 hits in 44 games for the Tigers of the Single-A Gulf Coast League; **1997:** Began the season with the Tigers of the Rookie Level Gulf Coast League before being promoted to Class-A Jamestown of the New York-Penn League. Hit in six consecutive games from June 26-July 5, batting .318 with five RBI during that span. Collected a pair of hits, including a homer, and drove in three runs in his final game for the Tigers. Went 3-for-4 with a double and two runs scored for the Jammers on August 15 at Vermont; **1998:** Hit .308 in 39 games for Jamestown of the Single-A New York-Penn League before being promoted to Single-A West Michigan of the Midwest League. Had 14 hits in 33 at-bats, hitting .424, from July 24-August 13 and closed out the season with a hit in each of his last seven games for the Jammers, going 14-for-34 with a .418 batting average. Got his only hit of the season at Single-A West Michigan in his last game of the year on September 7; **1999:** Appeared in 68 games with Class-A Oneonta of the New York-Penn League, gathering 57 hits with a .249 batting average. Had three hits, including a double, and a run scored against Pittsfield on June 29 and went 4-for-5 with an RBI and two runs scored at Hudson Valley on July 13. Had five RBI in four games, August 22-August 25; **2000:** Played in 88 games for West Michigan of the Single-A Midwest League, collecting 88 hits and posting a .278 batting average. Had career-highs with seven home runs and 44 RBI. Homered four-straight games from April 27-April 30, driving in seven runs, and belted a grand slam at Michigan on May 29. Went 4-for-5 with a double and three RBI against Burlington on June 3 and hit in 12 of 15 games from June 28-August 1. Committed only four errors in 131 total chances in the outfield and contributed seven assists

Year Club & League	AVG	G	AB	R	H	TB	2B	3B	HR	RBI	SH-SF	HP	BB-IBB	SO	SB-CS	GIDP	SLG	OBP
1996 Tigers (GULF)	.211	44	147	27	31	42	4	2	1	13	0-1	6	15-0	44	8-0	2	.286	.308
1997 Tigers (GULF)	.246	18	65	16	16	28	3	0	3	12	1-0	0	10-0	13	5-2	0	.431	.347
Jamestown (NYP)	.155	35	116	12	18	26	6	1	0	3	0-0	3	10-0	41	3-1	0	.224	.240
1998 Jamestown (NYP)	.308	39	130	26	40	55	9	0	2	17	1-0	1	12-0	26	11-3	3	.423	.371
W Michigan (MID)	.071	5	14	0	1	1	0	0	0	2	0-1	0	1-0	4	0-0	0	.071	.125
1999 Oneonta (NYP)	.249	68	229	36	57	74	9	1	2	20	1-1	8	18-0	60	26-4	1	.323	.324
2000 W Michigan (MID)	.278	88	316	48	88	125	12	2	7	44	1-1	7	26-1	70	23-2	8	.396	.346
Minor Totals	.247	297	017	165	251	351	43	6	15	111	4-4	25	92-1	258	76-12	14	.345	.323

McMillan, Joshua J.

Pitcher ... HT: 6-0; **WT:** 175 ... **B-T:** L-L ... **BORN:** 08 JUL, 1978, Fontana, CA **RESIDES:** Moreno Valley, CA ... **TRANSAC-TIONS:** Selected by Blue Jays in 17th round of 2000 draft; signed June 13, 2000. **PRO CAREER: 2000:** Was tied for second with 15 games pitched for Medicine Hat of the Rookie Level Pioneer League. Earned his first career victory with six-scoreless innings against Great Falls on July 22, scattering four hits, striking out three and walking just one. Two starts later, he allowed one run and four hits in six innings of work, tying his longest outing of the season and notching his second win.

Year Club & League	W-L	ERA	G	GS	CG	ShO	SV	IP	H	R	ER	HR	HB	BB-IBB	SO	WP	BK	OBA
2000 Medcine Hat (PIO)	3-3	4.34	15	15	0	0	0	64.1	72	47	31	5	2	29-0	56	5	0	.279

Medina, Frewing J. Perez

Pitcher ... HT: 6-2; **WT:** 170 ... **B-T:** R-R ... **BORN:** 08 OCT, 1980, Barquisimeto, VZ **RESIDES:** Lara, VZ ... **TRANSACTIONS:** Signed as non-drafted free agent by Blue Jays, Oct. 14, 1997. **PRO CAREER: 1998:** Pitched briefly for Lara of Venezuelan Winter League; **1999:** Led Chino of Venezuela Summer League in ERA (1.88) and opponents batting average (.202); second in saves (4); also tied for second in wins (5) and games (17); **2000:** Finished third in the Rookie Level Dominican Summer League with a 1.16 ERA for the Blue Jays. He went 10-0, finishing in a tie for fourth with the most wins, in 85 2/3 innings of work, spanning 14 appearances, including 11 starts. Struck out 81 and issued just 23 walks while holding the opposition to a .189 batting average.

Year Club & League	W-L	ERA	G	GS	CG	ShO	SV	IP	H	R	ER	HR	HB	BB-IBB	SO	WP	BK	OBA
1998 S Joaquin-2 (VSL)	2-4	2.79	16	9	0	0	1	58.0	43	26	18	2	7	28-0	53	1	0	.208
1999 Chino (VSL)	5-2	1.88	17	3	0	0	4	52.2	39	18	11	1	3	16-0	43	6	1	.202
2000 Toronto (DSL)	10-0	1.16	14	11	1	1	1	85.2	57	16	11	0	3	23-0	81	5	1	.189
Minor Totals	17-6	1.83	47	23	1	1	6	196.1	139	60	40	3	13	67-0	177	12	2	.198

Medina, Roberto Nicasio

Pitcher ... HT: 6-1; **WT:** 165 ... **B-T:** R-R ... **BORN:** 09 NOV, 1982, Sanba Grande de Boya, DR ... **RESIDES:** Santo Domingo, DR ... **TRANSACTIONS:** Signed as non-drafted free agent by Blue Jays, Sept. 3, 1999. **PRO CAREER: 2000:** Pitched two innings for the Blue Jays of the Rookie Level Dominican Summer League during the 2000 season.

Year Club & League	W-L	ERA	G	GS	CG	ShO	SV	IP	H	R	ER	HR	HB	BB-IBB	SO	WP	BK	OBA
2000 Toronto (DSL)	0-0	0.00	1	0	0	0	0	2.0	1	0	0	0	0	0-0	0	0	0	.167

Medina, Rodney A. Urdaneta

Infielder ... **HT:** 6-1; **WT:** 180 ... **B-T:** S-R ... **BORN:** 17 OCT, 1981, Maracaibo, VZ **RESIDES:** Maracaibo, VZ ... **TRANSAC-TIONS:** Signed as non-drafted free agent by Blue Jays, July 2, 1998. **PRO CAREER:** 1999: Appeared in 52 games for Chino of the Venezuelan Summer League, collecting 46 hits in 154 at-bats, driving in 22 runs and posting a .299 batting average; 2000: Collected 63 hits in 68 games for the Blue Jays of the Rookie Level Dominican Summer League. Posted a .452 slugging percentage and a .380 on-base percentage in 259 at-bats while hitting .282.

Year Club & League	AVG	G	AB	R	H	TB	2B	3B	HR	RBI	SH-SF	HP	BB-IBB	SO	SB-CS	GIDP	SLG	OBP
1999 Chino (VSL)	.299	52	154	21	46	58	10	1	0	22	1-2	6	25-1	15	10-5	0	.377	.412
2000 Toronto (DSL)	.282	68	259	63	73	117	11	6	7	43	1-3	6	37-1	26	5-5	4	.452	.380
Minor Totals	.288	120	413	84	119	175	21	7	7	65	2-5	12	62-2	41	15-10	4	.424	.392

Melgarejo, Vladimir G. Diaz

Pitcher ... **HT:** 6-3; **WT:** 180 ... **B-T:** R-R ... **BORN:** 14 FEB, 1983, Bella Vista, Panama **RESIDES:** Panama City, Panama ... **TRANSACTIONS:** Signed as non-drafted free agent by Blue Jays, Oct. 23, 1999. **PRO CAREER:** 2000: Appeared in 11 games out of the bullpen and went 3-0 for the Blue Jays of the Rookie Level Dominican Summer League, posting a 1.83 ERA. Gave up just eight runs — four earned — in 19 2/3 innings of work.

Year Club & League	W-L	ERA	G	GS	CG	ShO	SV	IP	H	R	ER	HR	HB	BB-IBB	SO	WP	BK	OBA
2000 Toronto (DSL)	3-0	1.83	11	0	0	0	1	19.2	13	8	4	0	2	11-0	13	2	0	.183

Montanez, Samir H. Ledda

Pitcher ... **HT:** 6-3; **WT:** 195 ... **B-T:** R-R ... **BORN:** 08 JUL, 1981, Barquisimeto, VZ **RESIDES:** Lara, VZ ... **TRANSACTIONS:** Signed as non-drafted free agent by Blue Jays, Oct. 22, 1999. **PRO CAREER:** 2000: Appeared in 12 games out of the bullpen for the Blue Jays of the Rookie Level Venezuelan Summer League.

Year Club & League	W-L	ERA	G	GS	CG	ShO	SV	IP	H	R	ER	HR	HB	BB-IBB	SO	WP	BK	OBA
2000 Chino (VSL)	0-1	7.32	12	0	0	0	0	19.2	23	19	16	1	4	27-1	8	2	0	.295

Mora, Ramon A. Yegues

Pitcher ... **HT:** 6-2; **WT:** 175 ... **B-T:** R-R ... **BORN:** 18 MAR, 1981, Monagas, VZ **RESIDES:** Monagas, VZ ... **EDUCATION:** HS ... **TRANSACTIONS:** Signed as non-drafted free agent by Blue Jays, Feb. 8, 1998. **PRO CAREER:** 1999: Led Chino of Venezuela Summer League in wins (6) and complete games (1); second in innings pitched (62); tied for second in games (17) and games started (8); 2000: Appeared in 11 games for Chino of the Rookie Level Venezuelan Summer League, posting a 6-2 record with a 2.95 ERA in 58 innings of work. He struck out 38 and issued 12 walks in his 11 appearances, including nine starts.

Year Club & League	W-L	ERA	G	GS	CG	ShO	SV	IP	H	R	ER	HR	HB	BB-IBB	SO	WP	BK	OBA
1998 S Joaquin-2 (VSL)	2-6	3.03	16	10	0	0	0	68.1	52	29	23	0	17	20-0	64	5	3	.208
1999 Chino (VSL)	6-3	2.47	17	8	1	0	0	62.0	55	25	17	1	4	15-0	45	2	2	.239
2000 Chino (VSL)	6-2	2.95	11	9	0	0	1	58.0	51	21	19	1	4	14-0	38	3	3	.241
Minor Totals	14-11	2.82	44	27	1	0	1	188.1	158	75	59	2	25	49-0	147	10	8	.228

Morrow, Alvin Scott

Outfielder ... **HT:** 6-4; **WT:** 240 ... **B-T:** R-R ... **BORN:** 28 APR, 1978, Kirkwood, MD **RESIDES:** St. Louis, MO ... **TRANSACTIONS:** Selected by Brewers in second round of 1997 draft; signed June 23, 1997; Traded by Brewers to Blue Jays for C Kevin Brown, July 25, 2000. **PRO CAREER:** 1997: Played in just two games for Ogden of the Rookie Level Pioneer League in his first season of professional ball; 1998: Appeared in 52 games for Ogden of the Rookie Level Pioneer League, posting a .221 batting average in 163 at-bats. Finished in a tie for third in the league with 50 walks. Knocked in three runs in his first game of the season June 18 and went 3-for-4 with a triple and two runs scored on June 27. Hit a homer and knocked in a season-high four runs on August 12; 1999: Played 82 games for Beloit of the Single-A Midwest League, delivering 69 hits for a .233 average, collecting 41 RBI in 296 at-bats. Went 2-for-5 with a double and a season-high five RBI against Cedar Rapids on April 26. Had two hits and three RBI on May 16 and went 3-for-6 with three RBI on May 22. Delivered a hit in 22 of his final 29 games; 2000: Began the season with Beloit of the Single-A Midwest League before being traded to the Blue Jays Organization, where he played the final 32 games for Hagerstown of the South Atlantic League. Hit a two-run homer during a four-run eighth inning as Beloit tried to rally from a five-run deficit against Wisconsin on April 9. The Snappers eventually lost the game, 8-7. Smacked a pair of doubles during an eight-run eighth inning at Michigan on April 28. Went 3-for-3 with two RBI as the Suns topped Charleston-WV, 5-2, in the first game of a doubleheader on July 29. He led off the second inning with a two-bagger and scored, doubled home a run in the fourth and launched a solo homer in the sixth.

Year Club & League	AVG	G	AB	R	H	TB	2B	3B	HR	RBI	SH-SF	HP	BB-IBB	SO	SB-CS	GIDP	SLG	OBP
1997 Ogden (PIO)	.250	2	4	1	1	1	0	0	0	1	0-0	0	1-0	2	0-0	0	.250	.400
1998 Ogden (PIO)	.221	52	163	35	36	61	8	1	5	26	0-0	0	50-0	65	7-2	3	.374	.404
1999 Beloit (MID)	.233	82	296	29	69	89	11	0	3	41	0-3	1	47-0	121	0-0	8	.301	.337
2000 Beloit (MID)	.260	64	204	32	53	99	17	1	9	27	0-1	4	37-2	77	0-3	4	.485	.382
Hagerstown (SAL)	.210	32	105	15	22	37	3	0	4	8	0-0	2	14-0	42	2-0	3	.352	.314
Minor Totals	.234	232	772	112	181	287	39	2	21	103	0-4	7	149-2	307	9-5	18	.372	.362

Mowday, Christopher Ross (Chris)

Pitcher ... **HT:** 6-4; **WT:** 210 ... **B-T:** R-R ... **BORN:** 24 AUG, 1981, Brisbane, Australia ... **RESIDES:** Strathpine, Queensland, Australia ... **TRANSACTIONS:** Signed as non-drafted free agent by Blue Jays, Oct. 23, 1997. **PRO CAREER:** 1998: Gained his first victory on June 21 against Lethbridge in a two innings relief stint in his first appearance; 1999: Tied for second on Medicine Hat in games finished (7); Third in games (16); on July 7, vs. Great Falls retired four of last five batters to pick up the save; on August 5 against Billings tossed three scoreless innings of relief to earn the win; went 2-2-1 with 3.93 ERA in nine games at home (18.1 innings); pitched for Queensland, Australian Baseball League, going 0-2, 6.75 ERA in five starts; 2000: Pitched in 15 games, making 13 starts, for Queens of the Class-A New York-Penn League. Held the opposition to a .233 batting average over 71 2/3 innings, going 5-2 with a 3.39 ERA. Threw eight scoreless innings in a 9-0 win at Vermont on August 4, scattering three hits and striking out five without issuing a walk. Closed out the season with a 3-0 record and a 2.77 ERA over his final seven starts August 4-September 5, allowing 12 runs in 39 innings of work.

Year	Club & League	W-L	ERA	G	GS	CG	ShO	SV	IP	H	R	ER	HR	HB	BB-IBB	SO	WP	BK	OBA
1998	Medcine Hat (PIO)	1-0	10.13	10	0	0	0	0	10.2	12	15	12	0	4	15-0	8	7	3	.267
1999	Medcine Hat (PIO)	2-6	5.97	16	1	0	0	1	28.2	34	25	19	3	2	12-0	28	7	1	.291
2000	Queens (NYP)	5-2	3.39	15	13	0	0	0	71.2	61	32	27	1	4	41-0	65	8	0	.233
Minor Totals		8-8	4.70	41	14	0	0	1	111.0	107	72	58	4	10	68-0	101	22	4	.252

Murray, Steven Richard (Steve)

Pitcher ... **HT:** 6-1; **WT:** 200 ... **B-T:** L-L ... **BORN:** 29 JUN, 1980, Peterborough, ON, Canada ... **RESIDES:** Ennismore, ON, Canada ... **TRANSACTIONS:** Selected by Blue Jays in ninth round of 1998 draft; signed June 4, 1998; On disabled list, June 23-Sept. 25, 2000. **PRO CAREER:** 1998: Ranked third among Pioneer League relievers in BB/9 IP ratio (1.84); from August 5-21 went 3-0, 3.27 ERA (22 IP, 18 H, 4 BB, 19 SO) in four starts; 1999: Tied for third on St. Catharines in games started (8); on June 23 vs. Batavia did not allow a run over the final two innings to notch the save; on July 14 against Mahoning Valley allowed just one earned run and struck out eight batters in five innings but was saddled with the loss; in his final game of the season yielded three runs in six innings to earn the win; posted 1-1-1 record while compiling 4.55 ERA in seven games at home (31.2 innings); 2000: Did not play in the 2000 season.

Year	Club & League	W-L	ERA	G	GS	CG	ShO	SV	IP	H	R	ER	HR	HB	BB-IBB	SO	WP	BK	OBA
1998	Medcine Hat (PIO)	4-1	5.71	14	10	0	0	0	58.1	77	46	37	9	1	11-0	41	5	2	.317
1999	St.cathrnes (NYP)	1-4	5.68	12	8	0	0	1	57.0	68	46	36	7	1	16-0	46	5	0	.294
2000								Injured — Did not play											
Minor Totals		5-5	5.70	26	18	0	0	1	115.1	145	92	73	16	2	27-0	87	10	2	.306

Negron, Miguel A.

Outfielder ... **HT:** 6-2; **WT:** 170 ... **B-T:** L-L ... **BORN:** 22 AUG, 1982, Caguas, PR **RESIDES:** Caguas, PR ... **TRANSACTIONS:** Selected by Blue Jays in first round (18th overall) of 2000 draft; signed June 12, 2000. **PRO CAREER:** 2000: Had 44 hits in 53 games for Medicine Hat of the Rookie Level Pioneer League in his first year of professional baseball. Began the season with nine hits and four RBI in his first 27 at-bats, spanning seven games.

Year	Club & League	AVG	G	AB	R	H	TB	2B	3B	HR	RBI	SH-SF	HP	BB-IBB	SO	SB-CS	GIDP	SLG	OBP
2000	Medcine Hat (PIO)	.232	53	190	26	44	49	5	0	0	13	2-0	3	23-3	39	5-3	2	.258	.324

Newman, Timothy Lee

Pitcher ... **HT:** 6-2; **WT:** 190 ... **B-T:** R-R ... **BORN:** 15 AUG, 1978, Mission Viejo, CA ... **EDUCATION:** Walla Walla (WA) ... **RESIDES:** Yakima, WA ... **TRANSACTIONS:** Selected by Blue Jays in 15th round of 1999 draft; signed June 3, 1999. **PRO CAREER:** 1999: Led Medicine Hat in games (23); second on team in games finished (7); made pro debut on June 19 and struck out a pair of batters in one inning; from July 15-August 1 went 1-0-1 with 2.25 ERA in seven appearances (8.0 innings); from August 1-6 saved back-to-back games; posted 3.00 ERA in eight games on the road; 2000: Did not play in the 2000 season.

Year	Club & League	W-L	ERA	G	GS	CG	ShO	SV	IP	H	R	ER	HR	HB	BB-IBB	SO	WP	BK	OBA
1999	Medcine Hat (PIO)	1-0	4.73	23	0	0	0	2	26.2	26	21	14	5	0	13-1	29	5	0	.248

Nunley, Robert D. (Derrek)

Pitcher ... **HT:** 6-1; **WT:** 185 ... **B-T:** R-R ... **BORN:** 13 SEP, 1980, Winchester, TN **RESIDES:** Jacksonville, FL ... **TRANSACTIONS:** Selected by Blue Jays in seventh round of 1999 draft; signed June 4, 1999. **PRO CAREER:** 1999: struck out two batters in first game of his career (2.0 innings); fanned at least one opponent in seven of eight games; compiled 1.93 ERA with five strikeouts in four games at home (4.2 innings); 2000: Split time between Medicine Hat of the Rookie Level Pioneer League and Class-A Queens of the New York-Penn League. Made eight appearances out of the bullpen, going 1-0 with a 2.63 ERA, holding the opposition to a .204 batting average. Tossed 4 1/3 scoreless innings of relief in his last appearance for Medicine Hat on July 14, scattering two hits, striking out four and walking a pair. Pitched in 11 games once being promoted to Queens, making one start, going 2-0 with a 5.12 ERA in 19 1/3 innings, striking out 20 and walking eight.

Year	Club & League	W-L	ERA	G	GS	CG	ShO	SV	IP	H	R	ER	HR	HB	BB-IBB	SO	WP	BK	OBA
1999	St.cathrnes (NYP)	0-0	3.12	7	0	0	0	0	8.2	8	3	3	1	1	2-0	10	0	1	.258
2000	Medcine Hat (PIO)	1-0	2.63	8	0	0	0	0	13.2	10	4	4	0	2	6-0	11	5	0	.204
	Queens (NYP)	2-0	5.12	11	1	0	0	0	19.1	23	12	11	1	0	8-0	20	0	0	.295
Minor Totals		3-0	3.89	26	1	0	0	0	41.2	41	19	18	2	3	16-0	41	5	1	.254

Ochoa, Damian A. Mendez

Pitcher ... **HT:** 6-2; **WT:** 175 ... **B-T:** R-R ... **BORN:** 26 MAY, 1982, Maracay, VZ **RESIDES:** Aragua, VZ ... **TRANSACTIONS:** Signed as non-drafted free agent by Blue Jays, Aug. 3, 1998. **PRO CAREER:** 1999: Tied for second on Chino of Venezuela Summer League in games (17); fourth on team in wins (3); 2000: Appeared in seven games for Chino of the Rookie Level Venezuelan Summer League, posting a 2-1 record with a 4.13 ERA.

Year	Club & League	W-L	ERA	G	GS	CG	ShO	SV	IP	H	R	ER	HR	HB	BB-IBB	SO	WP	BK	OBA
1999	Chino (VSL)	3-1	5.20	17	1	0	0	1	36.1	49	27	21	0	11	8-0	24	5	2	.318
2000	Chino (VSL)	2-1	4.13	7	4	0	0	0	28.1	33	15	13	0	2	9-0	19	1	3	.308
Minor Totals		5-2	4.73	24	5	0	0	1	64.2	82	42	34	0	13	17-0	43	6	5	.314

Orloski, Joseph Paul (Joe)

Pitcher ... **HT:** 6-3; **WT:** 180 ... **B-T:** R-R ... **BORN:** 17 MAY, 1979, Las Vegas, NV **RESIDES:** Las Vegas, NV ... **TRANSACTIONS:** Selected by Blue Jays in sixth round of 1998 draft; signed June 6, 1998. **PRO CAREER:** 1998: Tied for third in Pioneer League with 7 wins; from June 22-July 30 went 4-0, 1.32 ERA (34 IP, 30 H, 10 BB, 21 SO) in eight appearances; in four relief appearances went 2-0, 1.80 ERA (15 IP, 13 H, 3 BB, 10 SO); 1999: Led St. Catharines in innings pitched (64.2); second on team in strikeouts (57); tied for second in wins (3), and games (17); began the season as starter and went 0-6 with 5.40 ERA in seven games; moved to bullpen on July 24 against Mahoning Valley and earned victory in 4.1 innings of relief; from August 4-8 posted 2-0 record with 0.00 ERA while striking out 13 in three games (11.1 innings); fanned six in three innings on August 11 vs. Mahoning Valley; on August 25 against Williamsport pitched the final 2.2 innings and allowed no hits or runs for the save and combination shutuout; as a reliever, went 3-3-1 with 3.73 ERA and 36 strikeouts in 10 games (31.1 innings); 2000: Made 22 appearances out of the bullpen for Class-A Queens of the New York-Penn League, going 4-0 with a 1.38 ERA. He did not allow a run in four outings August 1-13, spanning 10 1/3 innings and he posted a 0.67 ERA in his final 11 games, allowing just three runs — two earned — in 27 innings of work. He fanned a career-high 66 batters and issued only 16 walks while holding opponents to a .173 batting average over 52 innings.

Year	Club & League	W-L	ERA	G	GS	CG	ShO	SV	IP	H	R	ER	HR	HB	BB-IBB	SO	WP	BK	OBA
1998	Medcine Hat (PIO)	7-1	3.92	14	10	0	0	0	59.2	71	37	26	5	2	18-0	42	6	1	.291
1999	St.cathrnes (NYP)	3-9	4.59	17	7	0	0	1	64.2	80	48	33	9	1	22-0	57	7	0	.301
2000	Queens (NYP)	4-0	1.38	22	0	0	0	3	52.0	32	13	8	2	2	16-1	66	2	0	.173
Minor Totals		14-10	3.42	53	17	0	0	4	176.1	183	98	67	16	5	56-1	165	15	1	.263

Ozuna, Francisco Zapata

Pitcher ... **HT:** 6-2; **WT:** 180 ... **B-T:** L-L ... **BORN:** 17 MAY, 1981, Santo Domingo, DR **RESIDES:** Santo Domingo, DR ... **TRANSACTIONS:** Signed as non-drafted free agent by Blue Jays, Nov. 20, 1997. **PRO CAREER:** 1998: Pitched in the Dominican Summer League; 1999: Tied for second on Dominican Summer Blue Jays in saves (1); had two games finished in five appearances; limited opposing batters to .167 batting average; 2000: Led the Rookie Level Dominican Summer League with 134 strikeouts over 92 innings and was third in the league with 11 wins for the Blue Jays. Francisco, who did not lose a game this season, made 14 of his 16 appearances in a starting role. He had a 1.27 ERA, which was fifth best in the league, allowed just 37 walks and held the opposition to a .148 batting average.

Year	Club & League	W-L	ERA	G	GS	CG	ShO	SV	IP	H	R	ER	HR	HB	BB-IBB	SO	WP	BK	OBA
1998	Blue Jays (DSL)	3-2	3.06	17	2	0	0	0	35.1	39	18	12	0	2	13-0	27	0	1	.287
1999	Sd Blue Jay (DSL)	2-0	1.29	5	3	0	0	1	21.0	11	5	3	0	2	6-0	17	2	1	.167
2000	Toronto (DSL)	11-0	1.27	16	14	0	0	1	92.0	46	15	13	3	5	37-0	134	5	0	.148
Minor Totals		16-2	1.70	38	19	0	0	2	148.1	96	38	28	3	9	56-0	178	7	2	.187

Patten, Lanny D.

Pitcher ... **HT:** 6-3; **WT:** 205 ... **B-T:** R-R ... **BORN:** 30 MAY, 1979, Whitecourt, AB, Canada ... **RESIDES:** Drayton Valley, AB, Canada ... **TRANSACTIONS:** Selected by Blue Jays in 30th round of 2000 draft; signed June 13, 2000. **PRO CAREER:** 2000: Pitched in 17 games for Medicine Hat of the Rookie Level Pioneer League in his first season of pro ball. Went 2-3 with a 3.71 ERA 43 2/3 innings of work, striking out 38 and walking 11. Allowed one run and five hits, striking out five and issuing just one walk, in five innings of work, his longest outing of the season, to pick up the win in one of his three starts this year.

Year	Club & League	W-L	ERA	G	GS	CG	ShO	SV	IP	H	R	ER	HR	HB	BB-IBB	SO	WP	BK	OBA
2000	Medcine Hat (PIO)	2-3	3.71	17	3	0	0	0	43.2	57	31	18	5	5	11-0	38	8	0	.318

Paulino, Armando (Guerrero)

Outfielder ... **HT:** 6-2; **WT:** 190 ... **B-T:** R-R ... **BORN:** 18 JAN, 1981, Bani, DR **RESIDES:** Bani, DR ... **TRANSACTIONS:** Signed as non-drafted free agent by Blue Jays, July 2, 1998. **PRO CAREER:** 2000: Collected 58 hits in 63 games for Medicine Hat of the Rookie Level Pioneer League. Tied for third in the league with six triples on the season. Went 2-for-4 with a double, triple, two RBI and a season-high three runs scored on July 15 and had a 14-game hitting streak July 17-August 2. Had a homer and a season-high three RBI on July 17 and July 22.

Year	Club & League	AVG	G	AB	R	H	TB	2B	3B	HR	RBI	SH-SF	HP	BB-IBB	SO	SB-CS	GIDP	SLG	OBP
2000	Medcine Hat (PIO)	.259	62	224	30	58	99	14	6	5	25	0-0	4	20-0	51	6-4	2	.442	.331

Paulino, Luis F. Guerrero

Infielder ... **HT:** 6-2; **WT:** 190 ... **B-T:** R-R ... **BORN:** 10 APR, 1982, Moca, DR **RESIDES:** Bani, DR ... **TRANSACTIONS:** Signed as non-drafted free agent by Blue Jays, March 8, 1999

Year	Club & League	AVG	G	AB	R	H	TB	2B	3B	HR	RBI	SH-SF	HP	BB-IBB	SO	SB-CS	GIDP	SLG	OBP
2000	Toronto (DSL)	.312	67	237	56	74	119	20	2	7	43	0-2	6	31-0	45	5-3	4	.502	.402

Payano, Wilson

Pitcher ... **HT:** 6-0; **WT:** 180 ... **B-T:** R-R ... **BORN:** 14 MAY, 1983, La Romana, DR **RESIDES:** La Romana, DR ... **PRO CAREER:** 2000: Appeared in just two games for the Blue Jays of the Rookie Level Dominican Summer League.

Year	Club & League	W-L	ERA	G	GS	CG	ShO	SV	IP	H	R	ER	HR	HB	BB-IBB	SO	WP	BK	OBA
2000	Toronto (DSL)	0-0	81.00	2	0	0	0	0	0.2	0	6	6	0	0	6-0	0	2	0	.000

Payne, Jerrod A.

Pitcher ... **HT:** 5-10; **WT:** 198 ... **B-T:** R-R ... **BORN:** 27 AUG, 1977, Elmira, NY **RESIDES:** Jacksonville, FL ... **EDUCATION:** North Florida ... **TRANSACTIONS:** Selected by Blue Jays in 10th round of 2000 draft; signed June 12, 2000. **PRO CAREER:** 2000: Made a pair of relief appearances for the Queens Kings of the Single-A New York Penn League before being promoted to Hagerstown of Class-A South Atlantic League. Went 0-2 with a 3.71 ERA in 19 appearances out of the bullpen for the Suns. Allowed 15 hits in 17 innings of work as the opposition hit .242.

Year	Club & League	W-L	ERA	G	GS	CG	ShO	SV	IP	H	R	ER	HR	HB	BB-IBB	SO	WP	BK	OBA
2000	Queens (NYP)	0-0	9.00	2	0	0	0	0	2.0	3	2	2	1	0	0-0	1	1	0	.375
	Hagerstown (SAL)	0-2	3.71	19	0	0	0	8	17.0	15	9	7	0	0	6-0	6	2	0	.242
Minor Totals		0-2	4.26	21	0	0	0	8	19.0	18	11	9	1	0	6-0	7	3	0	.257

Pearson, Shawn B.

Outfielder ... **HT:** 6-1; **WT:** 175 ... **B-T:** R-R ... **BORN:** 14 SEP, 1977, Guelph, ON, Canada **RESIDES:** Guelph, ON, Canada ... **EDUCATION:** Old Dominion (VA) ... **TRANSACTIONS:** Signed as non-drafted free agent by Blue Jays, Aug. 13, 1999. **PRO CAREER:** 2000: Split time between three levels of Class-A ball during the 2000 season. Played three games for Dunedin of the Florida State League, collecting six hits in 10 at-bats. Joined Queens of the New-York-Penn League in July and hit .351 in 20 games. Had a case one-hit in 16 of the 20 games and had a season-high three hits on June 22 and July 9. Went 13-for-28, hitting .464, in seven games July 2-11 and was second in the league in on-base percentage (.468) and was fourth in batting (.351) before his promotion on July 13. Struggled at the plate one joining Hagerstown of the South Atlantic League, delivering just 13 hits in 92 at-bats.

Year	Club & League	AVG	G	AB	R	H	TB	2B	3B	HR	RBI	SH-SF	HP	BB-IBB	SO	SB-CS	GIDP	SLG	OBP
2000	Dunedin (FSL)	.600	4	10	3	6	7	1	0	0	3	0-0	0	1-0	1	0-0	0	.700	.636
	Queens (NYP)	.351	20	74	18	26	27	1	0	0	3	0-2	0	18-0	8	7-4	1	.365	.468
	Hagerstown (SAL)	.141	33	92	9	13	15	0	0	0	5	1-0	1	15-1	20	4-2	3	.163	.269
Minor Totals		**.256**	**57**	**176**	**30**	**45**	**49**	**2**	**1**	**0**	**11**	**1-2**	**1**	**34-1**	**29**	**11-6**	**4**	**.278**	**.376**

Pereira, Ernesto J. Garcia

Pitcher ... **HT:** 6-3; **WT:** 170 ... **B-T:** L-L ... **BORN:** 06 MAY, 1982, Tovar, Merida, VZ **RESIDES:** Carabobo, VZ ... **TRANSACTIONS:** Signed as non-drafted free agent by Blue Jays, July 10, 1999. **PRO CAREER:** 2000: Pitched in 12 games for Chino of the Venezuelan Summer League, posting a 16.46 ERA in 13 2/3 innings of work.

Year	Club & League	W-L	ERA	G	GS	CG	ShO	SV	IP	H	R	ER	HR	HB	BB-IBB	SO	WP	BK	OBA
2000	Chino (VSL)	0-0	16.46	12	0	0	0	0	13.2	16	29	25	0	7	33-0	10	4	0	.296

Perez, Jersen Arnaldo

Shortstop ... **HT:** 5-10; **WT:** 185 ... **B-T:** R-R ... **BORN:** 20 JAN, 1976, Duverge, DR **RESIDES:** Lynn, MA ... **EDUCATION:** CC of Rhode Island ... **TRANSACTIONS:** Selected by Mets in 22nd round of 1996 draft; signed June 6, 1996; Traded by Mets to Blue Jays for future considerations, March 30, 2000. **PRO CAREER:** 1996: Began the season with the Mets of the Rookie Level Gulf Coast League, collecting 42 hits in 40 games. Batted .278 with a .351 slugging percentage and a .355 on-base percentage over 151 at-bats. Played in six games with Kingsport of the Rookie Level Appalachian League before being promoted to Pittsfield for the final game of the season; 1997: Appeared in 65 games for Kingsport of the Rookie Level Appalachian League before playing his final two games at Single-A Columbia of the South Atlantic League. Had 69 hits in 258 at-bats, which was third most in the league. After being promoted to Class-A ball, he went 4-for-6 with three doubles and two RBI; 1998: Played in 120 games for Class-A Columbia of the South Atlantic League, collecting 136 hits for a .279 batting average. Named to the South Atlantic League All-Star team as a short stop. Finished in a tie for first in the league with 10 triples. Began the season with a hit in 15 of his first 19 games. Fell a single shy of the cycle with a 3-for-6 and three RBI performance against Columbus on May 10 and went 3-for-4 with two triples, two RBI and three runs scored the following game. Hit in 16 straight games from May 21-June 9. Had six RBI in two games June 14-June 18 and hit a pair of home runs against Asheville July 5; 1999: Had 120 hits in 128 games for St. Lucie of the Single-A Florida State League. Delivered a hit in 31 of his final 41 games, going 47-for-151 for a .313 batting average. Went 4-for-5 with a triple, double and two RBI on August 17 and had four hits, an RBI and three runs scored at Vero Beach on August 30; 2000: Appeared in 126 games for Single-A Dunedin of the Florida State League, collecting 138 hits. He hit safely in 11 straight games as he raised his average from .277 to .291. Led the league with 24 doubles through June 14 and wound up third in the league with 35 two baggers. His two-out RBI triple capped a three-run top of the ninth inning as the Blue Jays edged Clearwater, 5-4, on June 19. Went 4-for-4 with four RBI in a 9-4 victory over Fort Myers on August 10.

Year	Club & League	AVG	G	AB	R	H	TB	2B	3B	HR	RBI	SH-SF	HP	BB-IBB	SO	SB-CS	GIDP	SLG	OBP
1996	Mets (GULF)	.278	40	151	24	42	53	5	3	0	12	0-0	1	17-1	18	7-2	2	.351	.355
	Kingsport (APPY)	.176	6	17	4	3	3	0	0	0	3	0-2	0	5-0	6	0-0	2	.176	.333
	Pittsfield (NYP)	.333	1	3	1	1	1	0	0	0	0	0-0	0	1-0	1	0-0	0	.333	.500
1997	Kingsport (APPY)	.267	65	258	45	69	92	10	2	3	29	0-2	3	7-0	41	12-7	4	.357	.293
	Columbia (SAL)	.667	2	6	3	4	7	3	0	0	2	0-0	1	0-0	0	1-0	0	1.167	.714
1998	Columbia (SAL)	.279	120	488	72	136	195	18	10	7	64	5-11	3	18-0	128	14-4	6	.400	.302
1999	St. Lucie (FSL)	.256	128	468	60	120	170	15	7	7	45	9-3	8	27-0	117	7-5	10	.363	.306
2000	Dunedin (FSL)	.271	126	509	69	138	211	35	7	8	64	8-5	4	20-0	106	8-4	11	.415	.301
Minor Totals		**.270**	**488**	**1900**	**278**	**513**	**732**	**86**	**29**	**25**	**219**	**22-23**	**20**	**95-1**	**417**	**49-22**	**35**	**.385**	**.308**

Perez, Randy F. Sequera

Second Baseman ... **HT:** 5-11; **WT:** 160 ... **B-T:** R-R ... **BORN:** 01 MAY, 1981, Caracas, VZ **RESIDES:** Miranda, VZ ... **TRANSACTIONS:** Signed as non-drafted free agent by Blue Jays, July 9, 1999. **PRO CAREER:** 2000: Collected 15 hits in 28 games for Chino of the Rookie Level Venezuelan Summer League.

Year	Club & League	AVG	G	AB	R	H	TB	2B	3B	HR	RBI	SH-SF	HP	BB-IBB	SO	SB-CS	GIDP	SLG	OBP
2000	Chino (VSL)	.214	28	70	14	15	16	1	0	0	5	2-0	0	10-2	14	4-0	2	.229	.313

Perez, Richard R.

Pitcher ... **HT:** 6-4; **WT:** 170 ... **B-T:** R-R ... **BORN:** 15 NOV, 1983, San Pedro De Macoris, DR ... **RESIDES:** San Pedro de Macoris, DR ... **TRANSACTIONS:** Signed as a non-drafted free agent by the Blue Jays, July 13, 2000 ... **PRO CAREER:** 2001 will be his first professional season.

Peters, Anthony Salvatore (Tony)

Outfielder ... **HT:** 6-0; **WT:** 210 ... **B-T:** R-R ... **BORN:** 28 OCT, 1974, South Newberry, OH ... **EDUCATION:** Miami-Dade So. (FL) ... **RESIDES:** Mesa, AZ ... **TRANSACTIONS:** Selected by Brewers in 45th round of 1994 draft; signed April 22, 1995; Selected by Blue Jays from Brewers from Rule 5 minor league draft, Dec. 15, 1997. **PRO CAREER:** 1997: Put together a ten-game hitting streak April 21-27, hitting .400 (10-25) during the streak; went 3-for-5 with a double, homer, three runs and six RBI on May 11 vs Cedar Rapids; strung together a seven-game hitting streak May 29-June 5; 1998: Collected four hits in four at bats with a run scored, a double and an RBI on May 23 against Cape Fear; had a nine-game hitting streak from May 25-June 3 where he batted .444 (16-36, 5 R, 3 2B, 2 RBI); hit a grand-slam and a solo homer while collecting five RBI on July 17 against Ashville; went 4-for-5 with two runs, one home run and three RBI against Charleston-WV on July 31; in May, June and July batted .347 (60-173, 31 R, 7 2B, 5 HR, 22 RBI); hit .316 (49-155, 30 R, 6 2B, 1 3B, 5 HR, 22 RBI) in games in front of the home fans; hit .313 (5-16) with a homer and 3 RBI in 5 SAL playoff games; 1999: Third on Dunedin in home runs (14) and fourth in stolen bases (15); drove in five runs with two home runs on April 14, vs. Daytona; hit three home runs on May 1, vs. Brevard County; through May 1, averaged one home run every nine at-bats; on July 2, vs. St. Lucie drove in five runs with a double and home run; hit in seven of eight games between August 6-16, batting .500 (9-18) with eight runs and six RBI; had seven game hit streak from August 18-27, batted .417 (10-24) scoring seven runs; batted .357 (20-56) in month of August; 2000: Delivered 122 hits in 127 games for Single-A Dunedin of the Florida State League. Finished second in the league with 97 runs scored. Went 4-for-4 with a homer, two RBI and two runs scored on May 30 and had three hits and three RBI against Charlotte on June 4. Peters hit safely in 11 straight games June 28-July 9, raising his average from .275 to .295. He went 4-for-5 with a grand slam and a season-high five RBI, scoring three times, in a 14-7 win over Tampa on July 9.

Year	Club & League	AVG	G	AB	R	H	TB	2B	3B	HR	RBI	SH-SF	HP	BB-IBB	SO	SB-CS	GIDP	SLG	OBP
1995	Brewers (ARIZ)	.244	51	172	25	42	60	8	2	2	24	1-0	2	29-0	55	9-3	2	.349	.360
1996	Beloit (MID)	.257	71	179	20	46	71	13	3	2	23	1-1	0	18-0	47	5-1	3	.397	.323
1997	Beloit (MID)	.235	113	375	50	88	143	16	6	9	43	5-1	1	31-0	110	21-7	8	.381	.294
1998	Hagerstown (SAL)	.303	104	327	58	99	143	12	1	10	35	3-0	3	25-0	72	15-7	8	.437	.358
1999	Dunedin (FSL)	.244	116	316	58	77	135	12	2	14	50	4-3	6	44-1	97	15-4	3	.427	.344
2000	Dunedin (FSL)	.268	127	455	97	122	201	30	2	15	61	4-3	7	71-1	164	23-8	9	.442	.373
Minor Totals		.260	582	824	308	474	753	91	16	52	236	18-8	19	218-2	545	88-30	33	.413	.344

Place, Eric H.

Pitcher ... HT: 6-0; **WT:** 205 ... **B-T:** R-L ... **BORN:** 27 MAY, 1975, Shelbyville, MI **RESIDES:** Torrance, CA ... **EDUCATION:** Western Michigan ... **TRANSACTIONS:** Selected by Blue Jays in 12th round of 1998 draft; signed June 7, 1998. **PRO CAREER:** 1998: During his first seven appearances went 2-0, 0.90 ERA (10 IP, 7 H, 3 BB, 11 SO) while not giving up a run in six of seven games; was converted to a starter in July and made eight starts going 2-4, 6.99 ERA (37.1 IP, 41 H, 14 BB, 28 SO); 1999: Appearing exclusively in relief for Hagerstown, cut 1998 ERA in half; did not allow a run during eight game stretch from April 15-May 7 going 2-0, allowing just six hits while striking out 22 in 17.1 innings; in seven games from May 13-June 5 compiled 1-0, 1.32 ERA giving up ten hits and striking out ten in 13.2 innings; from June 15-September 1, a 19 game stretch, allowed just 25 hits in 31.2 innings, compiling a 2.84 ERA; finished 13 games; in 22 games compiled home record of 4-2, 1.98 ERA; opponents batted .216 (55-255); 2000: Split time this season between Dunedin of the Single-A Florida State League and Hagerstown of the Class-A South Atlantic League. Pitched in 24 games, making one start, for the Blue Jays, posting a 5-2 record with a 4.24 ERA in 46 2/3 innings of work. Allowed one run in 10 2/3 innings, spanning three appearances August 3-14, allowing seven hits while striking out 11 and walking just one. Pitched in four games for Hagerstown in mid June, going 0-1 with a 5.40 ERA in five innings of work.

Year	Club & League	W-L	ERA	G	GS	CG	ShO	SV	IP	H	R	ER	HR	HB	BB-IBB	SO	WP	BK	OBA
1998	St.cathrnes (NYP)	4-5	6.51	19	8	0	0	0	55.1	59	47	40	6	4	22-0	40	4	2	.269
1999	Hagerstown (SAL)	6-4	3.13	40	0	0	0	0	72.0	55	34	25	2	2	38-1	56	3	1	.216
2000	Dunedin (FSL)	5-2	4.24	24	1	0	0	0	46.2	47	27	22	3	2	33-3	32	1	0	.269
	Hagerstown (SAL)	0-1	5.40	4	0	0	0	0	5.0	6	3	3	0	0	0-0	6	0	0	.300
Minor Totals		15-12	4.53	87	9	0	0	0	179.0	167	111	90	11	8	93-4	134	8	3	.250

Ponce, Arnoldo J. Tenorio

Second Baseman ... **HT:** 6-2; **WT:** 160 ... **B-T:** S-R ... **BORN:** 19 DEC, 1981, El Tigre, Anzoategui, VZ **RESIDES:** Anzoategui, VZ ... **TRANSACTIONS:** Signed as non-drafted free agent by Blue Jays, July 2, 1999. **PRO CAREER:** 2000: Delivered 23 hits in 83 at-bats for Chino of the Venezuelan Summer League, hitting one home run and collecting 15 RBI.

Year	Club & League	AVG	G	AB	R	H	TB	2B	3B	HR	RBI	SH-SF	HP	BB-IBB	SO	SB-CS	GIDP	SLG	OBP
2000	Chino (VSL)	.277	30	83	21	23	31	5	0	1	15	0-0	2	19-0	13	3-2	4	.373	.423

Porter, Scott Mitchell

Pitcher ... HT: 6-1; **WT:** 195 ... **B-T:** R-R ... **BORN:** 18 MAR, 1977, Roanoke, VA **RESIDES:** Doctors Inlet, FL ... **EDUCATION:** Jacksonville (FL) ... **TRANSACTIONS:** Selected by Blue Jays in fifth round of 1999 draft; signed June 3, 1999. **PRO CAREER:** 1999: Second in Pioneer League in SO/9 IP relief (13.27); fifth in league in saves (8); led Medicine Hat in saves and games finished (17); from July 2-19 was 1-0, 1.70 ERA with three saves, allowing just three hits and striking out eight in 5.1 innings; in his last seven appearances was 0-1, 3.25 ERA and three saves, allowing seven hits and just one base on balls while striking out 13 in 8.1 innings; finished 17 games in 18 appearances; allowed more than one earned run only once in 18 outings; 2000: Made 24 appearances out of the bullpen for Class-A Dunedin of the Florida State League, posting a 1-2 record with a 2.67 ERA. As a reliever, he finished second in the league with a .172 batting average against and was fifth with 10.96 strikeouts per nine innings. Struck out the side in order in the ninth inning to preserve a combined no-hitter against Fort Myers on April 22. Pitched 20 1/3 consecutive innings without allowing an earned run to begin the season April 7-May 20 (He surrendered two unearned runs at Vero Beach on April 29).

Year	Club & League	W-L	ERA	G	GS	CG	ShO	SV	IP	H	R	ER	HR	HB	BB-IBB	SO	WP	BK	OBA
1999	Medcine Hat (PIO)	1-3	5.49	18	0	0	0	8	19.2	23	16	12	1	1	10-0	29	2	0	.274
2000	Dunedin (FSL)	1-2	2.67	24	0	0	0	4	33.2	20	14	10	2	3	15-3	41	2	0	.172
Minor Totals		2-5	3.71	42	0	0	0	12	53.1	43	30	22	3	4	25-3	70	4	0	.215

Quiroz, Guillermo Antonio

Catcher ... HT: 6-1; **WT:** 202 ... **B-T:** R-R ... **BORN:** 29 NOV, 1981, Maracaibo, Zulia, VZ ... **RESIDES:** Maracaibo, Zulia, VZ ... **TRANSACTIONS:** Signed as non-drafted free agent by Blue Jays, Sept. 25, 1998. **PRO CAREER:** 1999: Led Medicine Hat with nine home runs; batted .500 (7-14) with two doubles and a home run in first four games; had six game hit streak from July 27-August 3, batted .286 (6-21) with six runs and six RBI; from August 25-September 1 batted .318 (7-22) in six game hit streak; road average 75 points higher than home average; named sixth best prospect in Pioneer League by Baseball America; played for Zulia, Puerto Rican League, batting .236 in 25 games; 2000: Split time between Single-A Hagerstown of the South Atlantic League and Class-A Queens of the New York-Penn League. Went 3-for-5 with two RBI and three runs scored against Augusta on June 12, his most prolific, statistical game for Hagerstown. Joined Queens in late June and went 6-for-12 in his first three games. RBI on four occasions and had 13 multi-hit games, including a stretch where he had six hits in nine at-bats July 24-25.

Year	Club & League	AVG	G	AB	R	H	TB	2B	3B	HR	RBI	SH-SF	HP	BB-IBB	SO	SB-CS	GIDP	SLG	OBP
1999	Medcine Hat (PIO)	.221	63	208	25	46	80	7	0	9	28	2-0	4	18-0	55	0-2	4	.385	.296
2000	Hagerstown (SAL)	.162	43	136	14	22	29	4	0	1	12	3-0	4	16-0	44	0-1	3	.213	.269
	Queens (NYP)	.224	55	196	27	44	68	9	0	5	29	0-1	4	27-0	48	1-2	4	.347	.329
Minor Totals		.207	161	540	66	112	177	20	0	15	69	5-1	12	61-0	147	1-5	11	.328	.301

Ramirez, Ismael J. Urvaz

Pitcher ... HT: 6-2; **WT:** 175 ... **B-T:** R-R ... **BORN:** 03 MAR, 1981, El Tigrito, Anzoategui, VZ ... **RESIDES:** Anzoategui, VZ ... **TRANSACTIONS:** Signed as non-drafted free agent by Blue Jays, July 30, 1998. **PRO CAREER:** 2000 - Went 2-0 with a 3.15 ERA in 20 innings for Chino of the Rookie Level Venezuelan Summer League.

Year	Club & League	W-L	ERA	G	GS	CG	ShO	SV	IP	H	R	ER	HR	HB	BB-IBB	SO	WP	BK	OBA
1999	Chino (VSL)	1-0	4.20	3	3	0	0	0	15.0	16	10	7	0	2	1-0	8	1	0	.281
2000	Chino (VSL)	2-0	3.15	4	4	0	0	0	20.0	20	7	7	4	1	2-0	13	0	0	.253
	Toronto (DSL)	3-1	3.72	11	7	0	0	2	46.0	51	24	19	1	3	6-0	26	0	0	.276
Minor Totals		6-1	3.67	18	14	0	0	2	81.0	87	41	33	5	6	9-0	47	1	0	.271

Ramos, Ubaldo E. (Ebaldo)

Catcher ... **HT:** 6-0; **WT:** 200 ... **B-T:** R-R ... **BORN:** 01 DEC, 1980, Aquadulce, Panama **RESIDES:** Aquadulce, Panama ... **TRANSACTIONS:** Signed as non-drafted free agent by Blue Jays, Feb. 10, 1998. **PRO CAREER:** 1998: led team in games (66) and RBI (57); led the Dominican Summer League in RBI (57); 1999: Led Dominican Summer League Blue Jays in home runs (7), RBI (44), doubles (9), slugging (.391), sacrifice flies (3), hit-by-pitch (9) and intentional base on balls (3); 2000: Did not play in the 2000 season.

Year	Club & League	AVG	G	AB	R	H	TB	2B	3B	HR	RBI	SH-SF	HP	BB-IBB	SO	SB-CS	GIDP	SLG	OBP
1998	Blue Jays (DSL)	.306	66	245	50	75	107	17	3	3	57	1-4	5	38-0	34	7-4	7	.437	.404
1999	Sd Blue Jay (DSL)	.249	64	225	25	56	88	9	1	7	44	1-3	9	25-3	49	0-0	5	.391	.344
2000	Medcine Hat (PIO)	.233	26	90	13	21	29	8	0	0	11	1-0	0	10-0	24	0-0	2	.322	.310
Minor Totals		.271	156	560	88	152	224	34	4	10	112	3-7	14	73-3	107	7-4	14	.400	.365

Reimers, Cameron Paul

Pitcher ... **HT:** 6-5; **WT:** 205 ... **B-T:** R-R ... **BORN:** 15 SEP, 1978, Missoula, MT **EDUCATION:** JC of Southern Idaho ... **RESIDES:** Missoula, MT ... **TRANSACTIONS:** Selected by Blue Jays in 35th round of June 1998 draft; signed May 25, 1999. **PRO CAREER:** 1999: Split season between starting and relief; picked up win in first outing with two scoreless innings, allowing one hit and striking out two; from July 21-August 20 compiled a 1.59 ERA, allowing six hits in 11.1 innings; picked up second save in last outing of year with two scoreless, hitless innings; home ERA 1.61, in 22.1 innings over six games; in relief compiled 1-1, 2.89 ERA with 17 strikeouts in 18.2 innings; 2000: Made 26 starts for Single-A Hagerstown of the South Atlantic League, going 7-11 with a 3.73 ERA in 154 1/3 innings of work. Closed out the season with three consecutive victories, including a complete-game win on August 25. Reimers allowed just one run and five hits while striking out three and walking one for his first career, complete-game victory. His 112 strikeouts led Hagerstown and he issued just 45 walks while holding opponents to a .265 batting average.

Year	Club & League	W-L	ERA	G	GS	CG	ShO	SV	IP	H	R	ER	HR	HB	BB-IBB	SO	WP	BK	OBA
1999	Medcine Hat (PIO)	1-5	3.25	13	5	0	0	2	44.1	39	21	16	2	2	12-0	29	7	3	.235
2000	Hagerstown (SAL)	7-11	3.73	26	26	2	0	0	154.1	158	79	64	10	21	45-0	112	14	2	.265
Minor Totals		8-16	3.62	39	31	2	0	2	198.2	197	100	80	12	23	57-0	141	21	5	.258

Renwick, Tyler Russell

Pitcher ... **HT:** 6-4; **WT:** 206 ... **B-T:** R-R ... **BORN:** 12 AUG, 1978, Surrey, BC, Canada **RESIDES:** Langley, BC, Canada ... **EDUCATION:** Hill (TX) JC ... **TRANSACTIONS:** Signed as non-drafted free agent by Blue Jays, June 23, 1998. **PRO CAREER:** 1998: Did not give up a run in his last two appearances throwing two innings, walking two and striking out three gaining two no decisions; 1999: Third on St. Catharines in games finished (6); in first six outings over nine innings compiled 3.00 ERA and allowed just four hits; started five of last six appearances; in last two games, both starts, was 1-0, 0.84 ERA giving up six hits and striking out ten in 10.2 innings; 2000: Made seven starts for both Queens of the Class-A New York-Penn League and for Single-A Hagerstown of the South Atlantic League. Began the season with two straight wins in his first two starts for Queens, surrendering just two runs and six hits in 12 innings of work, striking out 11 and walking five. He tossed six scoreless innings in his first start of the season June 22, notching the victory. He allowed three earned runs or less in his first three starts, giving up six runs — only two earned — and 10 hits, striking out 16 and issuing seven walks. After he was promoted to Hagerstown in late July, he won his first three starts, allowing eight runs — seven earned — and 16 hits in 16 1/3 innings of work June 29-August 8.

Year	Club & League	W-L	ERA	G	GS	CG	ShO	SV	IP	H	R	ER	HR	HB	BB-IBB	SO	WP	BK	OBA
1998	Medcine Hat (PIO)	1-1	21.38	9	0	0	0	0	8.0	10	20	19	2	2	20-0	7	2	1	.286
1999	St.cathrnes (NYP)	2-4	5.31	16	5	0	0	0	39.0	35	28	23	2	1	33-0	32	10	0	.241
2000	Queens (NYP)	2-2	2.55	7	7	0	0	0	35.1	26	19	10	1	1	23-0	31	5	0	.198
	Hagerstown (SAL)	3-2	5.40	7	7	0	0	0	35.0	44	28	21	2	5	21-0	17	11	0	.312
Minor Totals		8-9	5.60	39	19	0	0	0	117.1	115	95	73	7	9	97-0	87	28	1	.254

Reyes, Jose

Pitcher ... **HT:** 6-0; **WT:** 170 ... **B-T:** R-R ... **BORN:** 12 NOV, 1983, Estebania, Azua, DR **RESIDES:** Estebania, Azua, DR ... **TRANSACTIONS:** Signed as a non-drafted free agent by the Blue Jays, July 11, 2000 ... **PRO CAREER:** 2001 will be his first professional season.

Rikert, Wade C.

Outfielder ... **HT:** 5-10; **WT:** 175 ... **B-T:** L-L ... **BORN:** 21 AUG, 1976, Randolph, VT **RESIDES:** South Royalton, VT ... **PRO CAREER:** 2000: Split time between Medicine Hat of the Rookie Level Pioneer League and Queens of the Single-A New York Penn League. Went 3-for-5 with a homer and three RBI in his first game as a professional against Helena on June 16. Had three hits, including a solo home run, and two runs scored on July 1 and homered and drove in four runs versus Ogden on July 9. Collected seven hits in his first 23 at-bats for Queens, hitting .304 with three RBI and seven runs scored over seven games.

Year	Club & League	AVG	G	AB	R	H	TB	2B	3B	HR	RBI	SH-SF	HP	BB-IBB	SO	SB-CS	GIDP	SLG	OBP
2000	Medcine Hat (PIO)	.247	24	97	27	24	40	4	0	4	15	1-1	3	15-2	19	6-1	0	.412	.362
	Queens (NYP)	.250	36	108	19	27	32	5	0	0	14	1-1	1	18-0	22	8-3	1	.296	.359
Minor Totals		.249	60	205	46	51	72	9	0	4	29	2-2	4	33-2	41	14-4	1	.351	.361

Rincon, Daniel E. Soto

Pitcher ... **HT:** 6-3; **WT:** 165 ... **B-T:** R-R ... **BORN:** 11 OCT, 1982, Maracaibo, VZ **RESIDES:** Zulia, VZ ... **TRANSACTIONS:** Signed as non-drafted free agent by Blue Jays, July 2, 1999. **PRO CAREER:** 2000: Appeared in 19 games for Chino of the Rookie Level Venezuelan Summer League, going 3-1 with a 4.22 ERA in 42 2/3 innings of work.

Year	Club & League	W-L	ERA	G	GS	CG	ShO	SV	IP	H	R	ER	HR	HB	BB-IBB	SO	WP	BK OBA
2000	Chino (VSL)	3-1	4.22	19	0	0	0	2	42.2	31	24	20	0	3	29-2	35	4	1 .211

Rios, Alexis Israel

Outfielder ... **HT:** 6-5; **WT:** 185 ... **B-T:** R-R ... **BORN:** 18 FEB, 1981, Coffee, AL **RESIDES:** Guaynabo, PR ... **TRANSACTIONS:** Selected by Blue Jays in first round (19th overall) of 1999 draft; signed June 4, 1999. **PRO CAREER:** 1999: Led Medicine Hat in triples (3); collected four hits vs. Great Falls on July 7; had six game hit streak from July 23-29, batted .391 (9-23) with seven runs and four extra-base hits; batted .348 (16-46) with ten runs in 11 game hitting streak from August 5-17; home average (.324 36-111) 100 points higher than road average; named ninth best prospect in Pioneer League by Baseball America; played briefly for Caguas, Puerto Rican League, coming to bat just three times; 2000: Began the season with Single-A Hagerstown of the South Atlantic League but was sent down to Class-A Queens of the New York-Penn League after 22 games. Once the 19th overall pick of the 1999 draft started for Queens, he collected 19 hits in his first 52 at-bats for a .365 batting average. Finished second in the New York-Penn League with one strikeout every 10.18 plate appearances. Collected 14 multi-hit games and knocked in 25 runs, the most ever in his brief two-year career.

Year	Club & League	AVG	G	AB	R	H	TB	2B	3B	HR	RBI	SH-SF	HP	BB-IBB	SO	SB-CS	GIDP	SLG	OBP
1999	Medcine Hat (PIO)	.269	67	234	35	63	76	7	3	0	13	0-0	1	17-0	31	8-4	6	.325	.321
2000	Hagerstown (SAL)	.230	22	74	5	17	22	3	1	0	5	0-1	1	2-0	14	2-3	0	.297	.256
	Queens (NYP)	.267	50	206	22	55	71	9	2	1	25	1-2	4	11-2	22	5-5	5	.345	.314
Minor Totals		.263	139	514	62	135	169	19	6	1	43	1-3	6	30-2	67	15-12	11	.329	.309

Rivera, William

Infielder ... **HT:** 6-0; **WT:** 155 ... **B-T:** L-R ... **BORN:** 28 DEC, 1981, Caguas, PR **RESIDES:** Caguas, PR ... **TRANSACTIONS:** Selected by Blue Jays in 25th round of 2000 draft; signed June 12, 2000. **PRO CAREER:** 2000: Had 34 hits in 39 games for Medicine Hat of the Rookie Level Pioneer League. Went 13-for-31, hitting .419 with four RBI, in eight games from July 18-July 30.

Year	Club & League	AVG	G	AB	R	H	TB	2B	3B	HR	RBI	SH-SF	HP	BB-IBB	SO	SB-CS	GIDP	SLG	OBP
2000	Medcine Hat (PIO)	.274	39	124	22	34	39	3	1	0	8	4-0	0	24-0	29	0-0	2	.315	.392

Robles, Felipe G.

Pitcher ... **HT:** 6-4; **WT:** 170 ... **B-T:** R-R ... **BORN:** 09 AUG, 1982, San Pedro De Macoris, DR ... **RESIDES:** San Pedro de Macoris, DR ... **TRANSACTIONS:** Signed as non-drafted free agent by Blue Jays, Jan. 23, 2000. **PRO CAREER:** 2000: Pitched in three games in the Dominican Summer League (4.0IP).

Year	Club & League	W-L	ERA	G	GS	CG	ShO	SV	IP	H	R	ER	HR	HB	BB-IBB	SO	WP	BK OBA
2000	Toronto (DSL)	0-0	4.50	3	0	0	0	0	4.0	7	2	2	1	1	3-0	1	0	1 .412

Rodriguez, Julio A. Reynoso

Pitcher ... **HT:** 6-0; **WT:** 160 ... **B-T:** R-R ... **BORN:** 21 AUG, 1982, Monte Plata, DR **RESIDES:** Monte Plata, DR ... **TRANSACTIONS:** Signed as non-drafted free agent by Blue Jays, Feb. 1, 1999. **PRO CAREER:** 2000: Pitched in four games in the Dominican Summer League (3.1IP).

Year	Club & League	W-L	ERA	G	GS	CG	ShO	SV	IP	H	R	ER	HR	HB	BB-IBB	SO	WP	BK OBA
2000	Toronto (DSL)	0-0	8.10	4	0	0	0	0	3.1	5	3	3	1	0	1-0	3	0	0 .313

Rodriguez, Michael M. (Mike)

Catcher ... **HT:** 5-11; **WT:** 185 ... **B-T:** R-R ... **BORN:** 01 APR, 1975, Santo Domingo, DR **RESIDES:** Stephenville, TX ... **EDUCATION:** Tarleton St. (TX) ... **TRANSACTIONS:** Selected by Blue Jays in sixth round of 1996 draft; signed June 7, 1996. **PRO CAREER:** 1996: Led St. Catharines club with three intentional walks; hit safely in seven straight games August 9-19, hitting .360 (9-25) during streak; 1997: Compiled a ten-game hitting streak August 14-26, hitting .467 (14-30) during the streak; 1998: Hit safely in 6-of-7 games from June 24-July 3 batting .560 (14-25, 4 R, 4 2B, 9 RBI) with Hagerstown; was assigned to Dunedin for the remainder of the season; 1999: With Dunedin, hit in seven of eight games between April 28-May 8, batting .424 (14-33) with eight runs, seven RBI and six extra-base hits; in May, June and July combined to hit .310 (49-158); road average for season .319 (37-116); threw out 12% (3-26) of base stealers; 2000: Appeared in 73 games for Dunedin of the Single-A Florida State League.

Year	Club & League	AVG	G	AB	R	H	TB	2B	3B	HR	RBI	SH-SF	HP	BB-IBB	SO	SB-CS	GIDP	SLG	OBP
1996	St.cathrines (NYP)	.269	46	145	14	39	43	2	1	0	12	0-2	1	7-3	14	4-4	4	.297	.303
1997	Hagerstown (SAL)	.228	43	123	17	28	31	3	0	0	12	3-3	1	18-0	25	0-2	1	.252	.324
	St.cathrnes (NYP)	.286	2	7	0	2	3	1	0	0	1	0-0	0	0-0	1	0-0	0	.429	.286
1998	Hagerstown (SAL)	.303	50	132	20	40	53	10	0	1	17	6-1	4	8-0	20	1-1	3	.402	.359
	Dunedin (FSL)	.216	15	37	4	8	10	2	0	0	2	2-0	2	3-0	4	0-0	2	.270	.310
1999	Dunedin (FSL)	.281	80	260	36	73	104	17	1	4	30	3-0	2	17-0	40	3-2	9	.400	.330
2000	Dunedin (FSL)	.274	73	223	34	61	77	11	1	1	23	2-4	4	28-2	44	1-3	6	.345	.359
Minor Totals		.271	309	927	125	251	321	46	3	6	97	16-10	14	81-5	148	9-12	25	.346	.335

Rodriquez, Yuber A. Basabe

Outfielder ... **HT:** 6-1; **WT:** 170 ... **B-T:** S-R ... **BORN:** 17 NOV 83 ... **RESIDES:** Turmero, VZ ... **TRANSACTIONS:** Signed as non-drafted free agent by Blue Jays, Nov. 7, 2000 ... **PRO CAREER:** 2001 will be his first professional season.

Romero, Davis J. Rodriguez

Pitcher ... **HT:** 5-10; **WT:** 145 ... **B-T:** L-L ... **BORN:** 30 MAR, 1983, Panama **RESIDES:** Cocle, Panama ... **TRANSACTIONS:** Signed as non-drafted free agent by Blue Jays, July 3, 1999. **PRO CAREER:** 2000: Made 13 appearances for the Blue Jays of the Rookie Level Dominican Summer League in 2000. Allowed 10 runs and 15 hits in 34 innings of work, going 1-0 with a 2.65 ERA. Fanned 45 batters and issued just 10 walks as he held opposing batters to a .129 average.

Year	Club & League	W-L	ERA	G	GS	CG	ShO	SV	IP	H	R	ER	HR	HB	BB-IBB	SO	WP	BK OBA
2000	Toronto (DSL)	1-0	2.65	13	2	0	0	4	34.0	15	10	10	1	3	10-0	45	1	0 .129

Romero, Felix M. Aquino

Pitcher ... **HT:** 6-2; **WT:** 165 ... **B-T:** R-R ... **BORN:** 18 JUN, 1980, San Pedro De Macoris, DR ... **RESIDES:** San Pedro de Macoris, DR ... **EDUCATION:** HS ... **TRANSACTIONS:** Signed as non-drafted free agent by Blue Jays, July 20, 1997. **PRO CAREER:** 2000: Was second in the Rookie Level Dominican Summer League with three complete-game shutouts and was seventh with a 1.29 ERA in 77 innings pitched for the Blue Jays. Finished the year with an 8-2 record after making 10 starts and one relief appearance. He struck out 74 and walked just 15 while opposing batters hit only .162.

Year	Club & League	W-L	ERA	G	GS	CG	ShO	SV	IP	H	R	ER	HR	HB	BB-IBB	SO	WP	BK	OBA
1998	Blue Jays (DSL)	6-0	3.18	11	5	0	1	0	45.1	42	16	16	5	3	20-0	25	0	2	.261
1999	Sd Blue Jay (DSL)	1-6	5.65	12	6	1	0	0	43.0	41	33	27	3	7	33-0	26	14	2	.252
2000	Toronto (DSL)	8-2	1.29	14	10	3	3	0	76.2	45	14	11	4	6	15-2	74	1	0	.162
Minor Totals		15-8	2.95	37	21	4	4	0	165.0	128	63	54	12	16	68-2	125	15	4	.213

Rooney, Michael Richard (Mike)

Pitcher ... **HT:** 6-1; **WT:** 175 ... **B-T:** R-R ... **BORN:** 06 OCT, 1975, Suffern, NY **RESIDES:** Stony Point, NY ... **EDUCATION:** St. John's (NY) ... **TRANSACTIONS:** Selected by Diamondbacks in sixth round of 1997 draft; signed June 7, 1997; Selected by Blue Jays from Diamondbacks in Rule 5 minor league draft, Dec. 11, 2000. **PRO CAREER:** 1997: Made 13 starts for Lethbridge of the Rookie League Pioneer League in his first season of professional baseball. Posted a 5-2 record with a 5.49 ERA in 62 1/3 innings, striking out 40 and walking 24. Closed out the season with four straight wins August 14-31, allowing eight runs - seven earned — and 20 hits in 25 innings of work. He struck out 18 and issued just six walks during the streak; 1998: Pitched a career-high 105 2/3 innings for South Bend of the Single-A Midwest League, posting a 4-9 record with a 5.20 ERA. He struck out 72 and issued 35 walks while holding the opposition to a .288 batting average. Allowed just one run and seven hits, striking out seven without issuing a walk, in seven innings of work on July 26 to pick up the win in his longest outing of the season. After being promoted to Triple-A Tucson of the Pacific Coast League, Rooney made three starts, going 0-2 and giving up 10 runs — eight earned — over 15 2/3 innings; 1999: Appeared in just one game for Triple-A Tucson of the Pacific Coast League, facing just two batters and allowing both of them to reach via a base hit; 2000: Pitched in 17 games, making 15 starts, for High Desert of the Single-A California League. Had a 2-8 record with a 7.55 ERA in 70 1/3 innings, which includes a four-game losing streak August 11-27.

Year	Club & League	W-L	ERA	G	GS	CG	ShO	SV	IP	H	R	ER	HR	HB	BB-IBB	SO	WP	BK	OBA
1997	Lethbridge (PIO)	5-2	5.49	13	13	1	0	0	62.1	72	42	38	4	5	24-0	40	3	0	.291
1998	South Bend (MID)	4-9	5.20	21	20	1	0	0	105.2	122	75	61	6	7	35-0	72	2	1	.288
	Tucson (PCL)	0-2	4.60	3	3	0	0	0	15.2	20	10	8	3	2	9-1	6	0	0	.328
1999	Tucson (PCL)	0-0	0.00	1	0	0	0	0	0.0	2	3	1	1	0	2-0	0	0	0	01.000
2000	High Desert (CAL)	2-8	7.55	17	15	1	0	0	70.1	85	64	59	13	7	37-0	29	3	1	.308
Minor Totals		11-21	5.92	55	51	3	0	0	254.0	301	194	167	27	21	107-1	147	8	2	.298

Rosario, Francisco A. Divison

Pitcher ... **HT:** 6-0; **WT:** 160 ... **B-T:** R-R ... **BORN:** 28 SEP, 1980, San Rafael del Yuma, DR ... **RESIDES:** Del Yuma, DR ... **TRANSACTIONS:** Signed as non-drafted free agent by Blue Jays, Jan. 11, 1999. **PRO CAREER:** 1999: Led Dominican Summer League Blue Jays in saves (3); finished 11 games in 18 appearances; did not give up a home run the entire season; opponents batted .208 (26-125); 2000: Led the Rookie Level Dominican Summer League with 16 saves after making 26 appearances out of the bullpen for the Blue Jays. Surrendered just five runs over 37 1/3 innings, striking out 51 and walking just seven.

Year	Club & League	W-L	ERA	G	GS	CG	ShO	SV	IP	H	R	ER	HR	HB	BB-IBB	SO	WP	BK	OBA
1999	Sd Blue Jay (DSL)	1-0	3.06	18	0	0	0	3	32.1	26	16	11	0	2	11-2	38	3	1	.208
2000	Toronto (DSL)	2-0	1.21	26	0	0	0	16	37.1	21	5	5	0	1	7-0	51	8	0	.160
Minor Totals		3-0	2.07	44	0	0	0	19	69.2	47	21	16	0	3	18-2	89	11	1	.184

Sandoval, Marcos A. Escalona

Pitcher ... **HT:** 6-1; **WT:** 185 ... **B-T:** R-R ... **BORN:** 29 DEC, 1980, Valencia, VZ **RESIDES:** Carabobo, VZ ... **TRANSACTIONS:** Signed as non-drafted free agent by Blue Jays, July 2, 1997. **PRO CAREER:** 1998: Posted a 2.33 ERA in seven appearances pitched for Lara of Venezuelan Winter League; 1999: At Hagerstown, split season between starting and relief; in first three outing was 1-0, 2.08 ERA allowing 11 hits and striking out 11 in 13 innings; participated in two consecutive combination shutouts during span of three straight scoreless appearances from July 7-18 pitching eight innings; in last six appearances was 2-1, 2.11 ERA with one save in 21.1 innings; took part in five combination shutouts; compiled relief ERA of 3.89 in 17 appearances over 44 innings; pitched for Lara, Venezuelan Winter League, compiling 0-1, 2.89 ERA in 13 games; 2000: Pitched in 28 games, making 25 starts, for Single-A Hagerstown of the South Atlantic League, going 8-13 with a 4.56 ERA in 163 2/3 innings. Tossed a three-hit, 1-0 shutout against Charleston-WV in the first game of a doubleheader on April 19. It was the first career complete game and shutout for Sandoval, who struck out six and walked just one. He went 3-0 with a 1.62 ERA in six starts April 6-May 6 and snapped a personal three-game losing streak with a three-hit, 5-1, complete-game win at Charleston-WV in the first game of a doubleheader on May 29.

Year	Club & League	W-L	ERA	G	GS	CG	ShO	SV	IP	H	R	ER	HR	HB	BB-IBB	SO	WP	BK	OBA
1998	St.cathrnes (NYP)	1-2	6.15	16	4	0	0	1	41.0	33	32	28	4	7	22-0	39	3	1	.214
1999	Hagerstown (SAL)	4-3	4.55	27	10	0	0	4	83.0	89	47	42	6	15	32-0	53	8	1	.280
2000	Hagerstown (SAL)	8-13	4.56	28	25	2	1	0	163.2	188	105	83	20	15	49-3	100	3	2	.289
Minor Totals		13-18	4.79	71	39	2	1	5	287.2	310	184	153	30	37	103-3	192	14	4	.276

Sellier, Brian S.

Outfielder ... **HT:** 6-0; **WT:** 200 ... **B-T:** L-R ... **BORN:** 12 JAN, 1978, Tucson, AZ **RESIDES:** Phoenix, AZ ... **EDUCATION:** Grand Canyon (AZ) ... **TRANSACTIONS:** Selected by Blue Jays in 27th round of 2000 draft; signed June 16, 2000. **PRO CAREER:** 2000: Played in 66 games and had 54 hits for Queens of the Single-A New York Penn League in his first season of professional baseball. Had the game-winning sacrifice fly in the bottom of the ninth inning as the Kings beat Staten Island, 3-2, on August 6. Went 3-for-3 with a triple, homer, walk, three RBI and four runs scored against Pittsfield on August 26.

Year	Club & League	AVG	G	AB	R	H	TB	2B	3B	HR	RBI	SH-SF	HP	BB-IBB	SO	SB-CS	GIDP	SLG	OBP
2000	Queens (NYP)	.258	66	209	34	54	82	5	4	5	33	1-6	2	41-0	51	11-2	6	.392	.376

Singleton, Justin C.

Outfielder ... **HT:** 6-1; **WT:** 190 ... **B-T:** L-R ... **BORN:** 10 APR, 1979, Baltimore, MD **RESIDES:** Sparks, MD ... **TRANSACTIONS:** Signed as a non-drafted free agent by the Blue Jays, Aug. 23, 2000 ... **PRO CAREER:** 2001 will be his first professional season.

Siriveaw, Nom S.

Infielder ... **HT:** 6-3; **WT:** 195 ... **B-T:** S-R ... **BORN:** 09 DEC, 1980, Korat, Thailand **RESIDES:** Vancouver, BC, Canada ... **EDUCATION:** E. Oklahoma St. JC ... **TRANSACTIONS:** Selected by Blue Jays in ninth round of 2000 draft; signed June 13, 2000. **PRO CAREER:** 2000 - Had 57 hits in 63 games in his first season of professional baseball with Medicine Hat of the Rookie Level Pioneer League. Went 12-for-23 in six games June 19-27. Belted a grand slam against Idaho Falls on August 29 and collected a career-high four hits, including a pair of home runs, as the Blue Jays topped Great Falls, 14-3, on August 28.

Year	Club & League	AVG	G	AB	R	H	TB	2B	3B	HR	RBI	SH-SF	HP	BB-IBB	SO	SB-CS	GIDP	SLG	OBP
2000	Medcine Hat (PIO)	.243	63	235	40	57	93	8	2	8	40	0-0	0	35-1	64	7-0	2	.396	.341

Sisk, Aaron M.

Infielder ... **HT:** 6-0; **WT:** 185 ... **B-T:** R-R ... **BORN:** 17 SEP, 1978, Ft. Worth, TX **RESIDES:** Ft. Worth, TX ... **EDUCATION:** New Mexico ... **TRANSACTIONS:** Selected by Blue Jays in seventh round of 2000 draft; signed June 20, 2000. **PRO CAREER:** 2000: Appeared in 59 games for Medicine Hat of the Rookie Pioneer League, hitting .257 in his first season of professional baseball. Was fourth in the league with 13 home runs and finished third with one home run every 16.77 at-bats. Hit .520 in eight games July 12-23, going 13-for-25 with two home runs and eight RBI. Belted a pair of homers and knocked in eight runs in a 13-6 victory versus Helena on July 30.

Year	Club & League	AVG	G	AB	R	H	TB	2B	3B	HR	RBI	SH-SF	HP	BB-IBB	SO	SB-CS	GIDP	SLG	OBP
2000	Medcine Hat (PIO)	.257	59	218	32	56	109	10	2	13	50	0-2	3	34-1	56	4-0	7	.500	.362

Small, Chris (Buster)

Catcher ... **HT:** 6-0; **WT:** 200 ... **B-T:** R-R ... **BORN:** 27 JAN, 1978, Honolulu, HA **RESIDES:** Alpharetta, GA ... **TRANSACTIONS:** Selected by Blue Jays in 28th round of 2000 draft; signed June 13, 2000. **PRO CAREER:** 2000: Played in four games with Queens of the Class-A New York Penn League before joining Medicine Hat of the Rookie Level Pioneer League. Had 29 hits in 38 games for a .221 average with Medicine Hat.

Year	Club & League	AVG	G	AB	R	H	TB	2B	3B	HR	RBI	SH-SF	HP	BB-IBB	SO	SB-CS	GIDP	SLG	OBP
2000	Queens (NYP)	.133	4	15	2	2	3	1	0	0	1	0-0	1	1-0	5	0-0	0	.200	.188
	Medicine Hat (PIO)	.221	38	131	13	29	29	0	0	6	4-1	3	14-0	23	2-1	2	.221	.309
Minor Totals		.212	42	146	15	31	32	1	0	7	4-1	3	15-0	28	2-1	2	.219	.297

Smith, Michael

Pitcher ... **HT:** 5-11; **WT:** 195 ... **B-T:** R-R ... **BORN:** 19 SEP, 1977, Norwood, MA **RESIDES:** Westwood, MA ... **EDUCATION:** Richmond (VA) ... **TRANSACTIONS:** Selected by Blue Jays in fourth round of 2000 draft; signed June 15, 2000. **PRO CAREER:** 2000: Went 2-2 with a 2.29 ERA in 14 games, 12 starts, for Class-A Queens of the New York Penn League in his first season of professional ball. Was fourth among starting pitchers in the New York-Penn League with 9.91 strikeouts per nine innings. Struck out 55 and issued just 17 walks while holding opposing hitters to a .224 batting average in 51 innings of work. Tossed five-hitless innings at Mahoning Valley on July 5, striking out seven and walking two as he notched his first-career win.

Year	Club & League	W-L	ERA	G	GS	CG	ShO	SV	IP	H	R	ER	HR	HB	BB-IBB	SO	WP	BK	OBA
2000	Queens (NYP)	2-2	2.29	14	12	0	0	0	51.0	41	18	13	1	2	17-0	55	9	1	.224

Smith, Nielsen Taylor (Taylor)

Pitcher ... **HT:** 6-3; **WT:** 210 ... **B-T:** R-R ... **BORN:** 15 DEC, 1978, Salt Lake City, UT **RESIDES:** Henderson, NV ... **TRANSACTIONS:** Selected by Blue Jays in 33rd round of 1997 draft; signed Aug. 18, 1997. **PRO CAREER:** 1998: Tied for second in New York-Penn League with 15 games started; made one start for Dunedin before being sent to St. Catharines; won his first start in New York-Penn League on June 17 vs Jamestown (5 IP, 2 H, 1 R, 3 BB, 6 SO); won last start of the year on August 30 vs Erie (6 IP, 3 H, 0 R, 0 BB, 7 SO); went 2-2, 3.35 at St. Catharines' Community Park, but 2-3, 7.59 on the road; 1999: Led South Atlantic League in games started (28) and innings pitched (171.1); fifth in league in shutouts (1); named South Atlantic League Pitcher-of-the-Week June 11-17; led Hagerstown in starts, shutouts and innings; second on team in strikeouts (119); won back-to-back starts on April 18-23 allowing just two earned runs in 12 innings; on April 29, vs. Augusta pitched nine scoreless, two-hit innings striking out nine, walking just one but left with a no-decision; on June 16, vs. Charleston-WV pitched a two-hit complete game shutout; from June 29-July 16 made four consecutive quality starts, going 2-0, 1.55 ERA allowing 21 hits and striking out 18 in 29 innings; recorded the win on July 27, vs. Columbus with seven, two-hit shutout innings, striking out six; home ERA 3.32 in 108.1 innings; made 16 quality starts; 2000: Appeared in 13 games out of the bullpen for Class-A Dunedin of the Florida State League, posting an 0-1 record with a 3.52 ERA in 23 innings of work.

Year	Club & League	W-L	ERA	G	GS	CG	ShO	SV	IP	H	R	ER	HR	HB	BB-IBB	SO	WP	BK	OBA
1998	Dunedin (FSL)	0-0	2.70	1	1	0	0	0	3.1	3	1	1	0	0	4-0	4	2	0	.231
	St.cathrnes (NYP)	4-5	5.10	15	15	0	0	0	77.2	87	61	44	8	5	26-0	61	4	0	.275
1999	Hagerstown (SAL)	7-10	3.78	28	28	1	1	0	171.1	158	87	72	11	12	51-0	119	5	0	.242
2000	Dunedin (FSL)	0-1	3.52	13	0	0	0	0	23.0	21	19	9	1	0	10-1	20	2	0	.236
Minor Totals		11-16	4.12	57	44	1	1	0	275.1	269	168	126	20	17	91-1	204	13	0	.251

Snyder, Michael Craig (Mike)

Third Baseman ... **HT:** 6-5; **WT:** 230 ... **B-T:** L-R ... **BORN:** 11 FEB, 1981, San Dimas, CA **RESIDES:** Chino hills, CA ... **TRANSACTIONS:** Selected by Blue Jays in second round of 1999 draft; signed June 10, 1999. **PRO CAREER:** 1999: Third on Medicine Hat in walks (31); hit home runs in back-to-back games on August 15-16; hit in six straight games from August 14-20, batting .381 (8-21) with eight runs and six RBI; 2000: Split time between Single-A Hagerstown of the South Atlantic League and Queens of the Class-A New York-Penn League. Collected 30 hits in 54 games with Hagerstown before joining Queens in early July. Had a 10-game hitting streak July 16-July 28 and went 4-for-5 with a homer, two RBI and three runs scored August 4 against Vermont. Had 21 hits in 56 at-bats August 17-30, batting .375 during that span, raising his average 36 points.

Year	Club & League	AVG	G	AB	R	H	TB	2B	3B	HR	RBI	SH-SF	HP	BB-IBB	SO	SB-CS	GIDP	SLG	OBP
1999	Medicine Hat (PIO)	.209	62	196	30	41	57	7	0	3	19	0-0	1	31-1	47	3-4	3	.291	.320
2000	Hagerstown (SAL)	.182	54	165	26	30	43	8	1	1	13	0-0	1	32-0	48	4-1	2	.261	.318
	Queens (NYP)	.278	57	227	28	63	92	11	3	4	34	0-1	1	22-1	49	4-3	2	.405	.343
Minor Totals		.228	173	588	84	134	192	26	4	8	66	0-1	3	85-2	144	11-8	7	.327	.328

Spille, Ryan P.

Pitcher ... **HT:** 6-3; **WT:** 185 ... **B-T:** L-L ... **BORN:** 11 NOV, 1976, Cincinnati, OH **RESIDES:** Cincinnati, OH ... **EDUCATION:** S.E. Missouri St. ... **TRANSACTIONS:** Selected by Blue Jays in 19th round of 1999 draft; signed June 13, 1999. **PRO CAREER:** 1999: Made one start for St. Catharines, recording win, allowing two hits while striking out five in five scoreless innings; with Hagerstown won first three consecutive starts with 1.06 ERA, allowing ten hits with ten strikeouts in 17 innings; on August 14-20 won two straight starts, allowing four hits in 12 scoreless innings; in 12 starts between St. Catharines and Hagerstown, participated in six combined shutouts; made six quality starts with Hagerstown; opponent's leadoff hitters batted .197 (13-66); with runners in scoring position opponents batted .186 (8-43); 2000: Began the season with Dunedin of the Single-A Florida State League and was promoted to Double-A Tennessee of the Southern League in late July. Pitched his first career complete-game victory on July 14 in Dunedin's 8-1 victory over Brevard County. He surrendered just one run and three hits, striking out six and issuing a pair of walks, improving to 10-6 on the season. In his next start, he pitched seven scoreless innings but did not figure in the decision, scattering just one hit while tying a season-high with seven strikeouts. His next start came for Tennessee on July 26 where he gave up just one run and five hits as he did not figure in the decision in his first career Double-A start.

Year	Club & League	W-L	ERA	G	GS	CG	ShO	SV	IP	H	R	ER	HR	HB	BB-IBB	SO	WP	BK	OBA
1999	St.cathrnes (NYP)	1-0	0.00	1	1	0	0	0	5.0	2	0	0	0	1	0-0	5	0	1	.125
	Hagerstown (SAL)	7-1	2.20	14	11	0	0	0	69.2	49	20	17	3	4	15-0	49	1	1	.204
2000	Dunedin (FSL)	10-6	4.27	20	19	1	0	0	109.2	107	55	52	9	5	35-1	82	4	0	.264
	Tennessee (SOU)	1-1	4.18	4	4	0	0	0	23.2	23	11	11	1	0	10-0	8	0	0	.271
Minor Totals		19-8	3.46	39	35	1	0	0	208.0	181	86	80	13	10	60-1	144	5	2	.243

Spillman, Jeromie M.

Pitcher ... **HT:** 5-11; **WT:** 180 ... **B-T:** L-L ... **BORN:** 24 SEP, 1978, Beeville, TX **RESIDES:** Phoenix, AZ ... **EDUCATION:** Grand Canyon (AZ) ... **TRANSACTIONS:** Selected by Blue Jays in 37th round of 2000 draft; signed June 16, 2000. **PRO CAREER:** 2000: Appeared in 22 games out of the bullpen for Medicine Hat of the Rookie Level Pioneer League in his first professional season. Posted a 4-3 record with a 4.15 ERA in 39 innings of work, fanning 36 and issuing 18 walks. He allowed one run — unearned — over his final seven games, spanning 12 innings, striking out 11 and walking just one, compiling a 2-0 record and one save.

Year	Club & League	W-L	ERA	G	GS	CG	ShO	SV	IP	H	R	ER	HR	HB	BB-IBB	SO	WP	BK	OBA
2000	Medcine Hat (PIO)	4-3	4.15	22	0	0	0	1	39.0	34	22	18	4	0	18-3	36	2	2	.233

St. Amand, Reuben C.

Pitcher ... **HT:** 6-4; **WT:** 220 ... **B-T:** R-R ... **BORN:** 04 AUG, 1979, Glennallen, AK **RESIDES:** Olympia, WA ... **TRANSACTIONS:** Selected by Blue Jays in 17th round of 1998 draft; signed June 5, 1998. **PRO CAREER:** 1998: Longest outing of year came on July 5 vs Lethbridge (3 IP, 1 H, 0 R, 1 BB, 1 SO); 1999: finished four games in 15 appearances; did not give up an earned run in six straight appearances between July 20-August 14 allowing just seven hits while striking out 13 in 12 innings; 2000: Appeared in 17 games in his first ever season with Class-A Queens of the New York-Penn League. Gained his first career Class-A victory on July 7, allowing just one run and five hits in 4 2/3 innings of relief.

Year	Club & League	W-L	ERA	G	GS	CG	ShO	SV	IP	H	R	ER	HR	HB	BB-IBB	SO	WP	BK	OBA
1998	Medcine Hat (PIO)	0-0	9.82	10	0	0	0	0	11.0	11	16	12	0	0	13-0	2	3	0	.250
1999	Medcine Hat (PIO)	0-1	6.11	15	0	0	0	0	28.0	31	23	19	5	1	17-0	24	4	1	.274
2000	Queens (NYP)	2-4	5.87	17	5	0	0	0	46.0	65	42	30	1	2	22-0	28	8	0	.344
Minor Totals		2-5	6.46	42	5	0	0	0	85.0	107	81	61	6	3	52-0	54	15	1	.309

Stephenson, Eric D.

Pitcher ... **HT:** 6-4; **WT:** 180 ... **B-T:** R-L ... **BORN:** 03 SEP, 1982, Raleigh, NC **RESIDES:** Benson, NC ... **TRANSACTIONS:** Selected by Blue Jays in 15th round of 2000 draft; signed June 14, 2000. **PRO CAREER:** 2000: Made 19 relief appearances for Medicine Hat of the Rookie Level Pioneer League in his first season of professional baseball. Struck out 21 and issued 13 walks over 27 innings while compiling a 1-1 record with an 8.33 ERA.

Year	Club & League	W-L	ERA	G	GS	CG	ShO	SV	IP	H	R	ER	HR	HB	BB-IBB	SO	WP	BK	OBA
2000	Medcine Hat (PIO)	1-1	8.33	19	0	0	0	0	27.0	41	28	25	2	2	13-0	21	9	0	.353

Stevens, Joshua James (Josh)

Pitcher ... **HT:** 6-3; **WT:** 200 ... **B-T:** R-R ... **BORN:** 06 JUN, 1979, Glendale, CA ... **EDUCATION:** Riverside City (CA) ... **RESIDES:** Riverside, CA ... **TRANSACTIONS:** Selected by Blue Jays in 35th round of 1997 draft; signed May 24, 1998. **PRO CAREER:** 1998: His only decision came in his longest outing of the year, as he beat Helena on August 27 (5.1 IP, 1 H, 0 R, 0 BB, 3 SO); 1999: Second in Pioneer League in BB/9 IP relief (1.53); fourth in league in runners/9 IP relief (10.13); Led Medicine Hat in wins (5), games (23) and games finished (17); second on team in saves (4); in last nine appearances was 2-0, with two saves and a 0.75 ERA, allowing just eight hits and striking out 17 while walking only three in 12 innings; home record 4-1, 1.00 ERA with three saves (11 H, 4 BB, 20 SO, 18 IP); strikeout to walk ratio of 6.8/1; 2000: Pitched in 47 games for Single-A Hagerstown of the South Atlantic League, used primarily as a reliever in his 84 1/3 innings of work. Made three scattered starts during the year, posting an 0-3 record with a 2.77 ERA in his three starts while going 4-1 with five saves and a 3.03 ERA in 44 appearances out of the bullpen. Was fourth among relief pitchers in the league, allowing just 1.89 walks per nine innings. Worked three scoreless innings of relief, scattering a pair of hits, on May 2 to notch his first win of the season and picked up his second save of the year as he pitched three scoreless innings, giving up a hit and striking out a season-high eight batters, including six in a row between the seventh and ninth innings, on July 8. Allowed no earned runs in five consecutive games July 29-August 8, spanning 10 1/3 innings but suffered one loss.

Year	Club & League	W-L	ERA	G	GS	CG	ShO	SV	IP	H	R	ER	HR	HB	BB-IBB	SO	WP	BK	OBA
1998	Medcine Hat (PIO)	1-0	2.98	25	0	0	0	0	42.1	37	17	14	3	2	13-0	39	1	2	.226
1999	Medcine Hat (PIO)	5-1	2.45	23	0	0	0	4	29.1	27	14	8	2	1	5-0	34	2	0	.243
2000	Hagerstown (SAL)	4-4	2.99	47	3	0	0	5	84.1	97	42	28	4	3	19-1	95	9	0	.289
Minor Totals		10-5	2.88	95	3	0	0	9	156.0	161	73	50	9	6	37-1	168	12	2	.264

Tatis, Ramon Francisco Medrano

Pitcher ... **HT:** 6-3; **WT:** 185 ... **B-T:** L-L ... **BORN:** 05 JAN, 1973, Guayubin, DR **RESIDES:** Santo Domingo, DR ... **TRANSACTIONS:** Signed as non-drafted free agent by Mets, Sept. 6, 1990; Selected by Cubs from Mets in Rule 5 major league draft, Dec. 9, 1996; Selected by Devil Rays in expansion draft, Nov. 18, 1997; Claimed on waivers by Tigers from Devil Rays, Nov. 24, 1999; Released by Tigers, March 15, 2000; Signed by Yankees, March 21, 2000; Released by Yankees, May 27, 2000; Signed by Nippon (Japan), 2000. **PRO CAREER:** 1991: Made 12 starts for the Mets of the Rookie Level Dominican Summer League. Tossed 57 innings, posting a 2-6 record with a 4.26 ERA; 1992: Spent the season with the Mets of the Rookie Level Gulf Coast League, pitching in 11 games and making five starts. Went 1-3 with an 8.50 ERA over 36 innings, striking out 25 and walking 15; 1993: Pitched in 13 games in 42 2/3 innings for Kingsport of the Rookie Level Appalachian League, posting an 0-2 record with a 6.12 ERA; 1994: Made 13 appearances for Kingsport of the Rookie Level Appalachian League, going 1-3 with a 3.32 ERA over 40 2/3 innings; 1995: Split time between Single-A Columbia of the South Atlantic League and Class-A Pittsfield of the New York Penn League. Made 18 appearances for Columbia, 16 out of the bullpen, posting a 2-3 record with a 5.63 ERA in 32 innings of work. Joined Pittsfield in late June and went 4-5 with a 3.63 ERA in 13 starts in 79 1/3 innings. Pitched a complete-game shutout on July 16, allowing five hits while striking out 10 and walking only one; 1996: Pitched in 45 of 46 games out of the bullpen for St. Lucie of the Single-A Florida State League. Held opposing hitters to a .257 average in 74 1/3 innings of work. Tossed a string of 13 2/3 scoreless innings from May 7-31, spanning seven games, while scattering five hits; 1997: Spent the entire season with the Chicago Cubs; 1998: Split time between the Tampa Bay Devil Rays and Triple-A Durham of the International League. Began the season with Tampa Bay and joined the Bulls in early June. After being moved to the bullpen in mid/late July, Tatis yielded just one run over his final 12 1/3 innings of work before being re-called to Tampa Bay; 1999: Tied for the league lead with 28 starts for Durham of the Triple-A International League. Finished in a tie for third with 12 wins and was fifth in league with 74 walks. Struck out 97 and walked 74 in 155 1/3 innings of work. Allowed one run and five hits over seven innings for a win against Buffalo on June 1 and and matched his longest outing of the season with seven scoreless innings at Pawtucket on June 27. He scattered three hits and struck out six while issuing a pair of walks; 2000: Appeared in seven games for, making three starts, Columbus of the Triple-A International League, posting an 0-1 record with a 10.72 ERA over 22 2/3 innings.

Year	Club & League	W-L	ERA	G	GS	CG	ShO	SV	IP	H	R	ER	HR	HB	BB-IBB	SO	WP	BK	OBA
1991	Ny Mets (DSL)	2-6	4.26	12	12	0	0	0	57.0	59	41	27	4	3	34-0	43	13	2	.274
1992	Mets (GULF)	1-3	8.50	11	5	0	0	0	36.0	56	40	34	2	4	15-0	25	7	1	.341
1993	Kingsport (APPY)	0-2	6.12	13	3	0	0	1	42.2	51	42	29	1	5	23-0	25	4	0	.297
1994	Kingsport (APPY)	1-3	3.32	13	4	0	0	0	40.2	35	25	15	2	2	31-0	36	5	2	.232
1995	Columbia (SAL)	2-3	5.63	18	2	0	0	0	32.0	34	27	20	1	1	14-0	27	5	0	.279
	Pittsfield (NYP)	4-5	3.63	13	13	1	1	0	79.1	88	40	32	2	3	27-0	69	8	3	.285
1996	St. Lucie (FSL)	4-2	3.39	46	1	0	0	6	74.1	71	35	28	4	2	38-8	46	14	1	.257
1997	CHICAGO (NL)	1-1	5.34	56	0	0	0	0	55.2	66	36	33	13	3	29-6	33	4	2	.308
1998	TAMPA BAY (AL)	0-0	13.89	22	0	0	0	0	11.2	23	19	18	2	1	16-1	5	1	1	.418
	Durham (INT)	1-3	3.67	19	9	0	0	2	61.1	66	29	25	5	3	24-2	44	4	1	.278
1999	Durham (INT)	12-8	5.50	28	28	0	0	0	155.1	178	100	95	19	4	74-0	97	9	9	.293
2000	Columbus (INT)	0-1	10.72	7	3	0	0	0	22.2	31	30	27	2	0	18-1	15	1	1	.333
	Nippon (PL)	0-0	54.00	1	0	0	0	0	1.0	3	6	6	0	0	4-0	0	0	0	.500
Minor Totals		27-36	4.97	180	80	1	1	9	601.1	669	409	332	42	27	298-11	427	70	20	.285
MAJOR TOTALS		1-1	6.82	78	0	0	0	0	67.1	89	55	51	15	4	45-7	38	5	3	.331

Taylor, John H.

Pitcher ... **HT:** 6-4; **WT:** 220 ... **B-T:** R-R ... **BORN:** 15 MAR, 1978, Savannah, GA ... **EDUCATION:** Francis Marion (SC) ... **RESIDES:** Ridgeland, SC. **PRO CAREER:** 2000: Pitched 10 games out of the bullpen for Class-A Queens of the New York Penn League, tossing 8 2/3 innings and compiling an 0-1 record in his first professional season.

Year	Club & League	W-L	ERA	G	GS	CG	ShO	SV	IP	H	R	ER	HR	HB	BB-IBB	SO	WP	BK	OBA
2000	Queens (NYP)	0-1	9.35	10	0	0	0	0	8.2	13	10	9	0	2	6-0	9	4	0	.361

Thompson, Richard C.

Outfielder ... **HT:** 6-3; **WT:** 180 ... **B-T:** L-R ... **BORN:** 23 APR, 1979, Reading, PA **RESIDES:** Montrose, PA ... **EDUCATION:** James Madison (VA) ... **TRANSACTIONS:** Selected by Blue Jays in sixth round of 2000 draft; signed June 19, 2000. **PRO CAREER:** 2000 - Played in 68 games for Queens of the Rookie Level New York Penn League in his first season of professional baseball. Had 66 hits in 252 at-bats with a .349 slugging percentage and a .386 on-base percentage. Tied for fifth in the league with 45 walks and 28 stolen bases. Reached base safely by hit or walk in 20 consecutive games August 9-28. Went 4-for-5 with a double and a solo home run in the final game of the season September 6.

Year	Club & League	AVG	G	AB	R	H	TB	2B	3B	HR	RBI	SH-SF	HP	BB-IBB	SO	SB-CS	GIDP	SLG	OBP
2000	Queens (NYP)	.262	68	252	42	66	88	9	5	1	27	5-0	6	45-1	57	28-8	0	.349	.386

Thompson, Tyler Nathan

Outfielder ... **HT:** 6-0; **WT:** 200 ... **B-T:** R-R ... **BORN:** 28 AUG, 1975, Bloomington, IN **RESIDES:** Bloomington, IN ... **EDUCATION:** Indiana St. ... **TRANSACTIONS:** Selected by Blue Jays in seventh round of 1998 draft; signed June 7, 1998. **PRO CAREER:** 1998: Tied for second in New York-Penn League with 46 base on balls; led St. Catharines team in walks, runs (42) and doubles (17); hit .314 at St. Catharines' Community Park, but only .192 on the road; banged out four singles on August 5 vs Batavia; drew a season-high four base on balls on August 21 vs Hudson Valley; 1999: Third in South Atlantic League in walks (47); led Hagerstown in home runs (17), RBI (81), slugging (.455) and on-base percentage (.375); batted .477 (21-44) during ten game hit streak from May 6-21 with eight extra-base hits, nine runs and ten RBI; on May 13, vs. Macon collected six hits; on June 2, vs. Greensboro hit two home runs, part of two day spree in which he went 5-for-7 with two doubles, three home runs, four runs and four RBI; on July 7, vs. Delmarva hit two home runs; from July 10-26 hit in 14 straight games, batting .345 (19-55) with 16 RBI; road average for season .291 (68-234) with 50 runs, 29 extra-base hits and 46 RBI; in two playoff games hit .429 (3-7) with a home run; 2000: Collected 98 hits in 103 games for Single-A Dunedin of the Florida

State League, posting a .280 batting average with 39 extra-base hits. Had two home runs and eight RBI over three games May 4-6 and hit .406 with eight RBI in ten games June 13-28. Had three hits and four RBI August 15 and September 2 and went 3-for-4 with a season-high two home runs, three RBI and three runs scored August 22.

Year	Club & League	AVG	G	AB	R	H	TB	2B	3B	HR	RBI	SH-SF	HP	BB-IBB	SO	SB-CS	GIDP	SLG	OBP
1998	St.cathrnes (NYP)	.252	70	246	42	62	91	17	0	4	32	0-3	1	46-0	64	6-5	3	.370	.368
1999	Hagerstown (SAL)	.261	130	440	84	115	200	28	3	17	81	2-5	4	79-0	122	20-3	7	.455	.375
2000	Dunedin (FSL)	.280	103	350	51	98	161	26	2	11	57	2-2	4	45-1	93	20-5	5	.460	.367
Minor Totals		.265	303	036	177	275	452	71	5	32	170	4-10	9	170-1	279	46-13	15	.436	.371

Thorpe, Tracy R.

Pitcher ... **HT:** 6-4; **WT:** 254 ... **B-T:** R-R ... **BORN:** 15 DEC, 1980, Melbourne, FL **RESIDES:** Melbourne, FL ... **TRANSAC-TIONS:** Selected by Blue Jays in 11th round of 2000 draft; signed June 12, 2000. **PRO CAREER:** 2000: Pitched in 11 games, starting six, in his first season of baseball for Medicine Hat of the Rookie Level Pioneer League. Had a rough season, going 0-4 with an 8.54 ERA in 26 1/3 innings. Tossed five scoreless innings in his last start of the season on September 1, scattering one hit while striking out three without issuing a walk.

Year	Club & League	W-L	ERA	G	GS	CG	ShO	SV	IP	H	R	ER	HR	HB	BB-IBB	SO	WP	BK	OBA
2000	Medcine Hat (PIO)	0-4	8.54	11	6	0	0	0	26.1	28	28	25	3	3	17-0	15	3	0	.275

Umbria, Jose Leonardo

Catcher ... **HT:** 6-2; **WT:** 215 ... **B-T:** R-R ... **BORN:** 20 JAN, 1978, Barquisimeto, VZ **RESIDES:** Barquisimeto, VZ ... **EDUCATION:** HS ... **TRANSACTIONS:** Signed as non-drafted free agent by Blue Jays, Oct. 18, 1995. **PRO CAREER:** 1996: Threw out 39.1% of would-be basestealers; 1997: Threw out 37.8% of would-be basestealers, retiring 17 runners in 45 tries; 1998: Tied for St. Catharines team lead with four sacrifice hits; had three RBI on July 9 vs Lowell and repeated the feat on August 30 vs Erie; 1999: hit in seven straight games from May 22-June 2, batting .462 (12-26) with five runs and seven RBI; hit in eight of nine games between June 28-July 14, batting .357 (10-28); season average more than 60 points higher than lifetime mark; played just two games for Lara, Venezuelan Winter League; 2000: Began the season with Medicine Hat of the Rookie Level Pioneer League and played his way up to Hagerstown of the Single-A South Atlantic League, after a brief stop at Class-A Queens of the New York-Penn League. Had 19 hits in 14 games for Medicine Hat, including back-to-back, three-hit games June 21-22. Had a season-high five RBI in a 10-0 loss on July 3, his last game for Medicine Hat. Delivered five hits in his 10 at-bats for Queens before being promoted to Hagerstown in mid-July where he had 19 hits in 27 games.

Year	Club & League	AVG	G	AB	R	H	TB	2B	3B	HR	RBI	SH-SF	HP	BB-IBB	SO	SB-CS	GIDP	SLG	OBP
1996	Medcine Hat (PIO)	.189	36	122	9	23	26	3	0	0	10	2-0	1	7-0	23	1-2	1	.213	.238
	Dunedin (FSL)	.188	6	16	1	3	3	0	0	0	2	0-0	0	1-0	3	0-0	0	.188	.235
1997	Medcine Hat (PIO)	.175	49	126	4	22	24	2	0	0	15	1-3	0	6-0	24	2-1	2	.190	.207
1998	St.cathrnes (NYP)	.237	32	97	14	23	25	2	0	0	13	4-0	1	9-0	22	0-0	1	.258	.308
1999	Hagerstown (SAL)	.290	62	186	24	54	68	5	0	3	20	0-2	0	26-0	36	2-2	4	.366	.374
2000	Medcine Hat (PIO)	.345	14	55	11	19	30	2	0	3	14	0-0	0	11-0	10	0-0	0	.545	.455
	Queens (NYP)	.500	3	10	3	5	6	1	0	0	4	0-0	0	0-0	0	0-0	0	.600	.500
	Hagerstown (SAL)	.209	27	91	3	19	21	2	0	0	8	1-2	1	8-0	19	0-2	2	.231	.275
Minor Totals		.239	229	703	69	168	203	17	0	6	86	8-7	3	68-0	137	5-7	10	.289	.306

Valdez Gu, Suglar M. Guerrero

Outfielder ... **HT:** 6-3; **WT:** 190 **B-T:** R-R ... **BORN:** 07 OCT, 1981, Bani, DR ... **RESIDES:** Peravia, Bani, DR ... **TRANSAC-TIONS:** Signed as a non-drafted free agent by the Blue Jays, Aug. 26, 2000 ... **PRO CAREER:** 2001 will be his first professional season.

Valdez, Aneuris G.

Infielder ... **HT:** 5-10; **WT:** 152 ... **B-T:** S-R ... **BORN:** 20 AUG, 1982, San Pedro De Macoris, DR ... **RESIDES:** San Pedro de Macoris, DR ... **PRO CAREER:** 2000: Did not play in the 2000 season.

Year	Club & League	AVG	G	AB	R	H	TB	2B	3B	HR	RBI	SH-SF	HP	BB-IBB	SO	SB-CS	GIDP	SLG	OBP
2000	Toronto (DSL)	.138	31	65	14	9	11	0	1	0	1	3-0	0	8-0	20	2-2	1	.169	.233

Valdez, Santo Valdez

Pitcher ... **HT:** 6-1; **WT:** 170 ... **B-T:** R-R ... **BORN:** 30 MAR, 1982, Bani, DR **RESIDES:** Bani, DR ... **TRANSACTIONS:** Signed as non-drafted free agent by Blue Jays, March 8, 1999. **PRO CAREER:** 1999: Led Dominican Summer League Blue Jays in games started (13); third in innings (69.2) and strikeouts (60); gave up just one home run in almost 70 innings; 2000: Went 8-0 in 15 appearances, making 13 starts, for the Blue Jays of the Rookie Level Dominican Summer League. Struck out 106 and issued 20 walks in 82 2/3 innings of work while posting a 2.40 ERA and holding the opposition to a .216 batting average.

Year	Club & League	W-L	ERA	G	GS	CG	ShO	SV	IP	H	R	ER	HR	HB	BB-IBB	SO	WP	BK	OBA
1999	Sd Blue Jay (DSL)	3-4	3.36	15	13	0	0	0	69.2	59	32	26	1	2	34-0	60	3	0	.226
2000	Toronto (DSL)	8-0	2.40	15	13	1	1	1	82.2	66	33	22	2	3	20-0	106	8	0	.216
Minor Totals		11-4	2.84	30	26	1	1	1	152.1	125	65	48	3	5	54-0	166	11	0	.221

Vega, Vigri D. Real

Pitcher ... **HT:** 6-1; **WT:** 190 ... **B-T:** R-R ... **BORN:** 28 MAR, 1977, Aguadulce, Coche, Panama ... **RESIDES:** Cocle, Panama ... **TRANSACTIONS:** Signed as non-drafted free agent by Blue Jays, Oct. 19, 1996. **PRO CAREER:** 1999: Second on Dominican Summer League Blue Jays in innings (76), and strikeouts (63); third in ERA (2.84); 2000: Allowed just two earned runs in 11 innings of work for Medicine Hat of the Rookie Level Pioneer League. Struck out 15 and issued just two walks while allowing four total runs in 10 games out of the bullpen. Posted a 1.64 ERA and held opponents to a .190 batting average.

Year	Club & League	W-L	ERA	G	GS	CG	ShO	SV	IP	H	R	ER	HR	HB	BB-IBB	SO	WP	BK	OBA
1997	Sd Blue Jay (DSL)	5-1	1.67	9	9	1	1	0	54.0	27	14	10	1	1	17-0	40	1	0	.147
1998	Blue Jays (DSL)	6-2	4.94	12	12	1	0	0	54.2	62	40	30	2	1	23-0	45	3	0	.276
1999	Sd Blue Jay (DSL)	3-4	2.84	14	9	3	0	0	76.0	72	32	24	4	2	20-3	63	4	3	.247
2000	Medcine Hat (PIO)	2-0	1.64	10	0	0	0	1	11.0	8	4	2	0	1	2-0	15	2	0	.190
Minor Totals		16-7	3.04	45	30	5	1	1	195.2	169	90	66	7	5	62-3	163	10	3	.227

Weekly, Christopher Ryan (Chris)

Second Baseman ... **HT:** 6-2; **WT:** 195 ... **B-T:** L-R ... **BORN:** 04 DEC, 1976, Scottsdale, AZ **RESIDES:** Mesa, AZ ... **EDUCATION:** New Mexico St. ... **TRANSACTIONS:** Selected by Blue Jays in 12th round of 1999 draft; signed June 3, 1999. **PRO CAREER:** 1999: Fifth in Pioneer League in doubles (18); led Medicine Hat in batting (.300), hits (77), games (71), total bases (118), doubles and slugging (.455); had six game hit streak from July 5-11, batted .500 (11-22) with eight RBI; batted .560 (14-25) during seven game streak from August 2-10 with six runs and 12 RBI; on August 3, vs. Great Falls dorve in five runs with three hits, including a pair of doubles; hit in six of seven games between August 13-20, batting .393 (11-28) with six runs; hit home runs in back-to-back games on August 27-28; home batting average .336 (42-125) with 18 extra-base hits, 23 runs and 29 RBI in 36 games; had 23 multi-hit games; 2000: Played 66 games for Single-A Hagerstown of the South Atlantic League before finishing the season at Dunedin of the Single-A Florida State League. Batted .373 with 18 RBI during an 18-game stretch April 26-May 24, including a pair of multi-home run games. His second home run against Piedmont on May 10 capped a three-run bottom of the ninth, giving the Suns the victory. He followed that performance up by going 3-for-4 with two home runs, three RBI and two runs scored on May 20. Went 5-for-6 with a double, a homer and six RBI in a 16-3 victory over Cape Fear, June 1 and hit .367 with 22 RBI over 14 games May 30-June 17. Had five hits and four RBI in his first 11 at-bats with Dunedin and homered in back-to-back games August 10-11, driving in five runs.

Year	Club & League	AVG	G	AB	R	H	TB	2B	3B	HR	RBI	SH-SF	HP	BB-IBB	SO	SB-CS	GIDP	SLG	OBP
1999	Medcine Hat (PIO)	.300	71	257	43	77	117	18	2	6	42	1-2	1	29-0	43	12-2	6	.455	.370
2000	Hagerstown (SAL)	.291	66	234	21	68	106	15	1	7	49	0-3	1	22-0	53	2-5	8	.453	.350
	Dunedin (FSL)	.250	34	120	23	30	52	7	0	5	22	1-1	3	14-0	30	0-2	0	.433	.341
Minor Totals		.286	171	611	87	175	275	40	3	18	113	2-6	5	65-0	126	14-9	14	.450	.357

Weimer, Matthew Perry (Matt)

Pitcher ... **HT:** 6-2; **WT:** 202 ... **B-T:** R-R ... **BORN:** 21 NOV, 1974, Charlottesville, VA **RESIDES:** Annapolis, MD ... **EDUCATION:** Penn St. ... **TRANSACTIONS:** Selected by Blue Jays in 18th round of 1997 draft; signed June 4, 1997. **PRO CAREER:** 1997: Went 2-0, 0.60 ERA from July 2-August 2; 1998: Led Hagerstown staff in appearances (48); 1998: Went 3-1, 2.63 ERA in April; fanned all six batters he faced on May 10 vs Charleston-WV; did not allow a run over nine straight apperances (11.1 IP) May 22-June 19; never posted an ERA great than 3.09 in any month; 1999: Second on Hagerstown in games (46), games finished (26) and saves (6); did not allow a run in first five appearances over nine innings; from May 10-June 15 was 4-1, with one save and a 1.42 ERA in 14 games over 19 innings; finished April and May 4-0, 1.70 ERA allowing just 21 hits in 31.2 innings in 18 games; did not give up a run in six outings from July 10-27 picking up two saves, allowing just four hits and striking out 12 in nine innings without issuing a walk; home record was 4-1, 1.82 ERA in 24.2 innings over 18 games; pitched for Rancho Cucamonga, California Fall League, compiling 2-2, 6.60 ERA in nine games; 2000: Made 49 appearances out of the bullpen for Double-A Tennessee of the Southern League, going 4-3 with a 4.60 ERA in 62 2/3 innings of work.

Year	Club & League	W-L	ERA	G	GS	CG	ShO	SV	IP	H	R	ER	HR	HB	BB-IBB	SO	WP	BK	OBA
1997	St.cathrnes (NYP)	2-2	3.57	23	0	0	0	0	35.1	35	21	14	1	3	4-0	22	3	0	.250
1998	Hagerstown (SAL)	7-6	2.85	48	0	0	0	8	72.2	62	31	23	3	8	26-2	59	5	0	.230
1999	Dunedin (FSL)	6-3	2.89	46	0	0	0	6	65.1	60	23	21	5	5	20-3	37	3	0	.245
2000	Tennessee (SOU)	4-3	4.60	49	0	0	0	2	62.2	68	36	32	6	4	22-5	31	5	0	.281
Minor Totals		19-14	3.43	166	0	0	0	16	236.0	225	111	90	15	20	72-10	149	16	0	.251

Wenham, Michael A.

Pitcher ... **HT:** 6-1; **WT:** 170 ... **B-T:** R-R ... **BORN:** 31 MAR, 1983, Changuinola, Panama ... **RESIDES:** Boca del Toro, Panama ... **TRANSACTIONS:** Signed as a non-drafted free agent by the Blue Jays, Jan. 21, 2000 ... **PRO CAREER:** 2001 will be his first professional season.

Williams, Glenn David

Infielder ... **HT:** 6-2; **WT:** 195 ... **B-T:** R-R ... **BORN:** 18 JUL, 1977, Gosford, Australia **RESIDES:** Chipping North, Australia ... **TRANSACTIONS:** Signed as non-drafted free agent by Braves, Aug. 17, 1993; Released by Braves, March 23, 2000; Signed by Blue Jays, March 26, 2000. **PRO CAREER:** 1994: Split time between the Braves of the Rookie Level Gulf Coast League and Danville of the Rookie Level Appalachian League. Delivered seven hits in his first 15 at-bats for the Braves and went 3-for-4 with a double and two runs scored on June 25. After being promoted to Danville, Williams went 3-for-3 with three RBI on August 7 and hit a three-run homer against Princeton on August 12; 1995: Split time between Single-A Macon of the South Atlantic League and Class-A Eugene of the Northwest League. Began the season with Macon, playing in 38 games. Had a season-high three hits and three RBI on May 7 before being demoted to Eugene. Tied for third in the Northwest League with four triples and finished fifth in the league with 268 at-bats. Went 3-for-5 with a homer and three RBI July 1 and homered and knocked in three runs against Boise five games later. Fell a double shy of the cycle on July 17, going 3-for-4 with two RBI and hit three home runs and had nine RBI during a four-game stretch August 16-20; 1996: Appeared in 51 games for Single-A Macon of the South Atlantic League, collecting 35 hits, 13 for extra bases, in 181 at-bats. Had a season-high three hits and three runs scored against Piedmont on May 22; 1997: Played in 77 games for Class-A Macon of the South Atlantic League, collecting 79 hits in 297 at-bats for a .266 batting average. Went 3-for-4 with a double, triple four RBI and three runs scored on April 7 and went 3-for-3 with a pair of home runs and three RBI on June 19. Had two home runs and three RBI on July 13 and belted a pair of solo shots, going 3-for-4 with three runs scored on August 3. Went 3-for-6 with a homer and a season-high five RBI August 29. Batted .313 in 99 at-bats during the month of August after hitting just .242 in the first three months of the season; 1998: Tied for a league-high by appearing in 134 games for Class-A Danville of the Carolina League. Had five, three-hit games, including a season-high three doubles on June 5. Knocked in seven runs in two games June 26-27 and finished the year with at least one hit in 10 of his last 12 games August 24-September 5. Went 3-for-9 with a pair of doubles and eight RBI with the bases loaded during the 1998 season; 1999: Played in 57 games for Double-A Greenville of the Southern League in the Braves' organization. Had 46 hits and drew just seven walks in 204 at-bats. Delivered 13 hits in 35 at-bats for a .372 batting average May 2-May 10 and went 3-for-4 with a single, double, solo home run and three runs scored against Orlando on May 10. Had a season-high four hits and three RBI versus Jacksonville on June 2, going 4-for-5 with a double, homer and three runs scored to go along with his three RBI; 2000: Had 102 hits in 107 games for Single-A Dunedin of the Florida State League. Delivered 25 hits in 53 at-bats for a .472 batting average, April 18-May 5. Went 5-for-6 with a double, a home run and three RBI in a 14-inning loss against Kissimmee, 13-9, May 5. Collected two hits and knocked home four runs as the Blue Jays beat Sarasota, 11-7, May 21 and went 3-for-3 with a pair of doubles, a triple, three walks and four RBI in a 13-5 win over Tampa May 27. Hit the game-winning homer in the bottom of the 10th inning as Dunedin won its ninth straight game on August 11 and collected a season-high three doubles against Vero Beach on August 21.

Year	Club & League	AVG	G	AB	R	H	TB	2B	3B	HR	RBI	SH-SF	HP	BB-IBB	SO	SB-CS	GIDP	SLG	OBP
1994	Braves (GULF)	.202	24	89	8	18	26	2	0	2	7	0-1	0	9-0	32	4-1	0	.292	.273
	Danville (APPY)	.253	24	79	11	20	25	2	0	1	9	0-0	3	8-0	20	2-4	4	.316	.344
1995	Macon (SAL)	.175	38	120	13	21	25	4	0	0	14	1-3	1	16-0	42	2-1	3	.208	.271
	Eugene (NWST)	.224	71	268	39	60	100	11	4	7	36	0-2	5	21-1	71	7-4	4	.373	.291
1996	Macon (SAL)	.193	51	181	14	35	57	7	3	3	18	1-2	2	18-2	47	4-2	3	.315	.271
1997	Macon (SAL)	.266	77	297	52	79	143	18	2	14	52	1-4	5	24-1	105	9-6	4	.481	.327
1998	Danville (CARO)	.215	134	470	40	101	156	26	1	9	44	3-3	6	37-3	132	1-3	5	.332	.279
1999	Greenville (SOU)	.225	57	204	19	46	69	11	0	4	15	1-1	4	7-1	58	1-4	2	.338	.264
2000	Dunedin (FSL)	.261	107	391	53	102	175	26	4	13	77	0-6	6	33-1	91	4-2	11	.448	.323
Minor Totals		.230	583	099	249	482	776	107	14	53	272	7-22	32	173-9	598	34-27	36	.370	.295

Williams, Michael (Mike)

Pitcher ... **HT:** 6-3; **WT:** 190 ... **B-T:** R-R ... **BORN:** 09 AUG, 1978, Freeport, TX **RESIDES:** Cypress, TX ... **EDUCATION:** Galveston (TX) CC ... **TRANSACTIONS:** Selected by White Sox in 11th round of 1998 draft; signed June 3, 1998. **PRO CAREER:** 1998: Went 3-1 with a 3.49 ERA in 24 relief appearances for Bristol of the Rookie Level Appalachian League. Tied for second in the league with 31 relief points and tied for fourth with nine saves. Allowed just one run in his first eight appearances in professional baseball, spanning 11 innings, posting a 1-0 record with five saves. Struck out 43 and issued just 16 walks in 38 2/3 innings of work; 1999: Appeared in 37 games, making 16 starts, for Single-A Burlington of the Midwest League, posting a 6-7 record with a 4.45 ERA in 127 1/3 innings. Finished fifth in the league with a .167 batting average against when coming out of the bullpen. Pitched a complete-game victory over Lancaster in the second game of a doubleheader, allowing just an unearned run and six hits, striking out three and walking one. Tossed eight scoreless innings of relief July 25-August 9; 2000: Pitched in 46 games, 45 out of the bullpen, for Winston-Salem of the Single-A Carolina League. Struck out 79 and walked 37 in 70 innings, going 3-for-4 with a 3.73 ERA. Allowed no earned runs in six straight appearances from April 9-23 but he allowed an unearned run in each game and was saddled with defeats both times.

Year	Club & League	W-L	ERA	G	GS	CG	ShO	SV	IP	H	R	ER	HR	HB	BB-IBB	SO	WP	BK	OBA
1998	Bristol (APPY)	3-1	3.49	24	0	0	0	9	38.2	28	16	15	1	5	16-1	43	4	1	.200
1999	Burlington (MID)	6-7	4.45	37	16	2	0	2	127.1	119	78	63	9	14	65-1	83	11	2	.246
2000	Winston-sal (CARO)	3-4	3.73	46	1	0	0	1	70.0	62	39	29	4	13	37-1	79	14	0	.242
Minor Totals		12-12	4.08	107	17	2	0	12	236.0	209	133	107	14	32	118-3	205	29	3	.238

Wood, Stephen L.

Infielder ... **HT:** 6-4; **HT:** 215 ... **B-T:** R-R ... **BORN:** 10 DEC, 1977, Beverly Hills, CA ... **EDUCATION:** Cal-Poly-San Luis Ob ... **RESIDES:** West Covina, CA **TRANSACTIONS:** Selected by Blue Jays in 36th round of 2000 draft; signed June 13, 2000. **PRO CAREER:** 2000: Played in 21 games for Medicine Hat of the Rookie Level Pioneer League in his first season of professional baseball. Had a pair of doubles and scored two runs in his first game on June 16 and went 4-for-6 with two RBI and two runs scored in June 20. Hit his first-career home run against Butte on June 21.

Year	Club & League	AVG	G	AB	R	H	TB	2B	3B	HR	RBI	SH-SF	HP	BB-IBB	SO	SB-CS	GIDP	SLG	OBP
2000	Medcine Hat (PIO)	.227	21	88	14	20	34	8	0	2	14	0-0	0	9-2	16	0-0	3	.386	.299

Yepez, Jose R. Riera

Pitcher ... **HT:** 6-0; **WT:** 175 ... **B-T:** R-R ... **BORN:** 19 JUN, 1981, Carora, Lara, VZ **RESIDES:** Lara, VZ ... **TRANSACTIONS:** Signed as non-drafted free agent by Blue Jays, Oct. 30, 1997. **PRO CAREER:** 2000: Collected 33 hits in 115 at-bats for Chino of the Rookie Level Venezuelan Summer League.

Year	Club & League	AVG	G	AB	R	H	TB	2B	3B	HR	RBI	SH-SF	HP	BB-IBB	SO	SB-CS	GIDP	SLG	OBP
1998	S Joaquin (VSL)	.196	38	102	10	20	21	1	0	0	5	0-0	5	9-0	17	0-0	0	.206	.293
1999	Chino (VSL)	.188	6	16	0	3	3	0	0	0	1	0-0	1	1-0	2	1-0	0	.188	.278
2000	Chino (VSL)	.287	37	115	14	33	45	6	0	2	22	0-0	7	20-0	11	6-0	9	.391	.423
Minor Totals		.240	81	233	24	56	69	7	0	2	28	0-0	13	30-0	30	7-0	9	.296	.359

Player Development

TORONTO BLUE JAYS

American League

Manager: Jim Fregosi
Record: 83-79 (3rd in division)
All-Stars: Tony Batista, Carlos Delgado, David Wells
League Leaders: Tony Batista (35 double plays-3B), Jose Cruz (162 games, 405 putouts-OF, 417 total chances-OF), Carlos Delgado (162 games, 57 doubles, 378 total bases, 99 extra-base hits, 15 hit by pitch, 1416 putouts-1B, 1511 total chances-1B, 157 double plays-1B), Alex Gonzalez (16 scarifice hits), David Wells (20 wins, 35 games started, 9 complete games, 1.2 fewest BB/9 IP)

MOST USED LINEUP
(Most games at each position)

C	Darrin Fletcher (117)	
1B	Carlos Delgado (162)	
2B	Homer Bush (75)	
3B	Tony Batista (154)	
SS	Alex Gonzalez (141)	
OF	Jose Cruz (162)	
OF	Shannon Stewart (136)	
OF	Raul Mondesi (96)	
St	David Wells (35)	
Rel	Billy Koch (68)	
	Paul Quantrill (68)	

SYRACUSE SKYCHIEFS

International League -AAA

Managers: Pat Kelly, Omar Malave, Mel Queen
Record: 74-66 (7th)
All-Stars: Luis Lopez, Chad Mottola
League Leaders: Cesar Izturis (.981 fielding-SS, 231 putouts-SS, 87 double plays-SS), Luis Lopez (1/16.64 SO/TPA), Mark Lukasiewicz (11.32 SO/9 IP relief), Chad Mottola (33 home runs, 286 total bases, .566 slugging percentage), Kerry Taylor (2 shutouts), Andy Thompson (17 assists-OF)

MOST USED LINEUP
(Most games at each position)

C	Charlie Green (77)
1B	Kevin Witt (109)
2B	Brent Abernathy (90)
3B	Luis Lopez (54)
SS	Cesar Izturis (131)
OF	Chad Mottola (126)
OF	Vernon Wells (119)
OF	Andy Thompson (113)
St	Gary Glover (27]
Rel	Mark Lukasiewicz (42)

TENNESSEE SMOKIES

Southern League -AA

Manager: Rocket Wheeler
Record: 71-69 (4th)
All-Stars: Pasqual Coco, Bob File, Jay Gibbons, Robert Perez
League Leaders: Jay Gibbons (.525 slugging percentage, 58 extra-base hits), Chris McBride (1.20 BB/9 IP relief), Matt McClellan (27 games started), Robert Perez (547 at-bats)

MOST USED LINEUP
(Most games at each position)

C	Josh Phelps (39)
1B	Jay Gibbons (101)
2B	Mike Young (90)
3B	Mike Peeples (41)
	Tony Schifano (41)
SS	Felipe Lopez (127)
OF	Robert Perez (134)
OF	Scott Sollman (108)
OF	Selwyn Langaigne (69)
St	Matt McClellan (27)
Rel	Randy Espina (53)

DUNEDIN BLUE JAYS

Florida State League -A

Manager: Marty Peevey
Record: 84-54 (1st)
All-Stars: Joe Lawrence, Jarrod Kingrey
League Leaders: Jarrod Kingrey (23 saves)

MOST USED LINEUP
(Most games at each position)

C	Joe Lawrence (68)
1B	Matt Logan (117)
2B	Glenn Williams (99)
3B	Orlando Hudson (82)
SS	Jersen Perez (123)
OF	Tony Peters (109)
OF	Garrick Haltiwanger (89)
OF	Ryan Fleming (85)
St	Joe Casey (27)
Rel	Doug Dimma (43)

HAGERSTOWN SUNS

South Atlantic League -A

Manager: Rolando Pino
Record: 63-74 (11th)
All-Stars: Brandon Jackson
League Leaders: Shannon Carter (4 double plays-OF), Hugo Castellanos (.123 average against relief), Reed Johnson (.995 fielding-OF)

MOST USED LINEUP
(Most games at each position)

C	Kevin Cash (50)
1B	Mike Snyder (53)
2B	Jaime Goudie (99)
3B	Rob Cosby (70)
SS	Brandon Jackson (92)
OF	Shannon Carter (114)
OF	Reed Johnson (95)
OF	Auntwan Riggins (64)
St	Cameron Reimers (26)
Rel	Marc Bluma (48)

QUEENS KINGS

New York-Penn League -A (short)

Manager: Eddie Rodriguez
Record: 46-29 (3rd)
All-Stars: Dominic Rich
League Leaders: Brandon Lyon (0.95 BB/9 IP start, 7.99 Runners/9 IP start), Guillermo Quiroz (487 putouts-C)

MOST USED LINEUP
(Most games at each position)

C	Guillermo Quiroz (55)
1B	Mike Snyder (54)
2B	Dominic Rich (67)
3B	Rob Cosby (31)
SS	Raul Tablado (52)
OF	Richard Thompson (67)
OF	Brian Sellier (63)
OF	Alexis Rios (41)
St	Brandon Lyon (13)
	Diegomar Markwell (13)
	Chris Mowday (13)
Rel	George Perez (29)

MEDICINE HAT BLUE JAYS

Pioneer League -Rookie Advanced

Manager: Paul Elliott
Record: 36-40 (6th)
All-Stars: Jeremy Johnson, Andrew McCulloch
League Leaders: Tommy Callen (12 hit by pitch), Armando Guerrero (3 double plays-OF), Jeremy Johnson (.498 on-base percentage), Andrew McCulloch (15 saves, 45 relief points), Lanny Patten (1.63 BB/9 IP relief), Nom Siriveaw (15 double plays-3B)

MOST USED LINEUP
(Most games at each position)

C	Chris Small (38)
1B	Ron Davenport (42)
2B	Thomas Callen (46)
3B	Nom Siriveaw (51)
SS	Manuel Mayorson (53)
OF	Armando Paulino (62)
OF	Miguel Negron (52)
OF	Jeremy Johnson (48)
St	David Hanson (15)
	Joshua McMillan (15)
Rel	Andrew McCulloch (27)

TOPS IN THE ORGANIZATION

BATTING TOP 10 (Minimum 319 Plate Appearances) * played with more than one club

BATTER	CLUB	AVG	G	AB	R	H	HR	RBI
Lopez, Luis	SYR	.328	130	491	64	161	7	79
Gibbons, Jay	TEN	.321	132	474	85	152	19	75
Jackson, Brandon*	DUN	.312	116	407	77	127	5	54
Mottola, Chad	SYR	.309	134	505	85	156	33	102
Freel, Ryan*	SYR	.299	96	345	80	103	13	44
Johnson, Reed*	DUN	.298	131	457	92	136	12	98
Lawrence, Joe*	TEN	.291	140	508	91	148	13	76
Haltiwanger, Garrick	DUN	.291	100	354	57	103	10	56
Perez, Robert	TEN	.287	136	547	66	157	19	92
Peeples, Mike	TEN	.280	123	475	70	133	18	73

WINS

Coco, Pasqual	TEN	12
Spille, Ryan*	TEN	11
Cassidy, Scott*	TEN	11
SEVERAL PLAYERS TIED AT		10

SAVES

Kingrey, Jarrod*	TEN	30
File, Robert*	SYR	28
Dewitt, Matt	SYR	15
McCulloch, Andrew	MHT	15
Perez, George	QUN	12

STRIKEOUTS

Coco, Pasqual	TEN	142
McClellan, Matt	TEN	140
Cassidy, Scott*	TEN	128
Glover, Gary	SYR	119
Kusiewicz, Mike	TEN	115

Team Batting	Avg	AB	R	H	HR	BB	SO	SB	CS
DUNEDIN	.279	4642	760	1294	125	529	1026	127	57
TENNESSEE	.265	4686	640	1241	107	494	880	105	72
MEDICINE HAT	.264	2660	457	703	58	382	563	50	20
SYRACUSE	.264	4659	632	1230	149	384	798	136	63
QUEENS	.251	2538	364	637	25	328	530	88	40
HAGERSTOWN	.245	4444	621	1088	67	525	1056	152	65

PITCHING TOP 10 (Minimum 94 IP) * played with more than one club

PITCHER	CLUB	W-L	ERA	IP	H	BB	SO
Cassidy, Scott*	TEN	11-5	2.82	131	101	49	128
Baker, Chris	DUN	9-5	3.20	104	91	29	85
Taylor, Kerry	SYR	9-8	3.32	136	119	61	83
Dean, Aaron*	DUN	9-4	3.56	134	126	50	106
Kusiewicz, Mike	TEN	7-9	3.63	156	149	59	115
Reimers, Cameron	HAG	7-11	3.73	154	158	45	112
Coco, Pasqual	TEN	12-7	3.76	168	154	68	142
Estrella, Leo*	SYR	10-9	3.86	166	136	70	111
Kegley, Charles	DUN	3-9	3.88	111	96	74	66
Hubbel, Travis*	DUN	8-6	3.94	119	107	57	78

HOME RUNS

Mottola, Chad	SYR	33
Witt, Kevin	SYR	26
Thompson, Andy	SYR	22
Phelps, Josh*	DUN	21
SEVERAL PLAYERS TIED AT		19

RBI

Mottola, Chad	SYR	102
Johnson, Reed*	DUN	98
Perez, Robert	TEN	92
Lopez, Luis	SYR	79
Williams, Glenn	DUN	77

STOLEN BASES

Carter, Shannon	HAG	33
Freel, Ryan*	SYR	32
Mottola, Chad	SYR	30
Lawrence, Joe*	TEN	28
Thompson, Rich	QUN	28

Team Pitching	W-L	ERA	H	CG	ShO	Sv	HR	BB	SO
QUEENS	46-29	3.15	568	1	4	19	23	295	663
DUNEDIN	84-54	3.59	1089	3	10	47	87	573	887
SYRACUSE	74-66	3.89	1137	16	9	35	100	515	961
TENNESSEE	71-69	3.99	1169	7	8	34	85	524	896
HAGERSTOWN	63-74	4.05	1184	5	3	34	85	460	896
MEDICINE HAT	36-40	4.56	709	0	1	17	57	273	574

Player Development

2000 BLUE JAYS ORGANIZATION STATISTICS

– Switch-hitter   * – Bats/Throws left

Batter	Team	AVG	G	AB	R	H	TB	2B	3B	HR	RBI	SH-SF	HP	BB-IB	SO	SB-CS	DP	SLG	OBP
Abernathy, Bre	SYR	.296	92	358	47	106	143	21	2	4	35	3-3	1	26-1	32	14-13	7	.399	.343
# Alvarez, Jimmy	HAG	.232	50	155	19	36	52	5	1	3	15	1-0	2	25-0	44	12-5	0	.335	.346
Bernhardt, Jos	DUN	.250	3	4	0	1	2	1	0	0	3	0-0	0	1-0	1	0-0	1	.500	.400
Bernhardt, Jos	HAG	.125	2	8	1	1	2	1	0	0	0	0-0	0	0-0	3	0-0	0	.250	.125
Bernhardt, Jos	QUN	.136	17	59	1	8	10	2	0	0	3	0-0	0	4-0	10	0-0	5	.169	.190
TOTALS		.141	22	71	2	10	14	4	0	0	6	0-0	0	5-0	14	0-0	5	.197	.197
Blackburn, Joh	MHT	.193	18	57	5	11	19	3	1	1	8	1-1	0	10-0	9	0-0	0	.333	.309
Blake, Casey	SYR	.217	30	106	10	23	37	6	1	2	7	0-0	3	8-0	23	0-3	2	.349	.291
* Brosseau, Rich	QUN	.164	15	55	9	9	15	0	3	0	2	1-0	0	4-0	15	2-0	0	.273	.220
Brown, Kevin	SYR	.335	51	179	26	60	98	15	1	7	29	0-1	0	8-1	46	0-0	5	.547	.362
Brumfield, Jac	SYR	.233	11	43	5	10	18	3	1	1	4	0-0	0	2-0	7	1-0	2	.419	.267
Bundy, Ryan	DUN	.000	2	5	1	0	0	0	0	0	0	0-0	0	0-0	2	0-0	0	.000	.000
Bundy, Ryan	HAG	.230	25	87	10	20	32	6	0	2	13	1-0	0	11-0	31	2-2	1	.368	.316
TOTALS		.217	27	92	11	20	32	6	0	2	13	1-0	0	11-0	33	2-2	1	.348	.301
Callen, Thomas	MHT	.258	50	182	44	47	59	4	1	2	25	4-0	12	39-0	39	5-3	3	.324	.421
* Carter, Shanno	HAG	.273	123	443	74	121	150	15	7	0	39	1-0	11	45-0	129	33-6	5	.339	.355
Cash, Kevin	HAG	.245	59	196	28	48	90	10	1	10	27	1-1	1	22-1	54	5-3	7	.459	.323
Chiaffredo, Pa	TEN	.111	18	63	6	7	8	1	0	0	2	0-0	1	5-0	16	0-1	0	.127	.188
Chiaffredo, Pa	DUN	.289	11	38	7	11	18	1	0	2	6	0-0	1	5-0	9	0-0	0	.474	.386
Chiaffredo, Pa	HAG	.356	13	45	9	16	25	6	0	1	5	0-0	3	9-0	6	0-0	0	.556	.491
TOTALS		.233	42	146	22	34	51	8	0	3	13	0-0	5	19-0	31	0-1	0	.349	.341
* Clark, Chivas	HAG	.159	37	113	15	18	24	6	0	0	10	2-0	1	15-1	27	1-2	0	.212	.264
* Clark, Chivas	QUN	.220	15	41	9	9	12	1	1	0	5	2-1	0	17-0	9	2-1	0	.293	.441
TOTALS		.175	52	154	24	27	36	7	1	0	15	4-1	1	32-1	36	3-3	0	.234	.319
Cosby, Rob	HAG	.237	77	291	31	69	90	9	0	4	29	0-2	0	16-0	37	2-3	7	.309	.275
# Cosby, Rob	SYR	.270	42	163	15	44	52	8	0	0	22	0-1	0	14-1	22	4-2	3	.319	.326
TOTALS		.249	119	454	46	113	142	17	0	4	51	0-3	0	30-1	59	6-5	10	.313	.294
Dalesandro, Ma	SYR	.333	1	3	1	1	4	0	0	1	1	0-0	0	0-0	1	0-0	0	1.333	.333
Davenport, Ron	MHT	.345	59	229	37	79	111	16	2	4	46	0-2	3	21-0	28	5-2	7	.485	.404
* Dusan, Joe	DUN	.198	77	197	30	39	61	7	0	5	19	2-4	1	24-0	55	1-1	6	.310	.283
Fagan, Shawn	HAG	.279	45	172	20	48	64	8	1	2	23	0-0	1	18-0	28	5-1	2	.372	.351
Fagan, Shawn	QUN	.289	25	90	17	26	40	6	1	2	13	0-1	3	12-1	22	0-1	3	.444	.387
TOTALS		.282	70	262	37	74	104	14	2	4	36	0-1	4	30-1	50	5-2	5	.397	.364
Fera, Aaron	HAG	.241	50	166	22	40	63	11	0	4	32	0-2	6	20-0	53	5-0	1	.380	.340
Fera, Aaron	QUN	.167	10	36	3	6	13	1	0	2	7	0-2	0	1-0	9	0-0	0	.361	.179
TOTALS		.228	60	202	25	46	76	12	0	6	39	0-4	6	21-0	62	5-0	1	.376	.313
* Fleming, Ryan	SYR	.182	3	11	1	2	2	0	0	0	1	0-0	0	0-0	1	0-0	0	.182	.182
* Fleming, Ryan	TEN	.171	37	105	16	18	28	4	0	2	9	3-0	1	20-0	17	2-1	1	.267	.310
* Fleming, Ryan	DUN	.304	90	309	42	94	126	18	1	4	32	6-5	1	28-1	38	6-8	1	.408	.359
TOTALS		.268	130	425	59	114	156	22	1	6	42	9-5	2	48-1	55	8-9	2	.367	.342
Freel, Ryan	SYR	.286	80	283	62	81	135	14	5	10	30	4-2	9	35-1	44	30-7	3	.477	.380
Freel, Ryan	TEN	.295	12	44	11	13	18	3	1	0	8	0-2	1	8-0	6	2-3	3	.409	.400
Freel, Ryan	DUN	.500	4	18	7	9	19	1	0	3	6	0-0	0	0-0	1	0-0	0	1.056	.500
TOTALS		.299	96	345	80	103	172	18	6	13	44	4-4	10	43-1	51	32-10	6	.499	.388
* Gibbons, Jay	TEN	.321	132	474	85	152	249	38	1	19	75	0-7	10	61-5	67	3-1	10	.525	.404
* Giles, Tim	TEN	.264	115	397	43	105	162	18	0	13	56	0-5	1	53-6	98	1-6	11	.408	.349
Gonzalez, Alex	SYR	.000	1	5	0	0	0	0	0	0	0	0-0	0	0-0	2	0-0	0	.000	.000
Goudie, Jaime	HAG	.243	164	412	53	100	143	19	3	6	51	8-3	9	36-0	68	26-10	6	.347	.315
Greene, Charli	SYR	.225	77	267	23	60	87	12	0	5	26	3-0	3	17-0	46	1-3	5	.326	.279
Greene, Todd	SYR	.297	24	91	14	27	51	3	0	7	14	0-1	0	6-0	16	1-0	3	.560	.337
Greene, Todd	DUN	.200	5	20	2	4	8	1	0	1	4	0-0	1	2-1	4	0-0	0	.400	.304
TOTALS		.279	29	111	16	31	59	4	0	8	18	0-1	1	8-1	20	1-0	3	.532	.331
Haltiwanger, G	DUN	.291	100	354	57	103	166	27	3	10	56	0-1	3	37-1	67	18-4	10	.469	.362
Hamilton, Joey	SYR	.000	6	1	0	0	0	0	0	0	0	0-0	0	0-0	0	0-0	0	.000	.000
# Holliday, Josh	HAG	.220	74	218	46	48	81	13	1	6	29	3-4	7	52-1	64	2-0	2	.372	.381
# Hudson, Orland	TEN	.239	39	134	17	32	48	4	3	2	15	1-2	2	15-1	18	3-2	3	.358	.320
# Hudson, Orland	DUN	.285	96	358	54	102	143	16	2	7	48	4-1	2	37-1	42	9-5	15	.399	.354
TOTALS		.272	135	492	71	134	191	20	5	9	63	5-3	4	52-2	60	12-7	18	.388	.345
# Izturis, Cesar	SYR	.218	132	435	54	95	121	16	5	0	27	13-2	1	20-0	44	21-11	5	.278	.253
Jackson, Brand	DUN	.313	6	16	6	5	7	2	0	0	2	0-1	1	3-0	0	2-0	0	.438	.429
Jackson, Brand	HAG	.312	110	391	71	122	170	17	8	5	52	1-8	13	43-0	83	5-6	6	.435	.391
TOTALS		.312	116	407	77	127	177	19	8	5	54	1-9	14	46-0	83	7-6	6	.435	.393
# Jimenez, Richa	QUN	.219	9	32	5	7	8	1	0	0	3	0-0	1	3-0	9	0-0	0	.250	.306
* Johnson, Jerem	MHT	.376	67	245	66	92	149	24	3	9	58	1-1	6	55-3	29	5-3	8	.608	.498
Johnson, Reed	DUN	.316	36	133	26	42	67	9	2	4	28	1-3	11	14-0	27	3-2	1	.504	.416
Johnson, Reed	HAG	.290	95	324	66	94	152	24	5	8	70	2-3	14	62-1	49	14-2	9	.469	.422
TOTALS		.298	131	457	92	136	219	33	7	12	98	3-6	25	76-1	76	17-4	10	.479	.420
Keene, Kurt	HAG	.261	55	199	16	52	66	11	0	1	25	0-1	3	8-0	33	4-6	3	.332	.299
Keene, Kurt	QUN	.261	11	46	10	12	13	1	0	0	5	0-0	0	6-0	10	4-1	3	.283	.346
TOTALS		.261	66	245	26	64	79	12	0	1	30	0-1	3	14-0	43	8-7	6	.322	.308
Kimberley, Gly	MHT	.229	26	83	13	19	26	4	0	1	13	0-1	3	9-0	32	0-0	2	.313	.323
Kremblas, Mike	TEN	.275	30	69	16	19	26	4	0	1	6	5-2	10	9-0	14	1-1	2	.377	.422
Kremblas, Mike	DUN	.281	25	64	15	18	22	2	1	0	10	0-1	6	16-0	7	1-0	1	.344	.460
TOTALS		.278	55	133	31	37	48	6	1	1	16	5-3	16	25-0	21	2-1	3	.361	.441
* Langaigne, Sel	SYR	.239	16	46	3	11	16	5	0	0	3	1-0	0	1-0	8	0-1	1	.348	.255
* Langaigne, Sel	TEN	.244	76	213	26	52	58	4	1	0	22	2-1	1	21-1	43	1-5	7	.272	.314
* Langaigne, Sel	DUN	.600	5	10	2	6	7	1	0	0	1	0-0	0	1-1	2	0-0	0	.700	.636
TOTALS		.257	97	269	31	69	81	10	1	0	23	3-1	1	23-2	53	1-6	8	.301	.316

Batter	Team	AVG	G	AB	R	H	TB	2B	3B	HR	RBI	SH-SF	HP	BB-IB	SO	SB-CS	DP	SLG	OBP
Lawrence, Joe	TEN	.263	39	133	22	35	44	9	0	0	9	1-1	3	30-0	27	7-1	2	.331	.407
Lawrence, Joe	DUN	.301	101	375	69	113	186	32	1	13	67	0-3	5	69-6	74	21-7	9	.496	.414
TOTALS		.291	140	508	91	148	230	41	1	13	76	1-4	8	99-6	101	28-8	11	.453	.412
* Logan, Matt	DUN	.279	124	373	58	104	159	26	1	9	55	2-6	7	36-0	93	4-1	13	.426	.348
# Lopez, Felipe	TEN	.257	127	463	52	119	172	18	4	9	41	8-3	1	31-0	110	12-11	6	.371	.303
Lopez, Luis	SYR	.328	130	491	64	161	211	27	1	7	79	0-8	2	48-1	33	3-1	10	.430	.384
Loyd, Brian	SYR	.135	22	52	2	7	10	0	0	1	4	0-1	1	3-0	9	0-2	2	.192	.193
Loyd, Brian	TEN	.299	58	194	21	58	73	10	1	1	23	0-2	2	29-1	22	7-3	6	.376	.392
TOTALS		.264	80	246	23	65	83	10	1	2	27	0-3	3	32-1	31	7-5	8	.337	.352
Malpica, Marti	QUN	.278	55	216	30	60	80	14	0	2	34	1-0	2	7-0	35	0-3	5	.370	.307
Martinez, Case	QUN	.136	7	22	2	3	3	0	0	0	0	1-0	1	1-0	7	0-0	0	.136	.208
Martinez, Case	MHT	.280	9	25	5	7	13	3	0	1	3	0-0	1	6-0	7	0-0	1	.520	.438
TOTALS		.213	16	47	7	10	16	3	0	1	3	1-0	2	7-0	14	0-0	1	.340	.339
Mayorson, Manu	MHT	.220	56	218	39	48	52	2	1	0	12	2-0	1	33-0	27	3-2	6	.239	.325
Medina, Rafael	SYR	.000	33	1	0	0	0	0	0	0	0	0-0	0	0-0	0	0-0	0	.000	.000
Morrow, Alvin	HAG	.210	32	105	15	22	37	3	0	4	8	0-0	2	14-0	42	2-0	3	.352	.314
Mottola, Chad	SYR	.309	134	505	85	156	286	25	3	33	102	0-5	5	37-2	99	30-15	11	.566	.359
Mummau, Rob	SYR	.161	54	155	13	25	32	5	1	0	8	2-1	0	13-1	28	0-0	6	.206	.225
* Negron, Miguel	MHT	.232	53	190	26	44	49	5	0	0	13	2-0	3	23-3	39	5-3	2	.258	.324
Otanez, Willis	SYR	.171	22	76	6	13	22	3	0	2	14	0-1	0	6-0	15	0-0	4	.289	.229
Otanez, Willis	TEN	.320	27	103	13	33	53	5	0	5	19	0-1	1	10-1	16	0-0	2	.515	.383
TOTALS		.257	49	179	19	46	75	8	0	7	33	0-2	1	16-1	31	0-0	6	.419	.318
Paulino, Luis	MHT	.259	62	224	30	58	99	14	6	5	25	0-0	4	20-0	51	6-4	2	.442	.331
Pearson, Shawn	DUN	.600	4	10	3	6	7	1	0	0	3	0-0	0	1-0	1	0-0	0	.700	.636
Pearson, Shawn	HAG	.141	33	92	9	13	15	0	1	0	5	1-0	1	15-1	20	4-2	3	.163	.269
Pearson, Shawn	QUN	.351	20	74	18	26	27	1	0	0	3	0-2	0	18-0	8	7-4	1	.365	.468
TOTALS		.256	57	176	30	45	49	2	1	0	11	1-2	1	34-1	29	11-6	4	.278	.376
Peeples, Mike	TEN	.280	123	475	70	133	221	26	4	18	73	9-4	7	46-1	71	11-8	14	.465	.350
Perez, Jersen	DUN	.271	126	509	69	138	211	35	7	8	64	8-5	4	20-0	106	8-4	11	.415	.301
Perez, Robert	TEN	.287	136	547	66	157	249	33	1	19	92	2-3	6	26-3	82	8-7	12	.455	.325
Peters, Tony	DUN	.268	127	455	97	122	201	30	2	15	61	4-3	7	71-1	164	23-8	9	.442	.373
Phelps, Josh	TEN	.228	56	184	23	42	80	9	1	9	28	1-2	7	15-0	66	1-0	6	.435	.308
Phelps, Josh	DUN	.319	30	113	26	36	79	7	0	12	34	0-1	1	12-0	34	0-0	2	.699	.386
TOTALS		.263	86	297	49	78	159	16	1	21	62	1-3	8	27-0	100	1-0	8	.535	.337
Pugh, Dwayne	HAG	.133	6	15	2	2	2	0	0	0	0	0-0	1	5-0	9	2-0	0	.133	.381
Pugh, Dwayne	QUN	.000	8	16	2	0	0	0	0	0	0	0-0	0	1-0	5	1-0	0	.000	.059
TOTALS		.065	14	31	4	2	2	0	0	0	0	0-0	1	6-0	5	3-0	0	.065	.237
Quiroz, Guille	HAG	.162	43	136	14	22	29	4	0	1	12	3-0	4	16-0	44	0-1	3	.213	.269
Quiroz, Guille	QUN	.224	55	196	27	44	68	9	0	5	29	0-1	4	27-0	48	1-2	4	.347	.329
TOTALS		.199	98	332	41	66	97	13	0	6	41	3-1	8	43-0	92	1-3	7	.292	.305
Ramos, Ebaldo	MHT	.233	26	90	13	21	29	8	0	0	11	1-0	0	10-0	24	0-0	2	.322	.310
Rich, Dominic	QUN	.263	67	236	37	62	81	11	4	0	25	4-3	5	38-0	33	10-4	8	.343	.372
# Ridley, Jeremy	QUN	.000	1	2	0	0	0	0	0	0	0	0-0	0	0-0	0	0-0	0	.000	.000
# Ridley, Jeremy	MHT	.286	3	7	3	2	3	1	0	0	1	0-0	0	3-0	2	0-0	0	.429	.500
TOTALS		.222	4	9	3	2	3	1	0	0	1	0-0	0	3-0	2	0-0	0	.333	.417
# Riggins, Auntw	HAG	.221	67	195	25	43	48	5	0	0	9	4-0	2	12-0	56	16-4	4	.246	.273
* Rikert, Wade	QUN	.250	36	108	19	27	32	5	0	0	14	1-1	1	18-0	22	8-3	1	.296	.359
Rikert, Wade	MHT	.247	24	97	27	24	40	4	0	4	15	1-1	3	15-2	19	6-1	0	.412	.362
TOTALS		.249	60	205	46	51	72	9	0	4	29	2-2	4	33-2	41	14-4	1	.351	.361
Rios, Alexis	HAG	.230	22	74	5	17	22	3	1	0	5	0-1	1	2-0	14	2-3	0	.297	.256
Rios, Alexis	QUN	.267	50	206	22	55	71	9	2	1	25	1-2	4	11-2	22	5-5	5	.345	.314
TOTALS		.257	72	280	27	72	93	12	3	1	30	1-3	5	13-2	36	7-8	5	.332	.299
* Rivera, Willia	MHT	.274	39	124	22	34	39	3	1	0	8	4-0	0	24-0	29	0-0	2	.315	.392
Rodriguez, Mik	DUN	.274	73	223	34	61	77	11	1	1	23	2-4	4	28-2	44	1-3	6	.345	.349
# Roper, Douglas	HAG	.171	25	76	16	13	15	2	0	0	9	0-0	0	1-0	31	3-0	1	.197	.284
# Santos, Juan	HAG	.146	14	41	4	6	13	1	0	2	5	1-1	1	5-0	20	1-1	1	.317	.250
# Santos, Juan	QUN	.241	9	29	2	7	9	2	0	0	3	1-0	0	6-0	6	0-0	0	.310	.371
TOTALS		.186	23	70	6	13	22	3	0	2	8	2-1	1	11-0	26	1-1	1	.314	.301
Schifano, Tony	TEN	.233	87	275	24	64	78	11	0	1	24	8-2	7	19-2	53	6-4	4	.284	.297
* Sellier, Brian	QUN	.258	66	209	34	54	82	5	4	5	33	1-6	2	41-0	51	11-2	6	.392	.376
# Siriveaw, Nom	MHT	.243	63	235	40	57	93	8	2	8	40	0-0	3	35-1	64	7-0	2	.396	.341
Sisk, Aaron	MHT	.257	59	218	32	56	109	10	2	13	50	0-2	3	34-1	56	4-0	7	.500	.362
Small, Chris	QUN	.133	4	15	2	2	3	1	0	0	1	0-0	0	1-0	5	0-0	0	.200	.188
Small, Chris	MHT	.221	38	131	13	29	29	0	0	0	6	4-1	3	14-0	23	2-1	2	.221	.309
TOTALS		.212	42	146	15	31	32	1	0	0	7	4-1	3	15-0	28	2-1	2	.219	.297
* Snyder, Mike	HAG	.182	54	165	26	30	43	8	1	1	13	0-0	1	32-0	48	4-1	2	.261	.318
* Snyder, Mike	QUN	.278	58	227	28	63	92	11	3	4	34	0-1	1	22-1	49	4-3	2	.405	.343
TOTALS		.237	111	392	54	93	135	19	4	5	47	0-1	2	54-1	97	8-4	4	.344	.332
Solano, Fausto	DUN	.241	50	158	20	38	54	8	1	2	22	0-2	3	19-2	27	6-2	6	.342	.330
* Sollmann, Scot	TEN	.236	114	385	66	91	117	16	5	0	27	6-3	8	53-1	58	19-10	6	.304	.339
Speed, Dorian	TEN	.074	8	27	2	2	2	0	0	0	0	0-0	0	0-0	11	2-1	0	.074	.074
Stewart, Shann	DUN	1.000	1	3	2	3	4	1	0	0	0	0-0	0	2-1	0	0-1	0	1.333	1.000
Strange, Mike	DUN	.250	16	36	6	9	11	2	0	0	2	0-0	0	11-0	14	0-2	0	.306	.426
Tablado, Raul	QUN	.212	52	198	27	42	63	8	2	3	29	1-3	1	31-0	76	1-1	6	.318	.318
Thompson, Andy	SYR	.246	121	426	59	105	202	27	2	22	65	0-6	9	50-1	95	9-2	4	.474	.334
* Thompson, Rich	QUN	.262	68	252	42	66	88	9	5	1	27	5-0	6	45-1	57	28-8	0	.349	.386
Thompson, Tyle	MHT	.280	103	350	51	98	161	26	2	11	57	2-2	4	45-1	93	20-5	5	.460	.367
Umbria, Jose	HAG	.209	27	91	3	19	21	2	0	0	8	1-2	0	8-0	19	0-2	2	.231	.275
Umbria, Jose	QUN	.500	3	10	3	5	6	1	0	0	4	0-0	0	0-0	0	0-0	0	.600	.500
Umbria, Jose	MHT	.345	14	55	11	19	30	2	0	3	14	0-0	1	11-0	10	0-0	0	.545	.455
TOTALS		.276	44	156	17	43	57	5	0	3	26	1-2	1	19-0	29	0-2	2	.365	.354

Batter	Team	AVG	G	AB	R	H	TB	2B	3B	HR	RBI	SH-SF	HP	BB-IB	SO	SB-CS	DP	SLG	OBP
* Weekly, Chris	DUN	.250	34	120	23	30	52	7	0	5	22	1-1	3	14-0	30	0-2	0	.433	.341
* Weekly, Chris	HAG	.291	66	234	21	68	106	15	1	7	49	0-3	1	22-0	53	2-5	8	.453	.350
TOTALS		.277	100	354	44	98	158	22	1	12	71	1-4	4	36-0	83	2-7	8	.446	.347
Wells, Vernon	SYR	.243	127	493	76	120	213	31	7	16	66	1-5	4	48-1	88	23-4	4	.432	.313
Williams, Glen	DUN	.261	107	391	53	102	175	26	4	13	77	0-6	6	33-1	91	4-2	11	.448	.323
* Wise, Dewayne	TEN	.250	15	56	10	14	29	5	2	2	8	0-0	0	7-0	13	3-2	2	.518	.333
* Witt, Kevin	SYR	.247	135	489	58	121	233	24	5	26	72	1-0	4	45-6	132	1-1	9	.476	.316
Wood, Stephen	MHT	.227	21	88	14	20	34	8	0	2	14	0-0	0	9-2	16	0-0	3	.386	.299
Woodward, Chri	SYR	.322	37	143	23	46	78	13	2	5	25	1-0	0	11-0	30	2-0	2	.545	.370
Young, Mike	TEN	.275	91	345	51	95	147	24	5	6	47	4-6	1	36-1	72	16-5	5	.426	.340

Pitcher	Team	W-L	PCT	ERA	G	GS	CG	ShO	GF	SV	IP	H	AB	TBF	R	ER	HR	SH-SF	HB	BB-IB	SO	WP	BK
Abbott, James	MHT	2-1	.667	1.99	8	4	0	0	0	0	22.2	19	84	95	11	5	0	1-3	1	6-0	18	1	0
* Andrews, Clayt	SYR	8-7	.533	4.82	19	18	0	0	0	0	102.2	114	400	449	56	55	8	2-3	2	42-0	59	1	2
Baker, Chris	DUN	9-5	.643	3.20	41	6	0	0	10	5	104.0	91	403	440	50	37	11	2-1	5	29-2	85	9	1
* Bale, John	SYR	3-4	.429	3.19	21	12	0	0	2	0	79.0	68	291	338	35	28	4	1-3	2	41-0	70	4	0
Bauer, Pete	HAG	1-5	.167	5.06	9	9	0	0	0	0	32.0	37	125	141	27	18	2	2-3	3	8-0	22	4	0
Bell, Jason	SYR	3-4	.429	4.97	22	3	0	0	7	0	41.2	41	151	175	25	23	3	3-4	1	16-1	28	2	0
Bell, Jason	TEN	4-3	.571	3.53	12	2	0	0	3	0	35.2	30	129	151	19	14	2	6-4	2	10-1	32	0	0
TOTALS		7-7	.500	4.31	34	5	0	0	10	0	77.1	71	280	326	44	37	5	9-8	3	26-2	60	2	0
Birneal, Matt	MHT	1-0	1.000	6.02	21	0	0	0	8	0	43.1	55	181	199	40	29	8	1-3	1	13-0	50	8	2
Bluma, Marc	HAG	2-2	.500	4.28	48	0	0	0	19	1	67.1	75	267	306	48	32	3	3-4	5	27-3	52	1	0
* Bogott, Kurt	SYR	1-0	1.000	4.01	20	0	0	0	6	1	24.2	25	90	109	12	11	4	2-1	4	12-1	17	2	0
Bowles, Brian	TEN	4-4	.500	2.98	49	0	0	0	12	6	81.2	64	294	343	31	27	1	2-3	8	36-1	72	11	0
Cardwell, Bria	HAG	0-5	.000	9.09	11	6	0	0	2	0	31.2	41	131	154	38	32	7	0-1	1	21-0	29	2	1
Cardwell, Bria	QUN	2-4	.333	4.71	12	11	1	0	1	0	49.2	49	183	213	32	26	6	2-3	6	19-0	61	4	0
TOTALS		2-9	.182	6.42	23	17	1	0	3	0	81.1	90	314	367	70	58	13	2-4	7	40-0	90	6	1
Casey, Joe	DUN	10-8	.556	4.21	27	27	0	0	0	0	158.1	151	582	677	88	74	7	1-5	14	74-2	96	21	2
Cassidy, Scott	SYR	2-2	.500	3.76	8	7	0	0	0	0	42.2	48	166	190	30	28	7	1-4	4	15-0	39	3	0
Cassidy, Scott	DUN	9-3	.750	1.33	14	13	1	0	1	0	88.0	53	300	342	15	13	4	3-2	3	34-2	89	4	0
TOTALS		11-5	.688	2.82	22	20	1	0	1	0	130.2	101	466	532	45	41	11	4-6	7	49-2	128	7	0
Castellanos, H	DUN	0-0	.000	4.50	4	0	0	0	4	1	8.0	5	25	37	4	4	1	1-1	0	10-1	5	0	0
Castellanos, H	HAG	0-3	.000	1.64	29	0	0	0	19	7	38.1	16	130	155	11	7	1	2-0	5	18-1	30	5	0
TOTALS		0-3	.000	2.14	33	0	0	0	23	8	46.1	21	155	192	15	11	2	3-1	5	28-2	35	5	0
* Chacin, Gustav	TEN	0-2	.000	12.60	2	2	0	0	0	0	5.0	10	24	31	7	7	1	0-0	1	6-0	5	0	1
* Chacin, Gustav	DUN	9-5	.643	4.02	25	21	0	0	1	0	127.2	138	513	584	69	57	14	1-2	3	64-0	77	9	0
TOTALS		9-7	.563	4.34	27	23	0	0	1	0	132.2	148	537	615	76	64	15	1-2	4	70-0	82	9	1
Chulk, Charles	MHT	2-4	.333	3.80	14	13	0	0	0	0	68.2	75	271	295	36	29	5	0-2	2	20-0	51	3	0
Coco, Pasqual	TEN	12-7	.632	3.76	27	26	2	0	0	0	167.2	164	632	723	83	70	16	1-4	17	68-0	142	6	3
Cubillan, Darw	SYR	3-1	.750	0.55	24	0	0	0	14	6	32.2	14	108	123	2	2	0	1-0	1	13-1	41	1	0
Daneker, Pat	SYR	1-1	.500	3.29	2	2	0	0	0	0	13.2	18	54	58	6	5	2	0-1	1	2-0	4	1	0
Daneker, Pat	SYR	9-13	.409	5.54	29	27	0	0	0	0	157.2	186	629	691	108	97	28	2-4	5	51-1	73	5	4
Dean, Aaron	TEN	0-1	.000	1.50	1	1	1	0	0	0	6.0	5	22	28	1	1	0	0-0	1	5-0	4	2	0
Dean, Aaron	DUN	1-0	1.000	6.46	3	3	0	0	0	0	15.1	22	68	77	15	11	1	0-1	1	7-0	13	3	0
Dean, Aaron	HAG	8-3	.727	3.28	19	19	0	0	0	0	112.2	99	420	472	55	41	8	2-6	6	38-0	89	4	0
TOTALS		9-4	.692	3.56	23	23	1	0	0	0	134.0	126	510	577	71	53	10	2-7	8	50-0	106	9	0
* Detwiler, Jame	QUN	3-1	.750	2.83	20	0	0	0	8	1	35.0	25	123	146	12	11	0	2-0	2	19-1	38	3	1
Dewitt, Matt	SYR	4-5	.444	4.87	31	7	0	0	23	15	64.2	78	262	296	42	35	6	2-5	2	25-0	41	0	0
* Dimma, Doug	DUN	6-3	.667	3.84	43	0	0	0	17	1	79.2	74	300	361	46	34	6	1-3	8	48-4	42	7	0
Donnelly, Bren	SYR	4-6	.400	5.48	37	0	0	0	7	0	42.2	47	169	203	34	26	5	4-1	1	27-2	34	1	0
Eichhorn, Mark	SYR	1-0	1.000	1.10	17	0	0	0	4	0	16.1	5	55	57	2	2	2	0-0	0	2-0	17	0	0
Eichhorn, Mark	DUN	0-0	.000	0.00	5	0	0	0	4	0	5.1	3	19	20	0	0	0	1-0	0	0-0	8	1	0
TOTALS		1-0	1.000	0.83	22	0	0	0	8	0	21.2	8	74	77	2	2	2	1-0	0	2-0	25	1	0
Ellis, Robert	SYR	1-1	.500	4.50	16	0	0	0	10	2	18.0	17	65	85	10	9	2	3-0	2	15-1	18	3	1
* Espina, Rendy	TEN	6-1	.857	2.11	53	0	0	0	19	3	59.2	49	219	264	22	14	1	2-2	5	35-1	41	2	1
Estrella, Leo	SYR	5-4	.556	4.01	15	15	3	1	0	0	89.2	68	317	364	42	40	8	1-4	2	40-0	48	2	1
Estrella, Leo	TEN	5-5	.500	3.67	13	13	3	2	0	0	76.0	68	276	324	36	31	6	4-3	10	30-1	63	2	0
TOTALS		10-9	.526	3.86	28	28	6	3	0	0	165.2	136	593	688	78	71	14	5-7	12	70-1	111	4	1
File, Bob	SYR	2-0	1.000	0.93	20	0	0	0	11	8	19.1	14	66	69	2	2	1	0-0	1	2-0	10	0	0
File, Bob	TEN	4-3	.571	3.12	36	0	0	0	32	20	34.2	29	135	153	20	12	1	2-1	2	13-0	40	0	1
TOTALS		6-3	.667	2.33	56	0	0	0	43	28	54.0	43	201	222	22	14	2	2-1	3	15-0	50	0	1
Flores, Neomar	MHT	0-0	.000	12.00	1	1	0	0	0	0	3.0	6	13	14	4	4	1	0-0	0	1-0	2	0	0
* Ford, Matt	HAG	5-3	.625	3.87	18	14	1	0	0	0	83.2	81	310	353	42	36	5	0-4	3	36-0	86	5	0
Giles, Tim	TEN	0-0	.000	27.00	1	0	0	0	1	0	1.0	3	6	8	4	3	0	0-0	0	2-0	0	0	0
Glover, Gary	SYR	9-9	.500	5.02	27	27	1	0	0	0	166.2	181	661	731	104	93	21	2-4	2	62-0	119	5	1
* Gracesqui, Fra	HAG	0-1	.000	4.91	3	1	0	0	1	0	7.1	4	23	33	4	4	1	0-0	1	9-0	6	0	0
* Gracesqui, Fra	MHT	0-1	.000	2.63	8	4	0	0	0	0	24.0	15	81	105	11	7	1	1-0	2	21-0	20	5	0
TOTALS		0-2	.000	3.16	11	5	0	0	1	0	31.1	19	104	138	15	11	2	1-0	3	30-0	26	5	0
Gunderson, Eri	SYR	0-3	.000	2.67	33	0	0	0	10	2	27.0	26	102	117	12	8	2	2-1	1	11-0	17	4	1
Guzman, Alexis	MHT	6-8	.429	2.38	27	1	0	0	6	0	53.0	49	203	226	25	14	3	4-2	6	11-0	35	2	0
Halladay, Roy	SYR	2-3	.400	5.50	11	11	3	0	0	0	73.2	85	293	317	46	45	10	1-0	2	21-0	38	4	0
Hamann, Robert	DUN	2-1	.667	1.50	16	0	0	0	13	5	24.0	16	82	91	5	4	2	1-1	0	7-3	14	2	1
Hamann, Robert	HAG	8-4	.667	2.95	34	1	0	0	19	6	58.0	48	213	244	25	19	4	3-2	5	21-4	34	9	0
TOTALS		10-5	.667	2.52	50	1	0	0	32	11	82.0	64	295	335	30	23	6	4-3	5	28-7	48	11	1
Hamilton, Joey	SYR	3-2	.600	3.66	6	6	1	0	0	0	39.1	41	146	167	18	16	1	1-4	4	12-0	17	0	0
Hanson, David	MHT	7-3	.700	5.81	15	15	0	0	0	0	79.0	82	313	352	55	51	6	3-2	5	29-0	79	12	1
Heath, Woody	DUN	0-2	.000	6.30	8	1	0	0	3	1	20.0	27	78	97	17	14	1	0-2	1	16-0	11	4	0
* Hendrickson, M	TEN	3-1	.750	3.63	6	6	0	0	0	0	39.2	32	148	161	17	16	5	1-0	0	12-0	29	4	0
* Hendrickson, M	DUN	2-2	.500	5.61	12	12	1	0	0	0	51.1	63	200	235	34	32	7	1-5	0	29-0	38	1	0
TOTALS		5-3	.625	4.75	18	18	1	0	0	0	91.0	95	348	396	51	48	12	2-5	0	41-0	67	5	0
Houston, Ryan	HAG	5-1	.833	2.21	6	6	0	0	0	0	36.2	17	119	136	9	9	2	0-0	4	13-0	27	1	0
Houston, Ryan	QUN	1-2	.333	2.83	12	0	0	0	2	0	28.2	23	106	118	11	9	1	1-0	3	8-0	29	1	0

Pitcher	Team	W-L	PCT	ERA	G	GS	CG	ShO	GF	SV	IP	H	AB	TBF	R	ER	HR	SH-SF	HB	BB-IB	SO	WP	BK
TOTALS		6-3	.667	2.48	18	6	0	0	2	0	65.1	40	225	254	20	18	3	1-0	7	21-0	56	2	0
Hubbel, Travis	DUN	0-0	.000	3.38	3	0	0	0	1	0	5.1	4	17	20	2	2	2	1-0	0	2-0	3	1	0
Hubbel, Travis	HAG	8-6	.571	3.97	19	19	0	0	0	0	113.1	103	407	478	62	50	7	3-3	10	55-0	75	13	0
TOTALS		8-6	.571	3.94	22	19	0	0	1	0	118.2	107	424	498	64	52	9	4-3	10	57-0	78	14	0
Huesgen, Danie	QUN	2-1	.667	2.42	16	0	0	0	2	1	26.0	27	101	115	9	7	2	3-1	0	10-0	17	1	0
Huggins, David	TEN	1-1	.500	8.38	6	0	0	0	2	1	9.2	10	37	47	10	9	0	1-0	4	5-0	10	1	0
Kegley, Charle	DUN	3-9	.250	3.88	23	23	0	0	0	0	111.1	96	399	490	60	48	6	4-4	8	74-1	66	11	5
Kingrey, Jarro	TEN	2-0	1.000	2.12	16	0	0	0	15	7	17.0	11	57	76	6	4	0	2-1	1	15-2	16	1	0
Kingrey, Jarro	DUN	4-2	.667	2.97	37	0	0	0	34	23	39.1	33	147	177	20	13	2	2-2	3	23-1	35	5	1
TOTALS		6-2	.750	2.72	53	0	0	0	49	30	56.1	44	204	253	26	17	2	4-3	4	38-3	51	6	1
* Kozlowski, Kri	QUN	4-1	.800	2.82	21	0	0	0	3	0	44.2	38	172	194	21	14	2	1-1	0	20-0	58	3	2
* Kusiewicz, Mik	TEN	7-9	.438	3.63	27	26	1	0	1	0	156.0	149	603	684	83	63	14	8-4	9	59-1	115	10	0
* Lawrence, Clin	TEN	3-3	.500	5.30	34	1	0	0	18	0	54.1	63	219	268	33	32	7	3-2	1	43-2	31	6	0
LaChapelle, Ya	DUN	5-1	.833	2.60	18	7	0	0	3	0	55.1	42	201	234	22	16	4	2-2	2	27-1	49	2	0
Lewis, Peyton	HAG	0-3	.000	5.20	23	0	0	0	17	6	27.2	34	114	129	17	16	2	1-1	1	12-0	25	2	0
* Lukasiewicz, M	SYR	2-1	.667	3.48	42	0	0	0	12	0	41.1	34	149	176	17	16	7	2-0	0	25-1	52	3	0
* Lukasiewicz, M	TEN	0-0	.000	5.59	3	0	0	0	1	0	4.2	4	18	22	3	3	1	0-0	0	4-0	6	0	0
TOTALS		2-1	.667	3.72	45	0	0	0	13	0	46.0	38	167	198	20	19	8	2-0	0	29-1	58	3	0
Lyon, Brandon	QUN	5-3	.625	2.39	15	13	0	0	0	0	60.1	43	218	230	20	16	1	2-2	2	6-0	55	1	1
Malpica, Marti	QUN	0-0	.000	0.00	1	0	0	0	1	0	0.2	0	2	02	0	0	0	0-0	0	0-0	1	1	0
* Markwell, Dieg	HAG	0-1	.000	9.00	2	0	0	0	0	0	2.0	3	9	15	2	2	0	1-0	0	5-0	2	0	0
* Markwell, Dieg	QUN	4-3	.571	3.05	14	13	0	0	1	0	73.2	59	267	306	29	25	2	1-4	3	31-0	66	2	0
TOTALS		4-4	.500	3.21	16	13	0	0	1	0	75.2	62	276	321	31	27	2	2-4	3	36-0	68	2	0
McBride, Chris	TEN	2-2	.500	2.39	22	4	0	0	9	1	60.1	51	223	240	18	16	5	2-2	4	9-0	37	5	0
McClellan, Mat	TEN	6-12	.333	4.80	28	27	0	0	0	0	168.2	174	657	743	100	90	16	2-4	11	69-1	140	11	3
* McCullem, Ryan	MHT	2-2	.500	3.95	16	6	0	0	1	0	54.2	64	220	254	34	24	5	3-2	2	27-0	53	5	0
McCulloch, And	MHT	0-0	.000	2.67	27	0	0	0	24	15	27.0	24	105	112	9	8	3	0-0	0	7-0	26	2	0
* McFarland, Stu	QUN	2-2	.500	2.08	19	0	0	0	10	2	26.0	12	81	115	9	6	0	2-2	8	22-1	21	1	0
McGowan, Dusti	MHT	0-3	.000	6.48	8	8	0	0	0	0	25.0	26	95	129	21	18	2	1-5	3	25-0	19	8	0
* McMillan, Josh	MHT	3-3	.500	4.34	15	15	0	0	0	0	64.1	72	258	293	47	31	5	3-1	2	29-0	56	5	0
Medina, Rafael	SYR	3-1	.750	2.80	33	2	0	0	16	1	54.2	37	195	235	18	17	2	0-2	3	35-1	33	4	0
Morris, Willia	MHT	3-4	.429	5.52	24	0	0	0	8	0	44.0	46	168	192	33	27	4	3-3	1	17-1	29	3	0
Mowday, Chris	QUN	5-2	.714	3.39	15	13	0	0	2	0	71.2	61	262	310	32	27	1	0-3	4	41-0	65	8	0
Munro, Peter	SYR	4-3	.571	2.48	10	10	2	0	0	0	61.2	52	221	251	20	17	1	2-1	2	25-0	45	2	0
Munro, Peter	DUN	0-1	.000	5.56	3	3	0	0	0	0	11.1	11	43	47	7	7	0	0-0	0	4-0	12	1	0
TOTALS		4-4	.500	2.96	13	13	2	0	0	0	73.0	63	264	298	27	24	1	2-1	2	29-0	57	3	0
Nunley, Robert	QUN	2-0	1.000	5.12	11	1	0	0	2	0	19.1	23	78	88	12	11	1	0-2	0	8-0	20	0	0
Nunley, Robert	MHT	1-0	1.000	2.63	8	0	0	0	2	0	13.2	10	49	57	4	4	0	0-0	2	6-0	11	5	0
TOTALS		3-0	1.000	4.09	19	1	0	0	4	0	33.0	33	127	145	16	15	1	0-2	2	14-0	31	5	0
Orloski, Joe	QUN	4-0	1.000	1.38	22	0	0	0	8	3	52.0	32	185	206	13	8	2	2-1	2	16-1	66	2	0
* Painter, Lance	DUN	0-0	.000	0.00	1	1	0	0	0	0	1.0	0	3	03	0	0	0	0-0	0	0-0	0	0	0
Patten, Lanny	MHT	2-3	.400	3.71	17	3	0	0	5	0	43.2	57	179	196	31	18	5	0-1	5	11-0	38	8	0
Payne, Jerrod	HAG	0-2	.000	3.71	19	0	0	0	17	8	17.0	15	62	70	9	7	0	0-2	0	6-0	6	2	0
Payne, Jerrod	QUN	0-0	.000	9.00	2	0	0	0	1	0	2.0	3	8	8	2	2	1	0-0	0	0-0	1	1	0
TOTALS		0-2	.000	4.26	21	0	0	0	18	8	19.0	18	70	78	11	9	1	0-2	0	6-0	7	3	0
Perez, George	QUN	5-1	.833	0.78	29	0	0	0	25	12	34.2	21	116	138	3	3	1	2-2	3	15-2	35	3	0
* Place, Eric	DUN	5-2	.714	4.24	24	1	0	0	11	0	46.2	47	175	220	27	22	3	5-5	2	33-3	32	1	0
* Place, Eric	QUN	0-1	.000	5.40	4	0	0	0	3	0	5.0	6	20	21	3	3	0	0-1	0	0-0	6	0	0
TOTALS		5-3	.625	4.24	28	1	0	0	14	0	51.2	53	195	241	30	25	3	5-6	2	33-3	38	1	0
Porter, Scott	DUN	1-2	.333	2.67	24	0	0	0	12	4	33.2	20	116	135	14	10	2	1-0	3	15-3	41	2	0
Reece, Dana	HAG	0-0	.000	7.33	34	1	0	0	11	0	43.0	65	191	226	47	35	5	1-1	2	31-0	37	11	1
Reimers, Camer	HAG	7-11	.389	3.73	26	26	2	0	0	0	154.1	158	596	671	79	64	10	5-4	21	45-0	112	14	2
Renwick, Tyler	HAG	3-2	.600	5.40	7	7	0	0	0	0	35.0	44	141	170	28	21	2	2-1	5	21-0	17	11	0
Renwick, Tyler	QUN	2-2	.500	2.55	7	7	0	0	0	0	35.1	26	131	156	19	10	1	0-0	1	23-0	31	5	0
TOTALS		5-4	.556	3.97	14	14	0	0	0	0	70.1	70	272	326	47	31	3	2-1	6	44-0	48	16	0
Romano, Mike	SYR	6-3	.667	3.25	10	10	2	1	0	0	63.2	53	230	259	23	23	7	0-1	2	26-0	34	1	0
Sandoval, Marc	HAG	8-13	.381	4.56	28	25	2	1	0	0	163.2	188	651	721	105	83	20	3-3	15	49-3	100	3	2
Smith, Michael	QUN	2-2	.500	2.29	14	12	0	0	0	0	51.0	41	183	205	18	13	1	1-2	2	17-0	55	9	1
Smith, Taylor	DUN	0-1	.000	3.52	13	0	0	0	5	0	23.0	21	89	101	19	9	1	1-1	0	10-1	20	2	0
Sneed, John	TEN	5-9	.357	4.54	21	21	0	0	0	0	121.0	124	471	548	81	61	9	4-7	10	56-0	100	5	0
Southard, Lee	QUN	1-0	1.000	12.00	5	0	0	0	1	0	6.0	7	24	37	10	8	0	0-1	0	12-0	7	5	0
* Spille, Ryan	TEN	1-1	.500	4.18	4	4	0	0	0	0	23.2	23	89	99	11	11	1	2-2	0	10-0	8	0	0
* Spille, Ryan	QUN	10-6	.625	4.27	20	19	1	0	0	0	109.2	107	405	451	55	52	9	2-4	5	35-1	82	4	0
TOTALS		11-7	.611	4.25	24	23	1	0	0	0	133.1	130	490	550	66	63	10	4-6	5	45-1	90	4	0
* Spillman, Jero	MHT	4-3	.571	4.15	22	0	0	0	7	1	39.0	34	146	169	22	18	4	4-1	0	18-3	26	2	2
St. Amand, Reu	QUN	2-4	.333	5.87	17	5	0	0	3	0	46.0	65	189	219	42	30	1	1-5	2	22-0	28	8	0
Stephenson, Er	MHT	1-1	.500	8.33	19	0	0	0	8	0	27.0	41	116	134	28	25	2	1-2	2	13-0	21	9	0
Stevens, Josh	HAG	4-4	.500	2.99	47	3	0	0	15	5	84.1	97	336	363	42	28	4	3-2	3	19-1	95	9	0
* Stine, Justin	HAG	3-4	.429	3.13	41	0	0	0	9	1	54.2	53	200	229	28	19	2	2-1	0	26-1	46	3	0
Taylor, John	QUN	0-1	.000	9.35	10	0	0	0	3	0	8.2	13	36	47	10	9	0	1-2	2	6-0	9	4	0
Taylor, Kerry	SYR	9-8	.529	3.32	33	17	4	2	2	0	135.2	119	502	578	57	50	16	8-2	5	61-2	83	2	0
Thorpe, Tracy	MHT	0-4	.000	8.54	11	6	0	0	0	0	26.1	28	102	126	28	25	3	3-1	3	17-0	15	3	0
Vega, Vigri	MHT	2-0	1.000	1.64	10	0	0	0	7	1	11.0	8	42	47	4	2	0	1-1	1	2-0	15	2	0
Weimer, Matt	TEN	4-3	.571	4.60	49	0	0	0	20	2	62.2	68	242	273	36	32	6	2-3	4	22-5	31	5	0
Woodards, Orla	DUN	8-1	.889	2.27	41	1	0	0	16	7	87.1	65	314	353	26	22	4	1-3	3	32-1	69	2	0

SYRACUSE SKYCHIEFS
(AAA – International League)

(74-66, 4th, –9.5, North Division)

Team Highlights

- Finished above the .500 mark for the third straight season... Were a season high nine games above .500 on September 3 (74-65) after reaching a season low nine games below .500 on July 22 (43-52)... Won a season high six straight games from July 29 through August 3... Lost a season high four straight, four times... Under Mel Queen posted a record of 58-47, Pat Kelly was 15-19, while Omar Malave was 1-0... At the All-Star break were 41-44, post All-Star were 33-22... Over the final 39 games posted a record of 27-12, 31-13 over the final 44 games... Were second in the league in pitching with a 3.89 ERA and allowed the fewest hits (1137)...

Finished the final 74 games with a 3.41 ERA compared to a 4.44 ERA in the first 66 games... Were ranked 10th in the league in hitting with a .264 average and were fifth with 149 home runs as three players (Mottola, Witt and Thompson) hit more than 20, just the second time in franchise history (1954)... Tied a franchise mark with four players stealing 20 or more bases (Freel, Izturis, Mottola, Wells), done previously in 1987... Seven players and nine pitchers played for both Syracuse and Toronto... Ranked 11th in attendance with a total of 402,080 and an average of 6,001... Renewed working agreement with Toronto through the 2004 season.

International League Leaders

Batting

- **LUIS LOPEZ**, Batting Average 2nd (.328), Hits 2nd (161)... **CHAD MOTTOLA**, Batting Average 7th (.309), Hits 4th (156), Home Runs 1st (33), RBI 2nd (102), Slugging Percentage 1st (.566), Extra Base Hits 4th (61).

Pitching

- **GARY GLOVER**, Strikeouts 5th (119), Innings Pitched 3rd (166.2)... **KERRY TAYLOR**, ERA 4th (3.32), Shutouts T1st (2).

Individual Player Highlights

- **IF/OF RYAN FREEL** tied for the team lead with 30 stolen bases including 17 in August... Played 24 games at 2B, 12 at 3B and 23 in the outfield... Had five RBI, including a grand slam on August 24 vs. Rochester... Played at both Dunedin (A), four games, and then Tennessee (AA), 12 games, before joining the SkyChiefs... In August batted .371 with seven doubles, six home runs, 13 RBI and was named as the organization's Player of the Month.
- **IF/DH LUIS LOPEZ** batted .328 and had 161 hits, both good for second in the league... Led the SkyChiefs with a .384 on base percentage... Was named to the postseason All-Star squad as the DH along with Chad Mottola... Did not strike out in 25 consecutive games from May 12 to June 13, the second longest such streak in the minor leagues this season... Played 54 games at third base and 31 at first base... Was selected as both a mid-season and postseason IL All-Star.
- **OF CHAD MOTTOLA** was named as the International League's Most Valuable Player... Was the fifth player in franchise history to be named league MVP and the second since Syracuse's affiliation to the Blue Jays (Derek Bell, 1991) in 1978... Led the league with 33 home runs and slugging percentage at .566... Glenallen Hill was the last Syracuse player to lead the league in home runs with 21 in 1989... Was second in RBI with 102 and was seventh in batting with a .309 average... Became the first player in franchise history to steal 30 bases and hit 30 home runs in the same season... Is the first 30-30 player with one team since Derrick Gibson

accomplished the feat for Asheville (A) in the Rockies' organization in 1995... Was selected to play at the mid-season All-Star game... Was selected along with teammate Luis Lopez to the League's postseason All-Star team... Was named to the Triple-A All-Star team as an outfielder by Baseball America... Had a 14 game hit streak from June 13 through June 26... Had two two-homer games (Aug. 16 at Scranton WB & Aug. 23 vs. Rochester) and had a season high five RBI on August 23 vs. Rochester.

- **OF ANDY THOMPSON** 51 of his 105 hits went for extra bases... In May batted .313 with five home runs and 15 RBI... 22 home runs were third in the organization.
- **OF VERNON WELLS** for the second straight year represented the Blue Jays at the Futures All-Star Game during the ML All-Star break in Atlanta... Led the team with 31 doubles and stole 23 bases in 27 attempts... Was second on the team with 76 runs scored... Was 3-5 with a triple, two home runs and five RBI on August 8 vs. Scranton WB... Spent the entire season with Syracuse and was rated by Baseball America as the International League's "Best Defensive Outfielder"... Was named by Baseball America as the 7th best prospect in the IL.
- **1B KEVIN WITT** was second in the organization with 26 home runs including 11 in August and September (36 games)... Had a five RBI game on July 29 vs. Indianapolis... Had four two-homer games (May 29 at TOL, G2 July 7 at BUF, Aug. 6 vs. PAW, Sept. 2 at BUF).

Individual Pitcher Highlights

- **LHP CLAYTON ANDREWS** finished the season winning three straight games and pitched 7.0 plus innings in seven of his 18 starts... Allowed just one run in his first two starts of the year over 12.0 innings... Allowed a .250 average over his final six starts of the season.
- **LHP JOHN BALE** was named IL Pitcher of the Week from April 6 to 16 after starting the season with two starts of the season... Was 1-4 with a 3.41 ERA as a starter and 2-0 with a 2.45 ERA out of the bullpen.
- **RHP MATT DEWITT** led the SkyChiefs with 15 saves... Began the season as a starter before moving to the bullpen where he was 3-1 with a 1.33 ERA... In 27.0 relief innings fanned 24 batters, while walking five and allowing 21 hits.
- **RHP LEO ESTRELLA** tossed the 13th perfect game in IL history in a 5-0 win over Indianapolis in the first game

of a doubleheader on June 17 (7.0)... Was his first start at triple-A after starting the season with Tennessee (AA) where he threw a 6.0 inning no-hitter on May 27 vs. Orlando... Was the IL Pitcher of the Week for June 12 to 18... Was 3-0 in July with a 3.49 ERA in five starts.

- **RHP GARY GLOVER** led the team and was fourth in the league with 119 strikeouts... In six July starts was 3-3 with a 2.39 ERA.
- **RHP KERRY TAYLOR** ranked fourth in the league with a 3.32 ERA and was one of four pitchers to post two shutouts... Tied for the team lead with nine wins (Glover)... Was 7-7 with a 3.40 ERA as a starter and 2-1 with a 3.03 ERA in relief... Was the IL Pitcher of the Week from June 26 to July 2... Over his final 10 games, five starts, was 4-0 with a 1.29 ERA.

TENNESSEE SMOKIES
(AA – Southern League)

(First half, 33-37, 4th East Division; Second half, 38-32, 2nd East Division; Overall 71-69)

Team Highlights

- For the third straight season finished with an overall record of 71-69... Was the fifth straight season to finish above the .500 mark... Won a season high seven straight from May 22 through May 28 and were a season high three games above .500 at the end of the win streak on May 28... Were a season low eight games under .500 on June 13 and lost a season high seven straight from June 3 through June 10... Tied a SL record with 14 extra inning wins and had the best home record in the league at 42-27... Led the Southern League in batting at .265 and in hits with 1241... Were second in runs scored with 640 and third in home runs with 107... Were eighth in the 10 team league with a 3.99 ERA... Averaged 3,823 fans a game in the new Smokies Park for a total of 256,141 in attendance for 67 home dates, ranking fifth in the league... Were honored with the Southern League Award of Excellence as a result of an 114.2 percent increase in attendance over last season's total... Renewed their working agreement with the Blue Jays through the 2002 season... Were awarded the 2001 Southern League All-Star Game.

Southern League Leaders

Batting

- **JAY GIBBONS**, Batting Average 2nd (.321), Hits 3rd (152), Doubles 2nd (38), On-Base Percentage 4th (.404), Slugging Percentage 1st (.525), Extra-Base hits 1st (58), Runs Scored 2nd (85)... **ROBERT PEREZ**, Hits 2nd (157), RBI 3rd (92).

Pitching

- **PASQUAL COCO**, Wins 2nd (12), Strikeouts 5th (142)... **LEO ESTRELLA**, Shutouts T2nd (2), **ROB FILE**, Saves 5th (20), **MATT McCLELLAN**, Innings Pitched 5th (168.2).

Individual Player Highlights

- **1B JAY GIBBONS** was named as the Smokies MVP after leading the team with a .321 batting average and tied for the team lead with 19 home runs... Was second in the league in hitting and led the circuit with a .525 slugging percentage and was tied for the league lead with 58 extra-base hits... Was named Southern League Hitter of the Week from June 16 through 22 after batting .483 with 10 runs scored, four doubles, two home runs and eight RBI... In July batted a season high .435 and in August hit a season high six home runs and drove in 20 runs... Had a season high nine game hit streak from July 20 through 29... Was selected as the Topps Player of the Month for July for the third time in his career (Aug. 1998, May 1999)... Was selected to the Southern League postseason All-Star team at first base.

- **IF FELIPE LOPEZ** represented the World Team at the Futures All-Star Game in Atlanta during the Major League All-Star break... Was selected as a starter to the Southern League's Eastern Division mid-season All-Star team... Spent the entire season at Tennessee and batted .257 with nine home runs and 41 RBI... Played in 127 games, all at short stop... Was 5-14 with 10 RBI

- batting with the bases loaded... Baseball America rated him as the "Best Defensive Shortstop" in the league... Baseball America named him the 6th best prospect in the league.

- **IF/OF MIKE PEEPLES** who played 31 games at second base, 41 at third base and 52 in the outfield batted .280 with 18 home runs and 73 RBI... Was named as the league's Hitter of the Week from June 23 through June 29, hitting .429 with two homers and nine RBI to go along with an .810 slugging percentage... Batted .375 with five home runs and 26 RBI and was named as the organization's Player of the Month in June.

- **C BRIAN LOYD** was selected as the league's DH for the mid-season All-Star game after batting .299 with one home run and 23 RBI... Caught Leo Estrella's 6.0 inning no-hitter on May 27 and his 7.0 inning perfect game on June 17 with Syracuse (AAA), where he finished the season.

- **OF ROBERT PEREZ** returned to the organization and spent the entire season with Tennessee... Was second in the league with 157 hits and third with 92 RBI... Was named to the league's postseason All-Star team.

Individual Pitcher Highlights

- **RHP BRIAN BOWLES** was 4-4 with a 2.98 ERA in 49 games, all in relief... Did not allow an earned run in 35 of the 49 games pitched... Had a 1.17 ERA in April and May (23.0IP/3ER)... Struck out 10 batters in 4.2 innings of relief on August 2 at Jacksonville.

- **RHP PASQUAL COCO** was tied for second in the league with 12 wins and was fifth with 142 strikeouts... Also led the organization in wins and strikeouts... Was 3-1 in June with 2.67 ERA over six starts... May 23 pitched 7.1 innings of relief to pick up the win vs. Greenville (7H, 3R/2ER, 2BB, 3K)... Allowed two runs or less in five consecutive starts from July 22 through August 12... Was named to the league's end of season All-Star team as the best right-handed pitcher.

- **LHP RENDY ESPINA** pitched in a team high 53 games... Was 6-1 with a 2.11 ERA and allowed just one home run in 59.2 innings of work... Did not allow a run in his first 18 appearances, 16.1 innings, from April 6 through May 13... ERA in April was 0.00, July 0.79 and August 1.17... Allowed just one run in 24 outings (26.2) from June 25 through August 25.

- **RHP BOB FILE** was fifth in the Southern League with 20 saves and after finishing the season with Syracuse was second in the organization with 28 saves... Was selected to the league's mid-season All-Star team and was named to the Southern League's year-end All-Star team as best relief pitcher... Had 40 strikeouts in 34.2 innings of work, posting a 4-3 record with a 3.12 ERA... Had an identical 1.17 ERA in both April and June pitching in eight games each month... Right-handed hitters hit just .179 and he posted a 1.37 ERA on the road compared to a 5.40 ERA at home... Was named to the "AA" All-Star team at year end and was rated by Baseball America as the "Best Reliever" in the Southern League.

- **LHP MIKE KUSIEWICZ** led the staff with a 3.73 ERA in 27 game, 26 starts... Won his only relief appearance of the season on June 17 vs. Orlando with 3.0 shutout innings of work.

- **RHP MATT McCLELLAN** led the team in starts with 27 and was fifth in the league with 168.2 inning pitched... Was second in the organization with 140 strikeouts.

DUNEDIN BLUE JAYS
(A – Florida State League)

(First half, 40-29, 1st West Division; Second half, 44-25, 2nd West Division, Overall 84-54)
(West Division Playoffs, 2-0 vs. Fort Myers, Finals 0-3 vs. Daytona)

Team Highlights

- For the second consecutive season the Dunedin Blue Jays reached the Florida State League finals, before losing to the Daytona Cubs 3-0... Were crowned West Division champions after defeating the Fort Myers Miracle (Twins) 2-0... Had the most wins in the organization and the best overall record in the Florida State League for a second straight season... Have the best record over the last three season in the FSL with 215 wins and 163 losses resulting in a .607 winning percentage... Won a season high nine straight from August 2 through August 11... The final record of 84-54 was a season high 30 games above the .500 mark... Lost a season high

three straight on four different occasions... Were a season high two games under .500 four times and were last under .500 on May 12 at 17-18... Led the league with 760 runs scored and were T1st with a .279 batting average... The pitching staff allowed a league low 1,089 hits and were fourth in the league with 3.59 ERA... Ranked 12th among 14 teams with 34,908 in total attendance... Dunedin sent five players to the mid-season All-Star game along with skipper Marty Pevey and his coaching staff... Pevey was also named FSL Manager of the Year... 26 positional players and 22 pitchers saw game action during the season.

Florida State League Leaders

Batting

- **JOE LAWRENCE**, Batting Average 9th (.301), On-Base Percentage 3rd (.414)... **JERSEN PEREZ**, Doubles 3rd (35)... **TONY PETERS**, Runs Scored 2nd (97).

Pitching

- **JOE CASEY**, Innings Pitched 4th (158.1)... **JARROD KINGERY**, Saves T1st (23).

Individual Player Highlights

- **C JOE LAWRENCE** was selected as the team's MVP after batting .301 with 13 home runs and 67 RBI in his first full season as a catcher... Finished the season in Tennessee... Was selected to both the mid-season and year-end All-Star teams... Was ninth in the league in batting and third with a .414 on-base percentage... Named FSL Hitter of the Week from April 24 through 30 after batting .433 (13-30) with a double, two home runs and 10 RBI, while stealing four bases... Was the organization Player of the Month for April after batting .333 with seven doubles, eight home runs and 20 RBI... Scored in 12 consecutive games, the most in the league since July 1998... Reached base safely via a hit or a walk in 28 consecutive games from May 10 through June 6... Was named to the Baseball America High Class A Minor League All-Star Team at catcher... Named as the 8th best prospect in the league by Baseball America... Was named Mr. Baseball for the State of Louisiana.
- **OF RYAN FLEMING** played for both Tennessee and Syracuse after batting .304 in 90 games for Dunedin... Batted .326 (28-86) in May and in June batted .372 (29-76).
- **1B MATT LOGAN**, a native of Brampton, Ontario was named FSL Hitter of the Week when he hit .429 with three home runs and eight RBI for the week of July 10 through July 16.

- **SS JERSEN PEREZ**, who was third in the league with doubles with 35, batted .271 with eight home runs and 67 RBI... Led the team with 138 hits and 211 totals bases... Did not draw a walk from July 15 through August 31 (36 games) before drawing two on September 2 vs. St. Petersburg.
- **OF TONY PETERS** was awarded the Blue Jays' organization Community Service Award for his work within the Dunedin area... Was second in the league and led the organization with 97 runs scored... Stole a team high 23 bases and led the team with 15 home runs.
- **C JOSH PHELPS** played with both Tennessee and Toronto before finishing the season with Dunedin... Was named FSL Hitter of the Week from August 7 through August 13 after batting .478 with eight runs scored, three doubles, four home runs and nine RBI to go along with a 1.130 slugging percentage... Hit 12 homers in 113 at bats for Dunedin in 30 games... Batted .309 with 26 runs and 34 RBI... Led the Blue Jays in the playoffs batting .450 (9-20) with one home run and four RBI.
- **2B GLENN WILLIAMS** was batting .271 with 26 doubles, 13 home runs and a team high 77 RBI in 107 games before leaving the Blue Jays to play in the Australian Olympic Program.

Individual Pitcher Highlights

- **RHP CHRIS BAKER** was 4-2 with a 3.90 ERA as a starter and was 5-3 with five saves and a 2.92 ERA coming out of the bullpen... Allowed just two earned runs in 12.0 innings of work for a 1.50 ERA during the playoffs (2 games, 1 start).
- **RHP JOE CASEY** led the staff with 27 starts and posted a 10-8 mark with a 4.37 ERA... Was fifth in the league with 158.1 innings of work.
- **RHP SCOTT CASSIDY** finished the season at Tennessee after going 9-3 with a 1.33 ERA in 14 games, 13 starts for Dunedin... Was named FSL Pitcher of the Week from April 17 through April 23 after throwing a 6.0 inning no-hitter on April 22... Was again named FSL Pitcher of the Week from May 8 through May 14 going 2-0 with 0.00 ERA, while allowing just five hits and fanning 16 in 14.0 innings... Was the organization Pitcher of the Month and the Topps Player of the Month for May with a 6-0 mark and a 1.09 ERA, while allowing just 16 hits in 41.0 innings... Struck out 89 in 88.0 innings with right-handed hitters batting just .145 and lefties batting .234... Was rated by Baseball America as the "Best Control" pitcher in the league.

- **LHP GUSTAVO CHACIN** posted a 4.02 ERA with a 9-5 record... Won five consecutive starts from May 10 through May 31 with a 2.37 ERA (30.1IP/8ER)... Was 7-4 with a 4.23 ERA as a starter and was 2-1 with a 2.13 ERA out of the bullpen.
- **RHP JARROD KINGERY** tied for the league lead with 23 saves and led the organization with 30 after finishing the season with Tennessee... Finished with a 4-2 record and a 2.97 ERA in 37 games... On the road posted a 1.80 ERA, at home 4.19... Left-handed hitters batted just .114 while right-handed hitters batted .259... Was selected to the both FSL's mid-season and year-end All-Star teams as the best reliever.
- **LHP RYAN SPILLE** tied for the team lead with 10 wins in 20 games, 19 starts... Posted a 4.27 ERA in 109.2 innings of work before finishing the season at Tennessee.
- **RHP ORLANDO WOODWARDS** was 8-1 with seven saves and a 2.27 ERA after appearing in 41 games including one start... Was the organization's Pitcher of the Month for June, posting a 2-0 mark and a 1.80 ERA in nine games (15.0 innings)... On the road allowed just four earned runs in 37.1 innings for a 0.96 ERA.

HAGERSTOWN SUNS
(A – South Atlantic League)

(First half, 34-36, 3rd Northern Division; Second half, 29-38, 5th Northern Division, Overall 63-74)

Team Highlights

- The year 2000 commemorated the teams 20th season in Hagerstown... Was the first sub .500 finish since 1997... Won a season high six straight twice, from July 5 through July 12 and again from August 3 through August 8... Were a season high three games above the .500 mark on April 20 at 8-5 and again on April 26 at 11-8... Fell to a season low 12 games under .500 at 48-60 on August 2 and again on August 18 at 55-67... Lost a season high six straight on three different occasions, from June 18 through June 27, July 13 through July 18 and again from August 11 through August 18... On July 9 won by forfeit at Columbus after two bench clearing brawls left the RedStixx short position players... Were 12th in the 14 team league in hitting at .245 and were 10th in pitching with a 4.05 ERA... Ranked 12th in the league in total attendance at 102,443 for an average, over 64 home dates, of 1,601... Saw 26 positional players and 20 pitchers wear the Suns uniform.

South Atlantic League Leaders

Batting

- **BRANDON JACKSON**, Batting Average 4th (.312)... **REED JOHNSON**, On-Base Percentage 2nd (.422).

Individual Player Highlights

- **SHANNON CARTER** led the organization with 33 steals in 39 attempts... Led the team with 74 runs scored and finished the season second on the team with 121 hits, batting .273.
- **BRANDON JACKSON** finished the season with Dunedin after batting .312, second in the league, with a team high 122 hits... Hit in 19 straight games from July 21 through August 9 batting .432 (32-74) during the streak... Was the lone member of the Suns named to the SAL postseason All-Star team.

Individual Pitching Highlights

- **RHP HUGO CASTELLANOS** allowed just 16 hits in 38.1 innings, posting a 1.64 ERA... Finished the season with Dunedin after going 0-3 with seven saves... Recorded an 0.56 ERA on the road (16.0 innings)... He did not allow an earned run in 13 consecutive games from June 27 through August 2 (21.1 innings).
- **RHP AARON DEAN** was named SAL Pitcher of the Week from April 14 through April 20 after going 2-0 in 12.0 innings of work, allowing nine hits, two earned runs and striking out 17... Posted a record of 8-3 with a team low 3.28 ERA in 19 starts... Also pitched for both Dunedin and Tennessee this season.
- **LHP MATT FORD** was 5-3 with a 3.87 ERA in 18 games, 14 starts... Was the only member of the Suns to be named to the mid-season All-Star team... Had 86 strikeouts in 83.2 innings... Was 5-3 with a 3.88 ERA as a starter and 0-0 with a 3.86 ERA in relief.

- **REED JOHNSON** was named MVP of the Suns after hitting .290 with eight home runs and a team high 70 RBI and 24 doubles... Finished the season with Dunedin and combined to drive in 98 runs, second most in the organization... Was second in the SAL with a .422 on base percentage... Was 17 for 21 in stolen base attempts between the two clubs... Was the organization Player of the Month for May after batting .313 with 35 hits and 28 RBI in 31 games.

- **RHP ROBERT HAMANN** finished the season with Dunedin after 8-4 with six saves and a 2.95 ERA in 34 games, one start... Picked up four wins and three saves in his final 10 games with the Suns from June 12 through July 12.
- **RHP CAMERON REIMERS** led the team with 26 starts and 142 strikeouts... Posted a 7-11 record and was sixth in the organization with a 3.73 ERA.
- **RHP JOSH STEVENS** fanned 95 batters in 84.1 innings... Was 4-4 with five saves and a 2.99 ERA... Was 0-3 as a starter despite a 2.77 ERA in 13.0 innings... Had six strikeouts in a 4.0 inning save on August 22 at Savannah.

Baseball America's Best Tools

Syracuse – AAA
   Cesar Izturis, Best Infield Arm
   Vernon Wells, Best Defensive Outfielder
Tennessee – AA
   Felipe Lopez, Best Defensive Shortstop
   Bob File, Best Reliever
Dunedin – A
   Scott Cassidy, Best Control
   Orlando Hudson, Best Defensive Third Baseman

As an organization, the Blue Jays minor league affiliates finished sixth in all of organized baseball with a .530 winning percentage.

Syracuse SkyChiefs	74-66
Tennessee Smokies	71-69
Dunedin Blue Jays	84-54
Hagerstown Suns	63-74
Queens Kings	46-29
Medicine Hat	36-40
Total (.530)	**374-332**

QUEENS KINGS
(Short A – NY-Penn State League)

(46-29, 2nd, –0.5, McNamara Division)

Team Highlights

- In their inaugural season in Queen's, the Jays NY-Penn State League affiliate, finished above .500 for the first time since 1996... Lost in the Division finals to the Staten Island Yankees, 2-1... Finished the 2000 campaign a season high 17 games above the .500 mark... Won a season high five straight from August 14 through August 18... Started the year 0-1, the only time to be below .500 all season... From August 9 through the end of the season, posted a 21-7 record to reach the playoffs... Finished the season in the middle of the pack batting .251 as a team, however were second in the league with 328 base on balls... Were third in the loop with a 3.15 ERA and led the league with 663 strikeouts... Field Manager Eddie Rodriguez, his third year in the organization and second as manager, joined the US Olympic baseball team as first base coach... Geovanny Miranda, coaching with Medicine Hat, took over as Manager for Rodriguez... Played home games at St. Johns University and drew 38,662 fans in 38 home dates... 7 position players selected from the June draft debuted with the Kings, while five pitchers made their pro debuts. (see complete 2000 draft list)

NY-Penn State League Leaders
Pitching

- **BRANDON LYON**, ERA 8th (2.39)... **GEORGE PEREZ**, Saves 3rd (12), Games T4th (29).

Individual Player Highlights

- **3B SHAWN FAGAN** finished the season with Hagerstown after batting .289 with two home runs and 13 RBI in 26 games with Queens.
- **IF MARTIN MALPICA** was named as the team's MVP... Led the team with 14 doubles and 34 RBI... Batted .278, .350 on the road, while batting .192 at home... Had nine RBI in the first four games of the season (June 21 through June 24)... Led the team with one home run and four RBI in the playoffs.
- **OF SHAWN PEARSON** began the season with Queens and batted .351, scoring 18 runs in 20 games... Had hits in 16 of the 20 games he played in and reached base via a hit or a walk in all 20... Finished the season with Hagerstown.
- **1B MIKE SNYDER** tied for the team lead in batting at .278 and RBI with 34... Batted .302 (42-139) for the last 35 games of the season... Started the season at Hagerstown.
- **2B DOMINIC RICH** was named to the NY-Penn State League year-end All-Star team at second base... Batted .263 with 15 extra-base hits and 25 RBI in 67 games.
- **OF ALEXIS RIOS** batted .267 with one home run and 25 RBI... Fanned just 22 times in 224 plate appearances... Collected an RBI in five of his first six games with Queens after staring the season with Hagerstown.
- **OF BRIAN SELLIER** was third on the team with 33 RBI and was 11 for 13 in stolen base attempts.
- **OF RICH THOMPSON** led the team and was fourth in the organization with 28 stolen bases in 36 attempts... Reached base safely via a hit or a walk in 20 consecutive games from August 9 through August 20... Scored a team high 42 runs and led the team with 66 hits and 45 walks.

Individual Pitcher Highlights

- **RHP BRIAN CARDWELL** was named by Baseball America as the 10th best prospect in the league... Was 2-4 with a 4.71 ERA in 12 games.
- **LHP JAMES DETWILER** did not allow a run in eight consecutive outings from July 25 through August 19 (14.1 innings)... Was 3-1 with a 2.83 ERA in 20 games in relief.
- **RHP BRANDON LYON** was the organizational Pitcher of the Month for July after going 2-2 with a 1.21 ERA... Did not allow more than one earned run in any of his six July starts... Finished with a 5-3 mark and was eighth in the league with a 2.39 ERA... In 60.1 innings of work, allowed just one home run and six walks, while fanning 55.
- **LHP DIEGOMAR MARKWELL** started the season with Hagerstown before posting a 4-3 record and a 3.05 ERA with Queens... Picked up the only postseason win with 7.0 shutout innings vs. Staten Island.
- **RHP CHRIS MOWDAY** tied for the team high with five wins... Had a 3.39 ERA in 15 games, 13 starts, and was 3-0 in August with a 2.55 ERA in six starts.
- **RHP JOE ORLOSKI** in 22 games out of the bullpen was 4-0 with three saves and a 1.38 ERA... Had 66 strikeouts in 52.0 innings of work... Struck out six batters in 3.0 innings on August 10 at Oneonta.
- **RHP GEORGE PEREZ** was third in the league and fifth in the organization with 12 saves... Allowed a run in just two of the 29 games that he pitched in... Was 5-1 with a 0.78 ERA and opponents batted just .181 in 34.2 innings (116 at bats)... Was named as the organization's Pitcher of the Month for August after going 3-1 with five saves and a 0.66 ERA in 13 games.
- **RHP MIKE SMITH** posted a 1.64 ERA in five July starts, 22.0 innings of work... Overall finished with a 2-2 mark and a 2.29 ERA, fanning 55 in 51.0 innings.

The Toronto Blue Jays organization is second only to the Oakland Athletics in winning percentage over the past three seasons.

	Oakland	Toronto
1998	364-331	398-315
1999	398-296	381-332
2000	381-311	374-332
Total	**(.549) 1143-938**	**(.541) 1153-979**

MEDICINE HAT BLUE JAYS
(Rookie Advanced – Pioneer League)

(First half, 23-15, 1st North Division; Second half, 13-25, 4th North Division; Overall 36-40)

Team Highlights
- Won the first half of the schedule before struggling in the second half... Was the second consecutive season to finish with an overall record under .500... Were eliminated in the division finals of the playoffs, 2-1 by the Great Falls Dodgers... Won a season high seven straight from July 5 through July 12 and reached a season high 10 games above .500 on July 15 at 19-9... Lost a season high five straight three times, including the final five games of the regular season to finish a season high four games under the .500 mark... The pitching staff was third in the league with a 4.56 ERA and walked a league low 273 batters... Were fifth in the loop with a .264 average and were second with 382 walks... 13 position players and 10 pitchers made their pro debuts with the Blue Jays at Medicine Hat... 27,143 fans, over 38 home dates, saw Medicine Hat play... Renewed the player development contract with Toronto for an additional two years.

Pioneer League Leaders
Batting
- **RON DAVENPORT**, Batting Average 6th (.345)... **ARMANDO GUERRERO**, Triples T3rd (6)... **JEREMY JOHNSON**, Batting Average 2nd (.376), Hits 2nd (92), Doubles 2nd (24), RBI 5th (58), On-Base Percentage 1st (.498), Slugging Percentage 3rd (.608), Extra-Base hits T2nd (36), Runs Scored 4th (66)... **AARON SISK**, Home Runs 4th (13).

Pitching
- **CHARLIE CHULK**, ERA 6th (3.80)... **DAVID HANSON**, Wins T3rd (7)... **ANDREW McCULLOCH**, Saves 1st (15), Games T2nd (27)... **JOSH McMILLAN**, ERA 10th (4.34).

Individual Player Highlights
- **1B RON DAVENPORT** was named the organization's Player of the Month for July after batting .363 with nine doubles, two triples, four home runs and 32 RBI... Finished the season on a 14 game hit streak, .375 (21-56)... For the season batted .345 with four home runs and 46 RBI.
- **OF JEREMY JOHNSON** was named as the Pioneer League's MVP and was named by Baseball America as the 6th top prospect... Was second in the league with a .376 average, 92 hits and 24 doubles... Led the league with a .498 on base percentage after reaching base via a hit or a walk in 61 of the 65 games he started... Was third in the league with 36 extra-base hits and a .608 slugging percentage... Hit in 14 straight from June 18 through July 3 batting .385 (20-52) during that stretch... Hit .362 or better in each of the three months... Was the Pioneer League Player of the Week from July 17 through July 23 after hitting .520 (13-25) with 11 runs, five doubles, two triples and six RBI... Was the team MVP and was named to the league's postseason All-Star team... Was named as an outfielder to the Rookie League All-Star team by Baseball America.
- **IF AARON SISK** was fourth in the circuit with 13 home runs and batted .257 with 50 RBI... 25 of his 56 hits went for extra-bases... Was 4-5 with two home runs and eight RBI on July 30 vs. Helena... In a 19 game stretch from July 15 through August 7 hit .329 with five home runs and 23 RBI.
- **IF NOM SIRIVEAW**, the top Canadian pick by the Blue Jays in the 2000 draft, was a perfect 7-0 in steal attempts to lead the team... Overall batted .243 with eight home runs and 40 RBI in 63 games.

Individual Pitcher Highlights
- **RHP CHARLIE CHULK** was sixth in the league with a 3.80 ERA... Posted a 2-4 record in 14 games, 13 starts... In four July starts, was 1-0 with a 1.80 ERA.
- **RHP ALEXIS GUZMAN** was 6-8 with a 2.38 ERA in 27 games... Was 3-4 despite a 1.29 ERA in the month of August... Was T2nd in the league with teammate Andrew McCulloch with 27 appearances.
- **RHP DAVID HANSON** led the team with a 7-3 mark, while posting a 5.73 ERA... The seven wins T3rd in the league, while the 79.0 innings of work were a team high.
- **RHP ANDREW McCULLOCH** led the league with 15 saves and was named Rolaids Relief Man in the Pioneer League for the 2000 season with 45 points... In June had a 1.42 ERA and in August posted a 1.59 ERA.
- **LHP JOSH McMILLAN** posted a 3-3 record and was 10th in the league with a 4.34 ERA... Was 2-0 at home with a 3.57 ERA and on the road posted a 5.63 ERA with a 1-3 mark.

Player Development

2000 Minor League Club Leaders

SYRACUSE SKYCHIEFS

Batting Leaders

AVG.	Luis Lopez	.328
Runs	Chad Mottola	85
Hits	Luis Lopez	161
Total Bases	Chad Mottola	286
Doubles	Vernon Wells	31
Triples	Vernon Wells	7
Home Runs	Chad Mottola	33
RBI	Chad Mottola	102
Stolen Bases	Ryan Freel	30
	Chad Mottola	30
SLG.	Chad Mottola	.566
OBP	Luis Lopez	.384

Pitching Leaders

Wins	Gary Glover	9
	Kerry Taylor	9
ERA*	Kerry Taylor	3.32
Saves	Matt Dewitt	15
Games	Mark Lukasiewicz	42
Starts	Gary Glover	27
CG	Kerry Taylor	4
Shutouts	Kerry Taylor	2
Innings	Garry Glover	166.2
Strikeouts	Garry Glover	119
*Minimum 94.0IP		

DUNEDIN BLUE JAYS

Batting Leaders

AVG.	Joe Lawrence	.301
Runs	Tony Peters	97
Hits	Jersen Perez	138
Total Bases	Jersen Perez	211
Doubles	Jersen Perez	35
Triples	Jersen Perez	7
Home Runs	Tony Peters	15
RBI	Glenn Williams	77
Stolen Bases	Tony Peters	23
SLG.	Joe Lawrence	.496
OBP	Joe Lawrence	.414

Pitching Leaders

Wins	Joe Casey	10
	Ryan Spille	10
ERA*	Chris Baker	3.20
Saves	Jarrod Kingrey	23
Games	Doug Dimma	43
Starts	Joe Casey	27
CG	Scott Cassidy	1
	Mark Hendrickson	1
	Ryan Spille	1
Shutouts	NONE	
Innings	Joe Casey	158.1
Strikeouts	Joe Casey	96
*Minimum 94.0IP		

QUEENS KINGS

Batting Leaders

AVG.	Martin Malpica	.278
	Mike Snyder	.278
Runs	Rich Thompson	42
Hits	Rich Thompson	66
Total Bases	Mike Snyder	92
Doubles	Martin Malpica	14
Triples	Rich Thompson	5
Home Runs	Guillermo Quiroz	5
	Brian Sellier	5
RBI	Martin Malpica	34
	Mike Snyder	34
Stolen Bases	Rich Thompson	28
SLG.	Mike Snyder	.405
OBP	Rich Thompson	.386

Pitching Leaders

Wins	Brandon Lyon	5
	Chris Mowday	5
	George Perez	5
ERA*	Brandon Lyon	2.39
Saves	George Perez	12
Games	George Perez	29
Starts	Brandon Lyon	13
	Diegomar Markwell	13
	Chris Mowday	13
CG	Brian Cardwell	1
Shutouts	NONE	
Innings	Diegomar Markwell	73.2
Strikeouts	Diegomar Markwell	66
	Joe Orloski	66
*Minimum 60.0IP		

TENNESSEE SMOKIES

Batting Leaders

AVG.	Jay Gibbons	.321
Runs	Jay Gibbons	85
Hits	Robert Perez	157
Total Bases	Jay Gibbons	249
	Robert Perez	249
Doubles	Jay Gibbons	38
Triples	Scott Sollmann	5
	Mike Young	5
Home Runs	Jay Gibbons	19
	Robert Perez	19
RBI	Robert Perez	92
Stolen Bases	Scott Sollmann	19
SLG.	Jay Gibbons	.525
OBP	Jay Gibbons	.404

Pitching Leaders

Wins	Pasqaul Coco	12
ERA*	Mike Kulewicz	3.63
Saves	Rob File	20
Games	Rendy Espina	53
Starts	Matt McClellan	27
CG	Leo Estrella	3
Shutouts	Leo Estrella	2
Innings	Matt McClellan	168.2
Strikeouts	Pasqual Coco	142
*Minimum 94.0IP		

HAGERSTOWN SUNS

Batting Leaders

AVG.	Brandon Jackson	.312
Runs	Shannon Carter	74
Hits	Brandon Jackson	122
TB	Brandon Jackson	170
Doubles	Reed Johnson	24
Triples	Brandon Jackson	8
Home Runs	Kevin Cash	10
RBI	Reed Johnson	70
Stolen Bases	Shannon Carter	33
SLG.	Reed Johnson	.469
OBP	Reed Johnson	.422

Pitching Leaders

Wins	Aaron Dean	8
	Robert Hamann	8
	Travis Hubbel	8
	Marcos Sandoval	8
ERA*	Aaron Dean	3.28
Saves	Jarrod Payne	8
Games	Marc Bluma	48
Starts	Cameron Reimers	26
CG	Cameron Reimers	2
	Marcos Sandoval	2
Shutouts	Marcos Sandoval	1
Innings	Marcos Sandoval	163.2
Strikeouts	Cameron Reimers	112
*Minimum 94.0IP		

MEDICINE HAT BLUE JAYS

Batting Leaders

AVG.	Jeremy Johnson	.376
Runs	Jeremy Johnson	66
Hits	Jeremy Johnson	92
Total Bases	Jeremy Johnson	149
Doubles	Jeremy Johnson	24
Triples	Armando Guerrero	6
Home Runs	Aaron Sisk	13
RBI	Jeremy Johnson	58
Stolen Bases	Nom Siriview	7
SLG.	Jeremy Johnson	.608
OBP	Jeremy Johnson	.498

Pitching Leaders

Wins	David Hanson	7
ERA*	Alexis Guzman	2.38
Saves	Andrew McCulloch	15
Games	Alexis Guzman	27
	Andrew McCulloch	27
Starts	David Hanson	15
	Josh McMillan	15
CG	NONE	
Shutouts	NONE	
Innings	David Hanson	79.0
Strikeouts	David Hanson	79
*Minimum 60.0IP		

Through 2000

HOME RUNS

Full Season

1. Geronimo Berroa . . 36 - Knoxville, 1987
2. Chad Mottola . . . . . 33 - Syracuse, 2000
T3. Augie Schmidt . . . . 31 - Syracuse, Knoxville, 1984
T3. Glenallen Hill . . . . . . 31 - Knoxville, 1986
T3. Andy Thompson . . . 31 - Knoxville, Syracuse, 1999

Short Season

1. Gregory Morrison . . 23 - Medicine Hat, 1997
2. Jay Gibbons . . . . . . 19 - Medicine Hat, 1998
3. Darryl Landrum . . . . 17 - Medicine Hat, 1984
T4. Chris Johnston . . . . 15 - Medicine Hat, 1982
T4. Julian Yan . . . . 15 - St. Catharines, 1986
T4. Will Skett . . . . 15 - St. Catharines, 1996

RBI

Full Season

1. Tim Giles . . . . 114 - Knoxville, 1999
2. Peter Tucci . . . . 112 - Dunedin, Knoxville, 1998
T3. Geronimo Berroa . . 108 - Knoxville, 1987
T3. Jay Gibbons . . . . . . 108 - Hagerstown, Dunedin, 1999
5. Casey Blake . . . . . . 103 - Dunedin, Knoxville, 1998

Short Season

1. Jay Gibbons . . . . . . 98 - Medicine Hat, 1998
2. Gregory Morrison . . 88 - Medicine Hat, 1997
3. Chris Johnston . . . . 77 - Medicine Hat, 1982
4. Greg Wells . . . . 68 - Utica, 1977
T5. Mark Gerard . . . . . . 63 - Medicine Hat, 1983
T5. John Curl. . . . . 63 - Medicine Hat, 1995

BATTING AVERAGE

Full Season

T1. Rob Butler . . . . .358 - Dunedin, 1992
T1. Luis Lopez . . . . .358 - Hagerstown, 1997
3. Derek Bell . . . . .346 - Syracuse, 1991
4. Shawn Green . . . . . .344 - Syracuse, 1994
5. Robert Perez . . . . . . .343 - Syracuse, 1995

Short Season

1. Gregory Morrison . . .448 - Medicine Hat, 1997
2. Jay Gibbons . . . . . . .397 - Medicine Hat, 1998
3. Jeremy Johnson . . . .376 - Medicine Hat, 2000
4. Chris Johnston . . . . .358 - Medicine Hat, 1982
T5. Angel Ramirez . . . . .345 - Medicine Hat, St. Catharines, 1993
T5. Ron Davenport . . . . .345 - Medicine Hat, 2000

ERA

Full Season

1. Brian Smith . . . . 0.87 - Hagerstown, 1995
2. Travis Baptist . . . . . 1.44 - Myrtle Beach, 1992
3. Doug Linton. . . . . . . 1.55 - Myrtle Beach, 1987
T4. Mark Clemons. . . . . 2.04 - Kinston, 1985
T4. Chris McBride . . . . . 2.04 - Hagerstown, 1996

Short Season

1. Mike Halperin . . . . . 1.17 - St. Catharines, Hagerstown, 1994
2. John Sneed . . . . 1.29 - Medicine Hat, 1997
3. Tim Crabtree . . . . . . 1.43 - St. Catharines, Knoxville, 1992
4. Beiker Graterol . . . . 1.50 - St. Catharines, 1996
5. Bob Wishnevski . . . 1.53 - St. Catharines, 1987

SAVES

Full Season

1. David Sinnes. . . . . . 37 - Hagerstown, 1994
2. Randy St. Claire . . . 33 - Syracuse, 1994
T3. Mike Timlin . . . . 30 - Dunedin, Knoxville, 1990
T3. Jarrod Kingrey . . . . 30 - Tennessee, Dunedin, 2000
5. Rob File . . . . 28 - Syracuse, Tennessee, 2000

Short Season

1. Mike Toney . . . . 18 - Medicine Hat, 1994
2. Jim Mann. . . . . 17 - St. Catharines, 1996
T3. Bart Rich . . . . 16 - GCL Blue Jays, 1992
T3. Jarrod Kingrey . . . . 16 - St. Catharines, 1998
T3. Robert File. . . . . 16 - Medicine Hat, 1998

WINS

Full Season

1. Steve Davis . . . . 20 - Syracuse, Knoxville, 1985
T2. Tim Englund . . . . . . 18 - Florence, 1985
T2. Jimmy Rogers. . . . . 18 - Myrtle Beach, 1988
T4. Alex Sanchez . . . . . 17 - Knoxville, Syracuse, 1988
T4. Shannon Withem. . . 17 - Syracuse, 1998

Short Season

1. Alonso Beltran . . . . . 11 - St. Catharines, 1993
T2. Edwin Hurtado . . . . 10 - St. Catharines, 1993
T2. Charlie Puleo . . . . . . 10 - Utica, 1978
T2. Keith Gilliam . . . . . . 10 - Medicine Hat, 1982
5. Beiker Graterol . . . . 9 - St. Catharines, 1996

LOSSES

Full Season

T1. Mark Eichhorn. . . . . 17 - Knoxville, Syracuse, 1983
T1. Gary Glover. . . . . . . 17 - Hagerstown, 1997
T3. Mike Darr. . . . . 16 - Syracuse, 1978
T3. Scott Elam. . . . . 16 - Knoxville, 1982

Short Season

T1. Greg McCutcheon . 12 - St. Catharines, 1989
T1. Gary Glover. . . . . . . 12 - Medicine Hat, 1996
3. Rafael Pimentel . . . . 10 - Utica, 1979
T4. Gumercindo Diaz . . 9 - Bradenton, 1981
T4. Dan Dodd . . . . 9 - St. Catharines, 1988
T4. Mike Brady . . . . 9 - Medicine Hat, 1988
T4. Joe Orloski . . . . 9 - St. Catharines, 1999

1977-99 DRAFT (Still in Blue Jays Organization)

Player	Pos.	Year Drafted	Round Phase #		Player	Pos.	Year Drafted	Round Phase #	
Alex Gonzalez	SS	1991-June	REG.	13	Jarrod Kingrey	RHP	1998-June	REG.	10
Shannon Stewart	OF	1992-June	REG.	1	Eric Place	LHP	1998-June	REG.	12
Chris Carpenter	RHP	1993-June	REG.	1	Reuben St. Armand	RHP	1998-June	REG.	17
Andy Thompson	3B	1994-June	REG.	23	Ryan Fleming	OF	1998-June	REG.	18
Roy Halladay	RHP	1995-June	REG.	1	Robert File	RHP	1998-June	REG.	19
Ryan Freel	2B	1995-June	REG.	10	Franklin Gracesqui	LHP	1998-June	REG.	21
Billy Koch	RHP	1996-June	REG.	1	Ryan Houston	RHP	1998-June	REG.	31
Joe Lawrence	SS	1996-June	REG.	1	Aaron Dean	RHP	1998-June	REG.	38
Yan LaChapelle	RHP	1996-June	REG.	3	Cameron Reimers	RHP	1998-June	REG.	35
Mike Rodriguez	C	1996-June	REG.	6	Alexis Rios	OF	1999-June	REG.	1
Josh Phelps	C	1996-June	REG.	10	Michael Snyder	OF	1999-June	REG.	2
David Bleazard	RHP	1996-June	REG.	22	Matthew Ford	LHP	1999-June	REG.	3
Vernon Wells	OF	1997-June	REG.	1	Brian Cardwell	RHP	1999-June	REG.	4
Paul Chiaffredo	C	1997-June	REG.	6	Scott Porter	RHP	1999-June	REG.	5
Matt McClellan	RHP	1997-June	REG.	7	David Hanson	RHP	1999-June	REG.	6
Joe Casey	RHP	1997-June	REG.	8	Robert Nunley	RHP	1999-June	REG.	7
Travis Hubbell	RHP	1997-June	REG.	13	Ryan McCullem	LHP	1999-June	REG.	8
Matt Weimer	RHP	1997-June	REG.	18	Joshua Holliday	C	1999-June	REG.	9
Mark Hendrickson	LHP	1997-June	REG.	20	Robert Cosby	IF	1999-June	REG.	10
Perfecto Gaud	LHP	1997-June	REG.	25	Charles Kegley	RHP	1999-June	REG.	11
Juan Santos	C	1997-June	REG.	29	Christopher Weekly	SS	1999-June	REG.	12
Taylor Smith	RHP	1997-June	REG.	33	Brandon Lyon	RHP	1999-June	REG.	14
Joshua Stevens	RHP	1997-June	REG.	35	Timothy Newman	RHP	1999-June	REG.	15
Chivas Clark	OF	1997-June	REG.	38	Reed Johnson	OF	1999-June	REG.	17
Orlando Hudson	SS	1997-June	REG.	43	Ryan Spille	LHP	1999-June	REG.	19
Felipe Lopez	SS	1998-June	REG.	1	Robert Hamann	RHP	1999-June	REG.	21
Joseph Orloski	RHP	1998-June	REG.	6	Christopher Baker	RHP	1999-June	REG.	29
Tyler Thompson	OF	1998-June	REG.	7	Matthew Bimeal	RHP	1999-June	REG.	35
Michael Kremblas	C	1998-June	REG.	8	Douglas Dimma	LHP	1999-June	REG.	36
Steven Murray	LHP	1998-June	REG.	9					

CANADIANS IN THE BLUE JAYS SYSTEM

Ten Canadians have worn the Blue Jays uniform in the 24 year history of the franchise.

Players Who Have Played At The Major League Level

NAME	POSITION	HOMETOWN	YEAR(S)
Dave McKay	INF	Vancouver, BC	1977-79
Paul Hodgson	OF	Fredericton, NB	1980
Rob Ducey	OF	Cambridge, ON	1987-92; 2000
Denis Boucher	LHP	Lachine, PQ	1991
Vince Horsman	LHP	Dartmouth, NS	1991
Rob Butler	OF	Toronto, ON	1993-94; 99
Paul Spoljaric	LHP	Kelowna, BC	1994; 96-97; 99
Paul Quantrill	RHP	Cobourg, ON	1996-
Rich Butler	OF	Toronto, ON	1997
Steve Sinclair	LHP	Victoria, BC	1998-99

Other Canadians On The 40-man Roster

NAME	POSITION	HOMETOWN	YEAR(S)
Dave Shipanoff	RHP	Edmonton, AB	1982-1984
Nigel Wilson	OF	Ajax, ON	1991
Greg O'Halloran	C	Mississauga, ON	1992
Joe Young	RHP	Ft. McMurray, BC	1996-98

Players Currently In Toronto's Farm System

NAME	POSITION	HOMETOWN	2000 CLUB(S)
John Blackburn	C	London, ON	Medicine Hat
John Chadwick	RHP	Toronto, ON	Did Not Play
Jason Dickson	RHP	London, ON	Anaheim/Edmonton
Douglas Dimma	LHP	Richmond Hill, ON	Dunedin
Travis Hubbell	RHP	Edmonton, AB	Hagerstown/Dunedin
Mike Kusiewicz	LHP	Montreal, PQ	Tennessee
Yan Lachapelle	RHP	St. Laurent, PQ	Dunedin
Matt Logan	1B	Brampton, ON	Dunedin
Steve Murray	LHP	Ennismore, ON	Did Not Play—Injured
Lanny Patten	RHP	Drayton Vally, AB	Medicine Hat
Shawn Pearson	OF	Guelph, ON	Queens/Hagerstown/Dunedin
Tyler Renwick	RHP	Langley, BC	Queens
Nom Siriveaw	3B	Vancouver, BC	Medicine Hat

THE TORONTO BLUE JAYS JUNE 2000 FIRST YEAR PLAYER DRAFT

	Rd.	No.	Player	Pos.	Ht.	Wt.	B	T	D.O.B.	Hometown	School
S	1	18	Negron, Miguel	OF	6-2	165	L	L	08/22/82	Caguas, PR	Manuela Toro, High School
S	1*	33	McGowan, Dustin	RHP	6-3	190	R	R	03/24/82	Ludowici, GA	Long County, High School
S	2**	45	Bauer, Peter	RHP	6-7	247	L	R	11/06/78	Hagerstown, MD	University of South Carolina
S	2	58	Rich, Dominic	2B	5-11	190	L	R	08/22/79	Herndon, PA	Auburn University
S	3	88	Davis, Morrin	OF	6-2	190	R	R	12/11/82	Tampa, FL	Hillsborough, High School
S	4	118	Tablado, Raul	SS	6-2	175	R	R	03/03/82	Miami, FL	Southridge, High School
S	5	148	Smith, Michael	RHP	5-11	195	R	R	09/19/77	Westwood, MA	University of Richmond
S	6	178	Thompson, Richard	OF	6-2	185	L	R	04/23/79	Montrose, PA	James Madison University
S	7	208	Sisk, Aaron	3B	6-0	190	R	R	09/17/78	Forth Worth, TX	University of New Mexico
S	8	238	Abbott, David	RHP	6-4	225	R	R	10/19/77	Tucson, AZ	University of Arizona
S	9	268	Siriveaw, Nom	3B	6-3	200	S	R	12/09/80	Vancouver, BC	Eastern Oklahoma State College
S	10	298	Payne, Jerrod	RHP	5-11	195	R	R	08/27/77	Ocala, FL	University of North Florida
S	11	328	Thorpe, Tracy	RHP	6-4	232	R	R	12/15/80	Melbourne, FL	Melbourne, High School
S	12	358	Chulk, Charles	RHP	6-4	230	R	R	12/19/78	Melbourne, FL	St. Thomas University
S	13	388	Fagan, Shawn	3B/C	5-10	190	R	R	03/02/78	Levittown, NY	Penn State University
	14	418	Talanoa, Charles	RHP	6-4	215	R	R	12/29/80	El Segundo, CA	L.A. Harbor College
S	15	448	Stephenson, Eric	LHP	6-4	185	R	L	09/03/82	Benson, NC	Triton, High School
S	16	478	Brosseau, Richard	SS	5-11	180	L	R	09/22/78	North Oaks, MN	Minnesota University
S	17	508	McMillan, Josh	LHP	6-0	175	L	L	07/08/78	Moreno Valley, CA	Riverside City College
	18	538	Perkins, Mark	RHP	6-4	215	L	R	09/27/81	Victoria, BC	Lake City Community College
S	19	568	Blackburn, John	C	6-1	200	R	R	12/30/82	London, ON	AB Lucas Secondary School
S	20	598	McCulloch, Andy	RHP	6-1	200	R	R	02/26/78	Las Vegas, NV	University of Nevada Las Vegas
S	21	628	Harper, Jesse	RHP	6-4	195	R	R	11/11/80	Galveston, TX	Galveston Junior College
S	22	658	Davenport, Ulyses	2B-3B	6-2	185	L	R	10/16/81	Raleigh, NC	Leesville Road, High School
S	23	688	Cavey, Scott	RHP	6-5	205	S	R	03/20/78	Olathe, KS	University of Notre Dame
S	24	718	Keene, Kurt	C	6-0	190	R	R	08/22/77	Chattanooga, TN	University of Florida
S	25	748	Rivera, William	SS	6-0	150	L	R	12/28/81	Turabo Garden, PR	Turabo University
S	26	778	Johnson, Jeremiah	OF	6-1	185	L	L	05/06/78	Tamms, IL	South East Missouri State University
S	27	808	Sellier, Brian	OF	6-1	200	L	R	01/12/78	Phoenix, AZ	Grand Canyon University
S	28	838	Small, Chris	C	6-0	210	R	R	01/27/78	Alpharetta, GA	Princeton University
	29	868	Neuman, Christopher	LHP	6-1	190	L	L	10/02/81	Aledo, TX	Western Hills High School
S	30	898	Patten, Lanny	RHP	6-3	215	R	R	05/30/79	Drayton Valley, AB	Allan Hancock Junior College
S	31	928	Morris, Will	RHP	6-0	180	L	R	03/26/78	Rancho Cucamonga, CA	California State Poly University
S	32	958	Kozlowski, Kris	LHP	6-4	210	L	L	02/10/78	East Meadow, NY	Fordham University
S	33	988	Callen, Tommy	2B	5-11	175	R	R	01/11/78	Burlingame, CA	University of California
S	34	1018	Ridley, Jeremy	2B	6-2	195	S	R	11/21/77	Milton, ON	Ball State University
	35	1048	Gill, Michael	2B	5-10	180	L	R		Bradenton, FL	Manatee High School
S	36	1078	Wood, Stephen	1B	6-4	220	R	R	12/10/77	West Covina, CA	California State Poly University
S	37	1108	Spillman, Jeromie	LHP	5-11	185	L	L	09/24/78	Phoenix, AZ	Grand Canyon University
S	38	1138	Huesgen, Daniel	RHP	6-0	190	R	R	10/08/77	St. Louis, MO	South East Missouri State University
	39	1168	Zieour, Neesan	OF	5-11	185	R	R	11/02/80	Rocklin, CA	Sacramento City Junior College
	40	1197	McLane, Thomas	LHP	5-11	175	R	L	02/02/80	New Port Richey, FL	St. Petersburg Junior College
	41	1226	Gosch, Kirk	LHP	6-0	195	R	L	11/26/80	Hayden Lake, ID	Spokane Community college
	42	1255	Sorensen, Matthew	RHP	6-2	195	R	R	03/23/78	South Gate, CA	Cal State Fullerton University
	43	1283	Kniginyzky, Matthew	RHP	6-2	170	L	R	10/05/82	Mississauga, ON	Lorne Park Secondary School
	44	1310	McNeil, Derrick	3B	5-10	170	R	R	11/04/81	Lutz, FL	Land O'Lakes High School
	45	1336	Robinson Jr. Dennis	RHP	6-3	190	R	R	07/29/82	Putnam Valley, NY	Lakeland High School
	46	1360	Breen, Patrick	OF	6-2	170	L	L	06/23/82	Santa Ana, CA	Servite High School
S	47	1384	Martinez, Casey	C	5-10	190	R	R	08/31/77	Holmdel, NJ	Sacramento State University
	48	1404	Clark, Cody	C	6-3	180	R	R	09/14/81	Fayetteville, AR	Fayetteville High School
	49	1424	Bailey, Jacob	RHP	6-7	190	R	R		Fort Pierce, FL	Indian River Community College
S	50	1444	McFarland, Stuart	LHP	6-5	210	L	L	09/12/76	Arden Mills, MN	University of Florida

S – Signed

* 1st Round sandwich pick from Graeme Lloyd signing with the Montreal Expos as a Free Agent.

**2nd Round selection from the Montreal Expos for the signing of Free Agent Graeme Lloyd.

BLUE JAYS FIRST CHOICE IN JUNE DRAFT

1977	Tom Goffena-SS, #25	1989	Eddie Zosky-SS, #19
1978	Lloyd Moseby-OF, #2	1990	Steve Karsay-RHP, #22
1979	Jay Schroeder-C, #3	1991	Shawn Green-OF, #16
1980	Garry Harris-SS, #2	1992	Shannon Stewart-OF, #19
1981	Matt Williams-RHP, #5	1993	Chris Carpenter-RHP, #15
1982	Augie Schmidt-SS, #2	1994	Kevin Witt-INF, #28
1983	Matt Stark-C, #9	1995	Roy Halladay-RHP, #17
1984	Dane Johnson-RHP, #46	1996	Billy Koch-RHP, #4
1985	Greg David-OF, #25	1997	Vernon Wells-OF, #5
1986	Earl Sanders-RHP, #25	1998	Felipe Lopez-SS, #8
1987	Alex Sanchez-RHP, #17	1999	Alexis Rios-OF, #19
1988	Ed Sprague-3B, #25	2000	Miguel Negron-OF, #18

APRIL 2001

Week of April 1–7

Team	SUN 1	MON 2	TUE 3	WED 4	THU 5	FRI 6	SAT 7
TOR	@TEX (PR)	OFF	@TB	@TB	@TB	@NYY	@NYY
SYR					ROC	ROC	@ROC
TEN					@BIR	@BIR	@BIR
DUN					CLR	CLR	@SAR
CHWV					LEX	LEX	LEX

Week of April 8–14

Team	SUN 8	MON 9	TUE 10	WED 11	THU 12	FRI 13	SAT 14
TOR	@NYY	TB	TB	TB	KC	KC	KC
SYR	@ROC	@BUF	@BUF	OFF	SWB	SWB	SWR
TEN	@BIR	@WTN	@WTN	@WTN	@WTN	CHT	CHT
DUN	@SAR	@FTM	@FTM	@FTM	@FTM	TAM	TAM
CHWV	LEX	HKY	HKY	OFF	@DEL	@DEL	@DEL

Week of April 15–21

Team	SUN 15	MON 16	TUE 17	WED 18	THU 19	FRI 20	SAT 21
TOR	KC	OFF	NYY	NYY	NYY	@KC	@KC
SYR	OFF	BUF	BUF	@SWB	@SWB	@SWB	@SWB
TEN	CHT	CHT	@HNT	@HNT	@HNT	HNT	HNT
DUN	OFF	@CHA	@CHA	@CHA	@CHA	@TAM	@TAM
CHWV	@DEL	@KAN	@KAN	@KAN	@KAN	@HKY	@HKY

Week of April 22–28

Team	SUN 22	MON 23	TUE 24	WED 25	THU 26	FRI 27	SAT 28
TOR	@KC	OFF	TEX	TEX	OFF	ANA	ANA
SYR	@SWB	OFF	@PAW	@PAW	ROC	ROC	PAW
TEN	HNT	HNT	HNT	OFF	@MOB	@MOB	@MOB (DH)
DUN	SAR	SAR	CHA	CHA	CHA	CHA	CLR
CHWV	@HKY	@HKY	DEL	DEL	DEL	DEL	LKWD
AUB							
MED							

Week of April 29–30

Team	SUN 29	MON 30
TOR	ANA	OFF
SYR	PAW	PAW
TEN	OFF	@WTN
DUN	@CLR	@CLR
CHWV	LKWD	LKWD
AUB		
MED		

MAY 2001

Week of May 1–5

Team	TUE 1	WED 2	THU 3	FRI 4	SAT 5
TOR	@OAK	@OAK	@OAK	@SEA	@SEA
SYR	OTT	OTT	@DUR	@DUR	@DUR
TEN	WTN	WTN	WTN	@GRN	@GRN
DUN	@VER	@VER	@VER	@VER	GRN
CHWV	LKWD	OFF	GRN	GRN	GRN
AUB					
MED					

Week of May 6–12

Team	SUN 6	MON 7	TUE 8	WED 9	THU 10	FRI 11	SAT 12
TOR	@SEA	OFF	OAK	OAK	OAK	SEA	SEA
SYR	@DUR	@NOR	@NOR	@NOR	@NOR	RMD	RMD
TEN	@GRN	@GRN	@HNT	@HNT	HNT	HNT	@CHT
DUN	DAY	DAY	DAY	@TAM	TAM	TAM	TAM
CHWV	GRN	GRN	@LEX	@LEX	@LEX	KAN	KAN
AUB							
MED							

Week of May 13–19

Team	SUN 13	MON 14	TUE 15	WED 16	THU 17	FRI 18	SAT 19
TOR	SEA	OFF	@ANA	@ANA	@ANA	@TEX	@TEX
SYR	RMD	RMD	CHA	CHA	CHA	CHA	@IND
TEN	@CHT	@BIR (DH)	OFF	OFF	BIR	BIR	GRN
DUN	OFF	SAR	SAR	@CLR	CLR	FTM	FTM
CHWV	KAN	KAN	@GRN	@GRN	@GRN	@GRN	SAV
AUB							
MED							

Week of May 20–26

Team	SUN 20	MON 21	TUE 22	WED 23	THU 24	FRI 25	SAT 26
TOR	@TEX	CWS	OFF	CWS	CWS	@BOS	@BOS
SYR	@IND	@IND	@IND	OFF	@LOU	@LOU	@LOU
TEN	GRN	GRN	GRN	CAR	CAR	CAR	CAR
DUN	FTM	FTM	@DAY	@DAY	CLR	@CLR	@SAR
CHWV	SAV	SAV	SAV	AUG	AUG	AUG	AUG
AUB							
MED							

Week of May 27–31

Team	SUN 27	MON 28	TUE 29	WED 30	THU 31
TOR	@BOS	@CWS	@CWS	@CWS	BOS
SYR	@LOU	IND	IND	IND	IND
TEN	CAR	OFF	@ORL	@ORL	@ORL
DUN	@SAR	CLR	OFF	JUP	JUP
CHWV	OFF	@COL	@COL	@COL	@COL
AUB					
MED					

JUNE 2001

Week of June 1–2

Team	FRI 1	SAT 2
TOR	BOS	BOS
SYR	NOR	NOR
TEN	@ORL	@JAX
DUN	JUP	JUP
CHWV	@MAC	@MAC

Week of June 3–9

Team	SUN 3	MON 4	TUE 5	WED 6	THU 7	FRI 8	SAT 9
TOR	BOS	OFF	TB	TB	TB	FLA	FLA
SYR	NOR	NOR	@CHA	@CHA	@CHA	@CHA	@RMD
TEN	@JAX	@JAX	@JAX	OFF	MOB	MOB	MOB
DUN	STL	STL	STL	@BRE	@BRE	@BRE	@BRE
CHWV	@MAC	@MAC	OFF	HAG	HAG	HAG	HKY

Week of June 10–16

Team	SUN 10	MON 11	TUE 12	WED 13	THU 14	FRI 15	SAT 16
TOR	FLA	ATL	ATL	ATL	OFF	@MON	@MON
SYR	@RMD	@RMD	@RMD	OFF	COL	COL	COL
TEN	MOB	BIR	BIR	BIR	BIR	@CAR	@CAR
DUN	@BRE	@LAK	@LAK	@LAK	@LAK	-ASB-	-ASB-
CHWV	HKY	@LKWD	@LKWD	@LKWD	@LKWD	@HAG	@HAG
MED							GF

Week of June 17–23

Team	SUN 17	MON 18	TUE 19	WED 20	THU 21	FRI 22	SAT 23
TOR	@MON	@BAL	@BAL	@BAL	OFF	@BOS	@BOS
SYR	COL	LOU	LOU	LOU	LOU	@OTT	@OTT
TEN	@CAR	@CAR	-SL ASB-	-SL ASB-	JAX	JAX	JAX
DUN	-ASB-	@JUP	@JUP	@JUP	@JUP	@STL	@STL
CHWV	@HAG	-ASB-	-ASB-	-ASB-	HAG	HAG	HAG
AUB			BAT	BAT	BAT	@BAT	@PIT
MED	GF	GF	BILL	BILL	BILL	@MIS	@MIS

Week of June 24–30

Team	SUN 24	MON 25	TUE 26	WED 27	THU 28	FRI 29	SAT 30
TOR	@BOS	BAL	BAL	BAL	BAL	BOS	BOS
SYR	@OTT	@OTT	OFF	@BIR	@BIR	@BIR	PAW
TEN	JAX	OFF	DUR	DUR	DUR	DUR	@HNT
DUN	HAG	@STL	VER	VER	VER	@HAG	@FTM
CHWV	@PIT	HAG	LEX	LEX	@HAG	@HAG	@HAG
AUB	@MIS	@VER	@VER	@VER	WILL	WILL	WILL
MED		@IDF	@IDF	@IDF	@GF	@GF	@AUB

JULY 2001

Week of July 1–7

Team	SUN 1	MON 2	TUE 3	WED 4	THU 5	FRI 6	SAT 7
TOR	BOS	BOS	@TB	@TB	@TB	MON	MON
SYR	PAW	@COL	@COL	@COL	@COL	@TOL	@TOL
TEN	@HNT	OFF	@HNT	HNT	HNT	@CAR	@CAR
DUN	@FTM	@FTM	@FTM	TAM	@TAM	@CLR	CLR
CHWV	OFF	CHSC	CHSC	CHSC	CHSC	WLM	WLM
AUB	WILL	UTI	@UTI	UTI	@UTI	@BAT	BAT
MED	GF	GF	GF	@BILL	@BILL	@BILL	PROV

Week of July 8–14

Team	SUN 8	MON 9	TUE 10	WED 11	THU 12	FRI 13	SAT 14
TOR	MON	-ASB-	-ASB-	-ASB-	@PHI	@PHI	@PHI
SYR	@TOL	@TOL	-ASB-	-ASB-	@ROC	@ROC	BUF
TEN	@CAR	@CAR	-AA ASB-	-AA ASB-	BIR	BIR	BIR
DUN	CLR	@CLR	OFF	LAK	LAK	LAK	LAK
CHWV	WLM	WLM	OFF	@GRN	@GRN	@GRN	HKY
AUB	@WILL	@WILL	OFF	@LOW	@LOW	@LOW	VER
MED	PROV	PROV	OFF	CASP	CASP	CASP	@BILL

Week of July 15–21

Team	SUN 15	MON 16	TUE 17	WED 18	THU 19	FRI 20	SAT 21
TOR	@NYM	@NYM	@NYM	BOS	BOS	@NYY	@NYY
SYR	BUF	OTT	OTT	@OTT	@OTT	@PAW	@PAW
TEN	BIR	@WTN	@WTN	@WTN	@WTN	HNT	HNT
DUN	BRE	BRE	BRE	BRE	TAM	@TAM	@DAY
CHWV	HKY	@HKY	@HKY	@HKY	@LEX	@LEX	@LEX
AUB	VER	VER	VER	ONE	@ONE	@BRKN	@BRKN
MED	@BILL	@BILL	@BILL	@BILL	@BILL	MIS	MIS

Week of July 22–28

Team	SUN 22	MON 23	TUE 24	WED 25	THU 26	FRI 27	SAT 28
TOR	@NYY	@NYY	@BOS	@BOS	@BOS	NYY	NYY
SYR	@PAW	@PAW	TOL	TOL	TOL	TOL	OTT
TEN	HNT	HNT	@CAR	@CAR	@CAR	@CAR	MOB
DUN	OFF	@DAY	@DAY	TAM	@TAM	CLR	@CLR
CHWV	OFF	LKWD	LKWD	@BAT	BAT	@HKY	@LEX
AUB	@BRKN	@BRKN	@BAT	BAT	ONE	ONE	JAM
MED	GF	GF	@GF	@OGD	@OGD	@OGD	@PROV (DH)

Week of July 29–31

Team	SUN 29	MON 30	TUE 31
TOR	NYY	OFF	MIN
SYR	OTT	@OTT	@OTT
TEN	MOB	MOB	MOB
DUN	OFF	FTM	FTM
CHWV	@KAN	@KAN	@KAN
AUB	JAM	BRKN	BRKN
MED	OFF	@PROV	OFF

AUGUST 2001

	SUN	MON	TUE	WED	THU	FRI	SAT
				1	2	3	4
TOR				MIN	MIN	BAL	BAL
SYR				OFF	@ BUF	@ BUF	@ BUF
TEN				MOB	ORL	ORL	ORL
DUN				FTM	FTM	@ CLR	@ CLR
CHWV				@ KAN	HKY	HKY	@ LKWD
AUB				BRKN	@ MV	@ MV	@ ONE ***
MED				IDF	IDF	IDF	MIS
	5	6	7	8	9	10	11
TOR	BAL	OFF	@ SEA	@ SEA	@ SEA	@ ANA	@ ANA
SYR	@ BUF	SWB	SWB	@ SWB	@ SWB	BUF	BUF
TEN	ORL	OFF	DAY	DAY	@ WTN	@ WTN	@ MOB
DUN	OFF	DAY	DAY	DAY	DAY	@ SAR	@ SAR
CHWV	@ LKWD	@ LKWD	@ LKWD	LEX	LEX	GRN	GRN
AUB	@ ONE	MV	MV	OFF	UTI	@ UTI	@ WILL
MED	MIS	MIS	@ MIS	@ MIS	@ MIS	OGD	OGD
	12	13	14	15	16	17	18
TOR	@ ANA	OFF	OAK	OAK	OAK	TEX	TEX
SYR	BUF	OTT	OTT	ROC	@ BUF	@ BUF	@ ROC
TEN	@ MOB	@ MOB	OFF	HNT	HNT	HNT	HNT
DUN	OFF	@ CHA	@ CHA	@ CHA	@ CHA	@ TAM	TAM
CHWV	GRN	OFF	@ CC	@ CC	@ CC	@ CC	@ ASH
AUB	@ WILL	@ PIT	@ PIT	UTI	UTI	JAM	JAM
MED	OGD	OFF	@ CAS	@ CAS	@ CAS	@ GF	@ GF
	19	20	21	22	23	24	25
TOR	TEX	@ MIN	@ MIN	@ MIN	@ MIN	@ BAL	@ BAL
SYR	@ ROC	PAW	PAW	PAW	ROC	ROC	ROC
TEN	@ CHT	@ CHT	@ CHT	@ CHT	CAR	CAR	CAR
DUN	OFF	SAR	SAR	@ SAR	@ SAR	CHA	CHA
CHWV	@ ASH	@ ASH	@ ASH	OFF	DEL	DEL	DEL
AUB	@ MV	@ MV	LOW	LOW	LOW	LOW	ONE
MED	@ GF	MIS	MIS	MIS	GF	GF	GF
	26	27	28	29	30	31	
TOR	@ BAL	OFF	@ NYY	@ NYY	@ NYY	DET	
SYR	@ ROC	@ ROC	SWB	SWB	SWB	@ SWB	
TEN	CAR	WTN	WTN	WTN	WTN	@ CHT	
DUN	CHA	CHA	@ CLR	@ CLR	@ CLR	CLR	
CHWV	DEL	KAN	KAN	KAN	KAN	@ DEL	
AUB	ONE	@ JAM	@ JAM	OFF	MV	MV	
MED	GF	@ GF	@ GF	BILL	BILL	BILL	

*** GAME TO BE PLAYED IN COOPERSTOWN

SEPTEMBER 2001

	SUN	MON	TUE	WED	THU	FRI	SAT
							1
TOR							DET
SYR							SWB
TEN							@ CHT
DUN							SAR
CHWV							@ DEL
AUB							@ JAM
MED							@ MIS
	2	3	4	5	6	7	8
TOR	DET	NYY	NYY	NYY	OFF	@ DET	@ DET
SYR	@ PAW	@ PAW					
TEN	CHT	CHT					
DUN	SAR						
CHWV	@ DEL	@ DEL					
AUB	@ JAM	PIT	PIT	PIT			
MED	@ MIS						
	9	10	11	12	13	14	15
TOR	@ DET	OFF	@ BAL	@ BAL	@ BAL	CLE	CLE
	16	17	18	19	20	21	22
TOR	CLE	OFF	BAL	BAL	BAL	TB	TB
	23	24	25	26	27	28	29
TOR	TB	@ CLE	@ CLE	@ CLE	@ TB	@ TB	@ TB
	30						
TOR	@ TB						

KEY TO ABBREVIATIONS

SYRACUSE
BUF — BUFFALO BIISONS
CHA — CHARLOTTE KNIGHTS
COL — COLUMBUS CLIPPERS
DUR — DURHAM BULLS
IND — INDIANAPOLIS INDIANS
LOU — LOUISVILLE RIVERBATS
NOR — NORFOLK TIDES
OTT — OTTAWA LYNX
PAW — PAWTUCKET RED SOX
RMD — RICHMOND BRAVES
ROC — ROCHESTER RED WINGS
SWB — SCRANTON WILKES-BARRE
SYR — SYRACUSE SKYCHIEFS
TOL — TOLEDO MUD HENS

TENNESSEE
BIR — BIRMINGHAM BARONS
CAR — CAROLINA MUDCATS
CHT — CHATTANOOGA LOOKOUTS
GRN — GREENVILLE BRAVES
HNT — HUNTSVILLE STARS
JAX — JACKSONVILLE SUNS
MOB — MOBILE BAYBEARS
ORL — ORLANDO RAYS
TEN — TENNESSEE SMOKIES
WTN — WEST TENNESSEE DIAMOND JAXX

DUNEDIN
BRE — BREVARD CTY MANATEES
CHA — CHARLOTTE RANGERS
CLR — CLEARWATER PHILLIES
DAY — DAYTONA CUBS
DUN — DUNEDIN BLUE JAYS
FTM — FORT MYERS MIRACLE
JUP — JUPITER HAMMERHEADS
LAK — LAKELAND TIGERS
STL — St. LUCIE METS
SAR — SARASOTA RED SOX
TAM — TAMPA YANKEES
VER — VERO BEACH DODGERS

CHARLESTON
ASH — ASHEVILLE TOURISTS
AUG — AUGUSTA GREENJACKETS
CC — CAPITL CITY BOMBERS
CHSC — CHARLESTON S.C. RIVER DOGS
CHWV — CHARLESTON W.Va ALLEYCATS
COL — COLUMBUS REDSTIXX
DEL — DELMARVA SHOREBIRDS
GRN — GREENSBORO BATS
HAG — HAGERSTOWN SUNS
HKY — HICKORY CRAWDADS
KAN — KANNAPOLIS INTIMIDATORS
LKWD — LAKEWOOD BLUECLAWS
LEX — LEXINGTON LEGENDS
MAC — MACON BRAVES
SAV — SAVANNAH SAND GNATS
WLM — WILMINGTON WAVES

AUBURN
AUB — AUBURN DOUBLEDAYS
BAT — BATAVIA MUCKDOGS
BRKN — BROOKLYN CYCLONES
HV — HUDSON VLY RENEGADES
JAM — JAMESTOWN JAMMERS
LOW — LOWELL SPINNERS
MV — MAHONING VLY SCRAPPERS
NJ — NEW JERSEY CARDINALS
ONE — ONEONTA TIGERS
PIT — PITTSFIELD METS
STAT — STATEN ISLAND YANKEES
UTI — UTICA BLUE SOX
VER — VERMONT EXPOS
WILL — WILLIAMSPORT CROSSCUTTERS

MEDICINE HAT
BILL — BILLINGS MUSTANGS
CASP — CASPER
GF — GREAT FALLS DODGERS
IF — IDAHO FALLS BRAVES
MED — MEDICINE HAT BLUE JAYS
MIS — MISSOULA OSPREY
OGD — OGDEN RAPTORS
PROV — PROVO ANGELS

Player Development

NATIONAL BASEBALL HALL OF FAME AND MUSEUM

25 Main Street, Cooperstown, New York 13326
Web site: baseballhalloffame.org
phone: (607) 547-7200 fax: (607) 547-2044
e-mail address: info@baseballhalloffame.org

Public Relations: (607) 547-0215

Hours: Hours: May 1-Sept. 30: 9AM-9PM
Oct. 1-Apr. 30: 9AM-5PM
Closed: Nov. 26, Dec. 25, Jan. 1, 2002

Directory: Jane Forbes Clark (chairman), Joe Morgan (vice chairman), Dale Petroskey (president), Bill Haase (vice president, business and administration), Ted Spencer (vice president, chief curator), Jeff Idelson (vice president, communications and education), Scot Mondore (manager, museum programs), Jackie Brown (communications associate).

2001 Hall of Fame Weekend

Induction Ceremony: Sunday, August 5 1:30 PM, Clark Sports Center
Hall of Fame Game: Monday, August 6 2:00 PM, Doubleday Field

Hall of Famers to Have Played in Toronto

	Years with Blue Jays	Inducted		Years with Blue Jays	Inducted
Phil Niekro	1987	1997	Dave Winfield	1992	2001

Notable Blue Jays Artifacts at the Hall

- Baseball signed by Manager Roy Hartsfield and starting lineup from first Blue Jays game on April 7, 1977 against Chicago White Sox.
- Bat used by Cliff Johnson to set Major League record with 19th career pinch-hit home run on August 5, 1984.
- Ball used for first pitch of first game at Skydome on June 5, 1989.
- Cap and spikes worn and ball signed by Dave Stieb from his no-hitter on September 2, 1990.
- Ticket stub and press pin from July 9, 1991 All-Star Game at Skydome.
- Bat used by Joe Carter to hit two home runs in the 1992 World Series.
- Official 1992 World Series ball signed by World Champion Blue Jays.
- World Series Championship ring for 1992 Toronto Blue Jays.
- Bat used by Joe Carter to hit winning home run of 1993 World Series.
- Bat and helmet used by John Olerud during his batting title year of 1993.
- Ticket to all-Canadian Interleague Play game between the Expos and Blue Jays on June 30, 1997.
- Cap worn by Roger Clemens when he recorded his 3,000th strikeout on July 5, 1998.

A Look Ahead to 2002

Partial list of first-year candidates for Hall of Fame/BBWAA election in 2002 include Andre Dawson, Ozzie Smith and Alan Trammell. Notable upcoming Hall of Fame eligibles to have worn Toronto Blue Jays uniforms include: Joe Carter, Jimmy Key, Paul Molitor and Juan Samuel in 2004, and Tom Candiotti in 2005.

Notes From the Hall of Fame

The Hall of Fame opened on June 12, 1939. The first election occurred in 1936 and its class included Ty Cobb, Walter Johnson, Christy Mathewson, Babe Ruth and Honus Wagner. Not including the 2001 Veterans Committee election, the Hall of Fame is comprised of 251 members (62 living): 187 major leaguers, 23 executives, 17 Negro Leaguers, 16 managers and eight umpires.

Research Assistance

The Hall of Fame is pleased to provide assistance in baseball research and members of the media are encouraged to utilize this valuable baseball resource when ever necessary, by calling the Public Relations department at (607) 547-0215, or the Library Reference desk at (607) 547-0330.

THE CANADIAN BASEBALL HALL OF FAME AND MUSEUM

The Canadian Baseball Hall of Fame and Museum was formed in 1983 and was located on the Exhibition grounds in Toronto for several years. In 1994 individuals from the small picturesque town of St. Marys, just west of Stratford, relocated the Hall of Fame to its new permanent home. With the success of the grand opening in June of 1998, and its continuous growth from that date, the Canadian Baseball Hall of Fame and Museum is here to stay. With our 32 acres of land containing one regulation size ball field and two youth ball fields along with our one-of-a-kind museum, and walking trails throughout the property we have a strong beginning and an even stronger future. This past summer the Hall of Fame had the pleasure of hosting the Canadian National Junior team and would be more than pleased to host your team. Included in the Hall's 48 inductees are Blue Jay greats such as Ron Taylor (1985), Bobby Prentice (1986), Pat Gillick (1997) and Dave McKay in 2001. Jim Fanning was the lone inductee in 2000, joining past Expos Charles Bronfman (1984), Claude Raymond (1984), Ron Piche (1988), John McHale (1997) and Gary Carter, who will be inducted in 2001.

To contact the Canadian Baseball Hall of Fame and Museum:

P.O. Box 1838
140 Queen St.
St. Marys, ON N4X 1C2

www.baseballhof.ca
Email: baseball@quadro.net

Phone (519) 284-1838
Toll-Free 1-877-250-BALL
Fax (519) 284-1234

Executive Director: Tom Valcke
Director of Operations: Scott Crawford
Administrative Assistant: Marg Glover-Edgar

PLAYER LIMITS: 40 until opening day, when the number must be reduced to 25 until September 1, when it again becomes 40. The minimum number of active players maintained by each club throughout the championship season shall be 24.

TRADING REGULATIONS: The trading deadline is July 31.

Trades may be made with any other major league club in the period from the end of the championship season through July 31 (midnight) without waivers. Waivers are required, however:

1. If the assignment is to another major league club: From August 1 and ending at 5 pm EDT the day after the end of the season.

2. If assignment is to a minor league club, with right of recall, at any time after three years from the date the player first reported to a major league club during a championship season.

3. If assigned to a minor league club without right of recall, after acquiring three years service: At any time during the year.

4. If assigned to a minor league club, without right of recall, at any time prior to acquiring three years of service, special waivers are required between September 1 and the opening of the following season. If player is claimed, request may be withdrawn. If no claims are made, club has 7-day period in which to make assignment to minor leagues.

WAIVERS: a permission granted from all 30 clubs to assign a Major League player's contract to another Major league team or a minor league affiliate. Such permission is granted only for a specific period of time. The actual request is filed through the Commissioner's Office and is not disclosed to the public until the contract is rewarded.

PROCEDURES FOR OBTAINING WAIVERS:

- May request 7 players on any given business day.
- The waivers must be requested by 2:00pm ET on any business day.
- Waiver claiming period expires on the second business day after the initial request at 1:00pm ET.
- A Club desiring the assignment of a player on the waiver wire must submit a claim prior to 1:00pm ET on the last day of the claiming period.
- Priority for the waiver claim awards is given to the Club with the lowest winning percentage in the player's league when there are multiple claims submitted for the same player.
- If only one claim is entered, the claiming Club is eligible to be awarded the player contract.
- There is no specific limit on the number of claims that may be submitted on a particular day. However, no Club is permitted to exceed the 40-man or the 25-man roster limit.
- If a Club is awarded a player on a waiver claim which causes them to exceed the 40-man or the 25-man roster limit they must designate a different player for assignment.

THREE WAIVER PERIODS:

- November 11 through the 30th day of the following season.
- 31st day of the season through July 31
- August 1 through November 10

All waivers that have been granted expire at 5:00pm ET on the last day of a particular waiver period.

TYPES OF WAIVERS

- *OUTRIGHT WAIVERS (OR)* — this type of irrevocable waiver needs to be secured in order to Outright a player. An outright is to assign a player to a club's minor league affiliate without the right of recall. In other words, to remove a player from the 40-man roster. Also a player who has exhausted his options must clear this type of waiver if the club wishes to assign him to minor league affiliate. An outright waiver secured is good for entire waiver period. These waivers are needed from the 31st day of the season through August 31.
- *SPECIAL WAIVERS (SPL)* — also irrevocable, the special waiver is used for the same purpose as an outright waiver. One difference is these waivers are used from September 1 to the 30th day of the following season. A secured special waiver is good for seven days, as opposed to being good for an entire period like the outright waiver.
- *UNCONDITIONAL RELEASE WAIVER (UR)* — this irrevocable waiver is used for the purpose of an unconditional release of a player. At the time of the request the player shall be removed from all player limits. A player may be informed of the clubs intention to release him on a weekend, but the actual waiver process won't begin until the following business day. During the time a player is on an unexpired waiver request bulletin, he may discuss employment with other clubs but may not contract with another club. If the player has been claimed, he must be informed the end of the two-day period that his contract has been claimed. The player has five days from the time he was notified of the claim to either accept the assignment or terminate his contract. If the player terminates his contract he forfeits termination pay. Termination pay may vary depending on the time of year.
- *MAJOR LEAGUE WAIVER (ML)* — this type of revocable waiver is common and it is used to either option a player to a club's minor league affiliate or assign a player outright to another Major league club from August 1st to the end of the regular season. A player claimed on this type of waiver may be pulled back by the requesting club. This is known as a waiver withdrawal. Generally a club needs to secure this type of waiver in order to option a player if the date of the assignment is three or more years after the date the player first reported to a Major League club during a championship season. One year shall be deducted from the above three-year period for each season in which the player may have been charged with an option prior to first reporting to a Major League club during a championship season. A claimed player pulled back by the requesting club may not be assigned and cannot be placed on waivers again (except for UR waivers) for 30 days. When ML waivers are asked for a second time in the same period the request shall state that it is irrevocable.

ASSIGNMENT OF PLAYER CONTRACTS:

- Ten and Five Rule: Players with ten or more years of Major League service (MLS), the last five of which have been with one Club, shall not be assignable to another Major League Club without the Player's written consent.
- When a player with five or more years of MLS is asked by his club to consent to an assignment to the National Association, he has three choices;
1. Accept the assignment, 2. Refuse the assignment, 3. Elect Free Agency
- Any player who has at least three years of MLS and whose contract is assigned outright to a National Association club may elect, in lieu of accepting such assignment, to become a free agent.
- Any player whose contract is assigned outright to a National Association club for second time or any subsequent time in his career may elect, in lieu of accepting such assignment, to become a free agent. Unlike a player with five or more years of MLS, this type of player does not have the option of refusing the assignment.

OPTIONAL ASSIGNMENT: to assign a player from the active 25-man roster to a minor league affiliate with the right of recall. The player remains on the 40-man roster.

Miscellaneous

RECALL: to add a player from your reserve limit (40-man roster) to the 25-man roster. This player must serve at least 10 days on option in order to be recalled unless he is replacing a player placed on the disabled list.

OUTRIGHT ASSIGNMENT:

- MAJOR TO MINOR: to assign a player to the Club's minor league affiliate without the right of recall. The player is removed from the 40-man roster.
- MAJOR TO MAJOR: to assign a player from one Club's 40-man roster to another Club's 40-man roster. This transaction is more commonly known as a trade.

DESIGNATED FOR ASSIGNMENT:

- When a club that has reached it 40 and /or 25 man roster limit, either reinstates a player, or acquires a new player (through a selection, a signing, a trade or a waiver claim); they must designate a player for assignment or release. If they are going to assign the player, they must do it within 10 days.

WAIVER WITHDRAWALS:

- Waiver request may only be withdrawn on players who have been claimed on a Major League Waiver wire. If a player is claimed on a Major League Waiver wire, the request must be withdrawn within two business days or the contract will be awarded to the eligible club. During the two-day waiver withdrawal period the requesting Club can try to negotiate a deal with the eligible Club and make a waiver claim award under the terms of that deal.

WAIVER PRICES:

- Major League, Special and Outright Waivers are $20,000 or $25,000, while Unconditional Waivers are $1.00.

FREE AGENCY (RE-ENTRY): The 1985 collective bargaining agreement brought about changes in the free agency process. Following is the appropriate information:

Six years of Major League Service continues to be required to be eligible for free agency.

The Re-Entry Draft has been abolished.

A player has 15 days from the first day following the World Series to file for free agency.

By December 7, former club must offer to arbitrate or becomes ineligible to sign player. By December 19, player must accept offer or on January 9 former club becomes ineligible to sign the player. (Ineligible club regains eligibility the following May 1.)

If club and player proceed to arbitration, maximum salary cut rules do not apply.

Player who accepts former club's offer to arbitrate is not subject to repeater rights limitations.

SALARY ARBITRATION:

Beginning in 1987, three years Major League Service required for eligibility.

Beginning in 1987, maximum cut rules do not apply if in immediately preceding year player won arbitration increase of over 50%.

Three-man panels were scheduled to hear cases instead of single arbitrators in 50 percent of the cases in 1998, 75 percent in 1999 and 100 percent in 2000 and 2001.

Beginning in 1987, arbitrator is officially instructed to give particular attention for purposes of comparison to salaries of players with Major League Service no more than one annual service group higher than player who is arbitrating.

Beginning in 1991, a player with at least 2 but less than 3 years of Major League Service, shall be eligible for salary arbitration if: a)he has accumulated at least 86 days of service during the immediately preceeding season or b)he ranks in the top 17 percent in total service in the class of players who have at least 2 but less than 3 years of ML service, however accumulated, but with at least 86 days of service accumulated during the immediately preceeding season.

FREE AGENT DRAFT RULE (AMATEUR DRAFT) - REVISED FOR 1987: One selection meeting shall be conducted each year in June to be known at the "Summer Meeting".

Major League Clubs shall select in reverse order of their league standing at the close of the preceeding season (determined by the percentage of games it won). No club may transfer to another club its right to select.

A selected player shall be placed on a club's Negotiation List and shall remain, thereon until the start of the Closed Period (The seven days preceding the Summer Meeting) of the next selection meeting, unless at an earlier date he (1) signs a contract (2) is removed because he was not eligible for selection (3) becomes a College Player by entering or returning to college.

A club may not transfer its Negotiation Right to any other club.

REGULATION GAME: A regulation game consists of nine innings unless extended because of a tie score or shortened because (1) the home team needs none of its half of the ninth or only part of it; or (2) because the umpire-in-chief calls the game after five completed innings. A regulation game may be less than five innings if the home team is ahead after the first of the fifth, or takes the lead or ties the score while at bat in the fifth.

TIE GAME: A regulation game that is called by the umpire-in-chief when both teams have the same number of runs is a tie game. Individual player performances are official and are entered in the records, but the game does not count in the League standings and may be re-scheduled at a later date.

SUSPENDED GAME RULE:

Rule 4.12 SUSPENDED GAMES

(a) A league shall adopt the following rules providing for completion at a future date of games terminated for any of the following reasons:

   (1) A curfew imposed by law;

   (2) A time limit permissible under league rules;

   (3) Light failure or malfunction of a mechanical field device under control of the home club. (Mechanical field device shall include automatic tarpaulin or water removal equipment.);

   (4) Darkness because of any law, the lights may not be turned on.

   (5) Weather, if the game is called while an inning is in progress and before it is completed, and one of the following situations prevails:

     (i) The visiting team has scored one or more runs to tie the score, and the home team has not scored.

     (ii) The visiting team has scored one or more runs to take the lead, and the home team has not tied the score or retaken the lead.

(b) Such games shall be known as suspended games. No game called because of a curfew, weather, or a time limit shall be a suspended game unless it has progressed far enough to have been a regulation game under the provisions of Rule 4.10. A game called under the provisions of 4.12(a)(3) or (4) shall be a suspended game at any time after it starts.

(c) By amending NOTE to read as follows:

NOTE: Weather and similar conditions—4.12(a) (1 through 5)—shall take precedence in determining whether a called game shall be a suspended game. A game can only be considered a suspended game if stopped for any of the five (5) reasons specified in Section (a). Any legal game called due to weather with the score tied (unless situation outlined in 4.12(a)(5)(i) prevails) is a tie game and must be replayed in its entirety.

(d) A suspended game shall be resumed and completed as follows:

   (1) Immediately preceding the next scheduled single game between the two clubs on the same grounds;

or

(2) Immediately preceding the next scheduled double-header between the two clubs on the same grounds, if no single game remains on the schedule, or

(3) If suspended on the last scheduled date between the two clubs in the city, transferred and played on the grounds of the opposing club, if possible;

    (i) Immediately preceding the next scheduled single game, or

    (ii) Immediately preceding the next scheduled double-header, if no single game remains on the schedule.

(4) If a suspended game has not been resumed and completed on the last date scheduled for the two clubs, it shall be a called game.

(e) A suspended game shall be resumed at the exact point of suspension of the original game. The completion of a suspended game is a continuation of the original game. The lineup and batting order of both teams shall be exactly the same as the lineup and batting order at the moment of suspension, subject to the rules governing substitution. Any player may be replaced by a player who had not been in the game prior to the suspension. No player removed before the suspension may be returned to the lineup. A player who was not with the club when the game was suspended may be used as a substitute, even if he has taken the place of a player no longer with the club who would not have been eligible because he had been removed from the lineup before the game was suspended.

DISABLED LISTS:

15-Day: The player must remain off the active roster for a minimum of 15 calendar days, starting on the day following the player's last game.

60-Day: Same rules apply, however, this may only be used when the team's 40-man roster is full. Any player placed on the 60-day disabled list after August 1 may not play for the remainder of the season, including any post-season game.

EMERGENCY DISABLED LIST: Maximum number of players on list at one time-no limit. Minimum period of inactivity-sixty (60) calendar days. Players placed on this list after August 1st will remain there for the balance of the season. This list may only be used when a club is at the maximum limit of 40 players.

AMERICAN LEAGUE CURFEWS: No inning of an American league night game can start after 1:00 a.m., local time. Any inning started prior to 1:00 a.m. can be completed. Curfews shall be waived for the final series of the season between two teams in each of the cities.

Any game, regardless of length, called because of the time curfew, becomes a suspended game and must be completed from the exact point of interruption before the teams play their next scheduled game against each other.

DEFINITION OF NIGHT GAME: In the American League any game scheduled to start after 6:00 p.m. (i.e. 6:01 p.m., or later), will be considered a night game. If a game is scheduled to start at 6:00 p.m., and is delayed by rain or for any other reason, it will be considered a day game.

However, both games of a twi-night doubleheader shall be considered night games. When afternoon and night games are played on the same date and separate admissions are charged, they will be counted as one day and one night game, and will not be included in doubleheader statistics.

BATTING CHAMPIONSHIP QUALIFICATIONS: A batting champion must have 502 or more actual plate appearances. (The equivalent of 3.1 appearances for each of the 162 scheduled games.). If, however, there is any player with fewer than the required number of plate appearances whose average would be the highest if he were charged with the required number of official at bats, then the player shall be awarded the batting championship.

EARNED-RUN AVERAGE CHAMPION QUALIFICATIONS: To win the earned-run average championship a pitcher must pitch at least as many innings as the number of games scheduled for each club in his league that season and have the lowest earned-run average.

FIELDING CHAMPIONSHIP QUALIFICATIONS: The individual fielding champions shall be the fielders with the highest fielding average at each position, provided:

(1) A catcher must have participated as a catcher in at least one-half the number of games scheduled for each club in his league that season;

(2) An infielder or outfielder must have participated at his position in at least two-thirds of the number of games scheduled for each club in his league that season;

(3) A pitcher must have pitched at least as many innings as the number of games scheduled for each club in his league that season. **EXCEPTION:** If another pitcher has a fielding average as high or higher, and has handled more total chances in a lesser number of innings, he shall be the fielding champion.

DETERMINING THE MAGIC NUMBERS: Determine the number of games yet to be played, add one, then subtract the number of games ahead in the loss column of the standings from the closest opponent.

DETERMINING BATTING AVERAGE: Divide the number of at bats into the number of hits.

DETERMINING AN EARNED-RUN AVERAGE: Multiply the number of earned runs by nine; take the number and divide it by the number of innings pitched.

DETERMINING SLUGGING PERCENTAGE: Divide the total bases of all safe hits by the total times at bat. (At bats do not include walks, sacrifices, hit by pitcher, or times awarded first base because of interference or obstruction.)

DETERMINING ON BASE PERCENTAGE: Add the total of hits, walks and hit by pitches and divide by the total of at-bats, walks, hit by pitches and sacrifice flies.

DETERMINING FIELDING AVERAGE: Divide the total put-outs and assists by the total of putouts, assists and errors.

DETERMINING PERCENTAGE OF GAMES WON & LOST: Divide the number of games won by the total games won and lost.

CONSECUTIVE HITTING STREAKS: A consecutive hitting streak shall not be terminated if the plate appearance results in a base on balls, hit batsman, defensive interference or a sacrifice bunt. A sacrifice fly shall terminate the streak.

CONSECUTIVE-GAME HITTING STREAKS: A consecutive-game hitting streak shall not be terminated if all the player's plate appearances (one or more) result in a base on balls, hit batsman, defensive interference or a sacrifice bunt. The streak shall terminate if the player has a sacrifice fly and no hit. The player's individual consecutive-game hitting streak shall be determined by the consecutive games in which the player appears and is not determined by his club's games.

CONSECUTIVE-GAME PLAYING STREAK: A consecutive-game playing streak shall be extended if the player plays one-half inning on defense, or if he completes a time at bat by reaching base or being put out. A pinch-running appearance only shall not extend the streak. If a player is ejected from a game by an umpire before he can comply with the requirements of this rule, his streak shall continue.

SUSPENDED GAMES: For the purpose of this rule, all performances in the completion of a suspended game shall be considered as occurring on the original date of the game.

"SAVE" RULE: A pitcher shall be credited with a save when he meets all three of the following conditions:

(1) He is the finishing pitcher in a game won by his club, and

(2) He is not the winning pitcher, and

(3) He qualifies under one of the following conditions:

    (3) (a) He enters the game with a lead of no more than three runs and pitches for at least one inning, or

        (b) He enters the game regardless of the count, with the potential tying run either on base, at bat, or on deck (that is, the potential tying run is either already on base or is one of the first two batsmen he faces), or

        (c) He pitches effectively for at least three innings.

Miscellaneous

TOUGH SAVE: The reliever comes into the game with the tying runs on base and saves the game. Example: Reliever comes in with a 5-3 lead, two outs and the bases loaded in the ninth inning.

BLOWN SAVE RULE: When a relief pitcher enters a game in a save situation and departs or the game ends with the save situation no longer in effect because he has given up the lead, he is charged with a "blown save." (If the save opportunity still exists when he leaves the game, he is not charged with a save opportunity. If the pitcher has not given up the lead when he leaves the game, though the save opportunity may no longer exist, he is not charged with a save opportunity.

BAT AROUND: When all nine batters in a team's lineup come to bat during an inning.

DESIGNATED HITTER RULE: A hitter may be designated to bat for the pitcher in any spot in the batting order in any game without affecting the status of the pitcher. The designated hitter must be selected and be included on the lineup cards presented to the umpire-in-chief prior to the game. Failure to do so precludes the use of a designated hitter for that game.

The designated hitter is "locked" into the batting order but may be removed for a pinch-hitter or pinch-runner, who in turn becomes the designated hitter. The designated hitter, while still in the game, may be used defensively but the pitcher then assumes the batting order of the replaced defensive player, thus terminating the designated hitter role.

The designated hitter is eligible for all American League batting titles.

The designated hitter named in the starting lineup must come to bat at least one time, unless the opposition changes pitchers.

SCORING RULE ON PINCH-HITTERS: A player shall be considered a pinch-hitter only if he enters the game as a substitute batter and then only on his first time at bat which must be before he becomes a fielder. If the team bats around and a pinch hitter comes up a second time in the inning in which he first appeared he will not be considered a pinch hitter during that second time up.

A substitute hitter for a Designated Hitter is both a pinch hitter and a designated hitter on his first time at bat. On subsequent trips to the plate he is a Designated Hitter only.

EARNED-RUNS RULE: The determination of earned-run is as follows:

"An earned-run is a run for which the pitcher is held accountable. In determining earned-runs, the inning should be reconstructed without the errors and passed balls; and the benefit of the doubt should always be given to the pitcher in determining which bases would have been reached with errorless play."

Until 1969, the reliever could not be charged with an earned-run if he entered the game after the side could have been retired but for an error, no matter how many runs he subsequently gave up in that inning. Now, runs, scored by batters who reach base off the reliever are charged as earned on that pitcher's record. They are not, however, charged as earned against the team as a whole. Therefore, a discrepancy may occur between the total earned-runs charged against a team and the sum total of the earned-runs charged against the individual pitchers of that team.

DOCTORED BAT: A batter is out for illegal action when he uses or attempts to use a bat that, in the umpire's judgment, has been altered or tampered with in such a way to improve the distance factor or cause an unusual reaction on the baseball. This includes bats that are filled, flat-surfaced, nailed, hollowed, grooved or covered with a substance such as paraffin, wax, etc. No advancement on the bases will be allowed and any out or outs made during a play shall stand. In addition to being called out, the player shall be ejected from the game and may be subject to additional penalties as determined by his League President. (Rule 6.06d).

DETERMINING A "MAJOR LEAGUE YEAR": 172 days constitute a full year in the major leagues.

MAJOR LEAGUE SERVICE:

- is credited for each day the player appears on an active roster or major league disabled list or suspended list.
- in the case of a player called up from the minor leagues, is credited beginning with the date he physically reports.
- in the case of a major league player who is traded and reports in the normal course, service is not interrupted.
- in the case of a player sent down to the minor leagues, is credited through the date of the assignment.
- in the case of a player who is unconditionally released, is credited through the date waivers were requested.
- in the case of a player designated for release or assignment (MLR 2), is credited after the designation, through the date of the actual assignment or the request for unconditional release waivers.
- for a player who appears on his club's opening day roster, is credited as of the earliest scheduled opener, without regard to the actual opening date of his own club.
- is credited at the rate of 172 days per "year", though the season is actually 182 days long.
- is not credited during any period or periods of optional assignment totalling 20 days or more during a single season.

ROOKIE QUALIFICATION: A player shall be considered a rookie unless, during a previous season or seasons, he has (a) exceeded 130 at bats or 50 innings pitched in the major leagues; or (b) accumulated more than 45 days on the active roster of a major league club or clubs during the period of a 25-man limit (excluding time in military service) and time on the disabled list.

PLAYING RULES:

Spectator Interference—batter, runner and other runner(s) will be placed at the base(s) which the umpires feel they would have reached with no interference.

Time—ball is dead, play suspended. This sign used when ball is foul, umpire then pointing to foul territory.

Batted Balls Fair or Foul—if fair, umpire points to fair territory—if foul he raises arms overhead (as in "Time" above) and then turns and points to foul territory, and vocally calls "foul".

SCHEDULE: The American League schedule for the 2001 season will be the fifth year to incorporate Inter-League Play. The Blue Jays will also play an unbalanced schedule for the first time since 1978, including 76 games vs. AL East opponents. The 162 game schedule will include 144 games vs. the AL and 18 vs. NL opponents. The break down is as follows:

AL EAST	H	A
BAL	10	9
BOS	10	9
NYY	9	10
TB	9	10
Total	**38**	**38**

AL WEST	H	A
ANA	3	6
OAK	6	3
SEA	3	6
TEX	6	3
	18	18

AL CENTRAL	H	A
CWS	3	3
CLE	3	3
KC	4	3
MIN	3	4
DET	3	3
	16	16

NL EAST	H	A
ATL	3	0
FLA	3	0
MON	3	3
NYM	0	3
PHI	0	3
	9	9

MINIMUM SALARY: The minimum rate of payment to a player for each day of service on a Major League Club for the 2001 season is $200,000 U.S. Funds.

TERMINATION PAY: One full season's pay if player released opening day or later. Thirty days pay for player who is released on the 16th day before opening day or earlier. If player is released after that 16th day prior to opening day he receives one additional day's pay (over the 30 days) for each additional day.

CLUB/MEDIA CHAMPIONSHIP SEASON REGULATIONS

The following are Major League Baseball's regulations for Club/Media Relations. They are to be observed by all parties:

1. All accredited press, radio, TV representatives shall have pre-game access to the clubhouse. Clubhouses are to be open to accredited media from three hours and 30 minutes prior to game time until 45 minutes prior to game time.

2. The working media shall have access to both clubhouses no later than 10 minutes after the final out of the day's play — with the exception of day/night split admission games, when the media shall have access to both clubhouses no later than 10 minutes after each game.

3. Both clubhouses, the dugouts and field are off-limits except to appropriate club, League and Commissioner's Office personnel and media bearing appropriate credentials. Club credentials are not to be issued to unauthorized personnel. The Commissioner's Office and/or the League Offices reserve the right to revoke inappropriately issued credentials.

4. Players will be available to the media before and after games for interviews. These periods should not be limited except for the pre-game period described in #1 above. Upon request by the media, players who had key roles in the first game of a doubleheader are to be made available for a time between games.

5. The trainer's room and players lounge may be off-limits to the media but each club controls these areas, and it is vital they not be used as a sanctuary for players seeking to avoid the media. It is very important to our game that ALL players are available to the media for reasonable periods, and it is the player's responsibility to cooperate.

6. Ropes or other restraining barriers are not permitted to bar the media. A general code is to be observed by the media so uniformed personnel may do their work unimpeded. Media is to be allowed in foul territory, in an unrestricted manner, in an area which is not less than the territory between first and third bases, and which territory includes the area around the batting cage, except the dirt area around the batting cage.

7. Under no circumstances shall any club discriminate in any fashion against an accredited member of the media based upon race, creed, sex or national origin.

8. Physical abuse or threats directed to members of the media (and/or official scorers) by baseball personnel will not be tolerated. Disciplinary action, including fines and suspensions, will be considered in any cases which arise.

9. Visitors in the clubhouse should conduct themselves in a professional manner. There shall be no seeking of autographs, no removal of equipment and no sampling of players food spreads. Clubhouses are work places. Clubhouse business should be conducted as expeditiously as possible with a minimum of disruption of regular game routines.

10. Live TV and/or radio interviews with uniformed personnel during the course of a game are not authorized or permitted, nor is attaching a microphone to any uniformed personnel permitted without League approval. Microphones may not be placed in or adjacent to dugouts and/or bullpens in a manner that will allow uniformed personnel's remarks or conversation to be overheard during the course of a game without the prior approval of the League.

11. Live telephone interviews are not allowed from the clubhouse or the field without prior approval of the club.

12. Telephones from both dugouts to the press box are to be maintained in working order for the purpose of providing information regarding special circumstances to the media during the course of a game. Explanations of injuries should be made as soon as possible (to both the media and fans in the stadium).

13. Accredited media are not required to sign in for clubhouse access.

14. Any club whose personnel violates these regulations will be disciplined. Any member of the media who violates these regulations will lose his or her accreditation.

Miscellaneous

DIRECTLY TO THE MAJORS
Since the start of the amateur free-agent draft in 1965, 17 players have made their professional baseball debuts in the major leagues. The complete list:

N–Has never played in the minor leagues

DRAFT YEAR	PLAYER	TEAM
June '67 (secondary)	Mike Adamson, rhp	Baltimore
June '69 (regular)	Steve Dunning, rhp	Cleveland
June '71 (secondary)	Pete Broberg, rhp	Washington
	Rob Ellis, if	Milwaukee
	Burt Hooton, rhp	Chicago Cubs
June '72 (regular)	Dave Roberts, 3b	San Diego
January '73 (secondary)	Dick Ruthven, rhp	Philadelphia
June '73 (regular)	David Clyde, lhp	Texas
	N–Dave Winfield, of	San Diego
	Eddie Bane, lhp	Minnesota
June '78 (regular)	N–Bob Horner, 3b	Atlanta
	BRIAN MILNER, c	Toronto
	Mike Morgan, rhp	Oakland
	Tim Conroy, lhp	Oakland
June '85 (regular)	Pete Incaviglia, of	Texas
June '88 (regular)	Jim Abbott, lhp	California
June '89 (regular)	N–**JOHN OLERUD**, dh/1b	Toronto

Jan. 5-15	Period in which a player may make submission to arbitration. {Art. VI(f)}
Jan. 8	Last day for former Clubs to re-sign players who refused arbitration. {Art. XX(B)}
Jan. 18	Office of the Commissioner and MLBPA will exchange salary arbitration filing figures.
Jan. 19-22	Office of the Commissioner and MLBPA will schedule arbitration hearing dates.
Feb 1-20	Salary arbitration hearings held. {Art. VI(F)}
Feb. 15	First date injured players, pitchers and catchers may be invited to attend spring training workouts. {Art. XIV(A)}
Feb. 20	First date all other players may be invited to attend spring training workouts. {Art. XIV(A)}
Feb. 27	Mandatory date players are required to report for first spring training workout. {Art. XIV(A)}
March 2	First date to renew contracts. Ten day renewal period ends on March 11th. {U.P.C. Paragraph 10(a)}
March 7	First date Clubs may ask waivers on draft excluded players acquired after 8/15/00 or players chosen in the 2000 Rule 5 draft meeting (Special waivers required for all outright assignments to the National Association Sept. 1, 2000 through April 30, 2001.) {MLR 10(c)(6)}
March 11	Last date to renew contracts
March 12	First date draft-excluded/selected players may be assigned to a National Association Club. {MLR 6(e) & MLR 10(c)(6)}
March 14	last date to request Unconditional Release waivers (By 2 PM EDT) to be secured by March 16th, in order to owe only 30 days termination pay. {ART. IX B} *** In the case of a split contract: a – The N.A. rate of termination pay will be owed if U.R. waivers are requested by 2PM today. b – The Major League rate of termination pay will be owed if U.R. waivers are requested AFTER 2 PM today. {ART IX D} *** EXCEPTION TO SPLIT CONTRACT TERM PAY: THE ABOVE DOES NOT APPLY to players who cannot be assigned to the National Association without their consent and for players selected in the preceding Rule 5 draft.
March 15	Unconditional Release waivers requested today until 2PM ET March 28th will owe 45 days termination pay. {ART IX B}
March 16	Last day to assign an injured player to a National Association club until the close of the championship season (OUTRIGHT or OPTIONALLY) provided that: a) The player has less than 3 years of Major League Svc b) The assignment would not be the player's second (or subsequent) career outright since 3/19/90 c) The player had NO MAJOR LEAGUE SERVICE the prior championship season d) The player was not selected by the assignor Major League club in the immediately preceding Rule 5 Draft {Art. XIX C}
March 28	Last date to request U.R. waivers by 2 PM ET, if you will hand, telephone, or fax notice to player, without incurring full season salary. (Owe 45 days term pay)
April 1	Official opening of the 2001 championship season. All clubs are required to cut down to 25 men by midnight, April 1st.
April 30	Waivers secured on/after November 11th expire 5:00 pm EDT.

May 1	This is the 31st day of the 2001 championship season. New waiver period begins. Waivers secured on/after this date are good through 5:00 pm ET July 31st. {MLR 10(f)}
May 1	Earliest date former Clubs may re-sign free agent players who refused arbitration and were unsigned after Jan. 8th. {Art. XX B(3)}
May 15	Earliest date clubs may re-sign players whom they unconditionally released between midnight August 31, 2000 and April 1, 2001. (MLR 8(i)(2)}
May 29	Start of amateur free agent closed period re summer draft (at 12:01 a.m.)
June 5-7	Summer Free Agent Draft
July 10	All Star Game at Safeco Field, Seattle
July 31	Waivers secured on/after May 1, 2001 expire at 5:00 pm EDT. Players may be traded between major league clubs until MIDNIGHT tonight without any waivers in effect. {MLR 10(e)(1)}
August 1	New waiver period begins. Beginning this date and ending on the day following the close of the championship season, players may be assigned between major league clubs ONLY after major league waivers have been secured during the current waiver period. {(MLR 10(e)(1)}
August 15	Last date to bring player up for "full trial" to avoid draft excluded status. {MLR 6(e)}
August 31	Any player released after midnight tonight may not be resigned to a major league contract by the club that released him until May 15th of the following season {MLR 8(i)(2)} Post season rosters are established at midnight tonight. To be eligible, a player must be a bona fide member of a qualifying team on August 31st and must remain a bona fide member until the end of the season.
Sept. 1	Active player limit increased from 25 to 40. Beginning today outright assignments to the National Association may be made ONLY with special waivers in effect.
Sept. 30	Official closing of the 2001 championship season
Oct. 1	All players on optional assignment must be recalled.
Oct. 1	Beginning today, players may be traded between Major League Clubs without waivers in effect.
Oct. 9	Last date to request waivers on draft excluded players until 25 days prior to the opening of the following season. {MLR 10(c)(6)}
Oct. 10	The beginning of the closed period for Major League waiver requests. (Oct. 10th–Nov. 10) Special waivers may still be requested on players that are not draft excluded for the next Rule 5 draft. {MLR 10(c) 2}
Nov. 10	Waivers secured on/after Aug. 1, 2001, expire 5:00 pm ET. {MLR 10(f)}
Nov. 11	New waiver period begins. Major league waiver requests may be withdrawn by a club on a player only once in each waiver period; subsequent major league waiver requests in that period are irrevocable. Waivers (exclusive of special waivers) secured today and after shall be in effect until the 30th day of the following championship season. {MLR 10(f)}
Nov. (TBA)	Dates for filing Rookie, A, AA, AAA, and Major League reserve lists will be announced as soon as the dates are determined.
Dec. 20	Last date to tender contracts. {U.P.C. paragraph 10(a)}
NOTE:	The dates will be used unless notified differently.

TORONTO BLUE JAYS MEDIA SERVICES

TORONTO BLUE JAYS MEDIA RELATIONS
SKYDOME
ONE BLUE JAYS WAY
SUITE 3200
TORONTO, ONTARIO M5V 1J1

OFFICE: (416) 341-1303

FAX: (416) 341-1250

E-MAIL: MR@bluejays.ca

HOWARD STARKMAN, VICE-PRESIDENT, MEDIA RELATIONS
JAY STENHOUSE, MANAGER, MEDIA RELATIONS
MICHAEL SHAW, MEDIA RELATIONS COORDINATOR
JENNIFER MORRIS, MEDIA RELATIONS COORDINATOR
LAURA AMMENDOLIA, MEDIA RELATIONS SUPERVISOR
LEANNA ENGLAND, MEDIA RELATIONS ASSISTANT

CREDENTIAL APPLICATIONS: All news media will be asked to submit a written request for Blue Jays season media credentials on their official letterhead. All requests for season credentials must be received by Friday, March 23, 2001.

SEASON CREDENTIALS: Season credentials will be issued only to those legitimate newsgathering organizations who plan to cover the Blue Jays on a daily basis. Credentials will be issued only to members of the working media 18 years of age and older. NO SPOUSES, GUESTS or CHILDREN OF MEMBERS OF THE MEDIA WILL BE ISSUED CREDENTIALS. MEDIA PASSES ARE NOT TRANSFERABLE. Credentialed members of the media are prohibited from requesting or accumulating autographs or equipment on the playing field or in the dugout and clubhouse. Any violation of these guidelines will result in immediate revocation of the credential and future access. Only credentials issued by the Blue Jays, the American League or the BBWAA will be honoured. All credentials must be visible at all times.

DAILY CREDENTIALS: Daily credentials will be issued to those legitimate newsgatheirng organizations who do not qualify for season credentials. Any organization who anticipates the need for daily credentials must have a letter on file with the Blue Jays Media Relations Department. Requests may be sent via fax, but those requests must be made at least 24 hours in advance. Daily credentials are subject to the same restrictions as season credentials and any violation will result in revocation of the credential and any future access.

PHOTO CREDENTIALS: Credentials will be issued to those photographers on assignment for legitimate newsgathering organizations and those representatives of companies licensed by Major League Baseball. Photographers for licensees will only be granted daily passes. NO freelance photographers will be granted credentials and all photographs taken are to be used for newsgathering purposes or officially licensed products. Any other use of photographs taken will be considered a violation of existing trademark and copyright restrictions.

CLUBHOUSE ACCESS: The clubhouse is open to all media with proper credentials 3 1/2 hours prior to each game and then closes 45 minutes prior to the start of each game. It re-opens no later than 10 minutes after each game. Policies regarding access between games of doubleheaders will be determined by the Blue Jays Media Relations department. Access to the visiting clubhouse is subject to the visiting club's guidelines.

FIELD ACCESS: All credentialed members of the media will be given access to the playing field prior to each game. No media will be allowed in fair territory or beyond the first and third base bags. All non-uniformed personnel must clear the field at the conclusion of visitors batting practice unless that individual had credentials expressly for in-game field privileges (photo passes, pre-game ceremonies, etc.)

LIVE TRANSMISSIONS: Televisions and radio stations not holding broadcast rights for Blue Jays games will be allowed to transmit live reports prior to and after Blue Jays games. All live television shots will be done on the field. No live shots will be permitted from the clubhouses. No live transmissions inside the stadium by non-rightsholders will be permitted while the rightsholders are on the air or the game is in progress. Radio stations will be permitted to provide "scene setters" and score updates between innings but these reports may not continue once an inning is underway. Any violations of these policies will result in revocation of credentials.

ADMISSION TO SKYDOME: All media covering Blue Jays Baseball will enter the Skydome at Gate #9. All daily media credentials will be available at Gate #9, four hours prior to the game.

AUTOGRAPH REQUESTS: As noted earlier, no members of the media may use their access to solicit autographs or equipment from players or staff of either participating team. Any autograph needs should be directed to the Media Relations Department. Failure to do so will result in the revocation of credential privileges and forfeiture of any items obtained.

NOTES & STATISTICS: Game information is available in the press box two hours prior to first pitch. Play-by-play sheets, box scores and post-game notes will be distributed to your seat. As well, this information is available at www.bluejays.com.

MEDIA GUIDES: Are available upon request in the press box from club media relations representatives.

TELEPHONES: Seven charge-a-call phones are available for media use in the press box.

Miscellaneous

AC JOINT - Acromioclavicular joint; joint of the shoulder where acromion process of the scapula and the distal end of the clavicle meet; most shoulder separations occur at this point.

ANTERIOR - In front of; the front surface of.

ANTERIOR CRUCIATE LIGAMENT (ACL) - A primary stabilizing ligament within the center of the knee joint that prevents hyperextension and excessive rotation of the joint. A complete tear of the ACL necessitating reconstruction could require up to 12 months of rehabilitation.

ANTI-INFLAMMATORY - Any agent which prevents inflammation, such as aspirin or ibuprofen.

ARTHROGRAM - X-ray technique for joints using air and/or dye injected into the affected area; useful in diagnosing meniscus tears of the knee and rotator cuff tears of the shoulder.

ARTHROSCOPY - A surgical examination of the internal structures of a joint by means of viewing through an arthroscope. An arthroscopic procedure can be used to remove or repair damaged tissue or as a diagnostic procedure in order to inspect the extent of any damage or confirm a diagnosis.

BONE SCAN - An imaging procedure in which a radioactive-labeled substance is injected into the body to determine the status of a bone injury. If the radioactive substance is taken up by the bone at the injury site, the injury will show as a "hot spot" on the scan image. The bone scan is particularly useful in the diagnosis of stress fractures.

CARTILAGE - Smooth, slippery substance preventing two ends of bones from rubbing together.

CAT SCAN - Use of a computer to produce a cross-sectional view of the anatomical part being investigated from x-ray data.

CHARLEY HORSE - A contusion or bruise to any muscle resulting in intramuscular bleeding.

CONCUSSION - Jarring injury of the brain resulting in dysfunction. It can be graded as mild, moderate or severe depending on loss of consciousness, amnesia and loss of equilibrium.

CONTUSION - An injury to muscle and tissues cause by a blow from a blunt object.

DELTOID MUSCLE - Muscles at the top of the arm, just below the shoulder, responsible for shoulder motions to the front, side and back.

DISC - A flat, rounded plate between each vertebrae of the spine. The disc consists of a thick fibering which surrounds a soft gel-like interior. It functions as a cushion for the spinal column.

EPICONDYLITIS - Inflammation in the elbow due to overuse.

FEMUR - Thigh bone; largest bone in the body.

FIBULA - Smaller of the two bones in the lower leg; runs from the knee to the ankle along the outside of the lower leg.

FRACTURE - Breach in continuity of a bone. Types of fractures include simple, compound, comminuted, greenstick, incomplete, impacted, longitudinal, oblique, stress or transverse.

GLENOID - Cavity of the scapula into which the head of the humerus fits to form the shoulder girdle.

GRADE ONE INJURY - A mild injury in which ligament, tendon, or other musculoskeletal tissue may have been stretched or confused, but not torn or otherwise disrupted.

GRADE TWO INJURY - A moderate injury when musculoskeletal tissue has been partially, but not totally torn which causes appreciable limitation in function of the injured tissue.

GRADE THREE INJURY - A severe injury in which tissue has been significant, and in some cases totally, torn or otherwise disrupted causing a virtual total loss of function.

INFLAMMATION - The body's natural response to injury in which the injury site might display various degrees of pain, swelling, heat, redness and/or loss of function.

LABRUM (Labrum Glenoidule) - The cartilage of the glenoid cavity in the shoulder. A lip-edge or lip-like structure.

LATERAL - To the outside of the body.

LIGAMENT - Band of fibrous tissue that connects bone to bone, or bone to cartilage and supports and strengthens joints.

MAGNETIC RESONANCE IMAGING (MRI) - Imaging procedure in which a radio frequency pulse causes certain electrical elements of the injured tissue to react to this pulse and through this process a computer display and permanent film establish a visual image. MRI does not require radiation and is very useful in the diagnosis of soft tissue, disc, and meniscus injuries.

MEDIAL - To the inside of the body.

MEDIAL COLLATERAL LIGAMENT (MCL) - Ligament of knee along the medial aspect that connects the femur to the joint.

MENISCUS - Crescent shaped cartilage, usually pertaining to the knee joint; also known as "cartilage." There are two menisci in the knee, medial and lateral. These work to absorb weight within the knee and provide stability.

METACARPALS - Five long bones of the hand running from the wrist to the fingers.

METATARSALS - Five long bones of the foot, running from the ankle to the toes.

POSTERIOR - At the back part, or rear of the body.

POSTERIOR CRUCIATE LIGAMENT (PCL) - A primary stabilizing ligament of the knee that provides significant stability and prevents displacement of the tibia backward within the knee joint. A complete tear of this ligament necessitating reconstruction could require up to 12 months of rehabilitation.

QUADRICEP MUSCLES "QUADS" - A group of four muscles of the front thigh that run from the hip and form a common tendon at the patella; they are responsible for knee extension.

ROTATOR CUFF - Comprised of four muscles in the shoulder area that can be irritated by overuse. The muscles are the supraspinatus (most commonly injured), infraspinatus, teres minor and subscapularis.

ROTATOR CUFF IMPINGEMENT SYNDROME - A microtrauma or overuse injury caused by stress. The four stages are: 1) tendinitis with temporary thickening of the bursa and rotator cuff 2) fiber dissociation in the tendon with permanent thickening of the bursa and scar formation 3) a partial rotator cuff tear of less than 1 cm and 4) a complete tear of 1 cm or more.

SHIN SPLINT - A catch-all syndrome describing pain in the shin that is not a fracture or tumor, and cannot be defined otherwise.

SPRAIN - Injury resulting from the stretch or twist of the joint and causes various degrees of stretch or tear of a ligament or other soft tissue at the joint.

STRAIN - Injury resulting from a pull or torsion to the muscle or tendon that causes various degrees of stretch or tear to the muscle or tendon tissue.

STRESS FRACTURE - A hair-line type of break in a bone caused by overuse.

TENDINITIS - Inflammation of the tendon and/or tendon sheath, caused by chronic overuse or sudden injury.

TENDON - Tissue that connects muscle to bone.

TIBIA - Larger of the two bones of the lower leg and is the weight-bearing bone of the shin.

ULNAR NERVE - Nerve in the elbow commonly irritated from excessive throwing.

ULTRASOUND - An electrical modality that transmits a sound wave through an applicator into the skin to the soft tissue in order to heat the local area for relaxing the injured tissue and/or disperse edema.

NOTE: This list is not meant to be all inclusive, nor should it be used as a substitute for a physician's diagnosis and/or description of an injury or illness.

BROADCASTING

RADIO

THE TEAM — Canada's Sports Radio Network

A Division of CHUM Group Limited
1331 Yonge Street
Toronto, ON
M4T 1Y1

Main: (416) 926-8849   fax: (416) 926-2507
Contact: Gerald McGroarty, Program Director gmcg@theteamradio.com
        Janis Davidson Pressick, Media and Station Relations Manager — jdp@theteamradio.com
        Bruce Brenner, Engineer

'The Team' is Canada's first 24/7 all sports radio network with extensive coverage coast to coast, and stations in most of the major markets... has the radio broadcast rights for the TORONTO BLUE JAYS through the 2003 season... flagship station is 1050 AM in Toronto.

TOM CHEEK
PLAY-BY-PLAY ANNOUNCER

Returns for his twenty-fifth season as the BLUE JAYS' play-by-play man... Off-season functions include appearances and speaking engagements for the BLUE JAYS... 61 years old... Only person to see every BLUE JAYS game... Born in Pensacola, Florida... Attended the Cambridge School of Broadcasting in Boston... Began radio career in Plattsburg, New York and then moved to Burlington, Vermont where for nine years was corporate sales manager and sports director for a group of three radio stations in Burlington and Rutland... Play-by-play experience includes baseball, basketball, football and hockey for the University of Vermont... From 1974 to 1976 was the swing man on Montreal Expos radio broadcasts on television nights... Member of the broadcast team for ABC Sports at the 1980 Winter Olympics at Lake Placid and 1984 Olympics at Sarajevo... Has broadcast college basketball for Mutual Radio Network... Was instrumental in organizing the Burlington International Games (while living in Vermont in 1967)... Married and has three children... Wife Shirley, hails from Hemmingford, Quebec... Children Tom Jr., Lisa and Jeffrey... Resides in Oldsmar, Florida.

JERRY HOWARTH
PLAY-BY-PLAY ANNOUNCER

Back for his twentieth full-season as a member of the BLUE JAYS radio team... Worked a partial schedule of games in 1981 while still sports director and sports talk show host at KWMS radio in Salt Lake City prior to joining the sports department of CJCL radio in Toronto... Born in York, Pennsylvania and grew up in San Francisco... 55 years old... Graduated from University of Santa Clara in 1968... Served two years in the armed forces in West Germany... On return, attended Hastings Law School in San Francisco where he met his wife Mary... Started broadcasting career in 1974 with play-by-play of Tacoma Twins Triple A baseball and also for the University of Puget Sound's varsity baseball, basketball and football teams... Moved to Salt Lake City in 1976 and did play-by-play of Salt Lake City Gulls Triple A baseball for three years... Switched to basketball and was the Assistant General Manager of the Utah Pros of the Western Basketball Association and Group Sales Manager for Utah Jazz of the NBA prior to joining KWMS radio in 1980... Resides in Etobicoke with his wife Mary and two children Ben (24) and Joe (22).

GARY MATTHEWS
ANALYST

Returns for his second season as a broadcaster... Made his debut in 2000... Has also appeared on Headline Sports Television as a baseball analyst... The former major league all-star player spent 16 years in the majors with the San Francisco Giants (1972-1976), the Atlanta Braves (1977-1980), the Philadelphia Phillies (1981-1983), the Chicago Cubs (1984-1987) and the Seattle Mariners (1987)... After his playing career he worked in private industry and gained broadcasting experience before launching his coaching career... Was a minor league hitting instructor for the Chicago Cubs from 1995 to 1997... He joined the Toronto Blue Jays and served as their hitting coach for the 1998 and 1999 seasons... Son Gary, Jr. is a member of the Chicago Cubs organization and last year appeared in 80 games batting .190 with four homeruns and 14 RBI.

RADIO NETWORK

Flagship Station: The Team 1050 AM CHUM – Toronto

Affiliates: as of March 1, 2001

CITY	CALL LETTERS	FREQUENCY	CITY	CALL LETTERS	FREQUENCY
Vancouver, BC	The Team	1040	London, ON	CFPL	1290
Calgary, AB	The Team	660	Niagara Falls, ON	CJRN	710
Estevan, SK	CJSL	1280	Ottawa, ON	The Team	1200
Rosetown, SK	CJYM	1330	Owen Sound, ON	CFOS	560
Kindersley®, SK	CFYM	1210	Port Elgin®, ON	CFPS	1490
Weyburn, SK	CFSL	1190	Peterborough, ON	The Team	1420
Winnipeg, MB	The Team	1290	Sarnia, ON	CHOK	1070
Winkler, MB	CKMW	1570	Sault Ste. Marie, MI	WKNW	1400
Algoma/Manitoulin, ON	CKNR	94.1 FM	Stratford, ON	CJCS	1240
Hamilton, ON	CHML	900	Toronto, ON	The Team	1050
Huntsville, ON	CFBK	105.5 FM	Trenton, ON	CJTN	1270
Kingston, ON	The Team	1380	Halifax, NS	The Team	920
Kitchener, ON	Newstalk 570	570			

CBC

CBC-TV Sports and the Blue Jays have a three-year broadcast agreement (1999-2001) as the conventional broadcaster of Blue Jays games. The agreement will see the network broadcast 40 games a year during the course of the new three-year agreement. The CBC-TV Sports broadcasts of Blue Jays games will have the best weekend matchups - continuing its tradition of Friday, Saturday and Sunday coverage.

CBC-TV Sports relationship with the Blue Jays has been long and fruitful. The network was the original broadcaster of Jays games, beginning with their inaugural home opener at Toronto's Exhibition Stadium in 1977. CBC-TV Sports continued to televise Jays games until 1981, and carried the team's games again from 1993 to the present. The number of Blue Jays' games broadcast on CBC-TV Sports has increased throughout the years. From 1993-95 there were 25 games on the network; 1996 there were 35 games on CBC-TV Sports and in 1997 the network began broadcasting 40 games a season.

BRIAN WILLIAMS
Play-by-Play Announcer (CBC Network)

Will call all the action on CBC broadcasts of 2001 Blue Jays games... 1993 marked his first season as a regular Blue Jays broadcaster... Considered a sports commentator for all seasons, Brian has over 25 years of television experience... Brian broadcasted over 100 hours of live coverage during the 1988 Seoul Olympics and hosted the CBC Television Sports exclusive coverage of the 1992 Winter Olympics from Albertville, France and the 1998 Winter Olympics from Nagano, Japan... Also hosted CBC's coverage of the 1996 Atlanta Olympics and the 2000 Olympic Games from Sydney, Australia... As well, Brian has hosted an array of other major sporting events including: World Figure Skating Championships, The Canadian Open Golf Championship and Commonwealth Games... His broadcasting style has won numerous awards and praise from critics... He has twice won the Foster Hewitt Award for Excellence in sports broadcasting and is a five-time Gemini Award-winner for Best Perfomance by a Sports Broadcaster... He began his broadcasting career in Grand Rapids, Michigan, while attending Aquinas College where he was a Political Science graduate... In 1970, he returned to Canada and worked for four years in radio at CHUM and CFRB in Toronto... From there he moved to CBLT in 1974 as the anchor on the 6 PM news until 1983 when he moved to CBC Sports... The Winnipeg, Manitoba native resides in Toronto with his wife Geraldine and their three daughters.

JOHN CERUTTI
Colour Commentator (CBC Network)

2001 will be his fifth season as the Colour Commentator for CBC's telecast of Blue Jays games... The former major league pitcher pitched for the Toronto Blue Jays from 1985 through 1990 before finishing his career in 1991 with the Detroit Tigers... The Toronto Blue Jays selected the left-hand pitcher in the first round of the 1981 June Free Agent Draft... Appeared in 229 games with 116 starts and was 49-43 with four saves and a 3.94 ERA... The Albany, NY native was the winning pitcher in the Blue Jays first ever victory at SkyDome on June 7, 1989... The 40 year old currently resides in Oldsmar, FL with his wife Claudia and their three children.

CBC TELEVISION NETWORK

CBNT-TV	St. John's, NF	CKX-TV	Brandon, MB
CBHT-TV	Halifax, NS	CBWT-TV	Winnipeg, MB
CBCT-TV	Charlottetown, PEI	CBKT-TV	Regina, SK
CBIT-TV	Sydney, NS	CBKST-TV	Saskatoon, SK
CBAT-TV	Fredericton, NB	CBXT-TV	Edmonton, AB
CBMT-TV	Montreal, PQ	CBRT-TV	Calgary, AB
CBOT-TV	Ottawa, ON	CHAT-TV	Medicine Hat, AB
CBLT-TV	Toronto, ON	CKRD-TV	Red Deer, AB
CBET-TV	Windsor, ON	CKBI-TV	Prince Albert, SK
CKMI-TV	Quebec City, PQ	CJFB-TV	Swift Current, SK
CBLN-TV	London, ON	CKOS-TV	Yorkton, SK
CKWS-TV	Kingston, ON	CKSA-TV	Lloydminster, SK
CHEX-TV	Peterborough, ON	CBUT-TV	Vancouver, BC
CJIC-TV	Sault Ste. Marie, ON	CJDC-TV	Dawson Creek, BC
CKPR-TV	Thunder Bay, ON	CFJC-TV	Kamloops, BC
CKNC-TV	Sudbury, ON	CHBC-TV	Kelowna, BC
CBCL-TV	Timmins, ON	CKPG-TV	Prince George, BC
CHNB-TV	North Bay, ON	CFTK-TV	Terrace, BC

TSN

DAN SHULMAN
Play-by-Play Announcer (TSN)

2001 marks his seventh season as TSN's Play-by-Play man... The 34 year old Toronto native began his sportscasting career in 1986 while studying actuarial science at the University of Western Ontario... Broadcasted Mustang play by play for varsity basketball... Graduated from Western in 1989... Took radio job in Barrie, Ontario (CKBB) in 1990... Moved to CJCL (1430) in September 1991 working as a reporter/sportscaster... With "The Fan" from 1992-1995 beginning as a talk show host... Also hosted Jays Talk in 1992 & 1993... February 1993 moved to afternoon drive slot on "The Fan"... In 1994 worked the Winter Olympics in Lillehamer and the World Championships of Basketball for CTV... Broadcasts Major League baseball and NCAA basketball for ESPN, as well as MLB playoffs for ESPN radio... Came on board with TSN in February 1995... He and his wife Sarah reside in Thornhill with their sons Matthew, Alex and Ben.

PAT TABLER
Colour Commentator (TSN)

Replaces Blue Jays Manager and former analyst Buck Martinez in the 2001 season... Began with The Sports Network in 1993 as a studio analyst on TSN's half-hour pregame show, "Baseball Tonight"... Has also filled in occasionally as a colour commentator on TSN's live Blue Jays broadcasts... Was the New York Yankees first round pick in the 1976 free agent draft... Began his Major League career in 1981 with the Chicago Cubs and went on to play 12 seasons including stops with Cleveland (1983-87), Kansas City (1988-89), New York Mets (1990) and finally with Toronto (1991-92)... The former first baseman/designated hitter was a career .282 hitter with 47 home runs and 512 RBI... With the Blue Jays in two seasons, including the 1992 World Championship team, he batted .231 with one home run and 37 RBI in 131 games... Is known as one of baseball's greatest career clutch hitters, batting nearly .500 in bases loaded situations... The 43 year-old lives with his wife Susan in Cincinnati, Ohio and has three children, Tyler (20), Kathryn (16) and Troy (12).

CTV SPORTSNET

CTV Sportsnet, Canada's first 24-hour regional sports service, launched October 9, 1998 and the Toronto Blue Jays have a multi-year agreement to broadcast up to 42 games, starting in 1999. CTV Sportsnet will cater to viewers needs in four regions: East (Quebec and Atlantic Provinces), Ontario, West (Manitoba, Saskatchewan, Alberta and Northwest Territories), Pacific (British Columbia and Yukon Territories).

ROB FAULDS
Play-by-Play Announcer (Sportsnet)

The 2001 season will be the first full season for Rob as the play-by-play broadcaster for Spornet's Blue Jays telecasts... Over the last two seasons has worked on Blue Jays broadcasts on a fill-in basis... Serves as the play-by-play broadcaster for Ottawa Senators telecasts and is the host of Ford Raptors Basketball... Joined CTV in 1995 and has worked a variety of events including NHL, MLB, NBA, CFL, figure skating, two Olympic games, Junior Hockey, tennis, golf, track & field, curling and swimming... Began broadcasting while at Western University and then moved on to CFPL in London, Ontario in 1975... He then made stops in Sudbury, Winnipeg and Montreal before joining CTV... He has also worked as a radio broadcaster on Montreal Expos games in 1987 & 1988... The 45-year-old native of Hamilton, Ontario now resides in Toronto with his wife, Andrea and their son Ethan.

GAME DELAYS AT SKYDOME			
DATE	**TEAM**	**REASON**	**DURATION**
June 7, 1989	Milwaukee	Rain	6 minutes
August 27, 1990	Milwaukee	Bugs	35 minutes
August 10, 1991	Boston	Rain	14 minutes
July 21, 1994	Texas	Rain	7 minutes

SkyDome became the new home of the Toronto Blue Jays on Monday, June 5, 1989. The retractable roof stadium is the world's most advanced and luxurious ballpark. The stadium employs leading edge technology in both design and function. From the artificial turf to the 161 private SkyBoxes, the finest attention to detail was given.

At conception, SkyDome took an innovative approach to financing, construction and design. Until 1994, SkyDome had been owned by The Stadium Corporation of Ontario, a consortium comprised of both public and private funds. The Province of Ontario and the Municipality of Toronto each contributed 30 million dollars. Joining these two levels of government were 30 Canadian corporations including the Toronto Blue Jays Baseball Club. Each private company contributed 5 million dollars in exchange for preferred supplier status and a SkyBox. The final construction cost of SkyDome exceeded 500 million dollars.

Architects Rod Robbie and Michael Allen designed SkyDome and have patented its retractable roof system. Preparation of the site began in April 1986, with groundbreaking taking place in October of that same year. The last exterior concrete was poured in November of 1988 and the first test

of the moveable roof panels took place in January 1989. More than 10,000 person-years of employment were created by the construction of SkyDome.

The venue is located just to the south and west of the CN Tower, between John Street and Blue Jays Way. A five minute walk from Union Station, it is easily accessible by the TTC or Go Transit. Several public parking lots are within a ten minute walk of the stadium.

SkyDome is home to the Toronto Blue Jays Baseball Club and Toronto Argonauts Football Club as well as playing host to hundreds of other events during the year such as concerts, trade shows and charity functions. Also located in the building is the Renaissance Toronto Hotel at SkyDome, a 348-room hotel with 70 rooms overlooking the field. SkyDome houses several corporate offices for various companies including the Toronto Blue Jays.

One of the unique features of SkyDome is that it can be "transformed" from one mode (ie. baseball) to another mode (ie. football or concerts) within hours. The 100 level seating areas are situated on railway tracks that allow the seats to move for conversion purposes.

SKYDOME FACTS

ROOF
- SkyDome's roof system features a series of 3 moveable panels and 1 stationary panel. Panels 2 and 3 slide on parallel rails while panel 1 slides on a circluar rail "tucking" underneath 2 and 3
- the roof operates on a system of steel tracks and 54 drive mechanisms called "bogies" and is powered by a series of DC motors that generate over 750 horsepower
- roof area is 339,343 square feet or 31,525 square metres
- weight is 11,000 tons

- span at widest point- 674 feet or 209 metres
- height is 282 feet or 86 metres (from field level to highest point)
- covering is single PVC membrane on insulated acoustic steel deck
- 100% of the field and 91% of the seating area is exposed with the roof open
- open/close time- 20 minutes (71 feet or 21 metres per minute)

JUMBOTRON VIDEO DISPLAY BOARD
- largest video display board in North America, second largest in the world (Japan)
- the board was built by the Sony Corporation
- 67,200 Trinilights make up the viewing area

- dimensions are 33 feet high (10.0 metres) by 110 feet wide (33.6 metres)
- cost was $17,000,000

SEATING
- five levels: Esplanade, Club, luxury skyboxes on 2 levels, SkyDeck
- 50,516 for baseball
- 53,000 for football
- 55,00 for concerts

- 67,000 for other events
- SkyTent mode seats 10,000 to 30,000
- 41,000 seats are located between the foul lines
- Skyboxes range in price from $150,000 to 225,000 per year

HOTEL
- 348 distinctively decorated rooms

- 70 rooms overlook the playing field

FOOD SERVICES
- concessionaire- Ontario Sportservice, Inc.
- four counter service restaurants
- 19 locations
- 52 beverage stations
- five vending kitchens
- fine dining- SkyDome Food Services

- Windows on SkyDome is a 520 seat restaurant
- Sightlines- a 300 foot bar with all seats facing the playing field
- Hard Rock Cafe
- Bistro Club

SKYDOME PROVIDES BLUE JAYS WITH NEW TURF

The Toronto Blue Jays began playing on a brand new artificial surface (AstroTurf) beginning in 1997. Toronto's SkyDome provided the Blue Jays with a surface to be used for baseball only. The SkyDome now uses a dual turf system for baseball and football with football using the old turf.

The old system required painting football lines on the turf as well as cleaning up the base in-field areas and tobacco stains on the old turf in preparation for football games.

The new turf, AstroTurf stadium surface, was manufactured by Southwest Recreational Industries, Inc (formerly AstroTurf) based in Leander, Texas. The lifespan will now be increased to 14 years because it will only be used for one sport.

The product is the same as the previous turf with the following differences:
- the new underpad will be non-perforated and the fastening system is now velcro (instead of the zipper fasteners on the old turf);
- the velcro is easier to install, faster to install, requires lower maintenance and since the seam is tighter between the turf it will be safer for the players;
- the colour of the turf will be a slightly darker green in order to give it a more consistent look with natural grass and to add more colour contrast for television.

The total price including taxes and duties was $2,000,000 (CDN).

FIELD

- artificial turf system- Astro-Turf 8 (1 1/4 inches in thickness)
- dimensions for baseball are symmetrical, 328 down the foul lines, 375 to power alleys and 400 to dead centre
- diamond is centred two degrees off perfect north
- outfield wall is 10 feet high and padded

- bullpens are located just beyond the left and right field fences
- pitcher's mound is constructed on a fiberglass dish and can be lowered or raised by hydraulic system
- conversion takes approximately 10-12 hours to convert from baseball to football
- over 8 miles of zippers connect the strips of artificial turf

BLUE JAYS AT SKYDOME

	AT SKYDOME W-L	OPEN W-L	CLOSED W-L	CLOSED DURING GAME W-L
1989	34-20	22-20	10-0	2-0
1989 ALCS	1-2	–	1-2	–
1990	44-37	13-18	28-17	3-2
1991	46-35	26-22	19-10	1-3
1991 ALCS	0-3	–	0-3	–
1992	53-28	19-11	31-16	3-1
1992 ALCS	2-1	–	2-1	–
1992 WS	2-1	–	2-1	–
1993	48-33	15-14	30-17	3-2
1993 ALCS	1-2	–	1-2	–
1993 WS	2-1	–	2-1	–
1994	33-26	11-12	16-11	6-3
1995	29-43	17-26	12-16	0-1
1996	35-46	18-25	14-16	3-5
1997	42-39	20-20	18-16	4-3
1998	51-30	33-12	16-13	2-5
1999	40-41	17-34	19-5	4-2
2000	45-36	26-12	16-21	3-3
OVERALL	**508-424**	**237-226**	**237-168**	**34-30**

SKYDOME FIRSTS

GAME — Monday June 5, 1989 (Blue Jays-3, Milwaukee Brewers-5)
ATTENDANCE — 48,378
TIME/TEMP — 2:43/18°C
PITCHER — Jimmy Key, Toronto
BATTER — Paul Molitor, Milwaukee (doubled)
PLATE UMPIRE — Rocky Roe
PITCH — Fastball, called strike
HIT — Double by Molitor in 1st inning
RUN — Molitor in 1st inning
SINGLE — Kelly Gruber, Toronto, 1st inning

DOUBLE — Paul Molitor, 1st inning
HOME RUN — Fred McGriff, Toronto, 2nd inning
RBI — Gary Sheffield, Milwaukee, 1st inning
WINNING PITCHER — Don August, Milwaukee
LOSING PITCHER — Jimmy Key, Toronto
SAVE — Dan Plesac, Milwaukee
PUTOUT — Nelson Liriano, Toronto
ASSIST — Kelly Gruber, Toronto
STOLEN BASE — Fred McGriff, 6th inning
WALK — George Bell, Toronto, 2nd inning

FIRST GAME PLAYED AT EXHIBITION STADIUM

The Blue Jays slugged their way to a 9-5 triumph over the Chicago White Sox in their April 7, 1977, debut.

Despite snow flurries before the game and near-freezing temperatures, 44,649 fans witnessed the exciting contest, which featured 16 hits by the Blue Jays and 15 by Chicago.

Doug Ault smacked two homers and a single and rookie Al Woods hit a pinch-homer in his first big-league at bat for Toronto. Richie Zisk had four hits for the visitors.

The Blue Jays played 968-games from April 7, 1977-May 28, 1989 at Exhibition Stadium posting a record of 491-475 with 23,213,557 fans passing through the turnstiles.

TORONTO GROUND RULES—SKYDOME

1. Ball hitting any portion of fence or screen in back of home plate—in play.
2. Ball going into camera booth behind home plate: thrown by pitcher from rubber—one base; any other thrown ball—two bases.
3. Ball hitting padding and bouncing over fence—two bases.
4. A fairly batted or thrown ball lodged in the padding—two bases.
5. A fairly batted or thrown ball that goes into the dugout or strikes equipment on the dugout steps is considered in the dugout.
6. Ball hitting padding on outfield fence to foul or seating side of foul line—dead ball.

EXHIBITION STADIUM FIRSTS

GAME — Thurs. April 7, 1977 (Blue Jays 9, Chicago White Sox 5)
ATTENDANCE — 44,649
TIME/TEMP. — 3:22/0°C. (32°F)
PITCHER — Bill Singer, Toronto
BATTER — Ralph Garr, Chicago (walked)
PLATE UMPIRE — Nestor Chylak
PITCH — Called strike
HIT — Home run by Richie Zisk, first inning, none on
RUN — Ralph Garr (scored on sacrifice fly by Jorge Orta)
SINGLE — Jim Spencer, Chicago, April 7, 1977, first inning
DOUBLE — Richie Zisk, Chicago, April 7, 1977, second inning
TRIPLE — Ron LeFlore, Detroit, April 12, 1977, fifth inning
HOME RUN — Richie Zisk, April 7, 1977, first inning
FIRST RBI — Jorge Orta, Chicago, April 7, 1977, 1st inning
INSIDE-THE-PARK HOME RUN — Cecil Cooper, Milwaukee, May 5, 1977 (fifth inning)
GRAND SLAM HOME RUN — Hector Torres vs. New York, June 27, 1977 (ninth inning), off Ron Guidry)
TWO HOME-RUN GAME — Doug Ault, Toronto, April 7, 1977
THREE HOME-RUN GAME — John Mayberry, K.C., June 1, 1977
PINCH-HIT HOME RUN — Al Woods, Toronto, April 7, 1977 (fifth inning)
WINNING PITCHER — Jerry Johnson, Toronto (in relief), April 7, 1977

LOSING PITCHER — Ken Brett, Chicago (starter), April 7, 1977
SAVE — Pete Vuckovich, Toronto, April 7, 1977
PUTOUT — Steve Bowling, Toronto (fly ball to right field) April 7, 1977
ASSIST — Hector Torres, Toronto (ground ball to shortstop) April 7, 1977
ERROR — Rick Cerone, Toronto, April 7, 1977
SHUTOUT — Ferguson Jenkins, Boston, Sun. April 24, 1977 (9-0)
COMPLETE GAME — Dave Lemanczyk, Toronto vs. Chicago, April 9, 1977
WALK — Ralph Garr by Bill Singer, April 7, 1977 (first inning)
STRIKEOUT — John Scott by Ken Brett, April 7, 1977 (first inning)
FORFEIT — Baltimore, Thurs. September 15, 1977 (Blue Jays 9, Baltimore 0)
NIGHT GAME — Mon., May 2, 1977 vs. Milwaukee (Brewers 3, Blue Jays 1)
STOLEN BASE — Ralph Garr, Chicago, April 7, 1977 (first inning)
TRIPLE PLAY — Clancy to Mayberry to Gomez, April 22, 1978 (sixth inning)
BALK — Balor Moore, Toronto vs. Seattle, May 13, 1978
ONE-HITTER — Chris Knapp, California, September 3, 1978 (Angels 3, Blue Jays 1)
NO-HITTER — Never happened

EXHIBITION STADIUM LASTS

GAME — May 28, 1989 (Blue Jays 7, Chicago White Sox 5), 10 innings
ATTENDANCE — 46,120
TIME/TEMP. — 3:19/20°C. (68°F)
PITCHER — Bobby Thigpen, Chicago
BATTER — George Bell, Toronto, home run
PLATE UMPIRE — Dan Morrison
PITCH — fastball, home run
HIT — Home Run by George Bell, 10th inning
RUN — George Bell on home run

SINGLE — Steve Lyons, Chicago, 10th inning
DOUBLE — Kelly Gruber, Toronto 10th inning
HOME RUN — George Bell, 10th inning
RBI — George Bell, 10th inning
WINNING PITCHER — Tom Henke
LOSING PITCHER — Bobby Thigpen
PUTOUT — Fred McGriff, Toronto, 10th inning
ASSIST — Nelson Liriano, Toronto, 10th inning
ERROR — Matt Merullo, Chicago, 4th inning
STOLEN BASE — Steve Lyons, Chicago, 10th inning

SKYDOME FACTS AND FIGURES
SEATING CAPACITY FOR BASEBALL & SINGLE GAME PRICE

Seating	2001	Capacity	% of Capacity
Private Box Infield	$47.60	1,200	2.66%
Private Box Bases	$43.60	800	1.77%
Private Box Baselines	$41.25	400	0.89%
Club Level Infield	$44.00	2,700	5.99%
Club Level Baselines	$41.00	3,100	6.87%
Premium Dugout	$44.00	1,600	3.55%
Field Level Infield	$41.00	5,500	12.20%
Field Level Bases	$35.00	7,200	15.96%
Field Level Baselines	$29.00	2,900	6.43%
200 Level Outfield	$23.00	3,200	7.10%
100 Level Outfield	$23.00	3,300	7.32%
SkyDeck Infield	$23.00	4,700	10.42%
SkyDeck Bases	$16.00	2,600	5.76%
SkyDeck Baselines	$7.00	4,400	9.76%
Restaurants & Hotels	$3.00	1,500	3.33%
		45,100	**100.00%**

Distances From Homeplate	Feet	Metres
Leftfield	328	100
Left-Centerfield	375	114
Centerfield	400	122
Right-Centerfield	375	114
Rightfield	328	100

Height of Outfield Fence is 10 feet or 3 metres high.

BLUE JAYS SPRING TRAINING DIRECTORY

SITE

MINOR LEAGUE COMPLEX
Cecil P. Englebert Recreational Complex
1700 Solon Avenue
Dunedin, Florida 34698

DUNEDIN STADIUM
at GRANT FIELD
373 Douglas Avenue
Dunedin, Florida 34697

All home games will be played at Dunedin Stadium

MINOR LEAGUE DATES:
March 3 - Players Report

MAILING ADDRESS:
TORONTO BLUE JAYS
P.O. Box 957
Dunedin, Florida 34697

HOTEL HEADQUARTERS:
MINOR LEAGUE
RED ROOF INN
3200 U.S. 19 North
Clearwater, Florida 34684

TELEPHONES:
```
RED ROOF INN ....................................................... (727) 786-2529
DUNEDIN STADIUM OFFICE .......................................... (727) 733-9302
DUNEDIN STADIUM TICKETS ............... (727) 733-0429 or 1-800-707-8269
MEDIA RELATIONS OFFICE ........................... until Mar. 1 (727) 733-3339 ex. 35
                                                from Mar. 1 (727) 733-9302 ex. 5885
ENGLEBERT COMPLEX ................................................ (727) 733-3339
FAX-DUNEDIN STADIUM ............................ until Mar. 1 (727) 738-0349
                                                from Mar. 1 (727) 738-9829
PRESS BOX ................................................... (727) 733-9302 ex. 2584
```

TICKET DATA:
```
Ticket Office at DUNEDIN STADIUM, 373 Douglas Avenue, Dunedin ......... (727) 733-0429
Monday to Saturday: 10:00 a.m. to 5:00 p.m. for Phone Orders ........... (727) 733-0429
                                                                      1-800-707-8269
```

TICKET PRICES: Reserved $15.00, $14.00, $12.50 & $9.00 U.S. Funds

DUNEDIN STADIUM

Located at the corner of Douglas Avenue and Beltrees Street in Dunedin, Dunedin Stadium is the spring training home of the Toronto Blue Jays.

DIMENSIONS:
Left-field line	335 ft/102.1 m
Left-centre	380 ft/115.8 m
Centre field	400 ft/121.9 m
Right-centre	365 ft/111.3 m
Right field line	315 ft/ 96.0 m

Fence-12 feet high, chain link with screen cover (3.66 m high).
Warning track-12 feet/3.66 m.
Distance from baselines to out-of-play-60 feet at all points (18.29 m).
Batter's eye screen-40 feet by 60 feet/12.2 m by 18.3 m.
Capacity-6,106.

The largest spring exhibition crowd at Dunedin Stadium was 6,218 on Tuesday, March 27, 1990 for the game between the Blue Jays and Kansas City Royals and Wednesday, March 13, 1985 for a game with the New York Mets.

The first Blue Jays game ever played was on March 11, 1977 at Grant Field. The Blue Jays defeated the New York Mets 3-1.

The Blue Jays play their spring exhibition games at the newly expanded and modernized DUNEDIN STADIUM at GRANT FIELD.

From 1977 to 1989 the Blue Jays played at Grant Field with a seating capacity of 3,417.

The City of Dunedin, at a cost of approximately $2.4 million provided a new stadium in 1990 to be called Dunedin Stadium at the same location as Grant Field, at the corner of Douglas Avenue and Beltrees Street.

The stadium was designed by the architect firm of JOHNSTON DANA ASSOCIATES and was built by CASE CONTRACTING Company of Plant City, Florida.

The old structure came down in the first weeks of September 1989.

Some of the features of the current Dunedin Stadium:
- a symmetrical 'U'-shaped structure with four entrance ramps
- total capacity is 6,106
- seats are arm chairs (4480) with top eight rows under cover
- bleacher seats (1698) are located along first base/left field lines
- grade level area for wheelchairs (20 plus 20 for attendants)
- upgrade in lighting standards adequate for AA and AAA
- two new concession stands
- new public restroom facilities
- first-aid room
- security office
- ticket windows
- TV/photographer pits
- press box provides two radio booths, one television booth plus seating for 25 members of print and electronic media
- media workroom and lounge for hospitality
- umpires room
- padded outfield walls
- extended foul poles

The actual playing field remained the same as did Blue Jays and visitors clubhouses.

As well as the Toronto Blue Jays, the Dunedin Blue Jays of the Class A Florida State League play at Dunedin Stadium.

In the spring of 2002 the Blue Jays will see major renovations to Dunedin Stadium. This will include the removal of the current bleacher seats and the addition of 1,000 permanent seats to make the capacity 5,500. As well, a new two-story building will be constructed and will house a new clubhouse, training room and weight room on the ground floor with office space for the major league club on the second floor. A new minor league facility will also be constructed. The site for this facility is the current Van Ech Complex, which is located just north of the current minor league facility, the Englebert Complex. The new facility will feature new clubhouses, offices, weight rooms, five full fields and a half field. Four of the fields will be arranged in a cloverleaf formation with an observation tower in the center.

Spring Training

• **457**

Spring Training Record

1997-2000 OPPONENT	HOME			ROAD			OVERALL		
	W	L	T	W	L	T	W	L	T
BALTIMORE	7	7	0	3	5	0	10	12	0
BOSTON	8	6	0	5	13	0	13	19	0
CHICAGO (AL)	11	15	0	13	12	2	24	27	2
CLEVELAND	4	3	1	2	4	1	6	7	2
DETROIT	10	6	0	9	8	1	19	14	1
KANSAS CITY	10	6	0	10	8	0	20	14	0
MILWAUKEE	3	2	0	0	3	0	3	5	0
MINNESOTA	14	8	0	8	12	0	22	20	0
NEW YORK (AL)	7	8	0	6	12	0	13	20	0
SEATTLE	0	1	0	0	2	0	0	3	0
TAMPA BAY	3	1	0	1	1	0	4	2	0
TEXAS	9	9	0	6	12	1	15	21	1
ATLANTA	1	4	0	3	0	0	4	4	0
CINCINNATI	9	9	0	4	11	1	13	20	1
FLORIDA	0	0	0	0	1	0	0	1	0
HOUSTON	5	1	0	1	5	0	6	6	0
LOS ANGELES	2	3	0	0	2	0	2	5	0
MONTREAL	8	3	0	4	7	0	12	10	0
NEW YORK (NL)	9	8	0	6	6	0	15	14	0
PHILADELPHIA	24	20	2	22	29	1	46	49	3
PITTSBURGH	16	14	0	7	13	3	23	27	3
SANDIEGO	0	0	0	0	1	0	0	1	0
ST. LOUIS	20	11	1	13	16	1	33	27	2
vs NL	94	73	3	60	91	6	154	164	9
vs AL	86	72	1	63	92	5	149	164	6
TOTALS	180	145	4	123	183	11	303	328	15

Year-by-Year Breakdown

YEAR	OVERALL			HOME			ROAD			OTHER VENUES*			PCT
	W	L	T	W	L	T	W	L	T	W	L	T	
1977	8	16	0	5	8	0	3	8	0	0	0	0	.333
1978	8	17	0	3	8	0	5	9	0	0	0	0	.320
1979	12	12	0	6	6	0	6	6	0	0	0	0	.500
1980	10	7	0	5	4	0	5	3	0	0	0	0	.588
1981	13	13	1	7	6	0	6	7	1	0	0	0	.500
1982	15	12	1	7	7	0	8	5	1	0	0	0	.555
1983	16	10	0	9	4	0	7	6	0	1	1	0	.615
1984	13	16	0	8	6	0	5	10	0	2	2	0	.448
1985	19	9	1	11	4	0	8	5	1	1	2	0	.679
1986	15	12	0	10	3	0	5	9	0	0	0	0	.555
1987	9	11	2	5	5	1	4	6	1	0	0	1	.450
1988	18	10	2	9	5	0	9	5	2	1	1	0	.643
1989	21	10	0	12	4	0	9	6	0	0	0	0	.677
1990	4	10	0	1	5	0	3	5	0	0	0	0	.286
1991	9	19	2	6	10	0	3	9	2	1	2	0	.321
1992	13	18	0	12	4	0	1	14	0	1	3	0	.419
1993	11	19	0	8	8	0	3	11	0	2	2	0	.367
1994	12	18	1	7	10	0	5	8	1	0	4	0	.400
1995	5	5	2	4	2	1	1	3	1	0	1	0	.500
1996	9	22	1	6	8	1	3	14	0	0	3	0	.290
1997	17	14	1	12	4	0	5	10	1	0	0	0	.548
1998	16	16	0	7	10	0	9	6	0	2	0	0	.500
1999	12	20	0	8	9	0	4	11	0	0	0	0	.375
2000	18	12	1	12	5	1	6	7	0	2	2	1	.600
TOTAL	303	328	15	180	145	4	123	183	11	13	23	2	.480

* Other venues are included in home and road.

Spring Training Attendance

YEAR	HOME	ROAD	OTHER	TOTAL	YEAR	HOME	ROAD	OTHER	TOTAL
1977	21,728	22,093	—	43,821	1989	54,270	77,284	—	131,554
1978	20,009	36,334	—	56,343	1990	21,410	27,695	—	49,105
1979	21,420	26,496	—	47,916	1991	80,461	96,300	70,471	247,232
1980	15,377	18,499	—	33,876	1992	84,356	102,651	103,952	290,959
1981	24,180	33,391	—	57,571	1993	73,195	89,701	172,919	335,815
1982	26,442	37,237	—	63,679	1994	80,310	83,782	141,465	305,557
1983	27,662	31,590	28,871	88,123	1995	17,059	17,775	22,533	57,367
1984	32,869	53,900	110,990	197,759	1996	54,158	83,311	18,232	155,701
1985	39,022	45,268	67,007	151,297	1997	61,827	89,998	—	151,825
1986	43,263	62,936	—	106,199	1998	48,313	78,940	31,523	158,776
1987	35,101	38,383	16,620	90,104	1999	54,485	79,371	—	133,856
1988	42,673	73,234	39,570	155,477	2000	48,450	77,416	35,198	161,064
					TOTALS	1,028,040	1,383,585	859,351	3,270,976

2001 SPRING TRAINING SCHEDULE

DATE	LOCATION	VERSUS	TIME	R/TV
Thursday, March 1st	DUNEDIN	New York Yankees	1:05 p.m.	R
Friday, March 2nd	Tampa	New York Yankees	1:15 p.m.	
Saturday, March 3rd	DUNEDIN	Philadelphia Phillies	1:05 p.m.	R
Sunday, March 4th	Winter Haven	Cleveland Indians	1:05 p.m.	R
Monday, March 5th	Lakeland	Detroit Tigers	1:05 p.m.	
Tuesday, March 6th	DUNEDIN	Tampa Bay Devil Rays	1:05 p.m.	
Wednesday, March 7th	Ft. Myers	Minnesota Twins	7:05 p.m.	
Thursday, March 8th	Port Charlotte	Texas Rangers	1:05 p.m.	
Friday, March 9th	DUNEDIN	Philadelphia Phillies	7:05 p.m.	
Saturday, March 10th	DUNEDIN	Boston Red Sox	1:05 p.m.	R/TSN
Sunday, March 11th	Bradenton (ss)	Pittsburgh Pirates	1:05 p.m.	
	DUNEDIN (ss)	New York Yankees	1:05 p.m.	R
Monday, March 12th	Clearwater	Philadelphia Phillies	1:05 p.m.	
Tuesday, March 13th	DUNEDIN	Cincinnati Reds	1:05 p.m.	
Wednesday, March 14th	DUNEDIN	Cleveland Indians(SS)	1:05 p.m.	
Thursday, March 15th	Tampa	New York Yankees	7:15 p.m.	
Friday, March 16th	DUNEDIN	Texas Rangers	1:05 p.m.	
Saturday, March 17th	DUNEDIN	New York Yankees	1:05 p.m.	R/TSN
Sunday, March 18th	Lakeland	Detroit Tigers	1:05 p.m.	R/TSN
Monday, March 19th	OFF DAY			
Tuesday, March 20th	Baseball City	Kansas City Royals	1:05 p.m.	
Wednesday, March 21st	DUNEDIN	Houston Astros	1:05 p.m.	
Thursday, March 22nd	Sarasota (ss)	Cincinnati Reds	1:05 p.m.	
	Tampa (ss)	New York Yankees	7:15 p.m.	TSN
Friday, March 23rd	DUNEDIN	Minnesota Twins	1:05 p.m.	
Saturday, March 24th	St. Petersburg	Tampa Bay Devil Rays	1:05 p.m.	R
Sunday, March 25th	DUNEDIN	Detroit Tigers	1:05 p.m.	R
Monday, March 26th	Kissimmee	Houston Astros	1:05 p.m.	
Tuesday, March 27th	Clearwater	Philadelphia Phillies	7:05 p.m.	
Wednesday, March 28th	DUNEDIN	Pittsburgh Pirates	1:05 p.m.	
Thursday, March 29th	DUNEDIN	Tampa Bay Devil Rays	1:05 p.m.	
Friday, March 30th	Work out			
Saturday, March 31st	San Juan, Puerto Rico	Texas Rangers	7:05 p.m.	R

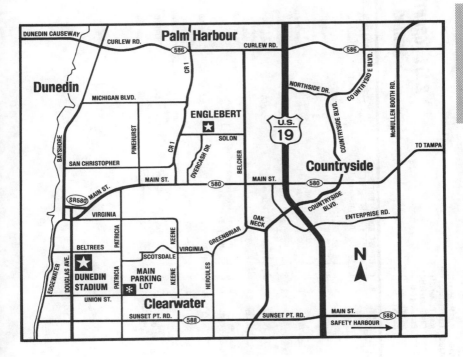

MANAGER: Buck Martinez (13)
COACHES: Terry Bevington (35)
Mark Connor (53)
Cito Gaston (41)
Garth Iorg (16)
Gil Patterson (47)
Cookie Rojas (1)

TRAINERS: Scott Shannon, George Poulis
STRENGTH AND CONDITIONING COORDINATOR: Jeff Krushell
TEAM PHYSICIANS: Dr. Ron Taylor, Dr. Allan Gross
EQUIPMENT MANAGER: Jeff Ross
MANAGER, TEAM TRAVEL: Bart Given
VICE-PRESIDENT, MEDIA RELATIONS: Howard Starkman

2001 TORONTO BLUE JAYS
SPRING ROSTER

NO.	PITCHERS (18)	B	T	HT.	WT.	BORN	BIRTHPLACE	RESIDENCE	2000 CLUB	W-L	ERA	G	GS	CG	SV	IP	H	R	ER	BB	SO	ML SER
51	BORBON, Pedro	L	L	6-1	224	11-15-67	Mao, DR	Houston, TX	TORONTO (AL)	1-1	6.48	59		0	0	41.2	45	37	30	38	29	6.045
40	BEIRNE, Kevin	L	R	6-4	210	01-01-74	Houston, TX	The Woodlands, TX	Charlotte (Int)	1-2	3.51	7	7	0	0	33.1	39	13	13	28	28	
									CHICAGO (AL)	1-3	6.70	29	1	0	0	49.2	50	41	37	20	41	0.135
26	CARPENTER, Chris	R	R	6-6	225	04-27-75	Exeter, NH	Bedford, NH	TORONTO (AL)	10-12	6.26	34	27	2	0	175.1	204	130	122	83	113	3.080
38	COCO, Pasqual	R	R	6-1	185	09-08-77	Santo Domingo, DR	Santo Domingo, DR	Tennessee (Sou)	12-7	3.76	27	26	2	0	167.2	154	83	70	68	142	
									TORONTO (AL)	0-0	9.00	1	1	0	0	4.0	5	4	4	5	2	0.002
45	ESCOBAR, Kelvim	R	R	6-1	220	04-11-76	La Guaira, VZ	Caracas, VZ	TORONTO (AL)	10-15	5.35	43	24	3	2	180.0	186	118	107	85	142	3.040
29	EYRE, Scott	L	L	6-1	200	05-30-72	Inglewood, CA	Bradenton, FL	Charlotte (Int)	3-2	3.00	13	0	0	12	48.0	33	18	16	20	46	
									CHICAGO (AL)	1-1	6.63	36	1	0	20	19.0	29	15	14	13	16	2.046
36	FILE, Bob	R	R	6-4	210	01-28-77	Philadelphia, PA	Philadelphia, PA	Syracuse (Int)	4-3	3.12	20	0	0	8	34.2	29	20	12	13	40	
32	HALLADAY, Roy	R	R	6-6	230	05-14-77	Denver, CO	Arvada, CO	Syracuse (Int)	2-3	5.50	11	11	0	0	73.2	85	46	45	21	38	
									TORONTO (AL)	4-7	10.64	19	13	3	0	67.2	107	87	80	42	44	1.127
50	HAMILTON, Joey	R	R	6-4	240	09-09-70	Statesboro, GA	Norcross, GA	Syracuse (Int)	3-2	3.66	6	6	1	0	39.1	41	18	16	12	17	
									TORONTO (AL)	2-1	3.55	6	6	0	0	33.0	28	13	13	12	15	6.132
44	KOCH, Billy	R	R	6-3	215	12-14-74	Rockville Center, NY	Clearwater, FL	TORONTO (AL)	9-3	2.63	68	0	0	33	78.2	78	28	23	18	60	1.152
21	LOAIZA, Esteban	R	R	6-3	215	12-31-71	Tijuana, MX	South Lake, TX	TEXAS (AL)	5-6	5.37	20	17	1	1	107.1	133	67	64	31	75	
									TORONTO (AL)	5-7	3.62	14	14	0	0	92.0	95	45	37	26	62	5.052
28	PAINTER, Lance	L	L	6-1	200	07-21-67	Bedford, England	Gilbert, AZ	Dunedin (FSL)	0-0	0.00	1	1	0	0	1.0	0	0	0	0	0	
									TORONTO (AL)	2-0	4.73	2	1	0	0	66.2	69	37	35	22	53	6.150
39	PARRIS, Steve	R	R	6-0	195	12-17-67	Joliet, IL	Plainfield, IL	CINCINNATI (NL)	12-17	4.81	33	33	0	0	192.2	227	109	103	71	117	4.016
54	PEREZ, George	L	R	6-4	220	03-20-79	San Pedro de Macoris, DR	San Pedro de Macoris, DR	Queens (NYP)	5-1	0.78	29	0	0	12	34.2	21	3	3	15	35	
19	PLESAC, Dan	L	L	6-5	217	02-04-62	Gary, IN	Valparaiso, IN	ARIZONA (NL)	5-1	3.15	62	0	0	0	40.0	34	14	14	26	47	15.000
48	QUANTRILL, Paul	R	R	6-1	195	11-03-68	London, ON	Tarpon Springs, FL	TORONTO (AL)	2-5	4.52	68	0	0	1	83.2	100	45	42	25	47	8.018
33	SIROTKA, Mike	L	L	6-1	200	05-13-71	Chicago, IL	Heathrow, FL	CHICAGO (AL)	15-10	3.79	32	32	1	0	197.0	203	101	83	69	128	3.131
49	WOODARDS, Orlando	R	R	6-2	200	01-02-78	Stockton, CA	Stockton, CA	Dunedin (FSL)	8-1	2.27	41	1	0	7	87.1	65	26	22	32	69	

CATCHERS (6)

NO.	PLAYER	B	T	HT.	WT.	BORN	BIRTHPLACE	RESIDENCE	2000 CLUB	AVG.	G	AB	R	H	2B	3B	HR	RBI	BB	SO	SB	ML SER
30	CASTILLO, Alberto	R	R	6-0	200	02-10-70	San Juan de la Magna, DR	Port St. Lucie, FL	TORONTO (AL)	.211	66	185	14	39	7	0	1	16	21	36	0	3.171
9	FLETCHER, Darrin	L	R	6-2	205	10-03-66	Elmhurst, IL	Oakwood, IL	TORONTO (AL)	.320	122	416	43	133	19	1	20	58	20	45	0	9.140
27	GREENE, Todd	R	R	5-10	208	05-08-71	Augusta, GA	Alpharetta, GA	Dunedin (FSL)	.200	5	20	2	4	1	0	1	4	2	4	1	
									Syracuse (Int)	.235	24	85	14	20	3	0	7	14	6	16	1	
									TORONTO (AL)	.297	34	101	11	27	2	0	5	10	5	18	1	3.119
6	LAWRENCE, Joe	R	R	6-2	190	02-13-77	Lake Charles, LA	Lake Charles, LA	Dunedin (FSL)	.301	101	375	69	113	32	1	13	67	69	74	21	0.000
17	PHELPS, Josh	R	R	6-3	220	05-12-78	Anchorage, AK	Rathdrum, ID	Tennessee (Sou)	.263	39	133	22	35	9	0	12	34	30	27	7	0.016
									Dunedin (FSL)	.319	30	113	26	36	7	1	9	28	12	34	1	
64	WERTH, Jayson	R	R	6-5	215	05-20-79	Springfield, IL	Chatham, IL	Tennessee (Sou)	.228	56	184	23	42	9	1	0	0	15	66	1	
									TORONTO (AL)	.000	1	1	0	0	0	0	0	0	0	0	0	
									Frederick (Caro)	.277	24	83	16	23	3	0	2	18	10	15	5	
									Bowie (East)	.228	85	276	47	63	16	2	5	26	54	50	9	

INFIELDERS (9)

NO.	PLAYER	B	T	HT.	WT.	BORN	BIRTHPLACE	RESIDENCE	2000 CLUB	AVG.	G	AB	R	H	2B	3B	HR	RBI	BB	SO	SB	ML SER
7	BATISTA, Tony	R	R	6-0	205	12-09-73	Puerto Plata, DR	Mao, DR	TORONTO (AL)	.263	154	620	96	163	32	2	41	114	35	121	5	4.072
18	BUSH, Homer	R	R	5-10	180	11-12-72	East St. Louis, IL	Keller, TX	TORONTO (AL)	.215	76	297	38	64	8	1	3	18	18	60	9	3.154
25	DELGADO, Carlos	L	R	6-3	230	06-25-72	Aguadilla, PR	Aguadilla, PR	TORONTO (AL)	.344	162	569	115	196	57	1	41	137	123	104	0	6.002
20	FULLMER, Brad	L	R	6-0	215	01-17-75	Chatsworth, CA	Henderson, NV	TORONTO (AL)	.295	133	482	76	142	29	1	32	104	30	68	3	2.155
14	FREEL, Ryan	R	R	5-10	185	03-08-76	Jacksonville, FL	Jacksonville, FL	Dunedin (FSL)	.500	4	18	7	9	1	1	3	6	8	1	2	
									Tennessee (Sou)	.295	12	44	11	13	3	0	0	8	8	6	2	
									Syracuse (Int)	.286	80	283	62	81	14	5	10	30	35	44	30	
2	FRYE, Jeff	R	R	5-9	160	08-31-66	Oakland, CA	Fort Worth, TX	BOSTON (AL)	.356	37	87	14	31	6	0	0	13	8	16	4	8.015
									COLORADO (NL)	.000	1	5	0	0	0	0	0	0	1	2	0	
8	GONZALEZ, Alex	R	R	6-0	195	04-08-73	Miami, FL	Coral Gables, FL	TORONTO (AL)	.252	141	527	68	133	31	2	15	69	43	113	4	6.055
3	IZTURIS, Cesar	S	R	5-9	175	02-10-80	Lara, VZ	Lara, VZ	Syracuse (Int)	.218	132	435	54	95	16	5	0	27	20	44	21	
5	WOODWARD, Chris	R	R	6-0	185	06-27-76	Covina, CA	Chino, CA	Syracuse (Int)	.322	37	143	23	46	13	0	5	25	11	30	2	
									TORONTO (AL)	.183	37	104	16	19	7	0	3	14	7	28	1	1.020

OUTFIELDERS (7)

NO.	PLAYER	B	T	HT.	WT.	BORN	BIRTHPLACE	RESIDENCE	2000 CLUB	AVG.	G	AB	R	H	2B	3B	HR	RBI	BB	SO	SB	ML SER
23	CRUZ, Jose	S	R	6-0	200	04-19-74	Arroyo, PR	Houston, TX	TORONTO (AL)	.242	162	603	91	146	32	5	31	76	71	129	15	3.063
43	MONDESI, Raul	R	R	5-11	230	03-02-71	San Cristobal, DR	San Cristobal, DR	TORONTO (AL)	.271	96	388	78	105	22	2	24	67	32	73	22	7.055
22	SIMMONS, Brian	S	S	6-2	190	09-04-73	Lebanon, PA	McMurray, PA	CHICAGO (AL)	DNP-INJURED												1.115
24	STEWART, Shannon	R	R	6-1	205	02-25-74	Cincinnati, OH	Miami, FL	Dunedin (FSL)	1.000	1	3	2	3	0	0	0	1	2	1	0	
									TORONTO (AL)	.319	136	583	107	186	43	7	21	69	37	79	20	3.121
15	THOMPSON, Andy	R	R	6-3	220	08-28-75	Oconomowoc, WI	Cottage Grove, WI	Syracuse (Int)	.246	121	426	59	105	27	2	2	65	50	95	9	
									TORONTO (AL)	.167	2	6	2	1	0	0	0	1	3	2	0	0.014
10	WELLS, Vernon	R	R	6-1	215	12-08-78	Shreveport, LA	Arlington, TX	Syracuse (Int)	.243	127	493	76	120	31	7	16	66	48	88	23	
									TORONTO (AL)	.000	3	2	0	0	0	0	0	0	0	0	0	0.066
11	WISE, Dewayne	L	L	6-1	180	02-24-78	Columbia, SC	Chapin, SC	Tennessee (Sou)	.250	15	56	10	14	5	2	2	8	7	13	3	
									TORONTO (AL)	.136	28	22	3	3	0	2	0	0	1	5	1	1.000

NON-ROSTER PLAYERS

NO. PITCHERS (9)		B	T	HT.	WT.	BORN	BIRTHPLACE	RESIDENCE	2000 CLUB	W-L	ERA	G	GS	CG	SV	IP	H	R	ER	BB	SO	ML SER
58	BAUER, Peter	R	R	6-7	250	11-06-78	Washington, DC	Hagerstown, MD	Hagerstown (SAL)	1-5	5.06	9	9	0	0	32.0	37	27	18	8	22	
72	CARRASCO, Hector	R	R	6-2	220	10-22-69	San Pedro de Marcois, D.R.	San Pedro de Marcois, D.R.	MINNESOTA (AL)	4-3	4.25	61	0	0	1	72.0	75	38	34	33	57	
									BOSTON (AL)	1-1	9.45	8	1	0	0	6.2	15	8	7	5	6	6.147
70	DANEKER, Pat	R	R	6-3	195	01-14-76	Williamsport, PA	Williamsport, PA	Charlotte (Int)	8-12	5.75	27	25	0	0	144.0	168	102	92	49	69	
									Syracuse (Int)	1-1	3.29	2	2	0	0	13.2	18	6	5	2	4	
34	DICKSON, Jason	L	R	6-0	195	03-30-73	London, Ontario	Chandler, AZ	Edmonton (PCL)	0-2	10.13	2	2	0	0	8.0	13	9	9	4	4	
									ANAHEIM (AL)	2-2	6.11	6	6	0	0	28.0	39	20	19	22	32	0.011
52	FRASCATORE, John	R	R	6-1	223	02-04-70	Queens, NY	Brookeville, FL	TORONTO (AL)	2-4	5.42	60	0	0	0	73	87	51	44	33	30	4.029
37	HENDRICKSON, Mark	L	L	6-9	230	06-23-74	Mount Vernon, WA	Mount Vernon, WA	Dunedin (FSL)	2-2	5.61	12	12	1	0	51.1	63	34	32	29	38	
									Tennessee (Sou)	3-1	3.63	6	6	0	0	39.2	32	17	16	12	29	4.057
59	McGOWAN, Dustin	R	R	6-3	195	03-24-82	Savannah, GA	Ludowici, GA	Medicine Hat (Pio)	0-3	6.48	6	6	1	0	25.0	26	21	18	25	19	
60	MICHALAK, Chris	L	L	6-2	195	01-04-71	Joliet, IL	Lemont, IL	Durham (Int)	0-0	5.68	6	0	0	0	6.1	4	4	4	1	7	
									Albuquerque (PCL)	11-3	4.26	23	21	1	0	133.0	166	72	63	55	83	0.038
71	NAVARRO, Jaime	R	R	6-4	250	03-27-68	Bayamon, P.R.	Mukwonago, WI	MILWAUKEE (NL)	0-5	12.54	5	5	0	0	18.2	34	31	26	18	7	
									Colorado Springs (PCL)	3-2	5.30	5	5	0	0	35.2	48	26	21	6	20	
									Buffalo (Int)	1-2	4.44	12	2	0	0	26.1	36	16	13	10	13	
									CLEVELAND (AL)	0-1	7.98	7	2	0	0	14.2	20	13	13	5	9	10.138

NO. CATCHERS (1)		B	T	HT.	WT.	BORN	BIRTHPLACE	RESIDENCE	2000 CLUB	AVG.	G	AB	R	H	2B	3B	HR	RBI	BB	SO	SB	ML SER
57	MOLINA, Izzy	R	R	6-1	200	06-03-71	New York, NY	Miami, FL	Omaha (PCL)	.235	90	311	39	73	9	1	10	36	14	55	5	0.170

NO. INFIELDERS (6)		B	T	HT.	WT.	BORN	BIRTHPLACE	RESIDENCE	2000 CLUB	AVG.	G	AB	R	H	2B	3B	HR	RBI	BB	SO	SB	ML SER
66	BALFE, Ryan	S	R	6-1	180	11-11-75	Cornwall, NY	Cornwall, NY	Mobile (Sou)	.262	130	462	61	121	21	4	12	66	46	120	3	
61	HOLBERT, Arron	R	R	6-0	160	01-09-73	Torrance, CA	Fontana, CA	Pawtucket (Int)	.252	80	294	38	74	13	1	2	23	15	54	8	
									Calgary (PCL)	.279	29	104	18	29	5	1	4	18	10	12	3	0.005
31	LINIAK, Cole	R	R	6-1	190	08-23-76	Encinitas, CA	Rancho La Costa, CA	Iowa (PCL)	.236	123	411	63	97	24	0	19	58	39	77	5	
									CHICAGO (NL)	.000	3	3	0	0	0	0	0	0	0	2	0	0.042
12	MORANDINI, Mickey	L	R	5-11	180	04-22-66	Leechburg, PA	Chesterton, IN	PHILADELPHIA (NL)	.252	91	302	31	76	13	3	0	22	29	54	1	
									TORONTO (AL)	.271	35	107	10	29	2	1	0	7	7	23	5	10.034
56	RICH, Dominic	L	R	5-10	190	08-22-79	Sunbury, PA	Herndon, PA	Queens (NYP)	.263	67	236	37	62	11	4	0	25	38	33	10	
67	TABLADO, Raul	R	R	6-2	175	03-03-82	North Bergen, NJ	Miami, FL	Queens (NYP)	.212	52	198	27	42	8	2	3	29	31	76	1	

NO. OUTFIELDERS (4)		B	T	HT.	WT.	BORN	BIRTHPLACE	RESIDENCE	2000 CLUB	AVG.	G	AB	R	H	2B	3B	HR	RBI	BB	SO	SB	ML SER
63	DAVIS, Morrin	R	R	6-2	190	12-11-82	Tampa, FL	Tampa, FL	Medicine Hat (Pio)	.222	40	162	17	36	6	2	5	16	11	59	3	
68	HUBBARD, Trenidad	R	R	5-9	203	05-11-66	Chicago, IL	Missouri City, TX	ATLANTA (NL)	.185	61	81	15	15	2	1	1	6	11	20	2	
									BALTIMORE (AL)	.185	31	27	3	5	1	0	0	0	2	3	2	4.066
62	LATHAM, Chris	S	R	6-0	198	05-26-73	Coeur D'Alene, ID	Las Vegas, NV	Colorado Springs (PCL)	.245	126	339	76	83	16	6	7	49	71	105	29	0.155
55	THOMPSON, Ryan	R	R	6-3	215	11-04-67	Chestertown, MD	Indianapolis, IN	Columbus (Int)	.285	86	326	45	93	23	3	23	75	27	72	9	
									NEW YORK (AL)	.260	33	50	12	13	3	0	3	14	5	12	0	3.081

2000 SPRING TRAINING STATISTICS

Batter		BA	SLG	OBP	G	AB	R	H	TB	2B	3B	HR	RBI	SH-SF	HBP	BB-IBB	SO	SB-CS	GDP	E
Abernathy		.250	.250	.250	10	12	1	3	3	0	0	0	2	0-0	0	0-0	1	1-0	0	0
Batista		.297	.649	.303	25	74	13	22	48	5	0	7	16	0-1	0	1-0	14	2-0	2	4
Blake		.375	.688	.353	11	16	4	6	11	2	0	1	6	0-1	0	0-0	3	0-0	1	1
Brown		.333	.778	.333	9	9	1	3	7	1	0	1	1	0-0	0	0-0	2	0-0	0	1
Brumfield		.292	.417	.320	11	24	4	7	10	3	0	0	3	0-0	0	1-0	3	3-0	0	0
Bush		.271	.400	.363	24	70	16	19	28	3	0	2	12	0-0	2	8-0	6	7-1	0	1
Castillo, A.		.234	.426	.265	20	47	5	11	20	3	0	2	11	0-0	0	2-0	9	0-0	1	1
Cordova	MLB	.319	.404	.347	16	47	8	15	19	1	0	1	7	0-0	1	1-0	10	0-0	1	1
Cordova	TM	.267	.467	.313	5	15	1	4	7	0	0	1	2	0-0	0	1-0	2	0-0	0	1
Cruz		.267	.507	.317	24	75	13	20	38	4	1	4	9	0-1	0	6-0	13	0-1	2	0
Dalesandro		.000	.000	.000	4	6	0	0	0	0	0	0	0	0-0	0	0-0	2	0-0	0	0
Delgado		.344	.563	.421	24	64	13	22	36	2	0	4	15	0-2	0	10-0	12	1-0	2	2
Fletcher		.216	.324	.256	12	37	2	8	12	1	0	1	5	0-0	0	2-0	3	0-0	0	0
Freel		.500	.500	.500	1	2	0	1	1	0	0	0	0	0-0	0	0-0	0	0-0	0	0
Fullmer	MLB	.304	.551	.359	24	69	12	21	38	2	0	5	20	0-2	0	7-0	7	0-1	1	0
Fullmer	LG	.306	.750	.381	13	36	8	11	27	1	0	5	13	0-1	0	5-0	2	0-1	1	0
Gonzalez		.143	.214	.213	20	56	8	8	12	1	0	1	5	0-0	0	5-0	18	0-0	2	4
Grebeck		.333	.500	.429	13	18	2	6	9	3	0	0	4	0-0	1	2-0	4	0-0	0	1
Greene		.500	1.071	.533	11	14	4	7	15	5	0	1	5	0-0	1	0-0	4	1-0	0	0
Izturis		.111	.111	.200	5	9	1	1	1	0	0	0	0	0-0	0	1-0	0	0-0	0	0
Lawrence		.000	.000	.000	1	1	0	0	0	0	0	0	0	0-0	0	0-0	0	0-0	0	0
Lopez, F.		.261	.609	.261	10	23	3	6	14	2	0	2	3	0-0	0	0-0	8	1-0	0	1
Lopez, L.		.400	.467	.438	13	15	2	6	7	1	0	0	3	0-0	0	1-0	1	0-0	0	0
Loyd		—	—	—	2	0	0	0	0	0	0	0	0	0-0	0	0-0	0	0-0	0	0
Mondesi		.236	.528	.291	24	72	17	17	38	1	1	6	16	0-1	3	3-0	19	7-0	1	0
Mottola		.154	.231	.214	7	13	1	2	3	1	0	0	2	0-0	0	1-0	5	0-0	0	0
Mummau		—	—	—	1	0	0	0	0	0	0	0	0	0-0	0	0-0	0	0-0	0	0
Otanez		.235	.353	.235	13	17	1	4	6	2	0	0	3	0-0	0	0-0	2	0-0	1	1
Perez		.000	.000	.000	2	2	0	0	0	0	0	0	0	0-0	0	0-0	0	0-0	0	0
Peters		.000	.000	.000	1	1	0	0	0	0	0	0	0	0-0	0	0-0	1	0-0	0	0
Phelps		.000	.000	.000	2	5	0	0	0	0	0	0	0	0-0	0	0-0	2	0-0	0	0
Sanders		.225	.325	.311	26	40	7	9	13	4	0	0	2	0-0	4	1-0	10	0-1	1	1
Segui	TM	.467	.767	.484	11	30	7	14	23	3	0	2	8	0-0	0	1-0	1	0-0	0	0
Stewart, A.		.000	.000	.000	3	5	0	0	0	0	0	0	0	0-0	0	0-0	0	0-0	0	1
Stewart, S.		.423	.731	.455	16	52	13	22	38	3	2	3	7	0-0	1	2-0	4	1-1	0	2
Thompson		.273	.591	.333	12	22	4	6	13	1	0	2	2	0-0	1	1-0	6	0-0	0	1
Wells, V.		.208	.292	.269	11	24	3	5	7	0	1	0	1	0-0	0	2-0	7	1-0	0	1
Wise		.162	.189	.295	22	37	6	6	7	1	0	0	3	0-0	2	5-0	8	5-0	1	1
Witt		.222	.444	.263	13	18	3	4	8	1	0	1	1	0-0	0	1-0	4	0-0	1	0
Woodward		.372	.488	.386	24	43	9	16	21	5	0	0	6	1-0	0	1-0	7	1-1	1	1
Young		.125	.250	.125	7	16	0	2	4	0	1	0	0	0-0	0	0-0	5	0-0	1	0
TEAM		.272	.475	.321	31	1027	172	279	488	59	6	46	166	2-7	15	63-0	190	31-6	18	28
OPPONENTS		.259	.421	.335	31	986	139	255	415	54	2	34	132	7-6	12	104-0	176	23-6	33	28

Pitcher		W-L	ERA	G	GS	CG	GF	SHO	SV	INN	H	BFP	AB	R	ER	HR	SH-SF	HBP	BB-IBB	SO	WP	BK	BA
Andrews		1-2	6.05	7	2	0	0	0	0	19.1	20	86	74	15	13	0	0-2	1	9-0	11	0	0	.270
Bale		0-0	9.00	3	0	0	0	0	0	6.0	9	29	26	6	6	1	0-0	0	3-0	4	0	0	.346
Borbon		0-0	1.42	14	0	0	2	0	0	12.2	8	50	45	3	2	1	0-0	0	5-0	13	0	0	.178
Carpenter		2-0	4.80	6	5	0	0	0	0	15.0	21	65	62	9	8	3	0-1	0	2-0	15	1	0	.339
Castillo, F.		3-1	2.81	6	6	0	0	0	0	25.2	21	105	91	8	8	3	1-0	1	12-0	17	0	0	.231
Coco		0-0	18.00	1	0	0	0	0	0	1.0	3	7	6	2	2	0	0-0	0	1-0	0	0	0	.500
DeWitt		0-0	9.00	3	0	0	0	0	0	5.0	7	23	20	5	5	1	1-0	0	2-0	2	0	0	.350
Donnelly		0-0	0.00	1	0	0	0	0	0	2.0	1	7	7	0	0	0	0-0	0	0-0	0	0	0	.143
Ellis		0-0	6.75	2	0	0	1	0	0	2.2	4	12	11	2	2	0	0-0	0	1-0	2	0	0	.364
Escobar		0-1	3.18	6	4	0	0	0	0	17.0	14	70	67	8	6	4	0-0	0	3-0	12	1	0	.209
Estrella		1-0	6.75	2	0	0	0	0	0	4.0	2	18	14	3	3	1	0-0	0	4-0	4	0	0	.143
Frascatore		1-1	4.11	12	0	0	2	0	0	15.1	15	67	57	9	7	2	0-0	1	9-0	8	0	0	.263
Glover		0-1	11.74	3	1	0	0	0	0	7.2	10	40	33	11	10	1	0-0	2	5-0	4	0	0	.303
Gunderson		0-1	3.52	9	0	0	4	0	3	7.2	4	31	27	3	3	1	0-0	0	4-0	7	0	0	.148
Halladay		3-1	3.60	7	6	0	0	0	0	30.0	32	131	115	12	12	3	1-1	1	13-0	15	0	0	.278
Koch		2-1	2.81	13	0	0	6	0	2	16.0	11	65	58	6	5	3	0-0	1	6-0	14	0	0	.190
Kusiewicz	MLB	0-0	0.00	3	0	0	1	0	0	5.0	1	18	16	0	0	0	0-0	0	2-0	3	0	0	.063
Kusiewicz	TM	0-0	0.00	1	0	0	1	0	0	1.0	0	5	3	0	0	0	0-0	0	2-0	0	0	0	.000
McClellan		0-0	11.57	2	0	0	2	0	0	2.1	4	11	9	3	3	1	0-0	1	1-0	2	0	0	.444
Munro		1-1	6.92	7	0	0	1	0	0	13.0	15	62	52	10	10	1	0-0	0	10-0	9	0	0	.288
Painter		1-0	3.00	13	0	0	5	0	2	15.0	13	56	55	5	5	3	0-0	0	1-0	17	0	0	.236
Quantrill		0-1	2.50	13	0	0	4	0	1	18.0	16	71	64	5	5	0	2-1	0	4-0	8	0	0	.250
Rodriguez		0-0	6.23	4	3	0	0	0	0	8.2	8	39	32	6	6	3	0-0	2	5-0	3	1	0	.250
Romano		0-0	9.00	1	0	0	0	0	0	2.0	4	12	10	3	2	0	1-0	0	1-0	0	0	0	.400
Sneed		0-1	6.75	3	0	0	3	0	1	1.1	2	10	6	1	1	0	1-0	2	1-0	2	0	0	.333
Wells, D.		3-0	2.25	4	4	0	0	0	0	12.0	11	43	42	4	3	2	0-1	0	0-0	7	0	0	.262
TEAM		18-12	4.39	31	31	0	31	0	9	260.1	255	1115	986	139	127	34	7-6	12	104-0	176	3	0	.259
OPPONENTS		12-18	5.41	31	31	0	31	1	4	256.0	279	1114	1027	172	154	46	2-7	15	63-0	190	7	1	.272

2001 TORONTO BLUE JAYS
SPRING ROSTER

BY POSITION, NUMERICAL & ALPHABETICAL

BY POSITION	NUMERICAL	ALPHABETICAL

BY POSITION

PITCHERS (27)
58 BAUER, Peter#
40 BEIRNE, Kevin
51 BORBON, Pedro
26 CARPENTER, Chris
72 CARRASCO, Hector#
38 COCO, Pasqual
70 DANEKER, Pat#
34 DICKSON, Jason#
47 ESCOBAR, Kelvim
29 EYRE, Scott
36 FILE, Bob
52 FRASCATORE, John#
32 HALLADAY, Roy
50 HAMILTON, Joey
37 HENDRICKSON, Mark#
44 KOCH, Billy
21 LOAIZA, Esteban
59 McGOWAN, Dustin#
60 MICHALAK, Chris#
71 NAVARRO, Jaime#
28 PAINTER, Lance
39 PARRIS, Steve
54 PEREZ, George
19 PLESAC, Dan
48 QUANTRILL, Paul
33 SIROTKA, Mike
49 WOODARDS, Orlando

CATCHERS (7)
30 CASTILLO, Alberto
9 FLETCHER, Darrin
27 GREENE, Todd
6 LAWRENCE, Joe
57 MOLINA, Izzy#
17 PHELPS, Josh
64 WERTH, Jayson

INFIELDERS (15)
66 BALFE, Ryan#
7 BATISTA, Tony
18 BUSH, Homer
25 DELGADO, Carlos
20 FULLMER, Brad
14 FREEL, Ryan
2 FRYE, Jeff
8 GONZALEZ, Alex
61 HOLBERT, Aaron#
3 IZTURIS, Cesar
31 LINIAK, Cole#
12 MORANDINI, Mickey#
56 RICH, Dominic#
67 TABLADO, Raul#
5 WOODWARD, Chris

OUTFIELDERS (11)
23 CRUZ, Jose
63 DAVIS, Morrin#
68 HUBBARD, Trenidad#
62 LATHAM, Chris#
43 MONDESI, Raul
22 SIMMONS, Brian
24 STEWART, Shannon
15 THOMPSON, Andy
55 THOMPSON, Ryan#
10 WELLS, Vernon
11 WISE, Dewayne

MANAGER
13 MARTINEZ, Buck

COACHES
35 BEVINGTON, Terry
53 CONNOR, Mark
41 GASTON, Cito
16 IORG, Garth
47 PATTERSON, Gil
1 ROJAS, Cookie

BATTING PRACTICE PITCHER
65 FIGUEROA, Jesus

BULLPEN CATCHER
46 STEWART, Andy

NUMERICAL

1 ROJAS, Cookie: Coach
2 FRYE, Jeff: IF
3 IZTURIS, Cesar: IF
4
5 WOODWARD, Chris: IF
6 LAWRENCE, Joe: C
7 BATISTA, Tony: IF
8 GONZALEZ, Alex: IF
9 FLETCHER, Darrin: C
10 WELLS, Vernon: OF
11 WISE, Dewayne: OF
12 MORANDINI, Mickey: IF#
13 MARTINEZ, Buck: Manager
14 FREEL, Ryan: IF
15 THOMPSON, Andy: OF
16 IORG, Garth: Coach
17 PHELPS, Josh: C
18 BUSH, Homer: IF
19 PLESAC, Dan: LHP
20 FULLMER, Brad: IF/DH
21 LOAIZA, Esteban: RHP
22 SIMMONS, Brian: OF
23 CRUZ, Jose: OF
24 STEWART, Shannon: OF
25 DELGADO, Carlos: IF
26 CARPENTER, Chris: RHP
27 GREENE, Todd: C-DH
28 PAINTER, Lance: LHP
29 EYRE, Scott: LHP
30 CASTILLO, Alberto: C
31 LINIAK, Cole: IF#
32 HALLADAY, Roy: RHP
33 SIROTKA, Mike: LHP
34 DICKSON, Jason: RHP#
35 BEVINGTON, Terry: COACH
36 FILE, Bob: RHP
37 HENDRICKSON, Mark: LHP#
38 COCO, Pasqual: RHP
39 PARRIS, Steve: RHP
40 BEIRNE, Kevin: RHP
41 GASTON, Cito: COACH
42 ***retired***
43 MONDESI, Raul: OF
44 KOCH, Billy: RHP
45 ESCOBAR, Kelvim: RHP
46 STEWART, Andy: Bullpen Catcher
47 PATTERSON, Gil: Coach
48 QUANTRILL, Paul: RHP
49 WOODARDS, Orlando: RHP
50 HAMILTON, Joey: RHP
51 BORBON, Pedro: LHP
52 FRASCATORE, John: RHP#
53 CONNOR, Mark: Coach
54 PEREZ, George: RHP
55 THOMPSON, Ryan: OF#
56 RICH, Dominic: IF#
57 MOLINA, Izzy: C#
58 BAUER, Peter: RHP#
59 McGOWAN, Dustin: RHP#
60 MICHALAK, Chris: LHP#
61 HOLBERT, Aaron: IF#
62 LATHAM, Chris: OF#
63 DAVIS, Morrin: OF#
64 WERTH, Jayson: C
65 FIGUEROA, Jesus: BPP
66 BALFE, Ryan: IF#
67 TABLADO, Raul: IF#
68 HUBBARD, Trenidad: OF#
69
70 DANEKER, Pat: RHP#
71 NAVARRO, Jaime: RHP#
72 CARRASCO, Hector: RHP#

ALPHABETICAL

66 BALFE, Ryan: IF#
7 BATISTA, Tony: IF
58 BAUER, Peter: RHP#
40 BEIRNE, Kevin: RHP
35 BEVINGTON, Terry: COACH
51 BORBON, Pedro: LHP
18 BUSH, Homer: IF
26 CARPENTER, Chris: RHP
72 CARRASCO, Hector: RHP#
30 CASTILLO, Alberto: C
38 COCO, Pasqual: RHP
53 CONNOR, Mark: Coach
23 CRUZ, Jose: OF
70 DANEKER, Pat: RHP#
63 DAVIS, Morrin: OF#
25 DELGADO, Carlos: IF
34 DICKSON, Jason: RHP#
45 ESCOBAR, Kelvim: RHP
29 EYRE, Scott: LHP
65 FIGUEROA, Jesus: BPP
36 FILE, Bob: RHP
9 FLETCHER, Darrin: C
52 FRASCATORE, John: RHP#
14 FREEL, Ryan: IF
2 FRYE, Jeff: IF
20 FULLMER, Brad: IF/DH
41 GASTON, Cito: Coach
8 GONZALEZ, Alex: IF
27 GREENE, Todd: C-DH
32 HALLADAY, Roy: RHP
50 HAMILTON, Joey: RHP
37 HENDRICKSON, Mark: LHP#
61 HOLBERT, Aaron: IF#
68 HUBBARD, Trenidad: OF#
16 IORG, Garth: Coach
3 IZTURIS, Cesar: IF
44 KOCH, Billy: RHP
62 LATHAM, Chris: OF#
6 LAWRENCE, Joe: C
31 LINIAK, Cole: IF#
21 LOAIZA, Esteban: RHP
13 MARTINEZ, Buck: Manager
59 McGOWAN, Dustin: RHP#
60 MICHALAK, Chris: LHP#
57 MOLINA, Izzy: C#
43 MONDESI, Raul: OF
12 MORANDINI, Mickey: IF#
71 NAVARRO, Jaime: RHP#
28 PAINTER, Lance: LHP
39 PARRIS, Steve: RHP
47 PATTERSON, Gil: Coach
54 PEREZ, George: RHP
17 PHELPS, Josh: C
19 PLESAC, Dan: LHP
48 QUANTRILL, Paul: RHP
56 RICH, Dominic: IF#
1 ROJAS, Cookie: Coach
22 SIMMONS, Brian: OF
33 SIROTKA, Mike: LHP
46 STEWART, Andy: BPC
24 STEWART, Shannon: OF
67 TABLADO, Raul: IF#
15 THOMPSON, Andy: OF
55 THOMPSON, Ryan: OF#
10 WELLS, Vernon: OF
64 WERTH, Jayson: C
11 WISE, Dewayne: OF
49 WOODARDS, Orlando: RHP
5 WOODWARD, Chris: IF

#-Non-roster